WITHDRAWN

THE CAMBRIDGE HISTORY
OF AFRICA

General Editors: J. D. FAGE and ROLAND OLIVER

Volume 8

from *c.* 1940 to *c.* 1975

THE CAMBRIDGE
HISTORY OF
AFRICA

Volume 8
from *c.* 1940 to *c.* 1975

edited by
MICHAEL CROWDER

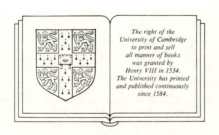

The right of the
University of Cambridge
to print and sell
all manner of books
was granted by
Henry VIII in 1534.
The University has printed
and published continuously
since 1584.

CAMBRIDGE UNIVERSITY PRESS

CAMBRIDGE

LONDON   NEW YORK   NEW ROCHELLE

MELBOURNE   SYDNEY

Published by the Press Syndicate of the University of Cambridge
The Pitt Building, Trumpington Street, Cambridge CB2 1RP
32 East 57th Street, New York, NY 10022, USA
296 Beaconsfield Parade, Middle Park, Melbourne 3206, Australia

First published 1984

Printed in Great Britain by the University Press, Cambridge

Library of Congress catalogue card number: 76–2261

British Library Cataloguing in Publication Data

The Cambridge History of Africa.
Vol. 8: From c. 1940 to c. 1975
1. Africa—History
I. Crowder, Michael
960   DT20

ISBN 0 521 22409 8

UP

CONTENTS

FIGURES

PREFACE

In the English-speaking world, the Cambridge histories have since the beginning of the century set the pattern for multi-volume works of history, with chapters written by experts on a particular topic, and unified by the guiding hand of volume editors of senior standing. *The Cambridge Modern History*, planned by Lord Acton, appeared in sixteen volumes between 1902 and 1912. It was followed by *The Cambridge Ancient History*, *The Cambridge Medieval History*, *The Cambridge History of English Literature*, and Cambridge Histories of India, of Poland, and of the British Empire. The original *Modern History* has now been replaced by *The New Cambridge Modern History* in fourteen volumes, and *The Cambridge Economic History of Europe* is now complete. Other Cambridge Histories recently undertaken include a history of Islam, of Arabic literature, of the Bible treated as a central document of and influence on Western civilisation, and of Iran, China and Latin America.

It was during the later 1950s that the Syndics of the Cambridge University Press first began to explore the possibility of embarking on a Cambridge History of Africa. But they were then advised that the time was not yet ripe. The serious appraisal of the past of Africa by historians and archaeologists had hardly been undertaken before 1948, the year when universities first began to appear in increasing numbers in the vast reach of the African continent south of the Sahara and north of the Limpopo, and the time too when universities outside Africa first began to take some notice of its history. It was impressed upon the Syndics that the most urgent need of such a young, but also very rapidly advancing branch of historical studies, was a journal of international standing through which the results of ongoing research might be disseminated. In 1960, therefore, the Cambridge University Press launched *The Journal of African History*, which gradually demonstrated the amount of work being undertaken to establish the past of Africa as an integrated whole rather than – as it had usually been viewed before – as the story of a series of incursions into the continent by peoples coming from outside, from the Mediterranean basin, the Near East or western Europe. This movement will of course continue and develop further, but the increasing facilities available for its publication soon began to demonstrate a need to assess both what had been done, and what still needed to be done, in the light of some general historical perspective for the continent.

The Syndics therefore returned to their original charge, and in 1966 the founding editors of *The Journal of African History* accepted a commission to become the general editors of a *Cambridge History of Africa*. They found it a daunting task to draw up a plan for a co-operative work covering a history which was in active process of exploration by scholars of many nations, scattered over a fair part of the globe, and of many disciplines – linguists, anthropologists, geographers and botanists, for example, as well as historians and archaeologists.

It was thought that the greatest problems were likely to arise with the earliest and latest periods: the earliest, because so much would depend on the results of long-term archaeological investigation, and the latest, because of the rapid changes in historical perspective that were occurring as a consequence of the ending of colonial rule in Africa. Therefore when, in 1967, the general editors presented their scheme to the Press and notes were prepared for contributors, only four volumes – covering the periods 500 B.C. to A.D. 1050, A.D. 1050 to 1600, 1600–1790, and 1790–1870 – had been planned in any detail, and these were published as volumes 2–5 of the *History* between 1975 and 1978.

So far as the prehistoric period was concerned, the general editors were clear from the outset that the proper course was to entrust the planning as well as the actual editing of what was necessary entirely to a scholar who was fully experienced in the archaeology of the African continent. In due course, in 1982, Volume 1, 'From the earliest times to *c.* 500 B.C.', appeared under the distinguished editorship of Professor J. Desmond Clark. As for the colonial period, it was evident by the early 1970s that this was being rapidly brought to its close, so that it became possible to plan to complete the *History* in three further volumes. The first, Volume 6, is designed to cover the European partition of the

continent, and the setting up of the colonial structures between
c. 1870 and *c.* 1905; the second, Volume 7, is devoted to the
'classical' colonial period running from *c.* 1905 to *c.* 1940; while
the focus of the third, Volume 8, is on the period of rapid change
which led from about the time of the Second World War to the
ending of formal control from Europe with the dramatic final
collapse of the Portuguese empire in 1975.

When they started their work, the general editors quickly came
to the conclusion that the most practical plan for completing the
History within a reasonable period of time was likely to be the
simplest and most straightforward. Each volume was therefore
entrusted to a volume editor who, in addition to having made a
substantial contribution to the understanding of the period in
question, was someone with whom the general editors were in
close touch. Within a volume, the aim was to keep the number
of contributors to a minimum. Each of them was asked to essay
a broad survey of a particular area or theme with which he was
familiar for the whole of the period covered by the volume. In
this survey, his purpose should be to take account not only of all
relevant research done, or still in progress, but also of the gaps
in knowledge. These he should try to fill by new thinking of his
own, whether based on new work on the available sources or on
interpolations from congruent research.

It should be remembered that this basic plan was devised
nearly twenty years ago, when little or no research had been done
on many important topics, and before many of today's younger
scholars – not least those who now fill posts in the departments
of history and archaeology in the universities and research
institutes in Africa itself – had made their own deep penetrations
into such areas of ignorance. Two things follow from this. If the
general editors had drawn up their plan in the 1970s rather than
the 1960s, the shape might well have been very different, perhaps
with a larger number of more specialised, shorter chapters, each
centred on a smaller area, period or theme, to the understanding
of which the contributor would have made his own individual
contribution. To some extent, indeed, it has been possible to
adjust the shape of the last three volumes in this direction.
Secondly, the sheer volume of new research that has been
published since many contributors accepted their commissions
has often led them to undertake very substantial revisions in their

work as it progressed from draft to draft, thus protracting the length of time originally envisaged for the preparation of these volumes.

At the time when the plan for Volume 8 was settled, 1975 seemed an ideal closing date. For the reason which has already been mentioned, it still *is* a very sensible date. But history does not stop at the points where its recorders and interpreters choose to draw their lines and, in the not inconsiderable space of time in which Volume 8 was being written and put together, it was inevitable that a number of events should occur which might be thought worthy of mention. Some of these have fitted nicely into the way some contributors chose to organise their chapters; some have not. Inevitably, therefore, the concluding line of the volume as a whole has become somewhat ragged. Secondly, not all historians are willing to write so close to the chronological frontier of their discipline as this volume aims to go. Its editor has therefore perforce sometimes had to seek contributions from scholars whose discipline is less history than political science or economics. The discerning reader will therefore recognise some differences of academic approach between chapters.

However, histories are meant to be read, and not to be commented on and analysed by their general editors, and we therefore present to the reader this concluding volume of our enterprise.

March 1984   J. D. FAGE
                                                      ROLAND OLIVER

Many people have assisted the Editor in the production of this volume. He would particularly like to express his debt to Professor Lalage Bown, Professor Robert Gavin, Dr Lorne Larson, Professor Robin Horton, and Dr Philip Shea.

INTRODUCTION

Whether the Second World War marked a decisive stage in the colonial history of Africa, unleashing forces that, with hindsight, we can see made political decolonisation by even the most reluctant of European powers inevitable, or whether it merely hastened a process that was already, if not very obviously, under way, will long remain a matter for debate. There is much to be said for both views. What is clear is that nearly all writers on the colonial period of Africa's past accept, or at least pay lip service to, the view that for whatever reason the Second World War represented a watershed in the history of the continent. Yet curiously few of them give its course or impact detailed attention. It is as though it were an interval between the two acts of a play in which the audience is asked to accept that there has been a passage of time but is given only the barest outline of what has happened meanwhile.

There are many serious studies of, on the one hand, the years 1919–1939 – the period of classic colonial rule – and, on the other, the years immediately following the war – the period of 'decolonisation' or 'the transfer of power'. Few historians have interested themselves in both periods, and the latter period has mostly been left to the attention of political scientists. Conversely, few political scientists have paid much attention to the years before 1945. The Second World War seems to represent a boundary between what is regarded as the proper territory of the historian and what is the province of the political scientist or journalist. Most historians apparently feel reluctant to bring the tools of their trade to bear on a period in which the chief actors are still practising their profession, and for which the archival evidence has, for the greater part of it, not yet been released. They prefer to let political scientists hazard judgements which they fear will fail the test of time.

Since *The Cambridge History of Africa* sets out to be an enduring historical survey, there might, therefore, seem to be a case for accepting the Second World War as a terminal event for the enterprise. At least for many of the countries that once ruled Africa, the archives are open for most of the period that preceded that war, though some still maintain the 50-year rule. As a result it will only be in 1990 that we shall learn the innermost secrets of some of the colonisers for the year 1940, the date with which this present volume begins.

Inevitably a volume that takes the history of Africa up to 1975, and the chapters of which were in some cases written as early as 1977 by those martyrs of collective enterprises – the prompt deliverers – does not have the advantage of perspective that even the preceding volume, covering the colonial period from 1905 till 1940, can have. Much of the evidence must of necessity be secondary or, where it is primary, the result of the direct experience of the contributor, using evidence assimilated from day to day in newspapers, conversation or interviews.

A more cautious scheme for a history of Africa would, then, have had its last volume conclude with the Second World War. But that would have been to leave the story without an ending. The Second World War may have been a watershed in African history, but it was more in the nature of a turning point within a period than the ending of one or the beginning of another. Whether the war is seen as having unleashed new forces or merely as having 'stimulated and given scope to forces already at play',[1] it did change the situation so radically in Africa that the conclusion of the change has to be seen if the significance of the war is to be understood. Indeed, one of the General Editors of *The Cambridge History of Africa* once criticised the writer for terminating his *West Africa under Colonial Rule* in 1945, 'thus excluding the most determining part of the colonial period'.[2] That was of course the dismantling of the European empires in the greater part of North and West Africa by 1960, and the rest of the continent by 1975.

In 1940 the vast majority of the inhabitants of the continent were under one form or another of European colonial rule. Of the three countries that were nominally independent, Liberia was enfeoffed to the Firestone Rubber Company of the United States, Egypt was severely limited in the exercise of her sovereignty by

[1] See Chapter 8.   [2] Roland Oliver in *The Observer*, 11 August 1968.

2

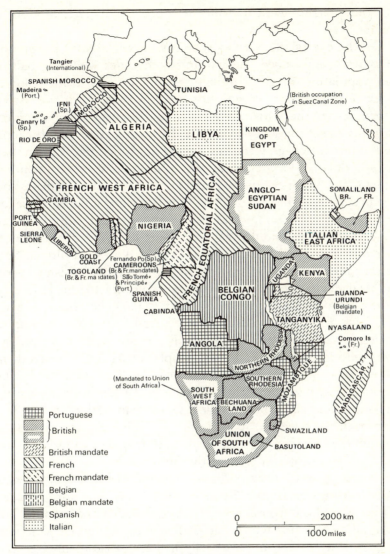

1 Africa, 1940.

the terms of the Anglo-Egyptian Treaty of 1936, while independence in the Union of South Africa was meaningful only for the white minority which had already embarked on a programme of stripping the non-white majority of the few political and social rights it did possess. Indeed, while most other black Africans during our period were to improve their political position, those of South Africa were to suffer a concomitant deterioration in theirs.

On the eve of the Second World War few, if any, Europeans or Africans envisaged that within two decades well over half of the population of the continent would be free from colonial tutelage. Despite the devolution of power in the major Asian dependencies, the British government did not yet think it necessary to apply that experience to Africa. By 1940 Ceylon had for long had internal self-government, while in India the British had already devolved a great deal of the business of government on Indians, retaining exclusive control only over external affairs and defence. Although the British Labour Party had independence for India on its programme, as far as the African colonies were concerned it considered self-government, let alone independence, a remote prospect. Malcolm MacDonald, Labour Colonial Secretary in the British National government, put the British view on political development in the African colonies to the House of Commons on 7 December 1938: 'It may take generations, or even centuries, for the peoples in some parts of the colonial empire to achieve self-government. But it is a major part of our policy, even among the most backward peoples of Africa, to teach them always to be able to stand a little more on their own feet.'[1] The Popular Front government of France had been no more daring in its thinking about political development in Africa, and the few reforms it had been able to introduce were basically assimilationist in intent, while the Belgians, Spanish, Portuguese and Italians did not give the subject a passing thought.

Far from decolonisation being a theme of these times, a new imperialism was in the European air. Italy had just invaded Ethiopia and incorporated it into her East African empire. The League of Nations, which had earlier voted economic sanctions against Italy in the hope of halting her invasion, once it was successful withdrew them, turning a deaf if embarrassed ear to the personal appeal by Emperor Haile Selassie for intervention on his country's behalf. Germany, still smarting under the humiliation of the Treaty of Versailles which had stripped her of her colonial empire, thrilled to Hitler's demands that the country regain its 'rightful place in the tropical sun'. Even in Spain there

---

[1] *Hansard*, 7 December 1938.

were expansionists who dreamed during the war of creating an empire taken from Nigeria and French Equatorial Africa.[1]

Not only was imperialism very much alive, but few Europeans questioned their right to possession of colonies. Conversely, the majority of Africans had come to accept the European presence, if only passively. Not a few of the educated élite shared the view of Isaac Delano who wrote in 1937: 'The people of Nigeria are very proud of the British Empire to which they belong, and of British statesmanship and equity. They realise that they cannot safely become independent of the British Government as things are today in the world.'[2] Some of the western-educated minority had, however, begun to articulate questions couched in terms of western political thought about the presence of the Europeans and their right to govern colonial peoples in an autocratic fashion. Thus for Lamine Guèye, who founded the Parti Socialiste Sénégalais in 1935, it was ironic that the same colonial power which imposed the *corvée* on its African subjects placed in the hands of their children at school books proclaiming that the 'colonies were an integral part of the very Republic whose founders had discovered and taught that "men are born and remain free" and which had as its motto "Liberty – Equality – Fraternity"'.[3] While the majority of the educated élite limited their demands to some form of participation in the institutions of government imposed on them by their colonial masters, with the various youth movements in West Africa demanding that this participation be granted more speedily, a minority in French North Africa was beginning to make overt demands for an early and complete independence that was not tied to some form of constitutional association with France. Even so, in the year before the outbreak of the Second World War the European imperial powers had good reason to be complacent about their long-term position in Africa. Yet within two years of the opening of hostilities in Europe Ethiopia had regained its sovereignty, and a decade later Libya became independent. Within another 25 years the last major European colony in Africa, Angola, had gained its independence on 11 November 1975, and the dismantling of the

---

[1] René Pélissier, 'Equatorial Guinea: recent history', in *Africa: South of the Sahara, 1977–78* (London, 1977), 301.
[2] I. O. Delano, *The soul of Nigeria* (London, 1937), 8.
[3] Lamine Guèye, *Itinéraire africaine* (Paris, 1966), 79.

Madeira (Port.)

Canary Is (Sp.)

SPANISH SAHARA

Ceuta (Sp.) • Melilla (Sp.)

MOROCCO

TUNISIA

ALGERIA

LIBYA

EGYPT

MAURITANIA

MALI

NIGER

CHAD

SUDAN

French territory of AFARS & ISSAS

THE GAMBIA

SENEGAL

GUINEA-BISSAU

GUINEA

SIERRA LEONE

LIBERIA

UPPER VOLTA

IVORY COAST

GHANA

TOGO

BENIN

NIGERIA

CENTRAL AFRICAN REP.

ETHIOPIA

SOMALIA

São Tomé & Principé (ind.1975)

Cape Verde Is. (ind.1975)

EQUATORIAL GUINEA

GABON

CONGO

ZAIRE

RWANDA

BURUNDI

UGANDA

KENYA

Cabinda

TANZANIA

Comoro Is (ind.1975)

ANGOLA

ZAMBIA

MALAWI

MOZAMBIQUE

MADAGASCAR

RHODESIA (ZIMBABWE)

NAMIBIA

SOUTH WEST AFRICA

BOTSWANA

SWAZILAND

SOUTH AFRICA

LESOTHO

Mauritius

Reunion (Fr.)

▨ Areas still under colonial rule

▦ UN Trust Territory under illegal South African rule

▦ Illegal independence from Britain declared by white minority government in 1965

--- Partitioned between Morocco and Mauritania, Nov. 1975

0   2000 km

0   1000 miles

2   Africa, 1975.

European empires in Africa was complete except for a few exotic enclaves and offshore islands. There were, of course, three major territories in which Africans were still subject to control by people of European origin but which no longer formed part of any European imperium. The white minority in the Republic of South Africa had gained virtual independence from Britain as long ago as 1910. The former German colony of South West Africa had been mandated to South Africa after the First World War. In Rhodesia the white minority had unilaterally and effectively taken its independence from Britain in 1965 so as to avoid any question of effective African participation in the political process of their country, let alone subjection to African majority rule, which was a prerequisite of the legal granting of independence by the mother country.

The political, social and economic consequences of this rapid collapse of the European colonial empires in Africa between 1940 and 1975 form the central theme of this volume. The first chapter will seek to assess the role of the Second World War in that collapse.

CHAPTER 1

THE SECOND WORLD WAR: PRELUDE
TO DECOLONISATION IN AFRICA

By 1939 the European colonial powers were as firmly in control
of their African territories as they ever would be. During the
preceding ten years there had been few major challenges to their
authority. Africans had come to accept the new political order and
to obey the rules laid down by the colonial administration. The
lesson had been learned that, although the colonial administration
was thin on the ground, in the last resort it had overwhelming
resources of power. Attempts to take advantage of the weakness
of some colonial administrations during the First World War and
to return to an independence based on pre-colonial political
structures, though temporarily successful, had failed. Such challenges to the colonial authorities as did take place during the 1930s
were made within the framework of the colonial state and were
by and large limited to protest against obnoxious features of the
administration; such protest took the form of riots against
taxation or strikes to obtain higher wages or better conditions of
service in the small colonial industrial sector. With the notable
exception of French North Africa, there were few violent demonstrations of a modern political character, that is, aimed at
securing greater participation by Africans, and more specifically
the small educated élite, in the governmental processes of the
colonial state. Nevertheless it was clear that if the educated élite
accepted the status quo it was a passive not an active acceptance:
they hankered after an independence, but, like the British, they
saw it as a goal whose realisation was distant. Yet when they saw
the one truly independent state of Ethiopia fall to colonialist
forces in 1936, their reaction was one of wide-scale protest.

By 1939 the imposed colonial states had gained legitimacy in
the eyes of their inhabitants, particularly among the educated
élites, who now identified their political and social ambitions with
them. This did not mean that they had abandoned their pre-colonial
identities; yet that part of the legacy of colonial rule that was called

less into question than any other by the nationalists was the framework of states superimposed on the pre-colonial polities by the invading European powers at the end of the nineteenth century. It was more the country-folk, particularly those whose lands had been arbitrarily split by the new European colonial frontiers, who tended to operate socially and even politically in terms of their pre-colonial structures.

On the eve of the Second World War, then, the *Pax Europaea* was firmly established in Africa. At one level it was a seemingly very tenuous peace, dependent on a handful of European administrators ruling over vast and populous areas with only a handful of African soldiers or para-military police at their disposal. Nigeria, for example, had only some 4000 soldiers and 4000 police in 1930, of whom all but about 75 in each force were black. Just how thin on the ground the European administrations were can be seen from the fact that in Nigeria in the late 1930s the number of administrators for a population estimated at 20 million was only 386, a ratio of 1:54000, and that included those in the secretariat. In the Belgian Congo the ratio was 1:34800 and in French West Africa 1:27500. It should not be forgotten, too, that in parts of the European colonial empire the colonial imprint was still very light. Many Africans had never personally seen a white man, while in Mozambique parts of the territory were not even administered by the government, but by concession companies.

The *Pax Europaea* established by the end of the 1930s was, of course, vital to the successful and intensive exploitation of the colonial estate by metropolitan capital. And by the 1930s the pre-colonial economic structure of Africa had been remodelled into a series of colonial economies whose common characteristic, whatever the nationality of their administration, was that they were producers of foodstuffs and raw materials for consumption or processing by the metropolitan and related economies; in turn they served as markets for the manufactured goods of European industry, many of them, like soap, processed from raw materials exported by these very colonial economies. The infrastructural pattern of the African colonies reflected clearly this function. Railways and roads were built primarily to link mines or areas of export-crop production with the coast; few were built to link one centre of production of crops or goods for internal consumption with another. The colonial administrations were handmaidens to

9

this exploitation, differing only in the degree of active assistance they gave in terms of taxation, forced labour or compulsory crop cultivation, and the extent to which they tried to protect the interests of their colonial subjects. Where private capital was unwilling to provide the infrastructural services it supplied in Europe, such as electrical power, railways and ports, the colonial governments raised the necessary funds for their establishment from the colonial budget either through taxation or loans. In short, by 1939 Africa had been integrated by colonial rule into the European capitalistic system and in turn had been impregnated with the capitalistic structure of the metropole, and such development that took place was mainly in those sectors producing for the export and import trade.[1] Any development of the internal exchange economy that resulted was largely co-incidental.

The extent and intensity of the incorporation of the African economy into the world capitalist system by 1939 varied from colony to colony and from region to region within individual colonies. This process had begun as early as the eighteenth century, but until the European occupation it affected principally those areas on the coast with which trade had already been opened up. The result of colonial occupation was to involve all Africans, however indirectly, in the world economy. The directness of their involvement was, of course, determined by the resources of the locality they lived in. By the beginning of our period the most intensively involved were the producers of crops such as groundnuts, palm-oil, cotton, cocoa, coffee and sisal for which there was a demand overseas. These crops had come to be produced in three distinct ways which were to have important effects on the course of the development of African nationalism. The first, predominant in West Africa, but also to be found in the Maghrib, Egypt and Uganda, was through the agency of peasant farmers. The second, predominant in Equatorial Africa and in parts of Central and southern Africa, was through company-owned plantations using wage and/or forced labour. The third was through farms run by white settlers using African wage-labour. Irrespective of nationality, the character of individual colonial administrations was deeply influenced by the modes of agricultural production to be found in their territories. Thus British admin-

[1] See the 'Introduction' to Peter C. W. Gutkind and Immanuel Wallerstein (eds.), *The political economy of contemporary Africa* (Beverly Hills and London, 1976), 11–12.

istration in Kenya with its settler-farmers, differed considerably from that in the Gold Coast, with its indigenous farmers. Where the principal means of agricultural production was through white settler-farmers, their interests were held paramount by the colonial administrations, as in Libya, Algeria and Southern Rhodesia. In colonies where settler-farmers and European-controlled plantations were jointly concerned as producers of export crops, as in Angola, Mozambique and the Belgian Congo, European interests were also held to be paramount. In colonies where there were substantial and influential settler groups who were not, however, seen as the principal or exclusive means of production of export crops, African interests were never entirely subordinated to them. Morocco, Tunisia, the Ivory Coast, Northern Rhodesia and Kenya fit into this category. Even with regard to Kenya, which in the popular British imagination was the white-settler colony *par excellence*, as early as 1923 a Conservative colonial secretary, the Duke of Devonshire, had laid down that:

Primarily Kenya is an African territory, and His Majesty's Government thinks it necessary definitely to record their considered opinion that the interests of the African natives must be paramount and that if, and when, those interests and the interests of the European races should conflict, the former should prevail... In the administration of Kenya, His Majesty's Government regard themselves as exercising a trust on behalf of the African population, and they are unable to delegate or share this trust, the object of which may be defined as the protection and advancement of the native races.[1]

In practice this of course only meant the protection of the African population from the more extreme forms of racial privilege exercised by the European settlers in Algeria and Southern Rhodesia, not from its overall subjection to the interests of the world capitalist economy. Nevertheless, in Tanganyika, for example, settlers were given financial support and preferential treatment even where it was clear from the statistics that African farmers were more productive.

Where white settlers and concession companies were insignificant compared with the African peasant farmer as a means of production of export crops, the political role of local Europeans was equally limited. It was in such colonies that decolonisation or disengagement was most easily achieved, as the cases of the Gold Coast, Nigeria, Upper Volta or Senegal witness. The most

[1] *Indians in Kenya*, Command paper No. 1922 (London, 1923), 9.

violent confrontations between Africans and colonial governments took place in those colonies where settler or concession-company interests were most deeply entrenched, as in Algeria, Southern Rhodesia or Mozambique.

Whatever the agency of production in a colony – white settler-farmer, plantation company or African farmer – those colonial dependencies most involved in the world capitalist economy and most directly subject to its fluctuations were those in which cultivation of crops for export had been most intensively developed.

By 1939, whatever the intensity of its production for the export market, three distinct zones of economic activity could be discerned in the continent.[1] The first, of course, was that devoted to the production of crops for export by whatever means, whether indigenous farming, forced-labour or wage-labour on European farms or concessions. Here African labour had been diverted from production of food for consumption for the home market to that for consumption overseas. A second zone, therefore, had developed in which a principal concern was production of food for consumption by the zone producing food for export. The third zone, which in other circumstances would have continued to concentrate on agriculture for domestic consumption, not having sufficient agricultural resources to produce surplus foodstuffs for the export or the internal market, had become the source of supply of labour for the farms of the first two zones. Such labour was forthcoming as a result of forced recruitment, as in the Portuguese colonies, the need to earn a wage in order to pay taxes, or through the desire of individuals who wished to take advantage of the economic opportunities provided by the colonial economy. This zone, of which Niger and Upper Volta or, on the other side of the continent, Nyasaland were obvious examples, was also a principal supplier of labour for mines, army, roads and railways. Thus few Africans escaped the impact of the colonial economy, whose most important political effect or by-product was the increasing peasantisation and proletarianisation of the erstwhile small-scale farmer. This was to be of crucial importance for the development of the nationalist movements which secured political independence from the colonial rulers. For it was from among this

[1] See Immanuel Wallerstein, 'Three stages of African involvement in the world economy', in Gutkind and Wallerstein, *Political economy*, 30–57.

class that an Nkrumah found his 'verandah boys' or a Samora Machel the recruits for the armies of FRELIMO.

Of equal importance, though sometimes disastrous in the effects on the well-being of those involved, were the long-term consequences of this massive transformation of the economies of Africa into dependent economies of the world capitalist system. In many cases this transformation led to an increase in production of crops for the export market that was detrimental, especially in the long-term, to the production of sufficient crops for domestic consumption.[1] A notorious example of this development was the Gambia, where a 'hungry season' resulted from over-concentration of labour and land on groundnuts, the chief export crop, to the detriment of rice, the main subsistence crop.

As Vieira da Silva and de Morais have shown for the Huambo District in Angola, the over-concentration on export crops led in the long-term to 'atrophy and decay' in the rural economy since the surplus derived from the production of the cash crop, maize, was not reinvested in the local eco-system, while soils that were allowed shorter and shorter fallows for regeneration deteriorated.[2] Such rural areas became less and less capable of supporting a local population that was in any case increasing as a result of improved and more readily available medical facilities, and their young men had increasingly to migrate in search of work. Huambo and the Gambia represent extreme examples of the effects of a colonial economic system whose principal concern was with meeting the demands of overseas markets for Africa's export crops, and which paid little, if any, attention to problems concerned with the production, distribution or improvement of subsistence crops.

This concern with cash-crop production was generalised throughout colonial Africa and reinforced by the taxation and labour policies of the colonial administrations, which compelled farmers to devote more and more energy, land and time to production of cash crops. Together these had important social consequences. They accelerated the growth of a plantation sub-proletariat and were a major factor in the massive migration

[1] See Chapter 5, where it is shown that by 1975 a majority of African countries were finding it increasingly difficult to feed themselves even though their economies were still primarily agricultural.

[2] Jorge Vieira da Silva and Julio Artur de Morais, 'Ecological conditions of social change in the central highlands of Angola', in Franz-Wilhelm Heimer (ed.), *Social change in Angola* (Munich, 1973).

to the towns that took place during the period covered by this volume and the consequent development of an urban sub-proletariat. They affected the relative roles of men and women in society: increasingly women were diverted from income-producing agricultural production to production of crops for domestic consumption.

If the long-term consequences of the colonial economic system were the impoverishment of many rural populations during our period and the increasing dependence of the farmer on crops whose prices were subject to wide fluctuations, for some sectors of colonial African society alien rule had brought positive benefits, in particular in the extension of education and ancillary social benefits. For while the main business of colonial rule may have been the exploitation of the resources of Africa for the benefit of the metropolitan economies, the colonial administrations in Africa were concerned, in differing degrees, to improve the lot of their populations. They certainly did not perceive, at the time, the long-term consequences of the economic structures that had developed by 1940. Indeed increases in export earnings by a colony seemed to augur well for it, since the duties imposed on these and the imports they made possible provided the where-withal to develop roads, and build bridges, hospitals and schools. It was these benefits as much as any distress caused by the colonial economic system that were to bring about the demise of colonial rule. Where the early opponents of colonial rule had been those who wished to regain their pre-colonial independences, the new opponents were those who had personally benefited most from the colonial system, the educated élite. The representatives of the pre-colonial polities – the chiefs – had now been absorbed into the colonial hierarchy as its most loyal collaborators. The educated élite, in challenging the colonial government, did not seek a return to the pre-colonial structures of Africa, but rather sought a share in the administration of the new colony–states. By 1940 few had gone as far as to demand control of the administration; independence was a word not openly bandied about except in the Maghrib and there only with caution. The western-educated élite, having reached, and in some cases surpassed, the intellectual attainments of their colonial administrators on those administra-tors' own terms, began to demand participation in the admini-stration. They were primarily concerned with the betterment of their position as a class, and paid little attention to the welfare of the rural masses, though they were to harness the rural by-product, the urban immigrants, to good effect in agitation against the colonial regime. The prevailing attitude of the educated élite in the late 1930s is summed up by the young lawyer, Obafemi Awolowo, who wrote in 1946 that 'the articulate minority is destined to rule the country. It is their heritage. It is they who must be trained in the art of government so as to enable them to take over complete control of the affairs of their country.'[1] It is this attitude that explains the hostility of the majority of the educated élite to the role of the chiefs in government, for they saw them as rivals for power, particularly in those British colonies, like Nigeria, where the system of indirect rule made it explicit that devolution of colonial power would be to the native authorities rather than to the educated élite.

Criticisms of the colonial structure, then, by 1940 had largely been limited to protests against its character, not its existence. These criticisms had been fuelled in part by the depressed level of the economy and consequent diminution of colonial services throughout the 1930s. At a time of rising expectations, based on the prosperity of the first two decades of the century when the terms of trade were in Africa's favour and peasant and trader had profited, the thirties, in which the terms of trade were dramatically reversed, brought disillusion with the positive aspects of colonial rule. This disillusion set in both among farmers who earned less and less from their crops and among the educated élite who found fewer openings in the colonial system – whether government or business – as diminishing revenues forced it to cut back its activities.

THE COURSE OF THE WAR ON AFRICAN SOIL

The extent to which the Second World War represented a turning point in the liberation of Africa from colonial rule, or merely acted as an accelerator to a process that was already under way, cannot be assessed without an appreciation of the impact of that war on the African continent itself.

Not long after the outbreak of war in Europe, the fighting was extended to Africa, just as it had been in the First World War.

[1] Obafemi Awolowo, *Path to Nigerian freedom* (London, 1947), 63.

Even before this, some 80000 African troops had been shipped from French Africa to Europe to fight against the Germans. Once Italy had entered the war on the side of Germany in May 1940 the security of the Suez route to the Far East was placed in jeopardy, with Italian forces in Libya posing a threat to Egypt, and those in the Horn of Africa to Kenya and the Sudan. With the fall of France in June 1940 the military situation in Africa became even more worrying to the British, as the administrations of French North and West Africa, Somali Coast and Madagascar opted for the Vichy regime, whose intentions as far as providing facilities for the German navy in its coastal colonies were not at all clear. The only coutervailing events were the decision by the black Guyanese Governor of Chad, Félix Eboué, to back General de Gaulle and the Free French, and his success in rallying the rest of Equatorial Africa and Cameroun to their cause with the assistance of military intervention from Free French forces based in Nigeria. The outcome was to secure an overland and air route for Britain and her allies from Accra and Lagos to Sudan and Egypt by way of Chad. This was to prove vital in the extended war in the Libyan desert. The destruction of the French fleet off the coast of Algeria at Mers-el-Kebir, and the shelling of the French battleship *Richelieu* in Dakar, relieved some of Britain's anxieties that the Germans might use the French fleet and increase the problems of communication with her colonies. However, the attempt by British and Free French forces to take Dakar in September 1940 failed ignominiously and did much to reduce de Gaulle's currency in the eyes of the Allies, though it did not, as feared, lead to Dakar being used as a German base as contemporary propaganda would have it.[1] Nevertheless the British in West Africa never felt secure on their borders until French West Africa declared for the Free French in November 1942.

In the Horn of Africa the Italians justified Britain's fears and invaded British Somaliland in August 1940, and also took Kassala in the Anglo-Egyptian Sudan and Moyale in Kenya. Despite the pathetically small British forces in this strategic area, the Italians were cautious in their invasion of both the Sudan and Kenya and did not prove the threat to the security of these colonies that they

[1] Michael Crowder, 'Vichy and Free France in West Africa during the Second World War', in *Colonial West Africa* (London, 1978), 274.

might have been. The initial British response, given their limited resources, was to order the recapture of Kassala and to give assistance to the Ethiopian patriots who were still resisting the recent Italian occupation. Kassala was taken in January 1941, and despite the four-to-one numerical superiority of the Italian forces over the British, the latter advanced into Italian East Africa and by 17 May they had effectively gained control over the Horn. Addis Ababa, which was taken in early April, was the scene a month later of the first act in the decolonisation of the European empires that was to take place over the next 35 years. On 5 May, 1941, Haile Selassie returned to his imperial capital, exactly five years to the day after it had been occupied by the Italians. It was, however, not uncharacteristic of the way decolonisation unfolded that the British insisted on retaining certain controls over his government, in particular in the Ogaden region. But it was also significant that this act of decolonisation was achieved with the assistance of African soldiers from both East and West Africa. The participation of Nigerian soldiers in this campaign was celebrated by the Hausa poet Sa'adu Zungur.

> The Nigerians cleaved through to the Somali corner without halting.
> The Ethiopians drank freely in city, in encampment and in village.
> Their enemy was knocked out. Ethiopia's troubles were over.[1]

With the expulsion of the Italians from East Africa, the main theatre of war became North Africa. There the Germans and Italians came close to occupying Egypt, almost reaching Alexandria. They were eventually driven back after the battle of El Alamein. Thereafter the war see-sawed back and forth in Libya, causing immense destruction in urban areas. The Germans and Italians were not finally expelled until after the joint American–British landings in North Africa in September 1942. While Morocco and Algeria were quickly taken from their Vichy administrations by the Allies, Tunisia, which for a short time was under German administration, became a battlefield suffering great devastation in its cities and towns. The last German and Italian forces were driven out of North Africa in 1943, and the Italian colonists in Libya were interned.

Madagascar was invaded by British forces and occupied between May and December 1942. The whole of French Africa was

---

[1] Sa'adu Zungur, 'Welcome to the soldiers', in Dandatti Abdulkadir, *The poetry, life and opinions of Sa'adu Zungur* (Zaria, 1974), 41.

eventually placed under Free French administration, though in North Africa de Gaulle ruled very much as a client of the Americans, a point not lost on the nationalists. France was given the administration of the Italian Saharan territory of Fezzan, which linked her Equatorial and North African colonies, while Britain administered the coastal territories of Tripolitania and Cyrenaica.

In contrast to the First World War, the Second did not lead to any redrawing of the map of Africa. Nor did any of the victors make long-term colonial acquisitions. However, during the war Britain did entertain ambitions with regard to the Italian colonies which she had conquered and which she certainly did not want returned to Italy or given to any power that might once again threaten the security of her imperial communications. But such ambitions were thwarted by American hostility towards any expansion of the British empire, or the granting to her of any open-ended trusteeship.[1] As it was, Ethiopia, as we have seen, regained an independence only recently lost; the Italian colony of Eritrea was placed under temporary British administration, and federated with Ethiopia in 1952. Somalia, administered by the British from 1941 to 1950, was given back to the Italians as a United Nations Trust Territory with a specific obligation to prepare it for independence within a decade; the Libyan provinces of Tripolitania and Cyrenaica were administered by Britain, and Fezzan by France until 1951 when, at the insistence of the United Nations, they became together independent as the Kingdom of Libya.

The majority of the African colonies controlled by Britain and France did not, of course, become directly involved in the hostilities. Yet they were much more obviously affected by the course of the war than they had been during the First World War. Apart from the increased sophistication of the technology available to the combatants, more particularly in the form of longer-range submarines and aircraft that made any territory potentially vulnerable, many cities and towns remote from theatres of war served as staging posts for soldiers and supplies. Improved means of mass-communication and the progress, albeit slow, of western education between the wars, meant that a much larger segment

---

[1] See William Roger Louis, *Imperialism at bay: 1941–1945: the United States and the decolonisation of the British Empire* (Oxford, 1977).

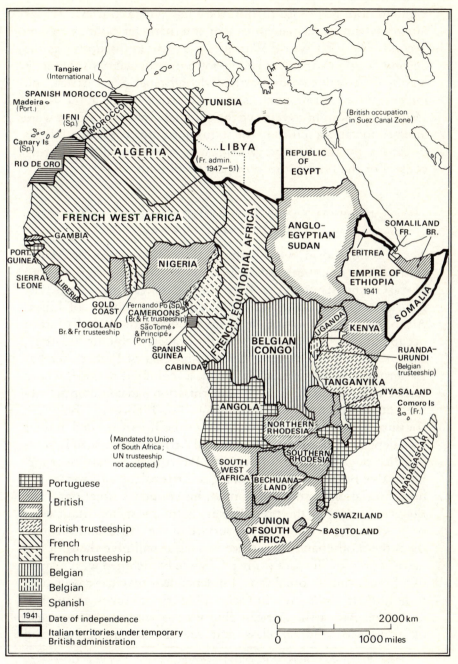

3   Africa, 1946.

of the African population was aware of the issues involved. In a much more real sense than in the First World War Africa was integrated into the mainstream of international politics by the Second. The First World War, it is true, was as disruptive as the Second World War in Africa, if not more so, accompanied as it was by wide-scale revolts, particularly in French West Africa, and millennial movements such as that of Garrick Braide in the Niger Delta which sought to remove the colonial power. But these were directed towards a return to the status quo ante. The forces stirred in Africa by the Second World War were aimed at securing control of the houses the Europeans had built.

THE IMPACT OF THE SECOND WORLD WAR ON THE COLONIAL POWERS

The Second World War shattered the colonial calm of Africa. Within a year of its outbreak Belgium and France had been overrun by the Germans. Soon after, Italy was dispossessed first of her East African empire and then of her North African colony of Libya. Although Britain did not suffer invasion and the humiliation of occupation by her opponents as did France, Belgium and Italy, she knew the bitter taste of defeat. Like that of France, her Far Eastern empire was seized by Japan, a 'coloured nation', whose earlier successes in the field of modernisation had contemptuously been attributed to skills of imitation. For France and Belgium, continued existence as independent entities briefly resided in their own dependencies: French Equatorial Africa in the case of France, and the Congo in the case of Belgium. Pierre Ryckmans, Governor-General of Belgium's Congo estate, was to declare with apparently no appreciation of the true irony of his country's situation: 'The Belgian Congo, in the present war, is the most important asset of Belgium. It is entirely at the service of the Allies, and through them the motherland. If she needs men, it will give them; if she needs work, it will work for her.'[1] While Frenchmen with visions of a France once more free and independent may have been able to hold their heads high in their Equatorial colonies, in the rest of French Africa the African élite was to witness the spectacle of a divided colonial class and see the recriminations and

[1] Pierre Ryckmans in June 1940, cited by George Martelli, *Leopold to Lumumba: a history of the Belgian Congo 1877–1960* (London, 1962), 201.

retributions visited upon those who had made the mistake of backing the Vichy horse too openly. In Dakar they were to be told that the venerable Marshal Pétain, who had led France to ultimate victory in the First World War with the massive assistance of African conscripts, was now a fallen idol, while General de Gaulle, presented as their liberator, had to be given special protection on his first visit to Dakar in case relatives of those killed during his abortive raid of 1940 should seek vengeance.

Of the European imperial powers in Africa only Spain and Portugal emerged from the war relatively unscathed, with the latter gaining some profit from the boom that the war generated in the demand for the products of its African colonies. The others, whose self-confidence had already received a body-blow as a result of the prolonged depression of the thirties, had now suffered the humiliation of defeat, a fact which they knew did not escape their better educated subjects. Subsequent victories were not sufficient to restore respect. The myth of colonial invincibility was destroyed, and the self-confidence of the colonial powers and administrators who sustained this myth dissipated. The colonial emperor had no clothes. This was a truth that was to be realised by the colonised Africans only dimly at first but with increasing clarity over the next thirty years. It was, however, a truth that was not at all apparent in the colonies of those two powers that were not directly involved in the war: Portugal and Spain. Their subjects were to remain insulated from the early winds of change that were blowing elsewhere in Africa by harshly repressive and economically backward regimes.

The dependence of the belligerent colonial powers on their colonies for survival was not only psychological and political, but military and economic, as Ryckmans made so clear. Even though Britain retained her territorial integrity, her continued existence and her struggle against the Germans and Japanese were dependent in some measure on supplies of produce and troops from her African colonies. After the fall of Malaya to the Japanese the raw materials of her African colonies became even more vital to her war effort. This dependence on her colonial empire was made quite explicit in the promises she made to the Indian peoples of independent dominion status after the war in return for cooperation during it, and in the propaganda designed to convince her African colonial populations that support during the war would reap its rewards in social, economic and political reforms after it had been won. Indeed, as we shall see, some of these reforms were actually initiated during the course of the war itself. France also was to make explicit her sense of obligation, of a debt that had to be repaid, to her African colonies at the Brazzaville Conference of 1944, where a bold outline for economic, social, legal and political reform was approved by the Free French administration. In the Belgian Congo, too, promises of social and economic reform were made, though political change was not on the agenda.

The official enunciations concerning the future of the colonial empires in Africa in no way questioned the basis of the colonial relationship. Winston Churchill specifically stated that the clause in the Atlantic Charter, which he signed with President Roosevelt, affirming 'the right of all people to choose the form of government in which they live' and hoping 'to see sovereign rights and self-government restored to those who have been forcibly deprived of them', did not apply to the African colonies. He also made it quite clear that he had not become 'the King's First Minister in order to preside over the liquidation of the British Empire'. Similarly the Free French stated categorically that the future of France's African territories was not to be 'self-government', but rather greater political freedom within the framework of a 'greater France'. Indeed the assurance of the survival of their colonial empires in the post-war world formed a bond between Churchill and de Gaulle,[1] who saw France's empire as the guarantee of her continuing status as a world power. There was, however, a basic difference between the two colonial powers in that Britain did accept that decolonisation of her empire was inevitable, even if this would take place only in some very distant future as far as her African colonies were concerned. Britain also had within the walls of its Colonial Office a group of 'reformers' who were determined to bring that future nearer.

Nevertheless both within the metropolitan countries themselves and increasingly in the United States of America, the whole colonial relationship and the right of one people to dominate another even in the short term was being questioned. In Britain, the war gave an edge to those within the Colonial Office who favoured reform and who, though they still believed that the

[1] Louis, *Imperialism at bay*, 27.

African colonies needed a great deal more social and economic development before they could be accorded even modest measures of self-government, felt that more positive steps should be taken to prepare them for political responsibility within a foreseeable future as distinct from one that had been merely nebulous. Within the government itself, Clement Attlee, Churchill's deputy and the leader of the Labour Party, protested against the holding of colonies for the financial advantage which 'mainly accrued to a capitalist group'.[1] The West Indian riots of 1938 had strengthened the hand of those who advocated reform in the Colonial Office and a former Indian State governor like Hailey had already perceived what many of the men on the spot had not yet seen, that Africa was a continent of 'rapid change, and greater changes impending'. He also asked the question as to whether the colonial authorities could 'be sure of the continuance of that degree of acquiescence in our rule which is a necessary condition of administrative progress'.[2] In the correspondence columns of *The Times*, Margery Perham regularly expressed the growing unease that thinking Britons concerned with the colonial empire were beginning to feel about their record. This unease was heightened by the open attacks made not only on that record but on the very idea of empire by the Americans, epitomised by the broadcast of Wendell Wilkie on his visit to London in November 1942 when he spoke of 'the necessity of abolishing imperialism'.[3] In this he was merely echoing the views of President Roosevelt and important elements within his administration who feared that the greatest danger to the stability of the post-war world would come from the re-establishment of a powerful British empire. The British, in turn, suspected that the motivation for American attacks on her empire came from a desire to secure freer access to her colonial markets. There was also the anomaly that America did not consider that her overseas possessions of Hawaii, the Philippines and Puerto Rico constituted an empire.

There was a certain bitterness that such attacks were directed primarily at the British, while the French seemed to escape unscathed. But this was not in fact the case. If anything, as William

[1] *Ibid.*, 33, citing minutes of ministerial meeting of 11 September 1942.
[2] Introductory chapter to *Native administration and political development in British tropical Africa*, confidentially printed, 1942, cited in John D. Hargreaves, *The end of colonial rule in West Africa* (London, 1978), 15.
[3] Margery Perham, *Colonial sequence 1930–1949* (London, 1967), 237.

Roger Louis points out, Roosevelt was more hostile to the French as a colonial power than to the British.[1] He did not want Indo-China to be returned to the French after the Japanese had been defeated, so poor a view did he have of France's colonial record there. At the very least he felt that restoration of Indo-China to French administration should be conditional on independence being made the long-term goal of policy there. American criticisms of French colonialism strengthened the position of those Free French politicians and administrators who wanted to see improvements in their economic and social policies in the African colonies, and it is significant that the promises of political, economic and social reform made at the Brazzaville Conference on the future of France's African colonies were a major factor in persuading a reluctant Roosevelt to accept the legitimacy of France's position in Indo-China.

In Britain the official mind never quite got over the shock of the realisation that the fate not only of the empire but also of the metropolis now hung militarily and financially on the whim of the ex-colonial ally.[2] The fear in Whitehall was that the Americans might make liquidation of the colonial empire a condition of support. And while this fear was not in the event realised, the threat was always there that anti-colonialism in America might put pressure on the colonial powers to prepare their subjects for independence under international supervision. And as Robinson points out, it was 'no accident that from 1943 the British began to liberalise their arrangements in order to appease American anti-colonialism'.[3] While in neither France nor Britain was there any intention of abandoning their African empires, an image that was so clearly tarnished in the eyes of Americans as well as of domestic critics of empire was given a polish and new names and formulae were produced to emphasise a change in the colonial relationship. In the case of Britain it was the replacement of the paternalistic concept of 'trusteeship' by that of 'partnership' and in the case of France the nominal transformation of the 'empire' into a 'union' and of 'colonies' into '*territoires d'outre mer*', and '*indigènes*' into '*autochtones*'.

[1] Louis, *Imperialism at bay*, Chapter 2.
[2] Ronald Robinson, 'Andrew Cohen and the transfer of power in Tropical Africa, 1940–1951', in W. H. Morris-Jones and Georges Fischer (eds.), *Decolonisation and after: the British and French experience* (London, 1980), 53.
[3] *Ibid.*, 54.

Whilst the political relationship was in neither case fundamentally altered during the war, political reforms were initiated that, as we shall later see, can be held with the advantage of hindsight to have led inevitably along the path to independence. And to prove to the Americans in particular that their empire really did have a new image, both France and Britain elaborated programmes of social and economic reform that marked a turning point in the history of their colonial rule. France introduced the ambitious FIDES (Fonds d'Investissement et de Développement Économique et Social) at Brazzaville, emphasising that the 'object of our colonial policy must be the development of the productive potential of the overseas territories and the growth of their wealth so as to assure the Africans of a better life by raising their purchasing power and improving standards of living...',[1] while Britain's Colonial Development and Welfare Act of 1945, reflecting the increased acceptance of the ideas of J. M. Keynes, set aside £120 million for post-war development and welfare in the colonies over a ten-year period. This greatly increased the £5 million a year set aside by the 1940 Colonial Development and Welfare Act. Here is perhaps the best illustration of a situation that was accelerated by the war rather than initiated by it. Although in 1929 the British government had made available through the Colonial Development Act up to £1 million a year in the form of loans or grants to the whole of the dependent empire, this was primarily designed to boost the British economy, and did not greatly affect the British policy that the colonies were to be economically self-supporting. It was the 1940 Act that marked the real turning point in the economic relationship between Britain and her colonies. And that Act of course had its roots in a pre-war situation and was being discussed within the Colonial Office before the outbreak of war. Nevertheless, as R. D. Pearce points out, it needed not only the recommendations of Lord Moyne in his report on the West Indian disturbances, but 'the ideological requirements of a war against Nazi Germany, to jolt the Treasury from its habitual parsimonious habits'.[2] As Malcolm MacDonald told the cabinet when presenting his proposals for colonial development and welfare: 'A continuation

[1] Cited in J. D. Hargreaves (ed.), *France and West Africa: an anthology of historical documents* (London, 1969), 239.

[2] R. D. Pearce, *The turning point in Africa: British colonial policy 1938–1948* (London, 1982), 21.

of the present state of affairs would be wrong on merit and it provides our enemies and critics with an admirable subject for propaganda...'[1] That this Act marked an end to a relationship between Britain and her colonies that was largely an extractive one, and one in which colonies had to pay for themselves, was made clear in Sir Bernard Bourdillon's speech as governor to the Nigerian Legislative Council when introducing the Colonial Development and Welfare Act in 1940. He assured his council that it was 'a development of the utmost importance', indicating that the doctrine of the self-sufficiency of individual colonies was now 'dead'.[2] FIDES on the other hand was much more specifically a by-product of the war and American pressures in particular, and represented a real *point de départ*, for although France had initiated a programme of public works in the colonies in 1931, this was done by means of a loan, not a grant. The Belgians, too, were affected by this concern to refurbish the image of empire, and whilst they had no intention of making political concessions in their Congo, they did initiate an ambitious development programme with a strong welfare content.

Russian critiques of empire gave the colonial powers less immediate concern than those of their American allies. Because of the political system from which they emanated, they were less morally wounding, though there was to be more concern as to their potential political effect on the colonial subjects themselves. The British had already been nervous about the Communist connexions of I. T. A. Wallace-Johnson in Sierra Leone and had placed him under restricted residence during the war. Though the French allowed *groupes d'études communistes* to be formed freely in their tropical African empire in the last years of the war, once the Communists had left the French government in May 1947, continuing affiliations between African politicians and the French Communist Party were the occasion for official repression of these politicians even though the party was as politically assimilationist as any other French party.

During the war there were widespread calls for placing the colonial empires under some form of international supervision. These were stoutly resisted by both Churchill and de Gaulle. Some Americans went so far as to suggest the establishment of

[1] *Ibid.*, 21.
[2] Jeremy White, *Central administration in Nigeria, 1914–1948* (Dublin and London, 1981), 233.

international trusteeships for all the colonial dependencies. Roosevelt felt that at least those colonial territories liberated by American arms should be placed under trusteeship. There was debate as to whether this trusteeship should consist of the supervision of the administration of the existing colonial power or the establishment of international administrations of which that in Tangier was cited as being a not very happy example. It was not only the Americans who advocated the extension of the idea of trusteeship to all colonial dependencies; support for such a move came from Australia, New Zealand, Russia, and Indian nationalists. As it was these plans never came to fruition. The Yalta Agreement specifically excluded such a solution. Even moves to put teeth into the existing mandates were resisted by Churchill, and in particular Jan Smuts, Prime Minister of South Africa, who feared the consequences for his own country's racial policies of close supervision of the South West African mandate. Nevertheless, the new United Nations Organisation, as successor to the League of Nations, was able to put some bite into its new system of trusteeships which replaced the former mandates. Where the Permanent Mandates Commission had had no right of inspection, the new Trusteeship Council had the right to send out Visiting Missions to the Trust Territories. Furthermore, inhabitants of these territories could appeal to the council over the heads of the colonial administering authority. Above all, in renewing the mandate as a trust, the United Nations gave the administering power the specific obligation of 'the progressive development towards independence' of its Trust Territory. Only South Africa refused to accept these innovations with regard to its South West African mandate.

As far as the colonial empires themselves were concerned, the United Nations charter nowhere specified independence as a goal for the 'non-self-governing territories', as the imperial dependencies were described. Yet the United Nations was to provide a forum in which the record of individual colonial powers could be challenged or condemned. But the sense of international accountability with which at least Britain, France, Holland and Belgium emerged after the war was not so much a structural as a moral one. Where before the war empire had still been a matter for pride, now it was increasingly seen as an embarrassment, something which needed constantly to be justified.

The Second World War, then, saw a dramatic change not only

in the standing of the great colonial powers in the world but also in their attitudes about their responsibilities towards their colonies. Britain, France and Belgium ended the war with their economies on the verge of ruin. Britain alone had overseas debts of over £3500 million. All three were dependent for their post-war rehabilitation on massive aid from America. Britain and France had lost their previous pre-eminence in international affairs to the two new super-powers, America and Russia, both of which, for different reasons, were hostile to the continued existence of the European colonial empires. And while France and Britain continued to be treated as world powers, they had in reality lost the strength to be so. Of the European imperial powers in Africa, only Spain and Portugal emerged relatively unscathed, and unaffected by the new and hostile international climate with regard to imperialism.

None of this, however, was immediately apparent. The immediate aftermath of the war saw a determined effort by the successful belligerent governments to renew their colonial missions. They were determined to be their own trustees as to the future of their colonial empires. Indeed in the British, French and Belgian colonies in Africa there followed after the war what might be called a second colonisation of Africa as technicians and experts flooded into the colonies to implement ambitious development schemes designed both to improve the lot of the colonial subjects and to help revitalise the metropolitan economies. Cathérine Coquéry-Vidrovitch has described the period from 1946 to 1952 as 'the great years of French colonial imperialism'.[1] Nevertheless, while both Britain and France may have fought the war to preserve their empires and, at least at the government level, continued to have faith in the imperial mission after the war, those who did the actual fighting, as A. J. P. Taylor has written of the British, 'had simpler aims. They fought to liberate the peoples of Europe from Germany and those of the Far East from Japan. The British did not relinquish their Empire by accident. They ceased to believe in it.'[2] And the post-war world proved this point; once the will to maintain empire was lost, colonial dependencies were either voluntarily ceded to their inhabitants or the empire

[1] Cathérine Coquéry-Vidrovitch, 'La Mise en dépendance de l'Afrique noire: essai de périodisation, 1880–1970', *Cahiers d'études africaines*, 1976, **16**, 39.
[2] Cited in the preface to Louis, *Imperialism at bay*, x.

collapsed. This latter was what happened in the Belgian Congo and was perhaps epitomised in the Portuguese African empire. There the very soldiers sent to defend it ceased to believe that it was either worth defending or even possible to defend.

After the war, then, the question appeared more and more to be how to extricate oneself from empire without losing the investment one had made in it, or else how to transform that empire into a political entity that could both withstand the critics of empire and satisfy the erstwhile colonial subjects themselves. The British chose the path of independence within a largely sentimental Commonwealth, the French that of political transformation of empire into a somewhat more structured community. The Italians had no choice in the matter when Somalia was returned to them. The Belgians stubbornly refused to read the signs of the times, with disastrous consequences. Significantly Portugal and Spain, the two powers least affected by the war, were as yet still insulated from these currents, both political pariahs in a democratic post-war world. Yet in 1952 when Portugal applied for membership of the United Nations, she reconstituted her colonies as overseas provinces in order that they should be immunised from UN discussion as being properly domestic concerns. When Spain was finally admitted to the United Nations on 14 December 1955, in the same year that Portugal was admitted, she was already preparing to divest herself of the most important part of her African empire, Spanish Morocco, whose independence she recognised the following April.

THE IMPACT OF THE SECOND WORLD WAR ON AFRICANS

Colonial historians, as Cherry Gertzel points out, like to see the transfer of power as a process whereby Europeans *granted* Africans independence, while African historians see it as one in which the nationalists *took* their freedom.[1] The truth of the matter in most cases lies somewhere in between. It is, however, fair to say that while the Second World War brought about demonstrable changes in the attitudes of the belligerent powers towards the way in which they administered their African subjects and placed them on the defensive about empire, generally it produced no

[1] See Chapter 7.

corresponding overt change in the attitudes of the colonial élites towards their imperial masters.

By and large in Africa, the war was an occasion for declarations of loyalty, coupled of course with the hope of reward in the form of a quickening of the pace of constitutional reform. Habib Bourguiba, who had been imprisoned by the French in 1938 for his nationalist activities, when brought back to Tunisia by the Germans in the hopes of playing off his nationalism against the Allies, made the following appeal in May 1943 to the Tunisian people:

Today you must close ranks behind France... Without France there is no hope of salvation; it is on her success that the future of our country depends. I am convinced that the French nation, once freed from the Nazi yoke, will not forget her true friends, those who stood by her in her hour of trial. What matters most now is to win the war.[1]

But even where independence was on the nationalist agenda as in French North Africa, demands for reform were still aimed at advance within a parliamentary framework to be achieved by negotiation rather than confrontation. Elsewhere the achievement of responsible government and independence were as yet still dimly perceived goals. Indeed the political reforms introduced during and immediately after the war by the British and French were generally in advance of those as yet envisaged by the colonial élites as attainable. But no sooner had these reforms been presented than they were declared inadequate. Colonial governments either had to respond with further concessions that hastened the pace of constitutional advance beyond that planned for, or resort to repression. They usually only took the latter course where such concessions appeared to jeopardise settler interests.

The solution to the conundrum of whether the imperial powers gave Africans independence or whether Africans took it lies, perhaps, here in the Second World War. There is a case to be made that, up until the conclusion of that war, Britain and France (except in her North African territories) were making the running constitutionally and that their concessions had till that time been sufficient to assuage the as yet limited demands of the colonial élites. Thereafter it was increasingly the nationalists who made the running, forcing the hands of the colonial governments to

[1] Cited in Henri Grimal, *Decolonization: the British, French, Dutch and Belgian empires, 1919–1963*, trans. Stephen de Vos (London, 1977), 117.

respond with concession or repression. The latter, as it turned out, in itself merely strengthened the determination with which these nationalists and their supporters pressed their demands.

The war may be said to have matured nationalism. It exposed its pioneers to a range of influences much broader than those that had been able to penetrate the enclosed colonial world of the 1930s. It created new social and economic conditions which the nationalists were able to exploit in order to persuade the colonial governments that they had growing support for their cause. In turn these new conditions put pressure on the nationalists to radicalise their programmes and make more urgent their demands for social reform and constitutional advance.

Those on whom the war had the most direct impact were, of course, those enlisted with the armies of the belligerent powers. As in the First World War, African soldiers drawn from every corner of the continent administered by the Allies played a vital role in the defeat of the Italians and Germans. As many as 80 000 French African soldiers had been fighting on the European front when France fell to the Germans. Soldiers from French Equatorial Africa, and later from French West Africa and Madagascar, when they rejoined the Allied cause, fought in the North African campaigns and the Middle East. The British recruited heavily in all their African colonies, including their mandated territory of Tanganyika, for service in the East African campaign. Recruits were required both as soldiers and as military labour. As demand for recruits rose, voluntary enlistment was increasingly replaced by some measure of conscription, in French, Belgian and British territories. Many potential draftees fled rather than face the rigours of military labour, so vivid were the memories in some areas of the hardships and mortalities resulting from the conscriptions of the First World War. African troops were also shipped by the British to India for service in the Burma campaign, where they were used both as infantry and carriers, and played a conspicuous part in the defeat of the Japanese. In all, around a million troops and carriers, including some non-white non-combatants from South Africa, were used in the war; allowing for casualties this meant that a huge number of young men returned to their homes with very much widened horizons, having in many cases learnt trades and other skills, in particular how to read and write. They returned with heightened expectations, and it is significant that the Accra riots of 1948 that led inexorably to the independence of Ghana were triggered by an ex-serviceman's demonstration against living conditions. There have been many testimonies to the educative impact of the war on African soldiers, forced from their villages by one form of compulsion or another – few were true volunteers even in those British territories where allegedly all recruitment was on a volunteer basis.

Joyce Cary, who had observed the impact of the First World War on remote Nigerian Borgu, also wrote about the impact of the Second World War on African troops:

But this war, far more than the last, must change Africa. The natives who now again come together belong to a new age and generation. Many more have the beginnings of education; nearly all have heard of cooperate and political action. Although as soldiers they may stand aside from revolutionary movements, they are making comparisons between wages, conditions and hopes. The Cape half-caste driver meets the Gold Coast farmer with free cooperatives and his independent status in a country without a colour-bar; the Nigerian Moslem sees, through the eyes of an Indian hillman, the fraternity of Islam; the Congo mechanic describes to some East Coast pagan the garden village built for him by the paternal despots of the 'Union Minière Belgique'.[1]

Their view of the colonial relationship was also altered by their experiences in the war. As Ndabaningi Sithole wrote:

World War II...has had a great deal to do with the awakening of the peoples of Africa. During the war the African came in contact with practically all the peoples of the earth. He met them on a life and death struggle basis. He saw the so-called civilised and peaceful and orderly white people mercilessly butchering one another just as his so-called savage ancestors had done in tribal wars. He saw no difference between the primitive and civilised man. In short, he saw through European pretensions that only Africans were savages. This had a revolutionising psychological impact on the African.[2]

The full impact of the return of the ex-servicemen on the nationalist movement in Africa has yet to be assessed. Though comparatively few took leading roles in the formation of political parties, and were in the case of French-speaking Africa to prove a conservative force politically in the late 1950s, they did fuel the social ferment in the urban centres, in which many of them settled in preference to returning to their villages. These urban centres were to prove the most fertile recruiting ground for mass parties. Where the colonial response to nationalist demands was repression,

[1] Joyce Cary, *The case for African freedom and other writings* (London, 1944), 152–3.
[2] Ndabaningi Sithole, *African nationalism* (London, 1959), 19.

and the reaction was armed uprising, it is not clear how far knowledge of modern weapons acquired during the war was a significant factor. Perhaps the most important result of the war for these soldiers and carriers was the broadening of their experience, particularly for those who had served in Europe and the Far East. Not only were they told that they were fighting to preserve freedom and democracy, but in India they witnessed fellow colonial subjects protesting against Britain's own restrictions on their political freedom. Many soldiers received rudimentary literary or technical education and a significant factor in the post-war enthusiasm for education, particularly in areas that had hitherto been indifferent to it, was the return of soldiers whose experiences in the world outside their villages had taught them its value.

Africa contributed manpower for the Allied war effort not only in the form of soldiers and military labour, but through the involvement of millions of men and women in the increased production of those crops which were needed to feed the troops as well as civilians in Europe. Once the Japanese had overrun the British and Dutch colonies in South East Asia, Africa became the only source of palm-oil for the Allies, while her tin, rubber and sisal came under increased demand. Even the neutral Portuguese territories were affected by the boom in demand for sisal. This demand for Africa's raw materials was secured not by higher prices, but in many cases by various forms of coercion, including conscription on to plantations or into the mines. Nomads were forced to sell cattle. But of course the increased demands for agricultural production conflicted with the requirements of the army, which sought the ablest-bodied young men who would normally have been involved in agricultural production. Coercion of labour was justified, where it was felt necessary to do so, in the name of Africa's contribution to the fight for freedom. Another equally important form of 'coercion' was inflation. Severe restrictions on important goods led to steep rises in their prices, while prices paid to farmers for agricultural exports were controlled. The result was that metropolitan companies and their local agents acquired cash crops cheaply and sold imported goods at high prices, while the farmer had to produce more if he were to be able to purchase them. Ironically the Vichy regime in West Africa, unable to export because of the Allied naval blockade, was much more benign from the point of view of the African peasant than its Free French successor, which was determined to secure a French stake in victory by contributions from its African territories, and did not hesitate to force peasants to produce the crops the Allies needed.

Once the Far Eastern colonies had been lost to the Allies, Africa became of increased strategic and economic importance. Freetown, with its deep-water port, and later Dakar, Monrovia, Accra, Lagos, Port Harcourt and inland towns like Kano and Fort Lamy provided staging posts to the Sudan and Egypt for the campaigns in North Africa. Later the campaign in the Far East involved considerable developments to the ports of Dar es Salaam and Mombasa, and Diego Suarez after the Vichy regime in Madagascar had been overthrown. These ports and other points strategic to the Allied war effort grew at a rapid rate with large-scale immigration from the countryside. The population of Léopoldville, for instance, increased from 40 000 inhabitants in 1939 to 110 000 in 1945. Workers required in airport and dock construction, and in the factories that processed goods that could not be obtained from Europe because of the submarine war, often lived in intolerable conditions in bidonvilles from Casablanca to Lagos. In North Africa these conditions were exacerbated by disastrous harvests from 1942 to 1945. The last was one-third or less than the pre-war harvest. That year Morocco lost half its sheep and Algeria almost three-quarters. The increasing proletarianism and peasantisation that accompanied the war effort, and in particular the often appalling conditions in the cities, created an unprecedented socio-economic situation ripe for nationalists to exploit.

Although the war brought with it heightened economic activity, from some perspectives the colonial economy underwent little change. Terms of trade, effectively, remained unfavourable to the African producer. In some parts of Africa the effects of the recession of the 1930s were intensified by the impediments to importing and exporting occasioned by the war at sea. And where demand for African produce rose it was not reflected in rises in price. Prices were strictly controlled by the colonial governments who retained the difference between the price paid to the producers and that obtained on the world market and used it to develop reserves that helped to finance the war effort. This was to set an important precedent for post-war governments, both colonial and independent, which continued to control the prices paid to farmers for their produce, usually to the latter's disadvantage. The reserves that were built up immediately after the war were used for development projects, many of them not of immediate benefit to farmers, and henceforth the latter carried an undue share of the tax burden in their countries.

In Belgian and French Africa much of the peasants' produce was requisitioned. The obnoxious forms of the pre-war colonial economy were intensified. Forced labour and compulsory crop cultivation, all imposed in the name of the war effort, meant that many African producers earned less than ever for their labour. Furthermore the cost of imported goods rose higher and higher as a result of shortages. Where prices for primary products and wages did increase they only served to reinforce an inflationary situation because of these shortages. In one respect, however, significant permanent changes did take place in the colonial economy. Before the war the processing of raw materials – mineral and agricultural–was carried out almost exclusively in Europe. During the war a substantial number of factories was established in the major African cities to process locally produced materials that hitherto had been imported in their finished state from Europe. These factories marked the beginning of the industrialisation that nationalists after the war became so anxious to develop as a way of lessening dependence on the metropolitan countries. In turn this industrial development led to the formation in many African cities of a significant wage-labour class which was to provide an important recruiting ground for the rising nationalist parties.

The expansion of the colonial economies during the war and the enlistment of many Europeans of war-service age into the armed forces led to an unprecedented expansion of business opportunities for Africans both on their own account and in the employ of the expatriate companies. These *nouveaux bourgeois* were to join forces with the nationalists and to provide the finances needed for sustaining the political movements that expanded in the wake of the political reforms made by the French and the British at the end of the war.

The aspirations of the African political élites were heightened by the war, but in sub-Saharan Africa at least these were still limited to reform of the colonial political process and an increase in the level of their participation in it. There were few demands for independence made by African political leaders as a result of the defensive position belligerent colonial powers now found themselves in. As Sylvia Leith-Ross, who was sent out to Nigeria during the war as an intelligence officer, observed: 'There were no loud protestations of loyalty to the British but equally no flagrant advantage was taken of our plight.'[1] In some colonies Africans actually made financial contributions to fund-raising schemes designed to assist the Allied war effort. In North Africa the situation was more delicate for the colonial powers. The nationalist cause, fuelled by Pan-Arabism, was much more advanced than in sub-Saharan Africa and had already resulted in violence in all three French territories. Independence as a goal, albeit still a long-term one, was already on the nationalist agenda. Although the initial reaction of the élites in French North Africa to the fall of France had been one of shock, and although the Vichy regime had been well received because of the prestige of Marshal Pétain, rationing and rises in prices increased discontent with the French authorities. To the propaganda of Pan-Arabism was added that of Germany. The Destour Party in Tunisia, as well as the country's new Bey, Moncef, flirted with the Germans. In nominally independent Egypt a number of politicians supported the Axis powers as a means of countering British political and military control. Once the Free French had taken over control in Tunisia as a result of the Allied landings in North Africa, Moncef Bey was deposed. But as Jean Ganiage has observed, 'plus que ses rélations avec l'Allemagne, Moncef avait payé de sa destitution ses manifestations d'indépendence à l'égard de la France'.[2] In Morocco Sultan Mohammed ben Youssef met with President Roosevelt as a fellow head of state on 22 January 1943, and the tenor of the meeting was such that the sultan foresaw a new future for his country as a result of Roosevelt's anti-colonial attitudes. A new party regrouping the hitherto divided nationalists and with discreet support from the palace was founded under the name Istiqlal, the party of independence. In Algeria in 1943, Ferhat Abbas issued the Algerian Manifesto calling for the creation of

[1] Sylvia Leith-Ross, *Stepping-stones: memoirs of colonial Nigeria 1907–1960* (London, 1983), 110.
[2] Jean Ganiage, 'L'Afrique du nord', in Jean Ganiage, Hubert Deschamps and Odette Guitard, *L'Afrique au XXe siècle* (Paris, 1966), 162.

an autonomous, democratic Algerian state which would have a federal relationship with France. In all three Maghrib territories, America's championing of the cause of subject peoples and the loss of respect for a fallen and divided France fanned the flames of discontent with the colonial situation.

These rising demands for independence in the Maghrib were not echoed south of the Sahara during the war. Nevertheless the war proved an accelerator in a political situation in which the majority of the educated élite had become disenchanted with the colonial vision of an association of Europe and Africa to their mutual benefit. Two decades of economic stagnation, the slow pace of political and social reform, as well as the excesses of the colonial system, had seen to that. And now the colonial masters themselves seemed in their propaganda to be reinforcing the reservations even the most devoted of African 'collaborators' had about the colonial record. The propaganda not only tried to *justify* that record, but insisted that in return for *collaboration* that record would be improved on after the war. It was also designed to counter the barrage of criticism of the colonial regimes made by the Nazis. In the French-controlled areas, Africans were subject to two rival sets of propaganda, directed not so much at securing the loyalty of the African subjects to France but pushing the claims of one view of France against another. For the British-controlled areas, a Colonial Film Unit was established whose purpose 'was to explain the war to unsophisticated colonial audiences: to tell them why Britain was fighting and invite colonial support'.[1] The wartime use of propaganda in both the French and British colonies proved to be a precedent, for thereafter both colonial powers continued to inform their colonial subjects about their policies and plans through the printed word, the radio and cinema. In the short run, the most significant aspect of this development was that Africans – at least those who were educated – were now being *invited* not forced or ordered, to cooperate with the colonial powers. And the reward was to be the granting of some of the requests the political élite had been making before the war, apparently in vain: greater political and administrative involvement by the educated élite in the machinery of government; and

[1] Peggy Medina Giltrow and David R. Giltrow, 'Films of the Colonial Film Unit', unpublished paper presented at the conference on 'The film as records of empire', 10 April 1981. I am grateful to Andrew Roberts for drawing my attention to this.

improvement of the social and educational facilities available to the colonial subjects. Britain was able, as a symbol of good faith, to make some of these concessions during the course of the war itself: thus in the Gold Coast the first appointments in the twentieth century of Africans to the field administration and the first appointments to the executive councils of both the Gold Coast and Nigeria were made in 1942–3. The wartime British administration of the West African colonies involved itself in large-scale planning for educational and social reform after the war. And if the Free French and Belgians, denied access to their metropoles, were less happily placed to introduce reforms during the course of the war, they did at least elaborate plans for reform. The Free French did so at the Brazzaville Conference in 1944. Pierre Ryckmans, who had attended the Brazzaville Conference, in his valedictory speech as the governor-general who had administered the Belgian Congo during the war, envisaged a change in the colonial policy of his country that would involve broad economic and social reform and a controlled participation by the élite in the political process.

The political élite, then, for the first time found its colonial masters trying to justify their rule to them. Furthermore, they were made aware that both America and Russia were deeply critical of the European colonial empires and their record. They were thus operating in a new international political climate in which their own criticisms of colonialism were becoming common currency and in which their aspirations seemed to be legitimised by the Atlantic Charter, whatever reservations Churchill may have had. The declaration about self-determination in that charter was to be an inspiration to educated Africans from Morocco to Madagascar.

But support for African ideas of political and social reform leading one day to self-government and independence came not only from the anti-colonial powers like America and Russia, but from within the colonial powers themselves. In Britain, the Labour Party, most explicitly through the Fabian Colonial Bureau, made clear its hostility to the long-term continuation of empire, and African nationalists could count on increasing support for their ideas from the Labour members of the wartime British government. Likewise within the Free French government, the Communists were a major force and *groupes d'études communistes* were established in a number of African colonial towns. They were to have a formative influence on the development after the war of French-speaking Black Africa's largest radical party, the Rassemblement Démocratique Africain. Here it must be said that the Communists did not favour independence as a goal for their African colonies, but rather association of the enfranchised African working classes with the international class struggle. Nor did the Socialists, who advocated reform of the colonial system, envisage a future for the colonies independent of a constitutional relationship with France.

The war brought Europeans and Americans out to Africa in greater numbers than ever before. What is more, many of them came from very different social backgrounds from those with whom Africans had hitherto generally come in contact. The exigencies of war, particularly the need to provision the supply routes to the Middle East and Far Eastern campaigns, resulted in the stationing in major African cities of large numbers of white soldiers and tradesmen, many of whom were much less well educated than the members of the growing African middle class of lawyers, doctors, teachers and clerical officers. More important still, these whites did not identify with colonial authorities but saw them as part of a class structure against which they voted overwhelmingly in the post-war elections in both Britain and France.

The myth of white superiority, of the separation of Africans and Europeans either informally, as in the case of the British West African and French colonies, or by formal rules approximating to a colour bar as in the Rhodesias and Kenya, were broken down by these temporary immigrants. While African soldiers who had served in France during the First World War had, as a result of coming into contact with the local population, 'quickly come to have doubts about the superiority of the coloniser',[1] and while in East Africa African troops who had fought alongside white soldiers had experienced similar doubts, this reaction was much more widely spread during the Second World War because of the sheer numbers of working-class whites who passed through the colonies. The educated Africans, particularly those who had never travelled abroad, gained a very different perception of their European rulers as a result of this wartime contact.

Perhaps no one perceived the impact of the war on the Africans'

[1] Paul Catrice, 'L'emploi des troupes indigènes et leur séjour en France', *Études: révue Catholique d'interêt général*, 20 November 1931, 401.

view of the European so acutely as Sylvia Leith-Ross, herself very much a member of the colonial class, who had first arrived in Nigeria in 1907. It is worth quoting her own observations *in extenso*:

Till then, and in spite of the 1914 war which had never really come very close to Nigeria, the mass of the people still thought of the white race as one, united by colour, education, religion... They thought of the white men as being 'brothers', with all the implications connoted in the African mind by that term, bound to assist each other and having the same aims and interests. All these white men were rich, and had come into the world with ready-made knowledge and skills. Therefore, for the time being, they dominated the African...

Every time we indicted Germany or Vichy France, we indicted ourselves as well. Except for the travelled or highly educated few, Europeans had been a mass conception for so long that whatever cruelty or treachery or injustice we attributed to our enemies was seen as a possible attribute of ourselves...

Further, outside and apart from our own propaganda directed against a section of fellow-Europeans, another and even more radical change, noted by few, was taking place in the black–white attitude of the masses. Perhaps for the first time, except in individual cases, an element of contempt had crept into their minds: these 'civilised' white men could nevertheless kill each other in great numbers, their rich towns could be destroyed, their expensive homes burnt down, they could be tortured and starved, they could cringe and beg for help and for money. And, a curious sidelight emerging from conversations with observant Africans who had been in contact with our troops or sailors, for the first time in their lives these Africans had met a number of Europeans *less educated than themselves*... They were careful to show no disdain, only sheer amazement that they should have been mistaken. You could not help feeling that this discovery was perhaps the final insidious blow which shattered the crumbling edifice of white superiority.[1]

COLONIAL REFORMS

The colonial reforms initiated by France and Britain are crucial to an understanding of the unforeseen speed with which the transfer of power took place in Africa following the war. These reforms, which as we have seen were conceived largely as a response to the changed political climate brought about by the war, were in turn to evoke a response by the African political class that was not one of gratitude for concessions – which in fact often surpassed their current expectations – but was rather a demand for yet larger and speedier concessions. It was as though the

[1] Leith-Ross, *Stepping-stones*, 116–17.

reforms themselves changed the political engine into a new gear that was to drive it inexorably towards independence, however hard the colonial rulers tried to apply the brakes, whether for fear of the consequences of too rapid a transition or to protect white minority interests. It is the journeys made by this machine, travelling very different roads in different parts of Africa, that form the central theme of the chapters of this volume. Suffice it to outline here the reforms that were introduced as a result of the war, for they can be picked up in detail on later pages, where their consequences and the responses to them are examined by regional specialists.

Not all the colonial powers responded in kind. Spain and Portugal, never directly involved in the war, made no modifications to their colonial policy. The Belgians initiated important social and economic reforms designed to ameliorate the standard of living of their Congolese subjects, believing that a full belly was the best antidote to nationalism. Some attempt was made to find a place in the Congo's colonial hierarchy for the minuscule educated élite, but plans for eventual political participation at the grass-roots level were years in preparation. The Belgians were in no mood for eventual disbandment of their rich African empire, and immediately after the war there was no thought of independence for their Congo even in the far distant future. Ideally they would have liked the withdrawal of the mandate over Ruanda–Urundi and its incorporation in the Congo as a seventh province. They particularly resented the specific obligation entailed in their subsequent UN Trusteeship to promote self-government and eventual independence and in fact did little about it.

The French and the British were still as much in the business of African empire as the Belgians. The French made it quite clear that the political reforms they initiated at Brazzaville in no way involved eventual *self-government* – and they did indeed use the English expression for want of an appropriate French one. Rather, the increased political rights accorded the Africans, as a result of the Brazzaville Conference and the deliberations of the two constituent assemblies, were to be held within the framework of an indissoluble and indivisible union of France and her overseas territories. Thus while de Gaulle and the Free French leaders accepted that it was necessary to initiate colonial reforms at Brazzaville – and de Gaulle himself was very conscious of the debt he owed Africans for their support during the war – the main aim of the conference was to make secure the links between the colonies and the metropolis. Through a strengthened empire the grandeur of France would be re-established. Acknowledgement of, and concessions to, local political identity were strictly within the framework of a Greater France. Accordingly the extension of citizenship to a limited number of Algerian Muslims without compromising their personal status as far as their religion and private law were concerned and the provision for representation of the colonies in the National Assembly were designed to bind the colonies more closely to France.

The reforms of the least palatable aspects of French colonial policy – the suppression of forced labour, the abolition of the *indigénat* or summary administrative justice, the change in status from *sujet* to *citoyen*, the legalisation of trade unions, were intended to give the colonial inhabitants renewed faith in the French mission. These reforms, though an immediate by-product of the war, had been mooted by the Popular Front government, which had permitted the formation of trade unions and professional associations by those with primary education in 1937. Even the extension of citizenship to Algerian Muslims along the lines of the *Ordonnance* of 7 March 1944 had been proposed but rejected during the government of the Popular Front. But although Brazzaville was not as innovatory as it has sometimes been characterised, it did initiate a major if unintended change in France's relationship with her colonies. As D. Bruce Marshall has emphasised:

> In the end, the reforms of Brazzaville did indeed contribute both to the desire for independence within the colonies and to the creation of a political system that tended to legitimise the pursuit of that aim. Yet nothing could have been further from the intentions of those responsible for Free French policy, especially Charles de Gaulle.[1]

Although self-government was a stock phrase in the British colonial vocabulary, and indeed had been accorded to India and Ceylon, there was still no intention in 1946, when the Burns constitution was introduced in the Gold Coast, of granting it to that or any other African colony except in the distant future. The

---

[1] D. Bruce Marshall, 'Free France in Africa: Gaullism and colonialism', in Prosser Gifford and William Roger Louis (eds.), *France and Britain in Africa: imperial rivalry and colonial rule* (New Haven and London, 1971), 748.

one country for which the British government appeared to perceive independence on the visible horizon was the Sudan, which in itself was a special type of colony administered by Britain as a condominium with Egypt. Pressures by nationalists who desired independence and those who saw their country's future in an independent union with Egypt had led the British Co-Dominus to declare in April 1946 that it 'was aiming at a free and independent Sudan which will be able as soon as independence is achieved to define for itself its relations with Great Britain and Egypt'.[1]

The Sudan may not have been so exceptional as it seems. For in the Colonial Office, according to Ronald Robinson, the thinking in 1947 was that within a generation most of the major British African colonies would become self-governing within the Commonwealth.[2] But public pronouncements indicated a much longer timetable. The Elliot Commission, which in 1945 recommended the establishment of university colleges in the Gold Coast and Nigeria, had seen them as training grounds for an independence that might be fifty or more years away. Before 1947 few colonial administrators in the field envisaged reforms as leading to anything more than increased representation. But in that year, with Indian independence, the inevitability of self-government for the African territories became evident.

Only for Italy, to whom the administration of her colony of Somalia was restored as a United Nations Trusteeship, was independence an objective with a specific term for its accomplishment. The UN, in agreeing in 1950 that Italy should continue to administer Somalia, did so on the condition that she prepare it for independence within ten years. Thus a colonial power, for the first time, had to work towards a fixed date for the independence of one of its colonies. The case of Libya was somewhat different. It achieved independence on 24 December 1951, without being formally restored to Italy or accepted as the domain of the British or French who were administering it, because of international wrangling over its future.

In taking over the Mandates of the League of Nations as

[1] P. M. Holt and M. W. Daly, *The history of the Sudan, from the coming of Islam to the present day*, 3rd ed. (London, 1979), 151.
[2] Ronald Robinson, 'Conclusion', in A. H. M. Kirk-Greene (ed.), *Africa in the colonial period: the transfer of power: the colonial administrator in the age of decolonisation* (Oxford, 1979), 179.

Trusteeships the United Nations introduced an important extraneous element into the political calculations of those colonial powers administering them in Africa. These powers – Britain, France and Belgium – were subject to inspection and criticism of their administration of these trusts and were obligated to develop them towards self-government though not after any specific length of time as in the case of Somalia. They were thus to be held internationally accountable for their stewardship in ways they had not been under the League of Nations Mandates, and colonial grievances could in the case of these Trusteeships be brought before the United Nations, an organisation by and large hostile to colonialism. Only South Africa refused to acknowledge the UN as successor to the League of Nations as far as its administration of South West Africa was concerned.

In retrospect, the political advances made by the French and British colonies at the end of the war, though perceived as generous by the donors, were considered paltry by the recipients, and of course seem so now. They did, however, represent the first hesitant steps in what was to prove a very rapid decolonisation of the African continent. In the case of the French, initial decolonisation was to be not within the framework of eventual independence; rather it consisted of the greater participation by what were now styled 'overseas territories' in the French political process. In the case of the British colonies, the aim was to prepare their inhabitants by gradual stages for an ever-increasing measure of participation in their own administration until they could be granted internal self-government as a prelude to independence within the British Commonwealth.

In 1946 the Gold Coast, considered at that time to be the most politically advanced of Britain's African territories, gained an elected African majority in its Legislative Council – the first such in colonial Africa. But only five of the eighteen members were directly elected by the people, the rest being elected by chiefs. In Nigeria, reflecting the colonial administration's continuing commitment to indirect rule, the new constitution introduced in 1946 provided for a majority of African unofficial members, all but four of whom were nominated from the Native Authorities. Only intervention of the colonial secretary had forced Sir Arthur Richards, the Governor, to retain the three elected members from Lagos and the one from Calabar provided for in the 1922 constitution. In Kenya, the first African member of the Legislative Council was only appointed in 1944. In Tanganyika, the first African member was not appointed until 1948. The Colonial Office may have had as its goal in 1947 the preparation of its major African colonies within a generation for self-government based on the educated African élite, once it had been sufficiently convinced that this élite had grass-roots support; but this was not manifest in its first experiments in devolution of power where the traditional élite was predominant in the legislatures of Nigeria and the Gold Coast.

As we have seen, political advances in the French Black African territories were directed at closer political integration with France. But even here, though all Africans were now granted citizenship, their actual status was that of second- and even third-class citizens. The majority still did not have the vote, and of those that did, a majority had to vote on a separate roll from that for the Europeans resident in the colonies, with the result that their votes were effectively worth much less than those of Europeans. Furthermore, their new territorial assemblies were only advisory.

These provisions also applied to Madagascar whose deputies to the Second Constituent Assembly had unsuccessfully demanded independence. The case of France's North African territories was different from that of her Black African territories. Algeria was treated as an integral part of France, while Morocco and Tunisia were protectorates where the sultan and bey were at least nominally sovereign. In Tunisia, because of the activities of Moncef Bey during the war, the French in fact imposed further control over the bey's administration, though the Tunisians were given some increases in electoral representation. Demands for independence made in Morocco were countered not with liberalisation of the political regime, but with modest economic reforms. In Algeria all Muslims became nominally citizens but, as in Black Africa, not all of them had the vote, so that the majority remained second-class Frenchmen in this North African 'France'. The failure to concede anything but the most modest of political reforms in North African territories was to be grist to the mill of the nationalist cause in Morocco and Tunisia, and to end all hope that Algeria could ever really be assimilated into France.

If any pattern emerges in these first tentative steps towards political decolonisation, it is that they were more adventurous in those French and British colonies where settler interests were not dominant. Where they were dominant, both countries had to confront a growing white nationalism, which was vociferously opposed to political concessions to the African majorities.

Much more important than these measures of political liberalisation introduced during and immediately after the war were the broad economic and social reforms made by the British, French and Belgians. While some reforms were altruistic, many were as much designed to assist in the rehabilitation of the motherland as with the development of the colonies themselves. The Belgians actually promulgated a ten-year plan that covered both the motherland and her African estate, while ambitious schemes like the Tanganyika groundnut scheme and the Gambia egg project were as much designed to alleviate the economic situation in Britain as to promote real development in Africa. Indeed during the postwar boom in agricultural prices, the surpluses earned by the colonies were held in metropolitan banks and thus helped finance the recovery of the motherlands as they had helped finance the war itself. The Belgians were quite explicit about the Congo's role in assisting the motherland's post-war recovery.

Thus the essential colonial economic relationship was not changed; but as far as the French, British and Belgian territories were concerned there were important modifications to it. In the first place all three powers immediately after the war introduced the idea of planning the economies of their colonies. Money was to be spent not only on aspects of the economy immediately beneficial to the import–export trade, such as new roads and railways, but on social welfare and education as well. The concept of the state's role as agent for the promotion of the welfare of its inhabitants was introduced to the colonies with increased educational and medical services as a major feature of the British, French and Belgian development plans. The concept of economic development was so new that Captain J. R. Mackie, the Director of Agriculture, was later to comment that Sir Bernard Bourdillon's statement on government policy for economic development in Nigeria following the passing of the 1940 Colonial Development and Welfare Act was the first that had 'ever been made publicly' in the country, and that in almost twenty years of service in Nigeria he had 'never seen such a statement of policy even in official papers'.[1]

[1] White, *Central administration in Nigeria*, 234.

The Colonial Development and Welfare Act can of course be seen as a self-interested measure, for it had been born out of the belated realisation, brought about by the Caribbean riots of 1938, that colonial neglect led to colonial disaster. Furthermore, it came to be perceived that economic development schemes would benefit the metropole as much as the colonies involved, for they increased the surplus that could be extracted from the colonial economies and would also enlarge the market for manufactured exports. But it would be cavalier to deny that the large-scale social welfare schemes introduced by France under FIDES, for instance, were not in part an attempt to repay a debt that, judging from the record and the public pronouncements of her officials and ministers, France sincerely felt she owed her colonial subjects for their wartime support. Furthermore, many of the administrators appointed to the colonial services of France and Britain after the war were not imbued with the innate sense of superiority of their pre-war colleagues, and espoused radical views about the colonial relationship. There was a growing sense of accountability to the administered as well as an increasing questioning of the morality of the colonial relationship. And even if independence was a distant goal for the British, and was excluded by the French in favour of greater eventual participation by Africans in the politics of a greater France, the consensus was that the foundations for this increased involvement of Africans in the government and administration of their countries had to be firmly sunk in an improved educational, social, medical and economic infra-structure.

CONCLUSION

The war, as Walter Rodney put it, 'called forth new responses from every section of the African population, from resident minorities, from colonial régimes and from the metropolitan capitalist class which had a stake in Africa'.[1] For all these reasons, the Second World War was a turning point, if not a watershed, in Africa's colonial history.

In the twenty years that followed the promulgation of the political reforms promised by Britain and France during the Second World War, the great majority of African colonial subjects gained their political freedom and the British, French and Italian

[1] Walter Rodney, *World War II and the Tanzanian economy*, Cornell African Studies Centre Monograph no. 3, 1976, 1.

colonial empires effectively ceased to exist. The Spanish, who had the smallest empire in Africa, reversed their previous policy of integration and assimilation when, in 1962, they began the political decolonisation of Fernando Po and Rio Muni which together became independent as Equatorial Guinea in 1968. The future of the Spanish Sahara was more problematic, being more than half the size of Spain itself, but with a population according to the 1960 census of only 23 793. In 1975, under pressure from King Hassan of Morocco, Spain agreed to divide it between his country and Mauritania. Only the Portuguese held steadfastly to their determination to incorporate their African dependencies in a perpetual union with the mother country. Significantly their two major colonies, Angola and Mozambique, were both settler colonies, for on the path to independence the greatest violence was experienced in those territories where white-minority interests opposed concessions to the demands of African nationalists, and where the metropolitan government either supported these settler interests, or delayed or modified the concessions they were prepared to make to African nationalists in non-settler territories in the hopes of reconciling the two nationalisms. Yet even in Southern Rhodesia, where the white nationalists, who had already had legal self-government since 1923, were able to declare their own unrecognised independence in 1965, the African nationalists were eventually to triumph in 1980 as they had in the former Portuguese territories. We may pause, then, to ask why the European empires in Africa collapsed so quickly and generally so easily in the quarter century after the Second World War, and to ponder how far the war was the dominant factor in this collapse.

We have argued that the war created a new international climate in which the leading colonial powers were put on the defensive and in which they felt obliged to introduce political as well as social and economic reforms, however tentative these may now appear to have been. Therefore, African nationalists, who had had limited goals before the war, and had been unsuccessful in gaining any major concessions from the colonial governments, found themselves operating in a new political climate. Their ideas and aspirations now found support not only in political circles within the relevant metropolis but in significant sections of the international community. What is more, the war had so changed the economic situation in many of their countries, in particular by swelling the number of immigrants to the towns, that the nationalists now had larger constituencies to call upon. And by conceding reforms which involved the establishment and significant extension of the franchise to Africans, either through direct or indirect elections, the colonial governments were also, consciously or unconsciously, accepting that they were responsible to their colonial subjects. The logic of granting suffrage to Africans, however limited and no matter what the criteria might be, was that it must later be extended. For either more people became qualified under the terms of the existing franchise, or else African nationalists protested that it was arbitrarily restrictive and that a France and Britain which held that universal suffrage was fundamental to good government could not justify limiting it in their African colonies. Where limitations on the suffrage were designed to protect the interests of a white minority, they easily became an issue that nationalists could use to rouse popular protest.

Of course until 1960 it was only Britain and France that made such concessions and then only when white-minority interests did not have to be protected. And even there they were caught in the dilemma, when engaging in the defence of white-minority interests as in Kenya or Algeria, that their practice was not consistent. But what of the colonial powers like Portugal and Spain which were not directly affected by the war, whose colonial economies stagnated by comparison with those of the French and British territories? Here the examples set by the French and British in decolonising made their own determination to hold on to their colonies invidious. However much they desired to retain control of them, however hard they tried to isolate them from the winds of change taking place in other parts of the continent, they were ultimately unable, in an age of mass communication, to insulate their African subjects from the ideas for independence that gained currency after the war. Even in French Black Africa, where for a time it seemed Africans would settle for a political freedom within a Franco-African Community and eschew independence as such, the example of Ghana and the special status of Togo and Cameroun which, as Trust Territories, did not fit into the grandiose plans for a Franco-African Community, had much to do with the decision by France in 1960 to grant independence to all its Black African territories. The collapse of Belgian authority in the Congo, whilst in part due to loss of will by the colonial authorities, was also a result of the influences of and examples set by other African territories, in particular the example of Ghana and of neighbouring Brazzaville, which enjoyed a great deal of political autonomy within the French Community and was only half-an-hour's ferry ride from Léopoldville. Where before the Second World War African leaders contemplating political concessions were operating in a world that accepted the fact of colonialism, after it they were to press their case in a world where the colonial dependencies were gaining independence by negotiation or violence in succession like the proverbial dominoes. And even where the colonial powers tried to resist these influences, as in Vietnam and Indonesia, and later in Algeria, it was demonstrated that their forces were no longer sufficient to maintain a control that had been apparently so easily retained before the war. Until then, the colonial powers had been able to keep control of their large populations with minimum force just because the latter accepted the colonial presence, even if only passively. But after the war, nationalists were able to harness not only the frustrations of the urban masses but also rural discontent to demand political concessions. Where these were resisted by the colonial powers, nationalists were able to mobilise armed resistance not only in the towns but in the countryside, where not even massive military force as used in Algeria and the Portuguese colonies could subdue people fighting on their own ground. The situation was made the more difficult for the intransigent colonial powers once countries like Morocco and Tunisia had gained independence and could support an Algerian independence movement, or as later Tanzania could support Mozambique.

That the colonial empires would be disbanded within less than two generations – an eventuality that seemed so unlikely in 1939 – is comprehensible in the context of the Second World War both as a result of the developments in the continent that it speeded up and the new economic, social and political forces it set in motion. Retrospectively, too, we can see that the gradual loss of will for empire on the part of the colonial powers was accompanied by a realisation that Africans, in seeking the political kingdom, had lost sight of the economic kingdom. Thus it suited the colonial powers, especially where they were not embarrassed by, or committed to, a rival white nationalism, to concede the political kingdom whilst retaining as much control as possible of their economic empire. For by and large, of course, it was the educated élite that inherited the colonial kingdom, so that in real terms the lot of the majority of inhabitants changed very little with the change from white to black control. The world capitalist system had deeply impregnated the colonial structures by the eve of independence and the élites who gained independence were loath to forgo the very obvious personal benefits that these structures immediately brought them. Indeed up until the end of our period very few African countries had sought alternatives to the economic structures they had inherited, however much socialist or Marxist window-dressing they may have displayed. The drama of the struggle for independence and the problems of the independent leaders after it, as the next chapter shows, is that the independence the Africans took, and the independence the colonialists gave, was in effect a qualified independence, for the reality of power, control of the economy, was still to be found overseas.

CHAPTER 2

DECOLONISATION AND THE PROBLEMS OF INDEPENDENCE

For millions of peoples in Africa – and those with liberal inclinations outside Africa – two decades of independence brought little but disillusionment. For the Africans, the nationalist agitations of the 1930s down to the mid-1950s promised a new era of political self-assertion and freedom from foreign imperialist domination. The vision of what was to come was well put by Kwame Nkrumah of Ghana when he said: 'Seek ye first the political kingdom and everything else shall be added unto you.' Independence was to be the millennium when the African, after decades of being exploited and oppressed, was to come into his own 'inheritance'. To the liberals of Europe and North America, the nationalist rhetoric of freedom and equality was a reassertion of the ideals they had cherished and proclaimed. But after two decades of independence these hopes and ideals were replaced by despair as pluralist institutions were supplanted by military rule in many states and the promise of plenty gave way, if not to the increasing impoverishment of the masses, then most certainly to relative stagnation. For example, it has been estimated that the average African state grew less food per capita in 1968 than it had done in 1956, while the per capita gross domestic product at market prices stood in 1970 at $200, a figure which had changed little from what it had been a decade earlier.[1]

Attempts at explaining the 'African predicament'[2] have been many and varied but perhaps the most perceptive are those of the 'structural analysts' or dependence theorists. As put by Osvaldo Sunkel, dependence is that system which links external pressures and constraints, often operating through 'hidden or subtle financial, economic, technical and cultural' mechanisms, with

[1] 'World hunger: causes and remedies', report by the Transnational Institute (Washington DC, 1974).
[2] Stanislao Andreski, *The African predicament* (London, 1968).

internal processes of underdevelopment characterised by the 'self-reinforcing accumulations of privilege' on the one hand and the existence of a 'marginal class' on the other.[1] Though there are different formulations of dependency theory, common to all the theorists is the postulation of a pattern of unequal, asymmetric exchange relationships which consistently and persistently operate to the advantage of the one partner and to the disadvantage of the other. The result is the emergence within the international system of dominant and dependent actors, or, in the language of Galtung, of a conflict between 'centre' and 'periphery' or between 'metropolis' and 'satellite' to use Gunder Frank's and Samir Amin's terminology.[2] The net outcome of dependent relationships 'is economic development for the centre and economic underdevelopment for the periphery; military ascendancy, highly developed means of communication and cultural expansion on the one hand, and military inferiority, primitive means of communication and cultural emulation on the other'.[3] As Gustavo Lagos has put it, the dependent actor suffers from absolute *atimia* or extreme deprivation.[4] While this broad characterisation is no doubt illuminating, it does not cover adequately the complexities and peculiarities of specific situations within the African predicament. We examine this predicament first by looking at the different ways in which African states obtained their independence and secondly by examining their constitutional legacy. This is followed by a discussion of some specific problems: those of the bureaucracy and the economy, the related problem of social mobilisation, the military and militarism and, finally, the problem of political leadership and political succession.

The choice of issues may seem arbitrary given the multitude of problems confronting African states before and particularly since independence. Nevertheless, it has some rationale. Basically, we could dichotomise the set of problems into two sub-sets. The first consists of issues inherent in the nature of African social and

[1] Osvaldo Sunkel, 'Big business and "dependencia"', *Foreign Affairs*, **50**, April 1972, 519. Quoted in Joseph A. Camilleri, *Civilization in crisis* (Cambridge, 1977), 71–2.

[2] A. Gunder Frank, 'Lumpen bourgeoisie and lumpen development', trans. Marian D. Berdecio (NU Monthly Review Press, 1972); J. Galtung, 'A structural theory of imperialism', *Journal of Peace Research*, 1971, **8**, 2; Samir Amin, *Neo-colonialism in West Africa*, trans. Francis McDonagh (London, 1976).

[3] Camilleri, *Civilization in crisis*, 72.

[4] Gustavo Lagos, *International stratification and underdeveloped countries* (North Carolina, 1963).

political systems antecedent to the imposition of colonial rule, for example, the heterogeneity of these systems, their socio-structural variety and the problems which these in turn created for state formation. The second sub-set is composed of difficulties which could be said to have arisen from, and be intimately bound up with, the dialectical logic of the colonial situation and the nature of the independence settlement, for example, bureaucratic style and leadership, and the framework of political contestation. Empirically, the sub-sets are closely interrelated, the one impinging on and shaping the other. Analytically, however, the pre-colonial and colonial dichotomy can be made with a degree of validity, and the choice of problems has been dictated by that dichotomy.

As outlined above, the basic problem confronting the African states – and third-world countries in general – is that of poverty, which in itself is to be explained in terms of a dependency relationship, which is a function of specific structural and behavioural variables. African states, it is contended, cannot expect to escape from the degradation of poverty unless they break the dependency relationship which binds them to the developed, industrial nations in an exploitative nexus. A break would require not only radical changes in the political and economic structures of these states but also attitudinal changes on the part of the élite – the bureaucratic-managerial and political élite, the military and the intelligentsia.

Thus, far from being arbitrary, there are cogent historical and theoretical warrants for the choice of problems for examination. Our analysis focuses on the problems that African states have experienced since gaining their independence; but, as we have already suggested, these cannot be understood without reference to the process whereby this independence was gained.

PATHS TO INDEPENDENCE

The year 1960 has been described, not without some justification, as 'the year of Africa'. Some 16 states – Cameroun, the Central African Republic, Chad, Congo-Brazzaville (now Congo), Congo-Léopoldville (now Zaire), Dahomey (now Bénin), Gabon, the Ivory Coast, Mali, Mauritania, Niger, Nigeria, Senegal, Somalia, Togo and Upper Volta – became independent, sovereign states

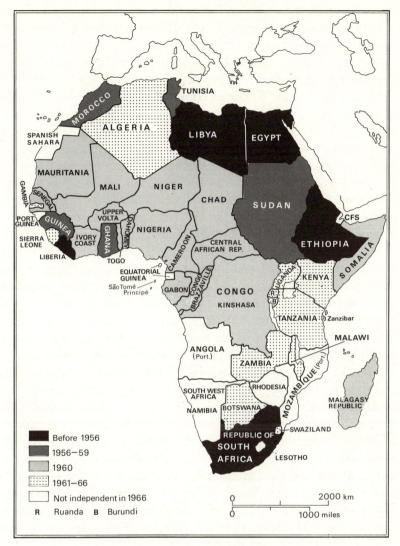

4   Africa: the path to independence, 1956–66.

in that year. Other states followed in quick succession: Sierra
Leone and Tanganyika in 1961, Burundi, Rwanda and Uganda in
1962, Kenya in 1963, Nyasaland and Northern Rhodesia in 1964,
the Gambia in 1965 and Bechuanaland and Basutoland in 1966.

The first colony to become independent in Africa was Liberia,
in 1847. It became independent soon after it was settled with slaves
repatriated from the United States. Over the next 60 years the rest

of the continent was occupied by the European colonial powers in one form or another and only Ethiopia remained effectively independent. And even she was invaded by Italy in 1935 and incorporated into the Italian East African empire until her liberation by Allied forces in 1941 during the Second World War. If we except Egypt, whose exercise of sovereignty continued to be constrained by the presence of British troops on the Suez Canal until 1956, the first European colony to gain independence after Liberia was Libya in 1951.[1] Over the next 26 years imperial rule in Africa was dismantled, the French Territory of the Afars and Issas gaining independence as the Republic of Djibouti in 1977. Rhodesia, South Africa and its dependency, South West Africa (Namibia), still remained as white-dominated territories but independent of imperial control from Europe.

Independence came to the different African states in a variety of ways, the process of decolonisation depending, in the main, first on the colonising power, and second on the nature of the colony itself, in particular whether or not it had a sizeable white-settler element. In West Africa – the stretch of territories extending from Senegal to Zaire – the colonising powers were Britain, France, Belgium, Spain and Portugal. In none of these was there a significant white-settler element. While Britain, Belgium and Spain administered their territories as separate political and administrative units, the French territories, other than those under United Nations Trusteeship, were governed as two 'federations' of states, Afrique Occidentale Française (AOF) and Afrique Equatoriale Française (AEF). Where Britain had followed a policy aimed at the ultimate attainment of complete independence by each of her colonies, France, Belgium, Portugal and Spain had maintained a system of 'Direct Rule', the long-term aim of which was to turn Africans into French, Belgian, Portuguese or Spanish 'citizens' as the case might be.

For the British territories in West Africa and elsewhere on the continent where there were no sizeable settler elements, the process of decolonisation became a graduated transfer of power to an emergent 'middle class' of lawyers, teachers, doctors and journalists, who spearheaded the various nationalist movements which had grown up in the second and third decades of the

---

[1] This does not of course take account of white-settler colonies; the Orange Free State gained independence in 1854 and the Union of South Africa in 1910.

twentieth century. The pattern was not unlike that which had occurred earlier in places like India and Ceylon. First, there was the creation of legislative institutions with limited powers, which was usually accompanied by the granting of a restricted franchise. This almost invariably encouraged the formation of political parties. The second stage followed with the extension of the area of discretion allowed to the legislative assemblies and a broadening of the franchise. This was succeeded by the third stage, the granting of internal self-government which led, often within a year or two, to the final stage of full independence and sovereign status.

Because the British-administered territories in western Africa were governed as separate entities, the process of the transfer of power involved minimum disruption. And herein lies the main contrast with the French territories. France had conceived of AOF (French West Africa) and AEF (French Equatorial Africa – Gabon, Chad, the Central African Republic, and Congo) as 'federations' to be united with France. For France, the future of her African territories was not to be full sovereignty but autonomy within a greater French Union, or Franco-African Community as it later came to be called. Not unexpectedly, this policy met with opposition from two main sources: first from the 'radical' politicians who rejected any idea of a 'qualified' independence; and secondly, from 'conservative' and rich states like the Ivory Coast and Gabon whose leaders thought that they stood to gain more by being directly associated with France than indirectly as members of a federation. In AOF, the Ivory Coast had provided the major part of the 'surplus' with which the 'federation' was maintained, while Gabon was in the same position with respect to AEF. The radical leaders of the poorer states wanted independence within the framework of the federations, seeing the proposal to devolve political power on the constituent territories rather than the group as a whole as one aimed at deliberate 'balkanisation'.

The turning point in French policy in both AOF and AEF came in 1958 when General Charles de Gaulle became President of France. He offered the constituent territories of both these federations, as distinct from the federations themselves, the choice of autonomy within a Franco-African Community or independence with all its consequences, which in effect meant the

Table 2.1. *Economic profile of former AOF states less Mauritania c. 1961.*

State	GDP 1961 in $ US million	Per capita GDP 1963	Index of agric. production 1960–1 (1954 = 100)	Growth rate GDP per capita 1961–8
Dahomey	160	70	111	1.1
Guinea	190	96	122	2.7
Ivory Coast	470	188	201	4.8
Mali	250	66	116	1.3
Niger	170	77	148	−1.6
Senegal	530	183	140	−1.4
Upper Volta	180	45	113	0.1

Source: Morrison *et al.*, *Black Africa* (New York, 1972), 50–3.

severance of all French aid. Guinea alone opted for the second alternative, and France pulled out, leaving in her wake a near-collapsing country. Guinea's fate at first served as a terrible warning to those who had voted to stay with France and continue to enjoy her considerable aid. At the same time her independence, and the forthcoming independence of the French UN Trust Territories of Togo and Cameroun as well as that of neighbouring British states proved irresistibly attractive and each Community state negotiated an independence with France that would ensure it continued to receive French aid.

If the move towards independence in the British West African states, AOF, AEF and the British East African states of Uganda and Tanganyika had been relatively peaceful, that in the Belgian territories was far from being so. In neither its Trust Territories of Rwanda and Burundi, nor its huge Congo estate, did Belgium, unlike Britain and France, attempt to create any national political institutions before 1959. And then, in the Belgian Congo, the proposed constitutional reforms allowed only for direct elections at the local-government level, though these had been introduced in 1956 in both Rwanda and Burundi. While these two countries had had some exposure to the outside world as a result of their status as UN Trust Territories, the Congo was for all practical purposes isolated from it by Belgium. With the independence of

Ghana in 1957 and the grudging offer by de Gaulle of independence to the francophone African states, Belgian administration of the Congo came to be seriously questioned by the handful of African nationalists, principal amongst whom was Patrice Lumumba, who had emerged as potential political leaders. A few days after Lumumba returned from the Pan-African Conference held in Accra in December 1958, rioting broke out in Léopoldville. The Belgian governor-general, who had advocated establishing a parliament for the Congo by the end of 1960 – an indication of the political vacuum in the country – and independence by 1963 (altered at the end of 1959 to independence in 1960), was forced by conservative protests to resign in 1959. Thereafter there was effectively a volte-face by the Belgian government and at the famous Table Ronde held in Belgium in January 1960 it was agreed to accede to Congolese demands for political freedom and grant independence within six months, although African delegates had talked in terms of independence within four years. In June 1960, with the political institutions of self-government barely established, the Belgians moved out of the Congo, only to return temporarily a month later to protect Belgian civilians still living there.

The too-hasty withdrawal of Belgium was the signal for all hell to break loose in the newly independent country. The Force Publique, which passed as the Congolese army, mutinied and Katanga, the richest region of the Congo, seceded under Moise Tshombe on 11 July. In the capital, Léopoldville (now Kinshasa), a game of musical chairs for the leadership began, while there were threats of further secession.

The United Nations, in response to appeals by the President, Joseph Kasavubu, and the Prime Minister, Patrice Lumumba, 'to protect the national territory of the Congo against the present external aggression which is a threat to international peace', sent a mission to the Congo on 14 July 1960. With its arrival began increased great-power involvement in the affairs of the Congo, an involvement which was to lead to the death of the UN Secretary-General, Dag Hammarskjöld, on 17 September 1961. The confused state of Congolese politics is discussed in detail in Chapter 14. Here, it is sufficient to note that the UN Security Forces, walking the tight-rope of international politics, finally succeeded in early 1963 in reuniting Katanga with the rest of the country and themselves pulling out of the Congo in 1964. Thus, though independence was proclaimed in June 1960, the semblance of a state did not begin to emerge in the Congo until four years later. The experience of the Congo thus marks an extreme case of one approach to independence by an African state.[1]

Portugal, unlike Britain, Belgium and France (except with respect to Algeria) saw her African territories as an extension of Portugal itself. Angola, Mozambique, Cape Verde and Guinea-Bissau were not just colonies, they were part and parcel of Portugal, or so they were regarded by the Portuguese government under Salazar, whether or not they had negligible settler populations as in Cape Verde and Guinea-Bissau, or large ones as in the case of Angola and Mozambique. From the Portuguese point of view there could be no question of independence for these territories. That would be like talking of independence for Portugal, which would be meaningless. But Portugal could hardly expect to keep its territories isolated from the political changes taking place all over Africa. With Portugal unwilling and unprepared to make any concessions, there was but one option open to the nationalist leaders – armed struggle. By the sixties, this had taken the form of organised guerrilla warfare, which is discussed in detail in Chapter 15. Within ten years, the cost of counter-revolutionary warfare was becoming unbearable for Portugal, which was then spending as much as 42 per cent of its budget on maintaining its armed personnel in these territories. Portugal was fighting a losing battle and in 1974 was finally defeated in Guinea-Bissau, Mozambique and Angola, in much the same way that the French had been in Indo-China two decades earlier.

Angola presented a different situation from Mozambique and Guinea-Bissau. First, it is more richly endowed by nature, and like the Congo was therefore expected to attract international interest. Second, because of its heterogeneous population, it was unable to produce a political leadership acceptable to all, with the result that the liberation movement splintered into three warring factions: the Movimento Popular de Libertação de Angola (MPLA); the Frente Nacional de Libertação de Angola (FNLA); and the União Nacional para a Independência Total de Angola (UNITA – initially a breakaway from the FNLA). The struggle

[1] See the classic study by Crawford Young, *Politics in the Congo* (Princeton, 1965).

for liberation thus became compounded by an internal civil war and was the signal for external, great-power involvement, with the Soviet Union, Cuba and a number of African states (Nigeria was one) supporting the MPLA; the United States, its African protégé, Zaire (which had ambitions towards the oil-rich enclave of Cabinda) and, interestingly, the Peoples' Republic of China supporting the FNLA; and UNITA appealing to South Africa for military support. Cuban soldiers, over 4000 of them, and Soviet and Yugoslav weapons ultimately won the day for the MPLA and Angola became an independent state in 1975, thus ending 400 years of colonial rule by Portugal in Africa.

In those territories that were politically dominated by white settlers, unlike the areas discussed so far, the dialectics of liberation had involved not just the coloniser and the colonised but also the white-settler element. In these territories, therefore, rather than a binary relationship, we are confronted by a triad. The classic case here was Algeria, which the French started occupying in 1834 after it had been occupied by a variety of conquering rulers in the preceding centuries. Though largely Muslim Arab and Berber in population, Algeria rapidly attracted non-Muslim European settlers. Within a decade of French colonisation, this element had grown to about 46000. By 1880 the figure was some 276000, rising in 1912 to 781000 and to over a million by 1960. With the influx of white settlers there followed the forceful acquisition of land and by 1868 the numbers dispossessed of land had grown so large that, in a nation-wide famine which broke out that year, some 500000 Muslims were feared to have died. By 1955, Algeria's settler element, which formed 11 per cent of the total population, owned more than 25 per cent of the arable land and earned over 50 per cent of the income derived from agriculture and some 90 per cent of that from exports.

The French, because of Algeria's proximity and the size of its settler population, regarded it as part of France and administered it as such. As in the Belgian and Portuguese territories, little if any attempt was made to evolve or develop local political institutions, while demands for these were met with brutal repression, as in the protest march in Sétif in 1945, a foretaste of revolt. Although the Algerian Statute of 1947 created a local assembly in which half the seats were held by Muslims, and provided for Muslim representation in the French National Assembly, settler interests ensured that nationalists did not profit from it (see Chapter 11). Demands by nationalists for effective participation in the government of their country were consistently blocked by the white-settler population and when they finally resorted to arms to press their case the settlers were backed by the French army in Algeria, which became a law unto itself and was prepared to defy the metropolitan government should the latter attempt any reform. The weaknesses and divisions of the governments of the Fourth French Republic did not improve matters, and the Algerian rebellion when it began led, in effect, to the collapse of that Republic. Rebellion finally broke out in 1954 and was led by young Algerian Muslims who had acquired some measure of cosmopolitanism and a knowledge of Marxist revolutionary techniques. They formed the Front de Libération Nationale (FLN), which had as its military arm the Armée Nationale de Libération. Their rebellion spread rapidly and by 1957 had grown into a full-scale war between the Algerian whites and the Muslim population. Attempts by different prime ministers of the Fourth Republic to find a solution to the Algerian war met with little success. At the end of May 1958, two weeks before the resignation of Premier Pierre Pflimlin, the last Prime Minister of the Republic, Algerian settlers had in fact rebelled against Paris and there was a plan to take over the Paris government through a coup to be led by commanders of the Algerian army. That the coup did not materialise can be attributed to General de Gaulle, who was invited to take power in France when the Fourth Republic collapsed. It was he who by careful manoeuvring succeeded in isolating the rebel generals and by skilful negotiations brought the war to an end.

De Gaulle's first move was to offer Algeria in 1959 a choice between independence, integration with France or association with France, which choice was to be made four years after the end of hostilities. This pronouncement precipitated a revolt in January 1960 by the European community, which rejected any talk of independence. The revolt failed and its leaders were subsequently arrested, but it was to be followed by another in April 1961. Out of the collapse of a third revolt emerged the Organisation de l'Armée Secrète (OAS), which resorted to terrorism and, creating fears of reprisals amongst the European population, forced an exodus of the settler community from Algeria. The liquidation of the OAS finally opened the way to negotiations which led in July 1962 to the independence of Algeria.

Dialectically, perhaps one should see the dilemma of white-minority rule in Africa as a play in three acts, the first act having been played in Kenya with the revolt of the Kikuyu (the Mau-Mau rebellion of 1952–6). As in Algeria, European-settler expropriation of good arable land was met with mounting resentment, especially by the dispossessed Kikuyu, a resentment which led to the formation of the Kenya African Union in the late forties under the leadership of Jomo Kenyatta (later to become prime minister and subsequently president of independent Kenya). With little opportunity of redress, what started as an ordinary political party soon grew into a revolutionary movement which was followed by open rebellion and the proclamation of a state of emergency which lasted until 1956. Even then country-wide political activity was not allowed until 1960, a restriction which was later to influence, in no small way, the post-independence pattern of politics. If Kenya can then be taken as the first act in the dialectics of white-settler–African relations, Algeria may be seen as the middle act, with white-dominated southern Africa providing the last act – after which the epitaph for white rule in Africa may perhaps be written. Before the end of our period, the curtain had risen on that last act. Part of the scenario for Algerian independence had a close parallel in Southern Rhodesia when in 1965 the white-minority settler group rebelled against London's efforts to pressure them to make concessions to African demands for participation in the country's government. They proclaimed their country independent as 'Rhodesia', and though their state was never recognised internationally they had the financial and military resources to defy London for 15 years. Indeed it was the success of the African guerrilla war against the forces of the illegal Rhodesian regime that finally brought it to the conference table and forced it to accept the transfer of power from the white minority to the black majority under Britain's supervision. But in 1975, at the close of our period, it seemed that London would never re-establish its authority and that the Algerian tragedy would be re-enacted there. As it was, despite much bloodshed on both sides, albeit on a proportionately much smaller scale than in Algeria, and despite the exodus of some settlers, the white minority remained in independent Zimbabwe under black-majority rule with entrenched political rights and a continuing economic role.

The process by which independence was won – whether through the 'peaceful' handing over of power or through revolutionary insurrectionist struggle – not only profoundly influenced post-independence events, it also engendered some of the problems which the independent states were to confront. Thus, one cannot begin to understand the nature of ethnic conflicts and the way they influenced the conflict between states over territorial boundaries, the problem of military intervention and rule, and the fragility of political leadership unless one fits them into the context of the independence settlement. Much of this is discussed below.

THE CONSTITUTIONAL INHERITANCE

The constitutional inheritance[1] of independence was not uniform but varied from one state to the other, the differences being due to the format of the decolonisation process, the nature of the political leadership to which power was transferred – the inheritors – and the character of the nationalist movements (which in most cases converted themselves into political parties) at the time of independence. In the main, three broad types of constitutional settlement can be distinguished:[2] states with a representative-parliamentary inheritance; states with radical-revolutionary regimes; and states with a conservative-monarchical settlement.

The states that entered on independence with representative parliamentary institutions were, in the main, those of anglophone and francophone East, West and Central Africa. Relative modernisation – one of the consequences of colonisation – had led to the emergence in these states of a 'new class', an educated élite who, either because they found themselves denied opportunities to which they thought themselves entitled became opposed to the colonial regime, or because of their exposure to new ideas

[1] On the notion of an 'inheritance' see Peter Nettl and R. Robertson, *International systems and the modernisation of societies* (London, 1968).
[2] The categorisation is quite arbitrary. For other categorisations, see, e.g., James S. Coleman and Carl G. Rosberg (eds.), *Political parties and national integration in tropical Africa* (Berkeley, 1964).

(many had been educated in Britain, France or the United States) rejected the whole notion of colonialism itself. They were, in essence, marginal men who, embracing the new, liberal ideas they had acquired from the various educational institutions they had attended abroad, had become alienated from their own society. Seeing themselves as prospective inheritors of the colonial mantle, with all the pomp and privilege that went with it, they spearheaded the early nationalist movements and became the leaders of the parties that emerged with the gradual liberalisation of the colonial regime, the granting of the franchise and the introduction of representative institutions in the decade following the end of the Second World War. Generally, their orientation to politics was conservative and gradualist, an orientation which fitted the predisposition of the colonial administrations.

Two models were in the main transferred. In the francophone territories, the model was, more often than not, the presidential parliamentarianism of the Fifth French Republic, while in the anglophone states it was the 'Westminster model'. In no case was any attempt made at achieving constitutional autochthony in the manner of India. But in every instance, no sooner had independence been won than constitutional and other changes were introduced which had the effect of radically modifying the spirit if not necessarily the form of the constitutional inheritance. In most cases, the pattern followed proved to be quite similar.

First, ruling parties sought a monopoly of political power by excluding or eliminating competing parties from the political arena. The tactics followed varied from the gerrymandering of constituencies and electoral manipulation, and the coercion and sometimes imprisonment of opposition candidates, to outright proscription of opposition parties. From a multi-party system, the regime became quickly converted into either a *de jure* or a *de facto* single party state: for example, the Parti Démocratique de la Côte d'Ivoire, led by Houphouët-Boigny, the United National Independence Party of Zambia, led by Kenneth Kaunda, or the Néo-Destour of Tunisia led by Habib Bourguiba.

The establishment of the single-party state was followed by the fusion of the roles of head of government and head of state in the person of the president, who was then often made 'president-for-life'. The legislature became increasingly emasculated as, under the single party, it was systematically subordinated to the executive while the executive itself was converted into an instrument for effecting the will of the president. Other changes followed as the judiciary was made to serve the interests of the executive and the security forces were converted into para-political extensions of the ruling party. Frantz Fanon gave a good description of this process of change when he wrote:

Before independence, the leader generally embodies the aspirations of the people for independence, political liberty and national dignity. But as soon as independence is declared, far from embodying in concrete form the needs of the people in what touches bread, land and the restoration of the country to the sacred hands of the people, the leader will reveal his inner purpose: to become the general president of that company of profiteers impatient for their returns which constitutes the national bourgeoisie.[1]

Independence and the paraphernalia of a constitutional settlement thus became no more than a restoration of the medieval dictum: *quod principi placuit, legis vigorem habet.*

The independent states of Africa with radical-revolutionary regimes can be divided into two sub-categories. In the first were states such as Ghana, Guinea, Mali and Tanzania (formerly Tanganyika and Zanzibar) which at the time of independence had a political settlement not unlike that of the 'representative-parliamentary' regimes. What differentiated them was the existence of mass populist-oriented political parties and a leadership espousing socialist or neo-Marxist ideology.

A good example was the Parti Démocratique de Guinée (PDG) led by Sékou Touré and built on the Confédération Générale du Travail, a federation of trade unions. As Ruth Schachter Morgenthau noted in her classic study *Political parties in French-speaking West Africa*, to the leaders of the PDG,

party and trade union were one. The trade union experience of many PDG leaders affected their ideas as well as their style of living, speaking, writing and acting. Since they held jobs low in the administrative hierarchy, they lived of necessity close to the people. Many had but irregular incomes; their housing was bad, few had cars, their clothes were simple. They relied on their colleagues or relations when in need, and made virtues of the labels pinned on them by their adversaries – 'illiterates', 'vagrants' and 'badly dressed'.[2]

[1] Frantz Fanon, *The wretched of the earth* (New York, 1963), 134.
[2] Ruth Schachter Morgenthau, *Political parties in French-speaking West Africa* (Oxford, 1964), 230.

Similarly, in Ghana members of Kwame Nkrumah's Convention People's Party were designated 'verandah boys' and 'prison graduates'.

But though radical and revolutionary in orientation, the pattern of immediate post-independence political development in these states did not differ, in essentials, from that in the 'representative-parliamentary' regimes. Representative institutions and the electoral process were progressively undermined as the supremacy of the party was proclaimed. In Nkrumah's Ghana, for example, no elections to the National Assembly were held after 1958. The assembly simply extended its life by legislative approval of its members. The pattern was similar in Guinea and Mali, where the party Congress met to ratify the list of candidates for the National Assembly drawn up by the president and the party executive. Tanzania, in this respect, proved to be an exception. Though a *de jure* one-party state with Nyerere, leader of the Tanganyika African National Union, as president, Tanzania[1] nevertheless maintained on the mainland the institutions she inherited at independence, with some freedom of electoral choice still being retained by the electorate. Unlike Ghana, Guinea or Mali, Tanzania made definite moves towards the realisation of its ideal of participatory democracy and in that respect was perhaps unique amongst African states.[2]

The second sub-category of the radical-revolutionary regimes comprised those states – Algeria, Mozambique, Angola, Guinea-Bissau and the Cape Verde Islands – which achieved independence not through bargaining but by 'internal war'.[3] These were states which at the time of independence had no inherited political institutions (Algeria being something of an exception, see above pp. 61–2) but came into existence as 'garrison states'[4] where the political rhetoric was that derived from the revolutionary experience of guerrilla warfare. That experience was oriented mainly at winning the sympathy and goodwill, or at the worst, the simple tolerance, of the peasantry in those areas which, before in-

---

[1] The reference here is specifically to Tanganyika. The union of that territory with Zanzibar is called Tanzania.

[2] *Socialism and participation*, the Election Study Committee, University of Dar es Salaam (Dar es Salaam, 1974).

[3] Harry Eckstein (ed.), *Internal war: problems and approaches* (New York, 1964).

[4] H. D. Lasswell: 'The garrison-state hypotheses today', in Samuel P. Huntington (ed.), *Changing patterns of military politics* (New York, 1962).

dependence, were held by the nationalist guerrilla leaders through force of arms. Though practice varied from one place to the other depending on the nature of the local communities and the state of the guerrilla war, nevertheless the principal thrust of effort was towards the formation of self-administering local committees representing groups of small villages, committees whose responsibilities were then progressively widened to cover functions such as local justice and security, education and health and cooperative production and marketing as the liberated areas were made more secure. From this there developed the model which the independent state eventually adopted, a model based at each level of organisation on an elected assembly of delegates which in turn elected an executive committee responsible for policy-making at that level and accountable – in principle – to the assembly which elected it. Generally, the aim was to maximise popular participation at each level of government and the organising principle could perhaps be described as a form of democratic centralism. Though this was the model established in Guinea-Bissau and Cape Verde, in essentials it is not unrepresentative of what obtained in Mozambique and Angola. It is far from certain how long such a neo-populist, 'neo-Marxist' framework can persist. Algeria – which also had a revolutionary experience and a colonial background not too dissimilar from that of Mozambique – had, under Ben Bella, sought to experiment with a socialist framework soon after it became independent. But within three years of independence Ben Bella was to be arrested and imprisoned by the military-backed Colonel Boumedienne, who castigated Ben Bella for calling for 'the withering away of the state' when the state was yet to be established. Twelve years later, after the coup that overthrew Ben Bella in 1965, Algeria had become, like many of the other African states, a one-man presidentialist state (see Chapter 11).

Thirdly, there was a group of states which embarked on independence with a conservative-monarchical settlement, notably Morocco, Ethiopia and Libya, to which may be added Lesotho and Swaziland and, for convenience, Zaire. (Technically Tunisia was a monarchy at independence but it was proclaimed a republic shortly afterwards.) The inclusion of Zaire may seem odd, but though, after the chaos of 1960–4, General Mobutu (who subse-

quently renamed himself Mobutu Sese Seko) emerged as President of Congo-Kinshasa (Zaire), the Zairean regime became
essentially monarchical in much the same sense as Morocco's
regime could be said to be so. Lesotho at independence could be
described as a 'constitutional monarchy' with Paramount Chief
Motlotlehi Moshweshwe II as king: four years after independence, Chief Leabua Jonathan, then prime minister, extra-legally
seized power and placed the king under house-arrest.

Morocco, even before its occupation and colonisation by
France, was a monarchy under the rule of a sultan. Under French
rule the monarchy was preserved and at independence Morocco
remained a monarchy under Mohammed V ben Youssef. In Libya,
the Sanūsī Emir of Cyrenaica emerged as King Muḥammed Idrīs
of Libya when the former Italian provinces of Fezzan, Tripolitania
and Cyrenaica were merged together in 1951 to form the new state.
But after just over a decade of independence, the monarchy in
Libya was to be abolished by the military, led by Colonel
Qadhdhāfī (Gadafi). The restored monarchy of Haile Selassie was
overthrown and replaced by a radical military regime at the end
of our period, by which time the conservative-monarchical regime
was an exotic form of government on the continent.

Independence – and the political settlement that came with
it – was not without its attendant difficulties. There was hardly
a state in Africa in which, within a decade of independence, there
was not a military coup or attempted coup. Dahomey (later the
Republic of Bénin) experienced no less than seven coups within
the first ten years of its independence. In fact, so prevalent were
military coups that civil governments became the exception rather
than the rule in the newly independent states. Not only coups;
independence also brought with it civil wars, as in Nigeria, Chad,
the Sudan and the ancient kingdom of Ethiopia. To civil wars must
be added the spate of inter-state wars over disputed boundaries:
between Algeria and Morocco; Kenya and Somalia; Somalia
and Ethiopia; the Sudan and Ethiopia; Algeria and Morocco and
Mauritania over Spanish Sahara; Zaire and Angola over sections
of Angola; and to a lesser extent between Nigeria and Cameroun.
The situation is in no way improved when we add internal
conflicts over ethnic boundaries. Of the 43 or more independent
African states, only Somalia can perhaps claim a homogeneous

population. Chad and the Sudan were almost from the time of their accession to independence confronted by secessionist wars while Nigeria had to fight a bitter civil war for close on three years to maintain her territorial integrity. When one realises that in a state such as Nigeria there are over two hundred ethnic groups, some with populations greater than those of, for instance, Gabon, Mauritania, Niger and Upper Volta, then one begins to appreciate the potential for internal conflict which the ethnic heterogeneity of African societies poses for the new states. This potential was all the more real by reason of the low level of institutionalisation of political structures, the parochial nature of political socialisation and the 'primitive' means of social communication and mobilisation which characterised these states. There is little doubt then that disputes over the borders created by colonial rule will remain to plague the newly independent states in the years to come. Be that as it may, it might be as well to take a closer look at some of the other problems that have arisen in the wake of independence.

THE BUREAUCRACY AND THE ECONOMY

In all the new states of Africa, the government was not only the largest single employer of labour, it was also the 'prime mover' economically and politically.[1] Because the public sector was so dominant, there can be no meaningful discussion of the problems of the new states that does not take into account the place and role of the bureaucracy in them. It has in fact been argued that it would be unreal to think of any type of national development in these states in which the bureaucracy, even if its role were limited to the provision of data, advice, and management expertise, was excluded.[2] Moreover, most of the independent African states exhibited a high degree of ethnic, religious and cultural heterogeneity, and as the histories of countries like Japan, after the Meiji Restoration, and Germany and Italy in the nineteenth century have shown, a centralised bureaucracy can be of crucial importance

---

[1] The percentages of wage and salary earners employed in the public sector in 1965 were: Somalia, 60; Sudan, 57; Togo, 48; Nigeria, 41; Ghana, 35; Senegal, 35; Tanzania, 32; Kenya, 29. Government spending as a percentage of GNP, 1961, gives the following figures: Somalia, 19; Sudan, 16; Togo, 13; Nigeria, 11; Ghana, 26; Tanzania, 18; Kenya, 17; Senegal, 24. (Source: Morrison *et al.*, *Black Africa*, tables 7.3 and 9.4.)
[2] Joseph La Palombara (ed.), *Bureaucracy and political development* (Princeton, 1969).

in the formation of a national entity out of a socio-cultural plurality. But though so central, the bureaucracy in the African states posed a number of problems.

With the exception of Egypt,[1] the bureaucracy was largely a new creation for most African states, an artifact of colonialism, which grew in most cases out of European military occupation, and most of its first members, as has been pointed out by one commentator, 'were military personnel drawn from the colonial regiments and occupation forces'.[2] Because of the need to maintain order in the colonised territories, this was the initial orientation of the civil servants in the new states. They were rarely development-oriented, an activity which before the Second World War was largely left to missionaries, trading companies, and, in the white-settled areas, to the immigrant European population. Even when, with increasing modernisation and rapid political change, particularly after the Second World War, the bureaucracy became involved in more complex administrative tasks, very little was done to develop indigenous participation in it at the policy-making level. Indeed, the expansion of the civil services after the war to meet the more complex tasks that the bureaucracy had to confront resulted in what has been described as a second colonial invasion.

As late as 1950 in the anglophone and francophone states, where more attention was given to the development of an indigenous bureaucracy than it was in the Belgian, Portuguese and Spanish territories, the managerial, supervisory, professional, senior technical and other upper levels of the administration were largely held by Europeans. The job of dismantling this racial structure was hardly begun in West Africa before 1948, and in East and Central Africa not before 1954 and 1960 respectively. As A. L. Adu noted, 'the pattern before the change [in the anglophone states] was that Europeans filled all "senior" service posts, that is, responsible posts in the administrative, executive, professional and technical grades. Local personnel were recruited to fill the "junior" service posts in the junior executive, clerical, semi-skilled and unskilled industrial and manipulative grades.' In East and Central Africa, he added, 'the situation was further complicated by the intervention

[1] Morroe Berger, *Bureaucracy and society in modern Egypt: a study of the higher civil service* (Princeton, 1957).
[2] A. L. Adu, *The civil service in the Commonwealth of Africa* (London, 1969), 17.

of the immigrant European, Asian and "coloured" communities who filled intermediate grade positions between the expatriate European and the Africans. They occupied what in West African terms may be described as the more junior of the so-called "European" appointments and the more senior of the African appointments.'[1]

The need rapidly to Africanise the bureaucracy in the African states meant that at independence most had civil services in which key decision-making posts had been filled either by relatively inexperienced, though educated, personnel, or by people who were experienced but not adequately educated. Even this generalisation has to be qualified. In states where one party was dominant before independence, it was not so much the relative competence of the individual as his ostensible loyalty to the party that became the prime consideration in the filling of posts. Africanisation thus became a method of ensuring that known party supporters were rewarded, and the notion of merit gave way to that of favouritism. The plums of independence were ready for the picking by the 'loyal'. In states such as Nigeria and Kenya, where ethnic considerations had been a very important factor in the struggle for independence, it was the individual's ethnic origin which mattered as the various ethnic groups competed to reap the fruits of independence. In either case, the end result was the same: efficiency was sacrificed to the demands of political expediency.

The anglophone and francophone states could, however, be said to have been relatively fortunate. The situation in the Belgian colonies was more dismal, as table 2.2 shows.

Zaire, once more, provides a classic example of the situation with respect to the bureaucracy in the Belgian territories. At the time of independence in 1960 there were only 30 Congolese (Zaireans) who had university degrees, while 350 were enrolled in the Congo's two universities. The total enrolment in secondary schools was 13 583. The result was that when independence came there were hardly any Congolese to man the bureaucracy (see table 2.3).

Prior to 1959, there had in fact been two civil services in the Congo: the civil service proper, which was restricted to the European population, and an auxiliary service in which Africans were to be found. When in 1959, by the Statut Unique, the

[1] *Ibid.*, 21.

Table 2.2. *Secondary school enrolment 1950 and 1966: selected countries.*

Country	Total estimated population (1969) in thousands	Secondary school enrolment	
		1950	1966
Kenya	10.9	8 000	49 223
Nigeria	56.7	21 437	202 683
Senegal	3.8	2 288	25 574
Central African Republic	1.5	237	4 668
Zaire	20.6	6 953	52 309
Rwanda	3.5	247	2 900
Burundi	3.5	350	2 932

Source: Morrison *et al.*, *Black Africa*, tables 5.9, 5.10, and 1.4.

Table 2.3. *Composition of the civil service in the Congo, 1960.*

Rank	Minimum educational requirement	Europeans	Africans
1	university	106	0
2	university	1 004	1
3	university	3 532	2
4	2 yrs university – complete secondary	5 159	800
5–7	four years primary – secondary	0	11 000

Source: Crawford Young, *Politics in the Congo*, 402.

bureaucracy was consolidated and seven grades established, only some 800 Congolese were found suitable for recruitment to the fourth rank, which had previously been exclusive to Europeans. Therefore, when the Belgians pulled out of the Congo at independence, the new African leaders found they barely had a civil service, for with only 30 graduates available to fill over 4000 vacated posts, one could hardly talk of the Congolese inheriting a bureaucracy.

It has been suggested that the bureaucracy has a crucial role to play in the political development of the new states in Africa. But this is a role for which the colonial bureaucracy was not designed and therefore it had to be considerably adapted to meet the demands of independent African states. Yet it was at the time when new orientations had to be formed for problem-solving that the bureaucracy had to face the dislocations caused by Africanisation and restructuring. In most cases, the 'new men' had neither the capabilities nor the experience to cope with the tasks they were confronted with – for example, formulating the new 'five-year development plans' which became fashionable with independence – while interference in matters pertaining to appointments and promotions by the new political leaders undermined what traditions of discipline, integrity and impartiality had existed previously in the civil service.

Besides being ill-equipped for the new role expected of them, the 'new men', as inheritors of the posts vacated by their erstwhile colonial masters, in most cases also fought to retain and to preserve the privileges and perquisites of the offices they had come to occupy, antithetical as these often were to the needs of the newly independent states. In seeking to maintain the aura of their offices, they succeeded only in cutting themselves off from the realities of their societies and in the process became, with the political leaders, a new breed of privileged élite, for whom, as in the colonial period, all else had to be sacrificed. Policy-making, in these circumstances, could not but be haphazard, as the priorities of the society were distorted to suit the demands of this élite. The bureaucracy, by the dialectics of independence, became, like the colonial system, a burden to the new states. In most of these, administrative costs soon accounted for more than sixty per cent of the recurrent budget. For these 'soft states', to use the language of Gunnar Myrdal, the distinguished Swedish development economist, with party structures which hardly extended beyond the main urban centres and barely existent local political structures, the dilemmas posed by a politicised bureaucratic system lacking the necessary techno-managerial skills became almost overwhelming. The situation was exacerbated by a wage structure and an educational framework which discriminated against the acquisition of managerial skills and expertise but placed a premium on a literary and 'liberal' education which was barely consonant with the technocratic requirements of a developing society.

SOCIAL MOBILISATION

Most African states proved not unmindful of the shortcomings of their public services and many initiated schemes for retraining and reorganisation. But if the problems posed by the bureaucracy – lack of (or inadequate) skills, inexperience, inefficiency – were partly solved by these schemes, it was not obvious that those posed by the structure of the society and the economy were so amenable.

One of the legacies of colonialism in the independent African states was the super-imposition of a new stratificational pattern on the traditional social structure. Since independence, not only did this new pattern (which owed itself more to western-type education than to any other single factor) displace and replace the traditional social structure, but the different strata tended in fact to rigidify, thereby creating what has been described by many observers as an 'élite–mass' gap, one of the main sources of instability in the independent African states.

In traditional society, status was defined either in kinship or lineage terms, or by age and sex. With the creation of new bureaucratic roles which required a formal education, the colonial state introduced a new criterion for status differentiation, and the acquisition of a formal education rapidly became the passport to upward mobility in the emergent stratification system. At independence, some five different levels of this stratificational system could be distinguished in the various African states.[1] The topmost stratum, which for purposes of convenience may be designated the 'upper class', and which was composed of approximately one per cent of the total population, was itself made up of two segments, the bureaucratic–professional and the commercial. The former was composed of the upper echelons of the bureaucracy (including parastatals), the military, lawyers, doctors, managers and university teachers, the educated élite who had had at least three years of university education; while the latter comprised the large farmers growing export crops and the big mercantile–contracting class, often linked with foreign financial interests and the 'political class' with whom they shared a

---

[1] E. De Kadt and G. Williams (eds.), *Sociology and development* (London, 1974); R. Sandbrook and R. Cohen (eds.), *The development of an African working class* (London, 1975); I. G. Shivji, *Class struggles in Tanzania* (Dar es Salaam, 1975).

common interest, that of furthering their economic ends through the manipulation and control of the machinery of state.

The second stratum, which might be termed the 'middle class', also formed two segments, the first consisting of the executive, technical and clerical cadres of the bureaucracy, the junior ranks of the military, school teachers and the like. These made up some two per cent of the total population, while the other segment, comprising some ten per cent of the population, could be defined residually as the *petite bourgeoisie*, those who were neither members of the 'upper class', nor of the third or fourth strata – the 'working class' (or proletariat) or the 'peasants'. These were the 'petty traders', usually self-employed, with little or no formal education and owning very little capital.

The proletariat was made up of the skilled, semi-skilled and unskilled labourers, who, like the *petit-bourgeois* members of the middle class had acquired little, if any, formal education. This stratum accounted for between five and eight per cent of the population, and in states where unionisation was permitted, was usually organised into trade unions. The fourth stratum, which formed something between 70 and 80 per cent of the population, consisted of the peasants, the 'subsistence farmers', who more often than not were illiterate and were usually to be found farming land not much more than an acre in area.

To the foregoing must be added a fifth stratum, the ever-growing class of unemployed – and possibly unemployable – primary-school leavers and school 'drop-outs'. This class was the creation largely of the post-independence era and a product of two main factors. The first was the explosion in formal education which generally accompanied the approach to, or the attainment of, independence. The second was the nature of the post-colonial 'administrative state'. Because of the need to provide the educated manpower required by newly independent states, most African states had rapidly to expand their educational systems. However, since the state was the main employer of labour, either job opportunities became quickly exhausted or the products of the schools became functionally obsolescent as the demand for labour became increasingly skill-specific. The result was the creation of a 'reserve army' – a veritable lumpenproletariat – of unemployed and unemployable youths who then began to constitute a real socio-political threat to the stability of the new state. This threat became all too real when the problem of the unemployable was considered in relation to the problem of urbanisation. In the past, the size of the city served as an index of 'progress' and 'development', so that by 1950 the urban population of the developed, rich countries was just about double that of the third-world countries. By 1975, however, half of the 15 largest cities in the world (measured in population) were situated in the poor states and it has been estimated that by 1990, 60 per cent of the world's urban population will be living in the cities of Africa, Asia and Latin America, a figure which is expected to rise to 75 per cent by the end of the century. Between 1970 and 1975, of the 106 million persons estimated to have moved from the rural into the urban areas, some 70 per cent (73 million) were in the nations of the Third World and a good proportion of these were school leavers moving into the cities in search of jobs.

Taking the Horn of Africa as an example of one of the poorest regions of Africa, the population of Addis Ababa, capital of Ethiopia, jumped from 560000 in the mid-1960s to over a million in 1974, a growth rate of about 7 per cent per annum. The comparable figures for Mogadishu and Asmara, capital cities of Somalia and Eritrea respectively, were 141000 in 1965 rising to over 250000 in 1974 for the former and 132000 rising to 296000 for the latter in the same time period. And these figures nowhere compare to the growth rates in the capital cities of some West African states. For example Lagos, the capital of Nigeria, between 1970 and 1975 recorded an annual growth rate of just about 14 per cent per annum. What was particularly striking about urban growth in African states was that growth occurred in states which were least capable of dealing with the multitude of problems associated with urbanisation. For the African states, far from being an index of 'progress', urbanisation began to be seen as an index of decay. To quote the third report to the Club of Rome, *Reshaping the international order,*

it is in the cities where the glaring disparities between the 'haves' and 'have nots' are most apparent. It is also in cities where poverty and disadvantage are the most concentrated. Migrants to the city are no ordinary people. They have taken the courageous decision to dig up their rural roots, to seek a 'new life' for themselves and their children. In coming to the city, they bring with them expectations and aspirations. If cities cannot meet these, if cities can offer no alternative to poverty, it will be in cities that future structural changes in national orders will be wrought. In the past modernization has tended to mean urbanization. In the future, it cannot do so.[1]

The pattern of social stratification described above, as one might expect, is a generalised and somewhat paradigmatic model which does not purport to be a faithful description of the concrete stratificational system as this exists in the different states. For example, Tunisia developed a much more homogeneous and coherent bureaucratic–managerial ruling class, which in fact profited proportionately more, compared to other sectors of society, from the acquisition of the landed properties previously owned by the small white-settler population, than either Morocco or Algeria. Algeria, on the other hand, by the agrarian reforms of 1972, succeeded better than Kenya in breaking up the emergent connexions between the landowning bourgeoisie and the top bureaucrats controlling the state apparatus. Equally Kenya had a much more visible class structure than Tanzania which, because of its proclaimed ideological stance and its previous history as a Trust Territory, together with its much smaller settler presence, was able to achieve greater success in its determined attempts to ameliorate class inequalities than other African states, with the possible exception of states like Guinea-Bissau, Mozambique and Angola. But whatever the variations, most African states were increasingly approximating to the paradigm given above so that it can be regarded as being not unrepresentative of the class structure of the African state during our period.

With any economy that remains mainly commodity–export-oriented long after independence, and whose surpluses go largely into the import of consumer goods to satisfy the demands of the élite, and with education as the principal avenue to upward social mobility and more and more students competing for the limited access to higher education, fewer and fewer make it into the ranks of the highly privileged upper class. As J. D. Barkan discovered in a survey of university students in Ghana, Uganda and Tanzania, states which were not untypical of many of the independent African states, 'the recruitment of university students, and hence the technocratic upper-middle class itself, is...becoming more and more restricted to sons and daughters of citizens with

[1] Jan Tinbergen (co-ordinator), *Reshaping the international order* (London, 1977), 31–2.

78

Table 2.4. *Degree to which ranks desired are expected to be fulfilled.*

	Ghana		Tanzania		Uganda	
	First job	Last job	First job	Last job	First job	Last job
	%		%		%	
Expect to obtain position at desired rank	79	58	76	40	66	37
Do not expect to obtain position at desired rank	9	22	12	33	15	30
Don't know	12	20	12	27	19	33
N =	(615)	(615)	(479)	(479)	(550)	(550)

Source: Barkan, *An African dilemma*, table 2.9.

relatively high educational backgrounds. Rather than bridge the élite–mass gap, students are consequently more likely to exacerbate this cleavage, and inhibit the process of vertical integration in their societies.'[1]

An obvious outcome of the élite–mass gap and the self-recruitment of the educated upper and middle classes was the alienation of the intelligentsia as expectations lagged behind the desired futures. Table 2.4 is sufficiently indicative of this. The educational system implanted by the metropolitan powers was intended to serve as a bridge between African traditional societies and western culture. But in bridging the gap between the 'traditional' and the 'modern', the system has not only undermined traditional culture but has also created a dilemma for the independent states: though purportedly change-inducing, it has produced a structure which had become perhaps the most important impediment to that change which it sought to bring about.

[1] Joel D. Barkan, *An African dilemma* (Nairobi, 1975), 188. See also David Court, 'The education system as a response to inequality in Tanzania and Kenya', *Journal of Modern African Studies*, 1976, **14**, 4; Richard Marvin, 'Why do African parents value schooling?' *Journal of Modern African Studies*, 1975, **13**, 3; Remi P. Clignet and Philip Foster, *The fortunate few* (Evanston, 1966); P. Foster, *Education and social change in Ghana*, (Chicago, 1965); David Abernethy, *The political dilemma of popular education* (Stanford, 1969).

Table 2.5. *Export and import trade: selected countries.*

Country	Principal export as % of total exports, 1966–8	No. of commodities making up 70% of exports, 1966–8	% of imports composed of 'machinery', 1962
Cameroun	28	4	16
Congo (Braz.)	48	2	42
Ethiopia	56	3	38
Guinea	64	2	40
Ivory Coast	35	3	32
Kenya	26	6	20
Lesotho	60	2	5
Liberia	73	1	55
Malawi	25	4	25
Niger	65	2	9
Sierra Leone	57	2	15
Tanzania	19	6	26
Zambia	94	1	30

Source: Morrison *et al.*, *Black Africa*, tables 13.2, 13.3 and 13.4.

The problem of the structure of the society was compounded by the structure of the economies of the African states. The colonial authorities saw these states essentially as sources of raw materials and markets for the products of European industry. Communications and other infrastructural developments were therefore carried out with these two aims in view, to the neglect of almost everything else. Africa thus inherited economies – enclave economies – in which the primary economic activity consisted in the production of export commodities for use in the factories of Europe and in the import of manufactures and other consumer goods. And since the price of manufactures rose quickly relative to agricultural commodities, both the balance of trade and of payments moved more in favour of Europe than of Africa. A structural dependence was thus created which barely changed during our period, as tables 2.5 and 2.6 show.

In these states, which are typical of the vast majority of states of independent Africa, the export of just about two commodities – which ranged from cotton, gum arabic, coffee, cocoa and sisal to

Table 2.6. *Direction of trade: selected countries.*

Country	Trade with African states, 1968		Trade with former colonial power		
	% Import	% Export	% Export, 1955	Total, 1962	Total, 1968
Cameroun	10	9	53	57	46
Congo (Braz.)	6	4	34	51	37
Guinea	1	9	63	17	13
Ivory Coast	10	8	58	54	41
Kenya	11	39	27	30	24
Lesotho	5	5	3	10	5
Liberia	2	2	n/a	n/a	n/a
Malawi	24	19	60	34	33
Niger	15	30	85	54	56
Sierra Leone	3	0	73	46	48
Somalia	11	1	2	38	40
Tanzania	17	18	33	45	23

Source: Morrison *et al.*, *Black Africa*, tables 13.5 and 13.6, 13.9–13.11.

copper, iron-ore, gold and petroleum – constituted approximately 70 per cent of total trade, while the import of 'machinery', which included vehicles and other mechanical devices, constituted less than a third of total trade.

Dependence was not just in terms of the export of commodities, it was also reflected in the pattern of trade. Close to a decade after independence, less than 10 per cent of all export and 14 per cent of all import trade was between African states as against 33 per cent with the previous colonial power. Trade between the African states in 1968 and eastern bloc countries ranged between one and 10 per cent with only four states, Guinea, Mali, the Sudan and Egypt, having a figure of more than 10 per cent. The mean figure of trade with the United States during the same period was 9.28 per cent with only three states, Burundi, Liberia and Ethiopia, having a figure of just about a third. In fact, at the time of the independence in 1960 of most of the African states (if trade between South Africa, Rhodesia/Zimbabwe, Zambia and Malawi, which accounted for over 40 per cent of total exports and imports, is ignored), about 35 per cent of total intra-African imports was

Table 2.7. *Percentage industrial composition of GDP at factor cost, 1965.*

Country	Agri- culture	Industrial activity	Con- struction	Transport and communi- cation	Trade	Other
Kenya	38	13	2	10	12	25
Morocco	32	22	5	—	22	18
Tanzania	55	7	3	5	13	17
Tunisia	22	18	9	8	15	27
Uganda	59	12	2	3	10	14
Zambia	10	48	7	6	13	16

Source: UN *Yearbook of national account statistics 1966,* 693–4.

absorbed by four countries, Algeria, Ghana, the Ivory Coast and Egypt, while 36 per cent of intra-African exports was provided by Kenya, Morocco, the Ivory Coast and Mali. Much of this trade was also limited to a restricted number of items, with food, beverages and tobacco forming about 59 per cent of the total in value with crude materials, fuels and manufactures making up 15, 3 and 22 per cent respectively.[1]

If the competitive nature of African exports can be taken to explain the low level of intra-African trade, the reliance on a few export commodities for foreign-exchange earnings and the higher price of imported manufactures relative to exports together accounted for the inability of the African states to transform their economies into more industrially based ones. Table 2.7 is illustrative of the industrial composition of the gross domestic product of some selected African states.

Even though the contribution of 'industrial activity' to GDP has been slowly rising in most African states during our period, there were certain peculiar characteristics of manufacturing which should be noted. For this purpose, Nigeria can be considered as a case study. For all the seemingly impressive growth rate of domestic manufacturing – 14 per cent between 1958 and 1963 and 15 per cent in 1971/2 – much of it remained largely characterised by low-level technology. On the other hand, the manufacture of

[1] P. Robson and D. A. Lury (eds.), *The economies of Africa* (London, 1969), 57.

Table 2.8. *Imported raw-material component in Nigerian manufacturing: selected industries, 1972.*

Industry group	% Raw material imported
Dairy products	40.85
Grain-mill products	99.75
Miscellaneous food products	60.35
Animal feeds	35.70
Beer brewing	46.00
Soft drinks	45.55
Made-up textile goods (except wearing apparel)	79.65
Carpets and rugs	100.00
Paper containers, boxes and board	44.95
Basic industrial chemicals	87.30
Fertilisers and pesticides	43.50
Drugs and medicines	45.45
Other chemical products	61.05
Tyres and tubes	44.75
Pottery products	92.10
Glass products	65.35
Concrete products (other than cement, bricks and tiles)	44.55

Source: Federation of Nigeria, third national development plan, 1975–80, 148.

agricultural and special industrial equipment, household electrical apparatus, and machinery and transport equipment, which required relatively more sophisticated technology, was a bare 2.3 per cent in 1972. Secondly, much manufacturing depended very largely on a high level of import components, as table 2.8 shows.

Whatever the rationale for industrialisation may have been – the creation of greater self-reliance through the diversification of the economy; the generation of more varied and increasing employment opportunities to meet the demands of a rapidly growing population; or the provision of greater welfare through overall economic development – the basic strategy in almost all the states was the process of introducing import substituting industries and therefore the conservation of foreign-exchange earnings for further investment. But as the Nigerian example shows, and it is not atypical, that strategy tended to prove more or less self-

Table 2.9. *Percentage expenditure p.m. GNP (at market prices): selected countries.*

Country	Year	Private consumption	General govt. expenditure on consumption	Fixed Capital formation	Increase in stocks	Exports Less Imports on goods and services		Net factor income from abroad
Algeria	1959	60	35	—	26	20	41	—
Cameroun	1963	72	15	11	—	23	21	—
Chad	1963	84	14	11	1	15	25	—
Congo (Braz.)	1964	67	23	14	1	—	—	-5
Ethiopia	1963	82	9	12	—	11	13	-1
Ghana	1965	80	13	16	—	16	24	-1
Malawi	1963	86	21	14	1	—	-21	-2
Morocco	1965	73	14	11	—	20	19	—
Sierra Leone	1964	85	9	13	—	30	34	-3
Sudan	1964	76	12	11	3	16	19	—
Tanzania	1965	72	14	14	—	31	30	-1
Tunisia	1965	72	17	27	1	20	35	-2

Source: UN Yearbook of national account statistics 1966, 681–2.

Table 2.10. *Total long-term and publicly guaranteed external debt: selected non-petroleum-producing states ($ billion).*

Country	End 1973	End 1974	End 1975	End 1976
Egypt	1.73	3.89	6.31	7.30
Tanzania	0.46	0.61	0.79	0.96
Zaire	0.89	1.31	1.68	1.90
Zambia	0.57	0.68	0.95	1.20

Source: H. van B. Cleveland and W. H. Bruce Britain, 'Are the LDC's in over their heads?', *International Affairs*, July 1977, 734.

defeating. The reason for this lay in the main with the government of the African states. First, despite grandiloquent five (or six or ten) year development plans, much of capital investment tended to be left to the small band of African entrepreneurs, with foreign financial links, whose main interest was the profitability of their investments, whatever the consequences for their countries. Secondly, because of their overriding desire to retain political power, government leaders found it inadvisable to tamper with the consumption habits of the élite on whom they relied for political support. The result was therefore for that élite to prefer to maintain their acquired taste for foreign consumer goods rather than to save, as table 2.9 shows.

The need to assuage élite consumption patterns, coupled with the necessity nevertheless to develop economically (and in the case of Egypt, to maintain defence requirements) not surprisingly led to heavy foreign indebtedness on the part of the African states, with some having as high a debt to GDP ratio as 0.80. With foreign indebtedness growing faster than the rate of growth of GDP, the capacity of these states to meet their foreign obligations became more doubtful. For some, unless the improbable were to happen, the long-term outcome seemed not unlikely to be complete bankruptcy.

That likelihood might have been obviated had African states agreed to cooperate or integrate to form larger units. For whatever the difficulties might be with regard to economic mobilisation, the simple fact remained that most of the independent African states were too small and too poor to form viable economic units. In 1964, for example, some 24 African states had populations of less than five million (four had populations of less than a million). Seven states had populations varying between 11 and 20 million, while Ethiopia had 22.2 million, Egypt 28.9 million and Nigeria 56.4 million. Of the 42 states listed as independent in 1972 (excluding Egypt), only 17 had a per capita GDP in excess of 200 dollars and only six – Algeria, Gabon, the Ivory Coast, Libya, South Africa and Tunisia – exceeded 400 dollars. Africa's share of the total world real income was just about 5 per cent, while its income from manufactures was approximately 2 per cent. In terms of trade in food, though by the mid-1930s Africa was exporting about one million tons of cereals per annum, by 1975 she was importing 10 million tons per annum. For most, then, the only hope of future progress seemed to lie in some form of economic union or the other. As Peter Robson rightly noted:

ultimately the character and pace of economic development in Africa may be considerably influenced for the better by the consolidation and development of economic integration arrangements. But although the long-term objectives of most African States can best be served by economic co-operation, short-term interests often lead to independent action. The future of economic co-operation in Africa will depend on which of these considerations becomes dominant.[1]

Given the competitive nature of African economies, the legacy of their colonial past and the character of their political leadership, one could not be sanguine about the prospects for integration.[2]

The evidence of two decades of independence showed that African leaders were more influenced by short-term considerations than by long-term interests. Few, if any, of the actual attempts at cooperation and integration – including the most promising East African Economic Community – survived the first twenty years of independence while many others remained either as proposals or as unions on paper only. In the last analysis, if there could be said to be a problem of independence, it was that independence gave to most of the African states a cover of spurious sovereignty with political power having been transferred to a political leadership whose sole aim – and achievement – was to have retained that power by preserving the myth of sovereignty.[3]

---

[1] Peter Robson, *Economic integration in Africa* (London, 1968), 21.
[2] See e.g. Hannu Nurmi, 'Public goods and the analytic theory of the state', in P. Birnbaum, J. Lively and G. Parry (eds.), *Democracy, consensus and social contract* (London and Beverly Hills, 1978).
[3] Arthur Hazlewood (ed.), *African integration and disintegration* (Oxford, 1967).

THE MILITARY AND MILITARISM

Independence not only brought to the fore the problem of economic dependency, but also that of the military, a problem that turned into a spectre haunting all the African states.[1] Having an armed force was as much part of the accoutrements of sovereignty as having a national flag or a national anthem. But though it could hardly be argued that most of these states faced any serious external threat to their sovereignty, they certainly were not hesitant about maintaining large military establishments – large, that is, relative to their resources and security needs, both external and internal. In fact, but for the problem of internal security, few of these states could be said to have required the size of armed personnel they established. (The colonial authorities, because they had to maintain their presence by armed force, had of necessity to create a military establishment requisite for that purpose though for the most part their armies were very small.) Thus, while the African states came to independence with quite small armies, there can be no escaping the fact that with independence the rate of increase in the size of the armed forces was quite phenomenal. And with the growth in size, there was a more or less corresponding increase in 'defence' expenditure (table 2.11).

Significant as the increases may have been, the full import of defence spending is perhaps only properly appreciated when it is compared with spending in other sectors, for example, on welfare services. The ratio of expenditure on defence to that on welfare in the African states when compared with the ratio in some of the developed countries or even other third-world states such as Venezuela, suggests that the choice of priorities in the African states was misplaced (tables 2.12 and 2.13).

The problem posed by the military in the new states of Africa was, however, not just one of numbers and costs, important as these may have been for the development of these states. There were also the related issues of dependency and instability. African armies, like their counterparts throughout the world, were in a narrow professional sense, 'modernity'-oriented. Being thus oriented, they were concerned about the state of their hardware, which tended to become outdated with rapid technological

[1] The literature on the military is quite extensive. There is a good bibliography in Claude E. Welch Jnr. and Arthur K. Smith, *Military role and rule* (Belmont, Cal., 1974).

Table 2.11. *Manpower and cost of African armies: selected countries.*

Country	Total man-power in hundreds, 1967	% change, 1963–7	Defence budget as % of govt. expendi-ture, 1967	% change in defence budget, 1963–7	Level of Africani-sation, 1965[a]
Nigeria	500	479	9.9	128	4
Zaire	354	10	14.5	118	3
Ethiopia	350	14	17.0	45	5
Sudan	185	54	17.7	67	5
Ghana	160	83	7·4	33	5
Somalia	95	85	18.1	33	5
Uganda	60	182	10.2	400	1
Senegal	55	103	11.6	107	4
Guinea	50	−4	8.1	87	5
Tanzania	50	11	3.8	150	1
Kenya	48	71	6.9	100	2
Ivory Coast	45	4	6.9	44	2
Liberia	41	10	6.7	28	5
Cameroun	35	21	19.5	35	1
Mali	35	6	21.2	17	4
Zambia	30	−6	5.7	110	1
Rwanda	25	153	9.7	182	1
Sierra Leone	19	1	4.9	33	2
Congo (Braz.)	18	143	8.9	80	2
Dahomey (Bénin)	18	64	12.0	15	2
Togo	15	569	13.5	350	2
Upper Volta	15	43	14.1	0	4
Niger	13	0	10.8	71	3
Burundi	10	15	6.9	−13	4
Mauritania	10	90	17.9	10	2
Chad	9	117	13.5	33	2
Malawi	9	−44	3.3	33	1
Gabon	8	30	7.6	41	3
Central African Rep.	6	11	7.9	83	2
Botswana	0	0	0.0	0	0
Gambia	0	0	0.0	0	0
Lesotho	0	0	0.0	0	0

[a] 0 = no army before independence; 1 = officer corps entirely foreign before independence; 2 = no indigenous officer corps before independence – mixed after independence with near-complete indigenisation at 1965; 3 = no indigenous officer corps before independence – total Africanisation thereafter; 4 = indigenous officers before independence; 5 = never a colonial territory, or indigenous officer corps at all levels by or shortly after independence.

Source: Morrison *et al.*, *Black Africa*, 116, 119, 120.

Table 2.12. *Comparative expenditure: selected countries 1972.*

Country	General economic		Public expenditures						Manpower					
	Pop. 1000	GNP $US million	Military $US million	% 3 of 2	Education $ million	% 4 of 2	Health $ million	% 5 of 2	Armed forces 1000	% 6 of 1	Teachers 1000	% 7 of 1	Doctors 1000	% 8 of 1
	1	2	3	2	4	2	5	2	6	1	7	1	8	1
Nigeria	69 500	10 585	566	5.35	204	1.92	30	0.28	274	0.39	119	0.02	3.1	0.004
Kenya	12 070	1 964	25	1.27	86	4.38	31	1.57	7	0.58	56	0.50	1.6	0.013
Ivory Coast	4 530	1 832	22	1.20	126	6.88	7	0.38	4	0.09	15	0.03	0.3	0.006
Ghana	9 700	2 572	34	1.32	97	3.77	27	1.05	19	0.02	61	0.06	0.8	0.008
Algeria	15 270	6 250	108	1.72	578	9.25	97	1.55	60	0.39	60	0.40	2.0	0.013
Zaire	22 860	2 378	100	4.20	132	5.55	18	0.75	50	0.22	88	0.38	0.9	0.040
Tanzania	14 000	1 522	37	2.43	55	3.61	23	1.51	11	0.08	24	0.17	0.6	0.043
USA	208 840	1 168 100	77 638	6.64	65 652	5.62	35 441	3.03	2 322	1.12	2 308	1.10	320.9	0.150
UK	56 790	154 308	8 186	5.30	8 962	5.80	8 641	5.60	372	0.07	530	0.90	73.6	0.130
Venezuela	10 970	14 097	270	1.91	663	4.70	310	2.20	34	0.31	71	0.65	10.9	0.010

Source: Ruth Leger Sivard: *World military and social expenditures* (Virginia, 1974).

Table 2.13. $ US Social and military indicators: per capita ranking, 1972 (rank in brackets).

Country	GNP per capita	Education		Health			Military expenditure	
		Public expenditure per capita	% illiteracy	Public expenditure per capita	Infant Mortality per 1000	Expenditure per capita	Expenditure per soldier	Pop. per soldier
Algeria	409 (4)	38 (2)	75(13)	6 (6)	86 (7.5)	7 (9.5)	1 800(22)	260 (5)
Botswana	119(18)	10(11)	67 (7)	4 (9.5)	175(38)	—	—	—
Burundi	66(41)	2(37)	90(25)	1(10)	161(32)	1(26.5)	1 500(25)	1700(31)
Cameroun	213(17)	9(13.5)	90(25)	2(22)	110 (9)	4(17)	6000 (3)	1520(29)
Central African Rep.	152(25)	5(21.2)	92(26)	2(22)	163(35)	4(17)	6000 (3)	1650(30)
Chad	82(36)	2(37)	94(28)	1(30)	155(29)	4(17)	4667 (7)	1260(23)
Congo	355 (8)	22 (5)	80(17)	5 (8)	148(24)	10 (4.5)	5 000 (6)	490(11)
Dahomey (Bénin)	104(31.5)	5(21.2)	80(17)	2(22)	150(26.5)	2(23)	2 500(17)	1440(28)
Eq. Guinea	264(14)	3(32)	80(17)	3(14)	140(21.5)	3(19)	1 000(29.5)	290 (6.5)
Ethiopia	78(37)	2(37)	93(27)	1(30)	162(33.5)	2(23)	1067(28)	580(14)
Gabon	916 (2)	19 (7)	70 (9)	12 (2.5)	184(41)	10 (4.5)	5 000 (6)	500(12)
Gambia	141(27)	5(21.2)	90(25)	3(14)	146(23)	—	—	—
Ghana	265(13)	10(11)	75(13)	3(14)	64 (3.5)	4(17)	1790(23)	510(13)
Guinea	105(30)	5(21.2)	90(25)	1(30)	155(29)	4(17)	2 500(17)	680(17)
Ivory Coast	404 (6)	28 (4)	80(17)	3(14)	138(20)	4(13)	5 500 (4)	1130(21)
Kenya	163(21.5)	7(16)	75(13)	3(14)	55 (1)	2(23)	3 571(10)	1720(32)
Lesotho	100(34)	4(28.5)	41 (2)	1(30)	137(18)	—	—	—
Liberia	222(16)	6(19)	85(19)	3(14)	137(18)	2(23)	1 000(29.5)	400 (8)

Libya	1982 (1)	101 (1)	73(10)	53 (1)	130(14)	48 (1)	4000 (9)	80 (1)
Malagasy Rep.	149(26)	5(21.2)	61 (5)	3(14)	55 (1)	2(23)	3000(14)	1780(33)
Malawi	99(35)	3(32)	78(14)	1(30)	119(12)	—	2000(21)	467(36)
Mali	67(40)	3(32)	90(25)	1(30)	168(36.5)	2(23)	2000(21)	1320(25.5)
Mauritania	174(20)	6(19)	95(30)	1(30)	137(18)	8 (7.5)	5000 (6)	620(15)
Mauritius	320(10)	10(11)	38 (1)	8 (4)	64 (3.5)	1(26.5)	—	—
Morocco	276(11)	14 (8)	80(17)	3(14)	149(25)	9 (6)	2556(16)	290 (6.5)
Niger	103(33)	2(37)	95(30)	1(30)	140(21.5)	1(26.5)	2000(21)	2100(35)
Nigeria	152(24)	3(32)	75(13)	—	58 (2)	8 (7.5)	2066(18)	250 (4)
Rhodesia	346 (9)	8(15)	75(13)	5 (8)	86 (7.5)	5(13)	6000 (3)	1140(22)
Rwanda	64(42)	2(37)	90(25)	3(14)	133(15)	1(26.5)	833(32)	650(16)
Senegal	252(15)	1(38.5)	90(25)	3(14)	67 (5)	5(13)	3333(12)	690(18)
Sierra Leone	183(19)	6(19)	90(25)	2(22)	136(16)	1(26.5)	1700(24)	1320(25.5)
Somalia	71(38)	1(38.5)	95(30)	1(30)	154(27)	4(17)	943(31)	210 (2)
South Africa	850 (3)	2(37)	60 (4)	4(95)	179(35)	19 (2)	25529 (1)	1350(27)
Sudan	125(28)	6(19)	90(25)	2(22)	121(13)	7 (9.5)	3139(13)	460 (9.5)
Swaziland	267(12)	12 (9)	64 (6)	5 (8)	168(36.5)	—	—	—
Tanzania	109(29)	4(28.5)	85(19)	2(22)	162(33.5)	3(19)	3382(11)	1270(24)
Togo	160(23)	5(21.2)	85(19)	1(30)	155(29)	2(23)	4400 (8)	2090(34)
Tunisia	405 (5)	30 (3)	68 (8)	7 (5)	78 (6)	6(11)	1258(26)	220 (3)
Uganda	163(21.5)	9(13.5)	75(13)	2(22)	113(10)	3(19)	2769(15)	800(20)
Upper Volta	69(38)	2(37)	95(31)	1(30)	181(40)	1(26.5)	2500(00)	2800(00)
Zaire	104(31.5)	6(19)	87(20)	1(30)	115(11)	4(17)	2004(19)	460 (9.5)
Zambia	359 (7)	21 (6)	59 (3)	12 (2.5)	159(31)	17 (3)	1250(27)	740(19)

Source: Sivard, *World military and social expenditures,* Rank ordering recomputed.

change. Weapons systems therefore had to be changed frequently, as the technology of war changed. But since most African countries (with the exception of South Africa) had neither the technological skills nor the resource base to maintain a modern armaments industry, it followed that all military hardware had to be imported from the arms merchants and manufacturers of Europe, the United States and the eastern-bloc countries. The need to ensure a regular supply of arms, both in terms of new acquisitions and the replacement and servicing of existing weapons, not infrequently led to a dependency relation which was further enhanced and consolidated through such devices as the giving of military aid, as the history of the United States' military aid to Ethiopia and the Soviet Union's supply of arms to Egypt (up till about 1973-4 in both cases) so clearly demonstrated. Dependency and aid were not infrequently accompanied by the intrusion of great-power rivalry into the domestic politics of the African states, introducing thereby further elements of instability. As examples of this, one could cite Soviet-American rivalry over Cuban intervention in the Angolan war of liberation; the intervention in Zaire by France, the United States, Belgium and Western Germany, through the surrogate provided by Morocco, when Cuban-trained Zairean mercenaries invaded the Shaba (former Katanga) province; Soviet-American rivalry in the Somalia-Ethiopia conflicts; Franco-Soviet rivalry in the Sahara, with France backing Morocco and Mauritania, and the Soviet Union supporting the Polisario, the nationalist movement fighting for the independence of the former Spanish Sahara – also supported by Algeria. Finally there was the special case of South Africa, where the struggle for African majority rule seemed a possible trigger for a third World War in which the drama of great-power rivalry would be played out between the west and the eastern-bloc countries.

Attempts at escaping from dependency through the diversification of supply sources were not very successful during the period covered by this volume. Not only did they prove costly and lead to inefficiency, but such attempts were countered by the withholding of supplies and replacements, so that, far from ending dependency, diversification only succeeded in replacing dependency on one or a limited number of supply sources by that on others. To this fact must be added the growth of a militaristic spirit fostered through the acquisition, from both the western and communist blocs, of arms. Most African armies, owing to lack of technological skills, a relatively low level of education, inexperience deriving from the escalation in numbers and the sometimes over-rapid indigenisation of the officer corps, were incapable of using the sophisticated products of the modern armaments industry. Much of the hardware therefore turned out not unexpectedly to be the redundant or discarded items of European armies, those already rendered obsolete through technological change. Thus African states became the dumping ground for such hardware (as indeed they had been in pre-colonial times), a dumping which tended to foster a new militarism, as seen in the increasing incidence of border wars, military coups and various other acts of aggression on the civilian populations of these states. The 'sovereignty of the people' proclaimed with the declaration of independence became, for many an African state, nothing more than tutelage under the military. Independence itself became a paradox.

POLITICAL LEADERSHIP AND POLITICAL SUCCESSION

The global changes which followed the end of the Second World War made independence for the various African states inevitable. It might be argued, however, that though independence was inevitable, these states were little prepared to cope with the numerous problems which went with the granting of a sovereign status.[1] But such an argument could be misleading, because of the ambiguity inherent in the notion of 'preparedness'. On the other hand, the argument about lack of preparedness could be taken to mean that the colonial authorities, by their various policies, failed to create in the territories they governed the conditions necessary for the assumption of sovereignty. It is not exactly clear how the 'necessary conditions' could be specified, but that interpretation has not been without its protagonists amongst African nationalist leaders, many of whom in fact used it to hasten the process of, and justify the demand for, independence.

On the other hand the argument about lack of preparedness

[1] B. B. Shaffer, 'The concept of preparation – some questions about the transfer of systems of government', *World Politics*, 1965, **18**; Ali Mazrui, 'Edmund Burke and reflections on the revolution in the Congo', in Ali Mazrui, *On heroes and Uhuru-worship: essays on independent Africa* (London, 1967), 3–18.

could be taken to mean that the African peoples were themselves unprepared for independence, implying that they were, in some sense, incapable of self-government. One of the grounds used to justify the original colonisation of Africa by the Europeans was that Africans were not capable of governing themselves, a notion that nationalist leaders quite properly rejected. For them the right to self-government also included the right to self-misgovernment. But as the African states continued to grapple with the problems of independence, the question of preparedness, irrelevant though it may now seem to be, continued to be raised. Africa's colonial heritage and the dependency which followed from that heritage has led to problems that must be overcome; the concept of 'preparedness' may throw light on these problems, but apart from its interest to historians, it can only usefully be employed as a challenge to African states to take decisions based on a rational assessment of possible solutions.

CHAPTER 3

PAN-AFRICANISM SINCE 1940

In 1940, Pan-Africanism seemed to be in a state of decay, yet was germinating new growth. One generation of leaders and organisations was fading. There had been no Pan-African Congress since the unimpressive New York Congress in 1927. The organiser of the four congresses between 1919 and 1927, W. E. B. DuBois, later acclaimed as the 'Father of Pan-Africanism', appeared to look back on them as a completed episode. His semi-autobiographical book, *Dusk of dawn*, published in 1940, showed minimal interest in Pan-Africanism. However, DuBois's contribution to Pan-Africanism was not only as the organiser and inspirer of occasional congresses, but also as an intellectual, making known the contribution of black people in both Africa and the African diaspora to humanity. In this respect, he was still fruitfully active. His *Black folk then and now*, published in 1939, was a lively and penetrating collection of essays on African and diaspora history and culture from ancient to modern times. It continued a genre he had pioneered as far back as 1915, with his book *The Negro*, and which he was to return to in 1947 with *The world and Africa*. In these works he showed himself capable of stimulating the intelligent general reader on vast, little-known themes. In spirit, these books were profoundly if not explicitly Pan-African. They dealt with Africa as a whole, defended the creativity and validity of African culture through the ages (as had the great nineteenth-century proto-Pan-Africanists, such as E. W. Blyden), and treated the history of the diaspora as a vital part of the history of Africa and Africans.

In the opening months of 1940, his great rival in fame – or notoriety – as a Pan-Africanist, Marcus Garvey, was dying in London. His Universal Negro Improvement Association (UNIA), the only mass-supported organisation till then in the history of Pan-Africanism, had long since divided into mutually hostile fragments. His remaining supporters were chiefly in distant North

America and the West Indies. His spirits were sinking; he was poverty stricken; and though respected by the younger generation of active Pan-Africanists in Britain, had held himself aloof from them. His magazine *The Black Man*, to which, largely, he devoted his last years, appeared at increasingly irregular intervals, and had petered out in June 1939. Despite his pugnacious attacks on other black leaders, the obituaries on his death contained some remarkably generous tributes, which recognised the uniqueness of his career and achievements. The organ of the League of Coloured Peoples, an essentially moderate or even conservative group based in Britain, described him as 'one of the greatest men our group has so far thrown up' and recognised that 'no other man operating outside Africa has so far been able to unite our people in such large numbers for any object whatsoever'.[1] Another of the older generation of Pan-African leaders, Duse Mohamed Ali, who had been one of Garvey's early mentors, but who later had disagreed with him, and had broken with the Universal Negro Improvement Association in 1922, came to much the same conclusion:

Perhaps no African, living or dead, had made such an impression on the world at large and quickened the desire for racial self-reliance and self-dependence in the breasts of Africans the world over, than the dead leader... It is to be deeply regretted that his dream of a permanent home for the peoples of African origin was not destined to be realised, but the fact remains that he altered the economic and political consciousness of the African the world over... He has unquestionably altered their outlook as no previous leader seemed capable of accomplishing.[2]

Ali was a representative figure in a third main strand of the Pan-African Movement in the period 1918–39. This was what might be called Commercial Pan-Africanism – the belief that large-scale commercial enterprise by people from Africa and the diaspora could prise resources from the hands of white imperialists, enrich the black race, and through the power of wealth win freedom. But by 1940, Ali had ceased to be an active Commercial Pan-Africanist, and had settled down in his last years as the proprietor and editor of *The Comet*, a locally influential magazine in Lagos. To a rising generation of Nigerians, he was a respected but rather remote old man, with a mysterious and exciting past. Like Garvey, he was much less fiery in his later years, especially

[1] *News Letter*, July 1940, **10**, 64.   [2] *The Comet*, 17 August 1940, 4.

over the evils of British imperialism. A man above local party divisions, he chaired the inaugural meeting of the National Council for Nigeria and the Cameroons (NCNC) in Lagos in 1944, almost his last public act before his death in 1945. His main rival as a Commercial Pan-Africanist, the spectacular Ghanaian, W. Tete-Ansa, was still attempting to carry through his latest grandiose commercial schemes in 1940, but with the outbreak of war the moment for such enterprises had passed. Indeed, even from the early 1930s, the younger successors of Ali and Tete-Ansa, West Africans like Eket Inyang Udoh, who had learned much from them, were much more commercial *nationalists* than Pan-Africanists.

Simultaneous with these declining careers and movements, there was from the mid-1930s a tough, resourceful and radical new generation of Pan-Africanists, some Marxist, such as the Trinidadians George Padmore and C. L. R. James and the Sierra Leonean I. T. A. Wallace-Johnson, others like the Kenyan Jomo Kenyatta and the Guyanan Ras Makonnen determinedly anti-imperialist. What bound them together ideologically was anti-imperialism, and the conviction that imperialism had a racial mode – that it was the exploitation of black men by white, and that the only way out, for the black world, was through racial solidarity and activism. This consensus enabled the anti-Marxist Makonnen, for example, to work harmoniously with the Marxist Padmore. What activated their radicalism, more than anything else, was the Italo-Ethiopian crisis, and the cynical abandonment of Ethiopia by the leaders of the League of Nations, Britain and France. Some, notably Padmore with his experience of the Comintern and Profintern, were also convinced that, with equal cynicism, the USSR merely regarded black movements as 're-volutionary expendables', and had jettisoned support for the black world in the interests of Popular Front policies. It should be noted that the first institutional expression of this group, the International African Friends of Abyssinia (IAFA), in 1935 had close contacts with the Paris-based *Ligue de la Défense de la Race Nègre*, at one time closely associated with the French Communist Party, and suppressed by the Popular Front government in 1937. One other factor bonding the radicals together was that despite diverse origins, they were geographically concentrated by their residence in Britain, which they felt 'to be at the centre of gravity as far as Africa was concerned'.[1] Sceptical about British free speech, they nevertheless recognised its utility for their own purposes; although determined to be neither smothered nor controlled, they appreciated the practical aid of British sympathisers. Dispersed around Britain by the blitz (Makonnen's restaurants in Manchester then becoming an important locale of the movement), they remained in close touch with each other. More than any other group, they were responsible for the Fifth Pan-African Congress in Manchester in 1945.

What saved them from being merely a small Pan-African discussion group of the sort that had long flourished in Britain was their ability to reach and penetrate other black circles. One of these was WASU, the West African Students Union, whose dominant figure, Ladipo Solanke, had long believed in the concept of a United West Africa, and whose hostel in London was a rendezvous for West African students and visitors, and other Africans, West Indians, black Americans and white sympathisers. Through friendly and informal contacts with WASU, the radicals were able to spread their influence. A British-based organisation with which they had more equivocal relations was the moderate League of Coloured Peoples (LCP), led by the Jamaican, Dr M. A. Moody. Makonnen regarded his group's relationship with the LCP as being 'one of convenience'.[2] However, in 1939, collaboration between the LCP moderates and the radicals was increasing, particularly in planning a World Conference to be held in London in 1940, which was to deal comprehensively with questions concerning Africa and the diaspora. The radicals were anxious that their organisation, the International African Service Bureau (IASB), which had replaced the IAFA in 1937, would not be swamped by the LCP, which had taken the initiative. War put paid to the conference, and the fragile cooperation between radicals and moderates. The former denounced the war as imperialist, and refused to support the British war effort. Moody, while continuing to work for black political and civil rights, felt that in that crisis it was necessary to rally behind the Union Jack. In consequence, by 1945 the intense radicalising effect of the Second World War made him seem irrelevant, while the radicals were in accord with the mood of the times. Despite wartime

[1] Ras Makonnen, *Pan-Africanism from within* (Nairobi, 1973), 152–3.
[2] Makonnen, *Pan-Africanism*, 127.

dislocation, the radicals, notably Padmore and Makonnen, remained organisationally effective. In 1944 they were able to create the Pan-African Federation (PAF) as an umbrella for a number of smaller organisations.

If Britain was the focus of Pan-African activity up to 1945, it would nevertheless be misleading to attribute all initiative between 1935 and 1945 to British-based groups and leaders. All over the black world, but most notably in West Africa and in the United States, people were aroused by the Italo-Ethiopian crisis. Thus, although only a handful of black Americans – such as the aviators John C. Robinson and Hubert Fauntleroy Julian – actually served in the Ethiopian forces, nevertheless many thousands expressed the wish to do so but were prevented by circumstances. The most important of these was the US State Department's ban on American citizens enlisting in Ethiopian forces. The black American press devoted enormous attention to the war, and to the appeals of various aid committees. Many black American organisations sought to aid Ethiopia; such, for example, was the Pan-African Reconstruction Association, founded by Samuel Daniels in Harlem in 1934. These press campaigns and aid organisations were paralleled in West Africa. The effect on both the younger and older generations of West Africans was often to make them aware in a way that was, at least implicitly, Pan-African. As Anthony Enahoro put it:

Our favourite newspaper, *The Comet*, was a weekly publication by [Duse Mohamed Ali]... From it I followed the fortunes of the Italo-Abyssinian War, about which Father and my teachers appeared considerably agitated. Fellow-feeling with other Africans was a newly awakened sentiment, much disappointment was felt about England's failure to go to the aid of the Ethiopians, and collections were taken for a 'Help Abyssinia Fund'.[1]

In other ways, the West African Pan-African response in the 1930s was less clear. This was the period of the decline of the National Congress of British West Africa and the rise of territorially based political parties. On the other hand Wallace-Johnson's West African Youth League had a Pan-African outlook, and tried to embrace French and Portuguese as well as British West Africa in the years after 1935. His detention on Sherbro Island for most of the period of the Second World War ended the League's effective life. The most spectacular of the new generation of West

[1] Anthony Enahoro, *Fugitive offender* (London, 1965), 45.

African political leaders, Nnamdi Azikiwe, proclaimed Pan-African ideas in his newspapers, the *African Morning Post* in Accra, and from 1938 the *West African Pilot* in Lagos; and in his book *Renascent Africa* (1937). He had a wide influence over the younger generation.

Azikiwe provided a model and personal encouragement to young West Africans to go to the United States for their university education, most notably in the case of Kwame Nkrumah, who in 1935 went to study at Lincoln University, Azikiwe's old school. In the 1930s and 1940s, several score West African students studied at Lincoln, not to mention numbers of other Africans who studied at other American universities, black and white. During the Second World War such students had opportunities to interact with a reviving black American interest in Africa, and to assess their own political position in a country which, if an ally of wartime Britain, was hostile to British imperialism. Among themselves, they formed an African Students Association (ASA), first mooted as an idea at Lincoln in 1939, which held its first general meeting in Harlem in 1941. Although its members were not many, they contained men who were later to make their mark in West Africa, such as K. O. Mbadiwe, A. A. N. Orizu, Mbonu Ojike, K. A. B. Jones-Quartey, and, of course, Nkrumah. It now appears that Nkrumah later exaggerated his role in the ASA, elevating himself retrospectively to the position of its first president, and claiming that he continued as president until he went to Britain in 1945. So far as is known he was the *second* president, and only held this post during 1942–3. Nevertheless, because the ASA affiliated itself to WASU in Britain, on reaching London in 1945 it was not difficult for Nkrumah, still a rather obscure person, to make himself known to the top leadership of Pan-Africanism in Britain. Additionally, he had a letter of recommendation to Padmore from C. L. R. James. But Nkrumah does seem to have played a part in radicalising the Council on African Affairs, a black American organisation which had been founded by Paul Robeson and Max Yergan. He played a prominent part in its Conference on Africa, held in New York in 1944, which in turn reflected the growing interest of politically conscious black Americans in the African continent.

THE 1945 PAN-AFRICAN CONGRESS

The 1945 Pan-African Congress was the culmination of the new growths in the movement, but also of a much longer process, stretching back to the eighteenth century, in which Pan-African consciousness had been germinating, especially in the diaspora, although also in Africa. After 1945, Pan-Africanism was to transfer its geographical centre, political priorities, and leadership, at long last, to the African continent itself, and the diaspora was to become peripheral in every sense. Nevertheless, despite the reiteration, especially by Nkrumah, that the Manchester Congress was the first to be dominated by Africans and African issues, it was very much the creation of diaspora leaders. It so happened that by 1944, DuBois had revived his active interest in Pan-Africanism and was planning another congress. Thus by early 1945, both DuBois and the radical Pan-Africanists in Britain were, unknown to each other, planning a Fifth Congress. This confusion was partly because DuBois's contacts in Britain were with WASU and the LCP, whose leader, Moody, had been contemplating some sort of Pan-African conference since 1943, rather than the IASB and the PAF. He hoped, as he had in 1919, to persuade the National Association for the Advancement of Colored People (NAACP) officially to support and finance his congress, which he wished to take place in Africa. When he became aware of the plans being made independently in Britain, at first he reacted icily. Two factors, however, prevented a disastrous split. As in the period between 1919 and 1927, the NAACP ultimately withheld official backing and finance, which reduced his power to dominate events or go his own way. More importantly, with masterly skill, Padmore soothed DuBois's susceptibilities, recognising his value as the embodiment of the movement's historical continuity and thus secured his cooperation. The congress that emerged reflected Padmore's radical ideas rather than DuBois's more cautious ones. Exploiting contacts with colonial trades-union leaders, and the meeting of the World Trades Union Congress in Paris in early October 1945, Padmore was able to ensure that Manchester was not merely a meeting of eminent black intellectuals and professional men. And, in another adroit piece of political management, not only was DuBois present, but also four delegates from the UNIA of Jamaica, thus symbolically reconciling the deepest antagonism within the movement. Neither did the presence of these UNIA delegates deter Amy Ashwood Garvey, Garvey's first wife, from attending, although the UNIA of Jamaica was headed by his second wife, Amy Jaques Garvey. The notable absences from the 1945 Congress were Moody and the LCP moderates, and any representative of francophone Pan-Africanism. It has been argued that political effort in French Black Africa, after the 1944 Brazzaville Conference, was directed (or misdirected) into the limited openings that became available in metropolitan French politics.[1] In personal terms, soon after the Manchester Congress, Nkrumah and Kenyatta returned to their own countries to take up the struggle for local independence. In sharp contrast, Léopold Senghor was acting as an official philological adviser on the language of the constitution of the French Fourth Republic. It could be said that the absence of francophone delegates in 1945 presaged one of the divisions in independent Africa from the late 1950s, that between francophone and anglophone Africa.

The Congress did not seize the world's headlines, yet undoubtedly it was an event of great importance. Nkrumah, reminiscing in 1963, asserted that 'we went from Manchester knowing definitely where we were going'.[2] As well as surveying the situation in various parts of Africa and the diaspora, the Congress issued two general statements, 'The Challenge to the Colonial Powers', and a 'Declaration to the Colonial Workers, Farmers and Intellectuals'. These contained the essence of its message. Both used Marxist-flavoured language – the 'Declaration' ended with the phrase 'Colonial and Subject Peoples of the World Unite!' – without being in reality Marxist statements. The 'Challenge' demanded independence for 'Black Africa' (although the congress had concerned itself with North Africa too), condemned 'the monopoly of capital', and envisaged the use of force to win freedom 'as a last resort', though not as inevitable. But what was perhaps the most characteristic and significant call of the Manchester Congress was for colonial freedom, 'the first step towards and necessary prerequisite to complete social, economic and political emancipation'.[3] Here was the first priority

[1] Imanuel Geiss, *The Pan-African movement* (London, 1974), 396–7.
[2] George Padmore (ed.), *The history of the Pan-African Congress* (2nd edition with new material, London, 1963), v.
[3] Padmore, *Pan-African Congress*, 5–7.

for the movement – national independence, a goal that had not clearly emerged from the earlier congresses. The question of what form Pan-Africanism might eventually take after the achievement of national independence was not considered. After all, despite the optimism of the moment, it is unlikely that the delegates foresaw national independence as not much more than a decade away for some African colonies. The issue of the relationship between national independence and supra-national Pan-Africanism was necessarily even more remote, although, inevitably, it was to arise in an acute form almost as soon as there was a sufficient nucleus of independent African states in existence.

Nkrumah had been the author of the 'Declaration to the Colonial Workers, Farmers and Intellectuals' of the congress. In the interval between October 1945 and his return to the Gold Coast in December 1947 at the request of the leaders of the United Gold Coast Convention (UGCC), no one was more active in implementing its decisions. He created, together with Wallace-Johnson and others, the West African National Secretariat (WANS), a small élite group of radically inclined West Africans in Britain. The tactic they advocated was mobilisation of the masses (unlike the conservative traditions of the UGCC leaders), and their objective was an independent United West Africa, an old West African dream, which can be traced back to the nineteenth-century proto-Pan-Africanist James Africanus Horton. Nkrumah and the WANS were not satisfied with the limited concept of a United *British* West Africa, but like the West African Youth League, wanted to include French and Portuguese colonies too. To this end, good relations were established not only with British West African political parties, such as the NCNC, but also with the only genuinely trans-territorial West African political party of the day, the Rassemblement Démocratique Africain (RDA), whose leaders, members of the French National Assembly, Nkrumah met in Paris in 1947. But his return to Africa in 1947, a year after Kenyatta had returned to Kenya, marked the beginning of the end of the period in which Britain was the most important geographical centre of Pan-African activity. For a time WASU continued to afford an umbrella under which Pan-Africanists could operate. In 1947–8, Makonnen (with help from British sympathisers and other Pan-Africanist radicals) produced and edited the journal *Pan-Africa*, perhaps the last in the line of influential Pan-African journals produced in Britain, which stretched back via Duse Mohamed Ali's *African Times and Orient Review* (1912–18) to S. J. Celestine Edwards's *Fraternity* (1892–4). But by the early 1950s, even those Pan-Africanists who remained in Britain seem, understandably, to have been swept along by heady events in Africa, especially in the Gold Coast; Pan-Africanism was not renounced but was subsumed in the national independence struggles. Thus Padmore published his book *The Gold Coast revolution. The struggle of an African people from slavery to freedom* in 1953. But this was, after all, quite consistent with the spirit of Manchester 1945, a spirit which as the 1950s advanced must have seemed more and more prescient.

THE AFRICAN DIASPORA AND POST-1945 PAN-AFRICANISM

One of the most poignant consequences of the post-1945 shift in Pan-Africanism was the increasing marginality of the diaspora. To begin with, in the early and mid-1950s, black Americans and British West Indians, the two diaspora communities who had historically been of most importance in the movement, had other and urgent preoccupations. In the United States, the older generation of black American Pan-Africanists, notably DuBois and Robeson, were sometimes victims of McCarthyism. Their Marxist sympathies made this inevitable. When the American Civil Rights movement began to get under way, with the historic confrontation with Governor Faubus in Little Rock, Arkansas, in 1953, it was the Frederick Douglass tradition in black American radicalism that was uppermost, demanding the rights of blacks as American citizens. As the Civil Rights movement began to cohere and gather strength under the leadership of Martin Luther King this, rather than a Pan-African perspective, remained uppermost until perhaps the mid-1960s. After all, King's most openly acknowledged political debt to any non-American was not to the new leaders of independent Africa, but to Gandhi. Apart from those who followed him, perhaps the most dynamic movement among black Americans, the Nation of Islam, proclaimed an Arabian rather than an African origin for black people. Meanwhile, in the British West Indies, the 1950s were years of struggles and negotiations for independence from Britain – and struggles within and among the West Indian colonies between federalists and anti-federalists. The latter, whose universal triumph began with the opting of Jamaica for separate independence, were hardly likely to subsume their hard-won local independence in a wider Pan-African identity. By the 1960s, Pan-Africanism in the West Indies became an ideology of dissident intellectuals, rather than of governments – although partial exceptions would be the interest shown by Forbes Burnham's government in Guyana in the 1970s, and Jamaica following the return to power of Michael Manley and his People's National Party in 1975.

In Jamaica, Amy Jaques Garvey, Marcus Garvey's widow, worked ceaselessly to keep her husband's memory and ideas alive and, as scholarly interest in Garvey began to grow in the mid-1950s, provided invaluable help to many scholars. It would not be an exaggeration to say that her part in the history of Pan-Africanism was in itself, for these reasons, a major one; she lived to see Garvey acknowledged as a hero again by black leaders in both Africa and the diaspora.

Africa in general, and Pan-Africanism in particular, continued to be of importance to the diaspora after the late 1940s. The advent of independent black African states, beginning with Ghana in 1957, and reaching a climax in the heady year of 1960, caused an immense stirring of interest and pride throughout the diaspora, and an understandable wish to relate to and emulate this movement. On the level of black popular culture, this found expression in the wearing of 'Afro' hairstyles and 'dashikis', the giving of African names to children, and even a vogue for attending beginners' classes in Swahili.

The younger generation of black political leaders, especially in the United States, who emerged from the Civil Rights movement, almost invariably emphasised the African heritage as part of their programme of Black Nationalism. Indeed, borrowing a leaf from the African nationalist leaders, or for that matter from the Manchester Congress, there were demands for national independence for black Americans. Thus the programme of the Black Panther Party in 1966 included as the party's 'major political objective', a call for 'a United Nations-supervised plebiscite to be held throughout the black colony (i.e. black Americans) in which only black colonial subjects will be allowed to participate, for the purpose of determining the will of black people as to their national destiny'.[1] Within the Black Panthers, by 1968, there was a split between those who stressed political black nationalism, and a wing led by Stokely Carmichael that put a strong emphasis on cultural nationalism. Carmichael's stance became increasingly detached from diaspora black nationalism and increasingly African inclined, until he decided to join the overthrown Nkrumah in exile in Guinea. Other black nationalists of the same generation became explicitly Pan-African in outlook, without leaving the United States. Thus the writer Imamu Baraka (the former LeRoi Jones), created the Congress of African Peoples, which held a meeting in Atlanta, Georgia in 1970, attended mainly by delegates from affiliated black American organisations, but also some Africans, such as the Guinean Ambassador to the United States, and a representative of Holden Roberto's Angolan National Liberation Front. Baraka regarded this gathering as 'one in a growing historical tradition of international gatherings of Pan-Africans'. Those present were an amazingly heterogeneous collection, representing what even he admitted were 'seemingly antithetical approaches to national and international African liberation'.[2] In his own address, he called for a World African Political Party: 'A Political Party that will function in South Africa like it will function in Chicago, where you know that if you are in Surinam or Jamaica, or New York City this World African Party will be functioning to get power, to bring about self-determination for Black people.'[3]

Another strand of diaspora life with a continuing interest in Africa and Pan-Africanism was the intellectual world. The black American contribution to the early growth of African studies was pioneering and seminal. Even if, in the massive expansion of African studies from the 1950s, the distinctively black American (or, one might add, West Indian contribution) no longer played quite such a central role, black American universities and scholars played a key part in initiating that expansion. Continuing interest among the black American intelligentsia in African culture was signalled by the creation of the American Society of African Culture (AMSAC) in 1956, which restricted membership to persons of African descent. Although its standing was seriously

[1] Bobby Seale, *Seize the time. The story of the Black Panther Party* (London, 1970), 89.
[2] Imamu Amiri Baraka (ed.), *African Congress: a documentary of the first modern Pan-African Congress* (New York, 1972), vii, viii.
[3] Baraka, *African Congress*, 94.

tarnished by the subsequent revelation of secret Central Intelligence Agency connexions, it would be unwise to dismiss this body, and its members, as nothing but puppets of covert American government policy. Its third annual conference, in Philadelphia in 1960, devoted itself to the discussion of 'African Unities and Pan-Africanism', and can be regarded as an event in the history of the movement. Some of those present had strong links with the Pan-African past, notably Rayford W. Logan, who had played an important part in the era of Pan-African congresses after the First World War; Jean Price-Mars, Haitian diplomat, philosopher of *négritude*, and President of the *Société Africaine de Culture* in Paris; and Jaja Wachuku, who had been at the 1945 Pan-African Congress, and who was in 1960 foreign minister of Nigeria.

One of the oldest dreams in the diaspora, that of the 'return of exiles' to Africa, found expression in the era of independent African states, not in mass migrations, but in the travel of many black American and West Indian individuals to Africa. Some went as visitors; some to work there; and yet others to make Africa their home. Of this last group, three of the most significant leaders of Pan-Africanism in 1945, DuBois, Padmore and Makonnen, were all to settle in Ghana, the bright 'Black Star' of the 1950s. For DuBois, his decision to settle in Ghana, where he was to die in 1963, was both a symbolical and a real renunciation of the United States and its dominant white culture. He and his wife spent the close of his life working on the *Encyclopaedia Africana*, a project which had official Ghanaian government backing, and whose first volume appeared in 1978. In some ways, Padmore's case is even more interesting, for in 1958 Nkrumah invited him to come to Ghana as his adviser on African affairs. Thus, in a brief final episode in his life, Padmore had the prospect of wielding power. Ironically, the last years in London were in fact more fruitful, as during that time he produced a steady series of major works, culminating in his *Pan-Africanism or Communism?* (1956), which as well as insisting on the need for Africa to be free from both western colonialism and subordination to Moscow's interests, also had encapsulated within it a major survey of the roots and history of Pan-Africanism. There can be little doubt that he intended this as a more or less 'official' history of Pan-Africanism; it stressed DuBois's alleged role as 'father' of the movement, ignored or underplayed contrary aspects of Pan-

Africanism's history, reconciled Garveyism with the rest of the movement, and glorified Nkrumah's policies in the Gold Coast as the supreme embodiment of Pan-Africanism in action. Yet in Ghana, he disliked the toadies and opportunists who surrounded Nkrumah, and they in turn were determined to keep him isolated from effective power. He helped organise the 1958 All-African Peoples' Conference, and was put in charge of a specially created Bureau of African Affairs; but the latter was merely a consolation prize for his exclusion from the cabinet. By July 1959 his health was failing, and in September 1959 he returned to London for medical treatment, only to die there.

This miserable close to Padmore's life illustrates the darker side of the position in modern independent Africa of committed Pan-Africanists from the diaspora. The most perceptive commentator on this is Padmore's old friend Makonnen, who gave Nkrumah loyalty to the end of his regime, suffering imprisonment for this after his overthrow in 1966. But his loyalty was not one of uncritical adulation. Thus, he found that after Padmore's death, even the Bureau of African Affairs was effectively controlled by Ghanaians, with non-Ghanaians being treated as 'outsiders', and the Bureau ceasing to be a 'truly Pan-African instrument of policy making'.[1] Worse still, he found the generality of Ghanaian politicians, and for that matter those in Kenya where he has lived since his release from prison in Ghana, to be hostile to New World blacks. Of course, not all diaspora visitors reached such gloomy conclusions; it is clear that Malcolm X found his brief visit to West Africa in 1964 an exhilarating experience, leading him to proclaim that 'Philosophically and culturally we Afro-Americans need to "return" to Africa – and to develop a working unity in the framework of Pan-Africanism.'[2]

As a phenomenon, the return of significant numbers of black individuals from the New World to Africa in modern times still remains to be explored fully. It is clear that at times, although never holding power, such people have been able to make an important contribution. Thus, the Martiniquan psychiatrist, Frantz Fanon, became one of the most important theorists of revolution in Africa in the 1960s, and a trenchant critic of those African rulers whom he regarded as accomplices of continuing

[1] Makonnen, *Pan-Africanism*, 209.
[2] Malcolm X, *The autobiography of Malcolm X* (London, 1976), 465–6.

imperialist control, roles which were taken on by the Guyanese scholar Walter Rodney in the 1970s. Perhaps the most spectacular 'return to Africa' of modern times in its impact on mass consciousness was that of the black American writer Alex Hailey. His quest for his family's origins in the Gambia led to the publication of his sensationally successful novel *Roots* in 1976, which was followed up by serialisation on television. The television version of *Roots* seized the attention of not only black, but also white, Americans, and signified the pride of the former and acceptance by the latter of the value of an African origin. In the aftermath, there was a boom in black American tourism to the reputed village of Alex Hailey's ancestors in the Gambia.

THE ROAD TO THE ORGANISATION OF AFRICAN UNITY

Undoubtedly the most visible aspect of Pan-Africanism after the 1950s was the attempt to create an all-African supra-national institution with the support of all independent African states. In a superficial sense, therefore, the creation of the Organisation of African Unity (OAU) in 1963 was the apotheosis of this phase of Pan-Africanism. This period is above all associated with the career of Nkrumah as leader of Ghana (although there were very few of his contemporaries as rulers of Africa who did not pay at least occasional lip-service to a vague Pan-African ideal). Even before Ghana became independent, he made some efforts to advance the cause of supra-national Pan-Africanism. However, it is worth recalling that before 1963, 'Kwame Nkrumah's voice and actions did not come out decidedly for a Union government for the whole of Africa'.[1] For some time his WANS dream of a West African Socialist Republic was his immediate aspiration, although he intended to hold a Pan-African Congress in the Gold Coast in 1954 to consider the affairs of the entire continent. This was prevented, however, by a political crisis within his country. Only from 1957 was he free to attempt the concrete realisation of his Pan-African dream. At the very celebrations for Ghanaian independence in 1957, he broached, to visiting representatives of other independent African countries, the idea of holding a Conference of Independent African States.

[1] S. K. B. Asante, 'Kwame Nkrumah and Pan-Africanism: the early phase, 1945–1961', *Universitas*, 1973, 3, 1, 45.

This conference, held in Accra in April 1958, was attended by heads of state or the foreign ministers of Libya, Ethiopia, the Sudan, Tunisia, Morocco, Egypt and Liberia, as well as the host country. It began the process leading to the OAU in 1963. It produced little more than a broad but vague consensus on foreign policy – that African states should be non-aligned in world power blocks and should stick together – but generated enough impetus to ensure further efforts. It also generated feelings of elation, among participants and more widely in Africa, that independent African countries were now meeting together to discuss the great questions of Africa and the world. The identity of the participants also ensured that in this new phase of Pan-Africanism the movement would be continental, including the lighter-skinned, mainly Arabic-speaking peoples of North Africa, rather than – as some of the leaders of the previous phase, such as Makonnen, would have wished – a Pan-Negro movement. A success within its own limitations, the conference fell short of the commitment to African independence and African unity that Nkrumah (or Padmore) had in mind – unlike the second Accra Conference of 1958, the All African Peoples' Conference in December. As V. B. Thompson had stated, this conference was a 'reaffirmation'[1] of the principles of the 1945 Manchester Pan-African Congress, for it called for a coordinated 'final assault on colonialism and imperialism in Africa', if necessary using violence in reply to colonialist violence. But where the All-African Peoples' Conference far transcended either 1945 or the first Accra Conference was in its decision to 'work for the ultimate achievement of a Union or Commonwealth of African States'.[2] Ambiguous though this phrase is (for there is a world of difference between the implied models of the American Union and the British Commonwealth), it unavoidably raised the question of the relationship of individual African sovereignty to overall African unity. The composition of the conference also raised thorny problems, as many delegates came from countries still under colonial or minority rule, and represented national and liberation movements rather than established governments. The clear implication was that Nkrumah was putting himself forward as the leader of African freedom

[1] V. B. Thompson, *Africa and unity: the evolution of Pan-Africanism* (London, 1969), 133.
[2] Kwame Nkrumah, *I speak of freedom. A statement of African ideology* (London, 1961), 174-5.

everywhere, a role that was for obvious reasons not very acceptable to many of his fellow heads of state.

In the years leading up to 1963, a parallel series of conferences took place: subsequent All-African Peoples' Conferences were held in Tunis in 1960 and Cairo in 1961, while further Conferences of African States were held at Addis Ababa in June 1960 and Léopoldville (now Kinshasa) in August 1960. Although the Addis Ababa Conference accepted the Algerian provisional government, as well as all independent African governments (excepting, of course, South Africa) as full members, and admitted observers from various other territories, nevertheless the Tunis and Cairo Conferences set the pace in increasing commitment to violent struggle against colonialism. Pan-Africanism came, once again, to have moderate and militant wings, expressing themselves through separate organisations. Naturally, those states that hosted and supported the 'Peoples' conferences', especially Ghana and Egypt, were regarded with increasing suspicion by the remainder.

Thus, when increasing numbers of African states were becoming independent, the Pan-African movement, which had committed itself to national independence and had, in 1957, glimpsed exciting further developments, had split. Not only was there a split between moderates and militants, but also, to some extent, between francophone and other states. This division was not, of course, linguistic in essence, but a consequence of the course of politics within French West and Equatorial Africa since 1946, and the way in which most of the colonies in those federations came to independence. In 1958, cutting short arguments among African political leaders as to whether a federal-type or a commonwealth-type relationship with France would be desirable, de Gaulle offered them the brutal choice of either complete secession, with the immediate cessation of all benefits, aid and links with France; or continuing association with the option of future full independence. Only Guinea, under Sékou Touré, chose immediate independence. But by 1960, the circumstances under which the remaining colonies could become independent had been made less harsh, as they were then permitted to do so and yet retain all the immediate advantages of continuing economic links with France, French technical and military aid, and firm French internal and external support for their governments. But these terms were applied to individual colonies, rather than to the two great federations of French West and French Equatorial Africa, which might have provided the bases for viable states. Many of the new states were either, like Chad, enormous in area, but minuscule in population and resources; or rich in resources, but minuscule in population and the skills necessary to develop their resources, like Gabon. Even the comparatively developed Ivory Coast, under the leadership of President Houphouët-Boigny (whose radical past was long behind him), found it advantageous to retain the closest links with France after independence. It is small wonder that the result of this process was the emergence of a bloc of conservative states, looking to France to maintain both their internal and external security, to provide capital and expertise for development, to provide a market for their agricultural and mineral produce, and to supply them with manufactured goods. Via this bloc, de Gaulle's preoccupation with keeping 'Anglo-Saxon' influence out of the European Common Market was imported into Africa, and took the form of suspicion of initiatives by anglophone states. The bloc signalled its existence by holding a major conference at Brazzaville in 1960, and became known as the Union Africaine et Malgache (UAM) or more commonly the Brazzaville group. Of the former constituent colonies of French West and Equatorial Africa, only Guinea and Mali were outside this group, and enthusiastic about Pan-Africanism.

From the Pan-African point of view, therefore, 1960 was the worst time for the Congo tragedy to have occurred; nothing could have served better to expose the divisions within the movement. To leaders like Sékou Touré and Nkrumah, it realised their worst fears about the dangerous weakness of a divided Africa in the face of malign outside intervention. As Patrice Lumumba, the Congolese Prime Minister, was a committed Pan-Africanist who had been much influenced by his attendance at the 1958 All-African Peoples' Conference, Nkrumah and Sékou Touré in particular felt personal loyalties to his government which anyway, whatever its defects, showed an unflinching determination to reject outside control and interference, especially from the Belgians. What is more, Lumumba looked to the Pan-African movement to buttress him in his country's hour of need, and even called a Conference of Independent African States in Léopoldville in August 1960, which, however, only revealed their weakness and division. All except Guinea affirmed wholehearted support for the United Nations' actions in the Congo, and insisted (in the name of keeping the Cold War out of Africa) that all aid to the Congolese government should be channelled via the UN. Only Guinea was willing to back Lumumba's wish to rid himself and his country of the UN, and to overthrow Moise Tshombe's secession in Katanga province (now Shaba) by force. In the aftermath, and as events unfolded, with the overthrow of Lumumba and the entrenchment of the Katanga regime, more divisions emerged. Thus, Nkrumah's adherence to working under United Nations auspices had the deeply ironic result that Ghanaian troops in the Congo were used to further the overthrow of Lumumba, whose government he wished to preserve. At the same time Guinea alone insisted that its Congo contingent should not be under United Nations command, despite the fact that at the outbreak of the crisis Nkrumah had spoken of the need for an African High Command to deal with the situation. As for the Brazzaville group, together with Liberia and Tunisia, they supported Lumumba's enemies, Kasavubu and Tshombe.

It is a tribute to the vitality of the Pan-African idea that the movement survived the Congo crisis, and was able to resolve some of its differences and put aside others in the creation of the OAU in 1963. Terrible though it was for the people of the country that became Zaire, the crisis was probably, in the long run, almost an asset to Pan-Africanism. To begin with, the dimensions of the tragedy, the clear involvement of the most sinister outside forces such as white mercenaries and international capital, the immense publicity generated by events, and the personalisation of the issues in the career, overthrow and death of Lumumba, created their own pressures for African unity. It is hard to be sure what part popular feeling played in all this but, to give what may be a significant example, in a country far from the Congo (albeit one which had supplied a contingent of troops for the UN force), in the early 1960s one of the most common names for humble bars catering to the Addis Ababa populace was 'Patrice Lumumba Bar'.[1] The third All-African Peoples' Conference in Cairo in March 1961 proclaimed Lumumba, who had been murdered only two months before, as the 'hero of Africa' – though within the conference, the governments represented were far more cautious than the liberation movements.

Despite these pressures, 1961 was a dismal year for Pan-

[1] Personal reminiscence of I. Duffield, who lived in Addis Ababa from January 1962 to July 1964.

Africanism, for not only did the divisions between independent African states seem to be formalising themselves, with the emergence of the Casablanca and Monrovia groupings, but also further deep divisions over major issues were becoming apparent. The Casablanca Conference, called in January over the Congo question, was attended by the North African states except Tunisia, but including representatives of the Algerian provisional government, plus Ghana, Guinea and Mali. Except for Libya, this was a grouping of the more radical African governments. Partly in reaction to this group, and reflecting suspicion at the predilection of the radicals (especially Ghana) to interfere in the affairs of their neighbours, as well as disagreements over Congo policy, the Monrovia Conference was held in May 1961. The core of the Monrovia group were the UAM countries, but Ethiopia, Liberia, Libya, Nigeria, Sierra Leone, Somalia, Togo and Tunisia also took part. With the exception of Libya, the Casablanca powers boycotted Monrovia. To the Monrovia powers, African unity was to be understood as in no way infringing on the sovereign independence of African states. Given the pro-French character of the majority of them, it is not surprising that they avoided any stance on the Algerian question that would have estranged France. At the second meeting of the group in Lagos in January 1962, the breach with the Casablanca powers seemed to widen. Fortunately for Pan-Africanism this breach was never total. Tunisia's determination that France should evacuate the Bizerta naval base won her support from both groups. The re-emergence of a united government in the Congo, acceptable to both, removed a major cause of dissension. Increasingly, powers on both sides, notably Guinea from the Casablanca group and Ethiopia from the Monrovia group, began actively to seek reconciliation and look for areas of cooperation. Gestures were made, such as the cancelling of the 1962 All-African Peoples' Conference, obnoxious to the Monrovia group as likely to promote interference in their internal affairs. Algerian independence and the overthrow by the UN of the Katangese regime removed major stumbling blocks. By the beginning of 1963, a meeting of all independent African states was possible, with every chance of the creation of a unified Pan-African state organisation as a result.

In this sense, the meeting in Addis Ababa in May 1963 that created the OAU was no surprise, although the atmosphere in

Addis Ababa was certainly euphoric, and even a little unreal, the city's streets having been whitewashed, and the destitute, beggars and other unwanted persons who normally inhabited them having been removed. Despite the atmosphere of goodwill, there was a genuine political duel at Addis Ababa between those who believed all Africa's other problems could only be solved within the framework of political union, and those who wanted a consultative body of African states, which would endeavour to promote African consensus certainly, but which would also guarantee unequivocally individual independence. Nkrumah was the great proponent of political union, but he had little support, even from the other radical states. Only Uganda totally supported his call for a Union Government of Africa. Given the over-whelming majority of countries either in favour of, or willing to acquiesce in, the opposite concept, and the skilful way in which the host country had prepared for the conference and emphasised the need both for unanimity and 'an organisation which will facilitate acceptable solutions to disputes among Africans'[1] (a manifest necessity), Nkrumah could only make the best of the situation by conceding with reasonably good grace. So from the outset, unity of the OAU was to be like that of the UN, a gesture towards idealistic aspirations, but in reality depending on the consensus of its members. Only sovereign African states were to be members – a total defeat for the Pan-Africanism of the All-African Peoples' Conferences. Article III of the OAU Charter, adopted at Addis Ababa, is in many ways the key to understanding the OAU's essential nature. It affirms:

(1) the sovereign equality of all member states;
(2) non-interference in the internal affairs of states;
(3) respect for the sovereignty and territorial integrity of each state and for its inalienable right to independent existence;
(4) peaceful settlement of disputes by negotiation, mediation, conciliation or arbitration;
(5) unreserved condemnation, in all its forms, of political assassination as well as of subversive activities on the part of neighbouring states or any other state;
(6) absolute dedication to the total independence of the African territories which are still dependent;

[1] Welcoming speech by Haile Selassie, in Z. Červenka, *The Organisation of African Unity and its Charter* (2nd edition, London, 1969), 8.

(7) affirmation of a policy on non-alignment with regard to all blocs.[1]

The conclusion, largely borne out by subsequent events, is that the OAU was essentially an organisation to defend the territorial and political status quo in independent Africa, a thing of governments and rulers rather than of peoples, though not necessarily immune to popular pressures. The issue on which its members found it easiest to agree – and here was a real continuity from 1945 – was that of support for decolonisation. Within its own ranks, despite the creation of OAU bodies to consider policies on such matters as health, education, economic cooperation, and even defence, individual sovereignty was to be supreme. It is not surprising that its highest governing body was to be the annual Assembly of Heads of State and Government.

Within these limits, the OAU proved to be by no means ineffective. For some years it had a good record in containing, if not solving, disputes between member states, although this was more usually achieved by *ad hoc* arbitration than through the Commission of Arbitration and Conciliation established in 1964. This kind of arbitration was of most use in preserving the status quo, when it came to territorial or boundary disputes. Thus, the question of Somalia's claims to large areas of Ethiopian and Kenyan territory was deferred by OAU foreign ministers' mediation in 1964 and 1973. As early as October 1963, Haile Selassie and Modibo Keita of Mali were able to mediate in the Moroccan–Algerian border clash of that year. The OAU was also often successful in reconciling states that had fallen out on various other grounds; thus in 1970 Haile Selassie reconciled Nigeria with Zambia, the Ivory Coast and Tanzania, all of which had supported the Biafran right to secession. But it could be said that by the mid-1970s, with escalation in the number and intensity of disputes within and between member states, and the tendency of many African governments to seek support in such disputes from one or other of the great-power blocs, the OAU was facing a crisis.

Furthermore, in time at least some Pan-Africanists had come to regard the OAU with suspicion as no more than the guardian of vested interests. Some of these suspicions were voiced at the Sixth Pan-African Congress, held in Dar es Salaam, Tanzania, in June

[1] 'Article III, Charter of the Organisation of African Unity', Červenka, *The Organisation of African Unity and its Charter*, Appendix A, 232–3.

1974, and following consciously in the traditions of the All-African Peoples' Conferences. There was strong representation from national and liberation movements in colonial territories and South Africa, and from the diaspora. Julius Nyerere in his opening address paid tribute to the Pan-African Conference of 1900, the Congresses of 1900 to 1945, and the early leaders of the movement up to 1945, as well as to Nkrumah (who had died in 1972 in exile). The conference was implicitly critical of the OAU.[1] However, the contribution of Walter Rodney to the congress went far beyond implied criticism, and constitutes probably the most fundamental and hostile criticism of OAU Pan-Africanism made by any committed Pan-Africanist. For him, 'The existing African régimes have helped create the illusion that the OAU represents the concretisation of African Unity. The OAU is the principal instrument which legitimises the forty-odd mini-states visited upon us by colonialism.' Indeed, beyond regulating 'a few internal conflicts between the petty bourgeoisie from different parts of the continent', its functions were also attacked by Rodney as maintaining the separation of African peoples within existing territorial boundaries, and stifling criticism of any 'exploitative, oppressive and autocratic African state... even when the most elementary civil and human rights are trampled on'.[2]

NATIONALISM, REGIONALISM AND AFRICAN UNITY

To understand the emergence of this kind of radical disillusion with the 'official' Pan-Africanism of the OAU, it is first of all necessary to explore a little further some of the contradictions and tensions engendered by a Pan-Africanism dominated by independent states, and attempting to exalt national independence *and* African unity simultaneously. To be fair to a number of leading Pan-Africanists of the late 1950s and early 1960s, this was not an unperceived problem. Nkrumah's eventual belief in an African Union Government has already been mentioned. Nyerere of Tanzania referred to the tension between national sovereignty and Pan-Africanism as 'the dilemma of the Pan-Africanist'.[3] For some

---

[1] *Resolutions and selected speeches from the Sixth Pan African Congress* (Dar es Salaam, 1976), 3–4. [2] *Resolutions and selected speeches*, 26–67.
[3] Julius K. Nyerere, 'The dilemma of the Pan-Africanist', in Nyerere, *Freedom and socialism* (Dar es Salaam, 1968), 207–17.

years there were efforts to approach an all-African supra-nationalism via an intermediate stage of regional unions. The pioneer in this approach was, of course Nkrumah. Provision was made in the constitution of Ghana for merging with other independent African states, although Nkrumah also demolished the common services Ghana had shared with other British West African territories in the colonial era. When France cut off all aid to Guinea in October 1958, however, Ghana at once offered practical aid in the form of a £10 000 000 loan, and within a month the two states had declared the existence of a Ghana–Guinea union, that was to be the beginning of a Union of West African States; in 1960, Mali joined the union, following its severance of ties with Senegal. But this union, which took the title of Union of African States (UAS) never had much substance in reality, and with the creation of the OAU in 1963 found liquidating itself in the name of wider African unity a painless process. The same cannot be said for the UAM, which also dissolved itself in response to OAU pressure, but was reborn in 1965 as the Organisation Commune Africaine et Malgache (OCAM), the Ivory Coast playing a leading role as midwife to this rebirth. In particular, OCAM reflected continuing resentment among Ghana's francophone neighbours at such manifestations as 'training camps' in Ghana for political dissidents from other African countries. Likewise, resentment was felt at the OAU for not preventing this, not surprisingly in view of the fact that the OCAM states had thought that the OAU charter gave cast-iron guarantees against such actions.

Naturally, the overthrow of Nkrumah in 1966, followed by that of Modibo Keita in Mali in 1968, leaving Guinea for some time as the sole radical West African state, removed some of these tensions. Nevertheless, when the impetus towards West African regionalism re-emerged on the economic level, practical advance was long delayed by francophone suspicions. As early as 1967 discussions were held in Accra under the auspices of a United Nations body, the Economic Commission for Africa (ECA), on the desirability of a West African Economic Community, along the lines of the European Economic Community (EEC). This was viewed with displeasure by France as yet another plan for 'Anglo-Saxon' economic domination, a view readily communicated to her friends in Africa, notably the Ivory Coast. Indeed, a purely francophone West African economic community was created in 1970, which not surprisingly looked to France and to the EEC, rather than to anglophone neighbours. This dismal situation began to improve with Nigerian initiatives towards the creation of a comprehensive West African economic community. Under the stimulus of the oil boom, Nigeria rapidly achieved a remarkable recovery from the destructive civil war of 1967–70, and by the mid-1970s was clearly the economic giant of West Africa, as well as having a population large and energetic enough to play, in relation to her neighbours, a leading role. In 1973, the Nigerian balance of payments went into substantial surplus, while the international oil crisis of that year put all her non-oil producing neighbours in a weaker position. Skilfully utilising this situation, and using Togo to sound out and soften up the francophone powers, Nigeria began to steer West Africa towards the creation of the Economic Community of West African States. Events within Europe helped, notably the accession of Britain to the EEC. Increasing (if not total) African unity was shown in the negotiations leading to the Lomé Convention of 1974, which regulated the relations of African, Caribbean and Pacific nations with the EEC. Finally, ECOWAS came into existence in Lagos in May 1975, the founder members being Mauritania, Senegal, the Gambia, Guinea-Bissau, Guinea, Sierra Leone, Liberia, the Ivory Coast, Mali, Upper Volta, Ghana, Togo, Dahomey (now Bénin), Niger and Nigeria – an exciting occasion, despite a salutary warning on the eve of the Lagos Conference by the Nigerian Federal Commissioner for Economic Development, Adebayo Adedeji, that 'it will take at least five years to develop a West African Economic Community'.[1] ECOWAS was in some ways clearly modelled on the EEC; it provided for the gradual diminution of customs duties and trade restrictions between members, the creation of common customs and commercial policy towards third-party countries, and the creation of common ECOWAS citizenship, which would confer freedom of movement, work and residence within the community.

The last was of direct importance to large numbers of ordinary West Africans, as migrant traders and migrant labourers moving across international frontiers are an important feature of many West African economies, yet such migrants had come under

[1] *West Africa*, 19 May 1975, 558.

unpleasant pressures. Early in 1970, Dr Busia's government in Ghana shocked Africa and the world by its sudden expulsion of large numbers of foreign Africans, mainly traders; by the end of January 1970, Ghana herself admitted 'repatriation' (or expulsion as many saw it) of 170 000 African foreigners. Nor was this unique, as the same period also saw mass expulsions from Ivory Coast. This kind of action – and there were examples elsewhere in Africa – contributed in no small amount to radical disillusion. Rodney used it as a stick with which to beat African governments:

> Pan-Africanism has been so flouted by the present governments that the concept of 'African' is dead for all practical purposes such as travel and employment. The 'Africanisation' that was aimed against the European colonial administrator soon gave way to restrictive employment and immigration practices by Ivory Coast, Ghana (under Busia), Zaire, Tanzania, Uganda, Zambia and others – aimed against ... all Africans who were guilty of believing that Africa was for the Africans.[1]

Given the sensitivity of the issues involved in free movement of labour, and the resentments that could be caused among *indigènes* at the presence of large numbers of either successful *or* unsuccessful foreigners, it is not surprising that by the April 1978 meeting of ECOWAS heads of state in Lagos, free movement of labour remained a matter for anxious discussion. The intermediate regional stage of Pan-Africanism represented by ECOWAS was still by 1978 an unproven venture (as Adedeji wisely predicted). The hope that Nigerian oil money could finance West African economic development in a more appropriate way, and on more easy terms, than traditional external aid from the developed nations or the World Bank, evaporated with the lapse of the Nigerian economy into serious balance-of-payments difficulties.

Thus, West African regional unity, despite being an aspiration dating back to the time of James Africanus Horton, and despite various attempts over the twenty years from 1958 to 1978 to bring it into existence in some form or other, produced a harvest mainly of frustrated hopes. Apart from the obvious practical problems, it is also necessary to take into account the fact that as well as being the region of Africa with the most persistent efforts to create a wider regional unity, it has also been the home of inveterate and effective opponents of regional unity. In this negative sense, the key state was certainly the Ivory Coast, and the key leader Houphouët-

[1] *Resolutions and selected speeches*, 25.

Boigny. In 1957–8 he was the most important leader, within the old Rassemblement Démocratique Africain, of the successful opposition to the idea of a united French West African independence. The subsequent watered-down plan for a Federation of Mali, to comprise Soudan (as the future Republic of Mali was still called in 1958–9), Senegal, Upper Volta and Dahomey, was further weakened by the Ivory Coast persuading Upper Volta and Dahomey to withdraw. Only a rump federation of the two remaining states came briefly into existence as an independent state in 1960. Within that federation, Soudan, under Modibo Keita, was enthusiastic for federal union as a basis for creating a transformed society, which was so little to the taste of Léopold Senghor of Senegal that he withdrew his country after only two months. The only wider grouping of former French West African territories that managed to establish itself securely in this era of transfer of power was the Conseil de l'Entente, formed in May 1959. But this was a creation dominated by the Ivory Coast (also comprising Dahomey, Upper Volta, and Niger), and very much the ancestor of the UAM and OCAM. African unity was certainly never one of its objectives, but rather a dedication to preserving the sovereignty of individual states even if by means of a loose economic or political association.

In other parts of Africa the regional idea had even less success. There were hopes in Egypt in the years immediately after the Egyptian revolution of 1952 that the Sudan might be at last reunited with Egypt, and support for this was canvassed energetically in the Sudan under the aegis of the Unity of the Nile Valley Movement, which was, however, perhaps more of a pressure group with a slogan than a genuine popular movement among the Sudanese. Sudanese achievement of independence in 1956 killed this 'movement'. In French-ruled North Africa the idea of the unity of the Maghrib (which as a geographical concept also includes Libya) was more than counterbalanced by the very different nature and outcome of the independence struggles in Algeria, Morocco and Tunisia. Thereafter, the main impetus for wider unions in North Africa came from Libya, whose abortive unions with Egypt and Tunisia underlined the lack of success of North African regionalism. These disunities in North Africa were further demonstrated by the acute confrontation between Morocco and Mauritania on the one hand, and the Polisario Front,

Algeria and Libya on the other, over the future of the former
Spanish Sahara, partitioned between Morocco and Mauritania by
agreement with Spain, but without consulting the wishes of the
Sahraouis, in 1975.

Regionalism in East and Central Africa was productive mainly
of disillusion. One problem faced by Pan-Africanists who favoured
regionalism in this part of Africa was the fact that historically
federalism was associated with settler pressures to maximise their
degree of local control. This was clearly so much the case with
the Central African federation of Southern Rhodesia, Northern
Rhodesia and Nyasaland, (officially known as the Federation of
Rhodesia and Nyasaland), created in 1953 against the wishes of
virtually all articulate African opinion, that African nationalists
in those territories inevitably opted for separate independence. In
the four British East African territories of Kenya, Uganda,
Tanganyika and Zanzibar, settler pressures for federation had not
succeeded, but there was a legacy from the colonial era of common
services in matters such as transport, currency, and customs.
Furthermore, on the personal level, in the late 1950s and early
1960s, there was perhaps no part of Africa where a greater
proportion of senior African political leaders regarded themselves
as Pan-Africanists. To name only some of the more obvious
examples, as well as Nyerere, there was Milton Obote of Uganda;
Jomo Kenyatta; Tom Mboya of Kenya who had chaired the
1958 Accra All-African Peoples' Conference; Oscar Kambona,
independent Tanganyika's first foreign minister; and Oginga
Odinga, Kenya's first vice-president. In other words, Pan-
Africanism was very much in vogue in the new ruling circles of
Uganda, Tanganyika and Kenya as they came to independence.
By comparison, from the three territories comprising the Federation of Rhodesia and Nyasaland, only one major figure committed to Pan-Africanism emerged in a position of power, Kenneth
Kaunda of Zambia, the former Northern Rhodesia. The East
African Pan-Africanists were aware of the dangers facing small
weak states in the modern world. For a number of years there were
hopes that these could be avoided by the creation of an East
African federation, which would be large enough in area, population and resources not to be the cat's-paw of outside powers,
and to tackle its internal social and economic tasks.

With East African regionalism, as with Pan-Africanism as a

whole, one of the central problems was that political forces had developed within individual colonial units, dedicated primarily to national independence, and with the possibilities of conflict between this aim and the wider regional ideal not confronted until too late. Not till 1958 was there a serious attempt to create a Pan-East African political party, which would unify all existing parties. The initiative was largely Nyerere's, and the outcome was disappointing. Instead of creating the unified East African party that Nyerere had hoped for, the 1958 Mwanza Conference created the Pan-African Freedom Movement of East and Central Africa (PAFMECA). This was nothing more than an *omnium gatherum* of existing East and Central African parties, with the object of furthering *national* rather than *regional* independence, and with all effective authority remaining with its constituent organisations. Furthermore, the Ugandans participated in the Mwanza Conference at only a minor and non-committal level, while the presence of Central African delegates made PAFMECA an ill-assorted body for furthering East African unity. In the years that followed, PAFMECA became an ever more diffuse body, as its conferences (more or less its only activity) were attended by delegates from a growing range of countries and movements. Accordingly, in 1961 it changed its name to the Pan-African Freedom Movement of East, Central and Southern Africa (PAFMECSA). Its growth was shown by the fact that its 1962 meeting was held in Addis Ababa, chaired by Kenneth Kaunda, with representation from 14 countries with 100 million inhabitants; its weakness by the fact that it was always chronically under-financed and in debt, with many of its constituent governments and parties failing to pay their dues.

The most spectacular initiative towards regional unity in East Africa came in June 1960, through Julius Nyerere offering to delay Tanganyikan independence until such time as all three major East African territories could become jointly independent as a federal unit. The first and only concrete achievement in the aftermath of this initiative was the replacement of the old colonial arrangements for East African common services by the East African Common Services Organisation (EACSO) in 1961. However, EACSO was very much controlled on a tripartite basis, with each of the three constituent nations having the right of veto. Very soon disagreements emerged among its members. Nevertheless, it was for some years, despite occasional friction, to be the best example of regional economic cooperation in the continent. The high point of expectation of an East African federation came in June 1963, when Obote, Nyerere and Kenyatta declared their intention to federate that year – although, significantly, Kenyan independence was not to be delayed until federation was arranged. The period of accord between the three leaders was brief; the Kenyans and Ugandans were more pre-occupied with internal affairs. Obote, who had taken a radical Pan-Africanist stance at the Addis Ababa Heads of State Conference in May, began to feel that East African federation was antithetical to continental unity. From the sidelines, Kwame Nkrumah made known his view that the proposed federation was not in accord with the OAU spirit, and a public controversy resulted between himself and Nyerere on the issue. The Ghanaians used their influence to stir up feeling against the federation, especially in Uganda. The failure to federate in 1963 soon soured relations between Tanganyika and her neighbours, and made for increasing friction in the running of EACSO. By the mid-1960s the feelings of Nyerere, who had in 1964 united Tanganyika with Zanzibar to form Tanzania, were shown by increasingly bitter comments on the failure to achieve East African federation, and the difficulties emerging within EACSO, in particular the wish of Tanzania not to have her nascent manufacturing sector flooded by imports from Kenya.[1]

Not only was regionalism, at best, a very limited success, but also the Pan-African movement was unable to prevent, in the period after 1960, two other kinds of challenge – separatist movements within existing states, and irredentist movements by national minorities wishing to join their kin in adjacent states. The Horn of Africa exhibited both tendencies. On the one hand, the Pan-Somali sentiments of all Somalia's governments since independence generated claims for a Greater Somalia, to include the Ogaden region of Ethiopia, the North-East Frontier area of Kenya, and Djibouti (the former French territory of the Afars and Issas). The Ogaden claim was promoted the most relentlessly, and by the mid-1970s OAU attempts at mediation had fallen down, and a major insurrection was taking place in the Ogaden, with sympathy and support from Somalia, escalating into full-scale war in 1978. Clearly, in circumstances like these, commitments to the

[1] Nyerere, 'Problems of East African co-operation', in *Freedom and socialism*, 64–5.

territorial integrity of member states on the one hand, and to the right of national self-determination on the other, became mutually contradictory. In a continent in which few states lack ethnic minorities, it is not surprising that the OAU, while wishing a peaceful resolution of this conflict, found Ethiopian territorial integrity of more importance than Ogaden Somali self-determination. Nor did the OAU find itself able to resolve the problem of the Eritrean secessionist movement, fighting for independence from Ethiopia ever since in 1962 Haile Selassie's government first abolished the federated status Eritrea had enjoyed since 1952. Irredentism struck the pacemaker of Pan-Africanism, Nkrumah's Ghana, at the very moment of independence. Many Ewes inside Ghana wished to be united with their fellow Ewes in neighbouring Togo. The incipient Ewe revolt on the eve of independence had to be suppressed by the use of troops. The still partially obscure events surrounding the invasion of Shaba province of Zaire (the former Katanga) in 1977 and 1978 by dissident elements based in Angola, seems to have been partly based on ethnic tensions. Examples could be proliferated of ethnic secessionism and irredentism, but undoubtedly the most serious crisis of this sort, to date, for the Pan-African movement – excepting the as yet unresolved multiple problems in the Horn of Africa – was that created by the Nigerian civil war of 1967–70.

The Nigerian civil war was a near disaster for the OAU, as not only did it provide the spectacle of its impotence to prevent foreign interference in the African continent, but it also split its members. A minority of four member states recognised Biafran independence in 1968, in the name of the right of the Ibo people to self-determination. It was an ill-assorted grouping – itself a comment on the complexities of the Biafran episode – consisting of Zambia and Tanzania, usually regarded as radical Pan-African countries, and the lukewarm enthusiasts for Pan-Africanism, Gabon and the Ivory Coast. The Nigerian federal government eventually received important supplies of arms not only from Egypt, but also from Britain, the Soviet Union and Czechoslovakia. On the other hand the Biafrans, no doubt equally feeling that necessity makes strange bed-fellows, received support from Portugal, France and, according to rumour, South Africa. Between 1967 and 1969, there was a series of attempts by the OAU to bring about peace, but the Biafrans were suspicious of a body that for the most part regarded the territorial integrity of its existing members as more important than minority self-determination; while the federal government was understandably anxious not to allow the OAU's efforts to take the form of mediation, let alone arbitration. The final collapse of Biafra in January 1970 was greeted with relief by almost all OAU members, and was a victory for the principle of territorial integrity – but it was a victory won by the Nigerian government, not by the OAU.

PAN-AFRICANISM AND THE ARMED LIBERATION STRUGGLES

If the issues of regionalism, secessionism and irredentism split or at least paralysed and to some extent discredited Pan-Africanism in the twenty years from 1958, support for national independence from colonial and white minority regimes was something everyone could agree on in principle. However, as we have seen, the issue of support for and recognition of the provisional government of Algeria, during the period when Algerian independence was yet being contested, divided the newly independent African states. Thus even national liberation could be a divisive issue. Nor was this the only problem faced by those engaged in armed liberation struggles at that time, in trying to engage the attention of those who had recently benefited from peaceful transfer of power. In a revealing anecdote, Amílcar Cabral, leader of the revolutionary liberation struggle in Portuguese Guinea until his murder by a Portuguese agent in 1973, remarked on:

An incident during the second All-African Peoples' Conference in Tunis during 1960, where we had some difficulty in being heard. One African delegate to whom we tried to explain our situation replied in all sympathy: 'Oh, its different for you. No problem there – you're doing all right with the Portuguese.' At least it helped us to see that we could count only on ourselves.[1]

At least in Cabral's country there was only one movement, the Partido Africano da Independência da Guiné e Cabo Verde (PAIGC), for the official Pan-African movement to recognise. In other places, notably Angola and Rhodesia, the spectacle of rival liberation movements complicated the whole problem of recognition and aid. The creation of the OAU's Liberation

[1] Amílcar Cabral, foreword to Basil Davidson, *The liberation of Guiné: aspects of an African revolution* (London, 1969), 9–10.

Committee in 1963 signified a serious determination to ensure that it would never henceforth be blandly assumed that any of those still under colonial and minority rule were 'doing all right', as well as to try to reconcile divided liberation movements, or at least to decide which of such movements ought to be supported. Based since inception in Dar es Salaam, though with regional bureaux in Lusaka and (till 1974) in Conakry, the Liberation Committee had its own bureaucracy and – though quite inadequately till 1974 – its own funds. Executive secretaries were Tanzanian, but its membership, drawn from OAU member states, fluctuated, and at times was fiercely contested. Its actions, necessarily often confidential or even secretive, soon aroused the suspicions of more cautious OAU members, and as a consequence its autonomy was restricted and all OAU states given observer status in its deliberations in 1966.

If this reduced opposition within the OAU, it cannot be said to have increased the Liberation Committee's ability to give effective aid, which remained, in the view of some, for some years an objective rather than a reality. In 1966 Cabral was 'convinced that Africa can and should do more for our struggle', whilst Basil Davidson, historian for the world-at-large of the independence struggles in Portuguese Africa, observed that in 1968 the Liberation Committee 'moved closer to at least a recognition of the need for more effective support...one might think, not before time'.[1] But it was in relation to the hard choices demanded by the liberation struggle in Angola that the Liberation Committee stumbled most. There, Holden Roberto's Frente Nacional de Libertação de Angola (FNLA) was officially recognised in 1963, rather than the Movimento Popular de Libertação de Angola (MPLA), partly because the MPLA's initial revolt, in Luanda in 1961, had been a disaster. Also, Holden Roberto was then better known to the leaders of independent Africa, having been at the 1958 All-African Peoples' Conference and having thereafter established his image. Recognition of the FNLA was withdrawn as its fortunes waned in 1964, and as it was identified as more of an ethnic Kongo than a Pan-Angolan movement, while official approval was now given to the MPLA. However, in 1972 the FNLA was recognised again, this time alongside the MPLA. Roberto's kinship to President Mobutu Sese Seko of Zaire, and

[1] Davidson, *The liberation of Guiné*, 141.

Zairean determination to further the FNLA's fortunes at the expense of the MPLA, influenced this confused policy as much as anything, although there were continuing attempts to reconcile the two movements. Then, at the moment of independence for Angola, the Liberation Committee also recognised the third Angolan movement, Jonas Savimbi's União Nacional para a Independência Total de Angola (UNITA), as a climax to OAU efforts through 1974 to persuade the three movements to nego-tiate jointly with the defeated Portuguese. The resolution of the resulting struggle for power after independence owed nothing to the OAU, and everything to the MPLA's military victory (aided by Cuban troops and Russian logistical support), over the forces of UNITA (backed by South African intervention) and the FNLA (backed by Zaire and employing western freelance mercenaries).

This Angolan situation displayed the Liberation Committee, and the OAU at large, in a situation of great disadvantage, which was to some extent redressed by the record elsewhere. Eduardo Mondlane, leader of the Frente de Libertação de Moçambique (FRELIMO), wrote, not long before his assassination in 1969, of the OAU's 'important work' towards achieving unity within the liberation movements (although stating, 'more work needs to be done along these lines'), and helping 'to get recognition and establish contacts with other parts of Africa'.[1]

In Namibia (South West Africa), the Liberation Committee consistently backed the South West Africa People's Organisation (SWAPO). From its inception in 1963, the OAU made a root-and-branch condemnation of the apartheid regime in South Africa and Namibia, and called for both its members and all United Nations members to sever diplomatic relations with, close their ports and airports to, and impose a trade and arms embargo on, South Africa. From 1963, the OAU made it its business to make life as difficult as possible for South Africa at the United Nations, and in 1974 almost succeeded in securing South Africa's expulsion, a move thwarted by British, French and American vetoes in the Security Council. Likewise, in 1963 the OAU called upon Britain not to transfer power in Rhodesia; when Ian Smith's illegal Unilateral Declaration of Independence (UDI) came in 1965, the OAU almost at once called on Britain to smash the rebellion

---

[1] Eduardo Mondlane, *The struggle for Mozambique* (London, 1969), 212–13.

immediately or face the breaking off of diplomatic relations by all OAU members.

Unfortunately, the implementation of these policies proved far more difficult than their promulgation, not only because the world at large, and especially the western world, continued to trade with and sell arms to South Africa, and covertly to support Rhodesia through sanctions-breaking companies, but also because of divided reactions and policies among OAU members themselves. In the case of some, there were recognised to be extenuating circumstances; thus Zambia's geographical position made it impossible for her to observe sanctions without causing her own economic collapse, and Botswana, Lesotho and Swaziland were even less able to break with South Africa. But the imposition of the various restrictions on South Africa's air and sea transport, and on trade with South Africa, were imposed piecemeal and in some cases tardily or not at all. The lead in defying OAU policy was taken by President Hastings Kamuzu Banda of Malawi, who in 1967 went so far as to establish diplomatic relations with South Africa, a move not universally unpopular with other OAU members, especially the Ivory Coast and a number of the other OCAM powers, and Ghana, then reacting strongly against the Pan-African militancy of the overthrown Nkrumah government. In 1970, Houphouët-Boigny took this line to its logical conclusion by advocating a policy of 'dialogue' with South Africa, arguing that the opening of diplomatic and trade relations would lead to a softening and peaceful resolution of racial oppression within South Africa. This was strongly rejected by the OAU at its 1971 Summit in Addis Ababa, but Gabon, Lesotho, the Malagasy Republic, Malawi and Mauritius supported the Ivory Coast, while Dahomey, Niger, Togo and Upper Volta abstained. In the aftermath, Malawi continued to have open relations with South Africa, President Banda making an official visit there in August 1971, and the Ivory Coast developed informal contacts up to the highest levels. The OAU had, however, some successes in the battle against South Africa, the most notable being its totally successful policy of African and international non-recognition of the Transkei Bantustan on its being granted so-called independence by South Africa in 1976, and of other Bantustans subsequently declared 'independent' by the Republic.

As for the Rhodesian question, by 1966 the OAU had already

been reluctantly forced to recognise the impracticability of its original reaction to Smith's UDI, and to accept the British and United Nations policy of sanctions, although without conviction. Furthermore, the Liberation Committee was faced with the split in the African nationalists' opposition to UDI, at that time between the Zimbabwe African National Union (ZANU) and the Zimbabwe African People's Union (ZAPU). Such divisions continued to bedevil the liberation struggle in Rhodesia, although in 1975 the Liberation Committee was able to recommend substantial assistance to the liberation movement, unified in 1974, under the aegis of the African National Council. On the other hand, it could not prevent sanctions-breaking, nor the rapid breakdown of the African National Council's precarious unity. After 1976 it supported the Patriotic Front (reflecting the increased influence in the Liberation Committee of President Samora Machel of Mozambique, who backed Robert Mugabe's faction). This turn of OAU policy in relation to Rhodesia represented a moving away from the policy of 'détente'. The thesis behind détente was that in a situation deteriorating for South Africa, with the collapse of the Portuguese in Mozambique and Angola, and the potentially exposed position of having to shore-up the weakening Smith regime in Rhodesia, realism would prevail in the Vorster government, which might be persuaded to put pressure on Ian Smith to concede an acceptable settlement. South African self-interest, therefore, was to be put at the disposal of Zimbabwe's liberation. The main architects and exponents of this policy were Tanzania, Botswana, Mozambique and Zambia. It was not totally without success, as South African pressure was widely believed to have been a factor in Ian Smith's apparent acceptance in September 1976 of the principle of majority rule. However, this was seen by the détente leaders and the Patriotic Front as little more than another white Rhodesian exercise in playing for time and dividing its internal and external opponents, of making apparent concessions while retaining the reality of power in white hands.

In general it would be true to say that from the Rabat Summit of 1972, the OAU policy declarations on liberation became more militant, even extending to the decision in principle that the armies of African countries ought to be committed to the armed struggle against colonial and white minority rule. Far from being welcome to either the OAU's radical critics, or to those leading liberation movements in the field, this was universally rejected as undesirable. Probably the most scornful comments were those of Walter Rodney in the paper he prepared for the Sixth Pan-African Congress in 1974:

The record to date exposes the gap between theory and practice on the part of OAU members as far as monetary support to the OAU Liberation Committee is concerned. Recently, the rhetoric has become seemingly more fiery... Take for instance the demagogic appeal that African governments should send armies to the combat zone. Such suggestion is completely out of touch with the concept of a people's war and out of sympathy with the process through which a people prepare themselves for self-liberation.[1]

If Rodney were to be dismissed as an armchair critic, then the continuing self-reliance in purely military matters of the liberation movements in the final phase of the wars against Portugal was even more eloquent. The liberation movements welcomed aid, but did not need or welcome crusading African armies, with their implications of outside leadership and control of the liberation process.

PAN-AFRICANISM AND WORLD AFFAIRS

Pan-Africanism after the advent of the era of independent African states became primarily the concern of Africa's leaders, movements, peoples and governments, yet it cannot be understood, before or since 1958, except in the context of certain global themes. Proto-Pan-Africanism had its roots in vast events: the transfer of African slave labour on a colossal scale across the Atlantic from the sixteenth to the nineteenth centuries, to work the plantations, mines and industries of the New World; the penetration of increasing areas of Africa by European commerce in the era of 'legitimate' trade that overlapped and succeeded the Atlantic slave trade; the European partition of Africa; and the transfers of power and liberation struggles since the late 1940s. By involvement in these events, Africa was taking part in an even vaster and world-wide historical process. In a few centuries, a small group of European states had risen to world-wide dominance, and created a plethora of doctrines, from crude racial superiority to paternalistic trusteeship for 'child races' or a 'duty'

[1] *Resolutions and selected speeches*, 31–3.

to develop the world in the name of 'progress', in order to justify their hegemony. Pan-Africanism was only one of a number of movements in the 'dominated' world to challenge that hegemony, ideologically and in practice, and take advantage of its internal contradictions and weaknesses. This was well understood by the pioneer Pan-Africanists of the earlier twentieth century, who often anticipated the post-1945 spirit of Afro-Asian unity. Thus, in his heyday after the First World War, Marcus Garvey supported Gandhi and the Indian National Congress. Duse Mohamed Ali was almost as much an activist for Pan-Islamism, Egyptian nationalism, and Indian and other Asian nationalisms, as for Pan-Africanism. He often spoke, as did W. E. B. DuBois, of 'the darker races', who had the same problems, enemies and tasks. Independence at its heady onset created the illusion that Africa easily and soon could be freed from external influences. The African states were to be non-aligned, plans for their joint economic development proliferated. All outside states accepting these things with goodwill were to be regarded as friends. Other realities have dispersed these ephemeral dreams.

In the economic sphere, modern, independent Africa still produced agricultural and mineral commodities for world markets, without much control over the terms of trade, and was heavily dependent on foreign capital and expertise (often from the old colonial powers) to produce and market them. In the starkest cases, this made for vitiated independence. Zambia's economy was almost totally dependent on the world price of copper, for which the market was almost wholly outside Africa; Mauritania was even more bereft of resources other than her French-developed mines which produced totally for export outside Africa; even revolutionary Angola retained, as of 1978, the services of Gulf Oil to develop off-shore oil, despite the use of American war materials by the Portuguese during the independence struggle, and widely alleged US Central Intelligence Agency support for the MPLA's enemies in the civil wars following independence. African road and rail systems still mostly followed colonial patterns, connecting an economic hinterland with the nearest port, from which the hinterland's primary commodities could be shipped to the advanced industrial countries. Africa still contained a high proportion of the world's poorest countries, the only clear exception to all this being the Republic of South Africa, still the economic, if no longer the political, metropolis of southern Africa. This was best illustrated not so much by the total dependence on selling cheap labour to South Africa of a country like Lesotho, small, poor in resources, and surrounded by South African territory, as by the continued economic relations with South Africa of independent and Marxist Mozambique.

Briefly after 1973 it seemed at least that African states with substantial oil resources could be exempt from poverty and dependency, and finance widespread development for themselves and also for less fortunate neighbours. The success of the Organisation of Petroleum Exporting Countries (OPEC) in vastly improving its members' terms of trade created hopes that producers of other primary commodities might do likewise. Such hopes were largely disappointed; improvements were invariably temporary and caused by factors beyond African control. Thus, African coffee producers, such as Ivory Coast, Ethiopia, Kenya and Uganda, benefited from the sudden steep rise in world coffee prices in the mid-1970s, but this was caused by frost in Brazil, the world's leading producer, rather than any coordinated African action. Subsequently, coffee producers were unable to maintain a price plateau. As for the OPEC's 'success' over oil prices, it led to serious problems for Africa. Most African states had no oil of their own, yet were peculiarly dependent on it for energy – as much as 95 per cent in the case of Tanzania, a by no means isolated example. The advanced industrial countries were in fact much better able to substitute other fuels, or in the case of Britain and Norway, domestically produced oil as well. On the other hand, their economies stagnated from 1973, and by 1978 the immediate market for oil had become depressed, and its real price had been dropping for some time, despite the likelihood of future oil-shortages. The more prodigal OPEC countries, whether in or out of Africa – Nigeria and Iran come to mind – found themselves facing not abundance but debt, with much diminished prospects of aiding (and influencing) others. Meanwhile, the industrial countries passed on to African customers for their manufactures the increased costs in oil.

These intrusive processes, functions of the world and not the African economy, inevitably were a profound political challenge to Pan-Africanism, with its optimistic doctrine that together Africans could solve all their problems. Even before the creation of the OAU, Nkrumah attacked the domination and manipulation of African countries by outside capital as 'neo-colonialism', and preached economic integration, even if political integration was his first priority. Yet under his guidance the Ghanaian economy was not integrated even with those of its neighbours. Internally Nkrumah's Ghana had 'socialist talk without socialist planning. The worst of both worlds'.[1] Likewise, once the hope of East African unity faded, Nyerere's Tanzania turned to a policy of *national* economic and social transformation. Tanzania's biggest regional economic project, the TanZam railway, linking the Zambian Copperbelt with Dar es Salaam, was constructed with Chinese capital, technical expertise, capital goods and even skilled labour, and by 1978 needed Chinese aid to restore efficient operation. As for the OAU, its Economic and Social Commission (ESC) from inception planned such things as a common external tariff, inter-African transport systems, increased inter-African trade, and better terms of trade; all, in 1978, still unrealised, with minor exceptions. Although largely dependent for expertise on the pre-existing United Nations agency, the Economic Commission for Africa (ECA), the ESC increasingly disliked the ECA's stance of being 'above' politics. Its first major victory – a paper victory – was UN acceptance in 1969 that the ECA should, broadly, cooperate with the OAU. In the 1970s the OAU enthusiastically followed the UN's call (1974) for a 'New International Economic Order' to benefit the developing countries. Its main action in that direction was the 1975 Lomé Convention. Though obtaining better terms for Africa from the EEC, this hardly transformed the nature of African economic relations. Subsequently, the OAU endorsed the creation of ECOWAS, and called for similar organisations to be created in other regions of Africa. None of this, even at its most useful, amounted to the economic unity that Pan-Africanism in theory stood for. In practice, national interests remained uppermost. In reality, most of Africa remained poor or very poor.

The original Pan-Africanist goal of political non-involvement with external power blocs proved as elusive as economic unity. Indeed insofar as commitment to Afro-Asian unity as a broad concept was concerned, outside involvement was in fact enthusiastically accepted. The 1955 Bandung Conference, though

[1] Makonnen, *Pan-Africanism*, 246.

dominated by already independent Asian powers, was also attended by African nationalists, and had some influence on the subsequent development of Pan-Africanism. It looked to the UN to safeguard universal human rights, and especially rights of national self-determination. Pan-Africanism in the era of independent states was to do the same. With the rise in the number of African members it became a formidable force in the UN. But the limits on the effectiveness of 'world opinion' as expressed in UN General Assembly majorities were the limits of what Africa could achieve by such means. As for the principle that African states should be 'non-aligned', this hardly survived. In the Africa of 1978, it was easy to make lists of powers that were very close to either the Soviet or the western blocs, even if not part of their formal systems of alliances. No one doubted that Kenya, the Ivory Coast, Liberia, Zaire, Chad, the Central African empire, Gabon, Morocco and Upper Volta, to name some obvious examples, were, with variations, close to the western world. Even Egypt under Nāṣir, one of the most formidable opponents of such involvement, subsequently inclined in many ways to the west. Equally, no one doubted the warmth of relations between the Soviet Union, Cuba and the German Democratic Republic (East Germany), and Ethiopia, Mozambique, Angola, Guinea-Bissau, Bénin, the Cape Verde Islands, the Congo Republic, and the Malagasy Republic. In the former Portuguese colonies, this closeness was a natural outgrowth of the substantial military and other aid given them during their independence struggles by the Soviet bloc; in the case of Angola, Cuban and Soviet aid was vital during the post-independence civil war. In Ethiopia, Russian logistic and material support and military advice, backed by troops from Cuba and Marxist South Yemen, enabled the Ethiopian government to win back control of the disputed Ogaden and hold onto the Eritrean port of Massawa in 1978. In the sphere of continuing liberation struggles, it was clear that the Patriotic Front and SWAPO were also receiving substantial Soviet-bloc as well as African aid. (The example of Albania is an exemplary caution against supposing that small states are invariably dominated by powerful friends and allies.) Furthermore, African states with strong western or eastern connexions would vehemently deny membership of, still less subordination to, foreign blocs. Good relations between African states were not always impaired by their differing non-African connexions, as was shown by Ethiopia and Kenya. Connexions with the same external friends might not ensure good relations, as was shown by the case of Somalia and Ethiopia. Formerly close to the Soviet Union, Somalia was estranged by Soviet and Cuban support for Ethiopia.

Revealingly, by the 1970s African states were increasingly looking to outside powers for support in both internal and external disputes, as was shown by the presence of foreign troops in increasing numbers of African countries. The Cubans were present in substantial strength in Angola and Ethiopia, and present in smaller numbers in several other countries, notably Mozambique. For many years France gave military support to Chad in its long war with its northern dissidents, and by 1978 there was disquiet even within France itself at the deployment of French forces there, and in the war against Polisario in Sahara and Mauritania. French forces remained in Djibouti after its independence. Most controversial of all, French troops intervened, together with the Belgians and with US logistic support, in the troubles of Shaba province in Zaire in June 1978. Once again, as in 1960–2 and the 'Stanleyville Drop' of 1964 when Belgian, American and British military intervention took place, Zaire posed the acutest, most complicated problems for Pan-Africanism. In both 1964 and 1978 the foreign military intervention was presented as a humanitarian rescue operation to save white residents from barbarous massacres, though the far more extensive massacres of Africans were more or less ignored, except to provide a propaganda picture of alleged African savagery. Shaba was invaded in 1978, as it had been in 1977, by insurgents based in Angola (although the Angolan authorities denied complicity), some of whom were former members of the Katangese gendarmerie, the military arm of Katangese secession in the early 1960s. For its part, the Zairean government had encouraged the MPLA's internal enemies, notably the FNLA, which had mounted raids into Angola from Zairean territory. The Zairean government was revealed by the Shaba intervention as so weak and unpopular that it had to rely on foreigners, including Belgians, to maintain its existence, and in the aftermath had to accept increased western control over Zaire's finances and economy as the price of continuing support. China also rushed to offer Zaire military aid, alleging that the episode was a Soviet–Cuban plot. Nothing could have more discredited the OAU, given its central function of preserving the inviolability of member states, and resolving disputes between them. Chinese involvement reflected increasing Chinese determination to persuade as many African states as possible to see the Soviet Union, Cuba and their African friends as the greatest threat to the continent's peace and security. In the immediate aftermath of the 1978 Shaba crisis, there was at least one improvement in the situation, with Angola and Zaire agreeing to prevent violations of each other's territory by resident exiles.

On one of the other great international issues of modern times, the conflict between the Israeli state and the Palestinians, Africa moved over the twenty years after 1958 from division to wide agreement. President Nāṣir of Egypt began the process of persuading the majority of African states to support the Arab powers over the Palestine question, using his influence within the Casablanca group and the OAU, and undoing the close relations that an intelligently administered aid programme had secured for Israel with many African countries, including Ghana. As late as 1967, the OAU refused to declare that Israel was an aggressor in the Six-Day war against Egypt. In the late 1960s and early 1970s this attitude changed, with continuing Israeli occupation of Egyptian territory, and a growing feeling that the plight of the Palestinians was analogous to that of Africans under colonial or white minority rule. A minority of African countries continued to resist the trend towards the anti-Zionist camp, prominent among these being the Ivory Coast and Malawi. But in 1973, all OAU members except Malawi, Botswana, Lesotho and Swaziland severed relations with Israel. The economic problem that confronted many African states after the oil crisis of 1973, and discontent at the level of Arab economic aid for Africa as a whole (as opposed to Muslim Africa), led to some feeling that Afro-Arab cooperation brought Africa only problems. Meanwhile, Middle Eastern oil continued to find its way to Rhodesia and South Africa. In 1976, however, a number of events rallied African support for the Palestinians. These included improved diplomatic relations between Israel and South Africa, the supply of Israeli war planes to South Africa, and the Israeli commando raid on Entebbe airport in Uganda to release Jewish hostages held there. Though many African leaders looked askance at Idi Amin's government in Uganda, such uninvited foreign armed intervention in Africa was a highly sensitive issue and totally unacceptable. At the same time, the supply of Arab funds to Africa was increasing, and in January 1977 at the Cairo Afro-Arab Summit vast new sums were pledged.

PAN-AFRICANISM AND CULTURE

From the days of proto-Pan-Africanism in the nineteenth century, a desire to defend and reassert the validity of African culture was a preoccupation of many within the Pan-African movement. As was stated at the beginning of this chapter, such matters continued as an important Pan-Africanist concern, notably exemplified in the work of W. E. B. DuBois, in the late 1930s to mid-1940s. Valuable though such efforts were as a counter-attack against the generally derogatory opinion of the then dominant white world about African culture and the African past, they nevertheless provided what was in some ways a confused and difficult legacy for Pan-Africanism in the mid- and late-twentieth century. To begin with, such thinking had come from men who, however much they desired to present a sympathetic interpretation of African culture, were nevertheless the products of European or North American education. There was nothing specifically African about the ways in which they attempted their task, which indeed only too self-evidently, as was bound to be the case, were based on the intellectual and cultural traditions of the white world. Secondly, their approach to the African past – and here the work of DuBois must particularly be born in mind – tended to be romantic, triumphalist, and devoid of any serious attempt to identify conflict and oppression within African societies. DuBois's readers were presented with a glorious past of great kings and kingdoms, disrupted by the slave trade and imperialism. At least one modern historian of Pan-Africanism, Imanuel Geiss, has rejected this legacy as romantic in a pejorative sense, reactionary, and incapable of providing present-day Pan-Africanism with the basis for a coherent and effective modernising ideology.[1] Thirdly,

[1] Geiss, *The Pan-African movement*, 114 and 197.

Pan-Africanism had a legacy, reaching back to the nineteenth century, and above all identified with the thought of E. W. Blyden, of assuming the existence of a generalised African culture based on racial identity; Blyden himself is credited with having originated the concept of the 'African personality'. Useful as such ideas were in making it more possible for peoples of African descent in the diaspora to identify with Africa, and for Africans within Africa to identify with fellow-Africans from other parts of the continent, they ignored the diversity of African cultures, and even the ethnic diversity of Africa, a continent which contains millions of indigenous people who are not black.

Easily the most determined effort to reproduce an ideology and art which would be determinedly authentic, which would exalt and glorify African culture and modes of thought as opposed to European, originated in the world of black students in Paris in the 1930s. This was the beginning of the concept of *négritude*, originally a search for identity by individuals who felt alienated from both their ethnic roots and from French society. Its most important leaders were the Martiniquan poet, Aimé Césaire, the French Guyanese poet Léon Damas, and the Senegalese Léopold Sédar Senghor who, years later, as President of Senegal, was able to give powerful patronage to the movement, although he was eventually to seem to lose interest in it. Under the aegis of *négritude*, which in the post-war era acquired a political dimension with claims to be an ideology of liberation, a whole school of francophone writers from both Africa and the New World emerged, as did the highly influential Paris-based magazine *Présence Africaine*. Yet it would be broadly true to say that *négritude* remained a force restricted to francophone black intellectuals (together with some white admirers such as Jean-Paul Sartre), and increasingly under attack not only from black intellectuals in non-francophone Africa, but even from some francophones themselves. Thus as early as 1952, the Martiniquan Frantz Fanon remarked that 'the man who adores the Negro is as sick as the man who abominates him', and described the educated Negro as the 'slave of the spontaneous and cosmic Negro myth'.[1] Twelve years later, in an ironic and perceptive critique of the relationship of the French West Indian élite to Africa on the one hand and

[1] Frantz Fanon, *Black skin, white masks*, tr. Charles Markmann (London, 1970), 12. Originally published as *Peau noire, masques blancs* (Paris, 1952).

to the French on the other, Fanon stated that 'the West Indian, after the great white error, is now living in the great black mirage'.[1]

The main lines of attack against *négritude* were that it romanticised African culture and society, and that it was meaningful only to a small élite of intellectuals who had lost touch, at least in part, with the African masses to whom such doctrines were of no concern, as they had never been assimilated to any degree to European culture. Such was the trend of argument against *négritude* of the South African, Ezekiel Mphahlele, who made a trenchant attack against the movement at the Dakar Conference on Black Literature of 1963, which had been sponsored by Senghor himself. Indeed, rather as the Pan-Africanists of the 1945 congress put the question of national independence first, Mphahlele asserted that national culture must come first. For Mphahlele, 'in a greater Africa, we may arrive at a point where Pan-African goals do determine certain national objectives, but cultures can only contribute to Pan-African ideals from a position of national strength'.[2] Another eminent anglophone writer, the Nigerian Wole Soyinka, had, however, changed his attitude to *négritude* by the mid-1970s. As he put it in 1976, 'from a well-publicised position as an anti-Negritudinist... it has been with an increasing sense of alarm and even betrayal that we have watched our position distorted and exploited to embrace a "sophisticated" school of thought which... repudiates the existence of an African world!'[3]

While these debates raged, cultural Pan-Africanism, like political Pan-Africanism, developed an institutional existence in the world of independent African states. Mention has been made of the Dakar Conference on Black Literature in 1963. By the 1970s, this kind of event was becoming a regular feature of what might be called official or semi-official culture in Africa, with such events as the Black Arts Festival in Dakar in 1966, and in Lagos in 1977. Cultural problems were also discussed at the UNESCO Conference on the Influence of Colonialism on African Cultures in Dar es Salaam in 1972, and the Sixth Pan-African Congress in Dar es Salaam in 1974. There remained, however, serious pro-

[1] Frantz Fanon, *Toward the African revolution*, tr. Haakon Chevalier (London, 1968), 37.
[2] Ezekiel Mphahlele, *The African image*. 2nd revised ed. (London, 1974), 92.
[3] Wole Soyinka, *Myth, literature and the African world* (Cambridge, 1976), ix–x.

blems; African writers still, for the most part, wrote in European languages, with a readership inevitably restricted to Africans fully literate in those languages or to interested white foreigners. Their works were usually published by European or American publishing houses, or their African subsidiaries. At the same time, the continent was being increasingly penetrated, even at the level of the masses, by foreign culture, spread through the media of the cinema, television and radio, despite sporadic attempts to use all these media to develop an authentic modern African popular culture.

In the view of one of the most perceptive leaders of the revolutionary liberation struggles of the 1960s and 1970s, the problem of culture in modern Africa was in a sense no problem at all. To Amílcar Cabral, this attempt to 'return to the sources' was no more than 'a means to attempt temporary advantages, a conscious or unconscious form of political opportunism' on the part of the African lower-middle classes under colonialism, unless it involved 'a genuine commitment to the fight for independence and a total, definitive identification with the aspirations of the masses, who contest not merely the foreigners' culture, but foreign rule altogether'.[1] Cabral was convinced – and this was certainly true of his native country – that the African masses had (with few exceptions) never lost their culture and traditions; and through the liberation movements they would universally gain the power not of restoring it or preserving it, but of using it creatively – in his own often repeated phrase, of 'making history'. This process, quite different from the search for a cultural identity usually associated with the cultural aspects of Pan-Africanism, was one whose outcome remained as yet undetermined.

[1] Amílcar Cabral, 'The role of culture in the liberation struggle', in *Guinea-Bissau: toward final victory. Selected speeches and documents from PAIGC* (Richmond, British Columbia, 1974), 42.

CHAPTER 4

SOCIAL AND CULTURAL CHANGE

The history of most African countries since 1940 seems to revolve around a single event: their gaining of political independence. But this climax of nationalism must be set within those social and cultural changes of which it was so much the product and which were, in the main, confirmed in their course for at least a decade or two thereafter. The Second World War boosted a whole variety of social changes: the intensification of cash-crop production, the acceleration of migration of all kinds and the rapid growth of cities, the diversification of the occupational structure and, eventually, the movement of Africans into its upper echelons, and the expansion of modern education at all levels. All these implied changes in areas more immediately constitutive of 'society', namely in how people identified themselves and in their patterns of social cooperation and conflict. Now the concept of 'social change' is more than a mere umbrella for several parallel, probably somehow-related changes in diverse aspects of social life; it denotes the systematic transformation of a particular society. But at what level do we set 'society'? The difficulty was that, though the prime source of these changes did not lie within them, it was still much easier, as late as the 1940s, to speak of local social systems like those of Asante or the Luo as being *societies* than whole colonies like the Gold Coast or Kenya. Thus the pioneering study, G. and M. Wilson's *The analysis of social change* (1945), took as its units of analysis these small-scale societies, even though the features of change which they described resulted from the progressive incorporation of these societies into wider units, of which the colonial social system was the most important. Though many of the elements of the future national societies were already then present, their full emergence, rather than their transformation, was to be *the* major aspect of social change in the decades that followed. This chapter, then, is a sociological commentary on one main aspiration of the nationalist movement: the creation of national societies within the boundaries of the colonial states.

We, like the nationalists, must begin from what colonialism created. Colonialism produced, besides the general 'increase in social scale', the implications of which for social relations the Wilsons analysed so clearly, a distinctive kind of societal integration. This had two aspects, which will be considered in turn at length below: a certain 'horizontal' integration of the various regions, natural and ethnological, within the state's boundaries; and a 'vertical' integration of emergent social strata in a social system corresponding to the state. These two dimensions were linked, however, since there tended to emerge a certain hierarchy of regions or communities, and the composition of the social strata was not random with respect to regional or ethnic origin.

An African colony's development was above all an aspect of its relations with the metropolitan power. Communications were an excellent indicator of the pattern of 'horizontal' integration: all tarred roads, so to speak, led to the capital, or at least to another entrepôt, a channel for material or symbolic interchange with the metropolis. Different parts of the regional and ethnic mosaic varied in the extent of their involvement with this centre, depending on what they could offer to the outside world, for example cash crops, or were interested in receiving from it, for example education. The primary integration, then, was that which developed between the regions and the centre, rather than that directly between the regions. The capital, as 'centre', was not the centre of a preformed system of joint relations, but imposed as the node through which all regions severally related to the outside. To the extent that direct inter-regional relations developed, they were, apart from some continuation of pre-colonial forms, an effect of one region's more direct relation with the centre, as with the relations between cash-cropping areas and the remoter areas which provided much of their labour. Otherwise, it was precisely at the outward-facing capital, and at other new centres established by colonialism, where some overall integration of the regions and their populations began to take place.

The colonial period also introduced altogether new kinds of social relations, especially those between employer and wage- or salary-earner. And it transformed, where it did not introduce, relations between officials and subjects. Hence developed the beginnings of a national system of social stratification. It does not necessarily follow that, because a certain kind of relationship, such as that entailed in wage-labour, was introduced with colonialism, we are at once dealing with a segment of a nationally integrated system. Because of the mode of regional integration that we have already outlined, a particular segment may be fairly unintegrated in any system of such relations going outside the locality and even fairly *un*differentiated from quite different kinds of purely local relations, for example those between members of two ethnic groups, or at the level of local political status, between chief and client. Thus class analysis, while an indispensable tool in examining the emergent social structures, must be combined with a lively appreciation of two features highly distinctive of most of sub-Saharan Africa: the enormous regional variety of class situations, underpinned by cultural diversity; and the crucial role of the state, which to a great extent formed, rather than reflected, the system of stratification. The most unified social strata were those located in the national centres, the cities, and especially those directly employed by the state itself. The 'primacy of politics', on which several social scientists have remarked,[1] is thus an effect of the loose, or rather distinctive, mode of societal integration bequeathed by colonialism. Nkrumah's injunction 'Seek ye first the political kingdom' shows that nationalist politicians appreciated it well.

Because Africa is so diverse and does not form a single social system, this account concentrates on the social processes typical of the 'normal' African country: an ex-colony of West, East or Central Africa which gained its independence in the 1950s or 1960s. The countries of southern Africa, and especially the Republic of South Africa, while sharing many cultural and local-level characteristics with those further north, differ, not merely because of the long-continued presence and power of whites and the existence of significant interstitial *mestiço* or coloured populations, but because their class systems were so much more dominated by wage-labour and locally based capital. But to see South Africa, for example, as economically 'advanced' or as politically 'backward' compared with a 'normal' African country – despite the attraction which such conceptions have for political actors – would be to impose an unjustified unilinear

[1] H. Spiro (ed.), *The primacy of politics* (New York, 1966).

pattern on a historical course which is likely to be as distinctive in the future as in the past. Ethiopia and the Arab countries of North Africa present a much greater problem, since they cannot be presented as variants of the sub-Saharan model. To the extent that their national societies were formed in a colonial mould, there are similarities. Thus because of a massive settler presence and extensive land expropriation from the indigenous population, it is helpful to draw parallels between Algeria's experience of rurally based national insurrection with similar movements in Angola and Mozambique. Ethiopia, of course, has as its core an ancient colonising, rather than colonised, nation, and it has been the responses of its periphery, rather than the form of its centre, which approach the model. But in other respects, the social and cultural forms of the North African societies are so much their own that their principal use will be as a foil to highlight the characteristic experiences of the bulk of Africa to the south.

PATTERNS OF MIGRATION

By 1940 the patterns of human migration characteristic of the colonial period were well established. Despite some continuities with pre-colonial movements and some origin in indigenous processes, such as nomad sedentarisation, they were dominated by the ways in which different regions of Africa had come to be related to the world economy. Three broad patterns of movement may be discerned: (i) to areas of cash-crop or export-oriented agriculture, (ii) to areas of employment in mines or industry, (iii) to general, heterogeneous employment in cities.

In West Africa any rural-to-urban movement was eclipsed by the vast flow of seasonal, unskilled agricultural labour from the poorer rural areas of the interior savanna to the areas where cash crops were grown by African farmers. There were also movements, continuing from the early colonial period or even before, of agricultural colonisation from areas of real land shortage into areas of land abundance, such as the Cross River area, the Nigerian Middle Belt and the northern Ivory Coast. Except for Nigeria, the movements in West Africa tended to be international in scope, the whole area presenting the aspect of a sub-continental labour-market.

Outside West Africa, something like this pattern evolved with the attraction of migrants from a wide area, but especially from Rwanda and Burundi, to the coffee and cotton farms of Uganda. Elsewhere plantations and European farms drew on local labour, much of it non-seasonal. But the major flows within southern Africa – from rural areas generally to the Copperbelt, the Rand and other mining centres, and the ports and cities of South Africa – were rather different in character. There were here no continuities with pre-colonial movements; there were much higher levels of involvement in migration than in West Africa generally; and men were absent from their rural homes for much longer, with periods of 10–15 years being common.

Both rates and incidences of migration are seen as effects of the relative opportunities that home or rural circumstances and potential target-areas offer potential migrants, endowed in particular ways. From the late 1940s, except for Portugal's colonies where it lasted until 1962, direct political compulsion to labour, such as existed earlier, was absent; and even where migration was initially compelled by the imposition of taxes, it was now undertaken in order to satisfy a variety of wants and needs which had become 'indigenous' to social life in the rural areas: cash to provide school fees, consumer goods, supplements to traditional diets, customary obligations like bridewealth or installation fees for chiefly office which had become monetised or inflated or both. Clyde Mitchell has shown clearly how gross *rates* of migration from different areas of Rhodesia were a function of levels of 'agro-ecological disadvantage', there being more migration from areas with poor soils, fewer European farms, and wages that were lower than the national average.[1] If an area developed a significant export product, migration flows might be reversed. Purely 'cultural' motives, such as the desire for 'bright city lights', seem quite subordinate to 'economic' ones.

The *incidence* of migration, however, was more dependent on a variety of social and cultural factors. Actual land shortage, the classic 'push' factor responsible for the exodus of the poorest rural classes in North Africa as well as in Asia and Latin America, remained uncommon in sub-Saharan Africa; though it developed where significant land-alienation had occurred, for example in Kenya and South Africa, and by the early 1950s was responsible

[1] J. C. Mitchell, 'Factors in rural male absenteeism in Rhodesia', in D. J. Parkin, *Town and country in Central and Eastern Africa* (London, 1975), 93–112.

for some seasonal migration, much of it fairly local, from the close-settled zones of northern Nigeria. It also largely accounted for the largest extra-continental migration flow, beginning in the First World War, of Algerians to metropolitan France, where they numbered over half a million by 1950. Usually the incidence of migration was higher among the better educated and the skilled, since the rewards of urban employment tended to be significantly higher for them. Where whole areas or populations were marked by relatively high levels of such attributes, rates of migration might be affected too, and complex patterns of population-shift might result. Thus many cash-cropping areas such as southern Ghana, where earlier prosperity had encouraged educational development, showed both high levels of out-migration (to urban employment) and high levels of in-migration of strangers from less-favoured areas as labourers or tenant farmers.

The migratory flow was also dependent on the costs of the migrants' absence from their home communities not rising too high.[1] The low wage levels of unskilled labour and the disincentives to permanent settlement which many migrants encountered, especially in their definition as 'strangers', or the absence, whether deliberate or unplanned, of housing facilities for their families, suggest that the subsistence sector continued to function. How could this be, granted the absence of so many young males? In broad areas of West Africa the dovetailing of the periods of peak labour demand in subsistence and in cash-crop farming areas permitted the migrant to move seasonally back and forth, so that the local subsistence economies were maintained at a minimum level, though they were not developed. In southern Africa such factors as the prevalence of female agricultural labour systems, the mobilisation of kin groups to carry out periodic male tasks such as bush-clearing, and the introduction of convenient new crops like cassava, contributed to a situation where proportions of adult males absent at any one time were commonly as high as 50 per cent and in some societies in Malawi even reached 70 per cent.

But no static equilibrium between the subsistence and the wage-earning sectors was ever attained. The increased world demand for both minerals and tropical agricultural products

---

[1] There is much disagreement on the costs of migration to the labour exporting area. For the 'optimistic' view, E. J. Berg, 'The economics of the migrant labor system', in H. Kuper (ed.), *Urbanization and migration in West Africa* (Berkeley, 1965); and opposed, S. Amin (ed.), *Modern migrations in Western Africa* (London, 1974).

Table 4.1. *Estimated population of selected African cities 1940s–1960s (population in thousands).*

	1940s		1950s		1960s	
Cairo	1947	2091	1960	3349	1966	4220
Algiers	1948	473	1954	570	1966	943
Dakar	1943	125	1955	300	1968	600
Kumasi	1948	78	[1960	218]	1966	301
Kano	[1931	89]	1952	130	1963	295
Lagos	[1931	127]	1952	267	1963	665
Addis Ababa	1948	402	1958	400	1968	620
Nairobi	1948	119	1957	222	1969	478
Dar es Salaam	1948	69	1952	99	1967	273
Kinshasa	1940	49	1950	191	1966	508
Salisbury	1940	67	1958	233	1968	380
Johannesburg	[1936	519]	1951	919	1960	1153

Source: W. A. Hance, *Population, migration and urbanization in Africa.*

induced by the Second World War, and the high commodity prices sustained for several years thereafter, at once stimulated greater employment in commerce and transport and yielded surpluses that could be devoted to educational and administrative expansion. In terms of the relative opportunities they offered, the stagnant subsistence economies tended to fall even further behind the cash-crop areas; and both fell behind the cities, where the new employment opportunities were concentrated. The years after 1945 saw a dramatic increase in rural–urban migration and in the rate of urban growth (cf. Tables 4.1, 4.2). From the mid-1940s, mining centres, like those on the Copperbelt, which had begun as labour camps and where settlement had been rigidly controlled by the authorities to prevent a stable urban population, began to assume more the character of towns, with new opportunities in the informal sector. The growing towns were equally magnets for the educated and the unskilled, labourers and petty traders. Where manufacturing industry was set up, this was also in or near the existing urban centres; both because of the same locational advantages that had earlier made them centres of the import–export trade and because the domestic markets for their manufactures were concentrated there among the urban wage-earners and the national élites. Thus urban growth since 1950 was particularly concentrated in the national capitals.'

Table 4.2. *Total population of selected African countries living in cities of (i) 20 000 inhabitants and (ii) 100 000 inhabitants, as proportion of total population.*

		(i)		(ii)	
		c. 1950	*c.* 1960	*c.* 1950	*c.* 1960
Egypt	1947–66	28.9	38.2	20.0	29.6
Algeria	1948–60	14.1	21.6	6.6	16.4
Senegal	1956–61	19.0	22.5	9.9	12.6
Ghana	1948–60	5.0	12.3	3.3	9.5
Nigeria	1952–63	11.4	14.0	4.1	8.7
Kenya	1948–62	3.8	5.9	2.2	5.2
Zaire	1957–9	7.1	9.1	3.5	5.9
South Africa	1951–60	30.8	35.1	23.1	26.5

Source: UN Economic Commission for Africa, in *Economic survey of Africa*, 1967.

A new feature of the expansion in the 1960s and 1970s was that migrants were less exclusively adult males in search of work. Women joining their husbands or migrating on their own account, and children seeking secondary education, accounted for a bigger share of rural–urban migratory flows than earlier, and the age and sex profiles of urban populations came to diverge less from the national norms.[1] Significant urban unemployment appeared in the 1960s, a reminder that urban job opportunities depended in the main on surpluses generated in the rural sector, which was depressed in many countries. In the late 1970s this led some African governments such as Ghana and Uganda to expel aliens, thus reducing the international character of earlier migration flows. Although migration might continue for as long as migrants could still reasonably expect, after a period of unemployment, to obtain a superior situation than was available in the countryside, it began to be evident that, without a new resource like Nigeria's oil, the rates of urban growth seen in the two decades after the Second World War could not be sustained for ever.

[1] This is especially well documented in J. C. Caldwell's analysis of the 1960 Ghana Census, *African rural–urban migration* (Canberra, 1969).

THE GROWTH OF TOWNS

The cities of sub-Saharan Africa tended to contain to a much greater extent than those of other regions of the Third World, including North Africa, a population that continued to move between town and country despite the sharp cleavage in terms of economic function, distribution of resources and formal institutions, between these two spheres. Migrants to all Third World cities bring rural attitudes, and retain for a while kinship links with their origins, but rarely have these links and identities continued as vitally as they did in Africa. The migrants' retention of rural land rights contributed very greatly to this; but so did the role of rurally based identities in adaptation to the demands of town life. This was no less true of the most capitalist cities – those of southern Africa with large proletariats – since official policy for long sought to prevent the consolidation of a stable urban population. Some towns in South Africa saw four or five generations that had returned to the rural areas after the period of their labour – a circulation which tended ultimately to be brought to an end by rural over-population as well as urban labour-demand. But everywhere some of the migrants stayed, so that a solely urban population grew, making it seem likely that high rates of immigration would also decline and ultimately create a permanent and firm division between townspeople and the rural populations, with all that this must imply for the character of national social structure.

The character of a colonial city was derived from the operation of four major factors: its predominant function, its occupational structure, its physical organisation and its ethnic composition. These factors were not independent of one another, since function has clear implications for occupational structure, mining and port towns having much larger true proletariats; while administrative centres have considerably higher proportions of both wealthier, educated strata and workers in the informal sector. Physical planning was better realised in the new towns established for a precise function in the colonial system, where there was no indigenous city of traders or craftsmen, for example Nairobi, which was an administrative and railway centre, or Port Harcourt, which was a port and railway terminus, and above all in the mining towns of the Copperbelt. Paradoxically, African urban studies took their rise from towns – Luanshya in Zambia being a classic case – which, being in their clear physical recognition of social-class boundaries almost models of the colonial system itself, were unusual in the 1950s and became more so later.[1] Here the town comprised three principal functional, physical and social-structural elements: the Mine Township, owned and organised by the company for its employees; the Government Township, with an occupationally heterogeneous population; and European residential areas housing those Europeans in supervisory or white-collar occupations.

Elsewhere, and especially where there was an indigenous landowning community, housing was less administratively controlled and there was less residential segregation by occupation. Instead, indigenous landlords and enterprising immigrants, where it was possible for them to buy land, built houses for themselves or to let, sometimes within the framework of a municipally planned layout, sometimes, as in the outer suburbs of Lagos or parts of Mengo–Kampala, subject to the minimum of such control. Some such city-areas recalled in their class heterogeneity – the rich and powerful living cheek-by-jowl with those of the lowest status – the social character of pre-colonial cities. But there also developed, especially from the 1960s and outside urban administrative boundaries, shanty towns which were more homogeneous in class terms, housing the lowest urban class of unskilled, casual and under-employed workers. The 1960s tended to bring a convergence of these two polar types of city. African governments were unwilling or unable to control urban settlement in the colonial way so that the 'informal' sector of cities tended to grow with continuing in-migration. But, on the other hand, as the African élites replaced expatriates in administrative posts and occupied the former European residential preserves, residential segregation by class continued. Indeed, it was extended, with the establishment of new housing estates for different income levels.

Ethnic composition affected urban social structure in several ways. Some cities clearly possessed a 'host' ethnic group, which was either the group that 'owned the land' or a group whose local preponderance was due to weight of numbers, education or

---

[1] A. L. Epstein, *Politics in an urban African community* (Manchester, 1958); G. Balandier, *Sociologie des Brazzavilles noires* (Paris, 1955).

political power in the national arena. These conditions coincided in the cases of the Kongo in Kinshasa, the Yoruba in Lagos or the Ganda in Kampala. But elsewhere, the Lebu, for instance, did not dominate their native Dakar nor the Ga Accra, while Port Harcourt, situated outside the homelands of any major ethnic group, was successively dominated by the Owerri Ibo (from the late 1940s to 1967) and thereafter, as the capital of the Rivers State of Nigeria, by the Ijo. Ethnically homogeneous neighbour-hoods or quarters were hardly to be found in Central or southern African cities and were not the rule elsewhere. They were more a feature of the older West African cities (e.g. the Vai, Kru, Bassa quarters of Monrovia), and attained the sharpest definition in the Hausa-speaking settlements of Muslim northerners in southern Ghana (*zongo*) or Western Nigeria (*sabo*). Even when developed in recent decades (like Sabo in Ibadan), they drew on pre-colonial cultural models as well as modern advantages. But elsewhere, and with the partial exception of the 'old towns' of indigenes, we find only a tendency towards the geographical concentration of fellow tribesmen. It was encouraged, to some extent, by chain-migration, as new arrivals sought out compatriots or kinsmen already established in town. Otherwise it tended to be a function of the income and educational levels, the status and occupational characteristics of the members of particular ethnic groups. It was most marked where they were occupationally homogeneous and of low status. Hence the concentrations of Haya women, many of whom were prostitutes, or Rwanda men, who were unskilled labourers, in 'urban villages' in parts of Kampala. Similar housing estates, such as Surulere in Lagos or Naguru in Kampala, attracted disproportionate numbers of Ibo and Luo respectively, since both groups included many young, moderately educated or skilled people, who as immigrants were free from many of the involvements of the locally dominant Yoruba and Ganda in the older parts of the town. But even these 'concentrations' were in ethnically mixed areas.

The classic studies of the Copperbelt towns in the 1950s demonstrated the existence of fairly unified urban social-status systems, in which ethnic groups were ranked in terms of ad-vancement in wealth, education and power in the modern sector.[1]

[1] See especially J. C. Mitchell and A. L. Epstein, 'Occupational prestige and social status among urban Africans in Northern Rhodesia', *Africa*, 1959, **29**, 22–39.

There was a limited divergence from this rule only in those West African cities like Freetown or Ibadan which had mixed Muslim–Christian populations and where some Muslim groups, considerably less advanced in modern education and its rewards, continued to stress alternative status values associated with Islamic learning. Because the specific problems and opportunities of urban life – residence in a slum-area, employment in a similar market situation, common need for recreation – severally affected many hitherto unrelated individuals, the *Gesellschaft* or voluntary association existing for a specific end was everywhere a characteristic urban institution. Trade unions and more informal organisations based on the work situation were vigorous within their particular spheres of relevance. The friendship groups existing on the basis of local neighbourhood, such as have been analysed in detail in Kisangani (Stanleyville) by Pons,[1] played an important role in enabling migrants to adapt to a very heterogeneous and transient environment; but because of this very circumstance, the neighbourhood or *quartier*, except in the case of well-established cities with stable populations, tended not to be the basis of enduring commitments and thus of long-term social mobilisation. Many social anthropologists have used the concept of *network* to characterise urban social relations. Each individual stands at the centre of a web of possible links (with, for instance, kinsmen, affines, neighbours, fellow tribesmen, age mates, fellow employees, fellow church-members, business contacts) and seeks to activate those particular ties which are significant.[2] But among them, ethnicity has a special importance. To understand it, we must move out from the city to the wider society within which it is set.

CHANGING BASES OF IDENTITY

These population movements, involving a great increase in both the scale of social relations and the amount of interaction within socially heterogeneous environments, had great effects on social identity and hence on emergent patterns of conflict and cooperation. Two such bases were especially significant: ethnicity and religion. These did not have any fixed relation to that other major

[1] V. Pons, *Stanleyville: an African urban community under Belgian administration* (London, 1969), esp. 127–212.
[2] Especially those of the 'Manchester' school who have worked in Central Africa; see the essays in J. C. Mitchell (ed.), *Social networks in urban situations* (Manchester, 1969).

source of identity – social rank or class – but might sustain or weaken it in various ways. It is the 'world religions' – Islam and Christianity – that are relevant here since, unlike Africa's 'traditional' religions – those practised uniquely by the members of particular small-scale societies – they confer an identity which is distinct from ethnic or communal identity as such, even when it is closely linked with it. Moreover, it is the very cosmopolitanism of the world religions which made them a social idiom which was relevant in the novel and heterogeneous situations of urban and national arenas.[1] Ethnicity, by contrast, seems to relate much more to the local and traditional, having a base in the many 'tribes' or 'ethnic groups' which comprise most African nations. As descriptive terms, and not very precise ones, these variously designate linguistic or cultural blocs, traditional polities or groups of peoples linked by some key identity-conferring social institution, such as an age-grade system or initiation rites. But here the issue is not how far the members of particular ethnic groups retained customary usages, but rather how identities based on some such usages and symbols became important in novel contexts. For there is no given fixity in the boundaries, necessity in the content, or uniformity in the significance of particular ethnic group labels.

Ethnicity

Ethnicity came to exist in two principal modes: where individuals interacted in urban or rural situations which drew people together from different ethnic origins; and where collective interest-groups, associated with particular areas of origin, competed to secure rewards for their members from the higher-order units within which they coexisted – the state and its subdivisions. The ties which initially linked kinsmen or fellow villagers in town, and the greater ease with which communication and hence new ties could be established between those of similar language and customs, led to the development in towns of new, broader stereotypes, which shaped how people thought of themselves as well as of others. They also provided them with a cognitive tool for organising social interaction in anonymous, multi-ethnic contexts. It was not

---

[1] For a convincing theory relating religious conversion to the increase in the scale of social relations see R. Horton, 'African conversion', *Africa*, 1971, **41**, 85–108 and 'On the rationality of conversion', *Africa*, 1975, **45**, 219–35, 373–99.

always much more than this. Though 'tribal elders' might apply particularistic norms within, say, the domestic sphere, or the network of 'home-boys' might be important for mutual aid and comfort, commercial and industrial relations were dominated by non-ethnic identities, such as those derived from occupational rank or control of resources in the market situation. The ethnic divisions among Africans were quite overshadowed by their common subordination, in all spheres, to Europeans, as in the Copperbelt towns of the 1950s, or urban South Africa and Rhodesia long after. Nor did ethnicity always dominate social relations in multi-ethnic rural situations. Its lack of saliency, for example in certain areas of eastern and central Uganda, where good land-population ratios attracted immigrants from many ethnic groups, seems to have been due both to the desire of established or potential big-men to attract followers and labourers of whatever origin, and to the importance of local residence as a basis of identity. In these contexts ethnicity had its significance, but it was highly situational: it was one of the ties an individual might activate in his support but not necessarily an overriding one, and always one that had to be invoked discreetly, if vital non-ethnic relationships were not to suffer.

Yet elsewhere ethnicity did bulk large in interaction between members of different groups – especially where it corresponded with economic function or residence, this typically being linked with inter-regional patterns of trade, as is common in West Africa. Thus ethnic identity, underscored in the 1950s by a greater emphasis on religious distinctiveness, has played a big part in the interaction of Hausa, as kola- or cattle-traders, with the peoples of the forest zone. Here ethnicity acted to improve the bargaining position of a group by excluding cultural outsiders and disciplining insiders. Rural parallels might exist where immigrants found a distinct ecological niche,[1] as Urhobo palm-wine tappers did in parts of Yorubaland, or where they provided wage-labour on cash-crop farms, the owners of which wished to exclude them, as 'strangers', from full proprietary rights.

[1] On the notion of 'ecological niche', see F. Barth, *Ethnic groups and boundaries: the social organization of culture difference* (Bergen–Oslo, 1969). This has deep historical roots in West Africa, as witness relations between Mandinka *dyula* and Akan, or Fulbe pastoralists and semi-servile Mandinka cultivators in Futa Jalon; for modern effects of the latter see W. Derman, *Serfs, peasants and socialists: a former serf village in the Republic of Guinea* (Berkeley, 1973).

But the ethnicity florescent in Port Harcourt and many other similar towns in other parts of Africa, in the late 1950s and 1960s, tells another story. It was not based on the economic specialisation or residential segregation of ethnic groups, but on their general competition for jobs, contracts and licences, indeed, access to any resources distributed by local or national government. Thus in Port Harcourt the ethnically mixed neighbourhoods played hardly any role in political mobilisation, this being dominated by ethnic interest-groups. This was a phenomenon not merely of certain kinds of cities but of a certain epoch in Africa's historical evolution, when, from the late 1940s and early 1950s, the nationalist movements began to mobilise popular political forces and to take control of state power. This is the second mode of ethnicity: an interaction, not of individuals in multi-ethnic contexts, but of organised ethnic-group interests rooted in their home areas. The major articulating role, before the creation of political parties, was played by formal and informal tribal associations that combined mutual aid for individual fellow tribesmen in towns with a general role of 'consciousness-raising' and lobbying in the interests of the home area. This dual role presupposes both the retention by town-dwellers of a source of security in their rural statuses and the state's serving as distributor of jobs and contracts to urban individuals, and of public amenities and development grants in the rural areas. These functions grew markedly after 1945, and so did their politicisation, both before and after national independence. Thus we have the paradox that 'tribalism' (to use a term of wide parlance in anglophone Africa) was both a product of nationalism and a threat to national integration; and while it might call on traditional symbols of ethnic identity, it was articulated by the educated and those in urban employment, acting both for themselves and their regions of origin.

The earliest formation of these ethnic groups usually preceded the development of 'tribalism'. In some cases, such as those of the Asante, the Ganda and the Lozi, a clear pre-colonial political and cultural identity was consolidated, with distinct privileges to be defended, in the colonial order. Other groups tended to organise in imitation of or in reaction to them, especially where they had suffered some form of 'sub-imperialism', as did the Tiv and other peoples of central Nigeria against the Hausa, or the Gisu and other peoples of eastern Uganda against the Ganda. In other cases, for example the Yoruba, Ibo and Ewe, the identity was fostered by the adoption by the Christian missions of a standard language form that was used in churches and schools, thus becoming a major source of fellow-feeling among an educated élite. Cultural associations, sometimes with welfare functions too, tended to be founded in the 1930s and 1940s.

By the 1950s ethnic group formation was shaped as much by the pressures of the national political environment as by prior patterns of association or cultural identity. Entirely new ethnic groups emerged, like the Luhya or Kalenjin of western Kenya, from two congeries of adjacent peoples, respectively Bantu-speaking and Nilotic-speaking. The exact boundaries of identity were shaped by considerations of strategy within the appropriate arena: within Nigeria as a whole the relevant identity was Ibo, within Port Harcourt it was Onitsha or Owerri, within Owerri it was Mbaise or... These identities, in the middle ranges, derived from the *colonial* administrative divisions of Nigeria, just as, after independence, nationality, for example as Kenyans in Uganda or as Malawians in Zambia, came to serve, in context, as a kind of 'tribe'. The principles of alliance-formation, tending towards a balance of roughly equivalent opponents at each level of the hierarchy, showed formal similarities to those operative in seg-mentary lineage societies. It is thus perhaps not accidental that some traditionally segmentary peoples, such as the Ibo and Luo, were among the most successful in adapting these principles to the organisation of tribal unions throughout their countries. And in the case of Somalia, perhaps the most culturally homogeneous of all African countries, the traditional segmentary clans or 'lineage confederations' themselves took on new roles as interest-groups relevant in political conflict and the state's distribution of reward. So ethnicity, sustained by the political environment of the state, came to be an important element in the national cultures of many African countries, acting back on patterns of individual association and action. Thus, second-generation Mossi migrants to Ghana were found in the early 1970s to have developed social identity as Mossi within Ghana, even though they had lost their cultural distinctiveness as Mossi as well as, very possibly, their ability to re-enter rural Mossi society. As a means of gaining political and economic power, they had to 'find ways of asserting their identity in a society where everyone, Ghanaian or non-Ghanaian, has an ethnic as well as a national identity'.[1]

Yet if it is impossible to dismiss ethnicity as mere false consciousness, an aberration from true consciousness of nation or class, equally it cannot be regarded as an ineluctable and eternal effect of the colonial imposition of states on ethnic mosaics. That is proved by its relative unimportance in some countries and contexts. Three general conditions have been stressed: the 'distributive state'; the specific ties between urban and rural areas; and the historical legacy of traditional cultures and identities. North Africa provides an instructive contrast to the situation in most of sub-Saharan Africa. Despite the existence of areas like the Kabyle region of Algeria which were distinct both in language and colonial experience, or of communities like the Mzabites, who preserved a special religious and occupational character, 'tribalism', as that is understood south of the Sahara, was largely absent. Cultural heterogeneity was indeed declining, with the steady Arabisation of Berbers and the attenuation of the old urban ethnic or religious minorities, Jews and others, once organised in *milets* under the Ottoman umbrella; but this was less significant than a divide of rural and urban populations much sharper than that found south of the Sahara, which restrained the growth of a joint interest, ethnic in idiom, of townsmen and rural regions. In the Maghrib the problem was more one, as Geertz points out for Morocco, of social particularism than of cultural heterogeneity;[2] and its model was the ancient antithesis between *makzin* (urban order) and *sibā* (tribal dissidence) that had been analysed centuries before by Ibn Khaldūn.

Generally, any cultural legacy seems to have been permissive and supportive, rather than decisive, as far as the presence or absence of ethnic consciousness was concerned. Thus Tanzania, celebrated as a country free of tribalism, enjoyed the absence of gross initial cultural divisions and of dominant ethnic groups. Furthermore it not only had in Swahili a supra-tribal mode of communication, but a ruling party, the Tanganyika African National Union, that was seriously committed to regionally

---

[1] Enid Schildkrout, 'Ethnicity and generational differences among urban immigrants in Ghana', in A. Cohen (ed.), *Urban ethnicity* (London, 1974), 124; on the wider context J. Rouch, *Migrations au Ghana* (Paris, 1956).

[2] C. Geertz, *The interpretation of culture* (New York, 1973), 246–9.

disinterested policies. Nevertheless TANU seemed only to have restrained ethnicity rather than to have nullified it.

If the 'distributive state' was a necessary condition for 'tribalism', it was far from being a sufficient one, since the distribution of jobs might go by other channels, for instance ethnically mixed factions or religious interest-groups, while liquid resources might be divided by class exclusively. Thus in Senegal there were 'clan politics', the 'clans' being shifting factions led by members of the political élite, but recruited through a variety of allegiances, of which the home-base was only one and religious fellowship another. This national political style grew from the urban politics of the *quatre communes* before 1940 and recalls other locales of factional politics such as the micro-politics of trade unions as reported from Uganda, or the small-town politics of Kita in Mali in the 1960s, where no single category of identity dominated. If it was particularly typical of parts of the West African savanna zone, there were good reasons for it: the universalist, homogenising ideology of Islam supported it, but more potent was the fact that these were areas, Senegal especially, which had experienced during the previous century a fair 'scrambling' of populations, with extensive movements of piecemeal agricultural colonisation and the loosening of customary tenures. There was thus less basis for the alignment of rural-regional and urban-ethnic interest which so underpinned the power of ethnicity elsewhere.

Religion

Religion may either be aligned with other identities or cross-cut and subdivide them. The imposition of colonial rule accelerated the spread of both Christianity and Islam.[1] Islam's advance, with some exceptions, such as parts of the West African forest belt or inward from the Swahili coast, was achieved through a deeper social penetration within areas where it had already existed, in some cases for centuries, as a religious idiom restricted to particular status groups – traders, members of royal courts, or religio-medical specialists. For Christianity, it was much more a geographical advance into fresh areas from its earliest bases along

---

[1] The relationship between colonisation and conversion was far from a straightforward one. For a comparative study, J. D. Y. Peel, 'Conversion and tradition in two African societies: Ijebu and Buganda', *Past and Present*, 1977, 77, 108–41.

the coasts and in a handful of interior kingdoms like Buganda, Merina, Lozi, and Kgatla, where prescient local rulers had sponsored it. But later, it too spread through the social structure to categories initially unattracted by it. Most nations included peoples at different stages of influence by the world religions and, except for peoples who were solidly Muslim or Christian well before the colonialist period, like the Kanuri or the Amhara, it was the peoples most involved in the colonial order who showed the greatest penetration by the world religions.

A fair religious variety came to exist in most African localities: in Muslim areas often several competing brotherhoods (*tarīqa*, pl. *turuq*), in mixed or exclusively Christian areas, usually the historically dominant missions – Catholic and one or more forms of Protestantism – as well as a variety of independent churches. There is some evidence that the various confessions might appeal to distinct status constituencies and together form a differentiated system of religious provision. But attempts to interpret that variety of religious expression primarily in terms of its correspondence, or 'elective affinity', to the ranked statuses or class positions of adherents, on an analogy with the religious stratification of Europe, are often misleading. Where social status differences came to exist between the members of different churches (or more importantly, between Muslims and Christians), they were most often the *consequences* of a variety of different, often accidental, attributes of the religions: the fact that they came early or late to an area; had a core of members from particular parts of the country; or possessed historical advantages such as Christianity's schools, Islam's role as an international trading network in certain areas, or the 'establishment' status accorded Catholicism in the Belgian Congo or Islam in Northern Nigeria. The case is easiest to make for some of the independent, locally developed churches – Zionists in South Africa, Aladura in West Africa – which typically enjoyed a lower standing and some of which were at times a vehicle for expressing class discontent.[1] But they frequently also attracted élite members and sympathisers, especially since independence; and their main religious aim was to relate Christianity to such indigenous religious concerns as

---

[1] For statements of this view and case studies, R. Kaufman, *Millénarisme et acculturation* (Brussels, 1964), and Part III, 'Religious expressions of discontent', of R. I. Rotberg and A. A. Mazrui (eds.), *Protest and power in Black Africa* (New York, 1970).

healing and divination. The trend of the period was rather for the various religious groups to come to resemble one another more in their membership, just as there was a tendency to offset the clash of specific doctrines and practices with the attitude that all were concerned with the same general morality and the same God.

Since the general level of personal religious observance continued so high in Africa, one might ask why religion was much less important as the basis of legitimation than it has been elsewhere, for example in Europe; or why religion, with some significant exceptions, was relatively unimportant as a general axis of social conflict. The main answer to the first question is straightforward: there was too much religious variety to permit religious legitimation except in the most vague terms. Significantly, while Islam was so used in the Arab countries of North Africa, especially Libya, Morocco and to a smaller extent Algeria, similar attempts to use Islam in the old Northern Region of Nigeria or Christianity in Ethiopia were, because of actual religious variety, probably counter-productive. The widespread Islam of countries like Senegal, Mali or Somalia, while linked to valued national traditions, contributed to a common social idiom, for instance the Swahili idiom of Tanzania, rather than furnishing an explicit ideology of legitimation.

The answer to the second question is more complicated. The churches, and to a lesser extent Islam, or Muslim brotherhoods, were organised and competing corporate interest-groups, sometimes in bitter rivalry for administrative support. Church schools were often a source of political conflict, as in Eastern Nigeria in the late 1950s, though increased government control of schools since independence tended to remove that important source of church politics. But beyond this, why were churches not more important as 'communal' interest-groups, acting on behalf of their members', rather than just their institutional, interests? It is worth recalling the case of Senegal, where religious allegiance, specifically to the Muslim brotherhoods, functioned in a way analogous to ethnicity, as a constituent of political interest-groups. Uganda was more exceptional, but its very divergence highlights the conditions of religion's small political weight elsewhere. Its pattern was an extension of that which developed decades earlier in the Buganda kingdom, its core region, where two conditions obtained: first, within the traditional order, local ties were eclipsed in importance by vertical ties of clientage focussed on the court, chieftaincy tending to be divorced from lineage or regional bases; secondly, conversion was led by rising members of the political élite and resulted in the formation of three confessional interest-groups – Anglicans, Catholics and Muslims. Religion and regional origin cross-cut, and in the relative unimportance of region, religion was able to emerge, at least for a time, as the dominant criterion of political allegiance.

But mostly, where religion and ethnicity cross-cut, it was the latter which predominated as a source of identity within the nation, since a common geographical base was so fundamental to the definition of group interests. Where a particular form of religion was strongly associated with one ethnic group to the exclusion of others, it often served as an idiom for, or an organisational aid to, an ethnic or regional interest-group, as the Tijāniyya order did for the Hausa of Ibadan against their Yoruba hosts, or the Kimbanguist church, linked with the ABAKO party, for Kongo interests within Zaire.

Because, in the main, most expressions of the world religions tended to be unidentified with the main interest-groups, whether ethnic or class, they were available in a diffuse form as a mediating element, relatively neutral ground, in social and political conflict. Religious institutions were therefore generally accorded respect by the political élite, provided that they did not appear as a rival focus of authority to the state. If they did, like Alice Lenshina's Lumpa church in Northern Zambia in the late 1960s or the Roman Catholic church in several countries (for instance, Zaire in the 1960s, Angola in the 1970s) since independence, they might expect to find the power of the state mobilised against them.

CLASS FORMATION

We turn now to that other, 'vertical', dimension of social structure, the consequence of the social division of labour and the hierarchy of political control that is so ambiguously coordinated with the system of regional and cultural divisions. Great though the effects of colonial rule had been on the social structures of Arab North Africa, we can still approach them as transformations of pre-existing systems of relations between social categories: peasants, pastoralists and nomads, landowners, urban 'bourgeois' groups like merchants, officials or Islamic intelligentsia (*'ulamā'*), and lower-class traders, craftsmen, labourers and the urban poor. To these have been added a modern-educated stratum, tending to be drawn from the old 'bourgeoisie', which has taken over the main part of running state and military institutions; and an industrial proletariat, especially in Egypt and in a city like Casablanca. Algeria, because of the heavy presence of the French settlers over many decades, has come nearest to a complete reworking of its pre-colonial social system, while Morocco, briefly and lightly colonised, has the least. But the national societies of sub-Saharan Africa were made, rather than remade. Such carry-over as there had been from pre-colonial systems of indigenous stratification, outside very local spheres, was most marked in the case of a few very coherent polities, notably the emirates of Northern Nigeria and Buganda, which managed to reach a privileged position as the 'core' of a colony; but beyond that, the continuity was more a matter of attitudes to rank and inequality (a notoriously elusive factor) or of such specific political roles as that of chief, which might radically change their contents. The alleged classlessness of much of pre-colonial Africa, while relating in many cases to some real differences between African and European or Asian societies,[1] was relevant as an ideology or an aspiration, not as an explanation of what developed with nationalism.

To the extent that class expresses occupation, gross employment statistics give some impression of the great regional variation in the size of particular class categories, as they had come to exist around 1960, and particularly of the extent to which, as measured by wage employment, especially outside agriculture, African populations had then moved from living in communities of predominantly subsistence cultivators (cf. table 4.3). The figures do not suggest any single path of change, in which this single indicator, the employment pattern, systematically correlates with other aspects of social change. West and Central Africa had relatively larger total labour forces, no doubt as a result of the greater economic role of women. Southern Africa, and above all

---

[1] L. A. Fallers, *Inequality: social stratification reconsidered* (Chicago, 1973) is a valuable discussion of the relations between traditional and modern stratification, both in Buganda and generally. See too, M. G. Smith, 'Pre-industrial stratification systems', in M. J. Smelser and S. M. Lipset (eds.), *Social structure and mobility in economic development* (Chicago and London, 1966).

Table 4.3. *Employment in Africa, by region, 1960.*

	North	East	Central	South	West
Labour force as % of total population	34.6	36.5	42.1	35.5	45.8
Wage-earners as % of labour force	33.2	15.4	15.2	63.3	6.1
Agricultural wage-earners as % of labour force	12.8	5.3	3.6	13.3	0.09
Non-agricultural wage-earners as % of labour force	20.4	10.1	11.6	50.0	5.2
Non-wage-earners, as % of labour force	66.8	84.6	84.8	36.7	93.9

Source: K. C. Doctor and H. Gallis, 'Size and characteristics of wage employment in Africa', *International labour review*, 1966, **93**, 166–7.

the Republic of South Africa, had easily the most wage-earners, predominantly in non-agricultural jobs, being followed here by North Africa. Within North Africa, Egypt, populous, highly urbanised and partially industrialised, contributed more than the others to this picture. Outside these areas, Mozambique with 30.5 per cent, and Angola with 27 per cent had the highest proportions of wage-earners. East and Central Africa had comparable profiles throughout, with levels of wage-earning, both in agriculture and outside it, well below North and South, but significantly above West Africa. West Africa, with few plantations and overall lowish levels of factory or mining employment, showed itself as the stronghold of the peasant farmer and the petty entrepreneur.

Peasantisation?

Discussion over the past two decades of the changing class character of the African rural population has largely been concerned with whether it is to be considered as composed of 'peasants'.[1] Such a claim goes beyond the unexceptionable

[1] Discussion took this turn in the 1960s, though the term *paysan* in the French literature, used earlier, never became the focus of debate about the character of rural transformation in quite the same way as it did in the English. See L. A. Fallers, 'Are African cultivators to be called "peasants"?', *Current Anthropology*, 1961, **2**, 108–10; R. Stavenhagen, *Social classes in agrarian societies* (Garden City, 1975), 64–71, 119–62 on

assertion that the vast majority of agricultural enterprises in Africa during our period – except for large capitalist estates, whether privately or state owned – tended to coincide with domestic units, so that the division of labour was still largely expressed through the kinship structure. It insists on the important consequence that most such producing units were, to an ever-increasing extent, politically and economically subordinated to non-producers, and, drawing an analogy with the large agrarian societies of Eurasia (as such categories as 'middle peasants' and even 'kulaks' declare),[1] implies that certain definite relations and actions would emerge. The central issues to be considered are, first, what kind of differentiation was occurring within rural communities and, secondly, the nature of the links between the rural communities and external or higher-order institutions.

In most areas of Africa at the beginning of the colonial period land was plentiful in relation to population needs, so control of it as a scarce resource was not the basis of social hierarchy. Since production was geared to the household's consumption needs, the amount of land required and worked tended to vary with the size of this unit, and family-failure, rather than land-shortage, was the source of economic difficulty. Chiefs and lineage-heads were 'owners' of the land only in that they held the right to allocate land to actual or potential members of their communities; but, with a few conspicuous exceptions like Ethiopia, Rwanda, Burundi or some societies in the western Sudan, they did not make heavy levies on agricultural production or maintain a radically different life-style. The authority of chiefs, as of household or lineage heads, required a high degree of redistribution of what resources came their way. As there was no landlessness, there was no wage-labour.

Something like these conditions prevailed in a good many areas of Africa as late as the 1950s, though it had begun to pass out

the Agni of Ivory Coast; K. Post, 'Peasantisation and rural political movements in Western Africa', *Archives Européennes de Sociologie*, 1972, **13**, 223–54.

[1] For 'middle peasants' (this being an allusion to the group whose support was claimed critical for Mao in China), G. Williams, 'Political consciousness among the Ibadan poor', in E. de Kadt and G. Williams (eds.), *Sociology and development* (London, 1974), 130–1. 'Kulaks' was used by G. Arrighi and J. S. Saul, 'Socialism and development in tropical Africa', *Journal of Modern African Studies*, 1968, **6**, 141–69, and since then very generally by Marxist writers on East Africa, such as M. Mamdani, *Politics and class formation in Uganda* (London, 1976), who makes the surprising claim that it 'is the popular usage in East Africa' (p. 10).

of existence as early as the 1900s in those parts of West Africa where cash-crop farming first developed on a large scale. Cash-crop farming, and the land shortage often linked with it, stimulated two kinds of differentiation within local communities: between farmer-employers and wage-labourers, and between richer and poorer farmers. Studies in Zambia and Kenya have shown how enter-prising cash farmers broke with many of the communal norms, which enjoined redistribution and so restrained economic polar-isation, and discerned parallels with Europe's 'Protestant Ethic'.[1] Land titles generally became more individualised, and labour systems less dependent on corporate kin groupings. Studies over a wide area have concluded that the advancement of successful farmers tended to be consolidated by the local intervention of the state, whose extension services, loan schemes and so on benefited them rather than the poorer farmers. But despite these tendencies, a marked rural polarisation was slow to emerge. This would be a process sustained over several generations and few adequate historical studies have been done. Polly Hill, however, has documented, in a Hausa village exhibiting land scarcity, com-mercial agriculture and a market in land, what has elsewhere been called 'cyclical mobility' – the rise and fall of farming families, as larger landholdings were broken up (a process greatly assisted in Africa by the polygyny of the wealthier farmers), while poorer farmers either dropped out of the rural community or built themselves up.[2] Even in Buganda, where something like a landed gentry was manufactured under the 1900 Agreement, the so-called *mailo* estates had been largely broken up by the 1950s, and, while there was considerable inequality in landholding, there was a spectrum from large to small owners, as well as a complex of other kinds of ties linking them. In many areas of West Africa, where cash-crop farmers employed strangers as wage-labourers, the migrants often went on to acquire land, either as tenants or unconditionally, to produce cash crops themselves. In most

[1] N. Long, *Social change and the individual* (Manchester, 1968) on the role of Jehovah's Witnesses among the Zambian Lala in legitimising a break with traditional uses of labour, or D. J. Parkin, *Palms, wine and witnesses* (London, 1972) on how successful Giriama copra-producers in Kenya use Islamic conversion to distance themselves from their fellows.

[2] Polly Hill, *Rural Hausa: a village and a setting* (Cambridge, 1972), especially chapters 10–13. Similar processes were noted in late nineteenth-century Russia, whose kulaks were less like English yeomen of an earlier period than has been assumed; cf. T. Shanin, *The awkward class* (Oxford, 1972).

African rural areas by the 1970s, then, where there had not been large-scale expropriation of land from Africans as a result of colonial policy, we find an overlapping and shifting of economic statuses: small farmers employing occasional migrant labour, migrants establishing quite large enterprises, individuals moving through different economic statuses.

So despite incipient class differences, a fundamental common-ality of conditions for all 'peasants' endured. In the bid for amenities such as a tarred road or a dam from the state, the more prosperous farmers inevitably provided, through cooperative movements or political parties or local government, general leadership of their communities. That leadership tended to be linked with some conformity to traditional norms of redistri-bution, secured perhaps by extensive kinship and affinal ties. It was ironic that Tanzania's ruling party, one of whose roots lay in the cooperative societies of the agriculturally advanced area near Lake Victoria, should commit itself, in the name of opposition to the polarisation of 'kulaks' and poor peasants, to policies which ignored this patterning of local interest *vis-à-vis* the state. Its *ujamaa* policies appealed less to the poorer peasants against the richer than to the poorer regions – those less advanced in cash-cropping – as against the richer ones like the Chaga or the Sukuma. It was misleading, particularly granted marked regional unevenness in development, to identify these rural gradations as the germs of national social classes.[1]

The wider national environment of the rural community, though it provided some support to the larger-scale peasant producers, also discouraged the emergence of a landed upper class in other ways. In general, so poor were the rewards of farming relative to some other occupations that prosperous farmers were soon likely to divert much investment outside agriculture, branching into transport or commerce and educating their children for bureaucratic employment. In sum, they or their children,

[1] The evaluation of the *ujamaa* policy is contentious, since much ideology has been invested in it, but see D. Feldman, 'The economics of ideology: some problems of achieving rural socialism in Tanzania', in C. T. Leys (ed.), *Politics and change in developing countries* (Cambridge, 1969), 85–111; L. Cliffe, 'The policy of *Ujamaa Vijijini* and the class struggle in Tanzania', in L. Cliffe and J. S. Saul (eds.), *Socialism in Tanzania* (Nairobi, 1972), vol. I, 195–211 and, a most useful comparison with rural policy in Nigeria in the light of theories of the peasantry, G. Williams, 'Taking the part of peasants', in P. C. W. Gutkind and I. Wallerstein (eds.), *The political economy of Africa* (New York, 1975).

without abandoning land-rights or social ties with the countryside (which might be politically valuable), aspired to join an essentially urban élite, not even dependent on rural rents. The main, and perhaps significant exception to the divorce of the national urban élite from significant direct involvement in agriculture occurred in Ghana, Kenya and some other countries in the late 1960s and early 1970s, where, with food shortages, inflation and consequent high prices, some members of the élite began to move into fairly large-scale capitalist farming of food crops, intended for urban consumption, using their influence to acquire surplus land and getting financial support from state institutions. For though nationalism derived its main rural support in cash-crop areas, and its leaders were often drawn from the families of prosperous peasant farmers (so that an affinity of the rural petty commodity producer and the nationalist state seemed likely), and though most states continued to be disposed to offer some, relative, reward to the larger peasant farmers (if only to secure the compliance of men who represented the organised local interests of peasants generally), the nationalist state was not the state *of* this rural stratum. The gap between the farmers and the non-agricultural sectors of society remained crucial.

The peasant movements of the 1960s must be set in a long tradition of rural unrest, whose ambiguous and protean character has made it difficult to interpret. There had been widespread opposition, of no particular class character, to the imposition of colonial rule – the chiefs' loss of wide discretionary powers, forced labour, levying of tax – of which the last remained a key feature of nearly all subsequent peasant opposition to the state, whether colonial or national. In the 1910s and 1920s these themes continued, often to blend with what were essentially movements of cultural reintegration after the first shocks of colonial social change. Their concerns had often been religious and included witch-finding, faith-healing and suchlike, but had sometimes assumed a more political tone if they were subject to harsh repression. The 1930s and 1940s had seen widespread resistance to tax, when income levels fell during the depression, as well as to the colonial regulation of agriculture in the form of compulsory crop-planting, and sanitary or inoculation measures. It had also seen the establishment by farmers of cooperatives to reduce their dependence on middlemen in marketing. The later colonial states had tried unsuccessfully to depoliticise cooperative societies, and also trade unions, which played, at least informally, a significant role in nationalist mobilisation from the late 1940s. This facilitated their virtual appropriation by the governing parties as an instrument to control the rural population. A further device for the exploitation of farmers, so convenient that it has been adopted very widely in sub-Saharan Africa, was the marketing board, by which the state, through monopsonist fixing of producer prices, could tax peasant farmers at will. There were several reasons why this exploitation initially met with so little protest: it was a well-concealed form of impost compared with rents or taxes; it was introduced at a time when, owing to the high level of world producer prices, sustained from the Second World War into the late 1950s, most farmers were absolutely better off than they had ever been. A proportion of what was taken was redistributed in the form of communal welfare goods valued by the farmers, and above all in the form of increased educational services. And there was a diffuse spin-off from the spending of the political parties and the non-agricultural sector.

But the 1960s saw a revival of agrarian discontent, especially in some of the earliest and wealthiest cash-crop growing areas like the Yoruba cocoa areas and the groundnut region of Senegal. World prices had slumped, and it was difficult for the governments to reduce the bureaucracies they had expanded with the marketing-boards' reserves. The situation in Nigeria was aggravated by the financial strain of its civil war. The Senegalese peasants responded by shifting back to subsistence crops, thus reducing the proportion of their output which could be taxed, and causing a major crisis in the national economy. The Yoruba peasants, reluctant to abandon the long-term investment which cocoa trees represent, backed up their demands for reduced taxes and better producer prices with attacks on government offices and a virtual take-over of the countryside round Ibadan. Such responses might be compared to the resistance of some rural areas to the *ujamaa* programme in Tanzania in the early 1970s, leading to violence both by and against the representatives of a 'socialist' state. It is very doubtful whether such actions should be taken to indicate the development of a widespread and solidary 'peasant' class consciousness, overriding other identities, or that peasants as such were in the process of becoming a distinct political force, rather than merely the source of sporadic pressures on the political élite. For the relations of the farming population with the rest of society were too complex and ambivalent. The urban sector and the agencies of the state might rest on resources extracted from farmers, but they provided crucial general conditions for the existence and development of the rural cash-economy to which the farmers were committed. At a more concrete and individual level, because of the ties which linked farmers and their kinsfolk in towns, farmers looked to the urban sector as one possible source of support. Because agrarian conditions tended to be regionally fairly specific, the demands of farmers blurred into the demands of regions and ethnic groups; and, in general, they depended on ethnic politicians or urban political brokers to negotiate their interests.

The entrepreneurial hierarchy

With the widespread development of small-scale export-oriented agriculture, an extensive trading hierarchy developed. It had two sides, buying agricultural produce and selling manufactured goods, which, by the 1920s and 1930s, both tended to be dominated by the same large European enterprises. In West Africa, where cash-cropping was most advanced, and rural incomes highest, the hierarchy typically had several tiers: (i) local head office, concerned with the actual import and export of goods; (ii) branches at key local centres for collection and distribution, run by Europeans who made arrangements with (iii) local agents, usually men of some standing, to whom they advanced cash to buy produce and goods to sell; and (iv) smaller men, without substantial capital or property, who actually contacted the farmers or hawked round the villages. In those areas, especially of East, Central and southern Africa, where rural cash-incomes were mostly derived from urban remittances, trading was more focussed on the small store that, along with the *boma* and later the dispensary, became the focal point of an area of dispersed settlement. The produce-collection side of the trading hierarchy in West Africa meant that the buying agents and the so-called 'middlemen' tended to be natives, that is, men with local connexions. But otherwise traders were often strangers; partly, no doubt, because the hierarchy was set up from outside and had penetrated into the rural localities, and partly because there were operational advantages in being culturally distinctive and free from local communal pressures. Some African peoples became known as traders, like the Kwahu in Ghana or the Ijebu in Nigeria. More conspicuous were the Syrians (Lebanese) in West Africa and Indians in East Africa. The Indians were found at every level from substantial shopkeepers in the large cities to tiny up-country storekeepers; the Syrians were more to be found in the middle-to-high levels of the hierarchy buying produce and selling cloth. In Angola, this kind of role was often taken up by small Portuguese traders, often recent immigrants.[1]

From the late 1930s this hierarchy began to change its character. The development of motor transport and better roads enabled some local buying agents to branch out into transport. The war caused a reorganisation of the marketing arrangements, and the large expatriate concerns tended to withdraw from the middle levels of the produce-buying hierarchy, leaving them to African or Asian enterprises. In the late 1940s rising entrepreneurs were an important base of the nationalist movement, through which they made accusations against both the colonial state and expatriate firms and banks for limiting their opportunities, especially by credit restrictions and oligopolistic agreements at higher levels. The same period in East Africa saw the emergence of a really significant African group of small traders and transporters, whose antipathy to the Asians became an enduring strand of nationalism. The nationalist success in the 1950s initially meant a definite improvement in the environment for traders: rapid urban growth which expanded their potential markets; loans made available for transport and other developments, provided from agricultural surpluses; and in East Africa, administrative measures against Asians. The arena for entrepreneurs at all levels shifted much more towards the middling and large towns.

The larger commercial magnates stood at the apex of a pyramid of wealth and status which ran down, with many gradations, to the urban poor; labourers, drivers, small traders and petty commodity producers of all kinds. Many traditional crafts were undermined by imported manufactures and changed needs, but the cities provided large markets for new, more informally

[1] D. L. Wheeler and R. Pelissier, *Angola* (London, 1971), 64, 143 emphasise that 'the ordinary Portuguese inhabitant of Angola was not a farmer or industrialist, but a petty trader, a *sertanejo* (storekeeper), whose ambitions were limited to owning a *taberna* or store'.

organised crafts, such as those concerned with supplying prepared food and clothing, servicing vehicles, constructing and maintaining buildings, furniture and other appliances. Here there were no formal educational barriers to entry, and little initial capital was needed. The master might have apprentices, and also employ some extra labour, in a situation of intense competition and small profit margins. Such were the capital, technical and management obstacles to expanding a single enterprise's scale of production beyond a certain point, that successful petty commodity producers aspired instead to move up the *distributive* hierarchy, to become traders in their own supplies, and then to branch out into transport, building contracting, and distribution of consumption goods like beer or tinned foods. Commercial success was largely a matter, at the upper end, of securing monopolistic advantage over competitors through contacts with expatriate suppliers and government officials, and also, at the lower end, of managing relations with a range of occasional or full-time employees, sub-contractors, apprentices, personal clients, junior partners and tenants. This had implications for the pattern of class relations within the informal urban sector. Despite the various ways in which the big entrepreneur might be said to exploit his subordinates, his continued operation did ultimately depend on his maintaining his network of subordinates and his wider reputation. Consequently he had to display personal generosity, offer help and loans to individuals and communal leadership, especially *vis-à-vis* the agencies of government. The commercial magnate, rather than the manufacturer or the bureaucrat, needed and was able to sustain in town something of the open-handed ethic of traditional chiefship. Despite his wealth, he was likely to be a man of humble origins and small education who served as a role-exemplar, a paradigm of success, to the youthful urban poor. A paradoxical development in South Africa in the 1950s was how such entrepreneurs tended to displace the old educated leadership of the African urban community, such as the teachers or clergy, since these latter were compromised by being made elements in the regime's system of control.

This account of the social structure of the informal urban sector has, it is true, largely been derived from the instance of Nigeria, whose size and wealth as a national economy created, from the 1950s and especially after 1970, a particularly complex entrepreneurial hierarchy. Something similar also emerged in other countries, such as Kenya or the Ivory Coast, which were relatively rich and espoused a 'capitalist' or 'mixed' economic policy. Poverty, perhaps more than professed 'socialism', limited its development in such countries as Tanzania or Mali. The nationalist epoch both gave scope to this indigenous commercial class and set bounds to it. A wheel came full circle: the entrepreneurs, having supported the nationalist movement to challenge the colonial state and the expatriate trading companies, again found themselves subordinated to the state, now Africanised, and to the expatriate enterprises.

Except for the smallest and poorest countries, after the 1940s internal markets came to be able to support some local manufacturing industries, and policies of import substitution were widely adopted. These were neither basic nor heavy industries but were concerned with light manufacturing and assembling, and depended to a great extent on foreign capital and the continued importation of parts or semi-raw materials. Few locals possessed the capital or the skills to develop such industries. Local entrepreneurs adapted to this as distributors of their products or as small-scale producers of cheap consumption goods for their workers and the rest of the urban population. As to indigenous social classes, the top salaried state officials far eclipsed local entrepreneurs. Nigeria, almost alone, provided a number of conspicuous exceptions. In the nationalist ruling parties of socialist countries like Mali and Tanzania, traders, despite their early support for the nationalist cause, consistently lost, in ideological and factional struggle, to bureaucrats and party officials. Even in countries which endorsed 'capitalism' in some form, the job-security, high salaries and above all state authority which officials possessed, endowed them with unchallenged advantages.[1] They allocated the resources of the state and they were the gateway through which expatriate enterprise had to enter the African country. High public office became a base from which

---

[1] On the cultural hegemony of the bureaucrat over the entrepreneur, P. Marris and A. Somerset, *African businessmen* (London, 1971), 224–6, speak of the entrepreneur's 'driving ambition to realise through his own enterprise an achievement that will command the same respect as the occupations of the highest status... the administrative and political élite from which he is excluded. He therefore emphasises those purposes which business shares with government... for him entrepreneurship expresses the spirit of African socialism'.

they could cut into capitalist enterprises, buying stock and acquiring directorships. Thus developed a 'national bourgeoisie', recruited from senior state officials, the African managers of wholly or partly foreign-owned enterprises, as well as the very élite of the minutely differentiated indigenous entrepreneurial hierarchy.

Workers and unions

In contrast with the variegated mass of people employed or semi-employed in the informal sector stood those in regular wage or salaried employment. A very high proportion of these, except for the mining and most highly industrial economies, were employees of the government or public corporations. Of these the unionised workers – those who most resembled the proletariat of a modern industrial country – maintained an ambivalent but important relationship to the urban poor.

A certain Fanonesque tradition, most convincingly represented by Arrighi, with primary reference to Central and southern Africa, held that these workers constituted an 'aristocracy of labour', a privileged group set against the rural and urban poor.[1] It argued that they enjoyed higher and securer incomes than other workers; that their very existence depended on the particular forms of exploitation of the rural population; that their strategic importance within the organs of the state enabled them to make effective demands on the national product; and that in consequence of these interests they identified upwards with those higher in the occupational hierarchy and even the political élite. But not all such claims were justified. Above all the evidence on wage-earners' living standards is not entirely clear. Some studies have suggested that, despite higher wage levels, higher urban living costs and the pressure of greater numbers of dependants on wage-earners meant that they had not been significantly advantaged;[2] on the other hand, the very fact of urban migration and the reported appeal

[1] G. Arrighi, 'International corporations, labor aristocracies and economic development in tropical Africa', in G. Arrighi and J. S. Saul, *Essays on the political economy of Africa* (New York and London, 1973); see too, responding to much criticism of the thesis, mostly from the left, J. S. Saul, 'The "labour aristocracy" thesis reconsidered', in R. Sandbrook and R. Cohen (eds.), *The development of an African working class* (London, 1975).

[2] Cf. G. Pfefferman, *Industrial labour in Senegal* (New York, 1968), discussed in R. Cohen, *Labour and politics in Nigeria 1945–1971* (London, 1974), 187–91.

of factory and other wage employment[1] seemed to indicate that most wage-earners were better situated than the mass of the rural and urban population.

But even if these advantages were secured in part at the expense of the rural or urban poor, it does not follow that their identification and action necessarily lay with the higher social classes. The distinction between wage-earners and peasants or those in the informal urban sector is easier to make analytically than concretely. Throughout the period, wage-earners remained closely linked by ties of kinship and residence with members of these other groups; households and wider corporate kin groups frequently derived income from several class sources; wage-earners moved in and out of other class situations, and frequently hoped to use their savings to enable them to become cash-crop farmers or entrepreneurs. In the towns all the non-élite groups – and this included many white-collar wage-earners, such as minor clerks or teachers as well as the great bulk of the entrepreneurial hierarchy – shared many of the same vexations: price inflation, wretched living conditions and poor public amenities. Despite the wage-earners' economistic pursuit of demands against their employers, where parallels with the behaviour of European workers were close, a distinctive and enduring 'proletarian' identity was slow to emerge; and, outside the industrial situation, merged in a diffuse popular consciousness, of the mass of ordinary people in the towns against the political élite. Here, as in the nationalist mobilisation against colonial rule in the late 1940s, unionised workers had a special role to play.

Unionised workers were the most organised segment of a work-force that, despite the homogeneity of its basic circumstances, was still very fragmented. To the prevailing culture of individualised, clientelist class-relations, they brought from their particular work situation a conception of confrontation together with the institutions to express it. Moreover, because the government was the principal employer and many of the most firmly established unions represented public-sector workers (railway, post and telegraph or electricity workers, teachers, lower salaried staffs), the pursuit of members' narrower occupational demands

---

[1] Cf. Margaret Peil, 'Aspirations and social structure: a West African example', *Africa*, 1968, **38**, 71–8.

against an employer could well broaden into a challenge to the government and become a vehicle for expressing the grievances of the larger mass of the non-unionised urban population against their rulers. This was first evident in late colonial Africa, where the employers, whether in the private or public sector were, in addition, identified with the European colonial power. In the late 1940s and early 1950s the several demands of workers in unions, and of cash-crop farmers and entrepreneurs, all ran parallel in the nationalist movement. In some cases, such as Guinea, the unions were *the* principal nationalist base, or, as in Kenya, a very major component; in others, such as Nigeria, where unions were fragmented in diverse ways, no clear relationship developed beyond a general contribution to nationalist awareness; in others again, such as Ghana or Zambia, an earlier close link between the unions and the nationalist party became attenuated, as, with the approach of independence, an indigenous élite began to take hold of the reins of state and its concerns diverged from those of the unionised workers. After independence, the ambiguous place of unions and their members in the social structure – which nationalism seemed for a while to have resolved – tended to re-emerge. The characteristics of the 1964 general strike in Nigeria, for example, were markedly like those of 1945. Workers, and especially those in key or strategic sectors, like miners or port and electricity workers, did have some power to push their own particular demands, at the expense of the government's own intentions, whether these stressed the privileges of the élite or a more widely redistributive programme. In some countries, such as Bénin – the former Dahomey – where they controlled the commercial centre of Cotonou, the unions played an effective role in national power politics. But union leaders, that is the leaders of national labour congresses rather than local shop-floor militants, could be coopted by the political élite and the unions used more as instruments of control by the government, especially where, as in Tanzania, only one centrally organised union was permitted; and this frequently led to the disaffection of ordinary members from union leaders. Whatever economic advantages unions might secure for their members, they did not go nearly far enough for the mass of wage-earners to be co-opted to the élite; and workers' organisations, if they were permitted reasonable freedom of action, were likely to conjoin the pursuit of their members' particular demands with the intermittent critique of government policies in the name of the 'common man'. Their stance was more a reaction to the evolution of urban conditions than the active presentation of a lower-class alternative to prevailing regimes. African economies were still too undeveloped, the wage-labour forces too small in most cases, for this to be possible. Conversely, as the disturbances at Soweto and elsewhere in the mid-1970s suggested, South Africa remained the one country where, owing to its occupational structure and the virtual exclusion of Africans from the ranks of capitalists, a social revolution based on the mass of wage-earners was at all likely. Here, unlike the countries to the north, mass African nationalism had no choice but to be, whatever its leadership, overwhelmingly a movement rooted among urban wage-earners.

The bureaucratic hierarchy

The bureaucracy did not form a class or an occupation as such, but an avenue of ascent, parallel to that of trade, but now greatly overshadowing it. The educational system was crucial here, for two reasons. First, because the colonial state, whose expatriate officials had no independent standing within local society, preceded and dominated the emergent national society, the ability to assume bureaucratic office, and hence education, was crucial for Africans to attain power. Secondly, in the absence of formed national social classes or status groups that were in a position to monopolise it, modern education was for individuals, over a generation or more, the gateway to social power rather than the fruit of it. The few cases where education was provided for recruits selected on other principles, such as membership of a traditional ruling estate, as in Northern Nigeria, only serve to underline this general rule for the colonial period.

Except for those, mostly Islamic, areas where colonial governments deliberately set out to provide some secular education, western education was for long overwhelmingly linked with the missions. At the beginning, the incidence of education among Africans was largely an effect of the vagaries of missionary presence and success – hence the early advancement of some coastal peoples like the Fante or those most receptive to the Gospel, like the Tonga of Malawi or the Ganda. Educated Africans in the late nineteenth century occupied a distinct niche, as political and economic go-betweens, but education did not confer a general social power. Indeed, for a generation from the

1890s, educated Africans, especially in West Africa and in Angola, suffered a setback, seeing themselves displaced either by European officials or by indigenous rulers. A general appreciation of the value of education, at least among the young, and a consequent attraction to the churches that provided it, began to develop with the penetration of the colonial administration and the commercial economy. Thereafter, and most particularly during the 1920s when both Britain and France produced key statements on colonial education policy, it developed among the wealthier cash-cropping peoples.

Education was needed to provide both government and the commercial companies with clerks, so mission schools, being the most ready means to produce them, were therefore subsidised by the colonial governments and greatly expanded. In the stratum of educated young men, conscious bearers of new values, the social impact of teachers was especially important, since they were most widely spread among the rural population. They tended to be amongst the most poorly remunerated of their stratum but, since teacher-training was the most common form of post-primary education, their profession was often a gateway to the more lucrative posts in government or commercial service. Their discontent was compounded by their exclusion, until the 1940s, from the local political structure, except in informal capacities, and there was often a divide, both cultural and generational, between the 'old élite', represented by chiefs who held local political authority, and the alternative status-hierarchy of the educated young. In French colonies at this time, the educated tended to be fewer and they were encouraged much more than in the British colonies to identify themselves with the colonial administrative hierarchy, from which they were not entirely excluded and which reached much further down, often displacing local chiefs from levels at which they were active in, say, Nigeria. In the Belgian Congo the évolués were contained for much longer, until the mid-1950s, when their numbers began to mount rapidly.

The Second World War created a much tighter vertical integration of the colonial societies: a higher level of interchange between local communities and the state and, in consequence, a greater rivalry between them for access to the resources of the state. This meant both that local communities came to depend on their educated sons, rather than on their more locally oriented chiefs, as representatives before the wider environment of the colonial state; and that the educated came to demand a larger place in the control of that state. Thus it was that the local rise of the educated led directly to their assumption of the key role in the movement for national independence. Since nationalism everywhere comprised a coalition of particular emergent class interests, the exact place within it of the educated varied considerably. It was not usually as clear-cut as in Tanzania, where TANU grew from the Tanganyika African Association, consisting of clerks and teachers, or Zaire, where the parties grew from associations of *évolués*. In the Gold Coast, older professionals, especially lawyers, joined with chiefs (many of whom were educated) in the United Gold Coast Convention, while a younger and generally less well-educated group formed the core of a more populist party in the Convention Peoples Party; teachers and ex-teachers dominated the Nigerian Action Group, and so on. The educated made a decisive contribution to nationalism in their articulation of a programme; and they were also its most definite beneficiaries, in that, whatever the general consequences of self-government for peasants, traders or workers, they would inherit the higher political and administrative posts vacated by expatriates and could create more posts of the same kind.

The Africanisation of the bureaucracy was thus a foremost component of decolonisation as well as nationalist advance; and since it meant the assumption by Africans of the highest posts, formerly occupied only by Europeans, it required the development of secondary and tertiary education. New universities were set up in East and West Africa shortly after the Second World War, and secondary-school expansion occurred steadily through the postwar period. Even so, the process was very uneven, the lead being taken by those parts of the English-speaking countries of West Africa which, in addition to being wealthier, had the longest traditions of secondary education. So while Tanzania, on its independence, had less than 100 graduates, Nigeria at the same time must have had several thousands, though these were most unevenly distributed within the country, and Ghana, relative to its population, counted even more. The process of Africanisation began late and went very fast. In the six years after independence, for example, the proportion of Nigerians in their country's officer corps rose from 18 per cent to nearly 100 per cent. With few

Table 4.4. *Educational expansion in selected African countries, c. 1950 to c. 1970; percentage of age-cohort enrolled in education institutions at appropriate level.*

	Primary, 6–11			Secondary, 12–18			Tertiary, 19–24		
	1950	1960	1970	1950	1960	1970	1950	1960	1970
Egypt	26	40	69	7	21	33	n/a	4.86	7.92
Algeria	15	28	75	5	8	11	n/a	n/a	1.70
Senegal	7	17	43	1	4	10	n/a	0.50	1.46
Ghana	19	40	61	1	3	9	n/a	0.24	0.83
Nigeria	16	37	34	1	3	4	n/a	n/a	0.30
Kenya	26	49	64	2	4	9	n/a	n/a	0.79
Tanzania	10	19	35	1	2	3	n/a	n/a	0.17
Zaire	33	43	88	1	3	9	n/a	n/a	0.65

Source: UNESCO, *Statistical Yearbooks*, 1963, 1964, 1975. The figures are subject to numerous notes and reservations expressed in this source.

exceptions in French Africa, Africans only rose to be ministers or top civil servants in the mid-1950s or even later. Regular senior technical and professional posts were Africanised more slowly, and Europeans continued to be engaged on a contract basis as the demand for such posts expanded. As Africans came in, they took over existing salary levels, as well as allowances and perquisites, and thus vastly outstripped their non-élite compatriots in income levels. A consequence of these signal rewards was that the general demand for education was greatly increased. The richest areas – Ghana and Nigeria's Western Region – used their cocoa revenues to provide free primary education for all and this major social policy fuelled further demand for secondary education since the numbers of primary leavers soon outstripped the supply of jobs. Countries like Kenya, with its Harambee schools of the 1960s followed fast behind the leaders; and even Tanzania, despite the deliberate attempt to reduce the financial privileges of government office after the Arusha Declaration in 1967, showed something of the same inflationary trend (cf. table 4.4). At the same time the pressure for jobs from the modestly educated tended to lead, in most countries, to sharp increases in the number of government personnel in the years after independence.

The social pre-eminence of those at the apex of this hierarchy had two complementary aspects: political, through the holding of governmental power, and cultural, through their 'modernity'. Of course there were variations, in time and place, in the precise composition of the élite. The civilian regimes which assumed power at independence were perhaps more heterogeneous in membership than those which developed later, including, as they did, party-bosses or communal champions who rose through trade, augmented by political influence, rather than through the bureaucracy. In some countries religious leaders, like the heads of Muslim brotherhoods, or traditional rulers of little western education, might be of national importance, though the general stance of the nationalist élites was against them – chieftaincy abolished in Guinea and Tanzania, the Ugandan kingdoms dissolved; the government in Zambia moving against both prominent chiefs and religious leaders. But political leaders were overwhelmingly men of some education, usually former clerks or teachers; and senior civil servants were more so. Though the élites at independence thus had these several points of entry, they became more homogeneous thereafter and their specifically *bureaucratic* component stronger. Independent traders who came to the political élite through party politics tended to be eclipsed by bureaucrats who branched into trade or property or by the African managers of expatriate enterprises, men more like bureaucrats than traders. The most striking new presence was that of the military, but soldiers were bureaucrats of a kind, and, under the gloss of the military ethos, shared the predilections of the educated generally. Military regimes either co-opted academics, lawyers and civil servants onto decision-making bodies as in Nigeria or, as was more the case in Ghana, tended to appropriate administrative functions themselves, thereby exciting inter-professional enmity. There was thus a general tendency for different sections of the élite to move into each other's spheres and to adopt common attitudes and life-styles. The touchstone was control of the resources of the state, through political office or employment in public institutions. Education provided the principal mode of access and, though taken as a badge of eligibility, was itself validated by the fruits which it conferred.

Although those at the top of the bureaucratic hierarchy were so distanced from the rest of the population, there still remained, as the widespread designation 'élite' implies, a marked reluctance to see them as forming a dominant social class, that is as a stratum whose attributes necessarily create an antagonistic relationship with lower strata. Rather, their distinctive attributes were conceived as being essentially cultural, and this enabled them to be at once both an example of what the non-élite might become and leaders of the whole society in its attempt to achieve a better life.

The intense pride shown by members of the élite in the appurtenances of their status is a token that, far from being members of an upper class with some genealogical depth and an established class culture, they were still, as many politicians' autobiographies detail, socially not far removed from the rural and urban poor. While they were not usually the children of subsistence farmers, still less of unskilled labourers, but rather of clerks, catechists, teachers, traders or cash-crop farmers, their grandparents were typically poor, rural and illiterate; and granted the extent of African kin groups, their wider range of relations usually covered a considerable social spectrum. Their own social ascent usually meant not just great personal effort and often parental sacrifice, but often contributions and support from other members of the kin group, to whom they were thus obligated. They remained linked to their origins in a variety of ways: by maintaining or 'training' poorer kinsfolk in their houses and by sending money home; by participating in family or community associations; by championing in urban and political arenas the interests of their regions and communities of origin; and by patronising individual co-originaires. There were, of course, limits as to how far this redistribution or communal responsibility went and there were no doubt many individuals who defaulted or performed only a shadow of what were felt as their obligations; but to the extent that élite members were thus responsive to the demands of their kin and their communities, it was not just from a personal residue of traditional norms but because this base of support continued to be of value to them. Only thus could they be sure of maintaining title to lineage land (an interest which was perhaps coming to seem of greater moment in the 1970s than it was in the 1950s), and only thus could they hope to achieve political office in elected regimes. The fact that a man was a 'leader of thought' or a recognised communal leader might significantly advance his chances even within a bureaucratic hierarchy where there was concern, in the name of 'national integration', to balance communal representation.

Yet undoubtedly there were strong tendencies for these links to become attenuated, and for the interests and experiences of the élite and the non-élite to diverge. Crucial to this were the combined effects of, first, a slowing down in the rate of growth of élite posts after the boom caused by belated colonial Africanisation and subsequent administrative expansion and, secondly, the élite's ability to ensure that its offspring got the lion's share of fresh or vacant élite posts in future. The latter derived from the élite's domination of the gateway to élite status: the educational system. It was already shown in the early 1960s, not only that children of professional parents had much better chances of completing secondary education than children of farmers or, even more so, of unskilled workers, but also that the chances of upward mobility through education could vary widely. They were, for example, significantly lower in Ghana than in neighbouring Ivory Coast – an effect of Ghana's then being more 'developed' in both the size of its élite and in the maturity of its secondary-education system. Education was demanded by the non-élite as the main key to upward mobility and its free provision at primary level, achieved in a few countries, seemed to preserve the original equality of opportunity. But since posts were limited in relation to the numbers of primary certificate holders, the critical level of selection shifted higher. It was at the level of secondary education that the real constriction of opportunity occurred and here the élite was able to provide the conditions – financial, cultural and whatever else – for the scholastic success of its children. There are no reasons to suppose that these basic mechanisms were in any way affected by a particular country's profession of 'socialism' or by such a policy as that of Tanzania attempting to limit the economic rewards of its élite.

So in all countries the élite tended to acquire a distinctive class-culture, shifting from being an aggregate of individuals from diverse communities who had acquired education and office, to being a fairly bounded social stratum. Increasingly its members, in addition to their wealth and power, had a distinct life-style, married among themselves, recruited from within their ranks and consolidated their order by material and cultural inheritance. A new social class was in formation. Attitudes to this process of those outside the ranks of the élite were deeply ambivalent. Within a few years of independence there was expressed, particularly among the youthful urban poor, sharp criticism of the rich and powerful and of the state policies associated with them; but there was also much acceptance of hierarchy provided that the superior showed patronage to community and individual clients. But it may be very misleading to interpret these divergent attitudes as definite evidence of a trend from a clientelist to an antagonistic pattern of class relations. Class action (as in strikes) was far from being a fresh development of the post-independence period; it could co-exist or alternate with clientelist responses by the non-élite. The system of regional integration, with a hierarchy of communities or regions oriented to improved access to the national centre, entailed the dependence of communities on educated-bureaucratic patrons. It was thus that the privileges of the élite, despite the class antagonism which they stimulated, were also combined with a pattern of conflict which cut across the axis of class.

STATE AND SOCIETY

In any society the designation given to those who hold power is usually symptomatic, but in sub-Saharan Africa the sheer variety of terms used – élite, political class or *classe dirigeante*, nationalist bourgeoisie or even *petite bourgeoisie* or new middle class – suggest the uncertainties. But of these terms, 'political class' is perhaps the most helpful since it points to the fact that social power was overwhelmingly the product of political or state bureaucratic office rather than of any material resource held independently of it. Capital and land were too exiguous, unconcentrated or localised – or else in the hands of foreign agents – for their possessors to be *nationally* powerful because of them; or those who held such resources within local arenas were too culturally heterogeneous, too much their possessors on purely local terms, or too devoid of the modern cultural resources necessary for operation as a truly national class. South Africa and Ethiopia, at least until its social revolution in the mid-1970s, were exceptions, in that they *were* thus controlled by such a property-owning class. The position in Arab states was historically more ambiguous. While, traditionally, there was no private property in land and the ruling élites were a political class of external provenance (Mamluk, Turk, Berber), the nineteenth century did tend to see the establishment of a landholding aristocracy of powerful families. But colonialism undermined or destroyed outright this social stratum, and social dominance tended to pass to a new *classe dirigeante*, the holders of political, military and bureaucratic office, as in sub-Saharan Africa.

The power of the political class did not just have the negative condition that no other coherent social classes existed at the national level. It involved more than its members' education and technical or administrative skills, important though these might be for the ascent of individuals; for these only conferred power because of the structural importance, even the 'overdevelopment',[1] of the state as the link between the national society and the outside world. For these external connexions, mediated through the state, were in diverse ways a prime source of the national society's integration – and that not only, as Marxist 'underdevelopment' theory implies, for those societies closely involved in trading links with the capitalist west. Local communities depended on external markets for their cash crops, and the state intervened to control this relationship; external alliances, more available to states than to forces of insurrection, yielded the means of coercive control when political classes were unable otherwise to dominate their societies. Oil, for a few states, was a resource which fell directly to the political class with no further intervention in society. The structural grounds for the hegemony of the political class were, *au fond*, the same for Algeria and Kenya, Liberia and Angola.

But internal features of society do seem to have had some effect on how the political classes influenced the course of social change. First, although the political class as such lacked its own constituency in society, it found the task of governing much easier when

[1] This is the formulation of Colin Leys, 'The "overdeveloped" post-colonial state: a re-evaluation', *Review of African Political Economy*, 1976, 5, 39–48, who thus confronts in an idiom of the left the same set of problems that other scholars denote by expressions like 'the primacy of politics'. See too J. S. Saul, 'The state in post-colonial societies – Tanzania', *The Socialist Register* (London, 1974) and 'The unsteady state: Uganda, Obote and General Amin', *Review of African Political Economy*, 1976, 5, 12–38. Saul's concept of a 'petit-bourgeois state' confuses, since it is never quite clear whether this state is considered 'petit-bourgeois' because of the political class's origins and/or internal connexions, or because it is 'petty' in relation to the real, overseas bourgeois (owners of multi-national corporations etc.) in whose real interests it is said to be governing.

it established alliances with particular formed interest-groups, some of which were more capable of forcing their attentions on the state than others. These might be ethnic groups, possessed of strategic resources such as educational advancement, which in turn was likely to be an effect of earlier prominence in cash cropping; or occupational or class categories. An indigenous bourgeoisie, for example, might be closely allied with the political class, as in Nigeria, or opposed by it, as in Tanzania; a major ethnic group, like the Luo of Kenya, might at one time be on good terms with the political class, at another time estranged from it. It is difficult to generalise across Africa about the general tendency of these alliances since they arose out of conjunctures that were highly specific as to both time and place. But such alliances had the potential for imparting a long-term effect on the pattern of social integration, as the political class became progressively committed to a particular pattern of ethnic and class support, and less and less able to take a purely uncommitted and pragmatic attitude to possible alliances.

Secondly, the political class might be inclined, because of its own social composition, to move in particular directions. To suggest this is to go back somewhat on the earlier point that one essential feature of a *political* class is precisely that its character derives from the structural position its members have come to occupy, rather than from their social origins. The 'plasticity' of élites in sub-Saharan Africa may no doubt be partly attributed to their heterogeneous origins. But the very inconclusiveness of the debate about Egypt's so-called 'new middle class', whose members' social origins clearly lay in the 'rural middle class and its urban offshoots', indicates how refracted the links between social class origins and potential for action at the level of the state could be. But if the interests generated by its members' particular class origin were likely, because local, to be fairly irrelevant to the directions of the political class's policy, the cultural values that derived from this origin could play a significant role at the national level. Thus the '*petit bourgeois*' background of the core of the Algerian political class was relevant to subsequent state policy less because of the direct operation of a '*petit bourgeois*' class interest than because that was the milieu of the religio-social reformist movement inspired by Ben Badis, whose ideology nicely sustained Islamic nationalism, as well as the legitimation of the urban political centre against the heterodoxy and dissidence of the hinterlands and the social hegemony of modernising functionaries. It is perhaps less likely that such socially specific existing cultural traditions should be as distinctly relevant to the direction of a political class's initiatives in Black Africa as in Arab Africa, where cultural idioms were more widespread. But the insistency of cultural debate in Black Africa – whether in novels and plays, in academic historiography or the pursuits of Institutes of African Studies – clearly testifies to the sense among the educated élite, from which the political class is largely recruited, and with whom it most needs to establish relations, that culture is highly relevant to the question: what kind of society do we want to create?

CULTURAL CHANGE

In this analysis of social change, one commonly held view has been deliberately avoided: that its essence has been the transmutation of 'traditional' societies into 'modern' ones through the ever wider adoption of modern cultural values, propagated among their co-nationals by a modernising élite.[1] Something like this has certainly been an important element in the self-representation of African élites. But there are too many ambiguities and difficulties for this account to be adequate as an explanation of social actuality. Many of the values alleged to be modern may also be traditional and 'traditional' behaviour may proceed less from traditional values than from rationally perceived advantages in the contemporary situation; the most 'modern' may retain powerful traditional attachments, and the 'traditional' may sometimes be harnessed for 'modern' ends; much of the empirical variation that we have to describe, for example in national policies regarding development strategy or wealth distribution or constitutional form, would seem to fall right outside any 'tradition–modernity' continuum. The theory tends to lift culture from its contexts and

---

[1] D. E. Apter has perhaps been the most influential proponent of such a perspective, both in his monographs on Ghana and Uganda and, more generally, in *The politics of modernization* (Chicago, 1965). See, too, D. N. Levine, *Wax and gold: tradition and innovation in Ethiopian culture* (Chicago, 1965), which presents a subtle descriptive account, using the 'tradition–modernity' framework, of the personal dilemmas of social change. R. A. LeVine, *Dreams and deeds: achievement motivation in Nigeria* (Chicago, 1966) seeks stimuli to modernisation in elements of traditional cultures, but his characterisation of the 'modern' seems unduly limited; cf. critique of S. R. Barrett, 'Model construction and modernisation in Nigeria', *Sociological Review*, 1969, 17, 251–66.

treats it as quite autonomous, whereas in fact the adoption of 'traditional' or 'modern' symbols is more often a function of context, rather than of individual predispositions. For Africa exhibits a hierarchy of social levels or contexts, from the local or regional in which a particular traditional idiom will tend to predominate, to the national where, as a rule, no such idiom will be able to prevail and where, in addition, social functions with no local or traditional analogue are performed. A general increase of 'modernity' in culture was thus largely an effect of the greater domination of all social relations by its source, the national sphere. Yet tradition is not wholly abandoned even by those whose lives are mostly passed in this sphere, for it remains a crucial source of personal identity; and because of the patterns of integration within the national society, it retains importance as one principal idiom of vertical communication between the élite and their rural dependants.

The educated élite is much more intensely concerned with culture – that is with the forging of a consistent cultural synthesis relevant to all levels and regions of the national society – than those ordinary people who move to and fro between social contexts creating their own personal balances, whether unified or compartmentalised, between the various cultural options open to them. Societal problems were echoed in the dilemmas of their personal experience. What balance was to be struck between local values, those associated with family and community of origin, and the more universal and cosmopolitan ones of formal education, work-place and the national political arena? How was the educated African to square those aspects of 'European' culture which depreciated Africa and legitimised its subordination, with those which had made him what he was, as an educated man, and underlay his claim to leadership roles within his own emergent national society? These personal and cultural questions became much more political in import when the nationalist movement came to maturity in the late 1940s and the educated began to move into positions of political responsibility. Négritude, the somewhat delayed response in French Africa to some of these issues, was from the beginning a synthesis of the narrowly 'cultural' with nationalist politics. Since the colonial state was now taken as given, the task was to define a level of national culture against both the micro-loyalties of the tribe and the cosmopolitan culture of the colonial powers. The position of the élite was intensely equivocal; for as representatives of the state, mediators between it and the outside world, they were sincerely committed to its integrity, but as communal representatives they were also susceptible to centrifugal or 'tribalist' attachments. One acute cultural problem was that the symbols of Africanness which could be most readily set against colonial culture were also in the main identified with particular ethnic sub-groups. Nowhere is this more evident than with that classic symbol of nationhood, a common and distinguishing language, for in sub-Saharan Africa linguistically homogeneous states and supra-ethnic languages such as Swahili are so few.

Yet undoubtedly the decades after the Second World War did see a definite enlargement of the common cultural stock within the national societies. Lingua francas continued to extend their range. Even ethnicity fostered and betokened it – despite its tendency to heighten *some* cultural differences as diacritical ethnic symbols – since it was essentially a competition between ethnic categories brought together under common conditions for common ends. And ethnic groups learnt from one another. The great spread of primary education generalised many concerns and experiences, and the continued expansion of the world religions indicated a progressive decline in the sufficiency of predominantly local religious symbols. It is significant that the most tenacious elements of 'traditional' religion, the most likely to survive migration to towns, were those that touched a common bedrock of African traditional religions: the individual's concern for divinatory and magico-medical assistance. The independent churches and new religious movements, which continued to expand well after the various diverse crises that begot them had subsided, were highly symptomatic of the dual aspect of general cultural change. On the one hand they represented an indigenisation of missionary religion, a closing of the cultural gap between theologies of élite and external origin and the religious concerns of ordinary people, an ecclesiastical forerunner to the movement among educationalists for a more truly vernacular curriculum. On the other, no doubt because they brought together a universal idiom with attention to widespread popular concerns, they showed a remarkable ability to attract members from different ethnic groups and to spread from one ethnic group to another.

It is no accident that the 1950s brought such an efflorescence of the novel – that cultural form which is so much 'about' modern social change, both a mirror and a guide – and that the novelists were so drawn to themes of culture contact: Ibo boy meets Yoruba girl, or the difficulties of meeting the expectations of one's kinsfolk as well as those of the civil service. Soyinka's first novel, about a group of intellectuals' responses to their society and to their social relations in and outside a university, was most aptly named *The interpreters*. And it is perhaps also indicative of a real socio-cultural advance that by the 1970s many of the most serious novelists – Soyinka, Achebe, Ngugi – had moved on to themes less purely 'cultural' and more political, less to do with the relations between Africans and 'European' culture, and more to do with those between the new political class and the mass of the population.[1]

'Cultural revival', with its echoes of *négritude*, became a rallying cry in the 1960s and 1970s, culminating in the Second World Black and African Festival of Arts and Culture held in Lagos in 1977. Despite its overt stance, this was highly ambivalent toward the traditions it celebrated; and necessarily so, since the national élite whose project it was had as a condition of its own existence the progressive destruction of those social contexts that had produced it. Conducted under the sponsorship of the state, it tended towards two major effects. First, it delocalised traditional cultural forms, wresting them from their proper contexts of use, subjecting them to the requirements of appeal to much wider groups, turning them into 'folklore' and giving them a more national character. Secondly, by thus appropriating forms whose most authentic bearers were still members of small rural communities and even making itself necessary to their survival, the élite legitimised itself in the eyes of those who were largely deprived of those 'modern' cultural and political resources which gave access to state power. Culture thus assisted a national integration against the incipient divisions of class as well as those of ethnicity.

There remains one important source of the emergent national culture that was neither universal nor purely ethnic or local in provenance: the ideas of the nationalist leadership about what kind of national society they wished to have. The general form

[1] E.g. C. Achebe, *A man of the people* (London, 1966); W. Soyinka, *Season of anomy* (London, 1973); Ngugi wa Thiongo, *Petals of blood* (London, 1977).

of the 'cultural problem', as sketched above, was common to most countries of sub-Saharan Africa; the origins and constitution of their élite groups were basically similar; they faced the same international environment and, with few exceptions, confronted similar obstacles to the development which they all desired. It may be asked here why the political cultures and development ideologies of Senegal and Guinea, Ghana and the Ivory Coast, Uganda, Kenya and Tanzania were so diverse. This diversity could not have been predicted in 1950. And it is not very enlightening in seeking an explanation merely to refer in general terms to the diverse circumstances in which particular countries won their independence and the equally diverse political conjunctures which developed since. But the very variety of responses suggests that we may have a notable case of the relative autonomy of ideas before which the determinism of social structure falters. What remains to be seen is whether this cultural autonomy will be matched by any long-term cultural influence on social structures; or whether it will turn out to be fairly epiphenomenal, while the intransigent weight of external circumstances forces African countries and peoples to advance in conformity to it.[1]

[1] In preparing this chapter, I received valuable help from Professor Ernest Gellner, who gave advice on North Africa, and from Dr A. J. Peace, who commented on an earlier draft.

CHAPTER 5

THE ECONOMIC EVOLUTION OF DEVELOPING AFRICA

The treatment of Africa as an economic entity needs to be approached with caution, for it is a continent of great natural diversity. Over and above this the differing political, social and economic policies imposed on the continent by the colonial powers left independent Africa with a poorly integrated economy. Intra-African trade was negligible; there was no continental transport and communications system; and the various independent African countries belonged to different monetary zones, each monetary area being linked with one or the other of the former metropolitan powers. It is, therefore, more accurate to talk about the evolution of the African economies rather than of *the* African economy; and necessary to trace how each has evolved during the period of 35 years covered by this volume. Such an approach, however, would do less than full justice to the economic history of Africa for in spite of the differences in the patterns of development of the various countries, certain overall themes and features are discernible. It will be our aim to highlight these while emphasising, as may be appropriate, the uniqueness of each economy. South Africa, being a developed economy, at least as far as its dominant white community was concerned, is not considered here except for comparative purposes; nor for that matter, unless expressly stated, is Rhodesia, due to lack of data, particularly during the period of the unilateral declaration of independence.

Without doubt this period is one of the most important in Africa's political as well as its economic history. But while by the end of our period only in four countries – the French Somali Coast (Djibouti), Rhodesia (Zimbabwe), South West Africa (Namibia) and South Africa itself – had political power not yet been transferred to Africans, in the economic sphere, by contrast, the reawakening process was still at the stage of assertion of rights and of a re-assessment of the relevance of the economic philosophy, strategy and policy inherited from the colonial powers. By 1975 no fundamental change had taken place in the economies which independent Africa inherited. In fact, in some areas there had been real setbacks.

THE COLONIAL ECONOMY ON THE EVE OF
THE SECOND WORLD WAR

The foundations of the national economies inherited by the newly independent governments were laid down in the first two decades of the twentieth century and elaborated in the succeeding two decades between the First World War and the Second World War, which marks the beginning of our period. By 1914, as J. Forbes Munro has put it, there had been 'a fairly dramatic strengthening of Africa's connections under the international economy, and possibly the final, conclusive transformation of its economies into peripheries of the industrialised capitalist centre of world exchange'.[1] Very few Africans now remained untouched by the demands of externally oriented production, or by a colonial philosophy that saw the colonies primarily as a source of raw materials for the metropolitan economies and as a market for imported manufactured goods.

Taxation was the principal lever that brought additional labour and produce on to the market; railroads provided a new transport infrastructure through which increased quantities of imported goods could be cheaply shifted into the interior and new areas opened for export production. By 1940 a particular pattern of dependency had developed in most colonies, and in some cases on a regional basis: at the centre of the colonial economic system was the export enclave; on the periphery were those areas that provided migrant labour for the export enclave. Very few Africans could now claim that they operated in a traditional 'subsistence' economy that was untouched by the demands of the international economy. Furthermore, as a result of the differing tariffs, currencies, legal systems, administrative policies and languages, as well as the direction of railway expansion, vertical links were forged between the metropolitan countries and colonies

[1] J. Forbes Munro, *Africa and the international economy 1800–1960* (London, 1976), 86.

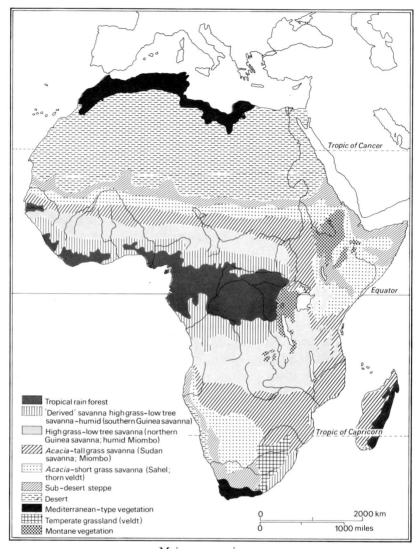

Tropic of Cancer

Equator

Tropic of Capricorn

■ Tropical rain forest
▥ 'Derived' savanna high grass–low tree savanna–humid (southern Guinea savanna)
▨ High grass–low tree savanna (northern Guinea savanna; humid Miombo)
▨ *Acacia*-tall grass savanna (Sudan savanna; Miombo)
▨ *Acacia*-short grass savanna (Sahel; thorn veldt)
▨ Sub-desert steppe
▨ Desert
■ Mediterranean-type vegetation
▦ Temperate grassland (veldt)
▨ Montane vegetation

0   2000 km
0   1000 miles

5   Major vegetation zones.

that discouraged both the continuation of pre-existing, and the
development of new, regional patterns of trade and
communication.

Within the export-led economy, European concerns generally
controlled the commanding heights of commerce and production,
with the Lebanese in West Africa and Asians in East Africa
occupying intermediate roles, and Africans restricted for the most

194

part to the least lucrative economic levels. This hierarchical pattern, however, had important regional variations. In West Africa there were few radical alterations in an economic system that had long-standing external contacts and where African participation in production and commerce remained very strong. In regions where mining, as in South Africa, or European-directed agriculture, as in Algeria, Kenya and Rhodesia, exerted a dominant influence, then the primary African role was increasingly seen as that of providing cheap labour. Between the extremes represented by these paradigms there was a variety of opportunity for African participation.

In at least two important respects economic self-sufficiency was being eroded. First, railroad expansion made it possible to distribute cheaply large quantities of imported goods; indigenous industries – particularly those involved in the manufacture of iron, salt and cloth – collapsed or were severely restricted in the face of this influx. Second, the quantity and variety of food production was adversely affected by the re-allocation of land and labour towards export production. This process was more gradual than the collapse of local craft industries. In the long term it was to have marked regional effects on nutrition, soil conservation and resistance to drought as well as initiating a growing dependence on imported foodstuffs.

The inter-war period, with a few brief exceptions, was a time of instability and depression in the international economy that had a profound influence on the economy of Africa at the beginning of our period. Between 1929 and 1932 the value of Africa's commerce had fallen by approximately 42 per cent and only recovered slowly over the next eight years. Indeed by 1938 many countries were still at lower levels of return from trade than they had been in 1929. In many colonies government direction of the economy (particularly in marketing) increased enormously during the 1930s in order to ensure that production was maintained, and even increased, in the face of falling commodity prices and wage-rates. Smaller firms and traders were forced out of business while a restricted number of large mercantile concerns reacted to insecurity by amalgamation, price-fixing and market-sharing thereby establishing a long-term oligopolistic influence on the colonial economies that was to continue in many cases long after independence. The white-settler communities, notoriously inefficient agricultural producers, were sheltered from disaster by preferential access to markets, credit, and government services. By 1940 African peasants and petty traders were having to pay a very heavy price – in absolute and relative terms – for their colonial subjugation and incorporation into the international economy.

THE PERFORMANCE OF THE AFRICAN ECONOMY, 1940–75

By 1940, then, the colonial economies of Africa had become firmly established. The colonial pattern of production, concentrating on primary products for export and importing most of the manufactured goods required, had become the established doctrine. Because of this external orientation, the pre-colonial African economies were distorted almost beyond recognition. They had lost their autonomy, and Africa's 'main function was to produce for the world market under conditions which, because they impoverished it, deprived [it] of any prospects of radical modernisation. This "traditional" society was not, therefore, in transition to "modernity"; as a dependent society it was complete, peripheral, and hence at a dead end.'[1]

Following the lean years of the depression, the war itself brought partial relief to the African economies. Although the demand for Africa's primary products increased substantially, particularly after the loss of South East Asia to Japan in 1942, there was no corresponding upward shift in prices because Africa's external commerce was subjected to a series of wartime marketing controls by the colonial powers. Indeed, it was not until the last two years of the war that significantly higher prices were paid for African primary produce. Thus for most of the war years African producers suffered substantial losses in their real incomes. For while their earnings from their agricultural products were stabilised, the prices of imported commodities, if they were available at all, rose. And in order to sustain, and possibly increase, production to meet wartime demands, colonial administrations adopted coercive measures. Whatever tactics were adopted, the net economic effect of the intervention of the colonial

[1] Samir Amin, 'Under-development and dependence in Black Africa – origins and contemporary forms', *Journal of Modern African Studies*, 1972, **10**, 4, 520.

powers in the marketing of agricultural commodities was to deprive African countries of the opportunity presented by the war to accelerate the pace of their development. The years between 1945 and 1949 saw no substantial improvement from wartime conditions. There continued to be trade controls, shortages of goods and high prices on imports. The post-war expectations of the African population were not met and this resulted in widespread labour, and to a certain extent agrarian, unrest.

Some of the agrarian discontent was directed at the operations of the produce marketing boards, direct descendants of the economic control boards established during the war. Originally conceived as instruments of long-term price stabilisation, the monopoly position of the boards was used increasingly to extract resources from the agrarian sector which were then diverted to other development sectors or, particularly in this period, whether expressly or not, to bolster the currency reserves of the metro-politan countries. Marketing boards continued to be prime instruments of government economic control throughout our period, even though their impact on agricultural production remained controversial.

What then was the economic situation in Africa by 1950 – the beginning of the pre-independence decade – and what changes took place during that decade? Because of the lack of reliable and comprehensive data, it is of course easier to pose than to answer this question. And whatever data are available, however frag-mentary, generally relate to individual countries. Quantitative data relating to the continent as a whole were, in the 1950s, unavailable. In fact, for this decade, indicators of total economic activity, such as domestic product and national income, are available for only 21 countries and in several of these countries the data are available for one year only. Extreme caution, therefore, needs to be exercised in attempting to draw valid conclusions from the data, particularly as their accuracy varies considerably from country to country, ranging from the highly probable to the merely conjectural.

But in spite of this limitation, it is still possible to identify, even if only in broad outline, the main features of the development in the economies of Africa between 1950 and 1960. Developments in Africa simply echoed developments in the industrialised market economies, particularly those of the colonial powers. Whereas the immediate post-war years saw the continuation of wartime restrictions in war-devastated Europe and labour and agrarian unrest in an expectant, demobilising Africa, with the progressive removal of wartime controls after 1948 and the resurgence in the international economy, the world demand for African produce expanded very rapidly. The reconstruction and re-equipment of the western industrial economies through Marshall Aid and the subsequent gradual removal of all forms of restriction and control, and the growth in real incomes in these countries, led inevitably to a commodities boom in Africa, particularly in Africa south of the Sahara. This boom was intensified by the outbreak of the Korean war in 1950 when the industrial countries stockpiled commodities. All these developments resulted in the prices for Africa's produce rising to unprecedented heights. For the first time since the First World War, the barter terms of trade moved strongly in favour of the Africa economies.

This boom had a considerable impact on the production of export commodities in Africa, particularly the annual crops. Thus in West Africa, groundnut production doubled between 1947 and 1957; cotton production more than trebled; coffee increased by one-and-a-half times; and cocoa, which takes between five and seven years after planting to yield, increased by 24 per cent during this ten-year period. Tea production doubled in southern Africa, while sugar production increased by 89.74 and 42 per cent in southern and eastern and central Africa respectively. Cotton enjoyed comparable increases in the three sub-regions while coffee production increased by 166 per cent in East Africa and by 83 per cent in Central Africa.

In the production of minerals, similar spectacular increases were achieved, as table 5.1 clearly shows. In 1938, Africa accounted for 97 per cent of the world output of diamonds; 95 per cent of cobalt; 46 per cent of gold; 40 per cent of chrome; 35 per cent of manganese; and 21 per cent of copper. In other minerals, the position of Africa was less pronounced – 12 per cent of total tin production; 6 per cent of iron ore; and 2 per cent of anthracite and bituminous coal. By 1950 Africa accounted for 52 per cent of world output of chromite and manganese; 22 per cent of copper; 56 per cent of gold and 13 per cent of tin concentrates. Although the output of diamonds, rock phosphates, cobalt, silver and asbestos expanded in absolute terms, the African share in the

Table 5.1. *Indices of output of principal minerals*
(1948–50, average = 100).

Mineral production	Level of production	
	1937–8 average	1955–7 average
Copper	91	155
Manganese	68	136
Iron ore	96	188
Lead	56	213
Zinc	31	224
Tin	91	112
Bauxite	—	404
Chromite	54	145
Cobalt	55	196
Asbestos	29	164
Calcium phosphate	72	167
Gold	132	120

Source: *United Nations economic survey of Africa since 1950*, table 2–1.

world production of these minerals declined during the pre-independence decade of the 1950s. Africa's share in world output increased in respect of copper, gold, tin concentrates, tungsten and zinc, and it remained constant in the case of iron ore, diamonds, and lead.

Thus in the 1950s most African economies were able to attain high rates of economic expansion, propelled as they were by the commodities boom of the post-war period. There were also inflows of private capital. Table 5.2 shows the changes between 1950 and 1957 in gross national products and gross capital formation in African countries, selected from the various sub-regions of the continent that enjoyed an average growth rate of 7.74 per cent per annum during the eight-year period covered. Their gross capital formation averaged 10.41 per cent per annum during the same period. As we have already pointed out, although comprehensive national income data are not available for most African countries for this period, the general picture is reasonably clear: gross national product grew on the whole at the rate of about 5–7 per cent per annum in real terms.

But the colonial structure of the African economies remained

Table 5.2. *Selected African countries; percentage changes in gross national product and gross capital formation, 1950-7.*

Country	Period	Gross national product			Gross capital formation		
		Total increase	Average yearly increase	Annual rate of growth	Total increase	Average yearly increase	Annual rate of growth
Belgian Congo	1950-7	78.7	11.2	8.64	145.4	20.8	13.68
Morocco	1951-6	49.5	9.9	8.38	—	—	—
Nigeria	1950-6	39.8	6.6	5.74	114.1[b]	19.0[b]	13.53[b]
Rhodesia and Nyasaland (Federation of)	1950-7	138.5	19.8	13.2	130.4[b]	18.6[b]	12.67[b]
Union of South Africa	1950-7	84.5	12.1	9.14	94.4	13.5	9.97
Gold Coast	1950-7	48.6	6.9	5.82	32.6	4.7	4.11
Mauritius	1950-7	57.6	8.2	6.72	40.0	5.7	4.92
Kenya[c]	1950-7	107.4	15.3	10.98	—	—	—
Tanganyika[d]	1954-7	16.9	5.6	5.33	8.0	2.4	—
Uganda[b]	1950-7	70.2	10.0	7.90	—	—	—
Uganda	1950-6	63.5	10.6	8.53	121.2[b]	29.2[b]	14.15[b]
Egypt (UAR)	1950-6	16.3	2.7	2.56	—	—	—

Source: United Nations economic survey of Africa since 1950.

[a] Cumulative rate
[b] Not including capital formation in peasant agriculture
[c] Net domestic product
[d] Gross domestic product

unchanged; if anything, it became consolidated. The rapid growth in the African economy had derived from the boom in the industrialised market economies. The peripheral nature of the African economies remained and their economic dependence intensified. It was also during this period that the colonial powers abandoned the policy of financial self-sufficiency for colonies and adopted instead the policy of responsible colonialism under which they provided the colonies with development funds. The adoption of the new policy was no doubt born out of a mixture of motives and intentions – a genuine humanitarian concern about poverty in Africa, a sense of moral obligation for Africa's wartime assistance, and a very large measure of enlightened self-interest. This was the rationale of the British Colonial Development and Welfare Act of 1945 and the French Fonds d'Investissement et de Développement Économique et Social (FIDES) of 1946.[1] These colonial aid programmes provided ready markets for metropolitan goods as well as finance for development in the colonies. More importantly, they enabled the colonial powers to achieve a greater measure of control over, and ability to coordinate and influence, the investment policies of the colonies. France went even further than the others. Because of its policy of assimilating the colonies to metropolitan France, as evinced in the constitution of the new French Union of 1946, its aid was linked to a public investment programme designed for the modernisation of France itself.

In concluding this review of development during this decade, it must be added that the flow of financial resources from the metropolitan countries, particularly Britain and France, and to a lesser extent Belgium, to the colonies was unsurpassed. It would help to put this development in proper historical perspective if it is pointed out that more resources were transferred in the decade 1946 to 1956 than during the entire period from 1903 to 1946. For example, between 1952 and 1957 France invested 579 billion French francs of public funds in the colonies. We shall come back to the question of aid later. But suffice it to add that neither Portugal nor Spain provided any substantial volume of aid to their African colonies.

Unfortunately, the boom in the demand for tropical primary products did not last long. Towards the end of the decade, there was a fall in their prices due to a world-wide economic depression.

[1] For a discussion of the significance of previous Development Acts see Chapter 1.

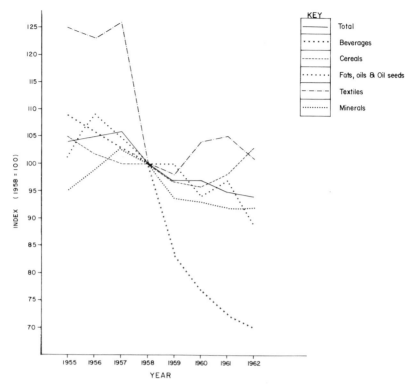

6   Primary commodities: export prices indices (1958 = 100)
(United Nations, Monthly Bulletin of Statistics, Sept. 1963).

There was consequently a considerable reduction in the rate of economic growth of the African economies by the beginning of the 1960s. Thus not only did the African countries, most of which had become independent by the first half of the 1960s, achieve independence with the colonial structure of their economy intact, but they also suffered the misfortune of taking over at a time when economic performance fell below that of the 1950s. To illustrate this, fig. 6 shows the magnitude of the reverses suffered by commodities' export prices. Consequently, the governments of the newly independent African states (and 17 of them became independent in 1960 alone) were faced with serious economic and financial problems soon after their assumption of power. The new leadership of these countries inherited not only underdeveloped economies with their colonial patterns of production and with the vast majority of their people ill-fed, ill-clad, ill-housed and illiterate, but they also faced the immediate problems of a slump in the prices of the commodities which were their main source of income. Public recurrent as well as development expenditure rapidly diminished. But the confidence and optimism generated by the crumbling of colonialism under the tidal wave of nationalism was enough to sustain the new leadership, which had promised improved economic and social conditions for their people and had thereby engineered a revolution of rising expectations among them.

Development planning was adopted by the African governments as the instrument not only for arresting the adverse trend in the terms of trade but also for accelerating the rate of growth and the pace of social and economic transformation and thus satisfying this revolution of rising expectations. Over and above their experience of post-war colonial development planning – itself based on the experience of wartime planning – the rapid transformation of the centrally planned socialist economies, particularly that of the USSR, influenced the newly independent countries in their reliance on centralised economic planning rather than on the operation of a free-market economy. The almost universal acceptance of planning as an efficient tool for policy formulation with regard to rapid economic development was also inspired by the example of the socialist countries. Even the United States, which for years had abhorred planning, was by 1960 actively encouraging aid-seeking countries to formulate national development plans. But the greatest single factor which strengthened the case for planning was the designation of the 1960s by the General Assembly of the United Nations as that organisation's First Development Decade.

The United Nations set down guidelines and objectives for accelerating progress towards the self-sustaining economic growth of individual nations and their social advancement so as to attain in each developing country a substantial increase in the rate of growth. Towards this end, it specified that each country set its own target, taking an annual rate of increase of 5 per cent in the gross domestic product (GDP) as the minimum growth rate to be achieved at the end of the decade. And this growth objective was to be achieved preferably through comprehensive planning. The achievement of the target rate of growth would, it was thought, be accompanied by an improvement in the economic conditions of the poorer sections of the population. It was also thought that there would be substantial social progress through the elimination of illiteracy, hunger and disease, through improvement in education and through a more egalitarian distribution of income.

The 1970s were similarly proclaimed as the Second United Nations Development Decade. The strategy for that decade called for an average rate of growth of GDP at constant prices of at least 6 per cent per annum. To achieve such an overall growth rate, an annual rate of expansion of 4 per cent in agricultural output and of 8 per cent in manufacturing production was necessary. The strategy also called for half a percentage point rise annually in the ratio of gross domestic saving to the gross product, so that the ratio would rise to around 20 per cent by the year 1980; and a rise of not more than 7 per cent in imports, or about one percentage point higher than the target set for GDP growth rate.

Even if African governments were otherwise inclined, there were forces impelling them to play a direct and pervasive role in the development process. It was a basic assumption of the UN First and Second Development Decades that developing countries would achieve the stated objectives through comprehensive planning. Bilateral donor agencies, particularly from industrialised market economies, together with such multilateral institutions as the International Bank for Reconstruction and Development (the World Bank) and the UN Development Programme, attached a great deal of importance to planning and the preparation of national plans as a precondition for providing investment finance, grants and technical assistance in the preparation of such plans. Unfortunately, instead of development planning becoming the instrument for engineering socio-economic change in Africa, a widening gulf soon began to emerge between planning and plan implementation. In an increasing number of countries, the development plan soon became, like the national flag and the national anthem, a symbol of sovereignty. More often than not it was unfortunately respected more in the breach than in the performance. In any case, the policies and programmes contained in such plans tended, with very few exceptions, to perpetuate the colonial pattern of production of the African economies. It is not surprising therefore that Africa's overall economic performance between 1960 and 1975 was poor.

As we have already stated, the boom in the demand for commodities had been replaced by a mild depression towards the end of the 1950s. Thus between 1958 and 1964 the total GDP of Africa increased by only 27 per cent or at about 4.2 per cent annually at compound rate. There was a slight improvement on this performance during the rest of the 1960s. For the whole of the UN First Development Decade, Africa achieved an average growth rate of 5.0 per cent in real terms. And during the first half of the Second Development Decade the performance was 4.5 per cent per annum. In all during the 15-year period, 1960–75, the overall African performance of 4.9 per cent fell below the targets of the First and Second Development Decades. The year 1975 was a particularly bad one for Africa mainly because of the world recession and real growth in GDP fell to 2 per cent, and thereafter was to become negative in not a few countries. As a periphery of the periphery, the African economies suffered considerably from the inflationary pressures which gripped the industrialised market economies in the latter part of the 1960s and the first half of the 1970s. Inflation coupled with recession led to an even sharper fall in the values of export commodities, thus seriously affecting government revenue from exports. The African governments also had no choice but to succumb to the demand for wage and salary increases and, in some cases, to the pressure to subsidise essential consumer goods, thus accentuating the inflationary process. Because of the consequential increases in government expenditure, most governments had to resort to deficit financing. These governments also perforce had to pile up external debts in order to pay for their imports, which increased from an estimated total of $US 5 billion in 1965, to about $US 22 billion in 1973 and $US 30 billion in 1975. This resulted in a growing demand for the rescheduling of external debts. Meanwhile, there was an increasing accumulation of arrears in international payments, and a growing number of countries became threatened with acute balance-of-payments difficulties due in part to heavy debt liabilities.

STRUCTURAL AND SECTORAL CHANGES

It has often been said that during this period developing Africa was running very hard to remain in the same place. This statement is borne out by the fact that it was the world's least developed

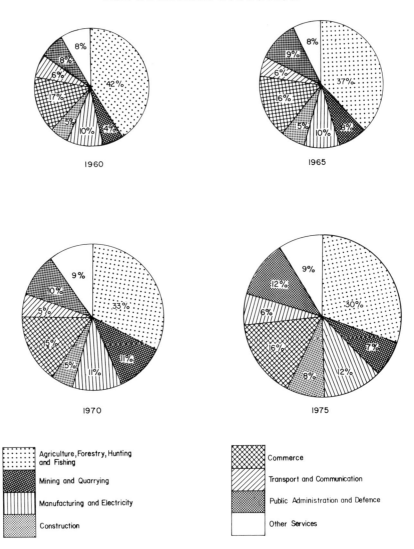

7 Developing Africa: structure of gross domestic product, 1960–75 (in million US$ at 1970 rate of exchange) (compiled from ECA computer national accounts print-outs, March 1977).

region, having 18 of the 25 least developed among developing countries and 27 of the world's most seriously affected countries while including 14 land-locked countries. In examining the structure of developing Africa, we shall perforce have to concentrate on the post-independence period for which data on national

Table 5.3. *Developing Africa: expenditure on gross domestic product, 1960–75 (in million $ US at 1970 rate of exchange).*

Expenditure	1960	1965	1970	1975	Percentage distribution			
					1960	1965	1970	1975
Total GDP at 1970 market prices	35 436.9	44 510.6	58 064.3	71 934.4	100.00	100.00	100.00	100.00
Private consumption	26 336.3	30 807.8	37 920.7	47 070.1	74.32	69.21	65.31	65.43
Government consumption	4 703.9	6 213.8	9 465.7	14 267.1	13.27	13.96	16.30	19.83
Fixed capital formation	5 705.3	7 074.6	9 664.1	18 748.3	16.10	15.89	16.64	26.06
Increase in stocks	145.4	512.6	732.2	687.2	0.41	1.15	1.27	0.96
Exports of goods and services	8 794.7	11 468.6	15 050.7	16 357.9	24.82	25.77	25.92	22.74
Less imports of goods and services	10 248.7	11 566.8	14 769.1	25 196.2	28.92	25.98	25.44	35.02

Source: ECA national accounts computer print-outs, March 1977.

accounts are available. The data in fig. 7 show that the economic structure of African countries underwent significant changes during this period. In particular, the share of agriculture in the GDP declined from 41.3 per cent in 1960 to 30.3 per cent in 1975. The share of mining increased from 4.4 per cent to 7.3 per cent, and the share of manufacturing and electricity increased from 10.0 per cent to 12 per cent. The share of construction also increased from 5 per cent to 8 per cent; while the share of public administration and defence increased from 8 to 12 per cent. Transport and communications did not change its relative share significantly. Despite these changes, agriculture remained the dominant sector in most developing African countries.

The economic structure over the period 1960–75 can also be examined by considering the evolution of the main components of expenditure on the gross domestic product (i.e. private consumption, government consumption, capital formation, exports of goods and services and imports of goods and services). The impression conveyed by the available information on private consumption in developing Africa (see table 5.3) is that private consumption absorbed a higher proportion of available resources in developing Africa than it did in other Third World countries. In 1960, private consumption accounted for 74 per cent of GDP in real terms, while in 1975 it accounted for 65 per cent. The situation is even clearer when we consider information on individual African countries. For instance, in 1960, private consumption accounted for more than 50 per cent in 44 of 48 developing African countries. The exceptions were Gabon (45 per cent) and Northern Rhodesia (48 per cent). In two countries, however, private consumption exceeded GDP by a significant margin – Libya (105 per cent) and Basutoland (108 per cent). In 1975, private consumption as a percentage of GDP was little changed from the 1960 levels, accounting for more than 50 per cent in 42 of the 48 countries. Libya did, however, achieve a substantial change in reducing the share from 105 per cent in 1960 to 48 per cent in 1975, thanks to oil production.

As is indicated in table 5.3, the share of government consumption in total GDP at 1970 constant market prices in developing Africa increased from 13 per cent in 1960 to 20 per cent in 1975. It is interesting to note that, in 31 of the 48 countries, the share of government consumption in GDP increased substantially in real terms from 1960 to 1975. The share decreased in 12 countries and remained constant in 5 others.

As regards gross fixed capital formation as a percentage of gross domestic product at constant 1970 prices, table 5.3 indicates an increase from 16 per cent in 1960 to 26 per cent in 1975. From the data on the individual countries, it appears that there was a rising trend in the share of the domestic product used for capital formation in all developing countries except Angola, the Congo, Ethiopia, the Gambia, Ghana, Kenya, Libya, Niger and Uganda.

Exports and imports of goods and services are considered in detail in the section dealing with Africa and the international economy. But it is important to point out here that the share of total exports of goods and services in GDP in developing Africa decreased from 25 per cent in 1960 to 23 per cent in 1975, while the share of imports of goods and services in GDP increased from 29 per cent in 1960 to 35 per cent in 1975.

The agricultural sector

Though there have been significant changes in the structure of the African economy, they have not been fundamental. Africa today still has *pro tanto* an agricultural economy. The fall in the relative contribution of agriculture to the GDP has been due not so much to increased productivity in the other sectors as it has been to the very low productivity in agriculture and to poor weather conditions. Under the UN First and Second Development Decades, a target rate of growth of 4 per cent per annum was assumed for agriculture. Production fell consistently very much below this target, averaging 2.5 per cent per annum. The worsening drought conditions in the Sudano-Sahelian region, particularly during the 1971–4 period, contributed in no small measure to this disappointing performance of the agricultural sector.

The pattern of agricultural production remained, for all practical purposes, unchanged. Crop production remained basically divided into production for export and production for domestic consumption. In sub-Saharan Africa, subsistence farming still co-existed with commercial or modern farming. Indeed, agricultural organisation in most African states was a mixture of the two. Traditional agriculture was still chiefly organised with the

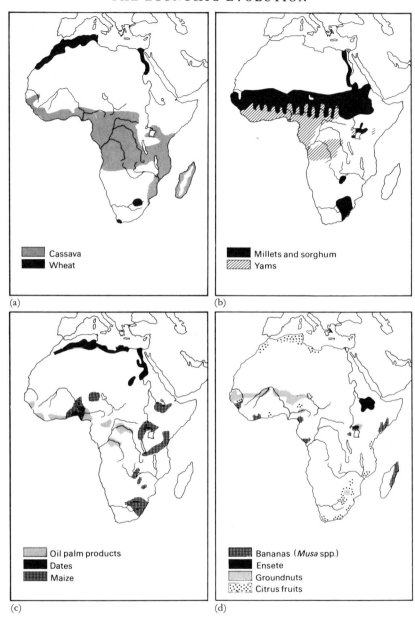

8   Staple and cash crops: main areas.
(a) Staple crops: cassava and wheat.
(b) Staple crops: millets, sorghum and yams.
(c) Staple and cash crops: maize, oil palm and dates.
(d) Staple and cash crops: groundnuts, citrus, bananas and ensete.
(Source: *Cambridge Encyclopaedia of Africa*.)

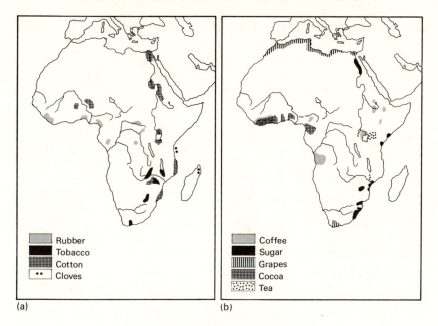

9   Cash crops: main areas.
(a) Rubber, tobacco, cotton and cloves.
(b) Coffee, tea, cocoa, sugar and grapes.
(Source: *Cambridge Encyclopaedia of Africa*.)

resources of and for the subsistence of the rural communities; it
was the basis for a way of life and an economy in which disposal
of produce by sale was incidental, depending on availability of
marketable surpluses. Modern agriculture, by contrast, was carried
on as a commercial undertaking entirely within the money economy, and its methods and objects were therefore different from
those of traditional agriculture. Traditional agriculture was heavily
predominant in West, Central and East Africa. In North Africa,
farming had become predominantly commercial. Until recently,
subsistence production accounted for between two-thirds and
three-quarters of the values of total production in tropical Africa.
However, with the increasing commercialisation of farming, the
relative share of subsistence production diminished progressively.
    We have already noted that, on the whole, agriculture was the
lagging sector responsible for dampening substantially the overall
growth of GDP. We must however go beyond the overall picture,
sombre as that is, to the main components of the agricultural

Table 5.4. *Indices of the volume of agricultural production in Africa* (*1952/3 = 100*).

	1948/9	1953/4	1958/9	1962/3	1965/6
All agricultural products	88	103	120	128	132
Food products	88	103	118	125	128
Non-food products	87	103	133	145	159
Livestock products	92	103	114	119	121
Per capita production					
All agricultural products	97	100	103	105	102
Food products	97	100	101	103	98
Non-food products	95	100	114	119	122

Source: ECA, *A survey of economic conditions in Africa.*

sector. Table 5.4 shows that whereas all agricultural products rose by 44 points between 1948 and 1966 (averaging 2.44 per cent annual increase), food and livestock products increased by 40 and 19 per cent respectively (averaging together 1.6 per cent). On the other hand, non-food products increased by 72 per cent during the same period (averaging 4.0 per cent per annum). On a per capita basis, the position did not improve very much; if anything it stagnated for all agricultural products and showed a marked tendency to deteriorate as far as food production was concerned. This is not surprising, since annual population increase averaged 2.2 per cent during this period.

The situation deteriorated considerably between 1966 and 1975. Climatic conditions were particularly unfavourable from 1971/2 to 1974 in the Sudano-Sahelian zone and in other parts of Africa. However, these were not the sole factors accounting for the poor performance in the agricultural sector. Weak administrative capacity and inadequate infrastructure support for agriculture, particularly in such fields as marketing, credit, transport, and extension services were also responsible. The producer-pricing policies also had a marked disincentive effect. The large-scale rural–urban migration affected agricultural production since the shortage of farm-hands which resulted from it did not in itself lend to the revolutionising of agricultural techniques and technologies.

Although much mechanisation had taken place, this was still rather marginal. And while the resources allocated for agricultural development in Africa increased substantially over the years, they were still far from being adequate. A supervised agricultural credit system was still a thing of the future.

The food situation deteriorated fast in the face of rising population and rapid urbanisation. The annual rate of increase in food production from 1970 to 1976 was 1.5 per cent, compared with the annual rate of increase in world production of 2.4 per cent during the same period. It also compared unfavourably with rates achieved by other developing regions. Consequently, the gap in nutritional requirements and per caput dietary energy supplies was wider in Africa than in any other developing region. On average, people in Africa received only 90 per cent of their nutritional requirements per day. This contrasted with many Latin American countries, where per caput dietary energy supplies were as high as 107 per cent of nutritional requirements. One of Africa's most serious problems remained a shortage of basic foodstuffs: due to harvesting techniques and poor and inadequate storage facilities, Africa still lost between one-quarter and two-fifths of its food production annually.

The mining sector

Unlike agriculture, the mining industry achieved considerable progress during the period under review. We have already referred to the spectacular increase in mineral production in the pre-independence decade of the 1950s. Table 5.1 illustrates these increases. During the period from 1960 to 1975, these growth rates were not only sustained but substantially improved upon. As we have already shown in fig. 7, mining and quarrying increased their contribution to GDP from 4.38 per cent in 1960 to 11.33 per cent in 1970, though this dropped to 7.25 per cent in 1975 due mainly to the world-wide depression beginning in that year. One of the most remarkable developments during this period was the entry of four countries into the rank of major oil-exporters: Algeria, Gabon, Libya and Nigeria. In 1960, Africa produced only one per cent of the world output of crude petroleum; by 1975 it produced 11 per cent.

One of the features of mining resources development in Africa was its uneven distribution as between individual countries and as between the various sub-regions into which the continent can be divided. We have already listed the major producers of crude petroleum. We must add to this list countries such as Egypt, Tunisia, Congo and Angola, which though not major oil-exporters, were nevertheless producers. The two major producers of natural gas were Algeria and Nigeria, while (if we except South Africa) Morocco and Rhodesia were the major producers of coal. Iron ore was produced mainly in Algeria, Guinea, Liberia, Mauritania, Sierra Leone and Swaziland, while Zaire and Zambia were the main producers of copper. Nigeria, Rwanda and Zaire were the main producers of tin concentrate; Ghana, Guinea and Sierra Leone were the main bauxite-producing countries; Morocco, Tunisia and Zambia produced lead ore; Morocco, Zaire and Zambia, zinc ore; while phosphate rock came primarily from Morocco and Tunisia. Zaire was the largest producer of diamonds in developing Africa, followed by Ghana and Sierra Leone. And the gold-producing countries were Ghana and Zaire, although small quantities were produced in Ethiopia, Gabon and Zambia.

As can be seen from table 5.5, mining and quarrying expanded most rapidly in North and West Africa during the period 1960 to 1970. Between 1960 and 1965, mining development was at its peak, growing at an annual average rate of 38.5 and 21.7 per cent in North and West Africa respectively. The slow-down in the growth of this sector between 1965 and 1975 and more particularly during the last five years was due to a variety of factors, including lack of capital and know-how as foreign capitalists became more and more cautious about investing in Africa in view of the growing economic nationalism, which was manifesting itself in the various indigenisation policies and programmes being pursued by an increasing number of African countries. In some of these there was outright nationalisation. There was also the problem of depletion of reserves in a number of countries while in a few there was a policy of conservation. The slow-down in the annual rate of growth in output of many minerals was due to the rising unit cost of production.

The 1960s witnessed the beginning of a substantial expansion of mineral processing industries. This encompassed petroleum refining; cement production; fertiliser production; the smelting

Table 5.5. *Structure and growth of mining and quarrying in developing Africa by sub-region 1960–75.*

Sub-region	Contribution of mining to GDP at 1970 factor cost (per cent)				Annual rate of growth of mining (per cent)			
	1960	1965	1970	1975	1960–5	1965–70	1970–5	1960–75
North Africa	3.1	10.5	18.1	8.0	38.5	18.4	−9.6	15.8
West Africa	2.5	5.2	7.7	9.0	21.7	16.8	9.1	15.9
Central Africa	4.6	3.7	6.6	7.9	−2.1	18.3	12.1	9.4
Eastern Africa	7.8	6.0	6.2	1.9	−0.8	8.6	−16.9	−3.0
Total	4.4	7.5	11.3	7.3	17.0	14.8	−4.3	9.2

Source: Compiled from ECA national accounts computer print-outs, March 1977.

of tin, lead and aluminium; and the establishment of steel plants in a number of countries.

The industrial sector

While traditional handicrafts and artisan-type industries were deeply ingrained in the history of North Africa and a number of sub-Saharan countries, the development of factory production was a fairly recent phenomenon, having its origins in the 1920s and 1930s. This is true even of the Republic of South Africa, where manufacturing industries grew at a much higher rate than in any other African country. The delayed entry of Africa into in-dustrialisation resulted from the reluctance of colonial powers to encourage it in their colonies lest it compete with metropolitan industry.

During the war years, there was an inevitable interruption of supplies from the industrialised countries. This encouraged the manufacture of consumer goods in the colonies. The scarcity of shipping space during the war also encouraged the processing of bulky raw materials. And for strategic reasons, the metropolitan countries established branches of some industries in the colonies and thus gave further impetus to manufacturing. But it was not until after the war, and particularly during the pre-independence decade of the 1950s and the first post-independence decade, that industrialisation was pursued vigorously and in a persistent manner by the governments of the emerging African nations. By 1960, the share of manufacturing in the total GDP of developing Africa had risen to 10.17 per cent. Industrial growth during the period 1960–75 averaged 6.4 per cent. This rate while higher than the rate of growth of the economy as a whole, and higher also than the rates achieved in such sectors as agriculture, electricity and transport, was much lower than the rates recorded by mining and construction. By 1975, industry contributed almost 12 per cent of the total GDP. The value added by manufacturing increased from $US 3.13 billion in 1960 to $US 7.09 billion in 1975 as table 5.6 shows. But compared with the other regions of the world, industrial development lagged behind; Africa was only able to increase its share of world manufacturing output from 0.5 per cent in 1960 to 0.6 per cent in 1975.

What were the main features of the manufacturing sector in

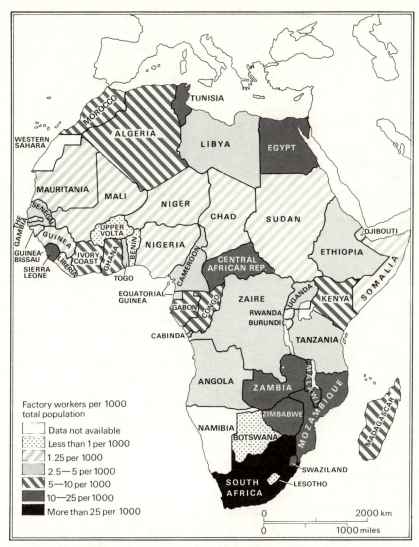

10 Factory workers as a proportion of the total population.
(Source: *Cambridge Encyclopaedia of Africa.*)

Africa during this period? First, there was the concentration of
industry in certain sub-regions and in certain countries. These
were countries which had a head start in industrialisation (like
Egypt) or had a high economic potential or mineral wealth (for
example, Nigeria and Algeria). Indeed, these three countries –
Egypt, Nigeria and Algeria – accounted for 41.7 per cent of

Table 5.6. *Some economic indicators of manufacturing industry in developing Africa by sub-region, 1960–75.*

	Value added by manufacturing (millions of $US)	Value added by manufacturing as percentage of total	Percentage of population	Percentage of GDP
1960				
North Africa	1690.5	54.0	25.9	37.1
West Africa	512.5	16.4	32.1	28.5
Central Africa	450.8	14.4	14.3	14.2
Eastern Africa	476.3	15.2	27.7	20.2
Total	3130.1	100.0	100.0	100.1
1975				
North Africa	3535.5	49.8	26.0	42.0
West Africa	1494.8	21.1	31.9	28.6
Central Africa	609.8	8.6	14.5	10.6
Eastern Africa	1453.3	20.5	27.6	18.8
Total	7093.4	100.0	100.0	100.0

Source: Compiled from ECA national accounts computer print-outs, March 1977.

developing Africa's total industrial output in 1975. And as is shown in table 5.7, these three countries together with seven others – Morocco, Zaire, Kenya, the Ivory Coast, Ghana, Zambia and Tunisia in that order – accounted for three-quarters of total African manufacturing output. The remaining 38 countries contributed barely 27 per cent of the total. Among these, 24 countries – half the total number of independent African countries in 1975, composed essentially of the least developed, land-locked or island countries – contributed less than 10 per cent. This imbalance in the distribution of industrial development is of course reflected sub-regionally. North Africa, with a quarter of Africa's total population and 37.1 per cent of its GDP, accounted for 54 per cent of its industrial output in 1960 and for 49.8 per cent in 1975.

Table 5.7. *Manufacturing value added (at factor cost in 1970 constant prices) in million $US.*

Country	1960 Amount	1960 Percentage of total African output	1975 Amount	1975 Percentage of total African output
Egypt	857	31.2	1180	16.8
Nigeria	184	6.7	1013	14.4
Algeria	210	7.6	738	10.5
Morocco	235	8.5	512	7.3
Zaire	246	8.9	509	7.3
Kenya	61	2.2	285	4.1
Ivory Coast	46	1.7	231	3.3
Ghana	61	2.2	222	3.2
Zambia	29	1.1	199	2.8
Tunisia	100	3.6	192	2.7
Total	2029	73.7	5081	72.4

Source: ECA Secretariat estimates, March 1977.

On the other hand, West Africa with almost a third of developing Africa's population and GDP accounted for only 16.4 and 21.1 per cent of its industrial output in 1960 and 1975 respectively. The relative shares of Central and eastern Africa were even smaller, if we except Rhodesia (Zimbabwe), which was of course still under white minority rule.

The second characteristic of African manufacturing output was its domination by light industry, although heavy industries increased their relative share significantly after 1960. Thus, whereas in 1960 the percentages of manufacturing value added by light and heavy industries were 77.5 and 22.5 respectively, the corresponding figures in 1975 were 60.2 and 39.8. Within the light industries group, food beverages and tobacco, textiles and clothing predominated and jointly accounted for 66.7 and 49.8 per cent of total industrial output in 1960 and 1975 respectively. The chemical and petro-chemical industry and basic metal industry represented only 12.3 per cent in 1960 and 21.6 per cent in 1975. Africa's share in the world output of metals and engineering products remained unchanged from 1955 to 1975 at 0.2 per cent. Of all developing regions, Africa had the lowest ratio of engineering production to engineering imports. The significance of this needs to be underlined. Engineering industries not only provide the means of production for themselves but also for virtually all other sectors. They serve not only as carriers of technology but also as the medium of technological invention and innovation. They contribute, possibly more than any other sector, to fostering labour, technical and management skills.

The third feature of industrialisation in Africa was that the industrial sector was composed of a heterogeneous collection of industrial products, many of which were of marginal significance for the achievement of self-sustaining growth. Industrialisation, rather than constituting an engine for growth in Africa, tended to accentuate the dualistic nature of the African economy. African governments had been led to believe that, through generous provisions of fiscal and other incentives combined with high protective duties, a dynamic and self-sustaining industrial sector would emerge. They therefore pursued an import-substituting industrialisation policy which more often than not depended on foreign capital, technology and skill with little or no backward and forward linkages with the agricultural and mining sectors, which were the backbone of the economy. Consequently, the heterogeneous industrial projects which were set up came to constitute islands of symbolic modernity surrounded by vast oceans of poverty and traditional agricultural sectors. Fortunately by the end of our period it was beginning to be recognised, if only slowly, that industry had an inner structural logic and that linkages within the industrial sector were as important to its vitality as linkages between it and the other sectors. An increasing number of governments had come to perceive that the importance of a sector depends not so much on its size as on its growth-promoting impact on other sectors.

The fourth characteristic feature of industrial development in the years 1960–75 was that these industries developed on a national scale. There were virtually no joint projects designed and implemented on the regional scale. As a result, most of the units set up served the local market and therefore had to operate in harmony with the size of that market, and experience its hazards and fluctuations, without being able to benefit from the economies of scale which characterise the production of the industrialised countries. The result was that a large number of industrial projects experienced difficulties, leading in most cases to prohibitive production costs and/or to poor uncompetitive quality with similar imported products.

Industrialisation in Africa proved a disappointment in spite of its relatively high rates of growth since independence. It did not bring about any reduction in the dependence of African countries on foreign countries. On the contrary – it contributed to the establishment of an industrial structure overly dependent on imported materials. Moreover, this policy did not encourage national savings nor prompt African entrepreneurs to enter the circuit of industrial investment since incentives provided were principally for the benefit of the foreign investor. The industrialisation pursued for most of this period was not part of an overall multi-sectoral strategy. It was not linked to agricultural and rural development, the main sector employing the largest section of the population and, as a result, it did not contribute to reducing the dualistic imbalances which characterised the African economy. Because the industrial projects were concentrated in the towns, industrialisation accelerated the process of urbanisation to the detriment of the rural sector and agricultural development. Some change in policy had taken place in the early 1970s, when an effort was made by some countries to establish industrial projects on a scale larger than the local market and oriented towards export. This was the case with the liquid or gaseous hydrocarbon industries; the agro-allied industries (textiles, leather, sugar, meat and oilseed processing); the construction industry; the ferrous and non-ferrous metals industry; and the wood industry (pulp and paper). Nevertheless Africa was by the end of 1975 still primarily exporting its raw materials and importing most of its requirements of manufactured goods.

Economic infrastructure

No country can develop properly without an adequate infrastructural support. Yet at independence all African countries were very short of social overhead capital. The economic and social infrastructures which they inherited were designed for a colonial type of administration which was concerned with the maintenance

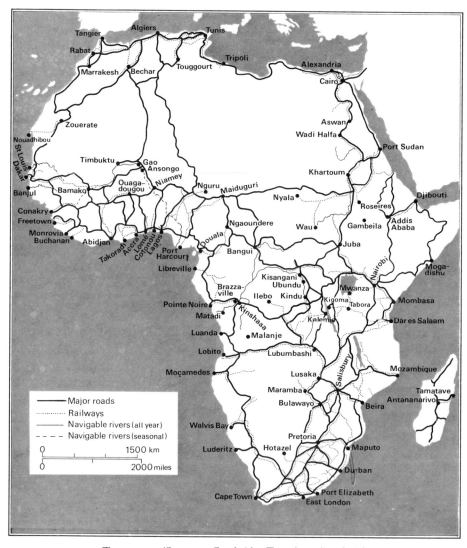

11 Transport. (Source: *Cambridge Encyclopaedia of Africa.*)

of law and order and the promotion of exports and imports. In the circumstances, therefore, the newly-independent countries had no alternative but to give priority attention to the development of their infrastructures. We shall presently concern ourselves with transport and communications; the social services will be considered later.

The total length (route kilometres) of African railways, exclud-

Table 5.8. *Transport and other economic indicators: percentage distribution of world totals, 1961.*

	Africa	South America	Europe (excl. USSR)	North America
Population	8.5	4.9	14.0	8.9
Area	22.5	13.2	3.7	18.0
Air transport capacity	2.0	5.0	23.0	62.0
Air traffic	2.3	5.3	24.0	60.0
Rail freight traffic	1.8	1.0	11.0	29.0
Commercial vehicles	2.9	4.8	24.0	55.0
Energy consumption	1.6	2.2	27.0	38.0
Gross domestic product (1958)	3.3	4.7	28.0	51.0

Source: UN *statistical yearbook.*

ing those in South Africa, is about 50000 km. If South African railways are included, it comes to about 73 000 km. In relation to the size of the continent these are very low figures. Indeed, the general impression of Africa's railway network is one of emptiness. In addition, the railways had different technical characters, such as gauges, couplings, brake systems and buffers and they were unconnected with one another. In Africa south of the Sahara, 76 per cent of the c. 60000 km of railroads were 3'6" gauge while about 20 per cent were of 1m gauge. In North Africa, on the other hand, over three-quarters of the 13 000 km of railroads were 4'8" (or standard) gauge, about 16 per cent were 1m gauge, while 8 per cent were 1.055m gauge (this being the 1320 km of line in the Republic of Algeria).

Because of the fragmentary composition of much of the railway system, road transport was of special importance, particularly as the scope of inland waterways was restricted to the comparatively few areas which have rivers and lakes navigable to anything larger than a canoe. Furthermore, few of the navigable rivers are navigable throughout the year. In 1963, developing Africa, excluding Angola and Mozambique, had a total mileage of 946 291 km of roads, less than 10 per cent of which were paved. The density of this network averaged 7.3 km per 100 km² which, even after due account has been taken of the great expanse of land occupied by deserts and therefore sparsely populated, was still very low. While, as in the case of the railways, there had been no attempt during the colonial period to build an all-African road system, unlike railroads there was no total isolation. There were highway links between neighbouring countries. But these were really *ad hoc* connexions rather than links in a planned system of regional or even sub-regional road networks. Thus road systems were essentially national and local in character.

Table 5.8 shows how relatively undeveloped Africa's transport system was at the beginning of the 1960s. Its share of world totals in air transport capacity, air traffic, rail freight traffic, and commercial vehicles was disproportionately smaller than its share of world population and land area while its share of the world transport system, using the above indices, was much smaller than its share of world income. This was also true of its share of energy consumption.

The social sector

We cannot end our analysis of structural and sectoral changes and trends without touching upon the all-important social sector – health, education, housing, water supplies – which in turn touches directly on the well-being of the citizens. Although for too long economists have been concerned with such quantitative parameters as GNP, income, savings, capital formation and per capita income as the indices for measuring economic progress, there is a growing feeling that these are far from being adequate in satisfactorily measuring the extent to which the human needs of the individuals are being met, particularly as there is no automatic policy relationship between any particular level or rate of growth of the GNP and improvement in such indicators as life expectancy, death rates, infant mortality, literacy, housing or water supplies. There has, therefore, recently been a search for a new kind of index, a Physical Quality of Life Index.

It is of course not difficult to understand or even appreciate why economists have favoured the easily quantifiable parameters in their measurement of progress. Social phenomena are not easily quantifiable and while social changes may be adopted as policy measures, the actual movement in the direction required may not be easily measurable except after a period of several years. Moreover, social conditions varied greatly from country to country and as a result any generalisation would in all probability be arbitrary and perhaps misleading. The following analysis is therefore limited to observable trends in social conditions.

African countries made great advances during the years between 1960 and 1975 in the social sectors in relation to what had been achieved in the colonial period. At the time of independence most of them had no more than very rudimentary social services. No country had well-established educational systems, health services or housing programmes. Indeed, many countries had only a handful of university graduates and only a few thousand high-school graduates. Pipe-borne water was a rarity and hospitals and health centres were few and far between. Even the schools which were established by the colonial administrations, or more usually by the Christian missionaries, were designed to produce clerks who were versed in the three Rs – arithmetic, writing and religious knowledge. Thus by 1960, countries such as the Gambia, Angola, Mali, Upper Volta, Mauritania, Somalia, Niger and Ethiopia – all of which are today classified as the most seriously affected by poverty and the least developed among the developing countries – had less than 10 per cent of their elementary school-age population enrolled in schools and less than 5 per cent of their secondary school-age population attending school. Indeed, by 1960 as many as 27 African states had less than a third of their primary school-age population enrolled, and almost all African states, particularly those south of the Sahara, had less than 8 per cent of their secondary school-age population enrolled. In 1960–1, the proportion of the population between the ages of 5 and 19 that was receiving formal education in Africa as a whole was only 16 per cent, compared with 44 per cent in South East Asia, 50 per cent in Latin America and 76 per cent in the Scandinavian countries. No comprehensive data are available with respect to the other services within the social sector, but the situation in these was hardly better. For example, a Colonial Office-sponsored economic survey of Nigeria in 1951 had this to report on health services:

Economic development is severely handicapped by the many health needs and problems of Nigeria. Outbreaks of relapsing and cerebro-spinal fevers are a serious problem in many of the Northern Provinces, and no province is entirely free from smallpox... Guinea worm infection prevails in many parts of the

North, and the incidence of yaws is widely spread throughout Southern Nigeria... Malaria is widespread... [1]

Thus, in evaluating performance during the period under review, it is important always to bear in mind the depths from which all African countries had to emerge in the social sector. And unfortunately, their task was not made easy by rapid increases in population. The estimated population of the continent in 1965 was about 220 million, or 8 per cent of the world's total. By 1975 it had increased to about 402 million, which represented about 10.1 per cent of the world population in that year. This represented an annual rate of increase of between 2.7 and 3.0 per cent, which was tending to rise. There is also the fact that Africa had the youngest age structure of any continent: over two-fifths of the population were below the age of 15. Thus, although there was phenomenal progress in absolute terms, relative to the needs of the rapidly increasing population the achievements were modest and in some countries even negative.

In the field of education, primary-school enrolments doubled between 1950 and 1964 for Africa as a whole; they increased fivefold after 1957 and fourfold after 1959. By 1963, the number of secondary-school pupils had increased by 2000 per cent over 1950; 700 per cent over 1957; and 500 per cent over 1959. Yet because of the high population growth rates and the age-structure, Africa was destined to continue for a long time to shoulder an unequalled enrolment burden.

Although marked improvements in health conditions were achieved between 1960 and 1975, health standards were still very low. The average death rate remained high at about 21 per 1000 and by the end of the period for most countries the average life expectancy was still under 50 years. The primary causes of morbidity and mortality were malnutrition, insanitary health environments, low health education and vector-borne disease. A long leeway still had to be made up by all states to increase the size of their medical and para-medical personnel. Although in most cases the situation greatly improved after the pre-independence decade – the improvement ranged from 2 per cent to 30 per cent over the figures for 1958 to 1960 – developments in different African states were uneven. Besides, the situation worsened in a

[1] Colonial Office, *An economic survey of the colonial territories, 1951 Vol. III. The West African territories* (London, HMSO, 1952).

number of states, for example Uganda and Ethiopia, due to a brain-drain caused by political upheavals.

One of the characteristic features of the African economy during this period was the rapid rate of urbanisation (see Chapter 4). Traditionally, Africans were country dwellers. Even around 1960, only 7–8 per cent of the population were living in towns of 100000 inhabitants and upwards. The proportion of urban population however varied from one sub-region to another, with North Africa being, by a very wide margin, the most urbanised, and East and southern Africa the least. After 1960 the annual rates of growth of urban population were consistently very much higher than the annual rates of growth of total population, and ranged from an average of 4.2 per cent to 15.5 per cent. By 1975, from 20 to 25 per cent of the people were living in urban areas. It must be added, however, that Africa remained the least urbanised of all the continents.

Rapid urbanisation put very severe pressures on such social services as housing, health and water supply. Housing conditions seem to have stagnated, if not deteriorated, during this period. For the whole continent the rate of increase in housing was approximately 3 units per 1000 people annually while basic needs were estimated at 10 to 13 units per 1000. The steeply rising costs of building materials aggravated the situation. In order to ameliorate the acute housing shortage, governments began to assume direct responsibility for providing housing, particularly low-cost housing, and giving incentives to private developers.

Although existing data are sketchy, there is enough evidence to show that the problems of open unemployment, underemployment and mass poverty assumed increasingly serious proportions. According to a recent International Labour Office estimate, unemployment and underemployment affected on the average 7.1 and 37.9 per cent of the total labour force respectively; that is to say, 45 per cent of the labour force was either openly unemployed or disguisedly unemployed. Little wonder Africa remained poor. For if we were to add to this figure the 44 per cent of the population below the age of 15 and therefore economically dependent, almost 240 million out of Africa's total population of 402 million in 1975 were contributing little or nothing to the GDP. Although a number of countries did embark on employment-creation programmes, on accelerated rural development, and on the restriction of migration of people without jobs from rural to urban areas, these proved no more than palliatives.

Income distribution is closely related to the problems of unemployment and underemployment. Empirical evidence on income distribution, scanty as it is, shows that inequalities worsened and were not significantly softened by social services and welfare benefits. The disadvantaged had very little opportunity for upward economic or social mobility owing to lack of employment and inadequate educational opportunities. According to a recent study by Adelman and Morris,[1] the poorest 40 per cent of the population received on average between 1965 and 1971 about 9 to 17 per cent of the national income, while the richest 20 per cent absorbed between 50 and 70 per cent. Still more striking, the richest 5 per cent of the population had between 17 and 34 per cent of the income. The implication of these estimates is very serious in terms of social justice (see Chapter 6). With per capita income being as low as it was in most African countries, and with the richest 20 per cent of the population having between 50 and 70 per cent of the total national income, it would seem that about 80 per cent of Africa's total population were around or below the poverty line; much of this poverty was to be found in the rural areas where most people still lived.

Sub-regional trends

To conclude this review of structural and sectoral changes let us examine very briefly any discernible sub-regional trends. The average annual growth rate of 4.9 for the years 1960–75 concealed large differences among the different sub-regions and groups of countries. The usual classification of Africa by region does not throw enough light onto the increasing economic disparity among African countries. In a recent assessment of trends and prospects[2] undertaken by the Economic Commission for Africa at the request of the UN General Assembly, as part of the study of long-term trends in the economic development of the regions of

---

[1] I. Adelman and C. T. Morris, *Economic growth and social equity in developing countries* (Stanford, 1973), 141–85.

[2] *Preliminary assessment of long-term development trends and prospects in developing Africa*, published by the UN Economic and Social Council as document E/5937/Add.3 of 29 March 1977, 7.

the world, African countries were classified into five economically more meaningful categories. There was, first, the group of major oil-exporters – Algeria, Gabon, the Libyan Arab Republic and Nigeria. The non-oil-exporting countries were classified into four groups on the basis of per capita income: $US 300–400; $US 200–300; $US 100–200; and below $US 100. Of the 41 non-oil-exporting countries on which data were available, five countries – Congo, the Ivory Coast, São Tomé and Principe, Tunisia and Zambia – belonged to the first per capita income category ($US 300–400); 11 countries – Cape Verde, Egypt, Equatorial Guinea, Ghana, Guinea-Bissau, Liberia, Mauritius, Morocco, Mozambique, Senegal and Swaziland – belonged to the second category ($US 200–300); another 11 countries – Botswana, the Central African Republic, the Gambia, Kenya, Madagascar, Mauritania, Sierra Leone, Sudan, Togo, Uganda and the United Republic of Cameroon – belonged to the $US 100–200 income-range group. The last group, with per capita incomes of below $US 100, consisted of 14 countries: Bénin, Burundi, Chad, Ethiopia, Guinea, Lesotho, Malawi, Mali, Niger, Rwanda, Somalia, the United Republic of Tanzania, Upper Volta and Zaire. The varying performance of these five groups of countries is most revealing (see table 5.9).

Whereas the four major oil-exporting countries and the five countries in the $US 300–400 group achieved average growth rates of 6.9 and 5.8 per cent per annum respectively between 1960 and 1975, the 14 countries whose per capita income was below $US 100 achieved only 2.6 per cent growth per annum. When due account is taken of population growth in these countries, this latter group achieved *no growth at all* on a per capita basis during the 15-year period; it is clear that their economies were declining. The 22 countries in the per capita income ranges of $US 100 to $US 300 achieved average growth of 4.1 per cent per annum, with a 1.4 per cent per annum increase in per capita income.

Table 5.9 provides data on the rate of growth of the 45 developing countries, first by geographical sub-region and, secondly, under the economically more meaningful classifications.

The performance of the different sectors of each group of countries is shown at table 5.10. The five non-oil-exporting countries proved through their performance that African countries did not have to wait for the discovery of crude petroleum before

Table 5.9. *Growth of real GDP in developing Africa, 1970*
(percentage per annum).

	1960–70	1970–5	1960–75
North Africa	5.6	6.1	5.8
West Africa	4.8	4.2	4.5
Central Africa (excluding S. Rhodesia)	3.2	2.9	3.1
East Africa	5.8	1.9	4.5
Total	5.0	4.5	4.9
Major oil-exporting countries (4)	6.9	7.0	6.9
Non-oil-exporting countries (41)	4.9	3.6	4.0
GDP less than $100 per capita	2.5	2.8	2.6
GDP $100 to under $200 per capita	4.3	3.8	4.1
GDP $200 to under $300 per capita	3.5	5.0	4.1
GDP $300 to $400 per capita	6.5	4.3	5.8

Source: Estimates from the Economic Commission for Africa.

Table 5.10. *Average growth rates by economic sector by groups of*
countries 1960–75 (percentage per year).

	Total GDP	Agriculture	Manufacturing	All industry	Services
Major oil-exporting countries	6.9	2.0	12.1	13.7	5.7
Non-oil-exporting countries	4.0	2.4	5.3	5.4	4.6
GDP less than $100 per capita	2.6	0.4	4.7	4.1	4.2
GDP $100 to under $200 per capita	4.1	2.7	6.6	5.5	5.7
GDP $200 to under $300 per capita	4.1	3.2	4.2	6.1	3.8
GDP $300 to under $400 per capita	5.8	4.0	9.7	4.8	7.3
Total	4.9	2.3	6.4	7.6	4.8

Source: Estimates from the Economic Commission for Africa.

development could get under way. For the region as a whole, the cumulative effect of this increasing disparity in economic performance among the different groups of countries is that a small number of countries would become increasingly economically dominant in Africa. We have already referred to the growing dominance of ten countries in the industrial sector. These countries, according to table 5.10, accounted for 72.4 per cent of Africa's total industrial output. In 1975, the four major oil-exporters accounted for 34.5 per cent of developing Africa's GDP; the five non-oil-exporting countries in the per capita income range of $US 300–400 accounted for 8.6 per cent; the 11 countries within the income range of $US 200–300 per capita accounted for 30.2 per cent; the other 11 countries within the per capita income range of $US 100–200 accounted for 13.6 per cent; and the 14 countries whose per capita income was below $US 100 accounted for 13.1 per cent. Thus nine countries shared between them 43.1 per cent of Africa's GDP in 1975 while 25 countries had only 26.7 per cent.

THE SEARCH FOR ECONOMIC INTEGRATION

As we have already emphasised, a principal legacy of colonialism in Africa was its consolidation of the continent into a number of politically distinct entities without regard to history and culture or political and economic viability. The colonial powers concentrated on forging vertical economic links between their metropoles and their dependencies rather than horizontal links among the colonies. They consistently discouraged the latter unless it served an imperial purpose. Yet paradoxically the genesis of economic integration is to be found in the policies of the colonial powers.

In East Africa, Kenya and Uganda formed a customs union as far back as 1917 and these two were joined by Tanganyika ten years later. Although this was designed to protect and further the interests of the white settlers in Kenya, it was also intended to give the three territories the benefit of economies of scale in the provision, improvement and administration of infrastructural facilities such as railways, roads, ports, and posts and telecommunications. In 1947 this common-market arrangement was developed into an institution for the administration of these infrastructural facilities – the East Africa High Commission. As the three countries approached independence, this arrangement encountered growing difficulties. With the independence of Tanganyika in 1961, the East African High Commission was replaced by the East African Common Services Organisation (EACSO). This was in turn replaced by the East African Community (EAC) with which we shall deal later.

The establishment of the Federation of Rhodesia and Nyasaland in 1953 had similar objectives to the East African High Commission – the protection of the economically dominant group, the white settlers. The only difference between the East African and the Central African approaches was that in the case of the latter the British colonial power was persuaded by the settlers that those interests were better served not merely through the economic integration of the three but also through their political integration. This gave the white settlers of the two Rhodesias the possibility of establishing economic and political hegemony over the three countries. Because of African opposition, the federation had a very short existence and fell apart in 1964. The common services were split up in 1963, ten years after they had been established.

The British dependences in West Africa were not contiguous; they were separated from one another by French colonies and Liberia. There were no settler interests to protect and therefore no compelling reason to set up a common market or customs union, or even a common services arrangement. However, in order to minimise the cost of administration, these countries had certain services in common, for example a common currency and a common income-tax policy, common research institutions and even a common school examination institution – the West African Examinations Council. The British High Commission territories of Bechuanaland (Botswana), Swaziland and Basutoland (Lesotho) were joined with South Africa, by which the last was surrounded, in a customs regime in 1910 with common external tariffs against third countries and with free movement of labour, capital, currency and goods.

The French organised their tropical African colonies into two administrative areas, French West Africa and French Equatorial Africa, as a means of establishing the most effective control. Each of these administrative areas was a kind of federation with appropriate federal institutions, a monetary system and a common policy in trade. Each federation had powers of taxation and all French financial assistance was channelled through it. The currencies of the two federations were freely transferable among the constituent colonies of the other federation with a par value being maintained with the metropolitan franc. They were also transferable to the Trusteeship Territories of Cameroun and Togo, as well as Madagascar and French Somaliland. These arrangements did not survive independence because France chose to grant independence not to each federation but to the constituent colonies.

The Belgians united their Trust Territory of Ruanda-Urundi with the Belgian Congo not only for the purposes of administrative convenience but also as a *de facto* common market. There was free movement of capital and labour and currency. With the approach of independence the Ruanda-Urundi Union split into two separate independent states, Rwanda and Burundi, and entered on a separate economic existence from the independent Congo (Zaire).

Although virtually all the economic groupings which were set up during the colonial period failed to survive colonialism, during this period the nationalists from all parts of Africa had advocated African integration and unity as the only means of bringing about self-rule and self-determination. The Fifth Pan-African Congress held in Manchester in 1945, for instance, recommended *inter alia* the establishment of a West African economic union as a means of combating the exploitation of the economic resources of the West African territories and for ensuring the participation of the indigenous people in the industrial development of West Africa. The Bandung Declaration of 1955 also urged economic cooperation among the African countries.

In 1958, a year after the Gold Coast had achieved independence as Ghana, the first conference of the leaders of political parties in Africa was held in Accra. This conference decided to establish a permanent organization, the All-African Peoples' Conference, among whose objectives was the promotion of intra-African trade through the removal of customs and other trade restrictions, the conclusion of multilateral payments agreements designed to facilitate intra-African trade, the formation of an African Transport Company for land, sea and air transportation; the setting up of an African Common Market; the creation of an African

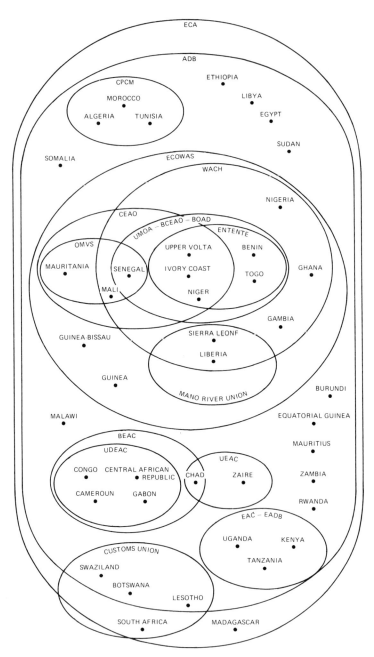

12 Regional and sub-regional organisations for cooperation and integration. (Source: UNCTAD, TD/B/609/Add.1 (vol. III).)

Investment Bank; and, the setting up of an African Institute for Research and Training whose primary task would be to promote the development of joint projects.

In 1960, the conference held its second meeting in Tunis where the recommendations of the first conference were endorsed. This was followed a year later by a third meeting held in Cairo. In the post-independence period, many meetings were held on the issue of economic cooperation and development. The United Nations Economic Commission for Africa, which was established in 1958, made determined efforts to foster economic cooperation among African states. From the beginning of the 1970s, particularly since the United Nations General Assembly passed the resolution in December 1972 calling for the developing nations themselves to take concrete action to promote technical cooperation, a series of sub-regional, regional and inter-regional meetings was held on the subject of cooperation, each meeting ending with a declaration and/or a programme of action.

It would be tedious to list all the declarations and pronouncements on the intention to cooperate. One thing that was clear was that the African states and, before independence, the nationalists, were not wanting in the right intentions. Yet, not only did they fail to build on the foundations laid by the colonial powers, whatever the motives of the latter, but they failed to achieve any significant breakthrough after independence.

Key to fig. 12

ADB	The African Development Bank
BEAC	Bank of Central African States
BOAD	West African Development Bank
CEAO	West African Economic Community
CPCM	Maghrib Permanent Consultative Committee
EAC	East African Community
EADB	East African Development Bank
ECA	United Nations Economic Commission for Africa
ECEAO	Central Bank of West African States
ECOWAS	Economic Community of West African States
ENTENTE	Council of the Entente States
OMVS	Organisation for the Development of the Senegal River
UDEAC	Central African Customs and Economic Union
UEAC	Union of Central African States
UMOA	West African Monetary Union
WACH	West African Clearing House

Judging from the number of economic groupings which have been established since 1960 (see fig. 12) one would be tempted to think that there had indeed been a breakthrough in economic cooperation and integration. According to an ECA directory of inter-governmental cooperation organisations in Africa, there were, in 1975, 6 economic communities, 20 inter-governmental multi-sectoral economic organisations and about 100 single-sector multi-national organisations meant to promote technical and economic cooperation in the continent. All these organisations had a chequered history; some were virtually moribund while others were no more than paper tigers. A few were earnestly trying to become effectively operational.

Why were the efforts at fostering economic cooperation in Africa not successful? To answer this question satisfactorily we would have to examine fully and in detail each economic grouping. All we can do here is highlight some of the major problems and issues involved.

The constraints facing economic cooperation in Africa were either internally generated or externally induced. The major internally-generated constraints included, first, the difficulty of agreeing on a formula for sharing the benefits and cost of economic cooperation; secondly, the over-sensitivity concerning national sovereignty; thirdly, the inadequacy of infrastructure and the absence of an appropriate institutional framework to promote economic cooperation; fourthly, differences in political ideology; and, finally, ambivalence in attitudes towards economic co-operation.

A series of under-capacities – inadequate physical infrastructure and lack of enabling institutional facilities – constituted the principal hurdles to effective regional cooperation. The real constraints were generated by the limited range of modern transport and communication links among member states. In the colonial period there was, of course, no intra-African clearing house arrangement nor a common currency and payments arrangement to facilitate commercial transactions, let alone the multi-national development institutions with the capacity for project identification, preparation, investment promotion and consultancy services in industrial and commercial ventures. These capacities are, however, the real nuts and bolts in the vehicle of multi-national economic cooperation, without which the latent power in the engine will not lead to forward movement. In this connexion, the Economic Commission for Africa tried to develop, in cooperation with African governments, physical infrastructural capacities on a continent-wide basis. Accordingly, plans were initiated for the development of a network of five trans-African highways: trans-Saharan roads from Algiers to Gao and Arlit and to Lagos; a trans-African highway from Dakar to Ndjamena; a coastal highway from Lagos to Nouakchott; and a trans-East African highway from Cairo to Gaborone. The Commission, in collaboration with the International Telecommunication Union and the OAU, established in 1963 the Pan-African Telecommunication Union (Panaftel) whose task was to develop a Pan-African telecommunications network.

In the years after independence, strong differences in political ideologies with consequential differences in economic organisation and policy appeared among different African countries. For example, the failure of the East African Community was due in part to the fact that Tanzania had a socialist ideology while Kenya followed the capitalist pattern. Furthermore, by and large the multi-national corporations had little sympathy with the aspirations for economic progress of African countries, but were only interested in protecting and extending the markets which they had dominated during the colonial era and maximising and repatriating profits for their metropolitan shareholders.

Finally, there was the constraint imposed by the failure of political initiatives and declared collective goodwill to be marked by concomitant practical action. In most African states there did not exist institutional arrangements and administrative machinery adequately equipped to translate collective declarations and political goodwill into operational development programmes and projects. More serious was the tendency for actions at national levels to be completely at variance with declarations in international forums and for some high-ranking public officials to allow themselves to be used as pawns on the chessboard of international power politics, thus delaying the economic progress of their own people.

Of course it can be argued that this dichotomy between internally generated and externally induced constraints is unrealistic, in that extra-African factors played direct and indirect roles in influencing the intensity, extent and direction of the operation of internally generated constraints, at individual country level. But Africa was still powerfully oriented to the outside world. And even more striking, it was still conditioned by strong attachment to pre-independence political, economic, social and cultural relations. This orientation and this attachment inhibited the development of concepts, policies and instruments essential for engineering the kind of domestic socio-economic change on which self-sustaining growth and self-reliance could be based and on which effective regional and sub-regional cooperation could be built. It was difficult, if not impossible, to achieve a significant measure of self-reliance, national and collective, while governments ran externally oriented and excessively open economies.

AFRICA AND THE INTERNATIONAL ECONOMY

Economic development was conceived in colonial Africa in terms of production for export and in terms of investment, technology and skilled personnel coming from overseas. Africa's dependence on the international economy, particularly that of the metropolitan countries, was almost complete. Indeed, the prevailing conventional wisdom during the colonial period supported this view. It linked the rate and direction of colonial socio-economic change with production for export and with the importation of skills, technology and capital goods and services and modern consumer goods. Thus, foreign trade was regarded as the prime engine of growth and development in the developing countries.

Foreign trade remained critically important to independent African governments, if they were ever to be in a position to maintain public services and attempt to fulfil their pre-independence promises. Yet in 1960, when so many African countries became independent, the values of Africa's imports and exports as percentages of world imports and exports were only 6 and 5.1 per cent respectively. Excluding South Africa, the figures were 4.8 and 4.1 per cent.

During the period 1960–75, Africa experienced phenomenal increases in its external trade. As is shown in fig. 13, the value of exports increased from $US 4920 million in 1960 to $US 33 012 million in 1975 – an increase by 6.7 times. Imports also increased 5.7 times in value during the period. In terms of volume, the exports of developing Africa increased annually at the average rate

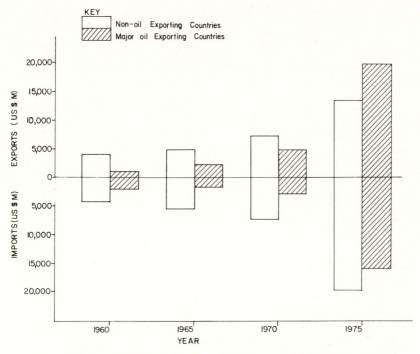

13   Exports and imports by groups of countries in developing Africa (excluding Angola and Rhodesia), 1960–75 (in million $ US) (United Nations, *Monthly Bulletin of Statistics*, various issues to Sept. 1976; IMF, *International Financial Statistics*, Dec. 1976).

of 4.5 per cent whereas the imports increased at the rate of 6.2 per cent during the same period. It will be recalled that during this period GDP increased on average at 4.9 per cent per annum. In other words, the growth rate of imports was about one percentage point higher than the growth rate of GDP. In annual values, as indicated in fig. 13, the non-oil-exporting countries achieved average cumulative increases of 8.3 per cent and 10.8 per cent for exports and imports respectively with the result that a very large trade gap developed for this group of countries over the period. Their deficit on external trade rose from $US 0.2 billion in 1960 to $US 6.3 billion in 1975. The major oil exporters turned their deficit of $US 1.1 billion in 1960 into a trade surplus of $US 3.8 billion in 1975.

Table 5.11 provides details of the growth rates of exports and imports by giving the annual averages for each five-year period

Table 5.11. *Average annual growth rates of export and import volume, by groups of non-oil-exporting countries, 1960–75 (percentage).*

	1960–5	1965–70	1970–5	1960–75
Exports				
GDP less than $100 per capita	−2.1	8.0	−6.0	−0.1
GDP $100 to under $200 per capita	6.8	4.1	−1.8	2.9
GDP $200 to under $300 per capita	2.6	2.6	4.3	3.2
GDP $300 to under $400 per capita	8.0	8.6	−0.3	5.3
Imports				
GDP less than $100 per capita	4.5	8.2	−1.4	3.8
GDP $100 to under $200 per capita	6.3	5.6	0.8	4.2
GDP $200 to under $300 per capita	5.5	1.3	9.5	5.4
GDP $300 to under $400 per capita	5.8	7.0	4.4	5.7

Sources: Estimates from the Economic Commission for Africa, based on data in the United Nations *Monthly bulletin of statistics* and International Monetary Fund, *International financial statistics*, various issues.

since 1960. The table shows that the annual growth rates of exports and imports from 1960 to 1975 increased as per capita GDP increased, and that the growth rate of imports was higher for each group of countries than for exports. At the lowest level (i.e. in the 14 countries with per capita GDP under $US 100 in 1970), the gap between the annual average growth rates of exports and imports was particularly marked. Exports failed to increase in volume for this group of countries during the period whereas imports rose by 3.8 per cent per annum. It should be noted that this group of countries included most of the countries of Africa hardest hit by drought in the years 1973 and 1974, and that by 1975 recovery of agricultural and livestock production was far from being complete. Finally, the export performance of all groups of countries, except those with per capita GDP of $US 200

Table 5.12. *Imports and exports by provenance or destination 1960–75 (percentages).*

Provenance or destination	Imports				Exports			
	1960	1965	1970	1975	1960	1965	1970	1975
Developed market economies	82	85	81	85	84	89	88	84
Developing market economies	11	8	13	10	10	5	5	10
Centrally planned economies	7	7	6	6	6	6	7	6
World	100	100	100	100	100	100	100	100

Source: UN, *Monthly bulletin of statistics*, IMF Directory of Trade.

to $US 300, was particularly disappointing during the first half of the 1970s.

The direction of Africa's trade did not undergo any significant change after 1960 as table 5.12 clearly shows. The principal trading partners of the region were countries with developed market economies. Chief among these were the members of the European Economic Community (EEC) which accounted for approximately 57 per cent of the trade of the region over the period, i.e. 55 per cent of imports and 58 per cent of exports. However, it should be observed that there was a steady relative decline in trade with EEC countries, particularly as regards export, in favour of the United States, the Latin-American Free Trade Association countries and Japan.

With regard to the patterns of trade some significant structural changes took place in exports particularly during the last ten years (1965–75). The most significant change was the rapid increase in the relative importance of exports of mineral fuels, lubricants and related materials and, to a lesser extent, of imports of machinery and transport equipment. The former increased from 19 per cent of total exports in 1965 to 55 per cent in 1975, while the latter increased from 31 per cent of total imports in 1966 to 39 per cent

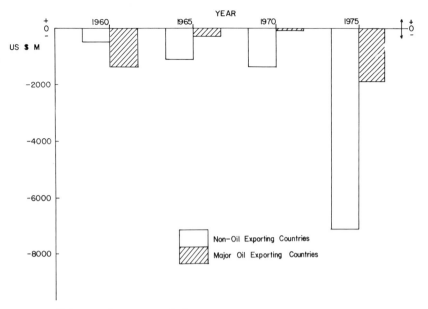

14   Balance of payments deficits on goods and services by groups of countries in developing Africa, 1960–75 (in million $ US). Note that the data for 1960 are much more unreliable than those for later years. (Estimates from the ECA.)

in 1975. On the other hand, the share of external trade attributed to food, drink and tobacco, and to exports both of manufactured goods and inedible raw materials, apart from fuels, declined considerably over the period. The net result of all these changes was that mineral fuel, lubricants and related materials became the most important group of exports in place of other crude inedible materials. These declined in importance to a level below that of foodstuffs, which continued to account for the second place in the share of total exports. Machinery and transport equipment continued throughout the period to be the most important group of imports, followed by manufactured goods. On the whole there was no significant change in the pattern of imports during the period under review.

   Let us now complete our review of Africa and the international economy by looking at the balance-of-payments situation from 1960 to 1975. As shown in fig. 14, the overall deficit for goods and services rose from $US 1970 million in 1960 to $US 9532 million in 1975. While there was little change in the deficit of the

Table 5.13. *Net transfers and net capital in-flows for oil-exporting and non-oil-exporting African countries (1960–75).*

	1960	1965	1970	1975
		(in million $US)		
(a) Net transfers				
Non-oil-exporting countries	135	224	735	2780
Major oil-exporters	210	191	252	69
Total	345	415	987	2849
(b) Net capital in-flows				
Non-oil-exporting countries	680	824	957	4477
Major oil-exporters	850	300	417	483
Total	1530	1124	1374	4960

Source: ECA Secretariat estimates, March 1977.

oil-exporting countries – it increased from $US 1400 million in 1960 to $US 1862 million in 1975 – the deficits of the non-oil-exporting countries increased from a mere $US 570 million in 1960 to $US 7670 million in 1975. In fact, for the poorest among this group of countries, the deficit rose from virtually nothing in 1960 to $US 1560 million in 1975. Although the level of deficit on goods and services account increased in the non-oil-exporting countries between 1960 and 1970, there was a very small limited rise in the size of the deficit between 1970 and 1975.

These deficits were covered by increasing in-flows of public transfers and capital, some rise in net receipts of private transfers and a running down of net foreign reserves. For example, the reserves of the non-oil-exporters fell by $US 410 million in 1975, while those of the major oil-exporters fell by $US 1310 million in the same year. The increase in the in-flows of net transfers and the level of the net capital in-flows since 1960 were as shown in table 5.13. Thus, the sharply-increased flows of resources into African countries, particularly during the 1970s, helped to contain the balance-of-payments problems. But it also increased their debt burdens to virtually unbearable proportions.

We must now turn to the role of foreign aid and investment in Africa's development. We have already noted the paucity of aid during the colonial period since the colonies were, in general, required to pay for themselves up until the Second World War. And private foreign investment was limited to mine development, plantations, and in some colonies, railways. The Second World War brought a fundamental change in the flow of aid and foreign investment. The establishment of the World Bank gave a fillip to this trend.

True enough, it was the urgency of reconstruction and rehabilitation in Europe after that war that pointed to the need for increased assistance to the developing countries. When the charter of the World Bank was drafted in 1944, it was in the hope that the Bank would be 'the principal instrument for restoring the war–torn nations of the world to economic life'. In 1946–7, the Bank's annual report confirmed that the most pressing calls upon the Bank were 'for purposes of reconstructing the war-damaged nations of Europe'. The same report, however, forecast that it would not be very long before the financing of development projects in the developing countries would tend to become the primary concern of the Bank. By June 1952, the Bank had granted a total of $US 1382 million as loans. Africa received only 9 per cent ($US 125 million). Out of this, $US 58 million was for electric power generation in Southern Rhodesia and the Union of South Africa, $US 20 million for the expansion of transportation facilities in the Union of South Africa – a total of 62 per cent – and $US 40 million or another 32 per cent for development programmes in the Belgian Congo. These three countries thus had nearly 95 per cent of total World Bank loans to the Africa region. By June 1958, the region received nearly 13 per cent of the total loans ($US 479 million). As much as 91 per cent of the loans to the African region were for electric power and transportation facilities. The Union of South Africa and the Federation of Rhodesia and Nyasaland again had the lion's share of the loans – about 63 per cent – while the Belgian Congo had 17 per cent. By 1966, total World Bank loans and International Development Association (IDA) credits to Africa (excluding the Union of South Africa) had reached $US 1224 million; IDA credits being $US 145 million. By 1970, World Bank loans had increased by $US 693 million and IDA credits by $US 403 million.

Official assistance, both financial and technical, also increased. Other developed countries besides the colonial powers began to give assistance to the developing countries. With the achievement of independence by the African territories, colonial funds gave way to bilateral assistance. At the end of 1961, the Development Assistance Committee (DAC) was organised by the aid-giving countries as a forum for consultation. The members of the committee soon provided most of the financial and technical assistance to the developing countries. By 1970, both the bilateral and the multilateral assistance to the continent (excluding the Union of South Africa) had expanded considerably.

From the data given in the *1976 Review of development co-operation* (OECD), total resource flows from the DAC countries and multilateral agencies increased from $US 3446 million in 1971 to $US 5160 million in 1974 and $US 8111 million in 1975. Total private flows, therefore, increased from $US 580 million in 1972 to $US 790 million in 1974 and $US 2680 million in 1975.

Resources were also made available by both the socialist and the OPEC countries. The annual commitment of bilateral development assistance from Centrally Planned Economies varied between $US 200 million and $US 400 million in the 1960–1 period, except in 1964 when it jumped to $US 870 million and 1962, 1966 and 1969 when it was less than $US 60 million. It is estimated that the commitment in 1972–4 was about $US 500 million a year. The financial assistance received from the OPEC countries became substantial after 1973. It is estimated to have been $US 587 million in 1973, $US 2167 million in 1974 and $US 2666 million in 1975, a total of $US 5420 million. But it did not offset oil price rises, and not all countries benefited from it.

Africa received much foreign assistance, both financial and technical. As shown in table 5.14, the external public debt of the developing countries of Africa south of the Sahara increased three-and-a-half times between 1967 and 1974. Even though suppliers' credit only doubled, private bank credit increased tremendously, especially after 1973 when official bilateral debt more than tripled and multilateral debt increased five-fold. As a result of the rapid increase of private resource flows in 1975, the DAC countries were able to achieve the target of 1.0 per cent of their GNP for total resource flows. Considering that most rapid increases took place after 1970, and that the greatest increase was in private resource flows, the debt service payments rose sharply and would thereafter continue to rise. Debt service payments

Table 5.14. External public debt classified by type of creditor, Africa south of the Sahara, 1967–74: amount in $US million (percentage in brackets).

	Total	Official		Private		
		Bilateral	Multilateral	Suppliers' credit	Banks	Others
1967	4629(100)	2261(48.8)	770(16.6)	737(15.9)	45(3.1)	716(15.5)
1968	5331(100)	2549(47.8)	939(17.6)	869(16.3)	206(3.9)	768(14.4)
1969	5884(100)	2789(47.4)	1241(21.1)	800(13.6)	245(4.2)	808(13.7)
1970	7327(100)	3666(50.0)	1628(22.2)	957(13.1)	292(4.0)	783(10.7)
1971	8345(100)	4304(51.6)	1929(23.1)	1118(13.4)	364(4.4)	631(7.6)
1972	9555(100)	4763(49.8)	2406(25.1)	1173(12.3)	638(6.7)	575(6.0)
1973	12582(100)	5923(47.1)	3295(26.2)	1327(10.5)	1653(13.1)	384(3.1)
1974	15957(100)	7349(46.1)	4019(25.2)	1599(10.0)	2640(16.5)	350(2.2)

Source: World Bank: Annual report, 1976.

increased four-fold between 1967 and 1973 with a great jump between 1972 and 1973, and these were only amortisation and interest payments.

Figures for total capital out-flow, including repatriation of profits and income, tell a different story. The out-flow of financial resources in the form of private transfers and payment for services for non-oil-producing developing African countries was substantially greater than capital in-flow in 1969, 1970 and 1973 while in 1971 and 1972 the out-flow and in-flow were about equal. The conclusion which emerges from this is very disturbing though not surprising. Aid to Africa was becoming increasingly more apparent than real. Looked at broadly, capital investment was coming to mean a recycling and extension of financial claims by foreign creditors on African resources without any net transfer of real value into Africa taking place. This was the cause of the growing demand for rescheduling of debt payments which reached a pitch at the Fourth Conference of the UN Conference on Trade and Development held in Nairobi in 1976. And that is why the action taken in 1977 by the Swedish and Canadian governments in writing off the debts owed to them by the most seriously affected states was welcomed. But these were mere palliatives. They did not solve the basic problems facing the African countries. In addition, much of the foreign aid was tied, with the donors stipulating that it must be used to purchase goods and services from their own countries. This could preclude the recipient countries from purchasing from low-cost suppliers and from developing economic relations that were in their best national interest. In particular, it tended to discourage economic and trade links with neighbouring countries and thereby hampered measures aimed at economic cooperation as well as links with the other developing regions where more suitable technology was available. Foreign loans thus had a substantial cost; the cost relating to repayment or amortisation and interest payment, the cost relating to foreign exchange for the service payment, as well as the cost arising from the restrictions placed on the ways in which aid could be used. Many countries were forced to borrow in order to be able to meet these increasing costs; so the loans and the repayments increased in a spiral.

CONCLUSION

We observed that the governments of the newly independent states were all determined to play a direct and pervasive role in the development process, and that through the United Nations the international community encouraged massive government involvement in development through the adoption of comprehensive planning. But in spite of all efforts by governments to accelerate the rate of progress, analysis of the economic evolution of Africa since 1940 has shown that no fundamental changes took place after independence. Indeed, the revolution of rising expectations which manifested itself among the masses at independence was overtaken by rising frustrations which were surfacing all over the continent, and which were potentially disturbing to political and social peace. There was no gainsaying the fact that Africa was facing an economic crisis of great portent which was rapidly assuming alarming proportions.

Why did government involvement in the development effort generally yield such disappointing results? Why did development planning fail to bring about the same fundamental and rapid transformation which it achieved in some centrally planned socialist economies? The answers to these questions are to be found partly in the planning techniques inherited from the industrialised market economies; partly in African policy-makers' perception of economic policy and the process of engineering socio-economic change; and partly also in the international community's conventional wisdom about the process of economic development, as was reflected in the objectives and targets set down for the First and Second UN Development Decades.

Early development planning, in the late 1950s and early 1960s, was limited to plans for government capital expenditure, or project-oriented plans, prepared within a framework of stated objectives which were in most cases limited to the provision of infrastructure, to capital investment in social services and to the expansion of agricultural production for export. A varying degree of comprehensive planning was later adopted by a growing number of countries. By 1968, upwards of 30 African countries had adopted development planning. Of 25 of these countries whose plans have been analysed, 9 countries had project plans, 13 countries made use of national accounts data and included sectoral analysis within a macroframework, while three countries made use of formal models. Planning was already becoming increasingly elaborate.

The hopes entertained in these plans were not realised.

Very few countries were able to achieve more than 70 per cent of the objectives set out in their development plans. Even fewer achieved a growth rate higher than the 5 per cent per annum set as a target for the First Development Decade. Nor, from the experience of those countries for which the appropriate data were available, could it be concluded that growth depended solely or mechanically on capital investment.

Apart from the fact that there was no unified approach to development, success was retarded by the inherited theories of development and economic growth which provided the intellectual basis from which African technocrats and policy-makers derived public policies. These theories, or at least some of them, linked the rate and direction of internal socio-economic change with export markets and with imports of skills, technology and capital goods and services and modern consumer products. Hence discussions centred on trade gaps, with insufficient attention to natural resources availability, local entrepreneurship, skilled manpower and technology and the domestic market. Most governments, in seeking to put these theories into practice and to accelerate economic development and diversify their economies, reinforced the existing pattern of production, exportation, and the import of factor inputs from abroad.

By continuing to produce what the international system wanted and not what they themselves needed, the dependence of African countries on the international community was increased and their capacity for self-reliance was reduced. Instability in export volumes, prices and export proceeds became a regular feature of the mono-cultural economies of most states. Unfortunately, African policy-makers thought that the solution to their excessive dependence – for such things as employment, foreign-exchange earnings, government revenue – on one or two export crops, was to pursue a policy of diversifying the production of agricultural export commodities. In a few years, this policy resulted in a greater number of agricultural export commodities in surplus supply in the 'world' market – the industrialised countries. This led to greater instability which was in turn worsened by inflation and periodic recessions in the industrialised countries, and rising payments to factor incomes abroad.

Multi-national arrangements for commodity management and price stabilisation were then sought as solutions to the growing price instability and worsening terms of trade for primary commodities. Experience, however, quickly revealed the limitations of this policy; first, because of the high cost involved; second, because many products concerned were susceptible to quality deterioration; third, because non-members (and even members) driven by necessity undermined the pricing formula by increasing production and selling below the price floor agreed upon by participants; and, finally, because of the intransigence of the industrialised countries which put one obstacle after another in the way of the successful conclusion of commodity agreements and, where such agreements were concluded, of their effective operation.

After more than two to three decades of negotiation between producers and consumers, agreements had been concluded on only six commodities – coffee, tin, cocoa, olive oil, sugar and wheat – and these were operated with varying degrees of success. This lack of success did not persuade developing countries to undertake an agonising reappraisal of their development strategies with a view to making a break from the past.

It would be wrong to conclude that because of this rather sombre picture, African governments failed altogether in their efforts to accelerate the development process. True enough, many of them made avoidable mistakes, most of them tended to behave as if the economic well-being of their people would be much advanced by symbolic modernisation, because of their politically motivated desire for convincing people that something was in fact being done. But the real cause of the disappointing results was that these governments and their advisers were ignorant of the dynamics of development in their own societies and simply extrapolated the experiences of other societies to their own. Besides, they failed to ask the fundamental question: development for what and for whom? They pursued the line of least resistance by continuing with inherited policies based on inherited theories.

CHAPTER 6

SOUTHERN AFRICA

In southern Africa, as in Ireland, history is formidably active in politics. What people believe about their past has been both a consequence and a cause of conflict, and also a source of political energy. People are not chess pieces. Their next move depends not only on where they are in relation to others but also on how they got there, and on how they *think* they got there. No matter how loaded it may be, the historical luggage which people carry in their heads, and in their school textbooks, is an important fact.

Such luggage is generally of three types. One is the moving symbol with which men seek 'to rally support for themselves or some cause, or to maintain a distinction'.[1] Secondly there is the searing event which has happened recently enough for many people to have experienced it themselves, or to have grown up in homes where parents or grandparents were still affected by its having happened to them. Thirdly there is the political myth whose supposed happening is used to justify certain political beliefs or actions. All three types of luggage are carried about everywhere but their weight, both relative and absolute, varies in different societies at different times. In southern Africa in the 1930s there was an abundance of such luggage although not everybody carried the same pieces.

For blacks the most important historic event was the loss of

Most of the facts and ideas contained in this chapter have been acquired over the years from my family, friends and colleagues. A few of the debts owed to the writing and conversation of others are acknowledged in footnotes and the bibliographical essay. I learned much from the opportunity of testing out ideas with colleagues at seminars in Cape Town, Stellenbosch and at the School of International Studies, Jawaharlal Nehru University, New Delhi. It was my good fortune that, during the writing of this chapter, another member of the family was preparing for publication the autobiography of Z. K. Matthews. Two fellow South Africans of my own generation, whose incisive criticism during the writing of this chapter I should particularly like to acknowledge, are Neville Alexander and the late Steve Biko. Many other friends were also generous with their time and their insights.

[1] Monica Wilson, 'Changing lines of cleavage', in Meyer Fortes and Sheila Patterson (eds.), *Studies in African social anthropology* (London, 1975), 51.

land to white conquerors. The hundred-year war in the eastern Cape, in Natal and elsewhere, culminating in the Land Act of 1913 which prohibited Africans from buying land outside the residual reserves was a bitter memory. So too for Herero and others in Namibia was the history of German annexation in 1884 and the subsequent thirty years of brutal conquest. Swazi remembered the signing away of their land to white settlers. In Lesotho the loss of the fertile Caledon plains to the burghers of the Orange Free State was tempered by the impregnability of Moshweshwe's mountain fortress. The skill of the old warrior-king retained honour, but not enough land, for his people.

Paradoxically it was this century of black defeat and dispossession which was also to be seen by South Africa's white rulers as their own dark vale. Smuts himself shifted from his early views but his people did not move with him. Dunbar Moodie has shown[1] how the hundred years from 1815 to 1914 became for the purified Afrikaner nationalists of the 1930s the sacred century. The Great Trek, the battle of Blood River, the concentration camps of the Anglo-Boer war, the humiliating poverty which uprooted them from the land, and Lord Milner's anglicisation policy were seen as a period of redemptive suffering at the hands of twin foes: the imperialist British with their capitalist tentacles, and the black 'heathens' in whose midst the chosen people had been set down and from whom God was miraculously rescuing them.

For another group of South Africans the important luggage consisted of the agonies of indenture in the latter half of the nineteenth century when their grandfathers had been shipped to Natal to work in the sugar plantations of the English-speaking settlers. But there was also some less burdensome history: the epic period – between 1893 and his departure from South Africa in 1914 – when the young Mohandas Gandhi forged his powerful tool of 'Satyagraha' and created a living tradition that became a source of inspiration not only to thousands of South Africans (see below) but also to countless Indians as they followed the Mahatma from the banks of the Sarbarnati to independence in 1946. For English-speaking South Africans, the British heritage of imperial power, wealth and culture bred a confidence which many others found patronising.

[1] T. Dunbar Moodie, *The rise of Afrikanerdom* (Berkeley, 1975).

Particular events gave rise to quite different memories. The First World War, for example, was remembered by the Coloured community for Square Hill and other battles in Palestine where members of the Cape Corps distinguished themselves, and by English-speaking South Africans for the nightmare battle of Delville Wood in the Somme mud. For nationalist Afrikaners, the war was remembered chiefly for the execution of Jopie Fourie whose blood was seen to be precious seed of the new nation. Africans were left with the loss of over 600 men in the sinking of the *Mendi*, a realisation that few had recognised their offering, and S. E. K. Mqhayi's haunting poetry. Many who held one of these memories dear had never heard of the others; and there were those who were indifferent to all four. So it was with all luggage. Few pieces were important to everybody and there were some in Southern Africa who travelled light. But the burdens which people bore and the different contents of their luggage were to play a significant role in the history of the period.

For the purpose of this volume, southern Africa has been defined as the region comprising the five countries of South Africa, Lesotho (Basutoland), Namibia (South West Africa), Botswana (Bechuanaland), and Swaziland. Such a definition makes sense for a constitutional historian but less so for an anthropologist or economist. The straight line separating Namibia from Angola tends to obscure the fact that people on either side of the boundary share common languages and customs. More restricting still is a definition which excludes Mozambique, whose southern parts are bound to South Africa by language, trade, and a long history of oscillating migration to the gold mines. No definition would eliminate such difficulties, but one should be conscious of the subtle bias which it introduces.

It is helpful to begin by examining the major divisions which separated people within the region. First, national boundaries: table 6.1 shows the size, both by population and area, of the five countries. Variations in the distribution of population were due primarily to the pattern of rainfall, but also to conquest, land legislation, the distribution of minerals, and the process of urbanisation. At the beginning of the Second World War, South Africa was an independent state whilst South West Africa, although a Mandated Territory, was ruled virtually as a fifth

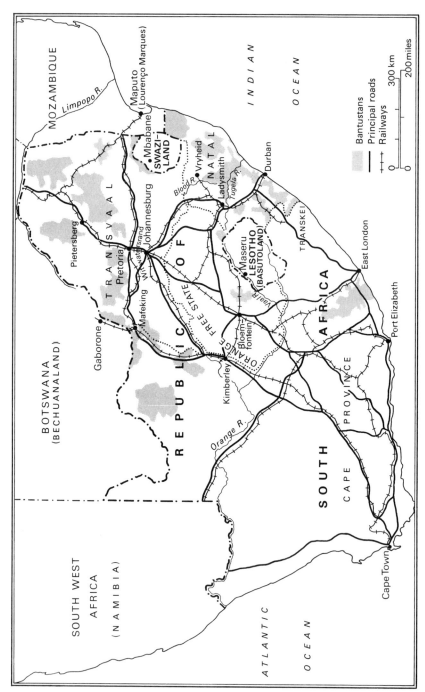

15   The Republic of South Africa, Swaziland and Lesotho.

Table 6.1. *Southern Africa: area and population (in thousands)*
1936–74; percentages in brackets.

Country	Population 1936	Population 1974		Area (sq. km)		Population density 1974 persons/ sq. km
South Africa	9590	24940	(88.7)	1222	(45.8)	20.4
Lesotho	562	1191	(4.2)	30	(1.1)	39.7
Namibia	318	860	(3.1)	823	(30.9)	1.0
Botswana	266	654	(2.3)	575	(21.6)	1.1
Swaziland	157	478	(1.7)	17	(0.6)	28.1
Total	10893	28123	(100)	2667	(100)	10.5

Sources: *World Bank atlas* (Washington, 1976); Union Office of Census and Statistics, *Official year book of the Union of South Africa and of Basutoland, Bechuanaland Protectorate and Swaziland, 1941* (Pretoria, 1937), 988; Philip, *The international atlas* (London, 1969).

province. Bechuanaland, Basutoland and Swaziland were all administered as separate United Kingdom dependencies by the British High Commissioner in Pretoria, but shared common currency, membership of the customs union, and much else with South Africa. Passports were not required by anybody crossing from one country to another. However, in subsequent decades these boundaries became increasingly important.

In societies where pigmentation is considered important, there is more to colour than meets the eye and even South Africa has been unable to produce an infallible definition of 'race' for purposes of population classification. Despite fuzziness at the edges, colour-caste divisions (and the ancestry they implied) were important primarily in terms of the distribution of power as reflected in long-entrenched racist legislation, such as the Mines and Works Act (1911), the Land Act (1913) and the Urban Areas Act (1923) but also in terms of peoples' perceptions of each other even within communities that were themselves subject to discrimination.[1]

[1] See, for example, Z. K. Matthews, *Freedom for my people* (London, 1980); Richard Rive, *Selected writings* (Johannesburg, 1977), 29–37; Martin E. West, *Divided community* (Cape Town, 1971).

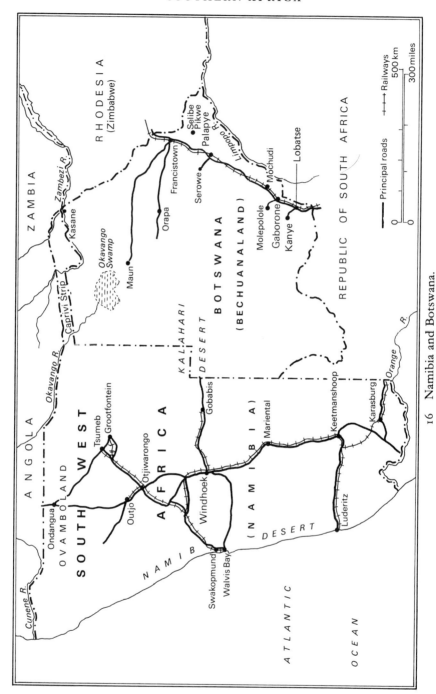

16 Namibia and Botswana.

Table 6.2. *Colour-castes in Southern Africa, 1936; number of persons (thousands), percentages in brackets.*

Country	African	White	Coloured	Asian	Total
South Africa	6597(69)	2004(21)	770(8)	220(2)	9590(100)
Basutoland	559(99)	1(—)	1(—)	0.3	562(100)
S W Africa	288[a](90)	31(10)	[a]	—	318(100)
Bechuanaland	260(98)	2(1)	4(1)	—	266(100)
Swaziland	153(98)	3(2)	1(—)	—	157(100)
Total[b]	7857(72)	2041(19)	775(7)	220(2)	10893(100)

Notes:
[a] For South West Africa, 'Native and Coloured' were enumerated together.
[b] Figures do not add up due to rounding.
Sources: Union Office of Census and Statistics, *Official year book, 1941*, 988.

Table 6.3. *Home languages in South Africa, 1946; number of persons (thousands), percentages in brackets.*

	Nguni[a]	Sotho[a]	Afrikaans[b]	English[b]	Other[c]
Africans	4772	2216	—	—	844
White	—	—	1375	949	49
Coloured	—	—	831	90	8
Asian	—	—	7	12	266
Total[d]	4772(42)	2216(19)	2212(19)	1051(9)	1168(10)

Notes:
[a] Languages are grouped according to mutual intelligibility. Nguni includes Ndebele, Swazi, Xhosa and Zulu. Sotho includes South Sotho, North Sotho (Pedi), and Tswana.
[b] Statistics for Afrikaans (and English) include one-half of those who speak the two official languages equally at home.
[c] Including Tsonga, Venda, Tamil, Hindi, Gujerati, German, Portuguese, Yiddish and a number of others.
[d] Figures do not add up due to rounding.
Source: Bureau of Census and Statistics, *Union statistics for fifty years* (Pretoria, 1960), A.18–19.

Table 6.4. *Urbanisation in South Africa, 1904–2000 (percentages).*

	1904	1936	1970	2000 (projected)
African	10.1	17.3	33.0	32 min./47 max.
White	52.7	65.2	86.7	(90)
Coloured	50.5	53.9	74.3	(85)
Asian	36.6	6.3	86.2	(91)
Total	23.4	31.4	47.8	47 min./58 max.

Sources: RSA Department of Statistics, *South African statistics, 1974* (Pretoria, 1974), 1.12. Charles Simkins, *Four essays on the past, present and possible future of the distribution of the black population of South Africa* (Cape Town, 1983), 143 ff.

A striking feature of southern Africa is the diversity of language. Some people, particularly Africans growing up in the urban crucibles, were fluent in several tongues but there were many, notably urban whites and rural blacks, for whom language was an impenetrable barrier. Second-language statistics are not available, but it seems that a higher proportion of Africans learnt Afrikaans or English in order to understand their employers than whites learnt Nguni or Sotho, despite the fact that the latter were the mother tongues of more people than spoke either of the official languages. The political importance of language as a frontier along which battles raged made itself explicitly felt in the Afrikaans language movement, which was a major source of energy for Afrikaner nationalism in its drive to power. It was not until 1976, and the revolt of the Soweto schoolchildren against the forcible imposition of Afrikaans as a medium of instruction, that language moved to the centre of the black political stage.

More than most countries, South Africa's urban–rural cleavage was blurred by the fact that a large proportion of workers moved to town as oscillating migrants who, though they might spend the best part of their working lives down a mine or in a factory, were not allowed to bring their wives or children with them, but returned regularly to their rural homes. Nevertheless the distinction between town and country is fundamental.

The figures of table 6.4 mask two important dimensions of the cleavage: one is the fact that by the 1930s most English-speaking whites had long since become urbanised whilst for many Afrikaners and blacks the towns were still new and bewildering places; the other is that the rural areas themselves were divided into the white-owned capitalist farms on which, in South Africa, more than one-third of the black population lived and the 'reserves' from which most of the South African migrant workers came.

Another boundary was the great gulf between rich and poor. Class divisions based on access to and ownership of land, of jobs and of capital in the form of livestock, mineral rights, business investments, and education were deeply embedded in the society of southern Africa. Although there were numbers of poor whites, and although some blacks were relatively well-to-do, the primary class division followed the colour line. In South Africa, ownership of private farm land was restricted almost entirely to whites by conquest as consolidated in the Land Act of 1913 whilst within the black reserves, which, after 1936, formed approximately 13 per cent of the country, the density of population on arable land was such that the level of income that could be derived from agriculture was far lower. In mining and manufacturing the better-paid jobs were effectively barred to Africans (and, in lesser measure, to Coloured persons and Indians) by direct legislative barriers and by the less visible but more pervasive obstacles of white conventions and the lack of opportunities for education and training. It is estimated that in 1936 the ratios of average white incomes per head to those of Africans, Coloureds, and Asians were 12:1, 7:1, and 5:1 respectively (see table 6.6). Rough though these figures are, they serve to illustrate clearly the enormous economic gap between black and white in South Africa.

This list of cleavages tells nothing of the tensions that existed between Afrikaners of the Cape and of the Transvaal; between Mfengu and Xhosa in the eastern Cape; between Christian denominations in various dorps; between 'borners' and migrants in the townships. Nor does it say anything about the important changes taking place in the relations between generations and between sexes. All these and more were there. But we have focussed on the boundaries of nation, 'colour', language, urbanisation and class because their interaction was a central feature of the history of the period. The divisions did not always overlap. Only two-thirds of those whose mother tongue was Afrikaans were white; those who spoke Swazi did not all live in Swaziland; not

Table 6.5. *Employment in South Africa by selected sectors 1936–76.*

	All employees			Blacks only		
	1936	1956	1976	1936	1956	1976
A. Numbers employed (thousands)						
Manufacturing	200	611	1273[a]	121	452	997
Mines and quarries	429	554	671	384	488	606
Construction	33	111	447	22	87	386
SAR and H	104	222	256	45	114	143
Agriculture[b]	na	843	(716)[c]	na	732	(602)
B. Index of employment (1936 = 100)						
Manufacturing	100	306	637	100	372	821
Mines and quarries	100	129	156	100	127	158
Construction	100	337	1360	100	403	1796
SAR and H	100	214	247	100	253	316

Notes:
[a] Reclassification in 1970 makes this figure not strictly comparable with previous years.
[b] Number of regular employees living on white, Coloured and Asian farms. Seasonal and occasional workers and domestic servants excluded.
[c] The figure is for 1975.
Source: South African statistics, 1978, 7.4 ff.

all the rich were white, nor was all the proletariat black. Yet part of the uniqueness of southern Africa is the extent to which the boundaries have been made to reinforce each other. Indeed, by the 1970s, the attempt to impose national boundaries to correlate with skin, language, and class differences was the central issue of South African politics.

INDUSTRIAL REVOLUTION IN SOUTH AFRICA, 1936–76

The first three years of the 1930s had been disastrous. But by the end of 1932 General Hertzog had abandoned the gold standard and by the summer of 1933/4 rain had fallen and President Roosevelt had devalued the dollar. The price of gold rose 47 per cent without causing inflation and the country was set for four decades of almost uninterrupted growth, its gross national product increasing at an average annual rate of approximately 5 per cent. Employment increased rapidly.

Between 1932 and 1939 total employment in the mining industry rose by over 50 per cent as 157000 new jobs were created. With the outbreak of war prospecting and development ceased, but in 1946 the richest gold ore ever found in South Africa was struck at Geduld in the Orange Free State and then, in 1949, Britain devalued sterling, thus raising the price of gold by 44 per cent. Between 1951 and 1969 the country's output almost trebled from 11.5 to 31.3 million fine ounces whilst employment on the gold mines rose to a peak of nearly 450000 in 1961. Between 1968 and December 1974 the price of gold, moving slowly at first, suddenly rocketed from $35 to $197 per fine ounce.[1] This spectacular change was accompanied by a marked increase in the rate of inflation which dampened, but did not eliminate, prospects of further expansions. But in breaking loose from its moorings which had held it stable for so long, the gold price was now subject to sudden fluctuations for the first time since the early 1920s. Increased exploitation of other minerals, notably platinum, offset the decrease in employment in the gold mines after 1961. Diamonds remained important as a source of both employment and foreign exchange. And coal, after the oil price rise in 1973, emerged as increasingly significant from both economic and strategic perspectives.

Stimulated by the growth of gold and the impact of war, industrialisation of the economy went on apace. Employment in manufacturing and construction between 1933 and 1939 had practically doubled and, during the war years, whilst construction declined temporarily, manufacturing increased by nearly 100000 (42 per cent) to 327000 persons in 1944. Only a fraction, approximately one in eight, of these wartime jobs went to whites, as many who would otherwise have claimed preference had been drawn into the armed forces. In the post-war years, rapid expansion continued until the onset of depression in the mid-1970s, by which time employment in manufacturing and construction together was greater than the total number of regular jobs in mining and agriculture combined. One of the most striking

[1] In the six years from 1970 to 1975 the annual average price received by the gold mines more than quadrupled from R26 to R112 per ounce fine.

features of the period was the increasing role of the state as employer, producer and investor in the South African economy. The first steel, produced by the government-owned iron and steel corporation (Iscor), was tapped in Pretoria in 1934. By 1961 output had risen to 2.4 million tons and by 1976 to over 5 million tons, which was 77 per cent of the country's total production of steel. In the civil service, including the railways and the post office, but excluding Iscor and other industrial corporations, employment in 1976 was 1.2 million, which was approximately one-quarter of all jobs outside agriculture and domestic service. It is estimated[1] that nearly one-third (30 per cent) of economically active whites were by 1977 employed in the public and semi-public sector. State involvement is also measured by the share of government investment, which increased as a proportion of gross domestic fixed investment from 35 per cent during 1950 to 53 per cent in 1976.[2]

On the farms too the period was one of expansion. Over the decade 1946/9 to 1956/9 the output of wool increased by 40 per cent, maize by over 50 per cent and wheat by over 60 per cent, whilst fruit and sugar doubled. Total employment of both casual and regular workers increased steadily until the end of the 1960s after which it started to fall. This was a turning point. Behind it lay changing techniques of production, the use of machinery and chemical weedkillers, which reduced demand for labour. The absolute number of whites on the land had been falling since the mid-1930s but it was not until the end of the 1960s that total farm employment, including that of Africans, began to decline.[3]

South African population in the generation before 1936 grew by approximately 2.1 per cent per annum but grew somewhat faster thereafter. Population growth varied considerably between the different countries. Over the period 1960–74, for example, the average annual percentage rates were: Botswana 1.9, Lesotho 2.2, South Africa 2.7, Swaziland 3.0 and Namibia 3.1.[4] The evidence suggests that, as elsewhere, growth was due primarily to falling

[1] Heribert Adam and Hermann Giliomee, *Ethnic power mobilized: can South Africa change?* (New Haven, 1979), 165.
[2] Dick Clark, *US corporate interests in South Africa* (Report to the Committee on Foreign Relations, United States Senate, Washington, 1978), 25.
[3] F. Wilson, A. Kooy, D. Hendrie (eds.), *Farm labour in South Africa* (Cape Town, 1977), 2.   [4] *World Bank atlas*, 1976.

death rates. Development of transport and the capacity to shift food in response to shortages contributed to this change, as did the work of churches in establishing and running medical services in many of the more densely populated rural areas of the country. The interaction between socio-economic factors and population growth is little understood, but in southern Africa population growth may prove the most significant change in the twentieth century. Projections in the 1970s estimated[1] that between 1970 and 2020 total population in South Africa might more than treble from 22 million to 79 million, with Africans quadrupling from 15.5 million to over 60 million and whites increasing in absolute numbers from 3.8 million to 7 million – but falling as a proportion of the total population from 17 to 9 per cent.

The expansion in mining and manufacturing output combined with the changing techniques of production in the capitalist agricultural sector and the rapid growth of population overall led to a rapid process of urbanisation as people poured off the land to take up jobs in town. The focus of much of the movement was the southern Transvaal, together with the five harbour towns from Cape Town to Maputo (Lourenço Marques) that served it. People came to the densely populated shanty-towns whose infinite capacity to absorb newcomers was a measure of human ingenuity and resilience under most trying conditions. Black Fordsburg, White Fordsburg, Sophiatown and Vrededorp were all polyglot ports of entry into the brash world of Johannesburg.[2] But not everybody came this way. Many men came alone to live in the vast labour compounds. Although their stay was temporary, in the sense that contracts varied from a few months to two years, it was for many the beginning of long-term commitment to urban employment.

In absolute terms the population of the Witwatersrand, Pretoria and Vereeniging increased from 1.2 million to 3.7 million between 1936 and 1970 whilst the urban population of the country as a whole grew from 3.0 million to 10.4 million. Peoples' responses, both as individuals and as groups, to the changes taking place, were shaped in no small measure by the distribution of political

[1] J. L. Sadie, 'The demographic forces in South Africa', *Transactions of the Royal Society of South Africa*, 1978, **43**, 1, 21.
[2] There is a wealth of literature, much of it banned in South Africa, describing the black experience. See, for example, Peter Abrahams, *Tell freedom* (London, 1954). Ezekiel Mphahlele, *Down Second Avenue* (London, 1959).

Table 6.6. *Income distribution by colour-caste in South Africa 1936–1970/1.*

A. *Income shares*

Income base	1936 Net national income		1970/71 Private consumption expenditure	
	% Population	% Income	% Population	% Income
African	68.8	19.7	70.0	19.1
White	20.9	74.5	17.8	73.7
Coloured	8.0	4.1	9.4	5.2
Asian	2.3	1.7	2.9	2.1

B. *Income per head ratios*

	1936	1970/71
White: African	12.4:1	15.2:1
White: Coloured	6.9:1	7.5:1
White: Asian	4.7:1	5.7:1
White: African-Asian-Coloured	11:1	12.9:1

Source: S. F. Archer, *South African Outlook*, December 1978. Peter Randall (ed.), *Power, privilege and poverty* (Report of the Spro-cas Economics Commission, Johannesburg, 1972), 116, Appendix C.

power and by the similarities and differences facing various groups as they moved to the cities. By the 1930s most English-speaking whites had long been urbanised and already occupied the commanding heights of the economy. Coming to the cities, poor whites, mainly Afrikaans-speaking, found themselves competing for scarce jobs with others whom, by virtue of conquest and skin-colour, they had always treated as inferior. For these others urbanisation was likewise a new experience born of rural impoverishment. But they found themselves struggling at the bottom of a pyramid whose base was well below the poverty datum line and which presented many barriers to prevent black people from rising.

Differences in access to jobs and to ownership of the means of production naturally implied differences in income (table 6.6). Throughout the period whites, who formed approximately one-fifth of the population, enjoyed some three-quarters of the total income; Africans, on the other hand, formed over two-thirds of the population and received approximately one-fifth of the national income. By international standards distribution of income in South Africa was particularly skewed. It has been estimated that the richest 20 per cent of the population earned approximately 75 per cent of total income in 1970. Comparative figures, though not all for the same year, of the share of income earned by the richest quintile in Brazil, India and the United States are 62, 52 and 39 per cent respectively.[1]

More detailed figures of salaries and wages paid in particular sectors enable us to obtain a slightly fuller picture of the impact of the industrial revolution on both relative and absolute living standards (table 6.7). The real earnings of black gold-mine workers in 1971 were estimated to be no higher and possibly slightly lower than they had been two generations previously in 1911. The sharp change over the next five years was due to an extraordinary combination of independent yet mutually re-inforcing events, including the increase in the price of gold, widespread industrial strikes centred in Durban in the summer of 1973–4, the decision by President Banda early in April 1974 to halt all South African recruiting in Malawi, and, later in the month, the collapse of the Portuguese empire. Despite the increase, wages on the mines (even after allowing for payments in kind) remained below the average earnings of black workers in the manufacturing sector where, largely because they did not have the access to labour from beyond the boundaries of South Africa, employers had long paid higher black wages.

In agriculture generalisations are more misleading, for there were wide variations across the country. But everywhere the gap in living standards between white farmers and their labourers was large and may well have increased over time. In some parts of the country farm wages increased, especially during the 1970s although, even allowing for wages in kind, they remained well below what were paid in other sectors. In subsistence agriculture,

[1] Source: S. F. Archer, 'The winter of our discontent: issues and policies of income distribution in South Africa', *South African Outlook*, December 1978.

Table 6.7. *Earnings in selected sectors 1936–76.*

A. *Gold mines 1936–76*

Date	Earnings (R/annum) White (W)	Black (B)	Earnings ratio W:B	Earnings difference W − B	Index of real earnings (1936 = 100) White	Black
1936	786	68	11.5 : 1	718	100	100
1956	2046	132	15.5 : 1	1914	119	89
1971	4633	221	21.0 : 1	4412	179	99
1976	8843	1103	8.0 : 1	7740	207	301

B. *Various Sectors, 1976*

	Earnings (R/monthly) White	Asian	Coloured	African	Average	Ratio W : Af
Mining[a]	713	275	186	88	151	8.1 : 1
Construction	557	297	217	112	187	5.0 : 1
Manufacturing	571	184	154	125	230	4.6 : 1
Retail trade	255	154	110	82	154	3.1 : 1
SAR and H	545	198	119	109	303	5.0 : 1
Banks	509	258	190	164	448	3.1 : 1
Central govt.	427	330	189	130	265	3.3 : 1
Local Authorities	540	174	161	98	218	5.5 : 1
Universities	597	272	182	122	427	4.9 : 1
Average[b]	489	197	157	106	220	4.6 : 1
Agriculture[c]	(330)	(92)	(35)	(18)	(27)	(17.9 : 1)

Notes:

[a] Including quarries.

[b] Including most sectors except agriculture, domestic service and self-employment.

[c] Figures for agriculture are less reliable and those cited are for the previous year (1975) and refer only to regular farm employees, thus excluding most farmers and all casual labourers. Nevertheless, they are instructive.

Sources: (A) Francis Wilson, *Labour in the South African gold mines 1911–1969* (Cambridge, 1972), 46; Chamber of Mines of South Africa, *Annual reports* (Johannesburg); *South African statistics*, 1978, 7.6 ff.

(B) S. F. Archer, App. C in Peter Randall (ed.), *Power, privilege and poverty* (Report of Study Project on Christianity in Apartheid Society, Johannesburg, 1972), 116.

the evidence points to a steady decrease in output per capita and hence for many, without adequate remittances from migrants, increasing poverty.[1]

Economic cleavages existed also within racial groups, as may be seen for example in the figures for income distribution amongst white South African taxpayers in 1976.[2] A few whites (0.8 per cent) had zero income or less, whilst nearly half (49 per cent) earned up to R5000 per annum. More than a third (37 per cent) earned between R5000 and R10000, whilst a further 173000 whites (12 per cent) earned between R10000 and R30000 with the remaining 8000 (0.6 per cent) earning more than R30000. For blacks no general figures are available, but a glimpse of the Ciskei at the grass roots in the 1960s is not atypical.[3] One third (33 per cent) of the 2082 households surveyed had no arable land at all. More than a quarter (28 per cent) had between 1 and 5 acres. Another third (35 per cent) had between 6 and 10 acres whilst 3 per cent of the households had between 11 and 30 acres of arable land.

Two further points are worth noting. There was a substantial shift, not unconnected with the rise of the National Party after the Second World War, in the ethnic distribution of wealth within the white community. The growth of big Afrikaner-led business was a particularly striking feature of the period. Per capita income of Afrikaners in 1946 was estimated to be less than half (47 per cent) that of English-speaking whites. By 1976 the proportion had risen to 72 per cent.[4] More significantly, despite the wide income gap between white and black, and despite grinding poverty, particularly in rural areas, one consequence of economic growth was a substantial increase in black buying power. By 1975 the total consumer market represented by blacks living in Johannesburg alone, for example, was estimated to be R638 million, approximately equal to the entire defence budget for that year.[5]

[1] For evidence of the decline in output in the reserves see J. B. Knight and G. Lenta, 'Has capitalism underdeveloped the labour reserves of South Africa?', *Oxford Bulletin of Economics and Statistics*, August 1980, **42**, 3, and F. Wilson, *Gold mines*, 189.

[2] House of Assembly debates (*Hansard*, Cape Town, 1977, **13**), col. 949. House of Assembly debates (*Hansard*, Cape Town, 1977, **16**), col. 1113.

[3] P. J. de Vos *et al.*, *A socio-economic and educational survey of the Bantu residing in the Victoria East, Middledrift and Zwelitsha areas of the Ciskei* (Fort Hare, 1970).

[4] Derived from Adam and Giliomee, *Ethnic power*, 174. The figures must be used with some care for other evidence (*ibid.*, 154) suggests that in 1936 the proportion was 61 per cent which implies a surprisingly large widening of the income gap between Afrikaners and other whites during the war years.

[5] M. Loubser, *Market potentials of consumer goods and services for non-white population groups in the main urban areas in the Republic of South Africa in 1975* (Bureau of Market Research, Pretoria, 1977).

As far as the infrastructure of the region is concerned, most of the important railways (see figs. 15, 16) in southern Africa were built in the half century between the mineral discoveries and the outbreak of the First World War; nevertheless in later years the state invested heavily in railway development. Between 1948 and 1972 the proportion of total track electrified rose from 4 to 21 per cent. During the early 1970s two new harbours were built at Richards Bay and Saldanha Bay and rail track was laid linking them, respectively, to the Witwatersrand and the iron-ore deposits of the northern Cape.

There was a great improvement in roads not least for defence purposes. Meandering gravel roads were resurveyed, and tarred highways laid down which connected the towns and also made farmers less isolated than they had been. The motorways driven through the hearts of the major cities during the 60s and 70s so transformed some of them that visitors and ex-prisoners, having been away for ten years, found themselves lost. Airports were built to serve the major industrial areas and the number of internal passengers (including some within the neighbouring countries) carried by South African Airways grew at an annual rate of 12 per cent from 115 000 in 1948 to 2.5 million in 1976.

The number of telephones grew at 7 per cent per year between 1936 and 1976 from 142 thousand to 2.1 million, but few of these went to black homes. During the same period the number of licensed radios grew slightly faster from 139 thousand to 2.5 million, thus reducing the average number of people per radio from 69 to 11. Television was not introduced until 1976 but by mid-1977 some 670 000 sets had been sold. The impact of these changes is difficult to assess but the spread of transistors, not least into the isolated homesteads of farm labourers, made many people aware of events outside their local area. At the same time skilful use by the state of its broadcasting monopoly did much, through heavy censorship, to influence white attitudes.

Considerable expansion took place in school-buildings and equipment, not only of material investment, but also of the less tangible but no less important investment in 'human capital', thus contributing to the rise in literacy which some perceptive observers regard as one of the most significant changes to have

Table 6.8. *Hospital beds 1936–62.*

	Population per bed		
	White	Black	Total
1936	207:1	521:1	395:1
1962	144:1	204:1	189:1

Sources: Union statistics for fifty years, A-3 and D-3; *Statistical year book 1966,* A-11 and D-3.

taken place during the period.[1] One consequence of this is the fact that between 1962 and 1977 the proportion of daily newspaper readers who were black rose from 33 to 45 per cent. At the same time the pattern of educational spending served – like so much of South Africa's public expenditure – to reinforce the existing maldistribution of wealth and opportunity. In 1960 only 2 per cent of white South Africans over the age of 19 had no education at all compared with 65 per cent of Africans. At the other end of the scale, where 23 per cent of whites over the age of 14 had passed standard 10 (i.e. 12 years of schooling) only 0.2 per cent of Africans had so so. Of those at school in 1974–5 it is estimated that per capita expenditure on African pupils was less than one-eighth the expenditure on all other pupils.

The picture for health was much the same. There was considerable expansion of the segregated medical services but this expansion was biased in favour of those who were urban, wealthy and white (table 6.8). Similarly whilst the population: doctor ratio between 1936 and 1970 fell from approximately 3400:1 to 2000:1 we find that, in 1975, two-thirds (65.5 per cent) of all doctors practised in the three metropolitan areas of the Witwatersrand, Cape Town and Durban, whereas only 5.5 per cent of all doctors practised in the rural areas where over half the population lived. In general, despite superb medical care in some areas, health services were not able to deal effectively with the existing pattern of disease, including widespread malnutrition amongst blacks.

[1] Between 1948 and 1970 the proportion of Africans aged 10 and older who could read and write increased from just over one-quarter (28 per cent) to a little under one-half (48–9 per cent). *Union statistics for fifty years,* A-22; *South African statistics, 1978,* **1**, 35.

Electricity, most of which was generated relatively cheaply from the coal of the southern Transvaal and Natal, was spread throughout the country by the network of Escom power-lines whose total area of supply rose from 20 000 sq. miles in 1936 to 139 000 sq. miles in 1958, thus bringing power to many towns and farms which previously had either generated their own or had none. Total production of electricity in the country grew at 7.7 per cent per annum from 3.8 thousand million KwH in 1935 to 80 thousand million KwH in 1976.[1]

During the 1960s, the Orange River drainage scheme with its great dams and its irrigation tunnels through the mountains was built with little public debate as to its effectiveness compared with other alternatives. On the western side of the Drakensberg there was much land but few people, whereas on the eastern escarpment imaginative irrigation and hydroelectric schemes on the various rivers that flowed through the Transkei to the sea could have revolutionised the farming potential in a densely populated rural area where people were desperately short of food. Other important decisions shaped by political considerations were South Africa's decision not to purchase water from Lesotho – thus spiking the Malibamatso scheme (see below) – but rather to pump water from the Tugela up the western escarpment to the Vaal from whence it was drawn to the Witwatersrand.

Possibly even more significant in the long run than the giant schemes were the multitude of small dams built on farms and in the reserves. This investment did something to offset the appalling loss of top soil as bad farming combined with heavy rain caused much of the country's most precious asset to be washed into the sea every year. Much soil was also taken by wind blowing over treeless miles of plough land, causing dust storms which reminded observers of the American dust-bowl. The speed with which the desert was encroaching from the south-west was an ominous sign of irreversible damage due to the loss of what economists, knowing only Europe, once called the 'indestructible powers of the soil'.

South Africa's infrastructure was not built in isolation. Roads, railways, air-routes, power lines and radio waves served not only to bind the countries of southern Africa more closely together

[1] Including net purchases outside the country. *South African statistics*, 1978, **14**, 3.

but also to link the region to the rest of the continent and the world. The Cabora Bassa Dam, built with limited interference from FRELIMO guerrillas in Mozambique on the lower reaches of the Zambesi, was joined to the Escom network and started to supply electricity in 1977. South Africa took care to ensure that she did not import too high a proportion of her total needs.[1] Moreover, the grid was designed in such a way that electricity from Cabora Bassa for Maputo itself had to pass through a transformer built on South African soil, near Pretoria. Across the sub-continent the other Portuguese–South African hydroelectric brainchild was designed to take water and power from the Kunene River to the new mines of the dry Namibian hinterland.[2] But construction was interrupted during the mid-1970s by the escalating war. Another link, this time spurred on by war, was the railway line built by the Rhodesian government in 1974 from Rutanga to Beit Bridge in order to connect directly with South Africa. The decline of passenger ships and the rise of jets shifted the gateway of southern Africa from Cape Town to Johannesburg and marked also a sharp increase in the number of international overseas travellers from under 9000 in 1948 to nearly 400000 in 1976. Radio programmes were beamed both ways across the Limpopo. The BBC, the Voice of America and, during the 1970s, Lusaka's Freedom Radio and the ANC's broadcasts from Maputo were all listened to in the Republic, as was the SABC elsewhere in Africa.

Stronger even than the infrastructural links were the international flows of labour which bound the region together into a single economy. As the mines expanded in the late nineteenth century the demand for labour grew voraciously and men were recruited from throughout the sub-continent and elsewhere. Thirteen years after the Witwatersrand gold discoveries, there were 100000 black miners at work in the area, large numbers of them drawn from outside South Africa. In 1896, for example, nearly two-thirds (60 per cent) of the black mineworkers came from Mozambique. In 1906 there were 80000 men recruited from

[1] Keith Middlemas, *Cabora Bassa: engineering and politics in Southern Africa* (London, 1975), 212, 233.
[2] Renfrew Christie, 'The political economy of the Kunene River hydroelectric schemes' (MA thesis, University of Cape Town, 1975). For a survey of the major dams in Africa south of the equator and of their interconnections see Henry Olivier, *Great dams in Southern Africa* (Cape Town, c. 1978).

Table 6.9. *Geographic origin of labour employed by the Chamber of Mines (in thousands); percentages in brackets.*

Area	1936		1973		1976	
Transvaal	22.2	(7.0)	10.8	(2.6)	26.2	(7.3)
Natal/Zululand	15.5	(4.9)	4.2	(1.0)	11.8	(3.3)
Cape Province	124.6	(39.2)	63.6	(15.1)	104.8	(29.0)
OFS	3.5	(1.1)	7.6	(1.8)	15.6	(4.3)
Lesotho	46.0	(14.5)	87.2	(20.7)	96.4	(26.7)
Swaziland	7.0	(2.2)	4.5	(1.1)	8.6	(2.4)
Botswana	7.2	(2.3)	16.8	(4.0)	15.5	(4.3)
Mozambique	88.4	(27.8)	99.4	(23.6)	48.6	(13.4)
Africa N of lat 22° S	3.4	(1.1)	128.0	(30.3)	33.8	(9.4)
Total	317.7	(100)	422.2	(100)	361.3	(100)

Source: Mine Labour Organisations (Wenela) Ltd., *Annual Reports* (Johannesburg).

Northern China and housed in compounds. Although the Chinese were repatriated within five years, the compounds were kept and expanded. By 1936 there were 318000 men housed on a single basis, working in the gold and coal mines of the Transvaal. Nearly two-fifths (39 per cent) of these men came from the Transkei and Ciskei; more than one-quarter (28 per cent) from Mozambique; 15 per cent from Lesotho and the rest from elsewhere (table 6.9). Between 1936 and 1973 the proportion (and after 1961 the absolute number) of black South Africans at work on the mines fell whilst those from elsewhere, notably tropical Africa north of latitude 22° S, rose steadily to a point when, in 1973, the proportion of non-South African blacks working on the mines had risen to over 80 per cent. Due to the combination of events already mentioned, important changes, including a marked increase in the real earnings of black miners, took place over the next four years. These combined with the sharp decline in the number of construction and manufacturing jobs meant that by 1976 the proportion of South Africans at work on the mines had more than doubled from 20 to 44 per cent. And the sources of labour from outside changed as well: Rhodesia became a significant supplier following the cut-off of all Malawians in 1974, whilst from

Mozambique the number of mineworkers fell (due primarily to pressure from South Africa) from an all-time peak of 120000 men in 1974 to 35000 men in 1977.

An important consequence of the long-term oscillating migration was the increased dependence of the rural communities upon the industrial core whose growth was made possible by the work of migrants. As economies develop, urban areas themselves become generators of income and employment through a twin process of both private and social capital accumulation and localised expansion of markets. The urban bias in the location of capital accumulation is likely to be even more pronounced where migrants cross national frontiers, because those who control the economy of the labour-receiving country are subject to few political pressures to use tax revenue collected in the wealthy core to finance roads, power stations, schools, or health services beyond the boundary. Thus, for example, Lesotho, which before 1914 was a net exporter of food and whose sons participated as diamond diggers, gold-miners, farm-workers, and schoolteachers in South Africa's century of economic growth, found itself after independence (1966) in a situation where less than one-tenth of its labour force was in paid employment inside the country, and nearly half outside. There was no prospect of providing jobs either for those working outside or for the growing population inside, and the people had no right of access to, nor voice affecting decisions concerning, the employment-generating capital which they had helped to form. Of course, oscillating migration embedded in a political–economic structure for a century or more is not the only cause of a country's chronic poverty but no analysis of southern Africa during the twentieth century can overlook the extent to which economic development in South Africa served to bias the whole process of capital accumulation against those rural areas, both inside and outside South Africa's boundaries, whence the flow of labour came, thus giving a geographic dimension to the distribution of wealth and poverty within the region.[1]

We turn now to the other links which helped shape South Africa's industrial revolution: the international flows of capital investment. From the opening up of the gold mines in 1887 until 1932, more than four-fifths (81 per cent) of the £148 million

[1] Francis Wilson, 'International migration in Southern Africa', *International Migration Review*, 1976, **10**, 4.

invested in the Rand came from outside Africa, mainly from Britain.[1] A generation later, in 1960, it was estimated that of the R940 million spent by the gold-mining industry on capital development since the Second World War approximately three-quarters (74 per cent) was new money from the public, of which half came from overseas, particularly from Britain and the United States. The remaining quarter (R240 million) came primarily from within the mining houses, whose internal resources had mushroomed after the opening of the OFS gold-fields. Over the years 1954–67 the investment income of the Anglo American Corporation alone more than quintupled from R5.2 million to R28.6 million. Not all organisations or individuals were so lucky. During 1935–63 the average rate of return from investment in the gold mines was 4.3 per cent compared with 7 per cent for United Kingdom equities. But the rewards of backing the right horse were such that the mines seldom had difficulty in raising their capital requirements.

Foreign investors did not confine themselves to the gold mines. Industrial companies in Britain, Germany, France, Switzerland, the United States and later Japan, found South Africa, with its strong infrastructure, cheap coal, cheap labour, and growing demand for both consumption and capital goods, to be a highly profitable area. However, apart from mining, much of South Africa's capital requirements were generated within the country. In the three decades before 1960, less than 15 per cent of total capital investment in a cross-section of manufacturing industries was derived from foreign sources, and almost two-thirds of that came from the sterling area, primarily the United Kingdom. Between 1960 and 1972 total foreign investment in South Africa rose from R3.0 billion to R7.8 billion, during which period the share coming from Western Europe (excluding the UK) rose from 14 to 25 per cent. But British investment, in some 600 companies, remained the largest proportion. Although foreign investment as a whole was relatively low (being less than 12 per cent of total investment in the thirty years after the Second World War) nevertheless it was widely seen as a vital component of the

[1] S. Herbert Frankel, *Capital investment in Africa* (London, 1938), 89. *Note*: these figures exclude reinvestment appropriated from profits. S. Herbert Frankel, *Investment and the return to equity capital in the South African gold mining industry 1887–1965* (Oxford, 1967), 8; and Wilson, *Gold mines*, 25.

economy.[1] As well as providing resources for growth, foreign investment often brought with it the technology and know-how used, not always appropriately, in new capital-intensive productive processes.

In addition to investments there were also loans, including the controversial revolving fund of $40 million guaranteed by a consortium of American banks in 1960 shortly after Sharpeville (see below) when the flight of capital threatened to bankrupt the South African economy. But the investors soon recovered from their fright and, despite new restrictions on the withdrawal of capital, returned more strongly than ever. Moreover, in the mid-1970s, the government and its parastatal arms such as Iscor, Escom, Sasol and Armscor sought to expand a number of security-related infrastructure projects rapidly in order to increase the country's self-sufficiency.

South Africa resorted to heavy borrowing abroad, particularly after the price of gold fell in 1975. This need for loans was reinforced by the virtual drying up of foreign private investment following the Soweto crisis of 1976, which came as the country was sliding into its second great depression. Before this South Africa had begun to export capital to such distant fields as Mauritania, Peru, Canada, Australia and Western Europe. Between 1960 and 1972 South African investments abroad[2] rose from R0.9 billion to R3.1 billion. The share of these funds that were invested in the sterling area fell from 60 to 42 per cent whilst the share in the rest of Western Europe rose from 5 to 20 per cent. Closer to home, where her businessmen had long been active, South Africa's investments, both private and public, were substantial. It has been estimated that in the mid-1960s approximately 40 per cent of total investment in the sub-continent (including also Zambia, Malawi, Rhodesia, Angola and Mozambique) was South African.[3] By 1976 nearly one-third (30 per cent) of South Africa's total foreign investment of R5.0 billion was in Africa.

[1] A. J. Norval, *A quarter of a century of industrial progress in South Africa* (Cape Town, 1962), 57; Aubrey Dickman, 'Investment – the implications for economic growth and living standards', *Optima*, 1977, **27**, 1; Clark, *US corporate interests*, 47. For a different view see Brian Kahn and Brian Kantor, 'Does South Africa need foreign capital?' (unpublished, University of Cape Town, 1977).

[2] *South African statistics*, 1974, **23**, 3. Investments abroad are defined as 'Liabilities towards South Africa of foreign enterprise "controlled" from South Africa'.

[3] Ruth First, Jonathan Steele, Christabel Gurney, *The South African connection* (London, 1972), 263. *South African statistics*, 1978, **23**, 3.

Table 6.10. *Southern Africa's foreign trade by continent and country, 1957–76.*

	Exports (%)		Imports (%)	
	1957	1976	1957	1976
Africa	19.2	10.8	6.8	5.2
United Kingdom	27.5	23.5	32.6	17.6
German Federal Republic	5.0	8.5	8.1	18.0
Other Europe	20.6	21.2	13.6	19.0
USA	6.3	9.7	19.6	21.6
Other North America	1.6	3.2	4.4	1.6
South America		2.6		0.7
Japan	2.3	12.6	3.2	10.2
Other Asia	2.8	6.1	11.2	4.0
Oceania (incl. Australia)	1.1	1.1	0.6	1.6
Unspecified	13.6	0.7	—	0.4
Total %	100	100	100	100
Total (R million)	(801)	(4194)	(1098)	(5859)

Source: *Statistical year book 1966*, Q.12-13; *South African statistics*, 1976, **16**, 18–19.

The involvement of South African mining houses in Zambia, of manufacturing companies in Rhodesia, and of the government itself in providing a soft loan to finance the building of Malawi's new capital in Lilongwe, and of helping Mozambique to keep the railways and harbours running after the Portuguese had withdrawn, all served to tie these countries more closely to the south. Elsewhere in the region, the South Africans were busy investing their capital and their expertise, particularly in minerals. Despite Botswana's active, and not unsuccessful, efforts to attract investors from further afield, South Africa remained dominant. For Namibia, still under South African control in the late 1970s, investors from all over the western world were jockeying for new mineral concessions which they hoped might prove as profitable as the coastal diamonds or the Rössing uranium deposits.

The invisible web spun by the capital investors and moneylenders was strengthened by the lines of trade which formed a similar pattern. South Africa, indeed, had a particularly open economy with trade in 1976 accounting for one-third of gross domestic product.

During the period for which statistics are available, a number of interesting changes took place, including the rise of Japan as a major trading partner. At the same time the share of South Africa's imports provided by the German Federal Republic increased markedly whilst Britain's share declined sharply. No less striking than these changes was South Africa's failure to expand trade with the rest of Africa which was seen to be her natural market, particularly after Britain's entry into the European Economic Community in 1973 and the subsequent raising of tariffs. Behind the South African foreign policy of dialogue and détente in the early 1970s lay the attempt not only to obtain African support (or neutrality at least) in voting at the United Nations but also to break the African boycott against South African goods and to penetrate the markets beyond Zambia.

Apart from economic gains to South Africa from the investment funds, and the technology and expertise that came with them, there were distinct political advantages to the Pretoria government of the flows, both in and out, of investments and trade. For although these increased South Africa's vulnerability to sanctions, particularly in the 1970s after Nigeria had begun to overshadow South Africa in importance as a trading partner with the west, nevertheless they served to dampen pressures which, in Britain and the Federal Republic of Germany particularly, could have caused considerable economic loss through reduction of the rich incoming flow of dividends and of employment in sectors exporting to South Africa.

It is against this background of urbanisation, capital accumulation, and the centripetal forces of industrialisation that we turn now to an examination of the political drama as it unfolded over the period.

POLITICS 1936–60

The emergence of the All Africa Convention on 16 December 1935 was as much a triumph as had been the founding conference in 1912 of the African National Congress. Arising in response to the white government's proposal to prevent all Africans, who

277

might in future qualify, from becoming ordinary voters in the Cape Province, where some 11000 Africans were already on the common roll, the AAC brought under its umbrella a wide spectrum of organisations dedicated to fighting the 'Native Bills' (see below). Under the chairmanship of Professor D. D. T. Jabavu and with Dr A. B. Xuma as Secretary, the Convention achieved an astonishing coalition – ranging from elderly, conservative rural African chiefs to young 'Coloured' Trotskyists from the western Cape.

However, the unity forged in the crisis did not last. Once the bills became law a new strategy had to be evolved. Members of the AAC debated the issue. Should they use the very institutions created by the Act in order to fight it? Or should they, as was being increasingly urged by I. B. Tabata, Goolam Gool and others, have nothing to do with such dummy bodies? Two organisations grew as the Convention collapsed in the early 1940s. One was the ANC which slowly re-gathered strength and, after Dr Xuma was elected president in 1941, began once again to make its presence felt. The other was the Non-European Unity Movement forged in 1943 out of a conference of delegates from the AAC, and the National Anti-CAD, a body established to fight the Smuts's government's intention to introduce a special 'Coloured Affairs' department.

Meanwhile the process of clarifying goals continued. From its foundation in 1912 the ANC had been clear as to where it stood; participation by all – albeit with a qualified franchise – in the political life of the common society to which everybody belonged irrespective of race, colour, or creed. This too was the basic belief of the Convention. As time went on, it became necessary to define the goals of the common society more clearly. The adoption by the Allied powers in 1941 of the Atlantic Charter suggested that even in South Africa there was hope. In 1943 the ANC published a manifesto on *African claims* and the Unity Movement announced its *Ten-point programme*. Common to these policy statements and the speeches which supported them was the premise that South Africa belonged to all who lived there. The fact that whites were included as equals – but not as masters – was continually reiterated.

The Freedom Charter adopted in 1955 by a 'Congress of the People' drawn from all race groups in the country and reflecting a broad spectrum of opinion, particularly in the African and Indian congresses, was a consensus document that could be supported both by those whose ultimate goal was a socialist society and those who were neither Marxist nor believed that the entire economy should be run by the state. All were agreed, however, that certain key industries, notably mining, should be nationalised.[1]

But not everybody who believed in a common society necessarily wished to alter the structure of ownership. Both in the Liberal and the Progressive Parties the emphasis was on the abolition of discriminatory legislation and the reorganisation of state expenditure to ensure equal education, better housing and welfare services. White radicals tended to move either into the Communist Party (until it was banned in 1950) or, later, into the Congress of Democrats until it too was proscribed in 1962. Despite vehement disagreement on many basic issues, there was a fundamental belief across the whole spectrum ranging from Moses Kotane, General Secretary of the Communist Party, to Helen Suzman of the Progressive Party that the country belonged to all those who lived in it, and that all South Africans had the right to equal opportunities irrespective of race or colour. But those who held power stood on the other side of this great divide. What was to be done?

'Who will deny,' said Chief Luthuli in 1952 'that thirty years of my life have been spent knocking in vain, patiently, moderately and modestly at a closed and barred door? The past thirty years have seen the greatest number of laws restricting our rights and progress until today we have reached the stage where we have almost no rights at all.'[2] His life and sense of frustration epitomised that of scores of leaders who for two generations and more had sought, via deputation and reasoned argument with cabinet ministers and government commissions, to persuade those in power to alter their policies. In 1936 the All Africa Convention sent a delegation to see the prime minister about his proposed Native Bills. In 1947, when Smuts summoned leaders to talk about the collapse of the Natives' Representative Council, they went. In 1959 a deputation from Fort Hare University

---

[1] For the full text see Thomas Karis and Gwendolen M. Carter (eds.), *From protest to challenge: a documentary history of African politics in South Africa 1882–1964*, Vol. III, 205.   [2] Cited in *Sechaba*, June 1969.

College, threatened with government control and ethnic segregation, appealed in vain to be heard at the bar of the house. The attempt to reason continued although, as time went on, belief in its ultimate efficacy was confined more and more to whites.

Not everybody, however, was content with knocking. Amongst the delegates to the founding conference of the AAC was Clements Kadalie, whose Industrial and Commercial Union, known amongst Africans as 'ICU Mlungu',[1] had mushroomed during the 1920s to a peak membership of 100 000 – sufficient to give both employers and government considerable food for thought. However by the mid-1930s, due to mismanagement, increasing state pressure and political disagreements, the movement had failed. But the need for an organisation to represent workers was greater than ever before. In 1941 the Transvaal African Congress called a conference which founded the African Mine Workers' Union. The government responded the next year by passing War Measure 145 which made all strikes by black workers illegal in all circumstances. In 1943, following a demand by the AMWU for higher wages, the government appointed a commission to investigate. In 1946, when average earnings for the mineworkers were no higher than they had been for the previous ten years, indeed for a generation, the AMWU, led by J. B. Marks, having attempted for months to negotiate, could get no response from the Chamber of Mines. So the AMWU finally called a strike. At its peak in mid-August 1946, some 74 000 men, approximately one-quarter of the total employed by the gold mines, downed tools and paralysed eight mines; five others were partially affected. The police were called out to force the men back to work at bayonet point if necessary. The Chamber of Mines issued a statement saying that 'the introduction of trade unionism among tribal Natives at their present stage of development would lead to abuses and irresponsible action'. Leaders of the strike were tried and the union was crushed. Five years later, after the price of gold had risen 44 per cent, the average real earnings of white mineworkers was 14 per cent higher than it had been at the time of the black strike. The real earnings of black miners were 3 per cent lower.

Other unions too were having a difficult time. From 1935, when he was appointed secretary of the African Laundry Workers'

[1] 'I see you white man'.

Union until he was interned in 1940, Max Gordon organised half a dozen unions for African workers in various industries in the southern Transvaal. He was a Trotskyist but held loosely to the finer points of doctrine with which members of the left so belaboured each other. His aim was to build a solid organisation without splitting hairs. Naboth Mokgatle draws a vivid picture of the trials and tribulations faced by union organisers at this time,[1] but under skilful and courageous hands the trade unions continued to grow despite constant police harassment. By 1947 it was estimated that there were almost a hundred African unions which, in Smuts's words, were 'unrecognised, unauthorised, but in existence'.[2] Like its political counterparts, the trade-union movement in South Africa was deeply divided between those for whom it was a movement to include all those struggling against poverty and exploitation, and those who saw it as an instrument of exclusion to benefit some, primarily white workers, at the expense of others, primarily black. In the Garment Workers' Union in the 1930s, most of the factory workers were young Afrikaans-speaking women recently come from the farms who were struggling to keep themselves and their families afloat. The union, led by Solly Sachs, fought strongly on their behalf and conditions improved greatly. In the war years, as the economy went on expanding, more and more people were drawn into the Witwatersrand factories. But when some Coloured women were hired, there were complaints to the union which stated that the new workers should stay. Union members who continued to object were expelled which meant, due to the closed shop agreement, that they lost their jobs. Afrikaans churchmen and politicians rushed to the rescue and formed the Blankewerkersbeskermingsbond (White Workers' Protection Society). During the 1950s, the new government cracked down on the labour movement (see below) and by 1960 membership of trade unions that were solidly on the side of the lowest paid workers was but a fraction of the total number employed.

In his presidential address to the AAC in 1936, Professor Jabavu who, like so many others, was influenced by events in India, where Gandhi was mobilising millions to boycott both British cloth and certain institutions, considered seriously 'a

[1] Naboth Mokgatle, *The autobiography of an unknown South African* (Berkeley, 1971).
[2] Karis and Carter (eds.), *From protest to challenge*, vol. II, 239.

complete boycott of all the new Acts'. However, he rejected it because 'a perfect organisation where there are no blacklegs'[1] did not exist. Yet the possibility of boycott remained. I. B. Tabata, whose analysis of boycott as a weapon in the struggle was to exert a profound influence, challenged those who maintained that, despised as they were, such bodies as the Natives' Representative Council and the Transkei Bunga had to be used.[2] He argued that non-collaboration would at least ensure that people did not help maintain the political instruments of their own oppression. Nevertheless there were many in the ANC, both on the left and the right, who thought they should give the institutions a try. But in 1946 members of the Natives' Representative Council, after 10 years of talking without the government paying any attention, could finally bear it no longer. Government refusal to allow the NRC – which happened to meet in Pretoria as the mine strike was beginning – to play any role in the matter was the last straw. Members of the NRC had, as Paul Mosaka put it, been playing with a 'toy telephone', and they would play no more. The council resolved to adjourn until further notice. Two months later they met again to hear Jan Hofmeyr, as Acting Prime Minister, accuse them of wanting to rush things. Z. K. Matthews, as chairman of the council's African caucus, delivered the measured reply and the council resolved to adjourn *sine die*.

This move was widely supported and the ANC resolved that further elections for the council should be boycotted. In the face of hardening white attitudes, as evidenced both by the crushing of the mine strike in 1946 and the victory of the National Party at the polls in 1948, the ANC became considerably more aggressive. In 1949, urged on by its increasingly influential Youth League (which had been founded in 1944 with Anton Lembede as first president), the ANC adopted a militant Programme of Action which set the stage for the next decade of persistent Congress attempts to change the policies of the government by means of mass action.

In 1955 the ANC sought to resist the introduction of Bantu Education by boycotting all the schools. Although the campaign was ill-prepared and received little support, it was the forerunner

---

[1] D. D. T. Jabavu, *All African Convention Presidential Address 1936* (Lovedale, 1936), 10.
[2] Later published: I. B. Tabata, *The boycott as a weapon of struggle* (London, 1960).

of a much tougher and more effective campaign, led by the school pupils themselves, 20 years later. More successful was the superbly organised bus boycott in 1957 when, by walking up to 20 miles a day for ten weeks or more, thousands of African commuters on the Witwatersrand from Alexandra, Sophiatown, and elsewhere, forced the Johannesburg Chamber of Commerce and subsequently the government itself to find ways other than raising fares to finance the increasing cost of transport.

A three-month potato boycott, organised in 1959 to draw attention to the system of farm gaols and the oppressive labour conditions found on farms in the potato-growing area of the eastern Transvaal around Bethal, made some impact, but the farm gaols were not abolished. It was not until later, when the boycott weapon was aimed from overseas, that it began, particularly in the field of sport, to make a visible difference to government policy.

Meanwhile another weapon was tried. In 1946 Smuts was pushed by his predominantly English-speaking Natal supporters to enact legislation to restrict Indian ownership to areas where they already owned land. Gandhi telegraphed his protest and India vigorously denounced South Africa at the opening session of the United Nations. Within the country itself the Indian community rallied behind the SA Indian Congress which, under the leadership of Dr Naicker, launched a passive resistance campaign. Two thousand people were sent to gaol but the campaign had little effect. In 1949 communal riots between Indians and Africans tore Durban apart in an episode which highlighted cleavages within the black community and demonstrated the difficulties of united resistance. Nevertheless Indian and African leaders were able subsequently to get together and plan a massive defiance campaign against unjust laws. Timed to coincide with the whites' tercentenary celebrations of the landing of Jan van Riebeeck, the campaign was launched on 26 June 1952 when resisters set out deliberately to break one of six laws relating to control of movement or to railway and post office segregation. During the four months (July to October) a total of 8000 volunteers, no less than two-thirds of them in the eastern Cape, went forward to be arrested. The government response was to pass legislation permitting the whipping of all those convicted of breaking a law for the purpose of demonstrating against it.

But the attempt to persuade those in power to mend their ways by means of Satyagraha actions was not finished. Seven years later another peaceful campaign, focussing once again on the hated pass laws, was mounted. Some jockeying for position between the ANC and the Pan-African Congress which, led by Robert Sobukwe, had recently broken away from the older body, prevented the campaign being properly co-ordinated, but this rapidly became a secondary consideration when on 21 March 1960 a large crowd of people responding to the PAC call gathered round the Sharpeville police station to hand in their passes and was shot at by police. Sixty-nine people lost their lives in an event which echoed round the world. A week later, nearly a thousand miles away, 30 000 Africans marched unarmed into Cape Town to demonstrate against the pass laws. A state of emergency was declared and the two African congress organisations were banned. An era had ended.

For white South Africans the second half of the 1930s was a honeymoon period. United behind the old warriors, Generals Hertzog and Smuts, the vast majority of Afrikaans- and English-speaking whites put aside the quarrels of the past and, basking in the glow of fusion, saw even the nightmare of white poverty begin to recede. But the price of unity was to be high. In 1936, having waited ten years for the two-thirds majority he needed, Hertzog was able to manoeuvre Smuts into supporting legislation to remove African voters from the common roll which had been open to those in the Cape Province with certain qualifications since 1853 and which had been entrenched, at the insistence of Cape delegates, in the South Africa Act, 1909. In place of the common franchise a Natives' Representative Council with advisory but no executive power was established and provision was made for those removed from the common voters' roll to elect three white representatives to the House of Assembly and two (also white) to the Cape Provincial Council. Another provision allowed Africans throughout the Union to elect four whites as additional members of the Senate. At the same time Hertzog was able to tidy some of the loose ends left in the Land Act of 1913 by finalising (at approximately 13 per cent of the total) the amount of land which was to be reserved for Africans. Smuts saw global dangers more clearly than those within his own country, thus, whilst he was not prepared to sacrifice white unity for the sake of black

South Africans, he was nevertheless willing to break it in order to take sides against Nazi Germany. When, on the outbreak of war in September 1939, Hertzog proposed that South Africa remain neutral Smuts argued that her interests as a small nation decreed that she should stand by her friends and go to war. The cabinet was evenly split but Smuts won the parliamentary vote with a majority of eleven. Hertzog crossed the floor to join D. F. Malan's 'purified' Nationalist Party, which had been in the wilderness since it opposed fusion of the (Afrikaner) Nationalist Party, led by Hertzog, and the (largely anglophone) United Party, led by Smuts, in 1933. South Africa, like Britain and her sister Dominions, entered the war 'dangerously unprepared',[1] although she too mobilised rapidly and sent troops first to East Africa where, with Indians, West Africans and others, they defeated the Italians and liberated Ethiopia. From there the South African army moved to North Africa where 11 000 South Africans were captured at Tobruk. Those not captured went on, after fighting at El Alamein, to Italy and the heart of Europe. Some 231 000 men were enlisted. More than one-third (37 per cent) of these were African or Coloured and were sent to war with spears but no guns.[2] Smuts himself played a key role in the war both as Commander-in-Chief of the South African armed forces and as a global strategist in close touch with Churchill and the British generals.

Another aspect of the war was its impact on the soldiers, both black and white, who went north to fight against Nazi racism and Italian Fascism. For blacks the experience of travelling outside the confines of a segregated society was profoundly liberating whilst for many whites the goals of the war as well as meeting all sorts and conditions of men and learning of a world far richer in culture than anything they had ever dreamed of made the social structures back home seem mean and petty. Smuts responded to these impulses when invasion threatened and, after remarking in 1942 that 'segregation had fallen on evil days', gave notice that if the Japanese landed he would arm blacks. But, as one of the most

[1] Neil Orpen, *South African forces, World War II* (Cape Town, 1968), vol. II, 338.
[2] For an illustration of the ambiguous nature of change in South Africa contrast the photograph of black troops doing parade drill with spears during the Second World War in Orpen, *South African forces*, vol. I, with that of the heavily armed black riot policemen in Johannesburg in 1976 in Peter Magubane, *Magubane's South Africa* (London, 1978), 104.

English of Smuts's supporters confided to his diary, 'Anything like a wholesale grant of the vote to our natives is utterly out of the question now and will remain utterly out of the question as long as anyone living can now foresee.'[1] As the threat of invasion receded and an election loomed, the hopes of trade-union representation, relaxation of the pass laws, and guns for black soldiers faded, and the 1943 election, though buoyed up on the tide of victory against Fascism in North Africa, was fought on the clear understanding that, at home, the black man should stay in his place.

Yet Smuts was still willing to negotiate and, who knows, with his willingness to *laat maar loop* (let things develop) he would later perhaps have seen the writing on the wall and moved to accommodate black aspirations. But Smuts was an old man. Moreover, despite all his knowledge and the breadth of his interests, despite the charisma which Hancock describes so vividly,[2] the harsh fact remains that Smuts was one of the chief architects of the South Africa Act, he had been second-in-command of the government which passed the Land Act in 1913 and was also the man without whose support Hertzog would never have been able in 1936 to remove Africans from the Cape common roll. He believed in evolution but did not discern the culs-de-sac of history. Perhaps he stretched as far as they would go the thongs which bound representatives of the white electorate. But at the end of his days, in the crisis of the African mineworkers' strike and the collapse of the Natives' Representative Council he, like Hofmeyr, failed to respond adequately to the hands that were being held out to him from across the widening chasm that divided South Africa. For the majority of his fellow countrymen Smuts was spokesman for the 'haves'; ruler of a country designed 'for whites only'; a man unable to see Africans as equals. He left no legacy on which those struggling for a common society could build. More immediately, however, the most damaging attack on Smuts came from the apostles of greater exclusiveness. In the post-war election of 1948 the United Party was defeated. The National Party, supported almost entirely by Afrikaans-speaking white voters, was returned to power.

[1] B. K. Long, *In Smuts's camp* (London, 1945), 106.
[2] W. K. Hancock, *Smuts* (Cambridge, 1962, 1968), 2 vols.

In 1938 the liturgical celebration of the centenary of the Great
Trek, with ox-waggons pulling slowly through the towns and
dorps of South Africa to a great climax in Pretoria, was instru-
mental in diffusing an Afrikaans-speaking whites-only group
consciousness, and in building up a reservoir of feeling which
'purified nationalists' were to harness effectively in their drive for
power. Despite this, and despite the coming together of Hertzog
and Malan in the opening days of the war, it was not all plain
sailing. Many of Malan's followers were not happy either with the
choice of leader of the new, Herenigde Nationale (United National)
Party, nor with Hertzog's insistence on soft-pedalling the policy
of making South Africa a Republic outside the Commonwealth.
A palace revolt was organised and the old general resigned.

Much more serious to the National Party, however, was the rise
of the Ossewa Brandwag (OB). Founded in the euphoria of the
centenary trek, it was a para-military organisation aimed at
rallying young Afrikaaners to the republican cause. Starting as a
cultural movement, it became increasingly committed to armed
subversion and was soon carving out a space for itself in the
political arena. Malan, in what he later described as one of the three
most difficult decisions of his life, decided to attack the OB head
on.[1] Helped by the turn of the tide in Europe, Malan was able
to defeat the rival organisation whose Nazi philosophy he
declared was a foreign import. In 1948, the National Party refused
to have anything to do with the OB and in the election the young
B. J. Vorster had to stand as a member of the Afrikaner Party
because Malan disapproved of his OB activities. He lost by two
votes, but by the election of 1953 the OB was dead, and the lost
sheep were back in the fold, with men like Vorster on their way
to the top of the party.

The power house which transformed Afrikaners from what
they were before the First World War into the 'organisation-men'[2]
they became after the Second was not, however, the National
Party as such. The Broederbond (League of Brothers), founded

[1] The two other decisions were whether or not to leave the Church ministry and
whether or not to follow Hertzog into 'fusion'.
[2] F. Van Zyl Slabbert, 'Afrikaner nationalism, white politics and political change
in South Africa', in Leonard Thompson and Jeffrey Butler (eds.), *Change in contemporary
South Africa* (Berkeley, 1975), 3–18.

in 1919 by Henning Klopper, went underground in 1922 where, save for those few occasions when it has emerged, blinking like a mole, in the harsh light of Sunday journalism, it remained until the late 1970s.[1] Hertzog was vehemently opposed to such a secret organisation, but from the time of his withdrawal from politics in 1940 until the assassination of Dr Verwoerd in 1966 and indeed right through the Vorster era, the evidence suggests that the Broederbond, whose leadership was drawn primarily from professional, political, religious and intellectual leaders, played a key role, especially in the Transvaal, in organising the Afrikaner nationalists' achievement and consolidation of power.

In 1944 the Federasie vir Afrikaanse Kultuur, an offshoot of the Broederbond, acted as host at a conference at which the new vision of 'Christian National' policy was put before the public. With the backing of the three Church denominations to which most white Afrikaans-speaking South Africans belonged, the programme stated explicitly that the first duty of a 'nation' (white-skinned and Afrikaans-tongued) was to save its own life, and laid the foundations of an ideology which was to serve the National Party for the next generation.

In the field of economics a number of young intellectuals, Albert Hertzog, Piet Meyer and others, after returning from study in Western Europe, established the Nasionale Raad van Trustees (National Council of Trustees) in 1936 in order to form trade unions with the specific objective of rescuing Afrikaans workers from the hold of class solidarity and of directing them along the paths of Afrikaner consciousness. In 1934 the Spoorbond (Railway Union) for white railway workers had been established by the Broederbond and, after a long battle, the Mine Workers' Union was taken over in 1948.[2] The threat of Coloured women in the Garment Workers' Union on the Witwatersrand led to the launching of the Blankewerkersbeskermingsbond to protect white workers from contamination by 'untouchables' of a different hue.

Across the class divide there was also need for organisation. The Reddingsdaadbond (RDB) (Rescue Action Society), formed

---

[1] J. H. P. Serfontein, *Brotherhood of power* (London, 1979); Ivor Wilkins and Hans Strydom, *The Broederbond* (New York, 1979); Charles Bloomberg, *The Broederbond and Christian nationalism in South Africa*, unpublished (1972).

[2] Dan O'Meara, 'The "Christian National" assault on white trade unions in South Africa', *African Affairs*, 1978, **77**, 306.

in the wake of the 1938 centenary celebrations, was designed to help Afrikaners develop some muscle within the English-dominated capitalist world. Nico Diedrichs, who with Geoff Cronje and others was one of the apostles of the new 'nationalism',[1] resigned his professorship in the Orange Free State to become full-time director of the RDB which collected funds (albeit not very successfully). The RDB enabled some small businesses to get off the ground and, more important, provided early support for the new investment house Federale Volks-beleggings (Federal People's Investments). Influential though these organisations were, it was not until the National Party had won the 1948 election that they had the opportunity of putting into practice the policies that had been so long in gestation.

The first actions of the new government were focussed on intensifying colour–caste cleavages where they were least visible. In 1949 marriage between 'European and non-European' was made illegal whilst, a year later, the illegality of sexual intercourse between whites and Africans was extended also against 'Coloured' and 'Asians' as well by an amendment to the 1927 Immorality Act. The Population Registration Act of 1950, hideously cruel in its effects, was used primarily to separate 'white' from 'Coloured' even within the same families. Attempts to justify these 'race' divisions on pseudo-scientific grounds drew heavily on Nazi thinking, but in remoter parts of the Karoo such refinements were dispensed with when, so the story goes, farm-labourer descendants of centuries of Bantu–Khoi interaction were lined up on local railway platforms before an official who glanced at each face pronouncing '*Jy's 'n Hotnot*' or '*Jy's 'n Kaffir*', as he thought the case might be. The Group Areas Act (1950) excluded black neighbours and entrepreneurs from preferred districts, thus extending urban segregation which had first been directed primarily against Africans, many of whom had been penned into 'locations' since before the First World War. The shabby procedures, 1951–6, to remove the franchise from Coloured voters in the Cape, reversed Hertzog's 1926 proposal that it be extended to the Coloured people in other provinces. Two reasons for rejecting the *bruin Afrikaners* were the National Party's fear of

---

[1] N. Diedrichs, *Nasionalisme as Lewensbeskouing en sy Verhouding tot internationalisme* (Bloemfontein, 1936).

losing its precarious hold on power due to the Coloured vote in a number of marginal Cape seats and, secondly, the increasing emphasis on racial purity which the young intellectuals brought back from Germany in the 1930s. The new Afrikaner nationalists used the fences of language and colour–caste both to give consciousness and cohesiveness to a group which was sufficiently numerous to win all elections confined only to whites, and also to foster division amongst everybody else.

A significant shift in the state's response to urbanisation came in 1948. The Smuts government had supported a proposal that the massive wartime movements of Africans to the manufacturing centres be accepted as inevitable. But the nationalists, harking back to policy enunciated in 1922 by a Transvaal local government commission that 'the native' should only enter the cities in order 'to minister to the needs of the white man and should depart therefrom when he ceases so to minister',[1] proposed a policy which not only made it more difficult for blacks to settle in town, but which also laid the foundations for extending the migrant labour system from the mining industry to the rest of the urban economy. The Prevention of Illegal Squatting Act (1951) prohibited squatting without permission, but did empower local authorities to proclaim emergency camps. The Native Abolition of Passes and Coordination of Documents Act (1952) streamlined the system of geographic control and introduced a single reference book, the *dompas*, which had to be carried at all times by all Africans of 18 years or older.[2] The Native Laws Amendment Act (1952) laid down the terms (birth in a town, or ten years continuous work with one employer, or 15 years continuous employment in the same town) under which a person might acquire rights to remain permanently in a particular town and, if a man, to bring in his wife and children to live with him. For those who did not yet fulfil these requirements family housing was not to be made available. Those wishing to seek work in town were allowed to come for 72 hours after which time, if they were not registered in employment they had to leave. Labour bureaux were established in 1951 to facilitate the co-ordination of labour flow, not least to agriculture. The *dompas*, containing information

---

[1] Transvaal Province, *Report of the Local Government Commission* (Stallard) (TP 1, Pretoria, 1922), para 267.

[2] The origin of the word is obscure. Possibly it is derived from 'where is your damn pass?'.

about an individual's place of residence, employment status and tax payments, had to be produced upon demand by any policeman. During the 1950s the average annual number of convictions for contraventions of the pass laws was double that during the 1940s (see table 6.12). Behind these statistics lay the indignities of arrogant arrest, and a development about which Africans felt particularly bitter: the extension of pass laws to women. Forty years previously a passive resistance campaign in the Orange Free State had successfully warded off a similar attempt, but now, despite massive protest culminating in a march of 10 000 women led by Lilian Ngoyi to Pretoria in 1956, the government extended the laws until by 1959 passes had to be carried by all African women. Such power led to abuse. For example a white policeman arrested a teenage girl for a pass offence.

After locking her in a police van he drove her to a remote place... He told her to get undressed. She told the court she had submitted because she was terrified. She did not voice any refusal but did everything he told her to do... The court accepted that she had not agreed to have intercourse. In view of the fact, however, that she silently submitted without being forced to, 'the policeman could have taken it as consent'. Therefore he would not be convicted of rape.[1]

He was, however, sentenced to two years imprisonment under the Immorality Act!

There were further controls on occupational mobility. The law bolstering the well-established conventional colour bar in secondary industry was used to ensure that the colour–caste pecking order was not upset by blacks giving orders to whites, and also as part of the white social system to reserve jobs in times of economic downturn. But the amendment to the Industrial Conciliation Act (1956), though drafted by men with memories of the depression, was passed long after the problem of poor whites had disappeared and the evidence suggests that, as the economy continued to expand, legal barriers to black advancement in manufacturing, as opposed to mining, were less significant than other obstacles such as white social custom, trade-union pressure, and the consequences of the education structure.

Political control was also increased. Legislation such as War Measure 145 of 1943 was already on the books to prevent African

[1] *Cape Times*, 8 August 1972.

workers from striking, and trade-union organisers had long been harassed by the state. But the real pressure on leadership did not come until 1950 with the Suppression of Communism Act and its subsequent amendments, which gave the state power to ban any individual who, in the opinion of the minister, was 'furthering the aims of communism'. Apart from the useful political mileage which could be gained both locally and internationally from such legislation at the height of McCarthyism and the Cold War, it provided the state with an instrument with which it was able, at the stroke of a pen, to turn an indispensable trade-union organiser, political leader, or creative writer into an impotent non-person. He became a social leper who was confined to a magisterial area, prohibited from addressing or attending any gatherings, from meeting more than one other person at a time, from visiting any factory, university or school premises, from writing or publishing anything and from being quoted either orally or in print for periods (which could be renewed) of between three and five years. Amongst the 1300 people banned over the years 1950–77 were some who were Communists and many, Roman Catholic priests, Quaker pacifists, and others, who were not.[1] The Act was an effective instrument of control. But it also, as we shall see, clogged the cybernetic channels by which a society grows in self-awareness and understanding.

No less far-reaching however than the banning of books and writers were the consequences of the Bantu Education Act (1953), which transferred control of African schools from churches and provincial authorities to the Department of Native Affairs (later Bantu Administration, later Plural Relations, later Co-operation and Development). There were essentially three components in the new thinking. One was the desire to have a syllabus more related to those jobs in the economy which government would permit blacks to take up. Another consideration was that the syllabus should be moulded by what the white rulers considered to be good for 'Bantu'. There was no question of blacks participating in debate about reform of education for the whole country. Effectively they were told that as blacks they had no right to train for more skilled jobs in the urban economy as there was 'no place for [them] in the European community above the level

[1] Sean Moroney and Linda Ensor, *The silenced: bannings in South Africa* (Johannesburg, 1979).

of certain forms of labour'.[1] Thirdly, the government sought also to destroy the influence of men and women whom it considered to be insidiously influencing Africans to hold ideas above their station as 'black Englishmen'. There is a sense in which the destruction of so much of what the missionaries had laboured for more than a century to build was a judgement on the arrogance of British imperial power, and the wounds it had inflicted on an earlier generation of Afrikaners, who found themselves often looked down upon by their wealthier, more self-assured, English-speaking neighbours. But the action, such as the dispersal of old school libraries and the destruction of all that for which proud institutions such as Lovedale, Adams College and Fort Hare stood, was wanton and deeply wounding. The legislation to segregate university education and to create ethnic institutions under state control was aimed, said a government spokesman, 'to produce native leaders who will accept and propagate Apartheid'. Nor was it only Africans who were casualties of the philosophy of Christian National Education. South Africans of Indian descent were segregated into Indian schools whilst 'Coloured' children had to go to schools taken over by the Coloured Affairs Department. Amongst whites too a policy of ethnic segregation was used to isolate Afrikaans-speaking children from others and to foster a narrow group identity so that the educational system entrenched group differences.

Other fundamental legislation during the 1950s laid the foundations for the policy that was to emerge during the following decades of separating from South Africa a number of politically independent archipelagos. In his meeting with some members of the Natives' Representative Council in 1947, Smuts had spelt out his ideas for future policy. These were to give the NRC executive powers – roughly equal to those of a provincial council – to run those rural areas set aside as 'Native Reserves'. The Bantu Authorities Act of 1953 executed this policy but with one crucial difference. Where Smuts had intended to place all the reserves under one black authority Verwoerd divided them according to language sub-groupings, with Nguni-speakers being split into four and Sotho-speakers into three. Six years later, during which time Ghana had become independent under Nkrumah whilst Verwoerd had become prime minister of South

[1] Pelzer A. N. (ed.), *Verwoerd speaks: speeches 1948–1966* (Johannesburg, 1966).

Africa, the Promotion of Bantu Self-Government Bill was introduced, thus opening the way, though not yet explicitly, to Bantustan independence within the Verwoerdian vision of a commonwealth of nations in southern Africa. The full implications of this policy as it evolved are analysed later.

As the 1950s drew to a close those who led white South Africa along the path of exclusion could feel well pleased with themselves as they looked back over the tracks of the previous quarter century. The economy was booming; investors, both local and foreign, were satisfied. Politically, not only was the policy of exclusion becoming clearer and, in the eyes of its supporters, more moral, but the time was ripe for the National Party's crowning achievement, the establishment of a white Republic. But this confidence was severely jolted in 1960 by a series of events including the 'Winds of Change' speech in Cape Town by Harold Macmillan, the Sharpeville tragedy, an assassination attempt which severely wounded the South African prime minister, a massive flight of capital, and the banning of the two major organisations representing African political aspirations. With Verwoerd's steely resolve and the breaking of a pledge to the leaders of the black protesters who marched on Cape Town, the government regained its nerve and pushed on with the referendum in which, by a narrow majority, whites voted for a Republic. In 1961 South Africa finally severed its long constitutional link with the British Crown and, even more telling as a measure of its increasing isolation in the world, withdrew from the Commonwealth in which, during previous decades, it had been so important a member.

SOUTH AFRICA'S NEIGHBOURS

Bechuanaland

Ever since the South Africa Act (1909), which made special provision for the later incorporation of the three High Commission territories, the Pretoria government had made periodic requests that this be done; but African opposition was firmly articulated by Tshekedi Khama, second son of Khama the Great, who had been installed as Regent[1] of the Ngwato people of the

---

[1] Tshekedi was Regent whilst his nephew, Seretse, was still too young to be Chief. Seretse's father Sekgoma II (Chief Khama's eldest son) died after a brief rule when Seretse was a child of four.

Bechuanaland Protectorate in 1926. In 1936 Hertzog tried again to incorporate the territories but Britain refused. On the outbreak of war Tshekedi and other chiefs offered Britain their resources and, after visiting Pretoria to examine conditions of Africans in the Union Defence Force, refused Smuts's suggestion that they encourage their men to join it. Instead a special corps of men from the territories was created and performed distinguished service around the Mediterranean. But again in 1949 the issue was raised when the young Seretse Khama returned home with his English bride. White South Africa, which had just made 'mixed' marriages illegal, was outraged and Malan announced that he would shortly be making a formal demand for the territories. Britain's response was to resist incorporation but to announce that recognition of Seretse as chief would be withheld for five years during which time he must live outside the Protectorate. At the same time Tshekedi Khama, who had done his best to stop Seretse's marriage to an unknown outsider, was banished from the Ngwato reserve, 'while the chieftainship is in suspense'.[1] The matter was not finally resolved until 1956 when, having renounced all claims to the chieftainship, the two men returned as private citizens to Serowe.

By this time, after years of parsimony, funds had been made available for the Protectorate. In 1955 a white paper was issued outlining a five-year development programme concentrating on water, roads, education, social services, and soil conservation. In 1958 negotiations began for mining in Ngwato country. In the same year the Joint Advisory Council, representing both blacks and whites, called for the establishment of a Legislative Council. By the year of Tshekedi's death in 1959, his nephew, for whom he had so long held the Ngwato land in trust as Regent, was on his way to becoming first president of an independent Botswana.

South West Africa/Namibia

By the end of the 1930s, South West Africa had been governed for almost two decades by South Africa under mandate from the League of Nations. In practice this meant that the territory was ruled under the same laws as applied to the Cape Province and was subjected to decisions which reflected primarily the interests of whites who, in South West Africa, formed less than 10 per cent

[1] Mary Benson, *Tshekedi Khama* (London, 1960), 198.

Table 6.11. *Land utilisation in South West Africa, 1936.*

	Million ha	Percentage
Farm land (3905 white-owned farms)	30.6	44.3
Desert (Namib)	12.0	17.4
Native reserves	9.9	14.3
Game reserves	9.6	13.9
Reserved for extension of native reserves	6.5	9.4
Urban areas	0.4	0.6
Total	69.0	100.0

Source: *Official year book 1937*, 1137.

of the population. The structure of political power was reflected most clearly in the pattern of land utilisation: nearly three-quarters (71 per cent) of the land, excluding the Namib Desert itself, was allocated either as white farm land or as game reserves (table 6.11).

The African population was heterogeneous, consisting of Ovambo, Damara, Herero, Kavango and other groups whose language differences were further accentuated by the government's policy of setting up more than 20 separate rural reserves. One aim of this policy was stated as being to create 'a potential labour-recruiting field for the future'.[1] At this stage the main employers of labour, apart from the white farmers, were the railways, a few mines (including diamond mines) and fishing companies. The economy of South West Africa grew very rapidly, particularly in the mining sector in the decade 1946–56. But the fact that national income as a proportion of gross domestic product fell from 92 to 60 per cent in the same period is a measure of the extent to which much of the increased wealth was taken out of the country in the form of dividend and other payments to foreign, especially South African, investors and property owners. By 1960 mining accounted for 34 per cent and agriculture for 15 per cent of GDP and the country's major exports were diamonds, copper, karakul pelts and cattle. The manufacturing sector, based largely on the canning of pilchards in Walvis Bay, was small and the economy

[1] *Official year book 1937*, 1155.

remained primarily rural with more than three-quarters of the population living on the land.

Like South Africa, South West Africa developed with an oscillating migrant labour system at the heart of the economy, but most migrants were drawn from within the country, particularly from the northern, Ovambo and Kavango, areas. Some workers came from Angola. Between 1938 and 1960–1 the annual number of workers recruited by the monopsonistic South West African Native Labour Association (SWANLA) rose from a little under 10 000 to 25 000, of whom one-third were employed by farmers, one-third by industry and government, one-quarter (27 per cent) by the mines and the rest in fishing and other activities.

Important political changes were also taking place. Having long considered the territory as effectively annexed to South Africa, Smuts applied to the new United Nations in 1946 for its formal incorporation. The Herero, led by Chief Hosea Kutako, rejected the referendum by which South Africa hoped to win African approval for the move. The Paramount Chief, Frederick Maharero, lived in the Bechuanaland Protectorate with 14 000 of his people who had fled from von Trotha's massacres in 1904 and he appealed to the Ngwato Regent for help. Tshekedi Khama responded immediately by cabling the United Nations to refuse South Africa's request. Soon afterwards, having found him living in a tent in a squatter camp outside Johannesburg, Tshekedi Khama commissioned the Revd Michael Scott to plead the South West African cause at the United Nations on behalf of Chief Kutako.

In 1949, the National Party government, seeking simultaneously to strengthen the South West connexion and its precarious majority, decreed that white *Suid-westers* should elect six representatives to the Cape Town parliament. South Africa's view that the mandate had lapsed with the collapse of the League of Nations was submitted by the UN General Assembly to the International Court of Justice which ruled that the mandate was still in force. South Africa however ignored the implications of this judgement and continued to govern the territory. Indeed it was the further extension of apartheid, with the forcible removal of blacks from the 'Old Location' in the centre of Windhoek to a new ethnically divided non-freehold township of Katatura some miles outside, that led to confrontation on the night of 10 December (the anniversary of the UN Declaration of Human Rights) in 1959 when police fired on unarmed demonstrators, killing 11 and wounding 54. This event, which preceded the Sharpeville massacre by three months, was no less far-reaching in its consequences. It led to the transformation of the Ovamboland People's Organisation, founded in 1957 by Toivo Herman ja Toivo to fight the migrant labour system, into the South West Africa People's Organisation (SWAPO) which had a broad national base and which was dedicated to ending South Africa's colonisation of the country. Sam Nujoma, who was to become first president of SWAPO, was banished to Ovamboland following the Windhoek shootings. Soon afterwards he left the country and in Dar es Salaam set up the headquarters of SWAPO in exile. Meanwhile, inside the country, the internal wing of the organisation, which was never banned although leaders were often harassed, quietly went on with the work of political mobilisation.

Swaziland

For more than sixty years, or two generations, the kingdom of Swaziland was dominated by King Sobhuza II who was installed as *ingwenyama* in 1921. At the time of the 1936 census, the total population was 157000, of whom 98 per cent were African, almost all Swazi-speaking. Less than 3000 were white, but whites, some of them domiciled in South Africa, owned nearly half the land. A sense of having been robbed by the Land Partition Proclamation of 1907, together with a steady curtailment of traditional power, created a deep sense of distrust of the colonial government by the Swazi people and led the king, an inherently conservative man, into muted but real conflict with Britain on these issues. Nevertheless Sobhuza found South African policies even more distasteful, particularly after the promulgation in 1926 of Hertzog's Native Bills, and he came down solidly against all attempts to incorporate Swaziland into the Union. But economic ties were strong and South Africa continued to exert its power over the tiny kingdom. Before the Second World War more than two-thirds of wage-paying jobs held by Swazi were outside the country, largely in the mines of the Witwatersrand. As time went on, however, relatively more jobs were generated within Swaziland. The Havelock asbestos mine, opened in 1937, became a major employer, whilst after the Second World War the afforestation programme, and the development of sugar planting (particularly after malaria had been brought under control) led to considerable expansion of the economy, so that by 1960 11 300 Swazi were employed within Swaziland, outnumbering the 7500 recruited during the year to the South African gold and platinum mines. Important though they were, the earnings of migrants formed a less substantial proportion of Swaziland's income than was the case in either Bechuanaland or Basutoland. Although nearly every Swazi adult male worked at some stage on the Witwatersrand, the people of Swaziland remained overwhelmingly rural in their outlook. Every year the people gathered for the great first-fruits ceremony of the *Ncwala* and the country, untroubled by constitutional crises or rivals to the king, retained its cohesiveness for longer than most other areas. But the conservatism of the king and his elderly councillors created strains in the years after the Second World War, when younger more educated men and women sought to modernise the social structure and to create a more democratically governed society.

Basutoland

Entirely surrounded by South Africa, the small mountain kingdom ruled, under Britain, by Moshweshwe's heirs had almost nothing which it could sell to the outside world except labour. In years gone by the Sotho had adapted quickly and efficiently to the opportunities presented by the opening up of the markets around the diamond and gold mines. Even after the fertile plains along the west bank of the Caledon River had been lost to the conquering white settlers in the Orange Free State they had grown and exported large surpluses of grain. However, by the end of the First World War, as a result of population pressure combined with the destructive effects of the widespread migrant labour system, Basutoland produced only just enough for its people to eat. This state of affairs continued until the great drought at the beginning of the 1930s, after which time the country became a steadily increasing net importer of grain. Over the 25 years from 1936 to 1961, the number of men engaged for work on the mines from Basutoland and the Orange Free State rose by two-thirds from 46000 to 69000. Over the same period the number of paid jobs within Basutoland remained a fraction of those held in South Africa.

Despite the internal poverty and lack of employment opportunities, Basutoland had a well-established infrastructure of education and one of the highest literacy rates in Africa. In 1945 the Roman Catholic Pius XII College was established where students could take degrees of the University of South Africa as could blacks in the Union. In politics too there was a great deal of activity. In 1952 the Basutoland Congress Party, closely modelled on South Africa's ANC, was founded by Ntsu Mokhehle. And in 1958 Chief Leabua Jonathan, later to be first prime minister of the independent Lesotho, established the Basutoland National Party with support from the somewhat surprising combination of Roman Catholics and the government of South Africa. It was supported also by the queen regent in her attempts to retain power after the young king came of age. Utterly dependent though it was on the South African economy, Basutoland by the end of the 1950s was being groomed, like Bechuanaland and Swaziland, for political independence.

South Africa was loath to accept this fact. J. G. Strijdom, who succeeded Malan as prime minister in 1954, was so anxious to achieve incorporation that he, the arch-republican, was willing to postpone a Republic if that would reduce opposition to transfer of the High Commission territories. But he died in 1958 without achieving either of his two goals. Paradoxically, it was the very failure of South Africa to achieve incorporation that enabled Strijdom's successor, Verwoerd, to play his master-stroke. Recognising that South Africa would have to live with the three territories as politically independent neighbours, Verwoerd turned this defeat into the springboard of a new strategy. Given that the three areas were dependent both for jobs and goods on a neighbouring country whose economic and military strength relative to theirs was overwhelming, there was no way in which their political independence could pose an effective threat to white control in South Africa itself. Indeed as Verwoerd saw, there were positive advantages in not incorporating the High Commission territories. For, as citizens of independent countries, the people living there would exert far less pressure to change South African society than if they were constitutionally part of it. Moreover South Africa would have international law and practice behind her in preventing them, as foreigners, from playing any role in her internal affairs. So despite one last appeal for incorporation in 1963, South Africa began to move towards a policy not only of welcoming the territories' coming independence but also of carving out and granting political independence to those parts of South Africa which, historically, had become labour reserves. The boundaries of the nation state were to be used to reinforce the barriers of language, colour and urbanisation. Blacks were to be further excluded by declaring them foreigners. Without wavering from the goal of maintaining control of the core of the economy, white South Africa's strategy gradually changed during the 1950s and early 1960s from incorporation to a policy of dispossession.[1]

MAINTAINING THE WHITE REPUBLIC, 1961–76

There were two sides to the coin with which the South African government sought to buy prosperity and security inside the laager of an all-white Republic. One was the migrant labour system, the other was the Bantustan policy. Both had deep historic roots. One was modelled almost entirely on the pattern which the gold-mining industry had evolved for itself over two generations before 1948. The other grew out of the nineteenth-century policies of Sir Theophilus Shepstone and the Land Act of 1913.

The Natives (Urban Areas) Act, as amended in 1952, had made the permanent urbanisation of black workers and their families more difficult but not impossible. However, government policy was aimed not only at slowing down but also at halting and ultimately at reversing the flow of black people to the cities. In 1968 labour regulations were promulgated which prohibited new workers from coming from the rural areas unless they had entered into a contract which had to be renewed annually back in the reserves. This break effectively nullified section 10(1)(b) of the Natives (Urban Areas) Act which had made it possible for workers to acquire residence rights for themselves and their families in town. The consequences of this policy became most clearly visible in the western Cape where, in 1966, employers were instructed that henceforth they must reduce the number of Africans on their payrolls by 5 per cent per annum. An immediate

[1] For further analysis see SAIRR, *Towards economic and political justice in South Africa* (Johannesburg, 1980).

consequence was the winding down of the local authorities' housing programmes to the point where, for some years after 1972, not one house was built for occupation by an African family. Meanwhile another goal of government policy, the fostering of economic growth, was assiduously pursued. Thousands of jobs were created during these boom years as new docks, roads, and buildings were constructed. Cape Town itself could not provide enough labour so, naturally, more workers were pulled off the land. But the Africans who were drawn in were not supposed to be there. Employers were permitted to erect only 'temporary' accommodation, which they did in the form of damp, windy, cold barns unfit for human occupation. The occupants referred to them as 'stables'. But the demand for labour continued to expand, not least in state sectors such as the railways and harbours, where between 1968 and 1974 the number of African workers more than quadrupled from 1400 to over 6000 men. By 1977, despite recession in the building industry where large numbers of migrants had been employed, the number of contract workers in Cape Town was approximately double what it had been in 1968. Somewhat more solid structures were built to house workers as time went on but, like the 'temporary' barns (still being used a decade later), they were designed for men only, without their families. Thus by 1976 the male:female ratio of Africans in Cape Town was, according to official statistics, almost 3:1. In Langa, a township where the heaviest concentration of migrants was housed, the proportion of men to women was over 12:1. The shortage of normal family housing both for the natural population growth of the 10000 African families who had acquired residence rights in Cape Town during earlier years, and also for more recent migrants from the country, was such that many people had no alternative but to build corrugated iron shanties for themselves wherever they could find some unused ground near the city. Concentrations of African squatter communities mushroomed, particularly after 1975, when the scattered dwellings were brought together in two major areas. One of these, Modderdam–Wekgenot–Unibel, where 25000 people lived, was destroyed by the government's bulldozers over six months beginning in the cold wet winter of 1977. The other, Crossroads, was continually threatened with demolition though later, after a unique combination of grass-roots resistance and international pressure, reprieved. Despite evidence of viable, well-organised communities, and despite the fact that, at Unibel, for example, the average household head had been in Cape Town for over 11 years and his spouse for more than five years, official policy was clear. With the special exception of Crossroads residents, wives and children illegally in Cape Town must return to the 'homelands'. Men with jobs had to go back to the labour compounds; those who had lost their jobs in the recession or who worked in the informal sector were required to leave the city and return to the reserves where there was virtually no prospect of work. Above all, restrictions were tightened to make it more difficult for people in the rural areas to move into the city, either to look for work or to join their husbands and fathers.

Not only in Cape Town but even more so in the industrial concentration in the southern Transvaal as well as in Durban, Port Elizabeth and other towns, the decade beginning in the mid-1960s witnessed an unprecedented expansion of single-sex barracks into which the workers of the country's economic miracle were directed as the migrant labour system became yet more firmly embedded as the centre-piece of apartheid's political economy. Precise figures are difficult to obtain, but it would seem that by the mid-1970s at least half the black men legally at work in the urban areas of South Africa were housed on a single basis in accommodation much of which had been built within the past decade.

But increasingly force had to be used to maintain the system. The number of cases sent for trial under the pass laws rose to a peak of 670 300 in 1968. Despite the subsequent downturn, the average annual number of prosecutions in the first half of the 1970s was still equivalent to more than one every minute of the day and night throughout the year. During the thirty years after the Second World War, the total number of prosecutions was more than 11.7 million (table 6.12). Despite this massive police net, many people managed to live in the cities illegally, either paying a fine or bribing the police whenever they were caught. Others lived in the vast shanty areas that mushroomed in those fragments of Bantustans within commuting range of cities (often involving long distances and arduous hours of daily travel) but where urban restrictions against housing and families did not apply. In Cape Town, over 1000 kilometres from the nearest 'homeland', the

Table 6.12. *Pass Law prosecutions, 1921–75.*

	Annual average number of contraventions (in thousands)
1921–9	54.7
1930–9	110.8
1940–9	157.7
1950–9	318.7
1960–9	469.1
1970–5	541.5

Note: Until (and including) 1962 figures are for convictions, which are slightly lower than prosecutions.
Source: *Union statistics for fifty years*, F.4; *Annual reports of the Commissioner of the South African police* (Pretoria).

inexorable logic of the policy led to the destruction of hundreds of homes by bulldozers. By using people as workers, argued Dr Verwoerd, one did not thereby integrate them into one's society any more than one integrated the ox, the ass, and the tractor which were also instruments of one's economic activity.

Parallel with the expansion of the migrant labour system went the unfolding of the Bantustan policy, that is, of constituting the Bantu homelands into self-governing or even nominally 'independent' territories. The Promotion of Bantu Self-Government Act (1959) was followed by the establishment in 1963 of the Transkei Legislative Assembly. This replaced the old *Bunga*, which, with a majority of elected voting members, had for so long been the forum for Transkei political debate. The TLA had roughly the same authority as a provincial council, with executive power over such matters as roads, education, and agriculture, but unlike the *Bunga* the Assembly can never be said to have been properly representative. Not only were elected members in a minority until 1976 but it was born, and lived its whole life, under the shadow of Proclamation 400. These emergency regulations ensured that no political gathering could take place without the express permission of a magistrate, and also empowered the police to detain without trial. The chief minister of the Transkei throughout this period was Chief Kaiser Matanzima, many of whose political opponents were arbitrarily arrested, notably on the eve of a vital pre-independence election. In at least one case the order to detain somebody for obstructing the cause of justice was signed before the police even asked him any questions.

Side by side with the political developments, whereby ten different 'homelands' were herded along the path towards constitutional independence, were the steps aimed first of all at reducing the movement of Africans to the major cities, and secondly, at stimulating some economic growth within the embryo states. In its white paper on the report of the Tomlinson Commission, which had been established to work out the Bantustan blueprint, the government rejected the possibility of white-controlled capital being invested within the 'homelands'. There emerged instead the policy of border industries whereby, through the carrot of tax railway-rating and other concessions, and the stick of the Physical Planning Act (1967) which empowered the Minister of Planning to prohibit an increase in the number of African employees in any particular factory, steps were taken to direct industrial expansion out of the existing urban areas to various decentralised growth points, many of them situated on the borders of the reserves. The evidence suggests that the policy of industrial decentralisation was not particularly successful in stimulating either border industries or, after the prohibition on white capital in black areas had been dropped, regional economic growth within the homelands. Indeed more jobs seem to have been destroyed by the application of the planning legislation than were created in the designated growth points.[1]

The truth was that those areas designated as Bantustans had long since become labour reserves on the periphery of, but with strong symbiotic ties to, the central core of the South African economy. Thus in the Transkei, for example, the number of migrants in the five years prior to independence doubled from 191 600 in 1971 to 377 800 in 1976. By this time no less than six out of every seven Transkeians earning a cash income were doing so in jobs outside the territory, notably on the Witwatersrand and in the western Cape. Furthermore, at least half the African population of the Republic did not have even that tenuous link with the Bantustans. By the 1970s the proportions of Africans

---

[1] Keith Gottschalk, 'Industrial decentralisation: jobs and wages', *South African Labour Bulletin*, 1977, **3**, 5.

living permanently on the white-owned farms and in the towns were of the order of one-quarter and one-third respectively. Those living on farms were in a particularly difficult situation, for the combination of population growth with changing techniques of agricultural production was pushing people off the land. Moving directly to town was illegal, so many families went to the densely populated rural ghettoes which mushroomed in the 'homelands'. There wives and children had to be left whilst the men went off to town as migrant workers.

Not everybody moved simply because of the decline in agricultural employment (see table 6.5). It is estimated that between 1960 and 1970 approximately half a million people were either endorsed out of towns or compelled to move from rural areas (called 'black spots') where the presence of Africans was considered undesirable by politicians and civil servants wishing to 'consolidate the homelands'. Another million or more were moved off white-owned farms where they lived as tenants of one sort or another paying their rent either in cash or, frequently, in labour. These removals created much hardship and bitterness, particularly amongst those who were moved to densely populated rural resettlement areas where there was no agricultural land and where people were miles from any employment opportunities.

Africans, whether they lived in the old reserves or not, were declared to be citizens of one of the 'homelands'. This meant that as each Bantustan became independent, starting with the Transkei in 1976, large numbers of blacks were formally deprived of their South African citizenship. The logical end of the policy, as government spokesmen proclaimed in the mid-1970s, was a Republic of South Africa in which all African inhabitants had been transformed into foreigners.

It is possible to interpret the policy of apartheid not so much as one which divides black from white, or even black from black, although it does both these things in full measure, but as one which divides the black man in half: he is a labour unit for the benefit and comfort of white people in towns and on farms, and a human being with his civic and political rights and, for many, even his family rights restricted to the rural Bantustans. Behind all the rhetoric of a constellation of states, a commonwealth of nations in southern Africa, each with its own 'homeland', lay the harsh reality of a single economy built on the assumption that four-fifths of those who worked in and drew their sustenance from it were no more than labour units and had no right to be there in any other capacity. Such was the fundamental flaw in the grand design of apartheid and such was the basic reason for black resistance to it.

Despite a proud tradition of judicial independence against arbitrary state power, the law in South Africa had, as has been convincingly argued, also long served as an instrument of political domination.[1] Pass laws, for example, did not apply to whites, but for Africans they were a cause of police harassment and, as has been shown, arrests on a massive scale. One significant development was that the law became increasingly determined by administrative fiat. Nowhere was this more evident than in legislation regarding where Africans might work and what jobs they might perform.[2] Proclamations and departmental circulars, which had never been debated in parliament, acquired the force of law. This growth of executive power, which bypassed both parliament and the courts and was not matched by any significant attempts to impose effective checks against its abuse, sprang not only from determination to redesign the society in accordance with ideological blueprints but also from the necessity of dealing with increasing resistance to the policies being imposed on blacks by means of the state's legal–administrative machinery.

Sometimes executive action was aimed against leaders and organisers, sometimes against writers and their ideas, thus reducing the flow of information and ideas. Blacks did not need Peter Abrahams, Alex la Guma, Ezekiel Mphahlele, or the young poets of the 1970s to tell them what life was like in the townships, although they did need them for their own self-awareness and understanding of the past. But whites did not know even the facts and became increasingly ignorant of what was happening in their own country. Indeed, not only readers of books but television viewers in London or New York often saw and heard more of life within Soweto or Langa than did whites living next door in Johannesburg or Cape Town. And so, over the years, the white electorate was led into an intellectual darkness that was to leave it grasping for a reality it could not see.

The denial of *habeas corpus* in several different Acts passed

---

[1] Albie Sachs, *Justice in South Africa* (Berkeley, 1973).
[2] G. M. Budlender, 'Administrative rule of African workers', *Responsa Meridiana*, 1975, **3**, 1.

between 1963 and 1976 empowered the police to detain people
without being obliged to bring them before any court, or to grant
them access to a lawyer, or even to inform their families where
they were. People vanished from anything between a few days to
periods of over a year without any charge having been laid against
them. Often, though not always, detention was used to extract
information. Disturbing reports, some given on oath, began to
emerge asserting the widespread use of torture in Namibia as well
as in South Africa.[1] In 1963 Mr L. Ngudle died after having been
detained under the General Laws Amendment Act. He was
alleged to have hanged himself. From this time until the death
in September 1977 of Steve Biko, first president of the South
African Students' Organisation and honorary president of the
Black People's Convention, at least 41 people, detained without
any charges having been brought against them, died in the hands
of the police.

But some political opponents were charged and the courts were
required to pronounce judgement on activities which in
democratic societies were part of the normal process of public
debate. In a pre-dawn raid in December 1956, 156 respected
citizens were arrested and charged with high treason. The nub of
the state's case was the Freedom Charter, a document in which
the African National Congress and others had sought to spell out
their political goals along the lines of social democratic parties in
the western world. The trial dragged on for over four years until
the remaining defendants were found not guilty and acquitted. By
this time however the ANC itself had been banned and many
of the treason trialists were soon to find themselves similarly
attacked by decrees against which there was no appeal to any
judge. In 1967 the Terrorism Act defined terrorism (retrospectively to 1962) so widely that, as the Dean of Law at the University
of Natal put it, nobody in South Africa could exist without doing
something which, in terms of the Act, could be construed as
terrorism.[2] One of the most publicised of the many trials that took
place in terms of this legislation was that of nine young 'black

---

[1] SA Institute of Race Relations, *Detention without trial in South Africa 1976–1977*
(Johannesburg, 1977); The Christian Institute of Southern Africa, *Torture in South
Africa?* (Cape Town, n.d.); H. Hunke and J. Ellis, *Torture: a cancer in our society*
(Windhoek, 1978); United Nations, 'Maltreatment and torture of prisoners in South
Africa', *Report of the Special Committee on Apartheid* (New York, 1973).

[2] A. S. Matthews, *Law, order and liberty in South Africa* (Cape Town, 1971).

consciousness' leaders whose trial in Pretoria from 1974 to 1976 on a number of all-embracing charges culminated in their being found guilty and sentenced to between 5 and 6 years imprisonment on Robben Island, where many of the older generation of political leaders were already incarcerated.

Another measure of social stress, albeit less directly political in nature,[1] was the astonishing number of murders, which rose from an average of seven per day in 1960 to twenty per day in 1977. Over this same period of time well over 1200 persons were executed, giving South Africa the unenviable reputation in the late 1960s of being responsible for almost half of the legal executions in the world.[2] A yet more striking manifestation of the rise of violence in the region was the rapid increase in South Africa's military budget in response to the ring of fire that began to spread round her borders in the mid-1960s as the various liberation movements from Mozambique, Zimbabwe, Angola, Namibia, and from South Africa itself embarked upon military, guerrilla, campaigns.

The increase in resources devoted to defence enabled South Africa to build up considerable military strength capable of dealing with any armies south of the Sahara that were not reinforced by military aid from outside the continent. In terms of manpower the armed forces were expanded by means of white conscription, from just under 10000 men in 1961 to 110000 men in 1974. In line with its increasing importance, the period of citizen-force training grew from three months in 1961 to an initial period of two years plus continuous training of 19 days a year for ten years. In addition to the citizen and permanent forces there was also the police, including the security police. The Bureau for State Security was established in 1969 to co-ordinate and complement police security and military intelligence. Supporting all these was a home-guard of 75000 commandos organised to defend their residential and industrial areas in case of civil disorder.

The hardware necessary to equip these forces was acquired no less rapidly. Despite a 1963 United Nations resolution calling for an arms embargo against South Africa, the Republic was able, by

[1] But see Frantz Fanon, *The wretched of the earth* (New York, 1963) for insight into the link between violence and a colonialist political structure.
[2] John Dugard, *Human rights and the South African legal order* (Princeton, 1978), 126.

shifting orders from Britain to France and elsewhere, over the next decade, to import and/or to build up her own capacity to produce (often under licence) a wide range of military equipment including aircraft such as Impala (the Italian Aermacchi MB326) and Mirages (French); helicopters (French); missiles, especially the Cactus/Crotale anti-aircraft system (SA/French); radar defence systems (UK and West Germany); herbicides, including two types used for military purposes in Vietnam (USA); as well as a variety of other equipment from Portugal, Spain, Israel, and Russia.[1] By the mid-1970s about a thousand contractors and sub-contractors were actively engaged in the local arms industry and the country was practically self-sufficient in the production of rockets, armoured cars, ammunition, bombs (including napalm), firearms and mines. Reserves of oil, estimated to be sufficient for five years, had been built up. In 1977 it was widely reported, though firmly denied by the government, that South Africa was building a nuclear testing site in the Kalahari Desert. In short, by the time of the mandatory arms embargo imposed by the United Nations in November 1977, South Africa was far more prepared for war than she had been in September 1939. Politically however, despite the extent of help from the west in providing arms, she was far more isolated.

THE STRUGGLE FOR LIBERATION, 1961–77

Resistance in South Africa after 1960 was inextricably linked with the wider events of decolonisation as they unfolded from Ghana's independence in 1957 to the collapse of the Portuguese empire in the mid-1970s. But the South African struggle was not the same as that in countries seeking to free themselves from control by a distant metropolitan power. It was an altogether tougher, more prolonged, and more difficult battle between people all of whom were firmly rooted in a country whose rulers had at their disposal the technology and organisation which makes modern authoritarianism possible. Such a situation led to the evolution of a number of different, and sometimes competing, strategies.

---

[1] Anthony Sampson, *The arms bazaar* (Sevenoaks, 1978), 167–8; Signe Landgren-Bäckström, *Southern Africa: the escalation of a conflict* (Stockholm International Peace Research Institute, Stockholm, 1976).

During 1961, within a year after the two African Congresses had been banned, no less than four different underground resistance groups emerged. Umkhonto we Sizwe (Spear of the Nation) led by Nelson Mandela, who had been Transvaal leader of the ANC, was formed with the aim of bringing about political change by means of selective sabotage against specific installations and buildings. Similarly Poqo (Alone) which had tenuous links with the PAC, the Yui Chui Chan Club[1] (which grew into the National Liberation Front), composed mainly of young black intellectuals who had broken away from the Unity movement, and the African Resistance Movement made up largely of young whites, began to plan and, in some cases to execute, militant forms of resistance. Between December 1961 and the end of 1964 there were more than 200 acts of sabotage or attempted sabotage primarily against state property, including police stations and railway lines. But the security police were well organised, and virtually all underground activity during this period seems to have been unearthed and crushed in a series of arrests and trials including that of the Umkhonto high command captured on a farm, Rivonia, outside Johannesburg in 1963. The majority of those jailed or hanged for their underground political activities were of course black, but resistance was by no means confined to any one group. Nguni lawyers; Afrikaans poets; Sotho journalists; English-speaking housewives; Marxists and Christians; Muslims and Jews; milkmen and engineers; all manner of South Africans and Namibians became caught up in dangerous underground work.

Others went into exile and from there began military training. In August 1966 the first major armed conflict south of the Zambezi since the wars of dispossession had ended two generations previously took place when SWAPO guerrillas clashed with South African forces in northern Namibia. Exactly a year later a combined ANC/ZAPU (Zimbabwe African People's Union) force fought Rhodesian troops in a series of engagements in the Wankie area. The insurgents were defeated and the ANC/ZAPU alliance was heavily criticised by both ZANU (Zimbabwe African National Union) and the PAC on the ground that it would draw South

[1] Named after the head of China's trade-union organisation, who led the Peking delegation to the Afro-Asian Solidarity Conference held in Tanganyika, February 1963.

African troops into Rhodesia and that it was bad guerrilla tactics to try and gobble up a regular army. In the event the failure, after two more similar attempts early in 1968 and 1970, to infiltrate South Africa via Rhodesia caused the ANC to turn to other methods until the victory of FRELIMO in Mozambique opened a shorter overland route via Swaziland into South Africa. By 1978 it was estimated that some 4000 black South Africans were undergoing military training outside the country.[1]

Closely allied with the resort to arms and the escalating guerrilla war was active international diplomacy. The ANC and the PAC established offices in different countries including Zambia, Tanzania, Algeria, India, Great Britain and the USA and, later in Angola and Mozambique. Diplomatic links were also established with other countries including Russia, China, and Nigeria, while the ANC in particular made sure that there was a regular South African anti-apartheid presence at the United Nations and meetings of the OAU. All this did much to mobilise world opinion against apartheid. In Africa the commitment to end white minority rule in the south was spelt out clearly in the Lusaka Manifesto (1969) which, whilst uncompromising in its attack on racism, nevertheless laid the basis for possible future negotiation.

Another important point of pressure was the campaign organised, largely from outside the country, by the South African Non-Racial Olympic Committee (Sanroc) to boycott segregated sports teams representing the country abroad. All players and administrators were anxious to get back into the international arena but there was some division between those who believed they should push ahead with integrating previously all-white clubs and leagues whilst leaving the rest of the society to catch up in its own time, and those who, arguing that 'You cannot play normal sport in an abnormal society', wanted the boycott to remain until apartheid had been dismantled.

Amongst those who believed that violent revolution was not possible given the military strength and determination of whites were some who argued that it was necessary to make use of such platforms as were available within the framework of apartheid in order to work to change that structure. Thus, Chief Gatsha Buthelezi, a former member of the ANC youth league, used the protection afforded by his position as chief executive councillor

[1] *Financial Mail*, 11 August 1978.

of the Kwazulu Legislative Authority to speak out on political issues in the late 1960s as no black politician had done since the banning of the African Congresses. Furthermore, he built up an organised and independent political base which extended beyond the boundaries of Kwazulu. He sought to shift the focus of action away from the Bantustan structure to a broader cultural movement, Inkhatha, which though Zulu-dominated was not, he insisted, an ethnic organisation. In 1977 the minister of police warned that he would take steps to ban Inkhatha if it opened its doors to non-Zulu members, but Buthelezi refused to comply. Nevertheless the chief was widely criticised, particularly by younger blacks who argued that his strategy served more to legitimise the policy of apartheid than to provide a fulcrum on which to lever the government away from its chosen path. Many feared the growth of an exclusive and destructive Zulu nationalism. But the possibility of Inkhatha emerging as a powerful vehicle of black resistance remained.

A similar strategy, though lacking Buthelezi's political skill, was followed by the Labour Party founded in 1966 to fight for those seats on the Coloured Persons Representative Council (set up by the government to replace direct representation in parliament) which were not nominated by the state president. This strategy, rejected 20 years previously by Africans when they withdrew from the Native Representative Council, was vehemently opposed, particularly in the western Cape, where the political descendants of the Unity movement still had considerable influence. Following Tabata and others, they maintained that all institutions created by the government were essentially established to side-track people from the real arena where the struggle for power had to be waged. When, in 1976, the government rejected the major findings of the Theron Commission, including one to the effect that 'Coloured' people should obtain direct political representation in the central parliament, the standing of the CRC fell to an all-time low.

After the Suppression of Communism Act had been used to mow down whole ranks of trade-union leadership by the simple process of banning them, the labour movement was fairly quiet for most of the 1960s. But early in 1973 a wave of strikes welled up in Durban and swept through the country pushing up wages in an unprecedented bout of employer self-examination. Then, in

September 1973, began the first of the major compound confrontations that were to rock the mining industry. In the four years up to September 1977 some 200 men were killed and over 1300 injured in approximately 78 different incidents caused in mines around the country by a variety of factors including wage grievances, inadequate structure of communication, and the migrant labour system.[1] There had long been instances of such disturbances but what was new was the frequency and the intensity of the confrontations which involved large numbers of miners.

During this period some employers, including major mining magnates led by Harry Oppenheimer, indicated a willingness, which had not existed in previous labour crises, to consider the prospect of unionisation of their black workers. The government too felt compelled to move and, in 1973, legislation was passed to make some provision for communication between workers and employers. However, the liaison committees which the state promoted were much criticised by trade unionists on the ground that by putting workers and management on the same committee effective power was left in the hands of employers. Works committees to which only workers were elected made some form of bargaining possible, but they were so constituted that workers were kept in isolation from the wider trade-union movement. No provision was made for full-time union organisers to participate in or guide the workers' negotiations. Despite the unwillingness of the state to concede much in the way of enabling trade unionism to flourish, and despite the continued harassment, sometimes even to death, of those assisting workers to organise, the labour movement continued to grow during the first half of the 1970s. Its potential power remained.

No less challenging was the thinking of a younger generation of black intellectuals who began to emerge in the second half of the 1960s with a philosophy of black consciousness, which argued the need to enhance black self-awareness by means of withdrawal into exclusive black organisations, of which the South African Students' Organisation (SASO), founded in 1969, was the most important. This movement was undertaken within the context of asserting the inclusive unity of the country as emphasised in the

[1] Dudley Horner and Alide Kooy, 'Conflict on South African mines 1972–1979' (Saldru working paper 29, Cape Town, 1980).

movement's slogan 'One Azania. One Nation' — Azania being the name by which they wanted a black-dominated South Africa to be known. The movement learnt a good deal — as their fathers and grandfathers had done before them — from blacks in the United States. Nor was it only American writing, by Malcolm X and others that was important; the work of Frantz Fanon, for example, though also banned, was obtained and avidly read.

For some years SASO, despite its militant criticism of the South African system, was given a surprising amount of rope by the government which, misunderstanding the sharp attack on the role played by white liberals, seemed to hope that at the bottom of black consciousness lay an acceptance of the whole philosophy of *eiesoortige ontwikkeling* (one's own sort of development) on which white control was based. The hope proved vain and by 1973 the government had started to ban its leaders, one of whom, Abraham Tiro, was the following year killed in suspicious circumstances by a parcel bomb that reached him in Botswana where he was co-ordinating black student activities in southern Africa. Later in the same year, following a rally to celebrate FRELIMO's victory in Mozambique, much of the black student leadership still left inside the country was swept up into gaol.

Coinciding with, and to some extent an expression of, the rise of black consciousness was a fresh burst of writing as people found ways of expressing their feelings publicly inside the country. But even poetry, oblique though its shafts often were, was not without its dangers and a number of poets and play-writers were banned. It is against this background that the eruption of events which surprised seasoned observers of the South African scene, black and white alike, can best be understood. The march on 16 June 1976 of schoolchildren in Soweto, so provocatively handled by the police, sparked off a wave of protest, including burning of buildings, throughout the country. Altogether about 700 people, a large proportion of them teenagers, were killed, most of them shot by police. Over 6000 persons were arrested and prosecuted.[1] The government was not unduly stretched by the revolt, for the army, while on standby, never had to be called in, but the episode marked the beginning of an altogether new mood of fearless self-assurance in a generation which had been raised within the framework of 'Bantu' and 'Coloured' education, yet had rejected

[1] John Kane-Berman, *Soweto* (Johannesburg, 1978).

it totally. The boycott of schools which the ANC had tried and failed to achieve at the introduction of Bantu Education in 1953 spread like a bushfire and continued to rage fiercely. By August 1977 in Soweto, not only had the pupils successfully organised a total boycott of all secondary schools but they had caused the mass resignation, in the midst of a deep economic recession, of more than half their teachers. Similarly members of the Soweto Urban Bantu Council were forced to resign. Although the scholars had won the battle against compulsory Afrikaans, the government had by no means yet lost the war over educational reform. In 1978 pupils were divided and some children returned to school. The teachers who remained continued to struggle with a heavy-handed bureaucracy whose lip-service to change was unmatched by action.

Another form of resistance was perhaps the most effective of all. Simply by disobeying certain legislation and ignoring its prohibitions people forced the government continually to face new realities that fell outside its plan. The most notable form of this 'informal' resistance was that against the pass laws, one aim of which was to prevent people settling in town. Precise figures are impossible to obtain but in Cape Town, for example, the actual African population was thought to be perhaps as much as 80 per cent above the official figure. And in Soweto, where the 1970 census counted 600 000 people, it was widely believed that there were more than a million. But even amongst those whose presence was illegal were many who had forced their presence to be recognised and accepted. Thus the squatter communities living around Johannesburg after the Second World War, led by men like James Sofasonke Mpanza, compelled reluctant local authorities to grant them effective rights to housing in town. A generation later African squatters were still doggedly battling against eviction but, as in Cape Town during the mid 1970s, meeting with the increasing force of government bulldozers and batons. Nor was it only in urban areas that government met with strong opposition. The reaction of African women in the remote western Transvaal to the introduction of passes in 1957 and the peasants' revolt in Pondoland during 1960 were but two manifestations of determined resistance which were crushed by superior might.[1]

[1] Charles Hooper, *Brief authority* (London, 1960); Govan Mbeki, *South Africa: the peasants' revolt* (Harmondsworth, 1964).

Those who struggled for liberation did not confine themselves to resistance. There was also a long tradition of affirmative action building up self-help community projects such as the Zenzele movement, which began to grow in the 1930s and later affiliated to the International Country Women of the World. And one of the immediate fruits of the black-consciousness movement were the community projects such as the Zanempilo Clinic in the eastern Cape and a cooperative clothing factory in Cape Town. But these latter two were regarded as subversive and they were banned by the state.

The line dividing the politics of exclusion from those of inclusion which has been traced through the history of this period ran also through the Church. This became most clearly apparent following a conference convened at Cottesloe in Johannesburg by the World Council of Churches at the time of the Sharpeville crisis in 1960. The Cottesloe statement by church leaders, including those of the Dutch Reformed Church, was repudiated by Verwoerd and subsequently by all the Afrikaans-speaking churches. But the split did not follow precise denominational or language lines. Some of the strongest opposition to the theory and practice of apartheid came from within the three Dutch Reformed churches, eleven of whose theologians had published a sharp attack on race discrimination shortly before the Cottesloe Conference in Johannesburg. And, from the time of its establishment in 1963 until it was banned in 1977, the Christian Institute led by the Revd Beyers Naudé, a former moderator of the southern Transvaal synod of the Dutch Reformed Church, played a major role in strengthening the opposition of individual Christians and of some denominations to the ideology of apartheid. No less important was the work of the Christian Institute in forging links between the established churches and the rapidly growing African Independent Churches which rejected white leadership, and which provided an appropriate structure for nurturing social security and cohesiveness in the turbulent process of economic and cultural transition.[1]

Besides the churches, universities and the press were also embroiled in the political arena. Legislation passed in 1959 authorising the government to impose restrictions on universities based on colour was vigorously opposed, particularly by the

[1] J. P. Kiernan, 'Poor and Puritan: an attempt to view Zionism as a collective response to urban poverty', *African Studies*, 1977, **36**, 1.

English-medium universities whose students were actively organised, through the National Union of South African Students, in their opposition to apartheid. A long tradition of press freedom in the country helped to strengthen the hand of editors whose newspapers came under increasingly frequent attack. But there was much the newspapers did not print for fear of state reprisals. Moreover, for the majority of papers, news was generally seen to be that which interested white readers. Nevertheless the role of several newspapers in facing both government and the general public with uncomfortable truths and with trenchant criticism was an important, although by itself inadequate, check on the increasingly arbitrary power of the state.

By the mid-1970s resistance in South Africa was stiffened by the astonishing fearlessness of children going out against bullets armed only with dustbin lids and stones. At the same time a process of clarifying targets could be traced by young blacks, one of whom pointed out that, 'In 1960 some 30 000 Africans marched peacefully into the centre of Cape Town; in 1976 their children burnt liquor outlets, and schools in the black townships; next time it will be white houses.' This new courage was not unconnected with the victory of FRELIMO in Mozambique and the guerrilla struggles in Rhodesia and Namibia which had an important psychological impact on all South Africans. Over the three years from the coup in Lisbon in April 1974 through the invasion of Angola in 1975, and the uprising in Soweto, Langa and elsewhere in 1976 to the killing of Steve Biko in 1977, South Africa crossed a watershed. In the face of mounting world pressure the government embarked on a limited programme of selective desegregation. But it showed no signs of yielding on the fundamental structure of apartheid which was designed to exclude black South Africans from effective political power. Not even the courage of the young could yet guarantee that sort of change from within.

Elsewhere in southern Africa, however, the two decades following Ghana's independence in 1957 were years of considerable political change as the process of decolonisation permeated the continent. For the three countries of Botswana, Lesotho and Swaziland the long struggle against political incorporation had almost been won by 1960. In 1962 Prime Minister Verwoerd acknowledged publicly that South Africa accepted the possibility of independence, although he still hoped that the three territories might yet see the benefits of becoming part of the South African Commonwealth of Nations. The first of the pre-independence elections took place in 1964 in Swaziland where, a year previously, widespread strikes had caused Britain to air-lift troops into the country. A number of political organisations emerged with broad agreement on three basic demands: that the king become a constitutional monarch; that independence be granted immediately; and that all racial discrimination be abolished. The king accepted the implicit challenge and formed his own Imbokodvo movement[1] to contest the elections which he won without a single opposition candidate retaining his deposit, let alone winning a seat. The election had taken place under a constitution which guaranteed an equal share of seats to the white community, to the Swazi hierarchy, and to voters on the national roll. But as soon as it had won the elections the Imbokodvo disfranchised all white South Africans in Swaziland, challenged the constitution as being racist, and demanded immediate independence. By February 1967 a new constitution acceptable both to the Imbokodvo (to which many of the young radicals had flocked after 1964) and to Britain had been drafted. The country gained its independence in 1968, two years after Botswana and Lesotho.

The problems of devising suitable institutions which would contain different interest groups and make orderly change possible were formidable. For Swaziland, particularly, the duality between loyalty to the king in whom was vested all the authority of the nation, and the emergence of a new set of loyalties to law and to the country, was a source of increasing tension. The king's power was being encroached upon and increasingly challenged by the younger more educated people who were moving into administrative and other jobs within the government and the private sector of the economy. In April 1973 the king issued an order in council which suspended the constitution, declared a state of emergency, vested all power in himself, and enabled him to detain persons for 60 days at a time, without trial. The leader of the opposition, Dr A. P. Zwane, President of the Ngwane National

[1] The full name, *Imbokodvo lemalabala*, means literally, 'the grinding-stone-that-brings-together-many-colours'. Hilda Kuper, *Sobhuza II, Ngwenyama and King of Swaziland* (London, 1978), 250.

Liberation Congress, was subsequently detained four times. By 1977 the king was still firmly in control. However, there were increasing signs, such as the teacher dissatisfaction of mid-1976, that the cleavage between the conservative, traditional hierarchy governing through the Swazi National Council and the more educated, urbanised people was deepening dangerously although the king, aged nearly 80, with his immense authority, was able to command a certain consensus.

In Lesotho Chief Jonathan won the pre-independence elections in 1965 with a minority vote. He had to face an immediate challenge from the young king who, though not possessing the same weight of authority as King Sobhuza, was none the less determined to retain some independence for the civil service and the police when independence came. However, in an historic decision the police obeyed Chief Jonathan's orders to prevent people gathering at a *Pitso* called by the king, whose power was thereby effectively curtailed although he remained titular head of the nation. In 1970 Chief Jonathan was defeated at the polls by the Congress Party but, refusing to concede defeat, he seized power illegally in a coup. A counter-coup failed in 1974. The leader of the Congress Party, Ntsu Mokhehle, escaped to Botswana but many political opponents were beaten up or killed whilst others were found guilty of high treason and gaoled for some years.

For Botswana the first decade of political independence was much smoother. Fusing in his person both the traditional and the modern, Sir Seretse Khama, the rightful heir of the Ngwato chieftainship, and the man who had risked his position and earned the disapproval of both the colonial power and the big neighbour by marrying the wife of his choice, was able to win and maintain the support of the vast majority of his people without being so threatened that he felt it necessary either to ban other political parties or to imprison his opponents.

But Botswana had other troubles which, by the mid-1970s, were becoming increasingly acute. Situated at the centre of southern Africa, she shared long borders with the three white-ruled countries where the struggle for liberation was becoming increasingly bitter and violent. For Botswana this meant first the problem of refugees as people streamed across at different times from Soweto, from Ovamboland, and from the south-western districts of Rhodesia. There was pressure too from the guerrilla movements to allow the passage of arms and men, but on this Botswana, like Lesotho and Swaziland, had to take a firm stand. Moral support was possible but more active involvement was suicidal. Botswana was not able to avoid being burnt by the war which raged particularly on the Rhodesian border, where Smith's troops, allegedly in hot pursuit, entered Botswana several times and killed a number of civilians. Although there was war both in Namibia and in Rhodesia there seemed to be some hope in the mid-1970s that the conflict would be resolved without further undue damage to Botswana. However, the long-term view to the south was far less promising. There the military struggle seemed only just beginning and the prospect for Botswana of finding itself in the no-man's land between guerrilla bases and the South African army was far from reassuring. Swaziland too was caught in a similar position: wedged between Maputo and the Witwatersrand, it was well situated for gun-running and the transit of guerrillas.

Lesotho's main problems centred around its economic bondage to South Africa. The country had long functioned as a labour reserve little different from the Transkei or the Ciskei. The difficulties involved in reducing its economic dependence on South Africa by creating employment opportunities and producing goods within its own borders were immense. Agricultural potential on the mountainous, overpopulated land was low. Apart from a relatively small pipe of diamonds, prospecting yielded little in the way of minerals. Development of manufacturing was constrained by the smallness of the internal market, effectively reduced still further by ready access to the shops and goods of the Republic. Any hopes of selling products within the wider market of the customs union were dashed by Pretoria's action in preventing investors from establishing either a motor-assembly plant or a fertiliser factory. Development of the Malibamatso water project was dependent upon an agreement with South Africa to buy the water, which for some years she declined to do. One remaining possibility was tourism. The chief attraction to the white South Africans who flocked across were the gambling casinos and soft-porn movies rather than the spectacular mountain scenery.

The renegotiation in 1969 of the customs agreement and the

sharp rise in earnings of gold-miners improved Lesotho's current account, so that by 1973–4 it was no longer dependent upon a grant-in-aid from the British government in order to balance the budget. Nevertheless the long-term prospects for Lesotho's economy were, if anything, worse at the end of its first decade of independence than they were at the beginning, for during this period the rate of growth of internal employment was well below the rate of natural population increase, and the emerging spectre of unemployment haunting South Africa itself was an ominous sign to the people of Lesotho, who found themselves increasingly behind black South Africans in the queue for jobs. While the South African mines were unlikely to dispense altogether with workers from Lesotho, there seemed little likelihood that demand for them would increase substantially in the foreseeable future or that Sotho workers would be drawn into the agricultural sector, where overall employment was on the decline, or into manufacturing which had never employed many foreign black workers. One consequence to Lesotho (and the other labour-supplying countries in the region) of the increasing importance of the national boundary was the extent to which it facilitated South Africa's policy of containing unemployment by the simple expedient of exporting it.

In contrast to Lesotho was Swaziland where, as we have seen, the economy was growing rapidly. By the 1960s the pine plantations were among the largest in the world and were producing both timber and paper in substantial quantities. The exploitation of iron-ore provided employment, as well as inducing the building of a railway, opened in 1964, which linked the country both to Maputo and to the Witwatersrand. Despite these developments Swaziland also continued to send migrants to work in South Africa.

Botswana's economy showed the most improvement in the first decade of independence. From the mid-1960s there was a good deal of prospecting and some notable finds. The most important of these were the two diamond pipes at Orapa and Jwaneng and the copper–nickel deposits at Selibe-Pikwe. The timing of these discoveries was important for, although in the early negotiations the Botswana government lacked the necessary experience to bargain adequately over the terms of the concessions, it was later able to renegotiate these and ensure that over 50 per cent of the profits were paid back, rather than being siphoned off abroad, as had happened in the neighbouring countries of Zambia and Namibia.[1] During the ten years from 1966 to 1975 the annual rate of growth of GNP averaged 5.1 per cent, and although technical difficulties at Selibe-Pikwe, combined with a sharp fall in the price of copper after 1974, deferred some of the hope invested in the mineral boom, the prospects for further substantial developments in that sector were good. Two important problems nevertheless accompanied this growth. One was that the major share of investment in this sector was South African; the other was the large amount of capital required to create one job in a country suffering severely from underemployment.

Growth in the agricultural sector, as in mining, was accompanied by serious difficulties. One was the uncertainty of exports following Britain's entrance into the Common Market with concessions against the new high tariffs having to be bargained for one year at a time. Less visible but no less important was irreversible ecological damage caused by extending grazing into unsuitable areas. Third were the longer term socio-economic implications of the apparently increasing skewness of rural income distribution, as the wealthy townsmen employed in the civil service and elsewhere invested in cattle, while countrymen with no stock were thus effectively disinherited of the land to which, theoretically, they had access.[2] Nor was the gap confined to the agricultural sector. In the civil service by the mid-1970s the ratio of salaries for super-scale posts was of the order of 10:1 compared with a ratio of approximately 5:1 in most developed countries. Thus, even within so homogeneous a country as Botswana, the cleavage between rich and poor was deep.

In Namibia the first lustrum of the 1960s was relatively uneventful. Attention was focussed on proceedings at The Hague where orders had been sought against South Africa for violation of the mandate. In 1966 the International Court of Justice refused to pronounce on the matters before it on the grounds that the applicant states, Liberia and Ethiopia, had no legal standing before the court. Following this a number of far-reaching decisions were made by interested parties. SWAPO issued a

[1] I am indebted to Charles Harvey for this point.
[2] Norman Reynolds, 'Rural development in Botswana' (Saldru working paper 13, Cape Town, 1977); Botswana, Ministry of Finance and Development Planning, Central Statistics Office, *The rural income distribution survey in Botswana 1974/5* (Gaborone, 1976).

statement from Dar es Salaam that there was now no alternative but 'to rise in arms and bring about our own liberation'. In August 1966 the first clashes between SWAPO guerrillas and South African security forces occurred in northern Namibia. Two months later the United Nations General Assembly resolved formally to terminate the mandate and to put Namibia under the direct responsibility of the UN. South Africa responded differently. Claiming incorrectly that the court's technical finding was a ruling in her favour, the South African government ignored the United Nations and proceeded virtually to complete the incorporation of the territory and to mould it more fully into its own image.

In 1968 legislation was passed enabling the establishment of Bantustans carefully modelled on South Africa's own emerging system.[1] The following year the South West Africa Affairs Act empowered the Republic to transfer the majority of fiscal and other powers still residing in the Windhoek Legislative Assembly to Pretoria. Statistics too became increasingly fused with South Africa's so that assessment of the direction in which net payments between the two countries were flowing became virtually impossible. Early in 1968 the Terrorism Act of 1967 was invoked for the first time to charge 37 Namibians for acts committed before the law was passed. The men were brought from Namibia to trial in Pretoria, where most were sentenced to long terms of imprisonment. Their leader, Toivo Herman ja Toivo, in a moving statement from the dock, firmly rejected South Africa's right to rule Namibia. This view was implicitly upheld by the International Court of Justice in June 1971 when it ruled that, in terms of the UN revocation of the mandate in 1966, the continued presence of South Africa in Namibia was illegal. The South African government rejected the judgement. A few days later the two boards of what were soon to join into the Evangelical Lutheran Church and which represented the majority of indigenous Namibians met to discuss the crisis and an Open Letter, signed by the two chairmen, Bishop Aula and Pastor Gowaseb, was sent to the prime minister outlining the extent to which South African policy infringed the Declaration of Human Rights, asserting that their country should be regarded as a single unit, and requesting the

[1] South West Africa, *Report of the Commission of Enquiry into South West African Affairs, 1962–1963* (Odendaal Report, 1964).

government to enable it to move peacefully to independence. These points were spelt out more fully to Mr Vorster by the two church leaders when they met him subsequently in Windhoek. The following month the Commissioner-General for Ovamboland, replying to increasing criticism of the contract-labour system, stated that it could not be regarded as a form of slavery because men reported voluntarily for recruitment. This proved to be the last straw and, in a well organised move, the Namibians struck. Starting in Windhoek on 13 December 1971 workers paralysed many parts of the economy by downing tools in protest against the labour system. Within a week more than 11 000 workers had come out and by mid-January at least 21 000 people had, it is estimated, been involved in some form of protest in 23 places, including 11 mines. Over 13 000 workers were transported by the government and others withdrew themselves to Ovamboland where their presence served to broaden the base of resistance by including peasant opposition. Over 100 km of border fence, for example, were destroyed in one night. The police and army moved in and early in February emergency regulations similar to those in the Transkei were proclaimed, furnishing authorities with wide powers to prevent meetings and to detain people without trial. Steps were also taken to alter the form of the recruiting system; SWANLA was abolished and replaced with 'homeland' labour bureaux; greater flexibility in the choice of job was introduced. But the essential features of the migrant labour system, which prevented a man from living with his wife and his children within commuting distance of his place of work, remained intact. By the end of February 1972 this round of internal resistance was broken.

Despite world pressure, SWAPO raids, and the practical logistics of creating a multitude of minute independent financial and administrative structures, the systematic application of the policy might have gone on for many years had not the April 1974 coup in Lisbon radically transformed the scene. The protective Angolan buffer along the northern Namibian border was swept away. Gone for the moment was the prospect of partitioning Namibia and carving out a new Ovambo state straddling the Kunene and supplying water, electricity and labour to the white-controlled economy further south. A new plan had to be made. In June 1974 the South African prime minister stated that it was up to the people of South West Africa to decide their future. After a year of negotiations led by the local leader of the National Party, a conference met in the Windhoek Turnhalle (Gymnasium) at the beginning of September 1975. The delegates represented ethnic groups (with whites as one group) and thus SWAPO, as a national party, was excluded. Nevertheless the declaration of intent, issued by the Turnhalle Conference, to move towards independence as a single state with the participation of all groups in a new government was a significant change from the direction in which Pretoria had previously been pressing.

Meanwhile the South African Defence Force which, since the early skirmishes with SWAPO, had built a substantial military base at Grootfontein and occupied much of the area south of the border, was ordered in July 1975 to enter Angola. South Africa's reasons included a desire to protect the Kunene scheme which was still being built, and the hope of strengthening anti-MPLA forces in the civil war then raging. In mid-October a South African army column marched rapidly north towards Luanda. But a month later the picture had changed radically. Soviet arms, including the 'Stalin organs' which halted Holden Roberto's FNLA army on the outskirts of the capital on the eve of independence, and Cuban troops were pouring into Angola. By mid-November the South Africans were stuck at Novo Redondo with no prospect of further advance without fearful escalation of a war that was rapidly becoming a nightmare to Pretoria strategists. But worse was to come: towards the end of the month two South African soldiers, captured in Angola, were displayed to the world's press in Lagos and, the next day, Nigeria, which in June had been backing UNITA, announced that it would recognise the MPLA government, citing the UNITA and FNLA acceptance of South African support as a major factor in the decision. By January 1976 South Africa had no option but to cut her losses and withdraw, having achieved nothing but the increase, if not the original intervention,[1] of Cuban troops in Africa.

In the same month the Security Council resolved unanimously that South Africa withdraw her illegal administration in Namibia and called for free elections under UN control. In August 1976 the Turnhalle Conference agreed on eventual independence and

---

[1] This point is unclear. For an attempt to sift the evidence see Johnson, *How long will South Africa survive?*, 137–54.

Table 6.13. *Employment in Namibia, 1975.*

Sector	Total	Percentage proportion of labour force	Percentage whites as proportion of total in sector
Agriculture			
Subsistence/communal	90 000	30.5	0
commercial/capitalist	52 800	17.9	13
Government and other services	28 300	9.6	51
Mining and quarrying	17 500	5.9	9
Manufacturing, electricity and water	13 200	4.5	35
Construction	12 500	4.2	23
Self-employed in subsistence areas	11 000	3.7	0
Commerce and finance	10 400	3.5	39
Transport and communication	9 300	3.1	19
Domestic service	8 000	2.7	0
Fishing	7 500	2.5	7
Defence/resistance/refugees	6 000	2.0	50
Unemployed and unspecified	29 000	9.8	0
Total labour force	295 500	100	13

Source: Wolfgang Thomas, *Economic development in Namibia* (Mainz, 1978).

the South African prime minister accepted the decision, thus formally marking the end of South Africa's long attempt to incorporate the mandated territory. But when colonialism ends neo-colonialism tends to begin, and the prospect of cutting formal political links by no means implied that South Africa renounced all interest in the shape of the emerging government. In order to understand the constraints within which Namibian politics would subsequently be played out it is helpful to glance at the structure of the economy – and its links with South Africa – at this time (table 6.13). In terms of contributions to the gross domestic product of the country it is estimated that the proportions in 1975 were: mining 27 per cent; manufacturing and construction 17 per cent; agriculture 16 per cent and the tertiary sector, including government services, 40 per cent. From mining, which was the major source of tax revenue, estimated gross earnings in 1973 comprised 61 per cent from diamonds; 18 per cent from copper; 9 per cent from zinc; and 8 per cent from lead. But, after some R 200 million investment by British and South African companies, uranium production started in 1976, and was expected to be much the largest source of export earnings by the early 1980s despite the fact that the Rössing mine was tied by long-term delivery contracts to the United Kingdom at a low price.

A measure of Namibia's economic subservience may be seen in the fact that, of the companies which between them controlled the 20 major mines in the country, 12 were primarily South African, while five were American, four were British, one was Canadian, and the rest of diverse ownership. Nor was it only in mining that South African interest was paramount. In the capitalist farming sector, which produced approximately nine-tenths of agricultural output, a substantial portion of the land was owned by South African individuals and companies, while the processing of meat (and fish) and the marketing of agricultural exports were largely in South African hands. And the government sector, including railways and other communications, was, of course, an extension of South Africa's own. Thus the two countries were bound tightly together although, as has been argued above, the absence of large-scale oscillating migration to South Africa over a long period of time left Namibia with one important degree of freedom not inherited by Mozambique, Lesotho, Botswana, or Swaziland when they became independent. Nevertheless of all the countries surrounding the Republic it was in Namibia that South Africa's vested interests were greatest and where, in the period of transition to independence, she sought to retain the greatest influence.

CONCLUSION

This chapter has focussed primarily on political and economic issues. Yet people also wrote poetry, composed and played music, danced, peered through microscopes, painted, designed bridges, built dams, healed the sick, and were creative in a myriad ways. There was indeed an exuberant vitality, a sense of energy, which ran through the society and found expression in many forms ranging from the lyrics of King Kong to the poetry of the *sestigers*; from the plays of Athol Fugard to the jazz of Dollar Brand. There was much of beauty and truth that grew on the dung-heap of South Africa's social system.

But one final question remains. Was South Africa in this period best seen as an aberration in the world of civilised people; an outcast from society? Or was it best understood as a microcosm of the world at large? There was much that was uncomfortably familiar about South Africa. American visitors found strong similarities to the pattern of segregation that existed in the Deep South as recently as the mid-1960s. Europeans saw aspects of the migrant labour system reflected in their own treatment of *Gastarbeiter*. The juxtaposition of comfortable wealth beside grinding poverty, which appalled visitors from Western Europe or North America, was familiar to those who lived in New Delhi or Rio de Janeiro. The tensions springing from ethnic and cultural differences were no more difficult than in Malaysia or the Sudan. Nor was the immense power of the state with its forcible interference with personal freedom something with which Chileans, Cambodians, or inhabitants of the Gulag Archipelago were unfamiliar. Many of the divisions and tensions which wracked South Africa during the twentieth century were to be found in other parts of the world: black/white; rich/poor; migrant/non-migrant; citizen/non-citizen; core/periphery; capitalist west/Third World; state power/individual freedom. And within the wider southern African region the relationship between a magnetic economy whose fields of force extended over an area which included other national states was itself an example of the one-way filter function of political boundaries in a world of uneven development. Indeed, with increasing awareness of the mutual interdependence of all countries in the 'global village', there was a profound sense in which the problems – as distinct from the solutions – facing southern Africa during this period of its history should be seen not only as those of a backward area still trapped in the past but also, paradoxically, as issues which would increasingly challenge the whole world in the future. And it was the attempt to understand these global issues in their particular South African context that gave a sense of urgency to the debate amongst historians, economists and others in the 1970s as they grappled with such questions as the nature of the relationship between class and race or between development and underdevelopment in a capitalist society.

Yet there was much that was unique about South Africa. No

other country, after the defeat of the Third Reich, built race into its legal structure so that whom a person might marry, where a person might live, be educated or swim in the sea, whether a person might vote, or how a person might work, were critically affected by ancestry and skin colour. No other country in the world had built its political economy explicitly on a system of oscillating migration which treated its workers not as persons but as labour units, and which made it a crime for women to live with their husbands. No other country in the world used the law quite so systematically to control the lives of those who lived within it. In no other society did so many people feel so demeaned by the structures of racism.

More and more, in the years after the Second World War, South Africa became the 'beloved outcast'; an extreme manifestation of all that other societies feared and rejected about themselves. A British television film of the Nazi concentration camps shocked those who saw it not least because of the way in which, in the hands of a South African script writer,[1] it showed how ordinary men and women could become caught up in the perpetration of a barbarism that was beyond belief. Similarly in South Africa the very normality of people seemed to blind them to the evil consequences of structures they had built up in pursuit of a goal which placed self-preservation, group security and prosperity before love of neighbour.

The troubled sub-continent in the mid-1970s seemed to be moving inexorably towards massive conflict as those excluded, not only from political power but increasingly from citizenship itself, sought military support to help them break loose from the oppression which gripped them. South Africa, proclaimed one of its generals in 1977, was at war. But the firing line did not lie, as the generals thought, along the national boundaries of the region. The truth was even more painful than that. As Saint-Exupéry has pointed out in a different context,[2] the firing line was invisible: it passed through the hearts of the people. For it was civil war.

---

[1] Charles Bloomberg in the Thames Television series, *The world at war*, produced by Jeremy Isaacs.

[2] Antoine de Saint-Exupéry, *Wind, sand and stars* (Harmondsworth, 1966), 145.

CHAPTER 7

ENGLISH-SPEAKING WEST AFRICA

Can the English-speaking countries of West Africa – Nigeria, Ghana, Sierra Leone, Liberia and the Gambia – be considered as a separate group? Apart from Sierra Leone and Liberia they are not contiguous and might seem to have little in common other than their imported official language; even this has very different status among different groups in each country. For the Creoles of Sierra Leone and Liberians of American descent it is their native language; for the Hausa-speaking peoples of Northern Nigeria it takes second place to their own language, reduced to writing long before the advent of the British.

The impact of colonial rule by Britain on its West African colonies was uneven. For some groups, in particular the coastal communities under British rule for over a century, it deeply affected their culture and gave them strong links with others similarly affected elsewhere in West Africa. Even for Americo-Liberians that British connexion was important because of their religious and educational links with Freetown. The real founder of Nigerian political journalism in the 1890s, for instance, was John Payne Jackson, an Americo-Liberian. The number affected by such links, however, was tiny. And in all five countries there have been 'two nations': small coastal communities with long connexions with Britain or, in the case of Liberia, America, and much larger communities which came under British rule only at the turn of the century.

Politically the development of the territories after independence showed marked divergencies. The Gambia remained a multi-party democracy. Ghana experienced one-party civilian dictatorship, multi-party democracy, 'dominant party' rule, and military government. Sierra Leone had multi-party, and two versions of one-party, rule, as well as a military regime. Nigeria experienced a period of turbulent multi-party government, followed by 13 years of military rule, and then an American-type presidential government. Liberia moved from personal, if benign, autocracy to a liberal form of one-party rule, and then to military rule. There was no unanimity in foreign policy, and there was sometimes deep enmity between these countries, particularly in Nkrumah's day. The interterritorial organisations for currency, research, airways and parallel functions once established for the four British colonies were dismantled, with the exception of the West African Examinations Council, which Liberia joined in 1969.

Trade between the countries continued to be as insignificant as it had been in the colonial era. The great British firms, such as the United Africa Company or Paterson Zochonis, which were household names in all of them, including Liberia, lost their commercial dominance. After independence, movement of staff by these firms between the territories ceased, although movement of individual citizens, including traders, continued on a considerable scale.

Yet, apart from historical convenience, there is still reason to treat these countries as a group. In a sense the merging of the 'two nations' in each country meant the movement inland from the coast of many of the external influences which the five countries shared. The national legal systems had a common origin and theoretical attachment to the rule of law continued to be strong. Their universities had strong links. Their administrative, police and military practices remained similar. A sense of a shared political past persisted. National politics began sooner in the anglophone than in the francophone countries and there were always strong links between the politicians of the British colonies. Dr Azikiwe, for example, first made his name in the Gold Coast. There lingered in anglophone countries the view not only that some francophone countries were not really independent of France but that their leaders did not want them to be. The importance of this political division diminished rapidly but it survived into the late 1970s.

Although the Commonwealth connexion had less and less to do with politics, it remained important in the fields of education and technical assistance. It brought together countless West Africans in organisations of many kinds, some non-governmental. Above all the English language itself, still little challenged as the language of government, law, higher education and big business, was not only regarded as a unifying force inside each country but facilitated cooperation among anglophone Africans. It linked them to a cultural system to which they themselves were making a significant contribution.

All this may be said to have affected only the élites and to be a dwindling imperial legacy. To the politicians it certainly mattered less than wider African links and in no way weakened these. But for an understanding of the recent history of these countries a knowledge of the anglophone links remains necessary, even if Liberia is a special case.

THE IMPACT OF THE SECOND WORLD WAR

No leading nationalist in English-speaking West Africa claimed that the 1939–45 war significantly changed his political outlook, though many testified to the effect on them of Mussolini's invasion of Ethiopia in 1935. In his autobiography, Kwame Nkrumah hardly mentions the 1939–45 war, during most of which he was in the United States, while Chief Awolowo, who was in London in the war years, gives it only passing mention in his political manifesto, *Path to Nigerian freedom*, published in 1947.[1] Although Dr Nnamdi Azikiwe constantly stressed the need for Britain to declare war aims for the future of the colonies and later deplored Britain's lack of gratitude to her colonial subjects who had helped her win the war, his own political philosophy had been formed long before, as his *Renascent Africa*, published in 1937, shows.[2] The same was true of the Sierra Leonean nationalist leader, I. T. A. Wallace-Johnson, whose previous radicalism and trade-union activity so alarmed the Sierra Leone government that he was interned for much of the war.

Is it then mistaken to see the 1939–45 war as a watershed in the history of West African nationalism? The answer is that the war did not create, but stimulated and gave scope to, forces already at play. Superficially, however, political activity in British West Africa on the eve of the war was still concerned with 'the ideals of early Victorian radicalism' as Lord Hailey put it.[3] Thus the Nigerian Youth Movement, whose leaders were not very young, demanded reform but not self-government at its confer-

---

[1] Obafemi Awolowo, *Path to Nigerian freedom* (London, 1947), 27–8, 36.
[2] Nnamdi Azikiwe, *Renascent Africa* (Accra, 1937, repr. London, 1968).
[3] *Journal of the Royal African Society*, April 1937, **36**, 140–1.

ence in Lagos in 1940. In the Gold Coast, politics was as much concerned with relations between chiefs and commoners as between the country and the colonial power. The only fundamental critiques of the colonial system in pre-war British West Africa had come from Azikiwe and Wallace-Johnson jointly in the Gold Coast, and separately in their own countries. But as Yaw Twumasi and others have shown, the urban and rural discontent on which Azikiwe and, after their return, both Awolowo and Nkrumah were able to draw in forming political parties with mass backing and demanding self-government had their roots in pre-war conditions, which were exacerbated by wartime inflation and restrictions.[1] This discontent had been manifested in the Gold Coast cocoa hold-up of 1938 against the 'pool' controlled by expatriate firms. The similar hold-up in Western Nigeria was less effective.

On the eve of the war Africans in all four British West African territories were a long way from the self-government demanded by Wallace-Johnson and Azikiwe. In Nigeria the northern provinces did not even come within the competence of the Legislative Council. No Nigerian sat on the Executive Council. The Legislative Council had a majority of officials, and of the African members only four were elected, and then on a restricted franchise. Only four Nigerians occupied senior posts in the administrative service, though others held senior appointments in the judicial and medical services. In the Gold Coast there were only three elected members of the Legislative Council, which could not legislate for Asante and the Northern Territories nor for British Togoland, which, although it was under League of Nations mandate, was administered as part of the Gold Coast.[2] In Sierra Leone, too, there were only three elected African members of the Legislative Council, which had an official majority. No Africans sat on the Executive Council. In the Gambia politics were confined to Bathurst (Banjul) municipal offices.

In all four colonies the outbreak of war produced protestations of loyalty from many quarters. Thousands volunteered for the forces. Money was raised for war charities, prayers were offered for an Allied victory. Educated West Africans realised what a Nazi

---

[1] See, for example, G. O. Olusanya, *The Second World War and politics in Nigeria 1939–1953* (London, 1973), 63–6.
[2] The Governor of the Gold Coast did, however, commonly apply laws passed by the Legislative Council to the whole country.

triumph might mean for them. Only in Nigeria, and there, until the NCNC was founded, largely through *The West African Pilot*, were the British constantly and sometimes bitterly reminded that Africans, too, expected some political rewards for their war services. *The West African Pilot* welcomed the Atlantic Charter in 1941, and attacked Churchill for his exclusion of the colonies from its ambit.

A few concessions were, however, made to African demands for a greater share in their government. In 1942 two African members were appointed to the Gold Coast Executive Council, one of them a chief, Nana Sir Ofori Atta, thus continuing British policy, strongly criticised by the intelligentsia, of placing heavy reliance on the chiefs as representatives of the people. In 1943 two Nigerians were nominated to the Nigerian Executive Council. In 1943 Sierra Leoneans were also appointed to that country's Executive Council. The appointment of two Gold Coasters, A. L. Adu and K. A. Busia, as district commissioners in 1942 was hailed as a major breakthrough. Gold Coasters had held such posts in the 1890s; but since 1900 field administration in all four colonies had been the exclusive preserve of the British.

These modest constitutional advances took place against a background of rapid economic and social change. During the war the British West African colonies became more closely integrated with the British economy than ever before. From 1942 a senior British cabinet minister was based in Accra to co-ordinate the colonies' war effort. For the first time the colonial administrations seriously concerned themselves with maximising production in all fields. For example, 18 000 labourers were forced to work in the mines in Nigeria, an official marketing-board system for export crops was established, and production drives were launched. As Peter Bauer puts it: 'leaflets were dropped from aeroplanes to explain to women and children cracking palm kernels in the remote African bush or growing groundnuts in the arid semi-desert south of the Sahara, that their produce was urgently required in the war for freedom'.[1]

State intervention, however, strengthened the position of expatriate firms, since it was easier to operate controls through them than through the rising class of African entrepreneurs and small traders, who were thus alienated and became after the war a main source of nationalist support. The controls placed by the

---

[1] P. T. Bauer, *West African trade* (London, 1954), 252.

colonial governments on prices paid to primary producers, the rapid inflation arising from shortages of imports and the increase in the number of people flocking into the towns seeking work in the new industries and construction projects resulting from the war effort added fuel to the nationalist fire. There was a multiplication of trade unions which were to prove in both the Gold Coast and Nigeria important supporters of the nationalist cause. In 1945, before the war's end, Nigeria experienced a 44-day general strike against the cost of living.

The war also encouraged local self-sufficiency not only in food but in such items as furniture and soap – the possibilities of producing these locally impressed nationalists. It also meant a construction boom in some areas, and significant improvements in communications, notably airfields, built and expanded in all four colonies, and in Liberia, as RAF and American staging posts (the presence of some 5000 well-paid US soldiers, many black, in Liberia is said to have had a 'marked impact' on 'tribal' people, still second-class citizens there).[1] For the first time the Sierra Leone Colony was connected with the Protectorate by a motorable road.

Parallel with the cautious constitutional advances, the British government also introduced the 1940 UK Colonial Development and Welfare Act expressing the concept, however feebly, of the duty of colonial powers to promote economic and social development in their colonies. Although it owed its origin partly to concern about conditions in the Caribbean, its introduction also owed much to wartime sentiment, and it insisted on trade-union freedom in affected colonies.

A major contribution of the British West African colonies to the war effort was the provision of troops and carriers. At the war's end West African forces numbered some 150000 – the majority of whom had volunteered for service and were not conscripted – against 8000 at its beginning. They had fought Europeans and helped to liquidate a colonial empire in Ethiopia, fighting beside white South Africans. Over half went to India and distinguished themselves against the Japanese in Burma; they served as Pioneers in the Middle East. A few, most Sierra Leoneans, obtained commissions in the Royal Air Force, but with one or two exceptions all West African soldiers, most illiterate,

[1] J. G. Liebenow, *Liberia: the evolution of privilege* (Ithaca, 1969), 77–8.

were commanded by British officers. Despite the fact that African rates of pay were much lower than those of the British, they brought cash to some subsistence economy areas and compared favourably with civilian rates. Army technical training also offered new opportunities. The contrast between pay and prospects in the army and civilian life led ex-servicemen to look for redress to the post-war politicians, most notably in the Gold Coast, which contributed proportionately far more to the forces than did Nigeria. But while in the Gold Coast ex-servicemen were prominent in the 1948 Accra disturbances, in Nigeria the majority came from the north and those in the south dissipated their influence in splinter organisations.

Few ex-servicemen became political leaders – Mokwugo Okoye, leader of Nigeria's Zikist movement, is one exception – and the first generation of anglophone African ministers were notably ignorant of military matters. Nor is it possible accurately to assess the political influence of their service overseas on ex-soldiers. From limited personal experience of serving with West Africans in Ethiopia, I could not go as far as Gabriel Olusanya, who declared, 'soldiers who went to war came back as new men with new ideas'.[1] War was primarily a matter of survival; relatively few soldiers from any nation can have seen it as an intellectually liberating experience of permanent value. Yet a wider experience and perspective had been gained, and if this seemed rather undramatic at an individual level, collectively it contributed to a critical evaluation of the post-war colonial situation.

The civilians, too, were no less conscious of the disasters to British arms than were the soldiers. But there was no land fighting in West Africa although after their success in the Ethiopian campaign of 1940–1, West African units temporarily returned home to guard against possible attacks from the Vichy-controlled French colonies. Yet the doubly artificial division between the francophone and anglophone countries resulting from the adherence to Vichy of the French colonial authorities – in many cases, putting people of the same ethnic group on different sides in a world conflict – must have bewildered and angered many Africans, including some technically 'Vichy' subjects serving in the British forces.

[1] Olusanya, *The Second World War*, 97.

One group of West Africans was politically active throughout the war: the students abroad, of whom by 1945 there were some 150 in Britain and some 30 in the United States. The West African Students Union (WASU) in London constantly raised African problems, including the need for substantial constitutional change, with British ministers and MPs. The corresponding body in the United States, included many, particularly Ibos, who were to become nationalist leaders. But in their case it was contact with new concepts and systems rather than the war itself which probably had the greater influence.

DECOLONISATION

Even after the war few in Westminster or Whitehall could foresee independence, even for West African colonies, within 20 years. But some Labour MPs could reconcile democracy and adult suffrage at home with colonial rule abroad, only because that rule was seen as a temporary trusteeship. It is a Labour Party myth, however, that the African colonies reached independence under Labour rule. Only the Gambia became independent under a Labour government, and it was the Conservative Ian MacLeod who showed the greatest enthusiasm for African self-government. The High Tory Oliver Lyttelton not only found himself urging an apparently complacent Kwame Nkrumah to speed up preparations for independence, but also established a close personal rapport with Nigerian politicians at the conferences that paved the way for Nigerian independence. Yet, as A. P. Thornton put it,

on both sides of the House of Commons more attitudes were being struck than principles expressed. Radicals read up on what radicals had been wont to say about the British Empire and said it again...but, remembering their responsibilities, said it in muted tones. Tories continued to strike the imperial note every so often, but more in nostalgia than from conviction.[1]

The change in world forces and Britain's weakness had taken the steam out of British imperialism by 1945. A door was ajar in West Africa which needed only firm pushing to open. In no case was independence in Commonwealth West Africa achieved as the result of violent struggle, even if the deaths following the ex-servicemen's demonstration in Accra in 1948 and the shooting

[1] A. P. Thornton, *The imperial idea and its enemies* (London, 1975), 332.

of 29 miners by the police during disturbances in Eastern Nigeria in 1949 encouraged political militancy, contributed to nationalist resentment, and provided powerful myths.

It was personal equality and participation in government service, in commerce, and in education which West African nationalists had first demanded, along with the redress of specific grievances. Such equality, it became clear to educated Africans, was always uncertain under colonial rule. So the demand for self-government – a more accurate term than independence at this stage – grew in the mid-1940s, at least in the Gold Coast and Nigeria. Even those who conceded that the British had not been oppressive felt that rule by white men was humiliating, and that Europeans could never prefer African over imperial interests. The impetus for West African independence was, in this worthy sense, racial. The nationalists, unlike those of Europe or much of Asia, could not seek to recreate a Poland or a Burma, or in general appeal to past polities. They demanded, instead, the right to rule themselves in the artificial units into which Europe had put them. They no longer sought independence for ancient Kano or Asante, or even for the Yoruba or the Wolof or any of the West African peoples numerous enough to deserve the name of nation.

Although the demand for self-government became increasingly vociferous and in the end, irresistible, in all cases in British West Africa independence followed prolonged negotiations and careful, though always inadequate, preparation. There were no European settlers and there were no strategic considerations to encourage British resistance to the demand, which, however, was never universal and was opposed by influential local groups in all four countries except, until the eve of independence, the Gold Coast. In the Gambia, earlier considered even by Gambian politicians to be too small to be self-sufficient, there was no demand for independence until the early 1960s. The National Council of the Colony of Sierra Leone opposed even the representation of the Protectorate, the greater part of the country, in the legislature, while the Sierra Leone People's Party, which was to take Sierra Leone to independence in 1961, arose in the Protectorate largely as a reaction to this contemptuous Creole attitude. In Nigeria the Northern People's Congress (NPC), which in 1950 became a political alliance between traditional forces and the majority of the, still very few, western-educated people in the Northern

Region, was concerned not with independence but with protecting northern interests from the political presumptions, as the NPC leaders saw them, of southern politicians.

The nationalist leaders who slowly moved to demand – 'request' is a better word in most cases – independence were in no case either prompted by outside forces or intent on internal social revolution. Indeed the conversion of the NPC to the cause of independence was seen by some as reflecting the views of those traditional forces which thought that British officials were now committed to policies which could only crode traditional power. They felt they should therefore support an independence under which a party of which they could approve would hold the reins.

The parties which took the Gambia, Sierra Leone and Nigeria to independence were all coalitions, embracing a variety of viewpoints. But the dominant elements were moderate, and sometimes conservative, closely connected with bourgeois families, or with chiefly houses. With the exception of Siaka Stevens in Sierra Leone none of the leaders had a base among the slowly growing trade unions. They sought a transfer of political power, not the transformation of society. To the extent that economic power had not been modified by institutions such as the marketing boards set up by the colonial government, they were content, at first at least, to allow it to remain undisturbed in the hands of overseas companies and market forces, while seeking greater opportunities for local businessmen.

The Gold Coast was generally thought, at least by western observers, to be different. But the Russians, before adjusting their sights to suit their international interests, originally, and from their point of view rightly, referred to and rejected all the West African leaders as 'bourgeois-nationalists'; and at first they included Kwame Nkrumah in this despised category. For even his Convention People's Party (CPP), as its 1951 election manifesto showed in its section on hire-purchase, could be more concerned with protecting traders than their customers and was concerned with consumers and with expanding African entrepreneurship rather than with the rights of workers and peasants.

Although reflecting real popular feeling, righteous resentment over racialism, and a conviction that only Africans could make just decisions about the use of African resources, the parties to which Britain's imperial power was transferred were parties in whose deliberations the rich and influential – and, it must be emphasised, the educated – predominated and which were in general financially supported by indigenous commercial interests rather than by the people's pennies. In this, if not always in their approach to external affairs or to the place of foreign enterprise in their economies, there was a significant similarity between the Gambia's People's Congress Party (PCP), the Sierra Leone People's Party (SLPP), and Nigeria's National Council of Nigeria and the Cameroons (later the National Council of Nigerian Citizens, NCNC), the Action Group, and the Northern People's Congress (NPC). Nor were there signs, outside Nigeria's Northern Region, of radical opposition to these triumphant organisations, all of which first came to power through elections – even if sometimes restricted or indirect – conducted by British officers.

The Gold Coast 1946–57

In 1946, the Gold Coast was still considered Britain's 'model colony' in Africa. The new constitution, introduced by the Governor, Sir Alan Burns, provided for an African majority, largely indirectly elected, in the Legislative Council. The chiefs, though often in serious conflict with their peoples, were still seen by the British as the people's representatives and as powerful partners of the administration. The greatest of them the *asantehene* of Asante, came to Accra to show his support for the new constitution. British officers still initiated policy; but ahead there seemed to stretch a peaceful road to a distant independence – perhaps in 15 years' time. This was a sort of date the Labour Colonial Secretary, Arthur Creech-Jones, or an influential Colonial Office civil servant like Andrew Cohen had in mind.[1] Improving infrastructure and a booming revenue suggested that once postwar shortages were overcome, the colony, the richest in Africa, would easily stand on its own feet. It was cocoa, of which the Gold Coast was the world's leading producer and whose world price was booming, that was the basis of prosperity, and which, in the south, had produced not only a class of thriving farmers, but numerous merchants and the means for education.

National unity, however, was tenuous even though the population was more homogeneous than that of most African

[1] See R. D. Pearce, *The turning point in Africa* (London, 1982), 166.

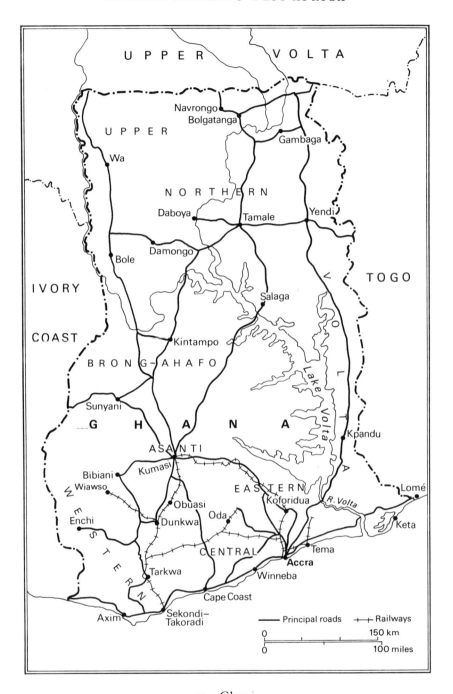

17 Ghana.

colonies. Southern politics had scarcely penetrated into Asante, which the new constitution had brought under the competence of the Legislative Council; far less the Northern Territories, which remained under direct control of the governor until 1951. And Africanisation of the senior posts in the civil services, particularly in the administrative service, was very slow; among heads of ministries and chief regional officers there was not a single African as late as 1954.

Twenty months after the inauguration of the Burns constitution, riots in many parts of the country, in which there were 29 deaths, shattered the illusion of peaceful change. The elementary-school leavers, the mainstay of the agitation against chiefs at popular level, transferred their antagonisms to the central government itself and to the big foreign firms, and joined with ex-servicemen and other discontented groups.

In the previous year the United Gold Coast Convention (UGCC) – the 'Convention' – had been founded, largely by successful professional men and merchants in the coastal towns, partly to express dissatisfaction with the powerful position of chiefs in the Legislative Council, partly to prepare the country as a whole for self-government – the first time this objective had seriously been discussed. Although UGCC leaders were briefly detained for their alleged responsibility for the 1948 disturbances, most of them were as surprised by these disturbances as were the British officials. While their detention at first gave them national popularity, the disturbances released forces they could not contain, in Asante as much as in the Colony. One UGCC leader, however, assessed the position accurately. Kwame Nkrumah, after ten years in the United States and a period involved in Pan-African politics in Britain, had been invited in 1947 to return to become full-time secretary of the UGCC. From the start it was clear that he was of a different stamp from the UGCC leaders, who were ready to use the disturbances as evidence to support their demand to the Colonial Office for self-government, but who never doubted that the government was destined to fall into the hands of people like themselves. Nkrumah, although he was later to become a dictator, at this time and for many years understood and could control the masses. He believed that one man's – or woman's – vote was as good and as valuable as another's and he was always accessible to any citizen – too accessible for the good of his government when he came to power. He also understood, together with men who later became his lieutenants, the importance of detailed organisation of political support, including that of newspapers.

He split with the Convention to form his own Convention People's Party (CPP) in June 1949. In the meantime, on the recommendation of a Colonial Office commission into the disturbances, an all-African committee under Mr Justice Coussey had drawn up a new constitution, which provided for a majority of African elected Ministers and an elected National Assembly. The CPP at once adopted the slogan 'Self-Government Now'; and although its leaders' approach was uncertain, the party in the end rejected the proposed new constitution, which still found a place for British officials in the Executive Council. At the end of 1949 the CPP threatened to take 'Positive Action' to oblige the British government to summon a constituent assembly, although it was clear that in the general election to be held in 1951 under the Coussey constitution the party could win power and largely achieve its objectives constitutionally. In January 1950 'Positive Action', in a half-hearted fashion, was declared, largely because the TUC proclaimed a general strike for industrial reasons. This time the Gold Coast government did not lose control and Nkrumah and other CPP leaders were charged on various counts and given gaol sentences.

While Nkrumah was in gaol the success of his party's attention to organisation and the demoralisation of the UGCC and its supporters were shown by the CCP's overwhelming victory in the Accra municipal elections of 1950, a victory which led to UGCC warnings about red revolution. The Governor, Sir Charles Arden-Clarke, and the Colonial Office, however, were sure that the CPP would win the 1951 general election and that Nkrumah would have to be released from gaol to lead a CPP government. After the party's overwhelming victory in 1951 (on a relatively small turn-out following low registration) he was released to become Leader of Government Business in a cabinet over which the governor presided.

It was to be another six years before the Gold Coast became independent. But there could now be no going back without the use of armed force. The delay was due partly to the CPP'S increasing emphasis on its ambitious social and economic reforms. By 1957 the number of pupils in primary and middle schools, for example, had more than doubled and those in technical and secondary schools had quadrupled, while there had been great improvement in communications, including the beginning of Tema Harbour. The party's realistic approach in some areas of administration was shown by the government's resumption of compulsory cutting-out of trees as the only means of controlling swollen-shoot disease in cocoa, a policy much resented by farmers and which the party itself had attacked in the 1951 election campaign. It can be argued, indeed, that the CPP's greatest contribution to Ghana's progress was made before independence. After independence increasing economic difficulties (there had been no real economic change), a growing obsession with external affairs, the loss of idealism as the government became entirely authoritarian, and a widening gap between profession and reality prevented the accomplishment of social reform.

More serious as an obstacle to the early achievement of independence, however, was the rise of the National Liberation Movement (NLM) after the 1954 election, which the CPP again won handsomely although at the cost of internal division in the party. The election saw the rise of independents and local groups, and the NLM, based in Asante, drew together CPP rebels, local leaders and chiefs in a movement, often violent and powerful enough to delay the negotiations with London for self-government which were expected to follow the election. Many chiefs had opposed the CPP, and now they felt that they could openly support – or in the case of the *asantehene*, lead – a crusade against independence under the party.

In Asante, too, particular bitterness was caused, or was fostered, by the NLM, over the government's fixing for four years of the price to be paid to farmers for their cocoa at a level less than a third of ruling world prices. The move was intended partly to combat inflation, partly to raise development funds from the difference between the world price and the local price. Half the country's cocoa was grown in Asante, and not only farmers but cocoa traders, merchants, and even landlords of booming Kumasi, resented this government restriction on the flow of money to Asante, which for some NLM leaders represented a heavy personal loss of income.

So powerful did the movement seem that to test CPP strength the British demanded a further election, which was held in 1956, before final negotiations. The election showed that the CPP had overwhelming strength in the colony, and in Trans-Volta Togo, with minority but still significant support in Asante and the north. But only 57 per cent of the voters out of a 50 per cent turn-out supported the CPP, representing perhaps 30 per cent of the adult population. It was the small size of this total vote, rather than its distribution, which did not reflect an insuperable north–south or any other kind of territorial or tribal division, that mattered for the future. For this was not the basis for declaring, as Dr Nkrumah was later to do, a one-party state; and Ghana was not again to experience a free and fair election until 1969.

Nigeria 1945–60

Politics in Nigeria came to life in 1945 with the publication of the proposals for the Richards Constitution, named after the then governor. While bringing Northern Nigeria into the central system and extending Nigerian representation in the Legislative and Executive Councils, this established three regions with representative bodies of their own. The proposals, however, were strongly criticised by nationalists, partly because the constitution had been imposed without consultation, partly because the elections were to be 'indirect'. Furthermore, when the Richards Constitution was debated in the House of Commons in 1945, a mere 29 minutes were devoted to it, which disgusted many Nigerians.

Before 1948, politics in Nigeria were more turbulent than those in Ghana. The NCNC – the National Council of Nigeria and the Cameroons, so-called because a part of Cameroun under UN Trusteeship was administered with Nigeria – was a mass move-ment, if only in limited parts of the country, of the kind which the CPP was to surpass. Nnamdi Azikiwe (Zik) was a popular leader, and an orator – if not organiser – whom Nkrumah might envy. But in contrast to the Gold Coast another force was wait-ing in the north which was to dominate politics until the soldiers took over in 1966. This was the Northern People's Congress (NPC), less a political party than the expression of an entrenched social and political system. The NCNC had, in fact, made political allies in the then Northern Provinces before the NPC, which was formally inaugurated in 1949 as a cultural organisation, had appeared on the scene. But because of the threatening influence

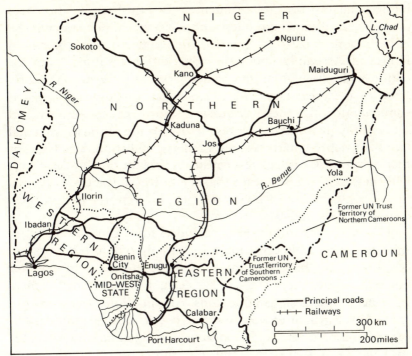

18   Nigeria, 1964.

of the Northern Elements Progressive Union (NEPU), an ally of the NCNC, leading northerners turned the NPC into an open political body in 1950.

In the meantime the British administration, largely under the influence of its Chief Secretary, Sir Hugh Foot, later Lord Caradon, had decided that the Nigerian government would not be 'overtaken by events' as the Gold Coast government had been in 1948.[1] So it proposed that a review of the Richards Constitution, the abrupt introduction of which, as well as its provisions, had excited nationalist antipathy, should be undertaken by a series of local conferences culminating in a national one. The government had also made important proposals to advance Africanisation of the senior civil service which, together with the constitutional consultations, helped to dampen the NCNC's fire.

For the first time the constitutional consultations really brought the Northern Provinces into Nigerian national politics, if only for leading northern representatives to protect what they saw as their

[1] Hugh Foot, *A start in freedom* (London, 1964), 103–6.

interests against southern influences. But this participation also provoked northerners to question their own emirate system. The NPC became a party in time for the elections to the Northern House of Assembly under the constitution resulting from the nation-wide discussions; its leader was the *sardauna* of Sokoto, scion of the great house of Usuman dan Fodio and a talented administrator. In these discussions northern spokesmen had successfully insisted that representation in the proposed national House of Representatives should reflect population, which meant that on the basis of the latest census figures the north would have half the seats.[1] It also meant that the northern leaders, confident in the conservatism of their own people, were relying on them to out-vote the radicals.

The new constitution also provided for a central council of ministers with a Nigerian majority, among whom the Northern Region would have one-third of those elected, and regional councils of ministers for the Western, Eastern, and Northern Provinces, now designated regions. Among those elected in 1952 to the four legislatures were few who could be called radicals. The administration's determination not to be taken unawares seemed to have been successful, and the subsequent long series of conferences which negotiated Nigerian independence were marked more by disputes among the Nigerians than disputes between them and the Colonial Office.

As well as the NPC, the elections produced another new force replacing the moribund Nigerian Youth Movement. This was the Action Group under Chief Obafemi Awolowo. Although he produced detailed programmes for it before the election, Chief Awolowo later formed the party out of those who had won election to the Western House of Assembly. Awolowo became leader of the new Western Region government.

The first constitution to provide for the appointment of Nigerian ministers found none of the leaders of the main parties in office at the centre. So the senior NPC federal minister and later Prime Minister, Alhaji Sir Abubakar Tafawa Balewa,[2] respected

---

[1] The last census had been taken in 1931, and gave the Northern Region 11.4 million against 8.6 million for the rest of the country. The 1953 census gave the Northern Region 16.8 million against 13.6 million for the rest of the country, excluding Southern Cameroons.

[2] Abubakar Tafawa Balewa was appointed to the newly created post of prime minister of the Federation in 1957 and was knighted in 1960. Before becoming prime minister he led the NPC in the House of Representatives as federal minister of transport. He was of relatively humble origin.

more for his integrity and his intelligence than for his decisiveness, always seemed to be inhibited by the fact that his NPC party leader, the *sardauna*, occupied the nominally inferior post of premier of the Northern Region.

The apparent unimportance of the central and – after the 1953 constitution conference – the federal, government in relation to the regions was the main feature of Nigerian politics up to independence. But the second most important feature had already become prominent; the demand for division of the country into smaller regions, called 'states'. Such demands were encouraged by the granting of regional status to the tiny South Cameroons Trusteeship in 1953. Above all it was maintained in the south that the allocation of half the seats in the federal House of Representatives to the Northern Region meant permanent domination of federal power by the NPC, which would always be assured of a great majority of these northern seats. Although voting for them was on the face of it democratic, southern resentment reflected the view that the NPC, because of its association with traditional authority to which northerners still deferred, would always find ways of maintaining its regional majority. In practice the NPC ruled centrally with allies, normally the NCNC, but sometimes including the Action Group.

'Tribalism', it is said, has dominated Nigerian politics. But some of the bitterest political disputes have been within ethnically related communities, some of which in Nigeria number many millions of people. This was particularly true among the Yoruba; but the 1953 crisis in Eastern Nigeria was the result of a dispute between Azikiwe and some Ibo ministers, while the Kano-based and Hausa/Fulani-led NEPU opposed its own Northern Regional government. Yet tribalism became more, not less, important as Nigerian politics developed. By the time of independence, in 1960, it was feared, rightly as it turned out, that a country which had come to independence as a result of compromises under British auspices might not indefinitely pursue these compromises after independence.

It was Alhaji Sir Abubakar Tafawa Balewa who appeared to many to be the guarantee that Nigeria would not split apart. For although, as we have said, he was regarded in the north primarily as a lieutenant of the *sardauna*, he was still widely respected in the south and beyond Nigeria. He was criticised by some Nigerian MPs for being too pro-western in external affairs and in particular for having made at independence a limited defence agreement with Britain. Yet immediately after independence he took a firm line at the UN about the Congo, demanding the exclusion of the great powers from the country's affairs, while his government soon after broke diplomatic relations with France because of her atomic tests in the Sahara.

Independence was, in the end, not the result of a mass movement, but of peaceful negotiation with the British. Nigeria's post-independence parties may have suffered in their own estimation, and that of many others, from this lack of militancy. But at independence, even if the élite who had inherited British power were intent on retaining their position, Nigerian politicians appear to have been determined to live down the divisions in their country between north and south, Muslim and Christian, Yoruba and Ibo, old and young, educated and uneducated. Yet it proved impossible, without further and bloody conflict, to erase from Black Africa's biggest and most complex country the legacy of its artificial creation.

Sierra Leone 1951–61

As late as 1951 Sierra Leone's Legislative Council still had a majority of British officials. Yet the long-established Freetown schools and Fourah Bay College had produced the most highly educated group in Black Africa. What caused this political underdevelopment?

Sierra Leone demonstrated in its most acute form the 'two nations' character of many African countries. The Creoles of Freetown and the tiny 'Colony' area were descendants of captives rescued from slave ships by the Royal Navy, or repatriated from London and the Americas. English was their language, they took English names, were mostly keen Christians, and had lost their ethnic affiliations. They were British citizens and proud of it. By contrast, in the Protectorate, which formally became part of Sierra Leone only in 1896, were peoples whose affinities lay with neighbouring Guinea and Liberia, the largest groups being the Mende of the south and the Temne of the north and west.

The constitution in operation in 1951 gave five legislative council seats to the Colony and three to the much bigger Protectorate, now known as 'the Provinces'. But there was Creole

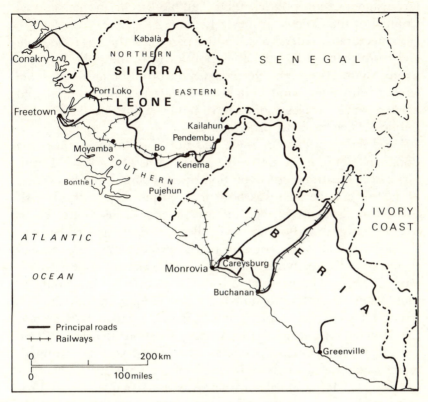

19   Sierra Leone and Liberia.

opposition to any increase in Protectorate representation, on the
ground that British 'protected persons', particularly illiterate
chiefs, could not legislate for British subjects. This delayed until
1951 the introduction of a constitution providing for an elected
Legislative Council most of whose members would come from
the Protectorate; and, in the Executive Council, for a majority of
unofficial members who would become ministers. Creole intransigence had some justification in view of the political domination
of the Protectorate by chiefs. It was supported by Sierra Leone's
most famous radical, I. T. A. Wallace-Johnson, a Creole who
frightened some of his own people because of his Moscow links.
His West African Youth League, established in 1938, was Sierra
Leone's first nationalist group and was suppressed during the war.
By 1951 Wallace-Johnson was in harness with the most

intransigent Creole politician, Dr Bankole-Bright, in the National Council of the Colony of Sierra Leone.

Protectorate leaders, too, had prepared for the 1951 election, and from then on Sierra Leone politics were the politics of the Protectorate. Although a vestigial Creole protest continued, some Creole politicians found an important place in Protectorate-based parties, while Creoles continued to hold a significant place in the public services and the professions.

Until independence in 1961, and until his death in 1964, the dominant figure in Sierra Leone politics was Dr Milton Margai. His career illustrates the evolution of the country's politics. Son of a Mende trader, he was born in 1896 just before the British Protectorate was established and was the first Protectorate person to take a degree at Fourah Bay College, and the first to become a physician. He was a founder of the Protectorate Educational Progressive Union, which gave birth to the Sierra Leone People's Party (SLPP). The party stood on the platform 'One Country, One People', and it included Creoles among its officers. Its strength lay in its association with 'big men', particularly among the Mende. Dr Margai, after an easy election victory, became Leader of Government Business in the new Executive Council, which included a cross-section of the community: a Muslim Creole, Dr Margai's half-brother Albert Margai, the first Protectorate lawyer and destined to become prime minister, and Mr Siaka Stevens, the leading trade unionist and destined to become president.

Without repression, Sir Milton, as he became, achieved an extraordinary personal ascendancy. He used the chiefs as agents. He conciliated the Creoles and appealed to all tribal groups. His age stifled criticism by younger politicians of his conservatism. Indifferent to ceremony and to theory, he was always ready to deal with troubles personally. To illiterate people, 'Pa' seemed to be infinitely wise, and to educated youngsters to be infinitely wily. When such a conservative man asked for independence, as he did in 1960, the Colonial Office could only agree.

His term of office, however, in spite of the appearance of stability, was troubled. A colonial mineral economy with a stagnant agriculture, Sierra Leone had the special problem of the illicit digging and smuggling of diamonds. This led to lawlessness and corruption, and gave some Lebanese traders, always relatively more important in Sierra Leone than in any other African country, an unhealthy power. Violent strikes for higher wages in Freetown in 1955 were directed against the ministers, as the new authority, as much as against employers; and there was a serious uprising in the north the following year against widespread malpractices by chiefs. After the independence agreement, Stevens went into opposition and at the time of independence in 1961 he and some of his followers were under detention. It was already clear that not even Protectorate unity could last. Later, however, people came to look back on the age of 'Pa' Margai as a golden one.

The Gambia 1951–65

For the Gambia, even the nationalist politicians sought some future other than independence until around 1960. It was felt that the country, with a population of only 300 000, was too small, poor and vulnerable to stand on its own. The Muslim Congress of Alhaji Ibraimah Garba-Jahumpa, for instance, in 1957–8 was asking for a permanent association with Britain. This, on Treasury prompting, Britain rejected. By 1960 the Gambia had become an embarrassment to Whitehall, for it was concluded that the country might not fit the 'self-government within the Commonwealth' rubric. It was hoped that its leaders could secure some arrangement with independent Senegal which would avoid it having to take complete independence on its own.[1] Such a link, however, was rejected for several reasons. It was feared that the partnership would be very unequal; the two had different legal and administrative systems, different official languages. Many Gambians working in Senegal profited from the artificially high value of the African franc. All feared that closer association would raise Gambian prices. Some, too, feared the end of their prosperous smuggling trade. Another influence was that of the chiefs, who could see that their counterparts in Senegal were largely powerless.

Although there had been Gambian members of the Legislative Council since 1888, the first political party, the Democratic Party,

[1] In fact the 'Confederation' established by the Gambia and Senegal in 1981, following the intervention of Senegalese troops to suppress an attempted coup in the Gambia, virtually achieved this. A monetary union was to be established and while it was agreed that each country could maintain its sovereignty, the Gambia was clearly the junior partner in the Confederation.

was not formed until 1951, and was virtually confined to the capital. The same year saw the establishment of the Muslim Congress. In 1954 Pierre Sarr N'Jie, a Bathurst lawyer of Wolof descent, formed the United Party with a Wolof base. It won control of the Legislative Council under a new constitution which provided for an elected majority with a form of ministerial government.

The most significant change came in 1959, when the Protectorate People's Society, a charitable organisation, was transformed into the Protectorate (later People's) Progressive Party to fight the 1960 election, in which there was direct voting throughout the country. The PPP won a clear Protectorate majority but only a minority of all elected seats. The chiefs welcomed the PPP cautiously but its support at first came from Mandinka men in the capital where senior jobs were in the hands either of the British, or of the local Creoles or urban Wolof. The Mandinka numbered about half the population and were evenly distributed throughout the country. Many Mandinka felt neglected and concluded that Bathurst and the Colony were favoured at the expense of the Protectorate, particularly in education.

To lead the new party there appeared a man who was to dominate Gambian politics for many years. Dauda Jawara was born in 1924, son of a prosperous farmer. He was educated at Achimota College in the Gold Coast, subsequently qualifying as a veterinary surgeon in Glasgow. He was principal veterinary officer, but abandoned this career for an uncertain political future. In the Legislative Council, a majority supported the appointment of Pierre N'Jie as chief minister – Gambians now for the first time had real executive authority. But in elections in 1962 Jawara won by a substantial margin, and became prime minister. He reverted to the Islamic faith in 1965 and was knighted in 1966, thus combining the heritage of two worlds. Thereafter the UP and its leader went into decline. After an amicably negotiated independence in 1965, political interest moved to divisions within the ruling PPP.

Liberia 1944–64

While British West Africa was moving towards independence, Liberia started a process of internal decolonisation. When William Tubman became president, in 1944, representation in the legislature was confined to the coastal counties where the descendants of America-Liberians and other immigrants tended to dominate affairs, while the hinterland majority was still ruled in colonial fashion with district commissioners supervising chiefs. Some hinterland peoples had been assimilated into America-Liberian society and into government service. But it was the 'unification policy' of President Tubman, who had an impeccable America-Liberian background, which began to erode the division of Liberia into two separate communities. In 1944 representation in the House of Representatives was extended to the hinterland, while in 1964 the Senate was opened to new hinterland counties and the 'colonial' administration was ended. President Tubman also strove to appoint people of 'tribal' (as they were known in local parlance) background to senior positions and he was the first president to travel regularly in the interior.

Since any real political contest still took place within the long-established True Whig ('With Hope in God') Party – the only one then tolerated, and under the firm control of coastal leadership – this political change at first was unremarkable. The old political and social distinction between America-Liberians and indigenes, however, proved increasingly difficult to maintain, even if the developing economic class division tended still to correspond to the old one. The citadels of the presidency and the vice-presidency, as well as leadership of the powerful Masonic order, perhaps alone remained firmly in America-Liberian hands.

President Tubman also brought Liberia fully into continental African politics, in which he played the role of elder statesman, particularly during the Nigerian civil war when he firmly supported the federal cause. His 'open-door' economic policy, while criticised by some as too generous to foreign concessionaires, ensured that Liberia no longer relied economically on the United States. The economy, however, remained heavily dependent on an export trade based on mining and primary production.

THE PROBLEMS OF INDEPENDENCE

Few West Africans expected independence itself to solve political, economic and social problems – except perhaps, in the early days, those CPP supporters who echoed Dr Nkrumah: 'Seek ye first the political kingdom and all things will be added unto it.'

Independence, instead, emphasised existing problems and brought forward new ones, in particular the fragile sense of national consciousness and the consequent manipulation of ethnic sentiment by politicians and others; corruption at all levels; weakness of the public services and lack of resources in face of the aspirations of the new governments; the nervousness of ruling groups who lacked the confidence of an established social order. There were the difficulties of adjusting imported, though not imposed, institutions to local conditions resulting in the establishment of one-party or military rule; the excessive rewards of political power, the fragility of independence when the economies depended so heavily both on the operations of foreign firms internally and on world market forces; and the incipient conflict between rich and poor, town and country, educated and uneducated. These divisions now displaced the old differences between chiefs and commoners, or between coastal and inland peoples, as well as between colonialists and colonials.

The weakness of national consciousness in Africa is easily exaggerated. Yet in all West African countries politicians were always in danger of yielding to the temptation to make tribal or particularist appeals. Yet the Nigerian civil war and its aftermath strengthened national consciousness. Large-scale corruption in all anglophone West African states except the Gambia has been well documented (it should be noted that this documentation is the work of the governments themselves). With the exception of the Gambia all anglophone states in West Africa during this period experienced military or one-party regimes, showing the difficulty of transplanting the Westminster and the Whitehall systems. But no workable indigenous alternative was devised, even if the American rather than the British system was ultimately preferred.

Protagonists of the one-party system claimed it as a truly African concept relying not on the continuous interplay of opposing groups but on an alleged search for compromise. They did not explain how a method for conducting affairs in a small chiefdom was appropriate for a large modern state. Clearly, however, the Westminster 'winner-take-all' principle might only produce bitter, and possibly violent, opposition since the rewards of political power were so great. West Africa witnessed victorious parties in nominally multi-party systems – in Sierra Leone as well as in Nigeria's regions – behaving as dominant one-party regimes and intruding party antipathies into daily life, into the award of scholarships, into appointments and even into the lower courts.

Behind all military coups in West Africa there lay army grievances as well as hostility to civilian governments arising from other causes. For example, in Ghana Colonel Acheampong was said to have overthrown Dr Busia in 1972 because he and other officers were incensed by that government's withdrawal of army privileges. Nevertheless army rule in anglophone West Africa in general was not oppressive and the courts, civil services and newspapers proved to have been in no more danger from soldiers than from civilians. Military rule, however, as shown by the series of coups and attempted coups in Ghana and Nigeria and the forcible overthrow of the one-year-old Freetown military regime by private soldiers in 1968, was no more stable than one-party rule.

In spite of ritual denunciation of foreign commercial enterprises by politicians, anglophone West African governments all sought to encourage foreign investment, though often in practice discouraging it. Even Dr Nkrumah had no antipathy to foreign private enterprise. It was Ghanaian private enterprise that he stifled, seeing its development as a threat to his theories as much as to his regime. All these countries, however, felt themselves to be at the mercy of the international market since, in spite of OPEC and other producers' organisations, demand and prices for their exports depended on economic decisions in the industrialised countries.

In West Africa, even among the Northern Nigerian aristocracy, birth conferred few privileges after independence. But in relation to the majority – particularly farmers – all officials, professional people and even industrial workers seemed privileged. State bodies in bewildering numbers had little to do with socialism but instead produced a kind of state-supported, if insecure, bourgeoisie. Education, at least of the higher kinds, still marked people out, and in Nigeria demands for the creation of new states tended to come from groups feeling at a disadvantage compared with more highly educated people in the existing states. Military rule in Nigeria and Ghana concealed social tensions. When they emerged, however, they were still more likely to be based on age or ethnic group than on social class.

Independent Ghana

Ghana entered independence with immense international good-will, with Dr Nkrumah as prime minister. He had won a decisive election victory, but with the votes probably of only 30 per cent of the adult population. Opposition MPs numbered 43 against the CPP's 57; so, in spite of the violence of the period when the NLM was campaigning against the CPP, it seemed possible that a multi-party parliamentary system could survive.

There were, however, ominous signs. During the independence celebrations, a violent uprising took place in Transvolta Togoland, the former Trust Territory of Southern Togoland, integrated with Ghana after a UN-conducted plebiscite whose results were challenged by some southern Togo leaders. The last executive act of Sir Charles Arden-Clarke as governor was to send the Ghana army in to quell the disturbances. The subsequent acquittal on a technicality of two opposition leaders accused of complicity in the violence led CPP leaders to question the efficacy of conventional legal machinery. Accra itself also experienced disturbances caused by a new movement among the area's Ga people.

The government took a series of measures which it declared necessary because of its opponents' violence. These included removal of chiefs who had supported the opposition, and they culminated in the Preventive Detention Act, passed in July 1958, after the alleged discovery of a plot led by an opposition MP. People could now be detained for periods of five years without appeal. The act was used first against 38 leading members of the opposition and then against opposition within the ruling party itself.

The fusion of state and party power now began, with the appointment of CPP members as regional and district commissioners in place of civil servants. A CPP organisation was given monopoly representation of farmers, while the TUC came under party control and independent cooperatives were crushed. MPs started to leave the opposition, which was now organised into the United Party under Dr Busia, and was beginning to lose local elections. By 1960 the number of opposition MPs had been halved. In that year Dr Nkrumah was elected executive president with overwhelming powers, but still by only a minority of the registered electors. He had earlier referred to the CPP as containing 'the vast majority of our country'.[1]

The CPP, once a genuinely popular movement, declined, increasingly reflecting the ideas of one man and the functionaries flourishing in his shadow. In 1961 a serious strike of railwaymen protesting against prices was summarily ended. But the strikers and others could see how functionaries were enriching themselves; and in his famous 'Dawn Broadcast' of 1961 Nkrumah himself accused the party's old guard of abusing their offices. Their places were then taken by people who owed their positions entirely to the president, and who echoed his theories. A number of the old guard returned when some of the new men were accused of complicity in attempts to assassinate Nkrumah.

In a plebiscite held in 1964 to confirm measures to give the president greater control over the judiciary and to turn Ghana officially into a one-party state, 93 per cent of the electorate were said to have voted for the president's measures. Only force could now remove him, and after many rumours the army, led by Colonel Kotoka, finally moved, on 24 February 1966, while the president was abroad in China.

Why did Kotoka undertake this risky venture? Many had said that if the president left Ghana he would never return; for the government's standing had sunk so low that it could not survive his absence. Kotoka had personal grievances about promotion and posting and shared the army's resentment that it was being reduced to an ill-equipped gendarmerie, while the Presidential Guard was pampered. But he also felt ashamed of his government, and was confident that public opinion would support him. Disgust with Nkrumah's regime was not the result so much of its authoritarianism or corruption, or of his extravagant political aims, as of its incompetence and profligacy. For Dr Nkrumah and his colleagues the answer to an economic problem was yet another costly board or corporation, with a new office block, overstaffed by party supporters, and with its own fleet of cars.

At independence Ghana had foreign reserves worth £190 million, adequate infrastructure, and an efficient government machine. When Nkrumah was overthrown the country was literally bankrupt, with external debts – some, it is true, inflated

[1] Dennis Austin, *Politics in Ghana 1946–60* (Oxford, 1964), 180.

by foreign companies – of some £250 million. Local food was prohibitively expensive and there was a chronic shortage of consumer goods turning the market women, for long powerful supporters, against the president. Frontiers with all Ghana's neighbours were closed, while the prisons were full. The world cocoa price had dropped to its lowest post-war point, and the effects were compounded by Ghana's marketing operations. Cocoa barter deals with Communist countries in fact probably strengthened the world market price; but Ghana received from the Communist countries only sub-standard or inappropriate goods.

Nkrumah wanted a planned, socialist, independent and non-aligned economy; but in practice there was little real planning. Import controls, necessary to provide foreign exchange for new industrial equipment, made operation of existing factories impossible. There was little socialism either, and no equality between party functionaries and the mass of people. There were state enterprises in plenty, but these served bureaucrats, or a favoured constituency, and the majority of them lost money heavily. In spite of stupendous waste, however, the Nkrumah regime had much to show. One of Dr Nkrumah's last public acts was to inaugurate the £120-million Volta hydroelectricity scheme, with which was associated the £50 million Valco aluminium smelter, the biggest non-oil private project in West Africa.

The new military regime was welcomed with enthusiasm and found a civil service eager to help it. For the pressing economic problems it faced the remedies were mostly clear; the difficulty was to apply them. Creditor countries, for example, concerned with setting precedents, were unready to go the whole way in rescheduling the Nkrumah debts, but speedy shipment of US surplus food and raw materials helped to peg the cost of living. The regime cut down spending, but it had to be careful not to inflate unemployment. The regime also turned to the World Bank and the IMF, whose advice Nkrumah had ignored, as well as to the UN. The frontiers were opened to food imports, and western governments provided credit. One controversial move was the offer to private enterprise of participation in some state enterprises. The object was to encourage Ghana's businessmen, who had been suppressed by Dr Nkrumah.

The military government dismissed party functionaries and

abolished various ideological bodies. But without creating unemployment it could not abolish the Workers' Brigade, which had originally been founded in 1957 as the Builders' Brigade to 'provide a useful occupation for the unemployed who are unable to secure either a formal apprenticeship or steady employment; to afford the youth of the country an opportunity to give patriotic service in the development of the country, and to assist in the execution of development projects, especially in rural areas'. Frequently, however, it had acted as a body of storm-troopers. The regime was lucky that its advent coincided with a world cocoa market recovery. But Dr Nkrumah's policies in his last years seem almost consciously to have been designed to reduce the economy to bankruptcy. Another regime could not fail to improve things even if – or perhaps particularly if – it did nothing.

Apart from arresting, but not really reversing, economic decline, the military regime's greatest achievement was to restore democratic civilian rule to Ghana in an election in 1969, which was a model of fairness. Unhappily the two main parties, the Progress Party (PP) and the National Alliance of Liberals (NAL) – although issuing sober election manifestos – backed their national demands with particularist tribal appeals in the southern regions. In the northern regions the national parties strongly championed differing sides in local disputes, such as succession to the Yendi chieftancy.[1]

Under Dr Busia, an administrator and intellectual turned politician, the PP formed a government whose record, in view of the intellectual calibre of its members, was disappointing. Its attempt, for example, to reduce unemployment in Ghana by expelling non-Ghanaians was not only harsh, as thousands of those affected had lived in Ghana for many years, but seriously disrupted commerce. In the end, however, it was the impossibility of controlling smuggling – together with the Ghanaian predilection for imported goods – and the weak, if politically dispassionate, world cocoa market which caused Dr Busia, under IMF prompting, to devalue Ghana's currency by 44 per cent in 1972.

Once more the army moved. But this time Colonel Acheampong could not use the justification used by Colonel Kotoka, since there

[1] This was one of the major chieftancies in northern Ghana. The death of the chief left a vacancy which could be filled by any of a number of candidates from ruling houses. PP backed one candidate and NAL another.

was no doubt that Dr Busia would have faced in due course a free and fair election. Acheampong's only justification might have been that the economic performance of his regime was greatly superior to Dr Busia's. Yet over six years later, after Acheampong's overthrow, his successors had to devalue by over 100 per cent. So, in spite of some earlier successes in campaigns to grow more food and industrial raw materials, the failure and the corruption of the Acheampong regime showed that military government had offered little to Ghana.

Independent Nigeria

Just as Ghana's independence celebrations three years earlier had been marred by a popular uprising in Transvolta-Togo, so, but to far less publicity, Nigeria's celebrations in October 1960 were accompanied by widespread disburbances among the Tiv of the then Northern Region. The Tiv had local grievances which their leaders felt could be met only by the creation of a 'Middle Belt' state out of the non-Muslim areas of the Northern Region. The demand for new states to separate minorities from the ethnic majorities of the three main regions was an important feature of pre-independence politics. Independence sharpened it, and it soon became clear that the findings of a Colonial Office commission, which had reported just before independence, that the creation of new states was undesirable and would not calm the minorities' fears, were mistaken. In any case, because in each region the largest ethnic group tended to dominate the ruling party, the demand for new states became a major cause of political instability, and each of the three main parties exploited it to the disadvantage of the others.

Only in the Mid-West area of the Western Region, however, was it found politically possible, in 1963, to separate a minority area from a region and create a new region. It was not until 1967, on the eve of the civil war, that General Gowon divided Nigeria into 12 states, including three in the Eastern Region, two of which were designed to detach the minorities there from the dominant Ibos who were the mainstay of the rebellion (fig. 20). Thereafter in 1976 came the division of the rest of Nigeria into 19 states, but even that left some significant ethnic groups dissatisfied.

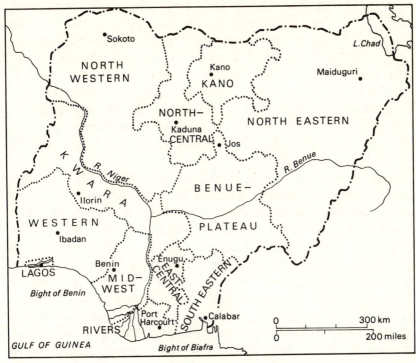

20   Nigeria: the 12 states.

So long as the Northern Region commanded half the seats in
the federal House of Representatives and contained well over half
the country's area, the Nigerian federation was at best unstable,
at worst unworkable. Southern fears of perpetual northern
domination were matched by the determination of northern
leaders not to allow the division of their region under any
circumstances. And although the NCNC found it convenient for
most of the pre-1966 period to join the NPC in the federal
government of Sir Abubakar Tafawa Balewa – Dr Azikiwe
became 'constitutional' governor-general in 1960, then president – the prospect of permanent 'northern domination' drove
some southern leaders to desperate acts, such as advocacy of
secession from the federation. In this sense, failure to meet the
demand for the sub-division of the regions, although it was a
self-interested demand, threatened the survival of the federation
as a whole.

It was the use of the army to deal with the violent opposition of Action Group supporters against the rigged elections which the NPC-supported government of the Western Region won in 1965, and the virtual breakdown of law and order in the region, which led directly to the military take-over in January 1966. It was believed in parts of the Northern Region that the military government had not only been installed as part of an 'Ibo plot', but would place Ibo officials in charge of the region. This led to the later murder of Ibos and subsequently, in 1967, to the civil war.

The war was never, as it was often represented, a conflict between Ibo and Hausa. The majority of the federal infantry came from the non-Muslim areas of the former Northern Region, and the Yorubas played a leading political role in the military government of General Gowon, himself a Christian from a non-Hausa ethnic group in the north. Nor was the civil war 'senseless'. It was seen on one side as a crusade to preserve national unity, and on the other as the only hope for physical security. It was, however, very much the result of miscalculation on the part of Colonel Ojukwu, military governor of the Eastern Region, who was convinced that he could win his struggle with Lagos to secure virtual autonomy for his Eastern Region only if the dispute were 'internationalised'. That meant secession, despite Gowon's declaration that he would maintain Nigeria's unity by armed force. In Enugu, it was calculated that 'progressive' governments, which could never declare support for the eastern cause while the region was part of Nigeria, would recognise an eastern secessionist government in preference to the Lagos government, dominated by the 'feudalists' of the Northern Region. This calculation proved quite wrong since some radical African governments – such as those of Guinea and Algeria – were among the strongest supporters of the federal cause, while the African states supporting the rebellion included, as well as Tanzania and Zambia, the Ivory Coast and Gabon. And while Ojukwu and his advisers had no sympathy with Communism, they could not have expected that Soviet arms – paid for by the federal government – would play a significant role in their defeat. If the rebel leaders miscalculated the international repercussions of the secession they were similarly at fault in their domestic calculations, seeing General Gowon and the federal military commanders, quite wrongly, as incompetent northerners who could not be effective in the absence of Eastern Region officers.

Success in the civil war immensely increased the self-confidence of federal civil servants and military commanders. The sacrifices necessary for victory were very unevenly shared but the victory itself immensely strengthened national consciousness, particularly as it was widely believed that outside support for the rebellion was based on a desire to see such a powerful country as Nigeria disappear. The defeated, for their part, conscious that they had conducted a brave fight against odds and had displayed great talent, were ready once more to take their place in the federation – although among them, too, the sacrifices had been most unevenly shared.

After independence genuine southern fears of 'northern domination' could not be substantiated; northern fears of southern intentions were equally vague. But there was one subject on which northerners and southerners not directly charged with the conduct of government could agree. At independence in 1960 all federal civil service heads of ministries and even the Secretary to the Prime Minister were British. 'Africanisation' for a time was now as controversial an issue as had been independence itself. The allegedly detailed preparation for the transfer of power was as deficient in this as in the matter of new states, but was even more unimaginative.

Yet, as in other Commonwealth countries, African civil servants soon took over the senior administrative posts and they did a magnificent job under mounting difficulties. I. F. Nicolson, however, maintained that, after the politicians had weakened their morale, 'confidence, leadership, decision and initiative were steadily drained' out of these administrators. The training given to young army officers, however, was expressly designed to bring out 'those qualities of leadership, confidence, initiative, and prompt decision which were being lost in the administrative service'.[1] This judgement proved true of the first military governors in Nigeria and was proved to be true of those appointed after General Gowon was peacefully removed in 1975 by senior officers impatient with his procrastination and ineffectiveness. The new military government (headed first by General Murtala Mohammed and, after his murder in an abortive coup in

[1] I. F. Nicolson, *The administration of Nigeria, 1900 to 1960* (London, 1970), 300.

1976, by General Obasanjo) embarked on a programme for a return to civilian rule in 1979 which was remarkable for its thoroughness and for the meticulousness of its execution in a country where public utilities and government services were notorious for their unreliability. This was facilitated by revenues from Nigeria's extensive oil-fields.

Oil started to make a substantial contribution to federal revenue in 1970, and in 1979 accounted for some 80 per cent of it. This gave immense new financial power to the federal government. The breakup of the regions into much smaller states greatly increased this federal strength, and, together with the advent of military rule, without which the breakup might never have happened, it was the most significant political development in post-independence Nigeria.

Independent Sierra Leone

After the death of Sir Milton Margai in 1964 two men dominated Sierra Leone politics – his brother, Sir Albert Margai, and Mr Siaka Stevens, earlier both senior lieutenants of Sir Milton. Both had left the SLPP before independence but Sir Albert returned to the party to succeed Sir Milton as prime minister.

Stevens formed his All People's Congress in 1960, a radical, democratic party, tied neither to the chiefs nor to the rich and influential. In foreign affairs it adopted a more radical stance than the SLPP. Few of its leaders would have been eligible at that time to become paramount chiefs; none then had a university degree. Except for Stevens, the APC leaders were also younger than the SLPP leaders; and the party was later to adopt a somewhat vague socialist ideology. To many in Sierra Leone, however, the outstanding feature of the new party was that its leaders were from the Northern Province, while those of the SLPP came from the south.

In the 1962 election, in which his APC won 16 out of the 62 seats, Stevens found some southern support. He was now leader of an effective opposition, and Sir Milton included him in Sierra Leone's UN delegation. Stevens also became Mayor of Freetown when his party won the city council elections in 1964. By 1967 his party had made such progress that, despite flagrant abuses in the general election of that year by the SLPP, the results were so close that the governor-general felt able to appoint Stevens, not Sir Albert Margai, as prime minister, as being the man most likely to command a majority. The force commander, Brigadier Lansana, intervened on the grounds that in these circumstances party conflict could produce disorder, and declared martial law to prevent Stevens taking over. Stevens and his lieutenants were confined by the army in State House where they had gone to be sworn in by the governor-general. The brigadier was then over-thrown by his military colleagues, who established a military government, and Stevens was briefly detained. There followed for him exile in London and in Guinea. In April 1968, after a counter-coup organised by private soldiers had overthrown the military regime – the first time in history that privates achieved such a feat – he was invited to return to take his rightful place as prime minister. In this counter-coup all serving army and police officers were arrested and imprisoned by their men; but a surprising degree of army and police discipline survived. It was almost a year before all army and police officers, except some who were to face court charges, had been released.

As prime minister, Stevens handled this crisis with diplomacy and courage. But scarcely less melodramatic were the events in 1971, which led to the rapid changes which made him first constitutional president and then executive president, following the attempt on his life in an abortive coup led by the then force commander, Brigadier Bangura. Troops from Guinea were brought in to act as his bodyguard. Their presence was widely resented, but he stoutly insisted on having them until 1973. His APC subsequently won two general elections, by means little different from those unsuccessfully employed by the SLPP and widely criticised; and after toying with the idea of a 'no-party' state, President Stevens, overriding all opposition, finally estab-lished by law a one-party state in the country where democratic notions first gained currency in West Africa.

Independent Gambia

After taking the Gambia harmoniously to independence in 1965, Sir Dauda Jawara's People's Progressive Party (PPP) never seemed in danger of losing power, although always holding free and fair elections at the prescribed intervals. In 1965 voters

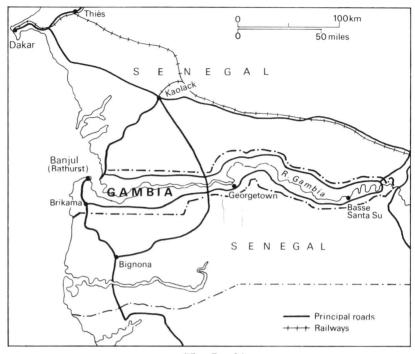

21   The Gambia.

rejected the proposal to turn the Gambia into a Republic. Sir Dauda waited five years to resubmit the proposal; it was accepted, and in 1970 he became executive president. His government slowly improved the economic and financial situation despite the fact that the Gambia was one of the victims of the Sahel drought and remained principally dependent on groundnuts, an increase in whose production the government has successfully fostered.

While the PPP reached power as a Mandinka-based party, and was accused of advancing Mandinka (as opposed to Protectorate) interests, Sir Dauda brought non-Mandinka into his cabinets and at times they were in a majority. Sometimes against the protests of his younger lieutenants, he placed confidence in non-Mandinka, or even British, senior civil servants; and there were still so few Mandinka at the top in the public services ten years after independence that some Mandinka were demanding a quota system of civil-service appointments. He also resisted party demands that the appointments of the five civil service commissioners 'up river', who for many people still represented 'the government', should become political.

The trade-union movement remained weak and divided. But if the small scale of corruption and the virtual absence of government extravagance limited the political targets available to the unemployed young, in the capital area they began to form a potential opposition to the government that was more menacing than the existing parties.

The Gambia was the clearest example of the division which has continued between the anglophone and francophone countries of West Africa after independence. All its peoples, except the small Creole community of the Banjul area, were kinsmen of ethnic groups in surrounding Senegal, and there was complete freedom of movement between the two countries. But, as we have seen, there was never any enthusiasm in the Gambia for any kind of merger with Senegal, although a 'special relationship' was established through joint institutions after independence.[1] In any case, as a member of ECOWAS and international groupings, as a signatory of the Lomé Convention covering all African states, and as recipient of aid from a range of Arab, Communist and western countries, the Gambia seemed neither isolated nor vulnerable, even though it had no army, but had made a security agreement with Senegal in 1965.

There were even smaller and less prosperous members of the OAU than the Gambia, and its president had the status of a senior statesman in Africa. He was, however, criticised inside his own party for leaning towards 'the West' and was one of the last African leaders to abandon recognition of Taiwan. The president's successful efforts to neutralise the United Party and other parties and to appeal to all sections of the country as a national figure weakened his appeal to some of his own Mandinka. But he survived opposition to himself and to his policies inside the PPP. Relaxed and paternal, he seemed likely to continue to survive in a state which, although democratic, offered little basis for a successful opposition party.

---

[1] Austin, *Politics in Ghana.*

Liberia 1966–76

In the years after its neighbour, Sierra Leone, became independent, the Liberian hinterland was finally, if still to some degree only formally, integrated into the national political system. In 1971, when President Tubman died in office, William Tolbert, long his vice-president, succeeded smoothly to the presidency. He dismantled swollen, and sometimes rival, security forces, ruled without repression, and instituted a less formal type of rule. After being elected president unanimously in 1975 he set a term to his period of office, in contrast to the regular extensions arranged for his predecessor, who had ruled for nearly 30 years.

Tolbert entered continental politics with even more enthusiasm than did Tubman and made sure that Liberia played a more prominent role in OAU initiatives. Liberia had also at last exchanged ambassadors with the Soviet Union – an exchange Tubman resisted, although he had agreed to it in principle as early as 1956 when the Soviet Union sought a diplomatic post in West Africa and Liberia, as the sole independent state, was the only one then available. President Tolbert visited Peking after severing relations with Taiwan. In 1973, with President Stevens of Sierra Leone, he formed the Mano River Union under which a customs' union and other forms of economic cooperation were to be established. So at last Sierra Leone, where Protectorate leaders had once seen Liberia as representing politically similar forces to those with whom they themselves were competing for power, forged close official links with its neighbour.

There remained a potential conflict over the issue of the holding of 'tribal' land by Liberian planters from the coast and by foreigners. But politically the 'settler-tribesman' issue, already waning, appeared to be giving way to a wider one that could excite real feeling. Although they were losing their privileged position, particularly with regard to taxation, the international mining and plantation enterprises, which loomed so large in the economy, together with the Liberians who, whatever their origin, were their partners and agents, were exposed as potential political targets. But although the benefits of economic growth were so unevenly distributed, Liberia still appeared to enjoy one of the most stable regimes in the region. Underneath, however, other forces were stirring. More people from the hinterland were gaining access to education, and thus were able to compete for power, and the general world recession began to affect the economy so that serious food shortages and high prices were to lead to discontent and rioting.

SOCIAL, CULTURAL AND EDUCATIONAL DEVELOPMENTS

For all anglophone West African states, the most important social development in the years since 1945 was the rapid spread of education. It was important for three reasons. So long as most of their citizens remained illiterate these countries could not be truly independent, since they would continue to require foreigners for administrative and technical posts as well as for teaching. So long as education, at any level, remained the privilege of the few, the 'tyranny of the clerks' would flourish and devotion to paper qualifications would distort judgements about individual merit. Above all, perhaps, the division into 'two nations' in all these states – between the relatively well educated coastal towns and the hinterland – would continue to impede national integration and produce bitter political divisions. The further argument that a high level of literacy is essential for democracy did not win universal acceptance. But, in this belief, all West African leaders attached great importance to the spread of education.

The educational division could be seen most sharply in Sierra Leone and Liberia, where in each case small communities – the Creoles and the Americo-Liberians – were highly educated while the mass of interior people had little or no education. But the political consequences in these cases, and in the almost similar one in the Gambia, were softened because the highly educated communities were so few in number that they clearly could not indefinitely dominate their countries politically.

In Ghana, enrolment in primary schools rose from 80 000 in 1946 to 255 000 in 1951, to 465 000 in 1957, and to 1 365 000 in 1972. But these impressive figures concealed a fall in standards, the imbalance – which all the countries experienced – between the number of boys and of girls in schools, and an imbalance also between the southern and the two northern regions which had significant political importance. The really serious division, however, was in Nigeria, where in the early 1960s only about five per cent of children of school age attended classes in substantial areas of the former Northern Region as against almost 100 per cent in certain districts of the three southern regions.

The division of Nigeria into states emphasised these differences, since the more southerly of the states carved out of the former Northern Region could themselves be seen to have a higher literacy and school attendance rate than the more northerly states. Inside the new states – some in the south as well as in the north – educational imbalance, which previously had not seemed important, also became significant. For it led to resentment from the less well educated on the ground that the better educated would monopolise government jobs. It was also felt that better educated areas would attract more support from the federal government.

The great expansion of primary education raised serious social problems. In the first place a high proportion of children left school prematurely (sometimes at their parents' insistence), having gained limited literacy but a conviction that this was enough to win a job outside agriculture. Of the children who finished the elementary course only a small proportion could go on to further training, the rest becoming the school-leavers whose inability to find jobs and whose disinclination to farm partly accounted both for increasing urban unemployment and crime and for the stagnation or decline of agriculture. Unemployment of secondary-school leavers and of graduates had not yet become an overwhelming problem but they could no longer, except in the most backward areas, suit themselves entirely in the matter of employment. In spite of considerable advances, secondary and technical education lagged behind the expansion of primary education, partly because of lack of funds and partly because of shortage of teachers. Many secondary schools, however, established and maintained high standards. If the elementary schools provided the troops for the nationalist movement, it was the secondary schools, even more than the universities, which provided the officers.

In 1942 there was no anglophone university in West Africa, although students of Fourah Bay College could be awarded Durham degrees in a limited range of subjects and the College attracted students from elsewhere in West Africa, such as Dr Robert Gardiner from the Gold Coast and Professor Kenneth Dike from Nigeria. Achimota College in the Gold Coast also offered a degree course in engineering for the London B.Sc., while in Nigeria, Yaba Higher College offered professional training but not degrees, an inferior status which in the 1930s and 1940s did more than any other single factor to arouse nationalist feeling among the Nigerian intelligentsia. By 1972 Nigeria had six universities with seven more in the offing; Ghana, three; Liberia one with, in addition, the degree-granting Cuttington College; and Sierra Leone with one campus in the capital, the long-established Fourah Bay College, and one campus up-country at Njala. And there were still thousands of anglophone West African students overseas.

Because at first they felt themselves to be – and were constantly told that they were – privileged, university students, although intensely political, seldom indulged, even against the colonial authorities, in the activities which have come to be associated with student politics elsewhere. Under the military regimes, however, students took over the opposition role vacated by politicians and frequently clashed with the authorities, often violently.

The great expansion of education was accompanied by efforts to maintain high standards; and while the universities were accused of being élitist or, because of their continued recruitment of expatriate staff and close connexions with English-speaking universities overseas, 'neo-colonial', they helped in the growth of an impressive body of West African scholars and in the inclination of curricula, at all levels, towards an African content, particularly in history.

The scholarly interest which for some years had been taken in their own history by West Africans was matched by a new interest in African art. But while there were important African historians of their race and countries even in the last century, for a long time, influenced more by missionaries than by those Europeans who had long seen the worth of African work, Africans with western education rejected African art and even crafts. People like the archaeologist, Dr Ekpo Eyo of Nigeria, or Professors Asihene and Nketia of Ghana, however, wrote expertly of their countries' traditional art.[1] Artists like Ben Enwonwu and Vincent Kofi drew on this art for inspiration for their own internationally esteemed

---

[1] Ekpo Eyo, *Two thousand years of Nigeria art* (Lagos, 1977); J. W. Kwabena Nketia, *Folk songs of Ghana* (Oxford, 1963); E. V. Asihene, *Introduction to the traditional art of western Africa* (London, 1972).

work. Archaeological finds, too, notably those at Nok and Igbo-Ukwu in Nigeria, showed that sophisticated work of high quality was produced in a remote past in areas which until recently had been assumed to 'have no history'. There also arose a lively interest among educated anglophone West Africans in traditional medicine.

English continued to be used as the language of instruction in post-primary and often in primary education, as it continued to be the language of politics, administration and large-scale commerce, only sharing this role with Hausa in parts of Nigeria's northern states. Widespread mortification at such use of an alien language did not produce, and seemed unlikely to produce, an alternative, as no single local language was generally acceptable in any country. So many West Africans, particularly novelists in Nigeria, showed a mastery of English that in a sense it was no longer an alien language. Such writers as Lenrie Peters of the Gambia, Eldred Jones of Sierra Leone, Ayi Kwei Armah of Ghana or Chinua Achebe of Nigeria, produced a distinct and significant branch of English literature; while Nigerian writers such as Tutuola and Okara adapted English to form a literature which can be called 'West African'.[1]

With the return, by no means complete, of cultural self-confidence, traditional dress also returned to favour. West African women combined traditional cloth and patterns to make attractive fashions in a modern style. West African cuisine was also becoming fashionable. Women, including those in Muslim areas, were never as maltreated in West Africa as they still were in some parts of the world; they gradually acquired the franchise to match their equality before the law. Few became political leaders, but there were now women judges and senior doctors, writers, scholars, civil-service heads of ministries, and ambassadors; and, as there had long been, enormously successful businesswomen and market traders.

The position of chiefs belongs to a discussion of politics. As they lost political power and influence, so they came in rural as well as most urban areas to be regarded by their people as the embodiment of their community, irrespective of their personal qualities. Few people in anglophone West Africa felt no allegiance

[1] See Amos Tutuola, *Feather woman of the jungle* (London, 1962) and Gabriel Okara, *The fisherman's invocation* (London, 1978).

to a chief of some kind, and social discipline was best maintained where traditional influences were strongest. Liberation from tradition, however, was not directly related to crime – much of it in urban areas the work of organised, ruthless gangs; but even radical young people began to wonder whether the retreat from chiefly authority had not gone too far.

Among the growing number of Muslims in West Africa, the world-wide trend towards greater orthodoxy became evident, though often accompanied by seeming political radicalism. Among Christians, divisions were sharper than in Europe, while there was an intensified search for African forms of the religion. But adherents of all religions deplored the fall in moral standards and hoped, no doubt unrealistically, that religion could reverse it.

Anglophone West Africa remained socially and culturally in transition from colonial status to full independence. But the transition did not psychologically injure its main agents. They and the people they represented showed a remarkable capacity for remaining their own selves while absorbing change.

REGIONAL RELATIONS

It is difficult to recapture the excitement with which Ghana's independence was greeted throughout Africa and the world. Although an irresistible movement towards independence throughout the continent was near, it did not look like that then. The date of Nigeria's independence seemed far away; for the Gambia and francophone countries independence was still scarcely discussed; while in other African colonies it was not yet even on the agenda. So one result of Ghana's pioneer status was the importance Nkrumah and his colleagues attached to the independence of other African states, and a belief in the capacity of their small state to exercise an influence which was beyond its capacity.

From his government's white paper on the 1960 Republican Constitution it was clear that Nkrumah thought that Ghana's task now lay in external affairs. Later it was suggested that, because a whole series of African countries became independent without Ghana's direct assistance, he did not recognise their liberation; and reserved the right, as he had as early as the first All-African Peoples' Conference in 1958 (which was not attended by the ruling parties of Nigeria, Sierra Leone or most francophone countries) to nominate the authentic liberation movement in any country.

Of Nkrumah's devotion to African unity and belief in the necessity and feasibility of an African continental government there is no doubt. And by the time he was overthrown all African leaders, however conservative or self-centred, were obliged to pay at least lip-service to African unity of a kind. It is one of Africa's tragedies, however, that the means he used to advance his ideal of Union Government and to oppose anything short of it included virulent newspaper campaigns against African leaders who differed from his views, diplomatic bad manners, harbouring dissidents and even training them in Ghana for subverting independent African governments of which he disapproved. This all seriously divided the continent, interfered with the establishment of the Organisation of African Unity and in the end virtually isolated Ghana.

Ghana's relations with Nigeria were often seriously strained. But what in his study of the two countries' relations Dr Olajide Aluko called 'the traditional jealousy, suspicion, competition and differences between Ghana and Nigeria'[1] were not ended by Nkrumah's overthrow. During the first Ghana military regime (1966–9), it is true, relations became cordial. The Nigerian military government at once recognised General Ankrah's new regime. Gowon readily accepted Ankrah's invitation to meet Colonel Ojukwu at Aburi, in Ghana, in January 1967. During the Nigerian civil war, however, relations between Accra and the Nigerian federal government deteriorated. Ghanaian newspapers sympathised with the secessionists, and Ankrah at times showed impatience with the Nigerian leadership. Ghana's change to civilian rule in 1969 actually worsened matters. The new Ghana government sent what was considered in Lagos as an impertinent offer to mediate in the civil war; later, as part of its 'indigenisation' policy, it expelled thousands of Nigerians long resident in Ghana.

Nkrumah's relations with Sierra Leone were also poor, particularly, before independence, with Sir Milton Margai, whose suspicion of Nkrumah was matched by that of President Tubman of Liberia. Sierra Leone's relations with Nigeria also became frigid towards the end of the civil war because of the open sympathy for the rebels expressed by spokesmen of Sierra Leone, which

[1] Olajide Aluko, *Ghana and Nigeria 1957–70* (London, 1976), 261.

seemed in danger of recognising the secessionist regime just as it collapsed. President Tubman's support of the federal cause, however, was much appreciated in Lagos.

For Nigerian diplomacy in Africa, the civil war was an acid test, successfully passed. Nigeria was to become the Black African country which Americans, in particular, always consulted about affairs in the continent. And its oil was also to make it a significant factor in international affairs.

No anglophone West Africa country, except Ghana briefly under Nkrumah, was influenced by the Soviet Union or China in its international relations. All to varying degrees sought that 'neutralism' or 'non-alignment', which it is so difficult to define. But if during the Nkrumah years Ghana sought an influence beyond her capacity, Nigeria in the early years of independence sometimes avoided exercising the influence which was hers. After 1970 Nigeria, militarily the most powerful country in Black Africa, which had been obliged to defer to Ghana on problems raised by the former Belgian Congo, the most important international issue for Black Africa until 1967, did not brashly assert the influence which her importance justified. On the contrary, as in the establishment of ECOWAS, she allowed and encouraged smaller countries to take full part in, and take credit for, its organisation.

ECONOMICS

During the Second World War, as we have noted, the economies of British West Africa were more closely integrated with the British economy than ever before. A recent book has claimed that the war years represented 'the heyday of the empire...at last the imperialism against which the critics of empire had railed so long actually existed'.[1] Before the war and particularly during the years of the great depression, colonial governments had primarily been concerned with administration and the maintenance of the conditions for trade and mining which their officials saw chiefly as the means for raising the taxes necessary to support their colonial government. Yet the degree to which the colonial economies stagnated in the years before 1939 is easily exaggerated, as is the indifference of the governments to economic development and the lack of enterprise shown by Africans.

[1] Pearce, *Turning point in Africa*, 220.

By 1939 the economies were largely monetised and currency notes were widely used. Railways, roads and ports facilitated movement of goods and people, and the initiative of hundreds of thousands of small farmers and traders (these latter both buying crops and providing farmers with 'incentive goods') had made the colonies major exporters of agricultural produce. The import and export trade, mining and timber extraction, were dominated by expatriate firms. But with the exception of the Levantine traders in Sierra Leone and Liberia, interior retail trade was largely in African hands, as was long-distance trade in, for example, kola nuts, cattle and dried fish. Agriculture was almost entirely the affair of small farmers.

The real change introduced by the war was the enlargement of state control over the colonial economies, a control which has since been extended. It included exchange and price controls, import licensing and restrictions on entry in various commercial activities. The major change, however, and one which many economists now see as having harmed the interests of African producers, was the establishment, in all four British colonies, of statutory marketing boards which were given a monopoly of the purchase, export and sales abroad of the major export crops, including cocoa, groundnuts, cotton and palm produce. The marketing boards used local firms as 'licensed buying agents', an arrangement which tended to favour expatriate firms. After the war the marketing boards were made permanent, on the ground that only thus could prices paid to farmers be 'stabilised' – a concept never properly defined.

In practice, by withholding part of the crops' export earnings in good years to create stabilisation funds for bad years, the marketing boards accumulated funds which were seldom disbursed to farmers but were ultimately plundered by independent governments. In addition, for years before independence, the investment of these funds in London bolstered sterling; and so long as Britain's Ministry of Food bought their crops it paid less than the world price to the marketing boards. At a time when there was talk of a 'revolution' in Britain's relations with her colonies under a Labour government, there was 'an enforced transfer of resources from the colonies to the metropolitan country such as had never occurred in British Africa before then'.[1]

[1] P. T. Bauer, *Equality, the Third World and economic delusion* (London, 1981), 183.

In addition to receiving low prices from the marketing boards, farmers were often paid in 'chits' or otherwise defrauded. The stagnation or fall in production of many marketing-board crops, or the large-scale smuggling of them into francophone countries and Liberia, it is now held, was the result of the marketing boards' practices. Nigeria, after the civil war, introduced genuine subsidies for marketing-board crops and considerable freedom for their marketing – but it was too late.

Whatever the consequences for export crops of the establishment of the marketing boards, local food production – in which until recently governments took little interest – also stagnated. This meant both higher prices – a major factor in the inflation which particularly affected Ghana and Nigeria – and a heavy drain on foreign exchange, particularly for the purchase of rice.

Disillusionment with public enterprises resulted from the deplorable record of their inefficiency and corruption in anglophone West Africa. But governments, except in Liberia, remained the chief agents of industrial development, and expanded their participation into petroleum production and refining, tourism, import of consumer goods, newspapers and publishing, steel production, mining, plantations, contracting, banking, insurance and other fields. Shortage of managerial experience was partly met by engaging foreigners or accepting foreign technical partners; but many government or semi-government enterprises seemed destined to be loss-makers.

Except in Nkrumah's case it was not devotion to socialist doctrines which moved governments into these activities, but a desire to ensure that control of them did not remain in the hands of non-citizens. Thus to different degrees and in different ways all governments, including Liberia, required that there be indigenous participation – whether private or public – in existing foreign enterprises. In the case of Nigeria, it was required that a majority of the shareholding should be indigenous. In nearly all cases these foreign enterprises were compensated for the enforced changes in the structure of their ownership.

There remained, however, a vigorous local private sector in trade and distribution, workshops, contracting and building, and road transport. Criticism of direct large-scale farming by government agencies grew on the grounds that government would be better employed in assisting, by provision of roads and storage, the millions of small farmers who still constituted the majority of the work-force, and whose output had to be greatly raised if a growing population was to be properly nourished.

With the exception of Nigeria (which did not always escape, and earned a reputation as a very slow payer overseas), independent African countries faced balance-of-payment problems and sought IMF help. Liberia continued to use the US dollar, whereas the four former British colonies, which once used a common currency closely linked to sterling, each established its own currency. Nothing better illustrates Ghana's economic tragedy, to which reference has been made, than the worthlessness of her cedi over much of the period. This led to vast smuggling of cocoa into neighbouring countries, and the smuggling into Ghana of goods bought with the francs the cocoa earned.

Smuggling became one of the most important commercial activities in anglophone countries. Whether ECOWAS, by harmonising produce prices and tariff levels in the area and by ensuring more realistic exchange rates, could diminish it seemed uncertain. But the drain of diamonds from Sierra Leone into Liberia, for example, and the ruin of some of Nigeria's industries by smuggled imports, were not marginal but were central features of the two economies. ECOWAS, it was hoped, would also facilitate the development of industries, for many of which Nigeria alone offered an adequate domestic market, in an increasing variety, ranging from car assembly to glass manufacturing and tyre production.

Yet even in Nigeria the structure of the economy did not fundamentally change after 1939. The oil industry was an 'enclave' industry, employing relatively few Nigerians; and although Nigerian entrepreneurs made much money in servicing the industry, or through foreign companies servicing it, very few participated in production, in which the state corporation was the predominant partner of the foreign oil companies. Nevertheless the oil boom produced in Nigeria a considerable class of very rich Nigerians, who became important in the London property market. Social mobility remained the great protection against social revolution.

'Seek ye first the political kingdom, and all things will be added unto it,' Kwame Nkrumah had assured his followers. That prophecy was still to be justified.

CONCLUSION

Because of Nigeria's immense population, the people of anglo-phone West African states outnumber those of all the rest of Black Africa. After independence, in spite of the violent disruptions which all experienced, they represented a relatively high degree of stability and order, internally and among themselves. Corruption was widespread and privilege was rife; nevertheless, democracy, if variously defined, was a general goal. One-party fashions did not become rooted, and after long experience of military rule Ghanaians and Nigerians returned to the uncertainties of civilian government and multi-party politics. Some West African states, including these, may have entered into a regular alternation between military and civilian rule; but in all anglo-phone states which experienced military rule, the civilians clearly showed their dislike of it.

Where a man came from, in many matters, remained more important than who he was or what he could do. There was no longer, however, even in the Nigerian emirates or in Liberia, any insuperable barrier to talent rising to the top. A combination of social mobility and access to land for almost everybody seemed likely to avoid the social tensions of many other parts of the world, provided that governments showed elementary competence in their economic management.

Class divisions were appearing, based on acquired – rather than inherited – wealth and on privileged access to state funds and facilities. With the passing of the anti-colonial struggle, the domestic social system was subjected to increasing scrutiny by young people. They could no longer believe that their countries' ills were a 'legacy of colonialism', a colonialism which was beginning to be seen as an episode, however significant, in a history which in many areas it scarcely interrupted. Nor, while bitterly denouncing racism in South Africa, did they attach to external political factors the sinister power ascribed to them in some other parts of the Third World. They joined, however, the Third World campaign against the rich countries.

Anglophone West African leaders themselves were mostly free of the double-thinking which allowed leaders of countries which had once been under colonial rule licence to indulge in corruption, tyranny and profligacy on the ground that they could not be blamed for deficiencies in behaviour which should be attributed to the colonial past – a sort of innocence by association. Real independence comes when citizens hold their leaders, not their history, responsible for their condition. Anglophone West Africans began to display that independence remarkably soon after the colonial rulers had departed.

CHAPTER 8

EAST AND CENTRAL AFRICA

In the 1940s it was the racial composition of the East and Central African societies that presented the critical obstacle to African advance. Although there was in 1940 a distinction in the British mind between the 'colonies of settlement', Kenya, Northern and Southern Rhodesia, on the one hand, and the 'colonies of administration', Uganda, Tanganyika and Nyasaland, on the other, the settler presence dominated the region in such a manner as to preclude the easy adoption of the 'West African' solution in the face of the demand for African independence. Power was nevertheless transferred to African not European hands, and by 1964 all these territories save Southern Rhodesia were independent African states. A year later, the settler rebellion in Southern Rhodesia dispelled any remaining illusions of Britain's effective control over that territory.

Independence, therefore, represented a fundamental landmark in this period, opening up new arenas for African participation and removing significant political, although not economic, constraints. The crucial effect, for the first post-colonial decade at least, was upon the internal balance of power once the colonial arbiter had withdrawn. The independence settlement conferred control of the institutions of state upon the dominant nationalist leadership, but it did not necessarily ensure its continued authority. Its legitimacy depended upon a complex internal political balance so that those who inherited the colonial mantle had both to nurture that legitimacy and to build the new state. The first decade of independence was therefore concerned primarily with the distribution of power in the post-colonial state, although the nature of the conflict was frequently obscured by the rhetoric of development.

While economics might necessarily take second place to the imperatives of politics, a significant acceleration of economic growth occurred in the 1960s, as well as an extension of the social

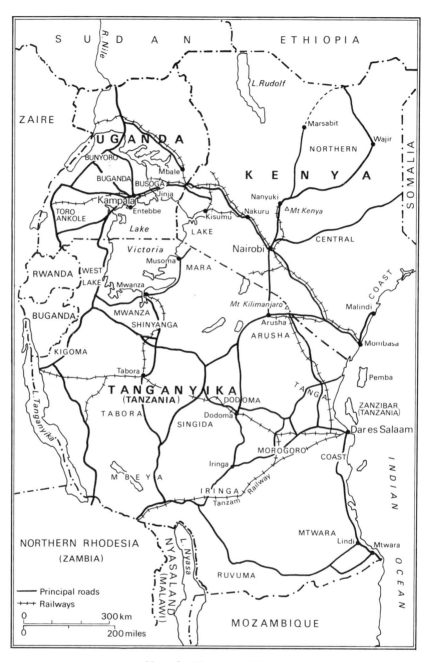

22   Uganda, Kenya and Tanzania.

infrastructure. Political independence did not, however, in the first instance change the pattern or the direction of economic development. There was a remarkable continuity in inherited institutions, in continued economic dependence, and in the inability to eliminate not only poverty but also the inequality that had been part of colonial society. The distribution of resources remained at best uneven, and at the worst grossly so. The difficulties of development were, moreover, compounded by the clear indications that the inherited model required serious alteration if self-sustaining growth was to become the norm.

As these states entered their second decade of independence they drew increasingly apart in their development strategies. That growing divergence reflected, at least in part, their different colonial legacies. While they shared the experience of political domination, the impact of colonial rule had varied from one state to the next. The process of change and of capitalist development had bitten deeper into some societies than others; they had adapted in different ways. Notwithstanding their common colonial origin, the economic foundations on which the leaders would build the post-colonial state were therefore in each case different. Two critical variables must be kept in mind as we seek to identify the major developments in this region over these years. On the one hand the particular socio-economic forces born out of colonial change and especially the extent to which capitalism had become rooted in indigenous society; on the other the nature of the leadership that emerged to assume power at independence. With these variables in mind, we turn to the political and constitutional changes that occurred.

POLITICAL AND CONSTITUTIONAL DEVELOPMENT

Any consideration of political and constitutional development must commence with the change from colonial to sovereign status, and the process of decolonisation from 1940 to 1964. In 1940 the European and Asian immigrant communities, especially the white minorities in Kenya and Rhodesia, were economically and politically dominant, and until 1960 they believed they would inherit power. While British post-war colonial policy generally recognised the forces of nationalism in the world at large, the presence of white settlers for whom Africa was home made it the more difficult for Britain to accept African majority rule as the necessary corollary for that region. Britain was therefore reluctant to commit itself to any policy on the timing and direction of constitutional change. Uganda's future as an African state was acknowledged from the outset and Tanganyika's status as a Trust Territory explicitly recognised African majority rule as the ultimate goal. Elsewhere the future was less clear, and the outcome in Southern Rhodesia, where in 1965 the white minority illegally seized power, emphasises the radical nature of the changes that occurred elsewhere between 1960 and 1964. In those years, after a decade of prevarication, Britain transferred power to African majorities and established six independent Black African states: Tanganyika in 1961, Uganda in 1962, Kenya in 1963, Malawi (Nyasaland) in 1964, Zambia (Northern Rhodesia) in 1964, and Zanzibar, which later joined with Tanganyika to form Tanzania, in 1963. The distinctive features of that decolonisation, therefore, were the sharp acceleration of pace at the end of the 1950s, and the transfer of power from white to black.

In the final analysis decolonisation was a synthesis of imperial design and nationalist pressure. On the one hand, the changes in British policy were undoubtedly influenced by international developments, and Suez, Cyprus and Malaya must all have played their part. Furthermore these were still the years of the Cold War; and while the British cautioned themselves not to confuse nationalism with Communism, Prime Minister Macmillan had pointed out, as he pushed Britain towards Europe, that the great issue in the changing international scene was whether Asia and Africa would swing to the east or to the west. On the other hand, the radical changes foreshadowed by the acceptance of majority rule for Kenya at the Lancaster House Conference in 1960 were made in response to a growing African political consciousness. Of a whole series of events we can highlight only the most portentous. It was the outbreak of urban and rural violence in Kenya known as Mau Mau, which resulted in the declaration of the state of emergency in 1952, that led finally to the British acceptance of majority rule. In Uganda it was the Ganda response to Governor Cohen's ill-conceived deportation of Kabaka Mutesa in 1953 that cemented the ties of Ganda nationalism and in 1959 stimulated the national movement that forced the British to retreat from their commitment to a unitary state. It was the emergency in Nyasaland in 1959 that forced a change of thought about the future of the Central African Federation. But beyond those crises it was the groundswell of resentment of ordinary human beings against the conditions of colonialism that ultimately created a situation where the colonial rulers could no longer rule without the excessive use of force.

Here we must enter a caveat. First, the political role of the immigrant communities, especially the Europeans, must not be discounted. The most bitter conflicts that occurred in these years did so where a white-settler community had been dominant. Second, account must also be taken of the implications for policy of the expansion abroad of corporate capital in the post-war years. Metropolitan economic interests and corporate power had a critical influence upon the final settlement reached in Kenya if not elsewhere. Nevertheless, while decolonisation in each territory owed more or less to the character of the colonialists' adaptation, a fact made clear by Rhodesia's Unilateral Declaration of Independence, it was the upsurge of African politics in the 1950s that made that adaptation necessary. If the point was reached where the cost of direct rule was too great, it was because of this new African challenge; and if the British objective was to retain the economic advantages of colonial relationships without the direct cost, this required collaboration with a new African élite. The essential ingredient in decolonisation therefore, and that which gave each new state its distinctive character, was the force of nationalism, and the character and identity of the African leadership that rode to power on its back.

Although African nationalism is said to have come 'later' to East and Central Africa than to West Africa, its roots lie deep in the past. There was a long record of protest and petition dating back to the 1920s in Kenya and Southern Rhodesia, and in Zambia the origins of nationalism are to be found in the first miners' strikes on the Copperbelt in 1935 and 1940. What changed was first the focus, which in the 1940s became national rather than local. Then, in the 1950s, a second change occurred as African politics became mass politics, and urban and rural dwellers united in a common support for a new generation of nationalist politicians whose objective was power at the national level.

The British had assumed they had almost indefinite time in which to achieve social development as the prerequisite for

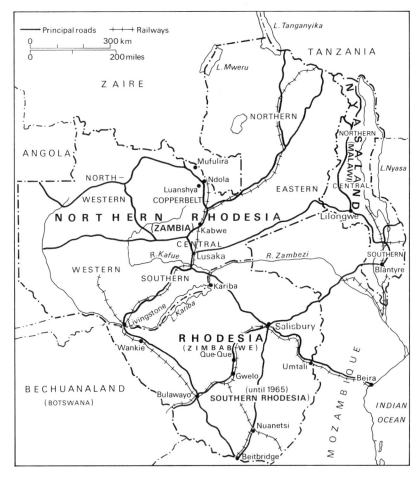

23   Rhodesia, Zambia and Malawi.

political change. The Labour Party's 1943 statement on post-war
aims for the colonies clearly saw the responsibilities as long term.
The more significant assumption, however, for the East and
Central African scene concerned the pattern of institutional
change. Official thinking, under the influence of post-war colonial
experience in Asia, accepted the need to accommodate nationalism,
and a major reassessment of constitutional and political policies
made in the Colonial Office between 1946 and 1949 acknowledged
the need to promote African advancement in the civil service and
in political representation. That strategy, however, was strongly

resisted by the East African governors, whose notions of political development were not those of the Secretary of State.[1] The colonial debate within East and Central Africa was about direct European enterprise as the basis for development, which assumed a continuing European political presence. The sabotage of a proposal in 1945 for equal unofficial representation of the three races in a new East African Legislative Assembly was a reflection of settler influence. The clearest demonstration, however, of settler power and of the character of official thinking was the decision by the new Conservative government to proceed in 1953 with the Central African federation, notwithstanding the almost unanimous opposition from the region's African inhabitants. Justified in terms of its economic potential, criticised as an abdication by Britain of her responsibility for the African people, this 'last attempt at Imperial consolidation' demonstrated that Britain still saw the Europeans as the most suitable agents for development.[2]

Seeing the European settlers as the 'most reliable collaborators' but unable to ignore either Asian minority or African mass, Britain attempted to identify political advance with multiracialism. Thus although Africans were appointed to the Legislative Council in Kenya in 1944, Tanganyika and Uganda in 1945, Northern Rhodesia in 1948 and Nyasaland in 1949, each new constitution 'involved a balancing of the racial composition of the unofficial side of the legislature', to provide representation for European, Asian and African. This was critical for the development of African political consciousness, since multiracialism failed to win African support. Africans rejected a partnership made infamous by Sir Godfrey Huggins' unfortunate reference to the partnership of rider and horse, and discredited more by the federation than by any other event. Over the length and breadth of East and Central Africa, Africans feared the extension of European domination. In Tanganyika in 1947 the controversy sparked off by Britain's proposals for interterritorial cooperation stimulated political feeling, and African resentment against colonial rule began to channel into the Tanganyika African Association. In

[1] C. Pratt, *The critical phase in Tanzania, 1945–1968: Nyerere and the emergence of a socialist strategy* (Cambridge, 1976), 14ff; Ronald Robinson, 'Andrew Cohen and the transfer of power in tropical Africa 1940–1957', in W. H. Morris-Jones and Georges Fischer (eds.), *Decolonisation and after: the British and French experience* (London, 1980).
[2] See Robinson, 'Andrew Cohen and the transfer of power'.

Uganda in 1950 a young Ganda leader pointed out that the proposed policy of federation further south was 'making it very difficult for Africans who would like to support British policy in East Africa'. It was this 'common colour platform emanating from Southern Africa that was disturbing the minds of Africans in East Africa today'.[1] and in 1957 the Tanganyika African Union (TANU) consolidated its growing mass base specifically as a result of opposition to multiracialism which became '*the* issue in Tanganyika in 1957–58'.[2] At the same time in Northern Rhodesia, politicians disagreed on the most appropriate strategy to adopt against both that federation and continued racial domination. The more militant elements founded the United National Independence Party (UNIP), which quickly became the dominant political force in the country.

Race and inequality were undoubtedly key stimuli to the growth of African nationalism. If the central issue was European political influence, there was also the crucial issue of Asian dominance in commerce and industry. The problem of race, it is true, presented itself in a different guise in Zanzibar, where the key issue was the dominance of the Arab minority on an island whose inhabitants were overwhelmingly African. Nevertheless on that island, as elsewhere, the 1950s saw the upsurge of African grass-roots political activity, which challenged racial domination and demanded power for the majority.

The aspirations that nationalism reflected were widespread, uniting Africans across colonial boundaries. For example, the Nyasaland African Congress, formed in 1944, and operating in Southern Rhodesia through the 117 000 Nyasa migrant labourers in that colony, gave an early impetus to Southern Rhodesian nationalist action and organisation. In 1956, the Nyasaland African Congress was in turn prompted to demand an African majority in the Legislative Council by recent developments not only in West Africa but also in Uganda. The wave of industrial unrest in East Africa's ports at the end of the war was influenced by news of the strike in Durban, and in East Africa news travelled easily and rapidly along the railway more than once to influence events in another territory.

[1] E. M. K. Mulira, *Troubled Uganda*, quoted in D. A. Low, *The mind of Buganda* (London, 1971), 154.
[2] Pratt, *The critical phase in Tanzania*, 35; John Iliffe, *A modern history of Tanganyika* (Cambridge, 1979).

The real test of nationalism was, however, the creation of state-wide political organisations with mass support. With hindsight we now appreciate the limitations of the political parties that emerged in the 1950s; but this should not lead us to underestimate their significance, in the context of their time, or the fundamental nature of the changes that their advent presaged. Three broad patterns of change emerged. The first was the rise of urban and proletarian discontent. The second was the growth of rural grievance. The third was the fusion of rural and urban protest into a national movement by a new nationalist leadership that articulated its own demands for political power in the sentiments of the aggrieved multitude. The desires and the discontents of the locality were translated into the idiom of national independence. We can do no better than quote the explanation given by Tanzania's President, Julius Nyerere, of the growth of nationalism to identify the heart of the process. 'National freedom – *uhuru* – was an uncomplicated principle, and it needed no justification to the audiences of the first few TANU speakers. All that was required was an explanation of its relevance to their lives, and some reasonable assurance that it could be obtained through the methods proposed by TANU.'[1]

The uneven incidence of industrial and urban protest reflected the uneven industrialisation and urban growth over the region as a whole; but in each case it was a protest against social and economic inequality and the deplorable conditions in which the bulk of the work-force lived and worked. Thus the post-war years opened with a succession of strikes in Mombasa, Dar es Salaam and Zanzibar; and a railway strike that involved both Rhodesias. The late 1940s saw a wave of strikes in Southern Rhodesia that made those years 'a period of African unrest of unprecedented intensity and scale'. Godfrey Huggins, then prime minister of Rhodesia, commented: 'We are witnessing the emergence of a proletariat and in this country it happens to be black.'[2] Whether or not it was a proletariat, the wage-labour force in Salisbury (the modern Harare), as in the other urban and industrial centres, challenged colonial rule (but not necessarily the capitalist system) to demand the improvement of their way of life, and to win steady increases in urban wages over the 1950s.

[1] Julius Nyerere, *Freedom and unity* (London, 1968), 1.
[2] L. Gann and M. Gelfand, *Huggins of Rhodesia* (London, 1964), 201.

The power of urban labour was most dramatically demonstrated on the Northern Rhodesian Copperbelt, where sustained militant action on the part of African miners through the 1950s ultimately wrested the dominant position from the white union. Their victory was finally signified by the dissolution of the European Mineworkers Union in 1964. The rolling strikes of 1956, which provoked the Northern Rhodesian government to declare a state of emergency, indicated the organisational ability of the miners that had first been demonstrated in 1935. The basis for trade unionism lay in this early and spontaneous response of African labour to relative deprivation and racial and economic inequality. The Northern Rhodesian copper-miners and the Mombasa dockers showed that illiterate workers could combine with some degree of success in defence of their interests and, in the Northern Rhodesian case at least, industrial action arising out of economic conditions essentially preceded political agitation directed at independence.

The trade-union movement that developed in the 1950s owed a good deal to the influence of British labour policy, to the support of the British and international trade-union movements, and also to changing employer attitudes towards organised labour. Beyond this, however, there was the direct stimulus of the nationalist struggle, and the growing African assertiveness that characterised the period from 1955. Union organisation offered a vehicle for the articulation of labour discontent but was also part of the drive towards independence; and the political environment of the late 1950s cannot be ignored as an important stimulus to trade-union activity in these latter years. Nor should we ignore the impact of the changing economic situation and the resulting unemployment.

The achievements of labour are difficult to measure. At independence there was a small labour movement in each territory. Membership covered only a small percentage of the wage-labour force, although this might reflect governmental constraints rather than union inaction. Thus Southern Rhodesia, with the largest wage-labour force in colonial Africa in the late 1950s, had the smallest trade-union movement. Northern Rhodesia, where union membership was just under 40 per cent of the wage-labour force, probably had the largest union membership. What distinguished Northern Rhodesia's labour movement, however, was the African

Mineworkers' Union, of which a Labour Department official commented in the late 1950s that 'over the past many years the idea has grown up amongst the Africans that once they enter the Copperbelt area the people they must obey in all things are the AMWU leaders...'.[1] The coincidence in Northern Rhodesia of a highly organised, centralised industry, with a concentrated work-force, a highly charged racial situation and powerful leadership in the persons of Lawrence Katilungu and, later, John Chisata, contributed to the emergence of a powerful union, whose trade-union tradition went beyond any other in the region. In Kenya a similar combination of a growing work-force in circumstances of racial inequality also stimulated the growth of a vigorous labour movement, and threw up an outstanding young labour leader in Tom Mboya. The Mau Mau emergency, and subsequently union involvement in the country's factional politics nevertheless precluded the development of autonomous unions.

The politics of nationalist protest required also the mass support of the rural majorities. Nationalism reflected the growing rural resentment at the increasing intrusion of colonial government into people's daily lives, which was a consequence of post-war policies for economic development and agricultural improvement. 'Purposive government action, in economic, educational and agrarian spheres, brought individual Africans, now more peasants than tribesmen, into much closer and more irritating contact with the colonial regime.'[2] The consequence, without exception, was an increased political consciousness rooted in anti-colonial sentiment at the grass-roots level. Thus, while George Nyandoro, one of the founders of the Southern Rhodesian National Congress, said of the Native Land Husbandry Act that it was 'the best recruiter Congress ever had',[3] Oginga Odinga, one of Kenya's major politicians, concluded that in Kenya 'resistance to government soil conservation measures and land consolidation gave the mass backing to the political movement...'.[4] The growth of nationalism in Northern Rhodesia, dominated as it was by the

[1] Richard Jacobs, *The relationship between African trade unions and political organisations in Northern Rhodesia/Zambia, 1949–61* (Geneva, 1971), 21, quoting the Northern Rhodesian government.
[2] John Lonsdale, 'Some origins of nationalism in East Africa', *Journal of African History*, 1968, 9, 1, 141.
[3] Quoted in L. W. Bowman, *Politics in Rhodesia: white power in an African state* (Cambridge, Mass., 1973), 49.
[4] *Not yet uhuru* (London, 1967), 107.

urban, industrial Copperbelt, was just as deeply rooted in the anti-colonial grievances of the villages, and the strength of rural protest contributed a great deal to the ultimate success of the nationalist movement. The Devlin Report's terse analysis of the roots of unrest in Nyasaland summed up the circumstances of rural protest over the region as a whole.

About ten years ago the Government enacted legislation under which rules were made to prevent soil erosion. [These rules] mean a good deal of labour, just before the rains come and when the ground is dry and hard... There are also veterinary rules...

Breaches of these rules lead to fines and in extreme cases imprisonment. They are very unpopular... Their object is little understood... The enforcement of these rules led to disputes and to a great deal of bitter feeling during the period we had under review...[1]

While the general groundswell of peasant discontent gathered momentum from opposition to enforced agricultural improvement, the most intense rural nationalism was born out of attachment to the land. Africans universally feared the loss of their land to Europeans. Even in Uganda, where there was minimal alienation of land to non-Africans, the Uganda government's attempt in 1956 to introduce land reforms which provided for individual tenure provoked a sharp opposition over almost the whole country. It was however in those territories where land had been alienated to Europeans that the most bitter resentment was bred. In Nyasaland the Abrahams Report in 1946 identified the strength of opposition to European planters, and the unrest of the 1950s owed a great deal to the bitterness created by the hardships of *thangata*, the African tenant system. In Southern Rhodesia, African action over land was checked only by the more repressive governmental controls that existed in that territory. In Kenya, where land had been the central political issue since the 1920s, it was the impact of land alienation upon the Kikuyu, the Africans most seriously disadvantaged by European settlement (although not those who lost the largest amount of land), that set in train the protest that erupted finally in 1952 into the violence of Mau Mau resistance and the state of emergency that lasted seven years and during which there were in excess of ten thousand African casualties.

[1] *Report of the Nyasaland Commission of Inquiry* (the Devlin Report), Cmnd 814 (London, 1959), 19. Compare resistance to the cutting-out of cocoa trees in the Gold Coast, Chapter 7.

The third characteristic pattern that we can identify is the emergence of a new style of leadership. The first stage began soon after the war when the earlier leadership of illiterate workers was replaced by that of younger, more educated men, like young Chege Kibachia in Mombasa, or Lawrence Katilungu on the Copperbelt. Those men, the clerks and the hospital orderlies, replaced the chiefs as leaders in the urban situation. A similar process of change occurred in the rural areas, although over a longer period of time, whereby the chiefs lost the role of communicators to a newer, younger generation of leaders: the school teachers, the clerks and the traders who were outside the chiefly and the Native Authority structure.

The second stage in this evolution occurred in the 1950s, a little later in some colonies than in others, with the appearance of a new type of politician, the nationalist, with a strong, more specific anti-colonial commitment. Young, many still in their twenties, they were generally more educated than the earlier leaders. Some, but by no means all, had been abroad for part of their education (which meant in many cases an experience of South Africa). There were exceptions, but the majority of these new leaders were the second generation of the emergent élite: teachers, cooperative officials, trade unionists, clerks, and a few of them professional men. These were the men who built the political parties; who started and edited the party newspapers; and who moulded rural and urban discontent into a coherent national protest which provided them with an institutional base from which, with apparently complete self-confidence, they demanded power.

The nationalists encountered a good deal of opposition in the 1950s from colonial governments which sought to direct political activity into a pattern of their own making, with a degree of coercion that was for the most part absent from the West African scene. In Kenya the emergency led to the prohibition of all political organisations and the complete cessation of normal political life for Africans until 1956, when the formation of political associations was permitted at the district level. Country-wide political activity was not again permitted until 1960, and that restriction, combined with the exclusion of the great majority of the Kikuyu from politics for the seven years of the emergency, had long-lasting consequences for the growth of the parties. In Central Africa the nationalists universally encountered vigorous official hostility throughout the 1950s, culminating in the 1959 state of emergency when the African parties were banned and the leaders detained in all three territories. In Tanganyika the fledgling party established in 1954, the Tanganyika African National Union (TANU), suffered early difficulties in a number of districts; and in Zanzibar neither Arab nor African nationalists went unscathed.

With the change in British policy by 1960 came a change in attitudes towards nationalist leaders, demonstrated dramatically by the sudden release of Nyasaland's nationalist leader, Dr Banda, early in 1960, apparently at the behest of the Secretary of State. It would be another year before Jomo Kenyatta's release, but from that date the colonial governments were forced to follow where the Colonial Office led, since as the Wild Report had pointed out apropos of Uganda:

If the aim, namely to establish a National Assembly on the House of Commons model, is accepted, then it follows that well-organised political parties commanding the confidence of the majority of the electorate are an essential part of the system...therefore our recommendations should be designed to encourage the development of political parties capable of operating the parliamentary system...[1]

Colonial policy decreed and the nationalists accepted that electoral support was a necessary prerequisite for the transfer of power. Hence the African people across the region went to the polls in a rapid succession of 17 different elections, some of them carried through with apparent haste, the last in each case on the basis of universal franchise, to determine the leaders who would assume office. The first direct elections were held in Kenya in 1957, the last in Nyasaland in 1964. The imperatives of the electoral process produced the modern mass movements which transformed political organisation at the territorial level. With the crucial exception of Southern Rhodesia, where settler control destroyed African politics in 1962, the African political parties held the centre of the stage for those seven years of electoral politics. TANU led the way; but in each state by 1964 the nationalists had established, with varying degrees of success, a new institutional framework for populist politics.

The parties that emerged could all trace their origins back to the earlier period of political activity. UNIP formed in Northern

[1] Uganda Protectorate, *Report of the Constitutional Committee 1959* (Entebbe, 1959), 33.

Rhodesia in 1960, and the Malawi Congress Party (MCP) established a year earlier, both succeeded the earlier congress-style movements established in the 1940s in response to the threat of federation. Both quickly built up massive support, although UNIP was unable to eliminate the old African National Congress (ANC), which continued as a small but vigorous opposition party until the introduction of the one-party state in 1972. In Kenya the dominant Kenya African National Union (KANU), traced its origins back to the Kikuyu Central Association formed in the 1920s, but was more immediately a confederation of district associations set up since 1956.

At the same time these parties were a new phenomenon: in terms of their objectives; their electoral functions; and their characteristic association of a new nationalist leadership with the discontented rural and urban mass. Their methods were also new. They used the techniques and symbols of the mass party and they emphasised recruitment at the grass roots and in the rural areas. Most of them performed considerable feats in mobilising large rural populations first to register and then to vote. In Nyasaland, for example, the registration of not far short of two million voters, in less than a week, before the 1964 elections, was a triumph for the MCP organisation. And everywhere they marshalled at the polls a massive, largely illiterate electorate, who made their marks for independence. Nor should it be assumed that illiterate voters were necessarily unaware of what was at stake. In Uganda, a significant drop in the poll in Bunyoro between the first and second general elections in 1961 and 1962, undoubtedly reflected grass-roots resentment at the unresolved Lost Counties issue.

The political parties therefore performed a major role in mobilising popular anti-colonial protest through the electoral machine. Yet notwithstanding their exhilarating electoral victories, the parties that took power shared one critical weakness that would have significant implications for the post-colonial state. Although many of the young nationalists demonstrated considerable organisational skill, the parties they created were organisationally weak. Their most serious weakness was perhaps their inability to control local-level activists in a situation where a good deal of nationalist activity occurred at the local level. While Kenya's KANU presented the most extreme problems of local autonomy, in fact all the parties, with the possible exception of the MCP, were characteristically more decentralised in practice than their constitutions allowed.

These weaknesses derived in part from the limitations of resources available. They also reflected the pluralistic character of the parties, which sought to mobilise a wide range of societal and economic interests within the one movement. Two particular internal problems need to be borne in mind. Where organised labour was a significant element in society, differing views as to the proper relationship between party and trade union created a potential source of conflict within the nationalist leadership. Although governments sought without exception to isolate the unions from politics, the political consequences of industrial action could not be avoided. Party politicians and radical young trade-union leaders saw industrial action as a legitimate weapon in the nationalist struggle, although there were in fact few politically motivated strikes across the region in these years. Labour's role in the nationalist struggle, however, notwithstanding the close relationship between party and union leaders, produced a potential rival to and thus a potential division within the party.

Second, the combination of different ethnic and regional interests within the same party was also a potential source of conflict. It was this association of regional interests, and therefore of a number of powerful national leaders exploiting regional grievances within the same party, that was one underlying cause of the inability of the centre to control the periphery in both KANU in Kenya and UNIP in Northern Rhodesia.

Such differences could not always be contained within the one party. Where more than one party emerged, it reflected the depth of cleavages within society that would not be subordinated to the nationalist objective, but were in fact exacerbated by the decolonisation process. Thus the success of the single party in Tanganyika and in Nyasaland was not least a reflection of the absence of deep-rooted divisions in those societies. In Kenya, by contrast, there were intense fears among the so-called minority tribes of their possible subjection, in the independent state, at the hands of the economically and politically dominant Kikuyu and Luo peoples. Reflected above all in the conflict between Kalenjin and Kikuyu over access to the settlers' land in the Rift Valley, this led to the formation in 1960 of a second party, the Kenya

African Democratic Union (KADU) to challenge KANU's drive for power, and to become, until shortly after independence, the parliamentary opposition. In Kenya also intra-party tensions reflected the conflict between landed and landless in Kikuyu society. In Uganda, the central political issue of Buganda's dominance, allied to the deep-rooted religious rivalry, resulted in the growth of a highly competitive two-party system.

It is important to bear in mind the role of violence in the decolonisation process. Radicalism in those years related to means rather than ends, and militancy and moderation referred to the use of force. Militant politics grew out of the juxtaposition of African deprivation and European privilege. Hence it was in the Kenyan Highlands and on the Northern Rhodesian Copperbelt, the two areas where colonialism bit deepest into African life, that African resentment against the indignities of colonialism produced the earliest and the most violent protest. These were not, however, the only areas of violent protest. Industrial unrest was a widespread theme during these years and rural populism carried with it undertones of violence. We may recall the successive crises of 1945, 1949 and 1959 in Buganda, all of which were marked by demonstrations against the Buganda government and colonial rule. UNIP militancy provoked serious rural violence in Northern Rhodesia in each successive year between 1958 and 1964.

Once the British changed their policy and became anxious, as they did from 1960, to 'guide the energies of the nationalists into constructive channels and to secure their cooperation in a programme of steady but not headlong political advance',[1] force was no longer necessary. The nationalist leaders who came to power at independence did so as a result of a bargaining process that proceeded through constitutional channels. All of them used the constitutional process to advance what they saw to be their country's and their own interests. But where there were rival elements within the nationalist movement, the bargaining process was not simply between colonial rulers and nationalists, but between those rival interests as well. The independence arrangements reflected those cleavages in society, as for example in Kenya's *majimbo* (regionalism) and Uganda's federalism, but they did not necessarily overcome them. Nationalist leaders in their demand for immediate independence made their bargains with the

[1] Sir Andrew Cohen, *British policy in changing Africa* (London, 1959), 61.

colonial power in the full knowledge that some of the provisions might prove temporary, but on the assumption that they themselves would determine any future alteration in the internal distribution of power. Before we consider that new phase, however, we must briefly consider Southern Rhodesia, where it was white, not black, nationalism that triumphed.

The most obvious difference between the settler communities in Southern Rhodesia and the other territories, especially Kenya, lay in the greater political autonomy the white Rhodesians had enjoyed since they were granted 'responsible government' (internal self-government) in 1923. The explanation for UDI therefore lay to some extent in the events before 1940, when the Southern Rhodesians had quietly developed 'a body of laws that not only protected white interests but generally inhibited Africans from developing their skills and demonstrating their capabilities'[1] and in the process established a firm institutional basis for racial segregation and white economic and political control. We need, however, to look further, for while the Kenyan settlers did not have control of the colony's government in 1940 they were then just as firmly entrenched as their Rhodesian counterparts. Of greater importance was the character of the white Rhodesian community itself. In the first place it was much larger than that of Kenya or Northern Rhodesia: 5 per cent of the population instead of 1 per cent. Second, it included an economically privileged white urban artisan class which was more permanently rooted in the country than were Northern Rhodesia's miners, and which enjoyed a greater political power derived from the country's greater political autonomy. That urban wage-labour force depended moreover for its privileged status on the racial segregation and the subordination of the African majority that were the cornerstones of the country's way of life. Third, the white farming community and the agricultural sector were economically more significant than was the case in Kenya. Southern Rhodesia's 7000 white farmers owned 49 per cent of the country's land, employed 42 per cent of the labour force, and were politically much more firmly entrenched than the growing business community – either the local or the international corporate interests. Thus while the business community might have favoured a more liberal conclusion to decolonisation, and the British might

[1] Robert Good, *UDI: the international politics of the Rhodesian rebellion* (London, 1973).

(as Huggins believed) have wished to give way to black nationalism as quickly as possible in order to sustain their trade links with African countries, it was the European farming community that dominated the internal power system. White farmers and artisans were politically more powerful than white businessmen, and it was they who determined the response to African nationalism in 1959–60, when a state of emergency was followed by new repressive laws. The most important factor was undoubtedly that the white Rhodesians controlled their own armed forces which the Kenyan whites did not. African militancy met its match, and we may therefore conclude that the initial failure of African nationalism in Southern Rhodesia was the result not of weaker Africans but of stronger Europeans.

Two other factors must also, however, be taken into account. If the nationalist movement in Southern Rhodesia developed along lines similar to those in other states, it carried within it the same weaknesses, not least the internal conflict within the leadership over tactics and strategy, and those internal divisions had serious consequences for the outcome of the African struggle, both before and after UDI. It might also be argued that the nationalists failed to identify the real nature of the struggle in Southern Rhodesia, misjudging both the potential for a liberal solution from within Rhodesia and the possibility of British intervention from outside. Just as Britain had never exercised her right of surveillance over Rhodesian legislation on behalf of the black population in the 42 years of responsible government, so in 1965 she failed to honour her colonial obligations. Whereas troops had been flown into Kenya in 1952 to quell the Mau Mau uprising among the Kikuyu, no force was used against Rhodesia's white settlers in 1965. While the underlying reasons for the British abdication of responsibility at this point remain a matter of debate, we must agree that, while the arguments for and against the use of force were impressive, the fact that force was not used

suggests that the issues at stake – reversing UDI and assuring ultimate majority rule in Rhodesia with all it entailed for the evolution of affairs in Southern Africa and Britain's position in Black Africa, the Commonwealth and the UN – were not worth the economic cost and the political risk involved in applying force. There was here a question of values and leadership...[1]

[1] Good, *UDI*, 65.

It was the overriding considerations of Britain's domestic policy that led to Britain's Rhodesian failure.

Post-colonial change

The politics of independence quickly focussed upon the allocation of scarce resources in a situation where the state was acknowledged as a direct agent of development, and government management of the economy was a long-established tradition. There was a strong continuity between colonial and post-colonial political postures, and the most powerful forces within the new state had been born during the nationalist struggle when colonial development policy had created new urban workers, new progressive farmers and a new African administrative class. There was a significant inequality of income not only between the races, but also between the small minority of African society which had found education and employment in the modern sector and the majority which had not. Colonial policy had also contributed to acute regional imbalances in economic development, where regions coincided to a greater or lesser extent with ethnic groupings. Hence although Tanganyika and Nyasaland were relatively free of ethnic conflict, elsewhere ethnic and/or regional inequality was a significant basis for political cleavage. In the independent state, the issues at the heart of the political debate therefore remained the same. In Zambia the transition to independence occurred against a background of industrial unrest that reached its climax in 1966 when the miners demonstrated their continuing power by taking the Copperbelt out on strike and won a 22 per cent wage increase which would exacerbate the urban–rural gap. In Kenya the Kikuyu hunger for land, while temporarily assuaged by the land settlement which restored the white highlands to African ownership, nonetheless remained the dominant political issue.

There were, however, two additional constraints, which would in due course have serious political consequences: first there was the burden of economic dependence that meant that expatriate capital was an additional influence upon the state. (All these states were dependent on external capital for development.) Second there was the conflict, already to some extent apparent, between the needs of the mass and the aspirations of the élite. While there was at the grass roots a healthy realism as to the possibilities that independence would bring, there were also the aspirations for a better life, and in particular for education and employment, that no government could satisfy in the short term. At the same time there were intense desires among the élite for the material standards of the expatriate society that they now replaced, but which no government could sustain except at the expense of the mass.

A remarkable number of issues was left unresolved by the independence settlements. In Uganda the 60-year-old conflict between Buganda and Bunyoro over the Lost Counties was left to be decided later by referendum, and the more recent but equally divisive Rwenzururu secessionist movement was holding down a significant part of Uganda's armed forces in the western kingdom of Toro. Kenya faced the Somali-oriented secessionist movement in her North-Eastern Province, and a potential disruption to security by those of the Kikuyu Mau Mau freedom fighters who remained in the forests. Zambia's security situation as the front-line state in southern Africa was critically affected by Rhodesia's illegal declaration of independence a year after her own, at a time when the country had scarcely overcome the bitterness generated by the Lumpa church uprising in Northern Province and when Lozi separatist feelings still made Barotseland a difficult area. In Zanzibar the revolution that swept the Arab minority from power in January 1964 no more than a month after that state's independence demonstrated the failure of constitutional arrangements to overcome racial fears. The independence constitution had provided for majority rule. Nevertheless, common-roll elections based on a universal adult franchise and single-member constituencies left the Arab oligarchy in power. That government's repressive measures towards the Afro-Shirazi Party (ASP) opposition, whose support derived from the African majority community, pushed Zanzibar towards a more authoritarian state. Anti-government elements drew together behind the Umma ('the masses') Party, formed in July 1963 by Abdul Rahman Mohammed (Babu). Whilst the catalyst for the revolution was provided by an outsider, it was Umma, with the radical elements of ASP, which assumed control a month later, and three months later joined Tanganyika to form the new Republic of Tanzania. Malawi suffered a major cabinet crisis soon after independence and subsequently an abortive invasion which, if it failed in the face of massive support for Dr Banda, nonetheless demonstrated the absence of consensus within the new government. But it was in East Africa that the limitations of power were most clearly demonstrated in 1964 by the army mutinies that occurred following the Zanzibar coup in swift succession in each state, and which were contained only with the assistance of the former colonial power.

The very integrity of the state was therefore at risk, and no government could claim effectively to command the use of force. The most important characteristic of the new states was their fragility. It is not therefore surprising that the prime concern of the new leaders was in each case to strengthen their control and to centralise power. They rejected secession as a legitimate solution to internal conflict, and reasserted the boundaries inherited with the colonial state. Where there had been a federal devolution of power it was revoked, although Kenya's regional structure (*majimbo*) was more easily abolished in December 1964 than Uganda's quasi-federalism, which was dissolved only after a violent confrontation between Obote's central government and Buganda in May 1966. Without exception, however, they set out to adapt the inherited structures through which they now exerted their power. The transfer of power had generally been on the basis of the Westminster model, and the independence constitutions characteristically had provided the new states with the institutions of representative parliamentary government, the underlying assumptions of which were those of a multi-party democracy. While the political pattern was generally that of the dominant party state, four of the new states, Uganda, Kenya, Zambia and Zanzibar, had an opposition party recognised under the conventions of parliamentary government. Yet within the first decade of independence each state adopted a single-party system, in which the dominant institution was a powerful presidential executive. As a result the 1960s marked important phases in institutional change, and in state-building, in which the dominant trend was away from the multi-party democracy envisaged in the independence settlements towards an authoritarian rule and the concentration of power at the centre.

The clearest demonstration of this concentration of power in the central executive was the progressive decline of the representative institutions of state. Notwithstanding the notion of parliamentary sovereignty, the right of elected assemblies to control the executive was not accepted, and each legislature in turn was reduced to a minor role in the political system. The Kenyan legislature was in the 1960s something of an exception, and articulate and frequently courageous MPs ensured a vital public forum for political debate that contributed a good deal to the openness of the Kenyan system. By 1970, however, presidential mediation between parliamentarians and government had given way to a more coercive control, demonstrated finally in 1975 by the arrest of two MPs within the precincts of parliament and their subsequent detention. In Uganda a viable two-party system at the outset ensured a vigorous parliamentary debate, but the decision of the parliamentary leader of the opposition Democratic Party to join the ruling Uganda Peoples' Congress (UPC) in 1964 marked the decline not only of the two-party system but also of the authority of the legislature itself. The constituent assembly that debated the new republican constitution in 1967 might have indicated a hankering for tolerance and discussion, but the National Assembly had some time earlier lost any genuine power. In Tanzania the hopes for a more vigorous parliamentary assembly within the one-party state failed to materialise, and in Malawi it was at no time contemplated. In Zambia, when the MPs attempted to establish for themselves a more positive role in the one-party assembly of 1974, they encountered the same party and presidential suspicion and opposition as their predecessors.

The concentration of power resulted also in the progressive emasculation if not abolition of elected local government institutions. The colonial attempt to build local governments on the British model had had limited success in East and Central Africa. While the urban and European-dominated local authorities in Kenya and Zambia had enjoyed significant power, only in Uganda and Kenya had African local authorities assumed an important governmental role, which they had performed with some degree of competence and success. Nevertheless, at independence all states were committed to a system of representative local government responsible, in varying degrees, for important functions of government at the district level. After independence, while the urban authorities grew in power, reflecting not least the urban growth that each state experienced to a greater or lesser degree,

the rural authorities were progressively shorn of their responsibilities and their functions transferred to central government – or,
as in Tanzania, to district development councils which, if they
preserved the element of local representation, ensured ultimate
government/party control.

Where traditional rulers had retained any significant constitutional authority, as in the case of Buganda and Barotseland, this
was in due course subordinated to the central authority and
ultimately abolished, although the procedure followed proved
different in each case. Everywhere there was a move away from
the formal use of traditional authority. Although tradition was by
no means dead the day of the chief had generally passed by 1975.
It was true that in Malawi the position of chief was to some extent
restored after independence, and traditional courts in 1967 were
given increased jurisdiction, including the right to pass death
sentences. Nevertheless no chief was permitted to build an
independent power base from which to criticise government or
party and President Banda was quite willing to depose chiefs
unpopular with his administration. So the paramount chief of the
Ngoni of Central Province was deposed for his anti-government
activities in 1967, as he had been suspended 14 years earlier by
the colonial regime for his opposition to agricultural rules.

The extension of executive power also resulted in the subordination of the labour movement and of interest groups – like
cooperatives – in general to government and to the party. Tanzania in 1964 led the way with the introduction of the National
Union of Tanganyika Workers. The pattern of a government-
controlled central organisation of unions, and industrial legislation that virtually prohibited strike action, was subsequently
introduced in each state, although in Zambia government control had up to 1975 stopped short of the same radical restructuring of the labour movement as occurred in East Africa.

The centralisation of power in the executive resulted in the
increased power and authority of the central bureaucracy, which
in each state was by 1975 vastly increased in size and staffed
predominantly by African nationals rather than expatriates. Their
power was no doubt most apparent in Kenya, where the president
had deliberately chosen to use the provincial administration as his
major agent of control as well as development; but a similar

extension of bureaucratic power occurred elsewhere as each state reinstated a paternalist and authoritarian bureaucratic machine.

This characteristic centralisation of control was in part a genuine attempt to grapple with the problems of development. The curtailment of local government and trade-union autonomy was justified in terms of the need to curb the consumptionist tendency of their members. It also, however, indicated the unwillingness of governments or individual rulers to share power. Thus notwithstanding President Kaunda's attempt in Zambia in 1968 to introduce 'decentralisation in centralism', it was only in Tanzania in 1972 that a genuine decentralisation of governmental authority had been attempted.

The authoritarian character of the post-colonial state was perhaps most obviously demonstrated by the refusal to tolerate opposition except on terms laid down by the ruling party itself. Yet although each state introduced and used a wide variety of constitutional and political measures, including Preventive Detention Acts, to control political opposition, they built very different kinds of parties and party systems. Thus, while the major institutional innovation after independence was the introduction of the one-party state, it was here that the greatest variations occurred both in the origins of the single-party system and in the character of the party itself. In each case the introduction of the one-party state was based on the argument that competitive party politics were wasteful, divisive and inappropriate in the circumstances of the independent but underdeveloped and (supposedly) classless state. Yet the resulting single-party system varied a great deal, and each independent state acquired its own distinctive character.

In Tanzania the absence at independence of any opposition to TANU paved the way for the easy transition to the one-party state. The critical events leading to its creation were the introduction of the Republic in 1962, the One-Party Commission in 1964, and the establishment of the constitutional one-party state in 1965. The Arusha Declaration of 1967 articulated Tanzania's objective of a socialist and self-reliant society and the strategy to achieve it, central to which was the public ownership of the major means of production. The *Mwongozo* or Guidelines, issued in 1971, stressed the importance of worker participation and refined the notions of leadership. The Union between Tanganyika and Zanzibar had enlarged the state in 1964, but the foundations of the system lay in TANU and in the Arusha Declaration.

The Tanzanian political system in the mid-1970s was still basically authoritarian. Political activity outside the party was firmly rejected and, as one perceptive and sympathetic writer observed, 'Whatever the longer term democratic potential for the new structures which [had been created], their immediate consequences have been to consolidate power in the hands of the present leaders, to silence their critics and to lessen the autonomy of previously independent institutions.'[1] Presidential power had been demonstrated by such decisions as the union with Zanzibar, made by Nyerere without reference to either cabinet or National Assembly, and the bureaucracy was (notwithstanding party rhetoric to the contrary) the dominant agent of development. At the same time Tanzania's socialist strategy and the institutional changes after 1965 indicated the desire on the part of some at least of the leadership to establish democratic controls over both national élite and middle-level party activists.

The procedures adopted for the introduction of the one-party state in Tanzania ensured a significant element of popular participation in that process. Three general elections showed that the electoral process and campaign rules provided a basis for genuine grass-roots electoral participation, and the first general election in the one-party state in 1965 was a milestone in African political history. Although the Arusha Declaration imposed some restrictions on recruitment, TANU remained in 1975 a mass party. The Leadership Code introduced under the Arusha Declaration in 1967 was a genuine attempt to prevent social and economic inequality, and while the small élite had not been eliminated it had been controlled. But the most significant changes for the growth of the democratic state had been within TANU itself, which had developed an important element of internal party democracy that was absent in other ruling parties. Following the extension in 1968 and 1969 of the parliamentary electoral system to the party, a wide range of posts in TANU were subsequently filled by an election process that followed closely the process for national parliamentary elections. Thus, while the prevailing characteristic of the Tanzanian political system was in 1975 the power of TANU, there

[1] Pratt, *The critical phase in Tanzania*, 193–4.

408

had been a significant development of internal democracy within the party.

Tanzania's post-colonial state obviously owed a good deal to President Nyerere's leadership and to his moral commitment to the principles of the democratic state. But the Tanzanian system in 1975 had also grown out of Tanzanian society, and reflected popular attitudes about party and society of a still predominantly egalitarian peasant society. If the Arusha Declaration was Nyerere's reaction to the early 'scramble of party members for status, income and personal power', it nevertheless struck a deeply responsive chord in an African society in which there was as yet no significant élite and few vested interests. In this respect it is important to bear in mind the much lower level of penetration of foreign capital in Tanzania compared with Kenya and Zambia and the much more diffuse impact of white settlement and of colonialism itself. Thus such stability as the Tanzanian system had achieved by the mid-1970s was the result not simply of the centralisation of power and authority, but of a significant consensus about the country's form of governance among a population in which there were still few deep economic or social cleavages.

Malawi won independence with a single party that enjoyed overwhelming mass support under President Banda's leadership, so that the move to a legal one-party state in 1966 also followed naturally upon earlier political developments. The emergent party system differed a great deal however from Tanzania's, for in Malawi political structures and associated values continued to ensure that instructions should be carried downwards. Banda's dominance was based both on his massive support, particularly among the more traditional elements of rural society, and also his intimate interaction with party networks. He became life president in July 1971, following a call from the party that the constitution be amended for this purpose, thus consolidating his control of all significant power. While the MCP, like TANU, had its little office in every town, and the party's tentacles stretched far and wide, the party remained subservient to its life president in the critical functions of policy-making and the choice both of parliamentary representative and of members of the party hierarchy. While the party organs, and especially the Malawi Young Pioneers, provided an important integrating force to offset potentially disruptive parochial loyalties, the party dependence on the centre remained a dominant characteristic of the system which inhibited any genuine decentralisation. While the influence of the leadership was as important as in Tanzania, President Banda's ideas and attitudes were very different from those of President Nyerere. Equally important, the cabinet crisis of 1964, when the young politicians who had earlier built Dr Banda up into a more than life-size figure, then challenged him unsuccessfully for control, made him wary of any colleagues and assistants. Thus Malawi's one-party state was a centralised autocracy, in which Dr Banda sustained the nation's unity with his appeal to the populace for personal support.

The evolution of the one-party system was a good deal more turbulent in Kenya, Zambia and Uganda, in all of which constitutional amendment was used to eliminate political opposition in an increasingly coercive state. Kenya's first experiment as a *de facto* one-party state followed the voluntary dissolution of KADU in 1964, on the occasion of the establishment of the Republic and the abandonment of the quasi-federal devolution of power. It lasted however only until 1966 by which time the enlarged KANU could no longer contain its divergent elements and the former Vice-President, Oginga Odinga, withdrew with a significant radical minority to form a new opposition, the Kenya People's Union (KPU). The KPU was itself banned in 1969, after a period of growing political violence, at which point Kenya became once more a *de facto* one-party state.

Until 1969 the mode of Kenyan politics was essentially that of a factional system focussed upon the presidency, and based on principles of patronage and clientage which required national leaders to sustain a local base if they wished to retain power at the centre. The party was, under those circumstances, essentially a machine to control and distribute patronage and, when necessary, to mobilise electoral support, rather than an institution to organise development or to ensure popular democratic control of the leadership. Paradoxically that factionalism, with its organised network of communications between centre and locality, resulted in a highly participant political system. Local political pressures were exercised through government 'right up to the President', and often through KANU which, notwithstanding its moribund state at the national level, at the local level was actively associated with local interests. The grass roots consequently remained highly politicised. The system, however, placed great pressure on resources, and resulted in a symbiosis between business and politics that provided the foundations for the dependent state.

At independence, uneven development reinforced the inherited ethnic cleavages in society to make ethnic rivalry a central issue of politics, in a situation where 'tribalism' meant essentially Kikuyu dominance. Ethnic loyalty was also however exploited to defuse economic discontent, most notably in a little general election in 1966, a strategy that progressively weakened Kenyatta's position as a symbol of Kenyan integration. The assassination in 1969 of Tom Mboya, Kenya's most controversial and probably most gifted political leader, led to a more intense polarisation of ethnic forces, and to the destruction of the KPU. It also resulted in the greater political dominance of the Kikuyu. By 1975 the Luo had been relegated to the periphery of the Kenyan political system which was now determined less by ethnic than by economic inequality. Mboya's assassination therefore also marked a distinctive change in the balance of power in Kenya and a new phase in politics. At that point, the rules of the political game changed. Although two remarkably open elections were held in 1969 and 1974, both of which resulted in significant changes in parliamentary membership, Kenyan politics had moved much more to palace clique and away from party, parliament or faction. As Kenyatta gathered power into the presidency, so the presidency became the prime resource in a political conflict that increasingly demonstrated the new class cleavages in society. The assassination in 1975 of J. M. Kariuki, a vigorous Kikuyu political leader who had openly challenged Kenya's increasing economic inequality and the self-aggrandisement of the small central Kikuyu élite, suggested the beginning of a further polarisation of forces on economic rather than ethnic lines. Whereas Mboya's death had united the Kikuyu in common defence against the Luo, Kariuki's death divided them, and this time they could not be held together by ethnic loyalty. Thus 1975 marked a qualitative change in the politics of a post-colonial Kenya.

In Zambia, UNIP's dominant position was apparent from the outset and President Kaunda had on many occasions expressed his confidence that the people of Zambia would vote the one-party state into existence. Nevertheless in 1968 the first general election disappointed him, particularly in Barotseland, where the Lozi, aggrieved at central government neglect, demonstrably withdrew their support from the ruling party. More serious was the intra-party conflict which between 1967 and 1971 pulled UNIP apart. In a manner reminiscent of Kenya, former Vice-President Kapwepwe in 1971 left the party to form a new opposition, the United Progressive Party (UPP) which represented the radical populist strain of UNIP's early days. As in Kenya the new opposition was short-lived. Following a period of violent inter-party conflict, President Kaunda in February 1972 banned the party, detained its leaders, and announced the decision to introduce a one-party state. The one-party constitution was passed in July 1973, and the first general election under the new system followed in December of that year. The low poll, averaging 39 per cent, and the marked absence of popular enthusiasm, suggested that there was in fact only a modest support for the party within the one-party state.

The similarities between the Kenyan and the Zambian experience are too important to be ignored. Both Kenya and Zambia became independent as two-party states, in which a dominant ruling party faced a small but vigorous opposition that represented essentially regional but also minority interests. In both, the dominant party proved unable to accommodate the deeply entrenched vested interests in society, and both used executive fiat to control and finally eliminate political opposition. The one-party state was therefore in both cases imposed upon societies characterised by deep cleavages that had produced a strongly factional system of politics. Under those circumstances the party was unable to act as an agent of integration, remaining instead a 'machine-like organisation' depending on material rewards rather than on political principle to maintain or extend political support.[1] The executive assumed a stronger authoritarian control, while it remained responsive to the pressures of factional networks and personal alliances that had been created in the colonial years.

Uganda's post-colonial experience demonstrated the fundamental problem of the new state. While the centralisation of power was an essential element in state formation, the concentration of power at the centre carried with it the danger of isolation, and the loss of communication between centre and locality. This was demonstrated first by Buganda, which remained the central political issue that faced the independent government. Milton

[1] Henry Bienen, 'Political parties and political machines in Africa', in Michael Lofchie (ed.), *The state of the nations* (Berkeley, 1971).

Obote, then president of the UPC and independent Uganda's first prime minister, had won independence on the basis of an electoral alliance with Buganda, and a quasi-federal constitution that challenged his own predilection for a powerful unitary government. He had not, however, resolved the underlying conflict between Buganda and the rest of the country over who should rule. Nor was he able to establish any genuine links between the central government and the Ganda populace, notwithstanding the election of the *kabaka* in 1963 as Uganda's first president. The Lost Counties referendum in 1964 might have demonstrated central government power, but it broke such fragile support as existed in Buganda for her association with the UPC. The crucial problem for Uganda however was that once Buganda acknowledged her stake in the new state, and the need to influence events from within, the logic of numbers gave her the crucial pivotal position in the state, both in its party and its governmental system. Between 1963 and 1966 what was at stake was less Buganda's future than that of the non-Ganda ruling party, and its leader, Obote. Buganda remained the most salient factor in Uganda politics not simply because it refused to accept a dispensation of power that challenged its past dominance, but because within a democratic system it enjoyed a very real chance of winning control. No one had ever governed Uganda without Buganda's support, so that when in 1966 Obote defeated Buganda he did so only by using armed force. The army thus became the crucial element in the political balance, its new significance symbolised by the mammoth army parade at the 1966 independence celebrations.

Buganda was not the only problem. The early growth of African local government at district level, which had made the district a significant political arena, combined with the long-held desires of those districts to catch up with Buganda, had resulted in a strong local political focus at the expense of the centre. There was moreover a coincidence between district and ethnic identity which further strengthened local ties. Uganda had had perhaps the most decentralised colonial administrative system in East and Central Africa; and her independence settlement had further enhanced district autonomy and given districts political resources not usually enjoyed by local authorities. The autonomy of the district as a political base had also had an important influence both on the development of the parties and on the limited control of the party centre over its branches. Thus the central government had found itself unable to control district authorities even where they were of the same party.

In the early years after independence, Obote achieved a good deal of control by mediation between district and centre. In his search for a greater centralisation of power however, his new Local Administration Act of 1967 destroyed not only the former regional administration, but also the network of links and checks and balances that had in the past knit locality and centre together. The change contributed a great deal to the circumstances of the coup in 1971 when the army commander, General Amin, assumed power. While the immediate cause of the coup was most probably Amin's fears for his own personal survival, the circumstances that made it possible related to the erosion of Obote's earlier district-level support. Although Amin's regime subsequently emerged as an aberrant even of military rule, his attempt in 1973 to break down the existing districts into smaller administrative units suggested that he was not unaware of the problems of local control.

While the search for more appropriate institutions had indeed led to a great assertion of central authority, it had therefore at the same time led the new African states along very different paths. Each of them had in the first decade of independence assumed a very different character and by 1975 the region encompassed a range of vastly different experiments and achievements. Tanzania's socialist experiment contrasted with Uganda's tragic decline under an anarchic military oligarchy. While Kenya and Malawi were the most clearly capitalist, Kenya's meritocracy had until 1975 shown a capacity to incorporate disparate elements of society in a way that Malawi had not. It was more difficult to identify a clear pattern underlying Zambia's sometimes bewildering succession of changes, and Zanzibar continued, notwithstanding union with the mainland, to hold herself aloof as she continued her revolutionary experiment. Nevertheless it was clear by 1975 that, despite the common problems of underdevelopment they shared, each state was moving along a different path in its search for development.

After its unilateral declaration of independence in 1965, the white minority remained firmly in control in Rhodesia although

isolated and under increasing external pressure. The ruling
Rhodesian Front, under its Prime Minister Ian Smith, remained
united in the face of trade sanctions imposed from without (see
Chapter 3), and the government shielded the white population
from their harmful effects. There was at the same time a
perceptible trend to increased white control and fresh discriminatory legislation. In March 1970 Rhodesia became a Republic with
a constitution that centred all political power in a lower House
of Assembly in which Africans had only 16 of 66 seats. African
representation was linked to contributions to total income-tax
payments which ensured that parity was impossible in the
foreseeable future. A new Land Tenure Act in 1969 permanently
divided the land into two equal portions, 45 million acres for five
million Africans and 45 million acres for fewer than 250000
Europeans, and introduced a rigid formula that precluded any
future significant transfer of European lands to African use or
ownership. Revenue allocations to social services for Africans
were decreased. The majority of African nationalist leaders were
in detention, restriction or exile, and security legislation ensured
control of any dissident political activity. African politicians in
exile, themselves still divided, were unable to turn either of their
national organisations, the Zimbabwe African People's Union
(ZAPU) or the Zimbabwe African National Union (ZANU) into
an effective liberation movement or to establish a joint military
command, notwithstanding the proddings from the Organisation
of African Unity's Liberation Committee in Dar es Salaam.
Although the first reported guerrilla attack took place in April
1966, African guerrilla action had been no more successful than
British negotiations up to 1971.

Beginning in 1972, however, certain critical changes occurred
which directly affected the internal situation in Rhodesia and led,
by 1975, to a fundamental weakening of the Rhodesian regime.
First, Africans in Rhodesia overwhelmingly rejected proposals for
a constitutional settlement agreed between the British and
Rhodesian governments in 1971, when they were given the
opportunity to voice their opinion to the Pearce Commission that
visited the country at the beginning of the year. This made a
constitutional settlement unlikely in the near future. Second, the
African National Congress (ANC) formed in Rhodesia in
December 1971 under the leadership of Bishop Abel Muzorewa

415

to oppose the settlement, now provided an organ within the country to articulate African opinion. It therefore stood as the only effective opposition within the country. As the economic situation became more difficult during 1972–3, so a dialogue between the Rhodesian Front and ANC slowly took shape, in which the latter demanded substantial changes to the 1971 proposals as a basis for a constitutional settlement. Third, a new phase began in the armed struggle, as ZANU, in particular, took the lead on the north-eastern frontier, and inside the country the rural population now proved much more willing to give support. The Rhodesian response was to extend military service obligations and to institute collective punishments on villages believed to have harboured guerrillas. Finally, the most critical change was the consequence of the Portuguese coup in 1974, and the subsequent decision to grant independence to the Portuguese African territories. This fundamentally changed the situation in southern Africa, and led directly to the attempts initiated within the region by the end of that year to find a constitutional settlement. It led at the end of 1974 to the dramatic changes climaxed in the meeting in Lusaka, under the guidance of the leaders of the Front Line states, of all the Rhodesian nationalist leaders, released by Smith from detention to seek the beginnings at least of a settlement, negotiated not by Britain and Smith, but by South Africa and Kaunda as the new brokers. It was not, however, until 1980, five years after the end of our period, and after a bitter guerrilla war, that Rhodesia was converted into an African-ruled state as Zimbabwe.

ECONOMIC DEVELOPMENT

There was a remarkable continuity of economic policy between colonial and post-colonial states, so that independence was less the watershed for economic than it was for political change. The 30 years after the Second World War are perhaps better viewed in terms of three short, successive phases in economic change, each merging into the other, each revealing more clearly than before the fundamental constraints upon development.

The first phase embraced the years from the end of the Second World War to the mid-1950s, during which time the colonial economic policies and practices that would have such long-term influence upon the region were laid down. The Colonial Development and Welfare Act of 1940 had given notice of Britain's commitment to a more positive programme of economic development, and from the end of the war she embarked upon vigorous state action to promote colonial welfare and economic improvement. Much more significant was the commodity boom and the increased prices for many cash crops that occurred between 1949 and 1953, and which produced a significant change in the terms of trade. Even if Britain's objective was metropolitan reconstruction as much as colonial progress, the years after 1945 were undoubtedly years of local expansion. A word of caution is necessary here: for many Africans the benefits of the world commodity boom were not obvious. The legacies of war – inflation, urban crowding, shortages of consumer goods, agricultural restrictions – persisted into the early 1950s and provided the resentment that was channelled into the organisation of trade unions, cooperative societies, and nationalist movements.

The second phase, which covered the decade from 1955, was also characterised by growth, but of a more erratic kind, so that economic progress was a good deal less stable. Commodity prices varied a good deal, after a sharp fall from the boom years, and that fluctuation, along with the vagaries of rainfall and the uncertainties of political change, produced a more sombre mood of financial stringency at independence. Unemployment became a significant issue. Nevertheless by any generally used criteria, all these states had achieved substantial growth since 1945. New infrastructures had been established across the region as a whole. The Owen Falls Dam in Uganda and the Kariba Dam on the borders of Rhodesia and Zambia had opened up new possibilities for development. Each new state inherited a budget a good deal larger than its colonial predecessor had enjoyed 15 years earlier, and the years immediately after independence were years of continuing growth and the expansion of social services.

As the 1960s gave way to the 1970s, however, unemployment and a slackening rate of growth emphasised the limitations of earlier achievements. Hence a new phase began, characterised by an increasing concern at the problems of growth without corresponding development. Two events in 1967 highlighted the changing situation. First, Tom Mboya, then Kenya's Minister for Economic Planning and Development, urged upon the Economic

Commission for Africa the necessity of a Marshall Plan for Africa; and if there was already strong disagreement as to the role of foreign capital in the development process, there was no disagreement as to his diagnosis of Africa's ills: unemployment, low productivity, inequality, export-oriented economies, dependence upon world markets and fluctuating prices, insufficient capital and inadequate resources of skilled manpower. Second, the Arusha Declaration gave notice of a radical change of strategy in Tanzania to socialism and self-reliance and thus provided the starting point for a new debate about the nature of development in Africa.

The colonial years: the search for increased productivity

With these changes in mind, we may turn to the colonial years when the dominant theme of post-war policy was increased productivity. This required the transformation of the African subsistence economy and the extension of cash-crop agriculture; and if the emphasis was upon cash crops for export there was also a concern for self-sufficiency in food. Increased productivity was also believed to require the application of European capital and expertise, and Europeans were accorded a critical role as agents of development, whether in the guise of administrators, settlers, planters or investors.

Certain assumptions underlying the general commitment to economic development need to be borne in mind, for they underline the nature of the strategies adopted. The first concerned the obstacles to be overcome. While nationalist leaders assumed that their countries' backwardness was the direct product of colonial exploitation, colonial officials at home and abroad saw it as rooted in the African condition. Development strategies were based on the assumption that western skills and technical knowledge would gradually be transferred to the indigenous peoples. Whereas this encouraged the Colonial Office to support a positive expansion of social research, it also produced a much more direct intrusion of colonial officials into African life. If the main contrast with pre-war days was the availability of funds for economic development, much greater demands were also made upon the African people by governments that set out to turn African cultivators into cash-crop farmers.

The second assumption concerned capital. The need for large-scale capital investment was accepted, and the somewhat ill-fated

Overseas Food Corporation and the more successful Commonwealth Development Corporation were both evidence of the
Labour government's faith in the public corporation as an
instrument of development. At the same time, successive British
governments acknowledged that much of the necessary capital
should come from private investment, and that this must play a
major role in the necessary diversification of the colonial economies. While there might be some debate about the meaning of
socialism in the colonies, colonial strategy was nonetheless seen
to require a managed economy in which government would
control private enterprise without discouraging it. Development
thus assumed the extension of the capitalist mode of production,
and the encouragement of the entrepreneur.[1]

We must also bear in mind the extent to which development
was viewed as a local responsibility. While the Colonial Office laid
down the broad lines of policy, it assumed that the initiative and
the financial responsibility remained with the man on the spot.
Ultimately, therefore, and notwithstanding new commitments to
colonial aid, a territory could advance only as far as its own
resources (including its ability to attract capital from abroad)
allowed. The strategies adopted therefore varied a good deal from
one territory to the next, as did the level of achievement. Since
the most striking contrasts were between those territories with
settlers and those without, it is important to bear in mind the
relative sizes of the non-African communities across the region.

The post-war commitment to African economic advancement
involved no alteration in either the existing pattern of peasant,
settler and plantation economy, or in the racial basis of land
ownership on which they were based. In Uganda the peasant
remained in the official mind the primary agent of development.
Tanzania maintained the same ambiguous mix of peasant, settler
and planter that had evolved before the war, although the
trusteeship system ensured a close watch on any further alienation
of land. But the dominant position of white settlers in Kenya and
the two Rhodesias, and the British acquiescence in federation,
indicated the importance attached to Europeans as the agents of
growth. Soldier settlements were an important item in post-war

[1] An important study in the development of corporate capitalism in Kenya and its
role in the process of economic development published after this chapter had been
completed is Nicola Swainson, *The development of corporate capitalism in Kenya, 1918–1977*
(London, 1980).

agricultural budgets, and the further development of large farms and plantations remained a central feature of agricultural policy in all three territories up to 1960.

European agriculture in fact made a significant contribution to production in those territories throughout the 1950s, although the plantation sector proved less vulnerable in Kenya than the settlers' farms to both economic and political crises. More critical in terms of its implications for long-term development was the privileged position of the European farming community that made this success possible. The European monopolist position in regard to land, agricultural inputs and the production of key cash crops imposed severe limitations upon the growth of African agriculture, as well as upon the prospects for balanced regional growth. The most extreme form of settler privilege applied of course in Southern Rhodesia, but generally, in all the territories involved, it was the African peasant farmer who paid for the European settler farmer's success.

European agriculture was thus a critical constraint upon African agricultural development in these years. Kenyan Africans demonstrated in due course, however, that this constraint could be overcome. More serious was the manner in which European control over large land areas contributed, from the late 1940s, to the deterioration of African lands. By 1955 the East African Royal Commission, warning of the dangers of inaction in the face of serious pressures upon the land, urged the abolition not only of racial but also of ethnic barriers to land ownership and land usage. Political events overtook its report, but when the white highlands were opened up to African ownership in Kenya, the difficulties of movement across tribal boundaries remained. While it was comparatively straightforward to transfer land from white to black, it was more difficult to overcome the serious regional imbalance of development to which European settlement had contributed so much. One result, by no means the least important, was an enhanced sense of regional consciousness among Africans determined to protect their own lands.

Another equally important legacy of the European sector was its influence upon prevailing ideas about agriculture itself. In Zambia, the commercial farmers and the federal Ministry of Agriculture (responsible for European agriculture in Zambia for the federal decade) created a set of attitudes that ten years after independence still led officials to define 'traditional' and 'modern' farming in terms of the patterns of usage that had been laid down for the European sector. Much more widely debated was Kenya's belief in the importance of large-scale farming. The so-called 'myth of the large-scale farms' both obscured the settler dependence upon monopoly and forms of state assistance, and sustained the large-scale farms whose economic size had been questioned since the Troup Report of 1953. Whether or not the transfer intact of large-scale farms to individual African owners was the key to the independence settlement, large-scale farming remained as a critical and highly controversial component of independent Kenya's agricultural strategy.[1]

The transformation of the African subsistence economy and the development of modern African agriculture were ultimately however the more significant thrusts of the colonial period. If the objective was the increased production of export crops, there was also a sense of urgency to take action against the effects of inadequate husbandry and soil erosion. This produced the compulsory conservation measures in both agricultural and pastoral areas that were to provide a powerful issue for nationalist politicians. There was in addition, however, a positive emphasis upon the expansion of agriculture itself. The conference on African land tenure in East and Central Africa held at Arusha in 1956 highlighted the basic assumption that increased productivity of the land would follow land reform and the introduction of individual land tenure. The strategies adopted for improved agriculture generally assumed the advantages of individual ownership, but in fact there was little uniformity of policy, and only Kenya set out with remarkable conviction and a good deal of compulsion to implement it.

The agents of change were the agricultural and the community development officers, although the provincial administration in each country generally assumed that the responsibility ultimately rested with itself. The strategies involved a variety of incentives as well as technical and institutional changes directed at turning the

---

[1] Colin Leys, in *Underdevelopment in Kenya: the political economy of neo-colonialism* (London, 1974), 37–9, argued that the economic settlement in 1963 which provided a protected position for foreign capital in independent Kenya was possible largely because of agreement by the British to transfer the former European lands to African ownership on the terms the African leadership wanted, and which ensured that mixed farms were available to African owners on easy terms.

cultivator into a cash-crop farmer. Improved farming schemes had a place in every territorial budget, and there were some notable showcase experiments. The Sukumaland ten-year development programme in western Tanzania, the first of its type and scale in post-war tropical Africa, spent approximately £2 million in a coordinated programme to maximise agricultural and veterinary development through careful land usage, livestock control and improved agricultural methods. It engaged Native Authority as well as provincial and departmental administration in a joint effort. In Tanzania, moreover, the Chaga farmers on Mt Kilimanjaro had long since demonstrated their ability to grow coffee, so that by 1961 the greater part of the country's coffee crop was produced by 120 000 coffee farmers typically on less than an acre each.

Uganda stood out as the classic peasant economy, sustained by peasant-grown coffee and cotton. In 1946, the Worthington Plan, in an effort at long-term and comprehensive planning, aimed at a vigorous expansion of African cash-crop production for the export market both of existing and also of new crops. Uganda's coffee and cotton farmers responded in the late 1940s to the dramatic rise in commodity prices, as the phenomenal expansion demonstrated. Cotton production increased from 264 000 bales in 1945 to 378 000 in 1952, and coffee from 20 000 to 37 000 tons. The value of the two cash crops rose from £9 938 000 to £47 704 000. Uganda's phenomenal growth between 1945 and 1955 was unambiguously based upon African peasant initiative and production.

Yet it was in Kenya, in the 1950s, notwithstanding settler privileges, that African agriculture achieved its most significant advances in terms not only of increased production but also of improved agricultural practice. The gross value of produce marketed by African farmers rose from £3.2 million in 1951 to £11.6 million in 1963. Whereas few Africans had derived an income from tea, rice, coffee or pyrethrum in 1950, in 1962 more than £4 million went to Africans growing these crops. The Kipsigis set this process in motion, having by 1953 on their own volition consolidated their beautiful hills and begun to grow pyrethrum; but the Kikuyu swiftly overtook them and it was the imperatives of the emergency and the enforced agricultural change in Central Province under the Swynnerton Plan that produced the most fundamental change.

Swynnerton set out in 1953 to accelerate African agricultural development on *existing* acreages by a concentrated programme of land reform and improved (and enforced) agricultural practice, and in the process to produce an African middle class. Consolidation, registration and individual land tenure, and the expansion of research, extension services and marketing, were part of a coherent programme of economic reform designed not least as an economic answer to the political pressures that produced the emergency. The relationship between land tenure and increased agricultural production was by no means proven and would be a source of debate for many years. But the Swynnerton Plan was a landmark in African agricultural development, which epitomised the objectives of agricultural policy over the region as a whole: the development of African cash-crop agriculture on the basis of the individual peasant farmer integrated into the market economy. Whether the programme was designed for 'progressive' or 'improved' or 'better' farmers, its objective was summed up for Malawi by the Jack Report in 1958: 'The ultimate aim in agriculture should be the evolution of the farmer who owns and works his own economic holding...'[1] The Kenyans would have added that he should employ his own farm labour.

This strategy produced a great many African peasant farmers whose level of production and whose material standard of living was visibly better than it had been in the past. In Kenya the 1950s were a period of tremendous development of African as well as European farming, which was sustained well into the 1960s, once the initial difficulties of the land-transfer programme had been overcome. Indeed Kenya's stronger agricultural cash economy, as compared with the other countries in the region, was based more on African potential than European past achievements.

It is nevertheless doubtful whether this impressive agricultural development constituted a revolution, even in Kenya, for it involved only a minority of the total population. Moreover, although there had been a dramatic expansion of production, it had for the most part been the result of the expansion of the acreages under cultivation rather than of structural or technological development. Outside Kenya it is also doubtful how much improvement of agricultural practice actually resulted from the 'Improved Farmers' schemes. The great majority of Africans in

[1] *Report on an economic survey of Nyasaland 1958–1959* (Federation of Rhodesia and Nyasaland, Salisbury, 1959), 44.

each territory were still in the early 1960s subsistence cultivators whose main implement was the hoe. They were in, but on the margins of, the new economy. Moreover the steady expansion of acreage under cultivation in the face of growing populations posed critical, unresolved questions about the future relationship of land and people.

This was the more disquieting in view of the limited industrial development that had occurred over these years. Although the colonial administrator tended to be suspicious of commerce and industry, fearing the social consequences for the African populations, he acknowledged the importance of industrialisation as a means to development. It was assumed that the impetus for change must come from outside and that external borrowing in one form or another was essential. With one exception, industrial development was left to the private sector.

The exception was Uganda where, in the post-war years, Governor Sir John Hall embarked upon a strategy of industrialisation that produced a group of large-scale industrial projects centred around the hydroelectric installation at Jinja. The Owen Falls Dam was completed in 1956, but the results of Hall's proposals, described as of 'a much wider scope than the limited programmes of government capital spending which formed the basis of most of the colonial development plans of the period',[1] were less impressive than expected. While the Uganda Development Corporation, formed in 1952, stood out as a unique example of state promotion of industrial development, it had limited success in attracting foreign finance and enterprise. Uganda did better perhaps in the long run with her own Asian entrepreneurs.

Indeed, concentration on an external impetus for industrialisation reflected an official indifference or hostility to Asian entrepreneurs, the only appreciable local source of venture capital. Nonetheless, Asian expansion into import-substitution industries proceeded apace in the 1950s and 1960s; capital was increasingly raised by inter-family alliances, often on an interterritorial basis. In practice this meant a growing penetration of Ugandan and Kenyan Asian capital into Tanganyika.

In Kenya and the Central African federation, however, where governments saw their role as primarily that of providing

---

[1] D. A. Lury, 'Dayspring mishandled? The Uganda economy, 1945–1960', in D. A. Low and Alison Smith (eds.), *History of East Africa*, vol. III (Oxford, 1976), 236.

encouragement and inducements to private enterprise, significant industrial expansion took place. In Kenya by 1955 the industrial contribution to GDP almost equalled that of commercial agriculture and by independence she had a nucleus of small industry and an established commercial sector. The Central African federation had also by 1973 achieved an impressive growth of industry, manufacturing output having risen in value from £26.9 million in 1954 to £65.4 million, and its share of GDP from 8.1 per cent to 11.7 per cent. By the early 1960s there was a significant industrial base on which future development could rest. That base was, however, for the most part located in Southern Rhodesia. Zambia's considerable economic development over the same period was distinctive, based on a copper industry that had given her one of the fastest growing economies in the world.

Kenya and Southern Rhodesia enjoyed certain important advantages derived from their strategic position, each at the centre of a growing economic region. Their critical advantage however was their ability to attract capital from abroad. Between 1950 and 1958, capital investment in Kenya was just over £300 million, of which 62 per cent was from the private sector. In the federation, over the decade of its existence, of a total gross investment of £1200 million, some £223 million, or one-fifth, was provided from external sources, the most conspicuous example being of course the Kariba Dam. Capital engineered growth, but it did so in response less to the African than to the European communities that had created economic enclaves which provided the stimulus for that growth. The result was not only industrial development, but also a larger and more firmly rooted foreign private sector and market economy in those territories than elsewhere. It was also grossly lopsided development. Regional distribution was uneven: in the federation by 1960 manufacturing accounted for 15.5 per cent of GDP in Southern Rhodesia, but only 8 per cent in Northern Rhodesia and 4.5 per cent in Nyasaland. Moreover, throughout its existence the federation was dependent on Northern Rhodesia's copper, and the Northern Rhodesian government calculated that its net loss to the federal government was £97 million. Although the copper industry created a booming economy, in Northern Rhodesia it was one characterised by a severe imbalance between a stagnant, neglected rural sector away from the line of rail and a fast-growing urban society. Finally, the benefits of industrial development were unevenly distributed between races, favouring primarily the European communities.

Industrial expansion contributed to the marked expansion of employment in the years up to 1955, so that each territory experienced an increase in its wage-labour force. At that point, however, the expansion slowed down, and indeed for a short period showed a positive decline. Labour departments began after 1956 to report increasing urban unemployment, as the expanding economies demonstrated their inability to absorb the growing numbers of men and women seeking wage employment. Hindsight enables us to identify the complex combination of factors that contributed to this critical change. Corporate capital was bound, as it extended its activities, to seek greater efficiency, and therefore the advantages of a more permanent, skilled labour force. The stabilisation of labour, in the interests both of a more efficient planned economy and better living conditions for workers, had been official policy at least since the 1949 Conference of East African Labour Commissioners. While there was a wide variation in territorial response, minimum wages legislation was gradually introduced in each state in the 1950s. Higher wages encouraged employers to an *ad hoc* importation of western technologies, and workers remained longer on the job, not least in the face of the increasing competition for employment.

Neither foreign capital, however, nor industrial growth produced an indigenous capitalism. In East Africa there were government programmes to encourage African trade, and in Kenya the Kikuyu had both thrown up a landed gentry and also already shown their propensity for business and commerce. Nevertheless at independence there were as yet few established indigenous capitalists.[1]

---

[1] The process of indigenous capital accumulation in colonial Kenya has received increasing attention in recent years. See the work of M. Cowen, especially 'Capital and peasant households' (mimeo, Nairobi, July 1976), and 'Notes on capital, class and household production' (mimeo, Nairobi, n.d.). Two more recent and critical studies are Apollo L. Njonjo, *The Africanisation of the 'White Highlands': a study in agrarian class struggles in Kenya 1950–1974*, Ph.D thesis, Princeton University, 1977, and Gavin Kitching, *Class and economic change in Kenya: the making of an African petite bourgeoisie 1905–1970*. (New Haven and London, 1980).

Post-colonial change

Once the political uncertainties that accompanied the transfer of power had been overcome, the economic development that followed was in the first place encouraging. In general, the initial post-colonial expansion and the Africanisation programmes that accelerated after independence defused the most serious tensions arising out of unemployment, and there was an impressive further increase in agricultural production. Malawi, perhaps the poorest country of all, nonetheless achieved an impressive 4.2 per cent rate of growth in the 1960s and eliminated its budgetary deficit. Kenya's smallholder agriculture demonstrated the ability of its peasant farmers to increase their surplus and to contribute to the country's average 6 per cent growth. The Million Acres Settlement Scheme significantly enlarged the area of land available for land-hungry Kikuyu and at the same time contributed to a considerable increase in agricultural surplus. Zambia, confronted with the constraints imposed by its land-locked position within the southern African region, and the indirect effects of the sanctions imposed on Rhodesia after UDI, nevertheless in the first four years of independence achieved a 13 per cent rate of growth and a remarkable expansion of social services, particularly education.

That early growth, however, obscured the underlying weaknesses of each state, which emerged more clearly as the 1960s progressed. Malawi's dilemma highlighted the issues that faced them all. Dr Banda's economic strategy was based on three prime assumptions: the need for large-scale foreign aid and private investment; the need to maintain the country's links with the south; and the primacy of agricultural development on the lines laid down in the colonial years, namely the encouragement of peasant agriculture. Although that strategy produced an impressive growth rate, by the 1970s it had failed to achieve any significant change in the country's basic poverty. Smallholder agriculture had contributed significantly to agricultural production, but the majority of Africans were still cultivators constrained by their low level of technology, and it was the estate sector that had enjoyed the strongest growth based on both improved technology and increased acreage. The inherent weakness of the country's position was demonstrated by the contin-

uing exodus of Malawians abroad: whereas there were 35 000
Malawians at work on the South African mines in 1964, in 1974
there were just under 100 000, whose remittances were the
country's third largest source of foreign earnings.[1] Moreover the
country's heavy dependence on external financing, while contributing to its growth, had also resulted in its growing problem
of external indebtedness.

Uganda's early, cautious planning as an independent state had
also emphasised the need for increased foreign aid to finance
development. Attempts to redress the inherited economic imbalance between the northern and southern parts of the country
produced political tensions before they brought economic
growth, but the government's second five-year development plan,
for 1966–70, indicated a major advance in economic planning
which grasped the need for diversification and industrialisation
much as Sir John Hall had done 20 years before. Despite the
exceptionally good seasons of 1968 and 1969 however, and a
variety of agricultural programmes, at the end of the 1960s there
had been little structural change. Uganda's peasants, like those of
Malawi, were still for the most part dependent upon the hoe; and
there were new areas of land shortage, and growing unemployment. Hindsight suggests the extent to which the Africanisation
programme and the failure to effect a wages policy had increased
the rural–urban gap in African incomes, while the growing
dominance of the military had already distorted expenditure.
President Obote's 'Move to the Left', however, which attempted
in 1969 to move Uganda to a more radical socialist strategy, was
his response to political rather than to economic pressures, as the
recurring theme of unity in the text made clear. His undigested
plans for nationalisation, while they were in conflict with his
proposals for the Africanisation of the retail trade, did little more
than promote a degree of economic uncertainty that undoubtedly contributed to the coup.

Although in 1964 the Seers Report was optimistic that Zambia
could use the great wealth inherited with her copper to overcome
her poverty and her unbalanced development, ten years later her
economy was in disarray. While she could point to an impressive
expansion of social infrastructure, the rural–urban gap had in fact
increased, notwithstanding the priority accorded to rural

[1] In 1974, however, following an air disaster in which 75 Malawians returning from
work on the mines died, Dr Banda suspended all mines recruitment.

development in each successive plan and in President Kaunda's 'Humanism', produced as a guide to planning in 1967. Many of the difficulties Zambia faced as a land-locked state were made worse by the consequences of UDI, but the country's fundamental weakness had been that up to 1974 she had failed to face up to policy alternatives. While aware of her overwhelming dependence upon copper, on those occasions when the government had begun to grapple with the issue a recovery in the price of copper had encouraged her to delay. Economic reforms in 1968 and 1969 provided for greater Zambian participation in the private sector and a major extension of state participation in the economy including a 51 per cent state interest in the mining industry. By the mid-1970s, however, the now overwhelming dominance of the state in the economy had failed to achieve any significant diversification of production. Having failed to save during the fat years that followed independence, Zambia found herself unprepared for the leaner 1970s. Moreover, having set out in 1964 with a proud financial independence, by 1975 she was weighed down by increasing external indebtedness, itself the product of the change in the international copper market.

The most significant experience however in these years was that of Kenya and Tanzania, for it was in those two countries that the fundamental issues of development were most clearly opposed. Kenya from the outset maintained its inherited policies, with their emphasis upon private enterprise and foreign capital as the necessary agents of growth. Confronted in 1965 with opposition to that strategy, the KANU government set out the objectives clearly in Sessional Paper no. 10 on 'African socialism and its application to planning in Kenya'. The objectives were political equality; social justice; human dignity including freedom of conscience, freedom from want, disease and exploitation; equal opportunities; and high and growing per capita income equitably distributed. The strategy was based on certain equally clear assumptions; that growth was the necessary prerequisite for development; that foreign capital, private and public, was essential for growth; and that the objectives of equity and justice could be achieved within a merit-based, achievement-oriented competitive society which recognised and rewarded individual initiative. While development programmes maintained from the outset a strong bias towards rural development, the central focus of Kenya's policies was the Africanisation of the private sector and the development of indigenous capitalism. The Trade Licensing Act of 1967, which provided the basis for an orderly transfer of ownership of expatriate trade and commerce to African hands, became the model for other African states seeking the same objective. That strategy produced impressive economic development and in the early 1970s a good many people were demonstrably better off than they had been ten years before. Certain weaknesses in this strategy had also however been demonstrated. On the one hand the growing presence of corporate capital retarded the growth of indigenous capitalism, although it did not resolve the problems of growing unemployment. On the other hand the Africanisation of the private sector contributed to an increased inequality in African society. In the mid-1970s Kenya appeared as a classic illustration of growth without development, which demonstrated the fundamental limitations of the inherited colonial economic model.

Tanzania also achieved a significant agricultural expansion in the mid-1960s, but neither that increased production nor attempts at 'transformation' had resulted in any significant structural change. The First National Development Plan failed moreover to achieve both its industrialisation objectives and the expected rapid rate of growth, not least as a result of its dependence upon a level of foreign investment that failed to materialise. That failure pushed Tanzania to review its inherited strategies, with their reliance on capital as the necessary agent of development. The Arusha Declaration of 1967 was, however, as much a response to inequality as to ineffective economic performance. Reflecting the Tanzanian leadership's concern with the social consequences of the capitalist model, it led to a radical change of strategy based on five principles articulated as the foundation for future planning: public control of the economy; development through self-reliance; rural development; social equality; and rural socialism. The Second Development Plan of 1966–70 therefore marked a radical change of priorities to rural development on the basis of *ujamaa*, or socialist agriculture. In the early 1970s, the combination of drought, structural change and the world energy crisis produced the country's most severe economic crisis since the 1930s and forced her into a greater dependency. Ten years after the Arusha Declaration, Tanzania was still therefore neither socialist nor self-reliant, but had, despite climatic and international difficulties, taken some important steps towards her goals. She had reduced, if not eradicated, the inequality that had been a major target of the socialist strategy which by 1972 President Nyerere argued was the rational choice for all African states.

As the first decade of independence drew to a close, it had become increasingly difficult for the post-colonial state to ignore the limitations of its resources and the underlying weaknesses that earlier growth might have obscured. Growth had failed to resolve the problems of increasing unemployment, as the massive expansion of urban and rural poor had demonstrated. A complex set of forces was pushing an increasing number of men and women to seek wage employment and the earlier measures were seen as short-term palliatives rather than long-term cures. The increased emphasis upon rural development as a strategy to absorb the rapidly growing population brought each state face to face at the same time with the continuing weakness of its agriculture. Kenya's Kericho Conference on Education, Employment and Rural Development highlighted as early as 1966 the size of the problem and the extent to which the agricultural revolution remained to be won. Nor had *ujamaa* resulted in Tanzania in any rapid spread of modern methods of agriculture. It was not only in Kenya moreover that the situation had changed from one of land surplus to one of land shortage. In each state the central issue of development strategy was clear: how to mobilise to greater productivity the growing African peasantry still on the periphery of the modern economy. At the same time, there was an increasing awareness of the constraints imposed by dependence not only on foreign capital, but on the capitalist model itself.

SOCIAL CHANGE

Both town and country experienced profound changes over these years. In 1940 the colonial state was essentially a caste society in which race determined both social and economic position. Europeans were dominant, whether as administrators, settlers or businessmen. The growing Asian population occupied the middle ranks of society except in Southern Rhodesia, and Northern Rhodesia where they numbered only some 2500 in 1950. While they were characteristically the shopkeepers, the traders and the businessmen, they also filled many of the clerical and middle-level administrative positions in both government and private sector. There was a small educated African élite, but the great mass of Africans who constituted the broad base of society were country dwellers, whose horizons were bound by homestead and subsistence. While the presence of government, church and school ensured that no rural community was isolated from the larger territorial society, the degree of interaction varied a great deal. Government demanded tax but otherwise did not impinge heavily on people's lives at the local level. Migrant labour, for the most part, sustained rather than destroyed the society from which it came. Rural life was characterised by a considerable autonomy and integrity, and traditional institutions and reciprocal relations prevailed for both the returning migrant and those who stayed at home.

Bearing in mind their rich diversity, we may identify the broad processes of change that encompassed these states in the years that followed. The most obvious change related to the racial fabric of society which (except in Rhodesia) was undermined by the political transformation that took place. While independence did not necessarily bring an end to expatriate privilege, it did remove much of the old racial dominance. The more fundamental changes, however, were those that occurred within African society itself, which became steadily more complex and more differentiated as Africans arrogated to themselves the opportunities as well as the responsibilities of the modern state. A new and enlarged élite grew steadily, in response first to the opportunities of education and the expanding bureaucracy, and second to the transfer of power. The result was the growth of a new inequality within African society. While the Second World War and the achievement of independence both in turn accelerated the growth of that inequality, it was essentially a cumulative process of change already set in motion long before the period began.

The colonial years

Perhaps the most important influence in the long run was the expansion of the cash-crop economy, which substantially increased rural cash incomes and produced noticeable improvements in standards of consumption for a significant section of the community. A cash income became a necessity, not only for tax, but also for the increasing range of new goods that appeared in the rural trade centres and the Asian stores. New houses with sheet-metal roofs became a good deal more common, and along with bicycles and, for a few, the new motor cars, contributed to the growing air of prosperity of a great many villages and homesteads. In the more fertile parts, particularly of East Africa, many villagers became prosperous peasants who, until the mid-1950s at least, enjoyed a substantial gain in real income as a result of their cultivation of cash crops: the Ganda, the Soga, the Kikuyu, the Chaga and Sukuma all enjoyed in common this new position of the better-off farmer. There were also, although in much smaller numbers, the larger cash-crop farmers, the burgeoning entrepreneurs. The prosperous land-owning class that had grown on the basis of the *mailo* land system in Buganda had developed a good deal further by the time of independence. In Kenya, where from the 1940s onwards chiefs were buying land, many of them emerged as prosperous farmers. The size of landholdings varied a great deal, so that the new more substantial farmers could be arranged on a continuum from prosperous peasants to successful large-scale farmers, all of them sharing certain attributes in common: they farmed for the market and they employed labour, if only on a seasonal basis. They were the new agricultural entrepreneurs, the *mulimi simpindi*, 'farmers for profit', as they were known among the Tonga of Zambia's Southern Province. They bought an increasing range of imported goods, they built better houses, they paid school fees for an expanding extended family, and they generally had more room for manoeuvre as a result of their greater economic resources. They constituted a new rural middle class.

Not every villager however became a prosperous peasant. The typical villager remained the man with an acre or two on which, with the help of family labour and the hoe, he produced a small quantity of cash crop in addition to his subsistence. His cash return was small and his resulting opportunities limited. Hence agricultural development produced a new rural inequality, and if this was less visible in some areas than others, nonetheless, no rural society remained unchanged in those years.

The growth of cash crops depended upon the fertility of the soil, the reliability of the rainfall and the availability of transport and marketing facilities. Some crops offered a better return than others, so that the man whose land would produce coffee or tea was found to do better than the man who could grow only cotton. Moreover there were areas of acute population pressure, which presented the ultimate constraint on development. The benefits of economic growth were therefore unequally enjoyed between regions, and rural inequality developed a marked regional dimension. In the mid-1950s, for example, at the peak of Uganda's new cash crop prosperity, in what was a peasant-oriented economy, the net annual farm income for the peasant farmer varied from 218 shillings in Buganda to 17 shillings in Kigezi. Moreover in Uganda as elsewhere there was a dramatic contrast between agricultural and pastoral areas, as the pastoral peoples were further left behind, while the agricultural regions pushed ahead.

An increasing number of men from the less fertile regions migrated elsewhere in search of employment, and this in turn had significant implications for rural life. Traditional agricultural practice was modified to take into account the changed labour resources, and the market became a permanent feature of rural society as rural self-sufficiency was broken down. When, for example, by the mid-1950s, 60 per cent of Zambia's rural male taxpayers were absent at any one time from home, their absence could not fail to affect agriculture. Not all those seeking wage employment were thinking only of the regular needs of tax. There were growing aspirations for improved material standards, and for the opportunities of modern life of which people were increasingly aware. Thus in Buganda in the mid-1950s wage employment for many Ganda had become a perpetual necessity, because 'cotton and coffee have created in Buganda customary standards of consumption which only a continuous money income can maintain'.[1] The same might have been said of the Copperbelt, whose growing population had adopted the characteristic lifestyle of a consumer society.

The 1950s witnessed an increasing search for urban wage employment, and a perceptible drift of Africans from country to town. Men travelled long distances, sometimes across territorial boundaries, so that there was in some respects an international labour force that could be found between the Southern Sudan and South Africa. In Uganda in 1957 39 per cent of wage labour in

---

[1] Walter Elkan, *Migrants and proletarians: urban labour in the economic development of Uganda* (London, 1961), 47.

the private sector was from outside the country, and in Southern Rhodesia in 1959, 50 per cent of the African labour force was foreign. Kenyans sought elsewhere in East Africa the opportunities refused them at home, and Malawians had always been known as great wanderers, forced abroad by the poverty of their home resources. Nevertheless, the majority of migrants remained within their own country and this internal migration gave each labour force its special character. In Uganda it was migrants from the poorer northern parts of the country who sought work in the southern estates and on Ganda farms; in Zambia mine labour was dominated from the outset by Bemba-speakers from the north, so that the Copperbelt could be referred to as an 'extension of Bemba-speaking society'[1] and the Bemba were by the 1950s the most proletarianised of Zambia's people.

Economic development produced a marked expansion of wage employment in the late 1940s and early 1950s, particularly in Zambia, Kenya and Rhodesia. The Royal Commission in 1955 reported an 'expanding volume of employment not restricted by labour shortage' in East Africa, and generally no evidence of unemployment. By that date employment had reached 558 000 in Kenya, 610 000 in Southern Rhodesia and 254 000 in Northern Rhodesia. Although this was still a small proportion of the total African population, nevertheless it changed the nature of the towns. In the 1940s they had been for the most part foreign enclaves whose dominant characteristic was racial inequality, and in which Africans fought a hard and continuing battle against poverty and appalling conditions. There was a small African educated élite: the teachers, clerks and hospital orderlies who organised the welfare associations and provided links with home; but the majority of Africans were unskilled workers. While most did not stay long, in Rhodesia the Land Apportionment Act had already gone a long way to creating a landless African working class, and in Mombasa and Zanzibar there was something akin to a permanent urban labouring class. Nevertheless workers in due course went home to the rural areas; they were migrants subject to the low wages and appalling conditions which were the characteristic lot of colonial labour.

During the 1950s that situation altered, as both the character of the towns and the conditions of employment began to change.

[1] George Kay, *A social geography of Zambia* (London, 1967).

While workers still went backwards and forwards between town and country there were many more of them and they stayed longer. From the mid-1950s the signs were of an increasingly stable labour force and a declining turnover. Slowly a casual and migrant labour force was being converted into a community of workers.

Three critical factors contributed to that change. The crucial influence was probably the introduction of minimum wages, which constituted a fundamental stage in the development of a more stable and skilled labour force, and in that respect the watershed was perhaps the Carpenter Report in Kenya in 1954, which proposed an urban family wage level that did not assume a rural subsidy. Equally important was the change in urban housing policy. Around 1957, and as the emergency drew to a close, the Nairobi City Council began to build family housing for workers instead of the old bachelors' quarters. At the same time Uganda, stimulated by Governor Sir Andrew Cohen, had introduced extended programmes in urban African housing, and for urban development in general. No housing programme could hope to meet the needs of the rapidly growing urban populations. In Kampala and Jinja, for example, where at least 50000 were employed by the late 1950s, there were fewer than 4000 tenants on government estates. Yet, despite the growing peri-urban squatter settlements, a change had begun, and it became possible for urban workers to contemplate a stable family life in town.

The third factor was the steady rise in wages that occurred through the 1950s. The change was perhaps most dramatic on the Copperbelt, where African real earnings rose approximately 300 per cent between 1945 and 1960; but everywhere the urban worker became better paid. The labour force also became more specialised. Increased wages not only persuaded workers to remain longer on the job, but also persuaded employers to offer training and to encourage a skilled labour force. Indeed much of the stimulus for change began with the employers themselves, and their concern for greater efficiency. Job specialisation and Africanisation, in spite of European opposition at the outset, slowly produced a new African skilled and semi-skilled labour force. And because the upward trend of wages benefited the skilled rather than the unskilled workers, so the urban wage-

earning population also became more differentiated. Urban inequality advanced among Africans, at the same time as
unemployment increased.

The colonial order also contributed to the rapid expansion of
a new élite. The word is unsatisfactory, but may be used with
caution to identify the growing body of Africans distinguished
by their better education, their greater wealth, and their position
in a society whose racial boundaries were being eroded. In 1946
Governor Sir Philip Mitchell appointed seven Africans as
administrative assistants to the Kenya provincial administration.
In 1947 the Holmes Commission on the East African civil services
recommended that all posts should be open to all candidates
regardless of race, and the Lidbury Commission in 1954 greatly
advanced the framework of Africanisation, not the least by
eliminating many wage inequalities based on racial grounds. The
process was slower in Central Africa, but in Zambia and Malawi
ultimately the direction was the same.

Over those years Africans also moved upwards in the teaching
service, at secondary as well as primary level; and the private
sector, more hesitantly in some territories than others, began
slowly to seek out promising young Africans to train as a new
executive class. There was also a slowly increasing number of
professionals. Africanisation in fact proceeded a good deal more
slowly than the commitment to political independence would
seem to require, held up not least by the early notion of
multiracialism. It also proceeded a good deal more slowly in
Central Africa than in East Africa. Nevertheless in each state,
there was to a greater or lesser degree by the early 1960s a
distinctive African élite who were increasingly taking up roles
previously restricted to the colonial ruling class. Their aspirations
were encouraged by the tremendous opportunities opened up to
them by decolonisation and the transfer of power, and society in
many ways encouraged them in the élitist assumptions of the
colonial order as well as their assumption that they would take
over control in the independent state.

Society, however, remained at independence remarkably egali-
tarian in terms of opportunity, still essentially open and fluid. In
East Africa the Bantu interlacustrine kingdoms and in Central
Africa Barotseland stood out as societies in which there was great

inequality and 'the language and gestures of deference were elaborated... in a quite fantastic way'.[1] Nevertheless, even in Buganda, upward mobility was a characteristic feature of life. Although many rural societies must have identified the new élite as did the Lugbara of north-western Uganda, as 'the educated and semi-educated protégés of the government',[2] appointment to the civil service was generally considered a highly desirable goal. Although in every society there were popular perceptions of social stratification based upon occupation, African society generally accorded the educated man respect, whether he was a village primary-school teacher or the new university graduate. The latter moreover was still in most cases as much at home in the village as the former. It was for the most part the older élite, especially the chiefs, whom the nationalists had discredited. The nationalist ethic and expanding opportunities obscured the potential conflict of interests and the dilemma of inequality posited by a strategy of development that assumed the capitalist model and emphasised the virtues of individual effort. The exceptions stood out clearly, and it was not insignificant that they occurred in those states where the market economy had made its deepest impact upon society. If capital had engineered growth, growth had engineered change, so that it was not surprising that in Kenya the process of economic development had produced not only an African élite but also an African property-owning class, primarily among the Kikuyu. The emergency had demonstrated the extent to which, by the 1950s, the Kikuyu were divided into landed and landless, with a land-owning gentry dominant within that society. In Zambia the mines had produced a distinctive urban industrial wage-earning labour force with clear perceptions of their interests as a working class; and UNIP had a distinctive anti-élitist sentiment.

Post-colonial change

During the first decade of independence a more complex set of social structures began to emerge. The objective conditions of inequality intensified while at the same time the population became occupationally more diverse and, almost imperceptibly,

---

[1] Lloyd A. Fallers, *Inequality: stratification reconsidered* (Chicago, 1973), 4.
[2] J. F. M. Middleton, 'Some effects of colonial rule among the Lugbara of Uganda', in V. Turner (ed.), *Colonialism in Africa*, vol. III (Stanford, 1971), 21.

the familial links between richer and poorer weakened. While in the great majority of cases the ties of the extended family prevented any rigid division between upper and lower income groups, nevertheless the social and cultural cleavages between them began to grow.

The expansion of the cash-crop economy had done most to hasten inequality after the Second World War, and perhaps the most significant influence 20 years later was the acceleration of Africanisation, first in government and then in the private sector, that followed independence. Africanisation and the need for skilled manpower meant an enormous expansion in the élite; and the retention of expatriate scales of remuneration produced the mandarin class against which the Holmes Commission had warned in 1947. The upper echelons of the bureaucracy, along with African ministers, the growing body of professionals and academics, and not least the army officers, swiftly emerged as a distinctive, privileged salariat distinguished by its wealth, its status and too often its élitist attitudes. Each salariat acquired its own distinctive traits. Dr Banda's cautious Africanisation meant that Malawi's top-level bureaucracy remained small in size, and in Tanzania the Arusha Declaration and the Leadership Code specifically challenged, although they did not eliminate, such an élite. In general élites showed a distinct preference for urban life, although for the most part keeping one foot in the countryside, and in Kenya especially having very deep roots in the rural areas.

The Africanisation of the private sector in due course reinforced this change. Although large-scale industry remained in expatriate hands, African trade and commerce greatly expanded, and in Kenya and Zambia at least there was also at the end of the period a distinctive group of new entrepreneurs and businessmen with deep interests in capitalist development.[1]

To focus exclusively on these upper levels of society is however to obscure the changes occurring elsewhere. Whether we identify them by employment, by wage levels or by material standards of living, it is clear that the middle levels of society were becoming

[1] In addition to work on indigenous capital accumulation cited above, see also for the ongoing debate on the emergence and nature of indigenous capitalism in Kenya Leys, *Underdevelopment in Kenya*; Leys, 'Capital accumulation, class formation and dependency: the significance of the Kenyan case', *Socialist Register*, 1978; Swainson, *Corporate capitalism*; and *Review of African Political Economy*, 1980, no. 17. Debate on 'Dependency' in Kenya, published after this chapter had been completed.

a good deal more differentiated. A whole range of new occupations was opening up to Africans, especially to the increasing ranks of educated, so that society became functionally a good deal more diverse. The industrial and commercial labour force, the workers, were also becoming more diversified, as they also acquired a more clearly defined status. Wage increases, new pension schemes and extended welfare services all contributed to the improved conditions of the urban working class, which became a good deal more stable and committed to wage employment. In Zambia it became much easier to retire on the Copperbelt, and by 1975 a growing number of miners were doing so. Presence in town did not necessarily mean an end to rural ties, especially in East Africa. In Kenya the aim of almost every urban worker, whatever his economic status, was to build a house on a piece of land at home, and the urban family in most cases had a second household in the rural area.

Increased internal migration swelled the urban populations in the independent state. The population of the Copperbelt had passed a million by 1974, but every urban centre had expanded as the growth of sprawling shanty towns and the informal sector demonstrated. There was a growing army of unemployed work-seekers whom the economy could not provide with jobs, especially the growing band of school-leavers. There was also a vigorous and expanding informal sector. By the 1970s the dominant feature of urban life had, however, become the visible inequality of African society. The rapid increase in African earnings after independence narrowed the gap between African and non-African, but widened the differences among Africans themselves. The colonial legacy of segregated residential areas contributed significantly to the development of distinctive social strata which urban life and wage employment invariably foster. The refinement in ranking of occupational category contributed also to the process of differentiation. By 1970 Uganda had altered her cost of living statistics to take account of high, middle and low income groups in urban society, and in Kenya the Third Development Plan acknowledged that in a society where individual merit must be rewarded, economic growth could not yet lead to equality. But what was most noticeable was the growth of a great body of working poor, many of them employed in the informal sector, receiving less than half the wages of the modern sector, and living in squatter housing.

Without exception, the wage increases of the 1960s benefited urban rather than rural wage-earners. At the same time the economic situation of rural dwellers varied a good deal both within and between countries in the region. At one extreme Zambia's rural inhabitants were absolutely worse off in 1975 than they had been in 1964, and that country's dramatic urban growth was itself a reflection of rural decline. At the other extreme, Kenya's 225 000 smallholders secured an impressive share of their country's development, and the cash inflow to smallholder farming had increased from £10 to £30 million between 1960 and 1968. The vitality of Kenya's rural economy was demonstrated not only by increased agricultural production but also by a self-help programme which, whatever its weaknesses, contributed £4 million to development in the 1960s. At the same time, however, that expansion sustained the existing rural inequality, and, in most cases, existing regional disparities. Moreover Kenya's land-transfer programme produced a new level of rural inequality with the emergence of African large-scale farmers who were also something of a landed oligarchy, and to whom the continuation of the large-scale farm strategy gave a disproportionately large share of development resources. The 1967 Land Control Act offered the opportunities for the accumulation of land in Uganda, although the demise of Buganda's political power in 1966 suggested that any new landed oligarchy that emerged as a result would have a different regional and political base. In Buganda itself the trend had been in fact towards the subdivision of the old *mailo* estates.

Large-scale landowners such as Kenya's were still however the exception rather than the rule. What was a good deal more significant was the changing pattern of landownership at the lower levels of rural society, especially in those areas of acute population pressure and land shortage. Tanzania was here the exception, since her *ujamaa* programme was a deliberate attempt to return to a communal landownership, although she did not in fact seek to disturb her Chaga coffee farmers from their landholdings. In Malawi also the dominant pattern remained that of a large number of very small plot holders. Elsewhere, however, it was possible to identify the development of a new market in land. In Kenya the land-reform programme significantly altered the pattern of land distribution in the peasant sector, largely to the disadvantage of the poorest levels of rural society. In a country where land was not only the major source of security but also the base for an aspiring entrepreneurial class, salariat and wage earners as well as wealthy farmers had begun to purchase land in the former 'African areas'. Although it would be some time before traditional rights would disappear, and although there were significant regional differences, nevertheless a fundamental change in land-ownership had begun. And while for the time being the process of subdivision and the further distribution of expatriate-owned land could absorb the expanding population, the inexorable advance of population in the 1960s and 1970s resulted in the continuous expansion of the rural poor. These were the great mass of Africans, not necessarily landless, but with too little land and too little education to acquire the surplus or the skills to supply their basic needs. If Kenya's rural poor were the best known, it was Malawi that presented the problem in its starkest form. Malawi's smallholder agriculture also expanded after independence, its value increasing from K15.9 to K26.0 million between 1964 and 1970. In a country whose dominant characteristic was the pressure of population upon land, only 2 per cent of the people had more than 12 acres, and the great majority of smallholders who contributed so much to the growth of the agricultural surplus typically had less than two acres. The individual return was small and in a country with a per capita income of K38, did not give the smallholder much room for manoeuvre. In the early 1970s it was the expatriate-owned estate sector that had unused land still to be taken up in the future for cultivation. Yet the increased migration to South Africa of the 1960s and the expansion of agricultural wage employment (some of it no more than seasonal) in the private sector on the estates, pointed to the evolution of a permanent, lowly paid, unskilled agricultural labouring class: the foundation of a rural proletariat.

Regional inequality added a marked ethnic dimension to the growth of social and economic inequality in these years. Least obvious in Tanzania, most marked in Kenya, the coincidence of regional and therefore ethnic associations with economic status and opportunity produced significant tensions. Hence in Kenya

442

by the late 1960s secondary-school children demonstrated a keen awareness of the greater advantages available to those from Central as compared with Nyanza province, an ethnic contrast that intensified no doubt the perceptions of Luo deprivation and Kikuyu advantage. Tribe and economic class acquired a direct association, illustrated dramatically by GEMA, the welfare association of Kikuyu, Embu and Meru people, established in 1968, and symbolising the dominance of the growing Kikuyu capitalist interests. The identification of economic and social status with regional and ethnic identity was, however, most tragically demonstrated in Uganda in the aftermath of the 1971 coup. By 1975 Amin's regime was best identified as that of a robber brigand who lacked the capacity to rule if not to exploit his prize. At the same time the pattern of purge and conflict suggested also that much of the behaviour of his followers derived from their perceptions of economic deprivation. Those followers were not only soldiers but also members of a minority for whom economic status coincided with ethnic and religious affiliations. The hard core of the Ugandan army in the mid-1970s was Muslim, drawn from the least educated of Uganda's smallest and least developed ethnic groups. Their economic desires were made clear not least by the manner in which they plundered the bulk of the economic spoils made available by the expulsion of the Asian community in 1972.

Ten years after independence the old notions of élite and mass were a good deal less apposite than before in the face of the changes that had occurred. Each state had responded differently both to its inherited economic inequality and to the process of post-colonial change. Something remarkably like a national identity was increasingly apparent to those who crossed national boundaries, and as governments and people responded differently to the process of change. The continuing process of Africanisation and training of high-level manpower had meant in Tanzania, as elsewhere, the absolute growth of the élite, the highest wage and salary earners. Yet Tanzania had narrowed, if she had not eliminated, the gap between rich and poor, and she believed that with the Arusha Declaration she had reversed the national drift towards the growth of a class-based society. In Kenya, the emergence of a property-owning class and a capitalist ethic epitomised the growing meritocracy and an achievement-oriented, class-based society. Regional and ethnic associations however, in the mid-1970s, still diffused perceptions of class, although they heightened awareness of economic inequality, in a situation of diminishing resources.

Ethnic diversity was therefore in the final analysis less important than the uneven rate of economic development. The addition of the term *wabenzi* (literally, 'those who drive Mercedes Benz cars', implying those with money and power) to Kenya's political vocabulary, as of *apamwamba* ('those nearer heaven', implying the important people) to that of Zambia, suggested that in those two countries at least there were powerful perceptions of inequality, and an increasing reaction to the coincidence between politics and material wealth. And in Uganda the continuing conflict that followed the coup was generated not least by the determination of a deprived religious and ethnic minority to keep what they had taken by force.

In general, society as a whole had more obviously divided into three strata: the salariat at the top, the great mass or urban and rural poor at the bottom, and in the middle, the better-off, including some farmers and urban wage-earners. There was much to suggest that the most far-reaching changes had been those in the middle; the new class of better-off farmers, the new urban working class, who were rapidly acquiring coherent perceptions of their own identity. What was equally significant was the extent to which access to education still determined one's place in society.

EDUCATION

The post-war years were characterised by a universal and insistent demand for education. The Kikuyu independent schools (started in the 1920s) dramatically enlarged Kenya's educational base, although at the same time they intensified its uneven ethnic distribution. Between 1943 and 1948 African school enrolments almost doubled in Southern Rhodesia, where education remained predominantly a mission responsibility. The Chaga Council petitioned the Visiting UN Mission to Tanganyika on the subject in 1948 as did the Nyasaland African Congress the Colonial Secretary in the same year. In Uganda, where government education proceeded apace, nevertheless in the 1950s, the private schools mushroomed to satisfy the demands of those who could not meet the requirements of the government educational system.

In Tanzania TANU and in Uganda the UPC, admittedly with only limited success, set up schools as part of their nationalist campaigns. There was no doubt about the desire for education, nor that it reflected the aspirations of Africans aware of the key relationship between education and economic opportunity.

The result was that the direction of post-war educational development was a good deal influenced by African pressures as well as by colonial design and settler controls. Colonial policy in the 1940s emphasised mass education for citizenship and self-government, and an integrated process that would train a smaller number of Africans for administration and also develop a civic consciousness. Priority was placed on the development of mass primary education for rural development, with a more limited secondary-school expansion sufficient to supply the then limited manpower needs. On that basis primary education undoubtedly expanded dramatically after 1945, although the extent and the quality varied from state to state. Uganda achieved a remarkable expansion under Governor Cohen, and on the basis of the de Bunsen Report on African Education of 1953, which was enthusiastically accepted, by 1959 half the children of appropriate age were at primary school. In Tanganyika, which had a good deal more ground to make up than the other East African territories, primary enrolments expanded from 142000 in 1950 to 375000 in 1960; but it was Kenya that moved further ahead with 726000 children in primary schools in 1960 compared with 300000 in 1949. Central Africa lagged a good deal behind, not least because of the constraints imposed upon African education by the settler-dominated federation. Zambia and Malawi (notwithstanding the latter's long history of mission education) in 1964, at independence, had achieved less primary expansion than even Rhodesia.

In the 1950s, however, priorities changed, and the emphasis shifted to secondary and post-secondary education. Part of the explanation related to the growing needs of government for African manpower as political change advanced, and the metropolitan power sought to create that new ruling class to whom they hoped to hand over power. At the same time much of the pressure for change was from Africans and nationalists unwilling to accept the constraints of the racially differentiated educational systems, and the pressures of the changing political climate. Hence the

1950s saw a significant expansion in secondary education, not-withstanding that it was meagre in comparison with the actual demand. Already the problem of wastage was serious, although primary-school leavers as yet found no difficulty in obtaining employment, as would be the case ten years later. In Central Africa and in Kenya, European and, to a lesser extent, Asian education still took precedence over African, which in Central Africa in particular lagged far behind. Zambia at independence conse-quently had only 1200 secondary-school certificate trained people (of whom a significant minority had obtained their training through South Africa) whereas Kenya had reached that stage in 1957 and Tanzania in 1960; and Uganda had six times as many at independence.

University education also saw its real beginnings in the 1950s. The Asquith Commission in 1945 had regarded the establishment of universities as the inescapable corollary of the commitment to political advance but tertiary education went ahead much faster in East than in Central Africa. Makerere College in Uganda, having started life in the 1920s as a school for artisans, in 1949 became a university college in special relationship with London University. Once again the force of nationalism and the dictates of manpower planning accelerated the pace of expansion: in 1956 Nairobi's Royal Technical College became the University College of Nairobi and the University of Dar es Salaam began life in quarters loaned by TANU in 1962, by which time all three had become constituent colleges of a University of East Africa. By that time, however, the opportunities for East Africans anxious for education to go abroad were greatly enlarged. In 1960, when there were 396 Kenyans at Makerere there were 1655 abroad. In Central Africa, in contrast, and notwithstanding the movement of a fortunate few abroad, higher education was a good deal slower to advance and, at the University College of Rhodesia and Nyasaland set up in 1956, a good deal more racially bound than it ever was in East Africa.

The achievement by the time of independence was therefore not inconsiderable. Moreover, sight should not be lost of the extent to which over these years it had been paid for by Africans themselves, through taxes and school fees. In Uganda, for instance, the African Development Funds based on the Price

Assistance Funds provided a great deal of the finance for the expansion of the 1950s.

The inherited educational systems nevertheless raised important questions as to the pattern of future development. In each case they absorbed a significant proportion of the recurrent budget, but came nowhere near satisfying either the popular demand or the national need. Nowhere was more than 50 per cent of the school-age population in primary schools, and in Tanzania and Central Africa it was a good deal less. The proportion of those who continued to secondary school was minute. The availability of education was geographically and therefore ethnically unbalanced. In Tanganyika in the early 1950s for example, 79 per cent of the Chaga of Kilimanjaro district were in primary school but only 7 per cent of the Masai. In each state the consequence of this regional imbalance in development was a visible identification of the new educated and privileged élite with a particular ethnic group: the Ganda, the Kikuyu, the Lozi as well as the Chaga, might not have had a monopoly of education, but they undoubtedly enjoyed a good deal more educational opportunity at a time when the rewards of education were very great. Finally education had become increasingly linked to examinations as the means of access to employment or further training. In the 1940s colonial governments had indeed emphasised the need to link education with rural life, but that early emphasis upon adaptation to the needs of an agricultural environment had been increasingly undermined, not least by the pressures of African opinion. Africans who had come to regard education as the key to greater affluence and the way out of rural poverty were bound to find such an agricultural bias unacceptable, and they rejected it as a form of discrimination in a racially structured educational system. For similar reasons African opinion defeated government attempts in the early 1950s to introduce a basic four-year education, complete in itself, along the lines recommended by the 1951 Binns Report for Tanganyika. No doubt these suspicions were strongest among the élite, and at that time it was racial inequality rather than the élitist and inegalitarian nature of the educational system that was under attack. Nevertheless the mass also had educational aspirations, and the tradition of a more academic education was strong. Moreover the demands for trained African manpower and the Africanisation programme that accompanied independence pushed educational expansion in the same direction.

Each state was committed at independence to the notion of planned educational development to overcome these inherited inadequacies. The first objective was the abolition of racial discrimination. As a Zambian report put it: 'There were certain things we had to do at independence, about which there was no argument whatsoever. For example the racist structure of the educational system had to be destroyed'.[1] Certain other administrative changes followed, as governments gradually assumed direct control over education, and the churches for the most part were required to transfer their schools to them. Priority was given in the first place to secondary-school expansion, and to a strategy of manpower planning that followed logically on the programmes and training laid down earlier by colonial governments. Ten years later the degree of Africanisation was impressive. Malawi stood out for her more cautious approach to Africanisation, but in Tanzania, by 1971, 90–95 per cent of senior and middle-level civil-service posts were held by citizens compared with 38 per cent in 1962. The first decade of independence however witnessed a remarkable acceleration of education as a whole. Perhaps this was demonstrated most dramatically in Zambia, which set out with a sense of urgency to redress the inherited colonial neglect, and doubled her primary-school enrolments between 1964 and 1972, increased her secondary-school numbers from 13 853 to 61 000 and set up the University of Zambia in 1965. Equally impressive, and demonstrating the same kind of immense popular enthusiasm for education, was the expansion in Kenya, where by 1975 there were two million children enrolled in primary schools and 300 000 in secondary schools, and a vigorous self-help programme had pushed the government far beyond its planned development.

This very expansion produced its own difficulties, however, and as the 1960s advanced, each state faced a new educational crisis, in which post-independence development compounded the weaknesses of the past. Educational expansion proceeded a good deal more rapidly than employment, so that by the end of the 1960s there was a school-leaver problem in each state. However, the crisis in education went a good deal deeper. In the first place there was a conflict between the need for skilled citizen manpower and

[1] *Education for development* (Government of the Republic of Zambia, 1976), 77.

the relevant high-level training, and the need to broaden educational opportunities, create a more egalitarian society, and satisfy popular demand. In the face of limited resources there was an intense competition for educational facilities which lay at the heart of the development process. This conflict of interest was also central to the process of differentiation and the growing inequality in each state. Thus the crisis of the late 1960s was not merely about the more efficient use of manpower (and hence the problems of wastage), school leavers, regional imbalances and the rural–urban gap; it was also about the process of social transformation. In a situation of growing social and economic differentiation, access to education remained the key to economic advance and to a privileged position in society. Access to education was thus a key political issue.

Each state responded differently to this crisis, demonstrating not only their different ideological commitments and styles of response to inherited inequality, but also the increasingly different social and economic pressures at work within the independent state. While the same popular aspirations could, for example, be identified in Kenya and Malawi, it was apparent that they could be held in check more firmly in the latter country than the former. Educational planning moreover encountered different obstacles. Hence while there was, as the 1960s progressed, a general shift back to a strategy centred on rural education, the manner in which it was approached varied a good deal.

In this respect Malawi most firmly based educational planning on the needs of agriculture as the key sector of the economy, and argued that expansion of secondary and higher education must be related directly and primarily to manpower needs rather than popular aspirations or demands. Tanzania also reasserted the needs of rural life and attempted a fundamental reorientation of her total education system. Prompted most of all by the arrogant reaction of university students in 1966 to National Service, which highlighted the dangers of a new élite, the Arusha Declaration spelled out the conflict between the inherited educational system and the goals of Tanzanian socialism. President Nyerere's subsequent *Education for self-reliance* outlined an educational strategy that would provide a seven years' basic education complete in itself, and appropriate for the rural life that the majority of Tanzanians would lead. Priority was thus returned in the late

1960s to primary education for rural development, a commitment further articulated in the Musoma Declaration of 1974 (which promised a four-year education for everyone), but still some way from achievement as our period came to a close.

Kenya's educational strategy was, in contrast, to accelerate the provision of educational services at all levels, to redress regional imbalances, but to equalise opportunities rather than rewards. In the first decade of independence government policy, pushed on by an infectious self-help or *harambee* movement, resulted in substantial expansion. At the same time gross disparities remained and unequal access to education had contributed a great deal to the growing social and economic class formation. Thirst for education continued as the big expansion in primary enrolment after the removal of fees in 1974 showed. The results of racial integration varied a good deal. Uganda and Tanzania had indeed begun the process prior to independence. Kenya, adopting a contrary line of action, maintained the existing tiered structure of schools inherited from the settler years, so that while racial segregation was abolished, the old system of high-and low-cost schools remained, and with it the inequality of access to education based increasingly on economic rather than racial strata. Moreover the continuing expansion presented significant budgetary problems to a government which in 1975 was spending 30 per cent of the state budget on education.

Kenya and Tanzania represented the two extreme responses to the educational crisis of the independent state. They shared with the other states, however, certain strategies that attempted to overcome educational problems, for example the National Service that attempted to absorb school leavers. The most famous and possibly the most successful was Malawi's Young Pioneers formed by President Banda in 1963, to give specialised training in agriculture to young men and women who then returned to the land.

Educational policy thus came full circle in these years, ending as it had begun with a firm emphasis on education for rural reconstruction. There was, however, a great difference in the notion of relevance as part of the process of colonial tutelage and relevance as the key to a more realistic, independent government's educational policy. Nevertheless the popular aspirations remained, and education was still in reality as well as in popular perceptions the means of upward mobility in the post-colonial state. Education remained, along with politics, the key to privilege and power.

Inter-state relations passed through three successive stages in the course of these 35 years. At the outset, in 1940, the political ties were essentially those created by colonial rulers and alien settler communities. Notwithstanding that the settlers in Northern and Southern Rhodesia felt a greater affinity with South than with East Africa, the notion of a confederation of British Central African states north of the Zambezi died hard. The war years strengthened the position of Europeans, and in 1945 the dominant issue in interterritorial relations was that of closer union, which had its climax with the creation of the Federation of Rhodesia and Nyasaland. By the 1950s, however, there were also many more links between Africans across the region, especially as a result of the movement of labour. In the 1950s also, as the nationalist movements advanced, so the new nationalist leaders forged new bonds with each other and established new, African-oriented political ties, and a significant degree of cooperation. Their associations fell short of political union, notwithstanding the aspirations for a federation in East Africa, so that independence saw a third stage in their relations, when inter-state relations became those of new, sovereign states. Sovereignty and statehood significantly altered the perspectives from which inter-state relations now were approached, and in the first decade of independence the demands of national interest began seriously to challenge earlier Pan-African loyalties. While the commitment to African unity did not disappear, the imperatives of national development made it a more difficult objective to achieve. A new conflict of interests emerged between national and regional associations and loyalties. Independence therefore constituted a significant watershed in inter-state relations which contributed to major realignments within the region in the years after 1970.

The most positive regional development in the colonial years was that in East Africa, which saw the emergence of a unique regional economic association. At the outbreak of the war the East African territories already shared a number of interterritorial activities, coordinated by an informal annual Conference of governors and its permanent secretariat. Those common activities increased greatly during the war years, out of which there emerged in 1948 the East African High Commission: a permanent executive authority created by Order in Council, having power to administer certain specified common services on an all-East African basis. It consisted of the governors of the three territories, who met two or three times each year, a High Commission secretariat, with its headquarters in Nairobi, and a central Legislative Assembly, part appointed by each governor and part elected by the representative element of the territorial Legislative Councils, with limited but not insignificant legislative powers over common services matters. Notwithstanding African fears that the East African High Commission would be used as a basis for settler domination (a significant influence upon the growth of nationalist politics in those years), that body provided a positive basis for economic cooperation and for regional development in the 1950s and established a set of interterritorial economic institutions of more positive value than those of the Central African federation. The three East African territories constituted a common market with a more or less uniform external tariff. They had a common currency. They shared a number of common services, jointly administered by the EAHC, of which the most important were the railways and harbours, airways, posts and telecommunications and research services. There could be no doubt that the economic development of the 1950s was greatly assisted by these common services, and it was the advantages of that economic association that the new nationalist leaders sought to preserve when Tanzania's independence necessitated changes in its constitutional base. Hence the High Commission was transformed in 1962 into the East African Common Services Organisation, created by the terms of an agreement entered into by the three East African governments.

In the 1950s African nationalists achieved a second significant level of political cooperation through the Pan-African Freedom Movement of East and Central Africa (PAFMECA) set up at Mwanza in Tanzania by the East African nationalist leaders in 1958. PAFMECA emerged as a loose but effective grouping of the political parties of all the East and Central African territories. Leaders met regularly in an annual conference. Their common front was a significant political force in the period of decolonisation; and they were able also to provide an important degree of assistance to territorial nationalist movements. PAFMECA provided significant assistance for UNIP in the first general elections in Northern Rhodesia in 1962, and for KANU in the Kenyan elections the following year. Its nationalist ideology was symbolised by the common recognition of Kenyatta (while still in restriction) as leader and its organisational capacity was assured by the dominant roles of Nyerere and Mboya. In 1962, when its regional embrace was enlarged to take in not only Ethiopia and Somalia but also the nationalist organisations of South Africa, it was renamed PAFMECSA, and UNIP's President, Kenneth Kaunda, was elected chairman, symbolising not least the common commitment to the liberation of southern Africa. Once Tanganyika became independent in 1961, Dar es Salaam became the natural base for the growing liberation movements of Central and southern Africa, and PAFMECSA, with Nyerere as its leading figure, became increasingly identified with the liberation of white-ruled southern Africa.

In the early 1960s PAFMECA was generally committed to the concept of an East African federation, as Nyerere first set it out to the Mbale (Uganda) PAFMECA meeting in October 1960, and again to the Conference of Independent African States at Addis Ababa in the same year. Nyerere offered to delay Tanganyika's independence until all three East African states could achieve independence, simultaneously, as a federation, but Tanganyika had in fact already become independent when, with Kenyatta and Obote, Nyerere pledged himself in the Federation Declaration of August 1963. From 1961 until 1964, East African relations were focussed essentially upon the federation issue. The causes of failure were complex, but ultimately the attempt at federation in the mid-1960s foundered on the fears of each state for its national interest, perceived increasingly from the vantage point of sovereignty and statehood.

Uganda especially in 1963 feared her future subordination as the smallest of the three states, but the central issue was and remained the belief that Kenya had achieved her development at Uganda's and Tanganyika's expense. East Africa's common market had without doubt made a positive and significant impact on the region's economic development in the years after 1945. It had produced a substantially unified market and a good deal of development of manufacturing. But the benefits of that development seemed to many in the 1950s to be unevenly distributed, with Kenya receiving the lion's share. Whether or not it was the common market that gave Kenya the distinct advantage that she enjoyed in the 1950s (rather than the accidents of geography and history and the attractions of the European community for international capital), Uganda and Tanganyika had increasingly become resentful at her greater development. Hence there followed a succession of attempts to reorganise the basis of the economic association, to provide for a great equality of development. In 1960 the Raisman Commission proposed a number of changes, principally the innovation of the Distributable Pool to facilitate redistribution between the three territories; and in 1964 the Kampala Agreement attempted to add new rules for an equitable distribution of industrial development. That agreement had not been implemented, however, when Tanzania's decision to withdraw from the common currency and to establish her own Central Bank set in train a sequence of events that seemed to presage the end of the association. In 1965, acknowledging the benefits for development for each of them, but aware of the dangers of disintegration, the three states set up the Philips Commission to evolve a more equitable basis for cooperation. Out of that emerged the East African Treaty for Cooperation, a new agreement, signed in December 1967 between three sovereign independent states seeking to re-establish the old economic association from which they all derived strength on a more equitable and acceptable basis.

In spite of the statesmanship of that decision, the 1970s saw the steady growth of disintegrative pressures from within each state. Ugandans, Kenyans and Tanzanians made demands upon their governments which required a national rather than an international solution. Foreign migrant labour, for example, became a threat to citizens seeking employment: Kenyans who had traditionally sought employment in Uganda became 'alien Africans', as did Ugandans in Kenya, or Kenyans in Tanzania. The most serious pressures upon the new East African Community emerged after the Uganda coup. On the one hand Tanzania's refusal to recognise General Amin as Head of State meant that the East African Authority, the executive body composed of the three heads of state, was unable to meet. On the other hand Uganda's growing isolation produced new difficulties for continuing economic cooperation. In 1972 Amin's expulsion of all Asians, citizens as well as non-citizens, as part of his 'economic war', had serious repercussions elsewhere in the region; but more serious was the abortive invasion of Uganda attempted by former President Obote's supporters from Tanzania in September of that year. Most fundamental, however, were the growing differences of outlook between the three states. National interests as perceived by leaders seeking to satisfy their citizens' aspirations pulled the three states apart, and by 1975 these had made it a good deal more difficult to contemplate the regional strategy for development on which ultimately the Community's future depended. The Community's attempts to regulate competition for resources within the region increasingly foundered on the domestic pressures exerted upon national leaders within each state. While there was an increasing and understandable tendency to identify the differences between the three states in terms of their ideological positions, the root of their dissension was in the final analysis the competition for scarce resources between states with significant disparities of economic development as well as differing political aspirations and priorities.

The central focus of inter-state relations in Central Africa in the post-colonial years remained the struggle for independence from white-minority rule in the south. Rhodesia's UDI highlighted Zambia's critical position as a frontline state, seeking to break the economic dominance of South Africa and reorient her economic as well as her political links to the north. As early as 1962 UNIP's party manifesto had included a commitment to build a railway to East Africa. The TanZam railway, linking the Copperbelt to the East African coast, built with Chinese assistance between 1967 and 1975, was thus a significant landmark in inter-state relations for the region. But by the time the TANZAM railway was finished in 1975, Zambia had paid a high price for her stand against Rhodesia and her consistent support of sanctions as well as of the liberation movements. Her economy had suffered increasingly from the constraints imposed upon her by her land-locked position, and her security was on successive occasions endangered by her consistent support as the frontline state for the liberation movements.

PAFMECSA disappeared as each participating colony gained

independence, but a new organisation of East and Central African heads of state, and heads of government meetings, attempted to create a new institutional base for regional relations and to coordinate their policies, especially on southern Africa. The Lusaka Manifesto of 1969 made their position on southern Africa clear, based as it was on a rejection of racialism and a commitment to non-racial government; but whereas it was then hoped that a peaceful solution to the problems of the white-ruled south might be found, the Mogadishu Declaration of 1971 acknowledged there was no way left for liberation except through armed struggle; a position to which all states save Malawi committed themselves.

Paradoxically the continuing commitment to the liberation of southern Africa and the active support given to the liberation movements imposed serious and increasing strains upon the relations between the now independent states of the region. This reflected changing ideological positions as well as differing national interests. Economic realities made President Banda reject a break with white-ruled Africa, and Malawi established diplomatic relations with South Africa in 1967 and Portugal in 1969. His conciliatory policy towards the south, however much it might be based upon a realistic assessment of the constraints of dependency, nevertheless earned him a good deal of opprobrium from his neighbours, and on successive occasions meetings of the East and Central African heads of state saw an attempt to expel Malawi from that body.

Zambia, Tanzania and Uganda drew closer together in the late 1960s, in what was known as the Mulungushi Club, informal meetings of leaders at party conferences, which took place between 1967 and 1973. The 1971 coup brought Uganda's association to an end for the time being. Moreover the need to coordinate their policies on Rhodesia, especially from 1974, meant that the Club itself was superseded by a similarly informal alliance of front-line states: Zambia, Tanzania, Mozambique and Botswana and later Angola. The changes in southern Africa following the Portuguese coup in 1974 meant therefore that the focus of interstate relations moved more firmly to the south.

Rhodesia evaded a solution, notwithstanding successive talks between the minority regime and a British government not unfairly described by Zambia's High Commissioner to London as a 'toothless bulldog'. By the mid-1970s much of the failure had to be attributed to the internal crises within the Zimbabwean movements in exile. Up to 1973 the incipient guerrilla war had been militarily unimpressive, not least because of the conflicts within the two Zimbabwean movements, ZANU and ZAPU. Nevertheless the Portuguese coup of 1974 and the end of Portuguese rule in Angola and Mozambique a year later constituted a fundamental watershed in the fight against white domination, and introduced a new, qualitatively different phase in inter-state relations in this region.

CHAPTER 9

THE HORN OF AFRICA*

Much more than most parts of sub-Saharan Africa, the Horn is a region with a historical and cultural identity of its own, created by the interactions – and often the conflicts – between its indigenous peoples, rather than by the imposition of an external colonialism. The forces which so drastically affected Africa during the mid-twentieth century certainly had their impact on the Horn. But this impact was mediated through indigenous social and political systems which softened some of its effects, and adapted it to local forms.

THE SETTING

The geographical configurations and historical developments which endowed the Horn with its peculiar character have been examined in earlier volumes in this series. In summary, they comprise the tensions between the social and political systems derived from the central Ethiopian highlands and those derived from the Red Sea, Gulf of Aden and Indian Ocean littoral, with a buffer zone of greatly varying width between the two. Ethnically, these tensions divide the Amhara and Tigrean peoples of the highlands from the nomadic Afar and Somali of the littoral, with the Oromo (Galla) by far the most important of the intermediate peoples. In religion, an analogous though by no means identical division separates the Orthodox Christian highlands from its Muslim periphery. Politically the long-established Ethiopian state, with a strength founded on arable agriculture, has continuously attempted to impose itself on surrounding peoples with smaller or more decentralised political structures.

These tensions did not change with the introduction into the region either of direct colonial rule, or of the technological, social and economic concomitants of European penetration. Most

* The spelling of proper names in this chapter is in accordance with current Roman usage.

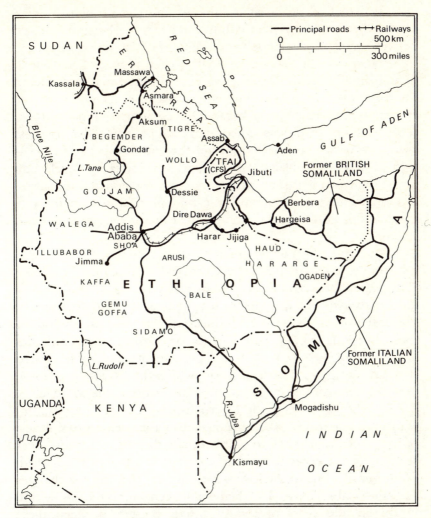

24   Ethiopia, Somalia and the French Territory of the Afars and Issas.

importantly, the Ethiopian empire was able to combine its
indigenous capacity for large-scale military and administrative
organisation with the rapid acquisition of imported firearms in
order both to maintain its independence and to expand its control
over large areas to the east, south and west of the highland core.
An African state thus remained independent at the centre of the
region until the invasion and conquest of Ethiopia by Italy in
1935–6. Around it, the fragmented littoral fell to various colonial

powers. The Red Sea coast and the northern tip of the Ethiopian plateau became the Italian colony of Eritrea. The short stretch between the Bab-el-Mandeb and the Gulf of Tajura was acquired by France as the French Somali Coast (CFS). The British Somaliland Protectorate occupied most of the Somali shore facing the Gulf of Aden. And the Indian Ocean coast down to the frontier with British Kenya became Italian Somalia. None of these territories, however, was to acquire any appreciable identity of its own, and none – at least until after the end of our period – was to follow the path usual in other parts of Africa by developing into an independent state within the former colonial boundaries. Regional linkages – especially the pull of Ethiopia on the one hand and of Somali unification on the other – were to prove too strong.

At the same time, developments were taking place which could not simply be regarded as extensions of the old regional rivalries. European penetration created resources which could be used by local actors to change, drastically, the nature and location of political power. Western-style education was the most obvious of these, but equally important were the organisational technologies which could be used to build permanent and differentiated structures of government of a sort which the Ethiopian empire, in all its centuries of existence, had never been able to develop. Those who controlled these structures – whether parties, bureaucracies or armies – became the automatic wielders of political power, and were able to differentiate themselves from other sections of the population. And even though the area remained, economically, one of the least developed in Africa, some changes had appreciable effects. The theme of this chapter is the interaction in the middle years of the twentieth century between these innovations and the underlying features of the Horn of Africa.

At the beginning of our period, the whole region (except for the French enclave) had the fortuitous and transient unity imposed by Italian conquest. The Italian occupation of Ethiopia after the war of 1935–6 led to the setting up of a unified government for the whole of Italian East Africa (Eritrea, Ethiopia and Somalia). This was based at Addis Ababa, and divided into six provinces with headquarters in Asmara, Gondar, Addis Ababa, Jimma, Harar and Mogadishu. In August 1940, shortly after Italy's entry into the Second World War, the Italians also overran the British Somaliland Protectorate.

The major legacy of this period, in material terms, was the system of roads which the Italian administration built throughout Ethiopia to link with those in Eritrea and – more tenuously – Somalia. Though allowed to decay during the 1940s, they remained highly important for the maintainance of central control. The political legacy was more ambivalent. On the one hand, Italian conquest helped to stimulate a new sense of Ethiopian nationalism, especially among some of those who had benefited from secondary education before the Italian invasion, while at the same time breaking down local autonomy more ruthlessly than an indigenous government could have done. The Ethiopian resistance – the 'Patriots' – helped to sustain a belief in Ethiopian independence, even though the Patriot forces themselves were politically fragmented and localised in leadership and outlook. As against that, the Italians attempted to mobilise local ethnic and religious interests so as to weaken the old highland hegemony. They encouraged Islam at the expense of Orthodox Christianity and, to the rudimentary extent that a non-participant political structure permitted, presented themselves as the protectors of formerly subject peoples against Amhara domination. For the first time, the great majority of Somalis were brought under common rule.

Italy's entry into the Second World War, however, left the Italian forces in the Horn isolated from the metropolitan country, among a generally hostile population. The rout of the Italian armies in North Africa in December 1940 completed their isolation, and released Allied troops under British command for an assault on Italian East Africa. One army invaded Eritrea from the Sudan, while another attacked Somalia from Kenya, and the Emperor Haile Selassie, who had flown from exile in England to the Sudan in December 1940, entered Ethiopia through Gojjam province with a small Anglo-Sudanese and Ethiopian force. The Italian forces were swiftly defeated, though only after heavy fighting at Keren in Eritrea, and the last Italian garrison, in Gondar, surrendered in November 1941.

THE RESTORED ETHIOPIAN EMPIRE, 1941-52

The British government had already made clear, in February 1941, that it would welcome the reappearance of an independent Ethiopian state, and would recognise Haile Selassie's claim to the throne. Haile Selassie made good this claim by his presence on the spot and the allegiance he received from the principal Patriot leaders. Five days after entering Addis Ababa, he asserted his position by making his first ministerial appointments. Thereafter, he proceeded steadily to extend his power at the expense of any potential rival. Haile Selassie, who had become regent of Ethiopia in 1916 and emperor in 1930, was already nearly 50 years old when he returned to his throne in 1941. He was to rule Ethiopia for another 33 years, unquestionably the outstanding individual in the Horn throughout this period, and one of the best known and respected Africans in the continent as a whole as well as outside it, not least as 'Ras Tafari'. That he was ousted from power in the mid-1970s is not perhaps so remarkable as the fact that he held it so long. Only partly could this fact be ascribed to the traditional legitimacy of the imperial office: emperors in the past had been under constant threat from would-be rivals, and Haile Selassie gained power, as he lost it, by *coup d'état*. It was due quite as much to his own political skills, which had enabled him to gain first the regency and then the throne from a comparatively junior position in the imperial family. His particular strength was in recognising potentially dangerous sources of political influence, and in reducing these to dependence on him by playing off rival factions and individuals. It enabled him to accommodate himself both to changing circumstances within Ethiopia and to the complexities of international politics, until he was into his eighties.

His first task in 1941 was to regulate his relationship with the British military forces, which effectively controlled the country pending the formation of a civil administration. This was achieved by the Anglo-Ethiopian Agreement of January 1942, under which Britain recognised Ethiopian independence, but retained special privileges which constituted in Ethiopian eyes an irritating slight on national sovereignty. These included the provision that no foreign advisers be appointed without British government consent, and that a British judge should hear any court case involving foreigners. This special status was abandoned in a second agreement of December 1944, though Britain still continued to administer the Somali-inhabited Haud and Ogaden areas of south-east Ethiopia. The recruitment of foreign advisers – at first British and subsequently of several nationalities, including notably a number of Americans – had been intended to promote the extension of the administrative reforms which Haile Selassie had initiated before 1935. To some extent, it did. Much of the formal administrative structure dating from the liberation period was to remain in force over the subsequent three decades. An official government gazette, *Negarit Gazeta*, was established for the publication of appointments, legislation and other official notices. The powers of government ministries were defined in 1943, and other imperial orders at the same period regulated provincial government, the judiciary, and the official status of the Orthodox Church. A start was made at formal budgeting. But these administrative arrangements made little difference to the effective allocation of political power, which remained tightly concentrated in the emperor's hands. The most important government agency of the 1940s and early 1950s was the office of the emperor's secretary, the *tsahafe tezaz*, who under his new title of Minister of the Pen was responsible for sending out the imperial orders on which the administration entirely depended. The holder of this office from 1941 to 1955, Tsahafe Tezaz Walda-Giyorgis, was Haile Selassie's closest confidant, and the principal manipulator of the court factions which manoeuvred for place and influence under the throne. The prime minister of the period, Ras Bitwoded Makonnen Endalkachew, was by contrast little more than a dignified figurehead.[1]

While the re-establishment of imperial control at the centre was a comparatively straightforward matter, the provinces presented more of a problem. Many of them, especially in the north, had well-established traditions of local autonomy, and in many areas also the Patriot leaders retained appreciable followings. Dissatisfied former Patriots were to lead most of the opposition movements against Haile Selassie in the 1940s and early 1950s. The emperor's first move was to systematise the patchwork of pre-war governates into 12 provinces, divided into some 75 sub-provinces, appointments to all of which were made from the centre. The governors were deprived of military initiative by the creation of a central standing army in place of the old provincial levies, and of financial control by a centralised tax collection and expenditure structure. However, it was still necessary to appoint to some of the governorships men with local prestige and

[1] C. Clapham, *Haile-Selassie's government* (London, 1969), 110–7.

connexions. The first troubles arose in 1942 in Gojjam, an Amhara province and centre of Patriot resistance, and were led by a Patriot, Dejazmach Belay Zeleke, who was evidently displeased with the sub-provincial governorship which he had been given, but could also draw on discontents with the new taxation system. His rebellion was defeated without difficulty, but to secure local quiescence taxation was restored to the pre-war level. The Tigre rebellion of 1942–3 was more serious, both because it received much greater support, and because some of its leaders aspired to separate from Ethiopia and unite with Eritrea, then under British military administration. Government troops sent to control the uprising were cut off, and rescued only after bombing by British aircraft based in Aden.[1] In southern Ethiopia, the central government had a freer hand to establish its own nominees, and governorships could be used as rewards for imperial protégés or northern Patriots whom it wished to remove from their home bases. Much of the exploitation which had characterised earlier Ethiopian administration in the area continued, most notorious being the acquisition of land by Ras Mesfin Sileshi, governor of Kaffa province from 1946 to 1955.

THE PERIPHERAL ADMINISTRATIONS

The Italian collapse in the Horn left the whole area (except for the French Somali Coast) under British control, and once Ethiopian independence had been re-established, Britain was left with responsibility for the periphery. British military administrations were established in Eritrea, former Italian Somalia, and British Somaliland, with an Administrator at Jigjiga, in Ethiopia, in charge of the Somali-inhabited areas of Ethiopia which had been reserved for British administration. After the war, the military administrations were gradually replaced by civilian ones, but the question of what should be done with the former Italian colonies remained open. Their disposal was undertaken by the four 'great powers' – the USA, USSR, Britain and France – who, failing to agree, left it to the General Assembly of the United Nations. Essentially, there were two alternatives. The first, association in some form with Ethiopia, was energetically pressed by the Ethiopian government for Somalia as well as for Eritrea.

[1] P. Gilkes, *The dying lion* (London, 1975), 187–91.

Over and above the formal reasons given for this claim – the alleged historic boundaries of Ethiopia, the invasions from the Italian colonies in 1896 and 1935, the desire for access to the sea – it reflected an intensely held historic mission to maintain and extend the frontiers of the state, which Haile Selassie shared with his predecessors as emperor and ruler of Shoa, as well as with his military successors. The second was some form of trusteeship, leading eventually to independence. In the event, one territory fell into each category.

In Eritrea, the question was complicated by the territory's ethnic and religious divisions, and by the connexions between these and outside actors. There were strong historic links between the highland Christians, who comprised about half of the population, and Ethiopia, and the Unionist Party (favouring union with Ethiopia) was first in the field. It was heavily supported by the Ethiopian government, and organised at local level through the Orthodox Church. Christian support for union with Ethiopia was however offset by the ancient rivalry between the Tigrean northern part of the Ethiopian plateau and the Amhara and especially Shoan south, which controlled the Ethiopian government. This ambivalence was embodied in the Christian Separatists, later called the Liberal Progressive Party (LPP), who wanted an independent Eritrea, ideally in association with the Tigre province of Ethiopia. The Muslim groups which comprised the other half of the population coalesced in 1946 into the Muslim League, which likewise campaigned for independence, and briefly joined with the LPP in 1949–50 to form the Independence Bloc. The Bloc soon fragmented, however, and the Unionists were able to present a strong enough front to help the General Assembly decide, in December 1950, that Eritrea should be federated with Ethiopia under the sovereignty of the Ethiopian Crown. The LPP leader, Woldeab Woldemariam, and several Muslim politicians, went into exile. The federal arrangements came into effect in September 1952, with the Ethiopian government assuming responsibility for defence, currency and external affairs, while a locally elected government in Asmara, headed initially by the Unionist leader Tedla Bayru, held residual powers.

While the main problem in Eritrea was the territory's fragmentation between hostile groups, in Somalia it was quite the opposite: the spread of Somalis across several territories. Since the Somali-inhabited parts of Ethiopia remained under British administration by the 1944 Agreement, the administrative unit established by the Italians was not upset. The British adminis-tration was for the most part willingly received by the Somalis, both as a deliverance from Fascism and because of the strong Somali sympathies of many of the officials involved in it, and a Somali police force was recruited under British officers. District and provincial advisory councils were created in 1946, and a number of clubs and associations were formed to express Somali aspira-tions, most important being the Somali Youth Club opened in May 1943. When the disposal of Italian Somalia came up before the four powers in 1946, the British Foreign Secretary, Ernest Bevin, suggested that the existing union of Somali territories be continued by creating a trusteeship, preferably under British supervision. This 'Bevin Plan', frequently to be invoked by supporters of Somali unification, found no favour with the other three powers – who regarded it merely as a pretext for extending British control – and was vigorously opposed by Ethiopia. Since Britain had acknowledged Ethiopian sovereignty in the Haud and Ogaden regions, there was little she could do to satisfy the Somali aspirations which the Bevin Plan had aroused, and in September 1948 these regions were transferred to Ethiopian control. The provisional administrative line established by the British became, in the absence of any demarcated boundary, the *de facto* frontier between Ethiopia and Somalia. The disposal of Somalia itself, meanwhile, was referred to the General Assembly of the United Nations, which decided in November 1949 – in defiance of the wishes of most Somalis – to entrust it for ten years to Italian trusteeship. The Somali territories were thus once more dismembered.[1]

The last and least significant of them all, the French Somali Coast, was involved only very indirectly with these developments. Its governors succeeded in maintaining its autonomy from both the Italians and the British in 1940–2, though it changed allegiance from the Vichy government to the Free French in December 1942. After the war, the absolute authority of the French governor was modified by the formation of a Representative Council, to which members were partly appointed, and partly elected on an extremely restricted franchise. Seats in the council were restricted, too, to

[1] I. M. Lewis, *The modern history of Somaliland* (London, 1965), 116–38.

466

members of specified ethnic groups – Frenchmen, Afars, Arabs and Issa-Somalis – and this arrangement persisted even after the appointment of members was abolished in 1950. It helped to ensure that politics in the territory were closely bound up with local ethnic rivalries, and scarcely concerned with wider developments in the region as a whole.[1]

POLITICISATION AND ITS OUTCOME

Throughout sub-Saharan Africa, the Second World War and its aftermath helped, directly or indirectly, to foment the growth in African political awareness which led to the formation of nationalist movements and ultimately to independence. In the Horn, which alone in Black Africa was actually fought over during the war, the effects might have been expected to be especially marked. So, in many ways, they were. However, while many of the basic processes at work were very similar to those in other parts of the continent, these necessarily interacted both with the underlying conflicts in the region and with the administrative structures already outlined. The results were varied. In some parts of the region, the growth of political awareness could be directed through existing structures to produce an outcome which reflected the aspirations of the peoples concerned; here, the channels of politicisation might be said to be 'open'. In other territories, they were 'closed' by structures which intervened either to prevent political awareness from arising, or to prevent it from fulfilling the aspirations to which it was directed, and which led eventually to violence.

The clearest example of open politicisation was in Somalia and British Somaliland, where the first stirrings of modern Somali nationalism were evident soon after the Italian defeat. A measure of Somali consciousness and opposition to alien rule had been present throughout the colonial period, most obviously in the campaigns of Sayyid Muḥammad ʿAbdille Ḥasan. In the post-war period, this was fanned by the events which brought almost all Somali territories under common rule, and reopened the question of their disposition. The new movement, which may be dated from the foundation of the Somali Youth Club in 1943, differed

---

[1] V. Thompson and R. Adloff, *Djibouti and the Horn of Africa* (Stanford, 1968), 38–45, 61–5.

from the old in the constitutionalist means through which it pursued its ends, in its readiness to accept innovations such as western education which traditionalists had regarded with suspicion, and in its conscious attempt to repudiate the clan divisions on which nomadic Somali society was based. The club's support spread rapidly, especially among educated Somalis, and by the time it changed its name to the Somali Youth League (SYL) in 1947 it had adherents throughout the Somali territories, including the Haud and Ogaden and north-east Kenya. In keeping with the egalitarian spirit of Somali nomadism, it had no single dominant leader, unlike most nationalist movements elsewhere in the continent.

Inevitably, the SYL came to be associated with some groups more than others in Somali society, and especially with the Darod who, as the largest and most widely spread of the Somali clan families, had greatest concern for unification. This left the way open for the formation of other parties based on sectarian interests, the most important of which in Somalia itself was the Hizbia Digil-Mirifle Somali (HDMS) founded in 1947 to represent the sedentary Digil and Rahanweyn peoples of the Juba and Shebele basin. A number of small pro-Italian groups were also formed, with active Italian support, to press for the restoration of Somalia to Italy. The SYL had strongly opposed Italian trusteeship, and several clashes between the League and the new Italian administration took place between 1950 and 1952. However, the Italians were strictly limited by the terms of their trusteeship, which was to last for only ten years, and both sides eventually realised the benefits of cooperation. The advisory territorial council formed in 1950 was transformed in 1956 into an elected legislature. Ten of the 70 seats were reserved for special interests, and of the remainder the SYL won 43 and the HDMS 13. The SYL formed a government under 'Abdillahi 'Ise from the Hawiye clan family.

After this success, the SYL was able to expand its support among the Digil and Rhanweyn groups. But as with many other successful parties, the more its supporters increased, the greater the divisions within it became. These divisions encompassed the whole range of issues facing Somalia, including clan rivalries, attitudes towards Somali unification and the Somali script, and relations with the Arab world. They were increased rather than diminished by the 1959 elections, which saw the SYL win 83 out of 90 seats in an enlarged Assembly and incorporate many former members of the HDMS. However, Somalis were at least able to discuss these issues within a constitutional structure which represented them, and which they had a large share in devising.

Within British Somaliland there was none of the urgency imparted by the ten-year trusteeship in Somalia, and in both political and social developments the territory tended to lag behind. The SYL spread into the territory and was especially strong among the Darod clans in the east, but the dominant party was the Somaliland National League (SNL), whose strength lay among members of the Isaq clan family which comprised most of the population. No burning issue appeared to foment political participation until 1954, when the relinquishing of the last vestiges of British administration in the Haud left the grazing lands on which many nomads in the territory relied under Ethiopian control. This caused an immediate outcry, and the political consciousness which had been aroused did not disappear, though even as late as 1959 the Legislative Council still had a majority of appointed official members. In the February 1960 elections, the SNL gained 20 of the 33 seats, its ally the United Somali Party (USP) 12 of the remainder, and the SNL leader Muhammad Haji Ibrahim Igal became Leader of Government Business. All parties favoured unification with Somalia in the cause of Somali unity, and there was considerable grass-roots pressure for this to take place as soon as possible. British Somaliland independence was hurriedly achieved on 26 June 1960, and when Somalia became independent on the ending of Italian trusteeship on 1 July, the two countries immediately united as the Somali Republic. Government posts were distributed among leading politicians from both territories, under the premiership of 'Abd al-Rashid 'Ali Shirmarke, a Darod SYL leader from the south.[1]

For Somalis in other territories, this painless route to nationhood was not available. The fact that Ethiopia was independent already, and Kenya was eventually to become so, was scarcely to the point. Somali aspirations were not only 'tribalist' – which did not bar them from political participation, at any rate in Kenya – but separatist, which did. Kenya lies outside the scope of this chapter. In Ethiopia, some efforts were made to win at least the semblance

---

[1] Lewis, *Somaliland*, 139–65.

of support from locally resident Somalis, largely through the manipulation of factional disputes in which one side would receive Ethiopian support in exchange for a declaration of allegiance. A few Somalis received government jobs in Addis Ababa or were elected to the Ethiopian parliament, and many more were given Ethiopian titles. The means available for expressing political participation of the kind that obtained in Somalia or British Somaliland did not, however, exist, and the possibility of allowing the area to secede to join the other Somali territories, repugnant as it was to the historic national mission which Haile Selassie felt himself to embody, was entirely excluded.

In the French Somali Coast, the political aspirations of the Issa Somalis remained for many years detached from those of the other territories, and were pressed through local institutions. The territory voted heavily to remain with France in the 1958 Referendum, and the Issa leader who had campaigned for union with Somalia, Muhammad Harbi, fled to Mogadishu. In the following years, the French helped to bring Afars to prominence in territorial politics, so that by the time the Issas had been fully mobilised to the cause of Somali nationalism they found the possibility of union with the Somali Republic blocked by an Afar majority, supported by the French and Ethiopians who had a common interest in preventing Somali control over the Jibuti–Addis Ababa railway. Differences between Afars and Issa-Somalis were further polarised when General de Gaulle, visiting the territory in August 1966, was confronted by Somali demands for independence. He reacted by calling a referendum on the territory's future in March 1967, in which the administration, by mobilising the Afar vote and expelling immigrant Somalis, succeeded in obtaining a 61 per cent majority for remaining with France. The territory, renamed the French Afar and Issa Territory (TFAI), was governed by this French–Afar alliance until 1976, when the French administration reversed its policy by seeking a broadly based coalition to take the territory to independence in 1977. The more numerous Afar living within Ethiopia were left almost entirely unadministered, and consequently unpoliticised, under the Sultan Ali Mirra of Aussa.

Whereas decolonisation in Somalia and British Somaliland led to ultimate union and independence, it was very different in

Eritrea. For a start, the process of politicisation under the British administration of 1941–52 had shown how divergent were the aspirations of different groups within the population. In addition, association with Ethiopia under the 1952 federation gave little opportunity for any of these aspirations to be satisfied. The Ethiopian government from the start regarded the autonomous Eritrean administration as a danger, both in its own right as a source of power independent of the highly centralised imperial regime, and for its possible effects on other areas of the empire. It therefore set itself to reduce Eritrea to central control, a process achieved over the ten years to 1962, when the Eritrean assembly was induced to dissolve itself. Eritrea was then reduced to the status of an ordinary Ethiopian province, ruled by a governor-general appointed from Addis Ababa. In the process, room was found for quite a number of individual Eritreans loyal to the government to be appointed to high positions in Addis Ababa. The machinery for group representation, on the other hand, was dismantled. Political parties disappeared. This left opportunities for those politicians who had fled from Eritrea at the time of federation to re-enter political life in the province as leaders of an underground movement which opposed Ethiopian rule by means of terrorism and guerrilla warfare. This movement, the Eritrean Liberation Front (ELF), was formed in the early 1960s and from about 1965 made its presence felt in Eritrea. Its activities in the early years depended heavily on the support it received from Arab states, especially Syria and Iraq, and were largely confined to the Muslim lowlands of the province. From the early 1970s, though divided into two and later three factions, it grew to be a considerable threat to the central government, tying down large numbers of Ethiopian troops, and extending operations to the Eritrean highlands.

In Ethiopia itself, finally, politicisation was consistently in-hibited both positively by the imperial government, and negatively by the absence of the stimulus to participation provided elsewhere by decolonisation. Whereas in every other territory in the region there was at least some period during which politicians were allowed to form parties, and to appeal for electoral support on the strength of their programmes or ethnic identity, this was not the case in Ethiopia outside Eritrea. Under the revised consti-tution of 1955, promulgated partly at least in response to the

Eritrean federation, the lower house of parliament was from 1957 elected by popular suffrage; but since parties were not permitted and the Chamber of Deputies exercised no control over the executive, it remained little more than a sounding board for local grievances. Unlike the position in Eritrea, there was neither the rural political consciousness nor the group of exiled politicians needed to mount a guerrilla challenge to the government. In these circumstances, demands for increased political participation came largely from the centre: from the students and younger educated officials who were trained to man the new centralising institutions of government. These, rather than provincial politicians, constituted the immediate potential opposition to the regime. Many of them were educated abroad, and returning home from the early 1950s onwards, came to see their own government, presided over by an ageing emperor and his courtiers, as uncommitted to the goals of dynamic modernisation which they saw their contemporaries in the nationalist movements pursuing in other parts of Africa. Many of the same ideas spread to the armed forces, which Haile Selassie had built up rapidly after the liberation, until by the late 1950s it comprised three infantry divisions, an Imperial Bodyguard, and a small air force and navy. A military academy established west of Addis Ababa before the Italian invasion was reactivated, and a second one set up at Harar in 1958. In keeping with Haile Selassie's policy of reducing his reliance on any single outside power, advisers were sought from several countries, including India, Israel, Norway and Sweden, but the main role from 1951 was taken by the United States. The military constituted an obvious danger to the regime, particularly as many of the junior officers were directly conscripted into the army from the secondary schools, which Haile Selassie tried to counter both by binding officers to him through grants of land and other favours, and by encouraging rivalries between units and individuals. Both the danger and the imperial counter-measures were illustrated by an abortive *coup d'état* by the Imperial Bodyguard in December 1960. A strange mixture of palace coup and would-be modernising revolution, this was led by the bodyguard commander and his brother, a radical young official recently returned from abroad. The rest of the armed forces remained loyal to Haile Selassie, who had been abroad on a state visit, and the revolt was crushed and its leaders killed.[1] It helped, however, to set a pattern of politicisation at the centre, at variance with the process of party formation in surrounding territories.

POLITICAL DECAY AND REVOLUTION

By the early 1960s then, the whole region except for the perennially anomalous French Somali Coast had been brought under the control of two indigenous independent governments. Two more contrasting regimes could scarcely be imagined. The Somali Republic could justly claim to be one of the very few African states which was built on a sense of nationhood shared by all its people. There were internal differences, certainly, derived partly from the legacies of British and Italian administration, and partly from divisions between Somali clan families, but these were contained within a common culture, language and religion, reinforced by a national genealogy in which all Somalis had a place. It was governed by a system founded on consent and participation, in which competing political parties made their ambitions relevant to the mass of the people through their close reflection of clan interests and alliances. Since this system was founded on an underlying national identity, moreover, it could dispense with the highly personalised leadership and intolerance of dissent found in nationalist parties whose principal *raison d'être* was simply the struggle against colonialism. It could thus, in response to electoral pressures or party manoeuvres, change both the prime minister, in 1964 and 1967, and the president, in 1967, peacefully and by constitutional means.

Ethiopia also possessed a strong sense of nationhood. This, however, was not common property as in the Somali Republic, but was rather the legacy of expansion from the highland core. Though it enjoyed some limited capacity for assimilating individuals, it made little pretence at assimilating social groups, with the result that political participation always held the risk of mobilising the identities of peripheral peoples in a way which threatened the whole structure of the state. Even disregarding the

[1] R. Greenfield, *Ethiopia: a new political history* (London, 1965), 337–452; C. Clapham, 'The Ethiopian *coup d'état* of December 1960', *Journal of Modern African Studies*, 1968, 6, 4, 495–507.

historic imperial legacy, therefore, the regime could not afford the open and democratic structure of government practised in Somalia. Instead, it continued to rely on the centralised control of an ageing emperor. The system of direct imperial supervision through the Minister of the Pen was to some degree dismantled after the dismissal of Tsahafe Tezaz Walda-Giyorgis in 1955, and administrative supervision was increasingly delegated, especially to the Prime Minister, Aklilu Habta-Wald; but political initiative continued to be reserved to the Emperor, who tolerated no source of independent authority. No mechanism therefore existed short of rebellion by which the government could be changed.

Yet these two contrasting systems were both to be overthrown not merely by *coups d'état*, but by military-led governments both of which could claim with some justification to be revolutionary. Of the two, moreover, it was the Somali regime which went first. The problems which it faced were certainly considerable. There were immediate difficulties in integrating the two regions, resulting in discontent especially in former British Somaliland, which as the smaller section naturally had most to lose. These difficulties came to a head in an attempted coup in the north in December 1961. The plotters lost support as soon as it became clear that their aim was the breakup of the Republic, but two northern ministers felt obliged to resign from the government the following year in order to preserve their local support. Political integration was however eased by the fact that the principal clan families straddled the north–south division. As a result, this division never wholly coincided with party lines, and opposition groups sought to overthrow the government in Mogadishu rather than dismember the Republic. Other problems were not so easily settled. The economy remained extremely poor, despite the receipt of aid from many sources, and attempts to secure the union with the Republic of the Somali-inhabited areas of Kenya, Ethiopia and the CFS/TFAI were all unsuccessful. These attempts will be described in a later section. What was important to domestic politics was the fact that they led not only to domestic disillusionment, but also to the formation, with Soviet aid, of an army very much larger than the Republic would otherwise have needed. This army, moreover, Soviet-trained and committed to a policy of territorial expansion, was to acquire an ideology and ethos very different from that of the colonially trained militaries of most other African states.

Support was equally alienated by a succession of increasingly frantic factional crises in Mogadishu, which appeared to reflect less the major issues facing the country, than the manoeuvres of individuals anxious to maintain their hold on office. In the first elections after independence, in March 1964, the SYL won a clear majority with 69 seats, followed by 22 and 15 for its two main rivals, the Somali National Congress and Somali Democratic Union, and 17 for independents, most of whom joined the government. Even then, however, a long government crisis followed, helped by splits in the SYL and the practice of secret ballot in the National Assembly, and the new government of 'Abd al-Razak Haji Husain was not confirmed in office until September. There were further crises in the first half of 1966, leading to the dismissal or resignation of several ministers. In July 1967, following the unexpected election of 'Abd al-Rashid 'Ali Shirmarke as president the previous month, Muhammad Haji Ibrahim Igal became prime minister, and tried to impose some order on the party, at the cost of weakening its representative capacity. The elections of March 1969, fought by 64 parties and over 2000 candidates, saw a further step towards breakdown and led to some 25 deaths. The SYL won 73 seats and its opponents 51, all but two of whom immediately crossed to the governing party in a search for posts. The dénouement came when President 'Abd al-Rashid was assassinated by a policeman – motivated, apparently, by clan rivalries – in October 1969. As the SYL caucus met to choose a successor, the army took control of Mogadishu, and turned over the government to a military council headed by Major-General Muhammad Siyad Barre.[1]

Insofar as the Ethiopian regime that fell in 1974 had been in power for over 30 years, and could be seen as the last representative of an imperial system of government which had ruled Ethiopia for many centuries, a more general analysis of its decline is called for than in the case of the Somali Republic. Certainly it was not jolted to its end by successive crises like its Somali counterpart. The years between 1961 and 1973 were generally uneventful, astonishingly so by comparison with most other African states during the same period. The same Prime Minister, Aklilu Habta-Wald, remained in office throughout, and ministerial posts circulated among much the same group of imperial protégés,

---

[1] I. M. Lewis, 'The politics of the 1969 Somali coup', *Journal of Modern African Studies*, 1972, **10**, 3, 383–408.

extended towards the end of the period to take in some of the younger generation of graduates returned from abroad. These ministers were not for the most part any less competent or well educated, nor any more corrupt, than their contemporaries elsewhere. What distinguished them was the fact that they had come to power within the imperial patronage network rather than through any source of support in the country at large, and needed to adapt themselves to this network if they were to survive. As a result, though capable of managing the administrative machinery of government, they were quite unable to perform the political function of rallying and associating social groupings – whether modern or traditional, central or regional – with the regime. When the crisis came in 1974, they could be brushed aside, imprisoned, and in many cases summarily executed, without being able to make any substantial difference to the march of events.

The regime's most critical weakness was its lack of links with Ethiopian society outside a narrow group in Addis Ababa. The centralising measures introduced by Haile Selassie after his restoration had decisively undermined the old provincial autonomy, and reduced the provinces to dependence on Addis Ababa. Provincial governors, as a result, became increasingly central appointees. In the process, they lost the capacity, which they had possessed up to 1935, to act as provincial spokesmen at the centre, backed if need be by an army drawn from their levies and retainers. No adequate machinery was developed in their place to link the government with provincial opinion. Political parties were not allowed to develop since they were seen, doubtless correctly, as a threat to the authority of the emperor: this in itself indicates the difficulty of reconciling social change with the imperial regime.[1] The Chamber of Deputies, elected by popular suffrage after 1957, did come to see itself as a forum for local interests, and since elections were held at four-yearly intervals, it remained fairly closely in touch with local opinion; it vigorously amended, for instance, the Agricultural Income Tax Proclamation of 1967. It was nonetheless very weak at both local and central levels: at local level because members had to stand for election on a purely personal basis, and could not organise the sort of backing for which a party would have been required; at the centre, because the parliament was entirely peripheral to the court and

[1] J. Markakis, *Ethiopia: anatomy of a traditional polity* (Oxford, 1974), 331.

the bureaucracy through which the government was carried on. The deficiencies of provincial representation were clearly shown by a rebellion in Gojjam province, in the Amhara heartland, in 1968. This was sparked off by opposition to assessments for the proposed agricultural income tax, but also reflected resentment at the actions of the Shoan governor-general. The government was not prepared to face the prolonged military action which would have been necessary to defeat the uprising, and instead replaced the governor-general.[1] Other small rebellions occurred in the south, especially in Bale province. The one attempt which was made to form a semi-political organisation to represent the Oromo peoples, named Mecha Tulama after two clan ancestors, was swiftly suppressed by the government in 1965. Although these attempts to mobilise rural opinion against the government were sporadic and of limited effectiveness, they underline the failure of integration which was most evident in Eritrea.

Having in effect deprived itself of political support from the periphery, the imperial regime was obliged to rely on central institutions which it had itself created, but which had no special reason to remain loyal to the emperor. Of these, the students were the most vocal, and the armed forces the most dangerous. Student opposition to the regime first became evident when university students in Addis Ababa supported the abortive coup in 1960. The first major demonstrations to provoke a confrontation with the regime took place in 1965. Thereafter they occurred almost annually, most violently in 1969–70, and involved secondary-school students in Addis Ababa and some of the provincial towns. These demonstrations, expressing an inchoate yearning for socialism and democracy, had few clearly defined goals and presented no direct threat to the regime, but they did much to weaken the aura of sacred authority which still surrounded the emperor, and hence indirectly helped to hasten the day when a more effective challenge would be possible.

This could only come from the armed forces, which by 1970 had come to include a four-division army, the Imperial Bodyguard, and an air force flying sophisticated jet aircraft. In 1961 and 1964 they had demonstrated their capacity to enforce demands for higher pay on a reluctant government, but any direct challenge to the regime required both a belief in alternative political

[1] P. Schwab, *Decision-making in Ethiopia* (London, 1972), 158–69.

objectives and the capacity to surmount divisions within the military. These requirements were met early in 1974. Within the armed forces, discontent over pay and conditions coalesced with a growing political awareness, especially among junior officers, which combined an intense nationalism with a contempt for the immobilism of the old regime. In the country at large, an economic crisis brought about by the rise in international oil prices combined with revelations of the government's incompetence, especially in dealing with a severe famine in Wollo province. From January onwards, a series of mutinies, strikes and demonstrations progressively challenged the government's control. Aklilu Habta-Wald resigned as prime minister in February, but his successor Endalkachew Makonnen never succeeded in establishing his authority. The emperor, resorting with his usual skill to his time-honoured tactics of factional manipulation, found himself dealing with social groupings which these tactics were powerless to control. Over the following six months, political initiative passed increasingly into the hands of a skilfully managed committee of the armed forces, known as the Derg. By July, the government was powerless to prevent the arrest even of its own ministers. The *coup de grâce* was delivered with Haile Selassie's deposition on 10 September 1974; he died in confinement the following year.

In both the Somali Republic and Ethiopia, and especially the latter, the military governments established in 1969 and 1974 were still too new at the end of our period to make possible anything more than a very provisional assessment of their role in the region's history. At first glance, the similarities between the two regimes were striking. Both claimed to be revolutionary, and aspired to cut through the paralysis which had afflicted their predecessors, in order to create states which were both nationalist and socialist. However, the very different structures of the two countries severely affected the ways in which these objectives could be achieved.

In the Somali Republic – renamed the Somali Democratic Republic after the coup – it soon became clear that the Supreme Revolutionary Council (SRC) would be more than merely a caretaker government, but its objectives were only gradually defined.[1] Its early appeals were directed largely against corruption

---

[1] I. M. Lewis, 'Kim Il Sung in Somalia: the end of tribalism?', in P. Cohen and W. Schack (eds.), *Essays in honour of Isaac Shapera* (Oxford, 1978).

and tribalism, a term which in the Somali context referred to the identification with clans and clan families on which political allegiances had largely been built. General Siyad Barre had also to establish his personal position, which he achieved after the exposure of alleged plots by his successive vice-presidents in 1970 and 1971. In January 1972, the SRC launched a campaign for 'scientific socialism', which involved state control of critical areas of the economy, combined with measures for national unification, economic development, the sedentarisation of nomads, and the introduction of a Somali script, over which previous civilian governments had argued inconclusively for the previous decade. These measures provoked some opposition, including a clash with conservative Muslim leaders over the emancipation of women, but the government was able to draw on an existing sense of Somali identity in order to sustain support. Though the ideology of the regime was explicitly Marxist–Leninist, and officials were sent for training to the Soviet Union and North Korea, political control remained in the hands of senior army officers. Despite a heavy emphasis on agencies of public indoctrination and control, no political party was established until after the end of our period, in 1976, and even then the new politburo mirrored the composition of the old SRC.

In Ethiopia, the socialist and nationalist objectives of the revolution could not be so easily reconciled. The early months, in mid-1974, were accompanied by liberalisation measures which included not only press freedom and the release of political prisoners, but also the granting of equal status to Islam with Christianity, and the relaxation of the old regime's insistence on the supremacy of the Amharic language. This liberalisation could not long survive the demise of the naive assumption that all groups had a common interest in the creation of a united, democratic and socialist Ethiopia. The Derg, elected from all units in the armed forces and all ranks from private to major, had little internal coherence once the removal of Haile Selassie was achieved, and the raising of political expectations and decline of authority evident in the military was equally clear in relations between landlords and peasants, between ethnic and regional groupings, and among urban groups. The Derg divided between those led by the titular head of state, General Aman Andom, who favoured a policy of reconciliation towards regional opposition and social groups associated with the old regime, and those led by Major

Mengistu Haile Maryam who sought an extreme Ethiopian nationalism and a decisive break with the past. The victory of the latter faction in November 1974 was accompanied by the execution of Aman and over 50 leading former civilian and military officials, and the despatch of additional troops to Eritrea, where bitter fighting continued until after the end of our period. By the end of 1975, the Derg retained power but had yet to establish its authority either in Addis Ababa or in the provinces, where conditions were as unsettled, and prospects as uncertain, as they had been 35 years before.

REGIONAL AND INTERNATIONAL RELATIONSHIPS

In contrast with many other parts of Africa, where foreign relationships continued even after independence to turn on the connexion with the former colonial power, in the Horn they have consistently been fuelled by tensions within the region. Both the intensity of regional loyalties and rivalries, and the weakness of extra-regional linkages, helped to account for this. Ethiopia, remaining uncolonised, did not acquire those cultural, economic and political bonds with a particular European state which characterised the colonial relationship. Elsewhere in the region, colonial links, though present, were weak. In both Eritrea and Italian Somalia, the Italian colonisers were militarily ejected in 1941; the British military administrations which replaced them were no more than temporary expedients, and though the Italians returned to Somalia in 1950, they did so under a United Nations Trusteeship which severely restricted both the duration and the nature of their administration. British Somaliland, always a neglected corner of empire, lost many of the normal post-colonial links with Britain on its union with Somalia at independence; a breach of diplomatic relations with Britain in 1963, over British policy towards the Somali-inhabited part of Kenya, further weakened the connexion. Only in the French Territory of the Afars and Issas did the metropolitan link remain critical, though even there the French remained largely because of the tensions created by intra-regional rivalries; for the Afar politicians who controlled the territorial assembly, the French presence was vastly preferable either to the association with the Somali Republic sought by their Issa rivals, or to the Ethiopian invasion which seemed likely to follow any French withdrawal.

These rivalries turned principally on the Ethiopian–Somali dispute, and secondarily on the status of Eritrea. The forms which they took developed during the period, in keeping both with changing domestic political structures and consciousness, and with the opportunities available for outside involvement. Immediately after the end of the Second World War, the principal concern was the disposal of the former Italian colonies, considered earlier in this account. The Ethiopian success at that time in securing control of Eritrea and fending off the Bevin Plan for Somali unification may be ascribed partly to the international sympathy Ethiopia received as an early victim of Fascism, and also to the fact that, as an independent state, she was able to become a founder member of the United Nations and take part in her own right at international conferences, whereas the Somalis had no such representation. The second object of Ethiopian diplomacy was achieved through the establishment of linkages with as many as possible of the western industrialised states, thus avoiding the isolation she suffered at the time of the Italian invasion in 1935. In the circumstances of the 1940s, this meant reducing her dependence on Britain, which as the author of the Bevin Plan and controller of almost all the peripheral territories was the prime target of Ethiopian suspicion. In the process, the United States became Ethiopia's most important source of outside aid, particularly through the Military Aid and Assistance Group which helped train and equip the new Ethiopian army. Ethiopian participation in the UN forces in Korea helped to emphasise these links, while at the same time publicising – in another legacy of 1935 – the emperor's commitment to international action against aggression.

The 1950s were a decade during which external relationships took second place to domestic political developments. Until 1960, Ethiopia was the only independent state in the region, and not until the late 1950s could she take advantage of the opportunities created by the easing of the Cold War and the emergence of other independent African states. Participation in the 1958 Accra Conference of Independent African States was Ethiopia's first venture into the new world of African diplomacy. Together with Haile Selassie's visits to the USSR and other Communist states in 1959, this could be seen as an extension of Ethiopia's traditional policy of multiplying and diversifying her diplomatic linkages. At the same time, it reflected a skilful awareness on the part of

Ethiopia's leaders of the need to adapt their foreign policy to a changing international system.

International relations became vastly more important to the region with Somali independence in 1960, because the Somali Republic's determination to unite all Somali peoples under a single flag automatically brought her into conflict with her neighbours in Ethiopia, Kenya and the CFS/TFAI. This goal, pursued in different ways by successive Somali governments, has consistently formed the base for Somali foreign policy.[1] In March 1963, the Somalis broke diplomatic relations with Britain over her refusal to allow the Northern Frontier District of Kenya to join the Republic; in May the same year, President Adan 'Abdullah Osman attacked Ethiopia at the inaugural conference of the OAU in Addis Ababa; and the following March, brief but intense fighting broke out on the Ethiopian–Somali frontier. Ethiopian involvement in African diplomacy, of which the 1963 Addis Ababa Conference was the outstanding achievement, was indeed partly a response to the threat presented to Ethiopia by a permanently hostile state on her south-east frontier. Although the democratic and anti-colonial Somali Republic might seem to have had more in common with the other new states in the continent than did his own anachronistic empire, Haile Selassie soon appreciated that almost every African state shared Ethiopia's interest in retaining the existing international frontiers, and that this could be used to isolate the Somalis. In addition, his own prestige as the senior African statesman and defender of Ethiopia against Italian Fascism could be used to promote a common continental organisation which other African leaders could not at that time achieve. For some ten years after 1963, through Haile Selassie's tireless travels round the continent, his mediation of disputes between African states, the location of the OAU head-quarters in Addis Ababa, and the championing of African causes in the UN and elsewhere, Ethiopia could claim to be the diplomatic leader of Africa.

The Somali Republic's response to the position of weakness in which those Ethiopian initiatives left her took two forms. The first, longer-term one, was to increase her military strength, and since the major western powers were already committed to defending the territories she sought to acquire, in Kenya, Ethiopia and

[1] J. Drysdale, *The Somali dispute* (London, 1964); S. Touval, *Somali nationalism* (Cambridge, Mass., 1963).

the CFS/TFAI, her natural allies lay in the Communist bloc. In November 1963, the Somalis announced their acceptance of Soviet military aid worth nearly £11 million, and began to form a large modern army. In the shorter term, however, the policy of confrontation with all her neighbours was both fruitless and expensive for so poor a country, and after Muhammad Haji Ibrahim Igal became prime minister in July 1967 he cultivated a policy of détente. Both aspects of Somali policy survived the 1969 coup, but the balance shifted gradually from the second back towards the first. The SRC sought no confrontation with Ethiopia, particularly while it was engaged in large-scale domestic social transformation and dealing with the effects of drought. But as a military government, it increased the strength of the armed forces, and at the same time greatly intensified the connexion with the USSR. This in turn increased the Ethiopian reliance for arms on the United States, which continued for a year or two after the 1974 revolution despite the change in Ethiopia's domestic political orientation. By 1977, both American reluctance to supply arms and the new Ethiopian regime's search for more congenial allies led to a dramatic reversal of alliances in the Horn, with both the USSR and Cuba heavily supporting Ethiopia during the 1977–8 Ethiopia–Somali war.

Though the Eritrean problem in a sense became a domestic one, following the incorporation of Eritrea into Ethiopia, it continued to have international ramifications both through the ELF's constant attempts to internationalise the conflict, and through the diplomatic means which the Ethiopians used to contain it.[1] The former included attempted hijackings of Ethiopian airliners on international flights, and the support which the ELF received from radical Arab regimes in Iraq, Syria, and Libya. The latter turned especially on Ethiopia's relations with the Sudan, whose long frontier with Eritrea was critical in any attempt to control supplies reaching the ELF, and to a lesser extent those with Egypt, as the most prominent African Arab state. Though there was no evidence of appreciable direct foreign involvement in the fighting during the period up to 1975, the successes of both Ethiopians and Eritrean guerrillas depended heavily on the support which each was able to mobilise from the international environment.

[1] T. J. Farer, *War clouds on the Horn of Africa: a crisis for détente* (New York, Carnegie Endowment, 1976), 29–35.

SOCIAL AND ECONOMIC CHANGE

In most of the Horn, indigenous social and economic structures retained a resilience which made them exceptionally resistant to change, and as a result made the shocks which they suffered at the end of the period, through drought and government action, all the more traumatic. Part of the reason for this was that in Ethiopia and British Somaliland, at least, the hand of government was light, concerned with basic maintenance functions rather than social transformation; the same could not be said to the same degree of the Italian territories. More important, existing structures retained a validity because of their adaptation to local circumstances, a lesson most clear in the case of Somali nomadism. For so long as most Somalis made their living through seasonal migrations in search of pasture for their herds, so long would the traditional system be the most appropriate way of organising society. This mode of life, ignoring roads, towns and international boundaries, equally placed great difficulties in the way of those who sought to impose the essentially stationary benefits of 'modern' life: the sedentary Somali of the Juba–Shebele basin were far more directly affected by both social and economic change. Although highland Ethiopian social organisation was very different from Somali nomadism, other elements in indigenous society contributed to a similar result, especially in the Amhara–Tigrean heartland from Addis Ababa north to the Eritrean frontier. Particularly important here were the strong conservative interests vested in the possession and use of land, with which the political structure at the local level and the Coptic Orthodox Church were also strongly associated. The combination was powerful enough to insulate the area from effective central-government intervention, as is most clearly shown by the imperial government's inability to exact taxes from Gojjam province, and the revolts which broke out when it attempted to do so. Eritrea and the southern and western parts of Ethiopia, where local social structures had been weakened by central conquest and land alienation, were more open to modernising influences.

Pressures for change, present though in some areas rudimentary before 1940, came from three main sources. The first and most direct was government, whether colonial or indigenous, which had an interest in achieving certain goals which could only be attained through modernisation: notably the establishment of an institutionalised structure of control, which called for a fixed capital housing the necessary agencies, both civil and military, the educational systems needed to produce appropriately qualified people to man them, the communications systems needed to extend their control to other parts of the territory, and the cash economy needed to finance them, which in turn required the encouragement of economic linkages with the outside world. Governments varied in the intensity with which, and the ways in which, they pursued this common goal. The colonial government of British Somaliland was unquestionably the most lackadaisical. Haile Selassie's government in Ethiopia, though intense in its search for control, was limited in the ways through which it could achieve it by the nature of its own political base, and the danger of creating forces which might – and eventually did – supplant it. The French regime in the CFS/TFAI was in a sense more passive, and was not under such pressure as the trustee administrations in the former Italian colonies to produce a balance sheet of progress achieved. The post-independence Somali government came closest to the generality of newly independent African regimes in its pursuit of conventional development goals; while from the two military regimes there emanated a genuine urge, however inarticulately conceived or inadequately executed, for revolutionary social transformation.

A second impetus for change came from the belief of individuals either in its intrinsic desirability, or at least in its capacity to improve their own circumstances. One indicator is the way in which oppositional movements to established regimes moved from the conservative to the radical side of the political spectrum. In British Somaliland, where as late as 1935 proposals for a governmental school at Berbera had been abandoned in the face of hostile riots, the post-war generation of Somali nationalists sought education and criticised the colonial regime for tardiness in providing it. Haile Selassie, who started his career as the leader of the modernising faction in Ethiopia, had from the 1950s constantly to adapt himself to demands for a faster rate of change, and by the 1970s was seen as the principal obstacle to it. Even the elected Somali government, which in the 1960s saw itself as being held back by the conservatism of the nomadic clans on which it relied for support, was overthrown by a regime which

Table 9.1. *Estimated populations of the Horn of Africa, 1937–74.*

	British Somaliland	Somalia	CFS/TFAI	Eritrea	Ethiopia	Total
1937	350 000	1 090 000	47 000	670 000	—	
1954	640 000	1 269 000	63 000	1 000 000	15 000 000	17 972 000
1958	1 980 000			20 000 000		
1961			81 200			
1964	2 420 000			22 200 000		
1970	2 550 000		95 000	24 626 000		27 271 000
1974	2 707 000		104 000	27 239 000		30 050 000

Note: all figures are estimates, and those for Ethiopia are especially subject to error.

Source: *United Nations demographic yearbooks*, 1955, 1965, 1974 (New York).

actively sought to resolve the problem by abolishing both clans and nomadism altogether. Thus the desire for change came to be espoused by important groups within indigenous society.

A third impetus for change was the simple pressure of population on resources. The total population of the region approximately doubled between 1940 and 1975 (table 9.1). Much of this increase was due to changes in health care, agriculture, and living conditions. The total increase would in any case have placed intolerable strain on existing structures, even without the 'revolution of rising expectations' by which some groups at least were affected. In addition, many people had to cope with – unless they succumbed to – the great drought in the eastern and southern parts of the Horn in 1972–4, which caused many thousands of deaths, especially in Ethiopia, and destroyed – temporarily at least – the basis of the Somali nomadic economy.

One other source of change the Horn of Africa was spared: it was not, unlike many parts of the continent, the scene of deep penetration by foreign companies bent on exploiting its mineral or agricultural resources. No large-scale mineral extraction took place, and agricultural penetration was largely restricted to a few plantations in the Awash and Juba–Shebele basins and in highland Eritrea. This in itself was a major factor accounting for the resilience of traditional institutions, and meant that, after the end of the colonial era, social and economic change was for the most part undertaken under the direction of indigenous people and governments.

URBANISATION AND EDUCATION

Though the Horn contained a number of long-established urban settlements, at Aksum, Gondar, Harar, Mogadishu and elsewhere, none of these had permanent populations of more than a few thousand. Urbanisation therefore very directly resulted from the establishment of permanent governmental headquarters in the late nineteenth century, and from new or improved communications links with the outside world. Into the first category came the territorial capitals, whether built by an indigenous government at Addis Ababa or by colonial regimes at Asmara, Jibuti, Hargeisa and Mogadishu, and the Ethiopian provincial capitals which mostly derived from the encampments of regional military governors. Into the second came the ports of Massawa, Assab and Berbera, as well as Jibuti and Mogadishu, and the railway town of Dire Dawa.

Although reliable figures for urban populations are not available for most towns until the 1960s, urban growth appears to have been fairly rapid, though not as meteoric as in some parts of the continent. Addis Ababa, estimated at about 100 000 inhabitants in the late 1930s, had reached 560 000 by the mid-1960s and over a million by 1974. Mogadishu's population similarly nearly doubled from 141 000 in 1965 to a quarter of a million in 1974. The Eritrean capital of Asmara stagnated after its Italian heyday, only expanding from some 100 000 in the late 1930s to 132 000 by 1965; the population then jumped to 296 000 by 1974, as drought and the worsening security situation drove people from the rural areas. Most provincial centres expanded more steadily, and by the mid-1960s eleven towns in the region (eight in Ethiopia, Mogadishu and Hargeisa in Somalia, and Jibuti) had populations over 30 000. In the mid-1960s, some 12 per cent of the Somali, and just over 5 per cent of the Ethiopian, population lived in towns of over 10 000, and by 1975 these percentages are likely to have drastically increased, especially as a result of drought. Two-thirds of the total population of the TFAI lived in 1970 in Jibuti.[1]

The reasons for these increases were much the same as elsewhere in Africa: government services, economic opportunities, and rural drift. Taking Ethiopia as an example, Addis Ababa

[1] *Demographic yearbooks*; R. K. P. Pankhurst, *Economic history of Ethiopia 1800–1935* (Addis Ababa, 1968), 689–715; Markakis, *Ethiopia*, 160–71.

had in 1970 about a third of the 100000 government employees in the country, a third of the secondary schools, and a third also of the hospital beds. Its position at the centre of the country and of its communications network (the road system radiated out from Addis Ababa, and roads bypassing the capital were non-existent or extremely poor) ensured for it a dominant trading role; and by far the greater part of industrial production was concentrated in the city and a string of smaller towns along the railway line to the south-east of it. The larger provincial capitals, such as Gondar, Dessie, Harar and Jimma, served in their turn as microcosms of Addis Ababa, attracting administrators from the centre as well as immigrants from the surrounding countryside. While the countryside continued to retain a considerable resilience, especially where it retained traditional social and political structures and a self-supporting economy, it was therefore in the cities that the main effects of modernisation were felt.

By comparison with many parts of Africa, the spread of formal education in the Horn was slow. In part, this was the result of an early lack of government action, since the Italian Fascist administration, the most dynamic of the colonial governments in the region, was the least anxious to train a rival élite of Somalis or Eritreans, while the British and French did very little indeed; the Ethiopian government was more committed to educational expansion than any of the colonial regimes, since from the time of Menelik it had recognised the need for a cadre of educated administrators, but the means at its disposal were very limited, and the schools established before 1935 were closed during the Italian occupation. In part, it was due to the existence in much of the region of established indigenous religious educational systems which understandably looked with suspicion on an imported alien rival; this was especially marked in British Somaliland, where local opposition prevented any schools from being opened before 1940, and in Ethiopia, where the Orthodox Church's fear of proselytisation by other Christian sects meant that missionary activity was largely restricted to the pagan areas of the south and west. In part, too, it was due to other difficulties, including the Second World War which severely disrupted education in the region and, more lastingly, Somali nomadism.

One result of the war, however, was to make people throughout the Horn aware of the efficiency of western technology and the consequent need to master it, so that opposition to formal education on traditionalist grounds was very much reduced. The Ethiopian school system was restarted after the liberation in 1941, though not until after the end of the war in 1945 could much be done to expand it, and the British military administrations in Somalia and Eritrea sympathised with local demands for education, and did their best to meet them within very limited resources. By 1952, Eritrea had the highest proportion of its population at school of any territory in the region, except for the CFS, where many of the pupils were French or Arab. The figures for this period indicate the progress made once the immediate effects of the war had faded, and show 15 000 schoolchildren (90 per cent primary, 1.5 per cent of the estimated population) in Eritrea in 1952; 1700 (91 per cent primary, 0.26 per cent of population) in British Somaliland in 1955; 11 000 (88 per cent primary, 0.86 per cent of population) in ex-Italian Somalia in 1954; and 2100 (85 per cent primary, 3.3 per cent of population) in the French Somali Coast the same year. The Ethiopian figures show over 99 per cent of the 68 000 schoolchildren claimed in 1952 (0.45 per cent of estimated population) as being in primary grades, and no more than 531 in secondary schools.

By 1962–3, the numbers at school had more than doubled in the Somali territories and more than quadrupled in Ethiopia (including Eritrea); they doubled again throughout the region between then and 1969–70, by which date there were 713 000 pupils at school in Ethiopia, 58 000 in the Somali Republic and 7800 in TFAI, 2.9, 2.3 and 8.2 per cent of the total population respectively. Although the imperial government in Ethiopia was to be criticised in later years for failing to institute a crash programme of education, the figures show that it did reasonably well by comparison with its colonial neighbours, despite the intensified education programme introduced by the Italian trust administration in Somalia after 1950. These figures represented only a small percentage of the potential school population – 14 per cent of the appropriate age group were estimated to be in primary school and 1.9 per cent in senior secondary school in Ethiopia in 1968–9 – but they nonetheless marked a very important force for change.[1]

Tertiary education at first depended entirely on opportunities

[1] *United Nations statistical yearbooks*, 1956, 1965, 1973 (New York); Markakis, *Ethiopia*, 143–59.

to study abroad, initially almost only in American and Western European universities, but subsequently in the Soviet bloc and elsewhere in Africa. The first such institution within the region, the University College of Addis Ababa, was founded in 1950, and combined with colleges of agriculture, public health and building to form the Haile Selassie I University in 1961; the name was changed to Addis Ababa University after the 1974 revolution. By 1969, there were 4600 students in tertiary education in Ethiopia, and nearly 2000 abroad. In Somalia, tertiary education got under way with the establishment of specialised institutes by the Italian trust administration in the early 1950s; the most important of these, the School of Politics and Administration, turned out a high proportion of senior Somali administrators and politicians. University education had to wait until the foundation of the University Institute of Somalia in 1960, and although there were nearly a thousand students in tertiary education in 1970, Somalis depended heavily on scholarships to study abroad, especially in Italy, Egypt, and latterly the USSR.

This process of educational expansion was accompanied by the characteristic problems and deficiencies common to the whole continent during the period. These included a heavy dependence on foreign teachers at the secondary level and upwards, a high drop-out rate, a very low proportion of female students, and a marked concentration of the available facilities in the cities as against the rural areas, in the sedentary as against the nomadic populations, and in the more developed provinces. In Ethiopia in 1962, for example, 38 per cent of secondary-school children were in Addis Ababa, and 67 per cent in the two provinces of Shoa (including Addis Ababa) and Eritrea. The problems of urban drift to which this gave rise, and the appropriateness of the syllabus for largely urban occupations (especially government service) were again common ones. In addition, both Ethiopia and Somalia experienced difficulties arising from their national languages. The desire for centralisation and national integration in Ethiopia led to the imposition of Amharic as the language of instruction throughout the country, at primary level from 1963 and junior secondary level from 1970. In addition to the resentment this aroused in non-Amharic-speaking areas, especially in Eritrea and some of the southern provinces, it created difficulties over the availability of qualified teachers and over transfer to the senior secondary and tertiary levels, in which the language of instruction was English. In Somalia, though the use of Somali was almost universal, there was no agreed script for writing it down, and the rivalry between the three contending possibilities – Roman script, Arabic script, and Osmaniya, a sophisticated indigenous Somali script invented in about 1920 – was so intense that the elected government before 1969 could make no decision on the issue at all. Even the military government delayed until October 1972 before deciding on the Roman version.

A further problem, of a different kind, arose from the strains in the relationship between students and the society of which they formed an awkward and atypical part. This presented itself in an acute form to the imperial regime in Ethiopia, where the students – initially in the university and subsequently in the secondary schools as well – were the only group which dared express open and fairly continuous opposition to the emperor and his government. The military government after 1974 closed the university altogether and sent the students to spread the revolutionary ideology in the countryside, at the same time removing a potential source of opposition in Addis Ababa, but this scheme was resented both by the students and in the countryside, and its success was mixed. A similar scheme to improve rural literacy, and involving schoolchildren as well as students, was instituted in the Somali Republic in 1974, and was rapidly converted, after the scale of the drought became apparent, into a drought rehabilitation service.

Both Ethiopia and the Somalia territories were fortunate, however, in possessing a rich and well-established literary culture which could serve as a source of pride and a point of reference to educated and uneducated alike, in the Republic through the Somali language and in particular its poetry, and in Ethiopia through the legacy of an ancient written language, Ge'ez, and its modern successor Amharic. As a result, writers in both countries continued to work in an indigenous medium which, even when their work took an imported form such as the novel, could adopt the subtleties of existing modes of thought; one example perhaps might be the novel *Fikr iska mekebir* (Faithful to the Grave) by the Ethiopian author and politician, Hadis Alamayahu. Analogously though less directly, something of the indigenous artistic tradition carried over into the work of Ethiopian artists of the 1950s and 1960s, such as Afework Tekle and Gabre-Christos Desta. Newspapers were also available in Amharic, Tigrinya (in Eritrea) and Somali, and though circulation as a whole was extremely small these outsold the European language press. At the same time, the resilience of Amharic did little for native speakers of other languages who had first to learn Amharic to be accepted into the national culture, and subsequently to learn a European tongue in order to gain access to the outside world. The dangers of a national language are, first, that it may not include all the peoples within the national boundary, secondly that it may restrict its speakers from communicating outside that boundary. Somali suffered from the second of these defects, Amharic from both of them.

Economic development is perhaps a misnomer for a region which remained among the poorest in Africa, and in which many people, especially in the lowland subsistence economy, were poorer at the end of the period than they had been at the start of it. Economic statistics for the Horn were always unreliable and often non-existent, especially in the early period and again after the military revolutions, but the per capita income estimates of \$US 90 for Ethiopia and \$80 for the Somali Republic in 1974 placed them no higher than 36th and 39th respectively among the then 42 independent African states.[1] Both countries continued to have a very high proportion of their populations in the subsistence sector, and relied for their exports almost exclusively on agricultural products, principally livestock and bananas in the Republic, and coffee, hides and oilseeds in Ethiopia. All but a very few manufactured items still had to be imported at the end of the period, though some simple import-substitution industries had by then been established, especially in Ethiopia.

However underdeveloped the economies of the Horn might have appeared in 1975, nonetheless by comparison with 1940 the changes were considerable. One difference with the pre-war era was that whereas then only the Italian Fascist administration had any firm commitment to promoting economic development, after 1945 this became one of the recognised responsibilities of govern-

---

[1] *Le Monde* (Paris), 4 February 1976.

ment, even though different regimes pursued it with varying degrees of intensity and all of them had to deal with the difficulties of the terrain, the weakness of the infrastructure, and the sometimes hostile attitudes of the people. As a result, the number of government agencies concerned with economic management and development proliferated, a process most clear in Ethiopia, where the establishment of Ethiopian Air Lines in 1948 was followed in the 1950s by the creation of specialised agencies for highways, telecommunications and electricity; ministries for community development, planning, and later land reform were set up, and the First Five-Year Plan, inaugurated in 1957, was succeeded by the Second and Third Plans; the fourth was still on the drawing board at the time of the revolution in 1974. A certain amount of this activity was simply window-dressing; the five-year plans never achieved the central position in government economic strategy which would have been necessary for their full implementation, and any substantial land reform programme would soon have run foul of the political bases of the imperial regime. The specialised agencies, on the other hand, did carry out new and important tasks for which there had been no place in the preceding millennia of independent Ethiopia. A similar process took place in Somalia.

In the immediate post-war period, none of the territories of the Horn possessed either the capital or the expertise needed to develop on their own, and though the lack of expertise was to some extent made good by education over the subsequent decades, the capital deficiency remained. Development therefore critically depended on outside assistance. In the Somali territories, this was provided until 1960 (or throughout the period in CFS/TFAI) by the colonial and trustee administrations. The British military administration in the 1940s was largely concerned with maintenance functions, and even in the 1950s the pace of change in British Somaliland remained slow, but the Italian trustee administration in Somalia promoted investment by both state and private interests, revived the banana industry, and encouraged production of cotton and cereals. Ethiopia meanwhile relied on advisers of many nationalities, and on development aid which came principally from the United States and from international institutions, which between them accounted consistently for some three-quarters of external aid; from the late 1950s onwards, Ethiopia further diversified the sources of assistance to include loans from Yugoslavia and the USSR, and subsequently China. External indebtedness, held steady at about $US 50m in the 1950s, thereafter rose precipitously to $US 76m in 1963, $US 130m in 1968, and $US 240m in 1973, in order to meet not only development expenditure but the increasing costs of the public service. The Somali Republic, too, diversified its sources of aid after independence in 1960, and became one of the largest recipients per capita in the world. Despite well publicised Russian and Chinese projects, most of it, even after the 1969 revolution, continued to come from western and international agencies.

Aid was largely used on infrastructural developments, especially communications. The core of the region's communications network continued to be the Italian road system built before 1941. This was extended and improved, especially in southern Ethiopia, and a new road was built to the Red Sea port of Assab, but very few feeder roads were constructed, and in most parts of Ethiopia produce had to be brought by mule to the nearest main road. But whereas Ethiopia at least had a fairly centralised network radiating from Addis Ababa, the Somali Republic had only the most meagre land communications between its two major centres of population, Mogadishu and the Shebele–Juba basin in the south, and the highlands round Hargeisa in the north. The most direct route between them, moreover, was barred by the great wedge of Ethiopian territory, and an all-weather north–south road was still under construction, with Chinese assistance, at the end of our period. No new railways were built in the region, but a network of local air services, especially in Ethiopia, linked outlying towns which were only with difficulty, if at all, accessible by road. Thus internal communications were appreciably better by the end of the period than they had been at the beginning. So were links with the outside world. International airports were built at Asmara, Dire Dawa and Addis Ababa in Ethiopia, at Jibuti, and at Hargeisa, Mogadishu and (in 1974) Kismayu in the Republic. Jibuti continued to be the largest port in the region, handling most of Ethiopia's trade even after the 1952 Federation which gave Ethiopia direct access to the Red Sea at Massawa and Assab, where a new modern port was built. The Somalis had no modern port facilities until 1968–9, when the Russian-built port at Berbera in the north, and the American-built one at Kismayu in the south, both came into operation. At Mogadishu a new port was nearing completion in 1975.

Industrial development within the region was largely confined to Ethiopia, and within Ethiopia to Shoa province and Eritrea. While the beginnings of industrialisation dated from the Fascist and liberation periods, its growth was slow until the late 1950s; from then onwards it expanded steadily until by the 1970s it accounted for some 5 per cent of gross domestic product. Industrial textile production got under way with Indian and Japanese investment in the mid-1960s, and other areas of large-scale production included building materials, shoes and cigarettes. It is not clear whether the very generous terms offered to foreign investors had any substantial effect on these developments. Shoa province contained 63.4 per cent of industrial employees in 1970, followed by Eritrea (23.6 per cent), and by Harar and Gojjam; the remaining ten provinces had 1 per cent of the total between them. An attempt at regional industrialisation in Tigre province energetically promoted by the Governor, Ras Mangasha Seyoum, after 1960, ended in failure. Somali industry was largely confined to processing agricultural products, including meat canning and sugar refining, though a more determined attempt to promote manufacture of basic goods such as building materials was undertaken after the revolution. The military revolutions in both countries, however, more directly affected ownership than production, since both of them had a strong ideological hostility to capitalism in general and foreign capitalists in particular. The Somali government nationalised banks and petrol companies soon after the revolution, and in early 1972 took control of all sectors of the economy, including medical facilities. In Ethiopia, banking became a state monopoly with the foundation of the State Bank of Ethiopia in 1942, and though private Ethiopian-owned banks were later permitted, and one was formed, banking remained overwhelmingly in state hands, and the insurance industry was also Ethiopianised from 1970; the state also owned or had shares in many other commercial ventures. From 1974, however, the tone and pace of nationalisation sharply changed, with the intention of creating a state-controlled economy in the shortest possible time.

These economic developments led to social change in the form of new kinds of association created by the new occupational structure. The earliest and most widespread of these were the urban versions of traditional self-help associations, known as *iqub*, *edir* and *mahaber* in Ethiopia, characteristic of newly urbanised societies. Labour unions were formed in Eritrea and among the employees of the Jibuti–Addis Ababa railway from the mid-1940s onwards, and the first strike was reported among railway workers in 1947. The Eritrean unions were actively involved in local politics during the federation period, and their leader, Woldeab Woldemariam, joined the ELF, but in the rest of Ethiopia they were much less prominent, and a legal framework allowing the formation of unions was not promulgated until 1962. The Confederation of Ethiopian Labour Unions, which was then formed, claimed some 80 000 members in over 160 unions by 1973, including not only urban but also plantation workers such as the employees of the Wonji Sugar Company. Regarded with some suspicion by the imperial government, they took an important part in the agitation which led to the revolution of 1974, and which was initially prompted by a strike of Addis Ababa taxi drivers.

AGRICULTURE

A limited number of themes encompass the main issues and developments in agricultural change in the Horn throughout our period. In Ethiopia, characterised by settled agriculture practised under archaic tenure systems in the northern highlands and generally exploitative ones elsewhere, the main issue was land reform; in the Somali territories, with their precarious nomadic economies, it was sedentarisation. Overlying both of these was the movement from subsistence to cash farming. Whereas in the last respect there was continuous though uneven change throughout the period, in the first two change came, with dramatic suddenness, at the end.

Commercial agriculture developed through a variety of agencies, both external and indigenous. What these had in common was a form of socio-economic organisation capable of operating a sustained commercial enterprise, combined with the essentially political ability to maintain control over a suitable area of land. The result, intriguingly, was that in both Ethiopia and the Somali region cash cropping developed on the peripheries of the locally dominant social and political groupings. In Somalia, this may obviously be ascribed in part to the ecological inadequacy of the Somali heartlands, though it may also be partly attributed to the resilience of the nomadic social structure; Somali agriculture thus developed principally among the atypical and somewhat despised Sab groups of the Shebele–Juba basin, and also in the highlands of the extreme north-west, around Hargeisa and Borama. In Ethiopia the pattern is still more striking, since the central Amhara highlands had been inhabited by arable agriculturalists for many centuries, yet remained almost entirely uncommercialised to the end of our period. One important pointer is the ability of the people of this area, comprising northern Shoa and much of the provinces of Gojjam, Wollo, Begemder and Tigre, to resist the payment of taxes, and thus the need for a cash income from which tax payments could be met; they thus avoided one of the main pressures for commercial agriculture in many parts of Africa. Equally important, peasant cultivators entrenched behind ancient systems of land tenure were able to prevent incursion by central landlords, such as happened in much of southern Ethiopia, or by foreign enterprises. Any threat to tax exemption or the land-tenure system was met by armed revolt, most clearly in the Gojjam rebellion of 1968. The areas of commercial cultivation thus formed a ring round the central highlands, from the Italian farms of Eritrea to the company plantations of the Awash valley, the coffee growing areas of the south and west, and the Humera district on the Begemder–Sudanese border.

The use of political power to generate agricultural development is most obvious in the Italian colonial plantations. Though these were founded before our period, they were revived after the war, and continued to be an important source of vegetable and dairy products in Eritrea, and of bananas in Somalia; the bananas enjoyed a protected high price market in Italy, which continued to take a very high proportion of the crop even after it had been brought under Somali state control through a National Banana Board formed in 1970. The only other important area of foreign-managed agriculture was the Awash valley in eastern Ethiopia, site of the sugar plantations of the Dutch HVA company dating from 1951, and of a British cotton plantation. Conditions in the sugar plantations, in which the Ethiopian government had a large holding, led to the formation of one of the most militant trade unions in Ethiopia, while at the same time the company, through its monopoly of the domestic sugar market, was able to secure profits amounting to some 24 per cent of turnover.[1] Elsewhere, commercialisation took place under indigenous control, though it made a very great difference whether this referred to the local peasantry or to landlords. Agriculture in the whole southern half of Ethiopia, from Harar in the east through southern Shoa to Walega in the west, was dominated by landlords, and this area produced by far the greatest part of Ethiopian exports. The land-tenure system resulted from the Ethiopian conquest in the late nineteenth and early twentieth centuries, with the granting of rights over land, which eventually became synonymous with ownership, to both high officials and individual settlers from the north; much land also remained in the hands of the emperor, and of some leading southern families. Land in southern Ethiopia continued to be alienated from the indigenous population throughout the reign of Haile Selassie, as a result both of expropriation by grasping governors, and of land grants made by the emperor as rewards for loyalty; many army officers were in this way given an economic stake in the maintenance of the regime.[2] In the southern provinces as a whole, some 50 to 55 per cent of landholdings were rented in the late 1960s, compared with less than 20 per cent in the northern highlands. These landowners naturally wished to reap a cash profit from their holdings, a goal most easily achieved in the Kaffa region by exploiting the existing wild coffee forest, and elsewhere by planting coffee, oilseeds, pulses, peppers, bananas and other crops. Coffee alone accounted for over half of Ethiopia's exports in every year from 1954 to 1972. Though attempts were made, principally by foreign-aid agencies, to encourage agricultural development by smallholders, the effect was generally to increase the payments to landlords, and, by promoting cost-effective mechanised agriculture, to promote evictions; this was the experience of the Chilalo Agricultural Development Unit run by Swedish aid in Arusi province, and a similar process of landlord control started to overtake the very rapid development of cash-crop farming at Humera on the Sudanese border.[3] The problem was recognised sufficiently for the

---

[1] Gilkes, *Dying lion*, 150-2.

[2] J. M. Cohen, 'Ethiopia after Haile Selassie: the government land factor', *African Affairs*, 1973, **72**, 289, 365-82.

[3] Gilkes, *Dying lion*, 124-31; M. Ståhl, *Ethiopia: political contradictions in agricultural development* (Stockholm, 1974).

imperial government to set up a Ministry of Land Reform in 1966, but since this was caught between the vested interests of the regime's supporters in the south and the intense hostility to central interference in land of all groups in the north, it is not surprising that it achieved little beyond some very useful survey work. The total nationalisation of land announced by the military government after the 1974 revolution was therefore greeted with enthusiasm in parts of the south, and with much greater reserve in the north, but its effects fall outside the period covered by this chapter.

In Somalia, a measure of commercialisation followed the gradual drift of nomadic herdsmen into agriculture in both north and south, but for the great majority nomadism remained the only practicable form of life, as well as one cherished for its own sake, until the great drought of the early 1970s. Drought was a recurrent danger throughout the low-lying parts of the Horn, with droughts of great severity perhaps once in a generation; in British Somaliland, 1927–8 and 1950–1 were particularly bad years. The drought which spread from north to south through the eastern part of the Horn in 1972–5 was exceptional not only for its intensity but also for the economic and political circumstances with which it coincided.[1] For the first time a major drought was seen not merely as a divinely inflicted punishment or as a catastrophe to be passively endured, but as something which governments might, and should be expected to, relieve. Moreover, it caught the two main governments of the region in very different postures. In Ethiopia, where many thousands of people died, especially in Wollo province, in 1973–4, the government greeted it with embarrassment, concealment, and then an ineffective display of imperial generosity; this picture of neglect, as it emerged from the revelations of foreign journalists, was very effectively used to discredit the monarchy during 1974. In the Somali Republic, which was worst struck in 1974–5, the military government used it as an opportunity both to appeal for foreign help, and to promote in drastic fashion its plans for sedentarisation. Destitute nomads were settled both on arable lands and – a great innovation – in fishing communities around the coast. These changes had scarcely got under way at the end of our period, and it was not yet clear whether they represented

[1] I. M. Lewis, *Abaar: the Somali drought* (London, 1975).

a temporary adjustment to the drought, or a revolutionary transformation of the nomadic self-sufficiency of traditional Somali life.

CONCLUSION

Much of the experience of the Horn during the central third of the twentieth century derived from developments which were common to the whole of Africa and, indeed, to much of the rest of the globe. The growth of population, the extension of a monetary economy geared principally to export production, the introduction of formalised educational systems and their provision of trained manpower to newly created state and private institutions whose members came in consequence to form an 'élite' superior in wealth, power and status to their fellows, were all of them familiar processes elsewhere. Rudimentary in 1940, these processes had by 1975 reached such a level that the contrast must have been staggering to any Somali or Ethiopian who had lived through the entire period, more so perhaps than in many other parts of the continent where the equivalent processes had begun earlier and continued more evenly; but in this respect the Horn may be said to have experienced no more than an accelerated form of a familiar revolution.

What was distinctive about the Horn was the absence of the colonial and post-colonial state as a mechanism for ensuring at least an administrative and to some extent also a normative continuity through a period of social and economic change. In Ethiopia and the Somali Republic, the state was not, as elsewhere, an alien framework externally imposed but subsequently accepted – indeed, largely taken for granted – as the matrix within which the various permutations of domestic political competition could be worked out. It embodied, rather, an internal and expansionist dynamic, for Somalis as the agency for achieving national unification, in Ethiopia as the expression of a central and imperial hegemony over surrounding areas, which made it part and parcel of domestic political conflict. In both countries, the takeover of the state by military regimes more clearly revolutionary than any found elsewhere in Africa was prompted – it is not too fanciful to suggest – by its failure to live up to the dynamic which was held to justify its existence. Beneath their Marxist rhetoric, both of the revolutionary governments expressed an intensified form of an existing national ideology: in the Republic that of unification, in Ethiopia that of assimilation to an essentially central conception of nationhood.

Where the two states differed from one another was in the implications of this ideology for the identities of other groups within the would-be nation. In the Somali Republic, the NRC's attempted destruction of clan identities was balanced by an emphasis on a homogenised Somali nationhood in which members of all clans had a part. In a way, the process was the reverse of that which had occurred during the period of party competition, when clan identities had been emphasised by politicians seeking support: since clans formed part of a Somali people, unified by language, literature, religion and traditional descent, neither the encouragement nor the suppression of clan directly threatened the national identity. By suppressing the clan, the NRC sought to remove an important source of domestic feuding over political and economic allocations, but because of the common Somali heritage it did not run too great a risk of popular reaction. The combined process of sedentarisation and homogenisation was indeed very similar, in a much speeded-up form, to that which had existed over a long period among the Sab groups of the Juba–Shebele basin.

Conversely in Ethiopia, just as the mobilisation of ethnic identities had been seen in the pre-revolutionary period as posing a serious threat to national unity, as was shown by the suppression of the Mecha Tulama association, so the accession of a revolutionary nationalist government in Addis Ababa prompted a localist reaction among many of the peripheral peoples. In the case of the cultivators of southern and western Ethiopia, commitment to the regime could be purchased through a policy of land nationalisation which conformed with the Derg's socialist aspirations without conflicting with its nationalist ones. Elsewhere, the policy of assimilation to the centralist ethic implicit in Ethiopian nationalism was not so easily accomplished, though its outcome at the end of the period was still extremely unclear. What was clear was that the processes of social, economic and political change in the region in the three decades after the Second World War had in many respects reinforced the tensions implicit in the make-up of the Horn.

CHAPTER 10

EGYPT, LIBYA AND THE SUDAN

Historically north-east Africa is rivalled in importance by no other region of the continent. Egypt, the focal point of this region, which also comprises Libya and the Sudan, has successively been one of the cradles of western civilisation, a major centre of Muslim culture, and in more recent times a base for Pan-Arab and Pan-Islamic resistance to political or cultural domination by the west. It was in Egypt that the first political and, more important, philosophical reaction against western tutelage in Africa took place.

Libya and the Sudan, Egypt's western and southern neighbours, have been closely linked to its destiny. This was particularly the case during our period, when the revolutionary change in Egypt that took place after the Second World War had percussive effects on the social, economic and political life of her neighbours. Historical links were reflected in similarities in the political and social sphere. The three states are predominantly Muslim and had all suffered under some form of western control, from which they only finally escaped during the period under review. They shared a background of anti-imperialist agitation and an identity with Pan-Islamism and Arab nationalism. They also experienced tensions between secular political ideologies and traditional Muslim notions of the polity. Many of these tensions were attributable to the rapid socio-economic changes taking place throughout the region but, because of the very different geographical and economic characteristics of the three states comprising it, they were varied in their nature. With a combined area of some two million square miles (*c*. five million sq. km) and a population of less than 60 million in 1975, there should have existed a very low population density. In reality, however, this was not the case, as most of the land was uninhabitable or unfit for cultivation.

Egypt, with some 40 million inhabitants, was the most populous of the three states. Although it had an area of 386 thousand square miles, only 3 per cent of the land was arable, which meant in real terms that it had one of the highest population densities in the world. Libya, although most of its 679 thousand square miles was also desert, had a population of only some two million. The Sudan, with 967 thousand square miles and a population of some 18 million, had a much more varied topography than its northern neighbours. Each differed greatly in its economic development. Libya, by far the richest of the three on account of its huge oil reserves, the impact of which was felt only after 1960, was hampered in its development by lack of population. Egypt, less favourably endowed with natural resources, especially minerals, was impeded in its economic progress by a rate of population growth that negated many of the gains made through increased industrialisation and irrigation. The Sudan remained by far the poorest region of the three.

Although the economies of the three states grew at different rates in the period 1940–75, their social effects were similar. Economic development, in particular industrialisation, stimulated both the increasing proletarisation of the urban masses and the increasing secularisation of the élite, with the polity in each case becoming increasingly polarised as a result. The development of trade unions, but more especially the growing importance of the military, joined at the level of the executive or officer class by precisely those who had been politicised and who had political experience, reflected this polarisation. From conservative Muslims to Marxists, the armies were inundated by young idealists, who wanted not only to defend the nation and the state, but also to step into the political arena. After 1952, the year of Egypt's *coup d'état*, the lines between civilian and military politics became blurred and the military eventually became the mainstay of the polity in all three states.

A further common political experience of the three countries in our period was the nature of their relations with the great powers. Although by mid-1950 they had all obtained political independence, they remained economically dependent on one or the other of the great powers, particularly the United States of America and the Union of Soviet Socialist Republics. Egypt attempted to steer a 'non-aligned' course, but failed to do so because the country needed both economic and military aid from external sources. Finally, the Palestinian problem, and the repeated wars between the Arab states and Israel left a profound, if not devastating, mark on the region. Apart from the massive human and material losses, the region on the whole was, as a result, ideologically traumatised, resulting in a period of self-criticism during which the causes of weakness and defeat were sought.

On the other hand the Israeli–Arab conflict contributed to the politicisation of the population of all three countries, and brought to power, or facilitated the emergence of, new social and political elements. Yet despite common religious and historical links and the shared struggle against colonialism and Zionism, the three states were marked by considerable political and ideological, as well as socio-economic, differences.

DECOLONISATION AND INDEPENDENCE

Egypt

The Anglo-Egyptian Treaty of 1936 had been intended both to secure Egypt as an ally of Britain in case of war because of her vital strategic position, and to assuage nationalist criticism of Britain's role in the country. Even so, the country continued to experience serious political unrest until well after the outbreak of the Second World War. Governments were frequently reshuffled, as the young and inexperienced King Fārūq (Farouk), who had only come to the throne in April 1936, attempted to exert his own authority in relation both to the ruling Wafd Party and the British High Commission by supporting radical politicians or movements. In the towns, the younger and politically articulate generation, organised into various political groups of conflicting ideological orientations – some nationalist and some ardently Islamist – battled against each other, and continued their agitation against the still considerable British military and political presence.

This political unrest reflected a growing politicisation of society, if not a nascent class conflict. Since the 1919 'revolution', and especially as a result of the depression, the socio-economic structure of the country had undergone considerable changes. During the 1920s, efforts at industrialisation had created an enlarged class of workers, as the growing numbers of trade unions indicated. More important, the nationalist movement had prompted the Egyptian bourgeoisie to invest in industry, headed

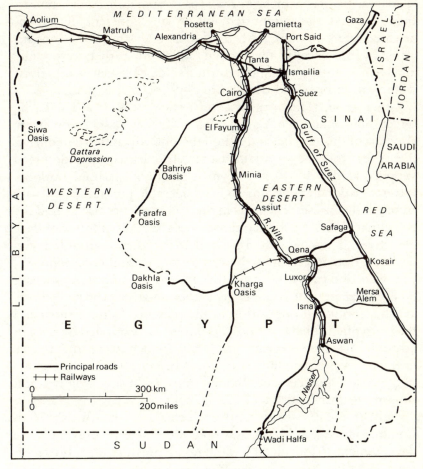

25 Egypt.

by the all-Egyptian Banque al-Misr, in order to gain greater independence from Great Britain and other foreign investors. By the early 1930s this economic nationalism also began to manifest itself in radical student groups and trade unions, which called for the boycott of foreign, and especially British, goods. Equally important at that time, and a contributing factor to the political turmoil, was the revival of Islam as a political force. To be sure this revival also took different forms – literary or economic, for instance – but its thrust was the resuscitation of pristine Islam. The political expression of this revival was the Muslim Brotherhood (al-Ikwān al-Muslimūn) headed by the popular Shaykh

Ḥassan al-Bannā', which, in the eyes of some observers, represented the first mass-supported and organised, essentially urban-oriented effort to cope with the plight of Islam in the modern world.[1] Intrinsically the Ikwān followed earlier (especially nineteenth-century) Islamic reform movements, but was activist where earlier ones had been more philosophical in nature.

Other groups and organisations, such as Miṣr al-Fatāt (the Green Shirts) and the Young Men's Muslim Association, were also part of this revival, and although politically important during the 1930s, they never attained the same degree of widespread support as Ikwān. Apart from a common Islamic outlook, extreme nationalist fervour and considerable political popularity amongst the masses, elements in these movements also shared the belief that violence was a legitimate tool for the attainment of their objectives. Thus between 1936 and 1939, when martial law was declared, riots and attempted assassinations became commonplace, and were indicative both of the underlying unrest in society, especially among the younger generation and the urban proletariat, and the continued opposition to the presence of the British and their Egyptian collaborators. This unrest was exploited by foreign powers such as Germany and Italy, which were themselves heading towards a conflict with Great Britain and France. Agents of the Fascist powers were actively engaged in soliciting political support against British and French control.

Neither the pro-British governments nor the British High Commissioner, Sir Miles Lampson, were able to prevent these developments. Considerable diplomatic pressure was, however, exerted by the British on the Wafd and the interim government at least to curtail violence, and there were fears that the British might intervene to protect their interests. In effect British threats imposed a secret and unilateral limitation on Egypt's sovereignty, which in the eyes of the British government was quite warranted. After 1936 events in Europe pointed to an international military conflict, and therefore 'imperial communications' had to be secured. Furthermore, the Middle East throughout that period was experiencing an increasingly violent nationalist reaction against Anglo-French control, especially in Palestine, Iran and Syria, which spilled over to other areas.

---

[1] For a history of the movement, see Richard P. Mitchell, *The Society of Muslim Brothers* (Oxford, 1969).

These events did not escape the notice of the more radical nationalist politicians, such as 'Alī Māhir and General 'Azīz al-Miṣrī, and their followers. It was they who turned Egypt increasingly toward its Arab neighbours by supporting Pan-Arab nationalism, and espousing a collective anti-Anglo-French stance. Although the British realised the implications of these developments, there was little that could be done other than to cajole and threaten, or in the last resort to intervene militarily, as was to be done in February 1942, an event that was only to fuel nationalist opposition further.

In August 1939, as Europe headed towards war, 'Alī Māhir, then the chief of the royal cabinet and an openly pro-Axis nationalist, was appointed prime minister after yet another government crisis. While nationalist forces were pleased, the British government was very concerned by this development, not necessarily because of Māhir's pro-Axis leanings, but on account of his association with the palace, and in particular his close ties with Shaykh al-Marāghī, the rector of Al-Azhar since 1935.[1] Al-Marāghī, a former supporter of the Wafd, had become the mentor of extreme Islamic elements, just as al-Miṣrī, then Egyptian commander-in-chief, was the inspirational leader of the extreme nationalists, especially among the young officers. Therefore it was not surprising that the rector, as well as the premier, resisted Britain's pressures on Egypt to declare war on Germany. Under the 1936 treaty, Egypt appeared to have had an obligation to do just that, but other than the declaration of martial law, the government refused to comply. At the same time the premier began to implement several important new policies. A territorial army (al-Jaysh al-Murābiṭ) was created, headed by 'Abd al-Raḥmān 'Azīz, as well as a Social Affairs Ministry, whose establishment had been repeatedly demanded by nationalists. In effect this brought into being an armed force outside the control of the British military mission. Moreover, the Ministry of War was given to another pro-Axis and staunch pan-Islamic sympathiser, Ṣāliḥ Ḥarb. The composition of the cabinet, therefore, augured ill for British interests, but appeared to reflect popular opinion. In terms of Egypt's foreign relations, it was significant that the premier visited the Sudan – the first Egyptian premier to do so – in 1940, thereby emphasising

---

[1] For a closer study of 'Alī Māhir's role in the crisis and his relations with the palace, see P. J. Vatikiotis, *Nasser and his generation* (London, 1978).

Egypt's rights in the area. Great Britain objected vehemently to this initiative.

In these circumstances the Wafd, fearful of losing its popularity, published a manifesto in April 1940. Whilst appearing to provide an alternative to the government's nationalist position by taking an anti-British stance, in reality it did little more than insist upon Egypt's political independence. It implicitly offered cooperation with the British in return for more satisfactory concessions in post-war Anglo-Egyptian relations. The Wafd tried to capitalise on Britain's precarious position in Egypt while at the same time exploiting the angry mood of the peasants and urban poor who were suffering under wartime economic restrictions and the generally abject economic situation. Cotton exports, the principal source of foreign income, had already been severely curtailed. During the war, real income and production per capita fell to the lowest levels recorded in the twentieth century. Further internal dissatisfaction and a growing mood of rebellion were the result. Even before 'Alī Māhir's and al-Miṣrī's removal by the British in the spring of 1940, the Ikwān and Young Egypt Party (known as the National Islamic Party – al-Ḥizb al-Waṭanī al-Islamī – from 1940), as well as many of the radical young officers, were said to have even contemplated a revolution, or at least a *coup d'état*.[1] 'Alī Māhir's dismissal was followed by two ineffective cabinets, both headed by independents who attempted to steer a course of neutrality. Meanwhile the Wafd was waiting in the wings to take power. This moment arrived in February 1942 after the military situation had deteriorated, and when the Axis forces were on the verge of conquering Egypt. With her own interests in Egypt about to collapse, Britain decided to intervene directly by presenting an ultimatum to the king demanding that Naḥḥās Pasha, the leader of the Wafd Party, should immediately form a cabinet, and backing this up with the threat of armed force.

The February 4 incident of 1942, as it became known, constituted a turning point in the annals of Egyptian as well as Arab history. Years later, after the July coup of 1952, Gamal 'Abd al-Nāṣir, Anwār Sādāt and General Nagīb (Neguib) were to declare that this event, together with the subsequent disarming of the Egyptian military, was a root cause of their determination to overthrow Fārūq's regime and rid the country of the British

[1] Vatikiotis, *Nasser.*

military presence. Equally important, and politically of particular consequence at the time, was the discrediting of the Wafd Party because of its alliance with British interests and the resulting growth in revolutionary elements, especially the left-wing ones, though most of them had of course to operate underground. As a result of the wartime situation Egyptian society was thus even further polarised, with these new socio-economic and political forces undermining the already important liberal—bourgeois parliamentary institutions. Moreover, the Wafd, placed in power with the help of the British, was increasingly estranged from both the palace and the extreme nationalist and Islamic forces.

Although the Wafd regime introduced legislation, such as a new budget, the suspension of penalties for hoarders, the introduction of agricultural subsidies and the legalisation of Arabic as the official language, all of which were intended as palliatives to the masses, it failed to recognise the need for land reform. Meanwhile, extreme nationalists, including General ʿAzīz al-Miṣrī, maintained contacts with the Axis powers. Those known to be publicly pro-Axis were either interned or politically isolated. Between 1943 and 1945 the struggle between the pro-palace factions and the Wafd continued, leading to internal party divisions and accusations of corruption. On 9 October 1944 the king dismissed Naḥḥās Pasha, undoubtedly in part as revenge for the February 4 incident, and appointed Aḥmad Māhir as prime minister. Aḥmad Māhir, the brother of ʿAlī, headed a group of former Wafdists, known as the Saʿadists, who had urged Egypt to declare war on the Fascists and who favoured progressive reforms at home. General elections were held in early 1945, but the Wafd boycotted them and many members transferred their support either to the Saʿadists or to the liberals. As a result the Saʿadists won their largest victory ever, gaining 42 per cent of the popular vote, while the liberals gained 24.1 per cent. However, in February 1945, when Egypt finally declared war on Germany, Premier Aḥmad Māhir was assassinated. He was succeeded by Maḥmūd Fahmī al-Nuqrāshī, another Saʿadist. The death of Māhir, unlike his brother a noted liberal, signalled a new wave of political violence and assassinations.

Despite the political vicissitudes that followed on the February 4 incident, the Wafd had initiated one important, and ultimately momentous, policy. Throughout the latter part of the 1930s it had become increasingly apparent that the radical elements supported Pan-Arabism. Until then their principal concern had been Egyptian nationalism, but with the unfolding of the Palestinian crisis, and Iraq's apparent championship of the Arab cause as 'the most independent' of Arab countries, Egypt also embraced Pan-Arabism. Throughout the war it became clear, even to the British, that some sort of regional organisation was needed, if nothing else, to channel growing Pan-Arabist sentiment. Thus, after prolonged negotiations, the Alexandria Protocol was signed in October 1944 and became the basis for the establishment of the Arab League. Significantly, Cairo became the seat of the organisation.

The years following the war up to the coup of 1952 saw the rapid disintegration of the Egyptian polity. With the Wafd out of power, the various splinter groups dissipated their political energies on inter-party squabbles, with none of them able to rule the country effectively. The Ikwān and radical nationalists on the right were confronted by considerably strengthened left-wing organisations, especially the trade unions. This was in line with the general trend in the Arab world in which the Soviet Union had gained exposure and some popularity, and in which leftist literature had become increasingly available. Among the more important of the left-wing groups was the National Committee of Workers and Students, founded early in 1945.

It was this popularly supported movement that was largely responsible for the mass demonstrations against the British and the government, such as the large-scale riots and demonstrations of February 1946, during which scores of people were killed. As a consequence Nuqrāshī's government was forced to resign. After further political violence Ismāʿīl Ṣidqī Pasha, who formed the new government, dissolved many of the left-wing organisations and ordered the arrest of many of their leaders in July 1946.

Political unrest did not abate. With the left suppressed, the right-wing political parties continued the struggle against the British and the government. A wave of assassinations followed, to which many prominent political figures fell victim. As a result frequent changes of cabinets and governments became a feature of the period; between 1945 and 1950 there were no less than seven different administrations. Against this background of disintegration, the radicalisation of practically all political forces, and the disastrous Palestine war of 1948–9, which not only exposed the weakness of the Arab armies, but clearly revealed the level of Egyptian domestic corruption and political decay, the Egyptian army prepared itself for a *coup d'état*. Two important political trends were now crystallised. One was the growth of leftist organisations, and the other the development of an 'Arab-Islamic dimension of nationalist agitation', which was to provide the basis of Gamal Nāṣir's programme. This programme, as Professor Vatikiotis has noted, was more amenable to exploitation by various political groups because it was more easily understood and more readily adhered to emotionally by the masses than an already discredited, complex, and essentially alien, constitutional democracy.[1]

The most important issues in the immediate post-war period, then, were the very nature of the country's political institutions, the growing poverty of the masses, the need for social and economic reform, and above all Britain's continued colonial role in the country. This last issue was focussed in the eyes of the masses on Egypt's claims in the Anglo-Egyptian Sudan. While Egypt insisted on the unity of the Nile Valley, Britain refused to acknowledge that Egypt had anything more than a nominal interest in the Sudan. After the disputed outcome of the Anglo-Egyptian negotiations in 1946, the matter was referred to the United Nations, which did not resolve the issue.

Egypt in this period was thus clearly heading towards a crisis that successive governments had done little more than postpone. None of the social and economic reforms they introduced constituted significant change. In 1950 the Wafd returned to power with a majority in parliament. In order to appease the urban proletariat and the peasants, several labour laws and land-reform acts were passed; none, however, increased the party's popularity sufficiently for the government to rule effectively. Nor were the radical nationalists appeased by the unilateral and sudden abrogation of the 1936 treaty in October 1951, after renegotiations had failed and the western powers had attempted to enlist Egypt into an anti-Soviet defence alliance. Indeed the nationalists saw this as a political victory over the old leadership of the upper bourgeoisie, and intensified their struggle against Britain, especially in the Canal Zone.

[1] Vatikiotis, *Nasser*; see also his *The modern history of Egypt* (London, 1969).

Early in 1952 the political crisis came to a head when British troops clashed with Egyptian police units in an attempt to take control of Government House in Ismailia, and killed over 50 policemen. In the following days, amidst strikes, mass demonstrations and a government threat to establish 'friendship ties' with the USSR, the centre of Cairo went up in flames. While it has never been established for certain who the arsonists were, several members of the Green Shirts and other extreme nationalist organisations were arrested and tried. Once again a revolutionary situation had arisen. Six months later, after continuous and ineffective government reshuffles, the Free Officers acted. On 23 July 1952, after four more governments, and after a futile attempt by the king to control the officers, the army seized power. A few days later King Fārūq was exiled.

The membership of the Free Officers' movement, ostensibly led by the grandfatherly and popular General Muḥammad Nagīb, who conveniently lent the young officers political legitimacy, was indicative of the ideological fragmentation of the Egyptian polity. Many of them had at one time or another been associated with radical groups of all the ideological persuasions.[1] In later years these early political commitments were reflected in their style of leadership as well as in their economic policies. In the initial phase of the 'revolution', however, the Free Officers did not follow any particular ideological orientation other than nationalism, vague notions of social egalitarianism and justice, as well as Islamic piety. In fact, the coup initially represented a rebellion by frustrated (and defeated) young officers who in the main came from the 'reasonably affluent middle class'.

The 'Revolutionary Command Council' appointed a temporary cabinet, headed by none other than 'Alī Māhir, complemented by two other extreme nationalist and erstwhile Green Shirt leaders, Fatḥī Riḍwān and Dr Nūr al-Dīn Ṭarrāf. The regime was primarily bourgeois nationalist in character, as was indicated by the suppression of all Communist as well as extremist Islamic and ultra-nationalist factions, such as the Green Shirts, by then known as the Islamic Socialist Party. Obviously the officers did not feel sufficiently secure to permit the existence of opposition parties, let alone involve them in the government of Egypt, as they

---

[1] Additional biographical material on the Free Officers is available in A. Abdel-Malek, *Égypte: société militaire* (Paris, 1962).

themselves were politically divided over their principal objectives. Instead, the council contented itself with seeking new solutions to old problems: for instance, what form of political institutions should the Republic adopt? Before the commissions that were convened to supply solutions could submit their findings, all parties were banned in January 1953, and replaced by a popular 'Liberation Rally', the first of three attempts by the Free Officers to mobilise mass political support. While they enjoyed widespread popularity, both inside and outside Egypt, there existed in many quarters and among some elements of the army considerable disquiet, mainly over the position of General Nagīb, but also over the shape of future political institutions and the nature of the polity itself. In the spring of 1954, in order to placate the opposition, the Revolutionary Command Council (RCC) lifted the ban on parties and decided to hold a general election. This decision, however, divided the council, and had even elicited some public opposition, mainly from the trade unions. As a result the RCC felt justified in purging the supporters of the *ancien régime*, both among officers and members of the public. With the exclusion of the Ikwān this process was therefore completed. However, the Ikwān's continued opposition to the military regime found its expression in its attempted assassination of Nāṣir in late 1954, with the result that it was driven underground, and all remaining opposition elements banned.

Despite the banning of opposition to the new regime, the success of the 'revolution' had not been assured, as the leadership was beset by rivalries within and continued public disturbances without. Even the soldiers were divided in their loyalties. In the end it was Lt-Colonel Gamal 'Abd al-Nāṣir and his supporters who succeeded in establishing effective leadership. Nāṣir, born in January 1918, was a shrewd, studious and reserved officer who had planned and led the coup. After the event he emerged as the most powerful among the original eleven conspirators. Only Nagīb, who enjoyed massive popular acclaim as a hero of the 1948–9 war with Israel, and who, in contrast to the officers, appeared moderate in his approach, overshadowed Nāṣir. Moreover, Nagīb favoured a return to parliamentary politics, which brought him into direct conflict with the 'revolutionary' officers. Consequently he was placed under house arrest in November 1954 and Nāṣir emerged as leader of Egypt.

Yet, while Nāṣir succeeded in eliminating opposition within the ruling circles and in the public arena, the 'young officers' still lacked popular legitimacy. Although in September 1952 the Agrarian Reform Law had been implemented and some modest egalitarian measures (anti-corruption laws, rent control, etc.) had been decreed, it was apparent that the officers had few, if any, precise economic or political objectives. If anything, it was the retention of power which was their main concern. The removal of General Nagīb in November 1954 was a major step in this direction.

The year 1955, therefore, proved to be of critical importance, as the 'young officers' set out to consolidate their control. Political events in the region came to their aid. Having just successfully concluded the negotiations with Great Britain about the withdrawal of British forces from Egypt, it was impossible for Nāṣir's government to join a western-sponsored defence alliance, the so-called Baghdad Pact, which Iraq and Turkey had agreed to enter. In any case the Anglo-Egyptian Treaty of 1954 provided for the return of British troops in case of global hostilities. Moreover, this NATO-related security arrangement was, in the eyes of the Egyptian regime, designed to maintain western hegemony in the area. For Egypt, western interests in the Nile Valley and the Sinai had always been a thorn in the flesh. Apart from nationalist and anti-imperialist sympathies, Egyptian leaders were keenly aware of the strategic importance of their country, a fact repeatedly stressed by history as well as by contemporary Western European politicians and military leaders. As the drama in Palestine unfolded and as Islamic-cum-nationalist forces challenged western colonial interests, and as Zionist forces succeeded in establishing a state of Israel, Egypt, as the most populous, powerful and economically advanced Arab state in the region, assumed its leadership. It was for this reason that the Arab League headquarters had been situated in Cairo, and that the new 'revolutionary' leaders of Egypt now assumed such a forceful role in Middle Eastern relations with the super-powers. In such circumstances a direct security arrangement with the western powers was anathema.

This rejection was taken as a serious and unacceptable rebuff by the partners in the western alliance and had serious implications for Egypt, as the west now held up the supply of arms and restricted the financial and other aid so urgently needed by the regime to carry out its plans for modernisation. During this period of worsening relations with the west, the government continued with the consolidation of its power base.

On 16 January 1956 a presidential republican system was instituted. The constitution formally linked Egypt to the Arab nation, and for the first time provided for sustained economic planning. The constitution was approved, and the Liberation Rally was replaced by the National Union, the only legal political organisation. The president broadened his new government by including a greater number of civilians and also removed several officers from the regime, including Anwār al-Sādāt.

Apart from the international pressures faced by Nāṣir, and the inability to secure large financial aid from the western powers for his development schemes, in particular the Aswan High Dam project, the government's most pressing problem internally remained economic development. Population growth had overtaken economic growth and it had become clear that Egypt must rapidly industrialise. With the end of the Korean war and the resultant slump in cotton exports, the country's already unfavourable trade balance became worse. It was for these reasons, and the growing association with the socialist countries, that the government became increasingly attracted to the notion of a socialist, or rather a planned, economy.

During the first three years of the revolution the old capitalist economy was permitted to function, mainly by default, as the Free Officers had little, if any, particular economic philosophy to hand when they seized power. While aware of the inequities existing in society, and driven by a fair amount of idealism, they had few practical answers. Marxism, moreover, was anathema to the regime and remained so even during the heyday of Arab socialism, despite the fact that throughout the 1930s and 1940s a considerable amount of Marxist literature had circulated in Egypt. The Land Reform Act, for example, was introduced not from any socialist idealism, but from a utilitarian recognition that liberation of the peasants was a prerequisite to continued industrial expansion.

If internal reforms and revolutionary aspirations constituted one element of Nāṣir's political and ideological aspirations, it was in the realm of foreign policy that he had some of his greatest successes. Unable to obtain financial support from the United

States for its development schemes, and unable to secure Western European support, the Egyptian government decided on a radical departure from past practices: it negotiated military and other aid from the eastern-bloc countries. Thus, when the Cold War was at its height, Egypt, potentially the most powerful and cohesive Middle Eastern Arab nation, chose to take this radical alternative course. The former regional colonial powers, Great Britain and France, and the recently established Israel, reacted by intervening militarily in 1956. This proved to be counter-effective.

Egypt's armed forces, ostensibly defeated, were rescued by international condemnation, principally from the USA and the USSR, and this forced the tripartite alliance to withdraw. Gamal 'Abd al-Nāṣir, as a result, emerged as a strong anti-imperialist and as the leader of Middle Eastern Arab–Islamic radical forces. After the Suez war, therefore, and in the context of Nāṣir's anti-imperialist crusade and his emergence as the Pan-Arab leader, his ideas assumed more substance and moved towards an Arab nationalism concerned not only with political unity, but with a socialist-inspired economic development plan. By the turn of the decade Egypt had become the leading exponent of Arab socialism. It is this achievement of Nāṣir's leadership, apart from his instilling a sense of purpose and a modern Egyptian identity into his people, for which the revolution must be noted. While many of these programmes either failed or did not meet expectations, they nevertheless constituted a marked and radical departure from previous economic and political attitudes.

The power of the bourgeoisie – and especially the landowners and foreign property-owners – was curtailed, if not destroyed. The attacks on foreigners and the sequestration of their property, especially after the 1956 Suez war, proved to be in many cases counter-productive, as their skills and services could not easily be replaced. Indeed, it has been argued that their departure left a great economic vacuum. Thus, while the Land Reform Law was little more than a political gesture, which had instantaneously popularised the regime amongst the peasants, the end of the decade witnessed the serious implementation of industrial development plans. Moreover, by 1960 the most powerful economic institutions began to be nationalised. Banking, transport, and even the Press (for obvious political reasons that had little to do with economics) were taken over by the state. Trade unions, which until then were an important source of political support – or opposition – were reduced in number and streamlined in organisation. In 1960 the first five-year development plan was instituted, and two years later, Nāṣir decided on a total reorganisation of the state. In May 1962, earlier trends were formalised with the promulgation of the 'National Charter', which aimed at a comprehensive restructuring of the political institutions and the economy of the country. The principal political party, the National Union, was abolished and replaced by the Arab Socialist Union. This was to consist of representatives from all strata of society. A new National Assembly was established. Essentially the political reorganisation provided for a mass party (the ASU) whose purpose was primarily to mobilise the masses in the service of the revolution and within the framework of the charter, while the state was run through a presidential system with sweeping powers legitimised by the National Assembly. The new constitution came into effect in March 1964.

While the country was moving into a new era, with hopes of some political stability and economic progress, regional events were once again determining Egypt's course. The president enjoyed considerable internal support until 1967, despite his repressive measures against political dissidents, but he found himself rapidly losing his Pan-Arab leadership. Moreover, Egypt was involved in a war in the Yemen, aimed at the eventual overthrow of all monarchical regimes in the peninsula, and this was draining the country's resources severely, even though the Soviet Union provided financial assistance. Several new power centres had arisen in the area to challenge Nāṣir's position during the 1960s as a leader of radical Pan-Arab thought and socio-economic reform. As a cardinal advocate of radical policies, he was attacked by Syria, Iraq, Saudi Arabia, and other countries, each representing diverse traditional and financial interests which had developed alternative political philosophies. Moreover, their nationalism was taking the increasingly virulent anti-Israeli position which since 1948 had become the hallmark of Arab nationalism. Nāṣir's attempt to reassert his authority brought him into conflict with Israel, which reacted by launching a pre-emptive air strike in June 1967 (see below). The resultant débâcle caused an upheaval of unprecedented proportions in the Arab world. Self-criticism and self-denigration followed. The roots of the whole Egyptian political system were threatened, and although Nāṣir offered to resign, the masses, whether by government orchestration or as a result of his charisma, recalled him.

In order to reassert his authority, Nāṣir ordered the reconstruction of the armed forces and especially the security machinery. He took direct control of all the principal ministries and instituted a virtual dictatorship. However, despite an attempted coup, Nāṣir survived, only to die of a heart attack in late September 1970. In the last three years of his rule, Nāṣir was mainly concerned with the maintenance of power, the rearming of the military and the search for a way out of the Arab–Israeli impasse. Meanwhile, the economic progress that had been made came to a standstill, with many factories closing down. Political demoralisation had set in, as was indicated by the irrepressible public criticism and rioting that followed the war. What became increasingly evident after 1967 was the priority given by the Egyptian leadership and people to Egyptian interests, even when these were clearly in conflict with Pan-Arab ideals.

Nāṣir had made no provisions for a successor. The Soviet Union, taken by surprise and unable to push forward a successor of its own choice, backed the compromise candidate, Vice-President Anwār al-Sādāt, who until then had lived in the shadow of power without any real and meaningful political duties – even his office as vice-president had been devoid of influence. The ensuing power struggle was mainly conducted behind the scenes. The divisions were along ideological lines. Some argued for continued association with the Soviet Union, others veered to the west, while a third group adopted an 'Egypt first' attitude, stressing the need for economic development. In order to consolidate his power, Sādāt continued his predecessor's policy, and only later began the 'demythologisation' of Nāṣir. Furthermore, he continued to pay lip service to Arab unity by signing an Agreement of Unity with Syria and Libya in April 1971. This he did without consulting the ASU or the National Assembly. And though there was opposition to this move, he had the support of the army, especially of General Ṣādiq. In May 1971 Sādāt neutralised his opponents by accusing them of plotting against the regime, thus establishing grounds for their dismissal and subsequent trial. He further secured his position by signing a Treaty of Friendship with the Soviet Union to ensure its support.

Yet discontent continued. The late 1960s and early 1970s were marked by a growing resentment against the regime as well as the Soviet Union. While Egypt's military and financial dependence on the eastern bloc precluded an immediate and abrupt break in relations, and although Sādāt appointed a vaguely pro-Moscow Prime Minister, 'Azīz Ṣidqī, he simultaneously developed contacts with the United States and with conservative states in the Arabian Gulf, especially Saudi Arabia. To demonstrate the intention of Egypt's new foreign policy – and to gain support from the anti-socialist elements within the country – Sādāt slowly initiated the *infitāḥ* (open door) economic policy, and expelled all Soviet advisers in July 1972. This move placated the military, who had become resentful of Soviet influence which had been in opposition to further military operations against Israel, an attitude based on an underestimation of Arab military capabilities as well as a desire to maintain a position of détente with the United States. The expulsion of the Russians also opened the way for urgent financial assistance from friendly rich Arab states and from the west.

Despite these changes in policy, including internal reforms – such as a new constitution in September 1971 followed by referendums and an election – designed to break with the past and to provide Sādāt with popular support, domestic opposition grew dramatically. Student riots throughout 1972 and early 1973 indicated opposition from the left as well as from conservative elements, while the historic differences between Muslims and Copts also reappeared. Opposition to Sādāt's regime stemmed not only from economic grievances, and the dismantling of socialism, but also from the widespread mood of hopelessness and impotence that resulted from the 1967 war. The public appeared to demand the resolution of the 'no peace, no war' stalemate. Against these internal pressures, Egypt with Syria decided to initiate an offensive against Israel.

The euphoria that followed the October 1973 (Ramadan) war and the resulting restoration of national pride were, however, insufficient to offset continued internal unrest. Western investments were not forthcoming as rapidly as expected, inflation was rampant (at least 25–30 per cent per annum) and the obvious re-emergence of the bourgeoisie (especially in Cairo and Alexandria) despite the government's declared intention of establishing a 'socialist' economy, gave rise to further strikes and riots throughout 1974 and early 1975. In consequence the government was reshuffled, and some salary increases were announced, mainly for civil servants. Despite these problems Sadat was able to maintain control of the situation and, in 1976, was re-elected president for a further term of six years though he did not complete it, being assassinated the year before it was to end.

The Sudan

The Sudan had been administered as a joint Anglo-Egyptian condominium since 1899. After 1924, when Britain forced the evacuation of Egyptian troops from the Sudan, Egypt had ceased to be an effective partner in the administration of the country. The Anglo-Egyptian Treaty of 1936, while confirming the condominium, merely restored to Egypt a façade of power, the reins of the government still being tightly held by the British. This formal reinstatement of Egypt as joint, if very junior, partner in the condominium did, however, permit Sudanese nationalists to play on Anglo-Egyptian differences to promote their own cause. It is in this context that all major political developments from 1940 up until independence must be seen.

In 1939, in the aftermath of the treaty, the educated élite formed their first political organisation, the Graduates' General Congress, which ostensibly proposed to 'assist the government in the progressive planning of the development of the country'. The congress became a political forum for both the educated élite and the different religious sects, an alliance which began to break up after 1940 as factions evolved into political parties.

As in Libya and Egypt, the outbreak of the Second World War and north-east Africa's involvement therein (by virtue of Italian and British confrontation in the area) stiffened nationalist resolve to attain self-determination. Egyptian Premier 'Alī Māhir's staunch nationalist position undoubtedly encouraged the congress, especially after his visit to the Sudan in February 1940. Two years later, in April 1942, and undoubtedly influenced by Britain's extremely precarious political and military situation in Egypt, the congress sent the Sudan government a memorandum of its

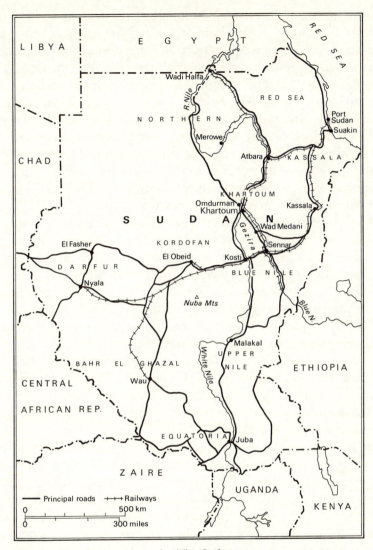

26   The Sudan.

political demands, namely self-determination and the right to
political expression. It also recognised – as a sign of appeasement –
Egypt's natural rights in the Sudan.

This latter demand was particulary significant since Egypt still
intended to advance its claim over the Sudan, and initially had
been hostile to the congress; but the war situation had spurred
on Pan-Arab sympathies, and Sudanese nationalists recognised the

importance of political and nationalist cooperation against the British. Sir Douglas Newbold, the Civil Secretary, further exacerbated the situation by his outright rejection of their demands. This was interpreted by many as a deliberate snub to the emerging Sudanese political élite. While, in private, British officials attempted to deprecate Newbold's policy, the political damage had been done. Not only were the nationalists incensed, but the congress's division deepened. One group, composed mostly of senior civil servants, was led by Ibrāhīm Aḥmad, the president of the congress and a tutor at Gordon College. It was willing to cooperate with the government and to await the conclusion of the war for political concessions. As such it constituted the basis for the Umma Party established in 1945. The other major group, led by Ismā'īl al-Azharī, also a tutor at the college and ex-president of the congress, formed the Unity Front, comprising hardliners who sought Egyptian support in order to exploit the differences between the condominium powers. This political division between those prepared to cooperate with the British administration in their quest for self-government, and those who sought Egyptian support even at the cost of eventual unification based on the old call for unity of the Nile Valley, was reflected in the principal sectarian and confessional conflict within the country. On the one hand were the Mahdists, or the *anṣar* as the Madhī had called his supporters, led by Sayyid 'Abd al-Raḥmān al-Mahdī, who gave their support to the Umma Party. On the other were their long-standing religious and political rivals, the members of the Khatmiyya *tarīqa*, who gave their support to the Ashiqqā' (Brothers) established by al-Azharī. The Ashiqqā' was effectively the first political party to be founded in the Sudan. The Ashiqqā' and their Khatmiyya supporters feared the establishment of a Mahdist-dominated state in the Sudan, especially one supported by the British. They therefore looked to Egypt for backing, though not always for the same reasons. Furthermore, these groups incorporated other diverse political factions, such as the unionists, socialists, and neo-Islamists, with little ideological homogeneity except their opposition to the British administration. In effect, however, these political groupings fragmented the already divided country further, or at least reinforced existing divisions.

Despite its rejection of the congress memorandum of 1942, the

Sudan government was still anxious to associate Sudanese with the administration of their country and to assuage the demands of the nationalists in a manner that was compatible with its own conception of the pace at which self-government should be achieved. Thus in 1944 an advisory council for the Northern Sudan was instituted, which consisted of 28 members to represent economic, social and professional interests. Eighteen others were elected or appointed from the provincial councils. The council, though able to discuss a wide range of issues, had only advisory powers. In itself an important development, the body was nevertheless widely criticised within and outside the Sudan. The extreme nationalists objected to its limited power and representation (especially the exclusion of the Southern Sudan), while Egypt considered it a threat to its own claims over the Sudan. In consequence the Ashiqqā' boycotted the advisory council, and throughout the remaining period of the war effective political activities were stifled by the emergency conditions.

With the conclusion of the war and the lifting of martial law, both Egypt and the Sudan witnessed a resurgence of nationalist agitation, resulting in the renegotiation of the Anglo-Egyptian Treaty of 1936, which necessarily had to deal with the Sudan. Thus in 1946, when the negotiations took place, a Sudanese delegation attempted to exert pressure on both Egypt and Great Britain by representing its nationalist cause in Cairo. It was, however, unsuccessful, since its members failed to agree on a common policy, a reflection of the political and religious differences within the delegation. Nevertheless, two important political successes were achieved. One was the British declaration admitting the Sudan's right to self-determination and to the establishment of further institutions of self-government. The second was the Sudan Administrative Conference held in Juba in June 1946, which effectively drew the south of the country into the process of political development. This was significant, as the south, economically and politically, had hitherto been isolated from the rest of the country under what was known as 'the Southern policy'. Thus the conference constituted an important, although belated, step toward the unification of the country.

If at this time the future looked brighter, it soon became clear that the struggle had just commenced. The Ashiqqā' boycotted the 1946 conference. Egypt, then under the premiership of Ṣidqī

Pasha, continued to insist on 'the unity of the Nile Valley', and thus repudiated the principle of self-determination for the Sudan. The problem was, therefore, once again shelved for future consideration. Only the proposals for a national legislature put up jointly by the Umma Party and the British (but opposed by the Ashiqqā') proceeded satisfactorily, even though there were some delays. In June 1948 the Sudan government, despite Egypt's opposition, established the new assembly. Consisting of 85 members, the majority of whom were drawn from the north, it became responsible for legislation in most domestic affairs, including the relations between the Sudan government and the condominium powers. Dominated by the Umma Party, the Legislative Assembly generally followed Britain's position, while the radical elements were increasingly driven to the fringe of the political spectrum.

In 1950, when once again the Anglo-Egyptian relationship was being renegotiated, renewed domestic unrest broke out in the Sudan, led mainly by the Ashiqqā', who attacked the assembly as a pawn of the British. These riots were effective insofar as they contributed to bringing about the revision of the rules governing the election of the assembly. Meanwhile, true to tradition, the Anglo-Egyptian talks were aborted and King Fārūq proclaimed the 'unity of the Nile Valley under the Egyptian Crown'. Shortly thereafter, in late 1951, the Egyptian Premier, Naḥḥās Pasha, announced the abrogation of the 1899 and 1936 agreements. Thus the three parties had arrived at another deadlock, which was only resolved after the Egyptian army coup of July 1952.

The new Egyptian regime, ostensibly led by General Nagīb, himself half-Sudanese, adopted a considerably more flexible attitude towards the Sudan question. It accepted the Self-Government Statute for the Sudan which had been enacted by the Umma-dominated Legislative Assembly in April 1952, as well as full Sudanisation of the administration within three years. In January 1953, Egypt and Britain arrived at a formal agreement of independence for the Sudan. However, the agreement was also criticised as being too hasty and for aggravating the political situation in the country, as it only dealt with structural and administrative issues. It did not account for the basic problems of the country, such as inter-ethnic hostilities, minority rights,

DECOLONISATION AND INDEPENDENCE

socio-economic development and the role of the religious orders. Consequently, the nationalist movement was further polarised.

Probably because the Ashiqqā' represented a wide spectrum of radical opinion, under the new name of the National Unionist Party (NUP), it won the elections of 1953, and al-Azharī was brought to power. In the lower and upper houses provided for by the new constitution the NUP won a majority of 50 and 31 seats respectively; the Umma Party obtained 23 and 8 seats, with the other four parties holding 24 and 7 seats.

To the surprise of the Egyptians al-Azharī followed a policy of complete independence instead of union with Egypt. The new democratic Sudanese regime feared Egyptian domination, especially after the ousting of Nagīb in 1954. Some writers argue that the historic animosity between the Mahdists and the Egyptians, which culminated in a bloody clash in March 1954 during Nagīb's state visit to open the Sudanese parliament, persuaded the Unionists to change their minds and to declare the Sudan independent in a joint session of the two houses in December 1955. A month earlier (at the request of the Sudan government) British troops had been evacuated and a plebiscite had approved independence. But al-Azharī's government was weak, rent as it was by personality conflicts and political disagreements. The strong Khatmiyya faction in the NUP seceded from it, forming the People's Democratic Party (PDP) in June 1956. The growing political unrest culminated in a 'holy alliance' between the Mahdist Umma Party and the Khatmiyya PDP, which replaced al-Azharī's government in July 1956, and elected 'Abd Allah Khalīl, the Secretary-General of the Umma Party and a participant in different British schemes for self-rule, as prime minister. The educated élite had succeeded, through playing on differences of the political powers, in attaining independence but, on the eve of that independence, the religious orders had gained the ascendancy. Confessional disputes and political factionalism were not the only problems faced by the new government in the Sudan. Another major difficulty concerned the north–south division within the country, in which the predominantly Christian southerners were pitted against the largely Islamic–Arab population of the north. From 1955 to 1972, when the Addis Ababa Agreement was signed, the Sudan was rent with violent conflict that degenerated into civil war, leaving hundreds of thousands homeless and the economy in ruins.

Although British policy toward the south had taken a dramatic turn at the time of the Juba conference, the effects of 'the Southern policy' could not be reversed overnight. The policy, which had deliberately involved massive population transfers and a purposeful destruction of the southern economy, had left the two halves of the country artificially divided. While British administrators later realised the futility of such a plan (which had been aimed at creating a 'buffer' state in the south that could later be linked to British dependencies in East Africa), the enmity and hatred which it had created between the two groups remained, and the negotiations over independence, which the southerners felt had been conducted without their full participation, further fanned the flames of bitterness. In August 1955 the government's decision to move southern soldiers from the Equatoria Corps to the north, and the dispatch of northern troops to the south, led to a mutiny by members of the corps that rapidly spread to the districts of Juba, Yei, Yambio and Maridi. Although it was quickly suppressed, the violence left 261 northerners and some 75 southerners dead.[1] Scores of soldiers from the corps subsequently refused to lay down their arms and fled into the forests, from whence they began sporadic resistance.

In Khartoum, the political changes in the post-independence period were not accompanied by any violent political confrontation or bloody take-overs of power. The two successful coups in 1958 and 1969 were peaceful, and these confrontations concerned clashes between personalities, and among the political groups in which the religious orders with their vast number of adherents were by far the most influential element. It appeared that the powers of the various religious orders were almost equal, and that balancing compromises and shifting coalitions among them were necessary for the continuity of the system. That is why coalitions were a symptom of Sudanese political life after independence.

Instability was, in part, a consequence of the failure of successive governments to achieve sufficient social and economic transformation to appease the different groups in the towns,

---

[1] Mohammad Omer Beshir, *The Southern Sudan: background to conflict*, 2nd ed. (Khartoum, 1970), 73.

especially the workers, whose demands for social equality, economic development and political participation continued to threaten the fragile politico-sectarian balance. The most important upshot of this instability was Khalīl's 'invitation' to the army to seize power. Khalīl's government not only found it increasingly difficult to secure a majority in parliament for its legislation, but also faced a growing economic crisis, border disputes with Egypt in 1957, and dissensions with its PDP coalition partner – especially after the spring 1958 election – because of their disagreement over the acceptance of American aid. Furthermore, the south began to assert its political power in parliament by siding with the NUP. Khalīl's government faced defeat over the aid issue in parliament, and it was believed that the government would also lose to a vote of no confidence scheduled for 17 November 1958. That morning, therefore, the Sudan found itself under its first military regime, though it was not the first attempt by the army to intervene in politics. In 1957 a military plot had been uncovered and its leaders dismissed or demoted. Among them were 'Abd al-Raḥmān Keibeida and Ja'fer Numayrī, who was to become Sudanese president in 1969 after leading a second coup.

From the outset the military regime tried to follow a policy of compromise, although it dissolved parliament and banished parties. Made up from senior ranks in the army and led by General 'Abbūd, head of the army, the new regime accepted American aid on the one hand and, on the other, appeased Nāṣir by concluding a Nile Waters Agreement in 1959 which favoured the Egyptian side. Yet, despite these apparent successes, the government became a victim of dissent within the ruling military junta. Major-General Aḥmad 'Abd al-Waḥhāb, a strong supporter of the Umma Party, and Brigadier Ḥasan Bashīr Nāṣir, with Khatmiyya affiliations, fell out with their colleagues. This resulted in 'Abd al-Waḥhāb's dismissal and the appointment of three new members to the junta; Brigadiers Muhyī al-Dīn 'Abd Allah, 'Abd al-Rahīm Shanan and Maqbūl al-Ḥājj. Muhyī al-Dīn and Shanan were both strong supporters of NUP and, after instigating a failed coup late in 1959, both were sentenced to life imprisonment.

From early 1960 the old politicians began to exploit the differences inside the military junta, and organised an opposition front which included al-Azharī, Khalīl, Ṣādiq al-Mahdī, Aḥmad Maḥjūb and the Communists. They demanded the election of a new parliament to draft a new constitution. The government reacted by arresting them, with the exception of the powerful Sayyed al-Mahdī, whose subsequent death affected opposition activities during 1961–2.

Despite internal opposition, the regime made some economic progress and successfully extended the scope of the civil service, which led to the adoption of the 1960 Provincial Administration Act. Although this Act provided for the establishment of provincial councils with legislative, executive and advisory powers, it also gave civil servants political powers as representatives of the government in their districts. This would explain why the demonstrators during the 'October 1964 revolution' demanded a purge of the civil service. Had it not been for the October revolution, the consolidation of the *effendiyya* (propertied and monied classes) would have been complete, as had occurred in some other Arab countries under military rule. To reinforce the Provincial Administration Act, a central council was established as the main political instrument legitimising the military base by involving civilians. Its membership was partly nominated by the president, partly directly elected, and partly selected by provincial electoral colleges. Most of the old parties boycotted its elections except the PDP and the Communists. The PDP had been strong supporters of the regime since 1961 while the Communists hoped to exploit the elections 'to weaken the regime through its own institutions'.

The weakest point of the regime was its southern policy, which eventually brought about its demise in October 1964. Severe repression by the army, which had begun attacking the civilian peasantry in the south as well as the 'rebels' and 'outlaws' who had fled after the 1955 mutiny, further increased the ranks of the armed dissidents. In September 1963 representatives of the various dissident groups involved succeeded in uniting their disparate forces into a new Land Freedom Army, which later adopted the name of Anyanya, a term which means 'snake poison' in the Madi, Moru and Lotuko languages.[1] Guerrilla attacks on police posts and army barracks in the south were stepped up and new training camps and supply lines were opened in the neighbouring countries of Ethiopia, Kenya and Uganda.

[1] Edgar O'Ballance, *The secret war in the Sudan: 1955–1972* (London, 1977), 59.

The government responded by increasing the army to more than 20 000 men, of whom an estimated 8000 were sent to the south. Foreign missionaries, whom General ʿAbbūd thought had encouraged the rebellion, were expelled, their schools closed and Koranic schools opened in their place. Southerners working in the civil service were forced to move north or resign; others, suspected of aiding the Anyanya, were arrested and imprisoned. The leaders of the newly formed Sudan African National Union, who had fled to Ethiopia, Uganda and the Central African Republic (the ex-French Oubangui-Chari), were ordered home, and efforts made to extradite those who refused to return voluntarily.

By early 1964 the conflict was beginning to have a severe effect on the economy. Hundreds of thousands of refugees had fled to the south, and relations with the neighbouring countries were strained. Trade and transport suffered, as did cultivation. In the north the government's need to finance the war played havoc with development plans and prevented them from increasing the wages of government workers and improving living standards. A decision by General ʿAbbūd in September 1964 to open discussions in the north on the situation in the south, coupled with the rising economic and social discontent, strengthened the hand of the opposition which formed a National Front of political organisations, trade unions and professional associations and called for a general strike on 24 October 1964. The president was forced to dissolve the military junta and to call for an emergency session of the Central Council. Nevertheless, the insistence of the demonstrators on the complete withdrawal of the military led to the formation of an all-party caretaker government with the strong representation of the National Front.

For the first time in the history of the Sudan, a Communist (Aḥmad Sulaymān), a Muslim Brother (al-Rashīd al-Ṭāhir), and representatives of trade unions (Shāfiʿī Aḥmad al-Shaykh) and peasant unions (al-Amīn Muḥammad al-Amīn) were chosen as members of the cabinet. The old parties were each represented by one member. Sir al-Khatīm al-Khalīfa, the new prime minister, was an independent moderate who was chosen for the office after the old parties' rejection of the nominations of the Chief Justice, Awad Allah, and Abdīn Ismāʿīl, the President of the Barristers'

Association, both of whom were accused of left-wing political affiliations. General 'Abbūd remained the head of the state with only titular powers.

The caretaker government began its activities by concluding a truce with the south. For the first time a southerner, Clement Moboro, was chosen as a minister, and given the vital portfolio of Interior Office Affairs. The government also prepared the way for an early election scheduled for April 1965. The representation of the workers in the government by the inclusion of their trade-union secretary-generals curtailed their economic demands. Yet, the weakening of the government came from the old parties who formed a second National Front, which, in January 1965, sent a letter to the prime minister demanding an early election and the government's resignation if these elections did not take place. The Umma Party concurred in this demand. Al-Khalīfa was forced to resign and a new government under his premiership was formed, favouring the old parties but with one minister each for the Communists and the Muslim Brothers.

In March al-Khalīfa opened a round-table conference in Khartoum aimed at resolving the southern question. It was attended by representatives of the Southern Front, a coalition of southern students, government officials and employees formed in October 1964, representatives of the various northern parties, and Elia Lupe, the leader of the Sudan African National Union, which represented those southern politicians in exile. Also in attendance was William Deng, a former government official from the south who had helped to set up SANU in 1962. His proposal for a federal constitution in the south had attracted the government's interest, but had also alienated a majority of the members of SANU, who continued to favour for the south either full autonomy or independence. Although the SANU delegation was eventually persuaded to agree to his participation in their delegation, their reluctance to accept his self-assumed role as a mediator with the al-Khalīfa government was a major factor in the conference's failure to reach a settlement. However, a 12-man committee, consisting of six representatives from the north and six from the south, was set up to study proposed solutions further.

While the establishment of the committee ostensibly held out hope that the conflict in the south might be ended in favour of negotiation, the failure of the conference to agree on more decisive action left the southern parties bitterly disappointed. On 21 March they announced that they would boycott the forth-coming elections, a move that was supported by the PDP. However, the government decided to proceed with a poll in the north, and the PDP then dropped their opposition to the election, and their candidates stood for office, winning three seats out of the 173 that were contested. The Umma Party gained 75 seats and the NUP 54 seats. The Communist Party, which was participating in general elections for the first time, took only eleven seats.

The election also marked the appearance of a new regional group, the Beja Congress Organisation, which won ten seats. Soon other regional groups appeared, notably in the Nuba Mountains and in Darfur, as a result of the failure of the first democratic experiment (1954–8) to introduce any degree of change in the poor rural areas. But even before their entry on to the national scene, it was clear that the continuing factionalism was making the Sudan almost ungovernable. The election figures gave no single party a workable majority, and the two big parties, the Umma and the NUP, were forced to form a coalition government under the premiership of Maḥjūb, who in the 1930s had been editor of the al-Fajr magazine group. Al-Azharī was elected permanent president of a Council of Five. The first action of the new government was to form a committee to draft a permanent constitution for the country, and a scramble began between the new partners for new alliances to win the elections under the proposed presidential system even before the new constitution was ratified. And in December 1965 the Constituent Assembly moved to dissolve the Communist Party after public demonstrations against it by Muslim Brothers who resented its alleged anti-Islamic attitudes. Eight of the eleven Communist members were dismissed from the assembly.

The second parliamentary period was dominated by two problems: the first was the bitter factionalism within parties and the deteriorating relations between them. The second was the south, where the disturbances were now taking on the character of a civil war. As early as 1966 the Umma Party, for the first time, faced a division in its ranks. Ṣādiq al-Mahdī, the President of the party, broke with his uncle, Imam al-Hādī al-Mahdī, over the question of demarcation between the Mahdist religious leadership and the control of the Umma Party. The schism resulted in a further division of the Umma Party into the Ṣādiq and al-Hadī factions. At the same time the leftist political forces also experienced serious divisions in their ranks. This factionalisation encouraged a system of dynamic and mobile coalitions. A basic factor behind the divisions and party regroupings after the 1964 revolution was the participation of the lower urban classes in politics through their trade unions, which acted as pressure groups. Their intervention forced the discussion of issues such as economic development, social change and the democratisation of party structures. As a result of the Umma Party split, Ṣādiq al-Mahdī was elected prime minister instead of Maḥjūb in May 1966. The NUP allied with Ṣādiq when he succeeded in mobilising most of the Umma to his side. This policy of playing on Umma Party differences was repeated by the NUP in 1967 when it brought down Ṣādiq and returned Maḥjūb to the premiership.

In the south conditions continued to deteriorate. On 8 July, after a minor incident in which a northerner was wounded, the Muslim garrison at Juba went on the rampage, murdering civilians and burning throughout the town. Three days later other soldiers surrounded a church at Wau, the capital of the Bahr al-Ghazal province, and opened fire on a wedding party. Casualties in the two events were estimated to include more than a thousand dead.[1] The southern parties claimed that the actions represented a deliberate attempt by the Maḥjūb government to depopulate the south, and argued that this meant that only a military solution to the problem was possible. Nevertheless representatives of the parties remained in Khartoum trying to reach a political solution with first the Maḥjūb and then the Ṣādiq al-Mahdī governments. The death of two southern leaders, Father Sabornino Lahure in 1967, and then of William Deng, who was ambushed by what was probably a military patrol in May 1968, further undercut the position of those seeking a political solution.

Within this context of parliamentary manoeuvring the 1968 elections were held before the Constituent Assembly had agreed on a permanent constitution for the country. These elections resulted in a small majority for the NUP and PDP, which had recently united as the Democratic Unionist Party (DUP). Although the DUP briefly joined with a faction of the Umma Party in May 1969, the army took power after less than five years of

---

[1] O'Ballance, *Secret war*, 80–1.

the restored parliamentary rule. The same reasons that lay behind the failure of the first democratic experiment sparked off this new army take-over, though this time it was not a 'handing-over of power'.

The military take-over in May 1969 was a direct result of the alienation of the radical forces after the dissolution of the Communist Party in 1965 and their subsequent infiltration of the armed forces. They now searched for extra-legal means by which to voice their protests. This radical note was clear in the first speech of the new military leader, General Numayrī, in which he described the old parties as 'wholly responsible for exploiting the state power for self-enrichment and for serving narrow partisan interests without caring for the interests of the masses'.

This *coup d'état* was different from that of 1958 in that it was led by the middle ranks in the army. The coup obtained wide support from the start because it identified itself with the popular forces and many of its first ministers were among the leaders of the 1964 October revolution. The new regime launched a programme to extend the public sector, to encourage the participation of international capital, and to introduce a five-year plan for social and economic development.

During its first year the regime was confronted by the militant *anṣar* (i.e. Mahdist) opposition, and after crushing this religion-based movement, the regime then began to distance itself from the Communist Party. The split of the Communists in September 1970 into the Muʿāwiya and Maḥjūb wings facilitated this. Thus, in November 1970, three of the Revolutionary Command Council, who were considered to be Communist sympathisers, were dismissed. The issues of contention in the RCC were the differences of opinion over the question of the proposed project of union between the Sudan, Egypt and Libya, and relations with the USSR. The worsening relations between the Communists and the RCC led in July 1971 to an attempted coup headed by a Major al-ʿAṭa, who had earlier been dismissed by Numayrī. The success of the regime in crushing this coup led to its severing relations with the eastern bloc and looking for help from the west. Internally a policy of institutionalising the regime was adopted. After a national referendum had been held in October 1971, Numayrī became president and dissolved the RCC, and a constitution was drafted in 1972.

That year Numayrī also turned his attention to the south. With the help of Ethiopia and the World Council of Churches, an agreement was concluded between the government and the Anyanya, led by General Joseph Lagu, to end the civil war. The 'Addis Ababa Agreement', as the pact came to be known, gave the south a form of regional autonomy within a federal structure of government. A regional people's assembly was set up with a High Executive Council, whose leader would also be a vice-president of the Republic. The Christian religion was to be recognised, together with the use of the English language, alongside Islam and Arabic. Although efforts to implement the ceasefire fully proved difficult, the agreement successfully ended the war and led to the return of most of the estimated 300 000 refugees who had fled the country during the fighting. Efforts to resettle the 800 000 other southerners made homeless by the conflict were undertaken with the aid of the United Nations Commissioner for Refugees, the Aga Khan, and numerous international aid organisations. Elections to the regional assembly were held without incident in November 1973 and Abel Alier, Numayrī's own nominee, was elected unopposed as president. Elections of southerners to the National Assembly followed in April 1974.

For Numayrī the conclusion of the agreement and the ending of the war, which had cost the lives of up to half a million Sudanese in 17 years and which had devastated the economy, was a major achievement.[1] Unfortunately it was not matched by success on the political front in the north, where the factionalism, both among the old party leaders and within the army, continued to grow. To help put an end to the discontent, Numayrī ordered the establishment of a one-party system. The Sudan Socialist Union (SSU), patterned on the Egyptian Arab Socialist Union, held its first conference in 1972. This conference adopted a national charter as its political manifesto along the lines of Nāṣir's Arab socialism.

The next three years witnessed a series of attempted coups against the regime. Student demonstrations in 1973 were the first signs of the growing opposition. In September 1975 and July 1976 the regime was able to crush two coups supported by the militant *anṣar*. Underlying these coups was a re-emergence of regionalism.

[1] Norman O'Neill, 'Sudan', *Middle East yearbook, 1980* (London, 1980), 223.

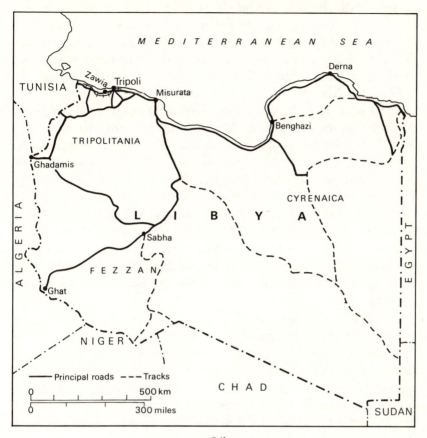

27   Libya.

Less-developed regions like the west began to use the presence of their men in the army seriously to affect the political system.

Libya

By 1944 the British had established their third and final occupation of Cyrenaica after the defeat of Rommel's forces in the desert. The British had already set up a military administration in neighbouring Tripolitania, and moves to facilitate the integration of the two territories had begun. In the south-west the Free French forces had occupied the Fezzan, after an advance from their headquarters near Lake Chad. Following an agreement between the French and the British military commanders in January 1943,

French authority was extended considerably north and east into the Tripolitanian Sahara. The regions of Ghat and Ghadamis, also occupied by the French were, however, to be administered by the French military authorities in the neighbouring territories: Ghat by the French in Algeria and Ghadamis by those in Tunisia.

With the liberation of the two northern provinces from more than 30 years of Italian rule came strong hopes of independence. After 22 years of exile in Egypt, the head of the powerful Sanūsiyya religious order in Cyrenaica, Sayyid Muḥammad Idrīs al-Sanūsī, returned to the wide acclaim of both townsmen and beduin. But his stay was not to last long. Having raised a Sanūsī force of 10000 men which fought with the British against the Italians, he insisted that Britain recognise the independence of Cyrenaica and the claims of the Sanūsī to govern it. He refused to return to Cyrenaica permanently until his demands were met, and continued to agitate for independence, albeit in a form that would permit the British to continue stationing troops in the country.

The British Foreign Office, however, had steadfastly refused to commit itself to independence, either for Cyrenaica or for Tripolitania, which some of Sayyid Idrīs's younger followers had insisted be included as part of Sanūsī demands. Instead, British policy remained bound to a statement made by the Foreign Secretary, Anthony Eden, in parliament in January 1942, in which he stated simply that 'His Majesty's government is determined that at the end of the war the Sanūsīs in Cyrenaica will in no circumstances again fall under Italian domination.'

In Tripolitania, where liberation from Italian rule had brought forth demands both for immediate independence and for national unification, the failure of Eden to mention Tripolitania in his statement led to fears that nationalist claims would be less favourably received than those of Cyrenaica. After a period of severe agitation, riots and demonstrations from 1943 to 1945, and the formation of several clandestine political clubs and organisations, a number of political parties emerged in the late 1940s, of which the Nationalist Party (al-Ḥizb al-Waṭanī), the United National Front (al-Jabha al-Waṭaniya al-Muttaḥida) and the Free National Bloc (al-Kutla al-Waṭaniya al-Ḥurra) were the most important. Led mainly by the urban notables and merchants of Tripoli, all the parties formed agreed on the fundamental principles of both independence and unity. Their main differences centred on recognition of Sanūsī claims to leadership once independence was achieved and on the future state's foreign policy.

Behind Britain's reluctance to commit itself formally to independence for either or both of the provinces lay a growing realisation of the strategic importance of the territories and an awareness of promises made to its wartime allies. Both the United States and the Soviet Union had come to have 'interests' in the future of the Libyan territories. The Italians, in return for their cooperation with the Allied powers in the later stages of the Second World War, hoped that at least some of their overseas colonies, including Libya, would be returned, or at the very least that they would have first claims to any trusteeships set up in them. The French were eager to preserve their rule in the Fezzan, Ghat and Ghadamis in order to create a link between their colonies further west and in Central Africa. The newly formed Arab League, speaking largely on behalf of Egypt, demanded that it be included in any plans to set up a trusteeship in the Libyan territories. Faced with all these considerations, British policy was to postpone a decision on the future of the three provinces until a peace treaty with Italy had been signed and the Allies had agreed on the disposition of Italy's former colonies. Meanwhile, Italian law, with some modifications in Cyrenaica, was to remain in force in the provinces occupied by Britain.

The election of a Labour government to power in Britain after the war, and the growing hostility between the western Allies and the Soviet Union, complicated negotiations for the final peace treaty. The new Labour Foreign Secretary, Ernest Bevin, favoured granting immediate independence to the territories, but the Soviet Union proposed that a joint Soviet-Italian administration be formed in Tripolitania. The United States countered this by suggesting that the whole country be placed under a United Nations Trusteeship for ten years, while the French remained opposed to independence for fear that this might further encourage rising nationalist sentiments in Algeria and Tunisia. The deadlock remained when the Allies finally signed a peace treaty with Italy in February 1947. At the time of signature, however, Britain, France, the United States and the Soviet Union declared their intention of continuing negotiations on the future of the Libyan territories. If no agreement were reached within a year of the treaty coming into effect, the matter was to be referred to the General Assembly of the United Nations. The four powers also stated their intention to 'accept the recommendation' of the General Assembly and 'to take appropriate measures for giving effect to it'.

When the General Assembly finally took up the issue in April 1949, it was startled to hear that Britain and Italy, supported by the United States had, in the meantime, drawn up a plan under which Libya was to become independent only after a period of ten years. Trusteeships were to be granted to the British in Cyrenaica, to the Italians in Tripolitania and to the French in Fezzan. News of the Bevin–Sforza plan (named after Bevin and the Italian Foreign Minister, Count Carlo Sforza) resulted in mass demonstrations throughout Libya and in other parts of the Arab world. In Tripolitania, the Nationalist Party, the United National Front and several other parties united to form the Tripolitanian National Congress Party. Its aims were to defeat the plan and forestall any further attempt to reimpose colonial rule in Libya.

In May 1949 the General Assembly failed, by one vote, to secure a two-thirds majority in favour of an Italian trusteeship over Tripolitania and a final resolution in favour of the Bevin–Sforza plan was defeated by a vote of 37 against 14 in favour with seven abstentions. Two weeks later, Sayyid Idrīs, with the support of Britain, declared Cyrenaica an independent state under a Sanūsī emirate, though Britain was to retain control over foreign affairs and defence. Six months later, on 21 November, the General Assembly, by a vote of 48 to one, with nine abstentions, adopted a resolution that the three provinces of Libya become jointly an independent state no later than 1 January 1952. Representatives of the local inhabitants were to meet to form a National Assembly and to draw up a constitution for the future state in consultation with a UN commissioner appointed by the General Assembly and advised by a ten-member council composed of Britain, the United States, France, Italy, Egypt, Pakistan and four representatives from the Libyan territories. On 24 December 1951, one week before the final deadline, Libya was declared an independent sovereign state and Sayyid Idrīs the new king. Britain insisted on his rule, despite considerable internal opposition.

Once Libya was independent, two fundamental problems presented themselves: the need to transform the declaration of national unity into reality and the need to develop a viable economy. While the latter problem was, at least in theory, overcome with the discovery of oil in the mid-1960s, the problem of unity continued to plague the monarchy until it was overthrown in 1969.

Despite their common struggle against the Italians, both Cyrenaica and Tripolitania retained a distinct identity, and each jealously guarded its own prerogatives. Cyrenaica was a network of tribal clans dominated by the Sanūsiyya. This Sufi brotherhood had been founded in 1837 by an Algerian scholar, Sayyid Muhammad ibn 'Alī al-Sanūsī al-Idrīsī. Originally based near Mecca, the Grand Sanūsī, as he was later to be called, re-established the brotherhood's headquarters at al-Zāwiya al-Baydā' on the central Cyrenaican plateau in 1843 after encountering political opposition in Arabia. Later the brotherhood's centre was moved to the Jaghbub Oasis, on the Libyan border with Egypt, which soon became a centre of learning in North Africa, second in importance only to Egypt's al-Azhar University. Like many of its fellow orders throughout the Islamic world, the Sanūsiyya espoused the cause of the common people, helping to set up 'schools, caravanserai, commercial and social focal points, law courts, banks, storehouses, poor houses and burial grounds',[1] as well as centres of learning which aimed at bringing the teachings of Islam to those often forgotten or neglected by the more orthodox 'ulamā'.

But while most Sufi orders were primarily religious groupings, the Sanūsiyya, like their counterparts, the Wahhābī in Arabia, rapidly became involved in politics as well. Under Sayyid Ahmad al-Sharif, who headed the Order from 1902 until his death at the hands of the Italians in 1933, the Sanūsiyya formed what Evans-Pritchard has called

an embryonic state. The Head of the Order was by this time less the religious Head of an Islamic fraternity than the leading representative of a nascent nationalism which became increasingly conscious of itself in the long struggle against the Italians... The Order became more and more a political organisation which directed, administratively, economically, and militarily, the entire Bedouin population, and morally the entire population of Cyrenaica, Bedouin and townsmen alike, against the common enemy.[2]

[1] Michael Gilsenan, *Saint and sufi in modern Egypt: an essay in the sociology of religion* (Oxford, 1973), 4.
[2] E. E. Evans-Pritchard, *The Sanussi of Cyrenaica* (Oxford, 1949), 228.

The military defeat of Sanūsī resistance to Italian colonisation, the destruction of the Sanūsī lodges and the banishment of its shaykhs, only served to increase the importance of the head of the Order as a symbol both of religious identity and of political resistance. When the British occupied Cyrenaica, the decision to resurrect the Sanūsī emir and to restore tribal rule found wide support throughout Cyrenaica. Tripolitania, on the other hand, was far more urbanised and settled. It contained about two-thirds of the population of the new state, the better part of the arable land, and a long history of commerce with the west as well as with sub-Saharan Africa and the Arab east. More closely akin to neighbouring Tunisia and Algeria, it had a large Berber minority, and about 30 000 Italians who had chosen to stay on despite the Italian withdrawal. Rent by political factionalism and rivalries among the urban merchants and notables, Tripolitania had taken the brunt of Italian settlement and had only reluctantly agreed to support Sayyid Muḥammad Idrīs as king of a united Libya for fear of the Italians coming back. In return for their support they demanded a centralised form of government under which the monarch would share power with a democratically elected parliament.

The third province, the Fezzan, possessed only about 40 000 inhabitants, divided between a negroid population and the nomadic Tuareg. Cut off from the sea by the desert on all sides, its links were mainly with the African states to the south and west (which like the Fezzan had been occupied by the French).

The final version of the constitution, which was approved by the newly formed National Assembly ten weeks prior to independence, established a federal system of government under which each of the provinces had its own governor, appointed by the king, an Executive Council, whose members were appointed or dismissed by the king on the recommendation of the governor, and a Legislative Assembly which could also be dissolved by the king on the recommendation of the chief of the Executive Council and after consultation with the governor. While the federal government retained the right to legislate and execute matters concerning foreign policy, defence and national finance, the provinces retained strong powers in matters of taxation, trade, civil, commercial and criminal law, education and the Press.

It was a situation which pleased the Cyrenaicans and the

Fezzanese who feared that a more integrated system would result in domination by Tripolitania; but it was bitterly opposed by large sections of public opinion in the western province. Opposition in that province became even more intense when, within the first two months of independence, the Tripolitanian National Congress Party was dissolved and its leader, Bashīr Saʿdāwī, was deported to Egypt after charging that elections to the house of representatives had been manipulated by officials of the federal government. Mass demonstrations against the election results broke out in Tripoli in February 1952 and were brutally put down by the police. It was a pattern which was to recur after all parties had been effectively banned by the king during the first year of independence. Throughout the 1950s and the 1960s, demonstrations challenged the monarch's rule and they continued, despite the enactment of an amendment to the constitution on 15 April 1953. The amendment dissolved the federal system and replaced it by a more centralised administration under which the country was divided into administrative units subject to the control of the Minister of the Interior. In October 1964 parliament was dissolved following widespread rioting and demonstrations against the American and British roles in Libya. A newly elected parliament, the fourth since independence, was dissolved by the king the following February. Elections were again held in May 1965, but by this time the number of voting constituencies had been reduced from 103 to 91. Sixteen candidates were returned unopposed and the remaining 75 elected members were all pro-government.

For the remaining period of monarchical rule, the country was torn by the centrifugal rivalry of the provinces, electoral disputes, conflict within the Royal Diwan, and disagreements both within and outside the cabinet concerning the powers of the king. With elections offering only a choice of a candidate and not of programme, votes were cast according to tribal, family and personal loyalties. Parliamentary deputies tended to put local interests above national ones and clandestine opposition movements grew increasingly active. Mass demonstrations organised by Baʿathists, various Marxist groups and workers' organisations were put down by force in 1962 and 1964, and in 1967 after the Six-Day Arab–Israeli war. Trade unions were dissolved and students arrested at the very time that their counterparts in Egypt and elsewhere in North Africa were gaining new rights under socialist regimes. By the autumn of 1969, the movement led by Colonel Mu'ammar al-Qadhdhāfī (Gadafi) and the Free Officers was but one of several groups secretly working to overthrow the regime. Qadhdhāfī's success was made possible by the discovery of oil in Libya and the rise of a tiny, but influential, middle class composed of technicians, urban tradesmen and civil servants.

Until the discovery of oil, the country was one of the poorest in the world. The decimation of the beduin population and of their herds by the Italians was a major cause of this, as was the appallingly low level of educational, medical and social services provided for the native population under Fascist rule. By 1951 Libya had only four preparatory and secondary schools with a total enrolment of 300 pupils. The 1954 census showed that 83 per cent of the population was illiterate. The war, in which the country had seen some of the fiercest battles recorded in modern history, left much of the population homeless and in a state of disease and starvation. The average life expectancy was little more than 30 years. Per capita income was about $35 a year; by 1962, despite an estimated eight-fold increase, it still stood at under $270 a year. By 1965, as the oil began to flow in, export earnings rose six-fold to £81 500 000; by 1969 they totalled more than 770 million dinars, just under £900 million. Although the government was making an effort to redistribute some of this new income, and to provide better education and social services, the bulk of the profits were drained overseas through the foreign oil companies operating on Libyan soil. Rapidly increasing inflation cut into income and Libya was becoming what Rémy Leveau has called 'a caricature of a consumer society'.[1] As the rural poor fled the dismal conditions prevailing in the countryside, the rate of urbanisation increased dramatically: in the 1960s the population of both Tripoli and Benghazi grew at around seven per cent per year, twice as fast as the population as a whole.

Abroad, Algeria, Tunisia, Morocco, Chad and Niger had become independent; Gamal 'Abd al-Nāṣir had become the hero of the Arabs and of the Third World; the Palestinians were becoming a new and powerful force in world politics. Isolated from Africa, Asia and the Arab world by their government's

[1] Rémy Leveau, 'Le Système politique libyen', in *La Libye nouvelle: rupture et continuité* (Paris, 1975), 85.

pro-western policies and increasingly aware of the potential power their oil wealth could bring, Libyans grew more and more impatient. The political system was unable to cope. As Leveau explained it: 'The administration found itself reduced to its distributive function, and this created more frustration among precisely those who had benefited. This incapacity of the Libyan political system explains the collapse of the monarchy and the relatively easy installation of the new regime.'[1]

Colonel Mu'ammar al-Qadhdhāfī and the Free Officers took power in a bloodless coup on 1 September 1969, although it was not until almost two weeks later that Qadhdhāfī was identified as the head of the government and of the armed forces; the names of the twelve members of the Revolutionary Command Council were not announced until the following December. King Idrīs, who was in Turkey at the time, refused to abdicate but eventually accepted exile in Egypt. With the western powers eager to retain their goodwill in a state that was now exceedingly wealthy and whose oil supplies were vitally important as shortages grew more imminent, foreign recognition quickly followed.

Of the twelve members of the RCC, only 'Umar 'Abd Allah al-Maḥā'ishī came from a relatively well-off family; his father was a provincial administrator under the old regime and of the Circassian Turkish stock which had ruled Egypt during the time of the Ottoman empire. He was later to defect to Egypt after allegedly attempting to overthrow Qadhdhāfī. Abū Bakr Yūnus and Muḥammad Abū Bakr al-Mgarief, who was killed in a motor accident in August 1972, came from important tribes – Yūnus from a tribe of the Aujila Oasis in Chad which had emigrated to Libya and al-Mgarief from the Maghāriba, one of the nine Saʿādī tribes of the Banū Sulaym. The remainder came from minor tribes and poorer families. Several, including Qadhdhāfī, came from oases in the interior where, as Ruth First has noted, 'they were the country's second-class citizens, the children of nomads or lowly cultivators who were born in the last days of the Italian occupation'.[2]

Owing no specific allegiance to any of the more noble tribes or to the urban notables of any of the three provinces, the RCC at its inception was seen to represent the interests of the country

---

[1] Leveau, 'Le Système politique', 84–5.
[2] Ruth First, *Libya: the elusive revolution* (Harmondsworth, 1974), 115.

as a whole. In a radio broadcast to the nation on the morning of the coup the RCC labelled the old regime 'reactionary and decadent...a hotbed of extortion, faction, treachery and treason'. It declared Libya a 'free, self-governing republic', and promised freedom, unity and social justice. The statement added that the coup was 'in no sense directed against any state whatever, nor against international agreements or recognised international law'.

Aside from the bulk of the armed forces, the new regime derived its main support from those sections of the middle class, many of them civil servants and technicians, who had been demanding a larger role for the country in determining matters concerning oil prices and production, and a more pro-Arab foreign policy. Their support explains the regime's subsequent success in carrying through its nationalisation of the oil sector, and the adoption of a wide-ranging development programme concentrated on agriculture, the infrastructure and the social services.

In addition, the new regime received the whole-hearted support of what Yolande Martin has described as the embryonic class of *petite bourgeoisie* and those who constituted a rural and urban lumpenproletariat,[1] whose employment was sporadic because the petroleum industry could only absorb a certain number of workers for a specified time. Once the construction work was finished, these workers went back to the cities, where they often could find no employment. They formed, together with the small *émigré* peasantry and the poor beduins, the class of people who inhabited the slums which surrounded the large cities. This class even now has very few political defenders.

Despite this support, the new regime was careful to emphasise its disavowal of the class struggle and of class distinctions. The new regime was to be based on the twin pillars of Islam and of Arab nationalism. Alcohol was banned, English disappeared from street signs and hoardings, and western advisers and consultants were replaced by Arabs. British troops were asked to leave and the giant American air base at Wheelus Field near Tripoli, the largest air base outside the US, was closed. Political parties, save for the Arab Socialist Union of Libya, which was modelled after that of Egypt, were banned. The natural resources of the country

---

[1] Yolande Martin, 'La Libye de 1919 à 1969', *La Libye nouvelle*, 48-9.

were to be mobilised for the struggle against imperialism and the development of the Arab nation as a whole.

In a speech delivered to the Libyan public on 15 April 1973, President Qadhdhāfī announced the beginning of a new cultural revolution in which the popular masses were invited to take power at all levels of government through the formation of popular committees. The population was to be mobilised into armed militia, the bureaucracy and administration dismantled and the centres of information turned over to the people. One month later, Qadhdhāfī outlined his 'Third International Theory' which he described as 'an alternative to capitalist materialism and Communist atheism'. It was a form of direct democracy, as he made an effort to explain in his *Green Book*, the first part of which was published in 1976. On 2 March 1977 a National Congress was held in Sebha; some 1000 delegates chosen by the people's committees, professional associations and trade unions attended to work out the details of a new political system and to select new secretaries who would supervise the reformed ministries. Libya adopted a new name, the Socialist People's Libyan Arab Jamahiriyah, which the government defined as a people's state.

Although the Libyan revolution managed to survive several attempted coups, including one in the summer of 1970 led by 'Abd Allah 'Abid al-Sanūsī, 'Umar al-Shalhī and other members of the old regime, the creation of the popular committees at the expense of the Arab Socialist Union, the arming of the militia – reportedly against the wishes of some of the more professional army officers – and the move to strengthen ties with the developing countries reflected the government's determination to repel any attempts, internal or external, to overthrow the regime.

Although the country's economic links with the United States had improved by the latter part of the 1970s, the government and the population were still aware of vivid newspaper accounts of US plans to invade Libyan oil-fields following the oil embargo of 1973 and early 1974. The defection of 'Umar al-Maḥā'ishī, then the Minister of Planning, dissension within the Revolutionary Command Council over the development of the Libyan state (as opposed to the Arab revolution) and student riots in Benghazi and Tripoli were signs of internal discontent as well.

Egypt

By the Second World War Egypt had already emerged as a leading Middle Eastern power, checked only by Iraq which, as the one recognised independent Arab state, attempted to assume leadership of all Arab states. But Egypt's geographical position, especially on account of both the size of her population and the Suez Canal, dictated her cardinal role in her relations with western and eastern powers. Egypt's importance was further emphasised by her cultural pre-eminence and the establishment of the Arab League in Cairo in 1944. From that time on Egypt's foreign policy exerted increasing influence in the region. Her military commitments during the 1948–9 war against Israel, and her struggle to contain Zionist/Israeli expansion (although unsuccessful until 1973) gained Egypt the role of Arab leadership. Indeed, by 1957, Egypt had become the principal spokesman for, and foreign policy pacemaker in, the Arab Middle East.

During the 1940s and early 1950s the principal foreign-policy objective remained the removal of British forces from Egyptian territory. Thus, in 1946, as well as after the coup of 1952, Egyptian leaders sought new, or revised, treaty arrangements with Great Britain. Furthermore Egypt's participation in the Arab–Israeli war of 1948–9 inextricably involved her in the development of this continuing conflict. Indeed, she became the principal protagonist in the Arab–Israeli confrontation.

Yet, until 1955, Egypt remained closely linked to the western powers. Only the vicissitudes of the Cold War and the shortsighted and rigid foreign policy of the United States of America – which demanded close military and political association in return for economic benefits – eventually caused Gamal 'Abd al-Nāṣir to give his support to the non-aligned Third World bloc, to turn to the Soviet Union for military aid, denied by the United States because of its commitments to Israel, and to recognise the People's Republic of China in 1956, while continuing Egypt's close economic relations with western powers. Great Britain, the USA, West Germany and France, in spite of great political and diplomatic differences, remained Egypt's principal trading partners throughout Nāṣir's rule.

In his *Philosophy of the revolution*, Nāṣir developed the notion of three intersecting circles encompassing the Arab, Islamic and African Worlds respectively. In these three worlds, Nāṣir believed, Egypt's role should lie. Egypt, in her relations with those countries outside these circles, should pursue a policy of non-alignment, and certainly non-military commitment. His aim was to steer clear of the Cold War. In this pursuit Nāṣir was consistent. But, given the nature of the Cold War and his conflict with Israel, he was forced to depend increasingly on the eastern bloc to obtain military aid and economic assistance.

In the early days of the revolution, the Revolutionary Council had few, if any, notions of ideology or any programme relating to foreign affairs. Situations, however, dictated its policy, making the regime 'pragmatist', or at least opportunist. It seized, in terms of national interests, those opportunities which would enhance Egypt's regional as well as global role. The 1954 negotiation securing Britain's withdrawal from Egypt heralded the latter's true independence and confirmed her leadership of the Arab World. Nāṣir then set about establishing himself as champion of the anti-colonial struggle. This development brought Egypt into direct collaboration with the Soviet Union and emphasised the reality of her own independence. The principal focus of Nāṣir's foreign policy of course remained his relations with Israel. Although in the first years of the revolution he had tried negotiating with Israel, the latter's intransigence and its involvement in the abortive Anglo-French invasion of the Suez Canal after Nāṣir had nationalised it in 1956, led to open confrontation. Although the USA as well as the USSR had opposed the tripartite invasion, it was to the latter world power that Nāṣir now turned for support. As a result of the invasion Nāṣir emerged as the champion of Arab nationalism and the anti-colonial and anti-Israeli struggle. Furthermore, Iraq had long lost any claim it had to leadership of the Arab World.

While championing Arab unity, Egypt's radical stance brought the country into confrontation with conservative regimes such as that of Saudi Arabia. In pursuance of the goal of Arab unity, Nāṣir persuaded Syria to join Egypt in a United Arab Republic in 1958. The union was short lived since the Syrians resented Egypt's attempts to dominate it and seceded in 1961. Even so, Nasir did not lose his role as leader of the Arab World and did not cease to strive for Arab unity. Egypt's new radical stance presented her with a dilemma. While pursuing the goal of Arab unity, she felt obliged to oppose Arab regimes such as that of Saudi Arabia. Egypt's military involvement on the side of the radical forces in the Yemen civil war further exposed the contradictions inherent in her foreign policy goals. Although she was receiving considerable aid from the USSR, on which she was becoming increasingly dependent, she still required further large-scale finance for her ambitious development projects, and this the conservative oil-rich Gulf states could provide. But ideologically she had placed herself in a corner. Her intervention in Yemen alienated her from the Gulf states, was divisive of the Arab World and tied down her military forces as well as diverting precious economic resources needed for her own development. By 1965 there were well over 75 000 Egyptian soldiers fighting in Yemen against the Saudi-supported Imam Muḥammad al-Badr.

This imbroglio resulted in Nāṣir losing his grip as a Pan-Arab leader. Other forces had entered the Arab political arena, challenging his authority: Baʿathism, the Palestinian movement, as well as the Saudi government. When in 1966 Israel succeeded in attacking Syria and Jordan without credible Egyptian military action, President Nāṣir was largely blamed for failing to thwart Israeli military might. Reacting to this situation Nāṣir produced a show of force by closing the Straits of Tiran and demanding the withdrawal of the UN Emergency Force from Sinai. Israel's reaction was totally unexpected. On 5 June 1967 the Israeli Defence Force destroyed most of Egypt's air force and followed up with a *Blitzkrieg* on the ground against the principal Arab armies of Egypt, Syria and Jordan, all of which were severely defeated.

The immediate effect of this débâcle was the re-entry into the region of the USA, while the USSR immediately re-armed her client states. The USA, however, became, with tacit Soviet support, the principal force in search of a political solution of the Arab–Israeli conflict. Moreover, Egypt's adherence to the UN Resolution 242 (22 November 1967) which implicitly recognised Israel's right to exist, marked a radical new departure in Egypt's foreign policy. Although subsequently a 'war of attrition' broke out during 1969 and 1970, mostly over the Suez Canal, the UN and other western powers pursued avenues for a peaceful settlement. And when by the summer of 1970, the Palestinian guerrilla forces clashed with the Jordanian military, it had become clear that the Arab–Israeli conflict had to be resolved. Although still heavily dependent on the USSR, Egypt's previous tough anti-US stance was dropped in favour of one seeking active US involvement in the area, as well as diplomatic accommodation. Nāṣir's sudden death in September 1970 and Anwār Sādāt's succession marked the return to a principally Egyptian-centred rather than a Pan-Arab-centred foreign policy.

Although Nāṣir had set the new trend in policy, it was Sādāt who subsequently implemented it. After the consolidation of his power base, he suddenly expelled Soviet military and technical advisers in 1972, pronounced the *infitāḥ*, or economic open door, policy which was designed to attract foreign, especially western, investors, and reached rapprochement with the conservative Arab Gulf states. Indeed it was they who supported Sādāt's military strategy by offering support and financial backing by means of a coordinated strategy of the Organisation of Arab Petroleum Exporting Countries (OPEC). All this led to his daring – yet highly successful – military offensive across the Suez Canal in October 1973. By doing this, he had forced western powers to take a stand, and once again to become an active partner in negotiating a settlement in the Arab–Israeli conflict. While Egypt's military established a beachhead on the eastern Suez Canal front, OPEC simultaneously announced the dramatic price rise for crude oil, giving OPEC's support to Arab states against Israel.

With the Soviet Union removed from Egypt, but still influential in Syria and Iraq, the USA made a dramatic initiative in the Middle East. The United States government (principally in the person of Dr Henry Kissinger) orchestrated the Geneva Conference on the Arab–Israeli dispute as well as the Sinai armistice agreements. Within a year Egypt had rejoined the western bloc, although pursuing an essentially Egypt-centred policy. Facing opposition, even hostility, from Arab states in response to her foreign policy, she became increasingly isolated in subsequent years. More and more it appeared that Egypt's problems could only be resolved with the assistance of the western powers. This was underlined by Nixon's visit to Egypt in 1974.

Sādāt's subsequent dramatic decision to negotiate direct with Israel to secure peace and release the Egyptian economy from the permanent threat of war was a logical development of a foreign policy which sought to consider Egypt's own interests, rather than regional interests, as paramount. In so doing Egypt, which had been the pacemaker for foreign policy in the Arab World, put herself out on a limb, in particular with her neighbour Libya, her Arab partner states, and to a lesser extent the Sudan.

The Sudan

Even before independence, the Sudan had tried to cultivate sympathy for her cause in the Third World. Her geographical position, however, produced a duality in her policy, namely one of identification with Arab as well as African causes. Thus, the Sudan joined the Arab League as well as attending the African Summit Conference in Accra in 1958. In 1963, the year of the creation of the Organisation of African Unity, the Sudan was one of its early participants and joined in the call for the preservation of the status quo in independent African states. However, this did not prevent Sudanese governments, at various times, from offering considerable political, economic and even military support to liberation movements seeking to overthrow governments in neighbouring states, or to establish their own states. The assistance given by Numayrī's regime to Hissan Habre in the Chadian civil war in the 1970s is one example; another is the support given by the same regime to the Eritrean liberation movements struggling to establish their independence from Ethiopia. Although relations between the Sudan and these movements were subject to considerable flux, Numayrī's regime in particular found it useful to use them to further his own interests in the region, foremost of which was his effort to prevent both Libya and Ethiopia from becoming too powerful.

Relations with the Arab states also fluctuated considerably over the years. After the disputes with Nāṣir's Egypt over the division of the Nile waters had been settled in 1959, Sudan and Egypt greatly extended their trading links and relations improved steadily. After the June war of 1967, Sudan also moved to re-establish closer links with the other Arab states and strongly supported the Palestinian cause. At the Arab Summit Conference held in Khartoum in November 1967, Sudan joined the other Arab League states in calling for 'no peace with Israel, no

recognition of Israel, no negotiations with Israel'.[1] In 1970
Numayrī headed a conciliation committee chosen by the Arab
states to mediate between King Hussein of Jordan and Palestinian
guerrillas and helped to bring about a ceasefire to end the civil
war in Jordan. After the July 1971 coup and counter-coup,
however, relations with both Libya and Egypt became strained
and the regime turned for support to the more conservative states
of the Arabian peninsula, Saudi Arabia, Kuwait and Abu Dhabi
in particular. The president called for an alliance of Arab money
with western technology and Sudanese resources, and both
political and economic ties increased considerably as a result. In
1975 the Abu Dhabi-based Arab Fund for Economic and Social
Development announced a ten-year plan to double output in the
Sudan and suggested a plan under which the Arab oil states would
contribute $6 billion to the Sudanese economy by 1985.
Henceforth the need to retain the goodwill of the Arab oil
producers became a major plank in Numayrī's foreign policy.

Sudan's relations with the Soviet Union and the eastern-bloc
countries began to improve significantly after the 1967 war, when
the Maḥjūb government broke diplomatic links with the United
States and the United Kingdom for their support of the Israelis
and concluded a major arms deal with the USSR. During his first
two years in power, these ties were also encouraged by Numayrī,
who also forged closer diplomatic links with China. However, the
events of July 1971 led the regime to question the wisdom of close
relations with the Soviet Union, who were thought to have had
a hand in the coup attempt, and although diplomatic ties remained
intact, relations became considerably more strained, while those
with the US and with other western countries in Europe were
improved.

Libya

Until the September coup of 1969 Libya had played but a modest
role in Pan-Arab affairs, and had kept a very low profile in the
world arena. In return for earlier help by Great Britain, the USA
and Italy, King Idrīs had leased the Wheelus air base and other
facilities to NATO, for which the country was financially rewarded. And although the kingdom officially supported the Arab
cause against Israel, without an effective military force her actual

[1] Anthony Sylvester, *Sudan under Nimeiri* (London, 1977), 193.

contributions were minimal. This changed dramatically in late 1969 when Colonel Qadhdhāfī came to power.

In 1970 Qadhdhāfī pressed ahead with his plans for wider Arab unity. In December 1969 the Tripoli Charter established an alliance of Libya, Egypt and the Sudan. It was followed by moves towards federation of the three countries and overtures towards Syria. Referendums held in Libya, Egypt and Syria approved the proposed constitution, and the Federation of Arab Republics was proclaimed on 1 January 1972. In August Egypt and Libya agreed in principle to merge their two countries, but Egypt, now led by President Anwār Sādāt, was hesitant about proceeding further. A 'march on Cairo' staged by some 40 000 Libyans to demonstrate support for the merger was turned back after it had crossed the border. Eventually the merger documents were signed on 1 September 1973, but severe disagreements over the military conduct of the October 1973 war, and Qadhdhāfī's rejection of Sādāt's negotiated settlement of the war, led not only to the end of the union plan, but also to increasing hostility between the two countries.

To the north and west, a proposed union with Malta was rebuffed, as was a parallel proposal made to Tunisian President Habib Bourguiba in December 1972. After the break-up of the union with Egypt, however, Tunisia and Libya agreed on a merger plan which was announced on 12 January 1974. Negotiated by Tunisian Foreign Minister Mohammed Masmoudi, it was violently opposed by his Prime Minister, Hedi Nouira, who dismissed him two days later on his return to Tunis from a trip abroad. Talks to outline the eventual union of the two countries' foreign and economic policies were indefinitely postponed.

The failure of the merger agreements and the proclamation of the Third International Theory (*The Green Book*) coincided with a noticeable increase in support for revolutionary movements abroad. Neighbouring Egypt and Sudan accused Libya of supporting Islamic revolutionary groups in their countries; other benefactors of Libyan arms and finance were believed to include such diverse groups as the Irish Republican Army, the Muslim Moro Liberation Front in the Philippines, and the black liberation groups in Zimbabwe (Rhodesia) and southern Africa. During the Lebanese civil war, the Libyans provided extensive supplies and funds to Nāṣirite groups as well as to the Palestinian rejection front.

After 1975, however, Libyan foreign policy was emphasising less the export of arms and more the importance of revolutionary unity. The government took its platform to international audiences through the United Nations, the North–South Dialogue Conferences and the non-aligned summit meetings, where it became a leading advocate of the New International Economic Order. Diplomatic and economic ties with African states were strengthened. The prime minister was dispatched to the Lebanon to mediate between the Lebanese Nationalist Movement and its right-wing adversaries. A major military and economic agreement was signed with Moscow in December 1976, but the government denied that it had granted the Soviet Union the right to set up military bases in the country. Relations with Eastern Europe, particularly Yugoslavia, with the southern Mediterranean countries and Malta, and with other Islamic countries, were also strengthened.

SOCIAL AND CULTURAL CHANGE

The profound political and economic transformation of northeast Africa which occurred after the Second World War also produced dramatic social change in Libya, Egypt and the Sudan. The exceedingly high rate of urbanisation was perhaps the most important development, but there were also major shifts in the deployment of the working population and in the role women played in society.

Despite its relatively small population, Libya saw its urban centres double in size in less then three decades: the population of Tripoli rose from just under 140 000 in 1954 to 269 000 in 1968; in Benghazi the figures were 70 000 and 191 000 respectively, giving it a rate of growth of 173 per cent over the 24-year period.[1] Cairo and Alexandria also experienced huge growth rates. By 1976 the population of Cairo had risen to 8.5 million, about one-fifth of the total population of the country. Another 2.5 million lived in Alexandria.[2] Ten years earlier the two cities had a combined total of only six million. Khartoum's population virtually tripled between 1973 and 1980, when it was expected to have reached one million. Altogether the population of Sudan's three main cities –

[1] B. Atallah and M. Fikry, 'Le Phénomène urbain en Libye. Problèmes juridiques et sociaux', *Villes et sociétés au Maghreb: études sur l'urbanisation* (Paris, 1974), 79–80.
[2] Janet Abu Lughod, 'The growth of Arab cities', *Middle East yearbook, 1980*, 43.

Khartoum, Khartoum North and Omdurman – was estimated to have risen to three million by 1980, or about one-sixth of the total population of the country.

The effects of such rapid urbanisation varied from country to country. With the huge rise in its oil revenues, Libya under Qadhdhāfī embarked on a massive development programme to improve housing and social services as well as industry and agriculture. Huge new estates, both public and private, were built in and around the major cities, while entirely new urban areas were planned for Misurata, Zawia, Derna and Sebha. However, the physical transformation of the cities brought with it disadvantages that the government did not anticipate. Foremost among these were the strains on family life that living in modern apartments produced in a society that remained tribal and traditional in outlook. While the rise in private incomes led to the accumulation of a host of consumer goods, ranging from western-style dining rooms to cars and television sets, the generation gap increased. So too did the sequestration of women whose productive role in the household was diminished as a result of the import of consumer goods and the mass immigration from the rural areas. In Cairo the rapid urbanisation produced immense strains on both the physical and social environment. Providing housing, social services and urban infrastructure, without the hard currency needed to finance such developments, defeated Nāṣir's attempts to remedy the problems caused by the rapid growth of the cities. However, the emphasis given to infrastructure and to the import of western goods and technology under President Sādāt led to even greater disruptions. Sewers, roads and communications facilities built prior to the Second World War were dismantled to make way for new construction programmes which were often delayed and aborted, as the problems of coping with congestion and the perennial lack of funds mounted. The influx of foreign capital for investment in new hotel and leisure complexes in Cairo and Alexandria added still further to the demands on existing services and to the social discontent. While parts of Cairo by the mid-1970s resembled New York or Paris, most of the urban residential quarters were neglected, overcrowded and/or destroyed to make way for new building.

The Sudan, despite its smaller urban population, faced similar problems. The huge influx of homeless refugees and of impoverished peasants to the town in the 1970s, coupled with the poor state of the country's finances, made urban life even more miserable for the many who lacked the income needed to buy basic necessities.

Aside from urbanisation, Libya, Egypt and the Sudan were also affected by the dramatic change in manpower supplies and requirements caused throughout the Arab world by the development of oil-fields. Both the Sudan and Egypt became major sources of labour supply for the oil-producing countries of Saudi Arabia and the Gulf, and the resulting emigration of able-bodied men left many villages depleted of skilled manpower. Libya, on the other hand, was forced to import labour, including hundreds of thousands of Egyptians, to provide the manpower needed for its huge development projects. This produced social and cultural strains in the major cities and, at times, political conflict as well.

While the status of many women in both Libya and the Sudan remained largely unchanged over the period, the destruction of household production in both countries – for varying reasons – adversely affected the lives of the rural women. However, in Egypt the spread of feminism in the cities improved the lot of those who were members of the upper and middle classes. Legal changes improving their position regarding divorce, inheritance and child custody, as well as their greater access to educational and employment opportunities, led to a significant change in their role in society.[1] By the mid-1970s the emancipation of urban women was also affecting the country's birth-rate, which had fallen slightly as a result of their greater access and receptivity to birth-control methods. But even these changes still left the majority of Egyptian women, especially those in the villages, plagued by the perennial evils of poverty and inequality.

ECONOMIC DEVELOPMENT

From the previous discussion it is clear that the political instability in all three states was caused to a large degree by their economic problems. Egypt in 1940 had already a considerable industrial base and a highly efficient agricultural sector. It also had a large manpower pool, with a considerable number of skilled workers. Thus the growth of organised labour unions contributed exten-

[1] Judith Tucker, 'Women in the Middle East', *Middle East yearbook, 1980*, 37.

sively to the reorganisation of the political structure, but they also tended to become clients of the large parties, such as the Wafd. Moreover, Egypt had little income other than from agricultural exports, principally cotton (which in 1952 accounted for 84 per cent of the total exports), thus making her economy highly vulnerable to international market fluctuations.

Although the nineteenth-century Egyptian rulers, and, after 1882, the British, provided a basic and modern economic infrastructure, substantial changes did not take place during the inter-war period. And during the war, with export restrictions on cotton, the economy came close to a standstill, fuelling anti-British resentment even further. The emphasis on agricultural expansion, therefore, must be regarded as one of the great errors of both the British and the Egyptian governments. But, as Mabro argues:

> Governments were in any case operating under severe financial constraints since their fiscal autonomy was constrained by the Capitulations [not abolished until 1938] which prevented them from taxing the rich foreign community and from imposing tariffs. Powerful vested interests became entrenched in land, trade and finance, and hence in the political structure; and they made sure that government policies would favour their sectional objectives.

Thus, as Mabro concludes, 'The conditions necessary for the transformation of an export economy into a modern, industrial and diversified economy did not exist.'[1]

The Revolutionary Council addressed itself in 1952 to the abolition of large estates and the redistribution of land, the removal of 'foreign vested interests' and the further extension of the industrial sector. But although the officers came to power with great idealism, the political realities prevented sweeping and immediate economic changes. They had no particular economic ideology to implement, and their initial decrees amounted in real economic terms to very little. Land reform, for example, affected only six per cent of the total cultivated land and was essentially a political measure to obtain greater public, but essentially *fallāh* (peasant), support.

Until 1956 – with the exception of the much publicised Aswan High Dam scheme – there were few signs of any real economic initiative. It was then that the Suez and other foreign companies were nationalised, 'which meant that the greater part of the foreign share in the Egyptian economy had been liquidated'. This

[1] R. Mabro, *The Egyptian economy 1952–1972* (Oxford, 1974), 23.

was followed by further nationalisations of indigenous companies, including the powerful Banque al-Misr, Egypt's first national bank. By 1960 the public sector was nearly the same size as the private sector.

As a result of growing Soviet influence, but especially of the failure of the Egyptian–Syrian union, Nāṣir proclaimed in May 1962 the National Charter which set out sweeping changes in the socio-economic structure of the country. Influenced by Soviet advisers and a growing socialist literature, this charter outlined the regime's plans for industrialisation: the expansion of the industrial infrastructure, the nationalisation of nearly all remaining private and financial enterprises, closer control of foreign aid, and a limit of 100 *feddans* each for agricultural owners.

The development plan of 1960–5 was followed by another covering the following five years. These were designed to establish an Arab model of socialist planned economy. By the mid-1960s, the 'old bourgeoisie' had been dismantled, as one author has asserted.[1]

Large-scale foreign loans, especially economic assistance from the Soviet Union and other eastern-bloc states, assisted this economic transformation. Although there was a noticeable improvement in the economy, with an average growth rate of about 6 per cent throughout this period, three factors militated against continuous growth. The first, and perhaps the most important, was the decrease in foreign private as well as public investment – no doubt on account of western fears of Soviet involvement. A second problem was that of an unwieldy and conservative bureaucracy, a problem which confounded successive generations of governments. Third was the high cost of maintaining the military establishment. Nevertheless, progress was made through the expansion of industrial exports. Cotton exports, for instance, in 1970 accounted for only 49 per cent of total exports. Exports of manufactured goods and of petroleum (from Sinai) had increased from about 7 per cent to about 40 per cent of the total export during the same period, with food processing and textiles predominating.

The 1967 war had serious consequences for the economy. Not only was Egypt deprived of revenues from the Suez Canal, but the substantial and rapidly expanding export revenues generated

[1] *Ibid.*

by the expanding oil production in the Sinai were also lost. In consequence, until after the October war of 1973, the Soviet Union and some Arab states, notably Libya and Saudi Arabia, assisted Egypt. After Sādāt had instituted his *infitāḥ* policy in 1971, and gradually dismantled the 'socialist' economy, western investors slowly began to return. However, western public investments remained cautious as long as the confrontation with Israel continued. In the private sector, however, Egypt continued to be heavily dependent on outside finance, now from such institutions as the World Bank and the International Monetary Fund, and the increasingly friendly OPEC countries. But, as in 1952, the core problem facing Egypt's economy was still the seemingly insurmountable demographic problem, with a population growth of 2.5 per cent per annum, but an annual GDP increase of only 1.3 per cent (1970–5).

Unlike Egypt, the Sudan had a small industrial base when it attained independence. Indeed, by 1960, only 2 per cent of the GDP came from manufacturing industries, which by 1973 had increased only to 7 per cent. The Sudan's major problems were its poor communication infrastructure and the lack of an integrated and efficient administrative structure and economic planning agencies. Moreover, the country lacked adequate funds for development until the mid-1970s. Yet the Sudan had great development potential which came to be recognised only in the latter part of our period.

The Sudanese, like the Egyptian, economy was largely dependent on the cultivation of cotton, amounting to about 45 per cent of the total income from exports. The Gezira irrigation scheme of 300 000 acres, which opened in 1925, continued to constitute the backbone of the country's economy. Yet less than 10 per cent of the cultivable land was being utilised agriculturally. Thus, during the 1970s the Sudan became increasingly attractive as a potential agricultural supplier to African, and especially Middle Eastern, states.

The period between 1936 and 1942 saw the rise of an indigenous commercial class due to the reinvestment of capital gained from the large private agricultural schemes in the White Nile area. These private schemes were primarily owned by the well-to-do religious families and pensioned civil servants who formed the bulk of the government's Sudanese supporters. Foreign communities, such as the Greeks and Syrians (who also had a large presence in Egypt), as well as the Egyptians, Europeans and *Muwalladīn* (Sudanese of Egyptian and Turkish origin) were not engaged in agricultural activities. They remained, however, dominant in commercial life and in the export trade.

The bulk of the Sudan's trade was carried on with the two Condominium powers, Egypt and the United Kingdom. The remainder of the Sudan's foreign trade was with neighbouring countries, and mostly consisted of cotton, gum arabic and sesame. The heavy dependence on cotton earnings was, as in the case of Egypt, one of the major income problems, as international cotton prices fluctuated with demand. Moreover, the country lacked any realistic policy for diversification of its revenue sources, nor did there exist a definite industrialisation policy. Only ginneries, soap, glass and vegetable-oil factories were established to satisfy the needs of the growing urban communities. The government's role in encouraging industrial development was limited to the production of spare parts for its transport network.

In 1956, on the eve of independence, an Act was passed to encourage industrial development by attracting domestic and foreign capital. The Act allowed for large tax exemptions and royalties, and it promised government subsidies. Despite this, industrial expansion in the private sector remained principally concentrated in traditional areas such as transport and agriculture. Indigenous capital, without backing from international companies, was unwilling to face the investment risks. Because of this fear, the governments in office always encouraged the promotion and expansion of the public sector. In 1961 'Abbūd's military regime launched a 'ten-year plan' which aimed at the diversification of the country's economy by establishing governmental industrial schemes, especially the canning sector, which was backed by the IMF and the World Bank. Nevertheless, expansion remained slow, and throughout the 1960s neither the military nor the civilian governments were able to improve the economy significantly.

In 1970 Numayrī's military regime introduced a five-year development plan. The target of the plan was to secure an increase in the GDP at an average annual rate of 7.6 per cent as against 4.9 per cent in the previous five years. But, like all previous schemes, it concentrated on increasing agricultural production by

60 per cent. But the plan was short-lived, as it depended on massive aid from the socialist bloc. The political changes that took place after the failure of the 1971 pro-Communist coup reintroduced western and especially Arab (principally OPEC) aid and led to the revision of the nationalisation decrees of May 1970. A new policy to link the Arab oil money and western technical know-how to exploit the Sudan's vast agricultural potential was pursued after 1973. However, due to the continuing political instability, the flow of capital was limited.

Libya was rated as one of the poorest countries in the world until the first major oil discoveries in the early 1950s, and even then the subsequent concessionary agreements (1955–6) took a decade to produce substantial profits. The country's principal income before the discovery of oil was derived from agriculture and from leasing fees from British and American military bases in the country. Other NATO countries provided additional financial assistance, which barely met the annual costs of running the state. It was this financial dependency, internal corruption and lack of economic development that prompted the military to intervene in late 1969.

By January 1970 the new government was ready to launch its campaign for higher oil prices. After a series of production cutbacks, and in the case of Royal Dutch Shell a shut-down of its Libyan terminal, the companies settled one by one. The new price was set at $2.53 a barrel, the highest outside the United States. The government then announced that it regarded this as a rectification of past injustices, not a new price, and that more demands were to come. Four months later the government gave notice of a new increase in oil taxes as well as a new price 'differential' to compensate both for the higher quality and the low sulphur content of Libyan crude and its proximity to western markets. In the face of a decision of the state-owned Italian company, ENI, and of France's ERAP, not to cooperate with a secret alliance of American, British, Dutch and other French firms formed to fight the Libyan demands, the companies agreed. In April 1971, the Tripoli Agreement raised the posted price of Libyan crude to just under $3.45 a barrel, an increase of 35 per cent. The agreement also provided for additional small rises each year until 1975, as well as an increase in the rate of income tax paid by the companies from 5 to 55 per cent. For the first time the threat of an embargo had been employed, but the agreement of the companies, and mediation by Egypt, made it unnecessary to translate the threat into action.

After the price rises of the early 1970s, the four-fold rise that followed the October 1973 war and the nationalisation of the oil sector, Libya's oil production dropped considerably, falling at one point to below one million barrels a day. By the end of 1975, however, world demand for higher grades of crude oil, which can produce more petrol than the heavier fuels needed to heat homes and industry, was rising and Libyan production was able to recover its normal level of two million barrels a day. By the end of 1977 the government was predicting an average of 2.4 million barrels a day. In line with this expansion the government signed new exploration and production agreements with several western companies to develop new oil and gas fields both onshore and in the Mediterranean. Libya also increased her participation in refining and marketing of crude oil – the so-called downstream operations – and expanded her refining capacity. Development of the petrochemical sector and the expansion of the country's own tanker fleet were also under way. In April 1972 the government instituted a provisional one-year development plan, followed in the next year by one for three years. With additional revenues after the autumn of 1973, this plan was amended to allow for increased expenditure on agriculture and social services.

CONCLUSION

The period from 1936 to 1975 heralded historic changes in north-east Africa that still continue to affect the region. Foremost among these were the achievement of independence in the case of Sudan and Libya and the rise of new class forces throughout the area. The take-over of power by the military after the failure of attempts at democratic rule, and the realignment of international relations, were also themes that marked the three countries during this period. Finally, while Egypt and the Sudan wrestled with the need to create a viable economy that would sustain independence, Libya gradually moved out of the orbit of the poorer states and by 1975 was able to use its oil-fed wealth to affect developments not only in the region but in other parts of Africa and the Middle East as well. In the Sudan and Libya the achievement of formal independence was followed by attempts to resolve internal differences that had been exacerbated during the colonial period. In the Sudan these differences were especially pronounced over the question of the south; in Libya they concerned the very different cultures of Tripolitania and Cyrenaica. Since each of these disputes focussed on the very nature of the state and indicated the difficulty of creating national loyalties in the wake of independence, they often cut across class lines and led to particularly bitter factional fighting that, as often as not, spilled over into the streets of the major cities. Although Egypt, with its long history of national unity, avoided clashes of this kind, the disputes over the Sudan in the early 1950s clearly played a role in the rise of the Free Officers and in the consolidation of Nāṣir's personal power.

In Egypt and the Sudan, the growth of industry and transport during the war created a new class of urban workers that by the end of the conflict was ready to challenge the traditional landowners and, to a certain extent, the newly enriched merchant class, for power. Although this process was delayed in Libya, the emergence of a new technocratic élite in the wake of the commencement of oil production, and the subsequent expansion of government administration, gradually destroyed the power of the monarchy and made possible the 1969 revolution. The combination of factional struggles against national unity with the emergence of class conflict led to prolonged internal dissension in the region in the 1950s and 1960s. This was met with repression and, at different times in the three countries, with a take-over of power by the military. Yet the failure of the regimes to come to grips with both economic and social change, and to create viable channels of political expression, had led by the mid-1970s to the emergence of new opposition against the military rulers in the Sudan, Egypt and Libya.

In foreign affairs, all three states moved closer to the Soviet Union and adopted various degrees of non-alignment in an attempt to further their efforts to remove the last vestiges of western domination. Like the experience with democracy, however, the close links with the Soviet Union proved to be temporary, as each regime discovered that alliances with Moscow carried unacceptable conditions. As a result Anwār Sādāt in Egypt, Numayrī in the Sudan and Qadhdhāfī in Libya by the mid-1970s had all reopened or extended their relations with the west, particularly on the trade and economic levels, in an attempt to gain more room for manoeuvre. The emergence of the Arab oil states in the Middle East helped to encourage this trend and, in addition, provided a new source of potential aid and comfort which each of the regimes sought to exploit to the fullest extent possible.

CHAPTER 11

THE MAGHRIB*

The Maghrib, which in Arabic means the place of the sunset, is not a precise geographical term. It has been construed at its narrowest as Morocco alone and at its broadest as all of northern Africa west of Egypt, including Mauritania, where Arabic is the national language. The present chapter excludes both Libya and Mauritania and focusses upon the political and economic development of the core countries, Algeria, Morocco and Tunisia, in a comparative perspective suggested by their similar colonial experiences. The French presence decisively reshaped all three societies, though in different ways, reflecting the particular colonial situations. In Algeria, where occupation by the French began in 1830, the indigenous economic and political order was most affected, whereas Morocco, the last to lose its independence, was least affected, especially in the northern zone, which in 1912 fell under Spanish rather than French control. In all three societies French education (and Hispano-Arabic education in Spanish Morocco) formed new élites imbued with nationalism and eager to take over the modern economic and political structures largely dominated by European settlers. Pre-colonial traditions influenced the independent regimes, established in Morocco and Tunisia in 1956, and in Algeria in 1962, only insofar as they were refracted through the prism of anti-colonial struggle.

The major influence upon these regimes was the struggle itself, which was more protracted and violent in the Maghrib than in most of colonial Africa because of the more extensive French and settler interests conditioning it. It generated political élites whose organisations and social followings in turn helped to define the new regimes and their respective strategies of development. The Second World War is a convenient starting point for a discussion of what happened after independence, for not only did it catalyse latent nationalist forces and generate an international climate more sympathetic to anti-colonial movements, but it also accelerated the

* The spelling of proper names in this chapter is in accordance with French and English usage.

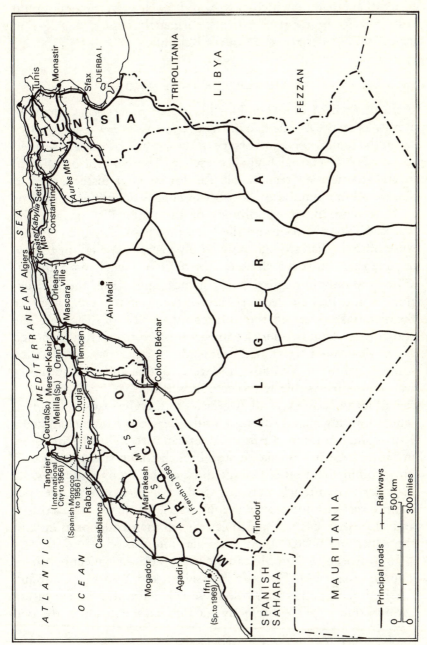

28   The Maghrib c. 1975.

MEDITERRANEAN   SEA

Tunis
Monastir
Sfax
DJERBA I.
TRIPOLITANIA
LIBYA
FEZZAN

TUNISIA

Aurès Mts

Setif
Greater Kabylia Mts
Constantine

Algiers

A L G E R I A

Oran
Mers-el-Kebir
Mascara
Orleans-ville
Tlemcen
Oudja
Ain Madi

Colomb Béchar

Ceuta (Sp.)
Melilla (Sp.)
Tangier
(International
City to 1956)
(Spanish Morocco
to 1956)
Fez
Rabat
Casablanca

M O R O C C O
M T S
A T L A S
(French to 1956)

Marrakesh

Mogador
Agadir
Ifni
(Sp. to 1969)

Tindouf

SPANISH
SAHARA

MAURITANIA

A T L A N T I C

O C E A N

Principal roads
Railways
500 km
300 miles

565

pace of political confrontation in the Maghrib to a speed that was faster than that to which post-war French governments could respond with appropriate reforms. Ultimately, in fact, the Algerian cancer was to destroy the Fourth Republic.

THE STRUGGLE FOR INDEPENDENCE

France's control over her North African possessions appeared almost as secure on the eve of the Second World War as in 1930, when the hundredth anniversary of the capture of Algiers seemed to portend an eternal French presence. The handful of Muslim politicians deemed responsible for earlier civil disturbances in Tunis and in a number of Moroccan cities were either in gaol or in exile, and the most militant of the nationalist parties, the Tunisian Néo-Destour and the Parti du Peuple Algérien (PPA), were officially banned and only barely visible. The fall of France in June 1940, however, shattered the myth of French invincibility. While the only immediate consequence, apart from the destruction of the French fleet at Mers-el-Kebir in Algeria, was the Spanish take-over of the international city of Tangier, the subsequent Anglo-American invasion of North Africa launched on 8 November 1942 had tremendous repercussions. French forces loyal to the Vichy regime were routed, and civil authority was temporarily subjected to an overwhelming military presence: the Allies in Morocco and Algeria, and the Germans in Tunisia, where fighting raged for six months between Rommel's Afrika Korps and a combined Anglo-American force. During this time, in Morocco as in Tunisia, the top French administrator remained only nominally in office, a lame duck of the Vichy regime, while in Algeria the French were engaged, as one Algerian leader put it, in 'a real race for power. Republicans, Gaullists, Monarchists, and Jews were each trying to cash in on their collaboration with the Allies and protect their particular interests.'[1]

In Morocco, Sultan Mohammed ben Youssef's meeting on 22 January 1943 with Franklin Roosevelt and Winston Churchill whetted his appetite for a role in world affairs and 'a new future for my country'.[2] He discreetly encouraged the fusion of the two

[1] Ferhat Abbas, 'Manifeste du peuple algérien', cited by Charles-André Julien, *L'Afrique du Nord en marche*, third ed. (Paris, 1972), 247.
[2] Roger Le Tourneau, *Évolution politique de l'Afrique du Nord musulmane, 1920–1961* (Paris, 1962), 206.

principal pre-war nationalist parties into the new Istiqlal (Independence) Party, which issued its first call for Moroccan independence on 11 January 1944. In Tunisia and Algeria wartime conditions encouraged their respective nationalist leaders, Habib Bourguiba and the more moderate Ferhat Abbas. In Tunisia, Moncef Bey exercised real sovereignty by appointing a cabinet of ministers on 1 January 1943 without the consent of the French resident-general. By exiling Moncef in May (with the agreement of the Allies) on unjustified charges of collaboration with the Axis, the French not only created a new national symbol but eliminated the only viable alternative to Habib Bourguiba's more militant brand of nationalism. And even in Algeria, where nationalism had seemed less deeply rooted, Ferhat Abbas issued a Manifesto of the Algerian People on 12 February 1943, after contacts with a high American as well as a French official.[1] The manifesto called for a separate Algerian constitution guaranteeing 'immediate and effective' political participation for the Muslim majority. After having confessed seven years earlier to his inability to discover an Algerian nation distinct from the France of which it was a part, Abbas now concluded that 'the hour has passed when an Algerian Muslim can ask to be anything but a Muslim Algerian', that is, of Algerian, not French, nationality.[2] Indeed, to contain the growing nationalist tide would have required substantial reform.

In theory the problem of reform was simpler in the two Protectorates than in Algeria. In Tunisia and Morocco the French had preserved the semblance of pre-colonial state institutions, with the bey and the sultan respectively exercising nominal sovereignty under treaties which accorded a French resident-general full control over their foreign relations. In practice, however, this French foreign ministry official had also extended his control, in the form of a direct administration which at the upper echelons was for the most part staffed by French nationals, over internal matters as well, on the strength of his authorisation in each treaty to carry out 'reforms which the French government considers useful'.[3] Significant reform after the war could have taken the form of expanding the effective jurisdictions of indigenous ministers and administrators. Instead the French Committee of National Liberation, after removing Moncef, imposed

---

[1] Julien, *L'Afrique du Nord*, 381.
[2] *Ibid.*, 247.   [3] *Ibid.*, 49–50.

a French secretary-general upon the Tunisian government to restrict its powers even further. However, in 1945 the Tunisians were given control of an additional ministry together with slight increases in electoral representation, but these limited reforms only served further to discourage Tunisian nationalists who might otherwise have accepted a programme that clearly led to self-government within the framework of the Protectorate. Indeed it was the French government's later refusal, on 15 December 1951, to countenance a meaningful, if gradual, transfer of power, that precipitated the final showdown between the Néo-Destour and the Protectorate authorities that led to independence. Likewise in Morocco, where fewer indigenous cadres had been trained, the French responded to nationalist demands for independence first by arresting leaders of the Istiqlal and then by initiating a programme of economic but not political reforms.

Algeria's legal framework was less susceptible than that of the Protectorates to incremental reforms that could have satisfied and reinforced moderate nationalists like Ferhat Abbas. Algeria was in theory an integral part of France, made up of three departments administered by the French Ministry of the Interior together with the Saharan territories which were under military rule. The three departments, headed by a governor-general appointed by the French council of ministers, also enjoyed a measure of budgetary autonomy not shared by their counterparts in metropolitan France. The only potential channels for Muslim participation were consultative municipal, departmental, and supra-departmental assemblies, dominated by European settlers and, after 1944, the French parliament. The logic of the system could permit measures mitigating inequalities of personal and civic status between Muslims and non-Muslims but not the sorts of political reform that recognised Algerian (Muslim) nationalism and offered it an institutional framework. Indeed, de Gaulle's deputy, General Catroux, indignantly rejected Abbas's manifesto, especially the specific recommendations added to it that the 'Algerian nation' be recognised and a constituent assembly be elected by universal suffrage to draft an Algerian constitution. The farthest de Gaulle would go was nominally to extend French citizenship to all Algerian Muslims, marginally to increase their representation in various local assemblies, and integrate several tens of thousands of them into the European electorate through the *ordonnance* of

7 March 1944. Such reforms, coming too late, could no longer satisfy Ferhat Abbas or most other relatively 'assimilated' Algerian Muslims who had wanted only to be French. Much less did they satisfy Messali Hadj's outlawed Parti de Peuple Algérien (PPA) or the reformist *'ulamā'* (religious scholars), who had affirmed the existence of an Algerian nation before the war. Virtually overnight Abbas's new movement, the Friends of the Algerian Manifesto, acquired half a million voting members (out of a possible Muslim male electorate of 1.7 million), and the PPA gained control of it.

While radicalising public opinion during the spring of 1945, the PPA had also been organising a clandestine *maquis*, the Arab Forces of the Interior, along the lines of the forces of the French Resistance. It seems that a general insurrection against French rule was already under consideration. On 8 May, following the official celebrations of the victory over Germany, violence erupted in Sétif when police tried to discipline Muslim demonstrators and a shot was fired. Bands began indiscriminately to kill Europeans, and the violence spread so quickly to other distant parts of the Constantine Department that it seems to have involved some degree of organisation, though no fully elaborated plan. Possibly some PPA militants had jumped the gun. The French reaction, in turn, probably ensured a future insurrection. The official vengeance for 103 French lives was perceived as verging on genocide: 6000 to 8000 Algerians killed, for the most part by French armed forces rather than by enraged or panicked settlers. 'On that day the Algerian people lost its illusions and understood that it would never be free and respected until it became strong...the Revolution had begun,' a spokesman of the Front de Libération Nationale (FLN) subsequently observed.[1] The impact of the French repression upon the future leaders of the Algerian revolution that erupted on 1 November 1954 cannot be overemphasised. A tragic cycle of terror, repression and counter-terror would finally involve substantial proportions of Algerian Muslims and settlers alike.

In the Moroccan and Tunisian Protectorates, by contrast, independence was achieved primarily by political processes that set limits to the use of violence. The underlying settler interests, which were not as great as those in Algeria, were more amenable

---

[1] *El Moujahid*, no. 23, 5 May 1958, cited by Julien, *L'Afrique du Nord*, 379.

to political mediation. In 1955 French North Africa's 1.7 million settlers constituted 11 per cent of Algeria's population but only 6.7 and 5.2 per cent, respectively, of Tunisia's and Morocco's. They had appropriated over one-quarter of Algeria's arable land and earned over half the income derived from agriculture, and 90 per cent of that derived from exports. In Tunisia they owned one-fifth of the arable land but only 7 per cent in Morocco. Most settlers lived in the cities, but in Algeria they monopolised the industrial and tertiary sector to a far greater extent than in the Protectorates. Industry developed more rapidly in Morocco after the war, but European industrial interests were less opposed to Muslim interests than was Algeria's racist *petite bourgeoisie*.

Algeria's million settlers were sufficiently powerful to prevent any French government from developing a coherent policy of reform or even properly implementing the Algerian statute of 1947, which gave Muslims half the seats in an Algerian assembly and representation in the French National Assembly. Elections were systematically rigged by a French administration that was 'colonised' by settler interests. Settlers also sabotaged French efforts to reform the Protectorates, for they enjoyed representation and political influence in Paris, notably through the Radical Party which participated in most government cabinets of the Fourth Republic. But they could not, as in Algeria, continually exclude indigenous nationalists from the exercise of power. The violence that engulfed Algeria after 1954 was in large measure the consequence of the settlers' power over weak governments in Paris to block any dialogue, let alone negotiation, with French-educated nationalists. Tunisians and Moroccans, by contrast, were in regular contact with French officials both in Paris and in their respective capitals of Tunis and Rabat.

Independently of the socio-economic stakes at issue, however, the strengths and structures of the nationalist forces in the three French territories of North Africa varied considerably and also conditioned the course of colonial conflict. Their relative strength and cohesion in Tunisia, for instance, explains the more economic use of violence there than in Morocco, despite relatively more entrenched and less adaptable settler interests in what was the older of the two Protectorates.

The nationalist movements, in turn, were largely conditioned by the élite structures of their respective societies. By the Second World War the 'traditional' élite used by the French in their 'native' administration had lost their moral authority in both Algeria and Tunisia. Although they remained strong in Morocco, their status depended increasingly on their having a French education. This French-educated Moroccan élite came predominantly from the bourgeoisie of Fez, the so-called Fassis. After this élite sealed its alliance with the palace by the formation of the Istiqlal Party, the French authorities came to rely increasingly upon rural notables, especially chieftains of Berber origin like Thami al-Glawi, Pasha of Marrakesh, as far as 'native' administration was concerned. Thus the French reinforced al-Glawi's authority at the expense of the sultan, although the French had originally pacified the country in the latter's name. Ultimately a coalition of these rejected urban notables was to triumph over the rural notables the French now co-opted, but not before urbanisation and industrialisation had generated other social forces in support of the nationalist struggle. The leaders of this coalition were insufficiently organised to keep these forces under political control, and their generally high traditional urban status, while giving them a certain homogeneity, hardly helped them in their efforts to enlist the support of a primarily rural society, or even of other urban strata.

The French-educated élites of Algeria and Tunisia were substantially larger than their Moroccan counterpart, due to the extension over longer time-periods of French education. By the Second World War their social origins were also more heterogeneous, due to a greater fragmentation of the traditional élites, the broader bases of recruitment into the French educational system, and to the opportunities for social mobility offered by colonial rule. Traditional social status did not, as in Morocco, cut individuals off from large segments of their respective societies. But, in the case of Algeria, education did. Whereas in the Protectorates the system of modern education gave a considerable place to Arabic, the Algerian system treated Arabic as a foreign language. The provision in de Gaulle's *ordonnance* of 1944 calling for greater infusions of Arabic into the educational system was not implemented. Consequently, French-educated Algerians did not, like their counterparts in Morocco and Tunisia, enjoy privileged access to a potentially national culture. In Tunisia, the tradition of a bilingual education, represented by Sadiki College, engendered élite cohesion without cutting it off from the Arabic-speaking masses. Tunisia, too, was linguistically much more homogeneous than either Algeria or Morocco, where Berber-speakers comprised respectively 25 and 40 per cent of the population. Consequently the élite not only enjoyed the distinction of being educated in French ways but also possessed a capacity for social communication that would ensure its cultural hegemony. In Algeria, on the other hand, the *évolués* were fit only for an assimilation into a French society that refused to accept them. The majority of this élite happened to be Kabyle rather than Arab; and any cohesion and mass followings it derived from shared ethnic origins boomeranged against its claim to be a national élite. In 1949, for instance, Aït Ahmed was dismissed as leader of the PPA's Secret Organisation (forerunner of the FLN) for espousing 'Berber particularism'. Berber–Arab rivalries should not, however, be overstressed in analysing political cleavages within the élite: but no shared Kabyle identity could hold it together, much less assure it cultural hegemony.

French-educated Tunisians in fact acquired considerably more cohesion than their Algerian or even their Moroccan counterparts. By the eve of the Second World War, half of those entering Sadiki College came from the Sahel, the agricultural area south of Tunis that concentrated one-tenth of Tunisia's population in closely interconnected but rival villages not too dissimilar, sociologically speaking, from those of Algerian Kabylia. These sons of peasant freeholders were by then taking over the élite Franco-Arab educational institutions that earlier, as in Morocco, had fallen by default to the sons of urban notables, the mamluks and *baldi* of Tunis. Upwardly mobile, the Sahelians could not find ready acceptance within the traditional urban élite. But their shared origins provided a ready source of solidarity in their new context – and coming from the Sahel did not, as in the case of the Kabyle of Algeria, prevent them from acquiring cultural hegemony. Through regional solidarity they were able to promote a national culture readily acceptable to other educated Tunisians, including sons of the traditional élite. Their organisational vehicle, the Néo-Destour, was historically rooted in the Sahel, but in the 1940s it acquired a strong base in Tunis, largely under the leadership of young members of established families.

The ultimate challenge to the educated élite in each North African territory was a political one. It could hardly avoid becoming involved in the nationalist struggle. Indeed failure to assert leadership would only allow other forces to capture it by default. The failure of the Algerian élite had already become apparent by 1945, when a congress of the Friends of the Algerian Manifesto proclaimed Messali Hadj 'the incontestable leader of the Algerian people' at the expense of Ferhat Abbas. Before the war Messali had organised many of the Algerian emigrants working in France, and his PPA had also acquired considerable strength in working-class districts of Algiers. Abbas, on the other hand, though representing a substantial portion of the educated élite, could not organise the spontaneous mass support his manifesto had suddenly aroused. A radical minority of the intellectuals joined the PPA, legally reconstituted as the Mouvement pour le Triomphe des Libertés Démocratiques (MTLD), to contest post-war elections. A further division that was not experienced to the same degree by the Moroccan or Tunisian élite was that between French-educated and Arabic-educated intellectuals. The latter, numerically weak but expressing the powerful ideal of a national Algerian culture, had created their own Islamic reform movement under the leadership of Abdelhamid Ben Badis. He had died in 1940 but his movement endured, further weakening the claims of the French-educated élite to national leadership. In the final phases of the independence struggle this French-educated élite, indecisive and wracked by internal divisions, was to prove itself marginal. Though many of its members had rallied to the FLN by 1956, it was to be subjected to the directives of the very different breeds of men who had organised the revolution.

In the Protectorates the élites were more cohesive and maintained command of their respective nationalist movements. Being culturally less cut off from their societies than the Algerian *évolués*, they also succeeded in mobilising substantial mass support. Both the Istiqlal and the Néo-Destour were able, for instance, to mobilise the Koranic 'free schools' similar to the ones Ben Badis established in Algeria. However, the Moroccans experienced considerably more difficulty than the Tunisians in controlling the social forces they helped to unleash. For one thing the Fassis did not possess a built-in peasant base like that of the Sahelians. More importantly, the Tunisians had a head start of roughly one generation not only in Franco-Arab education but also in political experience. In the post-war period their mass organisation was considerably more developed than was that of the newly founded Istiqlal. Perhaps, too, the relatively more modest class origins of the Tunisian élite contributed to its greater ability to assimilate organisational techniques from the French Socialist and Communist Parties and also, incidentally, from a settler community that had been more exposed than Morocco was to Fascism as well as the Socialist and Communist movements.

In addition to differences between the élites, the strength of linkages between élites and the masses also varied with the degree and types of social dislocation that made masses 'available' for nationalist activity. Native Algerian society had experienced the greatest dislocation before the outbreak of the revolution. By the mid-1950s at least half of the modern Algerian work-force was in France and the majority was no longer Kabyle. Even if the Algerian élite had been more cohesive, it would have had difficulty organising and controlling the proletariat. Only in 1956 was an Algerian trade union finally founded, though tens of thousands of Algerians had acquired some political experience in French trade unions. On the other hand Tunisia enjoyed a tradition of autonomous trade unionism. Though earlier attempts had failed, Farhat Hached successfully founded the Union Générale Tunisiens du Travail (UGTT) in 1946 in close cooperation with the Néo-Destour leadership. The Tunisian working force was relatively small and accessible, concentrated in Tunis, Sfax, and southern mining centres. By 1955 at least 80 per cent of the UGTT's 150000 members had also joined the Néo-Destour Party.

Even in Morocco substantial numbers of peasants were already being attracted to the new European cities before the Second World War. Morocco's post-war economic boom, relatively greater than those of other more developed colonial economies, permitted the process of urbanisation to catch up with and even surpass that of the other territories by 1955. The rapidity of the process itself contributed to instability. In the post-war period there was probably less unemployment or disguised unemployment in the new Muslim urban concentrations around European Casablanca than in either Algiers or Tunis. Miserable shanty towns of the kind that surrounded all North African cities were not necessarily potential tinderboxes of social unrest. But in

Casablanca they were to become so, in part because the Berber immigrants retained their rural roots while assimilating new roles and identities, and in part because in Morocco's expanding economy they were better off and could harbour rising aspirations. As in Algeria, trade-unionism was relatively underdeveloped, and the urban proletariat and sub-proletariat escaped the control and organisation exercised over them in Tunisia by the Néo-Destour. But their rising expectations were to coincide with those of Moroccan nationalism.

The efforts of the colonial authorities to stifle nationalist aspirations only intensified their appeal. The nationalist leaders, however, were faced with the problem of how to channel the burgeoning forces and how to direct the struggle. Their ability to do so depended on the scale reached by the conflict and their own organisational capacities.

Tunisia benefited from an élite that was better organised than those in the other two countries and from a French administration that was relatively more enlightened and able to avoid the excesses committed in Morocco and, more especially, in Algeria after the Second World War. Breakdowns in negotiations for reforms resulted not so much in widespread violence as in renewed Tunisian efforts to organise the rank and file so as to convince France that a modern Tunisian nation – Bourguiba's *pays réel* – really existed and had to be recognised. With negotiations for further reforms at a standstill in 1945, Bourguiba departed for Cairo to seek support from both the Arab League and international public opinion. His deputy, Salah ben Youssef, however, remained in Tunis to develop the organisation of the party, outlawed since 1938 and partly compromised by the wartime contacts of some of its secondary leadership with the Germans. As well as the UGTT, the Union Nationale des Agriculteurs Tunisiens and the Union Tunisienne des Artisans et Commerçants were also created in the late 1940s. The Néo-Destour was also able for a time to establish a National Front with the Destour, its pre-war rival that had clearly lost the contest for national leadership. The one sector recalcitrant to Néo-Destour control was that of the students and faculty of Zitouna, the traditional Islamic university of Tunis. One of the senior '*ulamā*', Fadhl ben Achour, tried with some support from the UGTT to develop an autonomous movement. The Néo-Destour youth organisation, however, was more than a match for Zitouna students on the streets, and by 1951 a majority of these, frustrated by lack of university reform and prospects for employment, were sympathisers with, or members of, Bourguiba's party.

The 'Supreme Warrior' himself returned to Tunis in 1949 with the consent of the French resident-general to stimulate new efforts at setting up an autonomous Tunisian government. The French government favoured further reforms, and two members of the Néo-Destour, including Salah ben Youssef, were mandated to join a 'homogeneous' (all Tunisian) government in 1951. However, late in the year negotiations over the granting of internal autonomy collapsed under settler pressures. Bourguiba's decision to precipitate matters by engaging in mass agitation against French attempts to introduce Franco-Tunisian co-sovereignty met with predictable police repression, including his own arrest on 18 January 1952. Mopping-up operations, notably on Cap Bon, resulted in scores of Tunisian deaths but could not compare with the operations launched against the Algerians in 1945. The Algerian deaths had not served the cause of any political organisation, whereas the Tunisian ones contributed to a national mythology of sacrifice and martyrdom incarnated by Bourguiba in prison and propagated by the party faithful.

Any eventual trade-union challenge to his or the party's authority was severely diminished on 5 December 1952, when Farhat Hached was assassinated 'under conditions that have never been elucidated' but which undoubtedly involved French (Corsican) hands.[1] Terror and counter-terror spread in 1953, while most of the Néo-Destour leadership was either in prison or exile. Nevertheless clandestine party networks managed to keep most of the 3000 armed *fellagha* (guerrillas), especially those recruited from the Sahel, under political control. Consequently, when the Mendès-France government indicated that it was prepared to grant internal autonomy to Tunisia, Bourguiba, transferred to France in 1955, was able to order them to lay down their arms. Tunisia's was the only national liberation movement in North Africa to enjoy some of the glamour of conducting a guerrilla struggle for independence without losing control of it – partly, no doubt, because Mendès-France acted before the violence got out of hand, selecting Tunisia, rather than Morocco, to test out

[1] Le Tourneau, *Évolution politique*, 130; cf. Julien, *L'Afrique du Nord*, 389.

his policy of reforming the Protectorates so as to preserve a French Algeria. Even before his surprise visit of 31 July 1954 to Tunis, however, the Néo-Destour had managed to build up a political apparatus of 100000 members wielding decisive moral authority over the population. Police repression, in modest doses over extended periods, had unintentionally helped the educated élite to forge a nation. When Bourguiba was finally allowed to return on 1 June, 1955, his moral authority seemed unlimited. Though he was challenged within the party by Salah ben Youssef, who was opportunistically calling for immediate independence, he triumphed over his former deputy by appealing to the political realism of a seasoned party and trade-union leadership. After the party congress held at Sfax in November, the party cadres were on Bourguiba's side and ben Youssef's only recourse was to terrorism. The last 'Youssefist' band was mopped up in the spring of 1956. Meanwhile Bourguiba had achieved independence and joined the new government as prime minister.

Neither in Morocco nor Algeria did there grow up a disciplined party organisation to match that of Tunisia. Too weak to develop autonomous leadership, the urban educated élite that founded the Istiqlal had to rely on the sultan for most political initiatives. In 1946 Sultan Mohammed ben Youssef obtained permission from the resident-general and the authorities of the Spanish zone to travel by land to Tangier, which had regained its 1923 status as an international city after its brief wartime occupation by Spain. By making this trip he provided the context for huge public demonstrations of loyalty affirming Morocco's national unity. While he was in Tangier, he also made an electrifying speech in which he omitted compliments to France, and by gestures of protocol, too, signalled to international opinion his impatience with French tutelage. In reaction, General Juin, the French Resident-General, ordered Istiqlal publications to be censored and in 1948 allowed his Director of Political Affairs, Colonel Jean Lecomte, to concoct abusive propaganda against the sultan and his family.[1] This only consolidated Sultan Mohammed's new authority as leader of the nationalist movement. The focus of Franco-Moroccan conflict became the sultan himself. Irritated by political criticisms voiced by Istiqlal notables, General Juin encouraged rivals of the sultan, led by a Berber chief, Thami

[1] Julien, *L'Afrique du Nord*, 393-4.

al-Glawi, to stage a tribal revolt. The French hoped, in fact, to weaken the forces of Arab urban nationalism by setting the predominantly Berber tribesmen against them. In 1951 the revolt was called off when the sultan capitulated under the threat of deposition and signed a protocol condemning 'the methods of a certain party'. But two years later, when he refused to sign decrees that would have accorded a share of Moroccan sovereignty to French citizens, a second revolt was staged. This time an exceptionally weak government in Paris caved in to pressure by local officials, French settlers, al-Glawi and other notables opposed to nationalism. The sultan was deposed on 20 August 1953 and exiled to Madagascar. But he still enjoyed religious as well as political legitimacy in the eyes of most Moroccans, and *Sidna* ('our Lord') would become the rallying cry of a nation ready to take up arms.

Even had they desired to prevent urban terrorism, the Istiqlal leaders could not have done anything because since December 1952 they had been gaoled for their alleged involvement in the uprising of Casablanca's proletariat in the wake of Farhat Hached's assassination. During the two years following the sultan's deposition Morocco experienced urban terrorism, counter-terror, and finally armed insurrection in the countryside from bases located in the Spanish zone. Meanwhile the Spanish authorities had embarked in 1952 upon a policy of collaboration with the nationalists, permitting freedom of the Press at least concerning activities in the French zone. The *khalifa*, the sultan's deputy in the Spanish zone, continued after Muhammad's deposition to exercise authority in his name, and the Spanish High Commissioner publicly supported Moroccan protests against the French action. In the French zone there was considerably more violence than there was in Tunisia after Bourguiba's arrest. The entire structure of local authority built up by the French in the countryside under tribal *caids* and their clients finally collapsed in 1955, once al-Glawi, realising that he was losing support, rendered obeisance to the sultan. To prevent further disorder, the French had to reinstate Sultan Mohammed, who, as King Mohammed V, became Morocco's indispensable arbiter, the one authority accepted by all Moroccan political forces – the urban and rural resistance movements, the urban notables of the Istiqlal and other minor parties, the proletariat, and rural notables compromised by French collaboration.

In stark contrast to both the Tunisian and Moroccan experiences, the Algerian revolution failed to engender a concrete locus of authority which all revolutionaries could accept. Before 1954 the politicians had been hopelessly divided as well as frustrated in their efforts to work within the elected bodies instituted by the Algerian Statute of 1947. In 1954 the PPA-MTLD suffered a further division between its leader, Messali Hadj, and a majority of the central committee. This division precipitated the outbreak on 1 November of armed insurrection. Having failed to reconcile the two factions, a self-styled Revolutionary Committee of Unity and Action, composed mostly of members of the party's para-military body, decided that existing parties and legal political processes were futile and that the only way to achieve Algerian independence was through violence. Indeed the decisions to engage in unlimited struggle and to organise only *after* launching the insurrection indicate a degree of political alienation among the leadership that was a major source of weakness. Once the revolution was launched, it was even more difficult to develop a political organisation for coordinating and ideologically shaping the raw guerrilla recruits who had spontaneously rallied to the Front de Libération Nationale. Furthermore, the only experiences shared by most of the revolutionary leaders were para-military ones. They tended to be less educated than the leaders of the Algerian parties they displaced and less educated than the Néo-Destour and Istiqlal leaders. Though the FLN managed in difficult wartime conditions inside Algeria to convene a congress, held in the Soummam Valley in August 1956, its resolution to accept the 'priority of the political over the military organisation' could not be implemented.

It was in the more isolated mountainous regions, such as Greater Kabylia and the Aurès, that the guerrillas, despite an improvised beginning, acquired the strongest roots. Here the FLN was able to develop a political as well as a military organisation, but communication with other parts of Algeria became difficult. The revolution acquired irreversible momentum on 20 August 1955, when guerrillas touched off a popular insurrection against 26 European centres in the region of Constantine, resulting in 123 dead, including 71 Europeans, many of them done to death with knives and sticks. French reprisals took 1273 lives by the official count and more than one thousand prisoners. The major consequence, however, was to sow a panic among European settlers throughout Algeria that would put pressure on French governments to build up an overwhelming military presence. By the following summer there were over 400 000 troops in the country. By the autumn of 1957 the French had fully regained the military initiative and had won the 'Battle of Algiers', eliminating the last effective guerrilla presences in the capital, including the leadership established by the Soummam Congress.

The French Fourth Republic was the first political victim of these ostensible victories. By condoning extensive use of torture, and by allowing the army to take over the administration of Algeria, the governments of Guy Mollet and his successors lost considerable moral authority in France without gaining the confidence of the settlers. After mass settler demonstrations in Algiers on 13 May 1958, in favour of keeping Algeria French under sympathetic military authorities, General de Gaulle was able to fill the resultant power vacuum in Paris. The French political system, however, was not the only victim of the Algerian war. Algeria's indigenous political forces were also disrupted by the massive French military presence, which even included electrified defensive lines on the country's borders with Morocco and Tunisia.

After the battle of Algiers, Abane Ramdane, the FLN's principal surviving leader and the organiser of the Soummam Congress, was strangled to death by members of his own party. Previous divisions within the FLN leadership had been mitigated in part by the ill-advised French kidnapping of one of its sections, which had included Ahmed Ben Bella. But thereafter the French military *quadrillage*, coupled with General Challe's mobile tactics, put the guerrillas continually on the run, preventing them from developing a political organisation inside their territory. The FLN was organised into six *wilayas*, or regional commands, which in theory covered the entire country including the Sahara, but it became increasingly difficult to communicate among or even within them,[1] much less between them and their arms depots and

[1] Colonel Amirouche, the commander of Wilaya III (Greater Kabylia), had hundreds of his men executed in 1959 to prevent security leaks.

sanctuaries in Tunisia and Morocco. The Gouvernement Provisoire de la République Algérienne (GPRA) was established in Tunisia under the nominal leadership of Ferhat Abbas, who had rallied to the FLN, but it could neither supply nor control the *wilayas*. Moreover, the general staff of the FLN, based near the Algerian frontier was outside the control of its ministries located in Tunis. The Chief of Staff, Colonel Houari Boumedienne, developed a well equipped standing army of 40000 men that proved in 1962 to be the only organised force capable of controlling independent Algeria.

The Evian Accords reached between the French and the provisional Algerian governments in March 1962, however, represented political victory for the FLN, as well as de Gaulle's triumph over the forces that had brought him to power. The agreement called for an immediate ceasefire followed by a referendum. This was held on 8 April, and an overwhelming majority of Algerians voted for independence. During the transition period from March to July the Algerians displayed remarkable discipline in the face of macabre provocations by extremist Europeans hoping to stir up mass violence and thus prevent independence. The constraining orders of FLN leadership hastily dispatched to Algiers by the provisional government were universally respected. But if the moral authority of the FLN was unquestioned (except perhaps by some of the 80000 Algerian Muslims who had fought on the French side and by other collaborators), its leadership remained seriously divided during the spring and summer of 1962. In institutional terms the FLN no longer existed. As the president of the provisional government subsequently explained, 'A military and political bureaucracy was forged in exile... [in] the absence of interior [political] life. Internal democracy, criticism and self-criticism, and serious criteria in the choice of leaders were all ignored, thus opening the door to *arrivisme* and flattery.'[1] His government watched helplessly as *wilaya* leaders, swelled by tens of thousands of new recruits parading as seasoned revolutionary veterans, jockeyed for position with the 'historic' chiefs of the revolution, such as Ahmed Ben Bella, just released from prison, and former political leaders like Ferhat Abbas. Boumedienne's army made Ben Bella's the winning

[1] Youssef ben Khedda, 'Contribution à l'historique du FLN', mimeo, April 1964, Algiers, cited by Elbaki Hermassi, *Leadership and national development in North Africa* (Berkeley and Los Angeles, 1972), 141.

coalition, and in the process mowed down hundreds of guerrillas in early September. 'The Summer of Shame', however, only reflected earlier developments within the FLN, for revolutionary leaders had liquidated many of their colleagues during the war. Despite brave fighting and brilliant diplomacy that won independence against incredible odds, the FLN failed to build political institutions, much less articulate a coherent ideology, as had the Néo-Destour in Tunisia, for guiding subsequent development and legitimating leadership. Yet eight years of fighting – compared with only two years of sporadic terrorism in the Protectorates – had utterly dislocated Algerian society. Whether or not as many as 1.5 million Algerians lost their lives, as the independent Algerian government claimed, the casualties were enormous. Roughly one-third of the rural population, moreover, was re-grouped into centres controlled by the French army, and many more escaped to other regions and moved to the cities. And in the final days before independence it was not just in the country-side, as in Morocco, that French authority collapsed. An estimated 90 per cent of the settler population, including much of the administration, failed to return from their summer 'holidays'.

THE INDEPENDENT REGIMES

However bitter the struggle for independence had been, the new regimes maintained many of the colonial legal and bureaucratic forms. One of the first acts of Ben Bella's government was to enact a decree, to be superseded only in 1973, revalidating most legislation of the colonial regime. The Algerians simply occupied the vacated French offices and re-enacted their routines – with some French technical assistance. Each regime displayed authoritarian characteristics inherited from its colonial predecessor, for conquest of the state machinery in each case weakened the nationalist movement. In power, the nationalists tried to prevent any countervailing institutions from encouraging and regulating conflicting interests. They almost unanimously valued national unity over political participation whenever the two seemed to be in conflict. Still, the particular mix of authoritarianism in each state varied with the degree of bureaucratic control that the French had exercised over society, the extent to which social groups were organised, and above all the sources of legitimacy available to each leader, with the constraints they might impose upon him. If power everywhere appeared concentrated, its scope varied, as did the extent to which it tolerated – or had to tolerate – opposition and the play of conflicting interests. And perhaps as important as the mix of authoritarianism for distinguishing the different regimes, were the respective loci of interests on which they seemed, ultimately, to rest. For these could define a regime's objectives just as political processes could reshape interests.

Curiously it was the Tunisian regime that most fully developed the bureaucratic–authoritarian tendencies of the colonial period. Although a more cohesive nationalist élite had built stronger political institutions than its neighbours before independence, these institutions would, in the last analysis, simply reinforce bureaucratic control and eventually wither away, so that the regime tolerated less pluralism and concentrated more power on itself than those of its neighbours.

Bourguiba inherited intact an administrative apparatus only slightly less elaborate than Algeria's. But because ben Youssef's revolt had verged on civil war, Bourguiba dismissed thoughts (publicly entertained earlier) of allowing factions (*tendances*) to compete within the Néo-Destour. In 1961 he was to have ben Youssef assassinated. Meanwhile, having benefited during the crisis of 1955 from UGTT support, he encouraged rivals of the trade-union leader, Ahmed ben Salah, to deprive the latter of his political base. The issue was not so much party control of the trade unions as intra-party politics. Ben Salah, who had been a party leader before becoming a trade-union official, was pushing for the Néo-Destour to adopt socialist economic policies that Bourguiba opposed. Once ben Salah had been neutralised, Bourguiba moved to reorganise the party, subjecting its local cells in 1958 to the regional and local administration of the Ministry of the Interior and purging a number of its more free-wheeling leaders, notably from the Federation of Tunis. Meanwhile he used his formal powers as head of government to modify the composition and functioning of the party's deliberative institutions at the national level.

After Bourguiba had been invested as prime minister in 1956 by the nominally sovereign bey, and gained the full support of an elected National Assembly nominated by the party's Political

Bureau, he was able the next year to eliminate all formal constraints upon his power by the simple expedient of having the National Assembly remove the bey and declare Tunisia a Republic, with Bourguiba its head of state. The new president acquired the bey's sovereign powers and limited the National Assembly to drafting a constitution. Meanwhile he appointed and dismissed ministers freely, and had the party's National Council modify the composition of the Political Bureau to reflect his changes. Gradually party institutions atrophied, for the effective locus of power became the administration controlled by a *de facto* presidential regime. The constitution of June 1959 reflected these realities and omitted any mention of those elements in the structures of the single-party system that in other one-party states sometimes place limits on the exercise of power.

The fusion of party and state temporarily generated an enormous capacity to mobilise, regulate, and extract resources from the society. Enthusiasm inspired by the independence struggle was effectively converted into support for the 'struggle against underdevelopment', especially after 1961, when Bourguiba decided to implement ben Salah's economic programme, which involved wide-scale regulation of the economy by the state. The experiment failed because ben Salah had been deprived of independent support within the party or trade union. In dismissing him in 1969, Bourguiba implicitly admitted the shortcomings of a political system that had placed no limits either on his choice of subordinates or on their exercise of power. But rather than implementing political reforms, he proceeded in the following three years to re-enact the course of events that had enabled him to concentrate power on himself in the first place. First he appealed to the liberals, headed by Ahmed Mestiri, who had opposed ben Salah and advocated a strengthening of the party's deliberative institutions through a limited exercise of internal democracy. The party congress held at Monastir in 1971 ratified these views, ruling that the central committee elected by the congress should in turn elect Bourguiba's Political Bureau. Bourguiba, however, had already dismissed Mestiri from the Ministry of the Interior and proceeded to appoint his own Political Bureau. Another congress held at Monastir in 1974 reversed the decisions of the earlier one, and meanwhile the liberals were purged from the party and even from honorific posts in the National Assembly.

The party in fact had become a hollow shell, and Bourguiba's legitimacy came to rest more on his historic role as founding father than on any consensus concerning social reform. In 1975 Bourguiba became president-for-life, but meanwhile his appointed successor, Prime Minister Hedi Nouira, was able to mobilise considerably less power than had Ahmed ben Salah. Opposition was developing, and the purged leaders – Mestiri inside the country and ben Salah abroad – were trying to organise it in the form of new parties. Meanwhile, a slightly younger generation of *apparatchiks* headed by Muhammad Sayah was trying to preserve the one-party system at a cost of increasing repression.

Bureaucratic–authoritarian tendencies also developed in the Maghrib's other single-party state, Algeria. But no Algerian enjoyed the solid support that the Néo-Destour had afforded Bourguiba, and consequently the consolidation of power in Algeria was a more complex process. Bereft of organised forces, other than Boumedienne's Armée Nationale Populaire (ANP), Ahmed Ben Bella made believe, and perhaps actually did believe, that he was consolidating power by having the FLN nominate a National Constituent Assembly that he could dominate. The constitution of September 1963 formally delineated a highly centralised presidential system and explicitly prescribed for the FLN a role not dissimilar from that practised by the Néo-Destour in Tunisia. Ben Bella completed his edifice in 1964 by convening a party congress that acclaimed his programme with few modifications, mostly concerning the role of Islam. The Charter of Algiers castigated the state for 'bureaucratism', while glorifying an ideal but intangible party. Boumedienne would sardonically observe that Ben Bella's advisers called for '"the withering away of the state" before it has been constructed'.[1]

Underlying the charter's 'theoretical intoxication'[2] was the fact of Ben Bella 'having to rely upon the army to remain in power while at the same time seeking to undermine Boumedienne's influence'.[3] Each time in 1963 and 1964 that guerrilla leaders took

[1] Cited by Jean Leca and Jean-Claude Vatin, *L'Algérie politique: institutions et régime* (Paris, 1975), 270.   [2] *Ibid.*, 270.
[3] William B. Quandt, *Revolution and political leadership: Algeria, 1954–1968* (Cambridge, Mass., 1969), 228.

up arms to pressure Ben Bella for a greater share of political influence, he called upon the ANP to put them down. The net result was greater influence for Boumedienne's Oujda group, which had been named after the Moroccan border town where Abdelaziz Bouteflika, Ahmed Medeghri, Ahmed Kaid, and Cherif Belkacem had served with Boumedienne in 1957. Ben Bella attempted to limit the group's influence by concentrating at its expense more formal powers in his own hands and by coopting some of the former *wilaya* leaders into the party. He even appointed Tahar Zbiri and Mohammed Chaabani to key posts in the ANP without Boumedienne's consent. The tactic did not work. Chaabani openly rebelled and was captured by the army and executed on orders from Ben Bella, against Boumedienne's wishes. Zbiri observed that Ben Bella 'constantly sought to create clans, opposing one to the other, so that when one clan was destroyed, he would create a new one to destroy those remaining'.[1] Once Boumedienne felt sufficiently threatened to stage a coup, Zbiri sided with him and led the squad that arrested Ben Bella without bloodshed in the early hours of 19 June 1965.

In 'readjusting' the revolution Boumedienne stressed collective leadership, but also the need for a strong state apparatus to fulfil revolutionary goals. In practice he had already concentrated considerable power by staffing the ANP with former officers of the French army. Without revolutionary credentials of their own, they were necessarily loyal. The higher civil service, too, was staffed in large part by Algerians who had worked under the French and their interests also converged with those of a regime determined to protect the state apparatus from interference by the FLN. Legislation was immediately passed guaranteeing the rights of civil servants. Communal elections in 1967 had the result of developing local clientèles that were dependent on the Ministry of the Interior (controlled by a member of the Oujda group) to the detriment of what was left of the party's influence.

Theoretically, collective leadership was exercised by the Council of the Revolution, a shadowy 26-man body, the composition of which was published only a month after the coup. It included substantial numbers of former guerrilla leaders, who were also

[1] Cited by Quandt, *Revolution*, 228. In Algerian political jargon a clan means a clique of politicians, not necessarily related by either family or ideological ties, but sharing tactical interests. The 'Oujda group' would be one exceptionally durable example.

co-opted into the party secretariat but excluded from the real power centres in the ANP, the security forces, and the key ministries. By 1967 collective leadership, other than that exercised by the closely knit Oujda group, was no longer functioning. A banal labour dispute triggered an uprising in the army, led by Tahar Zbiri, but forces loyal to Boumedienne easily suppressed it, and Zbiri's potential allies in the council and in the party were also removed from office. Zbiri escaped to Tunisia, but a senior fellow officer, Said Abid, was reported to have committed suicide. Having consolidated power, Boumedienne freely encouraged the development of an administrative state under leadership recruited primarily for its professional skills rather than previous political affiliations. Since, however, the party remained effectively an empty shell despite repeated attempts to 'restructure' it, the regime could not acquire the capacity temporarily generated in Tunisia to mobilise and regulate society. Until 1977 the only structures for eliciting political participation were 'popular assemblies' at the communal and, after 1969, *wilaya* level.

Boumedienne tried in 1972 to build up a popular base by embarking upon land reform, a lengthy process that succeeded in splintering the Oujda group. Ahmed Kaid was dismissed from his position as party director, and Interior Minister Ahmed Medeghri died in 1974 in circumstances that remain obscure. Possibly as a result of these events, Cherif Belkacem became politically inactive, and Abdelaziz Bouteflika, while remaining as foreign minister, appeared to play a somewhat independent political role by virtue of his personal connexions. In the face of increasing economic difficulties, Boumedienne hastily set about establishing constitutional structures that would formally concentrate political power on himself. First a new national charter was publicly discussed and ratified by plebiscite in June 1976. Then, with little discussion, a constitution was similarly ratified in November, followed by a presidential election of the single candidate, Boumedienne, and finally, in February 1977, by National Assembly elections. While granting more power to the president than the constitution of 1963 had accorded to Ben Bella, the new one also permitted Boumedienne to appoint a vice-president and prime minister. But from May 1977 he was ruling without organised political support. A plurality of fragile coalitions continued, as under Ben Bella, to compete for political

influence, but their power bases depended on personal relationships among officers and administrators rather than on guerrilla
networks or popular followings. As in one-party Tunisia, a
pervasive administration contained and muted conflict between
social forces, preventing them from organising.

In Morocco, by contrast, the monarchy encouraged political
competition among different social groups on the principle of
divide and rule. Not much stimulation was needed, as the political
forces unleashed by independence were heterogeneous but at the
same time relatively cohesive. They had been less fragmented by
colonial conquest and nationalist movements than those of
Morocco's more intensively colonised neighbours. The only
potential threat to Mohammed V's authority was the Istiqlal
Party. It advocated a constitutional monarchy but also urged the
formation of a 'homogeneous,' that is, one-party government to
take over the administrative apparatus of the Protectorate – and
in effect to subject the sovereign to a new Protectorate. Mohammed
V, instead, awarded cabinet positions to a splinter rival party
while reserving leadership of the new royal armed forces for his
son, Hassan, and other key security posts for unconditional
monarchists. Though he was unable to prevent the Istiqlal from
gaining some cabinet positions, neither did he discourage rural
expressions of discontent against administrators from the cities
imposed by the party.

The king pursued a strategy not unlike that attempted by the
administration of the French Protectorate. He encouraged
traditional rural notables, often of the same families as those
earlier thrust against him by the resident-general, to act as a
counterweight to the Istiqlal. When finally in 1958 he permitted
a 'homogeneous' government to be formed, a rural rebellion
obliged it to recognise the Mouvement Populaire, a party of
predominantly Berber supporters of the monarchy. Meanwhile
the Istiqlal itself split under the strains felt by the ministers
because of competing loyalties to king and party, and with the
backing of the Union Marocaine du Travail (UMT) a new,
ostensibly more radical party, the Union Nationale des Forces
Populaires (UNFP) was founded in January 1959. Subsequent
divisions between its radical intellectuals and its trade-union base
would also be exploited by the monarchy.

By the time he died in 1961, Mohammed V had consolidated

the monarchy's control of the countryside through networks of notables associated with the Ministry of the Interior. Communal elections held in 1960 further demonstrated that the Istiqlal, challenged in the cities by the UNFP, could no longer draw a majority of the votes. The time now seemed ripe to modernise the monarchy. Hassan II, who had studied law at the University of Bordeaux, was more reform-minded than his father and ready to transform his traditional authority as an arbiter into that of a plebiscitary monarch-president. With the collaboration of Ahmed Reda Guedira, who was a politically astute, French-trained lawyer, and more in the tradition of Napoleon III than of Charles de Gaulle, Hassan aimed to acquire a strong democratic majority by exploiting urban divisions while keeping his solid rural base, and then to undertake reforms that would undercut support for the UNFP. The first phase of the operation was a success. The constitution 'that I have made with my own two hands' (a Gaullist echo) was overwhelmingly ratified by popular referendum on 7 December 1962. Calls by the UNFP for abstention, moreover, were not fully endorsed by the UMT. The Istiqlal was then dismissed from the government, lest in the subsequent legislative elections it capitalise on its association with the triumphant palace.

The king, however, was not willing to compromise his non-partisan status by openly identifying with Guedira's new party, the Front Démocratique des Institutions Constitutionnelles (FDIC). Consequently the second phase failed. In boldly conceived but hastily arranged legislative elections Guedira was unable to win a majority of the seats. Moreover the FDIC was a heterogeneous coalition of palace personalities and traditional notables from the Popular Movement, which was also divided. With the help of scattered independent deputies it achieved a parliamentary majority, but the opposition played on its divisions rather than vice versa. Instead of bowing to a new parliamentary majority, the king brought the constitutional experiment to an end by declaring a state of emergency in June 1965. He continued to rely on rural support to rule the cities, but had to abandon any sustained efforts at reform lest they undercut the monarchy rather than progressive urban forces. Despite a new constitution promulgated in 1970, political life remained in suspense, increasingly subject to police repression ultimately backed by the royal armed forces. Hassan kept his Minister of the Interior,

General Oufkir, in power, despite his alleged part in the kidnapping and presumed assassination of Mehdi ben Barka, the principal leader of the leftist UNFP, in Paris in 1965, until the general turned against the king in 1972. Paradoxically, the attempted coups of 1971 and 1972 from which the king miraculously escaped with his life tended to fortify his legitimacy as an indispensable arbiter among urban forces fearful of military dictatorship. In May 1977, all the parties participated in legislative elections under a new constitution, promulgated in 1972, that offered less direct popular representation than that of 1962. The king continued to control the state apparatus inherited from the Protectorate while also determining to his tactical advantage the ground rules for political participation. But in relying for social control upon pluralistic competition, he exercised considerably less power to effect social change than the Maghrib's other authoritarian rulers could at times marshal.

Authoritarian governments that are neither fully constitutional nor buttressed by a totalitarian ideology usually have difficulty in acquiring legitimacy. The North African regimes were no exception. They each benefited initially from their respective leaders' involvement in the struggle for independence, but eventually they had to ground their authority in other forms of legitimation. Shortly after taking power, for instance, Ben Bella tried to acquire 'revolutionary' legitimacy by promoting an Algerian 'socialism' based on the idea of a self-managed industrial and agricultural sector. The myth of *autogestion*, however, was an unfortunate choice because it justified a privileged status for the workers of former colonial estates and small enterprises, rather than for the marginal peasants and others who had contributed much more to the revolution. Promoting self-management, moreover, did not seem quite compatible with building a strong state. Boumedienne scrapped *autogestion* in favour of a three-fold industrial, cultural, and agrarian revolution to be carried out under the direction of a strong state. In Tunisia, too, a thorough 'structural transformation' of the economy under the banner 'Destour Socialism' was supposed to engender economic take-off. Until Bourguiba halted the experiment in 1969, the myth conveniently justified state intervention. In Morocco, given its ostensibly liberal economy, there was less stress upon achievement. Instead, a peculiarly Moroccan synthesis of orthodox and maraboutic Islam enlisted politically strategic 'traditional intellectuals'[1] in support of the monarchy. So also in Tunisia, after 1970 an obsession with the history and mythology of the national movement was intended to refurbish Bourguiba's image.

With the exception of *autogestion*, the myths did not overtly express the interests of a particular class or social segment; Tunisian and Algerian socialism in their official forms rejected the inevitability of class conflict. Each regime seemed, however, to be conditioned by underlying social forces, even if each also enjoyed a measure of autonomy enabling it to reshape them. On balance the Moroccan monarchy, by encouraging social pluralism, seemed the most immobilised by the forces it had helped to create. Since social control depended upon maximising the number of contending forces, the regime could not systematically sacrifice the interests of any for the sake of an overall design. For instance, sufficient concessions had to be made to the urban proletariat to maintain the credibility of the Union Marocaine du Travail, because it served as a counterweight to the UNFP. Yet the commercial interests of the Fassi bourgeoisie also had to be respected, lest the Istiqlal rejoin its rival. Industrialisation at the expense of the countryside, or even agrarian reform, had to be ruled out because such policies would have endangered the royal control of the countryside exercised through traditional notables.

Moroccan society was in fact far more complex than party labels indicated. The notables of the Popular Movement, for instance, did not constitute a homogeneous social force. The monarchy was constrained by neither a landed 'feudal' nor an urban bourgeois class, but it had to buy off influential individuals and families to minimise the possibility of different interests coalescing. At first the royal patronage networks depended upon a judicious distribution of the spoils of settler society; subsequently under Hassan II, 'planned corruption' involved virtually all political actors with the supreme fixer, the king. The major constraint upon the monarchy was the moral as well as the financial expense, yet 'Morocco could undertake its own house cleaning only at the cost of reduced political control'.[2]

In Algeria, by contrast, social forces were considerably more fragmented by independence, and the regime managed to keep

[1] Rémy Leveau, *Le Fellah marocain défenseur du trône* (Paris, 1976), 91–4, stresses the political influence of these élites trained in traditional Islamic schools and universities.

[2] John Waterbury, 'Corruption, political stability and development: Egypt and Morocco', *Government and Opposition*, 1976, **11**, 4, 437.

corruption under control despite pumping considerable oil wealth into the public sector. Consequently neither organised pressure groups nor vertically integrated patronage networks put upon the regime constraints that were analogous to those existing in Morocco. Once Boumedienne had consolidated power, the regime, in fact, enjoyed considerably more autonomy than either of its neighbours. To be sure, social inequalities became visible after independence, despite an officially socialist ideology, but the spoils of settler society were distributed more spontaneously and widely than in Morocco, and did not consolidate either an Algerian bourgeoisie or any other organised social force.

There was no hard evidence that the state's managers and higher civil servants constituted or were in the process of constituting a self-perpetuating ruling class. However, some Marxist critics have argued that, once Boumedienne had crushed the Zbiri revolt and with it pressures for self-management, the regime consolidated an administrative bourgeoisie. Indeed, because of the earlier development of Algerian capitalism during the colonial era, the land was even less equitably distributed in Algeria than in Morocco. It is possible that the civil servants and technocrats recruited into the state apparatus by virtue of their educational qualifications came from the relatively more privileged landed families. Communal reform in Algeria may also have enhanced the influence of these families within the state apparatus, which, as in Morocco, was controlled and regulated through the Ministry of the Interior rather than the party. Within Boumedienne's core of professional officers important families were also represented, as is illustrated by the presence within the Oujda group of Ahmed Kaid and Ahmed Medeghri. But the agrarian reform of 1972, whatever its long-run impact, fulfilled one immediate short-term purpose. By wiping out absentee land-owners and limiting private property, it broke up nascent connexions between the landowning bourgeoisie and the official controlling state apparatus. As Boumedienne explained in introducing the reform, 'Either the agrarian revolution will succeed... or we will end up with a new Algerian bourgeoisie that will perhaps be tougher and more vile than the colonial bourgeoisie that used to exploit us.'[1] The other possible social base for an administrative bourgeoisie was the private industrial sector, but

[1] *Annuaire de l'Afrique du Nord*, 1972, **11**, 720.

administrative regulations and taxation laws were still stifling it in the mid-1970s. Collusion between the public and private sector might eventually generate a bourgeoisie, but meanwhile the regime enjoyed considerable autonomy and seemed constrained only by personal rivalries among the top leadership and perhaps, as a result of its military background, by its very detachment from civil society.

Until 1969 the Tunisian regime enjoyed greater coherence than either of its neighbours by virtue of its grounding in a political class created before independence. This class could be identified with an educated élite, but not with any of the social groups, such as workers, merchants or landowners, controlled by the party through the national organisations. It seemed for a while, in fact, that the only major constraint upon ben Salah's efforts to transform Tunisian economic and class structures was insufficient capital accumulation in what after all was the poorest of the three Maghribian societies. Possibly the hesitations of international organisations, notably the World Bank, to keep financing expensive state projects contributed to ben Salah's downfall.[1] But his ambitious attempts to regulate virtually all sectors of the economy cut deeply into the regime's political credit at home. For instance, the party replaced a veteran trade unionist, Habib Achour, with a provincial governor at the head of the UGTT, in order to punish the union for protesting against currency devaluation in 1964. Neither party nor union could retain plausible claims to represent anything other than the state apparatus.

As the party disintegrated under the impact of ben Salah's state capitalism, the social forces that had originally created it freed themselves from its discipline. If ben Salah could rely upon the party to implement reforms of wholesale and even retail commerce that primarily hit people from Djerba who played a dominant role in these sectors, he could not count on it to transform agrarian structures in its historic stronghold, the Sahel. It was a revolt of peasants from Ouardanine, a village that had once supplied *fellaghas* for Bourguiba, that sealed ben Salah's fate. Even so, the peasants probably had not demonstrated spontaneously, for leading members of the political class had accumulated property after independence, including some of the settlers' land and other small enterprises. After ben Salah's demise in 1969 parts of the

[1] Jean Poncet, *La Tunisie à la recherche de son avenir* (Paris, 1974), 96.

public sector, including land and import–export monopolies, also reverted to private and politically well connected hands. Contracting business and the tourist 'industry', already developing during the ben Salah era, subsequently flourished. It seemed possible that the new Tunisian bourgeoisie would begin to develop sufficient autonomy to undermine party hegemony. At the same time the trade-union movement was also becoming more independent under a leadership that had owed more to Farhat Hached than to Bourguiba. Regional rivalries seemed, too, to be intensifying in the mid-1970s; the party's leadership was increasingly Sahelian, as were the top ministers and other holders of strategic offices; moreover, conflict within the top leadership tended to reflect traditional rivalries among Sahel villages. If under Bourguiba the regime still enjoyed a certain autonomy, it seemed only a matter of time before the various social forces would produce a more pluralistic system.

STRATEGIES OF DEVELOPMENT

In the areas of economic and cultural policy, the three regimes pursued different strategies which reflected the differences in their underlying social bases. Algeria after 1967 and Tunisia until 1969 vigorously expanded their public sectors; in 1970 total public expenditures comprised 43 and 41 per cent of their respective GDPs, compared to a Moroccan total of only 26 per cent. Even discounting petroleum revenues, rates of public expenditure were considerably higher in Algeria and Tunisia than in Morocco. Boosted by petroleum revenues, Algerian public investment was almost triple that of Morocco after 1973, though Morocco had the slightly larger population. Clearly Algeria could afford to embark upon more ambitious development plans than its neighbours. To sustain its 'revolutionary' legitimacy, the state was to implant 'industrialising industries', or industries that would lead to further industrialisation, whereas Morocco, followed after 1969 by Tunisia, simply promoted enclaves exporting agricultural and mineral produce to Europe, and servicing its tourists. Yet it was hardly certain that importing expensive factories utilising the latest technologies would liberate the Algerian economy, much less result in self-sustaining industrial expansion. The success of the Algerian experiment depended also in part on its cultural and agrarian 'revolutions' – development in areas where Morocco and Tunisia had more coherent infrastructures.

In the ten years following independence it was Tunisia that placed the greatest stress on 'human investment', for the Bourguibist élite had been convinced that education was the key to progress. Even before engaging in systematic economic planning, Bourguiba urged a psychological revolution against 'retrograde' behaviour such as women wearing veils ('those filthy rags') and workers slacking off during the month of Ramadan (when Muslims are expected to fast between sunrise and sunset). In 1958 he virtually destroyed the bastion of the religious establishment, Zitouna University, together with its supporting Koranic schools, by integrating them with the national educational system. Bourguiba could wage his veritable cultural revolution, of course, only because of widespread support from a bilingual élite that in turn managed the apparatus of a mass party. Even so, he had to back-track over Ramadan. In retrospect, his major contribution to Tunisia may have been to unify and almost universalise an essentially bilingual form of instruction, thus perpetuating an open, Europe-oriented élite and giving it a mass base. Unlike Ataturk, however, he subsequently made peace with the Islamic establishment and appropriately appointed as *muftī* a bilingual scholar who headed the Islamic Studies department of the University of Tunis, thus furthering Tunisia's cultural interactions.

For different reasons neither Morocco nor Algeria was achieving such a balance. In Morocco the monarchy required the legitimation of traditional intellectuals; hence the Qarawiyine University at Fez and the Ben Youssef University at Marrakesh, though less developed than Zitouna at independence, were expanded rather than integrated into the national system. Within the state university system separate sections dispensed instruction in French and Arabic, systematically dividing the educated élite. Reckless efforts after independence to Arabise instruction in the primary schools resulted in serious deterioration at the secondary level, because Arabists were not available in sufficient numbers to teach technical subjects. Efforts in the mid-1960s to increase the hours devoted to French in the primary schools met, however, with the opposition of the Istiqlal, which was wedded to total Arabisation. The monarchy could not afford to sacrifice its roots in Arab–Islamic culture for the needs of an economy oriented to French markets.

In Algeria, by contrast, traditional intellectuals had no power base at independence, and the legitimacy of neither Ben Bella nor Boumedienne depended upon them. But Algeria had to create a national culture, whereas the former Protectorates had only to adapt theirs. Educated élites had articulated their respective Tunisian and Moroccan heritages before independence in ways that most of the Algerian nationalist leaders could not. After independence, consequently, cultural reconstruction had an urgency in Algeria that was not present in the other two countries. The fact, too, that the Kabyles had enjoyed disproportionate French educational opportunities made the problem of 'nation-building' even more urgent – and potentially divisive. As in Morocco, Arabisation of the colonial school system was encouraged, but more cautiously not only for lack of trained Arabists but also because many of the school teachers inherited from the French administration were Berbers from the Kabyle. Shortly after independence a Ministry of Religious Affairs was created, and by 1965 it was establishing a traditional system of schools and Islamic institutes, as though Algeria were determined to build up the obstacles to bilingualism that had already thwarted Morocco's educational planning. By 1976 one-quarter of the students in Algeria's state universities were following courses taught exclusively in Arabic, and in fields such as law and letters the French section appeared to have even less future than in Morocco. An ideological stress on national unity made cultural bifurcation less acceptable than in Morocco, yet Algeria's need for technically trained, bilingual or multilingual cadres was also greater, given its stress on industrialisation.

Indeed, fifteen years after independence Algeria remained the land of cultural paradox. Officially the National Charter established the principle of an Algerian *umma*, using for the first time a term Tunisians, Moroccans, and other Arabic-speaking peoples had hitherto reserved for the Arab, and originally for the Islamic, community. In its new context the terms perhaps placated the Berber Kabyles, much as belonging to an Arab *umma* had served the cultural interest of Arab Christians in the Near East. Yet the option of Arabisation was 'irreversible' and was eventually to 'exclude the existence of two juxtaposed sectors' in the educational system.[1] The traditional system of religious education was also to be superseded by a greater emphasis on Islam in the state schools. But meanwhile more university students were following exclusively French instruction in Algeria than in the rest of North Africa, and the graduates of the French sections were so favoured in career opportunities over those of the Arabic sections that the Arabists in law and letters went on strike in 1977, demanding that public-sector companies Arabise their administration so as to be able to hire them.

Of course student strikes had become commonplace in Morocco and Tunisia. Even before Hassan II succeeded to the throne, students represented by the Union Nationale des Étudiants Marocains (UNEM) had sided with Mehdi ben Barka in opposing the monarchy's consolidation of political power through the crown prince's control of the army. UNEM, with support from the majority of students, consistently supported the radical wing of the UNFP, and student opposition intensified after the kidnapping and presumed assassination of ben Barka in 1965. UNEM was dissolved in 1973 but the agitation continued. Tunisian students, too, acquired political grievances. A majority in the late 1960s objected to the party's rigid control of the student organisation, the Union Générale des Étudiants Tunisiens (UGET). From 1971 until 1976 the government did not even convene the annual UGET congress, and the students repudiated the leadership elected in 1976 in favour of other legally unrecognised representatives. If the Tunisians were involved in strikes and demonstrations less frequently than the Moroccans, their behaviour was even less tolerable to a political élite that placed a greater value on student solidarity with the regime. Underlying their respective political grievances, however, was a growing realisation shared by the students and regimes of both countries that the educational systems were not adapted to economic needs. After 1966 both governments had tacitly dropped their goal of universal primary education, but it was politically difficult to cut back or even prevent increasing enrolments in secondary and higher education despite the diminishing employment opportunities for graduates.

Table 11.1, comparing secondary and higher education enrolments for selected years in the three countries, shows that

[1] Front de Libération Nationale. *Charte Nationale* (Algiers, 1976), 67.

Table 11.1. *The evolution of secondary and higher education in the Maghrib (000s).*

		1961–2	1966–7	1970–1	1974–5
Algeria	secondary	47.5	134.7	287.7[a]	419.8
	higher	3.2	9.3	22.6[a]	35.9
Morocco	secondary	99.0	241.7	298.9	400.0
	higher	4.8	7.5	13.6	32.8
Tunisia	secondary	65.2	120.6	195.3	179.0
	higher	3.6	7.1	10.1	13.7

Note: Enrolments as percentages of eligible populations were not computed, but it should be noted that in 1974 the total populations of Algeria, Morocco, and Tunisia were respectively 16.3, 16.9, and 5.6 million.
[a] 1971–2.

Algerian enrolments were surpassing those of Morocco by the mid-1970s. The regime had successfully enlisted university activists to assist the agrarian revolution during vacations, but ironically they tended to come from the French sections, and at the Universities of Algiers and Constantine conflict with the Arabists erupted in 1975 because candidates for student elections were required to have participated as volunteers in the countryside. From a primary-school base in 1974 almost double that of Morocco, Algeria continued to expand education at all levels, with priority accorded to scientific and technical fields. But rapid expansion coupled with Arabisation was probably not so much meeting the country's needs in skilled manpower as increasing disguised unemployment in the burgeoning state apparatus.

If student unrest had underlying economic causes in all three countries, cultural life also tended to reflect a growing malaise. After independence most literature continued, except in Tunisia, to be written in French and published in France. Though the Algerian poet, Malek Haddad, lamented that they were 'direct victims of colonial aggression...expelled from their language just as the fellahs had been expropriated',[1] Algerian output increased after 1965. Despite efforts of the government to 'recuperate' such novelists as Mohammed Dib, and the young firebrand Rachid Boudjera, they preferred, like their young Moroccan counterparts, Mohammed Khair-Eddine and Tahar Ben Jelloun, to live abroad.

[1] Leca and Vatin, *L'Algérie politique*, 295–6.

In Dib's *Le Maître de chasse*, published in 1973, political authority in contemporary Algeria, while not explicitly condemned, seems as distant and alien as in the colonial era he described in an earlier trilogy. For Boudjera 'the Clan' rules 'Barbary', and it arrests and perhaps tortures the hero of *La Répudiation*, which appeared in 1969. Boudjera was no more polemical in his descriptions of Algeria than Khair-Eddine of Morocco in *Le Déterreur*, published in 1973. The better young writers in Arabic were also controversial. The Union of Tunisian Writers tried to exclude young formalists, but one of their leaders, Ezzedine Madani, wrote plays that criticised the regime by depicting autocracy in historical settings. Though a Tunisian propagandist boasted in 1973 of a 'new profession being created, that of cultural organisers',[1] a counter-culture also seemed to be developing, but within a national tradition that seemed more assured than that of Algeria.

As far as economic development was concerned, each regime concentrated on the modern agricultural, manufacturing, and mining sectors that had been largely in European hands before independence. Little was done in the traditional rural areas. Consequently urbanisation could not be controlled, despite efforts as early as 1958 in Tunisia to stem it by tearing up shanty-towns and sending squatters back to the countryside. The most important economic safety-valve was the European labour market. By the mid-1970s as many North African immigrants were living in Europe, for the most part in France, as there had been Europeans in North Africa two decades earlier – over a million and half. The majority came from Algeria, where the development efforts had been the most ambitious. Since the Algerian investments were highly capital intensive, centred on petroleum, iron and steel, and manufacturing industries involving a high level of technology, non-agricultural employment was not expanding rapidly enough to absorb natural increases in available manpower, much less rural migrants. But the European labour market dried up as a result of the world recession that began in 1975, and France banned further immigration.

Family planning was officially encouraged in Tunisia, with modest success, but was virtually abandoned in Morocco due to opposition by the Istiqlal. Algeria's hospitals did not publicise

[1] *Annuaire de l'Afrique du Nord*, 1973, **12**, 44.

contraception facilities, due to a combination of religious and ideological pressures. All three regimes did try, however, to dam the rural tide by undertaking public works projects: Promotion Nationale in Morocco, and similar 'worksites for the struggle against underdevelopment' in Tunisia, were financed largely with assistance from the United States until the mid-1960s but subsequently they dwindled, because of decreasing aid. Tunisia, followed by Algeria, then tried to stabilise its people on the land by building an extensive network of state cooperatives. All that remained of ben Salah's scheme of agrarian reform in Tunisia after 1969, however, were the cooperatives, in fact state farms, originally introduced on some of the former settler estates. Neither Morocco nor Tunisia was willing to embark on a real redistribution of indigenously owned property. By contrast, Algeria's 'agrarian revolution' effected some redistribution after 1972, but only a minority of the landless actually benefited. Moreover, at least one-quarter of these apparently refused in 1974 to stay on the land because traditional agriculture no longer appeared viable.[1] The regime had constructed some hundred 'socialist villages' by 1977, but at costs perhaps triple the budgeted $5000 per family dwelling. The second four-year plan (1974–7) continued to favour industry over agriculture, and new industrial projects were expected to cost five times as much as new agricultural and irrigation schemes.[2]

Morocco and Tunisia devoted proportionately more public resources to agriculture, but investments tended (despite some symbolic land distribution, notably in Morocco in 1972 after the second attempt on Hassan's life) to benefit established landowners producing for a modern export sector rather than the rural masses, only some of whom could be 'absorbed' into that sector as hired hands. In Morocco the national irrigation office was abolished in 1964 so that the Ministry of the Interior could exercise control over irrigated areas. Subsequently a series of dams, while developing Morocco's tremendous irrigation potential, principally improved the properties of medium and large landowners beholden to the regime. Tunisia's irrigated areas more than doubled after independence, but landowners benefiting from public investments were required to reimburse the government.

---

[1] Bruno Etienne, *L'Algérie, cultures et révolution* (Paris, 1977), 219.
[2] République Algérienne Démocratique et Populaire, *IIe Plan quadriennal 1974–1977, Rapport général* (Algiers, 1974), 89.

In Algeria, too, most of the public investment in agriculture until the early 1970s was channelled to the modern sector, especially for the upkeep of lands that had belonged to the settlers. Though some third of these seem to have been acquired after independence by private Algerian owners,[1] the rest were organised into cooperatives run in theory by former agricultural workers or, in some cases, by veterans of the war for independence. Most of these so-called self-managed farms ran at a considerable loss for several years after independence, and much of the state's agricultural budget was spent on an administration designed to supervise them, provide them with seeds, and fertiliser, and market their produce. Productivity dropped by as much as half in the first five years and national production subsequently stagnated or declined.[2] By the mid-1970s Algeria was spending at least one-third of its petroleum revenues on food imports. While Morocco and Tunisia also had to import wheat, their agricultural situations were not as catastrophic.

In all three countries, then, a rural sub-proletariat continued, as before independence, to move into the cities. Between 1966 and 1973, for example, Algeria's 'urban and semi-urban' population was estimated to have increased by almost 50 per cent, compared to a rural increase of only 14 per cent. Rural dislocation was least severe in Morocco, but by 1971 over one-third of the population was urban. Unemployment, perhaps highest in Algeria, was increasing everywhere, and none of the regimes seemed capable of damming the rural exodus.

In all three countries it was assumed in the early 1960s that the solution to this problem was rapid industrialisation. However, the Moroccan five-year plan elaborated in 1960 was never implemented, in part for lack of adequate financial resources, but in part, too, because of the monarchy's interest in shoring up its following among rural notables. In Tunisia, Bourguiba gave ben Salah full freedom in 1962 to implement plans that the French economist, Gerard Destanne de Bernis, had helped him elaborate in 1956. Heavy industry, including iron and steel, was to be created to generate a self-sustaining industrialisation process that would eventually absorb the rural migrants. The opportunity costs of

---

[1] Etienne, *L'Algérie*, 213.

[2] Kader Ammour, Christian Leucate and Jean-Jacques Moulin, *La Voie algérienne* (Paris, 1974), 73.

such industries were not carefully studied, for the value of an industrial infrastructure took precedence over 'capitalist' considerations of profitability. It was assumed that a steel industry operating at a loss would nevertheless in the long run save foreign currency and stimulate manufacturing industries. The experiment failed in Tunisia through a lack of capital needed for such expensive investment, and the regime turned instead to private foreign enterprise, offering favourable terms for investments in small enterprises geared to European markets. Morocco, too, attempted to internationalise its capital by stimulating joint ventures aimed at export markets, and both countries also generated considerable invisible foreign-exchange earning by encouraging foreign tourism.

Algeria, on the other hand, rejected dependence on foreign capital and readily accepted the myth of 'industrialising industries' propounded by de Bernis.[1] By acquiring in 1971 a majority interest in the major French oil producers operating in the country, the regime not only enhanced its revolutionary standing but acquired a painless means of accumulating capital. Revenues amounted to over $4 billion annually after 1973, and the regime was investing in gas liquefaction plants to export natural gas, of which Algeria held 5 per cent of the world's reserves. Meanwhile it was building a diversified industrial base centred on steel and petrochemicals, much as the French had projected in their 1959 Constantine Plan, but on a more ambitious scale. In 1975, for instance, work was begun on an integrated electronics industry which Algerians were simultaneously being trained to run. The government intended to leap into the technectronic era and master technology and production facilities currently available only in the most advanced industrial countries. But quick technological fixes seemed even less likely than dependent bourgeois development to resolve problems of unemployment. Algeria risked becoming more technologically dependent on the multinational companies, the more of their technology it imported. By 1976, with 14 per cent of its foreign-exchange earnings mortgaged by debt servicing, it was almost as indebted as Tunisia had been in 1971. The Algerian percentage was expected to reach 24.9 by 1982 and then decline, but the liquefaction projects expected to produce new

[1] Gérard Destanne de Bernis, 'Les Industries industrialisantes et les options algériennes', *Revue Tiers Monde*, 1971, **12**, 47.

revenues to pay off the debts were seriously delayed.[1] In fact administrative and human shortcomings were endangering much of the Algerian economic effort. Public sector management tended at intermediate levels to avoid taking initiatives, and administrative regulations tended in any event to obstruct action. Whether these were growing pains or congenital defects of state capitalism remained to be seen.

In the short run many of the new industries were operating, if at all, at considerably less than full capacity. Even so, between 1971 and 1973 more than four times as much fertiliser was being produced as could be consumed, and locally assembled tractors were saturating the rural markets. The agrarian revolution was designed in part to increase the purchasing power of the countryside sufficiently to absorb new industrial products, yet capital intensive industrialisation tended to increase inequalities of income distribution between urban and rural areas. The new Algerian industries continued to be heavily dependent on imports of capital goods and components; 70 per cent of the original investments and comparable proportions of operating expenditures in the early 1970s required foreign exchange.[2] The tripling of petroleum revenues between 1973 and 1974, however, provided opportunities for further industrialisation, though petroleum production appeared to have reached a plateau.

So also, the quintupling in 1974 of the price of phosphates, Morocco's and Tunisia's principal export, gave these liberal economies a shot in the arm, just as Tunisia was becoming a modest petroleum exporter. Neither regime was tempted, however, to risk 'industrialising' industrial development on its windfall export earnings, which remained modest by Algerian standards. Rather, the Moroccan five-year plan for 1973–8 appeared even to abandon import substitution for a policy of export-led growth that might maximise its comparative advantage in world markets. Industry was given priority, receiving almost 40 per cent of the projected public and private investments, but primarily to make of Morocco 'a base for assembling and completing' products manufactured elsewhere.[3] However, the

[1] *Le Monde*, 29 March 1977.
[2] Abdellatif Benachenhou, 'Forces sociales et accumulation du capital au Maghreb', *Annuaire de l'Afrique du Nord*, 1973, **12**, 336.
[3] Cited by Habib al-Malki, 'Chronique économique', *Annuaire de l'Afrique du Nord*, 1973, **12**, 594.

percentage of imported input in Moroccan industry did not appear to exceed Algeria's. Moroccan (and Tunisian) economic development seemed passively to conform to a new international division of labour, whereas Algeria was actively trying to change both the international order and its place in it. Neither approach to development, however, could come to grips with the basic demographic problem. Paradoxically, the least 'progressive' regime, that of the Moroccan monarchy, employed the largest proportion of the population in the secondary sector and the least in the over-staffed services sector. Colonial history and natural advantages as well as monarchical strategy explain, moreover, why a greater proportion remained rooted in the countryside.

FOREIGN AFFAIRS

Domestic politics largely conditioned the foreign policies of the independent regimes, especially with respect to the former colonial power. Morocco, for instance, avoided confrontations with France over economic issues during the first decade of independence because 'Moroccanising' European agricultural and commercial interests would have tended to benefit the Istiqlal rather than the clients of the monarchy who could subsequently be favoured. Conversely, Bourguiba belied his usual prudence in 1961 when he besieged French military installations at Bizerta, and again in 1964, when he nationalised remaining settler lands. He was attempting to keep up with Algerian progress in decolonisation, but he was also trying to buy support for unpopular state socialism at home. Similarly, Ben Bella was seeking support at home when he opted in 1963 for self-managed farms at the expense of those owned by absentee settlers, and Boumedienne marshalled sufficient legitimacy in 1971, when he nationalised French petroleum interests, to embark the following year upon an agrarian 'revolution' that divided his ruling coalition of state technocratic and landowning interests. The three regimes, however, experienced less conflict with France than with each other, and intra-Maghribian relations, in turn, were even more closely related to the internal politics of the respective regimes.

Despite the intermingling of Maghribian élites in French universities and the formation in Cairo of a Maghrib Bureau in 1945, the movements of national liberation were not coordinated. In fact elements of the FLN supported Salah ben Youssef, Bourguiba's rival, in 1955, and in 1962 Bourguiba favoured the Algerian provisional government that Ben Bella and Boumedienne then defeated. Before Algeria was independent, its struggle was a source of solidarity against a common colonial adversary, yet also an embarrassment to independent Tunisian and Moroccan governments committed to a variety of agreements and understandings with France. Leaders of the three dominant political parties met at Tangier in 1958 and proclaimed the principle of a North African Confederation, but not even a confederation of student unions got off the ground. In addition to differing political structures and divergent economic policies, shared borders were a more immediate obstacle to any sort of Maghribian union.

Borders established by France had naturally favoured its first colonised territory, Algeria. Morocco felt that France and Spain had sliced further territory from the historic homeland: not only the traditional Spanish enclaves of Ceuta and Melilla on the Mediterranean, but also Tarfaya, Ifni, and the Spanish Sahara, plus Mauritania and other portions of French West Africa extending into Mali and Senegal. Morocco peacefully recovered Tarfaya, in 1958, and Ifni, in 1969, from Spain, but France granted independence to iron-rich Mauritania in 1960. By recognising the new state, Tunisia incurred four years of Moroccan enmity. In 1961 Morocco and the Algerian provisional government agreed to form a confederation and also to discuss possible border rectifications after Algerian independence. Morocco was claiming considerable areas of French Algeria's western Sahara, including Tindouf and iron-ore deposits at Gara-Djebilet. Tunisia also claimed a piece of desert extending from its southern frontiers, in which oil was discovered.

Independent Algeria, however, was as intransigent in defence of its Saharan borders against its neighbours' claims as the FLN had been against earlier French plans to establish a separate Saharan entity. A border war with Morocco in 1963, in which perhaps 300 were killed, conveniently reinforced both regimes at home but did not resolve the underlying dispute. A subsequent agreement to ratify the existing frontier and to exploit the iron mines jointly was not implemented. In 1974, as in 1963, after weathering severe internal crises, King Hassan rallied virtually unanimous domestic support for irredentist claims, this time for the Spanish Sahara. He tried to obtain Algerian support in return for ratifying the Algerian–Moroccan border agreement of 1972, but Algeria instead supported self-determination for this territory inhabited by some 70 000 nomads. Morocco, however, persuaded Mauritania, with whom relations had finally been established in 1970, to accept Moroccan sovereignty over the northern half of the territory, which contained the world's largest reserves of phosphates, in return for Mauritanian sovereignty over the southern part which contained iron ore. In November 1975 Hassan mobilised some 350 000 civilians for a 'green march' in the name of Islam to 'liberate' the territory, ignoring an adverse ruling from the International Court of Justice concerning Morocco's historic claim. With Franco on his death-bed, Spain agreed to cede administration of the territory to Morocco and Mauritania pending a referendum. Much of the population fled to Algeria, which supported Polisario, the strongest of the Saharan political factions. Two years later Morocco was mired in a lengthy guerrilla war, its army being responsible for the security not only of the vast reaches of the former Spanish Sahara but also of Mauritania, which was under increasing pressure from Polisario. Algeria, backed by Libya, persisted in supporting the Saharan guerrillas despite Saudi and other efforts to mediate Algerian–Moroccan differences.

The root of the conflict lay not so much in either a Moroccan interest in the Bou Craa phosphate deposits or an Algerian one in an outlet from Tindouf to the Atlantic as in King Hassan's internal political needs and an Algerian interest in preserving a favourable regional balance of power. Maghribian economic integration, symbolised by the creation in 1964 of a Permanent Consultative Committee of economic ministers, also foundered – even when not disrupted by border disputes – against Algeria's determination to consolidate a dominant economic position before consenting to significant multilateral tariff reductions. Algeria, too, pressured Tunisia not to implement a union with Libya that had been proclaimed jointly by Presidents Bourguiba and Qadhdhāfī in 1974.

It was natural, with independence, that the Maghrib should reknit ties with other parts of the Arab world that the colonial conquests had largely severed. Moroccan and Tunisian independence co-incided, however, with the rise of Nāṣir, Egypt's union with Syria, and the unedifying struggles between Nāṣirists and Ba'athists over precedence within the vanguard of Arab unity. The Moroccan monarchy was wary of a movement that subverted monarchies, while Bourguiba and much of his French-educated élite viewed Pan-Arabism as a threat to their western-oriented variant of nationalism. The Tunisian president, too, had more immediate reasons for detesting Nāṣir. Egypt harboured Salah ben Youssef and appeared in 1958 to have been involved in a plot to assassinate Bourguiba. As late as 1966 the Tunisian foreign minister was accusing Nāṣir of 'micro-imperialism' and of using methods of 'intimidation, blackmail, and calumny' to impose his political line on other countries.[1] Tunisia as well as Morocco supported Saudi Arabia's campaign at this time for an Islamic summit to counter Nāṣir's influence.

On the other hand, personal relations between Ben Bella and Nāṣir were close, and Algeria was counted in 1963 as one of the four revolutionary Arab states, along with Egypt, Iraq, and Syria. Symbolic ties with the east reinforced Algeria's quest for national 'authenticity', and massive imports of Egyptian and Syrian schoolteachers contributed to its programme of Arabisation. Yet Algerians, considering themselves the only people in the Arab world to have carried out a real revolution, tended to share the Tunisian élite's disdain of Arab revolutionary posturing. Egyptian schoolteachers were resented. And while consistently supporting the Palestinian Liberation Organisation (PLO), Algerians scarcely concealed their impatience with the Palestinians' inability to purge their ranks, by physical liquidation if need be, to forge a coherent and rational strategy against the Zionist foe. Though Algeria was the only North African country actually to send combat units to the 1967 war, reactions to Egypt's agreement to a cease-fire were also symptomatic: there were demonstrations in Algiers not only against the British and American imperialists but also against the Russians for insufficient military aid to Egypt and Syria and against the Egyptians for giving up the fight.

The wave of Arab sympathies raised throughout the Maghrib by the June war did, however, stimulate the regimes into greater

---

[1] Cited by Wilfrid Knapp, *North West Africa: a political and economic survey* (London, third edition, 1977), 394.

subsequent involvement in Arab affairs. Tunisia's Prime Minister, Bahi Ladgham, played a central role in the efforts of the Arab League to mediate between the PLO and the Jordanian government. King Hassan dealt brilliantly with fractious military officers by sending an expeditionary corps to Syria in 1972. Its fortuitous presence and brave showing in the October war of 1973 gave the monarchy additional Arab–Islamic lustre at home, as did the convening of two Arab summit meetings at Rabat in 1969 and 1975. Moroccan contributions also ensured official Arab silence over the ex-Spanish Sahara, despite considerable Algerian aid to Egypt and Syria in 1973. With support from Sudan and Egypt, Morocco blocked Algerian efforts to have the Organisation of African Unity endorse its position on Saharan self-determination. Moroccan military assistance to Zaire in 1977 seemed an ingenious tactic for mobilising diplomatic support from conservative African regimes, and ensuring France's continuing favour.

The foreign policies of all three regimes continued, two decades after decolonisation began, to revolve about their respective French connexions. If the Common Market, with which each country signed a similar agreement in 1976, had broken France's virtual trade monopoly, the former Protectorates continued to rely heavily upon French military, economic, and cultural assistance, while Algeria looked above all to the Gaullist tradition of French foreign policy for support of its new world economic order and of a Mediterranean cleansed of super-power military presences. Each North African country went through a series of crises with France, and the breaks continued to be more traumatic than disputes with other industrial powers. Moreover the illusion usually persisted after a crisis that the antagonistic French policy that had precipitated it was an aberration that a subsequent French government would correct. Since the Second World War Bourguiba had consistently articulated such a perception; it was consonant with his step-by-step 'Bourguibist' tactics of national liberation and was apparently vindicated in 1972 by his first official visit, as president, to Paris: 'With what joy, with what pride, with what emotion I rediscover, in the evening of my life, France, and her friendship as I dreamed of it in my early youth. If I was the determined and loyal adversary of a certain France, it was in order to cooperate better with another, eternal France...'[1] If hardly a sentimental francophile like Bourguiba, Boumedienne also acted on the assumption of an eternal French debt. He blamed France for Algerian deficits in their 1975 balance of payments and for backing Morocco's diplomacy on the Spanish Sahara. Earlier King Hassan had considered de Gaulle to be misconstruing the French national interest in favouring Algeria.

As a counterweight to French influence, all three countries relied principally upon the United States, despite the latter's basic interest in countering not French but Soviet influence. In the cases of Morocco and Tunisia, dependence on United States aid, which totalled roughly $1 billion, was evident. When France cut off credits to Tunisia in 1957 because of its assistance to the FLN, the United States replaced them. When Franco–Moroccan relations were ruptured in 1965 over the ben Barka affair, the United States continued to support Morocco. Neutralist Algeria, by contrast, relied for much of its armaments upon the Soviet Union, not the United States. On most international issues, whether Vietnam, Angola, or economic relations between the industrial countries and the Third World, the Americans and the Algerians were at loggerheads, and diplomatic relations were officially severed from 1967 to 1974. But Algeria paid for its arms and for carefully limited Soviet military cooperation, ensuring just sufficient contact to reinforce anti-Communist biases among the Algerian officers, who continued to be largely French-trained. The naval base at Mers-el-Kebir remained in Algerian hands after the French departed in 1968, just as the Tunisian one at Bizerta, recovered in 1964, remained in Tunisian, not American, hands.

The one type of assistance Algeria really did need, however, in its struggles with France over economic issues, was managerial and technological. Shortly after independence the new state petroleum company, Sonatrach, enlisted private American consultants. By purchasing considerable private technological assistance, Sonatrach was able to manage progressively larger sectors of the petroleum industry, culminating in the nationalisations of 1971. One astute French observer also noted in 1977 that the principal threat to French cultural supremacy was perhaps not so much Arab as Anglo-Saxon culture.[2] Some of the public-sector

[1] *Ibid.*, 394.   [2] Etienne, *L'Algérie*, 177.

companies were sponsoring advanced training and entire under-graduate programmes taught in English. The United States, too, had become Algeria's largest export market, and was with West Germany second only to France as the prime source of imports, whereas the proportion of trade with Communist countries remained almost negligible and was declining.

Whether or not flags would follow trade in the final quarter of the twentieth century, the Algerian economy seemed at least as interlocked with those of the advanced capitalist countries as those of Morocco and Tunisia. 'Neo-colonial' or 'dependency' relationships are perhaps indefinable, subject to the persuasive definitions of countries like Algeria that try to restructure their economic relationships. But the more Algeria continued to import advanced technology into hastily improvised structures, the more dependent on continued injections of western capital it was likely to become, on terms that neither an ideology of autocentric development nor petroleum revenues could indefinitely soften. Ultimately the three regimes remained equally dependent on the political and economic evolution of the industrial world, especially of their European neighbours, and their degrees of dependence were perhaps proportionate to the variations in the character of their responses.

CHAPTER 12

FRENCH-SPEAKING TROPICAL AFRICA

French colonisation in tropical Africa resulted in the creation of
14 new countries, all of which became independent in 1960, with
the exception of Guinea which had become a sovereign state two
years earlier. Together these countries – namely Bénin,[1] Cameroun, the Central African Republic, Chad, Congo, Gabon,
Guinea, the Ivory Coast, Mali, Mauritania, Niger, Senegal, Togo
and Upper Volta – cover a vast area of over three million square
miles, but their combined estimated population in 1975 was only
just over 50 million. Thus though they are larger in size than
Europe less the Soviet Union, they have only a tenth of its
population.

To discuss francophone tropical Africa as if it were a unit is
misleading. Though all the states that comprise it were colonised
by France and still use French as their official language, these
facts cannot disguise the many differences among them that
have become much more pronounced since independence. Some
countries, such as Chad and Upper Volta, suffered during the
period under consideration from their land-locked position and
scarce resources, which resulted in low investment and a slow,
and sometimes negligible rate of economic growth. Others like
Gabon and the Ivory Coast, both relatively rich in agricultural and
mineral resources, enjoyed rapid economic growth. Their coastal
location and good port facilities helped them to sustain an active
foreign trade and to attract workers from poorer neighbouring
states. Guinea, by contrast, though rich in mineral and agricultural
resources and located on the Atlantic Ocean, had a government
which throughout our period proved incapable of harnessing
these advantages to the benefit of its people.

The states of francophone tropical Africa inherited a uniform
political system from France at independence, but within a short
time many of them had undergone institutional changes, some of

[1] At independence Bénin was still called by the name it was given as a French colony,
Dahomey. It changed to Bénin in 1975.

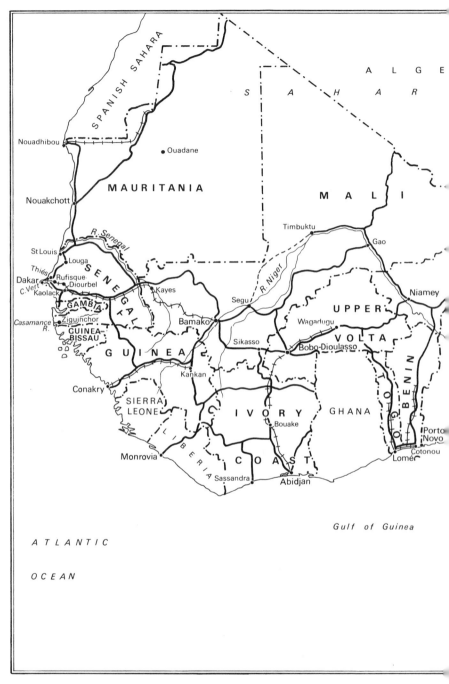

29 Francophone tropical Africa: the western states.

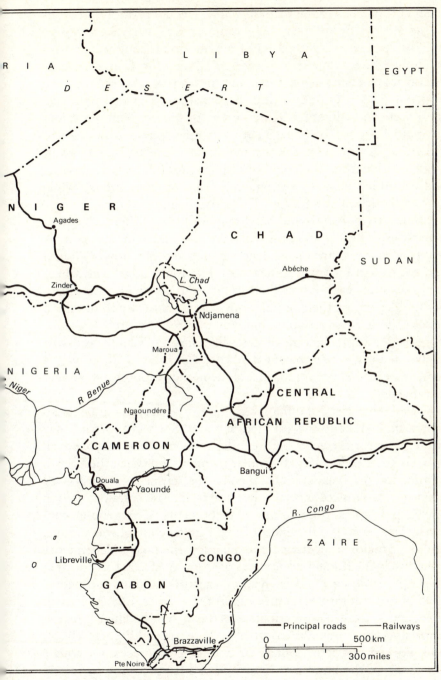

30   Francophone tropical Africa: the eastern states.

them abrupt ones in the form of military coups. Among governments led by the military there were striking variations. Some,
like that of General Lamizana of Upper Volta, sought to return
to civilian rule, while that of Marien Ngouabi in Congo tried to
establish a socialist state. Even among leaders who retained the
positions they acquired during the transfer of power by France,
there were wide divergences in the way they used them. President
Léopold Senghor of Senegal, for example, pursued policies of
moderate reform and cooperation with the former colonial power,
while President Sékou Touré of Guinea pushed for radical social
and economic change, keeping his distance from France while
actively courting the Eastern European countries.

Some states had large Muslim majorities, others Christian
majorities. Their populations differed markedly in many other
ways – density, place of residence, ethnic and social background
and sources of income. Some states, like Mali, Niger and Chad,
are enormous, each larger than France and Germany combined,
yet the density of their populations was pathetically thin. All 14
states together had a population that was only two-thirds that of
Nigeria. Per capita income in states like Mali and Chad was as low
as $80 in 1975, while that of the Ivory Coast and Gabon was as
high as $350, and urbanisation and the money economy were well
advanced.

Given the variety of differences among the 14 states, it becomes
increasingly difficult to treat them as a unit. Such an approach may
make sense for the years before independence when they were all
ruled by France in a largely similar manner, and when the French
administration was able to dictate the terms of the money
economy, to control their borders and to impose certain common
social, political and economic developments. The general consensus has been that the effect of this French control was unique,
and is of major importance in explaining the post-independence
situation in the francophone states of tropical Africa. It is true that
during the colonial era French administrators, soldiers and traders
did impose common structures upon these states, but the French
themselves were thinly spread on the ground. Their greatest
impact was on the small African élite that attended French schools
and worked in French offices or commercial houses. Of course
the depth of the impact of France varied from colony to colony
but, however deep it may have been, what has become increasingly

clear since independence is that many of the francophone tropical African states have as much in common with Arabic-, English- or Portuguese-speaking neighbours as with each other. Traditional pre-colonial relationships, masked by the colonial frontiers imposed by France, have begun to reassert themselves. New political and economic centres have strained the links forged among these states by the colonial experience. Nigeria and the countries of the Maghrib, for instance, began to exert an influence on the former Afrique Occidentale Française (AOF) inconceivable in colonial times. What was significant in the first 15 years of independence, then, was the emergence of a new state system in the region where the French connexion diminished in importance. Events since independence aggravated those differences among states that had been neutralised by colonial rule, while new economic and political relationships emerged in the region.

So, though we write about the francophone states of tropical Africa as a group, it is important to recognise that while this makes good sense for the period up to independence, during the 15 years that followed such a grouping became increasingly arbitrary.

FORMAL POLITICAL DECOLONISATION

The constitutional history of francophone tropical Africa during colonial times is relatively easy to describe because of the nature of French policy. Unlike English colonial administration, that of France was highly centralised, with all policy decisions being made by the Ministry of Colonies in France and passed on to the governor-general of the French West African Federation (AOF) with its capital in Dakar, and the governor-general of the French Equatorial African Federation (AEF) with its capital in Brazzaville, who in turn transmitted them more or less uniformly to the governors of the constituent territories. Togo and Cameroun, former German colonies and thereafter League of Nations Mandates and United Nations Trust Territories, were treated separately, although essentially the same policies were pursued in them. Of course the impact of those central decisions varied considerably depending on the environment, on existing social and economic conditions, on the state of African political organisation, and on such factors as the character of the colonial administrators themselves.

After the fall of France at the beginning of the Second World War, the Vichy regime appointed Pierre Boisson as High Commissioner for Black Africa. Effectively he was only governor-general of AOF for, under the leadership of the Guyanese Félix Eboué, Chad gave its support to the Free French of General de Gaulle and was soon followed by the other colonies of AEF as well as by Cameroun. After the Allied landing in French North Africa, Boisson threw in his lot with the Free French, though he was soon replaced by a Gaullist governor-general. Under the Free French administration, compulsory crop cultivation and extensive recruitment to help the Allied cause became the order of the day, but the wartime support of the African colonies was not ignored by de Gaulle: at the Brazzaville Conference in late January 1944 a number of major reforms were projected which gave a new character to the relationship between France and its tropical African colonies and, though it did not envisage self-government for them, permitted a measure of self-rule.

In retrospect, it is certain that France, like Great Britain and other colonial powers, would not have been able to hold on to its colonies. With the rise of the super-powers, the European states ceased to dominate the non-industrialised countries. Economic, social and political difficulties in France pushed French leaders to relinquish colonial control while, when it became clear that neighbouring British colonies were set firmly on the road to independence, francophone African leaders were less and less willing to accept French domination. The move to independence from France of the tropical African colonies was generally a peaceful one, though there were periods of violence, particularly in Cameroun. It can also be argued that the 14 francophone tropical African states benefited from decolonising victories won with bloodshed in other parts of the French empire – especially Algeria and Vietnam.

This largely peaceful transfer of power is partly explained by the post-war reforms stemming from the Brazzaville recommendations that were adopted by the French National Assembly. The reforms progressively extended citizenship to Africans and granted them freedom of assembly and association.

Before 1945, French colonial policy had oscillated between two formulae. The first was 'assimilation' – 'the fiction whereby the colonies were treated as integral parts of France'.[1] Assimilation had roots in the principle that all men are equal, asserted by Jean-Jacques Rousseau and expressed in the French Revolution of 1789. In their enthusiasm to translate the principle into law the French revolutionary leaders extended the legal rights of French citizenship to the few colonies France then possessed. However, the numbers of citizens in France's tropical African colonies remained small. Before the Second World War the policy of assimilation was applied only in the four communes of Senegal – Dakar, St Louis, Rufisque and Gorée. All persons, black and white, born in these communes were legally French citizens governed by French law, although Africans were allowed to follow Muslim personal law; they also had the right to elect one deputy to the French Chamber of Deputies. They elected their own mayors and municipal councillors and members of a local assembly with powers similar to those of the *conseils-généraux* in France.

The only other Africans who became legally eligible for French citizenship were some granted the privilege in the 1930s. Only a handful of highly educated Africans with the appropriate qualifications actually applied for the status of *citoyen*,[2] since it meant foregoing their cultural identity, family law and customs. Indeed this was the flaw of the assimilation policy even in theory – it had validity only for those few Africans whose background and values were similar to those of Frenchmen, that is for a mere handful of individuals who proved to be more concerned with their new French identity than with their African one.

The second colonial formula identified in pre-war French policy was 'association'. This policy was advanced at the end of the nineteenth century, when imperialism was on the rise in Europe. Where assimilation had been the demand of the French Left, association became that of the French Right. It implied a paternalist belief that it was right and proper for Frenchmen to care for 'backward' groups of 'associated' Africans – to protect them as well as control them. Association became the dominant theme of French colonial policy before the Second World War,

[1] See Thomas Hodgkin and Ruth Schachter, 'French-speaking West Africa in transition', *International Conciliation* (New York: Carnegie Endowment for International Peace, no. 528), May 1960, 389.
[2] In 1940, for instance, there were less than 2000 in French West Africa as a whole.

and under it Africans were 'subjects' of France with virtually no rights of representation, either in France or in the colonies. They had no access to higher civil service posts, or universities, which were only open to 'citizens'. Nor did they have much opportunity to gain a secondary education. 'Subjects' could be drafted into colonial forced labour brigades and the army, and could be tried and sentenced on the spot by French administrators under the *indigénat*, the colonial code of administrative justice, for whatever suspected offence. Thus they lived under the authoritarian rule of colonial administrators with virtually no legal recourse. Only the handful of 'citizens' had a right to judicial trial.

These two concepts of assimilation and association were invoked in the debates on decolonisation among French and African leaders after the Second World War. Both concepts excluded the possibility of the development of nationalism in the French African territories. Even the French Communists were assimilationists and had little sympathy for African nationalism. They believed the revolution in France had to take priority. Most African leaders were striving to achieve the promise of assimilation: equal, not separate, rights. Yet the logic of numbers made full equality among Frenchmen and Africans in a greater French polity impossible, for African voters, including those of North Africa, would outnumber metropolitan French voters. Furthermore, the economic costs of assimilation would have been prohibitive, given the disparity in levels of French and African economic development. Where could the funds be found to raise workers' compensation, welfare, education and other economic and social benefits in francophone Africa to the levels obtaining in metropolitan France? By the late 1950s, the French Left and many of the African nationalists were clear that assimilation was impracticable. Independent right of association with the mother country now became their goal, and the way was open to nationalist development and in time independence. To begin with, the post-war French governments initiated colonial reforms that conformed with the old assimilationist policies, rather than a separate national existence for their colonies. Liberal reforms, proposed by the first Constituent Assembly in April 1946, giving the colonies a degree of autonomy, were defeated in the subsequent referendum. The second Constituent Assembly drafted the more conservative October 1946 constitution of the Fourth French

Republic. It held that the Republic was 'indivisible' (Article I) and placed the 'overseas territories', as the colonies were now designated, firmly within the unitary Republic (Article 60). Although France and her colonies were called a 'Union', the eight territories in Afrique Occidentale Française and the four in Afrique Equatoriale Française (see fig. 29) had no separate international existence. Togo and Cameroun, in contrast, were 'associated territories' in the Union, and not an integral part of the French Republic, because of their UN Trusteeship status.

Power over legislation for the 'overseas territories' in matters of 'criminal law, the organisation of public freedoms, and political and administrative organisation' (Article 72) belonged to the French executive. The council of ministers had the right to adopt decrees not expressly contradicted by legislation – 'after previous consultation with the Assembly of the Union' (Article 72). Although this provision was enacted largely because delegates to the Constitutional Convention recognised that the French National Assembly was unlikely to spend much time over African problems, it resulted in a continuance of control over African affairs by the French government, which also had full control of the overseas civil service.

Yet the Fourth Republic made some significant changes in the rights of Africans. Forced labour was abolished. All African subjects received French citizenship (Article 81) though not all were enfranchised. At the same time, the abolition of the *indigénat* and a concomitant revision of the penal code gave all Africans access to courts and legal rights. Moreover, the extension of 'republican liberties' allowed Africans to form their own political organisations, which had not existed openly before, except in the four communes of Senegal. A further strong inducement to form African political organisations was the elections that took place on three levels of political representation. Those Africans with the vote elected delegates to territorial assemblies which met in the individual capitals of the 12 territories and two Trust Territories. Until 1957 they were elected by two electoral colleges in each territory. The first comprised Frenchmen and the handful of pre-war African citizens; the second comprised the new African citizens with the vote. In 1946 the criteria for the vote was status. Thus, for example, members of assemblies or cooperatives or unions, or holders of French decorations were enfranchised.

Literates and tax-paying heads of families were added later. The early franchise was severely limited, but was gradually expanded until the *loi-cadre* of 1956 granted virtually universal adult suffrage. In Senegal, for example, which, as a reflection of its special status had a single electoral college, only 2 per cent of the total population was registered to vote in 1945. By 1951 this had increased to 29 per cent and, in 1956, to 36 per cent. Universal adult suffrage in 1957 raised the percentage of the registered population to 46. By contrast, in the Ivory Coast, with a substantially smaller European population, the percentages registered were less than one per cent in 1945, 8 per cent in 1951, 36 per cent in 1956 and 60 per cent in 1957.[1]

Each territorial assembly in the 1945–56 period elected from its ranks five members of the two federal Grands Conseils of French West Africa or of Equatorial Africa, which met in Dakar and Brazzaville respectively. At the metropolitan level, Africans were represented in both houses of the French parliament, in the Assembly of the French Union and in the Economic Council. Togo and Cameroun were excluded from representation at the federal level because of their special status, but they did send deputies to Paris.

The number of African representatives in France was never large, since the logic of assimilation was never accepted, and one French vote never counted as less than the equivalent of ten African votes. African deputies were not numerous enough directly to decide major issues in the French assembly, but by collaborating on French issues with parties in the successive French multi-party governments, they managed to exact some concessions for Africa. The federal assemblies and the territorial assemblies were initially largely consultative and only had limited powers in the fields of finance.

Though African representatives were relatively powerless, the existence of three levels of representation was important for political developments in francophone Africa. Roughly every 18 months between 1946 to 1958, African voters turned out to elect representatives to one or other of the assemblies. Whether or not

---

[1] Percentages are calculated with the figures provided in Ruth Schachter Morgenthau, *Political parties in French-speaking West Africa* (Oxford, 1964), Appendixes 5, 7. The population figures for both countries are approximate for 1945 and are based on 1958 estimates for the other three years. Ivory Coast population figures are apparently substantially underestimated.

the political parties which developed in response actually organised the population on democratic lines over the long run, they did politicise it significantly. Africans became accustomed to acknowledging territorial issues and personalities. They became familiar with the notion that they or their leaders, and not only the French, could make decisions. Finally, the African élite gained significant political experience which led eventually to demands to govern their own countries. Thus, the post-war reforms prepared the way for the peaceful transition to independence. Nevertheless, for the first ten years after the Second World War, independence was seldom a matter of public debate. It was, after all, illegal under the French constitution. Africans elected to the French National Assembly pushed rather for reforms that went further to equalise the position of Africans and Frenchmen. The *deuxième loi Lamine Guèye* of 30 June 1950, named after the first *député* of Senegal, for example, gave African civil servants equal pay and conditions of work with their French counterparts, including vacations in metropolitan France. (The *première loi Lamine Guèye*, passed in May 1946, had extended citizenship to all African *sujets*, while allowing them to retain the use of customary law.) In 1952 African trade-union leaders obtained the *code du travail* which satisfied many union claims for minimum wage standards, limitation on hours of work, family allowances, holidays with pay, the right of collective bargaining and the validity of collective agreements, the cost of which was to prove far beyond the economic capacity of the African successor states.

On another level, African politicians consistently pressed for universal suffrage and the elimination of the dual electoral college. Step by step between 1945 and 1957 Africans achieved these goals. At the level of the territorial assembly there was a progressive reduction in the number of seats reserved for European voters. Finally, under the *loi-cadre* of 1956, the franchise for all direct elections became universal on the basis of a single electoral college. By this date pressures in metropolitan France and overseas had produced a change in attitudes of the European minority, such as planters and businessmen, with interests in Africa, who formed an influential lobby in France. They came to the view that they had more to gain from attempting to collaborate with dominant African groups than by trying to oppose them.

Indeed by 1956 African demands for self-government were very strong. African political parties, trade unions and youth movements were organised for, and experienced in, placing pressures on the French government. Simultaneously, the weakness of France was increasingly evident: defeated in Vietnam and facing a major war in Algeria, French leaders did not want trouble on yet another front, and were therefore prepared to consider a change in policy towards their increasingly restive tropical African territories.

The first sign of a change in French policy toward tropical Africa came when the 1954 Mendès-France government, under pressure from the United Nations, projected new constitutions for the Trust Territories of Togo and Cameroun, which allowed them a measure of autonomy. Although these did not satisfy either Togolese or Camerounian nationalists, they did raise the question in neighbouring French-speaking African territories as to why they too should not have internal self-government. Discussions escalated, and resulted in a redefinition of the position of francophone African territories in relation to France.

The *loi-cadre* of 1956, with implementing decrees in 1957, conceded a degree of autonomy to the francophone tropical colonies. The territorial assemblies acquired new legislative powers on specified matters – land, soil conservation, agriculture, forestry, fisheries, most mineral rights, internal trade, codification of customary law, primary and secondary education, health, cooperatives and urbanisation. Most important, the assemblies could elect predominantly African executives, known as Conseils du Gouvernement, which assumed control over the civil servants working in the fields enumerated above. The French governor remained in control of the other (French) 'state' services, possessed certain reserve powers and presided over the Conseil du Gouvernement. But the elected African vice-president acquired in practice the status and initiative of a prime minister – at least in the majority of territories where he was the leader of the party which effectively controlled the assembly.

The reforms of 1956–7 were a turning point in the relations between France and the overseas territories. By granting self-government, except in finance, defence and foreign relations, to the tropical African territories, the French government admitted that the 1946 constitution was impracticable. The reforms now divided the 'indivisible' Republic into component territories, and distributed power between them and France. The next step, total independence, was almost inevitable, although this was not immediately recognised by the moderate French leaders in power in France.

After the collapse of the Fourth Republic, the new 1958 constitution of the Fifth Republic reflected France's changed attitude towards the colonies. The referendum of 28 September 1958 gave African territories the option of voting '*non*' to the new constitution, and thus of choosing total independence. President de Gaulle emphasised that '*non*' meant an end to all French economic, technical and administrative aid. To vote '*oui*' meant accepting the status of an autonomous Republic in the new French Community and being assured of continued French aid. In spite of de Gaulle's threat, the choice was real, though the terms were set by France. In 1958 French politicians still believed autonomy was a feasible alternative to total independence. 'Autonomous Republics' were created which no longer sent deputies to France and had much more control over domestic affairs. The powers of the territorial assemblies became residual rather than enumerated, and the Councils of Ministers remained responsible to them (as they had been since the *loi-cadre* of 1956). Each Republic adopted its own constitution. Only certain enumerated matters – currency, common economic and financial policy, defence and foreign policy, higher education – were to be indirectly subject to continuing French control in that they were reserved for the Community. The French assumed that continued aid was sufficient inducement for the small and generally poor individual African territories to forgo complete independence.

Indeed, the French government had hitherto reinforced the dependence of those territories by *not* granting power or authority to the federal assemblies, which would at least have given these small territories some strength as a group. The reforms of 1956–7 had reduced their powers and did not provide for executives at the federal level. The 1958 constitution did not recognise the existence of the federations, and in 1959 they were officially dismantled. They were easy enough to break up – and the decision condemned the poor inland states in particular to greater poverty and isolation after the brief euphoric birth of the separate new nations. No wonder more powerful neighbours soon began to nibble at their borders after independence. By contrast, British policy in Nigeria transferred power to a federal government. Federation did not have an easy course after independence, for Nigeria suffered an agonising civil war when the oil-rich area of Biafra attempted to secede; yet afterwards the prospects of a large, populous and prosperous state made Nigeria into the dominant West African power, towering over its many francophone neighbours. It is hard to escape the conclusion that the French government wanted the tropical African states to be small, poor, weak, divided and thus dependent.

Full independence was at the time of the referendum nevertheless already under discussion in all African colonies, though most African leaders were not ready to give up French aid. Thus, of the 12 territories voting in the 1958 referendum, only Guinea voted '*non*'. Togo and Cameroun, as UN Trust Territories, were already scheduled for independence, and did not vote. Eleven territories then joined the French Community, presided over by the president of France, with a consultative Executive Council consisting of the heads of 13 constituent governments.[1] In principle, there was also a High Court of Arbitration and a Community Senate, consultative only, which included representatives of the constituent legislatures; but the Community never really took form, being overtaken by events.

By 1959–60 the tempo of political change all over the African continent had quickened. Radical African leaders were actively demanding independence from France, which faced a continuing war in Algeria and was threatened internally by the possibility of civil war. Beleaguered on all sides, the French gave way to the idea of independence for Africa, while clinging to the notion that aid would assure French influence, if not control, in the area. The French government sponsored an amendment to Title XII of the 1958 constitution, which permitted the 11 members to become independent yet remain with the Community and receive aid.

By the end of 1960 all the 14 territories of francophone tropical Africa had become politically sovereign states and members of the United Nations. The sovereignty was political only; it was hard to argue that any of the new states was viable in an economic sense and many of the borders appeared porous indeed. Creating viable nation states out of these nominally independent units became the difficult and challenging tasks of the African founding fathers.

[1] The other members were Malagasy and metropolitan France.

POLITICAL PARTIES AND LEADERS

POLITICAL PARTIES AND LEADERS, 1944–60

The constitutional advances made in francophone tropical Africa after the Second World War were accompanied by the development of political parties and other popular organisations, including trade unions and youth movements. Because of the special nature of the French colonial system, which rejected the idea of independence and for many years entwined political reforms with the concept of 'assimilation', many of the African organisations which eventually became part of the nationalist movements in Africa were born with labels made in France. There was a branch of the French Socialist Party (SFIO, Section Française de l'Internationale Ouvrière) in Senegal; there were African parties affiliated to the French Communist, Christian Democratic, and Radical Socialist Parties;[1] the African trade-union movements were similarly affiliated with metropolitan unions.

Given the alliance with French parties and the federal arrangements in Africa, political parties formed interterritorial networks at the outset. The most important was the Rassemblement Démocratique Africain (RDA), founded in Bamako in October 1946. Representatives of virtually all the territories went to the founding meeting. The conveners were six French West African deputies: Félix Houphouët-Boigny of the Ivory Coast, Lamine Guèye and Léopold Senghor of Senegal, Sourou Migan Apithy of Dahomey, Fily Dabo Sissoko of Soudan and Yacine Diallo of Guinea. Unfortunately, from the point of view of creating a common African front, opposition by the socialist minister for overseas France caused the Africans allied with the SFIO to withdraw, with the result that, although representatives appeared from most territories, some of the most important leaders of the time were excluded. Perhaps the most notable withdrawal was Senegal, whose leaders were then members of the SFIO. Thus began the rivalry between Senegal and the Ivory Coast.

The most powerful RDA leader was Houphouët-Boigny, though there were sections in all the territories of AOF, with the exception of Mauritania, and several of the AEF territories. The RDA was the dominant party in Soudan, Guinea, the Ivory Coast, Gabon and Chad, and its sections played an important role in politics (if not dominant) in Upper Volta, Niger, Cameroun

[1] Appendix 12 in Ruth Schachter Morgenthau, *Political parties*, 417 ff.

625

and Congo-Brazzaville. It existed as a minor party in Senegal and Dahomey. The unity of the RDA was not based on tight interterritorial organisation but rather on cooperation by the leaders, their common colonial experiences in education and employment, and their commitment to African emancipation. The weakness of interterritorial organisation became evident as, once the French government pushed for separate territorial autonomy under the *loi-cadre* reforms, leaders defended their separate territorial interests.

Two major internal crises in the RDA illustrate the competition which led to its demise. The first came to a head in 1950, when Houphouët-Boigny and the majority of the party's parliamentary representatives decided to break parliamentary ties with the French Communist Party, ties which dated from the time when the CP was in power in France. In the changed political climate of France the alliance with the Communists had become a serious liability for the RDA leaders who now wanted to adopt a policy of constructive collaboration with the French government. The crisis was eventually resolved at the cost of removing the secretary-general of the party, expelling dissident party sections in Cameroun, Senegal, and individuals on the left wing of the Niger section. As a result the official RDA faced strong criticism from the left for some years, particularly from trade unions, youth movements and student organisations.

The second crisis arose out of the *loi-cadre* decrees of 1956–7. It turned on the related issues of independence and federalism versus territorialism, and was brought into the open at the third RDA Congress, which also took place at Bamako in September 1957. By this time, the powerful Guinea and Soudan *sections* – which stood for moving rapidly toward total independence and for preserving the federation as the only meaningful framework for that independence – were in a position to challenge the leadership of the Ivory Coast. Houphouët-Boigny, reluctant to see his prosperous territory paying the greater part of the cost of an expensive federation of largely impoverished members, advocated the principle of territorial autonomy within a closely knit French–African community. This issue, and Houphouët-Boigny's attitude, brought about the disintegration of the interterritorial RDA, after the referendum of September 1958.

Other interterritorial groupings never acquired as much influence as the RDA. They took the form of temporary alliances among territorial parties; and the initiative in the formation of such alternative groupings generally came from the dominant mass party in Senegal. The first of these groupings was the Indépendants d'Outre-Mer (IOM), founded by Senghor in 1948 to project the influence of his newly founded Bloc Démocratique Sénégalais (BDS) at the level of the French parliament, including parliamentary representatives from Upper Volta, Dahomey and Guinea. For five years the IOM existed only as a parliamentary alliance with the French Christian Democrats. At its conference in Bobo-Dioulasso in 1953, it attempted to become an extra-parliamentary movement, emphasising the principle of African autonomy within a federal French Republic. The IOM was replaced in early 1957 by the Convention Africaine, and this in turn in 1958 by the Parti du Regroupement Africain (PRA), which united almost all non-RDA parties outside Mauritania. It then made strenuous, although unsuccessful, efforts to establish a single unified party covering all of the AOF through a merger with the RDA. The initiative failed; Senegalese leaders were unable to overcome a pattern of resistance against their claims to leadership which had its origins in resentments against the pre-war privileges of the 'old citizens'.

By 1958–9 the different leaders of AOF were openly clashing on strategies and goals. Sékou Touré and Modibo Keita wanted immediate independence, for example, but Touré was willing and able to push for it, even if it meant Guinea becoming independent on its own. Keita, in a land-locked country with few resources, believed independence should be achieved as a group. Thus Touré led Guinea to vote '*non*' to the 1958 referendum, while Keita voted reluctantly '*oui*', but led Mali into a union with Senegal by forming a new interterritorial party, the Parti de la Fédération Africaine (PFA) in March 1959, with the intention of reviving the now defunct federation. Initially the PFA had sections in Dahomey, Upper Volta and Niger, but its strongest opponent was Houphouët-Boigny who had more to offer these countries than either the Senegalese or Malian leaders. Houphouët-Boigny was not in favour of immediate independence, and more importantly he was not a federalist, since the Ivory Coast, as the wealthiest territory in the AOF, stood to lose from joining a strong independent federation. Houphouët-Boigny chose to tempt his weaker neighbours with promises of assistance and was able to form them into a counter-alliance as distinct from a federation. Thus the Entente came into being, to oppose the PFA and the Mali Federation. The Entente included the Ivory Coast, Upper Volta, Dahomey and Niger. Mali was composed only of Senegal and Soudan.

In AEF similar tensions existed. The strongest opponents of a federation were in Gabon which, being rich like the Ivory Coast, resented Congo-Brazzaville's pre-eminence in the federation, as the home of the capital of an otherwise poor federation which Gabon subsidised. Gabon's leaders preferred autonomy, although later on Gabon proved willing to join in unions for limited cooperation in both economic and political matters.

Thus the centrifugal tendencies set in motion by the *loi-cadre* prevailed. To most observers it seemed clear that the states of francophone tropical Africa would have been better off politically and economically had they continued to be organised on the federal basis that had been established by the French at the beginning of the colonial era. Whatever France's role in ensuring the break-up of these federations on the eve of independence, there can be no doubt that for the great majority of Africans the principle of autonomy within their given territorial borders was more attractive than federation. Indeed, however much their leaders may have been concerned with interterritorial affairs, as far as securing their home base was concerned, they were strictly national in organisation and appeal.

The struggle to create interterritorial alliances preoccupied only the handful of educated Africans who constituted the political élite. Most Africans had their own idea of what a political party should be. Indeed, in spite of the identity of labels, it would be a mistake to assume that the African organisations had the same characteristics as their metropolitan homonyms. Of necessity, the African institutions reflected their environments, and these were quite different from France. Most Africans who were educated had been 'subjects', and could only attend schools which discriminated against them. They acquired certificates which were not equal to those given in French schools and prepared them only for positions as subordinates to French officials or *commerçants*. Paradoxically, their experience with the inequalities of assimilation led them to place great value on equivalencies. Educated Africans, resenting colonial discrimination, took as their models French forms and institutions. It was natural for them to organise in the form of parties and natural that the constitutions adopted before and after independence were based on French tradition. Yet a broad gulf separated African reality from French reality. Most Africans were illiterate in French, though quite a few were literate in Arabic. Most were oriented to their ethnic communities and had never been exposed to national representative institutions. Traditional leaders still maintained an important role in directing the affairs of the mass of the population, who continued to live in rural areas. Even townsmen maintained contacts with traditional leaders in the countryside. Most traditional leaders were accustomed to having French-trained men act as intermediaries with the Europeans: these French-trained men were thus in positions of political prominence. But they, in turn, had to win the support of traditional and religious leaders, or devise a means of undercutting their power and reaching directly to individual men and women. Religious leaders like Muslim marabouts, chiefs, animist sages and official or 'separatist' Christian leaders could exact their price from the elected representatives. Their ability to block or control programmes, or influence party developments, depended on the number of people under their command or influence, and the resources they controlled.

The conditions facing the new party leaders varied widely from country to country. Even though many had shared such common experiences as being students at the École Normale William Ponty in Senegal or in territorial schools, the political orientations of the different leaders were not identical. They differed in ethnic origins and status, in religion, wealth, practical experience, ideology, and in the conditions under which they built their organisations. The 14 countries varied in the size and distribution of their ethnic groups, the size and experience of their western-educated élite, the presence or absence of large numbers of French colonisers, their geography and economic resources, their infrastructure and the modernising impact of colonial rule.

Thus the widespread rise of political parties in all the tropical African colonies obscured some real differences. Nevertheless, a pattern emerges. At the outset, when the franchise was limited, parties were dominated by the important people of the territory, often therefore by officially designated 'chiefs'. These 'patron' parties frequently had direct or indirect French official blessing and competed with 'mass' parties, which drew their leaders from among the more anti-colonial educated Africans, who made serious efforts to enroll the masses directly. In some territories, mass party leaders reached villages before the franchise became universal, and undercut the local leaders. By the early 1950s a mass party began to assume precedence in many territories, but did not become secure, except in Senegal, until after the *loi-cadre* reforms of 1956–7.

Thereafter most countries were dominated by a single party, which stressed direct participation in politics through the multiplication of local branches, parallel women's and youth organisations, regional, territorial and even interterritorial meetings and organs of the Press. These parties employed organisers, distributed party cards and collected dues. The Union Progressiste Sénégalaise (UPS), the Parti Démocratique de Guinée (PDG), the Parti Démocratique de la Côte d'Ivoire (PDCI) of the Ivory Coast, the Comité de l'Unité Togolaise (CUT), and the Bloc Démocratique du Gabon (BDG) all considered themselves to be mass parties, identified more or less with democratic reforms in their newly independent states. Even countries where it was difficult to discern a serious effort to organise the rural majority – such as Mauritania – developed one major controlling party under a French-educated leader who espoused modernising goals. Indeed, the distinction between patron and mass parties, best seen through a turnover of leadership at the local level before independence, usually faded away in the period after independence.

We discuss below two examples of mass party development, Guinea and Senegal, in order to illustrate the common trend in the 14 countries, and the diversities among them as well. Some 'mass' parties were led by nationalists who also supported radical social reform. Sékou Touré, the Guinean President, for example, had been involved in a Groupe d'Études Communistes (GEC), organised by French Communists in his country in the immediate post-war period, and in trade-union politics initially associated with the Communist unions in France. The imprint of the French presence, however, was less marked in Guinea than in countries such as Senegal or the Ivory Coast, because few settlers had established themselves there and there had been little capital investment. An African élite had not been able to organise politically in pre-war Guinea, but Sékou Touré, who had little formal education and had been a postal clerk before his rise to power, was able to create a successful mass party after the war.

Although the immediate impact of the French reforms under the Fourth Republic in Guinea was the creation of ethnic and regional parties, Touré's own Parti Démocratique de Guinée (PDG), however, had national pretensions and followed the organisational principles of its parent RDA. But when most RDA territorial branches broke their ties with the French Communist Party, Sékou Touré's trade union remained affiliated to the French Communist-dominated union. He rose to prominence as the territorial leader by organising a successful strike in 1953 against the insufficiency of the newly passed *code du travail*. Thereafter he consolidated his gains politically with a rapid national spread of his party which worked closely with his union – indeed, the leaders were mostly the same people. Although the PDG lost the 1954 elections, probably through interference by alarmed conservative French administrators, it continued to grow. A change in the French government in 1954 brought in a more tolerant colonial administration and the PDG won the 1956–7 elections. Meanwhile, Touré sought to appeal to varying regional and ethnic groups by noting his family ties to great traditional leaders of the past and emphasising the unifying principles of Islam, anti-colonialism and Marxism. At the same time he deplored ethnic divisions and the dominance of 'chiefs' or traditional leaders.

In 1957 he engineered a major change in territorial administration that removed official chiefs from their posts and he continued thereafter to undercut their power whenever possible. Still threatened by leaders of the remnant ethnic parties and by other Guinean intellectual groups, Sékou Touré was impelled by his urban union supporters to take a radical stand concerning independence. His own anti-French orientation and nationalism led him naturally to favour independence, but the penalities for Guinea's '*non*' vote in 1958 were very high. The lack of power of traditional leaders and the effectiveness of his organisation ensured a '*non*' vote in the 1958 referendum. Then, as it was still to be in the 1970s, communication was irregular and incomplete, even among close African political allies in the various franco-phone states. It is possible that Touré might not have called for a '*non*' vote had he not thought that other political leaders would follow his suit, as Djibo Bakary in Niger did, and had he not had an angry confrontation with de Gaulle, who was actively campaigning for a '*oui*' vote, on the occasion of the latter's official visit to Conakry in August 1958. Separate, early independence led to isolation for Guinea. It unintentionally reinforced the difficulty of territorial regrouping into one or more federations which were already unlikely to be realised, since the French had already dismantled the federal institutions of both AOF and AEF.

It was in fact the moderate leader – Léopold Sédar Senghor – who in 1959 created a new federation – the Mali Federation – with the radical Soudanese leader, Modibo Keita. Senghor was not identified with sweeping social reforms. He was not fiercely anti-colonial and not urgently Marxist in his economic programme. Nonetheless he, like all the other so-called moderates, developed into a nationalist.

Senegal was unique because of its long association with France, the early existence of a small 'citizen' class in the four communes, a relatively large number of educated people having at least secondary-school training, and its relatively extensive infrastructure, including a major port. Furthermore, it had been the capital of the AOF federation. Senegal had, however, only one export crop, groundnuts, and few mineral resources. Early contacts with France assured a relatively high degree of politicisation, even before 1948. It was not exclusively 'citizens' in the communes who entered politics. At a very early stage traditional leaders learned to put pressure indirectly on French administrators to obtain favours. African elected representatives, too, kept judicious ties with powerful traditional leaders outside the communes for the money and support they could obtain.

The first would-be national political party in Senegal, founded in 1936, was connected with the metropolitan French Socialist Party and headed by a 'citizen' lawyer, Lamine Guèye. His constituency was initially only the 'citizen' group, though his party did maintain ties with the unenfranchised interior. Therefore when the Brazzaville reforms were under discussion, he chose as his deputy a candidate who could appeal to the masses outside the communes, Léopold Sédar Senghor. In some ways Guèye's choice was ironic. Senghor was an intellectual, poet and grammarian, a naturalised citizen. Furthermore, he was a Catholic in a predominantly Muslim country, and a Serer rather than a member of the dominant Wolof group. But Senghor also proved a masterful politician. He immediately perceived the need to woo the rural masses and their traditional leaders directly, and was critical of Guèye for not doing this appropriately. A power struggle soon developed between the two men and in 1948 Senghor formed his own party, the Bloc Démocratique Sénégalais (BDS). Despite efforts by Guèye to win over rural leaders, it was Senghor who gained the reputation as the 'man of the people'. By 1951 his party had become dominant in Senegal.

Senghor, and his second-in-command, Mamadou Dia, stressed that theirs was a socialist mass party calling for reform. They built the BDS, which became the Bloc Populaire Sénégalais in 1956 and the Union Progressiste Sénégalaise in 1958, on the basis of ethnic and religious groups which asserted their power in relation to the 'old citizens'. Furthermore, they built alliances with some of the most powerful Muslim leaders in central Senegal. Yet, between 1951 and 1960, Senghor also took into account periodic demands of radical townsmen, 'young Turks', who wanted independence and revolutionary internal reforms, such as reducing the powers of traditional leaders. Senghor astutely gauged the moment when compromise was necessary and absorbed dissident groups in 1956 and again in 1958. By offering positions within the party, and later the government to the dissidents and taking at least nominally more radical stances, Senghor deflected the grievances of successive groups of 'young Turks'.

Intellectuals of the left continued to disagree with Senghor: at the 1958 referendum a left-wing group broke off from the UPS to form the Parti du Regroupement Africain (PRA), while a group of university students had formed the Marxist Parti Africain de l'Indépendence (PAI) the year before. Both parties campaigned for a '*non*' though Senghor successfully obtained a '*oui*' majority.

Senghor was consistently pragmatic in policy, and called only for a gradual move to state socialism. He joined with Modibo Keita, despite the radical ideology of the latter, to form the Mali Federation, since he believed the economic and political power of the two countries combined would be much greater than if they remained separate. Like imperial Austria, Senegal, as headquarters

Table 12.1. Francophone tropical Africa, 1960–75.

	Population	Size (sq.m)	Capital	Head of government
Bénin (Dahomey until 1975)	3 030 000	43 475	Porto Novo	1960 Hubert Maga 1963 General Christophe Soglo* 1963–4 Sourou Migan Apithy and Justin Ahomadegbe 1965 General Christophe Soglo* 1967 Colonel Alphonse Alley* 1968 Emile Zinsou 1969 Major Kouandete* 1970 Maga, Apithy, Ahomadegbe Lt-Colonel Mathieu Kérékou (president since 1972)*
Cameroun	6 600 000	183 736	Yaoundé	President Alhaji Ahmadou Ahidjo
Central African Republic (Oubangui-Chari until 1958)	2 100 000	240 535	Bangui	President David Dacko Field Marshall Jean-Bédel Bokassa (since 1966)*
Chad	3 950 000	495 750	Ndjamena	President François Tombalbaye General Félix Malloum (since 1975)*
Congo (Congo-Brazzaville)	1 300 020	132 000	Brazzaville	1960 President Abbé Fulbert Youlou 1963 President Alphonse Massemba-Débat* President Marien Ngouabi (since 1968)*
Gabon	978 000	103 347	Libreville	President Léon M'ba

Country	Population	Capital	President
Ivory Coast	5 600 000	Abidjan	President Félix Houphouët-Boigny
Mali (Soudan until 1960)	5 600 000	Bamako	1960 President Modibo Keita Colonel Moussa Traoré (since 1968)*
Mauritania	1 500 000	Nouakchott	1960 President Mokhtar Ould Daddah
Niger	4 500 000	Niamey	1960 President Hamani Diori Lt-Colonel Seyni Kountché (since 1974)*
Senegal	5 900 000	Dakar	1960 President Léopold Sédar Senghor
Togo	2 400 000	Lomé	1960 President Sylvanus Olympio 1963 President Nicolas Grunitsky General Etienne Gnassingbe Eyadema (since 1967)*
Upper Volta	5 900 000	Wagadugu	1960 President Maurice Yameogo General Sangoulé Lamizana (since 1966)*

* coup

of AOF, had the most to lose from a break-up of the federation. But Senghor was unwilling to tolerate the interference of Keita in Senegalese politics, or the possibility that radical Senegalese leaders might find an ally in the Soudanese president. This issue of political trust precipitated the break-up of the Mali Federation immediately after its independence in August 1960. Senghor remained in secure control in Senegal, based on his alliances with traditional leaders, while projecting a programme of gradual reform.

In all 14 states the 1950s were the high point of nationalism, when leaders rose to prominence, and built political parties to give substance to the liberation that decolonisation had brought to francophone tropical Africa. Up till the time of French withdrawal, the desire for independence unified Africans. Therefore they accepted the borders set by the French. When the French withdrew, the cleavages in African society began to come to the fore; independence seriously strained, indeed eroded, the weak new national institutions of the new nations. Independence demonstrated that leaders, even charismatic founding fathers, were barely skilful enough to cope with these cleavages. Independence came as a shock to moderate and radical leaders alike. The brief period of reforms, following the comparatively short period of colonial rule, had not prepared them or their people for sovereignty. The 14 new states were weak at birth.

THE DIFFICULTIES OF NATION-BUILDING, 1960–75

The colonial experience did little to prepare Africans for the multiple tasks of creating viable sovereign states where none had existed previously. The distance between the African élite and the rest of the people became quite evident, as in many countries political institutions withered. From the pre-independence period onwards, African leaders had been aware of the need to create a national loyalty. But to which African entity? The ethnic group, the territory, AOF, the continent? They used 'ethnic arithmetic' in an attempt to add up regional loyalties into national ones, choosing territorial party leaders, and later government officials, in a balance reflecting the ethnic composition of their states. Major ethnic groups were thus able to identify with leaders chosen for important national governmental offices, and in this way with national government. In varying degrees all the francophone leaders followed this policy which, however, revealed the new states' weaknesses, for it ran counter to the egalitarian currents in nationalist ideology. A radical leader like Sékou Touré did not wish to admit in public that he selected personnel partly for their ethnic attributes. He insisted that only merit counted, and moved firmly to undercut traditional leaders who had a following in the countryside among their own ethnic groups and could threaten the national government there.

In Senegal, a so-called democratic country, powerful traditional leaders existed in the form of Muslim marabouts who were firmly entrenched in the money economy, dominating the groundnut-producing zones in the central Wolof-speaking area. Although marabouts tolerated the appointment from Dakar of trained administrators who were carefully rotated to prevent them from forgetting their national vocation, these administrators were ineffectual if they were unable to deal with powerful regional Muslim leaders. This often meant giving them money or tempering a governmental programme which offended a marabout. It also meant administrative pleading for the support of the marabouts for agricultural production campaigns, health and vaccination programmes and for settling disputes, for example, between Fula nomads who were gradually being pushed off their grazing lands, and the encroaching Wolof, Serer or Tukolor farmers. The continued importance of the marabouts through the early 1970s ensured that governmental national reforms progressed at a snail's pace and reduced the prospects for a democratisation of local politics.[1] In Mali, by contrast, neo-traditional leaders were weaker and less entrenched in the money economy than in Senegal. Leaders of the national party, the Union Soudanaise (US), had come to power by appealing to opponents of traditional leaders rather than relying solely on marabouts or their equivalents. The Soudanese leader, first Mamadou Konate, and then his successor, Modibo Keita, obtained support from radical townsmen and from exploited groups in the countryside, such as fishermen who were barred from fish preserves, radical Muslims repressed by French officials, and former slaves of the northern Berbers. Yet Modibo Keita also emphasised ties to great

[1] See Lucy Creevey (Behrman), 'Muslim politics and development in Senegal', *Journal of Modern African Studies*, 1977, **15**, 2, 261–77.

leaders of the past, and paid homage to selected living neo-traditional leaders who claimed descent from pre-European Sudanic rulers. The platform of the Union Soudanaise called for elimination of the power of local traditional leaders, as well as reduction of the privileges of the newly emerging administrative class.

The Union Soudanaise attempted to follow a national programme of egalitarian reform and austerity, but was severely handicapped by poverty and communication problems. By 1968, when Modibo Keita was imprisoned by a military uprising, he had lost virtually all his support, urban and rural. Among the dissatisfied groups were leaders of the traditional trading families. Some, in pre-colonial times, had become wealthy in trans-Saharan trade, and others, in the colonial era, operated a West African trade network.[1] Keita's military successor, Captain Diakité, tried to give some encouragement to the West African traders, but was unable to overcome the barriers to trade established by his independent neighbours. Thus, although it had been a well implanted party, the Union Soudanaise disintegrated under the weight of economic problems and the dissatisfaction of important urban and rural families.

Senghor was forced to placate selected regional and religious leaders, while Keita lost office in part because he lost the confidence of powerful commercial families. In Congo-Brazzaville[2] Abbé Youlou and his successor, Marien Ngouabi, also had their problems balancing ethnic loyalties. Youlou had relied on support from the French administration, but he also had an ethnic base among a sub-group of the Kongo, the Lali, who were located in Brazzaville and had a long history of political activity. Youlou did not develop an elaborate national political party and was therefore unable to consolidate his power. His successor, after a military coup, was Alphonse Massemba-Débat whose base of support was among the Kongo. Youlou had been a conservative attacked by trade unionists and leftist intellectuals. Massemba-Débat's regime, therefore, took on the rhetoric of Marxism and pledged radical social reforms. Unrest continued –

[1] See Ruth Schachter Morgenthau, 'Strangers, nationals and multinationals' in William A. Shack and Ellis H. Skinner (eds.), *Strangers in African societies* (Berkeley, 1979).
[2] Called simply Congo after 1970 because the Belgian Congo was by then Zaire.

Congo's weak national institutions did not attract cooperation from the existing social groups, whether modern or traditional. Thus, when another military coup placed Marien Ngouabi in office in 1968, he had to rule a country which had never coalesced. His own support came from the northern Mboshi, and right through the early 1970s he indicated his fear of the powerful Kongo. He dismissed officials of Kongo origin and had uneasy relations with Zaire, which he feared might serve as the base for a Kongo conspiracy against him. Thus, even under a leftist military government rival ethnic groups were a threat to stability and a clear hindrance to modernisation. Moreover, ethnic considerations affected foreign relations with neighbouring African states, in particular Zaire.

These three national examples illustrate not only the importance of ethnicity, but also, more generally, the ephemeral quality of the parliamentary institutions left by the French colonisers. At independence, African leaders took control of political institutions left behind by the departing colonisers. This was a step in the transfer of power, but not to stability. In fact, the political institutions with which the 14 nations were born either disappeared or became empty forms. After independence, elections, if they took place at all, increasingly resembled loyalty parades. Party structures were eroded. The francophone countries went rapidly from multi-party to one-party states; many were subsequently supplanted by military regimes. Government rested in the hands of increasingly authoritarian leaders who, whatever their political ideology, if they kept legislatures, unions and parties, made sure they were weak and tried to build some kind of national stability around personal loyalty to themselves, as exemplified by Presidents Touré of Guinea, Senghor of Senegal, Houphouët-Boigny of the Ivory Coast and Ahidjo of Cameroun.

In some states, the consensus that had surrounded the founding fathers faded, partly due to pressures resulting from rapid but uneven economic growth. In other states the consensus dissolved altogether, partly because of economic stagnation or decline. Rapid change characterised the Ivory Coast, which attracted large-scale French investment, both because of its natural resource, and because the government favoured overseas investors. Senegal, although poorer, had enough in the way of ongoing commercial concerns to keep French money – and manpower – coming into the country. Cameroun had an injection of money from the discovery of oil; Gabon and Niger had revenues from uranium, and Guinea from bauxite. In these countries the government leaders could count, at least in part, on meeting expectations of urban as well as traditional rural leaders out of the steady growth of revenues. These countries became richer. But others became poorer, and governments in the poor states had to struggle much harder for stability than their affluent neighbours.

This of course did not mean that the richer states did not have problems. Félix Houphouët-Boigny's government in the Ivory Coast, for example, faced major political obstacles during the period in question. There were border problems in the north, partly caused by Upper Volta's dependence on the Ivory Coast, and the migrations of Mossi labourers who came to the Ivory Coast to work on the cocoa farms and returned home periodically. Within the Ivory Coast there were ethnic and regional problems. Before independence Houphouët-Boigny had created an alliance of traditional leaders from the rural areas; after independence, however, the alliance disintegrated. One important reason for this was that economic development spread very unevenly. The peoples in the burgeoning coastal area around Abidjan became better off than their neighbours in more remote interior sections; the cocoa-growing area, which was Houphouët-Boigny's home area, benefited greatly. In the towns and in the rapidly changing countryside there was tension between 'native' Ivoiriens and Dahomean and other 'strangers' from poorer neighbouring states: Mali, Guinea and Upper Volta, for example.

There were growing cleavages also between modern Ivoirien leaders, the new élite, and the rest of the people. This problem was common to all newly independent African countries, but it was more marked in the Ivory Coast because growth was more rapid and more resources were involved. An additional special feature of cleavages in the Ivory Coast and other francophone countries resulted from the French colonial assimilation policy. The *deuxième loi Lamine Guèye* and the *code du travail* left African governments with a tradition of high wages and benefits originally given to French citizens. Senegal and the Ivory Coast through the 1960s, for example, paid for vacations in France for their higher-level administrators. Government officials expected, and received, much better housing than that available to others, as well as cars and other valuable benefits. The small group of wage-earners in the private sector, through the *code du travail*, also received minimum-wage guarantees far above what rural workers could receive. Indeed, the state in western Africa was by far the largest employer, and produced little wealth, yet taxed the already hard-pressed African peasants to pay for the disproportionately high privileges of the frequently non-productive wage-earner. In the 1950s, the average wage of Africans in the public sector in Senegal was twice that of Ghana, even though the latter country was much richer.[1] Even though prices were higher in Senegal, and strict comparison was difficult, that difference underlines the financial problem in many francophone countries.

The Ivory Coast was no exception. Throughout the 1960s and 1970s, Houphouët-Boigny managed to contain periodic instability stemming from these many sources. Backed by the French, he disarmed dissatisfied élite members with a regular reshuffling of the government, co-opting, when he could, outspoken opponents. Occasionally he held state dialogues with ethnic leaders, ranging from civil servants to lorry drivers. These dialogues showed consummate political skill, yet even Houphouët-Boigny might not have been so successful over more than 30 years of leadership without the phenomenal growth in the wealth of his country.

The economic stagnation of Mali forms a striking contrast. When the Mali Federation split apart, Soudan took the name Mali and closed its borders with its former partner, despite the fact that it was now land-locked, with its major trade-routes to Dakar cut off. Its money economy was paralysed. To solve the problem resulting from this self-inflicted wound, its leaders sought alternative political unions, in particular a close link with Guinea. The left-wing ideology of the two governments made this a reasonable combination, but economically it did not help. The economy and infrastructure of Guinea were oriented to its coast, there was no rail-link with Mali, and Guinea itself was poor. Transport links with the Ivory Coast were inadequate and the distance to Abidjan was great. As dissatisfaction with the resultant economic hardships grew, Keita's government became increasingly authoritarian. He worsened the economic situation by withdrawing Mali from the French West African franc zone in 1962. The price of control of

[1] See Ruth Schachter Morgenthau, 'Old cleavages among new West African states: the heritage of French rule', *Africa Today*, April 1971.

his own currency was that the Malian franc was no longer transferable outside its borders with its seven different neighbours. As conditions deteriorated, Keita tried to return to the franc zone, but this did not help. Opposition grew, as Keita became more stridently Marxist and dictatorial, until his army arrested him in 1968.

Guinea fared slightly better economically than Mali, and Sékou Touré did manage to hold on to the leadership. When the French withdrew all their personnel after Guinea had voted to take independence, they left a weak modern infrastructure and a severely underdeveloped economy – no industrial structure and a poorly organised agricultural system. Touré, though a Marxist, called for economic help from western nations like the United States as well as from Communist countries. At the governmental level France ignored the appeal, while the Soviet Union and the eastern bloc began to try to fill the void left by the French. But it was private foreign investment in the development of Guinea's iron and bauxite, and the resulting revenues, that kept the government afloat. In 1960 Touré withdrew from the franc zone and established a national currency; changed four times by the early 1970s, it was almost without value in other countries. The Guinea government also sought to replace the African middlemen in the trading network with the nationalised distribution of goods. By the mid-1960s the Guinean domestic money economy was in disarray; the currency was severely devalued and there were few goods in the market place to buy with it in any case.

Guinea did not improve her economic position by turning to socialist countries for aid and trade. There were many problems with exchange and payment arrangements, which some critics argue actually made Guinea more dependent.[1] Guinea's economic problems and lack of effective administration disillusioned the élite, and produced a sense of hopelessness in the countryside. Many people left to live abroad, while it became difficult for foreigners to receive permission to come to Guinea. Touré emerged as an autocrat, removing his critics within the party, real or potential, allegedly for plotting against him. He attempted to rally national support by mobilising the population to resist numerous real or manufactured attempted coups, some of which

[1] Lansiné Kaba, 'Guinean politics: a critical historical overview', *Journal of Modern Africa Studies*, 1977, **15**, 1, 39.

he suggested were organised from abroad. In 1960 he accused the French, and in 1961 he expelled the Russian ambassador on such a charge. In 1965 he broke relations with France because of another anti-governmental plot. In 1969 he uncovered yet another, the 'Labé' plot, as a result of which 13 people were sentenced to death. In 1970 an attack was made on Conakry, supported by the Portuguese, according to a UN investigation. It was the largest-scale attempt at an overthrow of the Touré regime and as a result 91 people were sentenced to death. Other attempted coups were 'uncovered' between 1970 and 1974, and Touré frequently denounced foreign and domestic plotters. He did strike a more peaceful note in 1975 when, after his re-election for a third term in office, he announced that normal relations would be re-established with France.

Guinea after independence was, thus, often in political turmoil. Touré created a people's militia to fight 'subversion', to suppress plots against his government and to counterbalance the army. In Guinea, unlike Mali, the army barely existed, was kept divided, in motion, and out of sight. As many of the founding fathers were implicated in the 'plots', few remained in public life. Leaders in office came more and more from among those educated after independence. They received definite privileges in the form of excellent housing, access to scarce consumer goods and fine cars. Thus Touré kept in power, though the country stagnated politically and economically.

Nation-building in the 14 francophone states during the 1960s and early 1970s was not easy, as these case studies show. Senegal and the Ivory Coast had fewer difficulties than the others. Can it be argued that the relative stability of Senegal and the Ivory Coast, compared to Mali and Guinea, was in part the result of their different ideologies? The evidence is inconclusive. Both Mali's and Guinea's leaders adopted policies that discouraged local agriculture and commerce. Touré's government lived on foreign investment. However, some moderate governments had similar difficulties with agriculture and commerce. The drought of the early 1970s increased poverty in all the countries bordering the Sahara and exacerbated political instability in Mauritania, Chad, Niger and Upper Volta, whatever the type of regime.

In all 14 states creating the external national institutions was a struggle, and leaders from the modern élite were a minority that

Table 12.2.

	Population statistics			Education[b]					Religion[b] %	Major ethnic groups %
Population[a]	Size of largest city	% of pop.[a]	(Cities over 100000) % urbanised	Type	Schools	Pupils	% of pop.	% of age 6–14 in school		
Bénin										
3 030 000	180 000 Cotonou	6	10 (18)[d]	Primary	852	186 000	7	n.a.	Catholics 15	Fon 28[b]
				Secondary & technical	71	31 553			Muslims 13	Adja 7
				University	1	600				Bariba 6
										Yoruba 5
Cameroun										
6 600 000	340 000 Douala	5	8 (24)[d]	Primary	4137	938 071	16	80	Catholics 17	Bamileke 11[c]
				Secondary & technical	279	84 363			Protestants 17	Beti-Pahouin 10
				University	1	n.a.			Muslims 20	Tikar 5
Central African Republic										
2 100 000	350 000 Bangui	17	29 (36)[d]	Primary	778	178 550	9	55	Christians 35	Banda 33[a]
				Secondary & technical	38	10 960			Muslims 5	Baya 29

644

Population	Capital								Religion	Ethnic groups
3 950 000	Ndjamena	5	5 (14)	Primary	707	183 250	5	22	Christians 5	Arab 20[a]
				Secondary & technical	664	9762			Muslims 52	Sara
				University	1	n.a.				
Congo 1 300 020	Brazzaville	22	33 (40)[d]	Primary	1033	307 194	30	n.a.	Catholics 34	Kongo 45[a]
				Secondary & technical	122	87800			Protestants 10	Bateke 20
				University	1	1436			Muslims 1	Babangi 16
										Gabonese 15
Gabon 978 000	Libreville	9	0 (28)[d]	Primary	734	121 400	13	95	Catholics 42	Fang
				Secondary & technical	77	686			Protestants 18	Bakoto
				University	1	135			Muslims 1	Mitshogo
Guinea 4 310 000	Conakry	12	(19)[d]	Primary	1984	191 287	5	n.a.	Muslims 75	Susu[a]
				Secondary & technical	n.a.	2785			Catholics 1.5	Mandingo
				University	—	n.a.				Fulani

Table 12.2. *(cont.)*

	Population statistics			Education[b]					Religion[b]	Major ethnic groups
Population[a]	Size of largest city	% of pop.[a]	(Cities over 100000) % urbanised	Type	Schools	Pupils	% of pop.	% of age 6–14 in school	%	%
Ivory Coast										
5 600 000	600 000 Abidjan	11	13 (20)[d]	Primary	n.a.	681 735	14	65	Catholics 12	Akan
				Secondary & technical	n.a.	106 517			Muslims	Kru
				University 'Higher'	1	6 500				Mande
										Senufo
										Lagoon
										Lobe
Mali										
5 600 000	380 000 Bamako	7	7 (13)[d]	Primary	1222	254 634	5	22	Muslims 65	Mandingo
				Secondary & technical	14	6444			Christians 5	Soninke
				University 'Higher'	5	2 200				Dogon
										Songhai
Mauritania										
1 500 000	140 000 Nouakchott	9	9 (11)	Primary	n.a.	47 000	4	17	Muslims 99	Moors[a]
				Secondary & technical	26	7084			Christians 1	Fulani 75
										Tukolor etc. 25

Country (pop., capital)			Level					Religion (%)	Ethnic groups (%)
4 500 000 Niamey	3	3 (9)[d]	Primary	n.a.	139000	3	13	Muslims 85	Hausa[a]
			Secondary & technical	44	13810			Christians 1	Tukolor 6
			'Higher'		521				Fulani 7
			University	1					Fulani
Senegal 4 500 000 Dakar	13	13 (28)[d]	Primary	n.a.	269997	8	40	Muslims 80	Wolof 16[b]
			Secondary & technical	n.a.	68208			Catholics 10	Tukulor 6
			'Higher'	n.a.	5200				Fulani 7
			University	1	n.a.				Serer 7
									Diola 3
Togo 2 400 000 Lomé	10	10 (14)[d]	Primary	934	290000	13	60	Muslims 8	Ewe 8[b]
			Secondary & technical	90	31000			Christians 25	Ouatchi 6
			University	1	1385				Kabre 10
Upper Volta 5 900 000 Wagadugu	2	2 (8)[d]	Primary	1370	144376	3	11	Muslims 20	Mossi[a]
			Secondary & technical	58	14416			Christians 10	Fulani
			University	1	450				Dioula

[a] *Africa yearbook and who's who*, London: Africa Journal Limited, 1977. [b] *Europa yearbook*, 1977. [c] Gwendolen Carter, *Five African states*, Victor LeVine, 'The Cameroon federal republic', Cornell U. Press, 1963, 291. [d] Calculations by Richard Hay, 'Patterns of urbanisation and socio-economic development in the Third World: an overview', in *Third World urbanization*, R. Hay and J. Abu-Lughod (eds.), Chicago: Maaroufa Press Inc., 1977, 92–3: Hay's percentages depend on country reported 'urbanised' population in 1971 – it refers to % of population in cities of 20000 or over.

had to dilute the majority's traditional ties, even as they used them to reinforce national loyalties and institutions. As the capacity of the governments grew, as modern education and the money economy spread, groups with an interest in the national institutions also grew: such as planters in the Ivory Coast, migrant farm labourers in Upper Volta, miners in Gabon and Guinea, and, everywhere, civil servants and the urban population tied to wage-earning jobs. These groups had national interests that overrode or at least competed effectively with localised ethnic ones.

African national leaders also had difficulty reaching individual citizens except rhetorically, through radio, newspaper and word of mouth. In practice they often had to deal through intermediaries, chiefs and other traditional leaders, to assure results and implement programmes. Reaching the rural population became progressively more difficult for governments in countries where the value of the currency had drastically diminished, as in Mali and Guinea. There the governing urban élite, financed by injections of overseas aid, remittances or royalties, almost floated above the rural population. Few national institutions were suited to deal with such strains, and in some states, like Chad, even the army had difficulty holding together, and indeed eventually disintegrated.

In several cases only outside intervention by the former colonial power could shore up regimes unable to deal with the strains of independence. French troops stabilised President Senghor during his crisis with Mamadou Dia, and President Diori of Niger during his struggle with Djibo Bakary. Léon M'Ba remained president of Gabon in February 1964 solely because the French intervened on his behalf. In Chad, President Tomalbaye called upon French troops to help him fight northern separatists supported from Libya. This did not, however, stop his assassination in 1975.

The French did not try to prevent political revolutions from occurring in their former colonies, except in areas where their own direct interests were affected. Not surprisingly these were the most economically viable of the former colonies, or those having significant mineral potential.

SOCIAL, ECONOMIC AND CULTURAL CHANGE

The break-up of the AOF and the AEF federations shattered the cohesiveness, and reduced the horizons, of French-speaking tropical Africa. The separate states became weak rivals. The former federal capitals of Dakar and Brazzaville declined in importance. The land-locked states suffered severe economic declines, while the economies of most coastal states lost important traditional markets and sources of labour supply. The economies of stronger nations outside the area, like Nigeria, the North African states and even Zaire, attracted away trade and people. Within the francophone area new centres of economic dynamism emerged, most notably in the Ivory Coast, Gabon and Cameroun. Other economic shocks accompanied independence, in particular the drought in the early 1970s and the sharp rise in the cost of oil and imported goods. Inflation in France was automatically passed on to the franc-zone African states. Like their political institutions, the economic and social institutions of the francophone states were in crisis during the first 15 years of independence.

To determine the patterns that developed in the 14 francophone countries in the 1940–75 period, we shall look at some common indicators of change: religion, education, urbanisation and economic growth. These indicate the degree to which people living in villages organised on a traditional basis were drawn into institutions and activities which changed their orientations to their families, ethnic groups and to themselves. Second, these indicators were important for the African élite, who sought economic progress and a better life. Thirdly, they were important to those in political control for an understanding of problems they might have to confront. The spread of mass education, for example, raised expectations in states without the resources to fulfil them. Urbanisation, too, implied rapidly expanding populations in the cities, dissatisfied if there were no jobs or amenities. The spread of the universal religions, Islam and Christianity, could place people beyond the control of the political leaders, while eroding purely local ties and loyalties.

Because, during the colonial period, decisions for all territories were formulated in France, the official records of French tropical Africa show a deceptive uniformity, particularly before the

Second World War. In practice, of course, French colonial officials had to adapt to the special conditions of each territory, so that even before independence there were much greater differences between the territories in both their infrastructure and social composition than the colonial records suggest. Thus the role of Muslim leaders in different West African territories depended in part on their relative power at the time of the French conquest. Where the French came up against powerful Muslim leaders after subjugating them militarily they incorporated them and their successors into their administration. Where Muslim leaders were weak or few in number they were ignored or actively repressed. Senegal and the Ivory Coast respectively provide examples of these differing approaches.[1] Again, in practice the French invested their resources in territories where their returns were greatest, so that the remote and inaccessible land-locked territories like Chad or Soudan had fewer French officials and colonisers and received less attention as far as development of their social and economic infrastructure was concerned.

While economic development, the spread of education and urbanisation were objects of colonial effort – either to extract profit or to improve living conditions – the spread of religion was largely beyond the control of French officials. True, at times they favoured Muslims as superior to animists because they were literate, and used them therefore as clerks and interpreters: this is not the major explanation, however, for the rapid spread of Islam during the colonial period. Local political dynamics counted a great deal more. Adoption of one or another universal religion helped cement alliances or enmities. In the nineteenth century the spread of Islam was an answer, in part, to the social upheavals of the time – Islam bound together warring groups, which both fought the colonial invaders and attempted to conquer other African groups. Christianity, too, grew partly as a result of the desire by African groups to transcend limits set by traditional authorities or by social barriers, such as slavery.

In the late colonial period, however, when the monopoly of government institutions was in the hands of the modern élite, religion became important to them politically. Religion could be used to arouse the enthusiasm of potential supporters for leaders

[1] See Lucy Creevey (Behrman) 'The French Muslim policy in Senegal', in Daniel F. McCall (ed.), *Aspects of West African Islam* (Boston, 1971).

of new parties, or to close the ranks of a new political group against the attractions of outsiders from a different religion. In the AEF the Catholic Church was a powerful political force, although the substantial majority of the population never went to church and practised rituals mixing African pre-Christian beliefs with Christian doctrine. The Catholic Church had educated many members of the new élite in Dahomey, Togo, Cameroun and the Ivory Coast (and to a lesser extent Senegal). This training resulted in invisible but important social links between many leaders and the clergy. The Catholic Church sought to build on this relationship and to deepen its influence in Africa after independence by promptly appointing more African priests to high positions in the church. The clergy continued to have an important role in daily life, especially in rural areas, where parishioners would often seek the advice of their priest when confronted with a new problem. Individual clergymen continued to have considerable influence with members of the political élite whom they knew well. But the clergy had to tread warily to avoid, if possible, open clashes with other religious leaders or with secular groups which might label the church, with its headquarters in Rome, as neo-colonialist.

Muslim efforts to spread the faith were not so hampered. There were Muslims in all 14 countries, although they were a majority (in 1975) only in Chad (52 per cent), Guinea (75 per cent), Mali (65 per cent), Mauritania (99 per cent), Niger (85 per cent) and Senegal (80 per cent). Islam had continued to spread between 1940 and 1975 in all the territories. It was able to adapt to African social traditions, and to accept polygamy without demur. Moreover, Islam was unlikely to be identified with a European colonial presence, even by its detractors. After independence, when Middle Eastern and North African nations began to give gifts to support the extension of Koranic education and the construction of new mosques in various countries, Islam was still seen as indigenous, as a complement and extension to African traditions.

Muslim leaders, who were almost without exception Africans and not Arabs (or Europeans, as most Catholic clergy had been), usually were less hesitant than their Roman Catholic counterparts to support a political cause openly. In countries with a large Muslim majority, government leaders usually had to strike bargains with the Muslim leaders, especially in Mauritania and

Senegal. But the roles of Muslim leaders varied. In some localities established Muslim leaders were modernisers who acted as intermediaries between government leaders and the peasants. Thus, in Senegal, they helped to spread the cultivation of groundnuts, encouraged trade and urged their followers to vote in elections. Many were, however, wary of social reform, blocked health campaigns, objected to the creation of rural secular schools and were opposed to efforts to organise rural producing or selling cooperatives. Locally, thus, some Muslim leaders could slow down development schemes while other Muslim reform groups might support them.

Internationally, however, the Muslim leaders in francophone Africa had little weight. For francophone Africans, being Muslim rarely implied any feeling of solidarity with non-African Muslims – or indeed with Muslims in other African countries, whether English- or French-speaking. The notable exception was Shaykh Ibrahima Niass, the Tijāniyya leader of Kaolack in Senegal, who had considerable influence in Northern Nigeria, particularly Kano. Muslim unity in the area was rather symbolised by pilgrimages to Mecca or international congresses of Muslims; but no close inter-state unions of Muslims were formed. Furthermore, the historic tension between the Arabs and Berbers of the north and the Black African groups south of the Sahara made Muslim solidarity across this region more symbolic than real. This was to become very apparent in the civil war in Chad. Only a nominal policy of breaking relations with Israel after 1973 signalled a limited common front, and this was not confined to states having Muslim majorities.

Even the national political power of Muslim leaders was limited; it might slow down modernisation, but it never brought it to a halt. In particular, modern secular education, adopted by all the francophone leaders, undercut traditional Islamic values, and spread inexorably. In the pre-independence period few African children had the opportunity to go to school, although where schools were available they were filled. The French had instituted a system of primary and secondary schools which serviced first the French populations and secondly the Africans. After the Second World War the number of schools increased, and the University of Dakar was founded in Senegal. Primary schools remained concentrated in the larger towns and cities and very few were found in the countryside. The handful of secondary schools were also located in the larger towns. Supplementing this system were the Christian mission schools which, before independence, had been responsible in many territories for training a substantial element of the educated élite. The school system existing at independence, however, had left the overwhelming majority of school-age Africans with no access to education.

Francophone African élites, on the whole, defined modern education in terms of French standards, even if, as nationalists, they saw the negative impact of French schools on the sense of identity of African children. African children had to study history texts beginning with such immortal lines as 'Our ancestors the Gauls had blue eyes and fair hair...' and recounting with approbation the colonial feats of the European powers. They also had to study all subjects in a foreign language: French. The curriculum basically followed the French one, though French colonial administrators developed some technical programmes for specific purposes, such as a special diploma for medical assistants requiring less schooling and different topics from those taught in regular French medical schools. But African students – at primary and secondary schools, and the lucky handful at the university – wanted equality of standards and saw themselves as competing for the same goals and degrees as students in France.

When independence came, African leaders, many of whom had studied to become teachers, were faced with a dual problem. Most wanted to spread mass education. Yet they had to redefine educational goals to meet specifically African needs. They adopted new texts which included African history. By the mid-1960s, all 14 countries had either established technical schools, including schools for public administrators, teacher-training colleges, agricultural training programmes, and para-medical programmes for midwives and practising nurses, or added to those already in existence. They had not, however, sorted out how to Africanise academic programmes for African applicants to the universities, which remained for the greater part of our period under French academic direction. Most feared there would be a loss of standards as a consequence of the Africanisation of courses. The curriculum continued to lead to a *baccalauréat*, and resembled that of the French secondary school, so African students other than those from Guinea could still compete with their French peers for university entrance. Many continued to apply for entrance to university courses in France, even after most of the francophone states had built their own universities.

The French educational system was part of the colonial legacy, a product of assimilation, rigid and expensive, and required an unusually large number of expatriates to keep it going. With the possible exception of Guinea, the independent francophone states built on French precedents. Technical education was weak. Most of the African élite valued the same basic skills and advancements as did the French, and accepted industrialisation and modernised agriculture as necessary; so they emphasised education in the French language. Only Guineans departed from the precedent, with disastrous results. Even Mauritania, with Arabic as its lingua franca, maintained its French educational system intact, with Arabic merely being made a required subject. In the other countries French remained the official language. While there were numerous African languages, they were little used in the school systems, though there was some use of them on national radio and television.

All 14 countries attempted to spread education from the towns to the countryside, and they continued to import French teachers. It was many years after independence before there were enough Africans to staff primary schools and then in only a few countries. At the secondary school and university levels, French assistance continued to be required. In Guinea, Sékou Touré remained hostile to 'intellectuals', and refused therefore to see the need for arts as well as technical faculties in a university. Even Guinea, however, needed assistance in technical and secondary schools. Mauritania was also an exception; it did not have a university; lack of resources rather than ideology appeared to be the reason. It also did not have sufficient educated people to staff its schools.

The differing success in getting children into school in the 14 countries reflected varying governmental priorities. But the three richest countries also had the highest proportions of school-age children in school: Ivory Coast (75 per cent), Gabon (95 per cent), Cameroun (80 per cent). In 1975 countries which were the most urbanised also had high numbers of school-age children in school. Thus both the Central African Republic (55 per cent) and Congo (30 per cent) had more in school than most other countries.

Correspondingly, some of the lowest figures were in the least urbanised and poorest countries, such as Upper Volta (11 per cent), Niger (13 per cent) and Mauritania (17 per cent).[1] Togo (60 per cent) was an exception; neither highly urbanised nor very wealthy, it ranked fourth in schooling, having benefited both from a strong missionary presence and its Trusteeship status during the colonial period.

In francophone tropical Africa, as elsewhere on the continent, schooling was linked closely with urbanisation. Large-scale recorded urban growth in virtually all the 14 countries began with incentives provided by European colonisers. The money economy, however, supplied the most powerful stimulus: major trading posts, and later the major distribution centres for cash crops and imported goods, grew rapidly during the colonial period. Frequently the capital grew more rapidly than any other town, sometimes assuming the role of a 'primate' city, rivalled by no other urban centre and uniting all administrative, industrial, commercial and political power, as well as the most extensive infrastructure and service network. After the Second World War, and particularly after independence, the largest towns grew at an exponential rate.

Senegal provides an example of this pattern, although each country had its own idiosyncracies (table 12.3). In Senegal the trend towards urban concentration continued throughout 1940–75, without the benefit of an accompanying substantial growth in the economy. This resulted in a variety of predictable problems, among them an increase in unemployed or partially employed workers in the urban areas, primarily in Dakar. In 1972, for example, only 18 218 persons out of a population of 714 149 held wage-paying jobs. The rest were unemployed or engaged in the informal sector, where returns on work were typically very low. Many other francophone tropical African nations showed the same pattern of urban expansion without equally large economic growth. Migration to the city, and city growth due to natural causes, were very difficult to stop. Officials spoke of controlling

---

[1] Statistics in regard to children in school and urbanisation depend on governmental documents and in some cases appear to be gross estimates or are altogether lacking. Both percentage of the population in school and percentage of school-age in school are reported in table 12.2 because the latter figures were not always reliable and seem to be more of an estimate than the former (which were calculated directly, also from official figures).

Table 12.3. *Urban growth in Senegal.*

	1904	1930	1960–1	1974
Dakar (and Gorée)	25 100	64 000	374 000	714 149
Rufisque-Bargny	19 200	20 000	49 000	
Ziguinchor	700	8 200	29 800	49 003
Diourbel	500	11 300	28 600	38 574
Louga	1400	6 300	16 300	
St Louis	28 500	19 400	48 800	86 851
Kaolack	300	13 300	69 600	105 878
Thies	2 800	12 600	69 100	98 437
Urban population	78 500	155 100	686 600	
Total population	1 290 000	1 900 000	3 110 000	4 222 803
% urban	6.1	6.2	22.1	44

Source: Lucy Creevey, 'Religious attitudes and development in Dakar, Senegal',
World Development, July 1980, **8**, 504.

urbanisation and investing in rural areas, but they did little.
Léopold Senghor and Félix Houphouët-Boigny, among other
leaders, sought and received aid from international organisations
to improve rural areas, but the disparity between urban and rural
zones in this period actually increased, as the example of Senegal
demonstrates (see table 12.4).

Furthermore, the gap between the city poor and their new élite
neighbours appeared to be growing, despite efforts by some
leaders, such as Marien Ngouabi in the Congo, to improve the
living conditions of the city poor. And in the absence of rural
improvements to offset urban amenities, any improvements in city
services for the poor may even have helped attract urban
migration.

Other reasons, too, influenced the rate of urbanisation – among
them the Sahelian drought of the early 1970s. In the land-locked
countries of Chad, Niger, Upper Volta, Mali, and also to a lesser
extent in the coastal states of Mauritania and Senegal, the drought
led to a drastic agricultural decline. Where crops had formerly
grown they could grow no longer. Accurate estimation of the
consequences is not possible. Many people died and many more
migrated to the cities or to neighbouring agricultural zones where
water was available, and where they pushed other workers off the

Table 12.4. *Medical personnel and education in Senegal, 1964 and 1974.*

Regions	Population (thousands)		Doctors		Thousands of people per doctor		Midwives		Thousands of people per midwife		Nurses		Thousands of people per nurse		Education: percentage in schools, ages 6–14 Boys		Girls	
	1964	1974	1964	1974	1964	1974	1964	1974	1964	1974	1964	1974	1964	1974	1964	1974	1964	1974
Cap Vert	517	699	81	214	6.4	3.3	90	211	5.7	3.3	223	864	2.3	0.8	63	70	43	58
Casamance	562	619	10	10	56.2	61.9	9	16	62.4	38.7	106	320	5.3	1.9	21	42	10	21
Diourbel	538	635	8	10	67.3	79.4	10	19	53.8	33.4	92	250	5.9	2.5	6	15	3	10
River	371	389	15	15	24.7	25.9	12	19	30.9	20.5	147	310	2.5	1.3	14	33	6	27
Sénégal Oriental	162	245	4	5	40.5	49.0	1	5		49.0	45	127	3.6	1.9	6	22	1	16
Sine Saloum	766	814	11	14	69.6	58.1	14	26	54.7	31.3	146	297	5.2	2.7	26	23	14	17
Thies	442	556	15	13	29.5	42.7	2	34	54.7	16.4	95	289	4.7	1.9	20	31	13	23
Total	3358	3957	144	281	23.3	14.1	138	330	24.3	12.0	858	2457	3.9	1.6	23	45	14	26

Source: L. Creevey (Behrman), 'Muslim politics and development in Senegal', *Journal of Modern African Studies*, 1977, 15, 2, 267. The educational comparison between 1964 and 1974 is not exact – for example, Verrière excluded non-Africans, mainly found in Dakar.

Table 12.5. *Economic status.*

	Economically active population (EAP)	% of EAP in agriculture or herding	Agriculture % of GNP	Per capita GNP (US$) 1973[a]	Major exports	Imports/exports CFA million (1976 $1 = 250 FA)
Benin	1110000	75	30	110	Cocoa beans Palm oils Cotton lints	1974 I – 27200 E – 12621
Cameroun	(180482)[b]	75	35	250	Coffee Cocoa beans Cotton Wood Aluminium	1975 I – 128103 E – 102087
Central African Republic	(566500)[c] (43500)[d]	85	50	160	Coffee Cotton Diamonds	1975 I – 14614 E – 10112
Chad	1271000	89	& animal products 100	80	Cotton Animal products	1974 I – 22053 E – 9053
Congo	—	—	—	340	Wood products Sugar Palm oil Cocoa Tobacco Potash Petroleum	1974 I – 29658 E – 24970
Gabon	(381400)[c]	50+	—	1310	Wood products Manganese Uranium	1975 I – 100559 E – 201921
Guinea	—	80	(5 % of exports)	110	Aluminium Pineapples Coffee	1971[e] (million syli) I – 1076

658

				exports)		
			70		Cocoa Timber Petroleum	I – 241396 E – 254572
Mali	—	85	50	(75% of exports)	Groundnuts Cotton Animal products	1974[g] (million Mali francs) I – 60800 E – 16990
Mauritania	(360000 Agriculture (30000)[b])	70	200	(c. 50% of exports)	Iron ore Fish Copper concentrates	1974[g] (million ouguiya) I – 5345 E – 8175
Niger	—	90	100	(57% of exports)	Animal products Peanut products Uranium	1975 I – 26000 E – 20000
Senegal	1738000	70	280	(50% of exports)	Peanut products Phosphates	1975 I – 119876 E – 96151
Togo	—	90	180	40	Phosphates Cocoa Coffee	1974 I – 28612 E – 45174
Upper Volta	2855000	95	70	(100% of exports)	Animal products Groundnuts Cotton	1975 -I – 32386 E – 9369

Notes:
a Calculations by Richard Hay, 'Patterns of urbanisation', 92–3.   b Wage earners only.   c Employed.   d Unemployed.
e Guinea has its own unconvertible currency: 1972 $1 = 227.4 syli.   f Major export.   g Mali has its own currency: 1976
$1 = 500.0 Mali francs. Mauritania has its own currency: 1976 $1 = 214.73 ouguiya.
Source: *Europa yearbook*, 1977.

land and to the cities. In these, the poorest of the francophone tropical African countries, the drought accelerated the economic decline that followed independence. There was little that governments, with few resources at their command, could do to stem urban migration or to alleviate its impact.

The economic status of the 14 nations at the end of our period is illustrated by table 12.5. The Ivory Coast, Cameroun and Gabon demonstrated some modernisation of agriculture and eventual growth of industry.[1] In Cameroun, a growth in plantation agriculture – coffee, cocoa, cotton and wood production – was reinforced by mineral resources: bauxite and oil. Cameroun had one of the highest GDP per capita and, although wealth clearly was not evenly spread, there were new economic groups developing throughout the country who benefited from agricultural production.

Gabon also had a consistent growth in its GDP. It had great wealth in natural resources compared to the other countries and the highest GNP per capita – $1310 – but since the bulk of its national income came from oil, timber products, uranium and other minerals, it did not directly benefit the mass of the population who were directly engaged in subsistence agriculture. With its small population, it was the 'Yemen' of francophone Africa. It had the largest export surplus among the 14 countries and, next to the Ivory Coast, the largest amount of exports.

The Ivory Coast was the one agriculturally based economic success among the francophone tropical states. It had the second highest GNP per capita and the growth rate of the GNP was around 11 per cent per annum from 1960–75. The country drew the attention of foreign investors because of its rich resources in cash crops, lumber, oil products and minerals. Since success generated further success, the amount and kind of investments grew larger and more diverse; the economy was in active ferment. New groups emerged into the money economy. Although there was some trickle-down of benefits resulting in a rise in living standards for many people, a major criticism of the Ivory Coast's economy in this period was that it first of all benefited the members of the new and privileged élite, and much of its wealth was transferred to France.

[1] All GNP per annum growth rate figures come from *African yearbook and who's who*, 1977.

In the Congolese economy the bulk of trade was not large, but the Congo had considerable resources to exploit, including petroleum and potash. In the early post-independence period, the Congo's growth rate was slow but by the early 1970s it had jumped to a per annum GDP growth rate of 11.1 per cent. The Congo was relatively prosperous, even in the early post-independence period, by comparison with the countries bordering the Sahara.

Mali, Niger, Upper Volta and Chad, followed by the Central African Republic, were the poorest countries of the 14 with little developed infrastructure or resources for export. The first three suffered badly from the drought; but even previously their economies had not exhibited signs of growth. Mauritania in contrast had virtually its entire sparse population living as nomadic herders at the barest subsistence level, but its GDP multiplied by two and a half times from 1960 to 1970. This growth, however, was deceptive. It came from iron ore and copper exports begun in the 1960s and contrasted with the absence of any substantial exports before. Even with a positive balance of trade and relatively high GNP per capita, Mauritania was one of the poorest countries. The mineral exports had to cover heavy investment, and so there was little to distribute to people.

Bénin, Togo, Guinea and Senegal were also poor, although their economic plight seemed less desperate than the five countries just mentioned, because they had some mineral resources as well as export crops. Moreover, these states had fertile soil and, with the exception of Senegal, good rains, so subsistence farming could meet quite a few needs. Of the four, only Guinea had extensive resources – a potentially rich commercial agriculture, iron and very pure aluminium–bauxite reserves, as well as water-power potential. Senegal had a relatively high GNP per capita, but it exported little and had a large trade deficit. For all its long contacts with France and its advantages in the form of infrastructure, derived from having been capital of AOF, Senegal had severe economic problems. The expansion of the production of phosphates was a hopeful sign, but the major commercial crop and export, groundnuts, did not expand. Senegalese groundnuts suffered from competition in the world market into which they were thrust in the early 1970s, when France withdrew the subsidy she had continued to pay since colonial days.

The one area in which change seemed generally positive was in the field of culture. Throughout the last decades of colonial rule and immediately after independence, Francophone tropical African artists and writers began to reach an increasingly broader and enthusiastic audience in Africa and beyond. There had been outstanding early authors, such as the Senegalese writers Ousmane Socé, whose novel, *Karim*, was published in Paris in 1937, and Léopold Sédar Senghor, whose collection of poems, *Chants d'ombres*, was published, also in Paris, in 1945. Bernard Dadié of the Ivory Coast began writing in the 1930s and became a noted poet and playwright. All of them were heavily influenced by their French colonial past. They wrote in French perhaps in part because of their education, perhaps in part because the market for books was primarily French-speaking. Yet they often described African life and culture and the strains of adapting to the European presence and the accompanying destructive forces of modernisation. These African writers and artists maintained a lively dialogue in the pages of *Présence Africaine*, a cultural revue founded by Alioune and Cheikh Anta Diop of Senegal. Its headquarters, on the Rue des Écoles in Paris, also housed a bookstore and a publishing house specialising in African writings.

Other outstanding artists included Mongo Beti (*Ville cruelle*): Joseph Owono (*Tante Bella*), and Ferdinand Oyono (*Une vie de boy*), all from Cameroun; and Camara Laye of Guinea (*L'Enfant noir*). In Senegal, Cheikh Anta Diop attracted attention with his controversial interpretation of African history, *Nations nègres et culture* published in 1954. One of the best known African artists was Ousmane Sembène; his books, such as *Les Bouts de bois de Dieu*, published in 1960 and his films, beginning with *Borom Sarette*, generated worldwide interest.

Although some critics of the francophone tropical African authors, in particular some English-speaking African writers, have decried their work as too heavily influenced by French culture and literary traditions, many of their novels, poems, plays, films and treatises received international acclaim for their beauty, craftsmanship and distinctive assertion of an African cultural reality.

One point stands out from this examination of economic and social development from 1940 to 1975: the influence of France continued to be great. Although the individual nations moved away from each other as economic, social and political diversities increased among them, they all shared the same colonial legacy. The colonial period, while brief, had launched their modern economies. Except for Guinea, France continued to control foreign exchange and convertibility. The French had designed the network of roads, railroads and communication systems oriented to the coast and to France. Economic and population movements followed the new transport network which had replaced the system of trans-Saharan trade and migration of the pre-colonial era.

The technology of the modern economic system was French, and so, too, were the concepts of management. Although there were similar concepts in anglophone and former Belgian colonies, there was a special French character to institutions and practices in former French territories. The use of the French language and the continued importance of the French system of education gave depth to the French influence, even though traditional culture had deep roots. More important, however, as people left villages and went to the towns, or simply were drawn onto the fringes of a wage-based modern agriculture, they were touched by the French heritage, by French goods, currency, language and practices.

INTERNATIONAL RELATIONS

The colonisers of French-speaking tropical Africa departed reluctantly. Except in Guinea, the connecting economic, political and cultural ties, which were established in the colonial period, did not simply break at independence, but rather altered and faded.

Independence made possible changes in the pattern of international relations which had hitherto been controlled by the French; it opened direct access to all other countries, to the United Nations and other multilateral institutions. For the first time at independence the states of francophone tropical Africa had direct official contact, for example, with the United States and Russia, Japan, Germany, the United Kingdom and anglophone tropical Africa, with South Africa, China and India. Yet, in practice, poverty, the limits built into the monetary system by the rules of the franc zone, and the practical barriers to alternatives, kept relations with France preponderant. Most other nations recognised French hegemony in its former colonies.

The most persistent ties were the economic ones, since they rested on mutual necessities and advantages. In the colonial era, the French had redirected the bulk of trans-Saharan trade to the Atlantic coast, and turned the money economy towards the export of products which French consumers wanted. French investment flowed into potentially lucrative coastal regions – producing palm-oil in Dahomey, groundnuts in Senegal, coffee and cocoa in the Ivory Coast. These investments were made without any thought of meeting local needs, even in foodstuffs, or of producing the economic infrastructure that could eventually support independent states. Not until after the Second World War did the French government put a sizeable amount of aid into the development of the territories, though it was little in absolute terms or in terms of African needs. Only in 1947 was a development fund, FIDES,[1] established for the French African colonies. Between 1947 and 1956 French public capital investment in the AOF alone was between 750 million and one billion dollars, while the French, in addition, paid 27 per cent of the normal costs of civil administration. French funding was not enough for rapid development, except in the relatively wealthy territories of the Ivory Coast and Gabon. Rather, the dependence of all the colonies on the metropole resulted from French support for the territorial budgets and French insistence on being the dominant foreign economic partner.

With independence in 1960, France reviewed her economic obligations to her former colonies. After the devaluation of the franc in 1958 French-manufactured goods became more competitive on the international market. The need of French industry for protection in francophone tropical Africa became less, and many French industrialists sought outlets in other parts of Africa, particularly Nigeria. French industry became increasingly interested in competing for markets with Germany and the United Kingdom; global and European priorities took precedence over fading imperial ones. No French government, however, wanted to give away the decided advantage over other countries enjoyed by France in her relations with her former colonies. Even so, while French aid and assistance in the 1960s showed a relative stability in the total figure, there was a marked decline in the percentage

[1] Fonds d'Investissement et de Développement Économique et Social des Territoires d'Outre-Mer, succeeded in 1958 by the Fonds d'Aide et de Coopération (FAC).

this represented in the total French budget, and inflation cut into the effectiveness of the sum. The same pattern was evident in trade and monetary transactions.

Approximately half the French aid figures represented technical assistance personnel, of whom about half were teachers. The technicians took the place of the colonial civil servants and in countries like Senegal and the Ivory Coast the French 'advisers' continued to be a familiar sight, along with the *petits bourgeois* who had come out to work or try their fortune in colonial times and decided to stay on after independence. The fairly heavy technical assistance figures – except for the military contingent – were justified in France as an obligation to provide for former colonial civil servants.

Generally in the post-independence period the francophone tropical African territories received slowly declining assistance from France. All fourteen, therefore, faced a strong need to orient their economies in such a way as to attract investment from other countries and from multi-national corporations. A few African leaders took the position that French domination was more costly than it was worth. Thus, as already mentioned, Sékou Touré took Guinea out of the franc zone and sought aid and investment from eastern bloc countries; Modibo Keita pulled Mali out of the African franc zone and sought aid from Communist countries. Most other francophone leaders struggled for aid and trade wherever they could find it: they could not afford to do otherwise, and they were too weak to derive benefits from cooperating with each other. In the event France continued to be a major source of aid to her former colonies. Again Guinea was the exception, but Mali returned to the fold and made clear its desire for increased French assistance. Congo, for all its leftist rhetoric, remained heavily dependent on France for aid and technical assistance. Guinea, also, periodically gave indications of interest in resumed economic relations with France, though without taking concrete steps until 1978. Meanwhile, the United States gave Guinea and the other countries some aid. The European Development Fund and other donor organisations made increasing investments and gifts to these states. The Club du Sahel was a multi-donor effort to improve Sahelian conditions after the drought. Thus other donors entered the area.

After independence France remained the major trading partner

Table 12.6. *Trade between francophone tropical Africa and France.*

	Year	% Imports	% Exports
Cameroun	1975	46	29 (22 % Netherlands)
CAR	1971	61	56
Chad	1973	42	3 (6 % Nigeria, 5 % Congo, 3 % CAR)
Congo	1974	52	28
Dahomey	1972	40	38
Gabon	1973	56	37
Guinea	1969	14	2 (25 % Norway)
Ivory Coast	1973	44	26
Mali	1971	42	18 (24 % Ivory Coast)
Mauritania	1972	41	20 (18 % United Kingdom)
Niger	1973	35	49
Senegal	1974	41	51
Togo	1974	34	45
Upper Volta	1975	43	19 (48 % Ivory Coast)

Source: Calculated from import/export figures in *Europa yearbook*, 1977.

for the states of francophone tropical Africa[1] with the exception of Guinea. The countries which had the most wealth and the highest rate of growth were able to attract investment from and trade with other developed nations. Gabon, the Ivory Coast and, to a lesser degree, Senegal could and did receive investments from other nations, in particular Germany, the United States and Japan. The Camerounian government was even able to make decreasing dependence on French trade a matter of priority. In the other poorer francophone African countries there were also shifts from the sole dominance of France in 1940 to the situation shown in table 12.6. However, it is important to realise the figures are only relative, for there was a growing 'unofficial' sector of trade that did not show up in official records. It was based on smuggling across currency zones. Land-locked countries traded more with wealthier African neighbours than with France: Chad, Mali and Upper Volta had neither developed mineral deposits nor any other item to export to France. Niger exported uranium to France,

[1] The official figures, which are French in origin, do not include the 'unofficial' international trade, which is extensive.

otherwise she, too, would have had such a trade pattern; her 'unofficial' imports from Nigeria were heavy.

All the states, Guinea – and Mali for a time – excepted, used foreign exchange controlled by the Bank of France, and French materials inherited from the colonial era. It was easier to refurbish the railways, for example, by buying from the country of origin. The dominance of France in trade was stronger on the import than the export side of African ledgers.

As the Algerian war drew to a close, it became French policy to strengthen the franc zone by encouraging trading outside it. French officials believed their former tropical African colonies were not as rich as other parts of Africa, and initiated policies to allow French businesses access to the resources and markets of the rest of the continent.

These objectives followed from a vision in which Europe, led by France, would be more than just a good neighbour to Africa, but rather a big brother with a hegemony that could limit competition from other industrialised states. That meant seizing the moment following the end of colonialism to obtain economic opportunities previously held closely by European rivals. This policy explains why the French government did not hesitate to intervene actively in the Nigerian and Zairean wars, for example. Yet French policy at the same time sought to cooperate with the evolving European Community, so as to limit access by Japan, the United States, and of course Russia to francophone tropical Africa.

Though the number of French troops in tropical Africa declined, the French continued to be the self-appointed military guardians of the territorial integrity of the former colonies, and intervened from time to time to maintain the old colonial borders. French taxpayers grumbled, yet the policy continued of limited intervention to restore domestic balance within one or another African state, to maintain French hegemony, or to reinforce African borders against encroachment by more powerful neighbours.

The border between the Mediterranean African states and the Sahelian states was one zone of French intervention. The zone was thought to have mineral resources, such as uranium (in Niger) or oil; there were very few inhabitants, and no water. Pressure in France for mineral resources such as oil or uranium, led it to intervene in the zone after independence. Libya attempted to intervene, to a limited extent, in Niger, but more directly in Chad. French troops and planes were used to balk Libyan intervention almost from the time of independence itself. The population of the northern part of Chad, Muslim and often nomadic, resented the rule of Christian or animist southerners; Libyan reinforcement of separatism in northern Chad fed the controversy, and threatened the very existence of the state. Chad had the greatest cleavage between Muslims and non-Muslims, a difference which characterised in varying degrees all the people of the Sahel states.

Desire to keep hold of potential economic resources, such as uranium mines at Arlit and elsewhere in the Saharan zone, motivated French defence of Niger against encroachment by Libya. After the rise of OPEC, when uranium prices rose sharply in the world market, the French military advisers did nothing to prevent a coup against President Hamani Diori, who had ruled since independence. Diori's government was beset by economic troubles after the drought and had made moves to open Saharan uranium concessions to American and other non-French companies, thus threatening to reduce French influence.

Mauritania was another state in whose controversies the French intervened militarily. After Morocco and Mauritania had divided the former Spanish Morocco between them, the Polisario independence movement resisted the occupation of their country by these two states and were helped in this by Algeria. The Moroccans and Mauritania became allies and therefore the Moroccans were able to place their troops dangerously close to Nouakchott, the capital of Mauritania. This advanced King Hassan's territorial ambitions for a greater kingdom of Morocco, which had caused Morocco to challenge separate independence for Mauritania and even its entry into the United Nations. This threat to the borders of Mauritania concerned the Senegal government which did not want a powerful Morocco as a neighbour. Therefore the Senegalese government invited French troops and planes back into Dakar in the 1970s.

French aid to Biafra during the Nigerian war had a dual objective. One was to eliminate the threat of a potential Nigerian hegemony in Western Africa, by breaking up the most highly populated and richest African state which was attracting more and more migrants from its poorer neighbours. The other French objective was to gain access to Nigerian oil and markets. After the Biafran claim to independence failed, the French tried to make friends with the victorious government. A certain tension remained, however, and French power reinforced the wariness of Nigeria that was characteristic of that country's smaller, weaker francophone neighbours.

No country sought seriously to replace France in trade, in aid or strategically in francophone tropical Africa during the 1960–75 period. France saw no reason to cede its special place to any other power, including Russia. France shifted its strategy, however, from frequent internal interventions in the 1960s to greater emphasis in the 1970s on keeping encroaching outsiders away.

Among the francophone tropical African states, which had been bound together firmly during the French colonial era, ties faded, indeed more quickly than between them and France. For a while after independence some evidence of cooperation remained, such as common membership in the franc-backed monetary zone. Often reluctantly, out of sheer economic necessity, most states shared such luxury items as the airline, Air Afrique, and stayed in producers' unions to face the world market, or in customs unions to simplify border procedures and control. Yet when the leaders felt it necessary, they dispensed with these forms of cooperation. Thus, even conservative Mauritania moved out of the African monetary zone, Cameroun set up its own airline and various countries moved in and out of regional planning groups as their domestic situations dictated. Each nation sought to pursue its own self-interest as defined by its ruling élite. Each wanted a university, rather than to share the expense with a neighbour. No national government was willing to surrender any significant amount of national power or to share it. The history of the Mali Federation shows what most African leaders feared might happen in a political union or federation: intervention by one partner in the local affairs of the other. Another example of an unsuccessful effort to create a federation was the Ghana–Guinea–Mali union. Touré and Keita agreed with Kwame Nkrumah that a strong federal union was needed to fight neo-colonialism. Guinea accepted aid from and union with Ghana almost immediately after the French withdrew all their aid and services. After the break-up of the Mali Federation, in December 1960, the Republic of Mali joined in the union. The Ghana–

Guinea–Mali union, called the Union of African States (UAS) according to its charter issued in Accra in July 1961, was anti-colonial, anti-French and Marxist in tone. In addition, the charter called for the pooling of resources and a common orientation in domestic as well as foreign policy. The UAS had support from some North African leaders, who hosted the Casablanca Conference in 1961. In practice, however, the leaders of the three countries continued to run their own governments separately. The economies of the three countries were not complementary and the union did not last long enough to allow a real test of the avowed aim to unify the three states.

Meanwhile, leaders in the rest of francophone tropical Africa were trying to find their own formula for cooperation which was less ambitious. By the early 1960s the political differences between Léopold Senghor and Félix Houphouët-Boigny had diminished. To preserve existing borders and avoid alienating potential foreign donors, all the equatorial states, Cameroun, Madagascar and all the other West African francophone states with the exception of Togo, met at Brazzaville in December 1960 to form the Union Africaine et Malgache (UAM). They, too, condemned colonialism, but cautiously, and sought to advance their populations economically and socially by concerted action. But they vowed non-interference in each other's affairs and condemned subversion at the follow-up conference in Monrovia in May 1961.

The UAS and the UAM resolved their differences when they formed together the Organisation of African Unity (OAU) in Addis Ababa in early 1963. Nevertheless, the francophone tropical African states continued to feel the need for a regional grouping. The UAM states formed the African and Malagasy Common Organisation (OCAM) in February 1965, including all the francophone tropical states except Guinea. Madagascar, Rwanda and Zaire also joined. Mauritania withdrew in 1965, and Mauritius became a member in January 1971 when the OCAM became the OCAMM.[1] OCAMM called for cooperation, social and cultural as well as economic. Members reached economic agreements and undertook joint activities, such as a computer-training institute in Gabon, and the customs and economic union of Central

[1] The extra M stands for 'Mauricienne'. Cameroun also withdrew, finding more useful economic relations outside the OCAMM.

Africa, including all the former AEF states and Cameroun. At the United Nations and other international gatherings the franco-phone African states kept their distinct and separate network.

These moves towards cooperation among the francophone tropical African states were hardly wholehearted, however, and were in reality not very effective, since there was little follow-through of their plans, and there were often squabbles among member states. Though all fourteen largely retained the borders established by the French, they often disputed borders with each other, for example, Mali with Mauritania, Niger with Bénin, Upper Volta with Mali. They were rivals for French favours and for outside aid and investment. They were unable fundamentally to alter the economic patterns they had inherited with independence. Initiative for possible changes came from outside their borders. There were moves initiated by Nigeria, after it became wealthy from oil following the rise of OPEC, to create an economic community of West African states, which also included Bénin, the Gambia, Ghana, Guinea, Guinea-Bissau, the Ivory Coast, Upper Volta and Niger. Nigeria also intervened in Chad's internal difficulties and offered some aid to Niger and Bénin, whose port of Cotonou it used to relieve the congestion in the port of Lagos.

Another initiative came from Western Europe, as French policy changed. Gradually France transferred some of its economic responsibilities for the former colonies to the European Common Market. As long as Britain had stayed out of the Common Market, the existence of separate franc and sterling zones in Africa raised considerable barriers to regional integration and trade. Once Britain joined the Common Market, the barriers between anglo-phone and francophone tropical Africa became less rigid, and cooperation became much easier. By 1975 the Common Market and associated states (anglophone and francophone former colonies) had signed the Lomé Convention. From the European side the Lomé Convention marked an attempt to protect the former colonial markets against non-European competition. On the African side, the convention guaranteed the associated African states preferential treatment in the European market, promises of aid and cooperative trade arrangements, a programme to stabilise prices of exported commodities (STABEX), and foreign capital.

The African partners were not, however, prevented from accepting investment from other countries.[1]

There were also many changes in francophone tropical Africa, initiated by shifts in the structure of the international economy, coming from international institutions like the UN, from UNCTAD, currency changes, shifts in relations among donors, changes in energy patterns, in commodity prices or from world inflation. The initiative for most of these changes remained outside the hands of the francophone tropical African states.

Thus, independence brought a change in the pattern of francophone African international relations, a multiplication of diplomatic contacts and greater vulnerability to changes in the global balance of power. The change in the structure of the international economy that accompanied the rise of OPEC affected the 14 states. They suffered new and higher costs, and found some new sources of aid. Some tried to benefit from the split between China and Russia – Guinea, Mali and Congo, for example, all of which received Chinese aid. The intervention in Africa by Cuban troops worried many of the governments, particularly Senegal, the Ivory Coast and Cameroun. Many of the states tried also to benefit from the renewed rivalry that accompanied the search for raw materials in Africa by developing states, such as the United States, Japan and even South Africa.

In spite of difficulties, economic as well as political, all 14 states remained intact during 1960–75. They sought ways to develop, to strengthen their institutions and give substance to their newly acquired statehood. The cluster of French language, habits and institutions inherited from French colonial rule continued to define the area. '*Francophonie*', nurtured from France, remained a cultural as well as a political reality in tropical Africa.

Economically survival was still a question for the poorer states. Self-reliance was not around the corner. In agriculture imports were growing, and while the population grew, the potential was not realised. In commerce the market potential of the area could not be realised as long as frontiers were not open and free circulation of people and goods was hampered. In industry the

---

[1] For a more lengthy discussion of this subject, see Ruth Schachter Morgenthau, 'The developing states of Africa', *Annals of the American Academy of Political and Social Science*, July 1977, **432**, 80–94, and Morgenthau, 'African politics: background and prospects', in Frederick Arkhurst (ed.), *Africa in the seventies and eighties* (New York, 1970), 16–47.

start was slow. Separate independence may have appealed strongly to the leading political groups, but for most of the population the economic fruits of freedom remained out of reach.

For the future many development tasks could only be done through regional tropical African cooperation, across francophone-anglophone lines: such as developing the Sahel from the regional capital of Wagadugu, or making the inter-state rivers like the Niger, the Volta or Senegal navigable and harnessing them for electric power. Constraints in communications, agriculture, capital and human resources, pointed to many years of work ahead. The international transactions of the 14 states might in future become relatively less with each other (except culturally) and more with their other neighbours. The Mediterranean states, or states like Nigeria, Zaire and Angola, might become stronger poles of attraction – or they might not, should they threaten to overpower the weaker francophone states. In such a case the latter might group among themselves with smaller West African anglophone states. Meanwhile, the heritage of French colonial rule was fading in the mid-1970s, and the outlines of an African state system were becoming visible.

CHAPTER 13

MADAGASCAR

On the eve of the Second World War, the vast majority of Malagasy were French *sujets* who had extracted few political concessions from Paris. But political awareness was developing, especially among the urbanised Merina, whose leaders, Jean Ralaimongo and Joseph Ravoahangy, had agitated in favour of equal civil and political status with the Europeans and the reform of local labour regulations. Their campaign achieved Malagasy representation on a consultative body created in 1924, called the Délégations Économiques et Financières. The administration dominated the Délégations, quarrelled with the settlers' representatives, and ignored the Malagasy delegates. As a result the Malagasy gained limited knowledge of parliamentary procedure from them. Léon Cayla's term as governor-general (1930–9) witnessed the suppression of political activities and a decree establishing arbitrary arrest; anti-government newspapers were banned and labour was tightly controlled. Under pressure from the Popular Front government, he permitted the formation of the first trade unions in 1937. When he returned to France in 1939 he left a colony in which the mass of the population accepted French rule. But he also left behind an educated élite which harboured political and personal grievances against the administration.

The outbreak of the Second World War produced a wave of Malagasy patriotism, which the new Governor-General, Marcel de Coppet, used to mobilise Madagascar's resources. The collapse of France resulted in de Coppet's recall by the Vichy regime and the re-appointment of Cayla, who was forced to leave nine months later because he had reached retirement age. His successor was Armand Annet, who repressed all opposition, discriminated against the Malagasy, and abolished the Délégations. The Allies blockaded the island from late 1941, invaded it with a British force in May 1942, and forced Annet to surrender the following November. The British retained the Vichy administrators until January 1943, when they handed over power to the incoming Free French. In Allied hands, the island became a supplier of men and raw materials for the war. Between 1943 and 1945 the pressure on the Malagasy became intense, as the administration proceeded to conscript men for the army and forced labour, and to extract 150 million francs in 'contributions' for the war effort. Inflation rose rapidly, but wages hardly at all, while shortages became acute and the black market flourished. Farmers were forced in 1944 to sell their entire crop to the government's Office du Riz at a low and fixed price, and then when they needed rice for their own use to buy it back at a higher cost. Mass discontent became widespread. Governmental reforms were few, though the Free French did give the *fokonolonas* (village councils) some additional responsibilities and supported the concept of a new representative council. This body, which separated the settlers and Malagasy into two electoral colleges and pitted both against the governor-general's 30 appointees, was established in 1945. The council had no control over the budget; the settlers, who represented little more than one per cent of the population, were grossly over-represented on it; and the governor-general could dissolve it at will. Despite its flaws, it was an improvement over the Délégations, and it embodied the principle established at the Brazzaville Conference, whereby colonial representatives could sit in the French National Assembly and Senate. Membership of the French parliament gave Malagasy leaders important contacts with French officials and experience in the art of governing, both of which were later to prove invaluable.

The ideas articulated at Brazzaville and the principles of self-determination embodied in the Atlantic and United Nations Charters inspired Ravoahangy and Joseph Raseta, both of whom demanded that they be applied to Madagascar. The Malagasy voters elected the two Merina leaders to the first Constituent Assembly of the Fourth French Republic, but, once in Paris, the representatives discovered that all French parties were opposed to Malagasy independence or even autonomy. They therefore joined forces with Jacques Rabemananjara, a Betsimisaraka, who was elected to a third Malagasy seat in early 1946, to form the

31   Madagascar.

Mouvement Démocratique de la Rénovation Malgache (MDRM). They attempted unsuccessfully to introduce an independence bill in the assembly in 1946. In early October all Malagasy obtained French citizenship, though only some 10000 had the vote, when the island became an overseas territory. At the same time forced labour was abolished. A statute of 25 October divided the island into five provinces, each with its own budget and assembly, but the MDRM, dedicated as it was to national unity for independence, interpreted this reform as a French attempt to set the *côtiers* (coastal peoples) against the Merina. They were in part correct; the administration did view the MDRM as a Merina separatist party dedicated to the re-establishment of the former Merina monarchy, and for this reason it supported the Parti des Désherités Malgache (PADESM). The name of this party reflected very clearly the fact that it was composed of peoples who considered themselves socially, economically and politically underprivileged. Prior to the French conquest (1895) the island kingdom of the Merina spread from the high plateaux and established a hegemony over a number of other ethnic groups. Although the French destroyed the monarchy and attempted both to favour the *côtiers* and play them off against their former masters, nonetheless the Merina continued to dominate life in the island. They remained the most well educated, the largest and the most advanced ethnic group in terms of the assimilation of western ideas and technology, and thus the French found themselves forced to recruit them for positions in government, commerce and the military. This Merina monopolisation of key positions at all levels resulted in a form of sub-imperialism which has parallels with the situation in Rwanda and Burundi at the time of their independence. The French naively assumed, as did a number of *côtiers*, that the Merina leadership would attempt to turn back the clock and re-establish the old monarchy, and hence they favoured the PADESM. The MDRM gathered support rapidly among the Merina, but its membership also embraced two extremist groups born during the Second World War, the Jeunesse Nationaliste (JINA) and the Parti Nationaliste Malgache (PANAMA). Both contained some *côtiers*, were more aggressive and anti-French than the MDRM leadership, and desired a complete break with France, whereas the MDRM leaders wanted independence within the French Union. In the elections to the National Assembly held in November 1946, the three MDRM leaders were re-elected. Subsequent elections for the French Senate and Council of the French Union, as well as for Madagascar's provincial assemblies and National Representative Assembly, produced more MDRM victories. At the very height of its success, the party was struck a death blow when an anti-European rebellion broke out on 29 March 1947.

It is still not clear whether the revolt was coordinated by some central agency. Even if it was, the various attacks were badly organised and poorly executed. The attack on the Manakara military garrison was successful, but assaults on other posts and the major towns and cities were all abortive. The areas hardest hit by the rebels were on the east coast, where export crops and illegal exploitation of Malagasy labour were most prominent, although the rebellion also spilled over into the highlands. Some 28 European settlers and many more Malagasy were killed by the rebels; communications links were severed and public and mission buildings destroyed. Additional French troops arrived in the island, and by late 1948 the rebellion was over. The suppression of the rebellion was brutal. The administration claimed that 11 000 people of all races had died; the French Communist Party published a total of 90 000.[1] Governor-General de Coppet, during his second term of office from 1946 to 1948, accused the three deputies and the MDRM of master-minding the rebellion, and quickly banned the party. Raseta and Ravoahangy were condemned to death, although their sentences were later commuted, while Rabemananjara was given life imprisonment. Attempts to probe the rebellion's roots produced a variety of causes, ranging from the discontent over low wartime crop prices and labour abuses to the racism of French settlers and officials. What does seem clear is that the leadership lay not with the three deputies, but with the leaders of JINA and PANAMA, notably Rakotondrabe, Betrevola and Ravelonahina. The young extremists in these secret societies wanted a break with France. Once the revolt was under way the deputies, who were probably aware of the rebels' plans, disassociated themselves from it, but by then it was too late and all nationalists were branded traitors by the French.

The revolt shocked the French, and this feeling was shared by Governor-General Pierre de Chevigne (1948–50), who succeeded

---

[1] Estimates of the actual number of Malagasy killed vary widely. For example, N. Heseltine, *Madagascar* (London, 1971), 181 gives 60–80 000.

de Coppet and instituted surveillance of anti-French suspects, arbitrary arrest, and imprisonment without trial on a wide scale. PADESM split into quarrelling factions, and legitimate grievances against the administration went unheard until the arrival of Robert Bargue (1950–4), who did much to repair relations between the nationalists and the French. Bargue turned the attention of the island's assembly towards socio-economic questions and blunted the thrusts of the infant Communist movement, the Parti de l'Union du Peuple Malgache (PUPM), while his successor, André Soucadaux (1954–60), permitted the Malagasy to petition Paris for an amnesty and the release of those convicted of involvement in the rebellion. Paris arranged the requested amnesty and granted a pardon to those sentenced to more than 15 years' imprisonment, while Ravoahangy, Raseta and Rabemananjara were released from prison and exiled to France. In Madagascar, Soucadaux helped establish the socialist Parti Social Démocrat (PSD) in 1956, which was led by the *côtier* leader, Philibert Tsiranana. In the elections to the French National Assembly, Tsiranana was elected deputy just in time to witness the passage of the *loi-cadre*, which created a common electoral roll for the territory, introduced universal suffrage, granted a measure of internal autonomy, and inaugurated a system of ministerial government. Paris, however, continued to control defence, foreign relations, civil liberties, and finance through the governor-general.

Political parties emerged in numbers during 1956, and their support ranged from regionalist, to Christian, to socialist. The more stable parties were Norbert Zafimahova's Union Démocratique et Sociale Malgache (UDSM), the Aknonton'ny Kongres'-ny Fahaleoventenana Madagaskara (AKFM – Congress Independence Party), the Mouvement National pour l'Indépendence de Madagascar (MONIMA), the Rassemblement Chrétien de Madagascar (RCM), and the Renouveau National Malgache (RNM). Elections were held in 1957 for the new assembly and provincial councils. A *côtier*-PSD-UDSM alliance was carried to power in Majunga, Tuléar and Fianarantsoa provinces, thereby blocking any Merina domination of those provinces or the nation. Tsiranana was elected head of government on 1 May 1958. In August 1958, not long after he came to power, de Gaulle visited Madagascar to campaign for his constitutional proposals for the overseas territories. These envisaged full internal autonomy with the status of Republic within a French community. A vote against de Gaulle's proposal would result in Madagascar or any other territory that took this course being given independence 'with all its consequences' which would mean a withdrawal of all French aid and services. Tsiranana's party campaigned for a vote in favour of de Gaulle's proposals and in the referendum held in September 1958 Madagascar voted 77 per cent in favour of them. However, Tsiranana thereafter sought to undercut radical pressures, in particular those from the left-leaning AKFM which had campaigned for a 'no' vote, and he pressed France for a more definite separation. The Franco-Malagasy *Accords*, negotiated in April 1960, defined a new relationship and Madagascar achieved formal independence on 26 June 1960.

POLITICAL AND CONSTITUTIONAL HISTORY:
POST-INDEPENDENCE

The period 1960–72 did not witness any sudden changes in Franco-Malagasy relations. Although by 1960 there were a substantial number of trained Malagasy, Paris arranged to retain up to 1500 French technicians and teachers on the island, and ensured that key positions in most of the ministries were held by French nationals. Tsiranana's communications, financial, military and security advisers were all French. In the private sector, 36000 expatriates remained in commerce, agriculture or the professions because the PSD-UDSM alliance favoured foreign investment and the maintenance of good relations with France. At the inter-governmental level the two finance ministries cooperated closely. French aid continued at a high level throughout the 1960s, though much of it returned to France in the form of the repatriation of profits and purchases of capital equipment. In 1968 France was still supplying 63 per cent of Madagascar's imports and taking 45 per cent of her exports. At the military level, the French navy commanded Diego-Suarez, the French air force maintained a base at Ivato, and French nationals were training Malagasy soldiers well into the 1960s. Although Tsiranana possessed a 3000-man mobile police known as the Gendarmerie and a *côtier*-dominated para-military bodyguard, known as the Force Républicaine de Sécurité (FRS), to offset the power of the army, he nonetheless kept French forces nearby. In foreign affairs he remained a close supporter of France, and was wary of the Americans. On his initiative, links with South Africa were formed in 1968 in order to encourage tourists from that country. Close relations were established with the EEC, West Germany, Italy, Spain, Japan and Israel, but he discouraged contacts with Communist countries other than Yugoslavia, and did not show much interest in African affairs, though Madagascar became a member of the Organisation Commune Africaine et Malgache (OCAM). His attachment to France and his commercial relations with Pretoria angered the AKFM which advocated the expulsion of white settlers and servicemen, including some 50000 Comorans holding French citizenship, as well as the nationalisation of French firms and South African tourist facilities.

When Tsiranana came to power, he had recalled the three deputies exiled in 1954 and invited them to join his government. Raseta rejected the offer and became an independent, but Rabemananjara became Minister for the National Economy, while Ravoahangy, who died in 1969, was appointed Minister of Health. André Resampa became Minister of the Interior, and later in the decade the PSD's secretary-general. Through his efforts the PSD launched Syndicats des Communes (cooperatives), and PSD membership grew rapidly as thousands joined the party in search of jobs and favours. Changes in the structure of government were initiated, and the civil servants were brought to heel with anti-strike legislation and severe penalties for corruption. Within the party ranks, Tsiranana's attempts to impose obedience were less successful. The problem of party discipline and loyalty was partly solved by a constitutional amendment in 1962, which prevented the Senate from delaying legislation, and partly by a combination of coercion, bribery and flattery which won over troublesome regional leaders such as Jean François Jarison (Fianarantsoa), Justin Bezara (Diego-Suarez), and Jean Natai (Majunga). Tsiranana's policy of playing one faction off against another was largely successful, but an illness in 1967, and PSD in-fighting over posts, loosened his grip on the party leadership and opened the way for ministerial rivalries. The PSD, lacking any firm ideology, dependent upon one strong leader, and over-confident after a long term in office which witnessed no major changes of any kind, was beginning to fall apart. This lethargy was broken in 1970–1, when Tsiranana first demoted and then arrested his colleague Resampa, whom he claimed, somewhat curiously, was, with Jaona of MONIMA, a leader of a Peking–Washington sponsored anti-government revolt among the Antandroy. Resampa's removal highlighted the weaknesses of both the PSD and Tsiranana, who was heavily dependent on his organising abilities. It also marked the arrival of the students on the political stage.

Opposition to the PSD before 1970 had come from several weak parties whose followings were small and geographically restricted, and who shared only a feeling of nationalism and a distaste of Tsiranana. Raseta's Mouvement d'Union Nationale (MUN) eventually collapsed in the 1970 national elections; Jaona's MONIMA enjoyed support only in the Tuléar area; and Bezara's Parti Chrétien Démocratique (PCD) disintegrated in 1970 because of internal rivalries. Far more serious a threat was the AKFM. Unlike the PSD with its rural and *côtier* support, the AKFM was mainly bourgeois, Merina, urban, and intellectual. Its leader, a Protestant pastor, Richard Andriamanjato, had little familiarity with rural life and never managed to make any impact on the rural masses. All in all, the opposition was so ineffective that Tsiranana never found it necessary to curtail freedom of expression until 1970, and AKFM demands for expulsion of the French and nationalisation of their financial holdings fell on deaf rural ears. In order to curb its influence with Catholics and civil servants, Tsiranana labelled the Merina-dominated AKFM 'Communist'. For the Protestant Merina, Tsiranana came to represent everything they detested: a Catholic *côtier* attempting to govern those who viewed themselves as the natural rulers of the island.

It was the armed revolt in April 1971 of the impoverished Antandroy peasants, frustrated by the greed and corruption of the tax collectors, that gave Tsiranana's career its rudest jolt. The revolt, led by Jaona, was quickly supressed, and Tsiranana used it as an excuse for ridding himself of Resampa, a potential rival, and for reorganising his party for the January 1972 presidential elections. A number of reforms placed the reins of party power squarely in his hands and, when the voting was completed, government officials claimed that Tsiranana had won 99.9 per cent of the votes cast by 86 per cent of the population. But on 13 May, three weeks after his third inauguration, he was toppled from power as a result of fighting which took place between the FRS and the *zoam* (unemployed) of Antananarivo,[1] students and labourers. The rioting, which claimed 34 lives, was sparked off by student unrest at the Befalatanana medical school. The students demanded *équivalence* with French medical degrees and when this was not granted they went on strike. Tsiranana closed the school, and his officials later banned the medical students' union, while on 12 May the FRS arrested more than 400 students of the University of Madagascar who demonstrated in sympathy and imprisoned them on the island of Nosy Lava, off the north-west coast. An order by the Interior Ministry to return to their classes brought 50 000 demonstrators into Antananarivo's streets, where they were fired upon by the FRS. The demonstrators promptly went on strike on 15 May, forced the release of the 400 students, and demanded Tsiranana's resignation, a revision of the *Accords* with France and the removal of French troops. Tsiranana resigned on 18 May and the apolitical General Gabriel Ramanatsoa, a Merina, set up a military government. The students formed themselves into a 'committee of struggle' (KIM), while the teachers, trade unionists and *zoam* met separately. Both groups claimed to be determining the island's future, but Ramanatsoa drove a wedge between the KIM and the others by granting the teachers and trade unionists pay rises, whereupon most of them lost interest in politics. The KIM continued to press changes upon Ramanatsoa, such as a rupture of relations with France, and he gradually saw the need to create his own power base. He authorised the establishment of relations with Communist and Arab countries, began the 'Malagasisation' of education, re-negotiated the *Accords* with France and secured the withdrawal of French forces.

These moves won Ramanatsoa a short-lived popularity with the KIM and with Manandofy Rakatonorina's new 'Power to the People' (MFM), a seemingly Maoist group. The introduction of a reformed Supreme Court and a new national development council and government were accepted, but by early 1974 his popularity with the left had begun to wane, while his ability to deal with Merina–*côtier* friction was failing. The suppression of

[1] Under French rule it was known as Tananarive.

anti-Merina riots on the coast weakened his position in these areas, and he was forced to step down in February 1975, when he proved unable to put down a revolt by the *côtier*-dominated Groupe Mobile Policier (GMP). Composed of many former members of the FRS, as well as dissatisfied soldiers and police, the rebels were demanding a voice in national politics. Ramanatsoa could not meet their demands, and handed power over to the Interior Minister and head of the Gendarmerie, Colonel Richard Ratsimindrava, who formed a new government. But after a few days in office, Ratsimindrava was assassinated by unknown parties, and the suppression of the GMP revolt had to be carried out by the conservative General Gilles Andriamahazo, one of Ramanatsoa's former ministers.

A military directorate became the new form of government and when the internal bargaining was completed Ramanatsoa's former Foreign Minister, Captain Didier Ratsirika (Betsimisaraka), emerged as president of the Conseil Suprême Révolutionaire (CSR). To balance Ratsirika and the CSR there was a 'Military Development Committee' headed by Andriamahazo and dominated by Merina. The choice of a non-Merina appeared to be an effort once again to achieve a measure of national unity in the island; educated as Ratsirika was in France at the École Navale, and having spent considerable time at the Malagasy embassy in that country, he was acceptable to many intellectuals as well as *côtiers*. However, he seemed to have little understanding of rural life. In terms of political ideology he imitated a number of more radical African leaders. As Foreign Minister he had carried out measures which temporarily placated the KIM and MFM, and then later lobbied successfully for the abolition of the head tax, the nationalisation of banks, shipping lines and power companies, and the adoption of the *fokonolona* as the main instrument of national development. He nationalised cinemas, the Tamatave oil refinery and all mineral resources, closed down the American satellite-tracking station, and took over the holdings of the Compagnie Marseillaise de Madagascar (CMM). His policies were revealed to the public by radio and published as 'The Charter', or *The little red book of the Malagasy Socialist revolution*. In it he explained that he would use the *fokonolona* as the basis of agricultural and administrative reform. However, the armed forces and the youth movement were also to be employed to these ends. A referendum held in December 1975 approved the teachings of 'The Charter' and gave Ratsirika a seven-year term in office, though it remained to be seen whether he could retain the support of the armed forces and, at the same time, relieve regional disparity and improve the island's gloomy economic situation.

SOCIAL AND CULTURAL CHANGE

Society in Madagascar in 1940 was a rigid pyramid with the governor-general at the top and beneath him a hierarchy of civil and military authorities who together ruled the Malagasy. Most of the French in the island were transients serving with the military, civil service, or commercial concerns and had little interest in the local peoples. The Malagasy existed apart, with only a few of the educated élite being able to establish regular contact with the foreigners through professional organisations for writers and journalists, or through personal friendships. The mass of the Malagasy people lived simply on small farms or in villages, or engaged in cattle-herding in the southern part of the island. Contact with the French was not frequent, and the most visible person at the local level was the *chef de canton* or his French-speaking Malagasy interpreter. At the village level, the *fokonolona* took care of purely local matters. Composed of the elders of a village, it maintained local order and from time to time assisted the European administrator in his police duties. A conservative body, it did not act as an instrument of change, though indeed change was about to come as a result of wartime demands for men and raw materials. It was during the war that respect for traditional authority, particularly amongst the Merina, the Betsileo and people in urban centres, began to break down. A new force, nationalism, was on the rise. Historically, the Merina had been the first to experience change, and although they shared linguistic and traditional religious bonds with the other ethnic groups, their way of life was more exposed and receptive to French rule and culture.

In the years following the 1896 conquest, the Merina bourgeoisie (*Hova*) had continued to consolidate their position as businessmen and civil servants and to form an alliance with the aristocracy (*Andriana*) against the French. After independence, the *côtiers* replaced the French and the struggle continued. Official policy after 1945 aimed at rapidly educating and training numbers of *côtiers* in order to provide an alternative to continued dependence on Merina technicians, civil servants and teachers. But the Merina hold on the life of the island was too tight to be broken in only a few decades. They had traditionally been more receptive to education and change than the other ethnic groups and, because of their large numbers and central geographic location, they were able to exercise dominance in national life until 1960. The Merina adapted with relative ease to the evolution of modern civil law, which replaced many old traditions and customs, and it was in their society that the importance of the clan, the extended family and a large number of offspring had tended to decline most rapidly. Long-standing contact with Europeans produced in the Merina few feelings of cultural inferiority or racial antagonism, and many of the positive traditional values of the society were preserved. After independence other ethnic groups attempted to emulate and overtake the Merina, so that one began to see, for example, a change in attitude towards women in Betsimisaraka society similar to that found on the high plateaux. Among the Merina, women had undergone considerable intellectual development through education, and their evolution, as well as the evolution of other Malagasy women, was being accelerated by a rise in their standard of living. As education transformed the social structures of the *côtiers*, the various groups produced their own skilled and professional people, and the Merina grip on national life began to loosen. Another force at work in the island was inter-ethnic marriage. It was most frequent among the Merina and Antandroy, but spread among the *côtiers* because government officials from the high plateaux were increasingly being posted for long periods of time to centres away from their home areas. It was hoped by many of the younger generation that this practice would help to ease ethnic tensions.

A government estimate in 1975 placed the population of Madagascar at about eight million persons. Between 1950 and 1960 the population rose from 4 207 000 to 5 298 000 persons, while an estimate made in 1962 gave a total of 5 536 243 Malagasy and 121 358 aliens in the island. Of the foreign residents, Indians and Chinese had become more numerous since 1945, though the number of Europeans had declined, especially after the events of May 1972. There were 18 ethnic groups in the island, the largest of which was the Merina with over two million people, followed by the Betsimisaraka, Betsileo, Tsimihety and Antandroy. The population was not spread evenly throughout the island and its rapid growth both in cities and rural areas was due more to a decline in the death-rate than a rise in the birth-rate, though this, too, had occurred. The island's two main centres, Antananarivo (500000) and Majunga (76500) had more than doubled in population since 1945, though elsewhere there was little urbanisation. Antananarivo offered the rural resident opportunities for excitement, wage-earning, education and perhaps even a government job. But there was another side to the capital: the problem of the *zoam*, shortages in housing, water and sewage facilities, and a spiralling cost of living.

The position of the labour force in Madagascar differed little from that encountered in other Third World countries. In 1971 it was estimated that out of a working population of about 3 300000, there were some 300000 persons drawing regular salaries or wages. In that same year, however, an estimated 100 000 young people were about to come onto the job market. By the end of 1973 there were 40 000 unemployed young Malagasy, some with diplomas and degrees, others with only primary school education. In 1975 their impact was felt most acutely in the capital and Majunga, as well as the smaller urban centres of Tamatave (59 600) and Fianarantsoa (58 900), where they fed the extremist movements. These *zoam* were easily influenced by the indigenous press, which was very large for a nation where only about half of the population was literate. At independence there were about 200 titles in circulation in Madagascar. Most of these newspapers and periodicals had a small circulation, were limited to Antananarivo, and were politically oriented. Professionalism in the Malagasy press had always been lacking, with the exception of the Catholic weekly *Lumière*, and the news reporting was often slanted, inaccurate and frequently shot through with libellous statements. All newspapers had a faithful if small following and in the capital even the unemployed found money to support their favourite. Between May 1972 and the coup of February 1975, a truly free press was in existence for the first time in Madagascar's history. After that coup, however, rigid censorship was established, and papers were suppressed until there were only about 60 in circulation. *Lumière* had to cease production because of its objective reporting, and the Ratsirika regime carried censorship to the point that overseas mail was opened and incoming air passengers at Ivato were thoroughly searched for foreign papers. But other barriers were lifted, and it was perhaps indicative of Ratsirika's politics that the works of Plato, Rousseau, Marx and Mao, banned during Tsiranana's time, were introduced in 1973 into philosophy classes of the University of Madagascar.

Christianity, introduced initially to Madagascar in 1818, established roots among most Malagasy ethnic groups and by 1971 it was estimated that there were about 3 700 000 indigenous Christians in the island, representing 38 per cent of the population.[1] Protestant sects tended to predominate in Imerina, the Catholics in Betsileo and along the east coast, while the Lutherans had a monopoly in the south. However, much of the island was still untouched by Christianity, but it played a dominant role, as the majority of the élite were Christian and the churches provided an ancillary education system to that of the government.

During the colonial perod the Merina Protestant churches, because of their pre-1896 ties with the monarchy, were viewed with suspicion by the administration, a suspicion heightened by the Protestant colour of the emerging nationalist movement. White Protestant missionaries often attempted to ensure the neutrality of their Malagasy colleagues but their efforts were largely in vain. The Catholic Church, rightly or wrongly, had often been seen by the Malagasy as an appendage of the French colonial power, yet by 1953 even it had officially recognised the legitimacy of seeking independence. In 1956 there was a change from the earlier mission status to 'The Malagasy Catholic Church'. From that date onwards bishops and later archbishops were drawn from the indigenous clergy; and recruitment of missionary priests increasingly concentrated on countries other than France.

As control of the Protestant and Catholic Churches passed into Malagasy hands, many of the old sectarian animosities began to fade and in their place a new feeling of ecumenism began to appear. After 1960 the PSD demonstrated its impartiality towards the various Christian denominations and Islam, and by 1975 all religious bodies were largely ignored by the state and found it necessary to fall back on their own human and financial resources.

[1] 38 per cent Christian (20 per cent Catholic, 18 per cent Protestant); 5 per cent Muslim; 57 per cent traditional religions.

EDUCATIONAL DEVELOPMENT

The system of local, regional and national schools created by Governor-General Joseph Gallieni (1896–1905) existed virtually untouched until the end of the Second World War. The conflict put many French and Malagasy teachers into uniform, produced a scarcity of supplies and equipment, and brought about the physical deterioration of both state and mission schools. Access to the best schools, those reserved for French children, continued to be limited to the offspring of those few Malagasy with French citizenship. Both settlers and administrators ensured that few Malagasy ever went beyond the primary level to attend the *lycées* or French universities. The middle-grade Malagasy civil servants were trained at *écoles régionales*, of which the most important was the École Myre de Vilers in the capital. This institution produced many talented Malagasy, but most could never hope to advance to senior government posts. This restrictive system of education was broadened by the Brazzaville reforms, as a result of which the Befalatanana school of medicine, and then later a school of law and one of agriculture, were opened. Most of the secondary schools continued to be located in or around Antananarivo, and by 1951 two-thirds of all Malagasy were still without schooling. The highest proportion of these illiterates were *côtiers*. This dismal picture existed because the colonial administration was devoting a mere 8 per cent of the local budget to education in 1951.

The missions had established the first school system of education in the island during the early nineteenth century and their presence continued to be felt into the mid-1970s. The state schools continued to enrol most of the better students during the period under discussion. With the exception of two preparatory institutions, the École Paul Minault (Protestant) and the Collège St Michael (Catholic), the church schools usually had inferior facilities and charged higher fees. In spite of this some parents still sent their children to church schools. There were definite advantages: these schools, apart from offering a religious education, stressed Malagasy language and literature, and frequently offered French taught by French nationals. In some areas they absorbed the surplus students unable to gain entry to state schools. From 1960 onwards relations between the government and the churches remained good and there were no state take-overs, as was the case in many other African nations.

A five-year plan in education, launched in 1958, was under way when the *Accords* were signed, and one of its goals was a literacy rate of 70 per cent by 1972. In an attempt to alter the colonial pattern of educational opportunities, the PSD opened schools in *côtier* areas, a move which helped raise the overall number of children of school-age attending an educational institution to 53 per cent by 1967. On a geographical basis, however, only 10 per cent of the children in the extreme south were in school, as opposed to 35–50 per cent of all children in the highlands. The reduction of this disparity continued to be one of the Ministry of Education's key goals. The gradual rise in the national literacy rate, and the expansion of the school population in the 1960s was made possible in part by the increase in numbers and quality of local teachers. For many years Malagasy teachers had been poorly paid and trained, overworked, and relegated to a position of low social standing. Tsiranana, himself a former teacher, expanded the number of teachers very rapidly in the 1960s, and improved their lot by granting paid vacations and free housing or a housing allowance, by giving rises in pay, and by reducing the number of students per class. More teacher-training colleges were built, though in a number of cases the graduates went into professions other than teaching. The demand for schooling outstripped the number of Malagasy teachers, however, and French nationals still had to be employed. In the early 1960s more than 800 French teachers, financed by French aid, were giving instruction in 416 primary, 248 secondary, and 131 technical schools, as well as assisting youth and sports movements.

Technical education was neglected during the colonial era and continued to experience difficulties after 1960. Technical trades had low prestige and the education given in technical colleges did not always match governmental and industrial demands; while the stagnating economy found it difficult to absorb graduates after 1970. Higher education in Madagascar after independence was centred on the Befalatanana school of medicine and the University of Madagascar. At the close of the Second World War, Paris had begun to provide state scholarships for study in France in a wide range of disciplines, while educational reforms enacted in 1955 created an institute of law and natural sciences in the capital to

which a *faculté des lettres* was added four years later. As 'independence' drew nearer, Tsiranana began to plan a national university.
His motives were three-fold. The first was to keep Malagasy
isolated from what he considered the unsavoury political climate
of France, while the second was to foster the educational cause
of the *côtiers* within the island. Finally, Tsiranana wanted to reduce
the cost of overseas training, and during the 1960s and early 1970s
those Malagasy who went abroad were mainly educated in
disciplines connected with development plans. The University of
Madagascar began to hold classes in the 1960–1 academic year,
and the *Accords* provided for sending French professors and
administrators to Madagascar as part of the aid programme. It also
made provision for France to pay its operating costs. Until about
1966 a full one-quarter of the students were non-Malagasy, mainly
French nationals, who could obtain a degree equivalent to those
conferred in most French universities. The old educational/ethnic
divisions were, however, perpetuated at the university because the
bulk of the students were Merina or Betsileo. Most of the
undergraduates were in medicine (30 per cent), law and economics
(29 per cent), and science (28 per cent), with only 6 per cent in
agriculture. The number of students attending the university rose
from 3271 in 1968, of whom 2610 were Malagasy, 593 French and
148 of other nationalities, to 4000 in 1972, 7000 in 1973, and a
peak of 11000 in 1975. The demand for higher education had
become so great that two new university centres were opened in
Tuléar and Diego-Suarez, and some 200 Malagasy were sent to
study in the USSR.

Education changed the face of Madagascar, because the Malagasy, particularly the Merina, seized upon it as a tool for
modernisation and personal advancement. Students played a
significant part in the process of decolonisation, from the formation of the MDRM to the rise of Ratsirika and the breaking of
the French hold on the life of the island. It was the left-wing
students, many of whom were unemployed or faced bleak
employment prospects upon graduation, who were Ratsirika's
strongest supporters. If their career prospects in Madagascar
before 1972 had been bleak, they were now almost non-existent.
Uncertainty surrounded the new education programme in 1972,
as the government debated which aspects of the French system
should be retained or discarded. France refused to recognise the

Table 13.1. *School populations, 1972–4.*

	Population	Teachers
Primary schools		
1972	985 236	n.a.
1973	n.a.	9 927
1974	1 100 000	11 766
Secondary schools		
1972	35 000	1 165
1973	n.a.	n.a.
1974	57 000	1 478

equivalence of any new Malagasy system, whereupon the Malagasy retaliated by creating an indigenous as well as a French educational framework. The Malagasy system was orientated towards new curricula and new books, while the French system, restricted to 6000 pupils, remained as before and was supervised by 200 teachers from France. Many Chinese and Indian residents, as well as the French and some wealthy Malagasy, sent their children to the French schools. By 1973 the student body at the university was almost all Malagasy, the French students having departed. Increasingly, however, the relevance of the university was being questioned because it was graduating students for whom there were no jobs, and the standards had clearly dropped. Similarly, substantial numbers of secondary and primary students were ready to graduate and go out in search of employment.

The school system continued to expand after Tsiranana's downfall, as table 13.1 shows; but opportunities for these graduates were also few, and all but a handful eventually joined the growing and dissatisfied body of *zoam*.

ECONOMIC DEVELOPMENT

Madagascar's economy was based almost entirely on agriculture and 80 per cent of the island's population was on the land. In 1940 this economy was monopolised by four French trading and navigation companies, the Compagnie Marseillaise, the Compagnie Lyonnaise, the Compagnie Rochefortaise, and the Compagnie Générale. Their Chinese and Indian agents bought up agricultural products and had a virtual monopoly over the importation of and the wholesale trade in consumer goods and industrial equipment.

The island's economy received a significant boost during the Second World War and from 1942 exports rose rapidly. The mainstays of the agricultural exports were coffee, vanilla, sugar, tobacco, meat, rice, cloves, sisal, raffia and lima beans, and most were produced in the highlands, the homeland of the Merina and Betsileo. Attempts to integrate the peasant farmers' crops into an island-wide system of production and marketing failed. Little real planning took place until after 1945 when France introduced and financed an extensive series of projects designed in theory to benefit the farmers, but in fact merely tying the Malagasy economy closer to that of France. Few peasants gained any benefits. The schemes, known variously as Secteurs Expérimen-taux de Modernisation Rurale (SEMR), Zones de Développement (ZD), and from 1960 as Collectives Rurales Autonomes Modern-isées (CRAM), devoted 44 million francs to the improvement and modernisation of agriculture between 1947 and 1958, but their success was limited and only the seven most productive zones received adequate funding. When the *Accords* were signed, Madagascar was already part-way through the third (1958–62) colonial five-year plan, a development programme meant to improve the transportation and communication facilities in the island. 'Independence' brought with it no changes in this basic dependency of Madagascar on France; French firms failed to indigenise their senior staff positions and retained their head-quarters and boards of governors in France. Prior to Tsiranana's overthrow, these firms were not required to leave a share of the profits in the island. Thus, raw materials purchased in Madagascar could be sold in France and the profit used to buy goods for sale in the island. It is small wonder, therefore, that Tsiranana's successors were quick to abolish this classic colonial situation.

The first independent Malagasy five-year plan (1964–8) at-tempted to raise the standard of living, and money was set aside for transportation, agriculture, social affairs and industry. Some increases occurred in agricultural production, but few people experienced increased incomes. Industry, such as it was, did not fare much better. There was no complex of secondary industries in Madagascar and, apart from mining, industrial activity centred on the rather limited processing of agricultural products such as coffee, vanilla, cloves and perfume. The two most important mineral exports, graphite and mica, were also processed only at a basic level. From 1960 Tsiranana assisted firms which supplied local needs such as textiles, soaps, cigarettes, and shoe factories, breweries, plastics companies, and auto assembly plants, but all were dependent on foreign raw materials and were able to meet only half of the needs of local consumers. The development board which funded these ventures, the Société National d'Investissement (SNI), attempted to assist other schemes such as tourism, but none was very successful.

The very slow progress of these development ventures may be accounted for in part by the incompetence and corruption of Malagasy officials and managerial personnel, and in part by the lack of good roads, the high cost of energy, and the reluctance of the Malagasy to invest in anything other than land. In addition, the French trading companies that had been so important during the colonial period maintained their hold on the Malagasy economy until 1972; they failed to indigenise their senior staff positions or to localise their boards of directors. Since there were few restrictions on the transfer of currencies, company profits were routinely repatriated to France rather than invested in the Malagasy economy. The AKFM demands for nationalisation were countered by the PSD leaders, who argued that it would produce a break with France and that this would retard the island's economic evolution. The PSD's official policy was that, until such time as indigenous managers, capital and expertise developed, the expatriate firms had to be tolerated.

As a result of Ratsirika's post-1972 economic measures, the economic future of the country looked gloomy. Although it had the diversified base necessary to achieve self-sustained growth, and agriculture had the potential for making the island self-sufficient in food, the problems of economic potential were bound up with foreign investment, marketing, energy costs and managerial problems. At least two-thirds of French aid had gone into long-term projects, such as transport infrastructure, in the hopes that the discovery of a new resource would tempt foreign investors. But no new resource materialised. Neither the mining ventures produced much profit, nor were the high costs of oil exploration justified, for either the Malagasy or the expatriate firms. A sizeable budget and balance-of-payments problem emerged in 1969 but was alleviated somewhat in 1972 when prices for agricultural produce began to rise.[1] However, the demand for rice outstripped local production and from 1973 expensive imports had to be purchased. The revolution of 1972, the renegotiation of the *Accords*, new and very strict currency controls imposed on French firms, and a decree of November 1973 stipulating that all French companies had to establish their head offices in the island, shocked the French-dominated expatriate business community. New investment in the island became almost non-existent, and by 1974 the French population had sunk to 16 000. A few local industries operated behind high tariff walls and only the Japanese were now willing to invest in the country. With Malagasy participation, they established two plants for meat-extract production and fish processing.

In 1972 the state began reserving for itself, either on a full-ownership or a partnership basis, banking, insurance, transportation, external trade, power, mines, pharmaceutical products and the film industry. The agricultural Syndicats des Communes continued to prove unable to compete with the French export–import companies, while the Malagasy managers were often appointed without sufficient training or experience. In the months following the 1972 revolution it had become clear that the state import and export bodies (SINPA and SONACO) had not gained control over the island's economy. They used the CMM and Compagnie Lyonnaise as their main export and import branches, but the French firms continued to monopolise the key sources of credit, relations with shipping and insurance companies and links with foreign buyers. These two state bodies, like the many development boards inherited from the French or developed after 1960, were ineffective, top-heavy and costly. Lacking in administrative flexibility and financial autonomy, the various boards increased in number after 1972, and moved into all facets of internal and external trade, including mining, in 1975. Ratsirika nationalised the Compagnie Marseillaise in August 1975, took over its assets, and replaced the French board of directors by three Malagasy. By late 1975 investment in mining and industry had become stagnant and, with the exception of foreign-aid projects, foreign investment had all but ceased. Unfortunately Madagascar

[1] Agricultural prices began to fall again in 1974.

lacked persons trained in mining techniques and the ultimate success of this venture was open to question.

In the opinion of Ratsirika, however, the development boards were of secondary importance; it was the *fokonolona* which would bring about real economic growth and reform in the nation. Ratsirika believed that the local initiative of the *fokonolonas* would boost economic production, and from 1973 they were empowered to take over many of the duties of the district administration. Their functions were later expanded to include the expropriation and distribution of underdeveloped land to peasants organised into cooperatives. Other responsibilities involved the supervision of irrigation and road-building programmes, as well as the marketing and processing of agricultural products. For this last task the *fokonolona* organised *vatoeka* (technical committees) to which they delegated authority in economic matters. These committees were to have replaced the traditional Indian and Chinese produce buyers, but they were unable to buy and distribute sufficient goods for sale, and by the end of 1974 the local papers were filled with complaints concerning their inefficiency. Another of Ratsirika's reforms made the *fokonolona* independent of the local authorities – the *chef de cercle*, the *chef de canton* and the *chef de province* – and restricted local technicians to an administrative role. Squabbles between them and the civil servants became common. Further problems arose from the fact that the *fokonolona* were not universal in the island; they were found mainly in the highlands and not on the coast or in the south. The conservatism of the *fokonolonas'* members was another drawback to using them as the basic development cells, and in spite of government pronouncements the councils were not revolutionary bodies nor did they favour any particular ideology. Groups of revolutionary youth, sent out to work under the elders, left in disgust and returned to the urban centres. Thus, the island swung from French over-centralisation to Malagasy decentralisation, in which petty squabbling, a lack of organisation and incompetent management predominated. The only real changes the *fokonolonas* produced were negative ones: the disintegration and demoralisation of local agencies and authorities; an unsatisfactory network of food supply and distribution; roads which were allowed to deteriorate; and the slow demise of economic structures without any viable replacements. This string of failures was not an auspicious beginning for a body which was supposed to produce real economic growth and social reform in Madagascar.

The future of Madagascar was both bleak and uncertain. The economy was beginning to slow down and all indications were that it would soon grind to a halt. The general population was unhappy over the acute shortage of the staple food (rice) and consumer goods. Rural banditry was on the increase and the transportation system was beginning to break down. Foreigners whose presence was crucial to the effective functioning of the economy, the government and the educational system were leaving in ever-increasing numbers. Internal politics were in a state of turmoil with talk of plot and counter-plot, 'capitalists-imperialists', and other alleged 'subversive elements'. Ratsirika felt compelled to shift ministers to cope with what he considered to be the political realities of the situation. Ethnic rivalry was still very much alive, and though Ratsirika was attempting by various means to foster a stronger sense of Malagasy nationhood the old antagonisms were working against him. The future of the island seemed destined to be one of social, economic and political distress.

CHAPTER 14

ZAIRE, RWANDA AND BURUNDI

The apocalypse, an influential Belgian magistrate wrote at the end of his colonial career, was due in 2026. University graduates, mutinous soldiers, and messianic religious figures would sweep away the massive colonial edifice constructed by Belgium in Central Africa. Nationalism and Pan-Africanism were the ineluctable consequence of education and modernisation; the achievements of the colonial system, to our satirical jurist, contained 'the germ of their own destruction'.[1] Elements of this prophecy were to find their echo in the momentous transformations compressed into the third of a century from 1940 to 1975. A series of shock waves totally altered the political landscape: a nationalist explosion in Zaire[2] that engulfed the prudent calendars and Eurafrican visions of the coloniser, the turbulent eddies of which finally gave way to the would-be leviathan state of Mobutu Sese Seko (Joseph-Désiré);[3] an ethnic revolution in Rwanda, and a precarious ethnocracy in Burundi, with the liquidation of the historical monarchies in both. As the Second World War began, however, virtually no one had any premonition of the sea changes in store.

The formal structure of the colonial state was in many respects the logical prolongation of the absolutist Léopoldian state. The centralised personal control the monarch aspired to achieve had as its counterpart the pronounced concentration of powers in the

[1] Paul Salkin, *L'Afrique Centrale dans cent ans* (Paris, 1926).
[2] The Belgian Congo became known officially as the Republic of the Congo upon independence in 1960, then the Democratic Republic of the Congo under the 1964 constitution. To distinguish it from its northern neighbour bearing the same name, it was commonly referred to as 'Congo-Léopoldville', then 'Congo-Kinshasa' when the place-name of the capital city was altered in 1966. In 1971, the designation 'Zaire' was adopted for both the country and its principal waterway. To reduce confusion, 'Zaire' is used throughout here as the term for the independent state.
[3] In 1971, all Zairean citizens were required to drop forenames of European provenance in favour of names of African origin. For persons whose role extends beyond the name-change date, the former Christian name is indicated in parentheses.

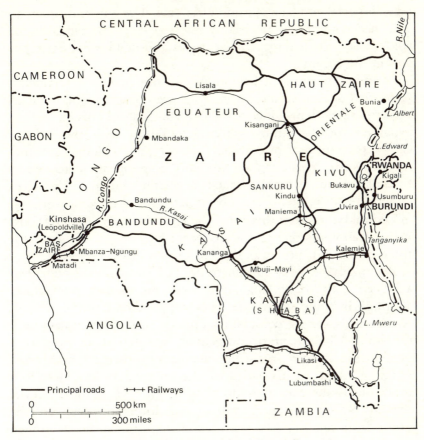

32   Zaire, Rwanda and Burundi.

metropolitan colonial organs in Brussels. Executive authority was
vested in the Ministry of Colonies, whose staff – and usually
minister – tended to be recruited from Catholic and conservative
milieux. The royal family also maintained an active interest,
political and economic, in colonial affairs. The king was on a
number of occasions the source of significant political initiatives.
The Chamber of Deputies received an annual report on the
administration of the colonies, and had to approve the colonial
budget, but its role as overseer was often purely nominal. Within
the colony, improving communications were making the concentration of power in the government-general in Léopoldville
(Kinshasa) more effective. The Tilkens reforms in 1933 had
sharply circumscribed the autonomy once enjoyed at the provincial

level, especially in Katanga and Orientale. The governor-general, who had come to be invariably selected from the ranks of the colonial service, had by 1940 clearly established his pre-eminence within the colony.

Ruanda-Urundi, as a League of Nations mandate, retained a somewhat special status, although it was roughly analogous in 1940 to a seventh province of the Belgian Congo. A decree of 1925 provided for its administrative integration with the Belgian Congo for purposes of currency, security, and colonial bureaucracy. Colonial legislation applied only if specifically extended to Ruanda-Urundi, which retained a separate budget. The vice-governors were, however, subordinate to the governor-general in Léopoldville. Parenthetically, the Usumbura (Bujumbura) post was a stepping-stone to the governor's palace in Kinshasa for three of the four post-war Belgian Congo governors-general.

By 1940, the field administration of the colonial state had achieved a thorough hegemony over the subject population, although in some areas, such as Kivu, Ruanda-Urundi, parts of Kasai and Kwango, colonial occupation was not complete until the 1920s. The reform of indigenous jurisdictions in 1933 completed the task of reorganising customary structures, and incorporating them as auxiliaries of the colonial order. Despite a proclaimed adherence to the doctrine of indirect rule, the territorial administration was peremptory and interventionist on the ground. Its capacity to sustain complete dominance was limited at some times by shortages of personnel and resources, especially during the peak Depression years and the Second World War, and at some places by the vitality and skill of some important chiefs, such as the *nyimi* of the Kuba or the *bami* of the Shi. The priority accorded to obligatory cultivation, begun in 1917 and generalised in the 1930s, and to public works, taxation, and labour supply for mine and plantation, was incompatible with real autonomy for customary leadership.

The infrastructure of colonial power was by no means limited to the administration; the missions and corporations were crucial elements in the imperial order. By 1930 there were as many Catholic missionaries as colonial functionaries. The impact of the church came through its control of the educational system; its critical though indefinable role as an agency for the transmission of an alternative value system; its related gate-keeping function in the allocation of opportunities for social mobility for the young, and the political weight of the more articulate and aggressive spokesmen in the senior hierarchy.

The basic framework of the capitalist sector was solidly implanted by 1940. Union Minière du Haut Katanga (UMHK) had achieved its pre-eminent role in the national economy. Although the heavy paternalism of the mining companies was most pronounced in Katanga, labour-intensive exploitation of diamonds in Kasai, tin in Kivu, and gold in the north-east cast a long shadow over the surrounding countryside. Agricultural capitalism was also powerful in its impact, whether organised primarily in plantation form with large labour demands in the case of palm-oil, or with the corporate power exercised through processing and marketing monopolies, whose supplies were assured through forced peasant cultivation, as in the case of cotton. A wage-labour force, exceptionally large in comparison with those of other African colonies at the time, had been generated by these developments; and the number of wage-earners had increased from 125 120 in 1920 to 536 055 in 1940.

The commanding heights of the evangelistic and capitalist sectors were resolutely Belgian. Although, in the religious sphere, Protestant missionary activity was tolerated, its non-Belgian character denied it access to subsidy (until 1946), state support, and political influence. The capitalist sector included Unilever, active in palm-oil, and Tanganyika Concessions which was the largest single share-holder in UMHK; basic control of the latter, however, remained in Belgian hands, and the economy was, fundamentally, a national enterprise. In Ruanda-Urundi, the relative weakness of the administrative sector was matched by the virtual absence of a corporate domain. A few small mines existed, tin ore being the most important, but their importance was minuscule. The population was far too great to permit a plantation economy to emerge. Only the mission infrastructure was comparable; the White Fathers, in particular, had by 1940 already created a remarkably thorough evangelistic structure with far-reaching social influence.

The scope for African initiative or mobility within the congealing structures of the colonial system was very limited. The adult African was a functional unit, as suggested by the customary census designation 'HAV' – *homme adulte valide* – to be harnessed to export-crop cultivation, or conscripted for mine or plantation service. Internal movement required administrative authorisation. Except for Catholic seminaries, full secondary education was non-existent, though some post-primary vocational institutes had appeared. Despite these handicaps, however, a new élite was just beginning to be visible, especially in the clerical ranks of the public and private bureaucracies.

Each element of the colonial power structure was confident of its capacity to direct the creation of a new society: Christian in its values, industrial in its rhythms and disciplines, Belgian in its orientation and loyalty. Achievement of these goals was very far in the future, and no one doubted the immensity of the task. At the same time, it served as full justification for the coercive weight of the colonial system. The presumed paternal benevolence of these ultimate ends was doubted by few of those who manned the hierarchies of state, church, or corporation, however heated might be the debate over particular pathways. To ruler and subject, the colonial apparatus was too powerful to imagine that it could be dismantled.

The German *Blitzkrieg* swept over Belgium in two weeks in May 1940, creating a moment of disarray in the colony. The government of Belgium fled to exile in Britain, and by autumn 1940 was operating from London. However, King Léopold III remained behind, and the civil service department heads continued to operate their ministries in Brussels. Confusion persisted for several months as to the status of the colony: residual focus of Belgian sovereignty; dependency of the exile government in London tied to a British alliance; or autonomous and neutral? By late 1940, the partisans of the London exile government had emerged victorious. Leadership in the colony was assured by the most vigorous and brilliant of Belgium's proconsuls, Pierre Ryckmans, a liberal Catholic. The London government, however, was in no position to assert strong authority over Kinshasa; the colonial administration became, for the first time, largely autonomous. The *effort de guerre* imposed severe sacrifices, which bore most heavily upon the African population. The Allies at first asked for increased production of tin and gold, with cobalt, tungsten, uranium and rubber subsequently added to the list. The number of required days of *corvée* labour on roads, public works, and forced cultivation was raised from 60 to 120, a figure in reality often exceeded. Coerced collection of wild rubber, abandoned since the 'red rubber' scandals of the Congo Free State, was resumed, raising rubber exports from 1142 tons in 1939 to 11 337 in 1944. Units of the Force Publique, funded by the colonial budget, were made available to Allied forces in the Abyssinian campaign, in West Africa, the Middle East, and even Burma. While the territorial service redoubled its pressure on the subject population, it was stripped of its cadres. In the words of a liberal jurist, the field administration 'was the great sacrifice of the war: decimated in its cadres, prostituted in its mission'.[1]

The war effort had serious consequences for the security of the colonial order, and engendered the most far-reaching disturbances since the early days of Léopoldian rule. Ironically, the first symptom appeared in the form of a revolutionary but racist white syndicalism on the Copperbelt as European employees revolted against the iron discipline of UMHK. In December 1941 a strike broke out among African UMHK workers at Lubumbashi, the first overt urban social protest movement. The immediate grievance was the blockage of wages in the face of a sharp increase in living costs resulting from war shortages. More general discontents had begun to be articulated in small discussion groups of African élites; these ideas formed a diffuse backdrop to this watershed event. Troops opened fire on demonstrators. The official death toll was 60, with most popular versions reporting a vastly greater number. Nor were ominous symptoms of a growing threat to colonial security limited to the Copperbelt. The Kananga (Luluabourg) garrison mutinied in February 1944, and several months were required before the last mutineers were rounded up. A major rural uprising occurred in the Masisi region of Kivu in 1944, expressed through the metaphor of religious protest. In November 1945, demonstrations by dock workers in the port city of Matadi produced an official toll of seven dead and 19 wounded when troops again fired on protestors. In its organisation and participation, the Matadi protest appeared to show signs of nascent working-class consciousness. A more generalised indicator of the social costs of the war effort lay in

[1] Antoine Rubbens, in *Dettes de guerre* (Elisabethville, 1945), 191.

the first appearance of rural exodus. By the end of the war, Belgian officials and missionaries began to note a marked reduction in the numbers of adult male cultivators in many areas.

Ruanda-Urundi lay on the margins of the war effort, and escaped most of its rigours. There was no wild rubber, nor large mines, to devour its manpower. The major preoccupation was the precarious balance between land and population. Mandate authorities were first sensitised to the dangers when a famine in 1928–9 claimed an estimated 300000 lives, or 10 per cent of the population. Poor rains in a number of areas brought renewed disaster in 1943–4, with again an estimated 300000 dead or uprooted.

In his last annual address as governor-general, Ryckmans declared firmly that 'the days of colonialism are over'. The future he foresaw had little in common with that which nationalist voices were coming to demand, but it was not a simple restoration of the pre-war system either. The time was at hand to engineer the first controlled participation of the African populace in local political organs. The awakening aspirations of the mass for a more satisfying existence were to find their fulfilment in a redoubled programme of economic development, joined to a panoply of social welfare measures. For the élite, a satisfying status within the colonial hierarchy was to be defined. In the post-war era, a delicate balance had to be maintained between the devolution of political responsibilities and the spread of mass education. A fundamental premise was that, in some way which only the unfolding future would define, a Belgian framework would remain.

When Ryckmans delivered his *Vers l'avenir* valedictory speech, most regarded it as a progressive statement. In Belgian circles, nearly all could agree that the priority for economic and social development was appropriate. Vast energies were deployed in preparing ten-year plans for colonial development, published in 1950–1. Further, the prolonged boom in the commodity markets from 1946 till 1957 meant that the colonial budget itself was generating ample revenues to support swift expansion of the educational system, health facilities, housing, water supplies, and similar social services. The proposition that a satisfying niche in colonial society had to be made available to the growing *évolué* class also commanded fairly general assent. Racial discrimination pervaded colonial life and legislation; responsible colonial officials were persuaded that these should be removed, at least for the élite, although many in the swiftly growing European population were not prepared to eliminate racism from their daily behaviour. But fulfilment of the Belgian Eurafrican dream depended, at some distant point, on the fidelity of the colonised.

During the early post-war years, when full initiative and control remained in the hands of the coloniser, several miscalculations hampered the application of the Ryckmans vision. The policy wheels turned exceedingly slowly, and reforms spent years on the drawing board. Until the late 1950s, the final product was the result of compromises between colonial interest groups; African views played almost no part in shaping the laboriously drafted decrees, which were for the most part overtaken by events almost before they appeared. In the case of Ruanda-Urundi, the growing United Nations pressure for political reform imposed unanticipated constraints. Finally, and most important, no one anticipated the speed at which political mobilisation would occur once it gained full momentum in the Belgian Congo and Ruanda-Urundi in 1959.

The failure of post-war reform in the political sphere in the Belgian Congo is epitomised in the fate of the two most prominent measures, the 1952 immatriculation decree, and the 1957 Statut des Villes. Immatriculation was intended as a solution to the problem of the status of the élite: the central postulate was that, as a number of Congolese intellectuals argued at that time, *évolués* represented a special social class, for whom a particular legal status had to be defined.[1] A commission was established in 1948 to develop legislative proposals. In the interim, a 'Carte de Mérite Civique' was created to offer special recognition to Africans deemed meritorious. The commission's initial proposals in 1949 were relatively generous to the élite. Passionate opposition from some colonial milieux, however, was sufficient to emasculate the eventual decree which emerged in 1952, which offered a few

---

[1] See the first published élite manifesto, issued in 1944, demanding exemption from measures 'which might be appropriate for the ignorant or backward mass', reprinted in Rubbens, *Dettes de guerre*, 128–9.

Congolese 'immatriculated' status, but linked it to very few concrete advantages. In the event, only 1557 Cartes de Mérite Civique and 217 immatriculation cards were issued.

Political participation was to be prudently introduced from the ground up. Congolese would begin to share responsibility at the higher levels of government only after a careful apprenticeship at the base. In pursuance of this principle, a commission was established in 1948 with a mandate to prepare a reform of municipal institutions, providing for some form of popular involvement. This legislation took no less than nine years in preparation, again encountering long delays while colonial interest groups sought guarantees for the rights of European residents. When the law was finally adopted in March 1957 it did make provision for 'consultations' which, in effect, were based on an adult male suffrage, but assured Europeans *de facto* parity in representation and maintained firm administrative tutelage. Although elections were organised in seven of the largest cities in 1957 and 1958, they were totally overshadowed by the January 1959 Kinshasa riots, and the sudden acceleration of events that ensued.

Post-war reform in Ruanda-Urundi followed a somewhat different path, reflecting the impact of United Nations Trusteeship. Belgium had been strongly opposed to the expansion of international jurisdiction over the former mandated territories which the United Nations Charter provided, in particular the specific obligation to promote self-government. The first Visiting Mission dispatched by the Trusteeship Council in 1948, while quite laudatory on the vigour with which economic and social welfare were promoted by the administration, expressed dismay at the absence of provision for political advance. After renewed criticisms on the political front by the 1951 Visiting Mission, a decree was issued on 14 July 1952 proposing a complex hierarchy of councils providing for limited African participation. The consultations were so indirect, and so filtered through the Tutsi chiefly hierarchy, that their impact was minimal.[1]

The 1954 Visiting Mission delivered a harsh verdict on the timidity of political advance. It was suggested that 20 to 25 years

[1] Ruanda-Urundi had an ethnically stratified society, with the command positions occupied primarily by the Tutsi, pastoralists who constituted about 15 per cent of the population. Except for an inconsequential number of Twa (Pygmies), the remainder were Hutu. Tutsi hegemony had been entrenched and systematised by 'indirect rule'.

would be sufficient time to complete the Trust mission. Stung to the quick, Belgium indignantly rejected the Visiting Mission's recommendations, with Ryckmans himself now mounting the counterattack. Nonetheless, in 1956 Vice-Governor-General Jean-Paul Harroy, in a move considered audacious at the time, reinterpreted the 1952 decree to provide for universal male suffrage for the sub-chiefdom councils. This did substantially increase the fraction of Hutu representation at the lowest level. However, the indirect election mechanism for the higher-level councils, allied to the *ex officio* representation of predominantly Tutsi chiefs at each level, meant that Hutu were progressively screened out in such a way as to leave, at the kingdom level, exclusively Tutsi membership in Ruanda, and only 3 Hutu members out of 31 in Urundi.

THE RISE OF NATIONALISM

If the title of nationalist is to be given to any movement of protest against alien rule and oppression, then origins of nationalism may be traced back to the early days of colonial rule: the great mutinies of 1895 and 1897; movements of religious dissent such as the Kimbanguist church; and regional uprisings such as the Pende revolt of 1931. If, however, nationalism must be restricted to a definition based upon the explicit demand for African political rights and self-determination, then Zaire, Rwanda and Burundi stand out for the tardiness of the nationalist challenge. The first public claim for independence appeared in Zaire only in 1956; in all three countries, large-scale politicisation of the population dates from 1959. In all three instances, mass mobilisation became intertwined with the crystallisation of ethnic self-awareness, which had a pronounced impact on the definition of political party alignments. A simple but fundamental starting point for understanding the belated appearance of African political movements, in comparison with countries to the north and east, is that the coloniser was not disposed to tolerate them. It was only in 1958 that the administration began to accept the formation of African parties, and not till 1959 did politicians have full scope for legal organisation. The policy of rigorously isolating Belgian Africa from external influences was quite effective. Only a handful of Africans was able to travel abroad till the middle 1950s; in 1958 there were still fewer than one hundred university students from the Congo and Ruanda-Urundi in Belgium. Nationalist literature was not allowed to enter the Belgian colonies, and the transistor revolution had not yet made radios widely available. The only African organ of opinion, *La Voix du Congolais*, was edited under the close supervision of the colonial authorities.

There were, however, harbingers of change. The future President, Joseph Kasavubu, in 1946 had spoken of the 'right of the first-occupant', a phrase referring to land issues in his native Bas-Congo, but carrying broader implications. By the middle 1950s, the aggressive tone of some statements from the Alliance des Bakongo (ABAKO) in Léopoldville won it increasing respect, not only in Kongo milieux; Kasavubu became its president in 1954. In Elisabethville, political effervescence was growing, especially in Kasaian intellectual circles. The fateful word 'independence' was first given public African expression in 1956. The debate was launched by a young Belgian professor, of liberal Catholic connexion, A. A. J. Van Bilsen, who published a 30-year plan for the independence of Belgian Africa. While the UN Visiting Mission's proposals for decolonisation within 20-25 years did not evoke immediate response from Ruanda-Urundi Africans, the Van Bilsen plan attracted close attention among Léopoldville intellectuals. A group of young Catholics in Léopoldville, with tacit encouragement from some sympathetic mission and university circles, published in mid-1956 the Manifeste de Conscience Africaine, putting forward a programme rather similar to the Van Bilsen scheme. The Conscience Africaine group was primarily composed of persons who had arrived in Léopoldville from up-river, loosely known in the local ethnic lexicon as 'Bangala'. ABAKO leaders, social rivals, riposted a few weeks later with a far more radical document, launching the lapidary but immensely powerful slogan of 'immediate independence'.

The debate on the future was now joined. The Catholic Church took a measured step away from its traditional role of moral buttress for colonial authority by announcing its support for an ill-defined emancipation. The 1957 Visitation of Ruanda-Urundi by the Trusteeship Council sparked off two major manifestos, which began to define more clearly the contours of decolonisation politics in the Trust Territory. A group of Ruanda Hutu intellectuals, led by future President Grégoire Kayibanda, issued a 'Bahutu Manifesto'. This warned that the Hutu, whom 'the departure of the Europeans might plunge into worse slavery than before', would at least have 'the right to refuse to co-operate in the efforts to attain independence' until the mechanisms of Tutsi domination were dismantled. The exclusively Tutsi High Council of Ruanda responded indirectly with a 'statement of views', which made no mention of the Tutsi–Hutu polarity, but urged the rapid training of an élite to whom power could be swiftly devolved.[1] In contemporary social perceptions, this meant the transfer of power to the Tutsi.

The urban elections of December 1957 in Léopoldville, Elisabethville and Jadotville (Likasi) reflected the growing African politicisation. The Léopoldville results, in particular, were a psychological shock. The Belgian administration sought to organise these elections without political parties; in the capital, candidates associated with the ABAKO won 133 of 170 seats in the African communes, which appeared to be a spectacular triumph for the partisans of 'immediate independence'.

The catalytic event which totally transformed terminal colonial politics occurred in Léopoldville on 4 January 1959. The administration sought to disperse a crowd gathered for an ABAKO political meeting, a move which escalated into a vast conflagration, spontaneous in its dynamics, massive in its participation. For three tense days mobs assaulted symbolic artifacts of the colonial system: social centres, administrative buildings, Catholic missions and Portuguese stores.

Nationalism in the Congo developed as a complex dialectic between the stunned and increasingly demoralised Belgian administration, an élite which swiftly raised its demands, and a mass which now began to play a major role. By mid-1959, the administration had simply lost its grip on the critical area between Léopoldville and the sea; by the end of the year, comparable politicisation of the rural mass had occurred in Kwilu and Maniema districts, and was present in germ in many other areas. Political leaders were taken by surprise at the scope of rural radicalism; rather than instigating it, the party organisers tried desperately to restrain it, harness it to their political goals, and avoid being swept away by it.[2]

[1] These two documents are reproduced in United Nations Visiting Mission to Trust Territories in East Africa, 1957, *Report on Ruanda-Urundi*, 6 December 1957, T/1346.
[2] The 'rural radicalism' thesis is expounded in Herbert Weiss, *Political protest in the Congo* (Princeton, 1967).

In Ruanda-Urundi, the development of nationalism was profoundly affected by the ethnic stratification of the two kingdoms,
and the interaction of events in each of them, despite their separate
identities. The absence of a major capitalist sector and the
mediation of colonial policy, through the traditional structures as
adapted by their use as instruments of indirect rule, meant that
the dislocating impact of colonialism was much more diffuse.
Rural radicalism did appear in Rwanda in 1959, but was focussed
on Tutsi hegemony rather than on the colonial system. The classic
language of anti-colonial nationalism was primarily articulated by
Tutsi leaders, heavily predominant in the ranks of the educated
élite in both countries.

The spread of political consciousness was accompanied by a
parallel process of ethnic mobilisation. The cultural categories
which served as foci for this newly politicised self-awareness were
by no means simple projections of the past; in many of the most
visible cases, such as Lulua, Mongo, or Ngala in the Congo, they
were units of identity which originated in the colonial period. In
other instances, such as the Hutu category in Rwanda and
Burundi, collective solidarity extended in a quite novel way to a
culturally related but historically fragmented grouping. In the
Congo, the politicisation of ethnicity in the era of nationalist
politics was strongly marked by the particular contours of social
competition in the principal cities: Kongo versus Ngala in
Léopoldville; Mongo versus Ngombe in Coquilhatville (Mbandaka); Shi versus Kusu in Bukavu; Lulua versus Luba/Kasai
in Luluabourg (Kananga); Kasaian versus 'authentic' Katangan
in Elisabethville. Particular aspects of the strategies of decolonisation contributed their part. In the Congo ethnic associations
were tolerated, though political parties remained banned until
1959. The first competitive elections were located in the urban
cockpit of ethnic social competition.

The early post-war reforms assumed that political evolution
would be slow, that it would remain under the full control of the
Belgian administration, provide long apprenticeship at local
echelons of governance, offer full partnership and participation
to the European residents in Africa, and would lead eventually
to a permanent linkage with Belgium. It was hoped that some
form of bond would tie Ruanda-Urundi to the rest of Belgian

Africa. In the event, none of these assumptions materialised. The 1958 elections in Belgium resulted in an unusual Christian Democrat–Liberal coalition, anxious to make a new departure in colonial policy. Governor-General Pétillon was brought to Brussels as a technocrat minister of colonies. He at once named a working group broadly representative of Belgian groups, but containing no Congolese members, to prepare a blueprint for political reform.

The Working Group Report was published on 13 January 1959, nine days after it had been made quite irrelevant by the Léopold-ville riots. A ponderous and complex plan was put forward, with directly elected councils only at the local level. These would then serve as electoral colleges for higher echelons, but with a dosage of nominated members. There was, to Congolese eyes, a disconcerting vagueness as to the attributes of these councils. There was no provision for a responsible executive, nor any mention of independence. Indeed, the wind was totally removed from the sails of the Working Group Report by the surprise broadcast of the same day by King Baudouin, the contents of which were known in advance only to the prime minister and colonial minister. The broadcast contained the specific pledge to lead the Belgian Congo to independence 'without undue precipitation or interminable delay'. During the course of 1959, confronted with the tumultuous mobilisation of broad sectors of the colonial populace, Belgium became increasingly aware of the weakness of its position. The Algerian war provided a frightening illustration of the cost of prolonged colonial conflict. Belgium was too small to withstand the foreseeable international pressures that would build up if sustained violence developed. Somehow the confidence of the Congolese nationalist leadership, itself fragmented, had to be won.

By the end of 1959, Belgium had decided that immediate political independence offered the best chance of retaining some influence in the Congo. It was possible to believe that the territorial administration and the chiefs it had installed could influence the outcome of elections in enough areas to assure a solid bloc of 'moderate' deputies. Further, the European administration remained intact, and security would depend upon the European-officered Force Publique. All of this underlay what became known as *le parti congolais*: placing an improvised, flimsy superstructure of elected legislative organs and councils of ministers to rest lightly atop the bedrock of the colonial state. On 25 January 1960, agreement was reached in Belgium at a Round Table Conference on independence for 30 June 1960 with national and provincial elections scheduled for May 1960. The twin processes of rural mobilisation and politicisation of ethnicity were given renewed impetus by the tumultuous electoral campaign. Power was to be defined by numbers, and aspirant politicians threw into the battle whatever resources they could discover: millennial promises, appeals to ethnic solidarity and fears, anti-colonial fervour, visions of national unity, and funds and advice from remarkably diverse sources. Two broad lines of cleavage, superimposed on many more regional ones, emerged: moderate versus radical, and federalist versus unitarian. The first involved, at one extreme, an indulgent attitude towards, and close association with, the colonial administration and, at the other, an aggressively anti-colonial stance. The other line of division separated those strongly committed to a centralised, unitary structure for the new state, from those who advocated provincial autonomy.

The elections yielded a psychological victory for the more radical nationalist parties. The initial hope of the administration, the Parti National du Progrès, won only 15 seats in the lower house. The major victor in most eyes was the Mouvement National Congolais–Lumumba (MNC/L) which made a major effort to offer its programme of radical, unitarian nationalism on a national scale. In the event it won 33 of the 137 seats, while a further eight were won by allied parties. The more dynamic regional parties, such as Parti Solidaire Africain (PSA) and ABAKO, swept their home areas but had only a limited bloc of parliamentary seats. The formation of a government out of this fractured parliament was a tortuous process, rendered even more difficult by the realisation that the numerous party groups were by no means disciplined, cohesive blocs. *In extremis*, a precarious formula was found, which seemed to offer a glimmer of hope: the two most prestigious leaders, Patrice Lumumba and Joseph Kasavubu, became prime minister and president respectively. The dangers of independence were reflected in the vote of confirmation on the Lumumba cabinet: though the parties represented in the Lumumba ministry represented 120 of the 137 seats, the government received only 74 votes, or five more than the bare minimum.

In Ruanda-Urundi, a working group similar to that for the Congo was sent out in the spring of 1959. Its report emerged in November 1959, and proposed a formula rather similar to that which had failed to take root in the Congo. The electoral principle, already introduced in 1956, was again to operate at the local council level, with elected burgomasters to replace appointed chiefs. The councillors would serve as electors for kingdom councils, with each *mwami* (king) becoming a constitutional figurehead, outside politics and parties. Political evolution was to proceed at the level of the two kingdoms. There was virtually no support in Rwanda or Burundi for maintenance of a common framework.

In Rwanda, the series of events which led to the establishment in January 1961 of the Hutu Republic began with the sudden and unexpected death of Mwami Rudahigwa Mutara III on 25 July 1959. The traditional royal council, the *biru*, convinced that foul play had been involved in the *mwami*'s death, convened at once without the knowledge of Belgian officials, and announced Jean-Baptiste Ndahindurwa as Mwami Kigeri V. This audacious coup was meekly accepted by the Belgians, thus apparently suggesting that real power now lay with the Tutsi monarchists. Sharpened apprehensions in Hutu circles at this development created a propitious climate for a *jacquerie* in November 1959: a week of rural violence, beginning with widespread burnings of Tutsi dwellings by Hutu peasant bands, followed by Tutsi assassination of a number of Hutu leaders. Although the death toll was not large (officially 13 Tutsi, 37 Hutu), the political impact was enormous. In the aftermath of the *jacquerie*, some 22 000, mainly Tutsi, fled into hastily created refugee camps in Burundi, Zaire, Uganda and Tanzania. In the following weeks, no fewer than 21 Tutsi chiefs and 332 sub-chiefs were killed, arrested, or forced out of office, over half of these in the north.[1] Hutu chiefs were appointed to fill these posts, often in disorderly conditions. Although the Belgian administration by no means controlled the direction of events, there is persuasive evidence that it had decided

---

[1] René Lemarchand, *Rwanda and Burundi* (London, 1970), 172–3.

to react to them by throwing its weight on the side of the Hutu, now organised in the Parti du Mouvement de l'Emancipation Hutu (PARMEHUTU). Tutsi interests were articulated by the Union Nationale Rwandaise (UNAR), radically anti-colonial in its lexicon, royalist and chauvinistic at its core. Communal elections were held in mid-1960s. With UNAR generally boycotting the elections, the result was an overwhelming triumph for PARMEHUTU, which captured 2390 of the 3125 local council seats. The structure of local power was radically altered by the installation of Hutu burgomasters in 210 of the 229 communes which replaced the sub-chieftaincies.

Legislative elections for a National Assembly were announced for January 1961. At the United Nations, where Belgian credibility was at low ebb and UNAR effectively portrayed itself as an anti-colonial movement, the General Assembly in December 1960 sought to head off an immediate PARMEHUTU monopoly of power by urging a Round Table Conference among the parties and the postponement of the elections. The conference was held in Ostend in early January 1961 and resulted in a predictable impasse. At this juncture, PARMEHUTU and the Belgian administration in Rwanda were anxious to go forward with the balloting, to pave the way for a swift transfer of power to PARMEHUTU. Brussels, however, while indignant over what appeared a systematic misunderstanding of Belgian motives, bowed to international pressures and postponed the elections. On 28 January 1961, trucks arrived in the small, central Rwandan town of Gitarama, bearing the 3126 communal councillors and burgomasters, furtively summoned by the PARMEHUTU leadership, certainly acting with the consent of the local Belgian administration, and possibly with the tacit approval of Brussels. By acclamation, this assemblage, acting as impromptu constituent assembly, declared the birth of the 'democratic and sovereign Republic of Rwanda', with Grégoire Kayibanda as prime minister, and Dominique Mbonyumutwa as president. The monarchy and all its symbols were declared abolished.

The Belgian administration, although it termed the coup illegal, accepted its results, claiming with some justice that it lacked the power to do otherwise. The Gitarama coup fixed the structure of power for post-colonial Rwanda; the 17 months which remained before independence on 1 July 1962 were devoted to formal legitimation of the new regime, both internally and at the United Nations. At UN insistence, a referendum was held on the issue of the abolition of the monarchy, and internationally super-vised legislative elections took place in September 1961. The PARMEHUTU, however, was already in power; the referendum yielded an 80 per cent vote in favour of the Republic, and assured the ruling party of 35 of the 44 seats. In a final compromise with the UN on 28 February 1962, two ministerial posts and some local administrative nominations were given to UNAR.

The building of an independent state in Burundi from 1959–62 set off very different lines of conflict between dynastic clan and generation. The monarchy, rather than being swept away, was momentarily reinforced as a reassuring symbol of unity. Historically, kings of Burundi took up in turn one of four dynastic names, Ntare, Mwezi, Mutaga, and Mwambutsa. The descendants of a king, or *ganwa* (princes of the blood), formed a clan carrying the dynastic name of the progenitor. Though intrigue within a royal clan was certainly possible, the existence of the structurally competing royal clans provided a relative continuity to factional struggle absent in Rwanda; to this must be added the much less centralised power of the *mwami*ship in Burundi until Belgian indirect rule enlarged its effective scope. During the twentieth century, dynastic rivalry had hinged around the Bezi and Batare clans, a competition intensified by the particular character of German intervention in Burundi politics in the early years. Throughout the Belgian period, Bangiricenge ruled under the dynastic name of Mwambutsa. He was enthroned in 1915, at the age of two, and died in European exile in 1977. The stakes of rivalry during the colonial period were primarily chieftaincy posts and seats on the kingdom council. With independence coming on the horizon from 1957, it was evident that the resources and power at issue would be greatly enlarged.

In the 1950s, the Belgian administration came to be identified with the Batare faction; thus, when nationalist vocabulary began to graft itself upon the Bezi–Batare rivalry, history cast the Bezi as radical anti-colonials (associated with the Parti de l'Union et le Progrès National/UPRONA) and Batare (linked to the Parti Démocratique Chrétien/PDC) as moderate collaborators with the administration. The new ideological costumes were brought into sharper focus by the dynamic role of Prince Louis Rwagasore, who became, in effect, the primary spokesman of UPRONA upon his return in 1958 from university studies in Belgium. UPRONA had been founded by a leading Bezi figure, Léopold Biha (his full name was Bihumugani); the PDC was launched by Pierre Baranyanka, great grandson of Mwami Ntare. Rwagasore stood somewhat outside the Bezi–Batare conflict as a real national figure. He was not the heir to the throne; as son of Mwambutsa, he belonged to the Bambutsa clan, and not the Bezi. His national appeal was also enhanced by his marriage to a Hutu woman, and by a charismatic political style, as well as by his tie to the palace. Belgian officials began to refer privately to the UPRONA leadership as crypto-Communist, and unmistakably sided with the PDC.

In March 1960 communal elections were announced for November of that year. Meanwhile, an interim council was named by the administration which was weighted toward Batare interests. Shortly after, Rwagasore was placed under house arrest in Bururi, in the south; other leading UPRONA figures were also hit by restrictive measures. The PDC, in alliance with several smaller parties, appeared to win a sweeping mandate, taking 2004 of the 2873 communal seats, compared with only 545 for UPRONA. Striking while the iron was hot, the administration at once announced that elections would be held for a legislature which would elaborate the central political institutions of an independent Burundi. The UN protested strongly, and the Belgians backed down on the question of legislative elections; however, a provisional council was created, with the new communal councils acting as an electoral college. A PDC-dominated interim central government was established, at once recognised by Belgium. However, under heavy UN pressure, Belgium partially retreated on 25 June 1961, reshuffling the interim government to confer two important ministries on UPRONA. Legislative elections were to be held in September, and Rwagasore was released. UPRONA succeeded in identifying itself as the party of both nationalism and the monarchy, and captured 58 of the 64 seats and 80 per cent of the vote. This verdict led to the investiture of Rwagasore as prime minister.

The euphoria of this triumph was short-lived. On 13 October 1961, a hired Greek assassin shot Rwagasore. The real conspirators were Batare leaders, in particular the PDC leader Baranyanka's sons, Jean Ntitendereza and Joseph Biroli, both of whom were convicted before independence, and hanged after. They apparently mistakenly believed they had the support of the Belgian Resident in this disastrous assassination, a conviction probably derived from contacts with some Belgian functionaries.[1] As Lemarchand notes, 'Only if one remembers the historical dimensions of the [Bezi–Batare] conflict can one understand the feelings of rage of the Batare in the face of a situation which denied them once and for all the opportunity to make good their traditional claims to power'.[2]

The demise of Rwagasore threw Burundi politics into disarray. Only the charisma of Rwagasore provided UPRONA with a unifying force; once this was removed, intra-party strife began to take on ominous new dimensions as for the first time Hutu–Tutsi conflict appeared. André Muhirwa, the only significant Batare figure in the UPRONA leadership ranks, succeeded Rwagasore as prime minister, perhaps somewhat blunting the intensity of the Bezi–Batare confrontation following the Batare role in the murder. Muhirwa, however, had social views tinged with Tutsi chauvinism, and soon became feared and hated by Hutu leaders. In January 1962, the first murders of Hutu intellectuals occurred in Bujumbura, carried out by the UPRONA youth, the Jeunesse Nationaliste Rwagasore (JNR), foreshadowing the deadly perils which lay ahead.

INDEPENDENCE AND CRISIS IN ZAIRE

What burst upon the world as the 'Congo crisis' in 1960 may be conveniently examined from four perspectives: the overlapping breakdowns of army; the administration; the problem of national unity; and the constitutional framework. The first flash-point was the army, riddled as it was with discontent when independence came. The political leaders had unwisely accepted a plan for Africanisation of the officer corps which kept this cadre exclusively European at the moment of independence, required a decade before much impact would be made, and above all excluded the current generation of other ranks from the prospect of swift promotion that was being enjoyed by the politicians. The first overt act of indiscipline occurred in Kinshasa on 4 July. Troops

[1] Warren Weinstein, *Historical dictionary of Burundi* (Metuchen, NJ, 1976), 223–4.
[2] Lemarchand, *Rwanda and Burundi*, 341.

in the nearest garrison at Mbanza-Ngungu (Thysville), ordered to Kinshasa as reinforcements to cope with possible trouble in the capital garrison, rose instead against their European officers.

Lumumba tried desperately to halt the mutiny, first by sacking the Belgian commander, and promoting all troops one rank, then, three days later, by announcing the total Africanisation of the officer corps, with acceptable Belgians remaining only as counsellors. This was to no avail: the mutual fears and suspicions between Europeans and Africans generated by the abrupt arrival of independence were too pervasive. The African mutineers were in mortal fear that the European officers would try to disarm them and exact lethal vengeance, while the European community in and out of the military camps was swept by lurid reports of rape and violence perpetrated by the troops, some of which were true. New officers were named, in some cases by election, in others by succession of the senior NCOs, in still others under the influence of the newly installed Zairean Commander-in-Chief, V. Lundula, or his Chief of Staff, Mobutu. However, weeks were to pass before anyone even loosely controlled very many troops. As it faced a crisis of survival, the new government was deprived of effective control over its instrument of security.

The backbone of the colonial state was its bureaucratic structure. Like the army, the administration carried its wholly European flavour into independence. Not until 1959 was there legal provision for the incorporation of Zaireans into the approximately 10000 executive-level posts in the bureaucracy. In 1960, the 4645 slots in the first three ranks still contained only three Zaireans. Furthermore, only the new generation of university graduates (the first Lovanium graduating class was 1959) was to have access to these. Those senior clerks who had not metamorphosed into politicians were as bitter as the old NCOs. Independence, it seemed, was only for politicians.

This malaise served as backdrop for the July panic. Amongst European functionaries, tales spread of 'black lists' of persons destined for sacking at the first opportunity after independence. Total panic gripped the European community in the wake of the mutiny, and by mid-July most Belgian functionaries save those in Katanga had fled. Of necessity, yesterday's clerks became today's director-generals. Many had long administrative experience and abilities far beyond those required for the posts in which they had been blocked by the discriminatory structure of the colonial service. Nonetheless, they were called upon to assume their new responsibilities in conditions of unprecedented disarray. For the moment, the administration was no more able than the army to fulfil its former mission of central control.

In Katanga the European community had long considered the province a distinctive entity, resenting centralised control from Kinshasa and Brussels and the siphoning of Katangan resources to finance development in the less-endowed regions. (In 1960, 45 per cent of state revenues, and over 50 per cent of the foreign exchange came from the Copperbelt, figures that have sharply increased since independence.) This essentially European particularism, in the final colonial days, spread to a segment of the African leadership through the prism of an intensifying social competition between immigrants from Kasai, especially Luba, who tended to predominate at the élite end of the African spectrum, and groups from the southern part of Katanga, who came to describe themselves as 'authentic Katangans', and organised politically behind the Confédération des Associations Tribales du Katanga (CONAKAT). As independence approached, the large Belgian firms, especially UMHK, increasingly disconcerted by the radical rhetoric of the more aggressive nationalist parties, found CONAKAT leader Tshombe's affirmations of close collaboration with Europeans reassuring. Lumumba viewed Tshombe and CONAKAT with great suspicion, both for their visible connexions with UMHK, and for their hints that secession was being seriously contemplated. CONAKAT received only two minor posts in the elephantine Lumumba government, while Tshombe became provincial president. On 11 July, profiting from the disruption in Kinshasa, Tshombe proclaimed Katanga's independence. Belgian troops disarmed the mutinous army garrisons in Katanga; Belgian functionaries were ordered to remain at their posts, in contrast to the flight elsewhere. A Katanga gendarmerie – a unit destined to serve many flags and causes – was recruited at top speed, with the help of Belgian officers. Although the African dimensions to the secession should not be overlooked, it could never have been undertaken without large-scale public and private Belgian support. On one crucial and ultimately fatal front, however, Belgian aid was refused: the new state of Katanga was not accorded official recognition by Belgium, nor by any other country.

On 8 August, Katanga was followed out of the national door by the Luba–Kasai region of South Kasai, in a more ambiguous and short-lived secession. The Luba provided the stereotypical success story in exploiting new opportunities for social advance presented by the colonial system. Luba had migrated in large numbers to focal points of modern activity: the Copperbelt, the Bas-Congo–Katanga (BCK) rail line, the Kasai provincial capital of Kananga, even to Kinshasa. Their apparent success made them objects of hostility – and by October 1959 of violent assault – in many places, particularly other areas of Kasai, and the Copperbelt. The final blow came in their virtual exclusion from both the national and provincial governments in June. Thus rejected on all sides, the Luba cradleland of South Kasai briefly claimed independence. As the site of most of the industrial diamond production, its loss in August 1960 deepened the crisis faced by the Lumumba government.

The final act in the drama of breakdown came with the split of the central government into two centres, each claiming to be sole repository of legality. The bifurcated executive established by the provisional constitution, with both President Kasavubu and Prime Minister Lumumba having important powers, was bound to lead to trouble. The two leaders could not have been more different, and the crisis laid bare certain flaws in both. Kasavubu had shown great courage at certain junctures in his political career; his 1946 speech on the 'right of the first occupant'; the 1956 ABAKO stance for 'immediate independence'; and a forthright political statement on the occasion of his inauguration as communal burgomaster in 1958. These had created a myth which proved larger than the man. Secretive, withdrawn, aloof, lacking in organisational talents, Kasavubu counted on events and other forces to work on his behalf. But Lumumba was a master organiser. In Kisangani (Stanleyville), where he first became visible, he had achieved leadership of virtually every organisation in sight by 1956. Of inexhaustible energy, charismatic style, immense charm, his political personality was almost irresistible in the final months of colonial rule. Yet joined to these talents were some fatal flaws: he suffered from an inability to collaborate with others on an equal political plane; he was distrustful; a mercurial, passionate and impatient man, he was prone to hasty judgement and susceptible to sycophants. By August 1960, he had become surrounded by an inpenetrable entourage of cosmopolitan ideological adventurers, whose ill-judged portrayals of political reality contributed to his growing isolation. Though Kasavubu and Lumumba remained quite close in the first phases of the crisis, by August a profound chasm of distrust separated them. Indeed, after mid-July they almost never met.

Kasavubu, on the basis of an ambiguous provision in the constitution, announced over the radio on 5 September that he was dismissing the prime minister, and proposing Ileo Songo-Amba (Joseph) in his place. He then retired to the presidential palace to await the further developments that many forces, external and internal, were by then anxious to help organise. Lumumba went into furious counterattack, announcing that he was removing Kasavubu. Parliament, hastily convened, annulled both sackings. On 14 September Colonel Mobutu intervened, announcing the establishment of his own College of Commissioners, composed of university students. The thread of constitutionality had been lost. Lumumba's residence was surrounded by UN troops as a measure of protection; the gesture was also, in effect, confinement.

Kasavubu had some decisive advantages. Mobutu continued to recognise his role as president, as did the UN. For a crucial few days, the UN froze the situation by closing the airport and radio station; Kasavubu's supporters benefited from continued access to Brazzaville radio. The western, especially American and Belgian, support for Mobutu and Kasavubu was far more effective than anything the Soviet Union was in a position to do for Lumumba.

By November 1960, the Lumumbist forces had concluded that it was not possible to recoup the situation from Kinshasa. They regrouped at Kisangani, gaining control of the provincial administration and army detachments. On 27 November Lumumba escaped from UN protection in Kinshasa and tried to join his backers in Kisangani. He was captured en route by the Kinshasa authorities, who transferred him to Katanga, where he was at once murdered. In the meantime, Lumumba's Vice-Premier, Antoine

Gizenga, had announced that Kisangani was the seat of the legal government. The nadir had been reached; torn into four fragments, with its administration paralysed, and the army, in the words of UN Special Representative R. Dayal, a 'disorderly rabble', prey to diverse external rivalries, the prospects for Zaire were dim.

INTERNATIONALISATION OF THE 'CONGO CRISIS'

The internationalisation of Zairean politics is the last immediate consequence of the crisis which requires consideration. This began with the intervention of Belgian troops on 10 July, with the ostensible mission of protecting the European population. On 11 July, Kasavubu and Lumumba were on the verge of agreeing to their presence, provided their mission was restricted to its announced purpose. However, that day was marked by the senseless Belgian bombardment of Matadi, and Belgian military support for the Katanga secession. Within three days, the Zaire government had appealed for American troops, UN forces, and a 'close watch' on the situation by the Soviet Union.

With remarkable speed, the United Nations put together an international force, which from then till 1964 was the most important coercive instrument in the country. The UN force, however, was responsible to the international body and not, as Lumumba apparently initially believed, to the Zaire government. Theoretically, it was intended to keep the peace without intervening in internal affairs, an impossible assignment in the conditions obtaining in 1960. Thus the complex patterns of international organisation politics – balances of power between the governing organs of Security Council and General Assembly, conflicts and rivalries between officers in the UN Secretariat and field command in Zaire – had considerable impact on political evolution in the country. The fatal dialectic of the Cold War set in very quickly. By August, the United States had concluded that Lumumba and his allies were dangerously susceptible to Soviet solicitations, and committed the considerable resources of its hyperactive intelligence agency to support political factions seeking his overthrow; then during the autumn months it dabbled in abortive assassination schemes. The Soviet Union, sensing an unanticipated opportunity to strike a serious blow to imperialist bastions in Central Africa, began delivering equipment and advisers to the Lumumba forces in late August. President Nkrumah of Ghana, in possession of a secret commitment from Lumumba to join the stillborn Ghana–Guinea–Mali union, mustered all the diplomatic resources at his command to keep him in power. In so unstructured and weakened a polity as the Zaire of the 'Congo crisis' epoch, the impact of such forces was considerable.

The first half of 1961 witnessed slow movement toward a formula of reconciliation, which might make possible a reunification of the fragments, and the formation of a compromise national government. The Lumumbist group at Kisangani wanted to preserve the essentials of the late prime minister's vision: a unitary state, weighted toward the radical 1960 parties. Katanga intimated willingness to re-enter the national community, provided that it were reconceived in a confederal image, permitting the runaway province to retain through internal autonomy what it was unable to gain as a result of absence of international recognition. Kinshasa wavered between the two, reflecting the changing international climate. With the UN as mediator, a new start was made in July 1961 by reconvening parliament; all but the CONAKAT deputies were in attendance. The assembly was almost evenly divided between Kisangani and Kinshasa blocs; however, former trade-union leader Cyrille Adoula was accepted by both as a compromise candidate. Many Lumumbists felt they had been out-manoeuvred; Mobutu remained commander of the now reunified army, while the security police were run by Nendaka Bika (Victor), both key figures in the 'Binza group', an informal clique of Kinshasa leaders enjoying strong western (especially American) backing.

Restoration of constitutional government eased the burden on the UN in dealing with *de facto* authorities without intervening in internal affairs. In New York, however, pressure was mounting on the UN Secretariat for some decisive action against the Katanga secession. On 28 August 1961, a first gesture of force was made in a smoothly executed operation aimed at 443 European officers and irregulars serving with the Katanga gendarmerie. Some 105, however, eluded the UN net, and others soon reappeared. The UN field representatives, without the knowledge of Dag Hammarskjöld, the Secretary-General in New York, devised a more far-reaching coup for 13 September, aimed at ending the secession. This plan, however, fizzled out, and UN forces found themselves engaged in an urban gunfight with the inevitable casualties and damage. The epitaph to this disaster was the tragic death of Hammarskjöld himself, when his plane crashed outside Ndola, Zambia, en route to a rendezvous with Tshombe to negotiate a cease-fire.

In December 1961, renewed fighting broke out between UN forces and the Katanga gendarmes. This time, the UN was able both to justify its action on grounds of self-defence, and also to thrash the Katangans. Tshombe had to seek a cease-fire, with an agreement that appeared to commit Katanga to end the secession. Tshombe's skill in dilatory manoeuvre was by no means exhausted, however, and much of 1962 was spent in sporadic and fruitless negotiations on the execution of the agreement. Finally, renewed conflicts in Lubumbashi between UN forces and Katanga gendarmes developed at the end of 1962. This time the UN command seized the occasion to pursue the military action to a full conclusion, by occupying all the major towns of South Katanga and putting the Katanga gendarmes to flight. Though local commanders exceeded New York instructions, the campaign was swift and decisive; on 14 January 1963, Tshombe declared the end of the secession.

The confusion which beset the central institutions in September 1960 had soon spread to the provinces. By 1962, the Kongo, Luba-Kasai, and North Katanga areas were de facto separate provinces. As provincial conflict escalated elsewhere, usually around regional cleavages, other candidates for separate provincial status appeared daily. Just possibly, many believed, a provincial structure based on smaller units, somewhat more homogeneous and created through the play of ethnic self-determination, could offer a more viable structure. Out of this came the fragmentation of the six old provinces into 21 during 1962 and 1963. Although ethnic affinity was accepted as a criterion, in fact the new units tended to follow the lines of the former districts, the colonial administrative echelon lying below the province. The hopes of greater cohesion of the new units were soon disappointed. The issue of the regional distribution of power was pivotal in the prolonged efforts to draft a permanent constitution to replace the provisional document hastily concocted on the eve of independence. When by 1963 parliament had reached an impasse in its constitutional labours, a special constituent assembly, composed of party, regional and interest-group representatives, was convened in Kananga in January 1964, to consider a draft prepared with UN assistance. The word 'federal' was carefully expunged, but the document contained many federal features. Beyond constitutional formality, a large degree of informal federalisation had occurred through the inability of the central government effectively to exercise powers in its domain.

By early 1964, troubles mounted for the Adoula regime. Tshombe, now in comfortable exile in Madrid, began to weave a coalition of the discontented. The Katanga days had left ample resources in his hands, plus friends who would provide more. Radicals were promised national unity, disavowal of the Lumumba murder, and an anti-American posture. Moderates were reassured by the actual performance of Tshombe in office in Katanga. European interests were told that he remained a friend of the west, and a defender of private enterprise in Africa. As the conviction grew in many quarters that the Adoula regime was no longer able to cope, the Tshombe alternative began to appear as a serious possibility, not least to President Kasavubu. On 6 July 1964, Kasavubu named Tshombe as *formateur* of a provisional government, while awaiting the organisation of elections for a new parliament and a permanent government as prescribed by the Kananga constitution which had just come into effect. In contrast to the industrious but colourless Adoula, who rarely made public appearances, Tshombe was gregarious and exuberant. The new prime minister enjoyed, for a time, astonishing popularity with the Kinshasa crowds. Tshombe did include one Lumumbist figure (André Lubaya) in his cabinet; otherwise it contained a full slate of persons who had never before held central ministerial office. But Lumumbist critics pointed to the continued control of the security apparatus by Mobutu and Nendaka, a former lieutenant of Lumumba from eastern Zaire, who had become a bitter enemy. By the end of the month, various Europeans once associated with the Katanga regime began to reappear in advisory roles. In its style of operation, the Tshombe regime soon took on the attributes of the old Katanga state.

Within two weeks of the installation of the Tshombe government, a wave of rebellion which had broken out in several parts of the country in early 1964 suddenly began to coalesce and extend rapidly. Six weeks later, a revolutionary government was proclaimed in Kisangani, about one-third of the national territory had been lost to the central government, and the Kinshasa regime seemed on the brink of collapse. However, the rebellions quickly began to give way before mercenary-led spearheads of the national army, and by the end of the year had broken into fragments, the rebel leadership in flight and all hopes of success vanished. The striking receptivity of the revolutionary appeal must be understood in the context of the hardships brought to many by the circumstances of independence. A few privileged categories – politicians, functionaries, officers – had enjoyed a spectacular social ascent; but most people suffered a sharp drop in well-being. The recollection, especially for the young, of the campaign promises, of the hopes that independence had awakened compared very unfavourably with the bitter reality. For older persons, there was a curious nostalgia for colonialism: not, of course, the vexations of European oppression, but for the order and predictability of life, for the reliability of services which accompanied the last years of *le temps des Belges*.

While these factors may suggest a generalised predisposition to insurrection, rebels did not find a ready audience everywhere. The reaction of a particular local community to a call to insurrection would depend upon its evaluation of the symbolic associations of those making the appeal. Who were the insurrectionaries? Brother, friend or foe? To this calculus was added a prudential estimate of risks and advantages. Who would win? Dare we oppose an approaching rebel band? What risks of vengeance from the national army would arise if we welcomed the rebels? Individuals, factions, communities, regions derived varying responses from these calculations.

The first embryo of rebellion appeared in October 1963, when a number of Lumumbist politicians crossed the Congo River and established a Conseil National de Libération (CNL) at Brazzaville, where a government prepared to provide sanctuary and facilitate revolutionary organisation by the Lumumbist opposition came to power in August 1963. A few months before, a relatively

726

little-known former Minister of Education from the 1960 Lumumba government, Pierre Mulele, had furtively returned to Zaire after three years in Egypt, China, and Eastern Europe. Quite independent of the CNL, he began to organise partisan bands in the valley forests of his native Kwilu district. More than in any of the other rebel groups there was a strong ideological content to the political and military instruction Mulele and his lieutenants provided, drawn primarily from Chinese theories of peasant revolution. The Mulele movement achieved remarkable success, for a time, in harnessing rural discontent in his own ethnic Mbundu zone, and among the neighbouring Pende. He had much more difficulty in penetrating other groups, and some saw themselves actively threatened by the Mulelists. Mulelist bands passed to the attack at the beginning of 1964, but by May the movement had become regionally encapsulated, and began to be torn by internal tensions. Mulelism became a political myth of formidable proportions, and it was many months before the last of the bands left the forest.

In February 1964 the CNL established a new office in Burundi, where the fluid political conjuncture had also become favourable. In the Ruzizi plain, bordering Burundi, factional dispute among the Fulero offered an initial base for rebel organisation, which soon exposed the weakness of the national army. On 15 May the frontier town of Uvira was taken by insurgents, opening the Burundi border. Rebels gained another foothold, when Kalemie (Albertville), capital of North Katanga, was captured on 19 June by youthful insurgents from the north. A scene to be re-enacted many times in the following weeks ensued; the national army simply evaporated, and small, lightly armed youth bands pushed south and east without encountering significant opposition. The situation in Kalemie itself soon became anarchic, and Gaston Soumialot, principal organiser of the eastern branch of the CNL, turned his own attention to regions north and east.

By mid-July, youth bands in Maniema were structured in more conventional form as an Armée Populaire de Libération (APL) under Nicolas Olenga. The APL snowballed as it moved toward Kisangani through zones of Lumumbist strength. In each town, new recruits were enrolled, commercial and state vehicles seized, bank and store vaults emptied, and sizeable stocks of equipment and ammunition captured from the fleeing national army. From quite modest beginnings, the APL when it reached Kisangani on 4 August had become a force which began to match the national army in numbers, vehicles, and small arms. In August, APL columns advanced in all directions: eastward from Kindu into Sankuru, north and west from Kisangani to Isiro (Paulis) and Bunia, east to Lisala and Boende, all of which were in insurgent hands by the end of August. Only one serious setback occurred; a column of 6000 men led by Olenga was driven back at Bukavu in mid-August by a national army garrison effectively led by Colonel (Léonard) Mulamba Nyunyi, with some American and Belgian advisers, and with the decisive support of Mwami Kabare, who at the last moment committed his Shi followers against the rebels.

Rebellion was at flood tide when CNL leader Christophe Gbenye proclaimed a revolutionary national government at the Lumumbist capital of Kisangani on 5 September. The decomposition of the People's Republic followed very swiftly after its establishment. The constitution of mercenary units and the incorporation of former Katanga gendarme units provided new resources for the national army; Belgian and American logistical support was increased. Relations between Gbenye, Soumialot and Olenga were always uneasy, and hierarchical control intermittent at best. The Kisangani regime found itself responsible for administering vast expanses of territory, with neither structure nor resources to respond to their needs. The expansion of rebel territory was accompanied by the application of revolutionary 'justice' to those associated with the central government, resulting in the massacre of thousands of persons.

By October, the national army counter-offensive began in earnest. The revolutionary government interned approximately 1800 Europeans who had remained in rebel-held areas and sought to use them as a bargaining counter, both as a shield against air raids, and to negotiate a halt of the advance on Kisangani. This led to the controversial American–Belgian parachute operation at Kisangani and Isiro on 24–26 November with American planes transporting Belgian troops. About 100 Europeans and many Africans were killed in connexion with this undertaking. Most African opinion was deeply offended by the racial arrogance implicit in the operation, which rested on the unstated assumption that European lives were more important than African ones.

Although the Tshombe government had not invited this intervention, it had accepted it, so reinforcing its political isolation in Africa.

By the end of 1964, as a collective threat to the central government the rebellions had failed. Leadership, never united, fell apart after the loss of Kisangani. However, many substantial pockets of rebellion remained, and many months passed before central authority was restored in a number of these. In some instances, their persistence was abetted by the belated arrival of external supplies: Soviet equipment, transferred by Algeria via the Sudan, and Chinese weapons across Tanzania into the Lake Tanganyika zone. Also, during 1965 the largest pocket of rebels, in the Fizi–Baraka zone on the Tanzania border, benefited from the assistance of the tireless revolutionary, Ernesto 'Che' Guevara, and a few dozen Cuban colleagues. They eventually became disillusioned, but the Fizi pocket became a zone of institutionalised dissidence from that time forward, and was never brought under central control. Elsewhere, the process of restoring the authority of Kinshasa was often accompanied by massacres comparable in scale to the assassinations by the rebels.

With the nightmare of rebellion largely over, political attention turned in 1965 to the contest for power under the Kananga constitution. National elections were scheduled for March. The evident challenge was to produce some sort of regrouping out of the rich florescence of parties which then claimed to exist; no less than 223 parties entered the 1965 campaign. It was, by now, exceedingly difficult to organise politically outside the structure and the resources of the state and this gave a decisive advantage to the incumbents. In February 1965 Tshombe launched a national political movement intended to underpin his bid for continued power, the Convention Nationale Congolaise (CONACO), containing 49 constituent parties. The Lumumbist bloc, which still functioned with some cohesion in the 1963 parliament, had fallen victim to multiple splits, and had lost a number of its leaders in the rebellions. Thus CONACO was the apparent victor in the parliamentary elections, taking 122 of the 167 seats.

Parliament did not meet till September, by which time the fragility of CONACO had become apparent. An opposition bloc of deputies, the Front Démocratique Congolais (FDC), emerged, led by security chief Nendaka and former Léopoldville provincial president Kamitatu Massamba (Cléophas). When parliament met, the first test votes showed the Tshombe and anti-Tshombe groups almost evenly divided. The crucial power contest was for the office of president, to be elected by parliament and the provincial assemblies. Kasavubu desired re-election, but Tshombe had decided to challenge him. As the evenness of the division became clear, tensions began to build. On 13 October, Kasavubu dismissed Tshombe as prime minister, and named Evariste Kimba as interim premier. On 14 November, the Kimba government failed to obtain a vote of confidence, by a vote of 121 to 134 (counting both houses). Kasavubu at once asked Kimba to make a second attempt at forming a government, but at this juncture there simply seemed no majority available for either side. Zaire appeared once again to be in a cul-de-sac. These were the circumstances in which the military high command decided to install General Mobutu as president on 25 November 1965. That same day, a suddenly chastened and united parliament convened, and approved the *coup d'état* by acclamation.

In a major address to the United Nations General Assembly on 4 October 1973, President Mobutu pronounced a harsh verdict on the First Republic:

The situation which we have experienced from 1960 to 1965 was cruel for our people. And we must recognize that anarchy, chaos, disorder, negligence, and incompetence were master in Zaire. Some of you look in the dictionary perhaps to understand the definition of the word 'anarchy', while in Zaire we have experienced it so thoroughly that many thought the word 'anarchy' was a Zairean invention.[1]

In fact, words such as 'chaos' and 'anarchy' really go too far to convey the reality of the period. Most of the time, in most places, the routines of life went forward. Many major economic enterprises continued to operate. UMHK, for example, hardly ever missed a day's work. Schools continued to function, indeed rapidly expanded, although an academic year was lost in many areas affected by the rebellions. Yet disorder was fatally lodged in the arteries of the system. Most Zaireans experienced in their personal lives some of its repercussions: the loss of a friend or relative; a brutal encounter with an ill-disciplined army patrol or

[1] *Études Zairoises*, September–October 1973, **2**, 79–102.

rampaging gang of youths; the depressing awareness that one's ethnicity defined the quarters of town it was safe to enter. This is why, in its unanimous acclamation of the New Regime, parliament was faithfully representing its constituents. The First Republic passed into history as a distasteful period which many people a decade later still did not wish even to discuss. It is this rejection of the legacy of the First Republic which serves as a point of departure for an understanding of the New Regime fashioned by President Mobutu.

THE NEW REGIME, 1965–75

Mobutu at once made his intentions clear by asking for five years in which to rebuild the country. The complete blueprint was not at hand; indeed, the coup had not been planned far in advance of execution. From the outset, however, certain themes were clear: depoliticisation, to cleanse the country of the political divisions of the First Republic; centralisation; creation of new political institutions; personal rule, with the presidency as the supreme institution. Mobutu intended to serve as a political leader, not as military caretaker; from the outset, few military personnel were called upon to serve in either political or administrative roles.

Political parties were dissolved; parliament was retained, and met occasionally for ritual approval of the budget for the remainder of its prescribed five-year term. Perhaps its major function was to serve as a well-remunerated sinecure for an important cross-section of politicians whose discontent would have been irritating, if not dangerous. At the end of 1966 provinces were reduced in number to eight plus a capital district of Kinshasa, and transformed into purely administrative organs. The perils of opposition were quickly demonstrated. On 30 May 1966, four leading figures of the First Republic (including ex-Prime Minister Kimba) were accused of conspiracy, tried in a five-minute court martial the following day, and hanged at once in a public square in Kinshasa. The benefits of collaboration, on the other hand, were seductive, as the president quickly developed exquisite skills in patrimonial distribution of benefices.

The mercenary elements and Katanga gendarmerie units were a serious menace, as Tshombe soon resumed plotting from Spanish exile. Mobutu could not at first afford the risk of expelling the former and disbanding the latter, until his hold on power was secure and the campaigns against the remaining pockets of rebels completed. The nature of the menace was made clear when 2000 Katanga gendarmes backed by a number of mercenaries mutinied at Kisangani in July 1966. A more serious mutiny occurred in July 1967, led by Colonel Jean Schramme, a former Belgian settler connected with the Tshombe faction. The conspiracy was partly aborted when Tshombe was kidnapped on the eve of the planned uprising, and imprisoned in Algiers, where he died two years later, officially of a heart attack. However, nearly 100 mercenaries and several hundred Katangans did seize control of Kisangani, then retreated to Bukavu, which they held until November.

By 1967, Mobutu was ready to give institutional form to his new regime. At the centre, effective power was concentrated in the office of the president. A single national party, the Mouvement Populaire de la Révolution (MPR), was created in May 1967. Generously endowed with government funds and vehicles, the party extended its structure throughout the country in the months that followed. There quickly appeared jurisdictional conflicts between the administrative and party representatives at different echelons of government, leading to a decision in October 1967 to fuse at each level the party and administrative responsibilities. The MPR role was extended to all organisational sectors: unions, youth and student organisations were converted into party organs, and cells were established in Catholic seminaries and army units. The apotheosis came in the 1974 revised constitution, which declared the MPR to be 'the nation politically organised', and 'the sole institution' of Zaire. The state itself, according to this constitutional theory, was simply a dependent emanation of the party. States, however, especially those cut from the cloth of the bureaucratic–authoritarian colonial tradition, do not wither away so easily. The more pervasive the party domain became, the more indistinguishable it became from the state.

Beyond the extraordinary definition of the party role, the 1974 constitution stands out for the breathtaking scope it gave to the power of the president. The leader of the party automatically became president of the Republic. He presided over all organs of the nation: the Political Bureau of the party (which determined broad policy goals and principles), the Council of Ministers (charged with the execution of Political Bureau decisions), the

National Legislative Council (which gave its views on budget and details of policy decisions, but could not challenge their essence), and the Supreme Court. Further, in effect the president named all the members of these various organs. The style of political rule under the Mobutu regime can be usefully described as 'patrimonial'.[1] Although initially he included in top posts many of the leading luminaries of the First Republic, they were progressively isolated from their sources of autonomous power and eventually thrust aside in favour of a new political generation which had hitherto played more secondary roles, or which had emerged after 1965, primarily from the growing ranks of university graduates. Few were permitted to keep a particular post very long, and there was constant rotation in the ruling organs. The increasingly personalist style of the regime was evident also in the evolution of its official ideology. The first MPR platform, the Nsele Manifesto, issued on 20 May 1967, had as its central theme 'authentic Zairean nationalism'. National dignity, non-alignment, an assertion of indigenous values in the place of imported doctrines, such as scientific socialism or capitalism, were its themes. In 1971, Mobutu unveiled the doctrine of 'authenticity'; Zairean nationalism had to reject the alienating overlay of imposed western values to fulfil itself through the Zairean cultural heritage. In the 1974 constitution, ideological evolution proceeded a further step by the establishment of 'Mobutuism' as the national doctrine. The content of this political thought was to be discovered in the writings, the speeches, and the actions of Mobutu.

The Mobutu regime in its first decade had undeniable accomplishments in the political realm. The vast country had been effectively reunited, and most disorder ended. When Mobutu sought a new mandate as unopposed presidential candidate in the 1970 elections, the regime and its leader had an undeniable élan. By the end of its first decade, the negative side of the personalist style of rule became more evident; with state resources as a vast patrimonial domain to be apportioned among the political élite, inequality and corruption spread throughout the body politic. By 1975, a deepening social malaise was again evident, compounded by a profound economic crisis beginning in 1974.

[1] This characterisation is advanced by Jean-Claude Williame, *Patrimonialism and political change in the Congo* (Stanford, 1972).

RWANDA: CONSOLIDATION OF THE HUTU REGIME

In comparison with its two neighbouring states of former Belgian Africa, the post-independence history of Rwanda was singularly uncomplicated, if not uneventful. The essential contours of the post-independence distribution of power were defined by the Rwanda revolution of 1959–61. These patterns worked themselves out more fully after 1962; in 1973, the legitimacy of the first-generation independence regime had eroded, and a reshuffling of actors though not of basic political structure occurred through the vehicle of a military coup.

In the aftermath of the revolution, a large-scale flight of Tutsi to neighbouring countries occurred; by 1963, an estimated 130000, or nearly one third of the Tutsi population, were refugees in Uganda, Tanzania, Burundi, and Zaire. A large part of the factionalised UNAR élite and the exiled *mwami* had not abandoned hope of reversing the revolutionary outcome. Perhaps 2000 Tutsi irregulars (*ingenzi*) were assembled in the neighbouring states to mount a seven-pronged assault on the Kayibanda regime in December 1963. Only one of the columns, 200 strong, advanced very far, reaching a point 12 miles from the capital of Kigali before they were destroyed by the Belgian-officered Garde Nationale Rwandaise. Savage vengeance was exacted on the Tutsi in Rwanda, with at least 10000 massacred by local Hutu bands. This disastrous invasion was the final postscript to the revolution. Outside the country the UNAR fell apart in the succeeding months, and internally it was removed from the posts negotiated for it by the UN in 1962. The Rwanda revolution was total and irreversible.

In the years that followed, the Kayibanda regime gradually lost its momentum. Regional tensions within the new Hutu political élite emerged; Hutu from the north, whose culture and history were quite distinctive, began to murmur that affairs were dominated by a clique from central Rwanda and that the Kayibanda regime permitted too high a fraction of Tutsi students in the university and secondary schools. President Kayibanda, whose withdrawn life earned him the nickname of 'hermit of Gitarama', offered no resistance to the military coup organised by army commander Juvenal Habyarimana in July 1973. Although the regional balance of Hutu domination was altered, with northerners now predominant, the fundamental character of the Rwanda revolution was maintained.

BURUNDI: FROM MONARCHY TO TUTSI REPUBLICANISM, 1962–75

Burundi politics in the first four years of independence are an extraordinary tangle, involving overlapping conflicts between *ganwa* clans, the monarchy and its opponents, *ganwa* and anti-royalist Tutsi, regional Tutsi and Hima groupings,[1] and an emergent politicisation of the polarity between Tutsi and Hutu. By 1975, fundamental transformations in political sociology had occurred. The monarchy had disappeared; the *ganwa* as a hegemonic élite had lost their role. A fundamentally unstable ethnocracy had emerged, but was yet to meet the need for a durable social formula compatible with the diffusion of egalitarian values and broadened self-awareness which inevitably accompany modernisation.

On the eve of independence, a fissure opened in the dominant UPRONA between what were, essentially, Tutsi and Hutu factions. Though Hutu mobilisation was limited at that point to Bujumbura and the Lake Tanganyika shoreline, this was the first time that the latent ethnic polarity became openly reflected in political structures. The Tutsi faction was led by Prime Minister Muhirwa, while the Hutu wing was headed by Paul Mirerekano, a Hutu merchant and mystic, who had once been an enthusiastic backer of Rwagasore, and remained a champion of Hutu rights. These factions became known as 'Casablanca' and 'Monrovia' respectively, after the radical and moderate groups of African states of the day. The horrifying example of Rwanda, not to mention Zaire, clearly exhibited the dangers contained in ramifying ethnic hostilities spilling over from the party into the administration. Mwami Mwambutsa, still a powerfully integrative symbol, tried to defuse the tensions by his increasing personal intervention in politics. In June 1963, Muhirwa resigned in disgust over the *mwami*'s intervention; Pierre Ngendandumwe,

---

[1] Some of the pastoralists in southern Burundi were known as Hima. Although they belong to the same original groups as the Tutsi, in Burundi they were believed to have migrated from a different direction, and to be of lesser status than the Tutsi. They did not participate in the structures of Tutsi hegemony over the Hutu.

a Hutu associated with the 'Monrovia' faction of UPRONA, was named as prime minister. From this point forward, however, successive governments were responsible to the court, and not to parliament. Executive functions were at best shared with an expanding palace entourage, largely composed of Bezi *ganwa* figures.

In singularly Byzantine fashion, Tutsi extremists were able to bring about the overthrow of the Ngendandumwe government by manoeuvring this 'Monrovia' regime into recognising the People's Republic of China, contrary to the preferences of the *mwami*, not to mention the Belgian and American embassies. In April 1964, Ngendandumwe was replaced by Albin Nyamoya, a Tutsi of noble (but not *ganwa*) lineage, linked to the 'Casablanca' group of UPRONA. The Nyamoya ministry coincided with the peak of the Zaire rebellions, and Bujumbura became a major focus of international intrigue. For some months Burundi politics were dominated by the 'Chinese factor', and tracts appeared warning of 'Communist penetration' of Burundi. In January 1965, the *mwami* again intervened to sack Nyamoya, alleging 'numerous errors and serious misjudgement...in foreign affairs as well as problems related to national progress'.[1] Ngendandumwe was reinstalled as prime minister, only to be murdered three days later by Rwanda Tutsi extremists. The *mwami* now turned to Joseph Bamina, a university-trained Hutu from a high-status lineage, and married to a Tutsi. Bamina had momentarily served as compromise UPRONA president in late 1962, acceptable at that point to both Tutsi and Hutu. At the *mwami*'s behest, relations with China were severed, and a paradoxical effort, endorsed by palace and *ganwa*, was made to drain by democracy the poisonous tensions which political instability had secreted. Elections were organised in May 1965, apparently without full calculation as to their implications. They were remarkably free and untrammelled, and resulted in a clear triumph for Hutu candidates. This was not at once apparent in the party labels; the pro-Hutu Parti du Peuple won 10 of 33 seats, while UPRONA won 21. But UPRONA was by now a shambles, with as many as five different UPRONA lists being presented in some constituencies. The crucial factor was that 23 of 33 winners were Hutu. Pending the naming of a new government, the *mwami* designated his private secretary and

[1] Weinstein, *Historical dictionary*, 227.

leading Bezi courtier, Biha, as interim prime minister in July. On 13 September 1965 the *mwami* confirmed his appointment, driving the Hutu parliamentarians to the conclusion that Mwambutsa intended to deny them the fruits of their electoral victory.

On 18 October 1965, a group of Hutu officers and men attempted a coup. This quickly failed in Bujumbura, but in the countryside Hutu bands attacked a number of rural Tutsi homes, killing and burning, especially in central Muramvya province. Vengeance was swift. Some 34 military participants in the coup were executed, and 86 Hutu political leaders were sentenced to death on charges of complicity. In the countryside, Tutsi bands with army support went on the rampage, slaughtering several thousand Hutu peasants. Until that point, all governments had contained relatively equal numbers of Hutu and Tutsi. Henceforth, although token Hutu representation continued, Tutsi hegemony was clearly affirmed. Biha, wounded in the attempted coup, no longer really functioned as prime minister. The *mwami*, who had withdrawn to the friendlier mountains of Switzerland, could not manage conflict by remote control. Radical Tutsi led a campaign against the Biha regime, which they labelled a Bezi clique. In March 1966, the *mwami* designated his 19-year-old son and heir apparent, Charles Ndizeye, to exercise his powers on the spot, but these were now rapidly ebbing.

In July 1966, Prince Charles announced his imminent succession to the throne; in September, he was crowned as Ntare V. Although 100000 attended his coronation, the new *mwami* was too young to have mastered the arts of political intrigue and manoeuvre. Yet his effort to do so rapidly brought him into fatal conflict with the Tutsi politicians. In November 1966, while he was on a state visit to Kinshasa, the monarchy was abolished.

Captain Michel Micombero, who had led the counterattack against the Hutu coup participants in October 1965, had been named prime minister in July 1966; his cabinet, like the abolition of the monarchy, represented a major turning point in Burundi's history. A new generation came to power, partly recruited from the army officer corps. Factional conflict continued to supply the inner dynamic of Burundi politics in the post-monarchy years, but now revolved around new foci. Micombero himself was representative of the new generation; of mixed Tutsi–Hima origins, and a family which did not rank highly in traditional prestige, he was far removed from the Bezi–Batare groupings of old. Regional affiliations, however, did play a growing role; Micombero and a number of his closest collaborators came from the Bururi district in southern Burundi. Tensions rose to the surface in 1969, when a number of Hutu intellectuals were killed, and again in 1971, when a number of officers from central Burundi were tried for plotting.

The next great watershed in Burundi politics was the holocaust of 1972, which took the lives of roughly 5 per cent of the population. On April 1972, Hutu attacks occurred simultaneously in three places – in Bujumbura, on the eastern border, and on the southern lakeshore, where really serious assaults occurred, with perhaps 2000 Tutsi murdered. The reaction was not long in coming, with the army coordinating the carnage carried out by armed Tutsi gangs of Rwagasore Revolutionary Youth. Educated Hutu were a particular target, as the architects of this slaughter were clearly determined to exclude forever a re-enactment of the Rwanda revolution. In such circumstances, the size of the death toll becomes a grisly secret of history; serious estimates run as high as 200000. Another victim was the deposed *mwami*, who returned from exile in March 1972; he was murdered by a radical Tutsi politician when the Hutu attack began.

When the weeks of terror had run their course, Micombero installed Nyamoya again as prime minister, in an effort to at least restore harmony among Tutsi factions. In 1974, Micombero dismissed Nyamoya, and the Bururi group returned to power. In November 1976, the Micombero era came to an end, with a military coup led by Colonel Jean-Baptiste Bagaza, a Tutsi related to the ousted president.

The lines of ethnic hegemony had hardened in Burundi, and it was difficult to see how the system could transcend the inherent limitations of a legitimacy limited to 15 per cent of the population. The ruling class was now caught in a gigantic trap. Many of its élite were deeply imbued with egalitarian, even revolutionary political values, and strongly rejected the older pattern of *ganwa* domination and court intrigue. Yet the threat of the servile insurrection, with the essentially contemporary idea of martyred Hutuhood, loomed as an omnipresent menace. At the moment of crisis, as in 1972, the fears and emotions tied to communal survival overcame rational thought and humane conviction, leaving the path clear for the most ruthless guardians of the ethnocratic order to pursue their macabre tasks.

ECONOMIC CHANGE

The period 1945–57 was one of extremely rapid economic growth in the Congo, whose major exports enjoyed buoyant markets. The most important single commodity was copper, accounting for from 50 to 60 per cent of the total value of minerals. Wartime production was about 150000 tons; this rose slowly to 250000 tons by the end of the colonial period. Of roughly equivalent importance, with exports during the 1950s worth $50–$60 million, were cobalt, diamonds, and tin, with gold and manganese not far behind. The Congo has been the world's largest producer of cobalt and industrial diamonds. Agricultural output also surged; in the best years in the 1950s, its total value came close to that of the mineral sector. The most important crops were cotton, palm-oil and coffee. Cotton, which peaked at 65300 tons in 1959, was grown, not wholly willingly, by peasant cultivators. Palm-oil was both produced on plantations and collected by peasant outgrowers, the latter system being particularly prevalent in Bandundu (Kwilu). Coffee became a major crop only after the Second World War, developing extremely rapidly during the price boom of the 1950s to reach 56541 tons in 1959.

The speed and turmoil of independence in the Congo had far-reaching economic consequences. Investment had ceased by 1958, to be replaced by a net capital outflow of $46 million in 1959. The capitalist sector endeavoured, as a holding operation, to maintain the use of existing installations, but not to expand until about 1967. Its expatriate staff, unlike those of the state, generally remained at their posts, so there was much less dislocation than in the public sector. Peasant agriculture was particularly hard hit, as the marketing infrastructure eroded, prices were unfavourable, and the coercive state apparatus which had been the major factor in cotton production could no longer enforce its cultivation; agriculture fell from 40 to 25 per cent of total GNP from 1958–66.

State finances were badly disrupted; indeed, in 1961 the government functioned without any budget at all. Smuggling and tax evasion deprived the state of much of its revenue; however, the bureaucratic establishment was expanded, and its remuneration increased. The scale of inflationary pressure is measured by an increase in money supply from an index of 100 in 1960 to 355 at the end of 1964, as compared with a decline in the volume of total production from 100 to 76. The Congo franc had declined to one tenth of its 1960 value at the time of the major currency reform of 1967. The budgetary deficit reached 30 billion Congo francs in 1965 ($170000000 at the official rate).

The New Regime of President Mobutu removed the obstacle of insecurity by 1967, which permitted renewed operation of extant installations and plantations throughout the country. The 1967 devaluation gave a five-year respite from inflation, and a period of favourable export prices plus a recovery of production to pre-independence levels produced buoyant exchange holdings; by 1970 Zaire was able to boast that it was one of the rare Third World countries whose currency was solid enough to be used in International Monetary Fund lending. State revenues surged from a low of $16600000 in 1962 to $250100000 in 1968, as public finances were brought for a time under relative control.

However, Mobutu's patrimonial politics came to require large outlays through a poorly controlled presidential account. By 1974, $100 million of just over $1 billion of government expenditures went officially through the presidency, and the real amount was in fact significantly higher. Linked to the large-scale distribution of public funds to reward fidelity was the institutionalisation of corruption; by one estimate, some 60 per cent of the 1971 state revenue was diverted to purposes other than those officially stated.[1] A period of record copper prices from 1972 till April 1974 produced a short-lived bonanza in public revenues, which in turn triggered a surge of expenditures; public outlays rose from $548.3 million in 1972 to $1183.8 million in 1974. Heavy external borrowing occurred in the early 1970s to finance an ambitious programme of development, and led to an external debt of more than $2 billion by 1975, placing the country on the brink of international bankruptcy.

Economic nationalism was a recurrent theme under the New Regime, beginning in 1966 with a decisive confrontation with the most powerful enterprise of the country, UMHK. Zaire insisted that UMHK be reconstituted as a Zairean corporation, rather than

[1] Jean-Philippe Peemans, 'The social and economic development of Zaire since independence: an historical outline', *African Affairs*, April 1975, **74**, no. 295, 162.

continuing as a Brussels-domiciled enterprise. With negotiations at an impasse, Mobutu suddenly published an ordinance on 1 January 1967 nationalising the Zairean-based installations of the company. Although rumours circulated for a time that Mobutu intended to bring in Japanese or French interests to manage the nationalised copper installations, a compromise very favourable to the former owners was soon arrived at. Another subsidiary of the Société Générale (the parent company of UMHK), the Société Générale des Minerais, was assigned management rights over the Zairean enterprise, which eventually was named the Générale des Carrières et des Mines (GECAMINES); by way of compensation, for 15 years it was to receive 6 per cent of gross sales, estimated to yield between $180 million and $360 million, depending on the prices. The net UMHK investment of external capital had been $200 million, nearly all of which had been completed by the 1920s. From 1950–66, UMHK profits totalled nearly $1 billion, of which roughly $320 million had been reinvested.[1]

The zenith of economic nationalism was the 1973–5 period. On 30 November 1973, the president announced a sweeping set of measures, prescribing the Zaireanisation of commerce, plantations, and many small and medium enterprises. The more attractive concerns wound up reserved to the top echelon of politicians and army officers, often acting through wives or relatives. Vast disruption of the commercial sector followed, as the Zairean *acquéreurs* generally lacked commercial experience, access to credit, and contacts with suppliers. Many were content to strip the assets of their businesses. The 30 November measures soon became intensely unpopular, and *acquéreur* a social epithet, the new owners being blamed for shortages and price rises.

At the end of 1974, Mobutu tried to defuse the rising resentment by a 'radicalisation of the revolution'. Party officials were told to abandon their businesses, and to repatriate their foreign bank accounts. The larger Zaireanised enterprises were placed under state control, along with a second wave of businesses that had not been covered by the measures of 30 November 1973. Radicalisation failed in its turn; the draconian measures were very unevenly applied and the state-directed reorganisation of large Zaireanised enterprises could not halt the economic haemorrhage. In March 1976, Zaireanisation was, for the moment, abandoned,

[1] *Unité* (Brussels), February–March 1970.

and former owners promised the 'retrocession' of their businesses.

Another major determinant of economic policy, joined to economic nationalism, was Mobutu's expansive vision of Zaire's manifest destiny: a mission of leadership in Africa, an example of what a new African state could achieve in spectacular development. Realisation of these ambitions necessitated a rapid increase in government resources. In the short run, this could only be accomplished by accelerating the exploitation of Zaire's treasure trove of minerals.

A generous investment code was promulgated in 1969. The major lure was the huge deposits of copper and allied metals in Shaba, previously held in reserve by UMHK. After vigorous competition among assorted international interests, the largest copper deposit was leased to a predominantly Anglo-American consortium, the Société Minière de Tenke Fungurumé (SMTF), headed by AMOCO Mines and Charter Consolidated (28 per cent each). A smaller copper concession was granted to a Japanese consortium, SODIMIZA. Other new investments included a Goodyear tyre factory and General Motors assembly plant in Kinshasa, a Continental Grain flour-mill in Matadi, and Gulf Oil development of offshore oil deposits, which began production in 1975.

A tremendous energy and transportation infrastructure was required to underpin these developments. Old Belgian plans to tap the enormous hydroelectric potential of the lower Zaire River, dating from 1910, were finally put into operation; Inga, phase I, was begun in 1966, and completed in 1968. By 1972, work had begun on Inga II, which would raise capacity to 1.3 million kilowatt hours (about half the capacity of Cabora Bassa); ultimate potential was 30 million kilowatt hours. By 1973, work had begun on the gigantic direct transmission line from Inga to Shaba, whose costs would exceed $400 000 000, with plans to complete the rail links from the copper mines to the sea.

By the early 1970s, the full implications of this strategy were becoming manifest. Dependency on copper was overwhelming; GECAMINES alone contributed 50 per cent of the state revenue, and two-thirds of the foreign exchange. Sharply deteriorating terms of trade for peasant producers demoralised the villages. Cotton output dropped from 63 000 tons in 1959 to an average of about 20000 tons in the early 1970s. By 1976, palm-oil exports were less than one quarter the pre-independence figure. By 1975, imports of the three major cereals, maize, rice and wheat, rose from 47000 tons in 1959 to an estimated 325000 tons by 1975.

For Rwanda and Burundi, the narrow limits set by geographic isolation from markets, high population densities, slight apparent mineral endowments, absence of industry, and shortage of land, ruled out the spectacular ambitions of Zaire. But with nothing but the rural sector to nurture, both accorded agriculture a higher priority, and avoided the pattern of rural deterioration which characterised Zaire.

Coffee, seriously promoted since the Second World War, averaged an annual production of about 10000 tons in both Rwanda and Burundi by the late 1950s. After a brief drop in production immediately after independence, output grew to an average annual level of 20000 tons each in the early 1970s. In 1975, this represented 90 per cent of Burundi's exports, compared to 72 per cent for Rwanda; the difference lay in the 2000 tons of tin which Rwanda exported yearly.

The Malthusian equation was an ominous preoccupation for both countries. Lethal famines in 1928 and 1943 demonstrated the precariousness of the equilibrium between man and the land. In Rwanda, by 1968 it was estimated that only 30 per cent of the cultivable land was fallow, with population projections suggesting that none would remain by 1980. The land shortage placed absolute limits on acreage which could be devoted to export crops; further pressure was exerted by the one million cattle in the two countries. No source of non-agricultural employment was in prospect for more than a fraction of the peasants. In the face of these austere circumstances, the post-independence economic performance of both countries was surprisingly good.

SOCIAL AND CULTURAL CHANGE

The period under review brought momentous transformations in the structure of society, and important ones in the cultural domain. We are doubtless too close to these changes to appreciate their full significance, particularly in the cultural domain. One important aspect of change, the crystallisation of new and enlarged patterns of ethnic self-awareness, has been considered in previous sections. We will focus here particularly upon urbanis-ation, inequality, and culture. In Zaire, the institutionalisation of a large urban sector stands out as a central contemporary trend. In 1940 Léopoldville, the largest city in Belgian Africa, had only 46 884 inhabitants; by 1975, there were an estimated two million. Kananga, Mbuji-Mayi, Bukavu and Mbandaka, with the 1970 census listed as having 429 000, 256 000, 135 000, and 108 000 inhabitants respectively, were in 1940, tiny towns of 10 000 or less.

The urban explosion began with the Second World War, and then slowly gathered force in the post-war years. Independence brought years of extraordinary growth, triggered by the end of controls on settlement, the rapid extension of the educational system from the 1950s, and the sharp decline in rural well-being after 1960. The 1970 census showed 15 per cent of the population living in 11 cities with populations of over 100 000. Although urbanisation is of slight impact in Rwanda and Burundi, even here the capital cities swiftly grew: Kigali from 5000 in 1962 to approximately 60 000 by 1975, and Bujumbura from 8000 in 1940 to about 130 000 in 1975.

The character of urban life had altered as a function of this growth. In 1940, the central parts of the towns were exclusively European, with African townships of modest dimensions on the periphery; where, as in the Copperbelt, large employers predomi-nated, company compounds for worker families, with their ordered paternalism, were common. By 1975, vast squatter communities girdled all the large towns. The former European quarter now also housed the top ranks of the public service, leading political figures and some successful African traders, as well as expatriates. Until 1957, unemployment was a marginal phenomenon in towns; those without jobs were simply returned to their home communities, and only a very small fraction were urban born. A modest recession in the western economies in 1957 brought retrenchment to the colony, including significant unemployment, which thereafter became a central feature of urban life. With it developed a vast and poorly measured sector of what became known as 'informal employment': hawking, providing small services, or performing domestic duties at the home of a somewhat more prosperous relative.

There were also rapidly changing patterns of stratification. In Zaire, before 1960 stratification had been above all racial. There was an absolute ceiling for Africans in the public service, and a *de facto* one in private bureaucracies. Restrictions on property ownership, access to credit, and entry to more profitable lines of sale made African success in commerce almost impossible. Social divisions among Africans were above all marked by prestige, as suggested by the very term *évolué*, which came into currency by 1940 to denote an educated African performing a white-collar function. As the word *évolué* suggests, social status was measured by European standards. An African worthy of esteem had to demonstrate his proximity to the domain of 'civilisation'. Education in the mission schools was certainly an indispensable prerequisite; however, more subtle criteria than the mere number of years in school were involved. 'Civilisation', operationally defined, meant European culture, values and behavioural mores. The status of *évolué* was conferred, in intangible ways, by the judgement of an informal jury of missionaries, administrators and other notables.

With independence, the top social category, the European population, fell sharply from its peak of 110000 in 1959, then stabilised at between 30000 and 40000. A highly remunerated group (except for the missionaries), their life style was influential in establishing the level of aspiration and expectation for the new African political–administrative class which, for the first time, commanded an income which made possible the attainment of these dreams. In the years after independence swift rise within the ranks of the élite depended on access to the main avenues of social mobility. Politics, the principal though newest avenue, drew its recruits mainly from the 25 to 35 age-group, and mainly from those employed in the bureaucracy of both the public and private sectors. This group had varying levels of secondary education (university graduates were not yet present in force). The point of entry was electoral office, or clientage ties with one who had achieved political success. The great year of recruitment was 1960; thereafter, access was more difficult, and criteria changed. Additional new opportunities opened under the New Regime, both through the apparatus of the party and technocracy.

The 10000 vacancies created at the top of the administration by the 1960 flight of Belgian functionaries provided a massive once and for all promotion opportunity for those poised just below. On the whole, the beneficiaries came from the category of relatively senior clerks who could lay plausible claim to these offices. Continued expansion of the administration made absorption of the university graduates on attractive conditions easily assured until the early 1970s. Private bureaucracies were much slower to open their managerial posts to Africans: GECAMINES, which continued to operate like a private firm after its ostensible nationalisation in 1967, in 1974 still had 1362 expatriates (concentrated in the technical domain), and 1135 Africans (holding the administrative posts).

For many, administrative and political income provided the starting capital which could be enlarged by extramural commercial activity, often managed by a member of the family. Especially profitable were urban undertakings which did not require full-time management: rental property, taxis, trucking, beverage sales. In the early 1960s, the imposition of import controls made the traffic in import licences extremely profitable, and brought about the emergence of a number of prosperous, politically connected, national import–export firms. The 1973 Zaireanisation edict had a powerful impact in enlarging the mercantile underpinnings of the politico-administrative class. It should be noted that very few of the new African businessmen emerged from the truncated, impoverished, largely illiterate pre-1960 Zairean trading community.

Beginning in 1940, the size of the urban labour force expanded quickly then stabilised. The number of wage-earners rose from 536000 in 1940 to 962000 in 1950; in 1972, the figure had fallen slightly to 905000. The colonial administration sought social peace after the Second World War through rising real wages, which tripled during the 1950–8 period. This in turn induced the large employers to mechanise their operations; GECAMINES in 1975 produced 450000 tons of copper with the same labour force which had turned out less than 180000 in 1950. Independence produced a short-lived further surge in real wages, which peaked in 1961 for those holding permanent wage employment. Inflation then swiftly eroded and nullified these gains; by 1965, real wages were back to the 1958 level. An effective price-stabilisation programme in 1967 aimed at both the external rates of exchange and internal price-levels. This and the introduction of a new currency permitted a halt to inflation and a brief recovery of wage levels. However, by 1972, deterioration had set in once again. The

International Labour Organisation reported that between 1964 and 1975 the real minimum wage (the effective remuneration level for the majority of workers) fell by 53 per cent.[1]

The rural sector experienced a comparable cycle. After the harsh phase of the *effort de guerre*, the 1950s saw a real improvement in rural well-being. Coercion, long the pillar of the colonial agricultural policy, slackened, and prices paid to producers rose. Schools, dispensaries, and clean water began to become available in the villages. The misfortunes after 1960 were particularly detrimental to the rural sector; by 1975, real prices paid to farmers for major crops such as cotton, coffee and palm fruits ranged from a quarter to a third of the 1960 level.

Thus a profound social malaise gripped the country. Though contained within the authoritarian structures of the state, periodic outbursts, such as the 1964–5 rebellions, or the wave of wildcat strikes in 1976, were symptomatic of the discontents generated by the contrast between the visible wealth of the administrative–political élite and the expatriate community, and the deteriorating situation of the mass of the populace. At the same time, a large element of fluidity remained in the emergent social stratification. The expanding educational system sustained the hope of mobility for those at the bottom, while those at the top enjoyed the momentary use of wealth rather than secure entrenchment as a propertied class.

The issues of stratification and inequality were differently posed in Rwanda and Burundi, and pivoted largely around the relationships between the two ethnic communities, Tutsi and Hutu. The impact of the first decades of colonial rule, German and Belgian, had been to generalise and entrench Tutsi socio-political hegemony. Early access to education had been largely restricted to Tutsi. The premise of inequality became administrative ideology through a doctrine of the natural superiority of the Tutsi ruling élite which was shared by the colonial administration and Tutsi leaders. A crucial institution of Tutsi domination, at the socio-economic level, was the widespread device of cattle clientage. A patron, generally Tutsi, would provide one or more cows to a client, normally a Hutu, in return for social and economic services. Historically, the cattle contract had developed

---

[1] Susumu Watanabe, 'Minimum wages in developing countries: myth and reality', *International Labour Review*, May–June 1976, **113**, no. 3, 353.

in several different forms. In central Rwanda, in the nineteenth and twentieth centuries, it had become generalised in a form (*ubuhake*) which entailed a caste-like relationship. In Burundi, the most widespread form of clientage, *ubugabire*, provided a wider range of social choice for the client. In the post-war years, it became an article of faith that abolition of cattle clientage was an absolute prerequisite of social change and political development. In 1954–5, the almost exclusively Tutsi kingdom councils in Rwanda and Burundi, with some prodding by the colonial administration, legally abolished cattle clientage. It later proved that this reform, which had appeared so critical in the 1950s, was simply overtaken by events. The issue of Tutsi–Hutu relationships, as independence approached, was translated to the political realm. The major avenue of social mobility after 1962 was the limited armature of the state itself – its administration, educational system and army. But this was too narrow a base to support a system of stratification comparable to that of Zaire.

The sphere of cultural change is the most difficult realm of all to understand. The mechanisms of transmission of western material culture are massive, yet the emergent cultural synthesis did not amount to 'acculturation', or the replacement of the historical cultural heritage by traits and values of western derivation. The school system, despite efforts to reform it, remained to a large degree western in form and content. The urban social environment provided a very different setting from the rural community within which the indigenous cultural heritage was formed. The transistor radio, which became available in the 1960s, brought a large sector of both urban and rural society within the reach of a world-wide communications system. Of particular importance was the role of the Christian Church. In all three countries, the Catholic Church in particular had been strongly implanted. Zaire already had 500 African priests by 1960, and by 1975 there were two dozen Zairean bishops, and one Cardinal. In 1968, the Catholic Church claimed the membership of 71 per cent of the Burundi population, and 55 per cent in Rwanda. A measure of the social influence of the church lay in its periodic political conflicts with the secular authorities in Zaire, beginning in 1971. The church, at that juncture, was the major social institution which lay outside the orbit of the state; the assaults upon it appear to have merely strengthened its attraction as an alternative to the existing socio-political order. Protestant churches were less potent, but claimed significant followings. After 1960, their number was increased by official recognition of African separatist churches, especially the Kimbanguists, rigorously suppressed by the colonial authorities as a political threat. Following independence, in Zaire the Kimbanguist church spread far beyond its initial Kongo cultural zone, especially in Kasai. In 1968 it was admitted to membership of the World Council of Churches.

Language was a particularly important arena and sensitive indicator of cultural change. In Zaire, the salient trend was towards the crystallisation of a multilingual society. The major regional languages, particularly Lingala and Swahili, spread rapidly during our period. Although no precise figures are available, it is safe to assert that, by the end of it, only the most isolated social categories of Zairean society (the elderly, rural women, young children) were not at least bilingual. In Rwanda and Burundi, the existence of Kinyarwanda and Kirundi as universally known indigenous languages made less necessary the diffusion of Swahili as the vehicular language, although the latter played an important role in Bujumbura. We may thus see symbolically enacted on the linguistic battlefield the drama of cultural change. The diffusion of regional languages represented the emergence of new forms of cultural synthesis, often urban-centred. These were also manifested in such domains as music and dance which formed an important part of urban leisure activities, or the syncretic forms of urban popular art. At the same time, the impact of western culture continued in the linguistic as well as other domains through the continuing spread of French.

EDUCATIONAL DEVELOPMENT

A central plank in the platform of post-war colonial reform was the serious commitment, for the first time, to a broad-based educational system. The educational pyramid was, however, to be constructed gradually, floor by floor. Accordingly, a vast primary network was established in the 1950s, which by the year before Zairean independence enrolled 70 per cent of the 6 to 11 age cohort. No less than 64 per cent were in the first two grades, and less than 3 per cent in the sixth grade. Secondary and higher education was much slower to develop. In 1959, only 29 000 pupils (less than 1000 girls) were in Zairean secondary institutions, with a mere 136 in the final-year graduating class. The foundation of the first universities was the occasion for bitter struggle within the inner walls of the colonial structure. The Catholic Church forced the issue in the early 1950s, and the administration reluctantly authorised the establishment of Lovanium University in Léopoldville in 1954. Anti-clerical forces had to be satisfied with the establishment of a second, state, university in Elisabethville in 1956. The pace of educational advance in Ruanda-Urundi was partly influenced by pressure from the United Nations. The first UN Visiting Mission in 1948, noting 'the concept of slowness which is one of [the] dominant characteristics of education in the territory',[1] was critical of the absence not only of any access to university training, but even of secondary schools. Though secondary schools were opened in the 1950s, it was only in 1963 (Rwanda) and 1964 (Burundi) that universities were founded, in both cases with the collaboration of the Catholic Church.

In the post-war years, strong pressure from the rapidly growing Belgian community forced the colonial administration to establish a state network of secular secondary schools, initially reserved for European children. The spillover of the *guerre scolaire* in Belgium (1954–8) led to the substantial expansion of a state network, now open to some Africans. Popular pressures for greater opportunities, as well as ideological conviction, led successive post-independence regimes to accord top priority to the expansion of education. Expenditures rose rapidly in this field, reaching 30 per cent of the Zaire national budget by 1969. In 1960, only 136 children completed their secondary schooling; in 1975 20 000 did so. That same year, a university which had awarded only 14 diplomas to Zaireans in 1960, awarded nearly 2000 degrees. To the two original campuses were added a Protestant university in Kisangani in 1963, and an array of specialised post-secondary institutes, sponsored by various international agencies.

A growing sense, in Zaire, that the state had inadequate control over its higher educational system led to a sudden and dramatic university reform in 1971, by which all units were merged into a single national university. The reform was accompanied by the

[1] United Nations Trusteeship Council, Fourth Session, supplement no. 2. United Nations Visiting Mission to East Africa, *Report on Ruanda-Urundi and related documents*, September 1950, 12.

nomination of Zairean university administrators to occupy the command positions on all the campuses; rationalisation and economy were to be achieved by regrouping each specialisation on a single campus. Though the goal of national direction and control was largely achieved, the haste and improvisation of the implementation brought serious dislocations.

In December 1974, Mobutu announced that the state would take over the Catholic and Protestant secondary and primary systems as well; though by this time the religious networks enrolled fewer students than the state schools, they were, on the whole, better staffed, directed and funded. Particularly at the secondary level, the Catholic schools were far superior to those of the state, as measured by the much greater percentage of graduates who passed the national state examination. This reform, at least in the short run, exceeded the capacities of the state to apply, and the Catholic and Protestant Churches were invited to resume operation of their networks in 1977.

INTERNATIONAL RELATIONS

The scale and resources of Zaire necessarily predestined it for a major role on the African stage and in world politics. Just as certainly the tiny size and poverty of Rwanda and Burundi limited their roles to virtual invisibility. Once independence became a familiar fact, Belgium became by far the most important diplomatic partner for both Rwanda and Burundi, and the source of most of their technical assistance, while the United States purchased most of their coffee. Periodic overtures came from France to incorporate them within the world of *francophonie*. Moments of sharp ethnic tension in either state almost necessarily translated into difficult relations with the other, as in 1963 or 1972. After 1966, both had close relations with Zaire, except for a period of rupture with Rwanda in 1968–9 created by Rwandan refusal to extradite mercenary mutineers from Zaire who took refuge in the country.

With the New Regime, Zaire moved to assert itself as actor in, rather than as mere object of, international politics. Other African leaders, exhausted and embarrassed by the endless convolutions of the 'Congo crisis', were prepared to accept Mobutu, despite reservations held by some deriving from his intimate American associations, and his suspected involvement in the decisions which sealed Lumumba's fate. Full entry of Zaire into the African family was symbolised by the holding in Kinshasa of the 1967 Organisation of African Unity summit conference. From this point forward, Mobutu had sufficiently consolidated his domestic position to move from the modest goal of full acceptance to a restless quest for African leadership. In 1970, he paid state visits to ten African states, and in 1972 attracted eight African heads of state to his party conference. 1973 was the high water mark; Mobutu spent no less than 150 days outside Zaire, including visits to 14 African states (and 12 others). In January 1973 he paid a spectacular state visit to China, returning with a pledge of $100000000 as aid for rural development. On 4 October 1973, he made a major address at the United Nations, highlighted by a surprise announcement of a rupture with Israel two days before the Yom Kippur war. Thereafter, some major reverses deflated the aspirations to African leadership of the New Regime. The rapid economic deterioration which became evident in 1974 made reconciliation with western creditor powers imperative. The civil war in Angola was disastrous for Zaire, which was deeply committed to the defeat of the MPLA. In September 1975, several Zairean battalions were operating inside Angola jointly with the FNLA, which was long dependent on Zairean support. The unforeseen entry of Cuban army units into the fighting in November quickly led to disaster for the Zairean and FNLA units. The simultaneous South African intervention in southern Angola placed Zaire in an impossibly exposed role, humiliated by defeat, and disgraced in Africa by complicity with apartheid and imperialism. Although the struggle against the MPLA was officially abandoned in February 1976, distrust between Angola and Zaire remained profound.

The two most important extra-African partners of Zaire between 1960 and 1975 were Belgium and the United States. Relations with Belgium followed a widely oscillating curve, with moments of fervent cordiality alternating with periods of bitter recriminations and even rupture. A Treaty of Friendship concluded just prior to independence was denounced two weeks later by a Zairean government outraged by the unsolicited intervention of Belgian troops, and the military and technical assistance rendered by Belgium to the secessionist state of Katanga. The removal of the Lumumba government on 5 September 1960 led to resumption of active ties between Kinshasa and Brussels, and by 1963 to very close relationships. Belgian military aid was critical in repulsing the 1964–5 rebellions. However, the UMHK nationalisation controversy of 1966–7 brought a new cycle of crisis. By 1970, restored intimacy was symbolised by a spectacular royal visit by King Baudouin. The 'radicalisation' period of 1973–5 brought renewed crisis; by 1975 financial disaster made warmer relations with Belgium again indispensable.

Although links with the United States were less dense and multiplex than those with Belgium, America served as international patron throughout most of the 1960–75 period, usually acting in concert with Belgium. Zairean independence coincided with a peak in global interventionism and Cold War preoccupation in United States foreign policy. Exaggerated fears of a 'Soviet take-over' drew the US deeply into Zairean politics in 1960, both directly in covert and diplomatic support for the removal of Lumumba, and indirectly through its substantial (though not determinant) influence in the United Nations operation in Zaire. Successive Zairean governments had intimate political ties with the United States. However, as President Mobutu became more self-confident, susceptibility to direct American influence diminished, giving way to a frigid period in 1974–5, culminating in allegations of American complicity in a confused conspiracy to eliminate Mobutu in June 1975. Common opposition to the MPLA in Angola and the exigencies of the economic crisis restored close relations.

Relations with the Soviet Union were predominantly hostile. The USSR made a short-lived bid at major military support to the Lumumba regime in late August 1960, but at that time – in contrast to the Angolan situation in 1975 – the USSR lacked the logistical capability to intervene swiftly and effectively. With the overthrow of Lumumba, Soviet diplomats were expelled. The USSR viewed Zaire as an American client state; Zaire accused the Soviet Union of meddling on successive occasions (1964 rebellions, 1971 student crisis at Lovanium University, Soviet–Cuban backing of MPLA in 1975, the Katanga gendarme invasions of 1977 and 1978). China, although viewed as a dangerous source of subversion in the early 1960s, became a warm friend a decade later with major state visits to Peking by Mobutu in January 1973 and December 1974. In early 1975, China was in many respects Zaire's closest ally, a remarkable episode (even if short-lived) which takes us conveniently back to our starting point: the unbelievable transformation of Central Africa in 35 short years. In 1940, Zaire, Rwanda and Burundi were so firmly embedded in the colonial domain that not even the most visionary prophet could have imagined what lay beyond.

CHAPTER 15

PORTUGUESE-SPEAKING AFRICA
With an appendix on Equatorial Guinea

Although modelled with local variations on the ideas and structures of Italian Fascism, and later stiffened by an admiration for German National-Socialism, Portugal's Estado Novo was constrained to neutrality during the Second World War. Geographical realities allowed no decisive preference for the Axis powers before the great turning points of 1942: unlike Franco's Spain, Salazar's Portugal sent no troops to aid the Germans on its eastern front. After those turning points the merest common sense ensured that Portugal's neutrality should be such as to prove acceptable to the western allies.

Portugal's colonies remained intact, but the overall influence of the World War, though less of a nexus of change than it proved elsewhere in colonial Africa, can now be measured as one of various and in some ways profound effect. On the side of the colonised, this influence constituted a formative prelude to the beginning of anti-colonial protest in modern forms; on that of the colonisers, it spurred the system to greater and more insistent exploitation of natural resources and African labour. Generally, the colonial governors anticipated hard times from interruptions to maritime transport. Arguing the economic dangers that lay ahead, the Governor-General of Angola, for example, told his council during its session of 9–14 September 1939 that 'he wished to see the installation of a war economy'. In fact, so far as most exports were concerned, the hard years were 1941–2, after which there came a recovery and expansion. Sisal exports from Angola fell by half between 1940 and 1941, barely improved in 1942, but more than doubled in 1943 and rose again in 1944. Though statistics were to remain gravely deficient in this sector as in others, it seems clear that these colonised peoples had to provide a productive 'war effort' by way of additional forced labour and other coercions, such as was imposed elsewhere, and especially in the Belgian Congo and French West Africa.

Steady expansion of the colonial economy began after 1945. This quickened through the 1950s and again later; but the future of Portuguese control was beginning by the early 1960s to be challenged by movements of African nationalism. So that although colonial economic expansion makes after 1945 a continuity except in Guiné and the islands, the whole period of 30 years can best be understood by dividing it into two phases, respectively from 1945 to 1960, and onwards from 1961: before and after, that is, the rise of effective movements of African contestation. The origins of these movements belong to the 1950s, even to the late 1940s; their action on the ground, and the great dramas to which it led, belong to the second phase.

The human arena of these events can be outlined by reference to the decennial census of 1950. Its findings were really little more than rough estimates, except in the counting of whites and assimilated non-whites, but show at least the broad composition of the peoples who were soon to become involved in long and large upheavals. Returns for Angola gave 4 036 687 Africans (with a slight excess of females), 78 826 'non-natives' (equivalent to whites), and 30 089 assimilados (or non-whites admitted to the status of 'civilised persons'). Those for Mozambique showed 5 732 317 Africans (again with a small excess of females), 91 954 'non-natives' (as well as 1613 listed as 'yellow' and 12 630 as 'Indians'), and 4349 assimilados. Guiné was thought to have some 503 970 Africans, together with 2263 whites, 6064 assimilados (of whom 4568 were listed as mestiços, and no doubt included a proportion of persons of Cape Verdean origin), and 11 'Indians'. The Cape Verde archipelago had at least 150 000 people, all of whom were formally outside the categories of the indígenato, although, for most of them, this was a narrow privilege within the system:[1] there were also some 4000 whites. São Tomé and

---

[1] In a survey of 1977 devoted to the history of Cape Verdean emigration, and containing much otherwise unanalysed statistical material, António Carreira finds that the term 'forced emigration' should be applied to the 73 056 Cape Verdeans listed in official records as having gone to work in São Tomé, Principe, Angola and Mozambique in the period 1941–70. He points out that these emigrants were, in practice, subjected to administrative coercions little different from the contract-labour system of the indígenato, whether in regard to wage-payment or other conditions of life and work. He doubts if the labour reforms of 1962, notably those of the Codigo de Trabalho Rural of 27 April of that year, could in any case be applied, in practice, by officials long accustomed to the 'deleterious and vitiated' systems that the Code was supposed to displace. A. Carreira, Migrações nas Ilhas de Cabo Verde (Lisbon, 1977), 216, 224, 235, 239.

Principe seem to have had about 60000 people, again including a few thousand whites; most of these were on São Tomé, much the larger island of the pair, while some 23000 were migrant 'contract workers' from Angola, Mozambique and the Cape Verdes. Portugal also possessed a couple of hectares at Whydah in Dahomey (now Bénin), the site of an old trading fort with a commandant and assistant, until shortly after the independence of that country in 1960.

The total number of Africans was thus of the order of ten and a half millions. This was probably an underestimate, but in any case the 1960 census was to show only a small increase on these numbers, a point that may of course be explained either by a merely arithmetical adjustment of 'traditional' census findings or by a very slow rate of natural increase. The 1970 census figures are of small value, given that large areas of all these mainland territories were debarred by this time to Portuguese enquiry, while very large numbers of rural people had fled into peripheral countries. Enumeration in the Cape Verde archipelago in 1970 could be less approximate since no fighting was in progress there, and gave a total population of 272000 or about 100000 more than in 1950. It may be noted in this context that whereas the Cape Verdean population appears to have suffered grievously in numbers from drought-induced famine during 1942–3 and 1947–9 – as with much else in Cape Verdean history, the facts remain to be established – no such famine struck again on any serious scale until 1969. Other useful points emerge from the census return. Surprisingly, in view of later settlement policies, there were more whites in Mozambique than in Angola; this situation would be rapidly reversed after 1950, and by 1975 the number of whites in Angola (counting only civilians) would be at least a third more than the number in Mozambique. Altogether, in the three mainland colonies where the status of *indígena* was applied to all not accepted as Portuguese, there were about 40000 *assimilados*, or considerably less than one half of one per cent of the indigenous population. Of this tiny percentage, a large proportion was *mestiço* (of mixed parentage originating from white male alliances with non-white females); and one may safely conclude that the number of assimilated Africans of 'unmixed' origin was a good deal less than one quarter of one per cent. Though statistics are lacking, this probably rose towards one per cent in Angola and Mozambique by about 1965, while an unknown but still small number of *indígenas* were by this time living as *assimilados* without being registered as such. Generally, these proportions portray the factual realities of Portuguese assimilation, and help to explain the continuing shallowness of Portuguese cultural impact even after administrative occupation was made complete in the 1930s.

COLONIAL CONTINUITY AND EXPANSION, 1945–60

In evaluating the record on the Portuguese side a large allowance has to be made for the propaganda of the Estado Novo, reflecting as this did the deep provincial isolation within which the regime had formed and contained its spokesmen. As late as 1967, when all three mainland territories were engulfed in widespread warfare, and the proportion of assimilated Africans was certainly no larger than one per cent, it would remain possible for Salazar's Foreign Minister, Franco Nogueira, to claim that Portugal 'alone' had 'practised the principle of multi-racialism, which all now consider the most perfect and daring expression of human brotherhood and sociological progress', so that 'our African provinces are more developed, more progressive in every respect, than any recently independent territory in Africa south of the Sahara, without exception'.[1]

Less unrealistic views were aired at home; and these confirmed the essential continuity of Portuguese colonial policy from the time of Norton de Matos's second governorship of Angola (1921–4) through the purely military dictatorship of the late 1920s and the practice of the Estado Novo after 1932. The essence of this continuity was well defined by Marcello Caetano, Salazar's eventual successor, when a professor of the University of Lisbon. During a series of lectures early in the 1950s, Caetano explained that

the blacks of Africa are to be governed and organised by Europeans, but are indispensable as the latters' auxiliaries... The Africans are themselves incapable of developing the territories they have lived in for millennia: they have made no useful inventions, discovered no profitable technology, conquered nothing that counts in the evolution of humanity, nothing in the fields of culture and technology to be compared with the achievements of Europeans or even of

[1] F. Nogueira, *The Third World* (London, 1967), 154–5.

Asiatics. The blacks of Africa are thus to be treated as productive elements organised or to be organised in an economy directed by whites... [1]

To which J. M. da Silva Cunha, for long the regime's prominent specialist on colonial affairs, could add with a characteristic self-assurance that 'the principles are good, and experience is not lacking. While mistakes have to be corrected, Portugal must continue to serve as the master and exemplar for those peoples who are the educators of other peoples.' [2]

Set against this background of an intense and often passionate attachment to economic and cultural discrimination against Africans, even if sometimes mitigated in sexual relationships between white males and non-white females, the task of 1945 was seen as being to extend the policies of the 1930s. More effectively than before, if possible more 'rationally', the maximum amount of labour was to be extracted from the largest feasible number of blacks at the lowest possible cost, whether directly in white-owned plantations and other enterprises, or indirectly in the provision of low-cost food produced by the rural African economy for the benefit of populations enclosed within the colonial economy proper. At the same time there was to be further centralisation of all effective controls in a reaffirmation of the Estado Novo's rejection of previous tendencies towards giving some measure of territorial autonomy to oversea whites.

To these ends, one may recall, the Estado Novo had taken over and modified the constitutional instruments of the pre-1926 parliamentary regime. That regime's regulations, providing for the coercion of labour on the principle that blacks were not considered to be working unless for wages – that is, for whites – were confirmed *in toto*. At the same time a Colonial Act of 1930, an 'imperial organic charter' of 1933, and some other regulations had reinforced Lisbon's control of the whole imperial system. In practice these modifications, during the 1930s, appear to have had far less effect upon the scene of action than the increasingly authoritarian attitudes of oversea governors and generals. Writing in 1938, Hailey could note that their intended results were 'not yet in full operation', and 'much indeed appears to have been left

[1] M. Caetano, *Os nativos na economia africana* (Coimbra, 1954), 16, author's translation.
[2] J. M. da Silva Cunha, *O sistema português de politica indigena* (Coimbra, 1953), 236–8, author's translation.

for determination by rules of practice'.[1] With an interval for the wartime years, these 'rules of practice' gradually knit together, after 1945, into the straitjacket which Salazar, concerned always to promote the identity of Portugal within a context of its medieval history, insistently envisaged. They were also assisted by other regulations, notably those of 1954 which further crystallised the differences in status between *indígena* and *assimilado*. The system accordingly did not develop, much less change; but it grew in size and coercive power.

No democratic politics being permitted to any community, one sees this growth in the economic and administrative fields. Many more men (with an unknown but probably not small number of women) were brought within a system of exploitation 'organised in an economy directed by whites'. This was achieved by an extension of labour recruitment on one hand, and of the obligatory cultivation of export crops on the other. Thriving on both, the colonial economy went steadily ahead after 1950: for example, Angolan coffee production rose from 38380 tons in 1951 to 168000 in 1961. The enlargement of obligatory cultivation of export crops was almost certainly very great in all three mainland territories. An independent observer in Mozambique during 1958 found that 'the actual number of men, women and children who are being forced to plant cotton (on acreage taken out of food production) probably exceeds one million. In 1956, the 519000 sellers received an average of $11.17 per person as their family's reward for an entire year's work.'[2] Comparable conditions existed in central and western areas of Angola, as also to a small extent in the groundnut zones of Guiné, and were to form a major factor in fuelling African discontent.

Forced labour formed another. Masked as 'contract labour', this appears to have become ever more prevalent. Designed initially by Norton de Matos during his first governorship of Angola (1912–15) as an improvement on surviving practices of domestic slavery,[3] contract labour had to be supplied by all fit adult males (but excluding *assimilados*) who could not otherwise show that they were 'employed', which meant working for a wage, during six months of the year. Reliable figures are again

[1] Lord Hailey, *An African survey*, 2nd ed. (London, 1945), 216.
[2] M. Harris, *Portugal's African 'wards'* (New York, 1958), 31.
[3] See N. de Matos, *A Província de Angola* (Porto, 1926), 15–16, 126–7.

lacking, but something of the prevalence of this system can be seen from the official returns of the Department of Native Affairs in Luanda, examined in 1954 by another independent observer. These showed, for all Angola, a total of about 379 000 *contradados* (those whom Norton's much earlier regulations had designated as *serviçais*) compared with about 400 000 *voluntarios* (those working for wages outside the 'contractual' system).[1] For the plantation economy, at that time, the Department of Native Affairs worked to a rough ratio of 33 *contradados* for each hundred hectares.

By the middle 1950s, in short, perhaps a quarter of all adult males in rural Angola were enclosed directly within the colonial economy under conditions of more or less coercion. It was evident, moreover, that regulations forbidding recruitment for private employers were a dead letter. An inspector-general of colonies, reporting in 1947, thought that the worst aspect of the labour position lay

in the attitude of the State to the recruitment of labour for private employers. Here the position is worse in Angola than in Mozambique: because in Angola, openly and deliberately, the State acts as recruiting and distributing agent for labour on behalf of settlers who, as though it were natural, write to the Department of Native Affairs for 'a supply of workers'. This word 'supply' [*fornecer*] is used indifferently of goods or of men... In some ways the situation is worse than simple slavery. Under slavery, after all, the Native is bought as an animal; his owner prefers him to remain as fit as a horse or an ox. Yet here the Native is not bought: he is hired from the State, although he is called a free man. And his employer cares little if he sickens or dies, once he is working, because when he sickens or dies his employer will simply ask for another.[2]

A continuity of policy was marked in the cultural field as well. Following a Concordat of 1940, a missionary statute of 1941 completed an earlier trend towards entrusting all education of Africans to Catholic missions (save for a small number of British Baptist and American or Canadian Methodist missions, these

[1] Figures supplied to the author, in mid-1954, by the Department of Native Affairs, Luanda. For a precise colonial restatement of the continuing policy on African labour, see *Relatorio do Gov.-Geral de Moçambique: Gen. Jose Tristão de Bettencourt* (covering period 20 March 1940 to 31 December 1941), (Agência Geral das Colonias, Lisbon, 1945), 77–85.

[2] This severely frank report was made by Henrique Galvão, then inspector-general of colonies. Kept secret, it was afterwards printed by the clandestine opposition. The passage in question is from the author's translation in B. Davidson, *The African awakening* (London, 1955), 205. Galvão subsequently published the report in full, in a slightly different and more abrasive translation, in H. Galvão, *Santa Maria: my crusade for Portugal*, tr. W. Longfellow (London, 1961), 53.

being tolerated because powerful governments could defend them). The education provided was of a merely primitive nature, being limited to a little literacy and the catechism, although white and *assimilado* children could have access to a few secondary schools run by the state. Yet even if the Portuguese cultural approach could have found a place for mass literacy – and as late as 1958, according to an estimate of UNESCO's, illiteracy in Portugal itself was still as high as 44 per cent – the economic system posed no educational requirement. So the 1950 statistical review offers no surprise in showing that illiteracy for all sectors of the population stood at 96.97 per cent in Angola, at 97.86 per cent in Mozambique, and at 98.95 per cent in Guiné, while even that of the Cape Verdean population, ostensibly all of 'civilised' status, stood at 78.50 per cent. Educational facilities for the 'civilised' minority were better, but still at a low level. Even in 1955–6, with an Angolan white population totalling some 110000 (not counting perhaps 35 000 *assimilados*), only 3729 students were registered in 'academic' education and 2164 in 'technical' education.[1] As late as 1958, only one Mozambican African had acquired a university degree.

However archaic the system, Salazar and those who followed him were determined to preserve it, seeing their empire not only as a vital means of assuring a favourable balance of payments for Portugal itself, but also, in their ideology of Lusitanian grandeur, as being crucial to Portugal's standing and importance in the world. On their view of the matter, any concession to liberalising reform must lead irrevocably to Portugal's gradual displacement by rival imperialist powers, and most probably by the controlling influence of the United States. A well-known declaration of Salazar's, perfectly representative of many others made about the colonies, may suffice to encapsulate an intransigence that was based on fear of Portugal's imperial weakness. 'We will not sell, we will not cede, we will not surrender, we will not share...the smallest item of our sovereignty', he declared at a time when stronger colonial powers had begun to withdraw their political controls. 'Even if our constitution would allow this, which it does not, our national conscience must refuse it.'[2]

[1] M. A. Samuels and N. A. Bailey, 'Education, health, and social welfare', in D. M. Abshire and M. A. Samuels (eds.), *Portuguese Africa, a handbook* (London, 1969), 187.

[2] Quoted by N. de Vasconcelos, *Não!* (Lisbon, 1961), preface. Author's translation.

Such was to remain the official philosophy to the end; but it acquired new life in the 1950s. Hoping for admission to the United Nations, the regime took measures to forestall outside enquiry into the conditions of the colonies. A constitutional change of 1951 declared that the colonies were henceforth to have the formal status of oversea provinces of the mother-country. Duly admitted to the United Nations in 1955, the regime denied having any obligation under Article 73 of the UN Charter, which concerns non-self-governing territories, since its oversea provinces were as much a part of Portugal, constitutionally, as the Algarve or Lisbon itself. This at least prevented any on-the-spot investigation by agencies of the UN, as well as releasing Lisbon from the need to make reports.

Generally, by 1960, the system had reached a point where its promoters could well believe, no matter what might be argued by sceptics, that they had reached an equilibrium capable of further economic enlargement, but calling for no structural change. Towards all but a minute fraction of the non-white population, this future might offer some eventual alleviation of 'native' status, but could allow for no development into a different system. There was quite a bit of internal criticism, notably from such men as Augusto Casimiro who had served as a provincial governor in Angola, but it made no difference. No scandals arising from coercion, and there were many of them, seem ever to have disturbed the certitudes of Salazar and his principal aides. No development of any oversea variants, much less of any non-Portuguese alternatives, could be allowed. What Albert Perbal told the Reale Accademia d'Italia in 1940, speaking to the theme of '*Comment former les Africains à la Civilisation?*', must hold unalterably firm. Perbal quoted as exemplary a statement by an inspector-general of education in French West Africa: 'Evidemment, dans ce domaine, je crois que nous sommes amenés à dire qu'il ne peut s'agir que d'une culture purement française, et je crois que l'idéal serait de faire des lycées qui soient le plus français possible.'[1] The difference, of course, was that the Portugal of Salazar wished or was able to form very few *lycées* of any kind at all.

Complacency marched hand-in-hand with repressive severity, and saw no reason save European and American jealousy or

[1] A. Perbal, 'Comment former les Africains à la civilisation?', *Reale Accademia d'Italia*, Rome, 1940.

subversion to doubt that the march could indefinitely continue. Thus Salazar in 1957:

We believe that there are decadent or – if you prefer – backward races whom we feel we have a duty to lead to civilisation: a task of educating human beings that must be tackled in a humane way. That we do feel and act like this is shown by the fact that there is no network of hatred and subversive organisations [in our territories] whose aim is to reject and displace the sovereignty of Portugal...[1]

Lesser men down the ranks hastened to echo the same assurance. Even in 1960 no concession to liberalising reform was on the programme, nor was any envisaged except as a betrayal of the Lusitanian mission. Yet by 1960 the ground was already shaking beneath their feet. The future was to be different from any that they had imagined.

THE RISE OF NATIONALISM

The last embers of an armed resistance by 'traditional' societies had flared and died by the early 1930s. Administrative control was at last complete, relatively strong in central and southern Mozambique and in central and western Angola, weak elsewhere and yet adequate to the government of sparse and scattered populations. Old hostilities to colonial rule might remain vivid in men's minds. New movements of rejection, messianic or ancestral or a mixture of the two, might whisper their message in the silence of the bush. But any further attempt to challenge the regime, head-on, seemed futile. At the present stage of research it is hard to be sure about this; but such is one's firm impression for the whole of the 1940s and the early years of the 1950s.

Any form of 'protest nationalism' was similarly long in taking shape among the literate few of the *assimilados* in the towns. Always divided by a cultural gulf from the *preto boçal*, the 'savage black' of the bush, their spokesmen since the 1880s had raged against the policies of Lisbon or at least against the representatives of Lisbon; but Norton de Matos and other governors of the early 1920s had stamped hard on these spokesmen and the Estado Novo had finally shut their mouths. For the literate few, however, the

---

[1] In a broadcast speech of 1 Nov. 1957, quoted here from E. de Sousa Ferreira, *Portuguese colonialism in Africa: the end of an era* (Paris, UNESCO, 1974), 113.

Second World War and its democratic victories were to contribute to a progress in their understanding of the colonial situation that made itself felt soon after the war. It may be doubtful how far such declarations as the Atlantic Charter, so influential among literate Africans elsewhere, were heard in these colonial towns of Portuguese Africa. But the downfall of Mussolini and Hitler, Salazar's own 'masters and exemplars', could not be concealed. The very patent lessons of that downfall penetrated even the Estado Novo's 'walls of silence'.[1] The will to protest gradually revived. In doing so, its thinking also changed.

The earliest clear manifestation of a new concern with protest was *Mensagem*, a cultural journal launched by a small group of *assimilados* of Luanda under the leadership of a 20-year-old poet, Viriato da Cruz. Appearing in 1948 – only two issues were ever permitted – *Mensagem* carried a masthead slogan whose meaning was to echo down the years, *Vamos Descobrir Angola*. In the circumstances this was equivalent to a political programme in itself, for its well-understood implication urged that literate Angolans must cease to be assimilated Portuguese and must find their way across the gulf which divided them from the *preto boçal*, now to be seen no longer as an object of contempt or charity but as the independent citizen of tomorrow. However elusively expressed in a poetry of 'going to the people', this was the assertion of a potential nationalism. 'What we wanted to revive', da Cruz recalled afterwards, 'was the fighting spirit of the African writers of the end of the nineteenth century,[2] but with quite other methods. Our movement attacked the overblown respect given to the cultural values of the West...[and] urged young people to "rediscover" Angola in every respect, and by an organised and collective effort...'[3] Although by often hidden channels, much would flow from *Mensagem*.

At about the same time another handful of *assimilados* or their Cape Verdean equivalents reached the same position while university students in Portugal, and strove to achieve 'a sharp aware-

---

[1] A description of A. Cabral's in his foreword to B. Davidson, *The liberation of Guiné* (London, 1969), 9.

[2] An interesting and vehement group, including such forceful figures as José de Fontes Pereira. See D. L. Wheeler, '"Angola is whose house?": early stirrings of Angolan nationalism and protest, 1822–1910', *African Historical Studies*, 1969, **2**, no. 1, 1; and M. de Andrade (ed.), *La Poésie africaine d'expression portugaise* (Paris, 1969).

[3] Andrade, *La Poésie africaine*, 12. Author's translation.

ness of the need to react against the Lusitanian idea of the black man, and to sketch out the route to a national affirmation'.[1] From their debates, too, much would flow. They secured permission to form a centre of African studies in Lisbon, took up the study of African languages while discussing how best they might 're-Africanise' themselves, and were able to publish a little of the 'poetry of rediscovery' now beginning to be written by themselves and their companions in all the Portuguese-speaking African territories. Among these students, certainly to be regarded as conscious nationalists by 1950, were three who would make history: Amílcar Cabral, who was to found the nationalist movement of Guiné and Cape Verde, as well as being an active participant in founding that of Angola; Agostinho Neto, who was to become the leading figure in Angolan nationalism; and Mário de Andrade, another Angolan who was to be the first among them all to reach a wide international audience in these difficult early years. Others joined them or followed much the same route: the Mozambicans Marcelino dos Santos and Eduardo Chivambo Mondlane (the latter, exceptionally, by way of an American university and a job at the UN), the Angolan Déolinda de Almeida (again, exceptionally, by way of colleges in the USA and Brazil) and, in the years that followed, many more.

Their political problem was twofold. How should they find their way back to African roots? Having done that, how could they then build broad movements aiming at independence? They were to solve both these bitterly difficult problems, though not easily; but it may bear emphasising here that one of their greatest assets, aside from clarity of mind and courage, would repeatedly be found to lie in what seemed their greatest obstacle. This was the complete and unrelenting denial by the regime of any demands for constitutional or administrative reform. Had the regime showed any real flexibility they would have had to meet their problems by accepting concessions; and the outcome in these Portuguese territories could then have followed the same grad-ualist road as in those of Britain and France. Denied this flexibility, they were obliged to think in terms of a radical alternative to the Portuguese system. What this alternative might really be, worked itself clear only in the action upon which they embarked. But this unquestionable need for an alternative remained, as it began, the essential basis of their thought and practice.

[1] Andrade, *La Poésie africaine*, introduction.

At that time the only Portuguese at all ready to consider an independent future for the colonies were members of the clandestine Communist Party of Portugal. Contacts with them were possible, whether in Lisbon or in colonial capitals, though also dangerous; and it was through these contacts, by such evidence as we now possess, that the early nationalists found their way to Marxist forms of analysis. These in turn reinforced the argument that any worthwhile alternative to the Portuguese system would have to become a non-capitalist and eventually socialist alternative. Meanwhile they wrestled with immediate difficulties. The position of the Portuguese Communist Party was analogous with that of the French, except for having to operate in a total clandestinity. It was the only party in the country that was pledged to end the colonial system, and so was often influential among African students in Portugal; but it tended to see itself as the directing force to that end. In the wake of the Second World War, accordingly, some attempt was made to form branch parties in the African colonies. None ever appeared, save very briefly in Angola around 1954–5, for this was the period in which radical Africans in the colonies were beginning to form nationalist organisations of their own. They thought that the Portuguese Communists should support these organisations rather than working in a separate organisation whose head and centre lay in Portugal. It appears that the issue was resolved at a secret congress of the Communist Party of Portugal in 1957. The handful of Africans who were present argued that the proposed slogan of 'Fight against Fascism' was meaningless in the colonies, at least for non-whites, and that any success would have to follow a programme aimed at decolonisation. It further appears that this was accepted. The Portuguese Communists agreed to desist from trying to promote Communist branch-parties, and to support the nascent movements of nationalism. In so far as these movements were influenced by Marxism, from the start they would have to come to terms with the realities of Africa.[1]

By 1957 these movements had already begun to take shape, tentatively, among small groups working their way out of 'cultural associations' and other permitted 'clubs' or 'gatherings' towards a direct challenge to colonial authority. Some were ephemeral and quickly suppressed. But a few, operating on the

[1] Private communication, African source. As was obvious, then and later, much remained obscure about these early debates and initiatives.

principle that any effective movement would have to emerge from a broad union of all possible adherents, and led by those who belonged to the radical mainstream deriving from the late 1940s, managed to hold their clandestine ground in face of a now alerted colonial police. Earliest among them was the Partido Africano de Independência da Guiné e Cabo Verde (PAIGC) formed in Bissau during September 1956 by Cabral and five others on a 'minimal programme' of national independence for Guiné and the historically and culturally related Cape Verdes. Next came the Movimento Popular de Libertação de Angola (MPLA) formed in Luanda in December 1956. Nothing quite parallel happened in Mozambique, where the first avowedly nationalist 'parties' took shape among exiles in Rhodesia and Tanganyika during 1960. But in the middle of 1962 three of these small groups came together in Dar es Salaam as the Frente de Libertação de Moçambique (FRELIMO) with Mondlane as president. Although formed outside Mozambique the component parts of FRELIMO, at this stage very much a coalition rather than a union of groups, already had active contacts in northern Mozambique among the Makonde people, and in most of the principal towns; and they were able, through these, to recruit volunteers and spread their message.

Insignificant in numbers, these little movements barely yet deserved the name. 'Nationalists without nations', as Cabral would afterwards say of them, they were obliged to substitute themselves for a public opinion which had yet to crystallise in their favour. The founding manifesto of the MPLA might well call for 'a revolutionary struggle' which would triumph through 'the building of a united front of all Angola's anti-imperialist forces, taking no account of colour, social situation, religious belief, or individual preference':[1] the work of building, as they well knew, had still to be begun.

Trying to get on with that, the militants of these early years threw themselves into the perilous labour of forming clandestine groups, distributing illegal pamphlets, and recruiting supporters who were ready to become participants. Perhaps peaceful forms of agitation might yet shift Lisbon? There were those who still hoped so, being duly encouraged by the independence of Ghana

[1] Quoted in M. de Andrade and M. Ollivier, *La Guerre en Angola: étude socio-économique* (Paris, 1971), 69–70.

in 1957 and of (French) Guinea in 1958, as well as by other signs of change outside the Portuguese territories. But they soon had reason to lose this hope, while others among them were already sure that insurrection, however problematical, could be the only way ahead.

Most of those then active in the Luanda leadership were to die in prison or in combat before recording any memoirs, while other evidence for this brief interlude of peaceful agitation remains scanty except in the case of Guiné. Writing a few years later, a group of Angolans then in Algiers recalled that 'pamphlet activity increased considerably in 1958. Everywhere, but particularly in Luanda, there was talk of armed revolution. Leaflets appeared that appealed for armed struggle for the liberation of Angola. They denounced colonialism, called on the masses to revolt. Besides this, legal or illegal anti-colonial struggle was more intense than ever in journals, existing organisations, football clubs, etc.'[1] That this information, recorded in 1965, was substantially accurate is confirmed by Portuguese reactions. Special sections of the political police (PIDE: Policia Internacional de Defesa do Estado) had been installed in the oversea territories as early as 1954.[2] And in April 1959 the Governor-General of Angola welcomed the arrival of air-force units and some paratroops with a warning that: 'We are living in the time of the leaflet... The leaflet has appeared in Angola...'[3] A little later that year the clash was already in the open, first in Guiné and then rapidly elsewhere.

Police repression put the match to the fuel in all three mainland territories. In August 1959 a strike of dockers in Bissau, organised by the clandestine PAIGC, was shot back to work with at least fifty dead and many wounded. In June 1960 a large gathering of peasants who assembled at Mueda, in the northern district of Cabo Delgado in Mozambique, so as to present complaints and claims to the local governor, was fired into by police and army units with

[1] Centro de Estudos Angolanos (ed.), *História de Angola* (Algiers, 1965), 153. None of these leaflets seems to have survived. Other materials clandestinely circulated included foreign criticisms of the Portuguese colonial system, as, for instance, translations of parts of my reportage of 1955, *The African awakening* (London, 1955) (information of 1970 from the late António de Melo, who was in Luanda at the time).
[2] Ministério do Ultramar, *Cinco anos: 2 Agosto de 1950 a 7 Julho de 1955* (Lisbon, 1956), 107, 165.
[3] Quoted in B. Davidson, 'The time of the leaflet', *New Statesman*, 21 November 1959.

the loss of several hundred killed.[1] In the same month of 1960 a demonstration in Angola in support of the nationalist leader, Agostinho Neto, arrested a few days earlier, was likewise assaulted by armed police and army, again with many killed. These shootings buried any lingering hope of progress by peaceful means. In a later summary of the position as it now appeared, the Mozambican leader Mondlane was undoubtedly speaking for his companions in MPLA and PAIGC:

Two conclusions were obvious. First, Portugal would not admit the principle of self-determination and independence, or allow for any extension of democracy under her own rule...Secondly, moderate political action such as strikes, demonstrations and petitions, would result only in the destruction of those who took part in them. We were therefore left with these alternatives: to continue indefinitely living under a repressive imperial rule, or to find a means of using force against Portugal which would be effective enough to hurt Portugal without resulting in our own ruin...[2]

Meeting secretly in Bissau a few weeks after the mass killing of August 1959, Cabral and his fellow leaders of the PAIGC had already drawn the same conclusion, and fixed their policy as struggle against the colonial system 'by all possible means, including war'. They then moved their base to Conakry, capital of the neighbouring Republic of Guinea, and set about their preparations. They were ready to launch their war in January 1963. The leaders of FRELIMO followed suit in September 1964. But the blaze of African counter-violence to the violence of the system came earlier in Angola, and had much that was spontaneous.

In January 1961 an Angolan called António Mariano, eponymous leader of a dissident Christian sect known as 'Maria', 'embarked on a campaign against European authority and the whole system of enforced cotton growing', burning seed, discarding tools, barricading roads, killing livestock, and chasing away such Europeans as they met while marching to the chant of hymns.[3] Enough troops were on hand to deal with this

---

[1] Evidence of Alberto-Joaquim Chipande, recorded by me in June 1968 and reproduced by E. Mondlane, *The struggle for Mozambique* (London, 1969), 117–8. Chipande was present at the occasion, and put the number of killed at 'about 600'.

[2] Mondlane, *The struggle for Mozambique*, 125.

[3] J. Marcum, *The Angolan revolution, I: The anatomy of an explosion (1950–1962)* (Cambridge, Mass., 1969), 125, drawing on UPA (Angolan) and Protestant missionary sources.

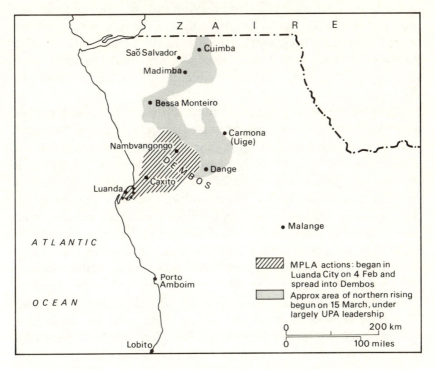

33   Angola: the risings of 1961.

outburst, but on 4 February the Portuguese found themselves
faced with another of a different order. At a time when most of
the recognised MPLA leaders in Luanda were in prison with the
certainty of long sentences or worse, others under MPLA
inspiration led an attack to free them. This failed, but signalled
both the onset of a wild repression by settlers, police and army,
and the origins of the great revolt that was to end with success
in 1975.

   While indiscriminate killing of Africans continued for weeks
in and around Luanda, a third rising of 1961, this time in March,
at first swept all before it. Moved partly by hatred of labour
coercion and partly by the leaders of a movement called União
das Populações de Angola (UPA), based in Léopoldville (Kinshasa) in the now independent Congo (Zaire), large numbers of
contradados and others seized control of wide areas of Uige and
Cuanza Norte, killing a large but unknown number of European

settlers, perhaps 200 in all,[1] and driving out such police and army posts as were then in the vicinity. Only in the following October were army reinforcements able to recover the bulk of this territory, but by then it was becoming apparent that they were dealing with a movement very different in its nature from the MPLA.

Originating in a lineage dispute within the Kongo people (divided between northern Angola and western Zaire, but with its traditional centres in Angola), the UPA had appeared as UPNA (União das Populações do Norte de Angola) in 1957. Initially, it brought together a number of kingmakers who supported a Protestant nominee to the 'throne' of the ancient Kongo kingship in opposition to those who supported a Catholic nominee selected and eventually enthroned by the Portuguese. From that it rapidly moved to a demand for the renewed independence of the Kongo kingdom, and then in 1959, as UPA, extended its claim to speak for an Angolan nationalism. But the UPA never escaped from its Kongo separatism, and soon, under the leadership of Holden Roberto, became increasingly an instrument of its immediate foreign backer, General (afterwards President) Mobutu Sese Seko of Zaire. It would thus remain throughout the liberation war a distraction, and often a destructive one, to the Pan-Angolan nationalist effort of the MPLA.[2]

DEVELOPMENTS IN COLONIAL POLICY, 1961–75

The evidence of a peculiarly savage Portuguese reaction to these risings of early 1961 brought Angola to a close international attention for the first time since the cocoa-slavery campaign of the early years of the century. This evidence was detailed and appalling, whether from newspaper correspondents, Protestant missionaries, or other non-Portuguese sources. In mid-June the British Baptist Missionary Society thought that a total of 20000 Africans killed might be a cautious estimate; and subsequent enquiry has done nothing to reduce it. Huge numbers meanwhile fled over the northern frontier; their total by 3 October, according

---

[1] Estimate of the Diamond Co. of Angola (Diamang) in its annual report of 30 June 1961; and see C. Parsons, 'The makings of a revolt', in *Angola: a symposium* (London, 1962), 67.

[2] See Marcum, *The Angolan revolution*; B. Davidson, *In the eye of the storm: Angola's people* (London, 1972); and bibliographies in both books.

to the International Red Cross, was about 141 000, the beginnings of a flood that would later mount towards 400 000. In London, faced with this catastrophe, a Conservative government defended its amicable attitude to the Estado Novo but deplored the intransigence of Lisbon's policy.[1] To this and other foreign criticism or comment, a badly shaken Portuguese government eventually responded with a number of constitutional reforms, but without shifting its essential position.

The first of these reforms, announced on 28 August 1961, repealed the Native Code of 1954 (an extension of earlier codes of the same nature), and formally abolished the distinction between *indígena* and *assimilado*, granting all inhabitants, in principle, the same civic status. In practice, however, this brought little change in the condition of African 'fit adult males', who remained legally subject to many labour obligations. Other decrees of the same period sought to promote white settlement and improve rural administration. Later measures of 27 April 1962 went a little further, though again chiefly on paper, by abolishing the 'moral obligation' on Africans to work for wages and, with this, the legal basis of the contractual system. If unfolded within a programme of liberalisation some ten years earlier, this reform could have made a considerable difference; as it was, it came much too late to be able to achieve any useful purpose.

Another ten years of African armed resistance induced in 1971–2 a further set of constitutional reforms, though once again designed primarily to reassure Portugal's now impatient allies that genuine changes of structure were to be attempted. Chief among these was a promise that the oversea provinces might accede in the course of time to the status of autonomous units, though with Lisbon retaining all effective control over finance and administration. At the same time some effort was made to widen the Estado Novo's extremely narrow franchise to include a number of black voters and representatives in provincial legislatures. But once again the tardy will to reform was overwhelmed by events, and in any case remained at best a feeble and uncertain one.

Various post-war pressures led to more realistic efforts to modernise the antiquated structures of the colonial economy: the rising world demand for coffee, cotton, and mineral ores; the steady

[1] E.g. *Hansard*, 15 June 1961, cols. 712 ff.

attrition of the wars set going by the nationalist movements; the growing interest of major foreign companies in the resources of Angola and Mozambique; and Lisbon's continuing drive to enlarge white settlement. Under this heading, there is little to be said about Guiné, where the nationalists had secured control over about half the country's productive area by 1968 and the colonial economy was nearing bankruptcy; or about the Cape Verdes, where a long cyclical drought set in with disastrous results during the second half of the 1960s, and where, in any case, funds for development were completely lacking; or about São Tomé, where a serious disturbance of 1953, motivated chiefly by fear of an extension of the contractual system to non-*indígenas*, was followed by a stiffened military control.[1] The people of Mozambique continued, as before 1940, to experience the relative stagnation of concession companies, together with a considerable extension of obligatory cultivation; generally, the Mozambican colonial economy grew much more slowly than that of Angola.

We have seen that Angolan output within the colonial economy, extended to the indigenous economy in terms of the obligatory production of export crops, picked up steadily after 1950. By a decade later it was rising at a much faster rate: through most of the 1960s, industrial output of all commodities and enterprises was said to have expanded at an average annual rate of about 17 per cent.[2] Mineral extraction accounted for much of this: between 1965 and 1970, for example, the volume of mineral exports was reported to have doubled to a total of about £170 million.[3] At the same time, the composition of investment changed. After 1964, now with the financial pressures of the colonial wars as a major factor, the Estado Novo's practical monopoly of all investment (save for a few exceptions, such as the British-owned Benguela Railway and the De Beers subsidiary, Diamang) had to be brought to an end. Most enterprises were now permitted to operate without a majority holding of Portuguese capital, while mining activity could be entirely foreign-owned and financed.

[1] For an account from the nationalist side, which put the number of Africans killed by troops under the orders of Governor Carlos Gorgulho at 1032 persons: CONCP, *L'Ile de São Tomé* (Algiers, 1968), 65. A Protestant missionary account at the time put the number of Africans killed at about 200: quoted in Davidson, *The African awakening*, 229–30. No official report, so far as is known, was ever published.

[2] *Financial Times*, 19 July 1971.

[3] Davidson, *In the eye of the storm*, 300.

Gulf Oil began drilling offshore from Cabinda in July 1966, and struck useful deposits. An international consortium under the coordinating hand of Krupp of Essen, with finance from Federal German, Danish, Austrian and US banks, agreed in June 1965 to produce $ US 100 million to mine iron ore at Cassinga, and went quickly into operation. Other large corporations, including the Anglo-American Corporation of South Africa, secured prospecting concessions. Most of these activities, confined to the centre and seaboard, were able to proceed with little or no interference from the nationalists who, for reasons both geographical and political, were limited to the east and north.[1] By 1974, Angola had become a major interest for many investing countries. The same trend was perceptible in Mozambique, though it was still at an earlier stage. There the symbol of the Estado Novo's lost monopoly was a major hydroelectric scheme at the Cabora Bassa gorge on the middle Zambezi. Built by international capital under South African organisation, Cabora Bassa was to provide power for the South African grid after its (post-war) completion in 1978.

White settlement continued to increase in Angola and Mozambique, though not in Guiné, under strong government pressure within Portugal itself, where legal emigration was now restricted largely to these African territories.[2] Costly and ambitious plans were made for rural *colonatos* (immigrant settler zones), but these came to little, no matter how much money was spent on them, because of a persistent unwillingness of immigrants to live outside the towns. This particular effort was largest in Angola, as was also its failure. A detailed study based on official figures showed in 1975 that the Junta Provincial de Povoamento de Angola,[3] created in 1962, was able to attract a total of only 1824

[1] Chiefly by reason of the continuing hostility to the Angolan national movement of the Zaire government and General (in 1965, President) Mobutu Sese Seko. See also page 793.

[2] But very large numbers of Portuguese workers emigrated to France and other Common Market countries, often by smuggling themselves over the Portuguese frontier (*o salto*). For an overall historical and sociological analysis, see E. de Sousa Ferreira, 'Ursachen und Formen der Auswanderung und ihre Bedeutung für die Entwicklung Portugals' (doctoral dissertation, Ruprecht-Karl University of Heidelberg, 1974). Also useful in this context, Huseyin Celik (ed.), *Les Travailleurs immigrés parlent* (Paris, 1970).

[3] Provincial Committee for Settlement in Angola: meaning, above all, 'white settlement from Portugal'. For a detailed analysis of the aims and work of the junta, see G. J. Bender, *Angola under the Portuguese: the myth and the reality* (London, 1978), at many points. Also, for the impact of settlement and other policies on the relatively densely populated areas of the High Plateau (notably Huambo): J. V. da Silva and

European settlers to *colonatos*, and that fewer than half of these remained in them at the end of 1968.[1] The high point of white settlement in Portugal's African territories was reached in 1973 with an approximate total of 550000.

More serious in its impact on African life, especially in Angola but also in Mozambique, was the continuing expropriation of African land in favour of European farms and plantations. In Angola, for example, the same careful study found that 'between the years 1968–70 the amount of land held by Europeans in Huambo district', relatively very fertile, 'more than doubled (from 249039 ha to 526270 ha) while the area cultivated by Africans was reduced by more than a third (36.5 per cent)', with gross income per African farm declining from $98.00 in 1964–5 to less than $35.00 in 1970.[2] This decline drove large numbers of farmers into a wage employment which effectively cancelled any advantages that had been supposed to derive from an end to the contractual labour system.

Such dislocations, spiralling from policies of 'development' which took no account of life outside the white-organised economy, and which plunged these territories into an ever deepening social crisis, were further enlarged by military policies aimed at containing the nationalist revolt. Of these the most influential was that of *reordenamento rural*, applied consistently to all three mainland territories after 1967. Rural populations in areas of 'nationalist infection', and gradually in most areas, were removed *manu militari* from their villages or homesteads and coralled within *aldeamentos* or other forms of 'guarded village', ranging in size from small annexes around fortified camps to large settlements within a military cordon. This was bad enough for sedentary cultivators; the evidence suggests that it was far worse for non-sedentary stock breeders. In the latter case, 'the resettlements represented cultural genocide and economic ruin for the pastoralists whose social and economic way of life is dependent upon the careful ecological balance they have evolved within their

J. A. de Morais, 'Ecological conditions of social change in the Central Highlands of Angola', in F.-W. Heimer (ed.), *Social change in Angola* (Munich, 1973). This concludes: 'The social consequences of these ecological conditions are disastrous. Not only is there a regression in the structural differentiation of rural Ovimbundu society, but the rural areas are no longer capable of supporting the population...' (p. 98).

[1] Bender, *Angola under the Portuguese*, 111.
[2] Bender, *ibid.*, 130.

annual transhumances'.[1] By 1974 more than one million rural people had been thrust into resettlements in Angola, not much less than a quarter of the country's whole population, while the position in northern and central Mozambique had become closely comparable. The plantation economy boomed, but its framework and foundations were now rotted to the core.

Undismayed by any evidence to the contrary, educational policies persisted in assuming that they need only continue in order to succeed. Their object remained as J. M. da Silva Cunha had defined it in 1957: 'We are attempting to accelerate the assimilation or complete "Portuguesation" of the natives, and to help improve their material situation by training them for more economically valued activities':[2] in other words, for a more effective entry to an 'economy organised and governed by whites'. The Missionary Statute of 1941 had laid down the since confirmed objective, and as late as 1964 da Silva Cunha glossed this once again when praising all those soldiers, missionaries and others 'who made this the land it now is, thoroughly Portuguese, with all the defects and virtues of the Portuguese: who made it what it is so that it could continue...and remain Portuguese, totally Portuguese, only Portuguese'.[3] That the instruction thus provided was of an extremely rudimentary nature was contested by no one who made serious enquiry: in 1969, for example, an official Lisbon institute drew attention to the fact that while teaching missionaries in Mozambique had increased from 44 in 1940 to 147 in 1960, the number of Mozambican Africans receiving rudimentary or functional instruction was said to have risen from 95 444 in 1942–3 to 385 259 in 1960–1. The same institute cast doubt on the figures for pupils, and added that 'in any case these figures, although partial, leave no margin for doubt as to the low level of progress'.[4] With due reservations on their accuracy, one may nonetheless offer the school-population figures for 1969–70 (but for 1968–9 in the case of Mozambique) in table

[1] Bender, *ibid.*, 138–9.

[2] J. M. da Silva Cunha, *Adminstração e direito colonial* (Lisbon, 1957), vol. I, 161: here tr. by Ferreira, *Portuguese colonialism*, 67–8.

[3] Quoted from Ferreira, *Portuguese colonialism*, 69.

[4] Instituto Superior de Ciências Sociais e Política Ultramarina (ed.), *Moçambique* (Curso de Extensão Universitária, Ano Lectivo de 1965–6, Lisbon), 645; quoted here from Ferreira, *Portuguese colonialism*, 70.

Table 15.1. *Numbers of pupils (all communities).*

Type of school	Cape Verde	Guiné	São Tomé and Príncipe	Angola	Mozambique
Infant teaching	—	—	209	2484	964
Primary	40685	26401	9089	384884	496381
Secondary					
Preparatory	2006	1254	901	25137	7307
Secondary	799	394	264	10779	10524
Technical/Occupational	302	415	113	14660	—
Arts	—	—	—	304	—
Ecclesiastical	69	27	—	720	600
Higher education (university, social service, ecclesiastical)	—	—	—	1757	1124
Teacher training	104	—	43	1402	1124

Source: *Annuário estatístico províncias ultramarinas*, Lisbon, 1970, vol. II; quoted here from Ferreira, *Portuguese colonialism*, 81.

15.1. In looking at the figures for secondary and higher education, one should bear in mind that the total number of white residents by this time was of the order of half a million. There were few places for their children, but almost none for the children of Africans. As for the latter, even the most rudimentary forms of this education had to be gained at the price of a more or less total alienation from their own cultures. What the Missionary Statute had laid down continued to be the rule: 'In the schools, the teaching of the Portuguese language and its use shall be obligatory. Outside school, missionaries and their assistants shall also use the Portuguese language...' The catechism might be learned and said in African languages; otherwise, these were to be treated as though they did not exist.

Little modified by the paper reforms of 1961–2, such attitudes and policies persisted through the 1960s. They were barely questioned from within the regime, so far as present evidence can show, and not at all by those who controlled the regime. This confidence in immobility appears to have derived from Lisbon's belief that the nationalist risings could and would be crushed without the need to make any serious concession to African grievances. Down to the early months of 1973 in Guiné, and in Mozambique and Angola even till the beginnings of 1974, little seems to have shaken this belief. Yet the actual course of events, by that time, had clearly pointed to another outcome.

THE FIGHT FOR INDEPENDENCE, 1961–75

If there was no political development on the Estado Novo's side, save of gestures which came too late or of second thoughts which lacked sincerity, there was much on the African; and it is probably in the development of African political thought that hindsight will always see the central interest of these years of warfare. As a prelude to considering that political development, this section will briefly review the military aspects and the chief events that led to independence.

Militarily, the Estado Novo was well placed in 1962 to cope with any form or scale of armed resistance on 'traditional' lines. Its security services were ruthless and experienced, its armed forces relatively large and well supplied. Whether politically or militarily, however, it was poorly prepared to deal with any use

34 Guinea-Bissau: launching the war of liberation. Cássaca in Quitáfine region was the locus of the crucial first congress of PAIGC in February 1964, where structures for political organisation and the mobile army were decided upon.

of irregular warfare that was powered by a modernising political analysis and leadership. In this respect the fact that none of Portugal's fighting men had seen active service, though a few senior officers had toured Hitler's battle fronts as guests of the Wehrmacht, mattered far less than another fact: that the Estado Novo's political leaders and military commanders were alike convinced of possessing an absolute and inherent intellectual superiority, and thought of their enemy either as a horde of savages or the otherwise helpless puppets of 'international Communism'. But the wars showed that the truth was the other way round, and the intellectual inferiority of the Portuguese commanders repeatedly swung the balance of strategic advantage to the African side.

These commanders tried to compensate in muscle for what they lacked in brain and, thanks to Portugal's allies, they found this easy to attempt. A complete record of western aid to the Estado

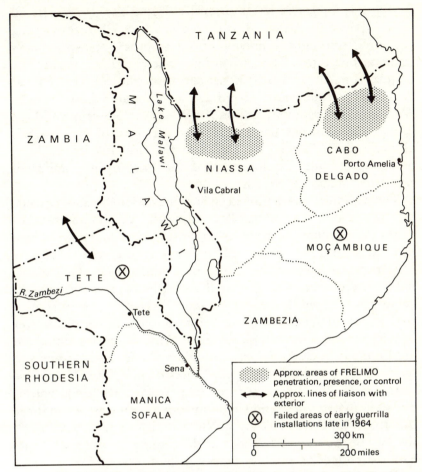

35   Northern Mozambique: the war situation in the wake of the earliest operations of September 1964.

Novo as a member-state of the North Atlantic Treaty Organisation (NATO) remained impossible in these years, but this aid was unquestionably large and continuous. It took the form of sympathetic diplomacy, going to the lengths of a formal celebration of the Anglo-Portuguese alliance and a state visit to Britain of Salazar's successor, Marcello Caetano, in July 1973, and many corresponding moves by the United States and other western powers; of commercial and financial support by means of a multiplicity of devices, chiefly arranged by the United States; and of a generous flow of arms and other forms of military aid, notably in this respect by France and West Germany. A reliable list of

Portuguese military aircraft in service during 1971–3, mostly on active service in Africa, showed ten types of US manufacture, ranging from light bombers to interceptors, transports and trainers; one type of Spanish origin; one of Italian origin; one of joint French and British manufacture (the SA-330 'Puma' helicopter); three more of purely French manufacture (chiefly 'Alouette' helicopters); and one of West German origin.[1] Much napalm and some defoliants were provided, probably by the USA, as well as a variety of sophisticated instruments such as bombsights, radio equipment and the like, by a number of countries, including Britain.

This armoury was deployed against the nationalist movements, and the zones they controlled, through the mobilisation of Portuguese military manpower on a rising scale to a point which had reached its feasible maximum by 1971. By that time the regime appears to have committed some nine-tenths of all its available military resources, whose overall totals, in 1972, were given as being 179 000 men in the army, 18 000 in the navy, and 21 000 in the air force. Together with the conscription of settler manpower in Angola and Mozambique, and of African service units and local militias (including a small number of African volunteers in 'commando'-type units at special rates of pay), the Portuguese then had in Africa a total force that was probably equivalent, by ratio of Portuguese and US populations, to at least seven times the largest US force deployed in Vietnam. By the same year, 1971, the Lisbon government was spending some 40 per cent of its national budget on military purposes, or a total of Esc. 15 311.7 million out of Esc. 36 647.8 million.[2] From an already high point in 1967, these expenditures in Africa rose steadily until the end (table 15.2).

While attempting to reduce areas of contestation or recover zones taken from their control, the Portuguese commanders also engaged in a variety of 'counter-insurgency' measures borrowed from British and American experience in South East Asia. The most important of these, and in the end the least well judged, was *reordenamento rural* in its several aspects, all of them concerned chiefly with driving peasant populations into guarded villages or

---

[1] UN General Assembly, A/9023 (Part IV) of 8 October 1973 (Report of Special Committee), 11, table 6.

[2] UN General Assembly, *ibid*: 8, official Portuguese sources.

Table 15.2. *Oversea territories: military budgets*[a] (*million escudos*).[b]

Year	Angola	Mozambique	Guiné	Cape Verde	São Tomé
1967	782.0	834.4	88.4	19.7	10.5
1968	951.3	910.3	92.8	25.2	10.4
1969	1289.6	945.0	106.1	33.8	11.4
1970	1746.9	1346.0	163.9	37.1	15.3
1971	2050.3	1204.3	189.7	37.3	14.5
1972	1925.1	1303.1	169.0	37.6	15.7
1973[c]	2037.3	2204.7	196.8	42.5	15.0

[a] Not including Timor and dependencies.
[b] For an approximate sterling equivalent at the time, divide by 65.
[c] Incomplete.
Source: UN General Assembly (Report of Special Committee), 9; official Portuguese sources.

within the perimeters of fortified camps. Much experience had already shown that this was a policy that could succeed if the operating power's armed forces were able to retain a firm and progressive strategic initiative, but that it would fail wherever this condition could not be met. For the most part, after 1967, the Portuguese commanders were unable to meet that indispensable condition; they nonetheless persisted with the policy. Gradually, Portugal's comparatively copious numbers of troops were swallowed up in guarding and supplying the *aldeamentos*, in garrisoning a multitude of fixed camps and isolated posts, in trying to keep open the bush tracks or dirt roads that led to and from such camps and posts, while deploying occasional 'offensives' against territory held by the troops of the liberation movements. This went hand-in-hand with regular and sometimes daily bombing of nationalist-held zones and villages and, increasingly after 1968, with helicoptered 'search and destroy' sorties by picked units.

Much of this was painful and destructive, but none of it was enough. A clear strategic initiative on the field of battle was never recovered. In April 1974 a movement of young officers of whom many had developed new political outlooks as a result of their experience in the wars in Africa, and perhaps especially in Guiné,[1]

[1] My impression from Portuguese and African sources in 1974. See also 'MFA na Guiné', editorial in Portuguese armed forces' bulletin, *Boletim Informativo*, Bissau, 1 June

overthrew the Lisbon regime on the twin slogans of 'Decolonisation and Democratisation'. There was little or no further fighting after that, either because the wars had come to seem futile or unwinnable, or because the troops had had enough. The regime preferred the second explanation. 'Our armed forces', General Costa Gomes told a press conference in May 1975, 'have reached the limits of psycho-neurological exhaustion.' The wars, in any case, were over. The nationalists had won.

There is almost nothing further to be said about the politics of this period on the Portuguese side, for the nature of the Estado Novo and its leaders prevented any intelligent response to African political initiatives that were inventive and continuous. Only General Spinola[1] appears to have glimpsed the potentials that could exist in political warfare. Finding he could not beat the PAIGC by military means, he embarked in 1970 on a programme of administrative propaganda designed to offer a 'better Guiné' (*Guiné melhor*) which might somehow yet emerge from reform of the colonial system. In April 1971, talking to a South African journalist, he explained that 'success is not to be hoped for in a war of this nature' unless one could mount what he called, in terms which perhaps only a man of Spinola's cultural formation could have devised, 'an anti-reactionary counter-revolution' to outbid the revolution of the nationalists. Little came of this in Guiné,

1974, no. 1, for details of structural organisation of MFA in Guiné; and statement in (MFA-edited) *Voz da Guiné*, Bissau, 19 August 1974 (my translation).

The colonised peoples and the people of Portugal are allies. The struggle for national liberation has contributed powerfully to the overthrow of Fascism and, in large degree, has lain at the base of the Armed Forces Movement whose officers have learned in Africa the horrors of a war without prospect, and have therefore understood the roots of the evils which afflict the society of Portugal...

This statement was the reproduction of a reportedly unanimous declaration by the assembly of the MFA in Guiné.

[1] Appointed to governor-generalship and military command in Guiné in the wake of General Arnaldo Schultz, who resigned in 1968, General (then Brigadier) António Sebastião Ribeiro Spinola had first seen active service as an operational commander in Angola during 1961. Some years earlier, and in line with the same ideas of structural reform, a minority trend within the regime (associated especially, it appears, with the then Overseas Minister Adriano Moreira) had looked with favour on a certain measure of devolution of control from Lisbon. This came to nothing, but gave rise for a while during the 1960s, at least among the more politically conscious of the Portuguese community in Angola, to a hope that something might be done.

Apart from Spinola, none of Portugal's senior commanders was prepared to admit that the wars were unwinnable by military means. They preferred, after the Lisbon coup, to claim that the 'home front', or whoever, had 'betrayed' them. For characteristic views, see (Generals) J. da Luz Cunha, K. de Arriaga, Bettencourt Rodrigues, S. Silvério Marques, *Africa, a vitória traída* (Lisbon, 1977).

but it is plain that Spinola was already thinking of Portugal itself, for he went on to say that 'to support a social counter-revolution in a developing region implies the setting-up of dynamic, solid and efficient structures; and to meet these needs Portugal is still encumbered with a slow-moving obsolescent bureaucracy...we must reform the structures on the home front'.[1] It was to become the Spinolist programme of 1974, but years too late.

The Africans, on their side, had to begin their wars in a posture of extreme weakness. They won because of their politics, but their politics could succeed only by steadily improving their military position. This was more than difficult. They had, to start with, no men of military experience, though they soon gained a few as African officers and non-commissioned officers joined them from the Portuguese army; and they had practically no weapons. Most of their earliest fighting volunteers were trained in Algeria: for the PAIGC in 1960–1, for MPLA a little later, for FRELIMO in 1963. Gradually as their international contacts improved, they were able to train others elsewhere: mostly in the USSR and one or two other countries in the East European bloc, some in Yugoslavia and Cuba, and a handful in China.[2] Initial supplies of small-arms, very meagre in quantity, came from the same sources.

Non-military aid was also sought in the west in line with the movements' policy of international non-alignment. Cabral spent many weeks in London during 1960; Neto visited old Methodist contacts in the USA during 1963; and Mondlane actually succeeded in securing some educational aid from the American Ford Foundation in 1964–5. But apart from winning the support of liberal and left-wing aid committees, notably in Holland, Britain, Italy and Sweden, such efforts proved largely fruitless save in the case of Sweden, whose government, onwards from 1967, gave

---

[1] A. J. Venter, *Portugal's war in Guiné-Bissau* (Munger Africana Library Notes, Pasadena, 19 April 1973), 190–1.

[2] Early in the 1960s, before its dispute with USSR, China provided military training for a few militants of the three movements (PAIGC, MPLA, FRELIMO). China then withdrew all direct aid, but provided small quantities of small-arms (chiefly light automatics and bazookas) for distribution through the Liberation Committee of the OAU and, from about 1967, helped to staff base-training camps in southern Tanzania in cooperation with Tanzania. In 1971 direct relations with the three movements were again renewed, and the leaderships of each were invited serially to Peking, although Chinese official propaganda continued, generally, to support the break-away or splinter groups in the case of each territory (UNITA in Angola, COREMO in the case of Mozambique and, briefly, the FLING group in Dakar in the case of Guiné). During the Angolan crisis of 1974–5, Chinese instructors trained FNLA troops in Zaire and provided FNLA with a substantial quantity of arms for use against the MPLA.

each of the movements considerable sums of money for non-military supplies through the para-statal Swedish International Development Authority. Aid from the Communist countries generally increased after about 1968, though at a rhythm that was always erratic, and extended also to many forms of non-military aid, including school holidays in the USSR for children living in badly bombed zones, as well as the training of nurses, doctors and the like. Weapons' supply, training aid and medical aid from Cuba was initiated on a small scale by Che Guevara during his African sojourn of the middle 1960s, (notably, at this stage, to the MPLA in Angola), and became steadily more important for the MPLA and PAIGC although, it appears, less for FRELIMO in Mozambique, as the years passed. Small Cuban medical teams and artillery-training sections served continuously in the liberated zones of the PAIGC in Guinea-Bissau from late in the 1960s, but no Cuban troops were committed to battle. By this time, too, many children from the territories were in schools in Cuba, while adult militants were also receiving military and other training there. And, as is well-known, Cuban troops served directly in Angola, against South African invasion, from late November 1975.

Fighting from internal forest or woodland areas linked to external sources of supply by guarded trails and head porterage, the armed units of all three movements worked generally towards the same concept:

In order to dominate a given zone, the enemy is obliged to disperse his forces. In dispersing his forces, he weakens himself and we can defeat him. Then in order to defend himself against us, he has to concentrate his forces. When he does this, we can occupy the zones that he leaves free and work in them, politically, so as to hinder his return there... [1]

This programme was as hard to carry out as it was simple to define; but it proved both possible and the key to success. These movements built up their slender forces, stage by stage, from numerically very small handfuls of fighters, each isolated in its 'zone of contestation' and barely capable of concerted action, until they were able to form large mobile units, or groups of mobile units, which attacked major targets. To such forces, onwards from 1968 or 1969 (somewhat earlier in Guiné, somewhat later elsewhere), there was added a variety of specialised units

[1] A. Cabral, quoted in *Afrique–Asie*, 1974, **66**, 25.

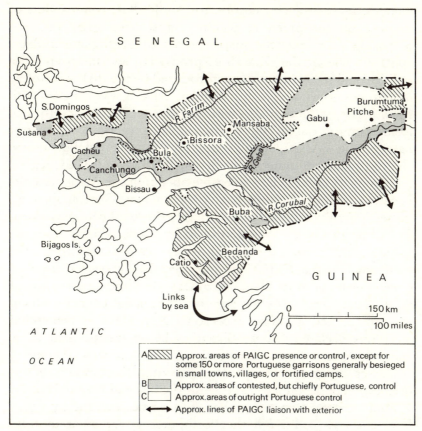

36 Guinea-Bissau: general position in late 1968 and after. The PAIGC
continued to improve its control of areas A, and its penetration into areas
B (with occasional raids into areas C).

able to deploy mortars, light artillery, a Russian-made 122 mm
'rocket' in 1971 and, after 1972, the similarly Russian-made
ground-to-air missile known as SAM-7. No fighting volunteers
from outside their own countries were accepted by any of the
movements.

By 1968 the PAIGC probably had some 4000 men in its regular
mobile units, as well as the beginnings of a network of local (that
is, non-mobile) village militias. Though outnumbered by about
nine to one, this small army had seized and held the strategic
initiative on the programme sketched above, and Lisbon's forces
were beleaguered in a large number of fortified towns, camps, or

villages. It was then a question for the PAIGC commanders of keeping up the pressure, picking off selected garrisons, and preparing to assault the major points of Portuguese military control while, at the same time, promoting and improving the political and social institutions introduced by the PAIGC into the large zones now under its firm control. All this was achieved with small losses,[1] although also with the disaster in January 1973 of losing Amílcar Cabral, assassinated at Conakry, the chief exterior base of the PAIGC, in a conspiracy launched by Portuguese African agents infiltrated from Bissau. To this the PAIGC replied by closing its ranks in new offensive operations. In March its units began to use SAM-7s with decisive effect against General Spinola's hitherto invulnerable air force. In July the key Portuguese forti-fied camp of Guileje was destroyed by bombardment from the ground, and the war, by the end of 1973, came largely to an end.

Meanwhile the PAIGC during 1972 had carried through a general election in its liberated zones – then some two-thirds of all the rural areas – for the election of regional councils which, in turn, elected a People's National Assembly; in September 1973 this declared Guinea-Bissau to be an independent state, and widespread international recognition followed. About 75 countries recognised the new Republic within three months of this declaration of September 1973, while the General Assembly of the United Nations, on 2 November of the same year, and by a very large majority, called on the Portuguese government to cease attacks on this sovereign republic and withdraw its armed forces. On 19 November, Guinea-Bissau became the forty-second member state of the Organisation of African Unity. Meanwhile hostilities continued on a small scale until May 1974.

After the Lisbon coup of April 1974 the new Portuguese government, now under the presidency of Spinola, asked the PAIGC, by way of President Senghor of Senegal, for an uncon-ditional cease-fire. The PAIGC refused this, but agreed to a truce that would enable Lisbon to prepare itself for unconditional evacuation. While Lisbon procrastinated, seeking to win time,

---

[1] Confirming the general rule that combatant losses in well-conducted irregular warfare are invariably small, official enquiries of the government of Guinea-Bissau made in 1975–6 showed, for military casualties, a total of about 345 seriously wounded, of whom 150 had suffered amputation; the number of military dead was not yet ascertained, but this figure for wounded could suggest that the number of killed, on the PAIGC side, was very small.

local Portuguese commanders made contact with their opposite numbers of the PAIGC. A consequent evacuation of Portuguese garrisons began in late July in spite of Lisbon's opposition, and continued without incident but now with Lisbon's agreement, until 14 October, when the last Portuguese units left. Lisbon had meanwhile recognised the independence of the whole country on 10 September. The new regime took over in circumstances of great economic difficulty but growing popularity. Fresh elections to the People's National Assembly, conducted in December 1976 throughout the country for the first time, showed large or very large majorities for PAIGC candidates in all except two of the country's ten electoral districts: in Gabu and Bafata, where PAIGC candidates gained only 56 and 50.4 per cent of the vote respectively.[1] The leaders of the PAIGC confirmed their posture of international non-alignment by seeking aid in the west as well as the east, and receiving some from both; its internal policies, however, assumed a non-capitalist model of development.

In the Cape Verde archipelago the clandestine network of the PAIGC, originating in 1957, came into the open during the middle months of 1974, and was reinforced in August and later by the return from Guiné of Cape Verdean political and military leaders. Pressure for independence became general, rivalry to the PAIGC being limited to two or three small urban groupings which proved to be too closely identified with the Portuguese system to enable them to win any ground. A general election held under Portuguese supervision on 30 June 1975 brought 85 per cent of the electorate to the polls; of this, just over 92 per cent voted for PAIGC candidates. An independent Republic under PAIGC leadership was proclaimed on 5 July, and recognised by Lisbon. Its Presi-

[1] This being a single-party system, votes against PAIGC candidates were signalled by a negative vote. No doubt some of these negative votes registered opposition to specific candidates, but in the case of the Gabu and Bafata districts the chief reason was certainly different. These districts, as the relevant map shows, had remained under Portuguese control almost till the end. Their populations are largely Fula and Mandinka whose chiefs, retaining much prestige, had almost all sided with the Portuguese against the PAIGC (cf. the general position of Fula chiefs in the nearby Futa Jalon in respect of the French colonial system during the mid-1950s, and the Parti Démocratique de Guinée led by Sékou Touré). The overall returns in these elections (of regional councillors, who in turn would elect members of the National Assembly) were as follows, compared with the similar returns in 1972 for all areas then liberated from Portuguese control: (1) *The 1972 (partial) elections.* Of 82032 voters, 79680 voted 'Yes', 2352 voted 'No'; percentage of 'Yes' voters, 97.1. (2) *The 1976 elections (whole country).* Of 193167 voters, 155542 voted 'Yes', 37625 voted 'No'; percentage of 'Yes' voters, 80.6. (From *O Militante*, Bissau, 1977, no. 1.)

dent was the secretary-general of the PAIGC, Aristides Pereira, while the party's deputy secretary-general, Luiz Cabral (younger brother of Amílcar Cabral), had become President of Guinea-Bissau. PAIGC policy had always aimed at an eventual union between the two countries; organisational steps towards union were taken in 1976 and 1977. These consisted of forming a Council of Unity whose principal task was to promote and supervise the work of joint commissions aiming at a complementary and convergent development of and between the two countries. Movement towards an eventual union would be 'step by step, and in practical and concrete ways'.[1]

In Mozambique, at the beginning of 1969, FRELIMO had been deprived of its initial leader, Eduardo Mondlane, by assassination in Dar es Salaam with a parcel bomb of enemy provenance (as later established by a Tanzanian police enquiry), but a new leadership under the army commander, Samora Moises Machel, was able to reinforce the movement's unity against a small faction, led by Lazaro Nkavadame and Uriah Simango, who favoured one or other form of negotiation for a compromise solution. While holding much of the northern districts of Cabo Delgado and Niassa, FRELIMO forces opened a new fighting front in the Tete district and made rapid progress southward into the 'waist' of Mozambique. After April 1974 the Spinolist government in Lisbon again tried for an unconditional cease-fire, evidently hoping to save some part of Portuguese control from the wreck of defeat, but FRELIMO, like its two companion movements, replied that it would continue the war unless the Portuguese withdrew. Frustrated of his hopes of gaining a compromise, Spinola resigned in September 1974, and the way was clear for negotiation on the technicalities of Portuguese withdrawal. Apprehensions that a South African force would enter southern Mozambique failed to materialise, partly no doubt because of the sheer speed of the Portuguese collapse and the impossibility, as it proved, of finding any alternative political organisation to FRELIMO such as might have invited South African entry (as was to happen in Angola); and an independent Republic under FRELIMO leadership was proclaimed and recognised on 25 June 1975.

---

[1] Spelt out in documents of Third Congress of PAIGC (Bissau, 15–20 November, 1977) and especially in Aristides Pereira, *Relatório do Conselho Superior da Luta*. In November 1980 a military take-over in Guinea-Bissau would reject union.

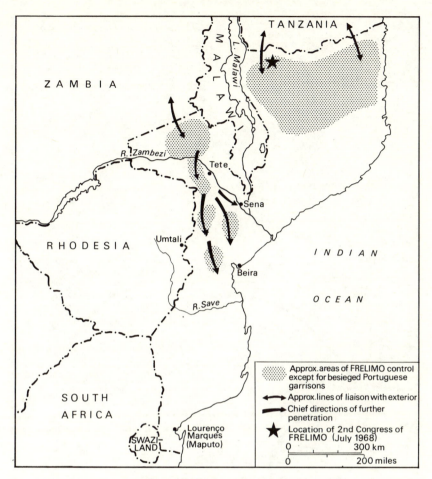

Approx. areas of FRELIMO control
except for besieged Portuguese
garrisons
Approx. lines of liaison with exterior
Chief directions of further
penetration
Location of 2nd Congress of
FRELIMO (July 1968)

0   300 km
0   200 miles

37 Mozambique: the war situation after late 1973.

Some rioting by Portuguese settlers in Lourenço Marques (now
renamed Maputo) was quickly quelled; most settlers left the
country; and the chief problem for the new administration
remained to instal its structures and institutions in all those
regions, but above all in the towns, which had not been brought
under FRELIMO control during the war. Initially, tolerable
relations were established with a South African government
which was now found to control electricity supply to southern
Mozambique, and agreement was given to the completion of the
Cabora Bassa Dam and power system. But the new government
moved at once to support the nationalist cause in Zimbabwe

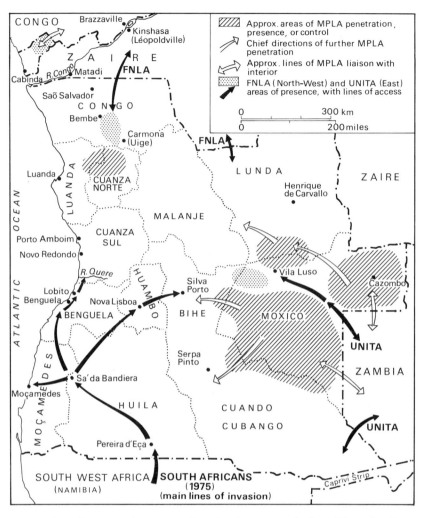

38   Angola: approximate war situation in 1970 and after. (Note that in 1973 the MPLA in central Moxico was weakened by the defection of part of its forces there.)

(Rhodesia), gave its adherence to UN sanctions on the illegal Rhodesian regime, and encouraged Zimbabwean fighting units to open external bases on its territory. Relations with South Africa rapidly deteriorated after 1978, when the South African government began to operate new policies of aggressive military 'destabilisation' aimed especially at Mozambique and Angola.

As at the onset of the fight for independence, Angola proved a special case, partly because of its larger white population and its proven wealth in minerals, and partly because rivals were found to set against the MPLA. The record here was unusually complex and confused, and can be sketched here only in the barest outline.

At the demise of the Estado Novo, in April 1974, the position of the MPLA was comparatively weaker than that of FRELIMO or PAIGC in Mozambique and Guiné. Three chief reasons could be detected. Probably the most significant of these lay in the long hostility of Zaire's President Mobutu, whose policy in Angola aimed at promoting the fortunes of his protégé, Holden Roberto, and the latter's Kongo-manned Frente Nacional de Libertação de Angola (FNLA, successor to UPA). This meant, in practice, that MPLA was barred from any logistical access to central and western Angola by way of the Zaire frontier, a major handicap that was suffered, in comparable geographical circumstances, neither by FRELIMO nor by PAIGC. A second reason lay in defections from the leadership of MPLA that were reminiscent of those from FRELIMO during 1968–9, the difference being that these MPLA defections occurred in 1972–3. A third reason, now of rising importance, lay in the existence of FNLA and of UNITA (União Nacional para a Independência Total de Angola), initially a breakaway from FNLA led by Jonas Savimbi, as proclaimed rivals to MPLA.

Neither of these two organisations had played any significant part in the war. The FNLA had adopted an *attentiste* position since the uprisings of 1961, and such warlike activities as it still engaged in were chiefly aimed at hampering or destroying the MPLA. Established after 1968 in a small zone on the borders of Moxico and Bihe south-east of the town of Luso, UNITA followed much the same line, and likewise made its peace with the Portuguese army on a joint anti-MPLA agreement.[1] Each, not surprisingly,

---

[1] There is much evidence for this. See, e.g. the exiled ex-Prime Minister Marcello Caetano, in his *Depoimento* (Rio and São Paulo, 1974), 180–1 (tr. O. Gjerstad): 'The enemy's [that is, the MPLA's] opening of the Eastern Front [in Angola] constituted a tremendous preoccupation, and [General] Costa Gomes, on assuming responsibility for Angola's defence, approached the case with intelligence and decisiveness. [General] Bettencourt Rodrigues received the task...to pacify the region, which he did by reaching an understanding with the people of UNITA...' An evidently genuine exchange of letters between the UNITA leader, Jonas Savimbi, and the Portuguese chief of staff in Eastern Angola, Lt.-Colonel Ramires de Oliveira, dating to late 1972 and concerning their collaboration, was published in *Afrique–Asie*, 8 July 1974, **61**, 7–18.

now found fresh external supporters and advocates, especially in South Africa and the USA.

This led directly to a struggle for power in which the Portuguese, holding the ring during 1974–5, sought to promote a 'tripartite government' of all three organisations. This proved only an exacerbation as FNLA tried to win a foothold, increasingly by violent means, in Luanda and other coastal towns where MPLA had an obviously overwhelming support, while Savimbi's organisation, UNITA, did the same in the Ovimbundu areas of the central districts where MPLA was comparatively weak. In July MPLA riposted by driving FNLA out of Luanda, and was then able to receive improved military supplies from the USSR and Yugoslavia (China by this time being a declared supporter of FNLA and its patron, President Mobutu).[1] In September 1975 MPLA had secured a dominant position in 12 out of the country's 16 districts, and appeared able to take the rest. Helped by US and Chinese aid, Mobutu then reinforced FNLA units with a considerable force from Zaire, partly of Zairean units with Portuguese officers, while a South African armoured force invaded southern Angola from Namibia in cooperation with Holden Roberto and Jonas Savimbi.[2]

Entering Angola on 23 October, this South African force pushed rapidly northward as far as a point beyond Novo Redondo, where it was halted. The MPLA now declared the independence of a People's Republic of Angola on the agreed date of 11 November, and set in motion an emergency plan for Cuban military support. At what appears to have been extremely short notice, a Cuban force eventually of some 13 000 men was shipped and airlifted to Angola. Joint MPLA and Cuban units then stopped the South African northern drive and went over to the offensive against the northern force from Zaire. The latter was driven out of the country in January 1976, at which point it became clear that Pretoria must either reinforce its own troops

[1] In point of fact, the first military supplies available to MPLA in that crucial month of July did not come from any part of Europe, but were sent (in a Yugoslav ship) by the PAIGC of Guinea-Bissau and Cape Verde. They included some armoured cars, which were landed with great difficulty, and were followed by a small contingent of PAIGC troops airlifted from Guinea-Bissau.

[2] See, for example, a report from the Johannesburg correspondent of *The Times*, 4 February 1977. This quotes South African official sources as saying that the maximum number of South African troops operating in Angola was 2000; outside observers had put this number as being closer to 6000.

794

or withdraw. South African government statements now declared that reinforcement would not be attempted without direct American support. But the Nixon administration and notably its Secretary of State, Dr Henry Kissinger, had by this time run into sharp Congress hostility to any further American involvement in support of FNLA or UNITA, and preferred to affirm that Pretoria had invaded Angola on its own initiative. Bereft of any direct and public American support, especially for the use of South Africa's powerful air force, Pretoria decided to withdraw. Its units pulled out of Huambo, Bihe and Benguela provinces early in February, and had crossed back into Namibia before the end of March. Behind them they left a scatter of demoralised UNITA and FNLA bands, weakened further by fighting between each other since December; these either fled, or were quickly mopped up, except in the mountains and forests of Huambo and Bihe, where a number of UNITA bands continued to be active,[1] and the 'second war of liberation', as it was now called, came to an end. With this, the new government of the MPLA was left to cope as well as it could with the confusions and dislocations which inevitably filled the scene. These were approached with policies of radical reorganisation similar in principle to the policies of FRELIMO and PAIGC.

São Tomé and Principe acceded to independence as a single Republic without fighting or political resistance from Lisbon. Nationalists of the Movimento de Libertação de São Tomé e Principe (MLSTP) reached an agreement with Portugal on 25 November 1974, providing that colonial rule should end with elections to a constituent assembly. These were held on 6 July 1975, and gave the MLSTP a 90 per cent majority of votes. On 11 July the last Portuguese troops and administrators were withdrawn, and independence was proclaimed the next day, Manuel da Costa becoming the country's first president.

[1] These bands were left with dumps of war material by the retreating South African army (pulling out of the High Plateau early in February) and continued a destructive warlike activity across a wide arc of hill country in northern Huambo and Bihe districts. By 1977 this activity was degenerating more and more into sporadic banditry. The army of the MPLA began systematic operations against them in June 1977, but fighting persisted. At this stage UNITA operations were mainly in South African-promoted raids across the Namibian border into southernmost Angola, and a continued air-lifted infiltration of sabotage groups for the wrecking of rail and other communications.

Lisbon allowed itself small room for manoeuvre in foreign relations during these years of warfare, but clearly thought that little or none would be required, and that the nationalist challenge could be contained with no substantial shift of posture. In this respect it relied upon its membership of the North Atlantic Treaty Organisation (NATO). The value of this membership was enhanced after the French withdrawal in 1966, when the Iberian–Atlantic command of NATO was moved from France to Portugal. But whereas the active support of individual NATO powers stayed practically complete until the end, Lisbon's real bargaining power diminished. An estimate of 1962 showed about 80 per cent of US oversea military air traffic as being dependent on the US base in the Azores, but another of 1968 (perhaps because so much US military air traffic was by then going to Vietnam) put this proportion at only 20 per cent.[1] Till late in the 1960s, however, long-range US air transports connecting with Western Europe appear still to have required some use of the Azores base.

The nationalist movements had nothing to oppose the powerfully supported colonial government save some rather scrappy African aid, unofficial but often weak links with sympathisers in the west and, after about 1960, a cautious though growing readiness of several governments in the Soviet bloc (then including China) to give material aid and facilities for training and education. So far as peripheral neighbours were concerned, the PAIGC had continuous support from Guinea and occasional support from Senegal; FRELIMO could count on Tanzania and afterwards on Zambia but not on Malawi; while MPLA found help in Congo-Brazzaville and afterwards (till 1973) in Zambia, to offset the unrelenting hostility of Zaire. The Liberation Committee of the Organisation of African Unity was sporadically able to collect military aid for each of the movements, but its total volume was always small.

The pioneering leaderships, drawn together from the first by their common cultural background and very comparable problems and policies, acted together in trying to evoke interest and raise support. In 1957 a handful of nationalists from Angola and Guiné met in Paris, at a '*réunion de consultation et d'étude pour le développement de la lutte*', and formed themselves into a Movimento Anti-Colónialista (MAC), largely for propaganda purposes. In January 1960, meeting at Tunis during the second All-African Peoples'

---

[1] Abshire and Samuels, *Portuguese Africa*, 436.

Conference, MAC was enlarged into a Frente Revolucionária Africana para a Independência Nacional (FRAIN). Its common action programme was signed by Abel Djassi (the pseudonym of Amílcar Cabral, PAIGC), Hugo Menezes (an Angolan specifically representing FRAIN), two MPLA leaders (Lucio Lara, Viriato da Cruz), and also, though he at once cancelled his adherence, by José Guilmor (the pseudonym of Holden Roberto, UPA, Angola).[1] Later in 1960 members of FRAIN went on support-seeking tours wherever they could gain access, notably in Britain and France; Cabral spent some months in London at this time, still under his *nom de guerre*. The government of Guinea, and afterwards that of Algeria, proved especially helpful with passports. Later again, in April 1961, FRAIN gave way to a Conferência das Organizações Nacionalistas das Colónias Portuguezas (CONCP) during a meeting in Casablanca; and CONCP remained as a coordinating body, based in Algiers, until the wars ended, though its activity dwindled as each movement developed its own external relations. By 1962 the refusal of cooperation by Holden Roberto (UPA, then FNLA, Angola) became constant, while the Mozambicans, up to now represented in the councils of the movements chiefly by Marcelino dos Santos, who was to become Vice-President of Mozambique in 1975, appeared as regular participants after the formation of FRELIMO in that year.

In 1976, after independence, the question was raised of forming a new type of coordinating body, but it became immediately apparent that this was regarded, by some if not by all, as undesirable. It was accepted that the five governments should not seek to form a 'lusophone grouping' within the OAU, and that basic political cooperation would in any case have to await the emergence of structured political parties, only then in prospect or course of formation. Even so, a three-day exploratory meeting of foreign ministers of the five governments met on São Tomé in May 1976, and some decisions were taken. The CONCP being now outdated, no other such organisation was formed, but the governments were recommended to agree on the principle of prior consultation before major internal gatherings. Some coordination in political and cultural questions, as well as in matters of technical, diplomatic, consular and telecommunicatory common interest, was likewise recommended.[2]

[1] Photocopy of programme, with signatures, in my possession.
[2] A. Pereira, *Relatório*, in *Nô Pintcha*, 4 September 1976, vol. 2, no. 47.

Each government reaffirmed its position of military non-alignment, and western apprehensions about east-bloc bases being established in these territories were not realised. While pursuing anti-capitalist domestic policies, each regime went out of its way to secure good relations with leading western countries, as well as with the UN and its agencies; only in the case of Angola, initially boycotted by the USA, was there delay in achieving such relations. Each government adhered to UN and OAU policy towards the illegal Rhodesian regime and the South African occupation of Namibia.[1] Relations with the Portuguese government improved after the latter had given up its demand that the new regimes should meet the debts to Portugal of the previous colonial administrations.

THE POLITICS OF LIBERATION: THEORY AND PRACTICE

With differences of emphasis or explanation, the founding leaderships of the three nationalist movements (the MLSTP not really counting till very near the end) each arrived at the same appreciation of the problems before them. The gruesome lessons of repressive brutality in 1959–60 confirmed the Lisbon regime's inflexibility, and reinforced their view that Portugal was a sub-imperialism incapable of practising a meaningful policy of reform. They saw well enough that if it had been thus capable, as one of them reminded his colleagues in 1965, 'we should surely not be at war with Portugal today'.[2] Things being as they were, however, Portuguese intransigence could be turned to advantage. For it eliminated the dangers of a compromise solution; and they were convinced, and found ever more confirmation in the newly-independent Africa of the early 1960s, that a compromise solution would leave the colonial condition of their peoples essentially unchanged. In eliminating those risks, moreover,

---

[1] This support for other movements seeking the end of racist regimes in southern Africa entered into the policies of non-alignment of the new regimes. Cf. a characteristic statement by Aristides Pereira, Secretary-General of the PAIGC and President of the Cape Verde Republic in *Relatório do CSL, 15 November 1977:*
'In creating our party, we knew very well that the aims of the struggle we were beginning could not be reduced to a mere liquidation of the colonial yoke upon our countries. This is so because it is impossible to destroy colonial domination without struggling against imperialism, which is the supporter of colonialism in all its forms. This anti-imperialist factor is a fundamental factor in our policy of non-alignment...'
[2] A. Cabral, in Proceedings of an inter-movement conference, Dar es Salaam, October 1965, *La Lutte de libération nationale dans les colonies portugaises* (CONCP, Algiers, 1965), 152.

Portuguese intransigence placed before them an absolute need to find an alternative not only to the colonial system but also, beyond that, to any possible derivative from that system. The wars would have to be used as an instrument to forge this alternative. 'We do not like war; but this armed struggle has its advantages. Through it we are building a nation that is solid, conscious of itself...'[1]

For the wars did indeed take hold of this starting theory of change, vague and unsure as it necessarily was, and continuously developed it further. Circumstances increasingly combined to show that successful movements could be built and maintained only from the ground of rural interests and of rural participation in serving those interests. A few townsmen might foresee a 'revolutionary future', but it very soon became clear that it was no good telling this to the peasants. What these saw, in their multitudes, were the 'small immediate facts' of a colonial coercion: the facts of contract labour, obligatory cultivation, a hated system of taxes, the pressures of the local *chefe do posto* and his *regulos* and police. Meaningful change would have to begin with things like those, and offer an alternative to things like those. To propose a mere change of masters from privileged white to privileged black would never be enough to justify the pains of war. In any and every case, the peasants would rally only to movements in which their interests and participation were seen and felt by them as paramount. To 'mobilise' the peasants meant to identify their grievances and show how these could be removed. A PAIGC internal directive of 1965 spoke for the general experience: 'Keep always in mind that the people are not fighting for ideas, for the things in anyone's head. They are fighting to win material benefits, to live better and at peace, to see their lives go forward, to guarantee the future of their children...' The alternative would have to be a modernising and egalitarian democracy, but easy words and promises would never achieve it: 'Practise revolutionary democracy...Hold frequent meetings...Hide nothing from the masses of our people. Tell no lies, claim no easy victories...'[2]

A further large conviction shaped itself. If the central objective

[1] A. Cabral, foreword to Davidson, *The liberation of Guiné*, 13.

[2] A. Cabral, *Palavras gerais*, 1965, quoted here from extract in Cabral, *Revolution in Guinea* (London, 1969), author's translation, 72. Complete French text, A. Cabral, *Unité et lutte* (Paris, 1975), ed. and tr. M. de Andrade, vol. II, 188–233; and in Cabral, *Unity and struggle* (London, 1979) tr. M. Wolfers.

was to create a movement in which the interests and participation of the vast majority were to be decisive – and fully rural populations were more than nine-tenths of these peoples – this could not be allowed to give paramountcy to the existing ideas of that majority. On the contrary, what was needed was 'a new culture, also based on our own traditions, but respecting everything that the world today has conquered for the service of mankind'.[1] And this need was an imperative; it could not be negotiable. Much bitter experience, right through the 1960s, proved again and again that allowing a free rein to the 'pre-colonial' or 'traditional' fund of ideas would lead straight to disaster by way of inter-ethnic disputes and rivalries, witchcraft practices, individualist ambitions, and one or other degeneration into terrorism.[2] It became unquestionably sure that a successful alternative system must arise from a fight on two fronts: against the past as well as against the present. This was the close grappling with absolutely local realities which always made it certain that these wars of liberation would lead to an alternative *sui generis*, no matter how otherwise glossed in revolutionary terms and titles.

Whatever the nationalists may have thought at the outset, they became aware that no imported examples could solve their problems. Much evidence from their documents and statements could illustrate this, and display the meaning they attached to a revolutionary as distinct from a reformist nationalism. 'We are trying,' Neto explained in 1970, 'to free and modernise our people by a dual revolution: against their traditional structures which can no longer serve them' – such as ethnic separatism, witchcraft belief, the oppression of women – 'and against colonial rule.'[3] When FRELIMO 'took up arms to defeat the old order', recalled Samora Machel a little later,

We felt the obscure need to create a new society, strong, healthy and prosperous, in which people freed from all exploitation would co-operate for the progress of all. In the course of our struggle, in the tough fight we have had to wage war against reactionary elements, we came to understand our objectives more clearly. We felt especially that the struggle to create new structures would fall within the creation of a new mentality...[4]

[1] A. Cabral, 'Resistência cultural', PAIGC seminar paper, November 1969.
[2] For evidence of this experience, see Davidson, *In the eye of the storm*, 29–32; and, for Guinea-Bissau, Davidson, *Africa in modern history: the search for a new society* (London, 1978), Chapter 30, and source references.
[3] Davidson, *In the eye of the storm*, 279.
[4] S. M. Machel, *Mozambique: sowing the seeds of revolution* (London, 1974), 39.

The styles might vary from dry realism to a vivid rhetoric; but the meaning was the same. The challenge was to overleap the colonial heritage but, just as much, the pre-colonial heritage as well. Against whatever obstacles of history or human nature, it had to be a matter of living differently in order to live better.

But how should the ideas of living differently be made to develop in men's minds? The field laboratories in which the answer was sought were the 'liberated zones'. These were more or less large areas taken out of Portuguese control and secured generally against Portuguese action except in aerial bombing and sporadic ground raids. As such, they were distinguished from 'zones of contestation' in which each side fought for control. In Guinea-Bissau the PAIGC was able to achieve its earliest liberated zones in 1964, progressively adding to them until 1974. FRELIMO reached the same position in parts of Cabo Delgado and Niassa in 1966 and in parts of Tete in 1970; while MPLA, though under exceptionally adverse conditions of terrain and sparse population, achieved it in areas of eastern Angola after 1967. These zones became a central and decisive feature in the life of the movements, although their extent and security greatly varied with the tides of war.

The chief effort of the leaderships in these zones was to develop an initial peasant sympathy, or at times a merely suspicious tolerance, into an active peasant participation. This effort took different forms. Of these the most important from first to last was the promotion of local committees of self-administration derived from assemblies, necessarily partial and inadequate at the start, representing large villages or groups of small villages. To these committees there were progressively given responsibilities arising from the needs of the war as well as from the need to exercise a local government in place of ousted colonial officials and colonial-appointed 'chiefs'; and these responsibilities were widened in the measure that the committees became more representative, elected, and efficient. In their mature form, in zones liberated over a long period, the best of these committees were elected bodies concerned with local justice, through the creation of village tribunals; with local security, through the manning of militias; with local education and health, through the supply of pupils and food to new elementary schools, and the provision of food and porterage to new bush clinics staffed by newly trained

PORTUGUESE-SPEAKING AFRICA

nurses with an occasional doctor making his rounds; and, above all, with the forging of the ideas of a democracy based on equality of status between all adults, and notably between women and men. Efforts were made at the same time to provide a substitute for banished Portuguese trading networks through sale-and-purchase shops; these bought local produce by barter exchange for goods imported from the exterior. Swedish aid was particularly useful in supplying such goods, which ranged from cloth and household utensils to transistor radios.

No doubt the results differed from zone to zone, and the mature form of this structural model could be achieved only in a few zones, while elsewhere the militants of the movements strove towards it as best they could. But the overall balance of evidence during the wars, and of what happened when the wars were over, combines to suggest that the essential structures of an alternative society, of a modernising and egalitarian culture, did indeed take shape in the experience of all three movements – if also, as one should perhaps emphasise, in widely varying degrees of maturity.

There set in, undoubtedly, a dual process of cultural development and convergence between 'the few' and 'the many'. The peasants learned new understandings and attitudes; but so did the originally urban leadership. Both aspects of this process helped to solidify the movements, broaden the scope of participation, and change the mentality of men and women; and it is in this elusive field of experience that one must look for the keys to their success, whether in making headway against their enemy or in preparing for the peace that would follow the enemy's defeat. In 1970 Cabral offered a sketch of this crucial process:

The leaders of the liberation movements, who are generally drawn from the 'petty bourgeoisie' (such as intellectuals, clerks) or urban workers (such as labourers, drivers, other employees), have to live day by day among various peasant communities in the heart of rural populations. They learn to know their people better. They uncover at its source the richness of their people's cultural values, whether philosophical, political, artistic, social or moral. They achieve a clearer perception of the economic realities, problems, sufferings and aspirations of the masses of their people. Not without a certain astonishment, they discover the richness of spirit, capacity for reasoned discussion and clear exposition of ideas, facility for comprehending and assimilating concepts, on the part of populations hitherto ignored, if not despised, and considered by the coloniser, and even by some nationals, as peoples of no kind of competence. The leaders thus enrich their own culture. They develop personally and free themselves from complexes. They reinforce their ability to serve their people through serving the movement.

On their side, the working masses and especially the peasants who are usually illiterate, and have never gone outside the boundaries of their village or region, also come into contact with other communities and, in their turn, lose the complexes which hampered them in their relations with other ethnic and social groups. They break the bonds of their village universe and integrate themselves progressively with their country and with the world. They acquire an infinity of new insights useful to their immediate and future action within the framework of the struggle. They strengthen their political awareness by assimilating the principles of national and social revolution that the struggle postulates. And so they become more able to play their decisive role of providing the chief force in the movement of liberation.[1]

All this being so, the armed struggle for liberation from colonial rule, as from restrictive traditional ideas, was to be seen not only as 'a product of the culture' promoted by that struggle, but also as 'a *determinant* of culture'; and this, 'without doubt, is our people's prime recompense for the efforts and sacrifices which war demands'. In thinking this, Cabral and his colleagues were giving the concept of 'culture' a multivalence applicable to societies in transition from one historical phase to another: in this case, to a regained self-rule and self-reliance, but within a world different from any that the past had known. They saw this in all-round terms. A new culture would be the fruit of insights gained by participation in this building of a new society. It would be independent, modernising, self-aware. It would induce between the individual and the collective a relationship of harmony; and this relationship of harmony would be such as to bind together all who worked or fought for common purposes. This was the developing harmony of understanding and purpose which, as a determinant, would open the way for, and accompany, organisational changes in the structure of existing society.

The cultural programmes of these movements accordingly began with the teaching of this politics of liberation, and of the morality associated with this politics: the morality, that is, of seeking individual self-realisation through service to these developing communities. The association of individuals and collectivities in decisions affecting their daily lives was one form of innovation; pressure against exploitative customs and attitudes

[1] A. Cabral, 'National liberation and culture' (Syracuse University, Eduardo Mondlane Memorial Lecture, 20 Feb 1970), 13; Cabral, *Unité et lutte*, vol. I, 332, and *Unity and struggle* (London, 1979).

derived from the pre-colonial heritage, such as polygamy and certain witchcraft beliefs, was another. Beyond such basic and decisive issues, affecting as they did the very capacity of these movements to make progress and develop, there evolved a modernising campaign against illiteracy, and in favour of the expansion of elementary forms of school education. Whenever zones could be sufficiently cleared of colonial control or military interference, bush schools were founded where few or none had existed before. Even by the end of 1968, leading the way in this respect, the PAIGC had some 14 000 children with an average age of twelve in about 150 schools with some 220 teachers in the zones of Guinea-Bissau which they controlled.

The few who were fully literate, meanwhile, saw it as a duty to use their talents in support of this cultural process, whether in poetry with a markedly political and social content, or, though less often, in writing stories that might lay foundations for a popular written literature.[1] Life in these movements became, as the years wore by, and in the broad sense indicated above, an increasingly cultural experience for growing numbers of those who participated.

Given the background of this subtle and continuous process of development pursued through years, the leaderships at the end of the wars were in no mind either to hasten or to modify their objectives. So far, through terrain often very harsh, their theory and practice had served well, and they could measure its strengths and weaknesses against a remarkable success. They now had strong movements behind them, movements which had become profoundly representative of their peoples, but the problems ahead were in many ways more complex, and therefore more difficult, than any that they had faced. The chief immediate task was to implant law and order into towns and other areas evacuated by the Portuguese (and, in Angola, evacuated also by

---

[1] For examples of the poets, see several collections: for example, M. de Andrade, *Antologia temática de poesia Africana: 1, la noite grávida de Punhais* (Lisbon, 1975); M. Dickinson (ed. and tr.) *When bullets begin to flower* (Nairobi, 1972) which, like the first, has resistance poetry from all the Portuguese colonies; Agostinho Neto, *Sacred hope*, tr. M. Holness (Dar es Salaam, 1974), one of Angola's leading poets (and President of Angola); and a Cape Verdean poet, Ovidio Martins, *Não vou para Pasárgada* (Rotterdam, n.d.). For examples of new writers in prose, see J. Luandino Vieira, *The real life of Domingos Xavier* (tr. M. Wolfers, London, 1977, but written *c.* 1960 in a rich language of Luanda slang and popular expression), and another Angolan, Pepetela, *As aventuras de Ngunga* (Lisbon, n.d., but written *c.* 1970). The list could be much extended.

South African and other invaders), and then, gradually, install throughout their countries the institutions and attitudes elaborated or projected in the wartime zones of liberation. This latter task was to stretch them to their utmost for a long period ahead.

The next immediate task was to cope with an invariably disastrous economic heritage. Production had collapsed in all urban and peripheral areas. Roads, bridges, railways were all much damaged, and huge numbers of land-mines had to be lifted. Every sort of technician, from book-keepers to plumbers, was in acutely short supply. There were few or no economic statistics, and no statisticians. They had to take into national ownership and management a large number of enterprises of whose nature they could at first know almost nothing. Beyond that, they had to found national banks, issue national currencies, and conclude a long series of basic international agreements on trade and exchange. It was rapidly clear that all this would take time, and that some years must pass before production could be generally restored even to pre-war levels.

The alternative they had begun to forge in the liberated zones of the war years predicated a non-capitalist and eventually socialist model. Yet they were careful, even with the wars behind them, to measure their words. If they remained insistent on emphasising their loyalty to a revolutionary objective defined in Marxist terms, they did so without demagogy. Some words of Neto's, when talking in 1976 to an Angolan trade union congress, may probably stand for their general attitude:

The long period of transition from a colonial society to a socialist society will call for a multi-sided form of economic organisation. The progress of our economic transformation towards socialism will be expressed by a steady growth of the state sector and of the co-operative sector in the rural areas, and by a steady reduction of the mixed sector, of the private capital sector... [1]

But there would be no hurry to collectivise property. 'Millions of Angolans own means of production. They have their bit of land. And we are very aware of how difficult it still is, in the rural areas, to transform these small properties into co-operative or state property.' Change could come only with peasant agreement: 'only when the peasantry fully understands the advantage and the meaning of this more advanced mode of production... This is a

[1] *Vitória Certa*, 23 October 1976, vol. II, no. 44, author's translation. Also in *People's Power* (London, 1976), Nov.–Dec. 1976, no. 5, 6–7.

matter of years of organisation and educative work . . .' As for the relations with major foreign enterprises, such as Cabinda Gulf Oil, Neto said that they would have to temporise, for such enterprises alone possessed the technology required to extract oil or other resources. But 'we do not wish to deceive foreign capitalist monopolies by concealing the fact that we intend to follow the road of socialising our means of production, of finance, of trade, of services, and of everything that can be socialised . . .'

Meanwhile they would press on with the further promotion and installation of the basic political structures of participation, whether in terms of party organisation or of the state organisation which called for assemblies and executive committees of self-rule at all levels of government. A beginning had been made, but the bulk of this task still lay ahead. Thus the central committee of the MPLA in Angola asserted in a programmatic statement of October 1976 that

The definitive forms of our state, considered as a whole and not merely as the apparatus of government, will arise from the representative institutions of power, from the organs of *Poder Popular* [People's Power], where the working class, the working people, participate institutionally in the command and government of society, in all activities and in every community throughout the national territory . . . [1]

Corresponding statements and definitions were available from FRELIMO and the PAIGC. These structures would take time to build. But they would represent, in the measure of their unfolding development, the groundwork of the society which these movements had set themselves to create.

EQUATORIAL GUINEA, c. 1940 to 1975

> . . . y alli, alegada de la verde masa africana,
> azotada por los vientos del Atlántico,
> orgullosa y solitaria, se erige una historia,
> un mundo, un destino . . .

Written of the island of Annobón, whose population in 1950 was 1403, these lines from a 'lament' of Francisco Zamora might seem to apply to all the parts of Equatorial Guinea, cut off from the rest of Africa by the heritage of a Spanish colonial culture

---

[1] *Documentos: 3ª Reunião do Comite Central do MPLA* (Luanda, 1976).

Table 15.3. *The census figures for 1950.*

	Whites	Non-whites	'Foreigners'	Totals
Fernando Po Is.	2161	14735	23579	40475
Rio Muni	1428	142316	12432	156176
Annobón Is.	6	1397		1403
Corisco Is.		513		513
Elobey Is.		96		96

unshared by any of its neighbours in 'a world, a destiny' of its own. It remains that this little territory played out the drama of rising nationalism in the same essential themes as its English- and French-speaking neighbours, although with peculiarities of its own and a *dénouement* both bizarre and tragic. One can divide its history in this period into three fairly distinct phases: up to 1959, when its status was raised from 'colonial' to 'provincial', taking a leaf out of Salazar's book; between 1960 and 1968, when Madrid went beyond Salazar's prescriptions and attempted a partial decolonisation which should, as it was hoped, conserve the territory as an integral segment of the Spanish system; and onwards from 1968, when the territory became an independent Republic. The first of these phases consisted of little more than a continuation of previous policies; these closely resembled the policies of Portugal and France, notably in dividing the population into a vast majority governed as 'natives' or non-citizens, and a very small minority (together with whites) admitted to civic status as *emancipados*, assimilation to the metropolitan culture being the only permissible means of advancement.

War stagnation in this phase was slightly lessened, at least in the case of Fernando Po, by a treaty of 1943 with the British in Nigeria, regulating the immigration of contract workers, most of whom came from the Niger Delta regions. But the arrival of Admiral Faustino Ruiz Gonzalez as governor-general in 1949 signalled the beginnings of a consistent effort to improve the colonial economy through the investment of budget surpluses in better communications, in the extension of elementary schools, and in some other initiatives. The whole phase showed a steady growth in population, though the relevant statistics are rough estimates save in the case of whites and, probably, of contract-workers in Fernando Po. In 1942 the territory was said to have

167158 people, including 4124 whites, most of whom were permanent settlers or urban residents, and 24321 non-white 'foreigners' who were mostly Nigerian immigrant workers on plantations, chiefly in Fernando Po. The 1950 census figures are set out in table 15.3.

By 1960 the whole population had grown from a total of about 200000 in 1950 to about 245000, with whites increasing to some 7000, nearly three-quarters of whom were on Fernando Po. No later figures of any value are available; but it appears that large numbers of Africans in Rio Muni fled abroad after about 1972, and that the number of whites in 1975 was only a small fraction of those who had lived in Rio Muni in 1960.

During the Second World War the Madrid regime had nourished some hope, at least until 1942, of being able to inherit British and French colonial territory. Disappointed in this, it responded slowly to the new political currents set going after the end of the war, but felt it wise during the 1950s to adopt a much more determined policy of assimilation. This took constitutional form on 30 July 1959, when the colony became the Región Ecuatorial de España, being divided into two provinces (Fernando Po and Rio Muni). Each of these provinces proceeded in 1960 to elect three deputies to the Spanish Cortes: two Africans and one European in the case of Fernando Po, two Europeans and one African in that of Rio Muni. At the same time, a little earlier than in the Portuguese system (and 14 years after the French system), the constitutional distinction between 'natives' and 'civilised' was abolished, while Admiral Gonzalez continued with his programme of cultural assimilation. Already by 1960 it was claimed that the whole territory had 118 pre-primary schools, 14 primary schools, four technical schools, one secondary school, and also, at Santa Isabel (capital of Fernando Po), a training centre for teachers and clerks. In addition, Catholic missions were operating 20 pre-primary schools, and two seminaries. The comparison with Portuguese practice was again apparent: 'Instruction is given in Spanish...Hygiene, Christian virtues, love of the fatherland and of the Caudillo [General Franco], the elements of Spanish language and culture, the rudiments of agriculture: these are what is mainly taught...'[1]

This 'provincial' phase saw the beginnings of nationalism, but

[1] R. Pélissier, 'La Guinée Espagnole', *Revue Française de Science Politique*, 3 September 1963, **13**, 631.

chiefly among small groups who had taken refuge from the Caudillo's paternal hand in Cameroun and Gabon. They formed two bodies: the Movimiento Nacional de Liberación de la Guinea (MONALIGE), and the Idea Popular de la Guinea Ecuatorial (IPGE). Their pressures were weak, but the general trend in West Africa was not; and Madrid now thought it well to seek its own *interlocuteurs valables*. A decision of 9 August 1963, approved by a referendum of 15 December 1963, introduced the territory to a measure of autonomy and the administrative promotion of a 'moderate' grouping, the Movimiento de Unión Nacional de la Guinea Ecuatorial (MUNGE). This proved a feeble instrument, and, with growing pressure for change from the UN, Madrid gave way to the currents of nationalism. Independence was conceded on 12 October 1968. The 'moderates' were now thrust aside, and Francisco Macías Nguéma emerged as the dominant figure.

Severely authoritarian from the start, Macías proceeded to silence his opponents or rivals one by one, revealing his preferred style in the renaming of Fernando Po, which became Macías Nguéma Byoga (while Annobón became Pigalu). A new constitution of 1973 deprived Macías Nguéma Byoga of its remaining provincial autonomy within the Republic, evidently to the advantage of the Fang supremacy on the mainland. Tensions with neighbouring countries were lessened by OAU and other mediation in the same year of 1973, but continued to disturb relations between the Macías regime and Nigeria and, at the time of writing, contacts between the two countries seemed uncertain.

Little can be said with confidence about economic and cultural change. In 1974 the country's production of cassava was estimated by the Food and Agriculture Organisation of the UN as being 46000 tons; of sweet potatoes 19000 tons; of bananas 12000 tons; of cocoa beans 12000 tons; of coffee 7200 tons; of palm-oil 4300 tons; of kernels 2100 tons; while power production in 1967 was recorded as being 9470000 kwh on Fernando Po and 5700000 in Rio Muni. In 1975 the Guinean peseta was replaced by the ekuele. Some aid had been sporadically achieved from Cuba, the USSR and China, but there is little reliable information as to its scale or use; and reports in 1975 suggested that the regime was close to bankruptcy, though some allowance may need to be made for the fact that most of such reports have emanated from refugees.

Towards the middle 1970s the Macías regime came under grave

accusations of being guilty of mass killings. In 1974 the World Council of Churches affirmed that large numbers of people had been murdered since 1968 in a 'reign of terror' which continued. The same body claimed that a quarter of the whole population had fled abroad, while 'the prisons are overflowing and to all intents and purposes form one vast concentration camp'. Early in 1975 refugees in Madrid published a list of 319 persons said to have been executed by the president's orders, and these sources placed the number of refugees as being between 55 000 and 75 000.[1] A year later, reports from Madrid also spoke of clashes within the country, and of growing opposition to the regime. Various coups were to follow.

[1] *West Africa*, 6 January 1975, 22.   [2] *The Times*, 28 June 1976.

BIBLIOGRAPHICAL ESSAYS

1. PRELUDE TO DECOLONISATION

2. DECOLONISATION AND THE PROBLEMS OF INDEPENDENCE[1]

This volume of *The Cambridge History of Africa* differs from the two volumes immediately preceding it in that when it was first planned in 1975 archival sources were available to its authors only for the first five years in those few record offices that operate the 30-year rule. By and large, then, this is a volume whose contributors have been unable to use archival sources directly or refer to works based on them. Indeed as far as Africa is concerned it is only very recently that work based on the Public Record Office at Kew, covering the first ten years of our period, has been published in journals and books. Notable among these have been William R. Louis, *Imperialism at bay 1941–1945: the United States and the decolonisation of the British Empire* (Oxford, 1977); Ronald Robinson, 'Andrew Cohen and the transfer of power in Tropical Africa, 1940–1951', in W. H. Morris-Jones and Georges Fischer (eds.), *Decolonisation and after: the British and French experience* (London, 1980); and R. D. Pearce, *The turning point in Africa: British colonial policy 1938–1948* (London, 1982).

If archival sources have been unavailable for most of the period covered by this volume, its authors have had to peruse a much greater wealth of newspaper reports, government publications, journal articles, sound recordings, photographs and films than for any other period of African history. Though here again the years covered by this volume are unevenly provided for: the impact of the Second World War on Africa is understandably scantily treated in newspaper reports and contemporary government

[1] Billy J. Dudley died before he was able to draft the bibliographical essay to accompany Chapter 2. It was therefore decided that the editor of this volume, who is also author of the preceding chapter, should write an essay to cover the literature available for both chapters with the selection and evaluation of books, articles and other sources being entirely his responsibility.

publications, while the attention it has received from scholars in both journal articles and monographs has been equally scant, as David Killingray has pointed out in his article on 'Military and labour recruitment in the Gold Coast during the Second World War', *Journal of African History*, 1982, vol. 23. Material for the period 1945–60 is much more abundant, but it can in no way compare with that available for the 15 years that succeeded it. Before 1960 a journalist visiting West Africa, politically the most advanced region of sub-Saharan Africa, was still something of a rarity and usually represented the 'serious' newspapers published in one of the metropolises of the colonial powers. This dearth of reporting on current events in Africa was compensated for in some countries like Nigeria and the then Gold Coast by a vigorous local press, and by a few specialist magazines like *New Commonwealth*, *African World*, *West Africa* and *The Times British Colonies Review*. It was only after 1960, the *annus mirabilis* of African independence, that the continent opened up to the international press. Similarly before 1960 relatively few scholarly works had been published on any African country relating to the period post-1940, and then for the most part they were written by nationals of the metropolitan country concerned. There were a few exceptions, such as the American scholar James S. Coleman's magnificent study, *Nigeria: background to nationalism* (Berkeley and Los Angeles, 1958). The great boom in doctoral dissertations on Africa did not begin in earnest until after 1960, and few of them touch on the Second World War, though many deal in depth with the period 1945–60. As far as the authors of many of the chapters in this volume are concerned, the period that has been most closely scrutinised in the press, in journal articles and monographs, and which is supported by a mass of sociological and economic data provided by both governmental and international agencies, is that of independence, as their bibliographical essays demonstrate. The period of independence of course differs in length for each African country, and only begins in the case of Portuguese-speaking territories at the date with which this volume ends. Generally we can say that by far the best served period from the point of view of scholarly coverage, documentation and availability of contemporary reportage is that from 1960–75.

There have, however, been drawbacks to this comparative glut of material for the years since 1960: some of it became available too late to be made use of by our contributors; a good deal of it, though scholarly in guise, is polemical and prescriptive in intent.

While there have been many excellent regional and national studies concerned with either whole or part of our period, there have been few continent-wide surveys of value. A number do, however, stand out. For the earlier years Lord Hailey's *An African survey (revised 1956)* (London, 1957), is an invaluable source with regard to the administrative, political, social and economic record of the colonial powers in Africa. As a study of African reaction to this record, Thomas Hodgkin's *Nationalism in colonial Africa*, published in the year the revised *Survey* was dated (1956), was seminal at the time and still has considerable value today. Immanuel Wallerstein's *Africa: the politics of independence* (New York, 1961) provides a useful overview of the problems different African states were then facing or had just faced in the struggle for independence. The role of political parties in this struggle and in the consolidation of the independence settlement thereafter is treated in Thomas Hodgkin's *African political parties* (Harmonds-worth, 1961) and James S. Coleman and Carl G. Rosberg (eds.), *Political parties and national integration in tropical Africa* (Berkeley and Los Angeles, 1964). René Dumont's *L'Afrique noire est mal partie*, translated as *False start in Africa* (London, 1969), expressed the fears of a sympathetic but concerned agronomist for the future of Africa under the leadership that inherited independence; as did also the various works of Frantz Fanon, notably *Les Damnés de la terre*, translated as *The wretched of the earth* (New York, 1963). Ater independence there were many attempts to explain the myriad problems faced by post-independence African states or, as Stanislas Andreski described it, *The African predicament* (London, 1968). Few were of more than passing interest, with the exception of the works of dependence theorists discussed by Billy Dudley at the beginning of his chapter. As general sources for the period 1960–75, *Africa Contemporary Record* (London, 1968 to date), the annual *Africa South of the Sahara*, and Roland Oliver and Michael Crowder (general eds.), *Cambridge Encyclopaedia of Africa* (Cambridge, 1981), are all useful.

No attempt is made here to treat either regional sources or the country-by-country sources which are adequately covered in the bibliographical essays relating to the regional chapters, except where they are of more than local interest. Nor is material relating to economic, social and cultural change considered except where it relates directly to Chapters 1 and 2, for it is fully covered in the bibliographical essays relating to Chapters 4 and 5.

As a background to the period covered by this volume, Lord Hailey's *African survey* provides a wealth of data. The chapters in John Fage's *A history of Africa* (London, 1978) covering the late colonial period and the problems of decolonisation are stimulating. More detailed coverage is given in regional surveys: W. Knapp (ed.), *A survey of North-West Africa* (Oxford, 1977), P. J. Vatikiotis *The modern history of Egypt* (London, 1969); D. A. Low and Alison Smith (eds.), *History of East Africa*, vol. III (Oxford, 1976); J. F. A. Ajayi and Michael Crowder (eds.), *History of West Africa*, vol. II (London, 1974), which can be supplemented by John Dunn (ed.), *West African states* (Cambridge, 1978); M. Wilson and L. Thompson (eds.), *Oxford history of South Africa*, vol. II (Oxford, 1971), which can be supplemented by T. R. H. Davenport, *South Africa – a modern history* (Johannesburg, 2nd ed., 1978). At the time of going to press no comparable regional symposium was available for Central Africa, though David Birmingham (ed.), *History of Central Africa*, vol. II (in press) promised to fill the gap.

French works translated into English that are valuable for an understanding of the colonial situation on the eve of decolonisation are J. S. Suret-Canale, *French colonialism in tropical Africa 1900–1945* (London, 1971), J. Berque, *French North Africa* (London, 1967), and Robert Delavignette, *Freedom and authority in French West Africa* (Oxford, 1950).

As already noted, there has been little written specifically about the impact of the Second World War on Africa and information about it has largely to be mined from national and regional histories. The course of the war on African soil can be traced in the official histories of the war, while the actual involvement of Africans in that war has been the occasion of a few in-depth studies, notably G. O. Olusanya, *The Second World War and politics in Nigeria 1939–1953* (London, 1973), and that by D. Killingray already cited. Walter Rodney, in *World War II and the Tanzanian economy* (Cornell, 1976), looks at the overall impact of the war – political, social as well as economic – on what was then Tanganyika. Michael Crowder does the same for West Africa in *West Africa under colonial rule* and in his chapter on the Second

World War in Ajayi and Crowder (*op. cit.*). There is useful material in Jean Ganiage *et al.* (eds.), *L'Afrique au XXᵉ siècle* (Paris, 1966). African reaction to the war can be studied in a number of autobiographies and political statements by African leaders, such as Lamine Guèye's *Itinéraire africaine* (Paris, 1966) and Ndabaningi Sithole's *African nationalism* (Oxford, 1968). Sylvia Leith-Ross, *Stepping-stones: memoirs of colonial Nigeria 1907–1960*, edited and with an introduction by Michael Crowder (London, 1983), has a fascinating chapter on the impact of the war on Nigerians as she perceived it. Eugene P. Schleh has compared 'The post-war careers of ex-servicemen in Ghana and Uganda', *Journal of Modern African Studies*, 1968, vol. 6, pp. 203–20. Joyce Cary, in *The case for African freedom and other writings* (London, 1944), also considered the impact of the war on African soldiers involved in it.

By far the most copious material available on the war concerns the impact it had on the colonial powers, particularly with regard to the introduction of more liberal political, economic and social policies in their African colonies. Examination of its role in the 'transfer of power' or 'decolonisation' has become something of an industry. The work of William R. Louis, Ronald Robinson and R. D. Pearce has already been referred to. Also important are John D. Hargreaves, *The end of colonial rule in West Africa* (London, 1978); D. Bruce Marshall, 'Free France in Africa: Gaullism and colonialism', in Prosser Gifford and William R. Louis (eds.), *France and Britain in Africa: imperial rivalry and colonial rule* (New Haven and London, 1971); and Margery Perham, *Colonial sequence 1930–1949* (London, 1967). Of vital importance to an understanding of the thinking of a man with influence in 'progressive' colonial circles is Lord Hailey's *The future of colonial peoples* (London, 1943).

Of the growing literature on 'decolonisation', Henri Grimal's *Decolonisation: the British, French, Dutch and Belgian empires, 1919–1963* (trans. Stephen de Vos, London, 1978) and Rudolf von Albertini's *Decolonisation: the administration and future of the colonies, 1919–1960* (New York, 1971) give respectively a French and German perspective on the problem. For a British point of view A. H. M. Kirk-Greene (ed.), *Africa in the colonial period: the transfer of power – the colonial administrator in the age of decolonisation* (Oxford, 1979), is useful though the contributions by many of the colonial officials show how bitter memories become tempered with time;

perhaps a more realistic view of just how traumatic the 'transfer' could be for British officials is presented by Sylvia Leith-Ross, *op. cit.* The African view of the 'transfer' has still to be gleaned from national rather than regional or continental studies, and these are unevenly distributed over the continent. Billy J. Dudley's own study of *Parties and politics in Northern Nigeria* (London, 1966) is a good example of a national's perspective on the problems of decolonisation. Generally informative are works by political leaders such as: H. K. Banda and H. M. Nkumbula, *Federation in Central Africa* (London, 1951), Edouardo Mondlane, *The struggle for Mozambique* (London, 1969), Patrice Lumumba, *Congo, my country* (New York, 1963) or J. Rabemananjara's *Le Nationalisme et problèmes malgaches* (Paris, 1958). Most of the new nations of Africa have had at least one study made by an American, French or British scholar of their struggle for independence, and these are noted in the bibliographical chapters for the regions into which they fall. A few of these studies are of more than local interest and those which Billy J. Dudley singled out for special mention are Crawford Young's *Politics in the Congo: decolonisation and independence* (Princeton, 1965) and Ruth Schachter Morgenthau, *Political parties in French-speaking West Africa* (Oxford, 1964). To these might be added Cranford Pratt's *The critical phase in Tanzania, 1945–1968* (Cambridge, 1976), Martin Kilson's *Political change in a West African state: a study of the modernisation process in Sierra Leone* (Cambridge, Mass., 1966), and Carl G. Rosberg and J. Nottingham's *The myth of 'Mau Mau'* (London, 1966). Generally useful for their country case studies – though these vary in quality – are the three volumes edited by Gwendolen M. Carter: *African one-party states* (Ithaca, 1962); *Five African states: responses to diversity* (Ithaca, 1963); and *National unity and regionalism in eight African states* (Ithaca, 1966).

The constitutional inheritance of the new African states is again the subject of a large number of national and regional studies, the more important of which are evaluated in the bibliographical essays relating to the regional chapters. The phenomenon of the one-party state, which in so many African countries replaced the metropolitan legacy of a multi-party democracy, was the subject of much debate and a large number of studies. Perhaps the best of these was Aristide Zolberg's *One-party government in the Ivory Coast* (Princeton, 1969). His book, *Creating political order: the party states of West Africa* (Chicago, 1966) and his article on 'The structure of political conflict in the new states of Africa', *American Political Science Review*, 62, 1968, provide helpful insights into the problems African states had in dealing with the constitutional inheritance. From the African point of view these problems are looked at from different perspectives by Tom Mboya in *The challenge of nationhood* (London, 1970); K. A. Busia in *Africa in search of democracy* (London, 1967); Bakary Traoré, M. Lô and J.-L. Alibert in *Forces politiques en Afrique noire* (Paris, 1966); and Ali Mazrui in 'Edmund Burke and reflections on the revolution in the Congo', an essay in his book *On heroes and Uhuru-worship* (London, 1967). The question of 'neo-colonialism' and 'dependence' is the subject of a vast and often polemical literature. A useful introduction by one who is very committed to the dependency theory is Samir Amin's *Neo-colonialism in West Africa* (London, 1976). The economic inheritance, whether seen in dependency terms or otherwise, is also the subject of a vast literature which is exhaustively discussed in the bibliographical essay for Chapter 5. Of more than national and regional interest are Giovanni Arrighi's 'Labour suppliers in historical perspective: a study of the proletarianisation of the African peasantry in Rhodesia', *Journal of Development Studies*, April 1970, vol. 3; Giovanni Arrighi and J. S. Saul (eds.), *Essays on the political economy of Africa* (London, 1973); Colin Leys, *Underdevelopment in Kenya* (London, 1974); Robin Palmer and Neil Parsons (eds.), *The roots of rural poverty in Central and Southern Africa* (London, 1977); Samir Amin's various studies of African states, such as *Trois expériences africaines de développement: le Mali, la Guinée et le Ghana* (Paris, 1965); and R. W. Clower, G. Dalton, M. Harwitz and A. A. Walters, *Growth without development: an economic survey of Liberia* (Evanston, 1966). On the question of regional integration of the former colonial economies, Arthur Hazlewood's *African integration and disintegration* (London, 1967) and his *African economic integration: the East African experience* (London, 1975), together with Peter Robson's *Economic integration in Africa* (London, 1968), provide a good introduction to the problem. Attempts by African economies to break out from dependence are examined in A. A. Adedeji (ed.), *The indigenisation of African economies* (London, 1981).

The administration of the new African states after the departure of the colonial rulers is the subject of a number of studies of which Morroe Berger's *Bureaucracy and society in modern Egypt: a study of the higher civil service* (Princeton, 1957) and A. L. Adu, *The civil service in Commonwealth Africa: development and transition* (London, 1970), may be cited. The continuing role of the traditional administration in the post-colonial state is examined in M. Crowder and Obaro Ikime (eds.), *West African chiefs: their changing status under colonial rule and independence* (New York, 1970).

Social change is again the subject of a vast literature, which is analysed in depth in the bibliographical essay for Chapter 4. The studies in Peter C. Lloyd's *The new élites of Tropical Africa* (London, 1967) provide a useful introduction to the class that inherited the colonial state, while R. Sandbrook and R. Cohen, (eds.), *The development of an African working class* (London, 1975) look at those most likely to challenge that inheritance. The role of the peasant in independent Africa is considered in Palmer and Parsons, *op. cit.*, Arrighi, *op. cit.*, Colin Leys, 'Politics in Kenya: the development of peasant society', *British Journal of Political Science*, 1971, vol. 1, D. C. O'Brien, *The Mourides of Senegal* (Oxford, 1971) and Polly Hill, *Studies in rural capitalism* (Cambridge, 1970).

Education as a factor for social mobilisation is the subject of many studies, notably those of Philip Foster for Ghana – *Education and social change in Ghana* (Chicago, 1965), and David Abernethy for Nigeria – *The political dilemma of popular education* (Stanford, 1969). For East Africa there is an interesting comparative study by David Court, 'The education system as a response to inequality in Tanzania and Kenya', *Journal of Modern African Studies*, 1975, vol. 13, no. 3. Revolution as a means of mobilisation is the subject of a number of studies by Basil Davidson with respect to the Portuguese territories, notably *In the eye of the storm: Angola's people* (London, 1972), and by Thomas H. Henriksen, 'Peoples' war in Angola, Mozambique and Guinea-Bissau', *Journal of Modern African Studies*, 1976, vol. 14, no. 3. The other end of the educational spectrum is brought out well in Pierre van den Berghe, *Power and privilege in an African university* (London, 1973).

The role of the military in the government of African nations succeeded the one-party state as the principal focus of political scientists over the last 15 years. There is a useful bibliography in

Claude E. Welch and Arthur K. Smith, *Military role and rule* (Belmont, Cal., 1974). Ruth First's classic *Through the barrel of the gun* (London, 1970) is the best introduction while useful local studies are D. Austin and R. Luckham, *Politicians and soldiers in Ghana* (London, 1975) and S. K. Panter-Brick, *Nigerian politics and military rule* (London, 1970). Alistair Horne's brilliant *A savage war of peace: Algeria 1954–62* (London, 1977) shows the Algerian soldiers as both military leaders and politicians intent on building up the successor state to the former French department.

No essay on the bibliographical resources for the period of decolonisation and independence can conclude without mentioning the many excellent journals and magazines which regularly have articles relating to the period, notably *The Journal of Modern African Studies, West Africa, African Affairs, Cahiers d'Études Africaines, Genève Afrique, Civilisations* and the invaluable *International African Bibliography*.

3. PAN-AFRICANISM SINCE 1940

The limitations in the primary sources as yet available for the study of Pan-Africanism in the period 1940–75 demonstrate many of the problems facing the historian of contemporary history. Many of those most involved are still living, some in positions of power; obvious inhibitions follow on the candour with which their friends and associates choose to enlighten the world as to parts played in recent, often controversial, events. Even in the case of those recently dead – the example of Jomo Kenyatta comes to mind – the same restraints still largely apply. Till the period of struggle for national independence in Africa, the movement and its leaders lived, for the most part, in comparative obscurity and had very limited resources; factors limiting the preservation and accumulation of future archival material. Much of the later material is interred in the archives of governments, African and non-African, or of institutions such as the OAU, the UAM, OCAM and ECOWAS. When the day comes when historians will have a wide degree of access to this material, they will find it to have been subject to the inevitable processes of accidental and deliberate decimation. Even so, they may well be almost overwhelmed by the sheer volume of paper that modern governments and international bodies generate. Official papers that have been published are useful, but normally portray official positions, agreed formulae and the surface of events, as well as giving useful information on non-controversial matters. The *Charter of the Organisation of African Unity* (1963) is an essential document, yet the inner debates and divisions from which it emerged can only be inferred from it.

For the period from the eve of the Second World War to the era of independent African states, there are a number of useful sources, mainly printed, though archival material is to be found in the W. E. B. DuBois papers, University of Massachusetts, the W. E. B. DuBois papers, Accra, and the Kwame Nkrumah papers, Ghana National Archives, Accra. Useful material, especially on West Africa, is to be found in the United States National Archives, Washington DC, scattered in Department of State decimal files; and Bureau of Commerce, Bureau of Foreign and Domestic Trade files. Mention should be made of the reminiscences of the late Professor K. A. B. Jones-Quartey, recorded by himself, the tapes of which are in the Centre of African Studies library, University of Edinburgh. A number of magazines run by Pan-Africanist leaders or institutions have survived, the chief of these being *The Black Man* (Millwood, NY), Marcus Garvey's last journalistic effort; *The Keys* and *The Newsletter*, both organs of the League of Coloured Peoples; and its successor *WASU Magazine*, both published in London by the West African Students' Union; the *African Interpreter* (New York), journal of the African Students' Association; the *New African* (London), organ of the West African National Secretariat; and *Pan-Africa* (Manchester), edited by Ras Makonnen, and replacing the International African Service Bureau's *International African Opinion*, library copies of which do not appear to exist. Mention should also be made of *The Comet* (Lagos), edited by the veteran Pan-Africanist Duse Mohamed Ali, and containing, in 1937–8, his serialised autobiography, 'Leaves from an active life'. In West Africa, too, Nnamdi Azikiwe's *West African Pilot* (Lagos), is important for its race consciousness and awareness of events in the African continent as a whole.

A number of autobiographies shed light on the period to the mid-1950s. For candour, none excel Ras Makonnen's *Pan-Africanism from within*, recorded and edited by Kenneth King (1973). Kwame Nkrumah's *Ghana: the autobiography of Kwame*

Nkrumah (Edinburgh, 1957) is valuable, despite its manifest intention of fostering his own cult of personality. Nnamdi Azikiwe's *My odyssey: an autobiography* (London, 1970) is much less directly useful to the student of Pan-Africanism, whilst W. E. B. DuBois's *Autobiography* contains almost nothing on his career as a Pan-Africanist, still less on anyone else's, and is mainly concerned with justifying the pro-Soviet stance on world affairs of his later years. However, his autobiographical work *Dusk of dawn* (New York, 1940) is useful in revealing his general outlook at that time. Outside the realm of autobiography, from the pre-independence period note should be made of DuBois's *Black folk then and now* (New York, 1939) and *The world and Africa* (New York, 1947), illustrating his essentially if not explicitly Pan-African concern for African and African diaspora culture and history. George Padmore's *Pan-Africanism or Communism?* (London, 1956) is an important document insomuch as it sought to propagate an official line on the history of the movement, as well as asserting the need for its freedom from Soviet control, and lauding Nkrumah's political achievements. Padmore's other works of his prolific post-1945 years, especially *Africa: Britain's third empire* (1949), *The Gold Coast revolution* (1953), *How Russia transformed her colonial empire* (1946), and *The life and struggles of Negro toilers* (1956), all published in London, illustrate the trend of thought of the man who was perhaps the most influential Pan-African ideologue and organiser of his generation. *The history of the Pan-African Congress* (second edition, London, 1963), which he edited, is a major source on the 1945 congress.

For the period from 1958 onwards, the student of Pan-Africanism will find useful documentation on rival African groupings in Louis B. Sohn (ed.), *Basic documents of African regional organisations* (New York, 1971). Primary documentation for the OAU includes the *Proceedings of the Summit Conference of independent African states*, volumes 1–4, Addis Ababa (1963); *Basic documents of the Organisation of African Unity*, Provisional Secretariat of the OAU, Addis Ababa (1963); *Assembly of Heads of State and Government resolutions, decisions and declarations of ordinary and extraordinary sessions*; and *Council of Ministers' resolutions and declarations of ordinary and extraordinary sessions*. These chart the surface of the OAU. Documents and resolutions of the OAU specialised commissions, and of its council of ministers, and assembly of

Heads of State and Government, exist in mimeographed form in the OAU Secretariat, Addis Ababa, and are issued in that form to member governments and sometimes to friendly governments, but are not made generally available.

Of the published works of Pan-Africanists in the era of independent African states, pride of place for sheer quantity must go to Kwame Nkrumah, although the many works published under his name after his overthrow have probably had little influence. More important are his pre-1966 works, principally his *Autobiography*, already mentioned; his attempt at a political philosophy of decolonisation, *Consciencism* (London, 1964); *I Speak of Freedom* (London, 1961); *Towards colonial freedom* (London, 1962); *Africa must unite* (London, 1963); and *Neo-colonialism: the last stage of imperialism* (London, 1965). It is plain even from these works that Nkrumah failed to provide Pan-Africanism with either a coherent ideology or plan of action. Of modern African Pan-African leaders, only Julius Nyerere could offer any rivalry to this flood of print, with works such as his *Freedom and unity* (Dar es Salaam, 1967); *Freedom and socialism* (Dar es Salaam, 1968); and *Freedom and development* (Dar es Salaam, 1973). These illustrate his trend away from an emphasis on regional and all-African unity, towards an internal solution to his peoples' problems. Of the revolutionary leaders in former Portuguese Africa, Amílcar Cabral's occasional writings show great insight into problems of African unity, although circumstances were not such as to allow him to address the question in a systematic manner. His *Revolution in Guiné. An African people's struggle* (London, 1969) contains such material, as does a reported interview with him in Basil Davidson, *The liberation of Guiné* (London, 1969). In a category of its own, apart from official documents and the writings of individual Pan-Africanists, is the *Resolutions and selected speeches from the Sixth Pan-African Congress* (Dar es Salaam, 1976), containing as it does some frankly critical material about the OAU and many African leaders and states.

Before passing over to secondary sources, mention should briefly be made of some published primary material on the relations of the diaspora to Pan-Africanism since the 1950s. Richard Wright's *Black Power* (New York, 1954) is a classic account of the problems faced by a sympathetic black American in coming to terms with both the old and the new Africa. Other accounts of visits to and sojourns in Africa are to be found in Malcolm X, *The autobiography of Malcolm X* (London, 1966) and Ernest Dunbar (ed.), *The black expatriates* (London, 1968). Imamu Amiri Baraka (ed.), *African Congress* (New York, 1972) gives insight into the fervent if ill-organised Pan-Africanism of many black Americans at that time, while the *Resolutions and selected speeches from the Sixth Pan-African Congress* contain material on the diaspora delegations at that meeting. The image of Africa held by an illiterate Afro-Cuban survivor into modern times from the slave era is given in Esteban Montejo, recorded and edited by M. Barnet, *Autobiography of a runaway slave* (London, 1968). However, of modern West Indians, the one who has most profoundly affected thinking about modern Africa has perhaps been Frantz Fanon; his *Toward the African revolution* (New York, 1967), and *The wretched of the earth* (second English edition, London, 1967) have been immensely influential, though perhaps more so outside than inside Africa. Finally, Alex Hailey's enormously successful novel *Roots* (New York, 1976), subsequently produced as a television serial, graphically demonstrates the sentiments of modern black Americans towards their African origins.

Secondary works comprise both a small number of general works, and a plethora of monographs, biographies and articles. Of the general works, the earliest were Philippe Decraene's *Le Panafricanisme* (Paris, 1959, second edition, 1961) and Colin Legum's *Pan-Africanism* (London, 1962). Both were journalistic works, and although useful in their day, now seem outdated. Like Adekunle Ajala's *Pan-Africanism, evolution, progress and prospects* (London, 1973) and V. B. Thompson's *Africa and unity* (London, 1969), both pay little attention to events before the post-Second World War period; likewise all four of these works pay most attention to the formal and institutional aspects of Pan-Africanism, and show little interest in the diaspora contribution. Imanuel Geiss's *The Pan-African movement*, the most scholarly of the general works, appeared in its English edition in 1974. It has only an epilogue on events after 1945, and is essentially a work on the historic roots of the movement. I. Wallerstein's *Africa: the politics of unity* (London, 1968), entirely relates to the era of African independence, as does Jon Woronoff's *Organising African unity*

(Metuchen, NJ, 1970). Woronoff and Wallerstein are in some ways closer to a batch of works specifically on the OAU than to the truly general works. In this category, a particularly important contribution has been made by Z. Červenka, with his works *The Organisation of African Unity and its Charter* (London, 1969) and *The unfinished quest for unity* (London, 1977). General surveys of the OAU are offered in Boutros Boutros-Ghali, *L'Organisation de l'Unité Africaine* (Paris, 1969), Michael Wolfers, *Politics in the Organisation of African Unity* (London, 1976) and Yassin El-Ayouty (ed.), *The Organization of African Unity after ten years* (New York, 1975). A more limited remit is thoroughly investigated in Berhanykun Andemicael, *The OAU and the UN* (New York, 1976).

Problems of regionalism have received the attention of several studies. On East Africa, there is A. J. Hughes, *East Africa: the search for unity* (London, 1963), J. S. Nye Jr, *Pan-Africanism and East African integration* (Cambridge, Mass., 1966) and Richard Cox, *Pan-Africanism in practice* (London, 1964). All are now somewhat out of date. In the case of West Africa, the books on regionalism overlap with works dealing with francophone Pan-Africanism. Although it only considers events up to 1945, J. A. Langley's *Pan-Africanism and nationalism in West Africa, 1900–1945* (Oxford, 1973) is nevertheless an essential introductory work. The first general look at West African regionalism was Claude E. Welch Jr, *Dream of unity: Pan-Africanism and political unification in West Africa* (Ithaca, 1966). More specifically on the francophone states are a number of works: W. Foltz, *From French West Africa to the Mali Federation* (New Haven, 1965); V. Thompson's *West Africa's Council of the Entente* (Ithaca, 1972) and Albert Tevoedjre's *Pan-Africanism in action: an account of the UAM* (Cambridge, Mass., 1965), which tends to uncritical sympathy with its subject. Because its author was Foreign Minister of Senegal, Doudou Thiam's *The foreign policy of African states* (London, 1965) has a certain air of authority, especially on the francophone sphere. Throwing light not only on West African Pan-Africanism, but an era in Pan-Africanism as a whole, are W. Scott Thompson's *Ghana's foreign policy, 1957–1966* (Princeton, 1969) and perhaps the best, and certainly one of the most sympathetic (though not uncritically so), of the biographical works on Nkrumah, Basil Davidson's *Black star* (London, 1973).

Basil Davidson has also made a most distinguished contribution to the understanding of the revolutions in tropical Africa in the 1960s and 1970s, and although these works are not primarily or directly on Pan-Africanism, they do offer a critique of the shortcomings of the formal Pan-Africanism of the OAU, and are therefore essential reading. They are *Which way Africa?* (London, 1967); *The liberation of Guiné* (London, 1969) and *In the eye of the storm* (London, 1972), as well as, with J. Slovo and A. R. Wilkinson, *Southern Africa: the new politics of revolution* (London, 1976). In the category of works on modern African revolutionary struggles, mention should also be made of Colin Legum and Tony Hodges, *After Angola* (London, 1976), and Eduardo Mondlane's *The struggle for Mozambique* (London, 1969).

A number of works throw light on the attitude to Africa of New World blacks. In this category come Harold Isaacs' distinguished work, *The new world of Negro Americans* (New York, 1964); Robert G. Weisbord's *Ebony kinship* (Westport, 1973); John A. Davis's *Africa seen by American Negroes* (Paris, 1958); A. C. Hill and Martin Kilson, *Apropos of Africa* (London, 1969), which is a collection of documents on 'sentiments of American Negro leaders on Africa from the 1800s to the 1950s'; and Richard Moore's 'Africa conscious Harlem' in J. H. Clarke (ed.), *Harlem, a community in transition* (New York, 1964).

Concerning economic aspects of African unity, mention might be made of two works. These are Reginald H. Green and Ann Seidman, *Unity or poverty?* (London, 1968), and I. W. Zartman, *The politics of trade negotiations between Africa and the E.E.C.* (Princeton, 1971). Zartman is also the author of *International relations in the new Africa* (Englewood Cliffs, NJ, 1966), which contributes to the literature on the relations of African states in the first decade of post-colonial Africa.

Concerning cultural Pan-Africanism, there is no work which deals with all aspects of the question. However, there is a considerable literature both on and of *négritude*; of fundamental importance here is the journal *Présence Africaine*, published in Paris since 1947, and which contains many contributions by such figures as Léopold Sédar Senghor, Aimé Césaire, and the Haitian Dr Jean Price-Mars (who was a great influence on the founders of *négritude*), as well as sympathetic commentaries on their writings and thought. The writings of both Senghor and Césaire are too voluminous for discussion here, but leaving aside the large corpus of poetry produced by both men, reference should at least be made to Césaire's *Discours sur le colonialisme*, published by *Présence Africaine* in Paris in 1955, and to the selection of Senghor's writings in *Liberté I; Négritude et humanisme* (Paris, 1964). The works on *négritude*, and especially on Senghor's role in it, are again far too numerous to list comprehensively here, but two useful studies in this area are Jacques Louis Hymans, *Léopold Sédar Senghor. An intellectual biography* (Edinburgh, 1971), written with considerable cooperation from its subject; and I. L. Markovitz, *Léopold Sédar Senghor and the politics of négritude* (London, 1969). A totally different approach to the role of culture in African liberation than that espoused by the *négritude* movement can be found scattered in the writings of Amílcar Cabral, and especially in the speech entitled 'The role of culture in the liberation struggle', given to a UNESCO Conference in Paris in 1972, and printed in *Guinea Bissau: toward final victory* (Richmond, BC, 1974). For Cabral, the search for authentic cultural 'roots' characteristic of *négritude* was irrelevant for the African masses, who had never lost their culture in his opinion, and was no more than a preoccupation of the alienated African *petite bourgeoisie* under colonial rule. The most noted anglophone critic of *négritude* is the South African Ezekiel Mphahlele; reference should be made to his works *The African image* (London, second revised edition 1974), *Voices in the whirlwind, and other essays* (New York, 1972), and 'Remarks on négritude', reprinted in his *African writing today* (London, 1967). From within the francophone world, the Martiniquan psychiatrist, political thinker and revolutionary, Frantz Fanon, produced perhaps the most trenchant attack on *négritude*, both in relation to the West Indies and Africa, and like Cabral saw it as a doctrine emanating from those intellectuals who belonged to neither the white world, which rejected them, nor the black world, which they turned to as they perceived that rejection. He first developed these ideas at length in his *Peau noire, masques blancs* (Paris, 1952). Finally, a reaffirmation in the mid-1970s of the concept of Africanity as central to the understanding of and development of modern African culture is outlined in Wole Soyinka's introduction to his *Myth, literature and the African world* (Cambridge, 1976).

4. SOCIAL AND CULTURAL CHANGE

The sources for Africa's social and cultural history since the Second World War are both vast and diverse, since they include virtually all writing on Africa in the social sciences in this period. Of great importance are the major journals: *Africa* (1930–), *Cahiers d'Études Africaines* (1960–), *Journal of Modern African Studies* (1963–), *Canadian Journal of African Studies* (1967–), and *African Affairs*, published for many years previously as the *Journal of the Royal African Society* but radically reshaped after 1972. There is also, of course, a host of journals specific to particular disciplines and particular countries or areas of Africa, mostly founded since 1960. The published papers from the series of International African Seminars, held intermittently since 1959, indicate how quickly scholarly perspectives, as well as the *actualités*, have changed since the burgeoning of modern Africanist scholarship in the early 1960s when the majority of African countries gained their independence. Of particular value here are A. W. Southall (ed.), *Social change in modern Africa* (London, 1961); P. C. Lloyd (ed.), *The new élites of tropical Africa* (Oxford, 1966); W. H. Whiteley (ed.), *Language use and social change* (London, 1968); S. Amin (ed.), *Modern migrations in Western Africa* (London, 1974) and D. J. Parkin (ed.), *Town and country in Central and Eastern Africa* (London, 1975).

Of the pioneer attempts to break from static anthropological models of African society and to understand the social sources of nationalism, several are still worth reading: M. Gluckman, 'Analysis of a social situation in Zululand', *Bantu Studies*, 1940, vol. 14, 1–2, G. Balandier, *Sociologie actuelle de l'Afrique noire* (Paris, 1955) and T. Hodgkin, *Nationalism in colonial Africa* (London, 1956). Many of the best studies of the nationalist movements in particular countries – such as J. S. Coleman, *Nigeria: background to nationalism* (Berkeley, 1958) or R. L. Sklar, *Nigerian political parties* (Princeton, 1963), D. Austin, *Politics in Ghana 1946–1960* (Oxford, 1964) or D. E. Apter, *Ghana in transition* (Princeton, 1955), and other such works mentioned in the regional chapters – contain original syntheses of local-level studies in relation to nationalism. For East Africa, J. M. Lonsdale's paper, 'Some origins of nationalism in East Africa', *Journal of African History*, 1968, vol. 9, 119–46, has been very influential.

J. Iliffe's masterly *Modern history of Tanganyika* (Cambridge, 1979) sets the nationalist period in the *longue durée* and achieves great sophistication in the integration of social, cultural, economic and political data. A number of useful collections of papers on social change, covering the period of nationalist mobilisation into independence, have been made: I. Wallerstein, *Social change: the colonial situation* (New York, 1966), P. L. van den Berghe, *Africa: social problems of change and conflict* (San Francisco, 1965), J. Middleton, *Black Africa: its peoples and their cultures today* (London, 1970), R. I. Rotberg and A. A. Mazrui (eds.), *Protest and power in Black Africa* (New York, 1970), R. Cohen and J. Middleton, *From tribe to nation in Africa* (Scranton, 1970). The genre continues with P. C. W. Gutkind and I. Wallerstein's *Political economy of contemporary Africa* (Beverly Hills, 1976) and other volumes in the Sage Series on African modernisation and development, where the Marxist perspectives which have become influential since the early 1970s are evident.

Migration and urbanisation have been pegs upon which every kind of argument about social change and development have been hung since the UNESCO volume edited by Daryll Forde, *Social consequences of urbanization and industrialization in Africa south of the Sahara* (Paris, 1956). The themes are linked in H. Kuper (ed.), *Urbanization and migration in West Africa* (Berkeley, 1965) and W. A. Hance, *Population, migration and urbanization in Africa* (New York, 1970), a general survey with extensive bibliography. The journal *African Urban Notes* (1964–) is specifically valuable here. To the already-mentioned IAI Seminar volumes on migration edited by Amin (1974) and Parkin (1976) may be added the special number of *African Perspectives* (Leiden, 1978/1) on theories of migration. For West Africa, A. L. Mabogunje's *Urbanization in Nigeria* (London, 1968) broke new ground in conceptualising what we mean by 'towns'; J. Gugler and W. G. Flanagan's *Urbanization and social change in West Africa* (Cambridge, 1978) has a useful bibliography. Studies of particular West African towns are too numerous to list: a number are reviewed in J. D. Y. Peel, 'Urbanization and urban history in West Africa', *Journal of African History*, 1980, vol. 21. East Africa has been less well-served (but see Parkin (1964) on Kampala), and several studies exist of towns in West Central Africa: G. Balandier's pioneer study, *Sociologie des Brazzavilles noires* (Paris, 1955), J. S. La Fontaine,

City politics: a study of Léopoldville (Cambridge, 1970), and V. Pons, *Stanleyville: an African urban community under Belgian administration* (London, 1969). Central and South Africa have both attracted notable work, as much concerned with rural/urban links as with urban forms in themselves: studies by A. L. Epstein, J. C. Mitchell, W. Watson, J. Van Velsen and others associated with 'Manchester social anthropology' and the former Rhodes-Livingstone Institute at Lusaka, and work from South Africa, notably the two-volume *Xhosa in town* (ed. P. Mayer, Cape Town, 1961) and M. Wilson and A. Mafeje's study, *Langa* (Cape Town, 1963). With the establishment of the 'Bantustans' in South Africa and the emergence of new radical schools of social science and history (see especially *Journal of Southern African Studies* (1976–)), the academic terrain changed greatly in the 1970s; for a recent study of migratory labour in the South African periphery, see C. Murray, *Families divided* (Cambridge, 1981) on Lesotho.

Ethnicity figures in nearly all accounts of nationalist or post-independence politics. Useful collections of regional studies are R. Melson and H. Wolpe (eds.), *Nigeria: the politics of communalism* (East Lansing, 1971), and P. H. Gulliver, *Tradition and transition in East Africa* (London, 1969). A. Cohen's account of the Hausa community in Ibadan, *Custom and politics in urban Africa* (Manchester, 1969) and J. C. Mitchell's *The Kalela dance* (Manchester, 1956), are both classic studies of urban ethnicity. D. C. O'Brien's *Saints and politicians* (Cambridge, 1975) is a witty, trenchant account of a country, Senegal, whose mode of political integration is relatively free of ethnicity.

Until recently, the literature on religion was oddly imbalanced. Independent churches were better covered than 'mission' ones – see the survey by D. B. Barrett, *Schism and renewal in Africa* (Nairobi, 1968), though its explanation is simplistic and untenable – and Islam was often better covered than Christianity – compare the IAI volume edited by I. M. Lewis, *Islam in tropical Africa* (Oxford, 1966, second edition 1980) with that on *Christianity in tropical Africa* by C. G. Baëta (Oxford, 1965). This is now largely redressed with the appearance of two major books: E. Fashole-Luke *et al.* (eds.), *Christianity in independent Africa* (London, 1978), and A. Hastings's remarkable synthesis, *A history of African Christianity 1950–1975* (Cambridge, 1979).

Discussion of stratification began, particularly for English-speaking Africa, with the analysis of élites: see the special issue of UNESCO's *International Social Science Bulletin*, 1956, vol. 8, devoted to 'African élites'; and the theme was picked up again by P. C. Lloyd, *The new élites*. French discussion was always more in terms of class, as in several papers, by J.-C. Pauvert, P. Mercier and G. Balandier, in *Cahiers Internationaux de Sociologie*, from 1954 (no. 16) to 1965 (no. 38). From the 1970s onwards, under the growing influence of Marxist ideas, class analysis of African societies became predominant, evidenced in at least one major new journal: *Review of African Political Economy* (1974–). In East Africa the work of G. Arrighi and J. S. Saul – see their *Essays on the political economy of Africa*, New York and London, 1973 – and C. T. Leys, *Underdevelopment in Kenya* (London, 1974) have been influential. Some of this work tends to a rather crude reductionism, e.g. M. Mamdani, *Politics and class formation in Uganda* (London, 1976); but G. Kitching's *Class and economic change in Kenya* (1980) is rich and subtle. Class analysis of such scope or scale has not yet been produced for West Africa; though R. Stavenhagen's analysis of the Ivory Coast, *Social classes in agrarian societies* (Garden City, 1975), G. Williams in various works (e.g. *Nigeria: economy and society*, London, 1976) and several contributors to J. Dunn (ed.), *West African states* (Cambridge, 1978), have shown the way.

Much writing on class formation focusses on particular sectors. As regards the rural sector, most of that on West Africa has concentrated on the rise and, latterly, the decline of small-scale commercial agriculture: S. S. Berry, *Cocoa, custom and socio-economic change in rural Western Nigeria* (Oxford, 1975); Polly Hill, *Studies in rural capitalism in West Africa* (Cambridge, 1970); D. C. O'Brien, *The Mourides of Senegal* (Oxford, 1971); and B. Beckman, *Organizing the farmers* (Uppsala, 1976). Studies of this genre on East and Central Africa are more limited; e.g. N. Long, *Social change and the individual* (Manchester, 1968), G. Lamb, *Peasant politics* (Lewes, 1974). There has been a large literature evaluating *ujamaa* policies in Tanzania: e.g. M. von Freyhold, *Ujamaa villages in Tanzania* (London, 1979) and G. Hyden, *Beyond Ujamaa in Tanzania* (London, 1980). Latterly the agrarian development of southern Africa has been seen anew in the light of its historical origins: see R. Palmer and N. Parsons (eds.), *The roots of rural poverty in Central and Southern Africa* (London, 1977), mostly relating to before 1930, but several contributions range into the independence period. Latterly too there has been important work on 'rural development' and its implications for rural class formation: see studies relating to Nigeria, Ghana, Niger, Senegal, Tanzania, Sudan and Kenya in J. Heyer, P. Roberts and G. Williams (eds.), *Rural development in tropical Africa* (1981). A fresh treatment of 'peasantisation' in a longer historical perspective is in M. A. Klein (ed.), *Peasants in Africa* (1980), with case studies of West and southern Africa.

The treatment of urban class formation has been fullest in respect of wage-earners. Apart from several excellent case studies: e.g. R. Grillo, *African railwaymen* (Cambridge, 1974), on East Africa; R. Jeffries, *Class, power and ideology in Ghana* (1978); A. Peace, *Choice, class and conflict* (1974), on Lagos, there are two useful collections, which extensively review earlier writing: R. Sandbrook and R. Cohen (eds.), *The development of an African working class* (London, 1975) and P. C. W. Gutkind, R. Cohen and J. Cooper (eds.), *African labor history* (1981). The informal sector has received less concentrated treatment, though it features throughout the literature on urbanisation, and in ethnographies of particular towns. For the miscellaneous urban poor, see K. Hart, 'Informal income opportunities and urban employment in Ghana', *Journal of Modern African Studies*, 1973, vol. 11, 61–89, and several papers in R. Bromley and C. Gerry, *Casual work and employment in Third World cities* (1979). An important marker for discussion has been the ILO report, *Employment, incomes and equality: a strategy for increasing productive employment in Kenya* (Geneva, 1972). Particularly in West Africa (but increasingly elsewhere) women play an important role in petty trade; see here N. Hafkin and E. Bey (eds.), *Women in Africa: studies in social and economic change* (Stanford, 1976). More studies of commercial groups are needed – but see Marris and Somerset (1971), E. O. Akeredolu-Ale, *The underdevelopment of indigenous entrepreneurship in Nigeria* (Ibadan, 1979), M. G. Schatzberg, *Politics and class in Zaire: bureaucracy, business and beer in Lisala* (New York, 1980).

Good institutional studies, ethnographies or social histories of the evolution of upper-class groups, as against the somewhat static studies of 'emergent élites' in the 1950s and 1960s, are rare. R. Luckham's study, *The Nigerian military* (Cambridge, 1971) and P. L. van den Berghe's study of academics, *Power and privilege in an African university* (London, 1973), are valuable; A. Cohen's study of the Freetown Creoles, *The politics of élite culture* (Berkeley, 1981) is unique of its kind. Anthropological studies of kinship may also be useful: e.g. for Ghana, C. Oppong's *Marriage among a matrilineal élite* (Cambridge, 1974). The literature on education and mobility is also very relevant (e.g. P. J. Foster, *Education and social change in Ghana* (Chicago, 1965); P. J. Foster and R. Clignet, *The fortunate few* (Evanston, 1966)). The best study conceived within the 'tradition-to-modernity' school, which transcends many of its limitations, is D. N. Levine's study of Ethiopia in the late 1950s, *Wax and gold* (Chicago, 1965). On questions of culture, identity and policy, however, it is usually best to turn directly to African writers themselves. A. A. Mazrui's writings eloquently cover most of the themes of concern to Africa's intelligentsia; see especially his *Political values and the educated class in Africa* (1978). The writings of political leaders, both theoretical (Nkrumah, Nyerere, Touré, Cabral) and autobiographical (Nkrumah, Awolowo, Kaunda, the *sardauna* of Sokoto) and, of course, African novels, are always illuminating. Finally, there are the major journals in which current political and cultural themes have been debated: particularly *Présence Africaine* (Paris, 1950–) and *Transition* (Kampala, 1961–197?).

5. THE ECONOMIC EVOLUTION OF DEVELOPING AFRICA

The subject matter of this presentation is very broad and the existing literature equally extensive, covering such wide-ranging themes as underdevelopment, imperialism, colonialism, Pan-Africanism, class struggle and revolution, accumulation and distribution of wealth and several other related economic and political issues in the equally broad field of planning and development in Africa. Obviously, such a bibliographic review has to be selective of only a few from the large corpus of books and articles in learned publications. The selection has been guided principally by the need to relate the review to the main strands of thought in the quest for understanding the economic and social development of Africa.

There exists a wealth of information on the economic development of Africa as a whole. The bulk of this relates to the period after the Second World War during which most countries of the region attained political independence. Some of the published

works were written in anticipation of the developmental relationships and problems that were to follow political emancipation,
while others were devoted to analysing Africa's economic
evolution and diagnosing the ills of the continent's slow pace of
development and consequent failure to uplift its masses from
poverty, ignorance, poor health and other common forms of
deprivation.

A detailed historical survey of useful background material for
studying and appreciating Africa's social and economic evolution
and the circumstances connected with this is provided by
R. W. July, *Precolonial Africa: an economic and social history* (New
York, 1975). Economic and social phenomena touching on issues
such as environment and economic adaptation, concepts of
private property, the idea of profit, the uses of surplus, and the
role of the state in mercantile development are dealt with in a
historical perspective.

G. Dalton, 'Traditional production in primitive economies',
Quarterly Journal of Economics, 1962, vol. 76, no. 3, 360–78 further
provided background information on the role of traditional
institutions in shaping the patterns of development, the receptivity
of Africans to innovations and the containment of the social costs
and dislocations of introducing new economic forms. This aspect
receives further treatment in the chapter by J. B. Elliot, 'The
character and prospects of African economies', in J. S. Uppal and
L. R. Salkever (eds.), *Africa: problems in economic development* (New
York, 1972), 5–26. The evidence for positive response to incentives and the particular circumstances responsible for lack of
response in the African setting are analysed by S. D. Neumark,
'Economic development and economic incentives', *The South
African Journal of Economics*, 1958, vol. 26, no. 1, 56–63.

The work by Charles Haines, *Africa today* (Baltimore, 1955) is
evidence of the development of intellectual interest in Africa after
the Second World War. About the same time, W. A. Hance, in
his book *African economic development* (New York, 1958) presented
a series of studies covering agricultural and industrial development, transport problems and case studies of Liberia, the Central
African Republic and Madagascar. Written before most countries
of the region achieved independence, the book reviewed the
underdeveloped state of the economy and the gradual transition
from subsistence to exchange economy.

Using the comparative method, Clive Dewey and A. G.

Hopkins (eds.), *Imperial impact: studies in the economic history of Africa and India* (London, 1978), discussed former imperial and colonial economic policy to illuminate their economic experiences and so contribute to the study of the developmental problems of new independent states. For whatever they were worth, efforts were made by governments in the colonial era to plan the economies of their colonies, as demonstrated by Barbu Niculescu, *Colonial planning: a comparative study* (London, 1958) in a survey of the development plans of some 60 dependent territories. Of the priorities common to all the plans, communication and agriculture ranked the highest, followed by education and health.

Global considerations of African development problems and processes have been the concern of many authors. Thus, Uppal and Salkever, *Africa: problems in economic development*, presented an anthology of articles and excerpts on the problems and processes of economic development in Africa as a whole. The article by A. M. Kamarck, 'African economic development: problems and prospects', *Africa Report*, 1969, vol. 14, no. 1, 16–20 is in the same vein and reflects some of the views also developed in his book *The economics of African development* (New York, 1967), which is an illuminating study of the economic development of Africa as a whole. The ties (economic, cultural and educational) with Western Europe are underlined along with the dependence for capital, personnel, technology and other infrastructural requirements long after political emancipation was attained.

Donald Rothchild and R. L. Curry, in *Scarcity, choice and public policy in Middle Africa* (Berkeley, 1978) assessed, among other issues, the benefits as well as the costs of multinational corporations' investments in Africa. That the MNCs, with their increasing oligopolistic powers, were creating a small, but relatively privileged 'labour aristocracy' of well-paid employees while restricting the growth of wage employment opportunities in the modern sector was put across by G. Arrighi, 'International corporations, labour aristocracies and economic development in Africa', in Robert T. Rhodes (ed.), *Imperialism and underdevelopment* (New York, 1970). S. Langdon, in the article, 'Multinational firms and the state in Kenya', *Institute of Development Studies Bulletin*, 1977, vol. 9, no. 1, 36–41, saw the state as an independent institution which was contriving a symbiosis between the multinational corporations and the auxiliary bourgeoisie.

In order to explain why Nigeria suffered from instability, the role of the state and its officials were examined in terms of their relationship to multinationals – the means by which Nigeria was incorporated into the global capitalist system. Thus T. Turner, in her paper, 'Multinational corporations and the instability of the Nigerian state', *Review of African Political Economy*, 1976, no. 5, 63–79, argued that the crucial nexus of the economy was a triad relationship between multinational corporations, commercial middlemen, and state officials.

The satellitisation and peripherisation of the African economy were all aspects of the growing significance of the interrelationship of external and internal factors of development in Africa. Such considerations sought to underline the dynamics of the structural changes in economic patterns which have evolved in the continent. This, for example, is evident in the treatise on African modern economic history by J. Forbes Munro in *Africa and the international economy 1800–1960: an introduction to the modern economic history of Africa south of the Sahara* (London, 1976). In a broader, more comparative perspective, he took as his central theme the integration of Africa into, and the subsequent structural shaping of African economies by, the modern international economy.

S. Amin, 'Development and structural change: the African experience, 1950–1970', *Journal of International Affairs*, 1970, vol. 24, no. 2, 203–23, set out to examine the concept of 'development'. For him, the African experience has shown that 'development' should be regarded as the continuation of the political struggle for independence. In the article, 'Underdevelopment and dependence in Black Africa – origins and contemporary forms', *Journal of Modern African Studies*, 1972, vol. 10, no. 4, 503–24, he showed how the forms of colonial penetration in Africa were conditioned by the social relations and structures met in the three macro-regions of Africa which he identifies as: Eastern and Southern Africa; West Africa, Cameroun, Chad and Sudan; and the Congo River basin. In all three macro-regions, he argued, the organisation of export production resulted in the abolition of traditional societies and conversion to their current status of dependent and peripheral formations.

R. Dumont, in *False start in Africa* (New York, 1969), subscribes to the same views and argues that the structural imbalance and dependence on exports was responsible for the present chronic trade deficits.

Structural dependence of African economies has been strengthened by the balkanisation of the continent. It has therefore been held that the present structure of underdevelopment in Africa stems from the incorporation of the continent into the expanding capitalist system over a period of some four centuries, a process completed during the nineteenth or early twentieth century with the partition of Africa and the imperialist expansionism of industrial capitalism. These are the views advocated in the work by Richard Harris and his colleagues in *The political economy of Africa: underdevelopment or revolution* (New York, 1975). In *New direction for economic development in Africa* (London, 1976), Emanuel A. Okwuosa traced economic thought and approach to development in Africa and the linkage of her economy to the economies of the western world and to the continent's colonial past; he argued that Africa should carve out her own path to development without necessarily breaking off the mutual interdependence between the different economic systems.

The economic consequence of the partition of Africa is well emphasised by Reginald Green and Ann Seidman in *Unity or poverty? The economics of Pan-Africanism* (Harmondsworth, 1968). They argued that balkanisation impeded economic growth and independence and as a result African countries were unable to achieve real economic growth and higher living standards on their own. Both authors further showed that the structural imbalance resulting from over-dependence on the export of one or a few primary products made economies extremely vulnerable, highly dependent and incapable of internal adjustment.

But why did efforts, especially after independence, fail to alter the inherited *status quo*? Once again Richard Harris, *The political economy of Africa*, offered some clues to this. The volume, restricted to Tanzania, Zambia, South Africa, Ghana, Nigeria and Kenya, provided an analytical perspective of the interrelationship of political and economic factors as a prerequisite for understanding the causes of underdevelopment and the condition for the development of the continent. His views are to some extent shared by Ann Seidman, *Planning for development in sub-Saharan Africa* (New York, 1974). She argued that, since independence, few countries succeeded in achieving their objectives of improvement in the lives of their people; she then explored the fundamental constraints inherent in the inherited institutional and resource allocation patterns which thwarted efforts to attain delayed development goals in 1960s.

5.   THE ECONOMIC EVOLUTION

Presenting the result of a symposium sponsored by the Haile Selassie I Prize Trust in 1966, R. K. Gardiner *et al.* (eds.), *Africa and the world* (Addis Ababa, 1970) agreed that Africa was passing through a critical phase in her economic development. Ideally agricultural development had to go hand in hand with industrial development, while educational and manpower planning and training should be undertaken concurrently.

As well as the global perspective, efforts have also been directed at assessing developments at the regional and country levels, touching on the same issues as those dealt with above. Thus, the articles in R. C. O'Brien (ed.), *The political economy of underdevelopment: dependence in Senegal* (Beverly Hills, 1979) were directed at refining the debate on African political economy. The contributors were concerned about the exploitative features of Senegal's dependence on France and the world capitalist system in general. The origin of the most acute of the present problems is to be found in the colonial and post-colonial relationships with France marked by unequal trade exchange and satellisation or peripherisation in terms of the metropole–satellite model.

In the same vein, Colin Leys in *Underdevelopment in Kenya* (London, 1975), postulated that colonialism led to the incorporation of the Kenyan economy into an increasingly global capitalist economy with the periphery subordinated to the centre. There was no free competition at the periphery, which was dominated by monopoly elements controlling the significant factors of production. Thus, the colonial period was marked by state activity for the benefit of European settlers creating conditions of monopoly.

The central theme in A. G. Hopkins's *An economic history of West Africa* (London, 1973), is the interaction of the various internal and external factors which have determined the structure and growth of the market economy of West Africa. He contended that Africans were 'economic men' responding to opportunities. Having discarded the stereotype of the 'traditional' he argued that the expansion of the domestic market was retarded not by institutional rigidities determined by anti-capitalist values, but by identifiable economic obstacles.

There is a general analysis of current and future evolution of the economy of the Maghrib in the literature. Works which also focus on economic integration include Samir Amin's *L'Économie*

du Maghreb, 2 vols. (Paris, 1966). Others are A. Tiano, *Le Développement économique du Maghreb* (Paris, 1968); C. F. Gallagher, *The United States and North Africa: Morocco, Algeria and Tunisia* (Cambridge, Mass., 1963); J. d'Yvoire, *Le Maghreb et la Communauté Économique Européenne* (Paris, 1965).

An important aspect of the situation in East Africa is clearly brought out in a series of writings covering the activities of the now defunct East African Common Market. These studies include: D. P. Ghai, 'Territorial distribution of the benefits and costs of the East African Common Market', in C. Leys, and P. Robson (eds.), *Federation in East Africa: opportunities and problems* (Nairobi, 1965), W. T. Newlyn, 'Gains and losses in the East African Common Market', *Yorkshire Bulletin*, November 1965; and Philip Ndegwa, *The Common Market and development in East Africa*, 2nd edition (Nairobi, 1968).

Education and manpower planning should, for maximum effectiveness, be dealt with *pari passu*, since the two sectors are highly interrelated. This linkage is very well demonstrated by Richard Jolly, in *Planning education for African development* (Nairobi, 1969). The author developed an ingenious new technique, based on intensive field experience, for showing the levels of educational attainment in a country and how they are built up by flows through the educational system. The technique is also used to bring out the basic manpower problems of Ghana, Uganda, and Zambia, and to show how current educational policies affect the level and composition of the stock of qualified manpower for the future.

Specific contributions directed mainly at the analysis of educational policies and problems are featured in several publications, among which the following can be cited: Julius K. Nyerere, *Education for self-reliance* (Dar es Salaam, 1967); W. W. Brickman, 'Tendencies in African education', *Educational Forum*, May 1963, vol. 27, 399–416; and Guy Hunter, *Education for a developing region: a study in East Africa* (London, 1963).

In his work, Harbison generally considered the relationship between education and manpower planning; F. H. Harbison and C. Myers, *Education, manpower and economic growth* (New York, 1964); F. H. Harbison, *Human resources as the wealth of nations* (New York, 1973). Problems of manpower development and diagnosis of the attendant problems have received the attention of several studies. R. G. Hollister, in 'Manpower problems and policies in Africa', *International Labour Review*, 1959, vol. 99, no. 5, 515–32, analysed, among other issues, the shortage of skilled manpower; rural–urban drift and unemployment; malfunctioning of the wage system and components of an integrated manpower policy.

Employment in Africa and related critical issues were the subject of an ILO contribution (Geneva, 1971), while P. De Briey focussed on 'The productivity of African labour', *International Labour Review*, 1955, vol. 72, 119–37. Labour migration has had significant economic and social consequences, particularly in the countries of southern Africa. This is the subject of the article by T. Soper on 'Labour migration in Africa' in the *Journal of African Administration*, 1959, vol. 11, 93–9.

In a historical study, R. Cohen, *Labour and politics in Nigeria, 1945–1971* (London, 1974), traced the history of the labour movement in Nigeria and tried to establish why factionalism prevailed; while G. Arrighi discussed the emergence of different forms of the *bourgeoisie* (*petite*, bureaucratic etc.) as a result of the investment policies of oligopolistic corporations and consortia (see G. Arrighi, 'International corporations, labour aristocracies, and economic development in Africa', in Robert T. Rhodes (ed.), *Imperialism and underdevelopment* (New York, 1970)).

The agricultural sector had a central role to play, particularly in the resolution of the food crisis that increasingly faced the continent in the period covered by this volume. K. R. M. Anthony *et al.* in *Agricultural change in tropical Africa* (Ithaca, 1979) concentrated on the process of agricultural change and on the factors that permit widespread increase in farm productivity and income.

S. C. Jain in the *Agricultural development of African nations*, 2 vols. (Bombay, 1965), presented a study of agro-economic structure, focussing on general agricultural development and on policies conducive to successful and rapid economic growth of the African countries covered. Considerations of the role of the state and mechanisation, crop and livestock production, land use and ownership in agricultural development are adequately covered by I. A. Svanidze in 'The African struggle for agricultural productivity', *Journal of Modern African Studies*, 1968, vol. 6, no. 3, 311–28.

Internal as well as external trade relations and conditions have been shown to be related to Africa's colonial and imperial heritage. Thus Claude Meillassoux (ed.), *Development of indigenous trade and markets in West Africa* (Oxford, 1971) adopted a Marxist perspective in his introduction. He considered the effects of the growth of markets on social relations, the intensity of long-distance trade, and the impact of European capitalism.

P. H. Turner made a comprehensive study of the workings of commercial institutions in Africa in *The commerce of new Africa* (London, 1969). Problems such as the supply of capital, the availability of skilled manpower, reform of outdated customs and practices are dealt with along with other more complex issues arising from the rapid pace of economic development and social change.

With the external orientation of African commerce, seaports assume a critical role. B. S. Hoyle and D. Hilling, in *Seaports and development in tropical Africa* (London, 1970) underline, through a collection of essays by geographers, the important role of seaports in the economic growth of underdeveloped areas. Maritime transport also affects the local level of industrialisation, mineral extraction and export. Thus the United Nations Economic Commission for Africa provided an assessment of the current state and past growth of industry in UNECA, *Industrial development in Africa: problems and prospects* (New York, 1967).

Studies on minerals are available and M. Bostock and C. Harvey have edited a collection of papers under the title: *Economic independence and Zambian copper* (New York, 1972). An early wartime study by Albert W. Postel, *The mineral resources of Africa* (Philadelphia, 1943), indicated Africa's annual production of each type of existing and known mineral along with the annual world production and the annual production of the world's chief producers. Similarly, N. de Kun in *The mineral resources of Africa* (Amsterdam, 1965), describes in detail the mineral wealth, the geology, and the various sources of energy, for all the countries of the continent.

It has been commonly realised in the literature that political freedom has not been matched by economic independence. D. P. Ghai edited a collection of essays titled *Economic independence in Africa* (Nairobi, 1973) which presented case studies of the policies pursued to obtain economic independence in Zambia, Kenya, Sudan and Egypt.

G. Arrighi and J. Saul in *Essay on the political economy of Africa* (New York, 1973), tried to demonstrate the extent to which 'structures of domination' (shaped by interaction of contemporary imperialism with patterns of domestic class formation) were the most important variables affecting the prospects for African progress and development. The authors argued that socialism was, in fact, becoming a real necessity in order to ensure the further development of the continent.

This socialist orientation, with variations on the theme of class struggle, coloured the works of several authors including African leaders. Such studies include: Kwame Nkrumah, *Class struggle in Africa* (New York, 1970), in which he held that the colonial period gave rise to the development of 'capitalist social structures' in Africa; and Frantz Fanon, *Les Damnés de la terre*, translated as *The wretched of the earth* (New York, 1963). Fanon perceives what Amin, Nkrumah and others correctly identified – that this new ruling class was dependent for its privileged position upon the intermediary role which it played in the neo-colonial framework. As Cabral put it, decolonisation made possible an alliance between the local bourgeoisie and the bourgeoisie of the capitalist metro-poles (Amílcar Cabral, 'The struggle in Guinea', *International Socialist Journal*, 442).

Other studies in the socialist/Marxist tradition include: E. J. Berg, 'Socialism and economic development in tropical Africa', *Quarterly Journal of Economics*, 1964, vol. 78, no. 4, 549–73; F. Burke, 'The Search for Ujamaa', in W. Friedland and C. Rosenberg (eds.), *African socialism* (Stanford, 1964); Kwame Nkrumah, *I speak of freedom* (London, 1961), and *Towards colonial freedom: Africa in the war against world imperialism* (London, 1962); Julius Nyerere, *Socialism and rural development* (Dar es Salaam, 1967); and *Freedom and socialism* (London, 1968). The related contribution of Léopold Senghor, *On African socialism* (New York, 1964), stressed the importance of culture in the task of nation-building, noting that it was not an appendage that could be dispensed with without damage to the entire fabric. The following three publications (among others) dwelt on the 'humanist' socialist views of the President of Zambia on development in his country: Kenneth Kaunda, *Zambia's economic revolution: the*

Mulungushi Declaration (Lusaka, 1968); *Humanism in Zambia* (Lusaka, 1967); and *Towards complete independence: after Mulungushi* (Lusaka, 1969).

It is now clear that the various attitudes represented either by socialist or capitalist thinking have been employed by governments in trying to reformulate their national development strategies. E. Marcus was concerned with this problem in 'The economic role of the government in independent tropical Africa', *American Journal of Economics and Sociology*, 1965, vol. 24, no. 3, 307–15.

The collection of papers edited by A. Adedeji under the title *Indigenization of African economies* (London, 1981), assessed the impact of government intervention in development planning, and gave a historical background to indigenisation.

U. G. Damachi in his book *Leadership ideology in Africa: attitudes towards socio-economic development* (New York, 1976), claimed that many leaders had propounded different ideologies – Kaunda's Humanism; Seretse Khama's *Kagisano*; Nyerere's *Ujamaa*; Gaddafi's Green Revolution, etc. As already implied above, the socio-economic development thinking of these leaders reflected a heavy reliance on socialist principles; all of them emphasised state control which necessarily limits the scope for private enterprise. Guy Hunter in *The best of both worlds? A challenge on development policies in Africa* (London, 1967) showed how the transfer of institutions, technology, and values from one society to another with completely different structures proved infertile or caused social distortions and precipitated a 'revolution or rising frustrations' with consequent social and military upheavals.

Even before the advent of political independence, and since then, there has been a growing body of opinion in support of integrating, in one form or another, the generally small economies of the equally small and balkanised states in Africa.

Arthur Hazlewood (ed.), in *African integration and disintegration: case studies in economic and political union* (London, 1967), presented a collection of papers on the way African states endeavoured to integrate their economies, and in some cases their political systems, in the face of powerful forces tending to pull them apart. The study is therefore concerned mainly with the politics as well as the economics of integration. Both R. H. Green and K. G. V. Krishna, in *Economic co-operation in Africa: retrospect and prospect* (Nairobi, 1967), reviewed developments in the field in 1965 and analysed the institutional framework for and the dynamics of economic union together with considerations of external influences on and opposition to African economic cooperation and integration. The work by A. M. Akiwumi on the *Judicial aspects of economic integration treaties in Africa* (Leiden, 1972) examined the general concept of international law in economic cooperation and analysed the various legal frameworks (treaties, conventions, etc.) adopted in the process, using to advantage the experiences of EAC, UDEAC and other such international organisations.

Other contributions on the problems of economic integration in the continent include, among others, P. N. C. Okigbo, *Africa and the Common Market* (London, 1967); F. V. Walker, 'Regional economic integration in Africa', in Uppal and Salkever, cited above; and P. Robson, *Economic integration in Africa* (Evanston, 1968).

Valuable surveys of economic and customs unions and the commercial policy of protectionism and tariff bargaining appeared in the following publications, which have both theoretical and practical interest: J. Viner, *The customs union issue* (New York, 1950); J. E. Meade, *Problems of economic union* (London, 1953); R. G. Lipsey, 'The theory of customs unions: a general survey', *Economic Journal*, Sept. 1960; G. H. Johnson, 'An economic theory of protectionism, tariff bargaining, and the formation of customs unions', *Journal of Political Economy*, 1965; and C. A. Cooper and B. F. Massell, 'Toward a general theory of customs unions for developing countries', *Journal of Political Economy* (Chicago), 1965, vol. 73.

Contributions on African sub-regional integration with a focus on the development, benefits and problems of the East African Common Market, are: D. V. Cowen, 'Towards a common market in Southern Africa', *Optima*, June 1967; D. P. Ghai, 'Territorial distribution of the benefits and costs of the East African Common Market', in C. Leys and P. Robson (eds.), *Federation in East Africa: opportunities and problems* (Nairobi, 1965); W. T. Newlyn, 'Gains and losses in the East African Common Market', *Yorkshire Bulletin*, November 1965; and P. Ndegwa, *The Common Market and development in East Africa* (Nairobi, 1965, second edition 1968). For the Maghrib sub-region, A. Robana wrote *The prospects for an economic community in North Africa: managing economic integration in the Maghreb states* (New York, 1973).

6. SOUTHERN AFRICA

The problem of assessing the significance of recent events is a major difficulty faced by anybody rash enough to attempt a brief history of southern Africa over so turbulent a period as the past forty years. Peoples' experiences and claims vary and their interpretations of what has happened differ widely. One contemporary, when asked what he thought were the most significant events to have occurred during the period, put high on his list the granting of constitutional independence to the Transkei in October 1976. Another contemporary regarded it as 'irrelevant; a mere book-entry'. Both people were young with acute political minds. One is white and a member of the ruling National Party; the other, black, has since died in prison for his political activities. To take two further examples, the great Xhosa poet and writer, S. E. K. Mqhayi, resigned as a teacher from Lovedale, an institution which prided itself on being particularly sympathetic to the African cause, because he felt the history he had to teach was unduly biased and uncritical of white conquest. On the other side of the fence, an Afrikaner nationalist in 1947 justified his party's attack on dual-medium schools where white children were taught in both Afrikaans and English. 'Our children', he complained, 'sit in dual medium schools which means that if you tell the one section its history, you hurt the other. Thus we paper over the cracks neatly, else we are race-haters.'[1] The way to a better understanding of events must, as a recent book[2] on ethnocentrism in historical writing points out, pass through the arena of conflict where historians with different interpretations and perspectives face each other and try to incorporate the others' views into their own work. New books had to be written in Europe when children in the international schools were first required to learn history in a language other than their own. That day is still a long way off in South Africa. Meanwhile one has to pick one's way forward, ever mindful of the extent to which one's own views, experiences and place in society filter not only the interpretation of events but also their selection.

Nor is perspective the only difficulty. Paradoxically, where a major problem lies in deciding what to leave out, there is an acute

---

[1] Cited by Dunbar Moodie, *The rise of Afrikanerdom* (Berkeley, 1975), 240.
[2] Roy Preiswerk and Dominique Perrot, *Ethnocentrism and history* (New York, 1978).

lack of information and of interpretation from some points of view. Much important writing is either banned or, for fear of police action, hidden away; sometimes destroyed; often never published. In a world of *Samizdat*, many facts will not emerge from their hiding places, including peoples' heads, for years to come. During the 1960s almost an entire generation of black writers went voluntarily or involuntarily into exile; bans were imposed so that their books could neither circulate nor be quoted in South Africa. Nor is it only black writers who have been thus 'erased from the scene'. Books ordered from outside do not always arrive; works read abroad cannot always be brought back and re-read when needed. Important material is published overseas of which scholars inside the country are not always aware.

Another barrier inhibiting the gathering of information is the diversity of languages in the region. Much has been printed – though not all of it preserved – in a wide variety of languages ranging from Afrikaans and Arabic through to Yiddish and Zulu. In addition, until 1979 state papers in South African archives were not open to the public until 50 (now 30) years after they had been written and thus the police records on such important political movements as the *Ossewa Brandwag* or *Umkhonto we Sizwe*, which were responsible for sabotage during the early 1940s and 1960s respectively, were not available and our information was limited to press cuttings, court records, or the memoirs of retired policemen. Until more monographs have been written which draw on this hidden wealth (including the fast-disappearing oral material), southern African history must remain fragmentary. Despite these difficulties, the area is one of the most richly documented in the continent and there is a mass of relevant writing, ranging from government commissions to unpublished student theses. What follows is simply an introduction to enable the reader to go straight to some of the most important of the source material and interpretative writing currently available in English.

It is best to begin with the bibliographical tools. Reuben Musiker's *South African bibliography: a survey of bibliographies and bibliographical work* (Cape Town, second edition, 1980) provides an admirable guide as to what is available. This is supplemented by his guide to important bibliographies and reference books published in the World Bibliographic Series as *South Africa*

(Oxford, 1979). For books in general the *SA national bibliography* which has been published regularly since 1959 is comprehensive. Government publications are listed in the House of Assembly's *Index to the manuscript annexures and printed papers of the House of Assembly including select Committee Reports and Bills and also principal motions and resolutions and Commission Reports 1910–1961* (Cape Town, 1963) which has a useful section on reports of government commissions. This is supplemented by the Library of Parliament's unpublished *Index to the printed annexures of the House of Assembly 1962–1971* (mimeo, Cape Town). In addition, there is the Department of Cultural Affairs, *Bibliography of the Department of Statistics 1910–1968* (Pretoria, 1969). Good bibliographies focussing on particular fields include G. E. Gorman, *The South African novel since 1950: an information and resource guide* (Boston, 1978) and University of the Orange Free State, Institute for Contemporary History, *Bibliography on South African political history, 1902–1974*, vol. I (Bloemfontein, 1978). Also important, not least as a measure of the amount of archival material now available is Susan G. Wynn, *African political material: a catalogue of the Carter–Karis collection* (Bloomington, 1977). The impact of censorship in the country is recorded in Jacobsen's *Index of objectionable literature* (Pretoria).

For a guide to unpublished research work scholars should consult Stefanus I. Malan, *Union catalogue of theses and dissertations of the South African universities, 1942–1958* (Potchefstroom, 1959), together with the *Annual supplements* compiled by the Ferdinand Potsmas Library in Potchefstroom. For theses written at other universities around the world the best guide is Oliver B. Pollak and Karin Pollak, *Theses and dissertations on Southern Africa: an international bibliography* (Boston, 1976). A rich quarry to be mined by historians of southern Africa is the periodical literature, most of which is recorded in the *Annual index to South African periodicals* compiled by the City of Johannesburg Public Library since 1940. Many of the books and articles cited in these bibliographies deal not only with South Africa but also with other countries in the region. But for references focussed specifically on these countries the best guides are: Richard P. Stevens, *Historical dictionary of Botswana* (Metuchen, 1975); John J. Grotpeter, *Historical dictionary of Swaziland* (Metuchen, 1975); Eckard Strohmeyer,

Namibian national bibliography 1971–1975 (Basle, 1978) and Shelagh M. Willett and D. Ambrose, *Lesotho* (Oxford, 1980).

We turn now to books (most of which themselves contain useful bibliographies) which may be regarded as starting points for those wishing to read more deeply. A wider, though by no means comprehensive, set of references is included in the bibliography at the back of this volume. The two volumes of the *Oxford history of South Africa* edited by Monica Wilson and Leonard Thompson (Oxford, 1969 and 1971) broke new ground and sparked off a lively debate about the interpretation of South African history. A good general work which takes account of this ferment amongst scholars is T. R. H. Davenport, *South Africa – a modern history* (Johannesburg, second edition, 1978) although Leo Marquard, *The peoples and policies of South Africa* (London, fourth edition, 1969, retitled *A short history of South Africa*) remains the best brief account. Two books which look specifically at the different interpretations of the various schools of thought are, for the earlier years, F. A. Van Jaarsveld, *The Afrikaners' interpretation of South African history* (Cape Town, 1964) and, for the 1970s, Harrison Wright, *The burden of the present* (Cape Town, 1977). There is as yet no major work by a black historian whose experience and perspective is so badly needed for a fuller understanding of the past.

For Swaziland there is J. S. M. Matsebulo, *A history of Swaziland* (Cape Town, second edition, 1976). In addition there is a major biography by Hilda Kuper, *Sobhuza II* (London, 1978). For Namibia the best introduction remains John H. Wellington, *South West Africa and its human issues* (Oxford, 1967) supplemented, for details of the subsequent decade, by J. H. P. Serfontein, *Namibia?* (Randburg, 1976). For the international aspects see John Dugard (ed.), *The South West Africa/Namibia dispute, documents and scholarly writings on the controversy between South Africa and the United Nations* (Berkeley, 1973). A major change in historical approach has been the change in time depth and archaeologists have provided evidence for this. It is summarised in R. R. Inskeep, *The peopling of Southern Africa* (Cape Town, 1978). Southern Africa has produced an unusually large number of in-depth studies of society in transition. Isaac Schapera's books on the Tswana, beginning with *Tswana law and custom* (London, 1938), Monica Hunter's

Reaction to conquest (London, 1936), E. J. and J. D. Krige's *The realm of a rain queen* (London, 1943) and Hilda Kuper's *An African aristocracy* (Oxford, 1947) laid the foundation.

Amongst more recent studies three books which demonstrate something of the depth and range of modern anthropology are Richard B. Lee and Irwen De Vore (eds.), *Kalahari hunter gatherers* (Cambridge, Mass., 1976); Axel Ivar Berglund, *Zulu thought patterns and symbolism* (Uppsala, 1968), and Colin Murray, *Families divided: the impact of migrant labour in Lesotho* (Cambridge, 1981). For the sociological contribution one might begin with Heribert Adam (ed.), *South African sociological perspectives* (London, 1971).

In the field of economics there are good general works on four of the five countries under consideration but in confining themselves to political boundaries of a single nation state all of them remain essentially partial descriptions. But taken together the following four books provide a comprehensive overview: D. Hobart Houghton, *The South African economy* (Cape Town, fourth edition, 1976); Wolfgang H. Thomas, *Economic development in Namibia* (Munich, 1978); ILO Jobs and Skills programme for Africa (Jaspa), *Options for a dependent economy: development, employment and equity problems in Lesotho* (Addis Ababa, 1979); and C. Colclough and S. McCarthy, *The political economy of Botswana: a study of growth and distribution* (Oxford, 1980). For those who find delving into statistical tables illuminating, two invaluable sources, albeit confined to one country, are published by the Department of Census in Pretoria: *Union statistics for fifty years 1910–1960* and the biennial *South African statistics* whose 1978 edition contains a number of tables covering a long run of years.

In labour there are two classics which complement each other. But both Sheila T. van der Horst, *Native labour in South Africa* (Cape Town, 1942) and Edward Roux, *Time longer than rope* (Wisconsin, second edition, 1964) focus primarily on the period before 1936 and are best read for understanding of the roots from which subsequent labour developments grew. More recent studies include Francis Wilson, *Labour in the South African gold mines 1911–1969* (Cambridge, 1972) and Eddie Webster (ed.), *Essays in Southern Africa labour history* (Johannesburg, 1978). Similarly, S. H. Frankel, *Capital investment in Africa* (London, 1938) laid the foundation for understanding the further development of international economic links during the period. This remained virtually the only study until, as with labour, a spate of books and articles were published in the 1970s. A guide, though it needs up-dating, to some of these may be found in Jan Edwards, *Bibliography on foreign investment in South Africa* (Johannesburg, 1975). Two books on some of the infrastructural links being forged in Africa south of the equator are: Guy Arnold and Ruth Weiss, *Stragetic highways of Africa* (London, 1977) and Keith Middlemas, *Cabora Bassa: engineering and politics in Southern Africa* (London, 1975) which together show something of the significance of links binding together South Africa and other parts of the continent which lie outside the regional definition used in this volume.

Given the very wide range of material available, it is difficult to reduce one's desert island list of political reading to less than a dozen books. The best descriptions of government in the decade before 1948 are to be found in two outstanding political biographies: W. K. Hancock, *Smuts: the fields of force 1919–1950* (Cambridge, 1968) and Alan Paton, *Hofmeyr* (Cape Town, 1964). A contemporary account of Afrikaner politics in the wilderness is to be found in Michael Roberts and A. E. G. Trollip, *A South African opposition 1939–1945* (Cape Town, 1947) whilst the best reference for the next decade is Gwendolen M. Carter, *The politics of inequality: South Africa since 1948* (London, second edition, 1959). Perceptive analysis of transformations within Afrikaner-dom since the 1960s is undertaken by Heribert Adam, *Modernising racial domination* (Berkeley, 1971), and by Heribert Adam and Hermann Giliomee, *The rise and crisis of Afrikaner power* (Cape Town, 1979). A longer-term perspective is well provided by T. Dunbar Moodie, *The rise of Afrikanerdom* (Berkeley, 1975), and W. A. de Klerk, *The Puritans in Africa* (London, 1975). For a view from inside the laager see A. N. Pelzer (ed.), *Verwoerd speaks: speeches 1948–1966* (Johannesburg, 1966).

The most important collection of original documents in politics from a black perspective is contained in Thomas Karis and Gwendolen M. Carter (eds.), *From protest to challenge*, of which vols. II and III (Stanford, 1973, 1977) cover the years 1935–64. For general accounts of African political resistance see Peter Walshe, *The rise of African nationalism in South Africa* (London, 1970), Gail M. Gerhart, *Black Power in South Africa* (Berkeley, 1978) and Tom Lodge, *Black politics in South Africa since 1945*

(Johannesburg, 1983). For the best detailed account of a specific confrontation between the state and its people see Charles Hooper, *Brief authority* (London, 1960), whilst accounts of the impact of apartheid on those affected by it are provided by Naboth Mokgatle, *The autobiography of an unknown South African* (Berkeley, 1971) and Z. K. Matthews, *Freedom for my people* (London, 1980). For a contemporary record of all political developments the *Annual survey of race relations*, published by the South African Institute of Race Relations in Johannesburg, is invaluable.

In the field of law, A. S. Matthews, *Law, order and liberty in South Africa* (Cape Town, 1971), Albie Sachs, *Justice in South Africa* (Berkeley, 1973), Muriel Horrell, *Laws affecting race relations in South Africa 1948–1976* (Johannesburg, 1978) and John Dugard, *Human rights and the South African legal order* (Princeton, 1979), provide a comprehensive overview. In military affairs Neil Orpen *et al.*, *South African forces, World War II*, 6 vols. (Cape Town, 1968–77) covers the early period in minute detail, whilst the best introduction to the later period is Basil Davidson, Joe Slovo and Anthony R. Wilkinson, *Southern Africa: the new politics of revolution* (Harmondsworth, 1976). In science the best book is A. C. Brown (ed.), *A history of scientific endeavour in South Africa* (Cape Town, 1977).

For education in general it is best to begin with E. G. Malherbe, *Education in South Africa* (Cape Town, 1977) whilst also reading I. B. Tabata, *Education for barbarism* (East London, 1960) to understand the depth of black opposition to the imposed education system. A preliminary guide to the confrontation between church and state during the period is John W. de Gruchy, *The Church struggle in South Africa* (Grand Rapids, 1979); two original sources from either end of the spectrum are Basil Moore (ed.), *Black theology: a South African voice* (London, 1973) and W. A. Landman, *A plea for understanding: a reply to the Reformed Church in America* (Cape Town, 1968). For discussion of the rapidly growing independent churches which lie outside the boundaries of the major traditional Christian denominations, see Bengt Sundkler, *Bantu prophets in South Africa* (London, second edition, 1961). Gabriel Setiloane, *The image of God among the Sotho-Tswana* (Rotterdam, 1976) is also illuminating.

It is not possible to select any one novel to represent the wealth of literature written during this period. Some of the more important books are listed in the bibliography. Here three anthologies may serve to whet readers' appetites. Nadine Gordimer and Lionel Abrahams (eds.), *South African writing to-day* (Harmondsworth, 1967); Richard Rive (ed.), *Quartet* (London, 1965); and Jean Marquard (ed.), *A century of South African short stories* (Johannesburg, 1978). In addition to prose, a lot of poetry welled up during the 1970s, some of which is in the anthology edited by Guy Butler and Chris Mann, *A book of South African verse in English* (Cape Town, 1979).

To conclude, it is perhaps worth making the point that those wishing to understand Southern Africa better will often learn more from the wide range of novels, plays, poetry and autobiographies written during this period than from much of the more academic analyses. Certainly twentieth-century South Africa cannot be understood, any more than nineteenth-century Russia, from the work of academics alone. But South Africa, as yet, has no Tolstoy.

7. ENGLISH-SPEAKING WEST AFRICA

Books covering several African territories are seldom more useful than those covering a number of European countries. There are exceptions. Thomas Hodgkin pioneered the serious study of African politics by foreign scholars with his *Nationalism in colonial Africa* (London, 1957). Concerned largely with Commonwealth West Africa this was a landmark. From the British side, in *The turning point in Africa* (London, 1982), R. D. Pearce chose the decade 1938–48, not the following years when independence was achieved, as the watershed in British colonial policy. For in 1947 the Colonial Office – if not the Labour government – decided, chiefly because of developments in the Gold Coast and Nigeria, that African colonies must become independent 'within a generation'. Hodgkin's and Pearce's books provide the background to political development in West Africa up to 1957.

Among books dealing with West African economies in general, two are classics: Peter Bauer's *West African trade* (Cambridge, 1954, second edition London, 1963) which is concerned with only Nigeria and Ghana, and Polly Hill's *Studies in rural capitalism in West Africa* (Cambridge, 1970), which is also concerned with these two countries, and analyses the way in which rural people, the great majority, 'order their economic behaviour'.

Nigeria

Four American 'blockbusters', of 500 pages or more, are essential for understanding Nigerian politics up to 1966. They are James S. Coleman, *Nigeria: background to nationalism* (Berkeley, 1958); Richard L. Sklar, *Nigerian political parties* (Princeton, 1963); C. S. Whitaker, *The politics of tradition* (Princeton, 1970) a fascinating and sympathetic analysis of the then Northern Nigeria by a black American; and J. N. Paden, *Religion and political culture in Kano* (Berkeley, 1973) whose discussion of the role of Muslim Brotherhoods in politics is significant far beyond Kano. A British contribution is *Nigerian government and politics* (London, 1966) by John P. Mackintosh *et al.*, while Billy J. Dudley, *Parties and politics in Northern Nigeria* (London, 1968) provides an interesting analysis by a Southern Nigerian.

A vast number of other books by Nigerians and outsiders deal with Nigerian politics. Books by or about individual politicians are essential for understanding the post-Second World War era. *My life* (Cambridge, 1962) by the Sardauna of Sokoto – believed to have been 'ghosted' by a senior administrative officer – covers the period up to self-government of the Northern Region in 1959. We await a biography of Sir Abubakar Tafawa Balewa. Chief Awolowo, the most prolific author among the Nigerian leaders, produced in 1946 *Path to Nigerian freedom* (London, 1946) and, among later works, his autobiography, *Awo* (Cambridge, 1960). Dr Azikiwe's autobiography *My odyssey* (London, 1970) takes his story up to 1947 – when he was already an experienced journalist and politician. *African revolutionary* (New York, 1973) is an inadequate biography (taking the story up to 1970) of Malam Aminu Kano, the NEPU leader and one of the most interesting of Nigeria's politicians. Chris Offodile's biography, *Dr M. I. Okpara* (Enugu, 1980), is too short to do justice to Azikiwe's successor as leader of the NCNC, and one of the most under-estimated politicians in Nigeria.

From countless books about Nigeria's economy one can recommend *Planning without facts* (Cambridge, Mass., 1966) by Wolfgang G. Stolper, an American who was briefly in charge of Nigeria's economic planning unit. In *Industrialisation in an open economy: Nigeria 1945–1966* (Cambridge, 1969) Peter Kilby argues that government efforts had little effect in promoting industrialisation. Professor W. Arthur Lewis's short *Reflections on Nigeria's economic growth* (OECD, 1967) is nevertheless the best of its kind.

Books that are more significant for understanding Nigeria than their titles suggest include: *Education in Northern Nigeria* (London, 1981) by Ozigi and Ocho; *Nigerian census, 1963* (Benin, 1972) by I. I. Ekanem; *The Second World War and politics in Nigeria* (Lagos and London, 1973) by G. O. Olusanya; and the *Willink report on minorities* (London, 1958). *The administration of Nigeria 1900 to 1960* (London, 1970) by I. F. Nicolson began, if with exaggeration, the 'demystification' of Lugard. It was taken a stage further by Jeremy White in *Central administration in Nigeria* (Dublin, 1971).

Of the memoirs of British officials the fullest is *But always as friends* (London, 1968) by Sir Bryan Sharwood-Smith, who retired as Governor of Northern Nigeria in 1957 after 36 years in Nigeria.

Two general books for the layman hold their places down the years: Michael Crowder, *The story of Nigeria* (London, many editions); and *Nigeria* (London, 1968) by Walter Schwarz.

For the civil war, John de St Jorre's *The Nigerian civil war* (London, 1972) is still the standard work. General Obasanjo's *My command* (Ibadan, 1980) is concerned mainly with war operations. Among many other books on the war and the secession, N. U. Akpan's *The struggle for secession* (London, 1971) is a valuable account of events leading to secession and of the administration of the rebel areas. A civil servant, he was head of the Biafran administration. Alexander Madiebo, commander-in-chief of the Biafran army, offered a somewhat different approach in *The Nigerian revolution and the Biafran war* (Enugu, 1980).

Ghana

No book on an African subject can have been recommended more often – or more properly – than Dennis Austin's *Politics in Ghana, 1946–60* (Oxford, 1964). A useful background is provided by *Ghana: the road to independence* (London, 1960 – new edition) by F. M. Bourret. Dr Nkrumah's numerous publications range from his *Autobiography* (London, 1957), believed to have been 'ghosted', to *Africa must unite* (London, 1963), *Neo-colonialism, the last stage of imperialism* (London, 1965) and the obscure philosophical work *Consciencism* (London, 1964). Study of these is necessary for understanding the course of Ghanaian politics until his death and after. In contrast are the scholarly works of Dr Kofi Busia, who became prime minister in 1969, in particular his standard work, *The position of the chief in the modern political system of Ashanti* (London, 1951).

Among books by Nkrumah's lieutenants are *Africa unbound* (New York, 1963) by Alex Quaison-Sackey, a considerably more balanced work than *Africa's golden road* (London, 1965) by Kwesi Armah. Inside the massive *Reap the whirlwind* (London, 1968) by Geoffrey Byng, Nkrumah's attorney-general and later adviser, a really good book struggles to get out. There is strong criticism of Nkrumah in *Kwame Nkrumah: the anatomy of an African dictatorship* (London, 1970) by Peter Omari, a Ghanaian university lecturer and international civil servant. In *Black star* (London, 1973) Basil Davidson produced, after Nkrumah's death, an appraisal which recognised his 'important failings' but claimed that his influence on the course of events would always seem significant. From its title the subject matter of *Political corruption: the Ghana case* (Stanford, 1975) by Victor T. Le Vine can be inferred.

Among studies of particular topics, *Organising the farmers* by Bjorn Beckman (Uppsala, 1974) describes the fluctuating relations between cocoa farmers and the CPP. *Uses and abuses of political power* (Chicago, 1971) by Maxwell Owusu analyses the relationship between wealth and local political power in Swedru in the south-central region, up to 1966. It concludes that the real object of politics in Ghana was power rather than wealth.

Among books describing Ghana's social scene are *Social structure of Ghana* (Accra, 1981) by Max Assimeng, a teacher at Legon, who tries to relate social phenomena in Ghana to those in the rest of the world; *Society and bureaucracy in contemporary Ghana* (Berkeley, 1975) by R. M. Price; and *Achimota in the national setting* (Accra, 1977) by Francis Agbodeka, published to mark the institution's golden jubilee, assesses the college's importance in the nation's life.

An American blockbuster, *Ghana's foreign policy, 1957–66* (Princeton, 1969) by W. Scott Thompson, overshadows all other books in this field. But for an understanding of Nkrumah's approach to external affairs a much shorter book, *The administration of Ghana's foreign policy 1957–65* (London, 1975) by Michael Dei-Annang, is essential. He was principal secretary, Ministry of

Foreign Affairs, 1959–61, and head of the African Affairs Secretariat, 1961–66.

Among many books on Ghana's economy, *Nationalism and economic development in Ghana* (McGill, 1969) by Roger Genoud is perhaps the most important. Of several studies concerned with the enterprise, *The Volta River Project* (Edinburgh, 1980) by David Hart is the most critical of the benefits it offered to Ghana. The two volumes of *A study of contemporary Ghana* (London, 1960) edited by Walter Birmingham, I. Neustadt and E. N. Omaboe, covers not only the economy but subjects such as land tenure and even religion. Tony Killick's *Development economics in action* (London, 1978) examines both the Nkrumah and the post-Nkrumah years. Nobody has written the essential study that will demonstrate that Ghana's economic decline was the direct result of the corruption of both the Nkrumah regime and those of his successors.

Sierra Leone

Scholars from a number of countries, as well as Sierra Leoneans themselves, have produced valuable studies of the country. There are, however, significant gaps: no biography exists, for example, of Sir Milton Margai.

A good introduction is Cyril P. Foray's *Historical dictionary of Sierra Leone* (Metuchen, 1977). John R. Cartwright, *Politics in Sierra Leone 1947–67* (Toronto, 1970) is a standard work, but Martin Kilson, *Political change in a West African state* (Cambridge, Mass., 1966), offers a more restricted but more stimulating study.

Because of the community's political as well as social significance, Leo Spitzer, *The Creoles of Sierra Leone* (Wisconsin, 1974), which takes the story up to 1945 and covers the emergence of Wallace-Johnson, is of general interest. I would put in a plea, too, for the delightful *A Krio-English dictionary* (Oxford, 1980) compiled by Clifford N. Fyle and Eldred D. Jones. N. A. Cox-George, *Finance and development in West Africa: the Sierra Leone experience* (London, 1961) is the first major study of the country's social and economic development. A later study is *The economic system of Sierra Leone* (Durham, NC, 1967) by Ralph Gerald Saylor, who concludes that the cost of government intervention in economic affairs far outweighed its benefit. A specialised but essential study is *The Sierra Leone diamonds* (London, 1965) by H. L. Van de Laan.

Liberia

Liberia is usually treated as a 'special case' in West Africa. It is not normally included in the multitude of works covering the whole area, since it is neither a francophone nor a Commonwealth state. There are, however, a number of good books – the best perhaps inevitably critical – dealing specially with the country. *Liberia: the evolution of privilege* (Ithaca, 1969) by J. Gus Liebenow, emphasises that in spite of Tubman's reforms the élite entrenched themselves in the new foreign enterprises. In *Tribe and class in Monrovia* (Oxford, 1964) Merran Fraenkel, whose fieldwork was done in 1958, rejected the analogy between Americo-Liberians and European 'settlers', but saw the correlation between ethnic origin and social class as still significant.

A member of the vigorous Kru tribe, Tuan Wreh, used the Liberian motto *The love of liberty brought us here* (London, 1971) as the ironic title of his critique of the Tubman regime. Another 'tribal' Liberian who, like Wreh, was in government service as a lawyer, Anthony Nimley, criticises the extortion practised by officials and the nepotism governing their appointments in *The Liberian bureaucracy* (Washington, DC, 1977). This emphasises that until 1934 the country had not even a nominally 'accountable' civil service.

The classic book on Liberia's economy is *Growth without development* (Evanston, 1966). The authors, R. W. Clower, G. Dalton, M. Harwitz and A. A. Walters, were university economists who carried out an economic survey of Liberia in 1960–2 for the government and USAID. The book, their 'unofficial' report, emphasised that unless political aims were changed, increased revenues would be irrelevant. Kinder judgements were made in books by two American writers: *The jet lighthouse* (London, 1960) by Galbraith Welch; and *Liberia: America's African friend* (Chapel Hill, 1962) by R. Earle Anderson. The official view is to be found in *Tubman of Liberia speaks* (London, 1959) and *The official papers of William V. S. Tubman* (Monrovia, 1968), well-produced collections of speeches.

The Gambia

Few books are devoted exclusively to the Gambia. Harry A. Gailey's *A history of the Gambia* (London, 1964) deals with events up to the eve of independence (1965). Information about the Gambia is, however, to be found in books concerning West Africa in general, Commonwealth West African states, or Senegal. *Senegambia* (Aberdeen, 1974), edited by R. C. Bridges, proceedings of a colloquium held at Aberdeen University in 1974, discusses issues which have since come to dominate Gambian politics. *The nature of poverty* (London, 1975) by Margaret Haswell deals with the Gambia's nutritional problems, and so agriculture.

Books about the intervention of soldiers in politics have become a secondary industry. Nigeria, Ghana and Sierra Leone are discussed in most of the general works, some of which seek a pattern which is not there. These include J. M. Lee, *African armies and civil order* (London, 1969). More specific, and relevant, are single-country studies, such as Robert Pinkney, *Ghana under military rule 1966–1969* (London, 1972); Robin Luckham, *The Nigerian military, 1960–1967* (Cambridge, 1971) and N. J. Miners, *The Nigerian army 1956–1966* (London, 1971). Victor O. Olusanya, *Soldiers and power* (Stanford, 1977) examines the 'development performance' of the Nigerian military. In *Soldiers and oil* (London, 1978) edited by Keith Panter-Brick, 13 scholars, Nigerian and British, discuss many different aspects of Nigeria under military rule. Thomas S. Cox, *Civil–military relations in Sierra Leone* (Cambridge, Mass., 1970) concludes that military intervention in politics complemented civilian intervention in military matters.

In Nigeria and Ghana participants in, or close observers of, military takeovers produced numerous memoirs. These include *Why we struck* (Ibadan, 1981) by Adewale Ademoyega, who sees events in Marxist terms; and *Nigeria's five majors* (Onitsha, 1981) by Ben Gbulie, another planner of the 1966 coup. For Ghana the most important book is *The Ghana coup* (London, 1966) by the then Colonel Afrifa, Brigade-Major to Colonel Kotoka who planned the 1966 takeover. *Politics of the sword* (London, 1977) is by General A. K. Ocran, who brought in the units under his command in support of the coup.

Several writers have been tempted to illuminate the affairs of one state by comparing it with another. We had a useful comparison, or contrast, in *Liberia and Sierra Leone* (Cambridge, 1976) by Christopher Clapham, covering the 1960s and early 1970s. Eleven papers on 'alternative strategies' appear in *Ghana and the Ivory Coast* (Chicago, 1971) edited by Philip Foster and Aristide R. Zolberg. In *Nigeria and Ghana* (Englewood Cliffs, NJ, 1966) John E. Flint discusses the two countries' differing political paths, while Olajide Aluko called his *Ghana and Nigeria 1957–70* (London, 1974) 'a study in inter-African discord'. A curiosity in this field is *The politics of pluralism* (New York, 1975) by David R. Smock and Audrey C. Smock. This contrasted, to Ghana's disadvantage, the policies pursued in the Lebanon and in Ghana, to deal with the two countries' common problem of 'pluralism'.

Trade unions played a more significant political than industrial role in both Ghana and Nigeria. *Class, power and ideology in Ghana* (Cambridge, 1978), by Richard Jeffries, analyses the Sekondi–Takoradi railwaymen's strike of 1961, which exposed the CPP government's claims to radicalism. *The role of trade unions in the development process* (London, 1974), by Ukandi Godwin Damachi, is concerned with Ghana. It traces the worsening relations between the CPP government and the workers, as well as union activities under both the Busia and military regimes. The title of *Labour and politics in Nigeria, 1945–71* (London, 1974) by Robin Cohen explains the book's scope. *The trade union movement in Nigeria* (London, 1969) by Wogu Ananaba was written by a leading actor in the drama. In *Choice, class and conflict* (Brighton, 1979), Adrian Peace analyses attitudes of workers after the civil war in the Agege and Ikeja industrial estates, and union disputes with the Gowon government.

Another category of books concerns relations between West Africa and Communist countries about which, at the time of independence, some western commentators were almost hysterical. An objective survey is provided by Robert Legvold in *Soviet policy in West Africa* (Harvard, 1970), which includes sections on Nigeria and Ghana. Books by disillusioned West African students include *Moscow diary* (London, 1967) by William Anti-Taylor, one of the first Ghanaian students to go to Moscow, and *On the tiger's back* (London, 1962) by the Nigerian Aderogba Ajao, who spent six years in East Germany.

The list of books about the English-speaking West African

states – many of them ephemeral – is being added to at an enormous rate each year. To this must also be added the huge number of articles published in scholarly journals of which the *Journal of Modern African Studies* is perhaps the most notable. An indispensable source for the course of political, social, economic and cultural events over this period is the weekly magazine *West Africa*.

The volume of source materials for the scholar of the recent history of West African states is swelled not only by the many published government reports but by the archives which in the case of the former British colonies are now open for the first decade of our period in Britain and in some cases can be consulted for more recent years in the individual states.

8. EAST AND CENTRAL AFRICA

Extensive documentary and secondary sources are available for the study of East and Central Africa, although not every country in the region has received equal attention, and the materials vary a great deal in value. A reasonably comprehensive guide to sources for East Africa is to be found in vols. II and III of the *History of East Africa* (Oxford, 1965 and 1976), while Tony Killick, *The economies of East Africa* provides a comprehensive guide to the sources on economic development of that region. For the East African Community see John Bruce Howell, *Subject guide to official publications* (Library of Congress, 1976).

Volume V of L. Gann and P. Duignan's *Colonialism in Africa, a bibliographical guide to colonialism in sub-Saharan Africa* (Cambridge, 1974) is the most useful starting point for Central Africa. Andrew Roberts' *History of Zambia* (London, 1976) contains an up-to-date bibliographical appendix which lists the main secondary sources for Zambia, and Robin Palmer's *Land and racial discrimination in Rhodesia* (London, 1977) should also be consulted for Rhodesia.

A great deal of valuable material is contained in the unpublished papers of the East African Institute of Social Research, now the Makerere Institute of Social Research, and of the research institutes of the Universities of Nairobi and Dar es Salaam.

Particularly useful are the mimeographed conference papers of the annual social science conference that has been held under one title or another since 1950. Reference should be made to Makerere

Institute of Social Research, Kampala, *Institute publications 1950–1970*, and *Research and publications, 1968–69*; also to University of Nairobi, Institute for Development Studies, *Research and publications* (annual); University of Dar es Salaam, Bureau of Resources Assessment and Land Use Planning, *List of publications*, and Economic Research Bureau, *List of discussion papers*. For the publications of the Rhodes-Livingstone Institute, see: University of Zambia, Institute for Social Research, *A complete list of the publications of the former Rhodes-Livingstone Institute*.

Each colonial government and Great Britain as the colonial power published a range of official materials which are an invaluable source of information for the colonial period. These include on the one hand annual departmental and other reports, and on the other the findings of a range of commissions of enquiry. Mention may be made here only of *East Africa Royal Commission, 1953–55: report* (Chairman Sir Hugh Dow) Cmd 9475, 1955; *Report of the Commission on the Civil Services of the East African Territories and the East African High Commission 1953–54* (Lidbury Report) (London, HMSO, 1954); *Report of the Uganda Relationships Commission, 1961* (Munster Report) (Entebbe, 1961); *Report of the Fiscal Commission* (Nairobi, 1963). For the Central African federation reference should be made to the Advisory Commission on the *Review of the Constitution of the Federation of Rhodesia and Nyasaland*, Cmnd 1151, 1960, 'Report and Evidence', 5 volumes (the Monckton Commission).

The *Proceedings* of the Legislative Council and the National Assembly which replaced it are an important source of information on political change for each state, although most especially for Kenya. Tanganyika, as a Trust Territory, was the subject of reports by the Visiting Missions (of 1948, 1951, 1954, 1957 and 1960). For Zambia a particularly useful study of conditions immediately prior to independence is United Nations, *Report of the UN/ECA/FAO economic survey mission on the economic development of Zambia* (the Seers Report) (Ndola, 1964).

In addition to the statistical publications of each territorial government, reference should be made to the *East African economic and statistical bulletin*, (quarterly from September 1948 to June 1961) succeeded by the *Economic and statistical review*, and to the Central African Statistical Office's *Federal monthly digest*. The availability of reliable economic data becomes more variable after independence. The *Annual economic report* remains the most authoritative statement of economic development for Kenya, Zambia, Tanzania and Malawi. For Malawi especial note should be made of the *Statement of development policies 1971–1980* (Zomba, 1971) and the *Compendium of statistics, 1955–65* (Ministry of Development and Planning, 1966). Economic data for Uganda since 1971 and for Rhodesia since 1965 is a good deal more difficult to obtain, and for Zambia at the time of writing the latest *Statistical yearbook* published was for 1971, although the *Monthly digest of statistics* remains a reliable source.

D. A. Low and John Lonsdale's Introduction to vol. III of the *History of East Africa* draws together the many threads of recent scholarship to provide a valuable introduction to colonial policy and decolonisation, although reference must also be made to Gary Wasserman's *The politics of decolonization* (Cambridge, 1976) which draws upon recently available settler archives to provide a significant reassessment of the role of settlers in Kenya's transfer of power. Cranford Pratt's *The critical phase in Tanzania 1945–1968* (Cambridge, 1976) provides not only a critical account of the failure of Britain's multiracial strategy in Tanganyika but also provides a perceptive analysis of Colonial Office thinking at this time. See also for the period of decolonisation and the transfer of power, David Goldsworthy, *Colonial issues in British politics 1945–1961* (Oxford, 1971); W. P. Kirkman, *Unscrambling an Empire, a critique of British colonial policy 1956–1966* (London, 1966); and J. M. Lee, *Colonial development and good government* (Oxford, 1967). More recent writing on the transfer of power, benefiting from additional official materials that have become available under the 30-year rule, has begun to probe further than was hitherto possible the underlying assumptions and motivations, and the influences upon policy changes after 1940–5, and to reassess the process of decolonisation. See, *inter alia*, W. H. Morris-Jones and Georges Fischer (eds.), *Decolonisation and after: the British and French experience* (London, 1980); John Hargreaves, *The end of colonial rule: essays in colonial history* (London, 1979); and James Morris, *Farewell the trumpets* (London, 1978). David John Morgan, *The official history of colonial development*, 5 vols. (London, 1980), written with full access to official sources, provides a good deal of information but is essentially a straightforward documentary account.

The role of white-settler communities in the decolonisation process is dealt with in A. Emmanuel, 'White settler colonialism and the myth of investment imperialism', *New Left Review*, May–June 1972. Gary Wasserman, in *The politics of decolonisation* (Cambridge, 1976), and 'The independence bargain: Kenya Europeans and the land issue 1960–62', *Journal of Commonwealth Political Studies*, July 1973, vol. 11, has documented the role of settler and commercial groups in the bargaining process that accompanied the transfer of power in Kenya, a story taken up by Colin Leys in *Underdevelopment in Kenya: the political economy of neo-colonialism* (London, 1974). See also A. Amsden, *International firms and labour in Kenya 1945–1970* (London, 1971). While there is as yet no comparable analysis for any of the other states in the region, the role of corporate capital in the decolonisation process had emerged at the end of the 1970s as a major issue for debate among historians, although one as yet unresolved.

The most useful general survey of the colonial period in East Africa is the *History of East Africa*, vol. II, edited by V. Harlow and E. M. Chilver (Oxford, 1965), covering the period from 1900 to 1945, and vol. III, edited by D. A. Low and Alison Smith (Oxford, 1976), from 1945 to 1963. There is a rich literature from which to supplement the country chapters in those volumes, but space allows mention of only a few. For Tanzania, essential reading is John Iliffe's *A modern history of Tanganyika* (Cambridge, 1979). Henry Bienen's *Tanzania: party transformation and economic development* (Princeton, 1970) must remain an indispensable source for the TANU Party, and G. A. Maguire's *Towards uhuru in Tanzania: the politics of participation* (Cambridge, 1969) is the best introduction to the dynamics of party politics and nationalism at the grass-roots level. For Zanzibar, Michael Lofchie's *Zanzibar: background to revolution* (Princeton, 1965) is the most comprehensive account of Zanzibar's politics in this period. Nelson Kasfir, in his 'Cultural sub-nationalism in Uganda' in Victor Olorunsola's *The politics of cultural sub-nationalism in African politics up to 1970* (New York, 1972), which takes the analysis up to the military coup of 1971, approaches Ugandan politics from the perspective of ethnic cleavage and conflict. While there is a rich array of ethnographic material for most parts of Uganda, it is Buganda that has been most richly served by scholars. Of the extensive studies of Buganda mention can be made here only of Christopher Wrigley's

Crops and wealth in Uganda (Kampala, 1959), D. A. Low and R. C. Pratt's *Buganda and British overrule 1900–1935: two studies* (Oxford, 1960), and *The King's men: leadership and status in Buganda on the eve of independence* (London, 1964), edited by L. A. Fallers, whose own contribution constitutes the most authoritative study of social change in Buganda.

The Kenyatta election: Kenya 1960–1961 by George Bennett and Carl Rosberg (London, 1961) must remain the most authoritative introduction to Kenyan politics in the nationalist period, as Rosberg and Nottingham's study of Mau Mau, *The myth of Mau Mau: nationalism in Kenya* (New York, 1966) remains indispensable on the role of the Kikuyu. The latter must now however be supplemented by more recent work on Kikuyu politics, especially Frank Furedi's 'The African crowd in Nairobi: popular movements and élite politics', in *Journal of African History*, 1973, vol. 14, no. 2. Four nationalist leaders have written autobiographical accounts of the nationalist years from very different political perspectives: Oginga Odinga's *Not yet uhuru* (London, 1967), Tom Mboya's *Freedom and after* (London, 1963), Josiah Kariuki's *Mau Mau detainee* (Oxford, 1963), and Bildad Kaggia's *Roots of freedom* (Nairobi, 1975). The most perceptive study of President Kenyatta is Jeremy Murray-Brown's *Kenyatta* (London, 1972).

Events in independent East Africa have generated a considerable literature. William Tordoff's *Government and politics in Tanzania* (Nairobi, 1967) provides a valuable analysis of changes in government and administration in the first five years of independence over the transition to the one-party state. Pratt's *The critical phase*, cited above, is a perceptive analysis of the emergence of Tanzania's socialist strategy, and of the central role played by President Nyerere; and Lionel Cliffe and John Saul have edited a valuable collection of essays in their two-volume *Socialism in Tanzania* (vol. I, *Politics*, vol. II, *Policies*) (Nairobi, 1972, 1973) covering the years from the Arusha Declaration to the early 1970s. Tanzania's one-party state has attracted a good deal of scholarly writing of which mention must be made of *One-party democracy* (Nairobi, 1967), the volume of essays on the first general election of 1965 edited by Lionel Cliffe. The three volumes of President Nyerere's speeches, *Freedom and unity* (Dar es Salaam, 1967), *Freedom and socialism* (1968) and *Freedom and development* (1973) provide a perceptive guide to the development of Tanzania's national ethic. While the Ugandan coup of 1971 has generated a good deal of literature none has provided an authoritative account of that event, although Ali Mazrui's *Soldiers and kinsmen: the making of a military ethnocracy* (Chicago, 1975), which seeks to place the 1971 coup and General Amin in Ugandan history, is a perceptive analysis of the post-colonial state. Michael Lee's *African armies and civil order* (New York, 1969) is the best source for information on the Ugandan military up to 1969, and Henry Kayemba, former private secretary to ex-President Obote and subsequently Minister of Health in Amin's regime, until his defection in 1977, has provided an inside account of the Amin regime in his *State of blood* (London, 1977).

For the post-colonial state in Kenya, Cherry Gertzel's *The politics of independent Kenya* (Nairobi, 1970) provides a detailed account of Kenyan politics up to 1968, and Colin Leys's *Underdevelopment in Kenya* is essential for its critical analysis of the Kenyan political economy up to the 1970s. Gerald Holtham and Arthur Hazlewood's study, *Aid and inequality* (London, 1976), while concerned primarily with economic development, provides an equally perceptive analysis of western influence in independent Kenya from a more sympathetic viewpoint. Former Vice-President of Kenya Oginga Odinga's *Not yet uhuru*, cited above, is a critical account of the first years of independence by one of the central actors, which provides useful insights into Kenya's factional politics. Richard Sandbrook's *Proletarians and African capitalism: the Kenyan case 1962–70* (London, 1975) provides not only an important study of the role of labour in Kenyan politics, but also contributes a good deal to an understanding of the factional basis of Kenyan politics. But perhaps the most important study of independent Kenyan politics is Geoff Lamb's *Peasant politics* (London, 1974), a case study of politics at grass-roots level in one Kikuyu district that illuminates the nature of centre-locality. C. J. Gertzel, M. Goldschmidt and D. Rothchild (eds.), *Government and politics in Kenya* (Nairobi, 1969), provides a useful guide to the working of government but two government reports are also essential reading: *Report of the Maize Commission of Inquiry* (1966), and *Report of the Commission of Inquiry (Public Service Structure and Remuneration) 1970–71* (Ndegwa report). Y. P. Ghai and J. P. McAuslan's *Public law and political change in Kenya* (Nairobi, 1970) is an authoritative account of the manner in which institutional change has assisted in the centralisation of power in Kenya, and Goran Hyden and Colin Leys's 'Elections and politics in single-party systems: the case of Kenya and Tanzania' in the *British Journal of Political Science*, October 1972, provides a critical analysis of the trend to authoritarian rule that characterises the region as a whole.

Of the extensive literature on East African regional association, mention can be made only of three books: Donald Rothchild's *Politics of integration: an East African documentary* (Nairobi, 1968) reproduces extracts from basic documents covering the history of East African association and is a useful guide to the literature. Colin Leys and Peter Robson's *Federation in East Africa* (Nairobi, 1965) covers the efforts to establish a federation in the early 1960s, and Arthur Hazlewood's *Economic integration: the East African experience* (London, 1975) surveys the strengths and weaknesses of the East African economic association up to the eve of its collapse in the mid-1970s.

The most succinct analysis of the East African economies up to 1963 is probably B. van Arkadie and D. Ghai's chapter in P. Robson and D. A. Lury, *The economies of Africa* (London, 1969), and for the post-colonial state, R. H. Green's article 'Ugandans prepare to work for progress', in *East Africa Journal*, August 1966, and B. van Arkadie's chapter on Tanganyika in M. Faber and D. Seers, *Crisis in planning*, vol. 3 (Sussex, 1972) are particularly useful. T. Szentes, 'Economic policy and implementation problems in Tanzania: a case study', in *African perspectives*, edited by C. Allen and W. Johnson (Cambridge, 1971), provides a perceptive critique of the impact of foreign capital on the Tanzanian political economy by a Marxist economist. Rural development in post-Arusha Tanzania is dealt with in a number of contributions to Cliffe and Saul's volumes on *Socialism in Tanzania* cited above, and in the volume on *Rural cooperation in Tanzania* produced by the Rural Development Committee at the University of Dar es Salaam. The most perceptive critique of *ujamaa* is Goran Hyden's 'Ujamaa, villagisation and rural development in Tanzania', in the *Overseas Development Review* for April 1975.

The ILO's *Employment, incomes and equality: a strategy for increasing productive employment in Kenya* (Geneva, 1972), provides a good deal of material on both social as well as economic change in independent Kenya, and Colin Leys's *Underdevelopment in Kenya* cited above is a perceptive critique from a neo-Marxist perspective of Kenya's capitalist development strategy and her neo-colonial dependency. The volume edited by Judith Heyer, J. K. Maitha and W. M. Senga, *Agricultural development in Kenya, an economic assessment* (Nairobi, 1971) is the most authoritative survey of the agricultural economy.

Christopher Wrigley's chapter on 'Changes in East African society' in vol. III of the *History of East Africa* must stand out for its sensitive and authoritative analysis of social change, drawing upon not only his own work but also on that of the outstanding group of social scientists associated with the East African Institute of Social Research at Makerere. Élite formation at the national level is the subject of Aidan Southall's chapter in P. C. Lloyd (ed.), *New élites of tropical Africa* (Oxford, 1966), and at grass-roots level in a fascinating study of grass-roots change in a northern district in Joan Vincent's more recent *African élite: the big man of a small town* (New York, 1971). M. P. K. Sorrenson's *Land reforms in the Kikuyu country* (Nairobi, 1967) provides an essential introduction to the history of land alienation and the independence land settlement which was the basis for the emergence of the Kikuyu bourgeoisie which R. van Zwanenberg identifies in his 'Neo-colonialism and the origin of the national bourgeoisie in Kenya between 1940 and 1973', in *Journal of Eastern African Research and Development*, 1974, vol. 4, no. 2. The best analyses of post-colonial society are Colin Leys's 'Politics in Kenya: the development of peasant society', in the *British Journal of Political Science*, July 1971, vol. 1, and Walter Elkan's 'Is a proletariat emerging in Nairobi?', in *Economic Development and Cultural Change*, *1965–75*, vol. 24.

For the role of labour in the colonial state, a wealth of detailed information is available in Anthony Clayton and Donald Savage's *Government and labour in Kenya 1895–1963* (London, 1974); in W. H. Friedland's *Vuta Kamba: the development of trade unions in Tanganyika* (Stanford, 1969); and Walter Elkan's *Migrants and proletarians: urban labour in the economic development of Uganda* (London, 1961). Finally the most sensitive introduction to the role of education in the process of class formation is David Court's 'Education as social control: the response to inequality in Kenya and Tanzania', in the *Journal of Modern African Studies*, January 1977. The source material for Central Africa is a good deal more uneven, and for Malawi a good deal more limited. Patrick Keatley's *The politics of partnership* (Harmondsworth, 1963) provides the most useful introduction; Richard Gray's *The two nations: aspects of the development of race relations in Rhodesia and Nyasaland* (Westport, Conn., 1974) is an analysis of economic and social history up to 1953, and Philip Mason's *Year of decision: Rhodesia and Nyasaland in 1960* (London, 1960) continues the story up to 1960. L. H. Gann's *History of Northern Rhodesia: early days to 1953* (London, 1964) is a detailed and complex account of that territory, and three studies of Rhodesia complement each other: Colin Leys's *European politics in Southern Rhodesia* (Oxford, 1959), Larry Bowman's *Politics in Rhodesia: white power in an African state* (Cambridge, Mass., 1973), and Giovanni Arrighi's *The political economy of Rhodesia* (The Hague, 1967), which is essential for its analysis of politics and class formation. Claire Palley's *The constitutional history and law of Southern Rhodesia* (Oxford, 1966) is a major contribution to our understanding of the law and working of the formal structure of government up to UDI.

Robert Rotberg's *Rise of nationalism in Central Africa: the making of Malawi and Zambia, 1873–1964* (Cambridge, Mass., 1965) remains the most informative introduction to the growth of African nationalism across the region as a whole. The most detailed and authoritative study of Zambian nationalism is David Mulford's *Zambia: the politics of independence, 1957–1964* (London, 1967). The most perceptive study of African politics on the Copperbelt remains however A. L. Epstein's *Politics in an urban African community* (Manchester, 1958) a study of Zambia's miners in the context of social change in the 1950s. Ian Henderson's unpublished Ph.D. thesis, 'Labour and politics in Northern Rhodesia 1900–1953' (Edinburgh University, 1977) adds significantly to but in no way supersedes Epstein's study. Elena Berger's *Labour, race and colonial rule* (Oxford, 1974) provides a detailed analysis of colonial labour policy for the Copperbelt.

There is as yet no full-length study of African politics in Rhodesia, although two useful accounts by Rhodesian African politicians are Ndabaningi Sithole's *African nationalism* (Cape Town, 1959) and Nathan Shamuyarira's *Crisis in Rhodesia* (London, 1965). Nor is there any major study of African nationalism in Malawi, although Clyde Sanger's *Central African emergency* (London, 1960) is a fascinating eye-witness account of the 1959 Emergency by one of Africa's most sensitive and experienced journalists; and the *Report of the Nyasaland Commission of Inquiry 1958–59*, Cmnd 814 (London, HMSO, 1959) (the Devlin Report) provides a vivid account of mass nationalism.

Richard Hall's *The high price of principles*, especially the second edition (Harmondsworth, 1973), identifies better than any other source the dynamics of nationalist politics and the basic issues at stake in independent Zambia, while William Tordoff edited *Politics in Zambia* (Manchester, 1974), a valuable collection of essays on political development between 1964 and the introduction of the one-party state in 1972. Donald Rothchild's 'Rural–urban inequalities and resource allocation in Zambia', in the *Journal of Commonwealth Political Studies*, 1972, vol. 10, no. 3, documents the rural–urban cleavages which remain the focus of Zambian politics, and Jan Pettman provides a useful study of the implications of her front-line position for Zambia's foreign and domestic policies. Although there is a good deal less available on the politics of Malawi, useful insights are provided by R. Hodder-Williams's 'Dr Banda's Malawi', in the *Journal of Commonwealth and Comparative Politics*, March 1974. *Banda* (London, 1974), Philip Short's stimulating biography of Malawi's president, is also a perceptive analysis of the country's political system.

The most perceptive study of Rhodesia focussed upon UDI is Robert Good's *UDI: the international politics of the Rhodesian rebellion* (London, 1973), and for the years since 1965, R. W. Johnson's *How long can South Africa survive?* (Oxford, 1977). William Barber's *The economy of British Central Africa: a case study of economic development in a dualistic society* (London, 1961) remains the most extensive treatment of the economy of the region as a whole, although his concept of dualism has been seriously challenged. W. L. Taylor's chapter, 'The economy of Central Africa', in Robson and Lury's *The economies of Africa* concentrates on the ten years of the Central African federation. Phyllis Deane's *Colonial social accounting* (Cambridge, 1953) is a detailed study of the economies of Northern Rhodesia and Nyasaland in the late 1940s which emphasises the village economy and its importance in Central African economic life, and at the same time provides important insights into the nature of social change. Deane's article, 'The industrial revolution in British Central Africa', in *Civilisations*, vol. 12 (Brussels, 1962) also provides an authoritative introduction to industrial development in Central Africa in the 1950s. Robert Baldwin's *Economic development and export growth: a study of Northern Rhodesia 1920–1960* (Berkeley, 1966) is the most authoritative study of the growth of that economy, and Arthur Hazlewood and P. D. Henderson's *Nyasaland: the economics of federation* (Oxford, 1965) is indispensable for an understanding of Malawi's colonial economic legacy. The most important, if not the most comprehensive, treatment of the Rhodesian political economy is Arrighi's *The political economy of Rhodesia* cited above, while his 'Labour supplies in historical perspective: a study of the proletarianization of the African peasantry in Rhodesia', first published in English in *The Journal of Development Studies*, April 1970, no. 3, challenges the basic assumptions of Barber's work quoted above and provides a radical analysis of the impact of European economic systems on the predominantly agricultural African societies of that territory.

Economic development in the early years of independence in Zambia is best followed in the collection of essays, *Constraints on the economic development of Zambia* (Nairobi, 1971), edited by Charles Elliot, although the most stimulating introduction to the Zambian political economy is surely Anthony Martin's account of the economic reforms of 1968–69, *Minding their own business* (Harmondsworth, 1975); while Richard Sklar in his *Corporate power in an African state* (Berkeley, 1975) has produced a major study of the mining companies which have dominated the economy.

A good deal less information is available for Malawi since independence. D. H. Humphrey's *Malawi since 1964: economic development, progress and problems* (Zomba, 1974) and Kathryn Morton's *Aid and dependence* (London, 1975) provide an overview, the latter with a good deal of basic data on Malawi's aid relations. The most useful introduction to Malawi's development strategies is however the government's own *Statement of development policies 1971–1980*.

As at Makerere in Kampala so at the Rhodes-Livingstone Institute in Livingstone and then Lusaka, a distinguished group of social scientists over the 1940s and 1950s produced an outstanding body of literature on social and economic change, in both rural and urban Central Africa. The crucial process of urbanisation is treated in a succession of fine monographs, of which mention here can be made only of G. and M. Wilson's *An*

869

essay in the economics of detribalisation (Livingstone, 1941–2) and Epstein's *Urban politics* cited above, while J. Clyde Mitchell's *The Kalela dance* (Manchester, 1956) must now stand as the classic analysis of ethnicity in the urban situation. For the post-colonial state, Robert H. Bates's *Rural responses to industrialisation: a study of village Zambia* (New Haven, 1976) provides a detailed analysis of the relations between town and country, and the effects of industrialisation on rural life.

The most useful introduction to the relationship between the Central African states and South Africa and their place in southern Africa is K. Grundy's *Confrontation and accommodation in southern Africa* (Berkeley, 1973), and to B. Mtshali's and A. Hughes's chapters, on Zambia and Malawi respectively, in Červenka's *Land-locked countries of Africa* (Uppsala, 1973). Malawi's relations with South Africa receive special attention in Caroline McMaster's *Malawi: foreign policy and development* (New York, 1974).

9. THE HORN OF AFRICA

There are good bibliographical guides to all of the territories in the Horn. H. G. Marcus, *The modern history of Ethiopia and the Horn of Africa: a select and annotated bibliography* (Stanford, 1972) covers the whole region. For Ethiopia, there are two further general bibliographies, A. Hidaru and D. Rahmato, *A short guide to the study of Ethiopia* (London, 1976) and C. F. Brown, *Ethiopian perspectives: bibliographical guide to the history of Ethiopia* (Westport, 1978). A separate brief bibliography of Eritrea is available in K. Chekole, 'Eritrea: a preliminary bibliography', *Africana Journal*, 1975–6, vol. 6. Somalia is covered in M. K. Salad, *Somalia: a bibliographical survey* (London, 1972), and the literature on Djibouti is discussed in W. S. Clarke, 'The Republic of Djibouti: an introduction to Africa's newest state and a review of related literature and sources', *Current Bulletin of African Affairs*, 1977–8, vol. 10.

The Second World War: The campaigns of 1940–1 and the subsequent British administrations of occupied territories have been described in contemporary official publications, notably *The Abyssinian campaigns* (London, 1942), *The first to be freed* (London, 1944), and Lord Rennell of Rodd, *British military administration of occupied territories in Africa, 1941–47* (London, 1948). George

Steer, *Sealed and delivered* (London, 1942) is a contemporary account of the campaign by a British journalist with a strong sympathy for the Ethiopian cause. No adequate history of the Ethiopian resistance has been published, the most detailed available account being in Richard Greenfield, *Ethiopia: a new political history* (London, 1965).

Ethiopia

The official gazette, *Negarit Gazeta,* has been published since 1942 in Amharic and English, and includes all legislation and major government appointments. Other useful series of official documents include *Statistical abstract* (Central Statistical Office, 1963 onwards), surveys of the various provinces (CSO, 1966–68), *Land tenure surveys* of the provinces (Ministry of Land Reform, 1967–70), and the *Administrative directory* produced by the Imperial Ethiopian Institute of Public Administration at two- or three-year intervals from May 1957 until the late 1960s. There are no census records or published parliamentary papers, and economic information is most easily gained from the regular series published by the United Nations, though *Economic progress of Ethiopia* (Ministry of Commerce and Industry, 1955) is useful for the post-war period. The International Bank for Reconstruction and Development has published *Ethiopia: a preliminary survey* (1950), *Economy of Ethiopia: main report* (1967), and *Economic growth and prospects in Ethiopia* (1970).

Ethiopian central government between 1941 and 1974 has been fairly fully covered. Margery Perham, *The government of Ethiopia* (London, 1948, second edition, 1969) is largely concerned with the period before 1936, but also discusses the changes made after 1941, and the second edition includes a postscript on developments in the intervening two decades. Christopher Clapham, *Haile-Selassie's government* (London, 1969) treats the development of the central government between 1941 and 1967 in some detail, while J. Markakis, *Ethiopia: anatomy of a traditional polity* (Oxford, 1974) is a more general analysis of the development of Ethiopian society and politics up to the eve of the 1974 revolution. P. Schwab, *Decision-making in Ethiopia* (London, 1972), deals only with a single issue, the agricultural income tax of 1967, but is particularly useful in following through its attempted implementation in the countryside.

871

G. A. Lipsky *et al.*, *Ethiopia: its people, its society, its culture* (New Haven, 1962), and Robert L. Hess, *Ethiopia: the modernization of autocracy* (Ithaca, 1970), are both useful general introductions drawn largely from secondary sources. The only general history of Ethiopia covering the modern period, Greenfield's *Ethiopia*, cited above, concentrates heavily on the two post-war decades and especially on the attempted *coup d'état* of 1960, an incident also discussed in Clapham, 'The Ethiopian *coup d'état* of December 1960', *Journal of Modern African Studies*, 1968. The only available biographies of leading Ethiopians during the period are, unsurprisingly, of Haile Selassie himself. L. Mosley, *Haile Selassie: the conquering lion* (London, 1964) is uncritical in treatment and almost entirely confined to the pre-1941 period, whereas P. Schwab, *Haile Selassie I: Ethiopia's Lion of Judah* (New York, 1979), takes a more critical end-of-reign perspective. Christopher Clapham, 'Ethiopia', in R. Lemarchand (ed.), *African kingships in perspective* (London, 1977) discusses his political role. His *Selected speeches 1918–1967* have also been published (Addis Ababa, 1967).

The dramatic events of 1974 and their aftermath have produced a large literature, amongst which may be mentioned C. Legum, *Ethiopia: the fall of Haile Selassie's empire* (London, 1975), and M. and D. Ottaway, *Ethiopia: empire in revolution* (New York, 1978). Patrick Gilkes, *The dying lion* (London, 1975) is despite its title largely concerned with the pre-revolutionary period, and includes useful material on the political economy of the imperial regime and on opposition to Haile Selassie. The often polemical literature on the nature and policies of the post-revolutionary regime lies beyond the period covered by this essay. Local and provincial government has been very little studied, the outstanding exception being J. M. Cohen and P. H. Koehn, *Ethiopian provincial and municipal government: imperial patterns and postrevolutionary changes* (East Lansing, 1980). Other material on local politics includes C. B. Rosen, 'The Governor-General of Tigre Province: structure and antistructure', in H. G. Marcus (ed.), *Proceedings* cited below, and P. T. W. Baxter, 'Ethiopia's unacknowledged problem: the Oromo' (*African Affairs*, 1978).

The ethnographic literature includes two outstanding studies of the Amhara, D. N. Levine, *Wax and gold: tradition and innovation in Ethiopian culture* (Chicago, 1965), and A. Hoben, *Land tenure among the Amhara of Ethiopia* (Chicago, 1973). Levine's *Greater*

Ethiopia: the evolution of a multiethnic society (Chicago, 1974) is a more speculative and controversial volume. Ethnographic writing on other Ethiopian peoples, including the Afar, Dassanetch, Gurage, Konso, Majangir, Mursi, Oromo (Galla) and Tigreans, falls beyond the scope of this essay. Rural society and economic change has been examined in several studies, the best general overview being J. M. Cohen and D. Weintraub, *Land and peasants in imperial Ethiopia: the social background to a revolution* (Assen, 1975). One particular development project, the Chilalo Agricultural Development Unit (CADU), has received a disproportionate amount of attention, including books by M. Stahl, *Ethiopia: political contradictions in agricultural development* (Stockholm, 1974) and B. Nekby, *CADU: an Ethiopian experiment in developing peasant farming*; and articles by J. M. Cohen in *Economic Development and Cultural Change*, 1974, and the *Journal of Developing Areas*, 1975. L. Bondestam, 'People and capitalism in the north-eastern lowlands of Ethiopia' (*Journal of Modern African Studies*, 1974) examines one of the most dynamic areas of Ethiopian cash-crop farming.

In addition to the IBRD reports already noted, a useful outline of the economy appears in Assefa Bequele and Eshetu Chole, *A profile of the Ethiopian economy* (Nairobi, 1969), while G. J. Gill, *Readings on the Ethiopian economy* (Addis Ababa, 1974) is a source-book for student use. J. Halpern, 'La Planification et le développement en Éthiopie après la deuxième guerre mondiale' (*Culture et Développement*, 1974) deals with government economic policy, and Teketel Haile-Mariam, 'The impact of coffee on the economy of Ethiopia', in S. R. Pearson *et al.*, *Commodity exports and African economic development* (Lexington, 1974) discusses the role of the principal export crop. Chapters on urbanisation in Ethiopia appear in several general collections, by B. Winid in R. Jones, *Essays on world urbanisation* (London, 1975), by J. J. Palen in A. H. Richmond and D. Kubat, *Internal migration* (London, 1976), and by P. and E. F. Koehn in R. A. Obudho and S. El-Shakh, *Development of urban systems in Africa* (New York, 1979). On education, Helen Kitchen (ed.), *The educated African* (London, 1962) provides the best general overview of the period up to 1960, while Teshome G. Wagaw, *Education in Ethiopia: retrospect and prospect* (Ann Arbor, 1979), gives a post-imperial perspective. For further appraisals see the articles by O. D. Hoerr in *East African*

Economic Review, 1974, and by M. N. Lovegrove in *Comparative Education*, 1973.

Periodicals on Ethiopia, publication of which was affected by the 1974 revolution and subsequent upheavals, include *Ethiopia Observer* (1957–), *Journal of Ethiopian Studies* (1963–), *Journal of Ethiopian Law* (1964–), and *Ethiopian Journal of Education* (1967–). Finally, the papers delivered at the occasional conferences on Ethiopian studies have been published in widely scattered places: the First International Conference (Rome, 1959), in E. Cerulli (ed.), *Atti del Convegno Internazionale di Studi Etiopici* (Rome, 1960); the Second International Conference (Manchester, 1963), in *Journal of Semitic Studies*, 1964, vol. 9, no. 1; the Third International Conference (Addis Ababa, 1966), in R. K. P. Pankhurst, ed., *Proceedings of the Third International Conference of Ethiopian Studies* (Addis Ababa, 1969–70); the Fourth International Conference (Rome, 1972), in *IV Congresso Internazionale di Studi Etiopici* (*Problemi Attuali di Scienza e di Cultura, Quaderno no. 191*) (Rome, 1974, 2 vols); this was followed by an American conference, published in H. G. Marcus (ed.), *Proceedings of the First United States Conference on Ethiopian Studies, 1973* (East Lansing, 1975); the Fifth International Conference was divided into two sections, the first (Nice, December 1977) published in J. Tubiana (ed.), *Modern Ethiopia: from the accession of Menelik II to the present. Proceedings of the Fifth International Conference of Ethiopian Studies* (Rotterdam, 1980), the Second (Chicago, April 1978) in R. L. Hess (ed.), *Proceedings of the Fifth International Conference of Ethiopian Studies, Session B* (Chicago, 1979). The Sixth International Conference was held in Tel Aviv in April 1980, and the Seventh in Lund, Sweden, in April 1982.

Eritrea

Material specifically on Eritrea falls into two groups, that on the post-war British administration and the disposal of the territory by the United Nations, and that on the liberation movements from the mid-1960s onwards. On the first period, G. K. N. Trevaskis, *Eritrea: colony in transition, 1941–1952* (London, 1960) was written by a British administrator, E. S. Pankhurst and R. K. P. Pankhurst, *Ethiopia and Eritrea: the last ten years of the reunion struggle, 1941–1952* (Woodford, Essex, 1953) by two dedicated supporters of unification with Ethiopia. Articles by L. Ellingson in the *Journal of African History*, 1977, and by Tiruneh Andargatchew in *Northeast African Studies*, 1980–1, look at the period with the benefit of hindsight. For two books on the later period, see A. Fenet *et al.*, *La Question de l'Erythrée* (Paris, 1979) and R. Sherman, *Eritrea: the unfinished revolution* (New York, 1980). A large number of pamphlets and articles cover much the same ground, as do several of the works noted under International Relations.

Somalia

The Somali Republic must rank among the lowest of African states in terms of its level of academic coverage, and material on many aspects of its modern history is sparse. The immediate post-war period is documented in the British official publications, and for the period of its trusteeship the Italian Ministry of Foreign Affairs published a detailed annual *Rapport du Gouvernement Italien à l'Assemblée Générale des Nations Unies sur l'administration de tutelle de la Somalie* (Rome, 1951–9); the British Colonial Office reports on the Somaliland Protectorate are much briefer and appeared biennially. Aspects of the transfer of power are also discussed in G. A. Costanzo, *Problemi costituzionali della Somalia nella preparazione all'Indipendenza, 1957–1960* (Milan, 1962), and D. Hall, 'Somaliland's last year as a Protectorate', *African Affairs*, 1961. The most useful Somali government publication is *Statistical abstract* (Mogadishu, 1964–   ).

There is, fortunately, an excellent general history, I. M. Lewis, *A modern history of Somalia* (London, second revised edition, 1980), and the same author has written extensively on Somali politics and society, including *A pastoral democracy* (London, 1961), 'The politics of the 1969 Somali coup', *Journal of Modern African Studies*, 1972, 'The nation, state and politics in Somalia', in D. R. Smock (ed.), *The search for national integration in Africa* (New York, 1975), and *Abaar: the Somali drought* (London, 1975). The strong connexions between Somali culture, society and politics are made clear by D. D. Laitin, *Politics, language and thought: the Somali experience* (Chicago, 1972), and also by B. W. Andrzejewski and I. M. Lewis, *Somali poetry* (Oxford, 1964). The fullest analysis of the changes undertaken by the post-1969 military government is P. Decraene, *L'Expérience socialiste somalienne* (Paris, 1977), but see also D. D. Laitin, 'The political economy of military rule in Somalia', *Journal of Modern African Studies*, 1976. V. G. Solodov-nikov, *Ucenye Zapiski Sovetsjo-Somalijskoj Ekspedicii* (Moscow, 1974) provides a Soviet view of post-1969 social and economic development during a period when relations with Somalia were close. A. A. Castagno, in Helen Kitchen (ed.), *The educated African* (New York, 1962) surveys educational development up to independence.

The considerable literature on Somalia's international relations, and especially on the 'Somali dispute', is surveyed in a later section.

CFS/TFAI

The available material on Djibouti is dominated by two substantial volumes, V. Thompson and R. Adloff, *Djibouti and the Horn of Africa* (Stanford, 1968), and P. Oberlé, *Afars et Somalis: le dossier de Djibouti* (Paris, 1971). The subsequent political development of the microstate can be followed in articles by Shilling (*Journal of Developing Areas*, 1973), Marks (*African Affairs*, 1974), Leymarie (*Revue Française d'Études Politiques Africaines*, 1977), and K. Shehim & J. Shearing (*African Affairs*, 1980).

International Relations

The international relations literature is overwhelmingly domin-ated by the conflict between Ethiopia and Somalia which, though breaking out into large scale warfare only after the period covered by this volume, was a consistent element in the politics of the region from 1941 onwards. E. S. Pankhurst, *Ex-Italian Somaliland* (London, 1951), provides an early Ethiopian viewpoint geared to the disposal by the United Nations of the former Italian colonies, while Saadia Touval, *Somali nationalism* (Cambridge, Mass., 1963) and J. Drysdale, *The Somali dispute* (London, 1964), both take it from the post-independence Somali perspective. C. Hoskyns, *The Ethiopia–Somalia–Kenya dispute 1960–1967* (Dar es Salaam, 1969), and V. Matthies' monumental *Die Grenzkonflikt Somalias mit Aethiopien und Kenya* (Hamburg, 1977) are concerned with the legal and diplomatic basis of the dispute. Finally, the war of 1977–8 gave rise to a substantial literature, much of it concerned with the Horn as a whole, and especially with the level of external intervention. Two volumes which go back into the historical bases for the conflicts both in the Ogaden and in Eritrea are T. J. Farer, *War clouds on the Horn of Africa* (second revised edition, New York, 1979) and Bereket Habte Selassie, *Conflict and intervention in the Horn of Africa* (New York, 1980), the latter being the work of a committed Eritrean nationalist.

10. EGYPT, LIBYA AND THE SUDAN

Two of the standard works on Egypt used by both scholars and general readers are *The history of Egypt* (London, second edition, 1980), by P. J. Vatikiotis and *Egypt: imperialism and revolution* (London, 1972) by the eminent French scholar Jacques Berque. The first is a revised version of *The modern history of Egypt*, which appeared in 1969, and contains chapters on the nineteenth-century history of Egypt and the British occupation as well as on the reaction against Europe during the period from 1930 to 1950. Additional chapters cover the period of the Second World War and the decline of the Wafd Party from 1939 to 1952, the coup by Nāṣir and the Free Officers and political and social developments to 1979. Interestingly, the revised version contains a new final chapter on educational and cultural developments in the modern period, including comments on the work of the playwright Tawfīq al-Ḥākim, the novelist Abd al-Raḥmān al-Sharqawī and the educational writings of Maḥmūd Amīn al-Alem. Jacques Berque's study poses a useful contrast to the work by Vatikiotis, in that it looks at the history of Egypt from the eyes of the indigenous citizens themselves. Sections on the history of imperialism and decolonisation are followed by a close examination of both peasant and village life, literature and social change as well as on political and economic developments.

Another work by Vatikiotis, *Nasser and his generation* (London, 1978) takes a closer look at the period following the 1952 revolution, but it also includes material on Nāṣir's origins, the Young Egypt society and the Muslim brotherhood not easily available elsewhere. *The Society of Muslim Brothers* (London, 1969), by Richard P. Mitchell, remains a classic work of its kind. Aside from discussing the origins, history and organisation of the brotherhood, it includes useful chapters on other Islamic organisations in Egypt and the debate about the nature of an Islamic state.

Students of class structure and class conflict will find two works of particular use: Mahmoud Hussein's *L'Egypte: lutte de classes et libération nationale* (Paris, 1975) and Anouar Abdel-Malek's *Égypte: société militaire* (Paris, 1962). Both cover the growth of the Communist Party in the 1940s and the development of class consciousness under Nāṣir, as well as the conflicts between Nāṣir, the party and the intellectuals. Finally, a new work, *Egypt: portrait of a president* (London, 1981), by an Egyptian sociologist resident in Paris, Ghali Shoukri, brings the history of Egypt up to date and includes very useful material on both Sādāt's domestic and foreign policies as well as on the growth of Islamic militancy in the late 1960s and early 1970s.

Few satisfactory works exist on the modern history of Libya, but two notable exceptions are John Wright's *Libya* (London, 1969) and Ruth First's *Libya: the elusive revolution* (Harmondsworth, 1974). The first contains a good overview of the struggle for independence and of political and economic developments during the reign of King Idrīs. The second also includes material on the resistance to Italian colonisation, the independence movement and the role of the United Nations, but in addition includes sections on the role of the army after the 1969 coup, the growth of religious ideology and Qadhdhāfī's relations with his Arab and African neighbours. *La Libye nouvelle: rupture et continuité* (Paris, 1975) contains essays by several notable French scholars on everything from the geography and history of Libya to the status of women and changes in rural society. Another work, published by CNRS a year earlier, *Villes et sociétés au Maghreb: études sur l'urbanisation*, includes an essay by B. Atallah and M. Fikry on 'Le phénomène urbain en Libye: problèmes juridiques et sociaux'.

P. M. Holt's *A modern history of the Sudan from the Funj Sultanate to the present day* (London, second edition, 1963) remains the classic work on the Sudan. More recent developments are covered by Anthony Sylvester, in *Sudan under Nimeiri* (London, 1977), although critics of the president will find little comfort for their views here. Two other works are essential for an understanding of the civil war: *The Southern Sudan* by Mohamed Omer Beshir (Khartoum, 1968) and *The secret war in the Sudan: 1955–1972* by Edgar O'Ballance (London, 1977). *Islam in the Sudan* (London, 1965) by J. Spencer Trimingham is invaluable for students of the Brotherhoods and their role in society and politics. *Islam, nationalism and communism in a traditional society* (London, 1978), despite its title, is mainly a history of the Communist Party in the Sudan and contains documents on the rise and decline of the party not obtainable elsewhere.

While many of the above-mentioned books cover economic development as well as politics and history, the works of two Middle Eastern economic historians, Robert Mabro and Patrick O'Brien, are also useful. The first has written an essay on 'Libya' in Wilfred Knapp (ed.), *North West Africa: a political and economic survey* (London, third edition, 1977), and together with Patrick O'Brien contributed an article on 'Structural changes in the Egyptian economy, 1937–1965', to a work edited by M. A. Cook entitled *Studies in the economic history of the Middle East* (London, 1970). O'Brien has also written an essay on 'The long-term growth of agricultural production in Egypt: 1821–1962', published in P. M. Holt (ed.), *Political and social change in modern Egypt* (London, 1968). Social anthropologists and students of tribal societies will fund the extensive works of E. E. Evans-Pritchard on the Nuer, Shilluk and Azande of the Sudan and on *The Sanussi of Cyrenaica* (Oxford, 1949) indispensable.

Finally, mention must also be made of the numerous annual reviews and yearbooks published on the Middle East and Africa, some of which contain useful general summaries of historical and economic developments in the post-war era. Among these are *The Middle East and North Africa* published annually since the early 1950s by Europa Publications, London, and *Africa Guide* and the *Middle East Annual Review* published each year by World of Information Ltd., Saffron Walden (England). The *Middle East Yearbook 1980* (International Communications Ltd., London), contains a series of valuable essays on political, economic and social change in Libya, Egypt and the Sudan in the 1970s by several well-known African, Arab and western scholars.

11. THE MAGHRIB

The most useful reference work on the contemporary Maghrib is the *Annuaire de l'Afrique du Nord*, published since 1962 by the Centre de Recherches et d'Études sur les Sociétés Mediterranéennes of the University of Aix-Marseille III. In addition to systematic and critical bibliographies, political, diplomatic, economic, and social commentaries on each country, and related documentation, it assembles academic articles each year around a common theme. *Maghreb*, published by the Documentation Française, was more useful between 1964 and 1973 than subsequently, when as *Maghreb-Machreq* its coverage of the Maghrib was progressively diminished.

The best general survey of the area is Wilfrid Knapp, *North West Africa: a political and economic survey*, (London, third edition, 1977), though Charles F. Gallagher, *The United States and North Africa* (Cambridge, Mass., 1963) is still worth consulting, as is Jean Despois, *L'Afrique du Nord* (Paris, 1964). The only works, however, that have attempted systematically to compare and explain national processes of development and political change in the three countries are Clement Henry Moore, *Politics in North Africa* (Boston, 1970) and Elbaki Hermassi, *Leadership and national development in North Africa* (Berkeley and Los Angeles, 1972).

Douglas Ashford, too, tried to attribute differences in specific policy areas to differences in the respective regimes treated in his *National development and local reform: political participation in Morocco, Tunisia, and Pakistan* (Princeton, 1967). Another promising approach to the area is that of political anthropology, best exemplified in Ernest Gellner and Charles Micaud (eds.), *Arabs and Berbers* (London, 1973).

The most stimulating political study of the pre-independence period remains Charles-André Julien, *L'Afrique du Nord en marche* (Paris, 1952), supplemented by an excellent critical bibliography in the third edition (1972). In an equally penetrating, but more phenomenological vein is Jacques Berque, *French North Africa*, translated by Jean Stewart (London, 1967), while standard political history, country by country, is covered by Roger Le Tourneau, *Évolution politique de l'Afrique du Nord musulmane, 1920–1961* (Paris, 1962). Nationalism in each country is also treated separately in L. J. Duclos, L. Duvignaud, and J. Leca, *Les Nationalismes maghrébins* (Études Maghrébines 7, Paris, Fondation Nationale des Sciences Politiques, 1966). Further case studies include, for Algeria: André Nouschi, *La Naissance du nationalisme Algérien* (Paris, 1962), Colette and Francis Jeanson, *L'Algérie hors la loi* (Paris, second edition, 1956), and William B. Quandt, *Revolution and political leadership: Algeria, 1954–1968* (Cambridge, Mass., 1969); for Morocco: John P. Halstead, *Rebirth of a nation: the origins and rise of Moroccan nationalism, 1912–1944* (Cambridge,

Mass., 1967); Robert Rézette, *Les Partis politiques marocains* (Paris, 1955), and Stéphane Bernard, *The Franco-Moroccan conflict* (New Haven, Conn., 1968); for Tunisia: Charles A. Micaud, Leon Carl Brown and Clement Henry Moore, *Tunisia: the politics of modernization* (London, 1964).

There have also been a number of political biographies of nationalist leaders. Jean Lacouture, *Cinq hommes et la France* (Paris, 1961) provides vivid portraits of Mohammed V, Habib Bourguiba and Ferhat Abbas, while Ania Francos and Jean-Pierre Séréni offer an informative if somewhat less than critical account of the career of *Un Algérien nommé Boumediène* (Paris, 1976). Even more adulatory are Attilio Gaudio, *Allal al-Fassi, ou l'histoire de l'Istiqlal* (Paris, 1972), misleading by its very title, and Félix Garas, *Bourguiba et la naissance d'une nation* (Paris, 1956). The figures in question have done better by themselves in their respective works, *Independence movements of North Africa* (Washington, 1954) and *La Tunisie et la France* (Paris, 1954). Their output of books and speeches has been prodigious; Al-Fassi's *Al-naqd al-dhati* (Cairo, 1952) appeared in French translation in the newspaper *Al-Istiqlal* during the month of March, 1957. The Tunisian Ministry of Information has regularly published Bourguiba's speeches since independence. A convenient selection of *Citations du Président Boumediène* was edited by Khalfa Mameri (Algiers, 1975). Opposition leaders have also published their reminiscences and analyses: Ferhat Abbas, *La Nuit coloniale* (Paris, 1962), Mohammed Boudiaf, *Où va l'Algérie?* (Paris, 1964), Mehdi ben Barka, *Option révolutionnaire au Maroc* (Paris, 1974), to cite but a few.

Élite transformation during the colonial period has not elsewhere received the remarkable treatment of Henri de Montety, 'Vieilles familles et nouvelle élite en Tunisie', translated by William I. Zartman for the volume he edited, *Man, state and society in the contemporary Maghreb* (London, 1973). Consequently there is no good baseline for subsequent comparisons, as Jean-Claude Vatin concludes from his monumental 're-reading' of the colonial period in *L'Algérie politique, histoire et société* (Paris, 1974). Jean Morizot, *L'Algérie kabylisée* (Paris, 1962) provides some indications of the disproportion of Kabyles occupying strategic positions, but the best sociological and anthropological studies of Algeria have focussed on societal rather than élite transformations. Pierre Bourdieu, *The Algerians* (Boston, 1962), discusses changes induced by the insurrection from a perspective somewhat similar to that of Frantz Fanon, *A dying colonialism* (New York, 1965), but both authors overestimated the changes in authority relationships within the family engendered by participation in the revolution. In Morocco, with the notable exception of André Adam, *Casablanca* (Paris, 1968), the countryside received more attention than urban strata. One of the more interesting monographs linking the two is John Waterbury's study of the Soussi merchants, *North for the trade* (Berkeley and Los Angeles, 1972). The straight ethnographic work of Julio Caro Baroja, *Estudios Saharianos* (Madrid, 1955), was of course more appropriate for the Spanish Sahara. The only comparative study of urban élites is found in Samir Amin, *L'Économie du Maghreb* (Paris, 1966), abridged in the translation by Michael Perl, *The Maghreb in the modern world* (London, 1970), but it is confined to indicators of employment and income distribution.

Yet despite such juridical works as Maurice Flory and Robert Mantran, *Le Régime politique des pays arabes* (Paris, 1967), the principal political studies of the independent regimes have focussed on élites and their interactions. Perhaps the most outstanding and certainly the most readable of these is John Waterbury, *Commander of the Faithful: the Moroccan political élite – a study of segmented politics* (London, 1970), but the first part of Rémy Leveau, *Le Fellah marocain défenseur du trône* (Paris, 1976), offers the explanation for the élite's apparently anachronistic behaviour that originally escaped Waterbury, namely the monarch's strategy with respect to rural élites. The most methodologically self-conscious of the élite studies is that of Quandt, cited above; in contrast Jean Leca and Jean-Claude Vatin suggest a variety of methods, from juridical and ideological to systemic analysis eclectically borrowed from Anglo-Saxon political scientists, for presenting their encyclopaedic study of independent Algeria, *L'Algérie politique: institutions et régime* (Paris, 1975). A somewhat uneven but provocative synthesis raising the question of a ruling class is Bruno Etienne's *L'Algérie, cultures et révolution* (Paris, 1977). Tunisia's one-party system permitted a blending of élite and institutional analysis; Clement Henry Moore, *Tunisia since independence: the dynamics of one-party government* (Berkeley and Los Angeles, 1965), was more sceptical of the party's mobilisational efforts than Lars Rudebeck, *Party and people* (New York, 1969), whose approach was functionalist.

More recently the Centre de Recherches et d'Études sur les Sociétés Mediterranéennes has published two studies of the three national élites, *La Formation des élites politiques maghrébines* (Paris, 1973), and *Élites, pouvoir et légitimité au Maghreb* (Paris, 1973). Michel Camau, *La Notion de démocratie dans la pensée des dirigeants maghrébins* (Paris, 1971) provides useful material for analysing their efforts to legitimate themselves; for Morocco, Clifford Geertz, *Islam observed* (New Haven, Conn., 1968), and Ernest Gellner, *Saints of the Atlas* (London, 1969), provide important clues.

Other than Moore, *Politics*, and Ashford, *National development*, there are no systematic comparative attempts to correlate regimes with policies and strategies of development, but Leveau, *Le Fellah*, presents a fascinating case study, while Algeria and Tunisia seem most honestly served, respectively, by Gérard Viratelle, *L'Algérie algérienne* (Paris, second edition, 1970) and, ideology aside, Jean Poncet, *La Tunisie à la recherche de son avenir* (Paris, 1974). André Tiano, *Le Maghreb entre les mythes* (Paris, 1967) offers useful comparative economic data, while Abdellatif Benachenhou, 'Forces sociales et accumulation du capital au Maghreb', *Annuaire*, 1973, vol. 12, 315–42, essentially concerns Algeria. A concise balance sheet of the performance of the Algerian economy since independence is given by Kader Ammour, Christian Leucate, and Jean-Jacques Moulin, *La Voie algérienne* (Paris, 1974) while the vagaries of self-management, which elicited a number of studies, are treated most exhaustively by Gérard Duprat, *Révolution et autogestion rurale en Algérie* (Paris, 1973), in regional and national political contexts. Useful policy studies in Morocco include André Tiano, *La Politique économique et financière du Maroc indépendant* (Paris, 1963), and William I. Zartman, *Morocco: problems of new power* (New York, 1964). Cultural trends and policies since independence constituted the focal theme of the *Annuaire*, 1973, vol. 12, and Jean Dejeux has provided an exhaustive guide and bibliography of *Littérature maghrébine de langue française* (Ottawa, 1973). Abdelkebir Khatibi, as perhaps befits a writer who is also a sociologist, limits his analysis to novels in *Le Roman maghrébin* (Paris, 1968), but has the advantage of including Arabic as well as French sources. Issues of Arabisation and cultural development have perhaps been discussed most extensively in Algeria, and Abdallah Mazouni, *Culture et enseignement en Algérie et au Maghreb* (Paris, 1969), presents balanced views, as in a more historical perspective does Mostefa Lacheraf, *Algérie: nation et société* (Paris,

1965). Contemporary Arabic thought may increasingly be shaped by Maghriban intellectuals such as Abdallah Laroui and Hichem Djaït, whose most mature works to date are, respectively, *La Crise des intellectuels arabes* (Paris, 1974) and *La Personalité et le devenir arabo-islamiques* (Paris, 1974), just as discourse about Islam benefited from an earlier work by the late Malek Bennabi, *Vocation de l'Islam* (Paris, 1954).

12. FRENCH-SPEAKING TROPICAL AFRICA

This is a brief selection of the numerous documents, books and articles of the 14 countries of francophone Africa. The early ones, written during or immediately after the colonial period, discuss the countries as a block – or frequently as two, AOF and AEF. General sources are few in the period after independence, as the countries themselves drew apart and built relations with neighbouring territories according to new social, economic and political imperatives, which had no reference to their former connexions in one of the two colonial federations. After the mid-1960s, bibliographic material tends to refer to individual countries, and to concentrate on but a few, ignoring others.

From 1940 to 1960, a number of sources provide useful information on French colonial policy and early political movements of the entire area, or one of the two federations. Among the classics on colonial policy are the books written by former colonial officials such as Lord Hailey and his French counterpart, Robert Delavignette (see Lord Hailey, *An African survey* (London, 1957) and Robert Delavignette, *Paysannerie et prolétariat* (Paris, 1948) or *Freedom and authority in French West Africa* (Oxford, 1950). In the same vein, Henri Brunschwig, *La Colonisation française* (Paris, 1949) and Henri Labouret, *Colonisation, colonialisme, décolonisation* (Paris, 1952) are also valuable sources of information on French colonial practices.

Documentation Française (Paris) periodically issued studies, in its Notes et études documentaires, such as *La République de Guinée* (no. 3202, 1965); *La République de Haute Volta* (no. 2696, 1960); *La République du Mali* (no. 2739, 1961); and *La République du Niger* (no. 2638, 1960). Background information on French policy, including geographic and economic data, may be found in Jacques Richard Molard, *Afrique Occidentale Française* (Paris,

1956). Books by French scholars represent different political orientations and therefore have different interpretations of events and policies; such as Jean Suret-Canale, *Afrique Noire, occidentale et centrale* (Paris, 1958), Gil Dugué, *Vers les États-Unis d'Afrique* (Dakar, 1960), Ernest Milcent, *L'AOF entre en scène* (Paris, 1958), Hubert Deschamps, *L'Éveil politique africain* (Paris, 1952) and André Blanchet, *L'Itinéraire des partis africains depuis Bamako* (Paris, 1958). Kenneth Robinson, 'Constitutional reform in French Tropical Africa', *Political Studies*, 1958, vol. 6, gave a valuable, although brief, perspective on the changing post-war institutions of the French colonies. Later sources with the advantages of more time to consider the content and impact of French colonial policy in this period provide invaluable material – see, for example, Michael Crowder, *Colonial West Africa: collected essays* (London, 1978); Catherine Coquéry-Vidrovitch, 'Mutations de l'impérialisme colonial français dans les années 30', *African Economic History*, 1977, vol. 4; A. S. Kanya-Forstner, *The conquest of the Western Sudan* (Cambridge, 1969); Amidu Magasa, *Papacommandant a jeté un grand filet devant nous: les exploités des rives du Niger 1900–1962* (Paris, 1978); and J. R. de Benoist, *La Balkanisation de l'Afrique occidentale française* (Dakar, 1978) and Lansiné Kaba's *Wahabiyya: Islamic reform and politics in French West Africa* (Evanston, 1974).

The most detailed analysis in English on political movements in French-speaking West Africa (which also includes analysis of French colonial policy), is Ruth Schachter Morgenthau's *Political parties in French-speaking West Africa* (Oxford, 1964). Another book which gives sketches of political movements and specific political events in the AEF in the immediate pre-independence period is by Virginia Thompson and her husband Richard Adloff, *The emerging states of French Equatorial Africa* (Stanford, 1960).

Debates among scholars, particularly those writing in English, over the organisation and impact of early African political movements, were sparked off by the works of Thomas Hodgkin, and Thomas Hodgkin and Ruth Schachter; see Hodgkin, *Nationalism in colonial Africa* (London, 1956), *African political parties* (London, 1961), and Hodgkin and Schachter, 'French-speaking West Africa in transition', *International Conciliation* (May, 1960). Politics in French-speaking Africa were also described using a development paradigm by James S. Coleman in 'The politics of sub-Saharan Africa', in Gabriel A. Almond and James S. Coleman (eds.), *The politics of developing areas* (Princeton, 1960). Many other writers provide valuable insights on late pre- (and early post-) independence politics. Among these are Kenneth Robinson and W. J. M. Mackenzie, *Five elections in tropical Africa* (Oxford, 1960), William J. Foltz, *From French West Africa to the Mali Federation* (New Haven, 1965).

Writers on the economic problems of the area in the immediate post-colonial period include Elliot Berg, who wrote 'The economic basis of political choice in French West Africa', *The American Political Sciences Review*, June 1960, and 'French West Africa' in Walter Galenson (ed.), *Labor and economic development* (New York, 1959). Economic information, as well as social and demographic data, was available from the *Annuaires statistiques*, published for the AOF and the AEF intermittently between the two world wars and in the pre-independence period. All countries published their own *Annuaires statistiques* in the post-independence period – not surprisingly countries with more administrative resources, including foreign assistance, produced statistics more regularly and reliably than their poorer neighbours. Thus, Senegal and the Ivory Coast offer considerable data, while Chad or Upper Volta do not. A general source on economic developments in the region is A. G. Hopkins, *An economic history of West Africa* (New York, 1973). C. Meillassoux wrote and edited useful anthropological studies, including *L'Esclavage en Afrique pré-coloniale* (Paris, 1975) and *Femmes, greniers et capitaux* (Paris, 1975).

A decade after independence, scholars produced a variety of economic studies including country studies at the World Bank and general ones, such as *Accelerated development in sub-Saharan Africa* (Washington, 1981), and the annual *World development report* (Washington, DC). I. Ouedrago, M. D. Newman and D. W. Norman produced *The farmer in the semi-arid tropics of West Africa: partially annotated bibliography* (ICRISAT, Patancheru, India, 1982). Elliot Berg's 'Reforming grain marketing systems in West Africa' is one of the interesting economic studies in *Proceedings of the International Workshop on Socio-economic Constraints to Development in Semi-arid Tropical Agriculture* (ICRISAT, Patancheru, India, 1980). Scholars with varying approaches to economic issues are increasingly focussing on specific sectors or regions. For example, some interesting recent studies are S. B. Baier's *An economic history of Central Niger* (Oxford, 1980); Jane Guyer's 'The food economy and French colonial rule in central Cameroun', *Journal of African History*, 1978, vol. 19; and J. M. Watts, 'A silent revolution: the nature of famine and the changing character of food production in Nigerian Hausaland', Ph.D. thesis, University of Michigan (Ann Arbor, 1979). Data on the export sectors of the various national economies is available; for example, on the effects of the Lomé Convention, see Paule Bouvier, *L'Europe et la coopération au développement* (Brussels, 1980).

Other post-independence works focus increasingly on specific countries. *L'Afrique Noire politique et économique* (Ediafrique, La Documentation Africaine, Paris, 1977) gives basic data. Analysis can be found in James S. Coleman and Carl G. Rosberg (eds.), *Political parties and national integration in tropical Africa* (Berkeley, 1964); or the series of three volumes edited by Gwendolen Carter, *African one-party states* (Ithaca, 1962), *Five African states: responses to diversity* (Ithaca, 1963), *National unity and regionalism in eight African states* (Ithaca, 1966). Also relevant are: Peter Gutkind and Immanuel Wallerstein, *The political economy of contemporary Africa* (Beverly Hills, 1976); Michael Lofchie, *The state of the nations, constraints on development in independent Africa* (Berkeley, 1971); and John Dunn (ed.), *West African states, failure and promise* (Cambridge, 1978).

Turning to each of the 14 countries, the material available is uneven, and often by journalists recounting political crises, appearing in such sources as *Le Mois en Afrique*, *Africa Report*, *Jeune Afrique*, *Présence Africaine* and *Marchés Tropicaux*. Articles can also be found in the *Journal of Modern African Studies* and other scholarly journals. *Jeune Afrique* puts out a useful yearbook (Paris); so does Colin Legum (ed.), *African contemporary record* (New York) and *Africa south of the Sahara* (London). Literature is substantial on the Ivory Coast, Senegal and Cameroun. In regard to the Ivory Coast, there are few studies on the pre-colonial and early colonial period; an exception is the study by F. J. Amon d'Aby *La Côte d'Ivoire dans la cité africaine* (Paris, 1951). Claude Meillassoux's *Anthropologie économique des Gouro de Côte d'Ivoire* (Paris, 1964) and T. Weiskel's *French colonial rule and the Baule peoples* (Oxford, 1980), are excellent additions to the literature. A thorough study of politics in the post-independence period was written by Aristide Zolberg, *One-party government in the Ivory Coast*

(Princeton, 1964). This book analysed one-party democracy as practised in the Ivory Coast and illustrated major shifts in the role of the political party after independence. Zolberg later co-edited, with Philip Foster, another volume including in-depth political analyses of the Ivory Coast and its neighbour Ghana, *Ghana and the Ivory Coast* (Chicago, 1971). Another interesting comparison between the impact of colonialism in an English colony and in a French one can be found in David Guyer, *Ghana and the Ivory Coast: the impact of colonialism in an African setting* (New York, 1970). More controversial is the critical study by Samir Amin, *Le Développement du capitalisme en Côte d'Ivoire* (Paris, 1967). Michael Cohen published a serious analysis of the growth of urbanisation in the Ivory Coast, *Urban policy and political conflict in Africa: a study of the Ivory Coast* (Chicago, 1974). Jean-Louis Fyot, *Méthode de planification: L'expérience de la Côte d'Ivoire* (Paris, 1972), took an early look at planning there. Bastiaan den Tuinden published an economic study for the World Bank, *Ivory Coast, the challenge of success* (Baltimore, 1978).

There is a wealth of sources on the pre-independence period in Senegal. Access to Senegal has been easy for scholars, particularly for English-speakers venturing into francophone Africa. Because it is the oldest colony with a special political history, it has attracted analysts and historians of all nationalities. The following books are only a selected few of those available. V. Monteil's books and articles on Senegal, based on his long years in the country at the Institut Français d'Afrique Noire (IFAN) provide interesting material on politics and social change with a special emphasis on religion; see Monteil, *Esquisses sénégalaises* (Dakar, 1966). Several authors focussed on the Muslim brotherhoods which are powerful economically and politically in Senegal. Among these are Cheikh Tidiane Sy, *La Confrérie sénégalaise des Mourides* (Paris, 1969), Lucy Creevey (Behrman), *Muslim Brotherhoods and politics in Senegal* (Cambridge, 1970) and Donal Cruise O'Brien, *Saints and politicians* (Cambridge, 1975). There have been a number of political histories of Senegal, among them one by Michael Crowder, *Senegal: a study in French assimilation policy* (London, 1962) and more recent political studies such as François Zuccarelli, *Un Parti politique africain: l'Union progressiste Sénégalaise* (Paris, 1970), Pierre Gonidec, *La République de Sénégal* (Paris, 1968), and Edward J. Schumacher, *Politics, bureaucracy and rural development in Senegal* (Berkeley, 1975). All political studies analyse the strength of the rural areas, particularly the dominant groundnut zone. Thus the particular rural concentration by Schumacher, a political scientist, is also the focus of works by V. Diarassouba, *L'Évolution des structures agricoles du Sénégal* (Paris, 1968) and J. L. Balans *et al.*, *Autonomie locale et intégration nationale au Sénégal* (Paris, 1975). The political philosophy of Léopold Sédar Senghor, *négritude*, has also received considerable attention, for example, by Irving Leonard Markowitz in *Léopold Sédar Senghor and the politics of négritude* (New York, 1969). W. A. E. Skurnik has written a study of foreign policy in Senegal, *The foreign policy of Senegal* (Evanston, 1972), concentrating on the conservative socialism of Senghor. Samir Amin wrote for Senegal, as he did for the Ivory Coast, a critical analysis from a radical perspective, see *Le Monde des affaires sénégalais* (Paris, 1964), and his *Trois expériences africaines de développement: le Mali, la Guinée et le Ghana* (Paris, 1965).

Cameroun has numerous published sources including Richard Joseph, *Radical nationalism in Cameroun* (Oxford, 1977), David Gardinier, *Cameroon: United Nations challenge to French policy* (Oxford, 1963), Edwin and Shirley Ardener, *Plantation and village in the Cameroons* (London, 1960), C. K. Meek, *Land tenure and land administration in Nigeria and the Cameroons* (London, 1957). Victor Azarya, *Dominance and change in North Cameroon: the Fulbe aristocracy* (Beverly Hills, 1976), R. Clignet, *The Africanization of the Labor Market: Educational and Occupational Segmentation in the Cameroon* (Berkeley, 1976), Willard Johnson, *The Cameroon Federation: political integration in a fragmentary society* (Princeton, 1970), David Kom, *Le Cameroun: essai d'analyse économique et politique* (Paris, 1971), Victor T. Le Vine, *The Cameroon Federal Republic* (Ithaca, 1971), Adamou Ndam Ngoya, *Le Cameroun dans les relations internationales* (Paris, 1976), Michel Prouzet, *Le Cameroun* (Paris, 1974), Neville Rubin, *Cameroon: An African Federation* (New York, 1971); and Nidva Kofele-Kale (ed.), *An African experiment in nation building: the bilingual Cameroon Republic since reunification* (Boulder, Colorado, 1980).

Bénin and Togo, like Niger, Upper Volta and Mauritania, and the four former Equatorial African States, are less well studied. Sources on these countries include Robert Cornevin, *Le Dahomey* (Paris, 1970); A. Akindélé and C. Aguessy, *Dahomey* (Paris, 1955);

Dov Ronin, *Dahomey: between tradition and modernity* (Ithaca, 1975); Maurice A. Glélé, *Naissance d'un état noir, l'évolution politique et constitutionelle du Dahomey de la colonisation à nos jours* (Paris, 1969); I. A. Akinjogbin, *Dahomey and its neighbours* (Cambridge, 1967); and Jacques Lombard, *Un système politique traditionnel de type féodal: les Bariba du Nord-Dahomey* (Paris, 1965). Niger sources include Pierre Bonardi, *La République du Niger: naissance d'un état* (Paris, 1960); Edmond Séré de Rivières, *Le Niger* (Paris, 1952), Pierre Donaint et François Lancrenon, *Le Niger* (Paris, 1972); Richard Higgott's 'Structural dependence and decolonisation in a West African land-locked state: Niger', *Review of African Political Economy*, Jan–April 1980, 43–58, gives a different point of view. R. Higgott and F. Fugelstad discuss 'The 1974 *coup d'état* in Niger' in the *Journal of Modern African Studies*, September 1975, vol. 13. On Upper Volta, see Elliott Skinner's *The Mossi of Upper Volta* (Stanford, 1964) and *African urban life: the transformation of Ouagadougou* (Princeton, 1974), as well as the essays edited by John Caldwell *et al.*, *Upper Volta* (New York, 1975). Sources on Mauritania include Christine Garnier and Philippe Ermont, *Désert fertile: un nouvel état, la Mauritanie* (Paris, 1960); Alfred G. Gerteiny, *Mauritania* (London, 1967); Richard M. Westebbe, *The economy of Mauritania* (New York, 1971) and Marcel Piquemol-Pastré, *La République Islamique de Mauritanie* (Paris, 1969); G. Désiré-Vuillemin, *Contribution à l'histoire de la Mauritanie de 1900 à 1934* (Dakar, 1962), and C. Moore, 'One-partyism in Mauritania', *Journal of Modern African Studies*, 1965, vol. 3. On Togo, see James Coleman, *Togoland* (New York, 1956), and Robert Cornevin, *Le Togo* (Paris, 1973).

Mali and Guinea received special attention for their proud independence and for their radical political language; numerous studies were carried out as a result. Recent material has been difficult to find on Guinea. A partial list includes Fernand Gigon, *Guinée, état-pilote* (Paris, 1959); Jean Suret-Canale, *La République de Guinée* (Paris, 1970); Maurice Houis, *Guinée française* (Paris, 1953); Ladipo Adamolekun, *Sékou Touré's Guinea: an experiment in nation building* (London, 1976), which includes a good bibliography; Claude Rivière, *Mutations sociales en Guinée* (Paris, 1971); Sékou Touré's *Oeuvres complètes* (Paris, n.d.) gives his interpretation of events. Lansiné Kaba gives another in his articles in the *Journal of Modern African Studies*: 'Cultural revolution, artistic creativity, and freedom of expression in Guinea', June 1976, vol. 14 and 'Guinean politics: a critical historical overview', March 1977, vol. 15.

For Mali, G. Snyder, *One-party government in Mali* (New Haven, 1965), K. Ernst, *Tradition and progress in the African village: the non-capitalist transformation of rural communities in Mali* (London, 1976); William I. Jones, *Planning and economic policy: socialist Mali and her neighbors* (Washington, 1976), Edmond Jouve, *La République du Mali* (Paris, 1974); Horeya T. Megahed, *Socialism and nation-building in Africa: the case of Mali, 1960–1968* (New York, 1970); and Nicholas S. Hopkins, *Popular government in an African town* (Chicago, 1972).

The four countries which formed the AEF have been relatively little studied in depth. Works include Jacqueline Bouquerel, *Le Gabon* (Paris, 1970); Brian Weinstein's *Gabon* (Cambridge, Mass., 1966); J. Cabot and C. Bouquet, *Le Tchad* (Paris, 1973); Georges Diguimboye, *L'Essor du Tchad* (Paris, 1969); Richard Westebbe *et al.*, *Chad: development, potential and constraints* (Washington, 1974); John Works, *Pilgrims in a strange land: Hausa communities in Chad* (New York, 1976); the bibliography by Philippe Frémeaux, *La Rébellion tchadienne* (Paris, 1973); Virginia Thompson and Richard Adloff's *Conflict in Tchad* (Berkeley, 1982); Samuel Decalo, 'Regionalism, political decay and civil strife in Chad', *Journal of Modern African Studies*, 1980, vol. 18. Other useful works are Marcel Soret's *Histoire du Congo, capitale Brazzaville* (Paris, 1978) and Pierre Kalck, *Central African Republic, a failure in decolonization* (London, 1971).

13. MADAGASCAR

The most noteworthy works on the period by Malagasy writers are R. W. Rabemananjara's *Madagascar, histoire de la nation malgache* (Paris, 1952), E. Ralaimhoitra's *Histoire de Madagascar* (Tananarive, 1965), and R. Rajemisa-Raolison's *Dictionnaire géographique et historique de Madagascar* (Fianarantsoa, 1966). All three should be used in conjunction with H. Deschamps' *Histoire de Madagascar* (Paris, 1972) and A. Spacensky's *Cinquante ans de vie politique de Ralamongo à Tsiranana* (Paris, 1970). Other French works of a general nature are M. de Coppet's *Madagascar et Réunion* (Paris, 1947), R. Pascal's *La République malgache* (Paris, 1965), and C. Cadoux's *La République malgache* (Paris, 1969). Pierre Boiteau, a French Communist and

MDRM sympathiser, wrote *Contribution à l'histoire de la nation malgache* (Paris, 1958) in which he makes the MDRM appear more nationalist than extremist, thereby playing down the role of PANAMA and JINA. In English the most valuable works are R. Adloff and V. Thompson's *The Malagasy Republic* (Stanford, 1965) and N. Heseltine's *Madagascar* (London, 1971). There are also several valuable periodicals, the *Bulletin de l'Académie Malgache*, the *Bulletin de Madagascar*, the *Revue de Madagascar*, and *Notes Reconnaissances et Explorations*. For the English-speaking world the 'Madagascar' section in *Africa Contemporary Record* (London) is an invaluable source of information on Malagasy affairs.

On the political side A. L. Annet reflects the Vichyite viewpoint in *Aux heures troublées de l'Afrique française, 1939–1942* (Paris, 1952), while in the post-war period one of the earliest protests against colonial rule came from J. Rabemananjara, author first of *Un malgache vous parle* (Paris, 1946) and then later of *Témoignage malgache et colonialisme* (Paris, 1956) and *Nationalisme et problèmes malgaches* (Paris, 1958). When used in conjunction with R. Rabemananjara's *Madagascar sous la rénovation malgache* (Paris, 1953) they give a clear picture of Malagasy grievances and aspirations prior to 1960. A good overview of political events is found in Spacensky's 'L'Evolution politique malgache, 1945–1966', in *La Revue Française de Science Politique* (1967) and R. Darsac's 'Contradictions et partis malgaches' in the *Revue d'Action Populaire* (1958). Explanations as to why the rebellion took place are few. B. C. Daniel's typescript, 'Les Événements de Madagascar' appeared at the École Nationale de la France d'Outre Mer (1948–9) but it is merely descriptive and not analytical. O. Mannoni attempted to explain the rebellion in terms of psychological dependency in his *Psychologie de la colonisation* (Paris, 1950), but the first scholarly work was J. Tronchon's *L'Insurrection malgache de 1947* (Paris, 1974). G. Althabe's earlier work, *Oppression et libération dans l'imaginaire* (1968), is also worth consulting, mainly because it influenced some of the people involved in the events of May 1972. Lastly there is P. Stibbe's *Justice pour les Malgaches* (Paris, 1954), a detailed account of the trial of the three deputies written by their left-wing lawyer.

For the years after 1960, studies on Malagasy politics are both highly legalistic in approach and careful in their treatment of Tsiranana. Spacensky's *Cinquante ans...* is rich, well-researched, and compulsory reading. R. Archer's *Madagascar depuis 1972 – la marche d'une révolution* (Paris, 1976), a clearly written synthesis of events since 1972, contains important material on the President and the bourgeoisie. Malagasy political parties are dealt with in a series of articles in the *Revue Française d'Études Politiques Africaines*, 1969 to 1975. Foreign policy before 1972 is explored by G. Cognac and G. Feuer in *Les Conventions de co-opération entre la République malgache et la République française* (Tananarive, 1963), while Madagascar's relations with the rest of the world are outlined by J. Maestre, author of *La République malgache et les organisations africaines* (Tananarive, 1968), and P. Decraene in his article 'La Diplomatie malgache à la recherche de nouveaux parténaires', which appeared in *Le Monde Diplomatique* (1969). The best overview of foreign policy after 1972 is found in *Africa Contemporary Record*. Material on local government can be gleaned from C. Cadoux's monograph on the subject, *La Commune malgache* (Mantasoa, 1967) and his article in *L'Actualité Juridique* (1965), 'Les Nouveaux Aspects de l'organisation locale à Madagascar'. Finally the trade union movement is dealt with in P. Delval's 'Le syndicalisme à Madagascar', *Pénant*, 1965. There are no serious studies of any of the pressure groups.

The social and cultural life of Madagascar has not received as much attention as it deserves: see, however, H. Berthier's *Notes et impressions sur les moeurs et coutumes du peuple malgache* (Tananarive, 1933), J. Faublée's *Ethnographie de Madagascar* (Paris, 1946), and R. Dandouau and G. Chapus's *Histoire des populations de Madagascar* (1952). O. Mannoni's *Psychologie de la colonisation* (Paris, 1950) contains useful material and should be read in conjunction with R. Ralibera's *Vazaha et Malgaches en dialogue* (Tananarive, 1966). Two important studies are P. Colin's *Aspects de l'âme malgache* (1959) and R. Andriamanjato's *Le Tsiny and le Tody dans la pensée malgache* (Paris, 1957), while a less scholarly work is D. Ramandriavohona's *Le Malgache: sa langue, sa religion* (Paris, 1959). Social change during the 1950s is discussed in O. Hatzfeld's article 'Évolution actuelle de la sociéte malgache', which appeared in *Monde non Chrétien* (1953), and in the 1960s by J. Lapierre in 'Problèmes socio-culturels de la nation malagache', *Cahiers Internationaux de Sociologie* (1966). The latter's conclusions are especially interesting when compared with those published by the Malagasy government's research bureau under the title *L'Enquête démographique – Madagascar, 1966* (1967). No study of Malagasy life would be complete without a consideration of the *fokonolonas*. No definitive study exists, but valuable information is found in C. Ranaivo's 'Les Expériences de fokonolona à Madagascar', which appeared in *Monde non Chrétien* (1949), F. Arbousset's *Le Fokonolona à Madagascar* (Paris, 1950), and G. Condaminas's *Fokonolona et communautés rurales en Imerina* (Paris, 1960). These titles are complemented by R. Dumont's *Évolution des campagnes malgaches* (Tananarive, 1959), a study on rural life. The role of women is considered by E. Radaody-Ralarosy in 'La Femme malgache dans la cité', which was published in the *Bulletin de l'Académie Malgache* (1960), while the *Annales de l'Université de Madagascar* (1967) printed 'La Femme, la société, et la droit malgache'. Several authors have written on the foreign elements in the island; G. Gayet produced 'Immigrations asiatiques à Madagascar' for *Civilisations* (1955), and J. Ratsima published 'Les Congrégations chinoises de Madagascar' in a 1960 issue of the *Revue de Madagascar*. D. Bardonnet wrote a similar article for the *Annuaire Française de Droit International* (1964) entitled, 'Les Minorités asiatiques à Madagascar' and which contains some useful material. The standard work on Christianity is H. Vidal's *La Séparation des Églises et de l'État à Madagascar, 1861–1962* (Paris, 1969), but of greater value is Père P. Lupo's *Église et décolonisation à Madagascar* (Fianarantsoa, 1973). As for the press, all that exists is R. L'Italien's unpublished thesis from the École des Hautes Études, 'Madagascar, 1950–1960: une étape vers la décolonisation' (1975).

The various issues of the *Revue Économique de Madagascar* and the *Travaux du Centre d'Études Rurales* carry useful articles on the economic life of the island. General studies worth consulting are M. Rudloff's *Économie du tiers monde*, vol. I (Tananarive, 1961), G. Bastion's *Madagascar, étude géographique et économique* (Paris, 1967), and the International Bank for Reconstruction and Development's substantial *Economy of the Malagasy Republic* (1968). French aid to Madagascar was outlined by R. Hoffer in his *Co-opération économique franco-africaine* (Paris, 1957). Other useful works were M. Gaud's *Les Premières Expériences de planification en Afrique noire* (Paris, 1967), and a book by R. Gendarme which revealed the stranglehold the large French companies had on Madagascar, *L'Économie de Madagascar* (Tananarive, 1960). Gendarme's study had an enormous impact on some Malagasy nationalists. Another helpful work by P. Ottino, *Les Économies paysannes malgaches du Bas-Mangoky* (Paris, 1963), provides a scholarly analysis of the economic structure of the south-west part of the island. Material on the economic functions of the communes is located in two books, one by M. Surbiguet entitled *Les Sociétés d'économie mixte à Madagascar* (Tananarive, 1966), and the other by A. Bergeret, *Les Sociétés d'aménagement agricole à Madagascar* (Tananarive, 1967). The most analytical study of economic life in the rural areas was Y. Prats's work, *Le Développement communautaire à Madagascar* (Paris, 1972).

14. ZAIRE, RWANDA AND BURUNDI

Abundant bibliographic and documentary sources are available for the study of contemporary Zairean, Rwandan, and Burundi history. Useful select but reasonably comprehensive bibliographies, covering the social and economic as well as political spheres, may be found in René Lemarchand, *Rwanda and Burundi* (London, 1970), and Crawford Young, *Politics in the Congo* (Princeton, 1965). For the colonial period, T. Heyse, assisted by J. Berlage, regularly produced the exhaustive *Bibliographie du Congo Belge et du Ruanda-Urundi*, appearing in *Cahiers Belges et Congolais*, nos. 4–22 (Brussels, 1953). The *Musée Royal de l'Afrique Centrale* has provided annual ethnographic bibliographies. For the 'Congo crisis', Dominique Ryelandt compiled a virtually complete listing, published as a supplement to *Études Congolaises* in 1963. The most recent period, for Zaire, is best covered by Edouard Bustin, in *Cahiers du CEDAF* (Brussels, nos. 3 and 4, 1971) (which also covers earlier periods).

Major Belgian documentary sources include the *Rapports Annuels sur l'Administration du Congo Belge, présentés aux Chambres Législatives*, and the analogous document for Ruanda-Urundi; the proceedings of the Conseil Colonial, which was required to debate all legislative enactments for the Belgian colonies; the records of the Conseil du Gouvernement and its provincial counterparts. The annual opening address of the governor-general to the Conseil du Gouvernement constitutes the most authoritative statement of official policy. Pierre Piron and J. Devos in their compilation of the *Codes et lois du Congo Belge* (last colonial edition 1959, with a 1970 post-independence update for Zaire), provide not only the legal texts, but also legislative histories and commentaries, which illuminate their intent and background.

The involvement of the United Nations with Rwanda and Burundi as a result of its Trust status, and Zaire as a consequence of its operation there from 1960 to 1964 leaves in its wake an important documentary deposit. For Rwanda and Burundi, the reports of the triennial Visiting Missions (1948, 1951, 1954, 1957, 1960), plus the several *ad hoc* commissions dispatched from 1960–1964, are an important source. For Zaire, in addition to the various reports of the secretary-general on the UN operation, several of the key participants have provided their personal accounts; these include H. T. Alexander, *African tightrope* (London, 1966), Rajashwan Dayal, *Mission for Hammarskjöld* (Princeton, 1976), Conor Cruise O'Brien, *To Katanga and back* (New York, 1962), and Carl von Horn, *Soldiering for peace* (New York, 1967). The major UN documents are conveniently assembled by the *Chronique de Politique Étrangère*, vol. XV, nos. 4–6 (1962).

For the post-independence period, government documents are abundant but of uneven value. For Zaire, government positions are diffused through the daily bulletins of *Agence Zairoise de Presse* (earlier *Agence Congolaise de Presse*). Proceedings of the national parliament and, for the First Republic, its provincial counterparts, provide some glimpses of what was happening, but the irregularity of the sessions, plus the narrow range of subjects considered during the Second Republic, limit their utility. The most valuable Zairean government document is the *Rapport Annuel* of the Banque du Zaire, issued since 1967. Current economic data is provided in *Conjonctures Économiques*, issued by the Departement d'Économie Nationale. Comparable bulletins of economic statistics are published by the Rwanda Ministère de la Coopération Internationale et du Plan, and the Institut Rundi des Statistiques.

A number of serials devoted to contemporary developments in the former Belgian colonies deserve mention. For the pre-independence period, these include *Zaire* (Louvain), *Problèmes d'Afrique Centrale* (Antwerp), *Problèmes Sociaux Congolais* (Lubumbashi, earlier *Bulletin de CEPSI*). For the 1960 to 1975 period in Zaire, the most important are *Études Zairoises* (Kinshasa, earlier *Études Congolaises*), *Zaire-Afrique* (Kinshasa, earlier *Congo-Afrique*), *Cahiers Économiques et Sociaux* (publication of the important Institut de Recherches Économiques et Sociaux at the Kinshasa campus of the Université Nationale du Zaire), *Courrier Africain* and *Travaux Africains* of the Centre de Recherche et d'Information Socio-Politiques (CRISP), from 1959 to 1971, then reorganised as *Cahiers du CEDAF* from 1971 (Brussels, Centre d'Études et de Documentation Africaine).

Major reference works include the *Encyclopédie du Congo Belge*, 3 vols. (Brussels, 1953), and the handbooks on each country prepared by the American University: *US Army area handbook for the Republic of the Congo (Léopoldville)* (Washington, 1962, revised edition, 1979); Gordon C. McDonald *et al.*, *Area handbook for Burundi* (Washington, 1969); Richard F. Nyrop *et al.*, *Area handbook for Rwanda* (Washington, 1969). For Burundi, invaluable political information is found in Warren Weinstein, *Historical dictionary of Burundi* (Metuchen, 1976). Documents pertaining to the Rwanda revolution are found in the CRISP publication, *Rwanda Politique 1958–1960* (Brussels, 1961). A magnificent record of Zairean current history is provided in the annual CRISP yearbooks, *Congo 1959* and successors, published from 1959 to 1967. In addition, special documentary histories were published by CRISP of two major political parties, the Parti Solidaire Africain and the ABAKO, as well as the Katanga secession and the 1964 rebellions.

The melodramatic events of 1955–65 in Zaire have generated such a vast literature that only a few of the most important can be mentioned here; conversely, serious treatments of the pre-decolonisation phase, or the New Regime since 1965, are far fewer. On the terminal colonial period, special note may be made of Roger Anstey, *King Leopold's legacy* (London, 1966), and Jean Stengers, 'La Belgique et le Congo', in *Histoire de la Belgique contemporaine* (Brussels, 1975), as well as Young (1965). Decolonisation and the crisis is given most authoritative analysis and documentation in the annual CRISP volumes noted above. For the international aspects, Cathryn Hoskyns remains the best source, *The Congo since independence* (London, 1965). The Belgian dimension is well represented in Ganshof van der Meersch, *Fin de la souveraineté belge au Congo* (The Hague, 1963), and in an interesting public debate by many of those most closely involved, edited by Pierre de Vos, *La Décolonisation* (Brussels, 1975). On the dynamics of Zairean nationalism and political parties, especially useful are Herbert Weiss, *Political protest in the Congo* (Princeton, 1967), and René Lemarchand, *Political awakening in the Congo*

(Berkeley, 1964). From a Zairean perspective, Thomas Kanza provides an autobiographical analysis in *Conflict in the Congo* (Baltimore, 1972). Biographies have appeared of three of the major leaders: Ian Colvin, *The rise and fall of Moise Tshombe* (London, 1968), Charles-André Gilis, *Kasavubu au coeur du drame congolais* (Brussels, 1964); Francis Monheim, *Mobutu, l'homme seul* (Brussels, 1962). On Lumumba, see René Lemarchand in Walter Skurnik (ed.), *African political thought: Lumumba, Nkrumah and Touré*, and Jean van Lierde (ed.), *La Pensée politique de Patrice Lumumba*. On the rebellions, in addition to the CRISP study, useful monographs have been contributed by Renée Fox, W. de Craemer, and J. M. Ribeaucourt in *Études Congolaises*, vol. 8 (January–February 1965), and Young, in Ali Mazrui and Robert Rotberg (eds.), *Power and protest in Black Africa* (London, 1970). On the early years of the Mobutu regime, the best study is Jean-Claude Williame, *Patrimonialism and political change in the Congo* (Stanford, 1971). Especially important for later Mobutu years are Michael G. Schatzberg, *Politics and class in Zaire* (New York, 1980) and Guy Gran (ed.), *Zaire: the political economy of underdevelopment* (New York, 1980). An overview of the first two decades of independence is provided in J. Vanderlinden (ed.), *Du Congo au Zaire 1960–1980* (Brussels, 1981). A leading politician and intellectual, Kamitatu Massamba (Cléophas), has published two sharply critical studies, *La Grande Mystification du Congo-Kinshasa* (Paris, 1971), and *Le Pouvoir au portée du peuple* (Paris, 1977).

The crucial process of urbanisation is treated in several monographs: Valdo Pons, *Stanleyville* (London, 1969); Jean La Fontaine, *City politics* (Cambridge, 1970), and Paul Raymaekers, *L'Organisation des zones de squatting* (Brussels, 1964), on Kinshasa; F. Grévisse, *Le Centre extra-coutumier d'Elisabethville* (Brussels, 1951); and the 1975 doctoral dissertation of Nzongola Ntalaja, 'Urban administration in Katanga'. In the ethnographic domain, Jan Vansina provides an invaluable reference work, in *Introduction à l'ethnographie du Congo* (Brussels, 1966). Major recent works providing an overview of the impact of colonial administration on particular societies are Wyatt McGaffey, *Custom and government in the Lower Congo* (Berkeley, 1970), and Edouard Bustin, *Lunda under Belgian Rule* (Cambridge, 1975).

Economic change is remarkably well covered. For the pre-independence situation, the best study is Fernand Bézy, *Problèmes structurels de l'économie congolaise* (Louvain and Paris, 1957). The outstanding team of economists gathered at Lovanium in the 1960s jointly produced *Indépendence, inflation et développement* (Paris, 1968), a comprehensive treatment of the political economy of the early independence years. Also important are Fernand Bézy, Jean-Philippe Peemans and Jean-Marie Wautelet, *Accumulation et sous-développement au Zaire 1960–1980* (Louvain-la-Neuve, 1981); Jean-Louis Lacroix, *Industrialisation au Congo* (Paris, 1967), and Christian Coméliau, *Conditions de la planification et du développement: l'exemple du Congo* (Paris, 1969). On the urban economy, viewed at the household level, Joseph Houyoux, *Budgets ménagers: nutrition et mode de vie à Kinshasa* (Kinshasa, 1973) is excellent. The best analysis of agricultural history is provided in the 1975 Brussels dissertation of Mulambu Mvuluya, 'Le régime des cultures obligatoires et le radicalisme rural au Zaire (1917–1960)'. Jean-Philippe Peemans has recently offered, in a series of contributions, an insightful overview of economic history, including the best treatment of the political economy of the Mobutu period; particularly valuable are *The political economy of Zaire in the seventies* (Louvain, 1974), and his chapter in Peter Duignan and L. H. Gann, *The economics of colonialism* (London, 1975).

Rwanda and Burundi have received far less attention, and have long suffered a tendency to generalise findings in a particular portion of one kingdom to all of both; especially the royalist model of ethnic caste relations derived from central Rwanda. The classic statement of this view is Jacques Maquet, *The premise of inequality in Rwanda* (Oxford, 1961), whose structural–functional model of Tutsi hegemony has been widely challenged (for example, in Helen Codere, *The biography of an African society, Rwanda 1900–1960*, Marcel d'Hertefelt, *Les clans du Rwanda ancien* (Tervuren, 1970), and Catharine Newbury's 1975 Wisconsin dissertation 'The cohesion of oppression: a century of clientship in Kinyaga, Rwanda'.

By far the most valuable overall political history is Lemarchand, *Rwanda and Burundi*, which focusses upon the decolonisation process and the tumultuous first half-decade of independence. For the 1972 Burundi tragedy, the best available analysis is Warren Weinstein and Robert Schrire, *Political conflict and ethnic strategies: a case study of Burundi*. Rural development issues are well analysed in Philippe Leurquin, *Le Niveau de vie des populations rurales du Ruanda-Urundi* (Louvain, 1960).

15. PORTUGUESE-SPEAKING AFRICA

On the Portuguese side, all administrative archives in Lisbon remained closed to inspection for the whole period under review, and what may be regarded as primary official sources are largely limited to the publications of such bodies as the Instituto Nacional de Estatistica and the Junta de Investigações do Ultramar, some of which are usefully factual but others not. Angola is generally better off than its companion territories in this respect as in others, thanks not least (for the most recent years) to the publications of the Missão de Inquéritos Agricolos at Luanda under the leadership of E. Cruz de Carvalho and J. Vieira da Silva; among these, attention may be drawn to an investigation into rural education conducted by F.-W. Heimer, *Educação e sociedade nas areas ruráis de Angola* (Luanda, 1972). On the other hand, there is a very large quantity of Portuguese books and ephemera, though of greatly varying interest. Some of these are officially sponsored surveys which, if invariably careful to offer no criticism, still contain valuable information. Among these may be mentioned a series of volumes sponsored by the Agencia Geral do Ultramar, and compiled for the most part by H. Galvão and C. Selvagem, *Império ultramarino português*; for instance, *Angola*, vol. III (Lisbon, 1952), and *Moçambique* (with India etc.), vol. IV (1953). The census returns of 1940 and 1950 are usefully considered by A. Moreira, *As élites das províncias portuguesas de indígenato* (*Guiné, Angola, Moçambique*) (Lisbon, 1956). Useful commentaries will also be found in C. F. Spence, *Moçambique* (London, 1963). Many memoirs, commentaries and controversies were also written or written about. A guide to much of all this is in two good bibliographies: G. J. Bender *et al.*, *Portugal in Africa* (Los Angeles, 1972), a catalogue of the extensive collection of Portuguese colonial materials assembled in the library of the University of California at Los Angeles; and G. J. Bender and A. Isaacman, 'The changing historiography of Angola and Mozambique', in C. Fyfe (ed.), *African studies since 1945* (London, 1976), a survey and listing of principal works.

Aside from the constitutional texts of the Estado Novo and from Salazar's rare but interesting speeches on African questions (see, for instance, a speech to the National Assembly of 30 Nov. 1960, which I myself have managed to read only in a Spanish

version: *Portugal y la campaña anticolonialista* (Santiago, Chile)),
several commentaries on the regime's theory and practice may be
singled out as being of especial value. One such is J. M. da Silva
Cunha, *O sistema português de politica indígena* (Coimbra, 1953),
where this veteran of the Estado Novo discusses the gap between
intentions and achievements; another, notable for its lapidary
identification of the regime's objectives, is M. Caetano, *Os nativos
na economia Africana* (Coimbra, 1954). These are representative of
a small group of authoritative texts produced for no propagandist
purpose, and may be compared with statements made *urbi et orbi*,
all merely polemical, such as A. Moreira, *Portugal's stand in Africa*
(New York, 1962), and F. Nogueira, *The United Nations and
Portugal* (London, 1963), or *The Third World* (London, 1967).

Against these may be set a number of critical studies from
within the regime or its dissident periphery, notably the writings
of H. Galvão in 1947 and after. This author's excoriating internal
report to a closed session of the National Assembly, made in 1947
while he was still inspector-general of colonies but moving into
strong dissidence, was published clandestinely in Portugal and
reproduced in part in English in B. Davidson, *The African
awakening* (London, 1955), and *in extenso* by Galvão himself in his
Santa Maria (London, 1961). Worth reading in the same context
is a memoir by the veteran Norton de Matos, written at the age
of 86 from a position generally critical of the Estado Novo's
policies: *Africa nossa* (Lisbon, 1953). Among immediate post-coup
studies, outstanding is E. de Sousa Ferreira, *Aspectos do colonialismo
Português* (Lisbon, 1974).

Compared with studies of Angola or Mozambique, Guiné,
Cape Verde and São Tomé fare poorly throughout the period. For
Guiné there is A. Teixeira da Mota, *Guiné Portuguesa*, 2 vols.
(Lisbon, 1954); but this should be compared with the ecological
survey of the later nationalist leader, Amílcar Cabral, while still
in Portuguese government employment, in *Boletim cultural da
Guiné Portuguesa* (Bissau, 1954–6), and reproduced in part in
A. Cabral (ed. M. de Andrade), *Unité et lutte*, vol. I (Paris, 1975).
Da Mota's book has a bibliography listing 387 titles. Cape
Verdean sources are notably defective, but something may be got
from A. Mendes Correia, *Ultramar Português*, vol. II (Lisbon,
1954), and a little from H. de Oliveira, *Cabo Verde: Quinto ano de
seca* (Lisbon, 1973), while the works of A. Carreira, writing

between 1966 and 1977, are continuously useful. Notable among the last is his *Migrações nas Ilhas de Cabo Verde* (Lisbon, 1977) which, apart from useful historical notes on the period here in question, offers the first serious published analysis of Cape Verdean emigration and its various motives; usefully, this book is also available in English. A first general bibliography of Guinea-Bissau and Cape Verde, incomplete but valuable, is J. M. McCarthy: *Guinea-Bissau and Cape Verde Islands: a comprehensive bibliography* (New York and London, 1977). São Tomé is the subject of a pioneering geographical and sociological survey by F. Tenreiro, *A Ilha de São Tomé* (Lisbon, 1961).

Among overall social studies for all territories, generally useful for its statistics and analyses, is E. de Sousa Ferreira on the cultural and educational aspects of the system, *Portuguese colonialism in Africa* (UNESCO, 1974). Cultural and economic issues are also discussed helpfully in some of the chapters in D. M. Abshire and M. A. Samuels (eds.), *Portuguese Africa: a handbook* (London, 1969); and, for Angola, see also W. Marques, *Problemas do desenvolvimento de Angola*, 2 vols. (Lisbon, 1965). A general historical survey of Angola in this period, strong on the Portuguese side but weak on the African, is in parts of D. L. Wheeler and R. Pelissier, *Angola* (London, 1971). This may be contrasted with a history written from the African side, *História de Angola* (Porto, 1974), and with B. Davidson, *In the eye of the storm: Angola's people* (London, 1972). The PAIGC has also produced a history from the nationalist side: *História: a Guiné e as Ilhas de Cabo Verde* (Bissau, UNESCO, 1974).

Generally, for the period of the liberation wars, the Portuguese bibliography dries to a trickle of descriptive or defensive works. The most useful among these, for Angola, is H. E. Felgas, *Guerra em Angola* (Lisbon, 1961), to which may be added journalistic reportages such as P. da Costa, *Um mês de terrorismo* (Lisbon, 1969). Of continuing value for these years is the long series of reports made by the relevant special committee to the General Assembly of the United Nations, covering all territories with detail from all available sources; while the research and records section of the UN Department of Political Affairs also published a valuable series of summaries of major developments, and these, though made for internal use, may no doubt be now generally available for study. To these should be added a book written by Salazar's exiled successor, M. Caetano, *Depoimento* (Rio and São Paulo, 1974), and General Spinola's revealing interview with A. J. Venter in the latter's *Portugal's war in Guiné-Bissau* (Pasadena, 1973). A notable study of the regime's military and administrative effort in wartime Angola, with an extensive bibliography, is G. J. Bender, *Angola under the Portuguese: the myth and the reality* (London, 1978).

For the period of the wars on the African side, by contrast, the bibliography of primary sources in ephemera, movement documents, and published (or unpublished) writings by nationalist leaders, is comparatively copious, while from 1966 onward there is a wide range of books, articles and papers by many foreign observers. As to the ephemera, a partial but useful collection is housed by the University of London, while a large collection going up to 1965 is at the Hoover Institute at Stanford; the latter is catalogued in R. H. Chilcote, *Emerging nationalism in Portuguese Africa* (Stanford, 1969), while the same author, in another publication under the same title (Stanford, 1972), has reproduced some of the more important documents in this collection. Essential writings by Amílcar Cabral are in his *Unité et lutte*, while a few of such writings appeared in A. Cabral, *Revolution in Guinea* (London, 1969), and about two-thirds, including most of the important items, in *Unity and struggle* (tr. M. Wolfers, London, 1979); by Eduardo Mondlane in his *The struggle for Mozambique* (London, 1969); by Samora Machel in a booklet, *Mozambique: sowing the seeds of revolution* (London, 1974); while, for Angola, see *Documentos da independência* (Department of Information, Luanda, 1975). Agostinho Neto's programmatic and other statements had yet to be collected, but see, for a small collection covering 1967–73, A. Neto, *Pensamento político* (Luanda, 1976). These sources are indispensable to an understanding of the development of nationalist theory and practice. For the period after independence, nationalist newspapers such as *Vitória Certa* and *Jornal de Angola* (Luanda), *Nô Pintcha* (Bissau), and *Tempo* (Maputo) have much valuble material, while *Nô Pintcha* has also published a very long run of extracts from Cabral's writings, some of them for the first time. By 1980, the whole bibliography was in rapid expansion.

External studies of the nationalist movements, often with the reproduction of interviews and documents, include: for Guinea, G. Chaliand, *Lutte armée en Afrique* (Paris, 1967; *Armed struggle in Africa*, New York, 1969); B. Davidson, *The liberation of Guiné*, with a foreword by Amílcar Cabral (London, 1969); R. Ledda, *Una rivoluzione Africana* (Bari, 1970); and L. Rudebeck, *Guinea-Bissau* (Uppsala, 1974). For Angola: R. Davezies, *La Guerre en Angola* (Bordeaux, 1968); J. Marcum, *The Angolan revolution, I: The anatomy of an explosion 1950–62* (Cambridge, Mass., 1969) and B. Davidson, *In the eye of the storm*. For Mozambique: L. Passerini (ed.), *Colonialismo Portoghese e lotta di liberazione nel Mozambico* (Turin, 1970; chiefly documents); B. Davidson, 'La Guerrilla africaine', in *Le Monde Diplomatique* (Paris, Nov. 1968); J. S. Saul, 'FRELIMO and the Mozambique Revolution', in G. Arrighi and J. S. Saul, *Essays on the political economy of Africa* (New York, 1973); S. Corrêa and E. Homem, *Moçambique: primieras machambas* (Rio de Janeiro, 1977); B. Munslow, 'The liberation struggle in Mozambique and the origins of post-independence policy', in University of Edinburgh (ed.), collected conference papers, *Mozambique*, Edinburgh, 1979; and the same author, *Mozambique: the revolution and its origins* (London, 1983).

Although merely introductory save in respect of basic nationalist writings, this brief list will at least serve to point the reader in useful directions, beyond which individual bibliographies in many of the studies cited, as well as the more general bibliographies mentioned above, will indicate the further scope of materials available by the early 1980s.

EQUATORIAL GUINEA

The historical sketch of this territory is based chiefly on A. de Unzueta y Yoste, *Guinea continental española* (Madrid, 1944), and *Islas del Golfo de Guinea* (Madrid, 1945); L. B. Corella, *Manuales del Africa española* (Madrid, 1950); documentation supplied for the purposes of the General Assembly (e.g. A/5078/Add. 3 of 26 March 1962); Documentation Française, *Notes et études documentaires, les territoires espagnols d'Afrique* (Paris, 1963); and R. Pelissier, 'La Guinée espagñole', in *Revue Française de Science Politique*, Paris, Sept. 1963, vol. 13, 3; as well as on a variety of ephemera. Information from the nationalist side is scanty, above all for the years after 1970, while Spanish official archives have not been inspected.

BIBLIOGRAPHY

I. THE SECOND WORLD WAR: PRELUDE TO DECOLONISATION
IN AFRICA

Ajayi, J. F. A. and Crowder, M. eds. *History of West Africa*, vol. II. London, 1974.

von Albertini, R. *Decolonisation: the administration and future of the colonies, 1919–1960.* New York, 1971. Originally published in 1966, as *Dekolonisation: die Diskussion über Verwaltung und Zukunft der Kolonien, 1919–1960.* Cologne.

Amon d'Aby, F. J. *La Côte d'Ivoire dans la cité africaine.* Paris, 1951.

Awolowo, Obafemi. *Path to Nigerian freedom.* London, 1947.

Azikiwe, N. *My odyssey; an autobiography.* London, 1970.

Bauer, P. T. *West African trade.* 2nd ed. London, 1963.

Berque, J. *French North Africa.* tr. Jean Stewart. London, 1967.

Brunschwig, H. *La Colonisation française.* Paris, 1948.

Cary, Joyce. *The case for African freedom and other writings.* London, 1944.

Coquéry-Vidrovitch, C. 'La Mise en dépendance de l'Afrique noire: essai de périodisation, 1880–1970', *Cahiers d'études africaines,* 1976, **16**.

Crowder, M. *West Africa under colonial rule.* London, 1968.
'The 1939–45 war and West Africa', in Ajayi, J. F. A. and Crowder, M. eds. *History of West Africa,* vol. II. London, 1974, 596–621.
'Vichy and Free France in West Africa during the Second World War', in Crowder, M. *Colonial West Africa,* London, 1978.

Delavignette, R. *Freedom and authority in French West Africa.* Oxford, 1950.

Fage, J. D. *A history of Africa.* London, 1978.

Fieldhouse, D. K. *Colonialism 1870–1945: an introduction.* London, 1981.

Frankel, S. H. *Capital investment in Africa.* London, 1938.

Ganiage, J. 'L'Afrique du nord', in Ganiage, J., Deschamps, H. and Guitard, O. *L'Afrique au XXᵉ siècle.* Paris, 1966.

Gann, L. H. and Duignan, P. eds. *Colonialism in Africa 1870–1960*: vol. II. The history and politics of colonialism 1914–1960. Cambridge, 1970.

Grimal, H. *Decolonization: the British, French, Dutch and Belgian empires, 1919–1963.* London, 1977. Originally published in 1965 as *La décolonisation.*

Guèye, L. *Itinéraire africaine.* Paris, 1966.

Gutkind, P. C. W. and Wallerstein, I. eds. *The political economy of contemporary Africa.* Beverly Hills and London, 1976.

Hailey, Lord. *An African survey.* London, 1957.
The future of colonial peoples. London, 1943.
Native administration in the British African territories, 4 vols. London, 1951.

Hargreaves, J. D. *The end of colonial rule in West Africa.* London, 1978.
Haywood, A. and Clarke, F. A. S. *The history of the Royal West African Frontier Force.* Aldershot, 1964.
Hinden, R. ed. *Fabian colonial essays.* London, 1945.
Hopkins, A. G. *An economic history of West Africa.* London, 1973.
Iliffe, J. *A modern history of Tanganyika.* Cambridge, 1979.
Joseph, R. A. *Radical nationalism in Cameroon: Social origins of the UPC rebellion.* Oxford, 1977.
Killingray, D. 'Military and labour recruitment in the Gold Coast during the Second World War', *Journal of African History*, 1982, **23**, 83–95.
Kirk-Greene, A. H. M. ed. *Africa in the colonial period: the transfer of power – the colonial administrator in the age of decolonisation.* Oxford, 1979.
Knapp, W. ed. *A survey of North-West Africa*, 3rd ed. Oxford, 1977.
Lee, J. M. '"Forward thinking" and War: the Colonial Office during the 1940s', *Journal of Imperial and Commonwealth History*, Oct. 1977, **6**.
Leith-Ross, S. *Stepping-stones: memoirs of colonial Nigeria 1907–1960.* London, 1983.
Louis, W. R. *Imperialism at bay 1941–1945: the United States and the decolonisation of the British Empire.* Oxford, 1977.
Low, D. A. and Smith, A. eds. *History of East Africa*, vol. III, Oxford, 1976.
Marshall, D. B. 'Free France in Africa: Gaullism and colonialism', in Gifford, P. and Louis, W. R. eds. *France and Britain in Africa: imperial rivalry and colonial rule.* New Haven and London, 1971.
Morris-Jones, W. H. and Fischer, G. eds. *Decolonisation and after: the British and French experience.* London, 1980.
Morrison, D. G., Mitchell, R. C., Paden, J. N. and Morrison, H. M. *Black Africa: a comparative handbook.* New York, 1972.
Oliver, R. and Atmore, A. *Africa since 1800.* 3rd ed. Cambridge, 1981.
Olusanya, G. O. *The Second World War and politics in Nigeria 1939–1953.* Lagos and London, 1973.
Padmore, G. ed. *The history of the Pan-African Congress.* 2nd ed. London, 1963.
Pearce, R. D. *The turning point in Africa: British colonial policy 1938–1948.* London, 1982.
Perham, M. *Colonial sequence 1930–1949.* London, 1967.
    The colonial reckoning: the end of imperial rule in Africa in the light of the British experience. London, 1961.
Rennell of Rodd, Lord. *British military administration of occupied territories in Africa, 1941–47.* London, 1948.
Robinson, R. 'Conclusion', in Kirk-Greene, A. H. M. ed. *Africa in the colonial period: the transfer of power – the colonial administrator in the age of decolonisation.* Oxford, 1979.
    'Andrew Cohen and the transfer of power in Tropical Africa, 1940–1951', in Morris-Jones, W. H. and Fischer, G. eds. *Decolonisation and after: the British and French experience*, pp. 50–72. London, 1980.
Rodney, W. *World War II and the Tanzanian economy.* (Cornell African Studies Centre Monograph, III.) 1976.
Schleh, E. P. A. 'The post-war careers of ex-servicemen in Ghana and Uganda', *Journal of Modern African Studies*, 1968, **6**, 203–20.

da Silva, J. V. and de Morais, J. A. 'Ecological conditions of social change in the central highlands of Angola', in Heimer F.-W. ed. *Social change in Angola*. Munich, 1973.

Sithole, N. *African nationalism*. 2nd ed. Oxford, 1968.

Suret-Canale, J. S. *Afrique noire: occidentale et centrale: vol. II. L'ère coloniale, 1900–1945*. Paris, 1964.

Wallerstein, I. 'Three stages of African involvement in the world economy', in Gutkind, P. C. W. and Wallerstein, I. eds. *The political economy of contemporary Africa*. Beverly Hills and London, 1976.

White, J. *Central administration in Nigeria, 1914–1948*. Dublin and London, 1981.

Wight, M. *The Gold Coast Legislative Council*. London, 1947.

The development of the Legislative Council, 1906–1956. London, 1964.

Wilson, M. and Thompson, L. eds. *Oxford history of South Africa*, vol. II. Oxford, 1971.

2. DECOLONISATION AND THE PROBLEMS OF INDEPENDENCE

Abernethy, D. B. *The political dilemma of popular education*. Stanford, 1969.

Aboyade, O. *Foundations of an African economy: a study of investment and growth in Nigeria*. New York, 1966.

Abshire, D. M. and Samuels, M. A. eds. *Portuguese Africa: a handbook*. London, 1969.

Adedeji, A. ed. *The indigenisation of African economies*. London, 1981.

Adu, A. L. *The civil service in Commonwealth Africa: development and transition*. London, 1970.

Amin, S. *Trois expériences africaines de développement: le Mali, la Guinée et le Ghana*. Paris, 1965.

'Development and structural change: the African experience, 1950–1970', *Journal of International Affairs*, 1970, **24**, 2, 202–23.

Neo-colonialism in West Africa, tr. F. McDonagh. London, 1976.

Andreski, S. *The African predicament*. London, 1968.

Arrighi, G. *The political economy of Rhodesia*. The Hague, 1967.

'Labour suppliers in historical perspective: a study of the proletarianisation of the African peasantry in Rhodesia', *Journal of Development Studies*, April 1970, **3**.

Arrighi, G. and Saul, J. S. *Essays on the political economy of Africa*. New York and London, 1973.

Austin, D. *Politics in Ghana 1946–1960*. Oxford, 1964.

Austin, D. and Luckham, R. eds. *Politicians and soldiers in Ghana, 1966–1972*. London, 1975.

Banda, H. K. and Nkumbula, H. M. *Federation in Central Africa*. London, 1951.

Barkan, J. D. *An African dilemma*. London and Nairobi, 1975.

Behr, E. *The Algerian problem*. London, 1961.

Bender, G. J. *Angola under the Portuguese: the myth and the reality*. London, 1978.

Berg, E. 'The economic basis of political choice in French West Africa', *American Political Science Review*, June 1960.

Berger, M. *Bureaucracy and society in modern Egypt: a study of the higher civil service*. Princeton, 1957.

van den Berghe, P. L. *Power and privilege in an African university.* London, 1973.

Berque, J. *Egypt: imperialism and revolution.* London, 1972.

Brockway, A. F. *The colonial revolution.* London, 1975.

Brunschwig, H. *French colonialism: myths and realities.* London, 1966.

Busia, K. A. *Africa in search of democracy.* London, 1967.

Cabral, A. *Revolution in Guiné. An African people's struggle.* London, 1969.

Carter, Gwendolen M. ed. *The politics of inequality: South Africa since 1948.* 2nd ed. London, 1959.

  ed. *African one-party states.* Ithaca, 1962.

  ed. *Five African states: responses to diversity.* Ithaca, 1963.

  ed. *National unity and regionalism in eight African states.* Ithaca, 1966.

Clapham, C. *Haile-Selassie's government.* London, 1969.

  Liberia and Sierra Leone – an essay in comparative politics. Cambridge, 1976.

Clignet, R. and Foster, P. *The fortunate few.* Evanston, 1966.

Clower, R. W., Dalton, G., Harwitz, M. and Walters, A. A. *Growth without development: an economic survey of Liberia.* Evanston, 1966.

Coleman, J. S. *Nigeria: background to nationalism.* Berkeley and Los Angeles, 1958.

Coleman, J. S. & Rosberg, C. G. eds. *Political parties and national integration in tropical Africa.* Berkeley and Los Angeles, 1964.

Court, D. 'The education system as a response to inequality in Tanzania and Kenya', *Journal of Modern African Studies,* 1976, **14**, 4.

Crowder, M. *Senegal: a study in French assimilation policy.* 2nd ed. London, 1967.

Crowder, M. and Ikime, O. eds. *West African chiefs: their changing status under colonial rule and independence.* New York, 1970.

Davenport, T. R. H. *South Africa – a modern history.* 2nd ed. Johannesburg, 1978.

Davidson, B. *In the eye of the storm: Angola's people.* London, 1972.

  ed. 'Portugal in Africa', *Tarikh* **24**, London, 1980.

Dumont, R. *L'Afrique noire est mal partie.* Paris, 1962.

  Afrique noire: développement agricole: reconversion de l'économie agricole: Guinée, Côte d'Ivoire, Mali. Paris, 1962.

Dunn, J. ed. *West African states: failure and promise.* Cambridge, 1978.

Fanon, F. *The wretched of the earth.* New York, 1963.

First, R. *Libya: the elusive revolution.* Harmondsworth, 1974.

Foltz, W. J. *From French West Africa to the Mali Federation.* New Haven, 1965.

Foster, P. J. *Education and social change in Ghana.* Chicago, 1965.

Foster, P. J. and Zolberg, A. eds. *Ghana and Ivory Coast: perspectives on modernization.* Chicago, 1971.

Gardinier, D. E. *Cameroon: United Nations challenge to French policy.* London, 1963.

Gertzel, C. J. *The politics of independent Kenya.* Nairobi, 1970.

Gonidec, P. F. *L'évolution des térritoires d'outre-mer depuis 1946.* Paris, 1958.

  Constitutions des états de la communauté. Paris, 1959.

Gray, R. *The two nations: aspects of the development of race relations in Rhodesia and Nyasaland.* Westport, Conn., 1974.

Green, R. and Seidman, A. *Unity or poverty? The economics of Pan-Africanism.* Harmondsworth, 1968.

Gutkind, P. C. W. and Wallerstein, I. eds. *The political economy of contemporary Africa*. Beverly Hills and London, 1976.

Gutkind, P. C. W., Cohen, R. and Jean Copans. eds. *African labour history*. London, 1978.

Hailey, Lord. *An African survey. (revised 1956)*. London, 1957.

South Africa and the High Commission territories. London, 1965.

Hazlewood, A. ed. *African integration and disintegration: case studies in economic and political union*. London, 1967.

Economic integration: the East African experience. London, 1975.

Henriksen, T. H. 'Peoples' war in Angola, Mozambique and Guinea-Bissau', *Journal of Modern African Studies*, 1976, **14**, 3.

Hodgkin, T. L. *Nationalism in colonial Africa*. London, 1956.

African political parties: an introductory guide. Harmondsworth, 1961.

Holt, P. M. ed. *Political and social change in modern Egypt*. London, 1968.

Holt, P. M. and Daly, M. W. *The history of the Sudan, from the coming of Islam to the present day*. 3rd ed. London, 1979.

Hopkins, A. G. *An economic history of West Africa*. London, 1973.

Horne, A. *A savage war of peace: Algeria 1954–62*. London, 1977.

Hoskyns, C. *The Congo since independence, January 1960 – December 1961*. London, 1965.

Iliffe, J. *A modern history of Tanganyika*. Cambridge, 1979.

de Kadt, E. and Williams, G. eds. *Sociology and development*. London, 1974.

Kilson, M. *Political change in a West African state: a study of the modernisation process in Sierra Leone*. Cambridge, Mass., 1966.

La Palombara, J. ed. *Bureaucracy and political development*. Princeton, 1969.

Lemarchand, R. *Rwanda and Burundi*. London, 1970.

Lewis, I. M. *A modern history of Somalia*. 2nd ed., revised. London, 1980.

Leys, C. *European politics in Southern Rhodesia*. Oxford, 1959.

'Politics in Kenya: the development of peasant society', *British Journal of Political Science*, July 1971, **1**.

Underdevelopment in Kenya: the political economy of neo-colonialism. London, 1974.

Lloyd, P. C. ed. *The new élites of Tropical Africa*. Oxford, 1967.

Lonsdale, J. 'The emergence of African Nationalism: an historiographical analysis', *African Affairs*, 1968, **67**.

Low, D. A. *Lion rampant: essays in the study of British imperialism*. London, 1973.

Low, D. A. and Smith, A. eds. *History of East Africa*, vol. III. Oxford, 1976.

Luckham, R. *The Nigerian military: 1960–1967*. Cambridge, 1971.

Lumumba, P. *Congo, my country*. New York, 1963.

Mabogunje, A. *The development process*. London, 1980.

Mazrui, A. A. *On heroes and Uhuru-worship*. London, 1967.

Soldiers and kinsmen in Uganda. London, 1975.

Mboya, T. *The challenge of nationhood*. London, 1970.

Mitchell, J. Clyde. *The Kalela dance*. (Rhodes-Livingstone Paper, no. 27.) Manchester, 1956.

Mondlane, E. *The struggle for Mozambique*. London and Baltimore, 1969.

Moore, C. H. *Politics in North Africa*. Boston, 1970.

Morgan, D. J. *The official history of colonial development*, 5 vols. London, 1980.

Morgenthau, R. Schachter. *Political parties in French-speaking West Africa.* Oxford, 1964.

Mortimer, E. *France and the Africans, 1944–60.* London, 1969.

Munro, J. Forbes. *Africa and the international economy 1800–1960: an introduction to the modern economic history of Africa south of the Sahara.* London, 1976.

Nettl, P. and Robertson, R. *International systems and the modernisation of societies.* London, 1968.

Nyerere, J. K. *Freedom and unity, a selection of writings and speeches, 1952–65.* Dar es Salaam, 1967.

O'Brien, R. Cruise. *White society in Black Africa.* London, 1972.

Odinga, O. *Not yet Uhuru.* London, 1967.

Palmer, R. and Parsons, N. eds. *The roots of rural poverty in Central and Southern Africa.* London, 1977.

Panter-Brick, S. K. ed. *Nigerian politics and military rule.* London, 1970.

Perham, M. *The colonial reckoning: the end of imperial rule in Africa in the light of the British experience.* London, 1961.

Colonial sequence 1930–1949. London, 1967.

Porter, B. *The lion's share.* London, 1975.

Pratt, C. *The critical phase in Tanzania, 1945–1968: Nyerere and the emergence of a socialist strategy.* Cambridge, 1976.

Rabemananjara, J. *Nationalisme et problèmes malgaches.* Paris, 1958.

Robson, P. *Economic integration in Africa.* London, 1968.

Robson, P. and Lury, D. A. eds. *The economies of Africa.* London, 1969.

Rosberg, C. G. and Nottingham, J. *The myth of 'Mau Mau': nationalism in Kenya.* London and New York, 1966.

Rotberg, R. I. *The rise of nationalism in Central Africa: the making of Malawi and Zambia 1873–1964.* Cambridge, Mass., 1965.

Sandbrook, R. & Cohen, R. eds. *The development of an African working class.* London, 1975.

Shivji, I. G. *Class struggles in Tanzania.* Dar es Salaam, 1975.

Smock, R. and Bentsi-Enchill, K. eds. *The search for national integration in Africa.* New York, 1976.

Thompson, V. and Adloff, R. *The emerging states of French equatorial Africa.* Stanford, 1960.

Thornton, A. P. *The imperial idea and its enemies.* London, 1968.

Tinbergen, J. (co-ordinator). *Re-shaping the international order.* London, 1977.

Traoré, B., Lô, M. and Alibert, J. L. *Forces politiques en Afrique noire.* Paris, 1966.

Walshe, P. *The rise of African nationalism in South Africa.* Berkeley, 1978.

Welch, C. E. *Dream of unity: Pan-Africanism and political unification in West Africa.* Ithaca, 1966.

Welch, C. E. Jr. and Smith, A. K. *Military role and rule.* Belmont, Cal., 1974.

Young, C. *Politics in the Congo: decolonisation and independence.* Princeton, 1965.

Zolberg, A. *Creating political order: the party-states of West Africa.* Chicago, 1966.

'The structure of political conflict in the new states of Africa', *American Political Science Review*, 1968, **62**.

One-party government in the Ivory Coast. 2nd ed. Princeton, 1969.

3. PAN-AFRICANISM SINCE 1940

Ajala, A. *Pan-Africanism, evolution, progress and prospects.* London, 1973.

American Society of African Culture. *Pan-Africanism reconsidered.* Berkeley, Cal., 1962.

Andemicael, B. *The OAU and the UN. Relations between the Organization of African Unity and the United Nations.* New York, 1976.

Asante, S. K. B. 'Kwame Nkrumah and Pan-Africanism: the early phase, 1945–1961', *Universitas*, 1973, **3**, 1, 36–49.

'The Afro-American and the Italo-Ethiopian crisis, 1934–1936', *Race*, 1973, **15**, 2, 167–84.

'The impact of the Italo-Ethiopian crisis of 1935–36 on the Pan-African movement in Britain', *Transactions of the Historical Society of Ghana*, 1974, **13** 2, 217–27.

Pan-African protest; West Africa and the Italo-Ethiopian crisis, 1934–1941. London, 1977.

Azikiwe, N. *Nigeria in world politics.* London, 1959.

The future of Pan-Africanism. London, 1961.

Renascent Africa. 2nd ed. London, 1966.

My odyssey: an autobiography. London, 1970.

Baraka, I. A. ed. *African Congress: a documentary of the first modern Pan-African Congress.* New York, 1972.

Boutros-Ghali, B. *L'Organisation de l'Unité Africaine.* Paris, 1969.

Broderick, F. L. *W. E. B. DuBois: a Negro leader in a time of crisis.* Stanford, 1959.

Cabral, A. *Revolution in Guiné. An African people's struggle.* London, 1969.

'The role of culture in the liberation struggle'. Speech by Amílcar Cabral to a UNESCO Conference in Paris, July 3–7, 1972. Repr. in *Guinea-Bissau: toward final victory. Selected speeches and documents from PAIGC.* Richmond, BC, 1974.

Červenka, Z. *The Organisation of African Unity and its Charter.* 2nd ed. London, 1969.

The unfinished quest for unity. Africa and the OAU. London, 1977.

Césaire, Aimé. *Discourse on colonialism*, tr. Joan Pinkham. New York, 1972.

Clarke, J. H. ed., with the assistance of Garvey, A. J. *Marcus Garvey and the vision of Africa.* New York, 1974.

Cox, R. *Pan-Africanism in practice – an East African study, PAFMECSA, 1958–64.* London, 1964.

Davidson, B. *Which way Africa?* London, 1967.

The liberation of Guiné: aspects of an African revolution. London and Baltimore, 1969.

In the eye of the storm: Angola's people. London, 1972.

Black star. A view of the life and times of Kwame Nkrumah. London, 1973.

Davidson, B., Slovo, J. and Wilkinson, A. R. *Southern Africa: the new politics of revolution.* London, 1976.

Davis, J. A. *Africa seen by American Negroes.* Paris, 1958.

Decraene, P. *Le Panafricanisme.* Paris, 1959.

DuBois, W. E. B. 'The African roots of the war', *Atlantic Monthly*, May 1915, 707–14.

The Negro. New York, 1915.

Black folk then and now: an essay in the history and sociology of the Negro race. New York, 1939.

Dusk of dawn: an essay towards an autobiography of a race concept. New York, 1940.

The world and Africa: an inquiry into the part which Africa has played in world history. New York, 1947.

Duffield, I. 'The business activities of Dusé Mohammed Ali: an example of the economic dimension of Pan-Africanism, 1912–1945', *Journal of the Historical Society of Nigeria*, 1969, **4**, 4.

'Pan-Africanism, rational and irrational', *Journal of African History*, 1977, **18**, 4, 597–620.

Dunbar, E. ed. *The black expatriates*. London, 1968.

El-Ayouty, Y. ed. *The Organization of African Unity after ten years*. New York, 1975.

Fanon, F. *Toward the African revolution*. tr. H. Chevalier. New York, 1967; London, 1980.

The wretched of the earth. 2nd English ed. London, 1967.

Black skin, white masks, tr. Charles Lam Markmann. London, 1970.

Foltz, W. J. *From French West Africa to the Mali Federation*. New Haven, 1965.

Garigue, P. 'The West African Students' Union', *Africa*, Jan. 1953, **23**, 55–69.

Garvey, M., with introductory essay by Hill, R. A. *The Black Man. A monthly magazine of Negro thought and opinion*.

Geiss, I. *The Pan-African movement*. London, 1974.

Green, R. H. and Seidman, Ann. *Unity or poverty? The economics of Pan-Africanism*. Harmondsworth, 1968.

Hill, A. C. and Kilson, M. *Apropos of Africa. Sentiments of American Negro leaders on Africa from the 1800s to the 1950s*. London, 1969.

Hooker, J. R. *Black revolutionary: George Padmore's path from Communism to Pan-Africanism*. London, 1967.

Horton, J. A. B. *West African countries and peoples*. 2nd ed. Edinburgh, 1969.

Hughes, A. J. *East Africa: the search for unity*. London, 1963.

Hymans, J. L. *Léopold Sédar Senghor. An intellectual biography*. Edinburgh, 1971.

Isaacs, H. R. *The new world of Negro Americans: the impact of world affairs on the race problem in the United States and particularly on the Negro, his view of himself, his country, and of America*. New York, 1964.

The Keys. The official organ of the League of Coloured Peoples, with introductory essay by Roderick J. Macdonald. Millwood, N.Y., 1976.

Kisogie, B. 'Report from Dar. State exhibitionists and ideological glamour', *Transition*, 1974, **9**, 47, 6–12.

Langley, J. A. *Pan-Africanism and nationalism in West Africa, 1900–1945*. Oxford, 1973.

Legum, Colin. *Pan-Africanism. A short political guide*. London, 1962.

Legum, Colin and Hodges, Tony. *After Angola. The war over Southern Africa*. London, 1976.

Macdonald, R. J. 'Dr Harold Arundel Moody and the League of Coloured Peoples, 1931–1947: a retrospective view', *Race*, **14**, 3, 1973.
Makonnen, Ras, recorded and ed. King, K. *Pan-Africanism from within.* Nairobi, 1973.
Markovitz, I. L. *Léopold Sédar Senghor and the politics of négritude.* London and New York, 1969.
Mazrui, A. A. 'Nkrumah: the Leninist Czar', *Transition*, 1966, **3**, 26, 9–17.
Towards a Pax Africana. A study of ideology and ambition. London, 1967.
Mboya, Tom. *Freedom and after.* London, 1963.
A development strategy for Africa. Ministry of Economic Planning and Development, Kenya, 1967.
The challenge of nationhood. London, 1970.
Mezu, S. O. *Léopold Sédar Senghor et la défense et illustration de la civilisation noire.* Paris, 1968.
Mondlane, E. *The struggle for Mozambique.* London and Baltimore, 1969.
Moore, R. 'Africa conscious Harlem', in Clarke, J. H. ed. *Harlem, a community in transition.* New York, 1964.
Mphahlele, E. 'Remarks on négritude', in Mphahlele, Ezekiel, ed. *African writing today.* London, 1967.
Voices in the whirlwind, and other essays. New York, 1972.
The African image. 2nd revised ed. London, 1974.
Murray-Brown, J. *Kenyatta.* London, 1972.
Nasir, G. A. *The philosophy of the revolution.* Cairo, 1954.
Egypt's liberation. Washington, 1955.
Nkrumah, Kwame. *The autobiography of Kwame Nkrumah.* London, 1957.
I speak of freedom. A statement of African ideology. London, 1961.
Towards colonial freedom: Africa in the struggle against world imperialism. London, 1962.
Africa must unite. London, 1963.
Neo-colonialism: the last stage of imperialism. London, 1965.
Nye, J. S. Jr. *Pan-Africanism and East African integration.* Cambridge, Mass., 1966.
Nyerere, Julius K. *Freedom and unity: a selection of writings and speeches, 1952–65.* Dar es Salaam, 1967.
Freedom and socialism. A selection from writings and speeches 1965–1967. Dar es Salaam, 1968.
Freedom and development. Dar es Salaam, 1973.
We are brothers in a common struggle: President Nyerere to the Mozambican people. Empresa Moderna, SARL, 1975.
Padmore, George. *The Gold Coast revolution. The struggle of an African people from slavery to freedom.* London, 1953.
The life and struggles of Negro toilers. London, 1956.
Pan-Africanism or Communism? The coming struggle for Africa. London, 1956.
ed. *The history of the Pan-African Congress*, 2nd ed. London, 1963.
Pan-Africa. A Journal of African Life, History and Thought, ed. Ras Makonnen. Manchester, 1947–8.
Présence Africaine, Paris, 1947.

Seale, B. *Seize the time. The story of the Black Panther Party.* 3rd ed. London, 1970.

Senghor, Léopold S. *Liberté I: Négritude et humanisme.* Paris, 1964.

Shepperson, G. 'Notes on Negro American influences on the emergence of African nationalism', *Journal of African History*, 1960, **1**, 2, 299–312.

'The Afro-American contribution to African studies', *Journal of American Studies*, 1975, **8**, 3, 281–301.

Soyinka, W. *Myth, literature and the African world.* Cambridge, 1976.

Spitzer, L. and Denzer, L. 'I. T. A. Wallace-Johnson and the West African Youth League', *International Journal of African Historical Studies*, 1973, **6**, 3, 413–51; **6**, 4, 565–601.

Tanzania Publishing House. *Resolutions and selected speeches from the Sixth Pan-African Congress.* Dar es Salaam, 1976.

Tevoedjre, A. *Pan-Africanism in action: an account of the UAM.* Cambridge, Mass., 1965.

Thiam, D. *The foreign policy of African states.* London, 1965.

Thompson, V. B. *West Africa's Council of the Entente.* Ithaca, 1972.

Africa and unity: the evolution of Pan-Africanism. London, 1969.

Thompson, W. S. *Ghana's foreign policy, 1957–1966.* Princeton, 1969.

Vaughan, D. *Negro victory. The life story of Dr Harold Moody.* London, 1950.

Wallerstein, I. *Africa: the politics of independence.* New York, 1961.

Africa, the politics of unity. An analysis of a contemporary social movement. London, 1968.

Weisbord, R. G. 'The British West Indian reaction to the Italo-Ethiopian war: an episode in Pan-Africanism', *Caribbean Studies*, 1970, **10**, 1, 34–41.

Ebony kinship: Africa, Africans and the Afro-American. Westport, Conn., 1973.

Welch, C. E. *Dream of unity: Pan-Africanism and political unification in West Africa.* Ithaca, 1966.

Wolfers, M. *Politics in the Organisation of African Unity.* London, 1976.

Woronoff, J. *Organising African unity.* Metuchen, NJ, 1970.

Wright, R. *Black Power. A record of reactions in a land of pathos.* New York, 1954.

X, Malcolm, assisted by Hailey, A. *The autobiography of Malcolm X.* London, 1976.

Zartman, I. W. *International relations in the new Africa.* Englewood Cliffs, NJ, 1966.

The politics of trade negotiations between Africa and the European Economic Community: the weak confront the strong. Princeton, 1971.

4. SOCIAL AND CULTURAL CHANGE

Abernethy, D. B. *The political dilemma of popular education.* Stanford, 1969.

Achebe, C. *A man of the people.* London, 1966.

Ajayi, J. F. A. and Crowder, M. eds. *History of West Africa*, vol. II. London, 1974.

Akeredolu-Ale, E. O. 'Socio-historical study of development of entrepreneurship among the Ijebu', *African Studies Review*, 1973, **16**.

Amin, S. ed. *Modern migrations in Western Africa.* London, 1974.

Apter, D. E. *Ghana in transition*. Princeton, 1955.
The political kingdom in Uganda: a study of bureaucratic nationalism. 2nd ed. Princeton, 1967.
The politics of modernization. Chicago, 1965.
Aronson, D. R. 'Ijebu Yoruba urban-rural relationships and class-formation', *Canadian Journal of African Studies*, 1971, **5**, 263–79.
Arrighi, G. 'International corporations, labor aristocracies and economic development in tropical Africa', in Arrighi G. and Saul, J. S. *Essays on the political economy of Africa*. New York and London, 1973.
Arrighi, G. and Saul, J. S. 'Socialism and development in tropical Africa', *Journal of Modern African Studies*, 1968, **6**, 141–69.
Austin, D. *Politics in Ghana 1946–1960*. Oxford, 1964.
Austin, D. and Luckham, R. eds. *Politicians and soldiers in Ghana 1966–1972*. London, 1975.
Baëta, C. G. ed. *Christianity in tropical Africa*. Oxford, 1965.
Balandier, G. 'La Situation coloniale: approche théorique', *Cahiers Internationaux de Sociologie*, 1951, **11**, 44.
Sociologie actuelle de l'Afrique noire. Paris, 1955.
Sociologie des Brazzavilles noires. Paris, 1955.
'Problématique des classes sociales en Afrique noire', *Cahiers Internationaux de Sociologie*, 1965, **38**.
Banton, M. 'Social alignment and identity in a West African city', in Kuper, H. ed. *Urbanization and migration in West Africa*. Berkeley, 1965.
Barrett, D. B. *Schism and renewal in Africa*. Nairobi, 1968.
Barrett, S. R. 'Model construction and modernisation in Nigeria', *Sociological Review*, 1969, **17**, 251–66.
Barth, F. *Ethnic groups and boundaries: the social organization of culture difference*. Bergen–Oslo, 1969.
Bascom, W. R. and Herskovits, M. J. eds. *Continuity and change in African cultures*. Chicago, 1959.
Beer, C. E. F. and Williams, G. 'Politics of the Ibadan peasantry', *African Review* 1975, **5**, 235–56.
Berg, E. J. 'The economics of the migrant labor system', in Kuper, H. ed. *Urbanization and migration in West Africa*. Berkeley, 1965.
Berg, E. J. and Butler, J. 'Trade unions', in Coleman, J. S. and Rosberg, C. G. *Political parties and national integration in tropical Africa*. Berkeley, 1964.
van den Berghe, P. L. ed. *Africa: social problems of change and conflict*. San Francisco, 1965.
Power and privilege in an African university. London, 1973.
Berque, J. 'L'idée des classes dans l'histoire contemporaine des Arabes', *Cahiers Internationaux de Sociologie*, 1965, **28**.
'Tradition and innovation in the Maghrib', *Daedalus*, Winter 1973.
Berry, S. S. *Cocoa, custom and socio-economic change in rural Western Nigeria*. Oxford, 1975.
Biebuyck, D. 'Introduction' to *African agrarian systems*. London, 1963.
Bienen, H. *Tanzania: party transformation and economic development*. Princeton, 1970.

Blair, D. S. *Post-independence literature in French.* Cambridge, 1976.

Brandel-Syrier, M. *Reeftown élite.* London, 1971.

Breese, G. ed. *The city in newly developing countries.* Englewood Cliffs, 1969.

Caldwell, J. C. *African rural–urban migration.* Canberra, 1969.

Charsley, S. R. 'The formation of ethnic groups', in Cohen A. ed. *Urban ethnicity.* London, 1974.

Cliffe, L. 'The policy of *Ujamaa Vijijini* and the class struggle in Tanzania', in Cliffe, L. and Saul, J. S. eds. *Socialism in Tanzania.* Nairobi, 1972.

Clignet, R. and Foster, P. 'Potential élites in Ghana and the Ivory Coast', *American Journal of Sociology,* 1964, **70**, 349–62.

The fortunate few. Evanston, 1966.

Cohen, A. 'Politics of the Kola trade', *Africa,* 1960, **36**, 18–36.

Custom and politics in urban Africa. Manchester, 1969.

'Cultural strategies in the organization of trading diasporas', in Meillasoux, C. ed. *Development of indigenous trade and markets in West Africa.* London, 1971, 266–81.

ed. *Urban ethnicity.* London, 1974.

Cohen, R. *Labour and politics in Nigeria 1945–1971.* London, 1974.

Coleman, J. S. *Nigeria: background to nationalism.* Berkeley and Los Angeles, 1958.

Coleman, J. S. and Rosberg, C. G. eds. *Political parties and national integration in tropical Africa.* Berkeley, 1964.

Colonna, Fanny. 'Le système d'enseignement de l'Algérie coloniale', *Archives Européennes de Sociologie,* 1972, **13**, 195–222.

Colson, Elizabeth. 'The impact of the colonial period on the definition of land rights', in Turner, V. W. ed. *Profiles of change: African society and colonial rule (Colonialism in Africa,* vol. III). Cambridge, 1971.

Deniel, R. *Croyances religieuses et vie quotidienne à Ouagadougou.* Études Voltaïques, 1970.

Derman, W. *Serfs, peasants and socialists: a former serf village in the Republic of Guinea.* Berkeley, 1973.

Dore, R. P. *The diploma disease.* London, 1976.

Dunn, J. and Robertson, A. F. *Dependence and opportunity: political change in Ahafo.* Cambridge, 1973.

Dupire, M. *Planteurs autochthones et étrangers en basse Côte d'Ivoire* (Études Éburnéennes, **8**). Abidjan, 1960.

Duvignaud, J. 'Classe et conscience de classe dans un pays du Maghreb: la Tunisie', *Cahiers Internationaux de Sociologie,* 1965, 185–200.

Epstein, A. L. *Politics in an urban African community.* Manchester, 1958.

Fallers, L. A. 'Are African cultivators to be called "peasants"?' *Current Anthropology,* 1961, **2**, 108–10.

Inequality: social stratification reconsidered. Chicago, 1973.

Fantoure, A. *Le Cercle des tropiques.* Paris, 1973.

Fashole-Luke, E., Gray, J. R., Hastings, A. and Tasie, G. eds. *Christianity in independent Africa.* London, 1978.

Feldman, D. 'The economics of ideology: some problems of achieving rural socialism in Tanzania', in Leys, C. T. ed. *Politics and change in developing countries.* Cambridge, 1969, 85–111.

Forde, D. ed. *Social consequences of urbanization and industrialization in Africa south of the Sahara*. Paris, 1956.

Foster, P. J. *Education and social change in Ghana*. Chicago, 1965.
'Education and social differentiation in Africa'. *Journal of Modern African Studies*, 1980, **18**.

Fraenkel, M. *Tribe and class in Monrovia*. Oxford, 1964.

Freyhold, M. von. *Ujamaa villages in Tanzania*. London, 1979.

Garlick, P. C. *African traders and economic development in Ghana*. London, 1971.

Geertz, C. *The interpretation of culture*. New York, 1973.

Gellner, E. and Micaud, C. eds. *Arabs and Berbers*. London, 1973.

Gluckman, M. *Politics, law and ritual in tribal societies*. Oxford, 1965.

Goddard, A. D. 'Population movements and land shortage in the Sokoto close-settled zone', in Amin, S. *Modern migrations in western Africa*. London, 1974.

Goody, J. *Production and reproduction*. Cambridge, 1977.

Grillo, R. D. 'The tribal factor in an East African trade union', in Gulliver, P. H. ed. *Tradition and transition in East Africa*. London, 1969.

Gulliver, P. H. ed. *Tradition and transition in East Africa*. London, 1969.

Gutkind, P. C. W. 'The view from below: political consciousness of the urban poor in Ibadan', *Cahiers d'Études Africaines*, 1974, **15**, 5–35.

Hance, W. A. *Population, migration and urbanization in Africa*. New York, 1970.

Hanna, J. L. and Hanna, W. J. *Urban dynamics in Black Africa*. Chicago, 1971.

Halpern, M. 'Egypt and the new middle class: reaffirmations and new explorations', *Comparative Studies in Society and History*, 1969, **11**, 97–108.

Harrell-Bond, B. E. *Modern marriage in Sierra Leone: a study of the professional group*. The Hague, 1974.

Heisler, H. *Urbanisation and the government of migration*. London, 1974.

Hermassi, E. 'Political traditions of the Maghrib', *Daedalus*, Winter 1973, 207–24.

Herskovits, M. J. and Harwitz, M. eds. *Economic transition in Africa*. London, 1964.

Hill, Polly. *Studies in rural capitalism in West Africa*. Cambridge, 1970.
Rural Hausa: a village and a setting. Cambridge, 1972.

Hodgkin, T. *Nationalism in colonial Africa*. London, 1956.

Hopkins, N. S. *Popular government in an African town: Kita, Mali*. Chicago, 1972.

Horton, R. 'African conversion', *Africa*, 1971, **41**, 85–108.
'On the rationality of conversion', *Africa*, 1975, **45**, 219–35, 373–99.

Hunter, G. *The new societies of tropical Africa*. London, 1966, 237–71.

Kaufman, R. *Millénarisme et acculturation*. Brussels, 1964.

Kilson, M. 'Nationalism and social classes in British West Africa', *Journal of Politics*, 1958, **20**, 368–87.
Political change in a West African state: a study of the modernisation process in Sierra Leone. Cambridge, Mass., 1966.

Koll, M. *Crafts and co-operation in Western Nigeria*. Freiburg-im-Breisgau, 1969.

Kuper, H. ed. *Urbanization and migration in West Africa*. Berkeley, 1965.

Kuper, L. *A black bourgeoisie: race, class and politics in South Africa*. New Haven, 1965.

La Fontaine, J. S. 'Tribalism among the Gisu', in Gulliver, P. H. ed. *Tradition and transition in East Africa*. London, 1969.
City politics: a study of Léopoldville. Cambridge, 1970.
Lamb, G. *Peasant politics*. Lewes, 1974.
Leonard, D. K. 'Bureaucracy, class and inequality in Kenya and Tanzania'. Paper presented to the Conference on Inequality in Africa, New York, October, 1976.
Levine, D. N. *Wax and gold: tradition and innovation in Ethiopian culture*. Chicago, 1965.
LeVine, R. A. *Dreams and deeds: achievement motivation in Nigeria*. Chicago, 1966.
Lewis, I. M. *Islam in tropical Africa*. 2nd ed. Oxford, 1980.
'Nationalism and particularism in Somalia', in Gulliver, P. H. ed. *Tradition and transition in East Africa*. London, 1969.
Leys, C. *Underdevelopment in Kenya: the political economy of neo-colonialism*. London, 1974.
'The "overdeveloped" post-colonial state: a re-evaluation', *Review of African Political Economy*, 1976, 5, 39–48.
Lloyd, B. 'Education and family life in the development of class identification among the Yoruba', in Lloyd, P. C. ed. *The new élites of tropical Africa*. Oxford, 1966.
Lloyd, P. C. ed. *The new élites of tropical Africa*. Oxford, 1966.
Africa in social change. Harmondsworth, 1967.
Power and independence: urban Africans' perception of social inequality. London, 1974.
Long, N. *Social change and the individual*. Manchester, 1968.
Lonsdale, J. M. 'Some origins of nationalism in East Africa', *Journal of African History*, 1968, 9, 119–46.
Low, D. A. *Buganda in modern history*. London, 1971.
Luckham, R. *The Nigerian military: 1960–1967*. Cambridge, 1971.
McGaffey, W. *Custom and government in the lower Congo*. Berkeley, 1970.
Maguire, A. D. *Towards 'Uhuru' in Tanzania: the politics of participation*. Cambridge, 1969.
Mamdani, M. *Politics and class formation in Uganda*. London, 1976.
Marris, P. *Family and social change in an African city*. London, 1961.
Marris, P. and Somerset, A. *African businessmen*. London, 1971.
Mayer, P. *Townsmen or tribesmen*. Cape Town, 1961.
Meillassoux, C. 'Class analysis of the bureaucratic process in Mali', *Journal of Development Studies*, 1970, 6.
Melson, R. and Wolpe, H. eds. *Nigeria: the politics of communalism*. East Lansing, 1971.
Merad, A. *Le Réformisme musulman en Algérie de 1925 à 1940*. Paris, 1976.
Michel, A. 'Les classes sociales en Algérie', *Cahiers Internationaux de Sociologie*, 1965, 207–20.
Mitchell, J. Clyde. *The Kalela dance*. (Rhodes-Livingstone Paper, no. 27.) Manchester, 1956.
ed. *Social networks in urban situations*. Manchester, 1969.
'Race, class and status in South Central Africa', in Tuden, A. and Plotnicov, L. eds. *Social stratification in Africa*. New York, 1970.

'Factors in rural male absenteeism in Rhodesia', in Parkin, D. J. *Town and country in Central and Eastern Africa*. London, 1975, 93–112.

Mitchell, J. Clyde and Epstein, A. L. 'Occupational prestige and social status among urban Africans in Northern Rhodesia', *Africa*, 1959, **29**, 22–39.

Morris, H. S. *Indians in Uganda*. London, 1968.

Murphree, M. W. *Christianity and the Shona*. London, 1968.

Murray, C. *Families divided*. Cambridge, 1981.

Ngugi wa Thiongo. *Petals of blood*. London, 1977.

Nieuwenhuijze, C. A. O. van. *Social stratification and the Middle East*. Leiden, 1965.

O'Brien, D. C. 'Co-operators and bureaucrats: class formation in a Senegalese peasant society', *Africa*, 1971, **41**, 263–78.
  Saints and politicians: essays in the organization of a Senegalese peasant society. Cambridge, 1975.

Oppong, C. *Marriage among a matrilineal élite*. Cambridge, 1974.

Ousmane, S. *Les Bouts de bois de Dieu*. Paris, 1976.

Owusu, M. *Uses and abuses of political power*. Chicago, 1970.

Paden, J. N. *Religion and political culture in Kano*. Berkeley, 1973.

Parkin, D. J. *Neighbours and nationals in an African city ward*. London, 1964.
  Palms, wine and witnesses. London, 1972.
  ed. *Town and country in Central and Eastern Africa*. London, 1975.

Peace, A. J. 'The Lagos proletariat: labour aristocrats or populist militants', in Sandbrook, R. and Cohen, R. *The development of an African working class*. London, 1975.
  'Prestige, power and legitimacy in a modern Nigerian town'. *Canadian Journal of African Studies*, 1979, **13**, 25–52.

Peel, J. D. Y. *Aladura: a religious movement among the Yoruba*. London, 1968.
  'Conversion and tradition in two African societies: Ijebu and Buganda', *Past and Present*, 1977, **77**, 108–41.
  Ijeshas and Nigerians: the incorporation of a Yoruba kingdom, 1890s–1970s. Cambridge, 1983.

Peil, Margaret. 'Aspirations and social structure: a West African example', *Africa*, 1968, **38**, 71–8.

Perlmutter, A. 'Egypt and the myth of the new middle class', *Comparative Studies in Society and History*, 1968, **10**, 46–65.

Pfefferman, G. *Industrial labour in Senegal*. New York, 1968.

Pons, V. *Stanleyville: an African urban community under Belgian administration*. London, 1969.

Post, K. 'Peasantisation and rural political movements in Western Africa', *Archives Européennes de Sociologie*, 1972, **13**, 223–54.

Prothero, R. M. *Migrant labour from Sokoto Province, Northern Nigeria*. Kaduna, 1959.

Quandt, W. B. *Revolution and political leadership: Algeria 1954–1968*. Cambridge, Mass., 1969.

Ranger, T. O. *Dance and society in East Africa*. London, 1976.

Richards, A. I., Sturrock, F. and Fortt, J. M. eds. *Subsistence to commercial farming in present-day Buganda*. Cambridge, 1973.

Roberts, A. D. 'The Lumpa Church of Alice Lenshina', in Rotberg, R. I. and Mazrui, A. A. eds. *Protest and power in Black Africa*. New York, 1970.

Roberts, P. 'The village school teacher in Ghana', in Goody, J. ed. *Changing social structure in Ghana*. London, 1975.

Rotberg, R. I. *The rise of nationalism in Central Africa: the making of Malawi and Zambia, 1873–1964*. Cambridge, Mass., 1965.

Rotberg, R. I. and Mazrui, A. A. eds. *Protest and power in Black Africa*. New York, 1970.

Rouch, J. *Migrations au Ghana*. Paris, 1956.

Sandbrook, R. and Cohen, R. eds. *The development of an African working class*. London, 1975.

Sangree, W. H. *Age, politics and prayer in Tiriki, Kenya*. London, 1966.

Saul, J. S. 'The state in post-colonial societies – Tanzania', *The Socialist Register*. London, 1974.

'The "labour aristocracy" thesis reconsidered', in Sandbrook, R. and Cohen, R. eds. *The development of an African working class*. London, 1975.

'The unsteady state: Uganda, Obote and General Amin', *Review of African Political Economy*, 1976, **5**, 12–38.

Schildkrout, E. 'Ethnicity and generational differences among urban immigrants in Ghana', in Cohen, A. ed. *Urban ethnicity*. London, 1974.

Shanin, T. *The awkward class*. Oxford, 1972.

Sklar, R. L. *Nigerian political parties*. Princeton, 1963.

Smith, M. G. 'Pre-industrial stratification systems', in Smelser, N. J. and Lipset, S. M. eds. *Social structure and mobility in economic development*. Chicago and London, 1966.

Smock, A. C. *Ibo politics*. Cambridge, Mass., 1971.

Southall, A. W. ed. *Social change in modern Africa*. London, 1961.

'From segmentary lineage to ethnic association: Luo, Luhya, Ibo and others', in Owusu, M. ed. *Colonialism and change: essays presented to Lucy Mair*. The Hague, 1975.

Soyinka, W. *Season of anomy*. London, 1973.

Spiro, H. ed. *The primacy of politics*. New York, 1966.

Stanley, W. R. 'Lebanese in Sierra Leone: entrepreneurs extraordinary', *African Urban Notes*, 1970, **5**, 154–74.

Stavenhagen, R. *Social classes in agrarian societies*. Garden City, 1975.

Sundkler, B. G. M. *Bantu prophets in South Africa*. 2nd ed. London, 1961.

Tessler, M. A., O'Barr, W. M. and Spain, S. H. *Tradition and identity in changing Africa*. New York, 1973.

Todaro, M. P. 'A model of labour migration and urban unemployment in less developed countries', *American Economic Review*, 1969, **59**, 138–48.

Tseayo, J. I. 'Tiv reaction to "pagan" status', in Williams, G. ed. *Nigeria: economy and society*. London, 1976.

Twaddle, M. '"Tribalism" in Eastern Uganda', in Gulliver, P. H. ed. *Tradition and transition in East Africa*. London, 1969.

Udo, R. K. *Migrant tenant farmers of Nigeria*. Lagos, 1975.

Van Velsen, J. 'Labour migration as a positive factor in the continuity of Tonga tribal society', in Southall, A. W. ed. *Social change in modern Africa*. London, 1961.

Vincent, J. *African élite: the big men of a small town.* New York, 1971.
Wallerstein, I. 'Élites in French West Africa: the social basis of ideas', *Journal of Modern African Studies*, 1965, **3**, 1–35.
   ed. *Social change: the colonial situation.* New York, 1966.
Watson, W. *Tribal cohesion in a money economy.* Manchester, 1958.
Welbourn, F. B. *Religion and politics in Uganda 1952–62.* Nairobi, 1965.
Wheeler, D. L. and Pelissier, R. *Angola.* London, 1971.
Whiteley, W. H. ed. *Language use and social change.* London, 1968.
Williame, J. C. *Patrimonialism and political change in the Congo.* Stanford, 1972.
Williams, G. 'Political consciousness among the Ibadan poor', in de Kadt, E. and Williams, G. eds. *Sociology and development.* London, 1974, 130–1.
   'Taking the part of peasants', in Gutkind, P. C. W. and Wallerstein, I. eds. *The political economy of Africa.* New York, 1975.
Wilson, M. and Mafeje, A. *Langa.* Cape Town, 1963.
Wolf, E. R. *Peasant wars of the twentieth century.* London, 1971.
Wolpe, M. *Urban politics in Nigeria: a study of Port Harcourt.* Berkeley, 1974.
Young, C. *Politics in the Congo: decolonisation and independence.* Princeton, 1965.
Zghal, A. 'Nation building in Maghreb', in Eisenstadt, S. N. and Rokkan, S. eds. *Building states and nations.* New York, 1973.
   'The reactivation of tradition', *Daedalus*, Winter, 1973, 225–37.

5. THE ECONOMIC EVOLUTION OF DEVELOPING AFRICA

Abangwu, G. C. ed. *Size and efficiency in African manufacturing; quantitative aspects of industrial development strategy in economic integration.* (African Institute for Economic Development and Planning.) Dakar, 1972.
Abbott, J. C. and Makeham, J. P. *Agricultural economics and marketing in the tropics.* London, 1979.
Adedeji, A. ed. *Africa and the international development strategy for the United Nations third development decade.* Addis Ababa, 1980.
Ake, C. *A political economy of Africa.* London, 1981.
Akiwumi, A. M. *Judicial aspects of economic integration treaties in Africa.* Leiden, 1972.
Allen, C. and Johnson, R. W. eds. *African perspectives, papers on the history, politics and economics of Africa, presented to Thomas Hodgkin.* Cambridge, 1970.
Anthony, K. R. M., Johnston, B. F., Jones, W. O. and Uchendu, V. C. *Agricultural change in tropical Africa.* Ithaca, 1979.
Assefa Mehretu. *Regional integration for economic development of greater East Africa, a quantified analysis of possibilities.* Kampala, 1973.
Babalola, S. O. *The emergent African nations and economic progress.* Ibadan, 1967.
Bairoch, P. *The economic development of the Third World since 1900.* tr. C. Postan. London, 1975.
Balassa, B. *The theory of economic integration.* London, 1961.
Barclays Bank DCO. *Overseas surveys.* London.
Bell, P. W. *African economic problems.* Kampala, 1964.
Benveniste, G. and Moran, W. E. *Handbook of African economic development.* New York, 1962.

Berlage, L. and Joris, G. eds. *The impact of the Association of African States and Madagascar on the origin of the imports of the European Economic Community.* (Antwerp University, Centre for Development Studies.) Antwerp, 1977.

Bongo, El Hadj Omar. *Dialogue of nations: Africa's political and economic role in the new world order.* Libreville, 1978.

Brett, E. A. *Colonialism and underdevelopment in East Africa: the politics of economic change, 1919–1939.* London, 1973.

Červenka, Z. *Land-locked countries of Africa.* Uppsala, 1973.

Chileshe, J. H. *The challenge of developing intra-African trade.* Kampala, 1977.

Clower, R. W. *Mainspring of African economic progress.* Edinburgh, 1969.

Cohen, D. L. and Daniel, J. eds. *Political economy of Africa.* London, 1981.

Convention of Association between the European Economic Community and the African and Malagasy states associated with that Community and annexed documents. Brussels, 1963.

Cowan, L. G., O'Connell, J. and Scanlon, D. G. *Education and nation-building in Africa.* New York, 1965.

Currie, D. P. *Federalism and the new nations of Africa.* Chicago, 1964.

Damachi, U. G. *Leadership ideology in Africa: attitudes towards socio-economic development.* New York, 1976.

Davidson, B. *Can Africa survive?* London, 1974.

De Wilde, J. C. ed. *Experiences with agricultural development in tropical Africa.* Baltimore, 1967.

Di Delupis, I. D. *The East African Community and Common Market.* London, 1969.

Fanon, F. *Toward the African revolution.* tr. H. Chevalier. London, 1980.

Franke, R. W. and Chasin, B. H. *Seeds of famine: ecological destruction and the development dilemma in the West African Sahel.* Montclair, NJ, 1980.

Galbraith, J. K. *The nature of mass poverty.* Cambridge, Mass., 1979.

Gardiner, R. K. A., Anstee, M. J. and Patterson, C. L. eds. *Africa and the world.* Addis Ababa, 1970.

Gavshon, A. *Crisis in Africa, battleground of East and West.* Harmondsworth, 1981.

Ghai, D. P. ed. *Economic independence in Africa.* Nairobi, 1973.

    The Association agreement between the European Economic Community and the partner states of the East African Community. (Council for the Development of Economic and Social Research in Africa.) Dakar, 1975.

de Graft-Johnson, J. C. *An introduction to the African economy.* (Delhi: School of Economics. Occasional papers no. 12.) New York, 1959.

Green, R. H. and Krishna, K. G. V. *Economic co-operation in Africa: retrospect and prospect.* Nairobi, 1967.

Green, R. H. and Seidman, A. *Unity or poverty? The economics of Pan-Africanism.* Harmondsworth, 1968.

Grove, A. T. and Klein, P. M. G. *Rural Africa.* Cambridge, 1979.

Gruhn, I. V. *Regionalism reconsidered: the Economic Commission for Africa.* Boulder, Col., 1970.

Hailey, Lord. *An African survey* London, 1957.

    Tomorrow in Africa. (The Africa Bureau. Anniversary address, 1957.) Southwick, Sussex, 1957.

Haines, C. G. *Africa today*. Baltimore, 1955.

Hance, W. A. *African economic development*. New York, 1958.

Hansberry, W. L. *Africa: the world's richest continent*, 1963.

Harris, R. ed. *The political economy of Africa: underdevelopment or revolution*. New York, 1975.

Harvey, C. *Macroeconomics for Africa: the elementary theory of the working of present-day African economies*. London, 1977.

Harvey, C. *et al. Rural employment and administration in the Third World: development methods and alternative strategies*. Farnborough, 1979.

Hazlewood, A. *The economy of Africa*. London, 1961.

ed. *African integration and disintegration: case studies in economic and political union*. London, 1967.

Economic integration: the East African experience. London, 1975.

Herskovits, M. J. and Harwitz, M. *Economic transition in Africa*. London, 1964.

Hicks, J. R. *Essays in world economics*. Oxford, 1959.

Hoyle, B. S. and Hilling, D. eds. *Seaports and development in tropical Africa*. London, 1970.

Hunter, G. *The best of both worlds? A challenge on development policies in Africa*. London, 1967.

Hunter, W. A. *Decision in Africa: sources of current conflict*. New York, 1960.

Iskenderov, A. *Africa, politics, economy, ideology*. Moscow, 1972.

Jain, S. C. *Agricultural development of African nations*, vol. I. Bombay, 1965.

Jolly, R. *Planning education for African development*. Nairobi, 1969.

Jones, W. O. *Economic man in Africa*. Stanford, 1960.

July, R. W. *Precolonial Africa: an economic and social history*. New York, 1975.

Kamarck, A. M. *The economics of African development*. New York, 1967.

Komorowski, S. M. *The impact of the choice of techniques on development in Africa, a preliminary study*. Addis Ababa, 1971–2.

de Kun, N. *The mineral resources of Africa*. Amsterdam, 1965.

Lawson, R. M. *The agricultural entrepreneurship of upper-income Africans*. Hull, 1977.

Legum, Colin, Zartman, I. W., Langdon, S. and Mytelka, L. K. *Africa in the 1980s: a continent in crisis*. New York, 1979.

Leistner, G. M. E. *Problems and patterns of economic development in Africa*. Pretoria, 1965.

Lewis, W. A. *Some aspects of economic development*. Aggrey–Fraser–Guggisberg memorial lectures, 1968. Accra, 1969.

Leys, C. and Robson, P. eds. *Federation in East Africa: opportunities and problems*. Nairobi, 1965.

Lozoya, J. and Cuadra, H. eds. *The Middle East and the new international economic order*. New York, 1980.

Makings, S. M. *Agricultural problems of developing countries in Africa*. Lusaka, 1967.

Mansell, B. F. ed. *East African economic union: an evaluation and some implications for policy*. Santa Monica, Cal., 1963.

Masefield, G. B. *A short history of agriculture in the British colonies*. Oxford, 1950.

Mazrui, A. A. *The African condition, a political diagnosis*. London, 1980.

Menon, B. P. *Bridges across the South: technical cooperation among developing countries.* New York, 1980.

MIT Fellows in Africa Programme. *Managing economic development in Africa...* Cambridge, Mass., 1963.

Munro, J. Forbes. *Africa and the international economy 1800–1960: an introduction to the modern economic history of Africa south of the Sahara.* London, 1976.

Mutharika, B. W. T. *Toward multinational economic cooperation in Africa.* New York, 1972.

Ndegwa, P. *The Common Market and development in East Africa.* 2nd ed. (Makerere Institute of Social Research, Kampala. East African studies, no. 22.) Nairobi, 1968.

Nellis, J. R. *A model of developmental ideology in Africa: structure and implications.* Beverly Hills, 1970.

Niculescu, B. *Colonial planning: a comparative study.* London, 1958.

Nielsen, W. A. *The great powers and Africa.* London, 1969.

Obone, A. E. *Economics: its principles and practice in developing Africa.* London, 1977.

Ochola, S. A. *Minerals in African underdevelopment.* London, 1975.

Okwuosa, E. A. *New direction for economic development in Africa.* London, 1976.

Organization of African Unity. *Lagos Plan of Action for the economic development of Africa, 1980–2000.* Geneva, 1981.

Paden, J. N. and Soja, E. W. eds. *The African experience.* Evanston, 1970.

Pearson, S. H., Pearson, A. R. and Cownie, J. *Commodity exports and African economic development.* Lexington, Mass., 1974.

Plessz, N. G. *Problems and prospects of economic integration in West Africa.* Montreal, 1968.

Postel, A. W. *The mineral resources of Africa.* Philadelphia, 1943.

Rivkin, A. *The African presence in world affairs: national development and its role in foreign policy.* New York, 1963.

Robana, A. *The prospects for an economic community in North Africa: managing economic integration in the Maghreb states.* New York, 1973.

Robson, P. and Lury, D. A. eds. *The economies of Africa.* London, 1969.

Rothchild, D. and Curry, R. L. *Scarcity, choice and public policy in Middle Africa.* Berkeley, 1978.

Schatz, Sayre P. *South of the Sahara: development in African economies.* London, 1972.

Schiffmann, C. *The developing countries and the enlargement of the European Economic Community.* Brussels, 1971.

Seidman, A. *Planning for development in sub-Saharan Africa.* New York, 1974.

Sewell, D. U. *Industrial development in tropical Africa.* Wellington, 1971.

Singh, V. B. *Studies in African economic development.* New Delhi, 1972.

Singleton, F. S. *Africa in perspective.* New York, 1967.

Stallings, B. *Economic dependency in Africa and Latin America.* Beverly Hills, 1972.

Todaro, M. P. *Economic development in the Third World.* 2nd ed. New York, 1981.

Turner, P. H. *The commerce of new Africa.* London, 1969.

UN Department of Economic Affairs, Bureau of Economic Affairs. *Structure and growth of selected African economies.* New York, 1958.

UN Department of Economic Affairs, Division of Economic Stability and Development. *Enlargement of the exchange economy in tropical Africa*. New York, 1954.

UN Department of Economic and Social Affairs. *Scope and structure of money economies in tropical Africa*. New York, 1955.

Economic survey of Africa since 1950. New York, 1959.

UN Economic Commission for Africa. *Report of the ECA mission on economic cooperation in Central Africa*. New York, 1966.

Intra-African economic cooperation and Africa's relations with the European Economic Community. Report by team led by K. Philip. Addis Ababa, 1972.

Attack on absolute poverty in Africa: the role of the United Nations Development Advisory Teams, UNDATS. New York, 1974.

UNESCO. *Survey of the natural resources of the African continent*. Paris, 1963.

UN Food and Agriculture Organisation. *Food and agricultural developments in Africa south of the Sahara*. Rome, 1958.

Uppal, J. S. and Salkever, L. R. eds. *Africa: problems in economic development*. New York, 1972.

Vilakazi, A. L., Fall, I. and Vilakazi, H. W. *Africa's rough road: problems of change and development*. Washington, DC, 1979.

Whetham, E. H. and Currie, J. I. eds. *Readings in the applied economics of Africa*, 2 vols. Cambridge, 1967.

The economics of African countries. Cambridge, 1969.

Zartman, I. W. *The politics of trade negotiations between Africa and the European Economic Community: the weak confront the strong*. Princeton, 1971.

6. SOUTHERN AFRICA

Suggestions for further reading in addition to titles mentioned in the bibliographical essay and in footnotes; asterisks indicate English editions of books originally published in another South African language.

Abrahams, P. *Mine boy*. London, 1946.

Ashton, H. *The Basuto*. London, 1952.

Ballinger, M. *From union to apartheid*. Cape Town, 1969.

Barber, J. P. *South Africa's foreign policy 1945–1970*. London, 1973.

Barker, A. *The man next to me*. London, 1962.

Bloom, H. *Episode*. London, 1956.

*Brink, A. *Dry white season*. London, 1980.

Benson, M. *The African patriots*. London, 1963.

Basutoland, Bechuanaland Protectorate and Swaziland. Report of an economic survey mission (Chairman C. Morse). London, 1960.

Brandel-Syrier, M. *Black women in search of God*. London, 1962.

Brookes, E. H. *Apartheid – a documentary study of modern South Africa*. London, 1968.

Brown, A. C. ed. *A history of scientific endeavour in South Africa*. Cape Town, 1977.

Brutus, D. *Letters to Martha and other poems from a South African prison*. London, 1968.

Bundy, C. *The rise and fall of the South African peasantry*. London, 1978.

Bunting, B. *The rise of the South African reich*. Harmondsworth, 1969. *Moses Kotane, South African revolutionary*. London, 1975.

Butler, J., Rotberg, R. I. and Adams, J. *The black homelands of South Africa*. Berkeley, 1977.

Butterfield, P. H. *A history of education in Lesotho*. Pretoria, 1977.

Carstens, W. P. *The social structure of a Cape Coloured reserve*. Cape Town, 1966.

Carter, G. M. and Philip, M. *From the front line: speeches of Sir Seretse Khama*. London, 1980.

Červenka, Z. and Rogers, B. *The nuclear axis*. London, 1978.

Clarke, E. and Ngobese, J. *Women without men*. Durban, 1975.

Cronje, G. *Regverdige rasse-apartheid*. Stellenbosch, 1947.

Davenport, T. R. H. & Hunt, K. S. *The right to the land*. Cape Town, 1974.

Davies, R. H. *Capital, state, and white labour in South Africa, 1900–1960*. Brighton, 1979.

Desmond, C. *The discarded people*. Johannesburg, c. 1967.

Devereux, S. *South African income distribution 1900–1980*. Cape Town, 1983.

De Vries, J. L. *Mission and Colonialism in Namibia*. Johannesburg, 1978.

Dikobe, M. *The Marabi dance*. London, 1973.

Driver, C. J. *Patrick Duncan: South African and Pan-African*. London, 1980.

Friedman, B. *Smuts: a reappraisal*. Johannesburg, 1975.

Fugard, A. *Three Port Elizabeth plays*. New York, 1974.

Goldblatt, D. *Some Afrikaners photographed*. Sandton, 1975.

Gordimer, N. *A world of strangers*. Harmondsworth, 1962.

The black interpreters. Johannesburg, 1973.

Gordon, R. J. *Mines, masters and migrants*. Johannesburg, 1977.

Gray, S. *A survey of English South African literature in the last ten years: research developments*. Johannesburg, 1982.

Greenberg, S. *Race and state in capitalist development*. New Haven, 1980.

Harvey, C. ed. *Papers on the economy of Botswana*. London, 1981.

Hellman, E. ed. *Handbook of race relations in South Africa*. Cape Town, 1949.

Hepple, A. *South Africa: workers under apartheid*. 2nd ed. London, 1971.

Verwoerd. Harmondsworth, 1967.

Hoernle, R. F. *South African native policy and the liberal spirit*. Johannesburg, 1945.

Holleman, J. F. ed. *Experiment in Swaziland*. Cape Town, 1964.

Horrell, M. ed. *Annual survey of race relations in South Africa*. Johannesburg, 1946–79.

Houghton, D. H., Wilson, M. *et al. Keiskammahoek rural survey*. 4 vols. Pietermaritzburg, 1952.

Houghton, D. H. and Dagut, J. eds. *Source material on the South African economy 1860–1970*. 3 vols. Johannesburg, 1973.

Huddlestone, T. *Naught for your comfort*. Johannesburg, 1956.

Hugo, P. *Quislings or realists? a documentary study of 'Coloured' politics in South Africa*. Johannesburg, 1978.

Hyam, R. *The failure of South African expansion 1908–19*. New York, 1972.

Inskeep, R. *The peopling of southern Africa*. Cape Town, 1978.

Jabavu, N. *Drawn in colour*. London, 1960.

Jones, D. *Aid and development in southern Africa*. London, 1977.

Jordan, A. C. *Towards an African literature*. Berkeley, 1973.

　The wrath of the ancestors. Lovedale, 1980.

Joseph, H. *Tomorrow's sun*. New York, 1967.

*Joubert, E. *The long journey of Poppie Nongena*. Johannesburg, 1980.

Khaketla, B. M. *Lesotho 1970: an African coup under the microscope*. London, 1971.

Khoapa, B. A. *et al.* eds. *Black review. Four annual surveys*. Durban, 1973-7.

Khopung, E. *Apartheid: the story of a dispossessed people*. Dar es Salaam, 1972.

Kotze, D. A. *African politics in South Africa 1964-1974*. London, 1975.

Kruger, D. W. *South African parties and policies*. Cape Town, 1960.

Kuper, A. *Kalahari village politics*. Cambridge, 1970.

Kuper, H. *Indian people in Natal*. Pietermaritzburg, 1960.

Kuper, L. *Passive resistance in South Africa*. London, 1960.

　An African bourgeoisie: race, class and politics in South Africa. New Haven, 1965.

Laclau, E. ed. *Capital accumulation and violence*.

La Guma, A. ed. *Apartheid*. London, 1971.

Lee, R. B. *The !Kung San: men, women and work in a foraging society*. Cambridge, 1979.

Legum, C. ed. *Africa contemporary record: annual survey and documents*. London, 1969- .

Lerumo, A. *Fifty fighting years*. London, 1971.

Lewin, H. *Bandiet*. London, 1974.

Luthuli, A. *Let my people go*. Johannesburg, 1962.

Malan, D. F. *Afrikaner volkseenheid en my ervarings op die pad daarheen*. Cape Town, 1961.

Mandela, N. *The struggle in my life*. London, 1978.

Manganyi, N. C. *Being black in the world*. Johannesburg, 1973.

Marais, J. S. *The Cape Coloured people*. Johannesburg, 1939.

Mayer, P. *Xhosa in town: townsmen or tribesmen: urbanisation in a divided society*. Cape Town, 1961.

　ed. *Black villagers in an industrial society*. Cape Town, 1980.

Mbeki, G. *South Africa: the peasants' revolt*. Harmondsworth, 1964.

Modisane, B. *Blame me on history*. New York, 1963.

Moorsom, R. *Transforming a wasted land*. London, 1982.

Muller, C. F. J. ed. *Five hundred years of history*. Pretoria, 1969.

Nash, M. *Ecumenical movement in the 1960s*. Johannesburg, 1975.

Nattrass, J. *South African economy: its growth and change*. Cape Town, 1981.

Ngubane, H. *Body and mind in Zulu medicine*. London, 1977.

Ngubane, J. K. *An African explains apartheid*. London, 1963.

Nkondo, G. M. *Turfloop testimony: the dilemma of a black university in South Africa*. Johannesburg, 1976.

Nkosi, L. *The transplanted heart*. Benin City, 1975.

Nolutshungu, S. C. *South Africa in Africa*. Manchester, 1975.

　Changing South Africa: political considerations. Manchester, 1982.

Nortje, A. *Dead roots*. London, 1973.

No Sizwe. *One Azania, one nation: the national question in South Africa*. London, 1979.

Nsekela, A. J. ed. *Southern Africa: towards economic liberation*. London, 1981.

O'Meara, D. *Volkskapitalisme: class, capital and ideology in the development of Afrikaner nationalism 1934–1948*. Cambridge, 1983.

Opperman, D. J. *Joernaal van Jorik*. Cape Town, 1949.

Palmer, E. *The plains of Camdeboo*. London, 1966.

Palmer, R. and Parsons, N. eds. *The roots of rural poverty in central and southern Africa*. London, 1977.

Patel, E. ed. *The world of Nat Nakasa: selected writings*. Johannesburg, 1975.

Paton, A. *Cry the beloved country*. London, 1948.

  Too late the phalarope. Cape Town, 1953.

Pienaar, S. *Getuie van groot getye*. Cape Town, 1979.

Pienaar, S. and Sampson, A. *South Africa: two views of separate development*. London, 1960.

Potholm, C. P. *Swaziland: the dynamics of political modernisation*. Berkeley, 1972.

Report of the commission for the socio-economic development of the Bantu areas within the Union of South Africa (Tomlinson). Summary. Pretoria, 1956.

Report of the Ciskei commission (Quail report). Silverton, 1980.

Report on the requirements for stability & development in KwaZulu & Natal (The Buthelezi report) (Schreiner). 2 vols. Durban, 1982.

Randall, P. *A taste of power*. Johannesburg, 1973.

Rhoodie, N. J. and Venter, H. J. *Apartheid*. Cape Town, 1959.

Russell, M. J. and Russell, M. *Afrikaners of the Kalahari: white minority in a black state*. Cambridge, 1979.

Sachs, A. *Jail diary*. London, 1966.

Sachs, E. S. (Solly). *Rebels' daughters*. Alva, 1957.

Sadie, J. S. *Projections of the South African population 1970–2020*. Johannesburg, 1973.

Sampson, A. *Drum*. London, 1956.

Schapera, I. *Migrant labour and tribal life*. Oxford, 1947.

Scott, M. *A time to speak*. London, 1958.

Selwyn, P. *Industries in the southern African periphery*. London, 1975.

Sepamla, S. S. J. *The Soweto I love*. London, 1977.

Sihlali, L. L. *The philosophy tenets and traditions of N.E.U.M.* Unknown, n.d.

Silk, A. *A shanty town in South Africa*. Johannesburg, 1982.

Sillery, A. *Botswana: a short political history*. London, 1974.

Simkins, C. and Desmond, C. eds. *South African unemployment: a black picture*. Pietermaritzburg, 1978.

Simons, H. J. and Simons, R. E. *Class and colour in South Africa 1850–1950*. Harmondsworth, 1969.

Small, A. *Kitaar my kruis*. Cape Town, 1962.

Spence, J. E. *Lesotho: the politics of dependence*. London, 1968.

Stevens, R. P. *Lesotho, Botswana and Swaziland*. London, 1967.

Stubbs, A. ed. *Steve Biko: I write what I like*. London, 1978.

Study project on external investment in South Africa and Namibia. ed. *Foreign investment in South Africa*. 5 vols. London, 1974–81.

Stultz, N. *Transkei's half loaf: race separatism in South Africa*. New Haven, 1979.

Surplus People Project. *Forced removals in South Africa: the SPP reports.* 5 vols. Cape Town, 1983.

Tabata, I. B. *The awakening of a people.* Nottingham, 1974.

Temkin, B. *Gatsha Buthelezi.* Cape Town, 1976.

Thoahlane, T. ed. *Black renaissance: papers from the black renaissance convention, December 1974.* Johannesburg, 1975.

Turner, R. *The eye of the needle.* Johannesburg, 1972.

Van den Berghe, P. L. *South Africa: a study in conflict.* Middletown, Conn. 1965.

Van der Merwe H. W. and Welsh, D. eds. *Student perspectives on South Africa.* Cape Town, 1972.

Van Wyk Louw, N. P. *Liberale Nasionalisme.* Cape Town, 1958.

Visser, G. and Cloete, O. B. *Traitors or patriots?* Johannesburg, 1976.

Voipio, R. *Kontrak soos die Owambo dit sien.* Johannesburg, 1972.

Wallman, S. *Take out hunger: two case studies of rural development in Basutoland.* London, 1969.

Watson, G. *Passing for white.* London, 1970.

Wickens, P. L. *The industrial and commercial workers' union of Africa.* Cape Town, 1978.

Welsh, D. *The roots of segregation.* Cape Town, 1970.

West, M. E. *Bishops and prophets in a black city.* Cape Town, 1975.

Wilson, F. *Migrant labour in South Africa.* Johannesburg, 1972.

Wilson, F. and Perrot, D. eds. *Outlook on a century: South Africa, 1870–1970.* Lovedale, 1973.

Wilson, M. and Mafeje, A. *Langa.* Cape Town, 1963.

Yudelman, D. *The emergence of modern South Africa.* Westport, 1983.

7. ENGLISH-SPEAKING WEST AFRICA

Ademoyega, A. *Why we struck.* Ibadan, 1981.

Adu, A. L. *The civil service in new African states.* London, 1965.

Afrifa, A. A. *The Ghana coup.* London, 1966.

Agbodeka, F. *Achimota in the national setting.* Accra, 1977.

Ajao, A. *On the tiger's back.* London, 1962.

Akpan, N. U. *The struggle for secession.* London, 1971.

Aluko, O. *Ghana and Nigeria, 1957–70.* London, 1974.

Ananaba, W. *The trade union movement in Nigeria.* London, 1969.

Anderson, R. E. *Liberia: America's African friend.* Chapel Hill, 1962.

Anti-Taylor, W. *Moscow diary.* London, 1967.

Armah, K. *Africa's golden road.* London, 1965.

Assimeng, M. *Social structure of Ghana.* Accra, 1981.

Austin, D. *Politics in Ghana, 1946–1960.* Oxford, 1964.

Awolowo, Obafemi. *Path to Nigerian freedom.* London, 1946.

  Awo. Cambridge, 1960.

Azikiwe, N. *Zik.* Cambridge, 1961.

  My odyssey: an autobiography. London, 1970.

Bauer, P. T. *West African trade.* London, 1954, 2nd ed. 1963.

Beckman, B. *Organising the farmers.* Uppsala, 1974.

Birmingham, W., Neustadt, I. and Omaboe, E. N. eds. *A study of contemporary Ghana*. London, 1960. 2 vols.

Bourret, F. M. *Ghana: the road to independence*. London, 1960.

Bridges, R. C. ed. *Senegambia*. Aberdeen, 1974.

Busia, K. A. *The position of the chief in the modern political system of Ashanti*. London, 1951.

Byng, G. *Reap the whirlwind*. London, 1968.

Cartwright, J. R. *Politics in Sierra Leone, 1947–67*. Toronto, 1970.

Clapham, C. *Liberia and Sierra Leone – an essay in comparative politics*. Cambridge, 1976.

Clower, R. W., Dalton, G., Harwitz, M. and Walters, A. A. *Growth without development: an economic survey of Liberia*. Evanston, 1966.

Cohen, R. *Labour and politics in Nigeria, 1945–1971*. London, 1974.

Coleman, J. S. *Nigeria: background to nationalism*. Berkeley and Los Angeles, 1958.

Cox, T. S. *Civil–military relations in Sierra Leone*. Cambridge, Mass., 1970.

Cox-George, N. A. *Finance and development in West Africa: the Sierra Leone experience*. London, 1961.

Crowder, M. *The story of Nigeria*. 3rd ed. London, 1973.

Damachi, U. G. *The role of trade unions in the development process*. London, 1974.

Davidson, B. *Black star. A view of the life and times of Kwame Nkrumah*. London, 1973.

Dei-Annang, M. *The administration of Ghana's foreign policy 1957–65*. London, 1975.

Dudley, B. J. *Parties and politics in Northern Nigeria*. London, 1968.

Ekanem, I. I. *Nigerian census, 1963*. Benin, 1972.

Feinstein, A. *African revolutionary*. New York, 1973.

Flint, J. E. *Nigeria and Ghana*. Englewood Cliffs, NJ, 1966.

Foray, C. P. *Historical dictionary of Sierra Leone*. Metuchen, NJ, 1977.

Foster, P. and Zolberg, A. eds. *Ghana and the Ivory Coast: perspectives on modernization*. Chicago, 1971.

Fraenkel, M. *Tribe and class in Monrovia*. Oxford, 1964.

Fyle, C. N. and Jones, E. D. *A Krio-English dictionary*. Oxford, 1980.

Gailey, H. A. *A history of The Gambia*. London, 1964.

Historial dictionary of The Gambia. Metuchen, NJ, 1975.

Gbulie, B. *Nigeria's five majors*. Onitsha, 1981.

Genoud, R. *Nationalism and economic development in Ghana*. McGill, 1969.

Hailey, Lord. *Native administration in the British African territories. Part III, West Africa*. London, 1951.

Native administration and political development in British tropical Africa. Leichtenstein (reprint), 1979.

Hart, D. *The Volta River Project*. Edinburgh, 1980.

Haswell, M. *The nature of poverty*. London, 1975.

Heussler, R. *The British in Northern Nigeria*. London, 1968.

Hill, Polly. *Studies in rural capitalism in West Africa*. Cambridge, 1970.

Hodgkin, T. L. *Nationalism in colonial Africa*. London, 1957.

Jeffries, R. *Class, power and ideology in Ghana*. Cambridge, 1978.

Kilby, P. *Industrialisation in an open economy: Nigeria 1945–1966*. Cambridge, 1969.

Killick, Tony. *Development economics in action*. London, 1978.

Kilson, M. *Political change in a West African state: a study of the modernisation process in Sierra Leone*. Cambridge, Mass., 1966.

Lee, J. M. *African armies and civil order*. London, 1969.

Levgold, R. *Soviet policy in West Africa*. Harvard, 1970.

Le Vine, V. T. *Political corruption: the Ghana case*. Stanford, 1975.

Lewis, W. A. *Reflections on Nigeria's economic growth*. OECD, 1967.

Liebenow, J. G. *Liberia: the evolution of privilege*. Ithaca, 1969.

Luckham, R. *The Nigerian military, 1960–1967*. Cambridge, 1971.

Mackintosh, J. P. *et al. Nigerian government and politics*. London, 1966.

Madiebo, A. A. *The Nigerian revolution and the Biafran war*. Enugu, 1980.

Miners, N. J. *The Nigerian army, 1956–1966*. London, 1971.

Nicolson, I. F. *The administration of Nigeria 1900 to 1960*. London, 1970.

Nimley, A. J. *The Liberian bureaucracy*. Washington, DC, 1977.

Nkrumah, Kwame. *The autobiography of Kwame Nkrumah*. London, 1957.
Africa must unite. London, 1963.
Consciencism. London, 1964.

Obasanjo, O. *My command*. Ibadan, 1980.

Ocran, A. K. *Politics of the sword*. London, 1977.

Offodile, C. *Dr M. I. Okpara*. Enugu, 1980.

Ogunsanwo, A. *China's policy in Africa*. Cambridge, 1974.

Okpu, U. *Ethnic minority problems in Nigerian politics 1960–1965*. Uppsala, 1977.

Olatunbosun, D. *Nigeria's neglected rural majority*. Ibadan, 1975.

Olusanya, G. O. *The Second World War and politics in Nigeria 1939–1953*. Lagos and London, 1973.

Olusanya, V. O. *Soldiers and Power*. Stanford, 1977.

Omari, P. *Kwame Nkrumah: the anatomy of an African dictatorship*. London, 1970.

Owusu, M. *Uses and abuses of political power*. Chicago, 1971.

Ozigi and Ocho. *Education in Northern Nigeria*. London, 1981.

Paden, J. N. *Religion and political culture in Kano*. Berkeley, 1973.

Panter-Brick, S. K. ed. *Soldiers and oil*. London, 1978.

Peace, A. *Choice, class and conflict*. Brighton, 1979.

Pearce, R. D. *The turning point in Africa: British colonial policy 1938–1948*. London, 1982.

Post, K. W. J. and Jenkins, G. D. *The price of liberty*. Cambridge, 1973.

Price, R. M. *Society and bureaucracy in contemporary Ghana*. Berkeley, 1975.

Quaison-Sackey, A. *Africa unbound*. New York, 1963.

Report of the Commission appointed to enquire into the fears of minorities and the means of allaying them. (Willink Commission). Cmnd. 505. London, 1958.

de St Jorre, J. *The Nigerian civil war*. London, 1972.

Saylor, R. G. *The economic system of Sierra Leone*. Durham, NC, 1967.

Schwarz, W. *Nigeria*. London, 1968.

Sharwood-Smith, B. *But always as friends*. London, 1968.

Sklar, R. L. *Nigerian political parties*. Princeton, 1963.

Smock, D. R. and Smock, A. C. *The politics of pluralism*. New York, 1975.

Sokoto, Sardauna of. *My life.* Cambridge, 1962.

Spitzer, L. *The Creoles of Sierra Leone.* Wisconsin, 1974.

Stolper, W. G. *Planning without facts.* Cambridge, Mass., 1966.

Stremlau, J. J. *The international politics of the Nigerian civil war.* Princeton, 1977.

Thompson, W. S. *Ghana's foreign policy, 1957–1966.* Princeton, 1969.

Tubman, W. V. S. *Tubman of Liberia speaks.* London, 1959.

  The official papers of William V. S. Tubman. Monrovia, 1968.

Van de Laan, H. L. *The Sierra Leone diamonds.* London, 1965.

Welch, G. *The jet lighthouse.* London, 1960.

Whitaker, C. S. *The politics of tradition.* Princeton, 1970.

White, J. *Central administration in Nigeria, 1914–1948.* Dublin and London, 1968.

Williams, D. M. *President and power in Nigeria.* London, 1982.

Wreh, Tuan. *The love of liberty brought us here.* London, 1971.

8. EAST AND CENTRAL AFRICA

Amsden, A. *International firms and labour in Kenya 1945–1970.* London, 1971.

Anderson, J. *The struggle for the school.* London, 1973.

Apter, D. E. *The political kingdom in Uganda: a study of bureaucratic nationalism.* Princeton, 1967.

Arrighi, G. *The political economy of Rhodesia.* The Hague, 1967.

Baldwin, R. *Economic development and export growth: a study of Northern Rhodesia 1920–1960.* Berkeley, 1966.

Barber, J. P. *Rhodesia: the road to rebellion.* London, 1967.

Barnett, D. L. and Karari, N. *Mau Mau from within: autobiography and analysis of Kenya's peasant revolt.* London, 1966.

Bates, R. H. *Unions, parties and political development: a study of mineworkers in Zambia.* New Haven, 1971.

  Rural responses to industrialisation: a study of village Zambia. New Haven, 1976.

Bennett, G. and Rosberg, C. *The Kenyatta election: Kenya 1960–61.* London, 1961.

Berger, E. *Labour, race and colonial rule: the Copperbelt from 1924 to independence.* Oxford, 1974.

Bienen, H. *Tanzania: party transformation and economic development.* Princeton, 1970.

Blundell, M. *So rough a wind: Kenya memoirs.* London, 1964.

Bowman, L. W. *Politics in Rhodesia: white power in an African state.* Cambridge, Mass., 1973.

Clayton, A. *The 1948 Zanzibar general strike.* Scandinavian Institute of African Studies Research Report no. 32. Uppsala, 1976.

Clayton, A. and Savage, D. *Government and labour in Kenya 1895–1963.* London, 1974.

Cliffe, L. ed. *One-party democracy.* Nairobi, 1967.

Cliffe, L. and Saul, J. eds. *Socialism in Tanzania* vol. I, *Politics;* vol. II, *Policies.* Nairobi, 1972, 1973.

Cohen, A. *British policy in changing Africa.* London, 1959.

Court, D. 'The education system as a response to inequality in Tanzania and Kenya', *Journal of Modern African Studies*, 1976, **14**, 4, 661–90.

Deane, P. *Colonial social accounting*. National Institute of Economic and Social Research, Economic and Social Studies no. 11. Cambridge, 1953.

'The industrial revolution in British Central Africa', *Civilisations* (Brussels), 1962, **12**, 3.

Ehrlich, C. 'The Uganda economy, 1903–1945', in Harlow, V. and Chilver, E. M. eds. *History of East Africa*, vol. II. Oxford, 1965.

'The poor country: the Tanganyikan economy from 1945 to independence', in Low, D. A. and Smith, Alison. eds. *History of East Africa*, vol. III. Oxford, 1976.

Elkan, W. *An African labour force*. East African Studies no. 7. Kampala, 1956.

Migrants and proletarians: urban labour in the economic development of Uganda. London, 1961.

'Is a proletariat emerging in Nairobi?', *Economic Development and Cultural Change 1965–75*, **24**.

Elliot, C. ed. *Constraints on the economic development of Zambia*. Nairobi, 1971.

Epstein, A. L. *Politics in an urban African community*. Manchester, 1958.

Fallers, L. A. ed. *The King's men: leadership and status in Buganda on the eve of independence*. London, 1964.

Finucane, J. *Rural development and bureaucracy in Tanzania*. Uppsala, 1974.

Friedland, W. H. *Vuta Kamba: the development of trade unions in Tanganyika*. Stanford, 1969.

Furedi, F. 'The African crowd in Nairobi: popular movements and élite politics', *Journal of African History*, 1973, **14**, 2.

Gertzel, C. J. *The politics of independent Kenya*. Nairobi, 1970.

Party and locality in Northern Uganda, 1945–1962. London, 1974.

Ghai, D. P. *Portrait of a minority: Asians in East Africa*. London, 1965.

Ghai, Y. P. and McAuslan, J. P. *Public law and political change in Kenya*. Nairobi, 1970.

Goldsworthy, D. *Colonial issues in British politics 1945–1961*. Oxford, 1971

Good, R. *UDI: the international politics of the Rhodesian rebellion*. London, 1973.

Gray, R. *The two nations: aspects of the development of race relations in Rhodesia and Nyasaland*. Westport, Conn., 1974.

Great Britain, Colonial Office, *Report of the Nyasaland Commission of Inquiry 1958–59* (the Devlin Report). Cmd 814. London, 1959.

Hall, R. *The high price of principles*. 2nd ed. Harmondsworth, 1973.

Harlow, V. and Chilver, E. M. eds. *History of East Africa*, vol. II (1900–1945). Oxford, 1965.

Hazlewood, A. *Economic integration: the East African experience*. London, 1975.

Hellen, J. A. *Rural economic development in Zambia, 1890–1964*. Munich, 1958.

Heyer, J., Maitha, J. K. and Senga, W. M. eds. *Agricultural development in Kenya, an economic assessment*. Nairobi, 1971.

Hodder-Williams, R. 'Malawi's decade under Dr Banda: the revival of politics', *Round Table* 1973, **252**, 463–70.

van der Hoeven, R. *Income distribution and employment programme. Zambia's income distribution during the early seventies*. Geneva, 1977.

Holtham, G. and Hazlewood, A. *Aid and inequality*. London, 1976.

Humphrey, D. H. *Malawi since 1964: economic development, progress and problems*. University of Malawi, Department of Economics Occasional Paper no. 1. Zomba, 1974.

Hutton, C. *Reluctant farmers*. Nairobi, 1973.

Huxley, Elspeth and Perham, Margery. *Race and politics in Kenya*. London, 1954.

Hyden, G. *Political development in rural Tanzania*. Nairobi, 1969.

    Beyond Ujamaa in Tanzania: under-development and an uncaptured peasantry. London, 1980.

Hyden, G. and Leys, C. 'Elections and politics in single-party systems: the case of Kenya and Tanzania', *British Journal of Political Science*, 1972, **2**, 4.

Iliffe, J. *A modern history of Tanganyika*. Cambridge, 1979.

International Labour Organisation (ILO). *Employment, incomes and equality: a strategy for increasing productive employment in Kenya*. Geneva, 1972.

Jacobs, R. *The relationship between African trade unions and political organisations in Northern Rhodesia/Zambia, 1949–61*. International Institute for Labour Studies, Geneva, 1971.

Kasfir, N. *The shrinking political arena*. Berkeley, 1976.

Keatley, P. *The politics of partnership*. Harmondsworth, 1963.

Kettlewell, R. W. 'Agricultural change in Nyasaland, 1945–1960', *Food Research Institute Studies* (Stanford), 1965, **5**, 3, 229–85.

Kyemba, H. *State of blood*. London, 1977.

Lamb, G. *Peasant politics*. London, 1974.

Lee, J. M. *Colonial development and good government: a study of the ideas expressed by the British official classes in planning decolonisation, 1939–1964*. Oxford, 1967.

Leys, C. *European politics in Southern Rhodesia*. Oxford, 1959.

    Politicians and policies: an essay on politics in Acholi, Uganda, 1962–65. Nairobi, 1967.

    Underdevelopment in Kenya: the political economy of neo-colonialism. London, 1974.

Leys, C. and Pratt, C. eds. *A new deal in Central Africa*. London and New York, 1960.

Leys, C. and Robson, P. eds. *Federation in East Africa: opportunities and problems*. Nairobi, 1965.

Lofchie, M. *Zanzibar: background to revolution*. Princeton, 1965.

Lonsdale, J. 'Some origins of nationalism in East Africa', *Journal of African History*, 1968, **9**, 1.

Low, D. A. *Political parties in Uganda, 1942–1962*. London, 1962.

Low, D. A. and Smith, A. eds. *History of East Africa*, vol. III. Oxford, 1976.

Lury, D. A. 'Dayspring mishandled? The Uganda economy, 1945–1960', in D. A. Low and Alison Smith. eds. *History of East Africa*, vol. III. Oxford, 1976.

McMaster, C. *Malawi: foreign policy and development*. New York, 1974.

Maguire, G. A. *Towards 'uhuru' in Tanzania: the politics of participation*. Cambridge, 1969.

Martin, A. *Minding their own business*. Harmondsworth, 1975.

Martin, D. *General Amin*. London, 1974.

Mason, P. *The birth of a dilemma*. London, 1960.

Mitchell, J. Clyde. *The Kalela dance.* Rhodes-Livingstone Paper, no. 27. Manchester, 1956.

Morris-Jones, W. H. and Fischer, G. eds. *Decolonisation and after: the British and French experience.* London, 1980.

Morton, K. *Aid and dependence.* London, 1975.

Mulford, D. *Zambia: the politics of independence, 1957–1964.* London, 1967.

Murray, D. J. *The governmental system in Southern Rhodesia.* London, 1970.

Murray-Brown, J. *Kenyatta.* London, 1972.

Odinga, O. *Not yet Uhuru.* London, 1967.

Palmer, R. *Land and racial discrimination in Rhodesia.* London, 1977.

Pratt, C. *The critical phase in Tanzania 1945–1968: Nyerere and the emergence of a socialist strategy.* Cambridge, 1976.

Roberts, A. D. *History of Zambia.* London, 1976.

Rosberg, C. G. and Nottingham, J. *The myth of Mau Mau: nationalism in Kenya.* London and New York, 1966.

Rotberg, R. I. *The rise of nationalism in Central Africa: the making of Malawi and Zambia, 1873–1964.* Cambridge, Mass., 1965.

Rothchild, D. 'Rural–urban inequalities and resource allocation in Zambia', *Journal of Commonwealth Political Studies,* 1972, **10**, 3.

Sandbrook, R. *Proletarians and African capitalism: the Kenyan case 1962–70.* London, 1975.

Short, P. *Banda.* London, 1974.

Sklar, R. *Corporate power in an African state.* Berkeley, 1975.

Sorrenson, M. P. K. *Land reforms in the Kikuyu country.* Nairobi, 1967.

Stren, R. 'Factional politics and central control in Mombasa, 1960–1969', *Canadian Journal of African Studies,* 1970, **4**, 1.

Swainson, N. *The development of corporate capitalism in Kenya, 1918–1977.* London, 1980.

Tordoff, W. *Government and politics in Tanzania.* Nairobi, 1967.

ed. *Politics in Zambia.* Manchester, 1974.

University of Dar es Salaam, Rural Development Committee, *Rural Cooperation in Tanzania.* Dar es Salaam, 1975.

Vincent, J. *African élite: the big man of a small town.* New York, 1971.

Wasserman, G. *The politics of decolonisation.* Cambridge, 1976.

Welensky, R. *Welensky's 4,000 days.* London, 1964.

Whisson, M. G. *Change and challenge: a study of the social and economic changes among the Kenyan Luo.* Nairobi, 1964.

Wrigley, C. C. *Crops and wealth in Uganda.* East African Studies no. 12. Kampala, 1959.

'Kenya: the patterns of economic life, 1902–1945', in Harlow, V. and Chilver, E. M. eds. *History of East Africa,* vol. II. Oxford, 1965.

'Changes in East African society', in Low, D. A. and Smith, Alison. eds. *History of East Africa,* vol. III. Oxford, 1976.

van Zwanenberg, R. M. 'Neo-colonialism and the origin of the national bourgeoisie in Kenya between 1940 and 1973', *Journal of Eastern African Research and Development,* 1974, **4**, 2.

van Zwanenberg, R. with King, A. *An economic history of Kenya and Uganda, 1800–1970.* London, 1975.

9. THE HORN OF AFRICA

Abir, M. 'The contentious Horn of Africa', *Conflict Studies*, 1972, **23**.

Accademia dei Lincei. 'IV Congresso Internazionale di Studi Etiopici (Roma 10–15 aprile 1972)'. *Problemi attuali di scienza e di cultura, Quaderno no. 191.* Rome, 1974.

Andargatchew, T. 'Eritrea, Ethiopia, and Federation, 1941–1952', *Northeast African Studies*, 1980–1, **2**, 3, 99–119.

Andrzejewski, B. W., and Lewis, I. M. *Somali poetry*. Oxford, 1964.

Assefa Bequele and Eshetu Chole. *A profile of the Ethiopian economy*. Nairobi, 1969.

Baxter, P. T. W. 'Ethiopia's unacknowledged problem: the Oromo', *African Affairs*, 1978, **77**, 283–96.

Beckingham, C. F. and Ullendorff, E. eds. 'Ethiopian studies: Papers read at the Second International Conference of Ethiopian Studies (Manchester University, July 1963)', *Journal of Semitic Studies*, 1964, **9**, 1.

Bereket Habte Selassie. *Conflict and intervention in the Horn of Africa*. New York, 1980.

Bondestam, L. 'People and capitalism in the north-eastern lowlands of Ethiopia', *Journal of Modern African Studies*, 1974, **12**, 3, 423–39.

Brown, C. F. *Ethiopian perspectives: bibliographical guide to the history of Ethiopia.* Westport, Conn., 1978.

Campbell, J. F. 'Background to the Eritrean conflict', *Africa Report*, 1971, **16**.

Cerulli, E. ed. *Atti del Convegno Internazionale di Studi Etiopici (Roma 2–4 aprile 1959)*. Rome, 1960.

Chekole, K. 'Eritrea: a preliminary bibliography', *Africana Journal*, 1975–6, **6**, 4, 303–14.

Clapham, C. 'The Ethiopian *coup d'état* of December 1960', *Journal of Modern African Studies*, 1968, **6**, 4, 495–507.

  Haile-Selassie's government. London, 1969.

  'Ethiopia', in Lemarchand, R. ed. *African kingships in perspective*. London, 1977, 35–63.

Clarke, W. S. 'The Republic of Djibouti: an introduction to Africa's newest state and a review of related literature and sources', *Current Bulletin of African Affairs*, 1977–8, **10**, 1, 3–31.

Cohen, J. M. 'Ethiopia after Haile Selassie: the government land factor', *African Affairs*, 1973, **72**, 289, 365–82.

  'Rural change in Ethiopia: the Chilalo Agricultural Development Unit', *Economic Development and Cultural Change*, 1974, **22**, 4, 580–614.

  'Effects of Green Revolution strategies on tenants and small scale landowners in the Chilalo region of Ethiopia', *Journal of Developing Areas*, 1975, **9**, 3, 335–58.

Cohen, J. M. and Koehn, P. H. *Ethiopian provincial and municipal government: imperial patterns and postrevolutionary changes*. East Lansing, Mich., 1980.

Cohen, J. M. and Weintraub, D. *Land and peasants in imperial Ethiopia: the social background to a revolution*. Assen, 1975.

Costanzo, G. A. *Problemi costituzionali della Somalia nella preparazione all'Indipendenza, 1957–1960*. Milan, 1962.

Decraene, P. *L'Expérience socialiste somalienne*. Paris, 1977.

Drysdale, J. *The Somali dispute*. London, 1964.

Dunning, H. C. 'Land reform in Ethiopia: a case of non-development', *UCLA Law Review*, 1970, **18**, 2, 271–307.

Ellingson, L. 'The emergence of political parties in Eritrea, 1941–1950', *Journal of African History*, 1977, **18**, 2, 261–81.

Ethiopia, Central Statistical Office. *Statistical abstract*. Addis Ababa, 1963 onwards.

Ethiopia, Imperial Ethiopian Institute of Public Administration. *Administrative directory of the imperial Ethiopian government*. Addis Ababa, 1957 onwards.

Ethiopia, Ministry of Commerce and Industry. *Economic progress of Ethiopia*. Addis Ababa, 1955.

Ethiopia, Ministry of Land Reform and Administration. *Report on land tenure survey of Arusi province* (1967), *Bale province* (1969), *Begemdir and Semien province* (1970), *Eritrea province* (1969), *Gemu Gofa province* (1968), *Illubabor province* (1969), *Kafa province* (1969), *Shoa province* (1967), *Sidamo province* (1968), *Tigre province* (1969), *Wallega province* (1968), *Wollo province* (1968). Addis Ababa, 1967–70.

Ethiopia, Ministry of the Pen/Secretariat of the Provisional Military Government. *Negarit Gazeta*. Addis Ababa, 1941 onwards.

Ethiopia Observer. Addis Ababa, 1957 onwards.

Ethiopian Journal of Education. Addis Ababa, 1967 onwards.

Farer, T. J. *War clouds on the Horn of Africa: a crisis for détente*. New York, Carnegie Endowment for International Peace, 1976, revised ed. New York, 1979.

Fenet, A. *et al. La Question de l'Erythrée*. Paris, 1979.

Gilkes, P. *The dying lion*. London, 1975.

Gill, G. J. *Readings on the Ethiopian economy*. Addis Ababa, 1974.

Greenfield, R. *Ethiopia: a new political history*. London, 1965.

Haile Selassie, Emperor. *Selected speeches of His Imperial Majesty Haile Selassie I, 1918–1967*. Addis Ababa, 1967.

Hall, D. 'Somaliland's last year as a Protectorate', *African Affairs*, 1961.

Halpern, J. 'La Planification et le développement en Éthiopie après la deuxième guerre mondiale', *Culture et Développement*, 1974.

Hess, R. L. *Ethiopia, the modernization of autocracy*. Ithaca, 1970.

Proceedings of the Fifth International Conference of Ethiopian Studies, Session B, April 13–16, 1978, Chicago, USA. Chicago, 1979.

Hidaru, A. and Rahmato, D. *A short guide to the study of Ethiopia*. London, 1976.

Hoben, A. *Land tenure among the Amhara of Ethiopia*. Chicago, 1973.

Hoerr, O. D. 'Educational returns and educational reform in Ethiopia', *East African Economic Review*, 1974, **6**, 2, 18–34.

Hoskyns, C. *Case studies in African diplomacy: the Ethiopia–Somalia–Kenya dispute 1960–1967*. Dar es Salaam, 1969.

International Bank for Reconstruction and Development. *Ethiopia: a preliminary survey*. New York, 1950.

Economy of Ethiopia: main report. New York, 1967.

Economic growth and prospects in Ethiopia. New York, 1970.

International Institute for Strategic Studies. *Conflicts in Africa* (Adelphi Papers, no. 93.) London, 1972.

Italy, Ministry of Foreign Affairs. *Rapport du Gouvernement Italien à l'Assemblée Générale des Nations Unies sur l'administration de tutelle de la Somalie.* Rome, annually, 1951–9.

Journal of Ethiopian Law. Addis Ababa, 1964 onwards.

Journal of Ethiopian Studies. Addis Ababa, 1963 onwards.

Karp, M. *The economics of trusteeship in Somalia.* Boston, Mass., 1960.

Kitchen, H. ed. *The educated African.* New York, 1962, 83–127.

Knutsson, K. E. 'Dichotomization and integration: aspects of inter-ethnic relations in Southern Ethiopia', in Barth, F. ed. *Ethnic groups and boundaries.* Bergen, 1969.

Koehn, P. and Koehn, E. F. 'Urbanization and urban development planning in Ethiopia', in Obudho, R. A. and El-Shakh, S. eds. *Development of urban systems in Africa.* New York, 1979.

Laitin, D. D. *Politics, language and thought: the Somali experience.* Chicago, 1972.

'The political economy of military rule in Somalia', *Journal of Modern African Studies*, 1976, **14**, 3, 449–68.

Legum, Colin. *Ethiopia: the fall of Haile Selassie's empire.* London, 1975.

Levine, D. N. *Wax and gold: tradition and innovation in Ethiopian culture.* Chicago, 1965.

'Class consciousness and class solidarity in the new Ethiopian élites', in Lloyd, P. C. ed. *The new élites of tropical Africa.* London, 1966, 312–27.

'The military in Ethiopian politics: capabilities and constraints', in Bienen, H. *The military intervenes: case studies in political development.* New York, 1968.

Greater Ethiopia: the evolution of a multiethnic society. Chicago, 1974.

Lewis, H. S. 'Wealth, influence and prestige among the Shoa Galla', in Tuden, A. and Plotnikov, L. eds. *Social stratification in Africa.* New York, 1970.

Lewis, I. M. *A pastoral democracy.* London, 1961.

'Nationalism and particularism in Somalia', in Gulliver, P. H. ed. *Tradition and transition in East Africa.* London, 1969.

'The politics of the 1969 Somali coup', *Journal of Modern African Studies*, 1972, **10**, 3, 383–408.

Abaar: the Somali drought. London, 1975.

'The nation, state and politics in Somalia', in Smock, D. R. ed. *The search for national integration in Africa.* New York, 1975.

A modern history of Somalia. 2nd ed., revised. London, 1980.

Leymarie, P. 'La République de Djibouti: entre l'Afrique Noire et le Monde Arabe', *Revue Française d'Études Politiques Africaines*, 1977, **173**, 58–72.

Lipsky, G. A. *et al. Ethiopia, its people, its society, its culture.* New Haven, 1962.

Longrigg, S. A. *A short history of Eritrea.* Oxford, 1945.

Lovegrove, M. N. 'Educational growth and economic constraints: the Ethiopian experience', *Comparative Education*, 1973, **9**, 1, 17–27.

Marcus, H. G. *The modern history of Ethiopia and the Horn of Africa: a select and annotated bibliography.* Stanford, 1972.

ed. *Proceedings of the First United States Conference on Ethiopian Studies, 1973.* East Lansing, African Studies Center, Michigan State University, 1975.

Markakis, J. *Ethiopia: anatomy of a traditional polity*. Oxford, 1974.

Marks, T. A. 'Djibouti: a strategic French toehold in Africa', *African Affairs*, 1974, **73**, 290, 95–104.

Matthies, V. *Die Grenzkonflikt Somalias mit Aethiopien und Kenya*. Hamburg, 1977.

Mesfin Wolde Mariam. 'The background of the Ethio-Somali boundary dispute', *Journal of Modern African Studies*, 1964, **2**, 2, 189–219.

Messing, S. D. *The target of health in Ethiopia*. New York, 1972.

Morrison, G. *The Southern Sudan and Eritrea: aspects of wider African problems*. London, 1971.

Mosley, L. *Haile Selassie: the conquering lion*. London, 1964.

Negussay Ayele. 'The foreign policy of Ethiopia', in Aluko, O. ed. *The foreign policies of African states*. London, 1977, 46–71.

Nekby, B. *CADU: an Ethiopian experiment in developing peasant farming*. Stockholm, 1971.

Oberlé, P. *Afars et Somalis: le dossier de Djibouti*. Paris, 1971.

Ottaway, M. and Ottaway, D. *Ethiopia: empire in revolution*. New York, 1978.

Ozay Mehmet. 'Effectiveness of foreign aid: the case of Somalia', *Journal of Modern African Studies*, 1971, **9**, 1, 31–47.

Palen, J. J. 'Urbanization and migration in an indigenous city: the case of Addis Ababa', in Richmond, A. H. and Kubat, D. eds. *Internal migration: the new world and the third world*. London, 1976.

Pankhurst, E. S. *Ex-Italian Somaliland*. London, 1951.

Pankhurst, E. S. and Pankhurst, R. K. P. *Ethiopia and Eritrea: the last ten years of the reunion struggle, 1941–1952*. Woodford, Essex, 1953.

Pankhurst, R. K. P. *Economic history of Ethiopia 1800–1935*. Addis Ababa, 1968. ed. *Proceedings of the Third International Conference of Ethiopian Studies, Addis Ababa 1966*. Addis Ababa, 1969–70.

Perham, Margery. *The government of Ethiopia*. 2nd ed. London, 1969.

Playfair, I. S. O. *The Mediterranean and Middle East vol. I: the early successes against Italy (to May 1941)*. (Official History of the Second World War.) London, 1954, 165–84, 391–450.

Rennell of Rodd, Lord. *British military administration of occupied territories in Africa, 1941–47*. London, 1948.

Salad, M. K. *Somalia: a bibliographical survey*. London, 1972.

Schwab, P. *Decision-making in Ethiopia*. London, 1972.
Haile Selassie I: Ethiopia's Lion of Judah. New York, 1979.

Shehim, K. and Shearing, J. 'Djibouti and the question of Afar nationalism', *African Affairs*, 1980, **79**, 315, 209–26.

Sherman, R. *Eritrea: the unfinished revolution*. New York, 1980.

Shilling, N. A. 'Problems of political development in a ministate: the French Territory of the Afars and Issas', *Journal of Developing Areas*, **7**, 1973.

Simoons, F. J. *Northwest Ethiopia: peoples and economy*. Madison, Wisconsin, 1960.

Solodovnikov, V. G. *Ucenye Zapiski Sovetsjo-Somalijskoj Ekspedicii*. Moscow, 1974.

Somali Republic, Central Statistical Department. *Statistical abstract*. Mogadishu, 1964 onwards.

Stahl, M. *Ethiopia: political contradictions in agricultural development.* Stockholm, 1974.

Steer, G. L. *Sealed and delivered.* London, 1942.

Teketel Haile-Mariam. 'The impact of coffee on the economy of Ethiopia', in Pearson, S. R. *et al.* eds. *Commodity exports and African economic development.* Lexington, 1974.

Thompson, V. and Adloff, R. *Djibouti and the Horn of Africa.* Stanford, 1968.

Touval, S. *Somali nationalism.* Cambridge, Mass., 1963.

The boundary politics of independent Africa. Cambridge, Mass., 1972.

Trevaskis, G. K. N. *Eritrea: a colony in transition, 1941–1952.* London, 1960.

Trimingham, J. S. *Islam in Ethiopia.* London, 1952.

Tubiana, J. ed. *Modern Ethiopia; from the accession of Menelik II to the present. Proceedings of the Fifth International Conference of Ethiopian Studies, Nice, 19–22 December, 1977.* Rotterdam, 1980.

UK, Colonial Office. *Somaliland Protectorate report.* London, usually biennially, 1944–60.

UK, Ministry of Information. *The Abyssinian campaigns.* London, 1942.

The first to be freed: the record of British military administration in Eritrea and Somalia. London, 1944.

Wagaw, Teshome G. *Education in Ethiopia: retrospect and prospect.* Ann Arbor, Mich., 1979.

Winid, B. 'Ethiopia', in Jones, R. ed. *Essays on world urbanisation.* London, 1975.

10. EGYPT, LIBYA AND THE SUDAN

Abd al-Rahim, M. *Imperialism and nationalism in the Sudan.* London, 1969.

Abdel-Malek, A. *Égypte: société militaire.* Paris, 1962.

Albergoni, G. *et al. La Libye nouvelle, rupture et continuité.* Paris, 1975.

Albino, O. *The Sudan – a southern viewpoint.* London, 1970.

Allan, J. A. *Libya: the experience of oil.* London/Boulder, 1981.

Allan, J. A., McLachlan, K. S. and Penrose, E. T. eds. *Libya: agriculture and economic development.* London, 1971.

Attiga, A. A. *L'Influence du pétrole sur l'économie Libyenne, 1959–1969.* Beirut, 1972.

Ayubi, N. N. *Bureaucracy and politics in contemporary Egypt.* London, 1980.

Baker, R. W. *Egypt's uncertain revolution under Nasser and Sadat.* Cambridge, Mass., 1978.

Barawy, R. *The military coup in Egypt.* Cairo, 1952.

Berger, M. *Islam in Egypt today: social and political aspects of popular religion.* Cambridge, 1970.

Berque, J. *Egypt: imperialism and revolution.* London, 1972.

Beshir, M. O. *The Southern Sudan: background to conflict.* London, 1968.

Revolution and nationalism in the Sudan. London, 1974.

The Southern Sudan: from conflict to peace. London, 1968.

Betts, T. *The Southern Sudan: the ceasefire and after.* London, 1974.

Bianco, M. *Kadhafi, messager du désert.* Paris, 1974.

Bleuchot, H. 'The Green Book: its context and meaning', in Allan, J. A. ed.

Libya since independence: economic and political development, ch. 10. London, 1982.

Bleuchot, H. and Monastiri, T. 'L'évolution des institutions libyennes (1969–1978)', in *L'Annuaire de l'Afrique du Nord*, 1977.

Cooley, J. K. *Libyan sandstorm: the complete account of Qaddafi's revolution.* London, 1982.

Collins, R. O. *Southern Sudan in historical perspective.* London, 1976.

Dawisha, A. I. *Egypt in the Arab world: the elements of foreign policy.* London, 1976.

Deeb, M. K. and Deeb, M. J. *Libya since the Revolution: aspects of social and political development.* New York, 1982.

The Democratic Republic of the Sudan, Ministry of Culture and Information. *The Southern Provinces Regional Self-government Act, 1972.* Khartoum, 1972.

Duncan, J. S. R. *The Sudan's path to independence.* Edinburgh, 1957.

Dupuy, T. N. *Elusive victory: the Arab–Israeli wars 1947–1974.* London, 1978.

El Fathaly, O. I. and Palmer, M. *Political development and social change in Libya.* Lexington, 1977.

Evans-Pritchard, E. E. *The Sanussi of Cyrenaica.* Oxford, 1949.

Fabunmi, L. A. *Sudan in Anglo-Egyptian relations: a case study in power politics, 1800–1956.* Westport, Conn., 1973.

Farley, R. *Planning for development in Libya: the exceptional economy in the developing world.* New York, 1971.

Fawzi, Saad ed Din. *The labour movement in the Sudan, 1946–1955.* London, 1957.

First, R. *Libya: the elusive revolution.* Harmondsworth, 1974.

Fowler, G. L. 'Decolonization of rural Libya', *Annals of the Association of American Geographers*, 1974, **63**, 4.

Guernon, H. *La Libye.* Vendôme, 1976.

Habib, H. *Politics and government of revolutionary Libya.* Ottawa, 1975.

Hansen, B. and Marzouk, G. A. *Development and economic policy in the UAR (Egypt).* Amsterdam, 1965.

Hartley, R. G. 'Libya: economic development and demographic responses', in Clarke, J. I. and Fisher, W. B. *Population of the Middle East and North Africa.* London, 1972.

Hasan, S. 'The genesis of the political leadership of Libya 1952–1969: historical origin and development of its component elements'. Ph.D. dissertation, George Washington University, Washington DC, 1973.

Hasan, Y. F. 'The Sudanese Revolution of October 1964', *Journal of Modern African Studies*, 1967, **5**.

Heikal, M. *Nasser, the Cairo documents.* London, 1972.
　　The road to Ramadan. London, 1975.
　　Sphinx and Commissar: the rise and fall of Soviet influence in the Arab world. London, 1978.

Henderson, K. D. D. *The making of modern Sudan* London, 1953.
　　Sudan Republic. London, 1967.

Hirst, D. and Beeson, I. *Sadat.* London, 1981.

Holt, P. M. *A modern history of the Sudan from the Funj Sultanate to the present day.* 2nd ed. London, 1963.
　　ed. *Political and social change in modern Egypt.* London, 1968.

Hopwood, D. *Egypt: politics and society*. London, 1982.
Hussein, M. *L'Égypte: lutte de classes et libération nationale*. Paris, 1975.
Issawi, C. *Egypt in revolution*. London, 1963.
Kerr, M. *The Arab Cold War, 1958–64*. Oxford, 1965.
Khadduri, M. *Modern Libya*. Baltimore, 1963.
Lacouture, J. *Nasser*. London, 1973.
Lacouture, J. and Lacouture, S. *Egypt in transition*. New York, 1958.
Lawson, D. *Libya and Qaddafi*. London, 1982.
Love, K. *Suez, the twice fought war*. London, 1969.
Mabro, R. *The Egyptian economy 1952–1972*. Oxford, 1974.
'Libya', in Knapp, W. ed. *Northwest Africa: a political and economic survey*. 3rd ed. London, 1977.
Mabro, R. and O'Brien, P. 'Structural changes in the Egyptian economy, 1937–1965', in Cook, M. A. ed. *Studies in the economic history of the Middle East*. London, 1970.
Marlowe, J. *Anglo-Egyptian relations, 1800–1953*. London, 1954.
Mead, D. *Growth and structural change in the Egyptian economy*. Homewood, Ill., 1967.
Meyer, G. E. *Egypt and the United States. The formative years*. London, 1980.
Mitchell, R. P. *The Society of Muslim Brothers*. London, 1969.
Moore, M. *Fourth shore: Italy's mass colonisation of Libya*. London, 1940.
Nasir, G. A. *The philosophy of the revolution*. Cairo, 1954.
O'Ballance, E. *The war in the Yemen*. London, 1971.
The secret war in the Sudan: 1955–1972. London, 1977.
O'Brien, P. 'The long-term growth of agricultural production in Egypt: 1821–1962', in Holt, P. M. ed. *Political and social change in modern Egypt*. London, 1968.
Pelt, A. *Libyan independence and the United Nations: a case of planned decolonization*. Yale, 1970.
al-Qadhafi, M. *The Green Book*, Part 1. London, 1976.
The Green Book, Part 2. London, 1977.
Radwan, S. *Agrarian reform and rural poverty 1952–1975*. Geneva, 1977.
Rejwan, N. *Nasserist ideology: its exponents and critics*. New York, 1974.
Sadat, A. *Revolt on the Nile*. London, 1957.
In search of identity: an autobiography. London, 1978.
Sanderson, G. N. 'Sudanese nationalism and the independence of the Sudan', *Symposium on Islamic North Africa*. London, 1971.
Schliephake, K. *Libyen: wirtschaftliche und soziale Strukturen und Entwicklung*. Hamburg, 1976.
Shoukri, G. *Égypte, la contre-révolution*, tr. M. Morgane. Paris, 1979.
Egypt: portrait of a president. London, 1981.
Stephens, R. *Nasser: a political biography*. London, 1971.
Sury, S. M. 'The political development of Libya 1952–1969: institutions, policies and ideology', in Allan, J. A. ed. *Libya since independence: economic and political development*. London, 1982.
Sylvester, A. *Sudan under Nimeiri*. London, 1977.
Trimingham, J. S. *Islam in the Sudan*. London, 1965.

Vatikiotis, P. J. ed. *Egypt since the Revolution*. London, 1968.
  The Egyptian army in politics: a pattern for new nations? Westport, Conn., 1975.
    Reprint of 1961 ed.
  Nasser and his generation. London, 1978.
  The history of Egypt. 2nd ed. London, 1980.
Waddams, F. *The Libyan oil industry*. London, 1980.
Wai, D. M. ed. *Southern Sudan: the problem of national integration*. London, 1973.
Warburg, G. *Islam, nationalism and communism in a traditional society: the case of Sudan*. London, 1978.
Waterbury, J. *Egypt: burdens of the past/options for the future*. Bloomington, Ind., 1978.
Wheelock, K. *Nasser's new Egypt*. London, 1975.
Wright, J. *Libya*. London, 1969.
  Libya, a modern history. London, 1982.
Ziadeh, N. *Sanusiyah: a study of a revivalist movement in Islam*. Leiden, 1968.

11. THE MAGHRIB

Abbas, F. *La Nuit coloniale*. Paris, 1962.
Adam, A. *Casablanca*. Paris, 1968.
Al-Fassi, A. *Al-naqd al-dhati*. Cairo, 1952.
  Independence movements of North Africa. tr. A. Gaudio. Washington, 1954.
Alleg, H. *et al. La Guerre d'Algérie*, 3 vols. Paris, 1981.
Amin, S. *The Maghreb in the modern world*, tr. M. Perl. London, 1970.
Ammour, K., Leucate, C. and Moulin, J.-J. *La Voie algérienne*. Paris, 1974.
Ashford, D. *National development and local reform: political participation in Morocco, Tunisia, and Pakistan*. Princeton, 1967.
Ayache, A. *Le Mouvement syndical au Maroc*. Paris, 1982.
Azzedine, Commandant. *En Algérie ne brûle pas*. Paris, 1980.
ben Barka, M. *Option révolutionnaire au Maroc*. Paris, 1974.
Baroja, J. C. *Estudios Saharianos*. Madrid, 1955.
Bedrani, S. *L'Agriculture algérienne depuis 1966*. Paris, 1982.
Benhouria, T. *L'Économie de l'Algérie*. Paris, 1980.
Benissad, M. E. *Économie du développement de l'Algérie*. 2nd ed. Paris, 1982.
Bennabi, M. *Vocation de l'Islam*. Paris, 1954.
Bernard, S. *The Franco-Moroccan conflict*. New Haven, 1968.
Berque, J. *French North Africa*, tr. Jean Stewart. London, 1967.
Bessis, J. *La Méditerranée fasciste: l'Italie mussolinienne et la Tunisie*. Paris, 1980.
Boudiaf, M. *Où va l'Algérie?* Paris, 1964.
Bourdieu, P. *The Algerians*. Boston, 1962.
Bourguiba, H. *La Tunisie et la France*. Paris, 1954.
Camau, M. *La Notion de démocratie dans la pensée des dirigeants maghrébins*. Paris, 1971.
Centre de Recherches et d'Études sur les Sociétés Méditerranéennes.
  L'Annuaire de l'Afrique du Nord, 1962 onwards.
  La Formation des élites politiques maghrébines. Paris, 1973.
Dejeux, J. *Littérature maghrébine de langue française*. Ottawa, 1973.

Despois, J. *L'Afrique du Nord*. Paris, 1964.

Djait, H. *La Personalité et le devenir arabo-islamiques*. Paris, 1974.

Documentation Française. *Maghreb*, 1964–1973, and *Maghreb-Machreq*, 1974 onwards.

Duclos, L. J., Duvignaud, L. and Leca, J. *Les Nationalismes maghrébins*. (Études Maghrébines 7, Fondation Nationale des Sciences Politiques.) Paris, 1966.

Duprat, G. *Révolution et autogestion rurale en Algérie*. Paris, 1973.

Étienne, B. *L'Algérie, cultures et révolution*. Paris, 1977.

Fanon, F. *A dying colonialism*. New York, 1965.

Flory, M. and Mantran, R. *Le Régime politique des pays arabes*. Paris, 1967.

Francos, A. and Séréni, J.-P. *Un Algérien nommé Boumediène*. Paris, 1976.

Gallagher, C. F. *The United States and North Africa*. Cambridge, Mass., 1963.

Garas, F. *Bourguiba et la naissance d'une nation*. Paris, 1956.

Gaudio, A. *Allal al-Fassi, ou l'histoire de l'Istiqlal*. Paris, 1972.

Geertz, C. *Islam observed*. New Haven, Conn., 1968.

Gellner, E. *Saints of the Atlas*. London, 1969.

Gellner, E. and Micaud, C. eds. *Arabs and Berbers*. London, 1973.

Halstead, J. P. *Rebirth of a nation: the origins and rise of Moroccan nationalism, 1912–1944*. Cambridge, Mass., 1967.

Harbi, M. *Les Archives de la révolution algérienne*. Paris, 1981.

Le F.L.N.: Mirage et réalité des origines à la prise du pouvoir (1945–1962). Paris, 1980.

Hermassi, E. *Leadership and national development in North Africa*. Berkeley and Los Angeles, 1972.

Horne, A. *A savage war of peace: Algeria 1954–1962*. London, 1977.

Jeanson, F. and Jeanson, C. *L'Algérie hors la loi*. 2nd ed. Paris, 1956.

Julien, C.-A. *L'Afrique du Nord en marche*. 3rd ed. Paris, 1972.

Le Maroc face aux impérialismes 1415–1956. Paris, 1978.

Khatibi, A. *Le Roman maghrébin*. Paris, 1968.

Knapp, W. *North West Africa: a political and economic survey*. 3rd ed. London, 1977.

Lacheraf, M. *Algérie: nation et société*. Paris, 1965.

Lacouture, J. *Cinq hommes et la France*. Paris, 1961.

Laroui, A. *La Crise des intellectuels arabes*. Paris, 1974.

Leca, J. and Vatin, J.-C. *L'Algérie politique: institutions et régime*. Paris, 1975.

Le Tourneau, R. *Évolution politique de l'Afrique du Nord musulmane, 1920–1961*. Paris, 1962.

Leveau, R. *Le Fellah marocain défenseur du trône*. Paris, 1976.

Mahsas, A. *Le Mouvement révolutionnaire en Algérie*. Paris, 1979.

Mameri, K. ed. *Citations du Président Boumediène*. Algiers, 1975.

Mazouni, A. *Culture et enseignement en Algérie et au Maghreb*. Paris, 1969.

Meynier, G. *L'Algérie révélée*. Geneva, 1981.

Micaud, C. A., Brown, L. C. and Moore, C. H. *Tunisia: the politics of modernization*. London, 1964.

Moore, C. H. *Tunisia since independence: the dynamics of one-party government*. Berkeley and Los Angeles, 1965.

Politics in North Africa. Boston, 1970.

Morizot, J. *L'Algérie kabylisée*. Paris, 1962.
Nouschi, A. *La Naissance du nationalisme Algérien*. Paris, 1962.
Poncet, J. *La Tunisie à la recherche de son avenir*. Paris, 1974.
Quandt, W. B. *Revolution and political leadership: Algeria, 1954–1968*. Cambridge, Mass., 1969.
Rézette, R. *Les Partis politiques marocains*. Paris, 1955.
Rudebeck, L. *Party and people*. New York, 1969.
Sivan, E. *Communisme et nationalisme en Algérie 1920–1962*. Paris, 1976.
Tiano, A. *La Politique économique et financière du Maroc indépendant*. Paris, 1963.
Le Maghreb entre les mythes. Paris, 1967.
Vatin, J.-C. *L'Algérie politique, histoire et société*. Paris, 1974.
Viratelle, G. *L'Algérie algérienne*. 2nd ed. Paris, 1970.
Waterbury, J. *Commander of the Faithful: the Moroccan political élite – a study of segmented politics*. London, 1970.
North for the trade. Berkeley and Los Angeles, 1972.
Zartman, W. I. *Morocco: problems of new power*. New York, 1964.
ed. *Man, state and society in the contemporary Maghreb*. London, 1973.

12. FRENCH-SPEAKING TROPICAL AFRICA

Adamolekun, L. *Sékou Touré's Guinea: an experiment in nation building*. London, 1976.
Africa South of the Sahara. London, annual.
L'Afrique Noire politique et économique. (Ediafrique, La Documentation Africaine.) Paris, 1977.
Akindélé, A. and Aguessy, C. *Dahomey*. Paris, 1955.
Akinjogbin, I. A. *Dahomey and its neighbours, 1708–1818*. Cambridge, 1967.
Amin, S. *Le Monde des affaires sénégalais*. Paris, 1964/1969.
Trois expériences africaines de développement: le Mali, la Guinée et le Ghana. Paris, 1965.
Le Développement du capitalisme en Côte d'Ivoire. Paris, 1967.
Amon d'Aby, F. J. *La Côte d'Ivoire dans la cité africaine*. Paris, 1951.
Ardener, E. and Ardener, S. *Plantation and village in the Cameroons: some economic and social studies*. London, 1960.
Arkhurst, F. ed. 'African politics: background and prospects', *Africa in the seventies and eighties*. New York, 1970, 16–47.
Azarya, V. *Dominance and change in North Cameroon: the Fulbe aristocracy*. Beverly Hills, 1976.
Baier, S. B. *An economic history of Central Niger*. Oxford, 1980.
Balans, J. L. *et al. Autonomie locale et intégration nationale au Sénégal*. Paris, 1975.
de Benoist, J. R. *La Balkanisation de l'Afrique occidentale française*. Dakar, 1978.
Berg, E. 'French West Africa', in Galenson, W. ed. *Labor and economic development*. New York, 1959.
'The economic basis of political choice in French West Africa', *The American Political Sciences Review*, June, 1960.
Beti, M. *Ville cruelle*. Paris, 1954.
Blanchet, A. *L'Itinéraire des partis africains depuis Bamako*. Paris, 1958.

Bonardi, P. *La République du Niger: naissance d'un état*. Paris, 1960.
Bouquerel, J. *Le Gabon*. Paris, 1970.
Bouvier, P. *L'Europe et la coopération au développement*. Brussels, 1980.
Brunschwig, H. *La Colonisation française du pacte colonial à l'Union française*. Paris, 1949.
Cabot, J. and Bouquet, C. *Le Tchad*. Paris, 1973.
Caldwell, J. *et al.* eds. *Upper Volta*. New York, 1975.
Campbell, B. 'Ivory Coast', in Dunn, J. ed. *West African states: failure and promise*. Cambridge, 1978, 66–116.
Carter, Gwendolen M. ed. *African one-party states*. Ithaca, 1962.
Five African states: responses to diversity. Ithaca, 1963.
National unity and regionalism in eight African states. Ithaca, 1966.
Clignet, R. *The Africanization of the labor market: educational and occupational segmentation in the Cameroon*. Berkeley, 1976.
Cohen, M. *Urban policy and political conflict in Africa: a study of the Ivory Coast*. Chicago, 1974.
Coleman, J. S. 'Togoland', *International conciliation*, 509. New York, 1956.
'The politics of Sub-Saharan Africa', in Almond, Gabriel A. and Coleman, James S. eds. *The politics of developing areas*. Princeton, 1960.
Coleman, J. S. and Rosberg, C. G. eds. *Political parties and national integration in tropical Africa*. Berkeley, 1964.
Coquéry-Vidrovitch, C. 'De la traite des esclaves à l'exportation d'huile de palme et des palmistes au Dahomey au XIX siècle'. Paper presented at the IAI Conference, Freetown, 1969.
'Le Blocus de Ouidah (1876–1878) et la rivalité franco-anglaise au Dahomey', *Cahiers d'Études Africaines*, 1962, 7.
'Mutations de l'impérialisme colonial français dans les années 30', *African Economic History*, 1977, 4, 103–52.
Cornevin, R. *Le Dahomey*. Paris, 1970.
Le Togo. Paris, 1973.
Creevey (Behrman), L. *Muslim Brotherhoods and politics in Senegal*. Cambridge, Mass., 1970.
'The French Muslim policy in Senegal', in McCall, Daniel F. ed. *Aspects of West African Islam*. Boston, 1971.
'Urbanization and development in Senegal'. Unpublished. September 1977.
'Muslim politics and development in Senegal', *Journal of Modern African Studies*, 1977, 15, 2, 261–77.
'Religious attitudes and development in Dakar, Senegal', *World Development*, July 1980, 8.
Crowder, M. *Senegal: a study in French assimilation policy*. 2nd ed. London, 1967.
Colonial West Africa: collected essays. London, 1978.
Dadié, B. *Climbié*. Paris, 1956.
Delavignette, R. *Paysannerie et prolétariat*. Paris, 1948.
Freedom and authority in French West-Africa. Oxford, 1950.
Deschamps, H. *L'Éveil politique africain*. Paris, 1952.
Désiré-Vuillemin, G. *Contribution à l'histoire de la Mauritanie de 1900 à 1934*. Dakar, 1962.

Diarassouba, V. C. *L'Évolution des structures agricoles du Sénégal.* Paris, 1968.

Diguimbaye, G. *L'Essor du Tchad.* Paris, 1969.

Diop, Cheikh A. *Nations Nègres et culture.* Paris, 1955.

Documentation Française. *La République de Haute-Volta.* (Notes et études documentaires, 2696.) Paris, 1960.

La République du Niger. (Notes et études, 2638.) Paris, 1960.

La République du Mali. (Notes et études, 2739.) Paris, 1961.

La République de Guinée. (Notes et études, 3202.) Paris, 1965.

Donaint, P. and Lancrenon, F. *Le Niger.* Paris, 1972.

Dugué, G. *Vers les États-Unis d'Afrique.* Dakar, 1960.

Dumont, R. *L'Afrique noire est mal partie.* Paris, 1962.

Ernst, K. *Tradition and progress in the African village: the non-capitalist transformation of rural communities in Mali.* London, 1976.

Foltz, W. J. *From French West Africa to the Mali Federation.* New Haven, 1965.

Foster, P. and Zolberg, A. eds. *Ghana and the Ivory Coast.* Chicago, 1971.

Frémaux, P. *La Rébellion tchadienne.* Paris, 1973.

Fyot, J.-L. *Méthode de planification: l'expérience de la Côte d'Ivoire.* Paris, 1972.

Gardinier, D. E. *Cameroon: United Nations challenge to French policy.* London, 1963.

Garnier, C. and Ermont, P. *Désert fertile: un nouvel état, La Mauritanie.* Paris, 1960.

Gerteiny, A. G. *Mauritania.* London, 1967.

Gigon, F. *Guinée, état-pilote.* Paris, 1959.

Glélé, M. A. *Naissance d'un état noir, l'évolution politique et constitutionelle du Dahomey de la colonisation à nos jours.* Paris, 1969.

Gonidec, P. *La République de Sénégal.* Paris, 1968.

Gutkind, P. C. W. and Wallerstein, I. eds. *The political economy of contemporary Africa.* Beverly Hills and London, 1976.

Guyer, D. *Ghana and the Ivory Coast: the impact of colonialism in an African setting.* New York, 1970.

Guyer, J. 'The food economy and French colonial rule in central Cameroun', *Journal of African History*, 1978, **19**, 577–97.

Hailey, Lord. *An African survey.* London, 1957.

Higgott, H. R. 'Structural dependence and decolonisation in a West African land-locked state: Niger', *Review of African Political Economy*, Jan–April 1980, 43–58.

Hodgkin, T. L. *Nationalism in colonial Africa.* London, 1956.

African political parties. London, 1961.

Hodgkin, T. L. and Schachter, R. 'French-speaking West Africa in transition,' *International Conciliation.* (Carnegie Endowment for International Peace, no. 528, 389.) New York, May 1960.

Hopkins, A. G. *An economic history of West Africa.* New York, 1973.

Hopkins, N. S. *Popular government in an African town.* Chicago, 1972.

Houis, M. *Guinée française.* Paris, 1953.

Johnson, W. *The Cameroon Federation: political integration in a fragmentary society.* Princeton, 1970.

Jones, W. I. *Planning and economic policy: socialist Mali and her neighbors.* Washington, 1976.

Joseph, R. *Radical nationalism in Cameroon: social origins of the UPC rebellion.* Oxford, 1977.

Jouve, E. *La République du Mali.* Paris, 1974.

Kaba, L. *Wahabiyya: Islamic reform and politics in French West Africa.* Evanston, 1974.

'The cultural revolution and freedom of expression in Guinea', *Journal of Modern African Studies*, June 1976, **14**.

'Guinean politics: a critical historical overview', *Journal of Modern African Studies*, March 1977, **15**.

Kalck, P. *Central African Republic, a failure in decolonization.* London, 1971.

Kanya-Forstner, A. S. *The conquest of the Western Sudan.* Cambridge, 1969.

Kimble, G. H. T. *Tropical Africa.* 2 vols. New York, 1960.

Kofele-Kale, N. ed. *An African experiment in nation building: the bilingual Cameroon Republic since reunification.* Boulder, Col., 1980.

Kom, D. *Le Cameroun: essai d'analyse économique et politique.* Paris, 1971.

Labouret, H. *Colonisation, colonialisme, décolonisation.* Paris, 1952.

Laye, C. *L'Enfant noir.* Paris, 1953.

Legum, C. ed. *African Contemporary Record.* New York, annually.

Le Vine, V. T. *The Cameroon Federal Republic.* Ithaca, 1971.

Lofchie, M. *The state of the nations, constraints on development in independent Africa.* Berkeley, 1971.

Lombard, J. *Un système politique traditionnel de type féodal: les Bariba du Nord-Dahomey.* Paris, 1965.

Magasa, A. *Papa-commandant a jeté un grand filet devant nous: les exploités des rives du Niger, 1900–1962.* Paris, 1978.

Markovitz, I. L. *Léopold Sédar Senghor and the politics of négritude.* London and New York, 1969.

Meek, C. K. *Land tenure and land administration in Nigeria and the Cameroons.* London, 1957.

Megahed, H. T. *Socialism and the nation-building in Africa: the case of Mali, 1960–1968.* New York, 1970.

Meillassoux, C. *Anthropologie économique des Gouro de Côte d'Ivoire.* Paris, 1964.

Urbanization of an African community: voluntary associations in Bamako. Seattle, 1968.

ed. *L'Esclavage en Afrique pré-coloniale.* Paris, 1975.

Femmes, greniers, et capitaux. Paris, 1975

Milcent, E. *L'AOF entre en scène.* Paris, 1953/1958.

Monteil, V. ed. *Esquisses sénégalaises.* Dakar, 1966.

Moore, C. 'One-partyism in Mauritania', *Journal of Modern African Studies*, 1965, **3**.

Morgenthau, R. Schachter. *Political parties in French-speaking West Africa.* Oxford, 1964.

'Old cleavages among new West African states: the heritage of French rule', *Africa Today*, April, 1971.

'The developing states of Africa', *Annals of the American Academy of Political and Social Science*, July 1977, **432**, 80–94.

'Strangers, nationals and multinationals', in Shack, William A. and Skinner, Ellis H. eds. *Strangers in African societies*. Berkeley, 1979.

Ngoya, A. *Le Cameroun dans les relations internationales*. Paris, 1976.

O'Brien, D. B. Cruise. *Saints and politicians: essays in the organization of a Senegalese peasant society*. Cambridge, 1975.

Ouedrago, I., Newman, M. D. and Norman, D. W. *The farmer in the semi-arid tropics of West Africa: partially annotated bibliography*. India, ICRISAT, 1982.

Owono, J. *Tante Bella*. Yaounde, 1959.

Oyono, F. *Une vie de boy*. Paris, 1956.

Piquemol-Pastré, M. *La République Islamique de Mauritanie*. Paris, 1969.

Proceedings of the International Workshop on Socioeconomic Constraints to Development in Semi-arid Tropical Agriculture. India, 1980. (Particularly Berg, E., 'Reforming grain marketing systems in West Africa (Mali)'.)

Prouzet, M. *Le Cameroun*. Paris, 1974.

Richard-Molard, J. *Afrique Occidentale Française*. Paris, 1956/1949.

Rivière, C. *Mutations sociales en Guinée*. Paris, 1971.

Robinson, K. 'Constitutional reform in French Tropical Africa', *Political Studies*, 1958, **6**.

Robinson, K. and Mackenzie, W. J. M. eds. *Five elections in tropical Africa*. Oxford, 1960.

Ronin, D. *Dahomey: between tradition and modernity*. Ithaca, 1975.

Rubin, N. *Cameroon: an African Federation*. New York, 1971/2.

Schumacher, E. J. *Politics, bureaucracy and rural development in Senegal*. Berkeley, 1975.

Sembène, O. *Les Bouts de bois de Dieu*. Paris, 1960.

Senghor, Léopold S. *Chants d'Ombres*. Paris, 1945.

Séré de Rivières, E. *Le Niger*. Paris, 1972/1952.

Skinner, E. P. *The Mossi of Upper Volta*. Stanford, 1964.

African urban life: the transformation of Ouagadougou. Princeton, 1974.

Skurnik, W. A. E. *The foreign policy of Senegal*. Evanston, 1972.

Snyder, F. G. *One-party government in Mali*. New Haven, 1965.

Socé, O. *Karim*. Paris, 1937.

Soret, M. *Histoire du Congo, capitale Brazzaville*. Paris, 1978.

Surêt-Canale, J. *Afrique Noire, occidentale et centrale*. Paris, 1958/1961.

La République de Guinée. Paris, 1970.

Sy, T. *La Confrérie Sénégalaise des Mourides*. Paris, 1969.

Thompson, V. and Adlof, R. *The emerging states of French Equatorial Africa*. Stanford, 1960.

Conflict in Tchad, Berkeley, 1982.

Touré, S. *Oeuvres complètes*. Paris, n.d.

den Tuinden, B. *Ivory Coast, the challenge of success*. Baltimore, 1978.

Wallerstein, I. *Africa: the politics of independence*. New York, 1961.

Watts, J. M. 'A silent revolution: the nature of famine and the changing

BIBLIOGRAPHY

character of food production in Nigerian Hausaland'. Ph.D. thesis, University of Michigan, 1979.

Weinstein, B. *Gabon*. Cambridge, Mass., 1966.

Weiskel, T. *French colonial rule and the Baule peoples: resistance and collaboration, 1889–1911*. Oxford, 1980.

Westebbe, R. M. *The economy of Mauritania*. New York, 1971.

Westebbe, R. M. et al. *Chad: development, potential and constraints*. Washington, DC, 1974.

Works, J. A. *Pilgrims in a strange land: Hausa communities in Chad*. New York, 1976.

World Bank. *Accelerated development in sub-Saharan Africa*. Washington, DC, 1981.

Woungly-Massaga. *La Révolution au Congo: contribution à l'étude des problèmes politiques de l'Afrique centrale*. Paris, 1974.

Zolberg, A. *One-party government in the Ivory Coast*. 2nd ed. Princeton, 1969.

Zuccarelli, F. *Un Parti politique africain: l'Union progressiste Sénégalaise*. Paris, 1970.

13. MADAGASCAR

Adloff, R. and Thompson, V. *The Malagasy Republic*. Stanford, 1965.

Althabe, G. *Oppression et libération dans l'imaginaire*. Paris, 1968.

Andriamanjato, R. *La Tsiny et le Tody dans la pensée malgache*. Paris, 1957.

Annet, A. L. *Aux heures troublées de l'Afrique française, 1939–1943*. Paris, 1952.

Arbousset, F. *Le Fokonolona à Madagascar*. Paris, 1950.

Archer, R. *Madagascar depuis 1972 – la marche d'une révolution*. Paris, 1976.

Bardonnet, D. 'Les Minorités asiatiques à Madagascar', *Annuaire Français de Droit International*, 1964.

Bastion, G. *Madagascar, étude géographique et économique*. Paris, 1967.

Bergeret, A. *Les Sociétés d'aménagement agricole à Madagascar*. Tananarive, 1967.

Berthier, H. *Notes et impressions sur les moeurs et coutumes du peuple malgache*. Tananarive, 1933.

Boiteau, P. *Contribution à l'histoire de la nation malgache*. Paris, 1958.

Cadoux, C. 'Les Nouveaux Aspects de l'organisation locale à Madagascar', *l'Actualité Juridique*, February, 1965.

La Commune malgache. Mantasoa, 1967.

La République malgache. Paris, 1969.

Colin, P. *Aspects de l'âme malgache*. 1959.

Comte, J. *Les Communes malgaches*. Tananarive, 1963.

Cognac, G. and Feuer, G. *Les Conventions de co-opération entre la République malgache et la République française*. Tananarive, 1963.

Condaminas, G. *Fokonolona et communautés rurales en Imerina*. Paris, 1960.

de Coppet, M. *Madagascar et Réunion*. Paris, 1947.

Daniel, B. C. 'Les Événements de Madagascar'. Unpublished, Paris, 1949.

Darsac, R. 'Contradictions et partis malgaches', *Revue d'Action Populaire*, July–August, 1958.

Delval, P. 'Le syndicalisme à Madagascar', *Pénant*, October–December, 1965.

Deschamps, H. *Histoire de Madagascar*. Paris, 1972.

Dumont, R. *Évolution des campagnes malgaches.* Tananarive, 1959.

Faculté de Droit. 'La femme, la société, et le droit malgache', *Annales de l'Université de Madagascar*, 1967, **4**.

Faublée, J. *Ethnographie de Madagascar.* Paris, 1946.

Gaud, M. *Les Premières Expériences de planification en Afrique noire.* Paris, 1967.

Gayet, G. 'Immigrations asiatiques à Madagascar', *Civilisations*, 1955, **5**.

Gendarme, R. *L'Économie de Madagascar.* Tananarive, 1960.

Hatzfeld, O. 'Évolution actuelle de la société malgache', *Monde non Chrétien*, July–September, 1953.

Heseltine, N. *Madagascar.* London, 1971.

Hoffer, R. *Co-opération économique franco-africaine.* Paris, 1957.

Institut National de la Statistique et de la Recherche Économique (INSRE). *L'Enquête démographique – Madagascar, 1966.* Tananarive, 1967.

Lapierre, J. W. 'Problèmes socio-culturels de la nation malgache', *Cahiers Internationaux de Sociologie*, 1966, **40**.

L'Italien, R. 'Madagascar 1950–1960: une étape vers la décolonisation'. Unpublished thesis, École des Hautes Études, 1975.

Lupo, P. *Église et décolonisation à Madagascar.* Fianarantsoa, 1973.

Maestre, J. C. *La République malgache et les organisations africaines.* Tananarive, 1968.

Mannoni, O. *Psychologie de la colonisation.* Paris, 1950.

Ottino, P. *Les Économies paysannes malgaches du Bas-Mangoky.* Paris, 1963.

Pascal, R. *La République malgache.* Paris, 1965.

Prats, Y. *Le Développement communautaire à Madagascar.* Paris, 1972.

Rabemananjara, J. *Un malgache vous parle.* Paris, 1946.
 Témoignage malgache et colonialisme. Paris, 1956.
 Le Nationalisme et problèmes malgaches. Paris, 1958.

Rabemananjara, R. W. *Madagascar, histoire de la nation malgache.* Paris, 1952.
 Madagascar sous la révolution malgache. Paris, 1953.

Radaody-Ralarosy, E. 'La Femme malgache dans la cité', *Bulletin de l'Académie Malgache*, 1960, **38**.

Rajemisa-Raolison, R. *Dictionnaire géographique et historique de Madagascar.* Fianarantsoa, 1966.

Ralaimhoitra, E. *Histoire de Madagascar.* Tananarive, 1965.

Ralihera, R. *Vazaha et Malgaches en dialogue.* Tananarive, 1966.

Ramandriavohona, D. *Le Malgache: sa langue, sa religion.* Paris, 1959.

Ranaivo, C. 'Les Expériences de fokonolona à Madagascar', *Monde non Chrétien*, April–June, 1949.

Ratsima, J. 'Les Congregations chinoises de Madagascar', *Revue de Madagascar*, 1960, 3.

Rudloff, M. P. *Économie du tiers monde*, vol. I. Tananarive, 1961.

Spacensky, A. 'L'Évolution politique malgache, 1945–1966', *La Revue Française de Science Politique*, 1967, 2 and 4.
 Cinquante ans de vie politique de Ralamongo à Tsiranana. Paris, 1970.

Stibbe, P. *Justice pour les Malgaches.* Paris, 1954.

Surbiguet, M. *Les Sociétés d'économie mixte à Madagascar.* Tananarive, 1966.

Tronchon, J. *L'Insurrection malgache de 1947.* Paris, 1974.

Vidal, H. *La Séparation des Églises et de l'État à Madagascar, 1861–1962.* Paris, 1969.

14. ZAIRE, RWANDA AND BURUNDI

Académie Royale des Sciences d'Outre-Mer. *Biographie coloniale belge.* 6 vols. Brussels, 1948–1967.

L'Apport scientifique de la Belgique au développement de l'Afrique Centrale. 3 vols. Brussels, 1962–1963.

Alexander, H. T. *African tightrope.* London, 1966.

American Council on Education. *Survey of education in the democratic republic of the Congo.* Washington, 1969.

Anstey, R. *King Leopold's legacy.* London, 1966.

Artigue, P. *Qui sont les leaders congolais?* 2nd ed. Brussels, 1961.

Aupens, B. 'L'Engrenage de la violence au Burundi', *Revue Française d'Études Politiques Africaines.* July 1973, **9**, 48–69.

L'Avenir politique du Congo Belge. Brussels, 1969.

Baeck, L. 'Léopoldville, phénomène urbain africain', *Zaire.* June 1956, **10**, 6, 613–36.

Étude socio-économique du centre extra-coutumier d'Usumbura. Brussels, 1957.

Bakonzi, A. 'The gold mines of Kilo-Moto in northeastern Zaire: 1905–1960'. Doctoral dissertation, University of Wisconsin, Madison, 1982.

Bézy, F. *Principes pour l'orientation du développement économique au Congo.* Kinshasa, 1957.

Problèmes structurels de l'économie congolaise. Louvain and Paris, 1957.

Bézy, F., Peemans, J.-P. and Wautelet, J.-M. *Accumulation et sous-développement au Zaire 1960–1980.* Louvain-la-Neuve, 1981.

Bianga, W., 'Peasant, state and rural development in postindependent Zaire'. Doctoral dissertation, University of Wisconsin, Madison, 1982.

Biebuyck, D. ed. *African agrarian systems.* London, 1963.

'La Société Kumu face à Kitawala', *Zaire,* 1957, **11**, 1, 7–40.

Biebuyck, D. and Douglas, M. *Congo tribes and parties.* London, 1961.

Bourgeois, R. *Banyarwanda et Barundi.* Brussels, 1958.

Bouvier, P. *L'Accession du Congo Belge à l'indépendance.* Brussels, 1966.

Braekman, E. M. *Histoire du Protestantisme au Congo.* Brussels, 1961.

Brausch, G. *Belgian administration in the Congo.* London, 1961.

Bustin, E. 'The Congo', in Carter, Gwendolen, ed. *Five African States.* Ithaca, 1963.

Lunda under Belgian rule. Cambridge, 1975.

Caprasse, P. *Leaders africains en milieu urbain.* Elisabethville, 1959.

Centre de Recherche et d'Information Socio-Politiques. *Rwanda politique 1958–1960.* Brussels, 1961.

Morphologie des groupes financiers. Brussels, 1962.

Parti Solidaire Africain (PSA). Brussels, 1963.

ABAKO 1950–1960. Brussels, 1963.

Congo 1959. Brussels, 1960. *Congo 1960.* 3 vols. 1961. *Congo 1961.* 1962. *Congo 1962.* 1963. *Congo 1963.* 1964. *Congo 1964.* 1965. *Congo 1965.* 1966. *Congo 1966.* 1967. *Congo 1967.* 1968.

Chomé, J. *La Crise congolaise.* Brussels, 1960.

L'Ascension de Mobutu. Paris, 1974.

Chrétien, J. P. 'Le Burundi', *Documentation Française*, no. 3364 (1967).
Chronique de Politique Étrangère. 'La Crise congolaise', 1960, **13**, 4–6. 'Évolution de la crise congolaise',1961,**14**,5–6.'L'ONU et leCongo',1962,**15**,4–6.
Décolonisation et indépendance du Rwanda et du Burundi, 1963, **16**, 4–6.
Clément, P. 'Patrice Lumumba (Stanleyville, 1952–1953)', *Présence Africaine*, 1962, **40**, 57–78.
Codere, H. *The biography of an African society, Rwanda 1900–1960. Based on forty-eight Rwandan autobiographies.* Tervuren, 1973.
Colvin, I. *The rise and fall of Moise Tshombe.* London, 1968.
Coméliau, C. *Conditions de la planification et du développement: l'exemple du Congo.* Paris, 1969.
Comité Zaire. *Zaire: le dossier de la recolonisation.* Paris, 1978.
Le Congo Belge. 2 vols. Brussels, 1958.
Cornevin, R. *Histoire du Congo-Léo.* Paris, 1963.
Davister, P. *Katanga enjeu du monde.* Brussels, 1980.
Dayal, R. *Mission for Hammarskjöld.* Princeton, 1976.
De Backer, M. C. C. *Notes pour servir à l'étude des "groupements politiques" à Léopoldville.* Brussels, 1959. 3 vols.
Decraene, P. 'Le "Coup" Rwandais du 5 juillet 1973 et ses suites', *Revue Française d'Études Politiques Africaines*, May 1974, **101**, 66–86.
Denis, J. *Le Phénomène urbain en Afrique Centrale.* Brussels, 1958.
Denuit, D. *Le Congo champion de la Belgique en guerre.* Brussels, 1946?
Dettes de Guerre. Elisabethville, 1945.
Doutreloux, A. *L'Ombre des fétiches. Société et culture Yombe.* Louvain, 1967.
Dumont, G. H. *La Table ronde belgo-congolaise.* Paris, 1961.
Durieux, A. *Institutions politiques, administratives et juridiques du Congo Belge et du Ruanda-Urundi.* 4th ed. Brussels, 1957.
Souveraineté et communauté Belgo-congolaise. Brussels, 1959.
Encyclopédie du Congo Belge, 3 vols. Brussels, 1953.
Feltz, G. 'Considérations sur l'histoire contemporaine du Rwanda', *Revue Française d'Études Politiques Africaines*, September 1971, 76–97.
Fetter, B. 'The Luluabourg revolt at Elisabethville', *African Historical Studies*, 1969, **2**, 2, 269–76.
Forde, Daryll. ed. *Aspects sociaux de l'industrialisation et de l'urbanisation dans l'Afrique au sud du Sahara.* Paris, 1956.
Fox, R., de Craemer, W. and Ribeaucourt, J. M. 'La deuxième indépendance: étude d'un cas: la rébellion au Kwilu', *Études Congolaises*, 1965, **8**, 1, 1–35.
Ganshof van der Meersch, W. J. *Fin de la souveraineté belge au Congo.* Brussels, 1963.
Gendebien, P. H. *L'Intervention des Nations Unies au Congo.* Brussels, 1967.
Gérard-Libois, J. *Sécession au Katanga.* Brussels, 1963.
Gilis, C. A. *Kasavubu au coeur du drame congolais.* Brussels, 1964.
Gould, D. J. *Bureaucratic corruption in the Third World.* New York, 1980.
Gran, G. ed. *Zaire: the political economy of underdevelopment.* New York, 1980.
Grévisse, F. *Le Centre extra-coutumier d'Élisabethville.* Brussels, 1951.
Guebels, L. ed. *Relation complète des travaux de la commission permanente pour la protection des indigènes au Congo Belge, 1911–1951.* Elisabethville, 1953.

d'Hertefelt, M. 'Les Élections communales et le consensus politique au Ruanda', *Zaire*, 1960, **14**, 403–38.

'The Rwanda of Rwanda', in Gibbs, James L. ed. *Peoples of Africa*. New York, 1965.

Hoare, M. *Congo mercenary*. London, 1967.

Hoffman, S. 'In search of a thread: the UN in the Congo labyrinth', *International Organization*, 1962, **16**, 2, 331–61.

von Horn, C. *Soldiering for peace*. New York, 1967.

Hoskyns, C. *The Congo since independence*. London, 1965.

Houyoux, J. *Budgets ménagers: nutrition et mode de vie à Kinshasa*. Kinshasa, 1973.

Hubert, J. R. '*La Toussaint Rwandaise et sa répression*. Brussels, 1965.

Ilunga Mbiya Kabongo, 'Ethnicity, social classes, and the state in the Congo, 1960–1965: the case of the Baluba'. Doctoral dissertation, University of California, Berkeley, 1973.

Institut de Recherches Économiques et Sociales. *Indépendance, inflation et développement*. The Hague, 1968.

Janssens, E. *J'étais le Général Janssens*. Brussels, 1961.

Joye, P. and Lewin, R. *Les Trusts au Congo*.

Kalanda, M. *Baluba et Lulua: une ethnie à la recherche d'un nouvel équilibre*. Brussels, 1959.

La Rémise en question, base de la décolonisation mentale. Brussels, 1967.

Kamitatu, C. *La Grande Mystification du Congo-Kinshasa*. Paris, 1971.

Le Pouvoir à la portée du peuple. Paris, 1977.

Kanza, T. *Conflict in the Congo*. Baltimore, 1972.

Katwala, G. J. 'Bureaucracy, dependency and underdevelopment in Zaire'. Doctoral dissertation, University of California, Berkeley, 1979.

Lacroix, J.-L. *Industrialisation au Congo*. Paris, 1967.

La Fontaine, J. *City politics: a study of Léopoldville, 1962–1963*. London, 1970.

Lefebvre, J. *Structures économiques du Congo Belge*. Brussels, 1955.

Lefever, E. *Crisis in the Congo: a UN force in action*. Washington, 1965.

Uncertain mandate: politics of the UN Congo operation. Baltimore, 1967.

Legum, Colin. *Congo disaster*. Baltimore, 1961.

Lemarchand, R. *Political awakening in the Congo*. Berkeley, 1964.

Rwanda and Burundi. London, 1970.

'Patrice Lumumba', in Skurnik, W. E. R. ed. *African political thought: Lumumba, Nkrumah and Touré*. Denver, 1968.

Leplae, E. 'Résultats obtenus au Congo Belge par les cultures obligatoires, alimentaires et industrielles', *Zaire*, 1947, **1**, 2, 115–40.

Leurquin, P. *Le Niveau de vie des populations rurales du Ruanda-Urundi*. Louvain, 1960.

van Lierde, J. ed. *La Pensée politique de Patrice Lumumba*. Brussels, 1963.

Louwers, O. *L'Article 73 de la Charte et l'anticolonialisme de l'Organisation des Nations Unies*. Brussels, 1952.

Lumumba, P. *Le Congo, terre d'avenir, est-il menacé?* Brussels, 1962.

Lux, A. 'Luluabourg. Migrations, accroisement et urbanisation de sa population congolaise', *Zaire*, 1958, **12**, 7–8, 675–724, 819–77.

McDonald, G. C. *et al. Area handbook for Burundi*. Washington, 1969.

McGaffey, W. *Custom and government in the Lower Congo*. Berkeley, 1970.

Magotte, V. *Les Circonscriptions indigènes*. La Louvière, 1952.

Malengreau, G. 'Le Congo à la croisée des chemins', *Revue Nouvelle*, 1947, 5, 1, 3–18; 1947, 5, 2, 95–108.

'La Situation actuelle des indigènes du Congo Belge', *Bulletin des Séances*, Académie Royale des Sciences d'Outre-Mer, 1947, 216–28.

Vers un paysannat indigène: les lotissements agricoles au Congo Belge. Brussels, 1949.

'Political evolution in the Belgian Congo', *Journal of African Administration*, 1954, 6, 4, 160–6.

Maquet, J. *The premise of inequality in Rwanda*. Oxford, 1961.

Maquet, J. J. and d'Hertefelt, M. *Élections en société féodale*. Brussels, 1959.

Markowitz, M. D. *Cross and sword: the political role of Christian missions in the Belgian Congo, 1908–1960*. Stanford, 1973.

Marres, J. and de Vos, P. *L'Équinoxe de janvier*. Brussels, 1959.

Marzorati, A. F. G. 'The political organization and the evolution of African populations in the Belgian Congo', *Africa*, 1949, 19, 4, 265–72.

Masson, P. *Dix ans de malheurs: Kivu 1957–1967*. 2 vols. Brussels, 1970.

Merlier, M. *Le Congo de la colonisation Belge à l'indépendance*. Paris, 1962.

Merriam, A. P. *Congo: background of conflict*. Evanston, 1961.

Miracle, M. P. *Agriculture in the Congo Basin*. Madison, 1967.

Monheim, F. *Mobutu, l'homme seul*. Brussels, 1962.

Monnier, L. *Ethnie et intégration régionale au Congo*. Paris, 1970.

Mosmans, G. *L'Église à l'heure de l'Afrique*. Paris, 1961.

Mpozagara, G. *La République du Burundi*. Paris, 1971.

Mukenge Tshilemalema, 'Businessmen of Zaire: limited possibilities for capital accumulation under dependence'. Doctoral dissertation, McGill University, 1974.

Mulambu Mvuluya, 'Le Régime des cultures obligatoires et le radicalisme rural au Zaire (1917–1960)'. Doctoral dissertation, Université Libre de Bruxelles, 1975.

Mwabila Malela, 'Prolétariat et conscience de classe au Zaire'. Doctoral dissertation, Université Libre de Bruxelles, 1973.

Newbury, C. 'The cohesion of oppression: a century of clientship in Kinyaga, Rwanda'. Doctoral dissertation, University of Wisconsin, Madison, 1975.

Nkrumah, Kwame. *Challenge of the Congo*. London, 1967.

Nyrop, R. F. *et al*. *Area handbook for Rwanda*. Washington, 1969.

Nzongola, N. 'Urban administration in Katanga'. Doctoral dissertation, University of Wisconsin, Madison, 1975.

O'Brien, C. Cruise. *To Katanga and back*. New York, 1962.

Peemans, J.-P. *The political economy of Zaire in the seventies: an essay in historical perspective*. Louvain, 1974.

'Capital accumulation in the Congo under colonialism: the role of the state', in Duignan, Peter and Gann, L. H. *The economics of colonialism*. London, 1975.

'The social and economic development of Zaire since independence: an historical outline', *African Affairs*, April 1975, 74, 295, 148–79.

Perrin, F. *Les Institutions politiques du Congo indépendant*. Brussels, 1960.

Pétillon, L. *Témoignages et réflexions*. Brussels, 1967.

Piron, P. and Devos, J. *Codes et lois du Congo Belge*. 4 vols. Brussels, 1959.

Pons, V. *Stanleyville: an African urban community under Belgian administration*. London, 1969.

Poupart, R. *Première esquisse de l'évolution du syndicalisme au Congo*. Brussels, 1960.

Raymaekers, P. 'L'Église de Jésus-Christ sur la terre par le Prophète Simon Kimbangu', *Zaire*, 1959, **13**, 7, 659-756.

L'Organisation des zones de squatting, élément de résorption du chomage structurel dans les milieux urbains en voie de développement. Brussels, 1964.

Romanuik, A. *La Fécondité des populations congolaises*. Paris, 1967.

Rubbens, A. 'Le Colour-bar au Congo Belge', *Zaire*, 1947, **1**, 5, 503-14.

'Political awakening in the Belgian Congo', *Civilisations*, 1960, **10**, 1, 63-76.

Ryckmans, P. *La Politique coloniale*. Brussels, 1934.

Étapes et jalons. Brussels, 1946.

Dominer pour servir. Brussels, 1948.

Salkin, P. *L'Afrique Centrale dans cent ans*. Paris, 1926.

Schatzberg, M. G. 'Bureaucracy, business, beer: the political dynamics of class formation'. Doctoral dissertation, University of Wisconsin, Madison, 1977.

Politics and class in Zaire. New York, 1980.

Schramme, J. *Le Bataillon Léopard: souvenirs d'un Africain blanc*. Paris, 1969.

Sénat de Belgique. *Rapport de la mission sénatoriale au Congo et dans les territoires sous tutelle belge*. Brussels, 1947.

Slade, R. *The Belgian Congo*. London, 1960.

Sohier, A. 'Le Statut des congolais civilisés', *Zaire*, 1950, **4**, 7, 815-22.

'La Politique d'intégration', *Zaire*, 1951, **5**, 9, 899-928.

Stengers, J. 'La Belgique et le Congo', in *Histoire de la Belgique contemporaine*. Brussels, 1975.

Combien le Congo a-t-il couté à la Belgique? Brussels, 1957.

Tempels, P. *La Philosophie bantoue*. Paris, 1949.

Tshombe, M. *Quinze mois de gouvernement du Congo*. Paris, 1966.

Turner, T. 'A century of political conflict in Saneuru'. Doctoral dissertation, University of Wisconsin, Madison, 1972.

'Congo-Kinshasa', in Olorunsola, Victor. ed., *The politics of cultural sub-nationalism in Africa*. New York, 1977.

UN Trusteeship Council. United Nations Visiting Mission to Trust Territories in East Africa, *Report on Ruanda-Urundi*, 1951 (T/1031); 1954 (T/1204); 1957 (T/1346); 1960 (T/1538).

US Army area handbook for the Republic of the Congo. Washington, 1962.

Van Bilsen, A. A. J. *Vers l'indépendance du Congo et du Ruanda-Urundi*. Brussels, 1958.

L'Indépendance du Congo. Brussels, 1962.

Vanderlinden, J. *La République rwandaise*. Paris, 1970.

Du Congo au Zaire 1960-1980. Brussels, 1981.

Van de Walle, B. *Essai d'une planification de l'économie agricole congolaise*. Kinshasa, 1960.

Van de Walle, F. J. *Odyssée et reconquête de Stanleyville, 1964. L'Ommegang.* Brussels, 1970.

Vansina, J. *Introduction à l'ethnographie du Congo.* Brussels, 1966.

Verhaegen, B. *Rébellions au Congo.* Brussels, 1966, 1969. 2 vols.

de Vos, P. *La Décolonisation.* Brussels, 1975.

Vie et mort de Lumumba. Paris, 1961.

Vers la promotion de l'économie indigène. Brussels, 1956.

Vwakvanakazi Mukohya, 'African traders in Butembo, eastern Zaire (1960–1980)'. Doctoral dissertation, University of Wisconsin, Madison, 1982.

Weinstein, W. *Historical dictionary of Burundi.* Metuchen, NJ, 1976.

Weinstein, W. and Schrire, R. *Political conflict and ethnic strategies: a case study of Burundi.* Syracuse, 1976.

Weissman, S. R. *American foreign policy in the Congo 1960–64.* Ithaca, 1974.

Wigny, P. *Ten year plan for the economic and social development of the Belgian Congo.* New York, 1950.

'Methods of government in the Belgian Congo', *African Affairs,* 1951, **50**, 201, 301–17.

Young, C. *Politics in the Congo: decolonisation and independence.* Princeton, 1965.

'Rebellion and the Congo', in Rotberg, Robert and Mazrui, Ali. *Power and protest in Black Africa.* London, 1970.

'Zaire: the unending crisis', *Foreign Affairs,* Oct. 1978, **57**, 169–85.

Zaire: a country study. Washington, 1979.

Abshire, D. M. and Samuels, M. A. eds. *Portuguese Africa: a handbook.* London, 1969.

Afrique-Asie. Paris, 1974, **25**, 66. Quoting A. Cabral.

Paris, 1974, **25**, 61, 7–18. On collaboration between J. Savimbi and Portuguese military command.

Alexandre, V. *Origens do colonialismo Português moderno.* Lisbon, 1979.

Andrade, M. de. *La Poésie africaine d'expression portugaise.* Paris, 1969.

Antologia temática de poesia Africana: 1, na noite grávida de punhais. Lisbon, 1975.

Andrade, M. de and Ollivier, M. *La Guerre en Angola: étude socio-économique.* Paris, 1971.

Anuário Estatístico: Colónia de Moçambique. Lisbon, various years.

Anuário Estatístico: Províncias Ultramarinas. Lisbon, 1970.

Bender, G. J. *Angola under the Portuguese: the myth and the reality.* London, 1978.

Bender, G. J. and Isaacman, A. 'The changing historiography of Angola and Mozambique', in Fyfe, C. ed. *African studies since 1945: a tribute to Basil Davidson.* London, 1976.

de Bettencourt, J. T. *Relatório do Gov.-Geral de Moçambique.* Lisbon, 1945, 77–85.

Boavida, A. *Angola: cinco séculos de exploração portuguêsa.* Rio de Janeiro, 1967.

Boletim Militar das Colónias. Lisbon, various years.

Brito, E. *A população de Cabo Verde no século XX.* Lisbon, 1963.

Cabral, A. Addresses in *La lutte de libération nationale dans les colonies portugaises*. CONCP, Algiers, 1965.
Foreword to Davidson, B. *The liberation of Guiné*. London and Baltimore, 1969.
Our people are our mountains. London, 1971.
Unité et lutte. (Collected writings.) 2 vols. I, *L'Arme de la théorie*; II, *La Pratique Révolutionnaire*. Paris, 1975.
Unity and struggle (collected writings). London, 1979.
Caetano, M. *Os nativos na economia africana*. Coimbra, 1954.
Depoimento. Rio and São Paulo, 1974.
Carreira, A. *Apreciação dos primeiros números discriminados do censo da população não civilizada de 1950 da Guiné Portuguesa*. Bissau, 1951.
Cabo Verde, formação e extinção de ume sociedade escravocrata. Bissau, 1972.
Migrações nas Ilhas de Cabo Verde. Lisbon, 1977. Eng. edn.: *The peoples of the Cape Verde Islands: exploitation and emigration*. Tr. and ed. Christopher Fyfe. London, 1982.
Cabo Verde: classes sociais, estrutura familiar, migrações. Lisbon, n.d.
Celik, H. ed. *Les Travailleurs immigrés parlent*. (Cahiers du Centre d'Études Socialistes, no. 94–98). Paris, 1970.
Centro de Estudos Angolanos. ed. *História de Angola*. Algiers, 1965.
Chaliand, G. *Lutte armée en Afrique*. Paris, 1967. (Published New York, 1969, as *Armed struggle in Africa*.)
Chilcote, R. H. *Emerging nationalism in Portuguese Africa*. Stanford, 1969.
Emerging nationalism in Portuguese Africa (Documents). Stanford, 1972.
CONCP. ed. *La lutte de libération nationale dans les colonies portugaises*. Algiers, 1965.
L'Ile de São Tomé. Algiers, 1968.
Corrêa, S. and Homem, E. *Moçambique: primieras machambas*. Rio de Janeiro, 1977.
Corella, L. B. *Manuales del Africa española*. Madrid, 1950.
da Costa, P. *Um mês de terrorismo*. Lisbon, 1969.
Davezies, R. *La Guerre en Angola*. Bordeaux, 1968.
Davidson, B. *The African awakening*. London, 1955.
Angola, 1961. London, 1961.
'La Guérrilla africaine', in *Le Monde Diplomatique*. Paris, Nov. 1968.
The liberation of Guiné: aspects of an African revolution. London and Baltimore, 1969. Enlarged edn. *No fist is big enough to hide the sky*. London, 1982.
'Angola in the tenth year', *African Affairs*, **70**, 278, Jan. 1971, 37.
In the eye of the storm: Angola's people. London, 1972.
'A report on the further liberation of Guiné', *Socialist Register*, 1973, 283.
'African peasants and revolution', *Journal of Peasant Studies*, 1974, **1**, 3, 269.
'The politics of armed struggle', in Davidson, B., Slovo, J. and Wilkinson, A. R. *Southern Africa: the new politics of revolution*. London, 1976.
The peoples' cause: a history of 'guerrillas' in Africa. London, 1981.
Dickinson, M. ed. and tr. *When bullets begin to flower*. Nairobi, 1972.
Documentation Française. *Notes et études documentaires: les territoires espagnols d'Afrique*. Paris, 1963.
Felgas, H. E. *Guerra em Angola*. Lisbon, 1961.

Ferreira, A. R. *O movimento migratório de trabalhadores entre Moçambique e a África do Sul.* Lisbon, 1963.

Ferreira, E. de Sousa. *Portuguese colonialism in Africa: the end of an era.* Paris (UNESCO), 1974.

Aspectos do colonialismo Português. Lisbon, 1974.

'Ursachen und Formen der Auswanderung und ihre Bedeutung für die Entwicklung Portugals'. Doctoral dissertation, Ruprecht-Karl University of Heidelberg, 1974.

Ferreira, V. *Estudos ultramarinos.* 2 vols. Lisbon, 1954.

Financial Times. 19 July 1971.

Freire, P. *Pedagogy in progress: the letters to Guinea-Bissau.* London, 1978.

Galvão, H. *Santa Maria: my crusade for Portugal.* London, 1961.

Por Angola (1945–49). Lisbon, n.d.

Galvão, H. and Selvagem, C. *Império ultramarino português.* 4 vols. Lisbon, 1952–53.

Government-General of Angola. *Conselho do Governo.* (Session reports.) Luanda, various years.

Government-General of Mozambique. *Relatório do Gov. Geral.* Lourenço Marques, various years.

Hailey, Lord. *An African survey.* London, 1957.

Harris, M. *Portugal's African 'wards'.* New York, 1958.

Heath, E. (British Lord Privy Seal.) Quoted in *Hansard*, 31 July 1961, col. 962.

Heimer, F.-W. *Educação e sociedade nas areas ruráis de Angola.* Luanda, 1972.

ed. *Social change in Angola.* Munich (in English), 1973.

Institute of Race Relations, London. ed. *Angola: a symposium.* London, 1962.

Instituto Superior de Ciências Sociais e Política Ultramarina. 'Moçambique. Curso de Extensão Universitária, Ano Lectivo de 1965–6. Lisbon, 1966.

Isaacman, A. F. *The tradition of resistance in Mozambique.* London, 1976.

Junta Províncial de Povoamento de Angola. *Alguns aspects de povoamento recente em Angola.* Lisbon, 1969.

Ledda, R. *Una rivoluzione Africana.* Bari, 1970.

Machel, S. M. *Mozambique: sowing the seeds of revolution.* London, 1974.

Marcum, J. *The Angolan revolution, I: The anatomy of an explosion 1950–1962.* Cambridge, Mass., 1969.

Martins, O. *Não vou para Pasárgada.* Rotterdam, n.d.

de Matos, N. *A Provincia de Angola.* Porto, 1926.

Africa nossa. Lisbon, 1953.

Militante, O. Bissau, I, 1, 1977 and subsequent numbers.

Ministério do Ultramar. *Cinco anos: 2 Agosto de 1950 a 7 Julho de 1955.* Lisbon, 1956.

Mondlane, E. *The struggle for Mozambique.* London and Baltimore, 1969.

Monteiro, J. *Os rebelados da Ilha de Santiago de Cabo Verde.* Praia, 1974.

Moreira, A. *As élites das províncias portuguesas de indígenato.* Lisbon, 1956.

Portugal's stand in Africa. New York, 1962.

Movimento das Forças Armadas. 'MFA na Guiné', in *Boletim Informativo* (da MFA), Bissau no. 1, 1 June 1974.

Munslow, B. 'The liberation struggle in Mozambique and the origins of post-independence policy', in University of Edinburgh. ed. *Mozambique*. (Collected conference papers.) Edinburgh, 1979.

Mozambique: the revolution and its origins. London, 1983.

Neto, A. *Sacred hope*. Dar es Salaam, 1974.

Pensamento politico. Luanda, 1976.

Nogueira, F. *The United Nations and Portugal*. London, 1963.

The Third World. London, 1967.

Okuma, T. *Angola in ferment: the background and prospects of Angolan nationalism*. Boston, 1962.

de Oliveira, C. *Tarrafal*. Lisbon, n.d.

de Oliveira, H. *Cabo Verde: Quinto ano de seca*. Lisbon, 1973.

PAIGC. *História: a Guiné e as Ilhas de Cabo Verde*. Bissau (UNESCO), 1974.

Parsons, C. 'The makings of a revolt', *Angola: a symposium*. London, 1962.

Passerini, L. ed. *Colonialismo Portoghese e lotta di liberazione nel Mozambico*. Turin, 1970.

Pelissier, R. 'La Guinée espagnole', *Revue Française de Science Politique*, 1963, **13**, 3, 631.

La Colonie du minotaure: nationalismes et révoltes en Angola (1926–61). Montamets, 1978.

People's Power. Pamphlet series of documentary materials of MPLA (Angola), PAIGC (Guinea-Bissau and Cape Verde), and FRELIMO (Mozambique), published by Mozambique, Guinea-Bissau, Angola Information Centre (London, 1976–   ).

Pepetela. *As aventuras de Ngunga*. Lisbon, n.d.

Perbal, A. 'Comment former les Africains à la civilisation?' *Reale Accademia d'Italia*, Rome, 1940.

Pereira, A. *Relatório*, in *Nô Pintcha*. Bissau, 4 Sept. 1976, **2**, 47.

Relatório do Conselho superior da Luta. Bissau, 1977.

Rudebeck, L. *Guinea-Bissau*. In English. Uppsala, 1974.

Salazar, A. de O. *Portugal y la campaña anticolonialista*. Santiago, Chile, n.d.

Samuels, M. A. and Bailey, N. A. 'Education, health and social welfare', in Abshire, D. M. and Samuels, M. A. ed., *Portuguese Africa: a handbook* London, 1969.

dos Santos, A. C. T. V. *Angola: coração do império*. Lisbon, 1955.

Saul, J. S. 'FRELIMO and the Mozambique revolution', in Arrighi, G. and Saul, J. *Essays on the political economy of Africa*. New York, 1973.

Scantamburlo, L., *Gramática e Dicionário da Língua Criol da Guiné-Bissau*. Bologna, 1982.

Secretariado do Propaganda Nacional. *Concordato e acordo misionario de 7 de Maio de 1940*. Lisbon, 1943.

da Silva Cunha, J. M. *O sistema portugues de politica indígena*. Coimbra, 1953.

Administração e direito colonial. Lisbon, 1957.

Spence, C. F. *Moçambique*. London, 1963.

Tenreiro, F. *A Ilha de São Tomé*. Lisbon, 1961.

Teixeira da Mota, A. *Guiné Portuguesa*, 2 vols. Lisbon, 1954.

UN General Assembly. Materials on Equatorial (Spanish) Guinea, A/5078/Add. 3 of 26 March, 1962.

Report of Special Committee. New York, A/9023 of 8 Oct. 1973. 11, Table 6.

US Army. *Area handbook for Angola.* ed. Herrick, A. B. *et al.* Washington, 1967.

de Unzueta y Yoste, A. *Guinea continental española.* Madrid, 1944.

Islas del Golfo de Guinea. Madrid, 1945.

Vail, L. and White, L. *Capitalism and colonialism in Mozambique: a study of the Quelimane District.* London, 1980.

Valkhoff, M. F. ed. *Miscelânea Luso-Africana.* (Linguistic studies.) Lisbon, 1925.

de Vasconcelos, N. *Não!* Lisbon, 1961.

Venter, A. J. *The terror fighters.* Johannesburg, 1969.

Portugal's war in Guiné-Bissau. (Munger Africana Library Notes, no. 19.) Pasadena, Cal., 1973.

Vieira, J. L. tr. Wolfers, M. *The real life of Domingos Xavier.* London, 1977.

Vitória Certá. Luanda, 23 Oct. 1976, **2**, 44.

Voz da Guiné. Bissau. 19 Aug. 1974.

Watkinson, H. (British Minister of Defence.) Quoted in *Hansard*, 15 June 1961, cols. 712 ff and 774.

West Africa. 6 Jan. 1975, 22.

Wheeler, D. L. '"Angola is whose house?"': early stirrings of Angolan nationalism and protest, 1822–1910', *African Historical Studies*, 1969, **2**, 1, 1 ff.

Wheeler, D. L. and Pelissier, R. *Angola.* London, 1971.

INDEX

Berry, S. S. 830
Bertier, H. 893
Beshir, Mohammad Omer 526n., 878
Beti, Mongo 662
Betravola 678
Betsileo people 685, 688, 691
Betsimisaraka people 675, 684, 686
Bevin, Ernest 465, 557; 'Bevin Plan' 465, 481; Bevin/Sforza Plan 538
Bezara, Justin 681, 682
Bezi faction, Burundi 715, 737
Bézy, Fernand 898; Bézy, F., Peemans, Jean-Philippe and Wautelet, Jean-Marie 899
Biafra secession 116, 125, 126, 169, 624; French aid 125, 668
bicycles 433
Bienen, Henry 412n., 862
Biha (Bihumugani) Léopold 716, 737
Bihe Province, Angola 793, 795 and n.
Biko, Steve 251, 308, 318
Binns Report (Tanganyika) 447
'Binza Group' 723
Birmingham, David (ed.) 814
Birmingham, Walter, Neustadt, I. and Omaboe, E. N. 855
Birnbaum, P., Lively, J., and Parry, G. (eds.) 86n.
Biroli, Joseph 716
biru (royal council, Rwanda) 713
Bissau 768, 771
Bitwoded Makonnen Endalkachew, Ras 413
Bizerta Naval Base 114, 604, 609
Black Arts Festival (Dakar 1966) 140; (Lagos 1976) 140
'black consciousness' 309, 314, 315
Black Fordsburg 263
Black Nationalism 105
Black Panther Party 105, 106
Black Peoples' Convention 208
black US soldiers (Liberia) 336
Blanchet, André 885
Blankewerkersbeskermingsbond (White Workers' Protection Society) 281, 288
Bloc Populaire Sénégalais 633
Blood River (battle) 252
Bloomberg, Charles 288n., 330
Blyden, E. W. 95, 139
Bobo-Dioulasso 627
Boende 728
Boisson, Pierre 616
Boiteau, Pierre 891
boma (government office) 170
Bonardi, Pierre 890
Bondestam, L. 873

boom, post-war 417
Borama 497
border industries (South Africa) 305
Borgu 32
Bostock, M. and Harvey, C. 840
Botswana 55, 129, 130, 137, 253, 315, 318, 319, 846; capital 276; independence 319, 320–1; per capita income 229; population 262; Rhodesian war 321
Bou Craa phosphates 600
Boudiaf, Muhammad 881
Boudjera, Rachid 598, 599
Boudros-Ghali, Boutros 824
Boumedienne, Col. Houari 68, 581, 585, 590, 592, 596, 604, 605, 609
Bouquerel, Jacqueline 891
Bourdieu, Pierre 881
Bourdillon, Sir Bernard 26, 46
bourgeois, urban 162; 'bourgeois-nationalists' 340
bourgeoisie, national 174; state-supported 357
Bourguiba, Habib 30, 65, 552, 567, 575–7, 583, 604, 605, 608–9; writings 881
Bourret, F. M. 853
Bouteflika, Abdelaziz 586, 587
Bouvier, Paul 887
Bowman, L. W. 393, 867
boycott (of South Africa) 277, 282, 283, 312, 316
Braide, Garrick 20
Brazil 133, 265
Brazzaville 50, 615, 649, 726
Brazzaville Conference (1944) 22, 24, 25, 38, 41–2, 102, 616, 632, 675, 689
Brazzaville Group see UAM
Brickman, W. W. 838
bridewealth 146
Bridges, R. C. 857
Briey, P. De 839
Britain: policy 4, 27, 97, 125, 128, 312; investment 201, 274; Second World War 20, 21, 28
Britain/France/Israel alliance (Suez) 516
British Somaliland 16, 460, 462, 464, 474, 480, 485, 489
British subjects (Sierra Leone Creoles) 350–1
British troops 401, 404
Broederbond (League of Brothers, South Africa) 287–80 and n.
Bromley, R. and Gerry, C. 831
Brown, A. C. 850
Brown, C. F. 870
Brunschwig, Henri 884

INDEX

Congo-Brazzaville (now Congo)
  independence 54, 611; economy
  209, 229, 244; education 72; ethnic
  problems 638, 639; parties, coups
  626, 638–9; external relations 135,
  639, 796
Congo-Léopoldville (later
  Congo-Kinshasa, now Zaire) 54,
  350, 698n., see also Zaire
Congress of Democrats (South Africa)
  289
Congress, Indian (South African) 283
Congress Party (Lesotho) 320
conquest, white South African 252, 253
Conscience Africaine
  (Congo-Léopoldville) 708
conscription, Second World War, 31, 33
Conseil de l'Entente 121
Conservative Party, British 338
conservative–monarchical states 64, 68–9
constituent assemblies 41, 45
construction industry, sector 208, 221,
  336
consumer goods, 146, 554; manufacture
  216
Continental Grain flourmill (Matadi)
  742
contract labour (Angola) 761, 771;
  (Namibia) 325
contradados (contract labour, Angola)
  761, 771
controls, trade 197
Convention Africaine (1957) 627
Cook, M. A. 879
Cooper, C. A. and Massel, B. F. 843
Cooperation and Development
  Department (South Africa) 292
cooperative societies 167, 168, 169
cooperative clothing factory (South
  Africa) 317
copper 81, 132, 198, 214, 296, 322, 323,
  328, 425, 428–9
Copperbelt 134, 146, 148, 387, 392–3,
  395, 399, 402, 435, 440; towns 150,
  152, 155; wages 436
Coppet, Marcel de, Gov. Gen. 674, 678,
  891
copra 66n.
Coptic Orthodox Church (Ethiopia)
  461, 463, 484, 488
Coquéry-Vidrovitch, Cathérine 28 and
  n., 885
Corella, L. B. 904
COREMO (Mozambique splinter
  group) 785n.
Cornevin, Robert 889, 890
Corrêa, S. and Homem, E. 904

Correia, A. Mendes 901
corruption 256, 362, 379, 381, 479, 855
corvée 5
Costa, Manuel da, Pres. 795
Costa, P. da 902
Costanzo, G. A. 875
côtiers (coastal peoples, Madagascar) 677,
  679, 682, 684, 685, 686
Cotonou 176
Cottesloe Statement (1960) 317
cotton 10, 80, 146, 198, 422, 434, 497;
  marketing boards 378
Council of the Revolution (Algeria) 586
Council of Unity (Guinea Bissau and
  Cape Verdes) 790
Council on African Affairs (Black
  American) 100
Court, David 79n., 818, 866
Coussey, Judge 344; Coussey
  constitution (Gold Coast) 344
Cowen, D. V. 843
Cowen, M. 426n.
Cox, Richard 824
Cox, Thomas S. 857
Cox-George, N. A. 855
CPP (Convention People's Party, Gold
  Coast/Ghana) 67, 179, 340, 344,
  345, 355, 358–9
Craemer, W. de 898
craft industries 171, 172, 195
craftsmen 163
CRAM (Collectives Rurales Autonomes
  Modernisées, Madagascar) 693
credit, agricultural 212, 213
credit restrictions 171
CRC (Coloured Persons Representative
  Council, South Africa) 313
Creech-Jones, A. 341
Creevey (Behrman), Lucy 637n., 650n.,
  656, 888.
Creoles (Sierra Leone) 331, 339, 350–1,
  352
Cronje, Geoff 289
Cross River 145
Crossroads (South Africa) 302, 303
Crowder, M. C. 814, 815, 853, 885, 888;
  Crowder, M. C. and Ikime Obano
  (eds) 818
Cruz, Viriato da 765, 797
CSR (Conseil Suprême Révolutionnaire,
  Madagascar) 684
Cuanza Norte (Angola) 771
Cuba aid 785, 786; Angola 61, 128, 135,
  136, 137, 326, 672, 786, 794;
  Ethiopia 136; Mozambique 136;
  Zaire 729
cultivation, compulsory 10, 35, 168

972

INDEX

diamonds 198, 214, 261, 276, 296;
    Lesotho 321; Botswana 322;
    Namibia 328
diamond smuggling 352, 380
Diarassouba, V. C. 889
diaspora (black) 95, 101, 104, 139; and
    Pan-Africanism 104–9, 117
Dib, Mohammed 598, 599
Dickinson, M. (ed.) 804n.
Dickman, Aubrey 275
Diedrichs, Nico 289 and n.
Diego-Suarez 34, 680, 681; province
    681
Digil people 468
Diguimboye, Georges 891
Dike, Prof. Kenneth 372
Diop, Anta 662; Diop, Alioune and
    Anta 662
Diori, Hamadi, Pres. 648, 668
'direct rule' 56
Dire Dawa 487, 894
disease 204, 269; vector-borne 226
Distributable Pool (East Africa) 454
distribution hierarchy 172
'distributive state' 158, 159
district development councils
    (Tanzania) 406
divination 189
Djait, Hichem 884
Djerba people 593
Djibouti (French Afars and Issas) 56,
    124, 136, 192; see also French
    Somali Coast
dompas (pass document) 290 and n., 291
Donaint, Pierre and Lancrenon,
    François 890
dos Santos, Marcelino 766
Douglass, Frederick 104
Dow Report (East Africa, 1955) 860
Drakensburg mts. 270
drought 209, 212, 240, 260, 299, 484,
    499; resistance to 195
Drysdale, J. 482n., 876
DuBois, W. E. B. 95, 101, 104, 107,
    132, 138, 820, 821
Duclos, L. J., Duvignaud, L. and Leca,
    J. 880
Dudley, Billy J. 881n., 813, 816, 852
Duffield, I. 113n.
Dugard, John 309, 847, 850
Dugué, Gil 885
Duignan, P. and Gann, L. H. 899
Dumont, René 813, 835, 894
Dunbar, Ernest 823
Dunn, John (ed.) 814, 830, 887
DUP (Democratic Unionist Party,
    Sudan) 532

Duprat, Gérard 883
Durban 265, 269, 283, 303, 313
Dutch HVA plantations (Awash) 497,
    498
Dutch Reformed Churches 317
dyula (Mandinka merchants) 155n.
D'Yvoire, J. 838

EAC (East African Community) 232
EACSO (East African Common
    Services Organisation) 123, 124,
    332, 452
EAHC (East Africa High Commission)
    232, 452
East African Authority 454
East African customs union 231, 285
East African Economic Community 86
East African Royal Commission (1955)
    420, 860
East African Treaty for Cooperation
    454
East and Central Africa 383–457; social
    change 431–44
Eastern bloc 81
Eboué, Félix 16, 616
ECA (Economic Commission for
    Africa) 118, 134, 228–9, 235, 237,
    417; publications 212, 215, 218,
    228, 230, 236, 240, 242
Eckstein, Harry (ed.) 67n.
École Myre de Vilers (Madagascar)
    689
École Paul Minault (Madagascar) 689
ecological damage 323; ecological niche
    155 and n.
economic development 46, 302, 383,
    417; East and Central Africa
    416–31
economic empire 51
economic evolution 192–250
economic integration 231–8
economic interests, metropolitan 387
economic nationalism 214
economic structure 80
economic union, unity 85, 86, 134
economies, metropolitan 28
economies, West African, monetised 378
economies of scale 220–1
ECOWAS (Economic Community of
    West African States) 119, 120, 134,
    369, 377, 380, 671, 819
edir (self-help associations, Ethiopia)
    496
education: colonial 14, 33, 46, 65, 225;
    expansion 76, 142, 169, 180, 189,
    225, 226; mission 177, 225; policy
    838

974

Enahoro, Anthony 99 and n.
enclave economies 80, 193
Encyclopaedia Africana 107
Endelkachew Makonnen 478
energy consumption 224
engineering production 219–20
English-speaking West Africa 331–81
English-speaking whites (South Africa) 259, 264
ENI (state-owned Italian oil company) 560
Enonwu, Ben 373
entrepreneurs 85, 170–4
entrepreneurship: African 335, 439; local 249
Enugu 364
Epstein, A. L. 151n., 829, 867
equality, personal 339
Equatorial Africa, company plantations 10
Equatorial Guinea 48, 806–10; assimilation 808; 'provincial' autonomy, independence 809; killings, refugees 808, 809, 810; economy 229, 807, 809; contract workers 807–8; education 809; nationalism 809
équivalence (of university qualifications) 683, 692
ERAP (French oil company) 560
Eritrea 874–5; Italian 459, 461; Second World War 18, 461; British administration 464; federation with Ethiopia 465, 471, 481; secession 125, 135; economy 495, 496, 497; education 489; urban growth 77
Ernst, K. 891
ESC (Economic and Social Commission, OAU) 134
Escom power lines (South Africa) 270, 271, 275
Estado Novo (Portugal) 758, 759, 764, 765, 773
Ethiopia 110, 114, 136, 145, 323; colonial rule 458; independence 5, 16, 18, 56; Italian invasion 4, 8, 97, 99, 459; liberation 285, 330
economy 209, 229, 492, 493, 495; aid 493; communications 485, 488, 493; crops 398; coffee 133, 492, 497, 498; oilseeds 492, 498; gold 214; hides 492; industry 495; trade 81
education etc.: education 225, 485, 488–91; language 490–1; literature and art 285, 386, 491–2; students 477; teachers, foreign 490

foreign relations: advisors, foreign 462–3, 472, 493; Eastern bloc 135, 136, 156; Ethiopia/Somali war 483; US aid 92, 481, 483
land 484; alienation 498; landlords 498; land reform 493, 496, 497, 499, 501; property-owning classes 165, 184; taxation 463, 464, 497; tenure 497, 498
political: constitution, revised 471; coups, rebellions 462, 476–8, 484; military government, Derg 478, 479, 480, 501
population 86, 486; cities 77, 485, 487–8; Muslims 161, 458; Somalis 496
Ethopian Agricultural Income Tax Proclamation 476
Ethiopian army 472, 477, 481; Imperial Bodyguard 472, 477; Korea 481; US aid 92, 481, 483
Ethiopian empire: centralisation 463, 476, 501; expansionism 124–5, 458–9, 461–4, 470, 501; provincial administration 476, 484
Ethiopian forces, black Americans in 99
Ethiopian highlands 458, 497
Ethiopian nationalism, resistance 461
Ethiopian Studies, Conferences 874
ethnicity, ethnic conflicts 64, 69–70, 152, 153, 154–9, 326, 402, 411, 800
Étienne, Bruno 600n., 609n., 882
European Common Market 112, 323, 608, 671
European Development Fund 665
European farms, enterprises 146, 170, 194, 195, 420, 425
European Mineworkers Union (Copperbelt) 392
Europeans in Africa 39, 418, 431, 559, 664
Evangelical Lutheran Church (Namibia) 324
Evans-Pritchard, E. E. 539 and n., 879
Evian Accords 581
évolués (educated Africans) 178, 179, 745
Ewe people 125
'excorporation' (South Africa) 301
executions (South Africa) 309
expatriate firms 335, 378
export/import trade 10, 378
export-led economy 194, 418
exports 12, 80, 209, 238–40, 500
ex-servicemen 32, 337
extension services, agricultural 166, 212

983

Maguire, G. A. 862
mahaber (self-help organisations, Ethiopia) 496
al-Maḥā'ishī, 'Umar 'Abd Allah 543, 545
Maharero, Chief Frederick 297
al-Mahdī, Ṣādiq 527, 531, 532
Mahdists 522, 533
Māhir, Aḥmad 509
Māhir, 'Alī 507, 508, 512, 520
Mahjūb Aḥmad 527, 531, 551; Mahjūb wing (of Communists, Sudan) 533
mailo estates (Buganda) 166, 433, 441
majimbo (regional structure, Kenya) 399, 404
Majunga province (Madagascar) 679, 681; town 687
Makerere College 446
makzin (urban order) 158
Makonde people 769
Makonnen, Ras 97, 98n., 99, 103, 107, 108 and n., 110, 134 and n., 820
Malagasy republic 129, 135
Malan, D. F. 285, 287, 295
Malan, Stefanus I. 846
malaria control 299
Malawi 55, 129, 137, 386, 428; economy, agriculture 81, 229, 427; labour recruiting, migration 147, 265, 272, 428 and n.; South African capital 275, 276
Malawi Young Pioneers 409
'Malawians' 157
Malaya, Malaysia 21, 329, 386
Malherbe, E. G. 850
Mali 114, 118, 159, 173, 611, 637; independence 54; Islam 161, 651; post-independence 66; traditional leaders 638
economy 229, 614; currency 641–2, 665; drought 656; trade, communications 81, 92, 641
external relations E. bloc 665; ECOWAS 119, France 665; Guinea 641
Malibamatso scheme (Lesotho) 270, 321
Mali Federation 627, 628, 632, 633, 636, 641, 669
al-Malki, Habib 603
malnutrition 226, 269
Malta 552, 553
Mamdani, M. 165n., 830
Mameri, Khalfa 881
Manchester 98, 101, 103, 104; *see also* Pan-African Congress
Mandates 27, 43, 253; S. W. Africa 296, 297; Togo, Cameroon 615
Mandela, Nelson 311

Mandinka people (Gambia) 155n., 354, 368
manganese 198
Mangasha Seyoum, Ras 495
Maniema district (Zaire) 709, 727
Manifesto of the Algerian People 567, 568
Manley, Michael 105
Mannoni, O. 892, 893
Mano River Union (Liberia/Sierra Leone) 370
manpower, skilled 249
Mantanzima, Chief Kaiser 304
manufactured goods 9, 80; exports 242; imports 171, 193
manufacturing industry, sector 173, 208, 217–21, 263
Maputo (Lourenço Marques) 263, 271, 321, 322, 791
Maquet, Jacques 899
al-Marāghī, Shaykh 507
Marcum, J. 904
Marcus, E. 842
Marcus, H. G. 870, 872, 874
Margai, Sir Albert 352, 366
Margai, Sir Milton ('Pa') 352, 366, 376, 855
'marginal class', 'marginal men' 53, 65
Mariano, António 731
Maridi 526
Markakis, J. 476n., 487n., 489n., 871
market, domestic 149
marketing 212; government control 195, 335
Marketing Boards 169, 335, 378–9; funds 378
market-sharing 195
Markovitz, I. L. 826, 889
Marks, J. B. 280
Marks, T. A. 876
Markum, J. 771, 772n., 904
Marquard, Jean (ed.) 851
Marquard, Leo 847
Marques, W. 902
Marrakesh 571
marriage laws (South Africa) 289; marriages, 'mixed' (South Africa) 295
Marris, P. and Somerset, A. 173n., 831
Marshall, D. Bruce 42 and n., 815
Marshall Aid 198
'Marshall Plan for Africa' 417
Martelli, George 20n.
Martin, Anthony 869
Martin, Yolande 544
Martins, Ovidio 804n.
Marvin, Richard 79n.

wabenzi (drivers of Mercedes-Benz cars) 444
Wachuku, Jaja 107
Wagaw, Teshome G. 873
wage labour, employment 10, 144, 163, 164, 165, 174, 175, 176, 426, 435; wage-labour class 35; wage relations 143, 144; wage structure 74, 146
wages 195, 205, 265, 391, 426, 436
Waḥḥābī order 539
Walda-Giyorgis, Tsahafe Tezaz 463, 474
Walker, F. V. 843
Wallace-Johnson I. T. A. 26, 97, 99, 103, 333, 334, 351–2, 855
Wallerstein, Immanuel 12n., 813, 823, 828
Walshe, Peter 849
Walvis Bay 296
WANS (West African National Secretariat) 103, 109
war-effort coordination 335
War Measure 145 (South Africa) 280, 291
wars: inter-state 69; secessionist 70; imperialist 98
wartime controls 197, 198
Wasserman, Gary 861, 862
WASU (West African Students Union) 98, 100, 101, 103, 338, 820
water, water supply 227, 325
Waterbury, John 591n., 882
waterways, inland 223
Watson, W. 829
Watts, J. M. 887
Wau 532
Webster, Eddie (ed.) 848
weedkillers 262
Weinstein, Brian 891
Weinstein, Warren 717n., 736, 897; Weinstein, Warren and Schrive, Robert 899
Weisbord, Robert G. 825
Weiskel, T. 887
Weiss, Herbert 709n., 897
Welch, Claude E., Jr. 824; Welch, Claude E., Jr and Smith, Arthur K. 87n., 818
Welch, Galbraith 856
welfare services, South Africa 279
Wellington, John H. 847
West, Martin E. 255
West Africa 819, 859
West Africa 10; decolonisation 56; industry 219; mining 214; peasant farmers 211
West African currency 232
West African Economic Community 118, 119; see also ECOWAS

'West African Economic Union' 233
West African Examinations Council 232, 332
West African income tax policy 232
West African Pilot 100, 335
West African research institutions 232
'West African Socialist Republic' 109
West African troops 285, 336
West African Youth League 99, 351
Westebbe, Richard M. 890, 891
West Germany 92
West Indies 23, 25, 47, 96, 104–5, 330
'Westminster model' 65
Wetanobe, Susumu 747n.
wheat 250, 262
Wheeler, D. L. 765n.; Wheeler, D. L. and Pélissier, R. 171n., 902
Whitaker, C. S. 852
White, Jeremy 26n., 46n., 853
White Fordsburg 263
Whiteley, W. H. (ed.) 827
white minority interests 49; nationalism 46
white-owned farms (South Africa) 259
White Republic (South Africa) 301–10
White Rhodesians 400, 401; South African 267, 307
whites, working class 39
white settlers, settler-farmers 10, 11, 71, 122, 145, 195–6, 232; decolonisation 12, 46, 48, 56, 61, 385–6, 862
wilaya (regional commands, Algeria) 580, 581; leaders 581, 586
Wild Report (1959, Uganda) 396 and n.
Wilkie, Wendell 23
Wilkins, Ivor and Strydom, Hans 288n.
Willett, Shelagh M. and Ambrose, D. 847
Williame, Jean-Claude 733n., 898
Williams, G. 165n., 167n., 830
Wilson, F. 266, 273n., 848; Wilson, F., Kooy, A., and Hendrie, D. 262n.
Wilson, G. and Wilson, M. 142, 143, 869–70
Wilson, Monica 251n.; Wilson, M. and Mafjie, A. 829; Wilson, M. and Thompson, L. (eds.) 814, 847
Windhoek 297, 298; Legislative Assembly 324; Turnhalle Conference 326–7
'winds of change' 294
Winid, B. 873
witchcraft, witchfinding 168, 800
Witwatersrand 263, 268, 269, 270, 282, 305, 321
Woldeab Woldemariam 465, 496